THE DIVINE OFFICE
revised by the decree of the Second Vatican Ecumenical Council and published
by the authority of Pope Paul VI

the Mundelein Psalter

The four-week cycle with pointed texts
for chanting the divine office:
Morning Prayer
Evening Prayer
Night Prayer
Office for the Dead

Approved for Use
in the Dioceses of the United States of America
by the United States Conference of Catholic Bishops

Douglas Martis, PhD, STD
Editor

Samuel F. Weber, OSB
Hymn Editor

HillenbrandBooks

Chicago/Mundelein, Illinois

Concordat Cum Originali
Monsignor James P. Moroney
Executive Director
USCCB Secretariat for the Liturgy

Published by Liturgy Training Publications, 1800 North Hermitage Avenue, Chicago, IL 60622; 1-800-933-1800, fax 1-800-933-7094, e-mail orders@ltp.org. See our Web site at www.LTP.org.

Hillenbrand Books is an imprint of Liturgy Training Publications (LTP) and the Liturgical Institute at the University of Saint Mary of the Lake (USML). The imprint is focused on contemporary and classical theological thought concerning the liturgy of the Catholic Church. Available at bookstores everywhere, or call 1-800-933-1800, or go to www.LTP.org. Further information about the **Hillenbrand Books** publishing program is available from the University of Saint Mary of the Lake/Mundelein Seminary, 1000 East Maple Avenue, Mundelein, IL 60060 (1-847-837-4542) or on our Web site at www.LITURGICALINSTITUTE.org or e-mail litinst@usml.edu.

Printed in the United States of America.

ISBN 978-1-59525-019-3

HMPSAL

CONTENTS

ACKNOWLEDGEMENTS

The English translation of the Concluding Prayers from *The Roman Missal* © 1973, International Committee on English in the Liturgy, Inc. (ICEL); the English translation of the General Instruction, Antiphons, Responsories, Intercessions, Introductory Verse, Psalm 95, Canticle of the Lamb, and Canticle from I Timothy 3:16 from *The Liturgy of the Hours* © 1974, ICEL. All rights reserved.

English translations of the Magnificat, Nunc Dimittis, Benedictus and Doxology by the International Consultation on English Texts.

Readings and Canticles from the *New American Bible* Copyright © 1970 by the Confraternity of Christian Doctrine, Washington, D.C. Used with permission. All Rights Reserved. No part of the *New American Bible* may be reproduced in any form without permission in writing from the copyright owner.

Psalm Translations Copyright © 1963 The Grail, England.

GIA Publications, Inc., exclusive North American agent, 7404 S. Mason Ave., Chicago, IL 60638 www.giamusic.com 800.442.1358 All rights reserved. Used by permission.

Hymns on pages 605, 725, 744, 859, 1312, 1314, © 2004 Reverend Thomas Buffer 4031 Clime Rd., Columbus, OH 43228. All rights reserved. Used with permission.

Hymns on pages 225, 230, from the Benedictine Nuns, Stanbrook Abbey, © 1975 Stanbrook Abbey . Used with permission. In some instances, the spelling and text have been altered by the editor to accord with U.S.A. use.

Hymns on pages 131, 136, 141, 146, 148, 163, 168, 177, 196, 206, 334, 336, 351, 360, 364, 371, 376, 381, 390, 482, 486, 513, 517, 546, 550, 563, 572, 576, 584, 588, 627, 671, 689, 693, 697, 702, 706, 711, 721, 730, 737, 766, 806, 823, 828, 832, 837, 841, 846, 855, 864, 868, 895, 898, 900, 904, 907, 918, 928, 938, 942, 956, 960, 962, 973, 976, 981, 986, 988, 992, 995, 998, 1002, 1010, 1012, 1014, 1018, 1019, 1020, 1021, 1022, 1026, 1030, 1035, 1037, 1038, 1041, 1045, 1052, 1054, 1055, 1056, 1059, 1061, 1064, 1065, 1067, 1070, 1074, 1076, 1080, 1082, 1086, 1089, 1091, 1095, 1096, 1098, 1102, 1107, 1109, 1114, 1115, 1119, 1130, 1131, 1136, 1140, 1144, 1146, 1150, 1162, 1164, 1166, 1177, 1182, 1188, 1200, 1203, 1206, 1214, 1220, 1228, 1231, 1238, 1242, 1246, 1248, 1253, 1256, 1263, 1267, 1274, 1278, 1288, 1294, 1329, 1332, 1333, 1334, 1336, 1337, 1338, 1340, 1342, 1343, from the Benedictine Nuns, Saint Cecilia's Abbey, Ryde, Isle of Wight, G. B. Used with permission. In some instances, the spelling and text have been altered to accord with U.S.A. use.

All other Hymns have been drawn from the common domain, using as sources *The Anglican Breviary*, 1955, *The English Hymnal*, 1933, and *The Monastic Diurnal*, 1963.

Gregorian chant melodies are those that tradition has assigned to the Office Hymns at Lauds and Vespers. Melodies have been taken from Roman, Benedictine and Sarum Use sources. For arrangement of Chant Tones for the Hymns, for the English Psalm Tones, Tone for "O God, come to my assistance," Tone for the Intercessions, and the Introduction to the Our Father composed by Reverend Samuel F. Weber, OSB. © 2007 Saint Meinrad Archabbey, St. Meinrad, IN 47577-1010. All rights reserved. Used with permission.

A PROJECT OF THIS MAGNITUDE reflects the dedication and work of many. The editor wishes to thank the following for their work and support: Rev. Samuel F. Weber, OSB, Karen Hopkins, Kevin Thornton, Barbara Nield, Dr. Denis McNamara, Linda Cerabona, Cardinal Francis George, OMI, Most Reverend Raymond Burke, Most Reverend J. Peter Sartain, Most Reverend Roger Kaffer, Msgr. James Moroney, Very Reverend John F. Canary, Very Reverend Dennis Lyle, Rev. Thomas Baima, Rev. Robert Schoenstene, Rev. John Szmyd, Rev. Alberto Rojas, Roger Gaura, Stephanie Jaeckel, José Maria Cabrera-Bustamante, Rev. Gregory Labus, Kevin Vogt, Rev. James Socias, John Thomas, Larry Cope, Anna Manhart, Deanna Keefe, Theresa Pincich, Maureen Como, Jeanne Troxel, Liturgical Insititute students, the students of University of St. Mary of the Lake/ Mundelein Seminary, and the priests, seminarians, and parishioners of *Saint-Louis-en l'Ile*, Paris, France.

Prot. no. 1000/71

DECREE

From ancient times the Church has had the custom of celebrating each day the liturgy of the hours. In this way the Church fulfills the Lord's precept to pray without ceasing, at once offering praise to God the Father and inteceding for the salvation of the world.

The Second Vatican Council showed the importance of the traditional discipline of the Church and desired to renew that discipline. It was, therefore, very concerned to bring about a suitable restoration of this liturgy of prayer so that priests and other members of the Church in today's circumstances might celebrate it better and more effectively (see Constitution on the Sacred Liturgy, *Sacrosanctum Concilium*, number 84.

Now that this work of restoration has been approved by Pope Paul VI in the apostolic constitution *Laudis canticum* of November 1, 1970, this Sacred Congregation for Divine Worship has published the Latin book for the celebration of the liturgy of the hours in accordance with the Roman Rite, and it declares that the present edition is the typical edition.
Anything to the contrary notwithstanding.

From the Office of the Sacred Congregation for Divine Worship, Easter Sunday, April 11, 1971.

Arturus Cardinal Tabera
Prefect

A. Bugnini
Secretary

GENERAL INSTRUCTION OF THE LITURGY OF THE HOURS

Chapter I: Importance of the Liturgy of the Hours or Divine Office in the Life of the Church

1. Public and common prayer by the people of God is rightly considered to be among the primary duties of the Church. From the very beginning those who were baptized "devoted themselves to the teaching of the apostles and to the community, to the breaking of the bread, and to prayer" (Acts 2:42). The Acts of the Apostles give frequent testimony to the fact that the Christian community prayed with one accord.[1]

The witness of the early Church teaches us that individual Christians devoted themselves to prayer at fixed times. Then, in different places, it soon became the established practice to assign special times for common prayer, for example, the last hour of the day when evening draws on and the lamp is lighted, or the first hour when night draws to a close with the rising of the sun. In the course of time other hours came to be sanctified by prayer in common. These were seen by the Fathers as foreshadowed in the Acts of the Apostles. There we read of the disciples gathered together at the third hour.[2] The prince of the apostles "went up on the housetop to pray, about the sixth hour" (10:9); "Peter and John were going up to the temple at the hour of prayer, the ninth hour" (3:1); "about midnight Paul and Silas were praying and singing hymns to God" (16:25).

2. Such prayer in common gradually took the form of a set cycle of hours. This liturgy of the hours or divine office, enriched by readings, is principally a prayer of praise and petition. Indeed, it is the prayer of the Church with Christ and to Christ.

I. Prayer of Christ
Christ The Intercessor With The Father

3. When the Word, proceeding from the Father as the splendor of his glory, came to give us all a share in God's life, "Christ Jesus, High Priest of the new and eternal covenant, taking human nature, introduced into this earthly exile the hymn of praise that is sung throughout all ages in the halls of heaven."[3] From then on in Christ's heart the praise of God assumes a human sound in words of adoration, expiation, and intercession, presented to the Father by the Head of the new humanity, the Mediator between God and his people, in the name of all and for the good of all.

4. In his goodness the Son of God, who is one with his Father (see Jn 10:30) and who on entering the world said: "Here I am! I come, God, to do your will" (Heb 10:9; see Jn 6:38), has left us the lesson of his own prayer. The Gospels many times show us Christ at prayer: when his mission is revealed by the Father;[4] before he calls the apostles;[5] when he blesses God at the multiplication of the loaves;[6] when he is transfigured on the mountain;[7] when he heals the deaf-mute;[8] when he raises Lazarus;[9] before he asks for Peter's confession of faith;[10] when he teaches the disciples how to pray;[11] when the disciples return from their mission;[12] when he blesses the little children;[13] when he prays for Peter.[14]

The work of each day was closely bound up with his prayer, indeed flowed out from it: he would retire into the desert or into the hills to pray,[15] rise very early[16] or spend the night up to the fourth watch[17] in prayer to God.[18]

We are right in thinking that he took part both in public prayers: in the synagogues, which he entered on the Sabbath "as his custom was;"[19] in the temple, which he called a house of prayer;[20] and in the private prayers that for devout Israelites were a daily practice. He used the traditional blessings of God at meals, as is expressly mentioned in connection with the multiplication of the loaves,[21] the last supper[22] and the meal at Emmaus.[23] He also joined with the disciples in a hymn of praise.[24]

To the very end of his life, as his passion was approaching,[25] at the last supper,[26] in the agony in the garden,[27] and on the cross,[28] the divine teacher showed that prayer was the soul of his

Messianic ministry and paschal death. "In the days of his life on earth he offered up prayers and entreaties with loud cries and tears to the one who could deliver him from death and because of his reverence his prayer was heard" (Heb 5:7). By a single offering on the altar of the cross "he has made perfect forever those who are being sanctified" (Heb 10-14). Raised from the dead, he lives for ever, making intercession for us.[29]

II. Prayer of the Church
Command to Pray

5. Jesus has commanded us to do as he did. On many occasions he said: "Pray," "ask," "seek"[30] "in my name."[31] He taught us how to pray in what is known as the Lord's Prayer.[32] He taught us that prayer is necessary,[33] that it should be humble,[34] watchful,[35] persevering, confident in the Father's goodness,[36] single-minded, and in conformity with God's nature.[37]

Here and there in their letters the apostles have handed on to us many prayers, particularly of praise and thanks. They instruct us on prayer in the Holy Spirit,[38] through Christ,[39] offered to God,[40] as to its persistence and constancy,[41] its power to sanctify,[42] and on prayer of praise,[43] thanks,[44] petition,[45] and intercession for all.[46]

Christ's Prayer Continued by the Church

6. Since we are entirely dependent on God, we must acknowledge and express this sovereignty of the Creator, as the devout people of every age have done by means of prayer.

Prayer directed to God must be linked with Christ, the Lord of all, the one Mediator[47] through whom alone we have access to God.[48] He unites to himself the whole human community[49] in such a way that there is an intimate bond between the prayer of Christ and the prayer of all humanity. In Christ and in Christ alone human worship of God receives its redemptive value and attains its goal.

7. There is a special and very close bond between Christ and those whom he makes members of his Body, the Church, through the sacrament of rebirth. Thus, from the Head all the riches belonging to the Son flow throughout the whole Body: the communication of the Spirit, the truth, the life, and the participation in the divine sonship that Christ manifested in all his prayer when he dwelt among us.

Christ's priesthood is also shared by the whole Body of the Church, so that the baptized are consecrated as a spiritual temple and holy priesthood through the rebirth of baptism and the anointing by the Holy Spirit[50] and are empowered to offer the worship of the New Covenant, a worship that derives not from our own powers but from Christ's merit and gift.

"God could give us no greater gift than to establish as our Head the Word through whom he created all things and to unite us to that Head as members. The results are many The Head is Son of God and Son of Man, one as God with the Father and one as man with us. When we speak in prayer to the Father, we do not separate the Son from him and when the Son's Body prays it does not separate itself from its Head. It is the one Savior of his Body, the Lord Christ Jesus, who prays for us and in us and who is prayed to by us. He prays for us as our priest, in us as our Head; he is prayed to by us as our God. Recognize therefore our own voice in him and his voice in us."[51]

The excellence of Christian prayer lies in its sharing in the reverent love of the only-begotten Son for the Father and in the prayer that the Son put into words in his earthly life and that still continues without ceasing in the name of the whole human race and for its salvation, throughout the universal Church and in all its members.

Action of the Holy Spirit

8. The unity of the Church at prayer is brought about by the Holy Spirit, who is the same in Christ,[52] in the whole Church, and in every baptized person. It is this Spirit who "helps us in our weakness" and "intercedes for us with longings too deep for words" (Rom 8:26). As the Spirit of the Son, he gives us "the spirit of adopted children, by which we cry out: Abba, Father"

(Rom 8:15; see Gal 4:6; 1 Cor 12:3; Eph 5:18; Jude 20). There can be therefore no Christian prayer without the action of the Holy Spirit, who unites the whole Church and leads it through the Son to the Father.

Community Character of Prayer

9. It follows that the example and precept of our Lord and the apostles in regard to constant and persevering prayer are not to be seen as a purely legal regulation. They belong to the very essence of the Church itself, which is a community and which in prayer must express its nature as a community. Hence, when the community of believers is first mentioned in the Acts of the Apostles, it is seen as a community gathered together at prayer "with the women and Mary, the mother of Jesus, and his brothers" (Acts 1:14). "There was one heart and soul in the company of those who believed" (Acts 4:32). Their oneness in spirit was founded on the word of God, on the communion of charity, on prayer, and on the eucharist.[53]

Though prayer in private and in seclusion[54] is always necessary and to be encouraged[55] and is practiced by the members of the Church through Christ in the Holy Spirit, there is a special excellence in the prayer of the community. Christ himself has said: "Where two or three are gathered together in my name, I am there in their midst" (Mt 18.20).

III. Liturgy of the Hours
Consecration of Time

10. Christ taught us: "You must pray at all times and not lose heart" (Lk 18:1). The Church has been faithful in obeying this instruction; it never ceases to offer prayer and makes this exhortation its own: "Through him (Jesus) let us offer to God an unceasing sacrifice of praise" (Heb 15:15). The Church fulfills this precept not only by celebrating the eucharist but in other ways also, especially through the liturgy of the hours. By ancient Christian tradition what distinguishes the liturgy of the hours from other liturgical services is that it consecrates to God the whole cycle of the day and the night.[56]

11. The purpose of the liturgy of the hours is to sanctify the day and the whole range of human activity. Therefore its structure has been revised in such a way as to make each hour once more correspond as nearly as possible to natural time and to take account of the circumstances of life today.[57]

Hence, "that the day may be truly sanctified and the hours themselves recited with spiritual advantage, it is best that each of them be prayed at a time most closely corresponding to the true time of each canonical hour."[58]

Liturgy of the Hours and the Eucharist

12. To the different hours of the day the liturgy of the hours extends[59] the praise and thanksgiving, the memorial of the mysteries of salvation, the petitions and the foretaste of heavenly glory that are present in the eucharistic mystery, "the center and high point in the whole life of the Christian community."[60]

The liturgy of the hours is in turn an excellent preparation for the celebration of the eucharist itself, for it inspires and deepens in a fitting way the dispositions necessary for the fruitful celebration of the eucharist: faith, hope, love, devotion, and the spirit of self-denial.

Priesthood of Christ in the Liturgy of the Hours

13. In the Holy Spirit Christ carries out through the Church "the task of redeeming humanity and giving perfect glory to God,"[61] not only when the eucharist is celebrated and the sacraments administered but also in other ways and especially when the liturgy of the hours is celebrated.[62] There Christ himself is present - in the gathered community, in the proclamation of God's word, "in the prayer and song of the Church."[63]

Sanctification of God's People

14. Our sanctification is accomplished[64] and worship is offered to God in the liturgy of the hours in such a way that an exchange or dialogue is set up between God and us, in which "God is speaking to his people ... and his people are responding to him by both song and prayer."[65] Those taking part in the liturgy of the hours have access to holiness of the richest kind through the life-giving word of God, which in this liturgy receives great emphasis. Thus its readings are drawn from sacred Scripture, God's words in the psalms are sung in his presence, and the intercessions, prayers, and hymns are inspired by Scripture and steeped in its spirit.[66]

Hence, not only when those things are read "that are written for our instruction" (Rom 15:4), but also when the Church prays or sings, faith is deepened for those who take part and their minds are lifted up to God, in order to offer him their worship as intelligent beings and to receive his grace more plentifully.[67]

Praising God With the Church in Heaven

15. In the liturgy of the hours the Church exercises the priestly office of its Head and offers to God "without ceasing"[68] a sacrifice of praise, that is, a tribute of lips acknowledging his name.[69] This prayer is "the voice of a bride addressing her bridegroom; it is the very prayer that Christ himself, together with his Body, addresses to the Father."[70] "All who render this service are not only fulfilling a duty of the Church, but also are sharing in the greatest honor of Christ's Bride for by offering these praises to God they are standing before God's throne in the name of the Church, their Mother."[71]

16. When the Church offers praise to God in the liturgy of the hours, it unites itself with that hymn of praise sung throughout all ages in the halls of heaven;[72] it also receives a foretaste of the song of praise in heaven, described by John in the Book of Revelation, the song sung continually before the throne of God and of the Lamb. Our close union with the Church in heaven is given effective voice "when we all, from every tribe and tongue and people and nation redeemed by Christ's blood (see Rv 5:9) and gathered together into the one Church, glorify the triune God with one hymn of praise."[73]

The prophets came almost to a vision of this liturgy of heaven as the victory of a day without night, of a light without darkness: "The sun will no more be your light by day, and the brightness of the moon will not shine upon you, but the Lord will be your everlasting light" (Is 60:19; see Rv 21:23 and 25). "There will be a single day, known to the Lord, not day and night, and at evening there will be light" (Zech 14:7). Already "the end of the ages has come upon us (see 1 Cor 10:11) and the renewal of the world has been irrevocably established and in a true sense is being anticipated in this world."[74] By faith we too are taught the meaning of our temporal life, so that we look forward with all creation to the revealing of God's children.[75] In the liturgy of the hours we proclaim this faith, we express and nourish this hope, we share in some degree the joy of everlasting praise and of that day that knows no setting.

Petition and Intercession

17. But besides the praise of God, the Church in the liturgy of the hours expresses the prayers and desires of all the faithful; indeed, it prays to Christ, and through him to the Father, for the salvation of the whole world.[76] The Church's voice is not just its own; it is also Christ's voice, since its prayers are offered in Christ's name, that is, "through our Lord Jesus Christ," and so the Church continues to offer the prayer and petition that Christ poured out in the days of his earthly life[77] and that have therefore a unique effectiveness. The ecclesial community thus exercises a truly maternal function in bringing souls to Christ, not only by charity, good example, and works of penance but also by prayer.[78]

The concern with prayer involves those especially who have been called by a special mandate to carry out the liturgy of the hours: bishops and priests as they pray in virtue of their office for their own people and for the whole people of God;[79] other sacred ministers, and also religious.[80]

Source and Summit of Pastoral Action

18. Those then who take part in the liturgy of the hours bring growth to God's people in a hidden but fruitful apostolate,[81] for the work of the apostolate is directed to this end, "that all who are made children of God by faith and baptism should come together to praise God in the midst of this Church, to take part in the sacrifice, and to eat the Lord's Supper."[82]

Thus by their lives the faithful show forth and reveal to others "the mystery of Christ and the real nature of the true Church. It is of the essence of the Church to be visible yet endowed with invisible resources, eager to act yet intent on contemplation, present in this world yet not at home in it."[83]

In their turn the readings and prayers of the liturgy of the hours form a wellspring of the Christian life: the table of sacred Scripture and the writings of the saints nurture its life and prayers strengthen it. Only the Lord, without whom we can do nothing,[84] can, in response to our request, give power and increase to what we do,[85] so that we may be built up each day in the Spirit into the temple of God,[86] to the measure of Christ's fullness,[87] and receive greater strength also to bring the good news of Christ to those outside.[88]

Harmony of Mind and Voice

19. Mind and voice must be in harmony in a celebration that is worthy, attentive, and devout, if this prayer is to be made their own by those taking part and to be a source of devotion, a means of gaining God's manifold grace, a deepening of personal prayer, and an incentive to the work of the apostolate.[89] All should be intent on cooperating with God's grace, so as not to receive it in vain. Seeking Christ, penetrating ever more deeply into his mystery through prayer[90] they should offer praise and petition to God with the same mind and heart as the divine Redeemer when he prayed.

IV. Participants in the Liturgy of the Hours
Celebration in Common

20. The liturgy of the hours, like other liturgical services, is not a private matter but belongs to the whole Body of the Church, whose life it both expresses and affects.[91] This liturgy stands out most strikingly as an ecclesial celebration when, through the bishop surrounded by his priests and ministers,[92] the local Church celebrates it. For "in the local Church the one, holy, catholic, and apostolic Church is truly present and at work."[93] Such a celebration is therefore most earnestly recommended. When, in the absence of the bishop, a chapter of canons or other priests celebrate the liturgy of the hours, they should always respect the true time of day and, as far as possible, the people should take part. The same is to be said of collegiate chapters.

21. Wherever possible, other groups of the faithful should celebrate the liturgy of the hours communally in church. This especially applies to parishes - the cells of the diocese, established under their pastors, taking the place of the bishop; they "represent in some degree the visible Church established throughout the world."[94]

22. Hence, when the people are invited to the liturgy of the hours and come together in unity of heart and voice, they show forth the Church in its celebration of the mystery of Christ.[95]

23. Those in holy orders or with a special canonical mission[96] have the responsibility of initiating and directing the prayer of the community; "they should expend every effort so that those entrusted to their care may become of one mind in prayer."[97] They must therefore see to it that the people are invited, and prepared by suitable instruction, to celebrate the principal hours in common, especially on Sundays and holydays.[98] They should teach the people how to make this participation a source of genuine prayer;[99] they should therefore give the people suitable guidance in the Christian understanding of the psalms, in order to progress by degrees to a greater appreciation and more frequent use of the prayer of the Church.[100]

24. Communities of canons, monks, nuns, and other religious who celebrate the liturgy of the hours by rule or according to their constitutions, whether with the general rite or a particular rite, in whole or in part, represent in a special way the Church at prayer. They are a fuller sign of the

Church as it continuously praises God with one voice and they fulfill the duty of "working," above all by prayer, "to build up and increase the whole Mystical Body of Christ, and for the good of the local Churches."[101] This is especially true of those living the contemplative life.

25. Even when having no obligation to communal celebration, all sacred ministers and all clerics living in a community or meeting together should arrange to say at least some part of the liturgy of the hours in common, particularly morning prayer and evening prayer.[102]

26. Men and women religious not bound to a common celebration, as well as members of any institute of perfection, are strongly urged to gather together, by themselves or with the people, to celebrate the liturgy of the hours or part of it.

27. Lay groups gathering for prayer, apostolic work, or any other reason are encouraged to fulfill the Church's duty,[103] by celebrating part of the liturgy of the hours. The laity must learn above all how in the liturgy they are adoring God the Father in spirit and in truth;[104] they should bear in mind that through public worship and prayer they reach all humanity and can contribute significantly to the salvation of the whole world.[105]

Finally, it is of great advantage for the family, the domestic sanctuary of the Church, not only to pray together to God but also to celebrate some parts of the liturgy of the hours as occasion offers, in order to enter more deeply into the life of the Church.[106]

Mandate to Celebrate the Liturgy of the Hours

28. Sacred ministers have the liturgy of the hours entrusted to them in such a particular way that even when the faithful are not present they are to pray it themselves with the adaptations necessary under these circumstances. The Church commissions them to celebrate the liturgy of the hours so as to ensure at least in their persons the regular carrying out of the duty of the whole community and the unceasing continuance of Christ's prayer in the Church.[107]

The bishop represents Christ in an eminent and conspicuous way and is the high priest of his flock; the life in Christ of his faithful people may be said in a sense to derive from him and depend on him.[108] He should, then, be the first of all the members of his Church in offering prayer. His prayer in the recitation of the liturgy of the hours is always made in the name of the Church and on behalf of the Church entrusted to him.[109]

United as they are with the bishop and the whole presbyterium, priests are themselves representative in a special way of Christ the Priest[110] and so share the same responsibility of praying to God for the people entrusted to them and indeed for the whole world.[111]

All these ministers fulfill the ministry of the Good Shepherd who prays for his sheep that they may have life and so be brought into perfect unity.[112] In the liturgy of the hours that the Church sets before them they are not only to find a source of devotion and a strengthening of personal prayer,[113] but must also nourish and foster pastoral missionary activity as the fruit of their contemplation to gladden the whole Church of God.[114]

29. Hence bishops, priests, and other sacred ministers, who have received from the Church the mandate to celebrate the liturgy of the hours (see no. 17), should recite the full sequence of hours each day, observing as far as possible the true time of day.

They should, first and foremost, attach due importance to those hours that are, so to speak, the two hinges of the liturgy of the hours, that is, morning prayer and evening prayer, which should not be omitted except for a serious reason.

They should faithfully pray the office of readings, which is above all a liturgical celebration of the word of God. In this way they fulfill daily a duty that is peculiarly their own, that is, of receiving the word of God into their lives, so that they may become more perfect as disciples of the Lord and experience more deeply the unfathomable riches of Christ.[115]

In order to sanctify the whole day more completely, they will also treasure the recitation of daytime prayer and night prayer, to round off the whole Opus Dei and to commend themselves to God before retiring.

30. It is most fitting that permanent deacons recite daily at least some part of the liturgy of the hours, to be determined by the conference of bishops.[116]

31. a. Cathedral and collegiate chapters should celebrate in choir those parts of the liturgy of the hours that are prescribed for them by the general law or by particular law.
In private recitation individual members of these chapters should include those hours that are recited in their chapter, in addition to the hours prescribed for all sacred ministers.[117]
b. Religious communities bound to the recitation of the liturgy of the hours and their individual members should celebrate the hours in keeping with their own particular law; but the prescription of no. 29 in regard to those in holy orders is to be respected.
Communities bound to choir should celebrate the whole sequence of the hours daily in choir;[118] when absent from choir their members should recite the hours in keeping with their own particular law; but the prescriptions in no. 29 are always to be respected.

32. Other religious communities and their individual members are advised to celebrate some parts of the liturgy of the hours, in accordance with their own situation, for it is the prayer of the Church and makes the whole Church, scattered throughout the world, one in heart and mind.[119] This recommendation applies also to laypersons.[120]

Structure of the Celebration

33. The structure of the liturgy of the hours follows laws of its own and incorporates in its own way elements found in other Christian celebrations. Thus it is so constructed that, after a hymn, there is always psalmody, then a long or short reading of sacred Scripture, and finally prayer of petition.
In a celebration in common and in private recitation the essential structure of this liturgy remains the same, that is, it is a conversation between God and his people. Celebration in common, however, expresses more clearly the ecclesial nature of the liturgy of the hours; it makes for active participation by all, in a way suited to each one's condition, through the acclamations, dialogue, alternating psalmody, and similar elements. It also better provides for the different literary genres that make up the liturgy of the hours.[121] Hence, whenever it is possible to have a celebration in common, with the people present and actively taking part, this kind of celebration is to be preferred to one that is individual and, as it were, private.[122] It is also advantageous to sing the office in choir and in community as opportunity offers, in accordance with the nature and function of the individual parts.
In this way the Apostle's exhortation is obeyed: "Let the word of Christ dwell in you in all its fullness, as you teach and counsel each other in all wisdom by psalms, hymns, and spiritual canticles, singing thankfully to God in your hearts" (Col 3:16; see Eph 5:19-20).

CHAPTER II: SANCTIFICATION OF THE DAY: THE DIFFERENT LITURGICAL HOURS
I. Introduction to the Whole Office

34. The whole office begins as a rule with an invitatory. This consists in the verse, Lord, open my lips. And my mouth will proclaim your praise, and Ps 95. This psalm invites the faithful each day to sing God's praise and to listen to his voice and draws them to hope for "the Lord's rest."[1]
In place of Ps 95, Ps 100, Ps 67, or Ps 24 may be used as circumstances may suggest.
It is preferable to recite the invitatory psalm responsorially as it is set out in the text, that is, with the antiphon recited at the beginning, then repeated, and repeated again after each strophe.

35. The invitatory is placed at the beginning of the whole sequence of the day's prayer, that is, it precedes either morning prayer or the office of readings, whichever of these liturgical rites begins the day. The invitatory psalm with its antiphon may be omitted, however, when the invitatory is the prelude to morning prayer.

36. The variation of the invitatory antiphon, to suit the different liturgical days, is indicated at its place of occurrence.

II. Morning Prayer and Evening Prayer

37. "By the venerable tradition of the universal Church, lauds as morning prayer and vespers as evening prayer are the two hinges on which the daily office turns; hence they are to be considered as the chief hours and celebrated as such."[2]

38. As is clear from many of the elements that make it up, morning prayer is intended and arranged to sanctify the morning. St. Basil the Great gives an excellent description of this character in these words: "It is said in the morning in order that the first stirrings of our mind and will may be consecrated to God and that we may take nothing in hand until we have been gladdened by the thought of God, as it is written: 'I was mindful of God and was glad' (Ps 77:4 [Jerome's translation from Hebrew]), or set our bodies to any task before we do what has been said: 'I will pray to you, Lord, you will hear my voice in the morning; I will stand before you in the morning and gaze on you' (Ps 5:4-5)."[3]

Celebrated as it is as the light of a new day is dawning, this hour also recalls the resurrection of the Lord Jesus, the true light enlightening all people (see Jn 1:9) and "the sun of justice" (Mal 4:2), "rising from on high" (Lk 1:78). Hence, we can well understand the advice of St. Cyprian: "There should be prayer in the morning so that the resurrection of the Lord may thus be celebrated."[4]

39. When evening approaches and the day is already far spent, evening prayer is celebrated in order that "we may give thanks for what has been given us, or what we have done well, during the day."[5] We also recall the redemption through the prayer we send up "like incense in the Lord's sight," and in which "the raising up of our hands" becomes "an evening sacrifice."[6] This sacrifice "may also be interpreted more spiritually as the true evening sacrifice that our Savior the Lord entrusted to the apostles at supper on the evening when he instituted the sacred mysteries of the Church or of the evening sacrifice of the next day, the sacrifice, that is, which, raising his hands, he offered to the Father at the end of the ages for the salvation of the whole world."[7] Again, in order to fix our hope on the light that knows no setting, "we pray and make petition for the light to come down on us anew; we implore the coming of Christ who will bring the grace of eternal light."[8] Finally, at this hour we join with the Churches of the East in calling upon the "joy-giving light of that holy glory, born of the immortal, heavenly Father, the holy and blessed Jesus Christ; now that we have come to the setting of the sun and have seen the evening star, we sing in praise of God, Father, Son, and Holy Spirit. . . ."

40. Morning prayer and evening prayer are therefore to be accorded the highest importance as the prayer of the Christian community. Their public or communal celebration should be encouraged, especially in the case of those who live in community. Indeed, the recitation of these hours should be recommended also to individual members of the faithful unable to take part in a celebration in common.

41. Morning prayer and evening prayer begin with the introductory verse, God come to my assistance. Lord, make haste to help me. There follows the Glory to the Father, with As it was in the beginning and Alleluia (omitted in Lent). This introduction is omitted at morning prayer when the invitatory immediately precedes it.

42. Then an appropriate hymn is sung immediately. The purpose of the hymn is to set the tone for the hour or the feast and, especially in celebrations with a congregation, to form a simple and pleasant introduction to prayer.

43. After the hymn the psalmody follows, in accordance with the rules laid down in nos. 121-125. The psalmody of morning prayer consists of one morning psalm, then a canticle from the Old Testament and, finally, a second psalm of praise, following the tradition of the Church.

The psalmody of evening prayer consists of two psalms (or two parts of a longer psalm) suited to the hour and to celebration with a congregation and a canticle from the letters of the apostles or from the Book of Revelation.

44. After the psalmody there is either a short reading or a longer one.

45. The short reading is provided to fit the day, the season, and the feast. It is to be read and received as a true proclamation of God's word that emphasizes some holy thought or highlights

some shorter passages that may be overlooked in the continuous cycle of Scripture readings. The short readings are different for each day of the psalter cycle.

46. Especially in a celebration with a congregation, a longer Scripture reading may be chosen either from the office of readings or the Lectionary for Mass, particularly texts that for some reason have not been used. From time to time some other more suitable reading may be used, in accordance with the rules in nos. 248-249 and 251.

47. In a celebration with a congregation a short homily may follow the reading to explain its meaning, as circumstances suggest.

48. After the reading or homily a period of silence may be observed.

49. As a response to the word of God, a responsorial. chant or short responsory is provided; this may be omitted. Other chants with the same purpose and character may also be substituted in its place, provided these have been duly approved by the conference of bishops.

50. Next is the solemn recitation of the gospel canticle with its antiphon, that is, the Canticle of Zechariah at morning prayer and the Canticle of Mary at evening prayer. Sanctioned by age-old popular usage in the Roman Church, these canticles are expressions of praise and thanks-giving for our redemption. The antiphon for each canticle is indicated, according to the character of the day, the season, or the feast.

51. After the canticle, at morning prayer come the petitions for the consecration of the day and its work to God and at evening prayer, the intercessions (see nos. 179-193).

52. After the petitions or intercessions the Lord's Prayer is said by all.

53. Immediately after the Lord's Prayer there follows the concluding prayer, which for weekdays in Ordinary Time is found in the psalter and for other days in the proper.

54. Then, if a priest or deacon is presiding, he dismisses the congregation with the greeting, The Lord be with you, and the blessing as at Mass. He adds the invitation, Go in peace. ℟. Thanks be to God. In the absence of a priest or deacon the celebration concludes with May the Lord bless us, etc.

III. Office of Readings

55. The office of readings seeks to provide God's people, and in particular those consecrated to God in a special way, with a wider selection of passages from sacred Scripture for meditation, together with the finest excerpts from spiritual writers. Even though the cycle of scriptural readings at daily Mass is now richer, the treasures of revelation and tradition to be found in the office of readings will also contribute greatly to the spiritual life. Bishops and priests in particular should prize these treasures, so that they may hand on to others the word of God they have themselves received and make their teaching "the true nourishment for the people of God."[9]

56. But prayer should accompany "the reading of sacred Scripture so that there may be a conversa-tion between God and his people: 'we talk with God when we pray, we listen to him when we read God's words.'"[10] For this reason the office of readings consists also of psalms, a hymn, a prayer, and other texts, giving it the character of true prayer.

57. The Constitution on the Liturgy directs that the office of readings, "though it should retain its character as a night office of praise when celebrated in choir, shall be adapted so that it may be recited at any hour of the day; it shall be made up of fewer psalms and longer readings."[11]

58. Those who are obliged by their own particular law and others who commendably wish to retain the character of this office as a night office of praise (either by saying it at night or very early in the morning and before morning prayer), during Ordinary Time choose the hymn from the selection given for this purpose. Moreover, for Sundays, solemnities, and certain feasts what is said in nos. 70-73 about vigils must be kept in mind.

59. Without prejudice to the regulations just given, the office of readings may be recited at any hour of the day, even during the night hours of the previous day, after evening prayer has been said.

60. If the office of readings is said before morning prayer, the invitatory precedes it, as noted (nos. 34-36). Otherwise it begins with the verse, God, come to my assistance with the Glory to the Father, As it was in the beginning, and the Alleluia (omitted in Lent).

61. Then the hymn is sung. In Ordinary Time this is taken either from the night selections, as already indicated (nos. 34-36), or from the morning selections, depending on what the true time of day requires.

62. The psalmody follows and consists of three psalms (or parts in the case of longer psalms). During the Easter triduum, on days within the octaves of Easter and Christmas, on solemnities and feasts, the psalms are proper, with their proper antiphons.
On Sundays and weekdays, however, the psalms and their antiphons are taken from the current week and day of the psalter. On memorials of the saints they are similarly taken from the current week and day of the psalter, unless there are proper psalms or antiphons (see nos. 218ff.).

63. Between the psalmody and the readings there is, as a rule, a verse, marking a transition in the prayer from psalmody to listening.

64. There are two readings: the first is from the Scriptures, the second is from the writings of the Fathers or church writers, or else is a reading connected with the saints.

65. After each reading there is a responsory (see nos. 169-172).

66. The scriptural reading is normally to be taken from the Proper of Seasons, in accordance with the rules to be given later (nos. 140-155). On solemnities and feasts, however, it is taken from the proper or the common.

67. On solemnities and feasts of saints a proper second reading is used; if there is none, the second reading is taken from the respective Common of Saints. On memorials of saints when the celebration is not impeded, the reading in connection with the saint replaces the current second reading (see nos. 166 and 235).

68. On Sundays outside Lent, on days within the octaves of Easter and Christmas, and on solemnities and feasts the Te Deum is said after the second reading with its responsory but is omitted on memorials and weekdays. The last part of this hymn, that is, from the verse, Save your people, Lord to the end, may be omitted.

69. The office of readings normally concludes with the prayer proper to the day and, at least in recitation in common, with the acclamation, Let us praise the Lord. ℟ And give him thanks.

IV. Vigils

70. The Easter Vigil is celebrated by the whole Church, in the rites given in the relevant liturgical books. "The vigil of this night," as St. Augustine said, "is of such importance that it could claim exclusively for itself the name 'vigil,' common though this is to all the others."[12] "We keep vigil on that night when the Lord rose again and inaugurated for us in his humanity that life ... in which there is neither death nor sleep.... Hence, the one whose resurrection we celebrate by keeping watch a little longer will see to it that we reign with him by living a life without end."[13]

71. As with the Easter Vigil, it was customary to begin certain solemnities (different in different Churches) with a vigil. Among these solemnities Christmas and Pentecost are preeminent. This custom should be maintained and fostered, according to the particular usage of each Church. Whenever it seems good to add a vigil for other solemnities or pilgrimages, the general norms for celebrations of the word should be followed.

72. The Fathers and spiritual writers have frequently encouraged Christians, especially those who lead the contemplative life, to pray during the night. Such prayer expresses and awakens our expectation of the Lord's Second Coming: "At midnight the cry went up: 'See, the bridegroom is coming, go out to meet him... (Mt 25:6). "Keep watch, then, for you do not know when the master of the house is coming, whether late or at midnight or at cockcrow or in the morning, so that if he comes unexpectedly he may not find you sleeping" (Mk 13:35-36). All who maintain the character of the office of readings as a night office, therefore, are to be commended.

73. Further, since in the Roman Rite the office of readings is always of a uniform brevity, especially for the sake of those engaged in apostolic work, those who desire, in accordance with

tradition, to extend the celebration of the vigils of Sundays, solemnities, and feasts should do so as follows.

First, the office of readings is to be celebrated as in The Liturgy of the Hours up to the end of the readings. After the two readings and before the Te Deum canticles should be added from the special appendix of The Liturgy of the Hours. Then the gospel should be read; a homily on the gospel may be added. After this the Te Deum is sung and the prayer said.

On solemnities and feasts the gospel is to be taken from the Lectionary for Mass; on Sundays, from the series on the paschal mystery in the appendix of The Liturgy of the Hours.

V. Daytime Hours

74. Following a very ancient tradition Christians have made a practice of praying out of private devotion at various times of the day, even in the course of their work, in imitation of the Church in apostolic times. In different ways with the passage of time this tradition has taken the form of a liturgical celebration.

75. Liturgical custom in both East and West has retained midmorning, midday, and midafternoon prayer, mainly because these hours were linked to a commemoration of the events of the Lord's passion and of the first preaching of the Gospel.

76. Vatican Council II decreed that these lesser hours are to be retained in choir.[14]

The liturgical practice of saying these three hours is to be retained, without prejudice to particular law, by those who live the contemplative life. It is recommended also for all, especially those who take part in retreats or pastoral meetings.

77. Outside choir, without prejudice to particular law, it is permitted to choose from the three hours the one most appropriate to the time of day, so that the tradition of prayer in the course of the day's work may be maintained.

78. Daytime prayer is so arranged as to take into account both those who recite only one hour and those who are obliged, or desire, to say all three hours.

79. The daytime hours begin with the introductory verse, God come to my assistance with the Glory to the Father, As it was in the beginning, and the Alleluia (omitted in Lent). Then a hymn appropriate to the hour is sung. The psalmody is next, then the reading, followed by the verse. The hour concludes with the prayer and, at least in recitation in common, with the acclamation, Let us praise the Lord. ℟. And give him thanks.

80. Different hymns and prayers are given for each of the hours so that, in keeping with tradition, they may correspond to the true time of day and thus sanctify it in a more pointed way. Those who recite only one hour should therefore choose the texts that correspond to the true time of day.

In addition, the readings and prayers vary in keeping with the character of the day, the season, or the feast.

81. Two psalmodies are provided: the current psalmody and the complementary psalmody. Those who pray one hour should use the current psalmody. Those who pray more than one hour should use the current psalmody at one hour and the complementary psalmody at the others.

82. The current psalmody consists of three psalms (or parts in the case of longer psalms) from the psalter, with their antiphons, unless directions are given to the contrary.

On solemnities, the Easter triduum, and days within the octave of Easter, proper antiphons are said with three psalms chosen from the complementary psalmody, unless special psalms are to be used or the celebration falls on a Sunday, when the psalms are those from the Sunday of Week I of the psalter.

83. The complementary psalter consists of three sets of three psalms, chosen as a rule from the Gradual Psalms.

VI. Night Prayer

84. Night prayer is the last prayer of the day, said before retiring, even if that is after midnight.

85. Night prayer begins like the other hours, with the verse, God, come to my assistance, the Glory to the Father, As it was in the beginning, and the Alleluia (omitted in Lent).

86. It is a laudable practice to have next an examination of conscience; in a celebration in common this takes place in silence or as part of a penitential rite based on the formularies in the Roman Missal.

87. The appropriate hymn follows.

88. After evening prayer I of Sunday the psalmody consists of Ps 4 and Ps 134; after evening prayer II of Sunday it consists of Ps 91.

On the other days psalms are chosen that are full of confidence in the Lord; it is permissible to use the Sunday psalms instead, especially for the convenience of those who may wish to pray night prayer from memory.

89. After the psalmody there is a reading, followed by the responsory, Into your hands. Then, as a climax to the whole hour, the Canticle of Simeon, Lord, now you let your servant go in peace follows, with its antiphon.

90. The concluding prayer then follows, as it appears in the psalter.

91. After the prayer the blessing, May the all-powerful Lord is used, even in private recitation.

92. Finally, one of the antiphons in honor of the Blessed Virgin Mary is said. In the Easter season this is always to be the Regina caeli. In addition to the antiphons given in The Liturgy of the Hours, others may be approved by the conferences of bishops.[15]

VII. Combining the Hours With Mass or With Each Other

93. In particular cases, if circumstances require, it is possible to link an hour more closely with Mass when there is a celebration of the liturgy of the hours in public or in common, according to the norms that follow, provided the Mass and the hour belong to one and the same office. Care must be taken, however, that this does not result in harm to pastoral work, especially on Sundays.

94. When morning prayer, celebrated in choir or in common, comes immediately before Mass, the whole celebration may begin either with the introductory verse and hymn of morning prayer, especially on weekdays, or with the entrance song, procession, and celebrant's greeting, especially on Sundays and holydays; one of the introductory rites is thus omitted.

The psalmody of morning prayer follows as usual, up to, but excluding, the reading. After the psalmody the penitential rite is omitted and, as circumstances suggest, the Kyrie; the Gloria then follows, if required by the rubrics, and the celebrant says the opening prayer of the Mass. The liturgy of the word follows as usual.

The general intercessions are made in the place and form customary at Mass. But on weekdays, at Mass in the morning, the intercessions of morning prayer may replace the daily form of the general intercessions at Mass.

After the communion with its communion song the Canticle of Zechariah, Blessed be the Lord, with its antiphon from morning prayer, is sung. Then follow the prayer after communion and the rest as usual.

95. If public celebration of a daytime hour, whichever corresponds to the time of day, is immediately followed by Mass, the whole celebration may begin in the same way, either with the introductory verse and hymn for the hour, especially on weekdays, or with the entrance song, procession, and celebrant's greeting, especially on Sundays and holydays; one of the introductory rites is thus omitted.

The psalmody of the hour follows as usual up to, but excluding, the reading. After the psalmody the penitential rite is omitted and, as circumstances suggest, the Kyrie; the Gloria then follows, if required by the rubrics, and the celebrant says the opening prayer of the Mass.

96. Evening prayer, celebrated immediately before Mass, is joined to it in the same way as morning prayer. Evening prayer I of solemnities, Sundays, or feasts of the Lord falling on Sundays may not be celebrated until after Mass of the preceding day or Saturday.

97. When a daytime hour or evening prayer follows Mass, the Mass is celebrated in the usual way up to and including the prayer after communion.

When the prayer after communion has been said, the psalmody of the hour begins without introduction. At the daytime hour, after the psalmody the short reading is omitted and the prayer is said at once and the dismissal takes place as at Mass. At evening prayer, after the psalmody the short reading is omitted and the Canticle of Mary with its antiphon follows at once; the intercessions and the Lord's Prayer are omitted; the concluding prayer follows, then the blessing of the congregation.

98. Apart from Christmas eve, the combining of Mass with the office of readings is normally excluded, since the Mass already has its own cycle of readings, to be kept distinct from any other. But if by way of exception, it should be necessary to join the two, then immediately after the second reading from the office, with its responsory, the rest is omitted and the Mass begins with the Gloria, if it is called for; otherwise the Mass begins with the opening prayer.

99. If the office of readings comes immediately before another hour of the office, then the appropriate hymn for that hour may be sung at the beginning of the office of readings. At the end of the office of readings the prayer and conclusion are omitted and in the hour following the introductory verse with the Glory to the Father is omitted.

Chapter III: Different Elements in the Liturgy of the Hours
I. Psalms and Their Connection With Christian Prayer

100. In the liturgy of the hours the Church in large measure prays through the magnificent songs that the Old Testament authors composed under the inspiration of the Holy Spirit. The origin of these verses gives them great power to raise the mind to God, to inspire devotion, to evoke gratitude in times of favor, and to bring consolation and courage in times of trial.

101. The psalms, however, are only a foreshadowing of the fullness of time that came to pass in Christ the Lord and that is the source of the power of the Church's prayer. Hence, while the Christian people are all agreed on the supreme value to be placed on the psalms, they can sometimes experience difficulty in making this inspired poetry their own prayer.

102. Yet the Holy Spirit, under whose inspiration the psalms were written, is always present by his grace to those believers who use them with good will. But more is necessary: the faithful must "improve their understanding of the Bible, especially of the psalms,"[1] according to their individual capacity, so that they may understand how and by what method they can truly pray through the psalms.

103. The psalms are not readings or prose prayers, but poems of praise. They can on occasion be recited as readings, but from their literary genre they are properly called Tehillim ("songs of praise") in Hebrew and psalmoi ("songs to be sung to the lyre") in Greek. In fact, all the psalms have a musical quality that determines their correct style of delivery. Thus even when a psalm is recited and not sung or is said silently in private, its musical character should govern its use. A psalm does present a text to the minds of the people, but its aim is to move the heart of those singing it or listening to it and also of those accompanying it "on the lyre and harp."

104. To sing the psalms with understanding, then, is to meditate on them verse by verse, with the heart always ready to respond in the way the Holy Spirit desires. The one who inspired the psalmist will also be present to those who in faith and love are ready to receive his grace. For this reason the singing of psalms, though it demands the reverence owed to God's majesty, should be the expression of a joyful spirit and a loving heart, in keeping with their character as sacred poetry and divine song and above all with the freedom of the children of God.

105. Often the words of a psalm help us to pray with greater ease and fervor, whether in thanksgiving and joyful praise of God or in prayer for help in the throes of suffering. But difficulties may arise, especially when the psalm is not addressed directly to God. The psalmist is a poet and often addresses the people as he recalls Israel's history; sometimes he addresses others, including subrational creatures. He even represents the words as being spoken by God himself and individual people, including, as in Ps 2, God's enemies. This shows that a psalm is

a different kind of prayer from a prayer or collect composed by the Church. Moreover, it is in keeping with the poetic and musical character of the psalms that they do not necessarily address God but are sung in God's presence. Thus St. Benedict's instruction: "Let us reflect on what it means to be in the sight of God and his angels, and let us so stand in his presence that our minds are in harmony with our voices."[2]

106. In praying the psalms we should open our hearts to the different attitudes they express, varying with the literary genre to which each belongs (psalms of grief, trust, gratitude, etc.) and to which biblical scholars rightly attach great importance.

107. Staying close to the meaning of the words, the person who prays the psalms looks for the significance of the text for the human life of the believer.

It is clear that each psalm was written in its own individual circumstances, which the titles given for each psalm in the Hebrew psalter are meant to indicate. But whatever its historical origin, each psalm has its own meaning, which we cannot overlook even in our own day.

Though the psalms originated very many centuries ago among an Eastern people, they express accurately the pain and hope, the unhappiness and trust of people of every age and country, and sing above all of faith in God, of revelation, and of redemption.

108. Those who pray the psalms in the liturgy of the hours do so not so much in their own name as in the name of the entire Body of Christ. This consideration does away with the problem of a possible discrepancy between personal feelings and the sentiments a psalm is expressing: for example, when a person feels sad and the psalm is one of joy or when a person feels happy and the psalm is one of mourning. Such a problem is readily solved in private prayer, which allows for the choice of a psalm suited to personal feelings. The divine office, however, is not private; the cycle of psalms is public, in the name of the Church, even for those who may be reciting an hour alone. Those who pray the psalms in the name of the Church nevertheless can always find a reason for joy or sadness, for the saying of the Apostle applies in this case also: "Rejoice with the joyful and weep with those who weep" (Rom 12:15). In this way human frailty, wounded by self-love, is healed in proportion to the love that makes the heart match the voice that prays the psalms.[3]

109. Those who pray the psalms in the name of the Church should be aware of their full sense (sensus plenus), especially their Messianic sense, which was the reason for the Church's introduction of the psalter into its prayer. This Messianic sense was fully revealed in the New Testament and indeed was affirmed publicly by Christ the Lord in person when he said to the apostles: "All that is written about me in the law of Moses and the prophets and the psalms must be fulfilled" (Lk 24:44). The best-known example of this Messianic sense is the dialogue in Matthew's Gospel on the Messiah as Son of David and David's Lord,[4] where Ps 110 is interpreted as Messianic.

Following this line of thought, the Fathers of the Church saw the whole psalter as a prophecy of Christ and the Church and explained it in this sense; for the same reason the psalms have been chosen for use in the liturgy. Though somewhat contrived interpretations were at times proposed, in general the Fathers and the liturgy itself had the right to hear in the singing of the psalms the voice of Christ crying out to the Father or of the Father conversing with the Son; indeed, they also recognized in the psalms the voice of the Church, the apostles, and the martyrs. This method of interpretation also flourished in the Middle Ages; in many manuscripts of the period the Christological meaning of each psalm was set before those praying by means of the caption prefixed. A Christological meaning is by no means confined to the recognized Messianic psalms but is given also to many others. Some of these interpretations are doubtless Christological only in an accommodated sense, but they have the support of the Church's tradition.

On the great feasts especially, the choice of psalms is often based on their Christological meaning and antiphons taken from these psalms are frequently used to throw light on this meaning.

II. Antiphons and Other Aids to Praying the Psalms

110. In the Latin tradition of psalmody three elements have greatly contributed to an understanding of the psalms and their use as Christian prayer: the captions, the psalm-prayers, and in particular the antiphons.

111. In the psalter of The Liturgy of the Hours a caption is given for each psalm to explain its meaning and its import for the personal life of the believer. These captions are intended only as an aid to prayer. A quotation from the New Testament or the Fathers of the Church is added to foster prayer in the light of Christ's new revelation; it is an invitation to pray the psalms in their Christological meaning.

112. Psalm-prayers for each psalm are given in the supplement to The Liturgy of the Hours as an aid to understanding them in a predominantly Christian way. An ancient tradition provides a model for their use: after the psalm a period of silence is observed, then the prayer gives a resume and resolution of the thoughts and aspirations of those praying the psalms.

113. Even when the liturgy of the hours is recited, not sung, each psalm retains its own antiphon, which is also to be said in private recitation. The antiphons help to bring out the literary genre of the psalm; they highlight some theme that may otherwise not attract the attention it deserves; they suggest an individual tone in a psalm, varying with different contexts: indeed, as long as farfetched accommodated senses are avoided, antiphons are of great value in helping toward an understanding of the typological meaning or the meaning appropriate to the feast; they can also add pleasure and variety to the recitation of the psalms.

114. The antiphons in the psalter have been designed to lend themselves to vernacular translation and to repetition after each strophe, in accordance with no. 125. When the office of Ordinary Time is recited, not sung, the quotations printed with the psalms may be used in place of these antiphons (see no. 111).

115. When a psalm may be divided because of its length into several sections within one and the same hour, an antiphon is given for each section. This is to provide variety, especially when the hour is sung, and also to help toward a better understanding of the riches of the psalm. Still, it is permissible to say or sing the complete psalm without interruption, using only the first antiphon.

116. Proper antiphons are given for each of the psalms of morning prayer and evening prayer during the Easter triduum, on the days within the octaves of Easter and Christmas, on the Sundays of the seasons of Advent, Christmas, Lent, and Easter, on the weekdays of Holy Week and the Easter season, and from the 17th to the 24th of December.

117. On solemnities proper antiphons are given for the office of readings, morning prayer, the daytime hours, and evening prayer; if not, the antiphons are taken from the common. On feasts the same applies to the office of readings and to morning prayer and evening prayer.

118. Any memorials of the saints that have proper antiphons retain them (see no. 235).

119. The antiphons for the Canticles of Zechariah and of Mary are taken, during Ordinary Time, from the Proper of Seasons, if they are given there; if not, they are taken from the current week and day of the psalter. On solemnities and feasts they are taken from the proper if they are given there; if not, they are taken from the common. On memorials without proper antiphons the antiphon may be taken at will either from the common or from the current week.

120. During the Easter season Alleluia is added to all antiphons, unless it would clash with the meaning of a particular antiphon.

III. Ways of Singing the Psalms

121. Different psalms may be sung in different ways for a fuller grasp of their spiritual meaning and beauty. The choice of ways is dictated by the literary genre or length of each psalm, by the language used, whether Latin or the vernacular, and especially by the kind of celebration, whether individual, with a group, or with a congregation. The reason for using psalms is not the establishment of a fixed amount of prayer but their own variety and the character proper to each.

122. The psalms are sung or said in one of three ways, according to the different usages established in tradition or experience: directly (in diredum), that is, all sing the entire psalm, or antiphonally, that is, two choirs or sections of the congregation sing alternate verses or strophes, or responsorially.

123. At the beginning of each psalm its own antiphon is always to be recited, as noted in nos. 113-120. At the end of the psalm the practice of concluding with the Glory to the Father and As it was in the beginning is retained. This is the fitting conclusion endorsed by tradition and it gives to Old Testament prayer a note of praise and a Christological and Trinitarian sense. The antiphon may be repeated at the end of the psalm.

124. When longer psalms occur, sections are marked in the psalter that divide the parts in such a way as to keep the threefold structure of the hour; but great care has been taken not to distort the meaning of the psalm.

It is useful to observe this division, especially in a choral celebration in Latin; the Glory to the Father is added at the end of each section.

It is permissible, however, either to keep this traditional way or to pause between the different sections of the same psalm or to recite the whole psalm and its antiphon as a single unit without a break.

125. In addition, when the literary genre of a psalm suggests it, the divisions into strophes are marked in order that, especially when the psalm is sung in the vernacular, the antiphons may be repeated after each strophe; in this case the Glory to the Father need be said only at the end of the psalm.

IV. Plan for the Distribution of the Psalms in the Office

126. The psalms are distributed over a four-week cycle in such a way that very few psalms are omitted, while some, traditionally more important, occur more frequently than others; morning prayer and evening prayer as well as night prayer have been assigned psalms appropriate to these hours.[5]

127. Since morning prayer and evening prayer are particularly designed for celebration with a congregation, the psalms chosen for them are those more suited to this purpose.

128. For night prayer the norm given in no. 88 has been followed.

129. For Sunday, including its office of readings and daytime prayer, the psalms chosen are those that tradition has particularly singled out as expressions of the paschal mystery. Certain psalms of a penitential character or connected with the passion are assigned to Friday.

130. Three psalms (78, 105, and 106) are reserved for the seasons of Advent, Christmas, Lent, and Easter, because they throw a special light on the Old Testament history of salvation as the forerunner of its fulfillment in the New.

131. Three psalms (58, 83, and 109) have been omitted from the psalter cycle because of their curses; in the same way, some verses have been omitted from certain psalms, as noted at the head of each. The reason for the omission is a certain psychological difficulty, even though the psalms of imprecation are in fact used as prayer in the New Testament, for example, Rv 6:10, and in no sense to encourage the use of curses.

132. Psalms too long to be included in one hour of the office are assigned to the same hour on different days so that they may be recited in full by those who do not usually say other hours. Thus Ps 119 is divided in keeping with its own internal structure and is spread over twenty-two days during daytime prayer, because tradition has assigned it to the day hours.

133. The four-week cycle of the psalter is coordinated with the liturgical year in such a way that on the First Sunday of Advent, the First Sunday in Ordinary Time, the First Sunday of Lent, and Easter Sunday the cycle is always begun again with Week I (others being omitted when necessary).

After Pentecost, when the psalter cycle follows the series of weeks in Ordinary Time, it begins with the week indicated in the Proper of Seasons at the beginning of the appropriate week in Ordinary Time.

134. On solemnities and feasts, during the Easter triduum, and on the days within the octaves of Easter and Christmas, proper psalms are assigned to the office of readings from those with a tradition of use at these times and their relevance is generally highlighted by the choice of antiphon. This is also the case at daytime prayer on certain solemnities of the Lord and during the octave of Easter. At morning prayer the psalms and canticle are taken from the Sunday of the Week I of the psalter. On solemnities the psalms at evening prayer I are taken from the Laudate Psalms, following an ancient custom. At evening prayer II on solemnities and at evening prayer on feasts the psalms and canticle are proper. At daytime prayer on solemnities (except those already mentioned and those falling on Sunday) the psalms are taken from the Gradual Psalms; at daytime prayer on feasts the psalms are those of the current week and day of the psalter.

135. In all other cases the psalms are taken from the current week and day of the psalter, unless there are proper antiphons or proper psalms.

V. Canticles From the Old and New Testaments

136. At morning prayer between the first and the second psalm a canticle from the Old Testament is inserted, in accordance with custom. In addition to the series handed down from the ancient Roman tradition and the other series introduced into the breviary by St. Pius X, several other canticles have been added to the psalter from different books of the Old Testament, in order that each weekday of the four-week cycle may have its own proper canticle and on Sunday the two sections of the Canticle of the Three Children may be alternated.

137. At evening prayer, after the two psalms, a canticle of the New Testament is inserted, from the letters of the apostles or the Book of Revelation. Seven canticles are given for each week of the four-week cycle, one for each day. On the Sundays of Lent, however, in place of the Alleluia Canticle from the Book of Revelation, the canticle is from the First Letter of Peter. In addition, on the solemnity of the Epiphany and the feast of the Transfiguration the canticle is from the First Letter to Timothy; this is indicated in those offices.

138. The gospel Canticles of Zechariah, of Mary, and of Simeon are to be treated with the same solemnity and dignity as are customary at the proclamation of the gospel itself.

139. Both psalmody and readings are arranged in keeping with the received rule of tradition that the Old Testament is read first, then the writings of the apostles, and finally the gospel.

VI. Readings From Sacred Scripture
Reading of Sacred Scripture in General

140. The reading of sacred Scripture, which, following an ancient tradition, takes place publicly in the liturgy, is to have special importance for all Christians, not only in the celebration of the eucharist but also in the divine office. The reason is that this reading is not the result of individual choice or devotion but is the planned decision of the Church itself, in order that in the course of the year the Bride of Christ may unfold the mystery of Christ "from his incarnation and birth until his ascension, the day of Pentecost, and the expectation of blessed hope and of the Lord's return."[6] In addition, the reading of sacred Scripture in the liturgical celebration is always accompanied by prayer in order that the reading may have greater effect and that, in turn, prayer - especially the praying of the psalms - may gain fuller understanding and become more fervent and devout because of the reading.

141. In the liturgy of the hours there is a longer reading of sacred Scripture and a shorter reading.

142. The longer reading, optional at morning prayer and evening prayer, is described in no. 46.

Cycle of Scripture Readings in the Office of Readings

143. The cycle of readings from sacred Scripture in the office of readings takes into account both those special seasons during which by an ancient tradition particular books are to be read and the cycle of readings at Mass. The liturgy of the hours is thus coordinated with the Mass in

such a way that the scriptural readings in the office complement the readings at Mass and so provide a complete view of the history of salvation.

144. Without prejudice to the exception noted in no. 73, there are no readings from the Gospel in the liturgy of the hours, since in the Mass each year the Gospel is read in its entirety.

145. There are two cycles of biblical readings. The first is a one-year cycle and is incorporated into The Liturgy of the Hours; the second, given in the supplement for optional use, is a two-year cycle, like the cycle of readings at weekday Masses in Ordinary Time.

146. The two-year cycle of readings for the liturgy of the hours is so arranged that each year there are readings from nearly all the books of sacred Scripture as well as longer and more difficult texts that are not suitable for inclusion in the Mass. The New Testament as a whole is read each year, partly in the Mass, partly in the liturgy of the hours; but for the Old Testament books a selection has been made of those parts that are of greater importance for the understanding of the history of salvation and for deepening devotion.

The complementarity between the readings in the liturgy of the hours and in the Mass in no way assigns the same texts to the same days or spreads the same books over the same seasons. This would leave the liturgy of the hours with the less important passages and upset the sequence of texts. Rather this complementarity necessarily demands that the same book be used in the Mass and in the liturgy of the hours in alternate years or that, if it is read in the same year, there be some interval in between.

147. During Advent, following an ancient tradition, passages are read from Isaiah in a semicontinuous sequence, alternating in a two-year cycle. In addition, the Book of Ruth and certain prophecies from Micah are read. Since there are special readings from 17 to 24 December (both dates included), readings for the Third Week of Advent which fall on these dates are omitted.

148. From 29 December until 5 January the readings for Year I are taken from the Letter to the Colossians (which considers the incarnation of the Lord within the context of the whole history of salvation) and the readings for Year II are taken from the Song of Songs (which foreshadows the union of God and humanity in Christ): "God the Father prepared a wedding feast for God his Son when he united him with human nature in the womb of the Virgin, when he who is God before all ages willed that his Son should become man at the end of the ages.[7]

149. From 7 January until the Saturday after the Epiphany the readings are eschatological texts from Isaiah 60-66 and Baruch. Readings remaining unused are omitted for that year.

150. During Lent the readings for the first year are passages from Deuteronomy and the Letter to the Hebrews. Those for the second year review the history of salvation from Exodus, Leviticus, and Numbers. The Letter to the Hebrews interprets the Old Covenant in the light of the paschal mystery of Christ. A passage from the same letter, on Christ's sacrifice (Heb 9:11-28), is read on Good Friday; another, on the Lord's rest (Heb 4:1-16), is read on Holy Saturday. On the other days of Holy Week the readings in Year I are the third and fourth Songs of the Servant of the Lord and extracts from Lamentations; in Year II the prophet Jeremiah is read, as a type of Christ in his passion.

151. During the Easter season, apart from the First and Second Sundays of Easter and the solemnities of the Ascension and Pentecost, there are the traditional readings from the First Letter of Peter, the Book of Revelation, and the Letters of John (for Year I), and from the Acts of the Apostles (for Year II).

152. From the Monday after the feast of the Baptism of the Lord until Lent and from the Monday after Pentecost until Advent there is a continuous series of thirty-four weeks in Ordinary Time.

This series is interrupted from Ash Wednesday until Pentecost. On the Monday after Pentecost Sunday the cycle of readings in Ordinary Time is resumed, beginning with the week after the one interrupted because of Lent; the reading assigned to the Sunday is omitted.

In years with only thirty-three weeks in Ordinary Time, the week immediately following Pentecost is dropped, in order to retain the readings of the last weeks which are eschatological readings.

The books of the Old Testament are arranged so as to follow the history of salvation: God reveals himself in the history of his people as he leads and enlightens them in progressive stages. This is why prophetic books are read along with the historical books, but with due consideration of the period in which the prophets lived and taught. Hence, the cycle of readings from the Old Testament contains, in Year I, the historical books and prophetic utterances from the Book of Joshua as far as, and including, the time of the exile. In Year II, after the readings from Genesis (read before Lent), the history of salvation is resumed after the exile up to the time of the Maccabees. Year II includes the later prophets, the wisdom literature, and the narratives in Esther, Tobit, and Judith.

The letters of the apostles not read at special times are distributed through the year in a way that takes into account the readings at Mass and the chronological order in which these letters were written.

153. The one-year cycle is shortened in such a way that each year special passages from sacred Scripture are read, but in correlation with the two-year cycle of readings at Mass, to which it is intended to be complementary.

154. Proper readings are assigned for solemnities and feasts; otherwise the readings are taken from the respective Common of Saints.

155. As far as possible, each passage read keeps to a certain unity. In order therefore to strike a balance in length (otherwise difficult to achieve in view of the different literary genres of the books), some verses are occasionally omitted, though omissions are always noted. But it is permissible and commendable to read the complete passage from an approved text.

Short Readings

156. The short readings or "chapters" (capitula) are referred to in no. 45, which describes their importance in the liturgy of the hours. They have been chosen to give clear and concise expression to a theme or an exhortation. Care has also been taken to ensure variety.

157. Accordingly, four weekly series of short readings have been composed for Ordinary Time. They are incorporated into the psalter in such a way that the reading changes during the four weeks. There are also weekly series for the seasons of Advent, Christmas, Lent, and Easter, In addition there are proper short readings for solemnities, feasts, and some memorials, as well as a one-week series for night prayer.

158. The following determined the choice of short readings:
in accordance with tradition, exclusion of the Gospels;
respect for the special character of Sunday, or even of Friday, and of the individual hours;
use only of the New Testament for the readings at evening prayer, following as they do a New Testament canticle.

VII. Readings From the Fathers and Church Writers

159. In keeping with the tradition of the Roman Church the office of readings has, after the biblical reading, a reading from the Fathers or church writers, with a responsory, unless there is to be a reading relating to a saint (see nos. 228-239).

160. Texts for this reading are given from the writings of the Fathers and doctors of the Church and from other ecclesiastical writers of the Eastern and Western Church. Pride of place is given to the Fathers because of their distinctive authority in the Church.

161. In addition to the readings that The Liturgy of the Hours assigns to each day, the optional lectionary supplies a larger collection, in order that the treasures of the Church's tradition may be more widely available to those who pray the liturgy of the hours. Everyone is free to take the second reading either from The Liturgy of the Hours or from the optional lectionary.

162. Further the conferences of bishops may prepare additional texts adapted to the traditions and culture of their own region,[8] for inclusion in the optional lectionary as a supplement. These texts are to be taken from the works of Catholic writers, outstanding for their teaching and holiness of life.

163. The purpose of the second reading is principally to provide for meditation on the word of God as received by the Church in its tradition. The Church has always been convinced of the need to teach the word of God authentically to believers, so that "the line of interpretation regarding the prophets and apostles may be guided by an ecclesial and catholic understanding."[9]

164. By constant use of the writings handed down by the universal tradition of the Church, those who read them are led to a deeper reflection on sacred Scripture and to a relish and love for it. The writings of the Fathers are an outstanding witness to the contemplation of the word of God over the centuries by the Bride of the incarnate Word: the Church, "possessing the counsel and spirit of its Bridegroom and God,"[10] is always seeking to attain a more profound understanding of the sacred Scriptures.

165. The reading of the Fathers leads Christians to an understanding also of the liturgical seasons and feasts. In addition, it gives them access to the priceless spiritual treasures that form the unique patrimony of the Church and provide a firm foundation for the spiritual life and a rich source for increasing devotion. Preachers of God's word also have at hand each day superb examples of sacred preaching.

VIII. Readings in Honor of Saints

166. The "hagiographical" readings or readings in honor of saints are either texts from a Father of the Church or another ecclesiastical writer, referring specifically or rightly applicable to the saint being commemorated, or the readings are texts from the saint's own writings, or are biographical.

167. Those who compose particular propers for saints must ensure historical accuracy[11] as well as genuine spiritual benefit for those who will read or hear the readings about the saints. Anything that merely excites amazement should be carefully avoided. Emphasis should be given to the individual spiritual characteristics of the saints, in a way suited to modern conditions; stress should also be laid on their contribution to the life and spirituality of the Church.

168. A short biographical note, simply giving historical facts and a brief sketch of the saint's life, is provided at the head of the reading. This is for information only and is not for reading aloud.

IX. Responsories

169. Its responsory follows the biblical reading in the office of readings. The text of this responsory has been drawn from traditional sources or freshly composed, in order to throw new light on the passage just read, put it in the context of the history of salvation, lead from the Old Testament to the New, turn what has been read into prayer and contemplation, or provide pleasant variety by its poetic beauty.

170. A pertinent responsory also follows the second reading. It is less closely linked with the text of the reading, however, and thus makes for a greater freedom in meditation.

171. The responsories and the portions to be repeated even in private recitation therefore retain their value. The customary reprise of the whole responsory may be omitted when the office is not being sung, unless the sense requires this repetition.

172. In a similar but simpler way, the responsory at morning prayer, evening prayer, and night prayer (see nos. 49 and 89), and the verse at daytime prayer, are linked to the short reading as a kind of acclamation, enabling God's word to enter more deeply into the mind and heart of the one listening or reading.

X. Hymns and Other Nonbiblical Songs

173. A very ancient tradition gives hymns the place in the office that they still retain.[12] By their mystical and poetic character they are specifically designed for God's praise. But they also are an element for the people; in fact more often than the other parts of the office the hymns bring out the proper theme of individual hours or feasts and incline and draw the spirit to a devout celebration. The beauty of their language often adds to this power. Furthermore, in the office hymns are the main poetic element created by the Church.

174. A hymn follows the traditional rule of ending with a doxology, usually addressed to the same divine person as the hymn itself.

175. In the office for Ordinary Time, to ensure variety, a twofold cycle of hymns is given for each hour, for use in alternate weeks.

176. In addition, a twofold cycle of hymns has been introduced into the office of readings for Ordinary Time, one for use at night and the other for use during the day.

177. New hymns can be set to traditional melodies of the same rhythm and meter.

178. For vernacular celebration, the conferences of bishops may adapt the Latin hymns to suit the character of their own language and introduce fresh compositions,[13] provided these are in complete harmony with the spirit of the hour, season, or feast. Great care must be taken not to allow popular songs that have no artistic merit and are not in keeping with the dignity of the liturgy.

XI. Intercessions, Lord's Prayer, and Concluding Prayer
The Prayers or Intercessions at Morning and Evening Prayer

179. The liturgy of the hours is a celebration in praise of God. Yet Jewish and Christian tradition does not separate prayer of petition from praise of God; often enough, praise turns somehow to petition. The Apostle Paul exhorts us to offer prayers, petitions, intercessions, and thanksgiving for all: for kings and all in authority, so that we may be able to live quiet and peaceful lives in all reverence and decency, for this is good and acceptable before God our Savior, who wishes all to be saved and to come to the knowledge of the truth" (1Tm 2:1-4). The Fathers of the Church frequently explained this as an exhortation to offer prayer in the morning and in the evening.[14]

180. The general intercessions, restored in the Mass of the Roman Rite, have their place also at evening prayer, though in a different fashion, as will be explained later.

181. Since traditionally morning prayer puts the whole day in God's hands, there are invocations at morning prayer for the purpose of commending or consecrating the day to God.

182. The word preces covers both the intercessions at evening prayer and the invocations for dedicating the day to God at morning prayer.

183. In the interest of variety and especially of giving fuller expression to the many needs of the Church and of all people in relation to different states of life, groups, persons, circumstances, and seasons, different intercessory formularies are given for each day of the four-week psalter in Ordinary Time and for the special seasons of the liturgical year, as well as for certain feasts.

184. In addition, the conferences of bishops have the right to adapt the formularies given in the book of the liturgy of the hours and also to approve new ones,[15] in accordance with the norms that follow.

185. As in the Lord's Prayer, petitions should be linked with praise of God and acknowledgment of his glory or with a reference to the history of salvation.

186. In the intercessions at evening prayer the last intention is always for the dead.

187. Since the liturgy of the hours is above all the prayer of the whole Church for the whole Church, indeed for the salvation of the whole world,[16] universal intentions should take precedence over all others, namely, for: the Church and its ministers; secular authorities; the poor, the sick, and the sorrowful; the needs of the whole world, that is, peace and other intentions of this kind.

188. It is permissible, however, to include particular intentions at both morning prayer and evening prayer.

189. The intercessions in the office are so arranged that they can be adapted for celebration with a congregation or in a small community or for private recitation.

190. The intercessions in a celebration with a congregation or in common are thus introduced by a brief invitation, given by the priest or minister and designating the single response that the congregation is to repeat after each petition.

191. Further, the intentions are phrased as direct addresses to God and thus are suitable for both common celebration and private recitation.

192. Each intention consists of two parts; the second may be used as an alternative response.
193. Different methods can therefore be used for the intercessions. The priest or minister may say both parts of the intention and the congregation respond with a uniform response or a silent pause, or the priest or minister may say only the first part of the intention and the congregation respond with the second part.

Lord's Prayer

194. In accord with ancient tradition, the Lord's Prayer has a place suited to its dignity, namely, after the intercessions at morning prayer and evening prayer, the hours most often celebrated with the people.
195. Henceforth, therefore, the Lord's Prayer will be said with solemnity on three occasions during the day: at Mass, at morning prayer, and at evening prayer.
196. The Lord's Prayer is said by all after a brief introduction, if this seems opportune.

Concluding Prayer

197. The concluding prayer at the end marks the completion of an entire hour. In a celebration in public and with a congregation, it belongs by tradition to a priest or deacon to say this prayer.[17]
198. In the office of readings, this prayer is as a rule the prayer proper to the day. At night prayer, the prayer is always the prayer given in the psalter for that hour.
199. The concluding prayer at morning prayer and evening prayer is taken from the proper on Sundays, on the weekdays of the seasons of Advent, Christmas, Lent, and Easter, and on solemnities, feasts, and memorials. On weekdays in Ordinary Time the prayer is the one given in the four-week psalter to express the character of these two hours.
200. The concluding prayer at daytime prayer is taken from the proper on Sundays, on the weekdays of the seasons of Advent, Christmas, Lent, and Easter, and on solemnities and feasts. On other days the prayers are those that express the character of the particular hour. These are given in the four-week psalter.

XII. Sacred Silence

201. It is a general principle that care should be taken in liturgical services to see that "at the proper times all observe a reverent silence."[18] An opportunity for silence should therefore be provided in the celebration of the liturgy of the hours.
202. In order to receive in our hearts the full sound of the voice of the Holy Spirit and to unite our personal prayer more closely with the word of God and the public voice of the Church, it is permissible, as occasion offers and prudence suggests, to have an interval of silence. It may come either after the repetition of the antiphon at the end of the psalm, in the traditional way, especially if the psalm-prayer is to be said after the pause (see no. 112), or after the short or longer readings, either before or after the responsory.
Care must be taken to avoid the kind of silence that would disturb the structure of the office or annoy and weary those taking part.
203. In individual recitation there is even greater freedom to pause in meditation on some text that moves the spirit; the office does not on this account lose its public character.

CHAPTER IV: VARIOUS CELEBRATIONS THROUGHOUT THE YEAR
I. Mysteries of the Lord
Sunday

204. The office of Sunday begins with evening prayer I, which is taken entirely from the four-week psalter, except those parts that are marked as proper.
205. When a feast of the Lord is celebrated on Sunday, it has a proper evening prayer I.
206. The way to celebrate Sunday vigils, as circumstances suggest, has been discussed in no. 73.
207. It is of great advantage to celebrate, when possible, at least evening prayer with the people, in keeping with a very ancient tradition.[1]

Easter Triduum

208. For the Easter triduum the office is celebrated in the way set forth in the Proper of Seasons.

209. Those who take part in the evening Mass of the Lord's Supper or the celebration of the Lord's passion on Good Friday do not say evening prayer on either day.

210. On Good Friday and Holy Saturday the office of readings should be celebrated publicly with the people before morning prayer, as far as this is possible.

211. Night prayer for Holy Saturday is said only by those who are not present at the Easter Vigil.

212. The Easter Vigil takes the place of the office of readings. Those not present at the solemn celebration of the Vigil should therefore read at least four of its readings with the chants and prayers. It is desirable that these be the readings from Exodus, Ezekiel, St. Paul, and from the Gospel. The Te Deum follows, then the prayer of the day.

213. Morning prayer for Easter Sunday is said by all. It is fitting that evening prayer be celebrated in a more solemn way to mark the ending of so holy a day and to commemorate the occasions when the Lord showed himself to his disciples. Great care should be taken to maintain, where it exists, the particular tradition of celebrating evening prayer on Easter Sunday in honor of baptism. During this there is a procession to the font as the psalms are being sung.

Easter Season

214. The liturgy of the hours takes on a paschal character from the acclamation, Alleluia that concludes most antiphons (see no. 120), from the hymns, antiphons, and special intercessions, and from the proper readings assigned to each hour.

Christmas Season

215. On Christmas eve it is fitting that by means of the office of readings, a solemn vigil be celebrated before Mass. Night prayer is not said by those present at this vigil.

216. Morning prayer on Christmas Day is said as a rule before the Mass at Dawn.

Other Solemnities and Feasts of the Lord

217. In arranging the office for solemnities and feasts of the Lord, what is said in nos. 225-233 should be observed, with any necessary changes.

II. The Saints

218. The celebrations of the saints are arranged so that they do not take precedence over those feast days and special seasons that commemorate the mysteries of salvation.[2] Nor are they allowed to break up the sequence of psalms and biblical readings or to give rise to undue repetitions. At the same time, the plan makes proper provision for the rightful honoring of the individual saints. These principles form the basis for the reform of the calendar, carried out by order of Vatican Council II, and for the plan for celebrating the saints in the liturgy of the hours that is described in the following paragraphs.

219. Celebrations in honor of the saints are either solemnities, feasts, or memorials.

220. Memorials are either obligatory memorials or, when not so classified, optional memorials. In deciding on the merits of celebrating an optional memorial in an office to be celebrated with the people or in common, account should be taken of the general good or of the genuine devotion of the congregation, not simply that of the person presiding.

221. When more than one optional memorial falls on the same day, only one may be celebrated; the rest are omitted.

222. Only solemnities are transferred, in accordance with the rubrics.

223. The norms that follow apply to the saints entered in the General Roman Calendar and to those with a place in particular calendars.

224. Where proper parts are not given, they are supplied from the respective Common of Saints.

1. ARRANGEMENT OF THE OFFICE FOR SOLEMNITIES

225. Solemnities have an evening prayer I on the preceding day.

226. At evening prayer I and II, the hymn, the antiphons, the short reading with its responsory, and the concluding prayer are proper. Where anything proper is missing, it is supplied from the common.

In keeping with an ancient tradition, at evening prayer I both psalms are as a rule taken from the Laudate Psalms (Ps 113, 117, 135, 146, 147A, 147B). The New Testament canticle is noted in its appropriate place. At evening prayer II the psalms and canticles are proper; the intercessions are either proper or from the common.

227. At morning prayer, the hymn, the antiphons, the short reading with its responsory, and the concluding prayer are proper. Where anything proper is missing, it is supplied from the common. The psalms are to be taken from the Sunday of Week I of the four-week psalter; the intercessions are either proper or from the common.

228. In the office of readings, everything is proper: the hymn, the antiphons and psalms, the readings and the responsories. The first reading is from Scripture; the second is about the saint. In the case of a saint with a purely local cult and without special texts even in the local proper, everything is taken from the common.

At the end of the office of readings the Te Deum and the proper prayer are said.

229. At daytime prayer, the hymn of the weekday is used, unless other directions are given. The psalms are from the Gradual Psalms with a proper antiphon. On Sundays the psalms are taken from the Sunday of Week I of the four-week psalter and the short reading and concluding prayer are proper. But on certain solemnities of the Lord there are special psalms.

230. At night prayer, everything is said as on Sundays, after evening prayer I and II respectively.

2. ARRANGEMENT OF THE OFFICE FOR FEASTS

231. Feasts have no evening prayer I, except those feasts of the Lord that fall on a Sunday. At the office of readings, at morning prayer, and at evening prayer, all is done as on solemnities.

232. At daytime prayer, the hymn of the weekday is used. The weekday psalms with their antiphons are said, unless a special reason or tradition requires a proper antiphon; this will be indicated as the case occurs. The reading and concluding prayer are proper.

233. Night prayer is said as on ordinary days.

3. ARRANGEMENT OF THE OFFICE FOR MEMORIALS

234. In the arrangement of the office there is no difference between obligatory and optional memorials, except in the case of optional memorials falling during privileged seasons.

Memorials During Ordinary Time

235. In the office of readings, at morning prayer, and at evening prayer:

a. the psalms and their antiphons are taken from the current week and day, unless there are proper antiphons or proper psalms, which is indicated as the case occurs;

b. the antiphon at the invitatory, the hymn, the short reading, the antiphons at the Canticles of Zechariah and of Mary, and the intercessions must be those of the saint if these are given in the proper; otherwise, they are taken either from the common or from the current week and day;

c. the concluding prayer from the office of the saint is to be said;

d. in the office of readings, the Scripture reading with its responsory is from the current cycle. The second reading is about the saint, with a proper responsory or one taken from the common; if there is no proper reading, the patristic reading for the day is used. The Te Deum is not said.

236. At daytime prayer and night prayer, all is from the weekday and nothing is from the office of the saint.

Memorials During Privileged Seasons

237. On Sundays, solemnities, and feasts, on Ash Wednesday, during Holy Week, and during the octave of Easter, memorials that happen to fall on these days are disregarded.

238. On the weekdays from 17 to 24 December, during the octave of Christmas, and on the weekdays of Lent, no obligatory memorials are celebrated, even in particular calendars. When any happen to fall during Lent in a given year, they are treated as optional memorials.

239. During privileged seasons, if it is desired to celebrate the office of a saint on a day assigned to his or her memorial:

a. in the office of readings, after the patristic reading (with its responsory) from the Proper of Seasons, a proper reading about the saint (with its responsory) may follow, with the concluding prayer of the saint;

b. at morning prayer and evening prayer, the ending of the concluding prayer may be omitted and the saint's antiphon (from the proper or common) and prayer may be added.

Memorials of the Blessed Virgin Mary on Saturday

240. On Saturdays in Ordinary Time, when optional memorials are permitted, an optional memorial of the Blessed Virgin Mary may be celebrated in the same way as other memorials, with its own proper reading.

III. Calendar and Option to Choose an Office or Part of an Office
Calendar to be Followed

241. The office in choir and in common is to be celebrated according to the proper calendar of the diocese, of the religious family, or of the individual churches.[3] Members of religious institutes join with the community of the local Church in celebrating the dedication of the cathedral and the feasts of the principal patrons of the place and of the wider geographical region in which they live.[4]

242. When clerics or religious who are obliged under any title to pray the divine office join in an office celebrated in common according to a calendar or rite different from their own, they fulfill their obligation in respect to the part of the office at which they are present.

243. In private celebration, the calendar of the place or the person's own calendar may be followed, except on proper solemnities and on proper feasts.[5]

Option to Choose an Office

244. On weekdays when an optional memorial is permitted, for a good reason the office of a saint listed on that day in the Roman Martyrology, or in an approved appendix to it, may be celebrated in the same way as other memorials (see nos. 234-239).

245. For a public cause or out of devotion, except on solemnities, the Sundays of the seasons of Advent, Lent, and Easter, Ash Wednesday, Holy Week, the octave of Easter, and 2 November, a votive office may be celebrated, in whole or in part: for example, on the occasion of a pilgrimage, a local feast, or the external solemnity of a saint.

Option to Choose Texts

246. In certain particular cases there is an option to choose texts different from those given for the day, provided there is no distortion of the general arrangement of each hour and the rules that follow are respected.

247. In the office for Sundays, solemnities, feasts of the Lord listed in the General Calendar, the weekdays of Lent and Holy Week, the days within the octaves of Easter and Christmas, and the weekdays from 17 to 24 December inclusive, it is never permissible to change the formularies that are proper or adapted to the celebration, such as antiphons, hymns, readings, responsories, prayers, and very often also the psalms.

In place of the Sunday psalms of the current week, there is an option to substitute the Sunday psalms of a different week, and, in the case of an office celebrated with a congregation, even other psalms especially chosen to lead the people step by step to an understanding of the psalms.

248. In the office of readings, the current cycle of sacred Scripture must always be respected. The Church's intent that "a more representative portion of the holy Scriptures will be read to the people in the course of a prescribed number of years"[6] applies also to the divine office. Therefore the cycle of readings from Scripture that is provided in the office of readings must not be set aside during the seasons of Advent, Christmas, Lent, and Easter. During Ordinary Time, however, on a particular day or for a few days in succession, it is permissible, for a good reason, to choose readings from those provided on other days or even other biblical readings - for example, on the occasion of retreats, pastoral gatherings, prayers for Christian unity, or other such events.

249. When the continuous reading is interrupted because of a solemnity or feast or special celebration, it is allowed during the same week, taking into account the readings for the whole week, either to combine the parts omitted with others or to decide which of the texts are to be preferred.

250. The office of readings also offers the option to choose, with a good reason, another reading from the same season, taken from The Liturgy of the Hours or the optional lectionary (no. 161), in preference to the second reading appointed for the day. On weekdays in Ordinary Time and, if it seems opportune, even in the seasons of Advent, Christmas, Lent, and Easter, the choice is open for a semicontinuous reading of the work of a Father of the Church, in harmony with the biblical and liturgical context.

251. The readings, prayers, songs, and intercessions appointed for the weekdays of a particular season may be used on other weekdays of the same season.

252. Everyone should be concerned to respect the complete cycle of the four-week psalter.[7] Still, for spiritual or pastoral advantage, the psalms appointed for a particular day may be replaced with others from the same hour of a different day. There are also circumstances occasionally arising when it is permissible to choose suitable psalms and other texts in the way done for a votive office.

CHAPTER V: RITES FOR CELEBRATION IN COMMON
I. Offices to be Carried Out

253. In the celebration of the liturgy of the hours, as in all other liturgical services, "each one, minister or layperson, who has an office to perform, should do all of, but only, those parts which pertain to that office by the nature of the rite and the principles of liturgy."[1]

254. When a bishop presides, especially in the cathedral, he should be attended by his college of priests and by ministers and the people should take a full and active part. A priest or deacon should normally preside at every celebration with a congregation and ministers should also be present.

255. The priest or deacon who presides at a celebration may wear a stole over the alb or surplice; a priest may also wear a cope. On greater solemnities the wearing of the cope by many priests or of the dalmatic by many deacons is permitted.

256. It belongs to the presiding priest or deacon, at the chair, to open the celebration with the introductory verse, begin the Lord's Prayer, say the concluding prayer, greet the people, bless them, and dismiss them.

257. Either the priest or a minister may lead the intercessions.

258. In the absence of a priest or deacon, the one who presides at the office is only one among equals and does not enter the sanctuary or greet and bless the people.

259. Those who act as readers, standing in a convenient place, read either the long readings or the short readings.

260, A cantor or cantors should intone the antiphons, psalms, and other chants. With regard to the psalmody, the directions of nos. 121-125 should be followed.

261. During the gospel canticle at morning prayer and evening prayer there may be an incensation of the altar, then of the priest and congregation.

262. The choral obligation applies to the community, not to the place of celebration, which need not be a church, especially in the case of those hours that are celebrated without solemnity.

263. All taking part stand during:
   a. the introduction to the office and the introductory verses of each hour;
   b. the hymn;
   c. the gospel canticle;
   d. the intercessions, the Lord's Prayer, and the concluding prayer.
264. All sit to listen to the readings, except the gospel.
265. The assembly either sits or stands, depending on custom, while the psalms and other canticles (with their antiphons) are being said.
266. All make the sign of the cross, from forehead to breast and from left shoulder to right, at:
   a. the beginning of the hours, when God, come to my assistance is being said;
   b. the beginning of the gospel, the Canticles of Zechariah, of Mary, and of Simeon.
   The sign of the cross is made on the mouth at the beginning of the invitatory, at Lord, open my lips.

II. Singing in the Office

267. In the rubrics and norms of this Instruction, the words "say ... recite," etc., are to be understood to refer to either singing or recitation, in the light of the principles that follow.
268. "The sung celebration of the divine office is more in keeping with the nature of this prayer and a mark of both higher solemnity and closer union of hearts in offering praise to God. . . . Therefore the singing of the office is earnestly recommended to those who carry out the office in choir or in common."[2]
269. The declarations of Vatican Council II on liturgical singing apply to all liturgical services but in a special way to the liturgy of the hours.[3] Though every part of it has been revised in such a way that all may be fruitfully recited even by individuals, many of these parts are lyrical in form and do not yield their fuller meaning unless they are sung, especially the psalms, canticles, hymns, and responsories.
270. Hence, in celebrating the liturgy singing is not to be regarded as an embellishment superimposed on prayer; rather, it wells up from the depths of a soul intent on prayer and the praise of God and reveals in a full and complete way the community nature of Christian worship. Christian communities of all kinds seeking to use this form of prayer as frequently as possible are to be commended. Clerics and religious, as well as all the people of God, must be trained by suitable catechesis and practice to join together in singing the hours in a spirit of joy, especially on Sundays and holydays. But it is no easy task to sing the entire office; nor is the Church's praise to be considered either by origin or by nature the exclusive possession of clerics and monks but the property of the whole Christian community. Therefore several principles must be kept simultaneously in mind if the sung celebration of the liturgy of the hours is to be performed correctly and to stand out in its true nature and splendor.
271. It is particularly appropriate that there be singing at least on Sundays and holydays, so that the different degrees of solemnity will thus come to be recognized.
272. It is the same with the hours: all are not of equal importance; thus it is desirable that those that are the true hinges of the office, that is, morning prayer and evening prayer, should receive greater prominence through the use of singing.
273. A celebration with singing throughout is commendable, provided it has artistic and spiritual excellence; but it may be useful on occasion to apply the principle of "progressive solemnity." There are practical reasons for this, as well as the fact that in this way the various elements of liturgical celebration are not treated indiscriminately, but each can again be given its connatural meaning and genuine function. The liturgy of the hours is then not seen as a beautiful memorial of the past demanding intact preservation as an object of admiration; rather it is seen as open to constantly new forms of life and growth and to being the unmistakable sign of a community's vibrant vitality.
   The principle of "progressive solemnity" therefore is one that recognizes several intermediate stages between singing the office in full and just reciting all the parts. Its application offers the

possibility of a rich and pleasing variety. The criteria are the particular day or hour being celebrated, the character of the individual elements comprising the office, the size and composition
of the community, as well as the number of singers available in the circumstances.

With this increased range of variation, it is possible for the public praise of the Church to be
sung more frequently than formerly and to be adapted in a variety of ways to different circumstances. There is also great hope that new ways and expressions of public worship may be found
for our own age, as has clearly always happened in the life of the Church.

274. For liturgical celebrations sung in Latin, Gregorian chant, as the music proper to the Roman
liturgy, should have pride of place, all other things being equal.[4] Nevertheless, "the Church does
not exclude any type of sacred music from liturgical services as long as the music matches the
spirit of the service itself and the character of the individual parts and is not a hindrance to the
required active participation of the people."[5] At a sung office, if a melody is not available for the
given antiphon, another antiphon should be taken from those in the repertoire, provided it is
suitable in terms of nos. 113 and 121-125.

275. Since the liturgy of the hours may be celebrated in the vernacular, "appropriate measures are
to be taken to prepare melodies for use in the vernacular singing of the divine office."[6]

276. But it is permissible to sing the various parts in different languages at one and the same
celebration.[7]

277. The decision on which parts to choose for singing follows from the authentic structure of a
liturgical celebration. This demands that the significance and function of each part and of
singing should be fully respected. Some parts by their nature call for singing:[8] in particular,
acclamations, responses to the greetings of priest and ministers, responses in litanies, also
antiphons and psalms, the verses and reprises in responsories, hymns and canticles.[9]

278. Clearly the psalms are closely bound up with music (see nos. 103-120), as both Jewish and
Christian tradition confirm. In fact a complete understanding of many of the psalms is greatly
assisted by singing them or at least not losing sight of their poetic and musical character.
Accordingly, whenever possible singing the psalms should have preference, at least for the major
days and hours and in view of the character of the psalms themselves.

279. The different ways of reciting the psalms have been described in nos. 121-123. Varying these
ways should depend not so much on external circumstances as on the different genres of the
psalms to be recited in the same celebration. Thus the wisdom psalms and the narrative psalms
are perhaps better listened to, whereas psalms of praise and thanksgiving are of their nature
designed for singing in common. The main consideration is to ensure that the celebration is not
too inflexible or elaborate nor concerned merely with formal observance of rules, but that it
matches the reality of what is celebrated. The primary aim must be to inspire hearts with a
desire for genuine prayer and to show that the celebration of God's praise is a thing of joy (see
Ps 147).

280. Even when the hours are recited, hymns can nourish prayer, provided they have doctrinal and
literary excellence; but of their nature they are designed for singing and so, as far as possible, at
a celebration in common they should be sung.

281. The short responsory after the reading at morning prayer and evening prayer (see no. 49) is of
its nature designed for singing and indeed for congregational singing.

282. The responsories following the readings in the office of readings by their very nature and
function also call for their being sung. In the plan of the office, however, they are composed in
such a way that they retain their power even in individual and private recitation. Responsories
set to simpler melodies can be sung more frequently than those responsories drawn from the
traditional liturgical books.

283. The longer readings and the short readings are not of themselves designed for singing. When
they are proclaimed, great care should be taken that the reading is dignified, clear, and distinct
and that it is really audible and fully intelligible for all. The only acceptable melody for a
reading is therefore one that best ensures the hearing of the words and the understanding of the
text.

284. Texts that are said only by the person presiding, such as the concluding prayer, can be sung gracefully and appropriately, especially in Latin. This, however, will be more difficult in some languages, unless singing makes the texts more clearly audible for all.

ENDNOTES

Chapter I

1. See Acts 1:14, 4:24, 12:5 and 12. See also Eph 5:19-21.
2. See Acts 2:1-15.
3. SC art. 83.
4. See Lk 3:21-22.
5. See Lk 6:12.
6. See Mt 14:19, 15:36; Mk 6:41, 8:7; Lk 9:16; Jn 6:11.
7. See Lk 9:28-29.
8. See Mk 7:34.
9. See Jn 11:41ff.
10. See Lk 9:18.
11. Lk 11:11.
12. See Mt 11:25.ff; Lk 10:21ff.
13. See Mt 19:13.
14. See Lk 22:32.
15. See Mk 1:35, 6:46; Lk 5:16. See also Mt 4:1 and par.; Mt 14:23.
16. See Mk 1:35.
17. See Mt 14:23 and 25; Mk 6:46 and 48.
18. See Lk 6:12.
19. See Lk 4:16.
20. See Mt 21:13 and par.
21. See Mt 14:19 and par.; Mt 15:36 and par.
22. See Mt 26:26 and par.
23. See Lk 24:30.
24. See Mt 26:30 and par.
25. See Jn 12:27ff.
26. See Jn 17:1-26.
27. See Mt 26:36-44 and par.
28. See Lk 23:34 and 46; Mt 27:46; Mk 15:34.
29. See Heb 7:25.
30. Mt 5:44, 7:7, 26:41; Mk 13:33, 14:38; Lk 6:28, 10:2, 11:9, 22:40 and 46.
31. Jn 14:13ff., 15:16, 16:23ff. and 26.
32. See Mt 6:9-13; Lk 11:2-4.
33. See Lk 18:1.
34. See Lk 18:9-14.
35. See Lk 21:36; Mk 13:33.
36. See Lk 11:5-13,18:1-8; Jn 14:13, 16:23.
37. See Mt 6:5-8, 23:14; Lk 20:47; Jn 4:23.
38. See Rom 8:15 and 26; 1 Cor 12:3; Gal 4:6; Jude 20.
39. See 2 Cor 1:20; Col 3:17.
40. See Heb 13:15.
41. See Rom 12:12; 1 Cor 7:5; Eph 6:18; Col 4:2; 1 Thes 5:17; 1 Tm 5:5; 1 Pt 4:7.
42. See 1 Tm 4:5; Jas 5:15ff.; 1 Jn 3:22, 5:14ff.
43. See Eph 5:19ff.; Heb 13:15; Rv 19:5.
44. See Col 3:17; Phil 4:6; 1 Thes 5:17; 1 Tm 2:1.
45. See Rom 8:26; Phil 4:6.
46. See Rom 15:30; 1 Tm 2:1ff.; Eph 6:18; 1 Thes 5:25; Jas 5:14 and 16.
47. See 1 Tm 2:5; Heb 8:6, 9:15, 12:24.
48. See Rom 5:2; Eph 2:18, 3:12.
49. See SC art. 83.
50. See LG no. 10.
51. Augustine, *Enarrat. in Ps. 85*, 1: CCL 39, 1176.
52. See Lk 10:21, the occasion when Jesus "rejoiced in the Holy Spirit and said: 'I thank you, Father...'".
53. See Acts 2:42 Gr.
54. See Mt 6:6.
55. See SC art. 12.
56. See SC art. 83-84.
57. See SC art. 88.
58. See SC art. 94.
59. See PO no. 5.
60. CD no. 30.
61. SC art. 5.
62. See SC art. 83 and 98.
63. SC art. 7.
64. See SC art. 10.
65. SC art. 33.
66. See SC art. 24.
67. See SC art. 33.
68. 1 Thes 5:17.
69. See Heb 13:15.
70. SC art. 84.
71. SC art. 85.
72. See SC art. 83.
73. LG no. 50; SC art. 8 and 104.
74. LG no. 48.
75. See Rom 8:19.
76. See SC art. 83.
77. See Heb 5:7.
78. See PO no. 6.
79. See LG no. 41.
80. See no. 24 of this Instruction.
81. See PC no. 7.
82. SC art. 10.
83. SC art. 2.
84. See Jn 15:5.
85. See SC art. 86.
86. See Eph 2:21-22.
87. See Eph 4:13.
88. See SC art. 2.
89. See SC art. 90. *Rule of St. Benedict* ch. 19.
90. See PO no. 14; OT no. 8.
91. See SC art. 26.
92. See SC art. 41.

93. CD no. 11.
94. See art. 42. See also AA no. 10.
95. See SC art. 26 and 84.
96. See AG no. 17.
97. CD no. 15.
98. See SC art. 100.
99. See PO no. 5.
100. See nos. 100-109 of this Instruction.
101. CD no. 33; see also PC nos. 6, 7, 15; AG no. 15.
102. See SC art. 99.
103. See SC art. 100.
104. See Jn 4:23.
105. See GE no. 2; AA no. 16.
106. See AA no. 11.
107. See PO no. 13.
108. See SC art. 41; LG no. 21.
109. See LG no. 26; CD no. 15.
110. See PO no. 13.
111. See PO no. 5.
112. See Jn 10:11, 17:20 and 23.
113. See SC art. 90.
114. See LG no. 41.
115. See DV no. 25; PO no. 13.
116. See Paul VI, Motu Proprio *Sacram Diaconatus Ordinem*, 18 June 1967, no. 27.
117. See SCR, Instr. InterOec no. 78b.
118. See SC art. 95.
119. See Acts 4:32.
120. See SC art. 100.
121. See SC art. 26, 28-30.
122. See SC art. 27.

Chapter II
1. See Heb 3:7-4:16.
2. SC art. 89a; see also art. 100.
3. Basil the Great, *Regulae fusius tractatae* resp. 37, 3: PG 31, 1014.
4. Cyprian, *De oratione dominica* 35: PL 4, 561.
5. Basil the Great, *Regulae fusius tractatae* resp. 37, 3: PG 31, 1015.
6. See Ps 141:2.
7. John Cassian, *De institutione coenob.* 3, 3: PL 49, 124, 125.
8. Cyprian, *De oratione dominica* 35: PL 4, 560.
9. RP, Ordination of Priests no. 14.
10. Ambrose, *De officiis ministrorum* 1, 20, 88: PL 16, 50. See also DV no. 25.
11. SC art. 89c.
12. Augustine, *Sermo Guelferbytanus* 5: PL Suppl 2, 550.
13. Ibid.: PL Suppl 2, 552.

14. See SC art. 89.
15. See SC art. 38.

Chapter III
1. SC art. 90.
2. *Rule of St. Benedict* ch. 19.
3. See *Rule of St. Benedict* ch. 19.
4. See Mt 22:44ff.
5. See SC art. 91.
6. SC art. 102.
7. Gregory the Great, *Homilia 34 in Evangelia*: PL 76: 1282.
8. See SC art. 38.
9. Vincent of Lerins, *Commonitorium* 2: PL 50, 640.
10. Bernard of Clairvaux, *Sermo 3 in vigilia Nativitatis* 1: PL 183 (ed. 1879) 94.
11. See SC art. 92c.
12. See SC art. 93.
13. See SC art. 38.
14. Thus, for example, John Chrysostom, *In Epist. ad Tim 1*, Homilia 6: PG 62, 530.
15. See SC art. 38.
16. See SC art. 83 and 89.
17. See no. 256 of this Instruction.
18. SC art. 30.

Chapter IV
1. See SC art. 100.
2. See SC art. 111.
3. See General Norms for the Liturgical Year and the Calendar no. 52.
4. See ibid. no. 52c.
5. See ibid. Table of Liturgical Days nos. 4 and 8.
6. SC art. 51.
7. See nos. 100-109 of this Instruction.

Chapter V
1. SC art. 28.
2. SCR, Instr. MusSacr, 5 March 1967, no. 37. See also SC art. 99.
3. See SC art. 113.
4. See SC art. 116.
5. SCR, Instr. MusSacr no. 9. See also SC art. 116.
6. SCR, Instr. MusSacr no. 41; see also nos. 54-61.
7. See ibid. no. 51.
8. See ibid. no. 6.
9. See ibid. nos. 16a and 38.

LITURGICAL CALENDAR FOR
THE UNITED STATES OF AMERICA

JANUARY

1. The Octave Day of Christmas
    THE BLESSED VIRGIN MARY,
    THE MOTHER OF GOD
    Solemnity
2. Basil the Great and Gregory
    Nazianzen, bishops and doctors
    Memorial
3. Most Holy Name of Jesus
4. Elizabeth Ann Seton, religious
    Memorial
5. John Neumann, bishop
    Memorial
6. Blessed André Bessette, religious
7. Raymond of Penyafort, priest
8.
9.
10.
11.
12.
13. Hilary, bishop and doctor
14.
15.
16.
17. Anthony, abbot   Memorial
18.
19.
20. Fabian, pope and martyr
     Sebastian, martyr
21. Agnes, virgin and martyr   Memorial
22. Vincent, deacon and martyr
23.
24. Francis de Sales, bishop and doctor
     Memorial
25. The Conversion of Saint Paul, apostle
     Feast
26. Timothy and Titus, bishops
     Memorial
27. Angela Merici, virgin
28. Thomas Aquinas, priest and doctor
     Memorial
29.
30.
31. John Bosco, priest   Memorial

Sunday between January 2 and January 8:
   EPIPHANY   Solemnity
Sunday after January 6: Baptism of the Lord
                          Feast

FEBRUARY

1.
2. The Presentation of the Lord   Feast
3. Blaise, bishop and martyr
    Ansgar, bishop
4.
5. Agatha, virgin and martyr   Memorial
6. Paul Miki, martyr, and his companions,
    martyrs   Memorial
7.
8. Jerome Emiliani, priest
    Josephine Bakhita, virgin
9.
10. Scholastica, virgin   Memorial
11. Our Lady of Lourdes
12.
13.
14. Cyril, monk, and Methodius, bishop
15.
16.
17. The Seven Founders of the Order of
     Servites, religious
18.
19.
20.
21. Peter Damian, bishop and doctor
22. The Chair of Saint Peter, apostle
     Feast
23. Polycarp, bishop and martyr
24.
25.
26.
27.
28.

MARCH

1.
2.
3. Katharine Drexel, virgin
4. Casimir
5.
6.
7. Perpetua and Felicity, martyrs
8. John of God, religious
9. Frances of Rome, religious
10.
11.
12.
13.
14.
15.
16.
17. Patrick, bishop
18. Cyril of Jerusalem, bishop and doctor
19. JOSEPH, HUSBAND OF THE BLESSED
     VIRGIN MARY   Solemnity
20.
21.
22.
23. Toribio de Mogrovejo, bishop
24.
25. THE ANNUNCIATION OF THE LORD
     Solemnity
26.
27.
28.
29.
30.
31.

APRIL

1.
2. Francis of Paola, hermit
3.
4. Isidore, bishop and doctor
5. Vincent Ferrer, priest
6.
7. John Baptist de la Salle, priest   Memorial
8.
9.
10.
11. Stanislaus, bishop and martyr   Memorial
12.
13. Martin I, pope and martyr
14.
15.
16.
17.
18.
19.
20.
21. Anselm, bishop and doctor
22.
23. George, martyr
     Adalbert, bishop and martyr
24. Fidelis of Sigmaringen, priest and martyr
25. Mark, evangelist   Feast
26.
27.
28. Peter Chanel, priest and martyr
     Louis Mary de Montfort, priest
29. Catherine of Siena, virgin and doctor
     Memorial
30. Pius V, pope

MAY

1. Joseph the Worker
2. Athanasius, bishop and doctor   Memorial
3. Philip and James, apostles   Feast
4.
5.
6.
7.
8.
9.
10. Blessed Damien Joseph de Veuster of Moloka'i, priest
11.
12. Nereus and Achilleus, martyrs
    Pancras, martyr
13. Our Lady of Fatima
14. Matthias, apostle   Feast
15. Isidore
16.
17.
18. John I, pope and martyr
19.
20. Bernardine of Siena, priest
21. Christopher Magallanes, priest and martyr, and his companions, martyrs
22. Rita of Cascia, religious
23.
24.
25. Bede the Venerable, priest and doctor
    Gregory VII, pope
    Mary Magdalene de Pazzi, virgin
26. Philip Neri, priest   Memorial
27. Augustine of Canterbury, bishop
28.
29.
30.
31. Visitation of the Blessed Virgin Mary   Feast

First Sunday after Pentecost:
    HOLY TRINITY   Solemnity

Thursday after Holy Trinity:
    CORPUS CHRISTI   Solemnity

Friday following Second Sunday after Pentecost:
    SACRED HEART   Solemnity

Saturday following Second Sunday after
    Pentecost: Immaculate Heart of Mary

JUNE

1. Justin, martyr   Memorial
2. Marcellinus and Peter, martyrs
3. Charles Lwanga and companions, martyrs   Memorial
4.
5. Boniface, bishop and martyr   Memorial
6. Norbert, bishop
7.
8.
9. Ephrem, deacon and doctor
10.
11. Barnabas, apostle   Memorial
12.
13. Anthony of Padua, priest and doctor   Memorial
14.
15.
16.
17.
18.
19. Romuald, abbot
20.
21. Aloysius Gonzaga, religious   Memorial
22. Paulinus of Nola, bishop
    John Fisher, bishop and martyr and Thomas More, martyr
23.
24. THE NATIVITY OF JOHN THE BAPTIST   Solemnity
25.
26.
27. Cyril of Alexandria, bishop and doctor
28. Irenaeus, bishop and martyr   Memorial
29. PETER AND PAUL, APOSTLES   Solemnity
30. The First Holy Martyrs of the Holy Roman Church

JULY

1. Blessed Junipero Serra, priest
2.
3. Thomas, apostle   Feast
4. Elizabeth of Portugal
5. Anthony Mary Zaccaria, priest
6. Maria Goretti, virgin and martyr
7.
8.
9. Augustine Zhao Rong, priest and martyr, and his companions, martyrs
10.
11. Benedict, abbot   Memorial
12.
13. Henry
14. Blessed Kateri Tekakwitha, virgin   Memorial
15. Bonaventure, bishop and doctor   Memorial
16. Our Lady of Mount Carmel
17.
18. Camillus de Lellis, priest
19.
20. Apollinaris, bishop and martyr
21. Lawrence of Brindisi, priest and doctor
22. Mary Magdalene   Memorial
23. Bridget of Sweden, religious
24. Sharbel Makhluf, priest
25. James, apostle   Feast
26. Joachim and Ann, parents of the Blessed Virgin Mary   Memorial
27.
28.
29. Martha   Memorial
30. Peter Chrysologus, bishop and doctor
31. Ignatius of Loyola, priest   Memorial

AUGUST

1. Alphonsus Liguori, bishop and doctor   Memorial
2. Eusebius of Vercelli, bishop
   Peter Julian Eymard, priest
3.
4. John Mary Vianney, priest   Memorial
5. Dedication of St. Mary Major
6. The Transfiguration of the Lord   Feast
7. Sixtus II, pope and martyr, and his companions, martyrs
   Cajetan, priest
8. Dominic, priest   Memorial
9. Teresa Benedicta of the Cross, virgin and martyr
10. Lawrence, deacon and martyr   Feast
11. Clare, virgin   Memorial
12.
13. Pontian, pope and martyr, and Hippolytus, priest and martyr
14. Maximillian Mary Kolbe, priest and martyr   Memorial
15. ASSUMPTION OF THE BLESSED VIRGIN MARY   Solemnity
16. Stephen of Hungary
17.
18. Jane Frances de Chantal, religious
19. John Eudes, priest
20. Bernard, abbot and doctor   Memorial
21. Pius X, pope   Memorial
22. Queenship of the Blessed Virgin Mary   Memorial
23. Rose of Lima, virgin
24. Bartholomew, apostle   Feast
25. Louis of France
    Joseph Calasanz, priest
26.
27. Monica   Memorial
28. Augustine, bishop and doctor   Memorial
29. The Martyrdom of John the Baptist   Memorial
30.
31.

SEPTEMBER

1.
2.
3. Gregory the Great, pope and doctor
4.
5.
6.
7.
8. Nativity of the Blessed Virgin Mary
                                        Feast
9. Peter Claver, priest   Memorial
10.
11.
12. The Most Holy Name of the Blessed
    Virgin Mary
13. John Chrysostom, bishop and doctor
                                        Memorial
14. The Exaltation of the Holy Cross   Feast
15. Our Lady of Sorrows   Memorial
16. Cornelius, pope and martyr, and Cyprian,
    bishop and martyr   Memorial
17. Robert Bellarmine, bishop and doctor
18.
19. Januarius, bishop and martyr
20. Andrew Kim Taegon, priest and martyr,
    and Paul Chong Hasang, martyr,
    and their companions, martyrs   Memorial
21. Matthew, apostle and evangelist   Feast
22.
23. Pio of Pietrelcina, priest   Memorial
24.
25.
26. Cosmas and Damian, martyrs
27. Vincent de Paul, priest   Memorial
28. Wenceslaus, martyr
    Saint Lawrence Ruiz, martyr, and his
    companions, martyrs
29. Michael, Gabriel, and Raphael, archangels
                                        Feast
30. Jerome, priest and doctor   Memorial

OCTOBER

1. Thérèse of the Child Jesus, virgin and
   doctor   Memorial
2. The Guardian Angels   Memorial
3.
4. Francis of Assisi, religious Memorial
5.
6. Bruno, priest
   Blessed Marie-Rose Durocher, virgin
7. Our Lady of the Rosary   Memorial
8.
9. Denis, bishop and martyr, and his
   companions, martyrs
   John Leonardi, priest
10.
11.
12.
13.
14. Callistus I, pope and martyr
15. Teresa of Jesus, virgin and doctor
                                        Memorial
16. Hedwig, religious
    Margaret Mary Alacoque, virgin
17. Ignatius of Antioch, bishop and martyr
                                        Memorial
18. Luke, evangelist   Feast
19. John de Brébeuf and Isaac Jogues, priests
    and martyrs,
    and their companions, martyrs   Memorial
20. Paul of the Cross, priest
21.
22.
23. John of Capistrano, priest
24. Anthony Mary Claret, bishop
25.
26.
27.
28. Simon and Jude, apostles   Feast
29.
30.
31.

NOVEMBER

1. ALL SAINTS   Solemnity
2. The Commemoration of all the Faithful
    Departed
3. Martin de Porres, religious
4. Charles Borromeo, bishop   Memorial
5.
6.
7.
8.
9. The Dedication of the Lateran Basilica in
    Rome   Feast
10. Leo the Great, pope and doctor
                                         Memorial
11. Martin of Tours, bishop   Memorial
12. Josaphat, bishop and martyr   Memorial
13. Frances Xavier Cabrini, virgin   Memorial
14.
15. Albert the Great, bishop and doctor
16. Margaret of Scotland
    Gertrude, virgin
17. Elizabeth of Hungary, religious
                                         Memorial
18. Dedication of the churches of Peter and
    Paul, apostles
    Rose Philippine Duchesne, virgin
19.
20.
21. The Presentation of the Blessed
    Virgin Mary   Memorial
22. Cecilia, virgin and martyr   Memorial
23. Clement I, pope and martyr
    Columban, abbot
    Blessed Miguel Agustín Pro, priest and
    martyr
24. Andrew Dung-Lac, priest and martyr, and
    his companions, martyrs   Memorial
25. Catherine of Alexandria, virgin and
    martyr
26.
27.
28.
29.
30. Andrew, apostle   Feast

Last Sunday in Ordinary Time:
    CHRIST THE KING   Solemnity

DECEMBER

1.
2.
3. Francis Xavier, priest   Memorial
4. John of Damascus, priest and doctor
5.
6. Nicholas, bishop
7. Ambrose, bishop and doctor   Memorial
8. THE IMMACULATE CONCEPTION OF THE
    BLESSED VIRGIN MARY   Solemnity
9. Juan Diego, hermit
10.
11. Damasus I, pope
12. Our Lady of Guadalupe   Feast
13. Lucy, virgin and martyr   Memorial
14. John of the Cross, priest and doctor
                                         Memorial
15.
16.
17.
18.
19.
20.
21. Peter Canisius, priest and doctor
22.
23. John of Kanty, priest
24.
25. THE NATIVITY OF THE LORD   Solemnity
26. Stephen, first martyr   Feast
27. John, apostle and evangelist   Feast
28. The Holy Innocents, martyrs   Feast
29. Thomas Becket, bishop and martyr
30.
31. Sylvester I, pope

Sunday within the octave of Christmas or if
    there is no Sunday within the octave,
    December 30: Holy Family   Feast

INTRODUCTION AND PASTORAL GUIDE

> Wherever possible, other groups of the faithful should celebrate the liturgy of the hours communally in church. This especially applies to all parishes – the cells of the diocese, established under their pastors, taking the place of the bishop; they "represent in some degree the visible Church established throughout the world."
>
> *The General Instruction on the Liturgy of the Hours,* 21.

THE MUNDELEIN PSALTER intends to be a contribution to the continuing renewal of the liturgy. It highlights a new realization of the value of this type of prayer, especially for Catholic communities today. With its roots sunk deep in the daily prayer of Judaism, the diurnal, public recitation of the Psalms has been the daily companion of Christians through the history of the Church. The structuring of the liturgical year, of the week, and of the day gives a profound meaning and stability to the Church's desire to keep the mysteries of faith ever before us. The important value of the public, communal celebration of the Divine Office must not be underestimated, especially in communities that do not have the daily celebration of the Eucharistic Liturgy.

The deep, sober beauty of the chanting of the psalms provides an oasis of calm and peace in the often hectic and frenzied pace of people today. And so, this volume does not intend to offer anything flashy or flamboyant. It does not boast of any innovation; it does not introduce the next fad. The Church's prayer must be allowed to speak for itself, to express the joy and grief, the anguish and elation of God's children across the ages and around the globe. This volume hopes to offer an opening to the radical beauty of Judeo-Christian prayer, in an accessible, comprehensible way. This, after all, is the prayer of the Church.

This Psalter does, however, signal a rediscovery in a way: it is simply the Church's prayer, not charged with any political agenda, not aimed directly at social reconstruction. It harbors no hidden motive of changing the world or the Church or even ourselves, (these changes occur by grace). Its sole intent is to foster fidelity in the praise of God by joining our prayer to those of other cultures and generations which offer the same sacrifice of praise. The Divine Office is the expression of the Church, the Body of Christ, at prayer.

HOW DOES THIS WORK? There have been many images used to describe what happens during the singing of the Psalms. The pace and rhythm of it can be likened to waves that constantly wash over us with the Biblical prayer, bathing us in the images and emotions of the Psalms, wearing a path in the stone of our hearts by its constant, gentle force. A hymn for the Common of Holy Men and Women gives marvelous expression to this idea: "May all that splendid company/whom Christ our Savior came to meet,/ help us on our uneven road/ made smoother by their passing feet."

The regularity of this prayer and fidelity to it, afford its participants a different kind of appreciation. Christians come to live with the praise of God, abide with it. In the frenzied pace of the contemporary world, people rush from "thing to thing" or activty to event, like tourists rushing from monument to monument for the "souvenir snapshot" without really seeing or experiencing the genius of a place. Those who engage in the Liturgy of the Hours, on the other hand, gradually come to *know* the Scriptures, become one with the culture of the Bible and of the Church. It is only then that the Christian cultural symbols begin to reveal their richness and a new depth of meaning.

Christian prayer is bound up inextricably in the weave of the liturgical year and the mysteries of faith. The fundamental connection between the Paschal Mystery and human life unfolds in the rhythm of each day, week, and year as each sunrise promises resurrection and each dying day begs for mercy.

HOW TO INTRODUCE THE LITURGY OF HOURS IN THE PARISH

Because the Liturgy of the Hours is the official public prayer of the Church, certain members are bound to celebrate it: those in Holy Orders, religious communities and secular institutes are required to celebrate all or part of the office for the good of the whole People of God. This, however, does not mean that the Catholic faithful should think it reserved to a religious elite. This prayer belongs properly to the people. And so the Church has insisted that the people be given access to it.

Many parish communites celebrate some form of the office during the more solemn seasons of the year, especially Advent, Lent and Holy Week. The Second Vatican Council encouraged *at least* a weekly celebration of Sunday Vespers.

Beginning the public celebration of the Liturgy of Hours need not be a complicated project. A pastor might celebrate one or more hours with parishioners before or after the daily Mass. Pastoral Council meetings might begin with the communal recitation or singing of all or part of the office. Parish staffs might adopt the structure given by the Divine Office to provide rhythm to the daily engagement in ministry. Choirs could begin their rehears-

als with this form of prayer as a reminder of the ministry of sacred music and its relation to the Paschal Mystery. Christian families can find a center and source of stability in praying the office daily, paying particular attention to the rhythm of the liturgical year, the celebration of saints' days, and night prayer. The Office for the Dead can provide an important structure for families in grief or can be used as a regular reminder of deceased relatives. Even two people, praying together publicly in church, can be an important witness of Christian fidelity and offer an invitation to others to join.

The prayer requires no particular expertise. The following fundamental principles can easily be learned, understood and gradually adopted.

1. The office begins with the sign of the cross, indicated by the symbol (✠), and the OPENING VERSE. Notice that the verse, "O God, come to my assistance," even in communal celebration uses the word "my" instead of "our". This signals that those assembled for prayer join together as the Body of Christ, praying in him, through him praising the Father. The first task then is to foster the unity that goes beyond individual or personal prayer. Not "our" assistance as if we were a group of disconnected individuals in a recitation of personal prayers, but "my" assistance as members of one body already seeking unity and wholeness.

2. The HYMN follows. The hymn is an integral part of the celebration of the office, as made evident by the care with which the Church has developed proper texts especially for the feasts of the saints and the seasons of the year. Three aspects of these hymns can be noted. 1) Most of the hymns are arranged to be sung to any Long Meter tune (such as *Iesu dulcis memoria* or Old Hundreth.)

Traditional chant tunes have been provided for the cycle of Ordinary Time so that the ancient hymn texts (most of which date from the first eight centuries of Christianity) can be chanted with their traditional tunes. 2) The texts provided for certain feast days are proper to these celebrations. They are frequently biographical and thus provide a treasury of reflection. 3) From the earliest days of the Church, these hymn texts have been chanted so that the faithful might constantly have on their lips the orthodox faith.

3. The PSALMODY is generally composed of two psalms and a canticle. The antiphon is first intoned by the cantor or leader and then continued (after the *) or repeated by the participants. Alternation of the verses can be done in a variety of ways: side to side, between cantor and assembly, men alternating with women.

4. The READING follows the psalmody. The text is read without introduction or concluding verse. During the seasons of Advent, Christmas, Lent and Easter the readings are taken from the Proper of Seasons.

5. The RESPONSORY is chanted or recited.

6. All stand and make the sign of the cross for the GOSPEL CANTICLE and its proper antiphon.

7. The INTERCESSIONS are intoned by the cantor or leader. They may be recited or sung with the assembly repeating the response after each petition.

8. THE LORD'S PRAYER with its invitation follows the petitions.

9. The CONCLUDING PRAYER, without invitation, follows immediately after the Lord's Prayer. At Compline (Night Prayer) the invitation "Let us pray" is said before the concluding prayer.

10. A priest or deacon may give the BLESSING and DISMISSAL. In the absence of an ordained minister, a lay person sings or says, "May the Lord bless us, protect us from all evil and bring us to everlasting life. ℟. Amen."

11. At Compline, the blessing is said, even in individual recitation: "May the all-powerful Lord grant us a restful night and a peaceful death. ℟. Amen." An antiphon in honor of the Blessed Virgin follows.

NOTES FOR CHANTING THE OFFICE

The singing of chant must be characterized by the three virtues of sobriety, simplicity and restraint. This requires on the part of the singer a mind disciplined in the art of prayer as well as in the art of music. There must never be a sensation of dragging in the rendition of the chant. It must be sung *lightly* and it must *move*.   *Chants of the Church*, 1953.

THIS EDITION OF THE DIVINE OFFICE is arranged to foster the communal singing of the prayer. It uses Gregorian notation which might at first seem intimidating, but is actually more flexible and more accessible than modern notion. Many new resources are becoming available to help with understanding chant. The following basic information can provide a starting point for novices:

1. The Gregorian staff is composed of four horizontal lines. The first signal for

chanting is given at the beginning of the staff; is called the clef. In the *Mundelein Psalter*, the "Do clef" and the "Fa clef" are used. The Do clef indicates on which line the first note of the diatonic scale is to be sung; the Fa clef indicates the fourth note of the scale. In the song made famous by Julie Andrews in *The Sound of Music* the diatonic scale is given: do, re, mi, fa, so, la, ti, do. In the following example, the Do clef is on the third line, thus the notes to be chanted are: Do, ti, la, do; do, ti, la.

IIA

Do,   ti,   la, do ; do,   ti,   la.

In the second example, the Fa clef is
shown on the third line, thus one
chants: Fa, mi, re, do; do re.

IID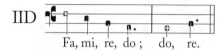

Fa, mi, re, do ;   do,   re.

2. The open note, usually found at the
   beginning of each phrase, indicates the
   reciting tone; it can include many words
   or syllables.
3. Text in *italics* indicates the syllable on
   which the recitation note changes.
4. In chant, the principle is that the "many
   voices become one." In this way the
   assembly is formed into the one Body of
   Christ. The soft human voice of individual singers, joined together, is aided by
   the acoustics of the chapel to create a
   rich, full sound.
5. Special notions in the text help the
   assembly to sing in unison. While in
   general, one sings to the end of the
   phrase, a dagger (†) in the text signals a
   short pause within a phrase. An asterisk
   (*) indicates the second half of the
   chanted phrase.
6. Chant is designed to sustain and
   highlight the text; music serves the
   prayer so that the participants may reflect
   on the mystery revealed in the text.
7. In general, the cantor will intone the
   antiphon; all repeat it.
8. The cantor intones the first phrase of the
   psalm, the left side of the assembly joins

to finish the verse. The right side alter-
nates with the left side through the
doxology (*Gloria*), then all join together
to repeat the antiphon.

Prayer of this kind requires patience,
practice, humility and charity. The
richness of the liturgy is revealed
gradually. It is over the course of the
liturgical year, and week and day that we
attend the mystery of our faith.

The General Instruction of the Liturgy
of the Hours, included in this volume,
pages 7-36, provides a rich theological
and liturgical introduction to the Church's
public prayer and more ample instruction
on the implementation of the Divine
Office. Those who use the Mundelein
Psalter are urged to read and meditate on
it regularly as a source of spiritual enrich-
ment.

For chanting the hymns in Latin, see the
Liber Hymnarius, Solesmes, 1983. The
Latin texts provided here are for refer-
ence.

Additional information, audio files and
other helpful tools can be found at
www.mundeleinpsalter.com.

THE BENEDICTINE SISTERS of Saint
Cecilia's Abbey, located on the Isle of
Wight, (U.K.) are owed our profound
gratitude for their selfless work at
translating from the Latin the majority
of hymns that appear in this volume.
Please pray for them, that Lord will
reward their efforts in this life with
growth in holiness and in the members
of their community, and grant they they
may sing in the presence of the Lamb for
all eternity. May every celebration of this
Office be an implicit prayer for them.

THE ORDINARY
OF THE LITURGY OF THE HOURS

OPENING VERSE
All stand and make the Sign of the Cross.

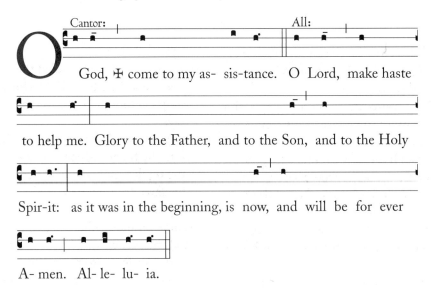

O God, ✠ come to my as- sis-tance. O Lord, make haste
to help me. Glory to the Father, and to the Son, and to the Holy
Spir-it: as it was in the beginning, is now, and will be for ever
A- men. Al- le- lu- ia.

Or, during Lent:
All stand and make the Sign of the Cross.

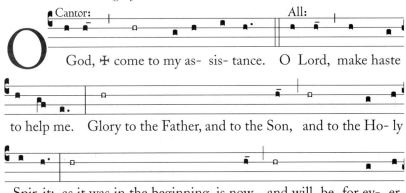

O God, ✠ come to my as- sis- tance. O Lord, make haste
to help me. Glory to the Father, and to the Son, and to the Ho- ly
Spir-it: as it was in the beginning, is now, and will be for ev- er

A- men.

RESPONSORY

VI F

Weeks I and III

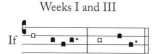

Weeks II and IV

Benedictus

Blessèd ✠ be the Lord, the *God* of Israel; * he has come to his people and set *them* free.

He has raised up for us a *mighty* savior, * born of the house of his ser*vant* David.

Through his holy prophets he promised of old † that he would save us *from* our enemies, * from the hands of all *who* hate us.

He promised to show mercy *to* our fathers * and to remember his ho*ly* covenant.

This was the oath he swore to our *fath*er Abraham: * to set us free from the hands of *our* enemies,

free to worship him without fear, † holy and righteous *in* his sight * all the days of *our* life.

You, my child, shall be called the prophet *of* the Most High; * for you will go before the Lord to prepare *his* way,

to give his people knowledge *of* salvation * by the forgiveness of *their* sins.

In the tender compassion *of* our God * the dawn from on high shall break *up*on us,

to shine on those who dwell in darkness and the sha*dow* of death, * and to guide our feet into the way *of* peace.

Glory to the Father, and *to* the Son, * and to the Ho*ly* Spirit:

as it was in the begin*ning*, is now, * and will be for ever. *A*men.

Magnificat

My soul ✠ proclaims the greatness *of* the Lord, * my spirit rejoices in God *my* savior

for he has *looked* with favor * on his low*ly* servant.

From this day all *gen*erations * will call *me* blessèd:

the Almighty has done great *things* for me, * and holy is *his* Name.

He has mercy on *those* who fear him * in every gen*er*ation.

He has shown the strength *of* his arm, * he has scattered the proud in their *con*ceit.

He has cast down the mighty *from* their thrones, * and has lifted up *the* lowly.

He has filled the hungry *with* good things, * and the rich he has sent a*way* empty.

He has come to the help of his *servant* Israel * for he has remembered his promise *of* mercy,

the promise he made *to* our fathers, * to Abraham and his children *for* ever.

Glory to the Father, and *to* the Son, * and to the Ho*ly* Spirit:

as it was in the begin*ning*, is now, * and will be for ever. *A*men.

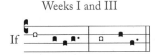

Weeks I and III — If

Weeks II and IV — VII d

Benedictus

Bendito ✠ sea el Señor, Dios de Israel,* porque ha visitado y redimido a su pueblo,

suscitándonos una fuerza de salvación * en la casa de David, su siervo,

según lo había predicho desde antiguo * por boca de sus santos profetas.

Es la salvación que nos libra de nuestros enemigos * y de la mano de todos los que nos odian;

ha realizado así la misericordia * que tuvo con nuestros padres,

recordando su santa alianza * y el juramento que juró a nuestro padre Abraham.

Para concedernos que, libres de temor,* arrancados de la mano de los enemigos,

le sirvamos con santidad y justicia,* en su presencia, todos nuestros días

Y a ti, niño, te llamarán profeta del Altísimo, * porque irás delante del Señor a preparar sus caminos,

anunciando a su pueblo la salvación, * el perdón de sus pecados.

Por la entrañable misericordia de nuestro Dios, * nos visitará el sol que nace de lo alto,

para iluminar a los que viven en tiniebla * y en sombra de muerte,

para guiar nuestros pasos* por el camino de la paz.

Gloria al Padre, y al Hijo, * y al Espíritu Santo.

Como era en un principio, ahora y siempre, * por los siglos de los siglos. Amén.

Magnificat

Proclama ✠ mi alma la grandeza del Señor, * se alegra mi espíritu en Dios, mi salvador;

porque ha mirado * la humillación de su esclava.

Desde ahora me felicitarán * todas las generaciones,

porque el Poderoso ha hecho obras grandes por mí: * su nombre es santo,

y su misericordia llega a sus fieles * de generación en generación.

El hace proezas con su brazo: * dispersa a los soberbios de corazón,

derriba del trono a los poderosos * y enaltece a los humildes,

a los hambrientos los colma de bienes * y a los ricos los despide vacíos.

Auxilia a Israel, su siervo, * acordándose de la misericordia—

como lo había prometido a nuestros padres— * en favor de Abrahám y su descendencia por siempre.

Gloria al Padre, y al Hijo, * y al Espíritu Santo.

Como era en un principio, ahora y siempre, * por los siglos de los siglos. Amén.

INTERCESSIONS

Introduction:

Response:

The Lord's Prayer

Celebrant :

WITH longing for the coming of God's kingdom,

let us offer our prayer to the Father: *All:* Our Father, who art

in heaven, hallowed be thy name; thy kingdom come; thy will

be done on earth as it is in heaven. Give us this day our dai- ly

bread; and forgive us our trespasses as we forgive those who

trespass a- gainst us; and lead us not in-to temp-ta-tion, but

de-liv- er us from e- vil.

Pater Noster

Celebrant :

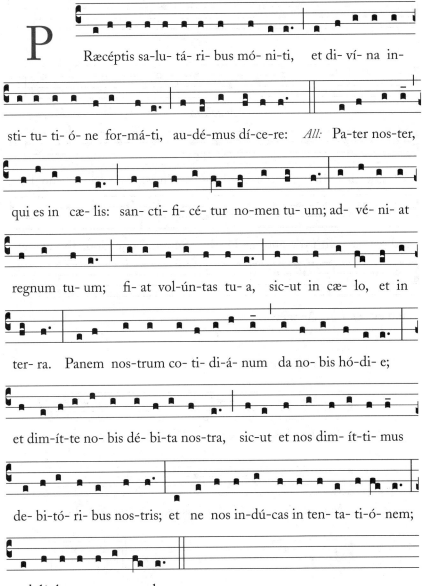

Ræcéptis sa-lu- tá- ri- bus mó- ni-ti,   et di- ví- na in-

sti- tu- ti- ó- ne for-má-ti, au-dé-mus dí-ce-re: *All:* Pa-ter nos-ter,

qui es in cæ- lis: san- cti- fi- cé- tur no-men tu- um; ad- vé- ni- at

regnum tu- um; fi- at vol-ún-tas tu- a, sic-ut in cæ- lo, et in

ter- ra. Panem nos-trum co- ti- di-á- num da no- bis hó-di- e;

et dim-ít-te no- bis dé- bi-ta nos-tra,   sic-ut et nos dim- ít-ti- mus

de- bi-tó- ri- bus nos-tris; et ne nos in-dú-cas in ten- ta- ti-ó- nem;

sed lí- be-ra nos a ma- lo.

PRAYER TONE

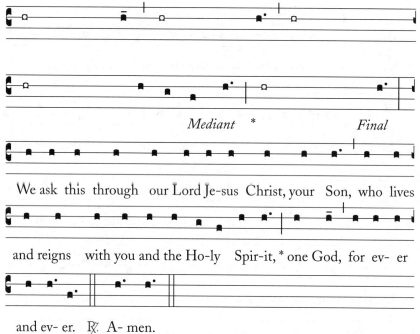

Mediant   *   *Final*

We ask this through our Lord Je-sus Christ, your Son, who lives

and reigns with you and the Ho-ly Spir-it, * one God, for ev- er

and ev- er. ℟. A- men.

DISMISSAL, when a priest or deacon is present:

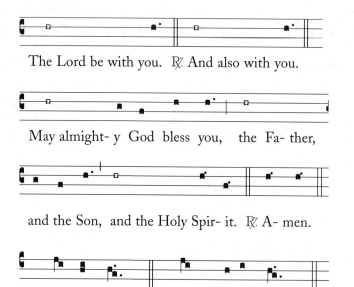

The Lord be with you. ℟. And also with you.

May almight- y God bless you, the Fa- ther,

and the Son, and the Holy Spir- it. ℟. A- men.

Go in peace. ℟. Thanks be to God.

DISMISSAL, when no priest or deacon is present:

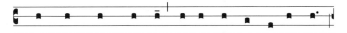

May the Lord bless us, protect us from all e- vil

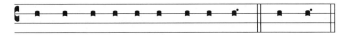

and bring us to ev- er- lasting life. ℟. A- men.

At Night Prayer, the blessing is said, even in individual recitation:

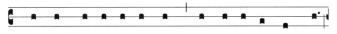

May the all-powerful Lord grant us a rest-ful night

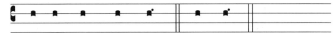

and a peace- ful death. ℟. A- men.

Alternate modes

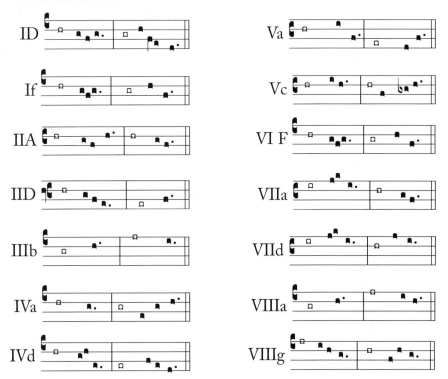

Proper of Seasons
Advent

FIRST SUNDAY OF ADVENT

PSALTER, WEEK I, 600.

Evening Prayer I

READING   1 Thessalonians 5:23-24

May the God of peace make you perfect in holiness. May he preserve you whole and entire, spirit, soul, and body, irreproachable at the coming of our Lord Jesus Christ. He who calls us is trustworthy, therefore he will do it.

RESPONSORY (VI F)

Lord, show *us* your mercy, * your mercy *and* love.
— Lord, show *us* your mercy, * your mercy *and* love.
And grant us *your* salvation,
    your mercy *and* love.
Glory to the Father, and *to* the Son, * and to the Ho*ly* Spirit.
— Lord, show *us* your mercy, * your mercy *and* love.

CANTICLE OF MARY

Ant.   See the Lord coming *from* afar; * his splendor fills *the* earth.

INTERCESSIONS

Jesus Christ is the joy and happiness of all who look forward *to* his coming. * Let us call upon *him* and say:
*Come, Lord, and do not de*lay!*
In joy, we wait *for* your coming,
— *come*, Lord Jesus.
Before time began, you shared life *with* the Father,
— come *now* and save us.
You created the world and all who *live* in it,
— come to redeem the work *of* your hands.
You did not hesitate to become man, sub*ject* to death,
— come to free us from the pow*er* of death.
You came to give us life *to* the full,
— come and give us your un*end*ing life.
You desire all people to live in love *in* your kingdom,
— come and bring together those who long to see you *face* to face.

Our Father . . .

Prayer

All-powerful God,
increase our strength of will for doing good
that Christ may find an eager welcome at his coming
and call us to his side in the kingdom of heaven,
where he lives and reigns with you and the Holy Spirit,
one God, for ever and ever.

Morning Prayer

READING   Romans 13:11-12

It is now the hour for you to wake from sleep, for our salvation is closer than when we first accepted the faith. The night is far spent; the day draws near. Let us cast off deeds of darkness and put on the armor of light.

RESPONSORY (VI F)

Christ, Son of the *living* God, * have mercy *on* us.
— Christ, Son of the *living* God, * have mercy *on* us.
You are the one who *is* to come,
— have mercy *on* us.
Glory to the Father, and *to* the Son, * and to the Ho*ly* Spirit.
— Christ, Son of the *living* God, * have mercy *on* us.

CANTICLE OF ZECHARIAH

Ant.   The Holy Spirit will come upon you, Mary; † you have no need to *be* afraid. * You will carry in your womb the Son of God, al*le*luia.

INTERCESSIONS

To God our Father, who has given us the grace to wait in joyful hope for the revelation of our Lord *Jesus* Christ, * let us *make* our prayer:
*Show us your mer*cy, *Lord.*
Sanctify us in *mind* and body,
— keep us without sin until the coming *of* your Son.
Make us walk this *day* in holiness,
— and live upright and devout lives *in* this world.
May we be clothed in our Lord *Jesus* Christ,
— and filled with the *Holy* Spirit.
Lord, help us to stand watch*ful* and ready,
— until your Son is revealed in *all* his glory.

Our Father . . .

Prayer

All-powerful God,
increase our strength of will for doing good
that Christ may find an eager welcome at his coming
and call us to his side in the kingdom of heaven,
where he lives and reigns with you and the Holy Spirit,
one God, for ever and ever.

Evening Prayer II

READING   Philippians 4:4-5

Rejoice in the Lord always! I say it again. Rejoice! Everyone should see how
unselfish you are. The Lord is near.

RESPONSORY (VI F)

Lord, show *us* your mercy, * your mercy *and* love.
— Lord, show *us* your mercy, * your mercy *and* love.
And grant us *your* salvation,
— your mercy *and* love.
Glory to the Father, and *to* the Son, * and to the Ho*ly* Spirit.
— Lord, show *us* your mercy, * your mercy *and* love.

CANTICLE OF MARY

Ant.   Do not be afraid, Mary, † you have found fa*vor* with God; * you
                will conceive and give birth to a Son, al*le*luia.

INTERCESSIONS

To Jesus Christ, our Redeemer, the way, the truth, *and* the life, * let us make our
    *hum*ble prayer:
Come and stay with us, *Lord.*
Son of the Most High, your coming was announced to the Virgin Mar*y* by
    Gabriel,
— come and rule over your peo*ple* for ever.
Holy One of God, in your presence John the Baptist leapt in Eliz*a*beth's womb,
— bring the joy of salvation to *all* the earth.
Jesus the Savior, the angel revealed your name to Jos*eph* the just man,
— come and save your people *from* their sins.
Light of the world, for whom Simeon and all *the* just waited,
— come and *com*fort us.
O Rising Sun that never sets, Zechariah foretold that you would visist us *from*
    above,
— come and shine on those who dwell in darkness and the shad*ow* of death.

Our Father . . .

Prayer

All-powerful God,
increase our strength of will for doing good
that Christ may find an eager welcome at his coming
and call us to his side in the kingdom of heaven,
where he lives and reigns with you and the Holy Spirit,
one God, for ever and ever.

MONDAY

Morning Prayer

READING   Isaiah 2:3
　　Come, let us climb the Lord's mountain,
　　　　to the house of the God of Jacob,
　　That he may instruct us in his ways,
　　　　and we may walk in his paths.
　　For from Zion shall go forth instruction,
　　　　and the word of the Lord from Jerusalem.

RESPONSORY (VI F)
Your light will *come*, Jerusalem, *
the Lord will dawn on you in radi*ant* beauty.
— Your light will *come*, Jerusalem, *
the Lord will dawn on you in radi*ant* beauty.
You will see his glo*ry* within you;
— the Lord will dawn on you in radi*ant* beauty.
Glory to the Father, and *to* the Son, * and to the Ho*ly* Spirit.
— Your light will *come*, Jerusalem, *
the Lord will dawn on you in radi*ant* beauty.

CANTICLE OF ZECHARIAH
Ant.　　　　　Lift up your eyes, Jerusalem, † and see the great power *of* your
　　　　　　　King; * your Savior comes to set *you* free.

INTERCESSIONS
Christ the Lord, Son of the living God, light from light, leads us into the light
　　and re*veals* his holiness. * With confidence let us *make* our prayer:
Come, Lord *Jesus.*

Light that never fades, dispel the *mists* about us,
— awaken our *faith* from sleep.
Guard us from all *harm* today,
— may your glory fill *us* with joy.
Give us unfailing gentleness *at* all times,
— toward every*one* we meet.
Come to create a new *earth* for us,
— where there will be jus*tice* and peace.

Our Father . . .

Prayer

Lord our God,
help us to prepare
for the coming of Christ your Son.
May he find us waiting,
eager in joyful prayer.
We ask this through our Lord Jesus Christ, your Son,
who lives and reigns with you and the Holy Spirit,
one God, for ever and ever.

Evening Prayer

READING   Philippians 3:20b-21
We eagerly await the coming of our Savior, the Lord Jesus Christ. He will
give a new form to this lowly body of ours and remake it according to the
pattern of his glorified body, by his power to subject everything to himself.

RESPONSORY (VI F)
Come and *set* us free, * Lord God of power *and* might.
— Come and *set* us free, * Lord God of power *and* might.
Let your face shine upon us and we *shall* be saved,
— Lord God of power *and* might.
Glory to the Father, and *to* the Son, * and to the Ho*ly* Spirit.
— Come and *set* us free, * Lord God of power *and* might.

CANTICLE OF MARY
Ant.   The angel of the Lord brought God's mes*sage* to Mary, * and she
                conceived by the power of the Holy Spirit, al*le*luia.

INTERCESSIONS
We cry *to* the Lord, * who will come to bring *us* salvation:
Come, Lord, and *save us.*

Lord Jesus Christ, our God, Sav*ior* of all,
— come swift*ly* and save us.
Lord, by your coming in*to* this world,
— free us from the sin *of* the world.
You came *from* the Father,
— show us the path that *leads* to him.
You were conceived by the *Ho*ly Spirit,
— by your word renew the same Spirit *in* our hearts.
Lord, be mindful *of* all men,
— who from the beginning of time have placed their *trust* in you.

Our Father . . .

Prayer

Lord our God,
help us to prepare
for the coming of Christ your Son.
May he find us waiting,
eager in joyful prayer.
We ask this through our Lord Jesus Christ, your Son,
who lives and reigns with you and the Holy Spirit,
one God, for ever and ever.

TUESDAY

Morning Prayer

READING   Genesis 49:10
   The scepter shall never depart from Judah,
         or the mace from between his legs,
   While tribute is brought to him,
         and he receives the people's homage.

RESPONSORY (VI F)
Your light will *come*, Jerusalem, *
the Lord will dawn on you in radi*ant* beauty.
— Your light will *come*, Jerusalem, *
the Lord will dawn on you in radi*ant* beauty.
You will see his glo*ry* within you;
— the Lord will dawn on you in radi*ant* beauty.
Glory to the Father, and *to* the Son, * and to the Ho*ly* Spirit.
— Your light will *come*, Jerusalem, *
the Lord will dawn on you in radi*ant* beauty.

CANTICLE OF ZECHARIAH
Ant.   From the root of Jesse a flower will blossom, † the glory of the
                        Lord will *fill* the earth, * and all creation shall see the saving
                        power *of* God.

INTERCESSIONS
God the almighty Father stretches forth his hand again to take possession of the
    remnant *of* his people. * Let us make our *prayer* to him:
*Lord, may your king*dom *come.*
Lord, grant that our works of pen*ance* may please you,
— and that we may be ready for your kingdom which *is* so near.
Prepare a path in our hearts for the coming *of* your Word,
— and let his glory be re*vealed* among us.
Bring low the mountains *of* our pride,
— and fill up the valleys *of* our weakness.
Break down the wall of hatred that di*vides* the nations,
— and make level for mankind the *paths* to peace.

Our Father . . .

                                    Prayer
        God of mercy and consolation,
        help us in our weakness and free us from sin.
        Hear our prayers
        that we may rejoice at the coming of your Son,
        who lives and reigns with you and the Holy Spirit,
        one God, for ever and ever.

                        Evening Prayer

READING   See 1 Corinthians 1:7b-9
    We await the revelation of our Lord Jesus Christ, who will strengthen us to
    the end, so that we will be blameless on the day of our Lord Jesus Christ.
    God is faithful, and it was he who called us to fellowship with his Son.

RESPONSORY (VI F)
Come and *set* us free, * Lord God of power *and* might.
— Come and *set* us free, * Lord God of power *and* might.
Let your face shine upon us and we *shall* be saved,
— Lord God of power *and* might.
Glory to the Father, and *to* the Son, * and to the Ho*ly* Spirit.
— Come and *set* us free, * Lord God of power *and* might.

CANTICLE OF MARY
Ant.   Seek the Lord while he *may* be found; * call on him while he is
                        near, al*le*luia.

INTERCESSIONS
To the eternal Word who became man to reveal to us the new and *living* way, * let
     us make our *hum*ble prayer:
Come, Lord, and save us.
God, in whom we live and move and *have* our being,
— come and teach us that you have made *us* your own.
You are not *far* from each of us,
— show yourself to all who *search* for you.
Father of the poor and consoler of *the* afflicted,
— set captives free, give joy to *those* who mourn.
You hate death *and* love life,
— free all mankind from e*ter*nal death.

Our Father . . .

Prayer

     God of mercy and consolation,
     help us in our weakness and free us from sin.
     Hear our prayers
     that we may rejoice at the coming of your Son,
     who lives and reigns with you and the Holy Spirit,
     one God, for ever and ever.

WEDNESDAY

Morning Prayer

READING   Isaiah 7:14b-15
     The virgin shall be with child, and bear a son, and shall name him Immanuel.
     He shall be living on curds and honey by the time he learns to reject the bad
     and choose the good.

RESPONSORY (VI F)
Your light will *come*, Jerusalem, *
the Lord will dawn on you in radi*ant* beauty.
— Your light will *come*, Jerusalem, *
the Lord will dawn on you in radi*ant* beauty.

You will see his glo*ry* within you;
— the Lord will dawn on you in radi*ant* beauty.
Glory to the Father, and *to* the Son, * and to the Ho*ly* Spirit.
— Your light will *come*, Jerusalem, *
the Lord will dawn on you in radi*ant* beauty.

CANTICLE OF ZECHARIAH
Ant.   The One who is coming after me is greate*r* than I; * I am not
                worthy to untie the strap of *his* sandals.

INTERCESSIONS
The Word of God humbled himself to dwell with us so that we might *see* his
    glory. * Rejoicing in hope, let us *call* upon him:
Emmanuel, be with *us.*
Ruler, *just* and righteous,
— bring justice to the poor and *the* oppressed.
King of peace, you beat swords into plowshares and spears *in*to pruning hooks,
— turn hatred into love and our grievances in*to* forgiveness.
You do not judge *by* appearances,
— recognize those who *are* your own.
When you come with power and might up*on* the clouds,
— grant that we may come before you *with*out shame.

Our Father . . .

Prayer

Lord our God,
    grant that we may be ready
    to receive Christ when he comes in glory
    and to share in the banquet of heaven,
    where he lives and reigns with you and the Holy Spirit,
    one God, for ever and ever.

Evening Prayer

READING   1 Corinthians 4:5
    Stop passing judgment before the time of the Lord's return. He will bring to
    light what is hidden in the darkness and manifest the intentions of hearts. At
    that time, everyone will receive his praise from God.

RESPONSORY (VI F)
Come and *set* us free, * Lord God of power *and* might.
— Come and *set* us free, * Lord God of power *and* might.

Let your face shine upon us and we *shall* be saved,
— Lord God of power *and* might.
Glory to the Father, and *to* the Son, * and to the Ho*ly* Spirit.
— Come and *set* us free, * Lord God of power *and* might.

CANTICLE OF MARY
Ant.   The law will go *forth* from Zion; * the word of the Lord from
                        *J*erusalem.

INTERCESSIONS
Let us pray to *God* the Father, * who sent his Son to bring us *end*less peace:
*Lord, your king*dom *come.*
Father most holy, look kindly on your Church,
— come and visit this vine which your own right *hand* has planted.
Be mindful, Lord, of all the *sons* of Abraham,
— fulfill the promises you made *to* their fathers.
Merciful God, look kindly upon men and women of *every* race,
— may they honor you *for* your goodness.
Eternal Shepherd, visit the sheep *of* your flock,
— and gather them together *in* one fold.
Remember those who have gone forth from this world *in* your peace,
— lead them into glory *with* your Son.

Our Father . . .

Prayer
Lord our God,
grant that we may be ready
to receive Christ when he comes in glory
and to share in the banquet of heaven,
where he lives and reigns with you and the Holy Spirit,
one God, for ever and ever.

THURSDAY

Morning Prayer

READING   Isaiah 45:8
Let justice descend, O heavens, like dew from above,
    like gentle rain let the skies drop it down.
Let the earth open and salvation bud forth;
    let justice also spring up!

RESPONSORY (VI F)

Your light will *come*, Jerusalem, *
the Lord will dawn on you in radi*ant* beauty.
— Your light will *come*, Jerusalem, *
the Lord will dawn on you in radi*ant* beauty.
You will see his glo*ry* within you;
— the Lord will dawn on you in radi*ant* beauty.
Glory to the Father, and *to* the Son, * and to the Ho*ly* Spirit.
— Your light will *come*, Jerusalem, *
the Lord will dawn on you in radi*ant* beauty.

CANTICLE OF ZECHARIAH

Ant.   I shall wait for my *Lord* and Savior * and point him out when he
is near, al*le*luia.

INTERCESSIONS

Christ is the wisdom and power of God, and his delight is to be with the child*ren*
    of men. * With confidence *let* us pray:
Draw near to us, Lord.
Lord Jesus Christ, you have called us to your *glo*rious kingdom,
— make us walk worthily, pleasing God in *all* we do.
You who stand un*known* among us,
— reveal yourself to *men* and women.
You are nearer to us than we *to* ourselves,
— strengthen our faith and our hope *of* salvation.
You are the *source* of holiness,
— keep us holy and without sin now and until the day *of* your coming.

Our Father . . .

Prayer

Father,
we need your help.
Free us from sin and bring us to life.
Support us by your power.
Grant this through our Lord Jesus Christ, your Son,
who lives and reigns with you and the Holy Spirit,
one God, for ever and ever.

Evening Prayer

READING   James 5:7-8, 9b

Be patient, my brother, until the coming of the Lord. See how the farmer awaits the precious yield of the soil. He looks forward to it patiently while the soil receives the winter and the spring rains. You, too, must be patient. Steady your hearts, because the coming of the Lord is at hand. See! The judge stands at the gate.

RESPONSORY (VI F)

Come and *set* us free, * Lord God of power *and* might.

— Come and *set* us free, * Lord God of power *and* might.

Let your face shine upon us and we *shall* be saved,

— Lord God of power *and* might.

Glory to the Father, and *to* the Son, * and to the Ho*ly* Spirit.

— Come and *set* us free, * Lord God of power *and* might.

CANTICLE OF MARY

Ant.   Blessèd are you *a*mong women, * and blessèd is the fruit of *your* womb.

INTERCESSIONS

To Christ, the great light promised by the prophets to those who live in the shad*ow* of death, * let us raise our *voice* in prayer:

Come, Lord *Jesus.*

Word of God, in the beginning you created all things and in the fullness of time as*sumed* our nature,

— come and deliver *us* from death.

True light, shining *on* mankind,

— come and dis*pel* our darkness.

Only-begotten Son, dwelling in the *Fa*ther's heart,

— come and tell us of God's *loving* kindness.

Christ Jesus, you come among us as the *Son* of Man,

— transform those who know you into the *sons* of God.

You welcome all who call upon *you* in need,

— bring into your wedding feast those who beg *at* the door.

Our Father . . .

Prayer

Father,
we need your help.
Free us from sin and bring us to life.
Support us by your power.
Grant this through our Lord Jesus Christ, your Son,
who lives and reigns with you and the Holy Spirit,
one God, for ever and ever.

FRIDAY

Morning Prayer

READING   Jeremiah 30:21-22

Thus says the Lord:
His leader shall be from Jacob
    and his ruler shall come from his kin.
When I summon him,
    he shall approach me.
You shall be my people,
    and I will be your God.

RESPONSORY (VI F)

Your light will *come*, Jerusalem, *
the Lord will dawn on you in radi*ant* beauty.
— Your light will *come*, Jerusalem, *
the Lord will dawn on you in radi*ant* beauty.
You will see his glo*ry* within you;
— the Lord will dawn on you in radi*ant* beauty.
Glory to the Father, and *to* the Son, * and to the Ho*ly* Spirit.
— Your light will *come*, Jerusalem, *
the Lord will dawn on you in radi*ant* beauty.

CANTICLE OF ZECHARIAH

Ant.   Our God comes, born as man of *Da*vid's line, * enthroned as
                king for ever, al*le*luia.

INTERCESSIONS

Through his Son, God the Father revealed his glory to *men* and women. *
    Therefore, let our joyful *cry* resound:
Lord, may your name be *glorified.*
Teach us, Lord, to *love* each other,
— as Christ loved us *for* God's glory.

Fill us with all joy and *peace* in faith,
— that we may walk in the hope and strength of the *Ho*ly Spirit.
Help all mankind, Lord, in your *lov*ing mercy,
— be near to those who seek you *with*out knowing it.
You call and sanctify *the* elect,
— though we are sinners, crown us with e*ter*nal happiness.

Our Father . . .

Prayer

Jesus, our Lord,
save us from our sins.
Come, protect us from all dangers
and lead us to salvation,
for you live and reign with the Father and the Holy Spirit,
one God, for ever and ever.

Evening Prayer

READING   2 Peter 3:8b-9
In the Lord's eyes, one day is as a thousand years and a thousand years are as
a day. The Lord does not delay in keeping his promise— though some
consider it "delay." Rather, he shows you generous patience, since he wants
none to perish but all to come to repentance.

RESPONSORY (VI F)
Come and *set* us free, * Lord God of power *and* might.
— Come and *set* us free, * Lord God of power *and* might.
Let your face shine upon us and we *shall* be saved,
— Lord God of power *and* might.
Glory to the Father, and *to* the Son, * and to the Ho*ly* Spirit.
— Come and *set* us free, * Lord God of power *and* might.

CANTICLE OF MARY
Ant.   Out of Egypt I have *called* my Son; * he will come to save *his*
                people.

INTERCESSIONS
With confidence let us call *up*on Christ, * the shepherd and guardian *of* our souls:
Lord, have mercy on *us.*
Good shepherd *of* God's flock,
— gather all in*to* your Church.
Lord Jesus, help the shepherds of your *pil*grim people,
— until you come again may they zealously *feed* your flock.

Choose from among us heralds *of* your word,
— to proclaim your Gospel to the ends *of* the earth.
Take pity on all who struggle and fall a*long* the way,
— may they find a *friend* to help them.
Show your glo*ry* in heaven,
— to those who listen to your *voice* on earth.

Our Father . . .

Prayer

Jesus, our Lord,
save us from our sins.
Come, protect us from all dangers
and lead us to salvation,
for you live and reign with the Father and the Holy Spirit,
one God, for ever and ever.

SATURDAY

Morning Prayer

READING   Isaiah 11:1-2

A shoot shall sprout from Jesse,
    and from his roots a bud shall blossom.
The spirit of the Lord shall rest upon him:
    a spirit of wisdom and of understanding,
A spirit of counsel and of strength,
    a spirit of knowledge and of fear of the Lord,
    and his delight shall be the fear of the Lord.

RESPONSORY (VI F)
Your light will *come*, Jerusalem, *
the Lord will dawn on you in radi*ant* beauty.
— Your light will *come*, Jerusalem, *
the Lord will dawn on you in radi*ant* beauty.
You will see his glo*ry* within you;
— the Lord will dawn on you in radi*ant* beauty.
Glory to the Father, and *to* the Son, * and to the Ho*ly* Spirit.
— Your light will *come*, Jerusalem, *
the Lord will dawn on you in radi*ant* beauty.

CANTICLE OF ZECHARIAH

Ant.   Banish your fears, O people of Zion; † God, *your* own God, * is coming to you, al*le*luia.

INTERCESSIONS

Let us pray to *God* our Father, * who from of old has called his people *to* salvation:
Lord, protect your *people.*

You promised to plant the seed of justice a*mong* your people,
— protect the holiness *of* your Church.

Lord, teach all men and women to listen *to* your word,
— and help believers to perse*vere* in holiness.

Keep us in the love *of* your Spirit.
— that we may receive the mercy of your Son who *is* to come.

Father most merciful, strengthen us *to* the last,
— until the day of the coming of Jesus *Christ* our Lord.

Our Father . . .

Prayer

God our Father,
you loved the world so much
you gave your only Son to free us
from the ancient power of sin and death.
Help us who wait for his coming,
and lead us to true liberty.
We ask this through our Lord Jesus Christ, your Son,
who lives and reigns with you and the Holy Spirit,
one God, for ever and ever.

SECOND SUNDAY OF ADVENT

Evening Prayer I

READING   1 Thessalonians 5:23-24

May the God of peace make you perfect in holiness. May he preserve you whole and entire, spirit, soul, and body, irreproachable at the coming of our Lord Jesus Christ. He who calls us is trustworthy, therefore he will do it.

RESPONSORY (VI F)

Lord, show *us* your mercy, * your mercy *and* love.
— Lord, show *us* your mercy, * your mercy *and* love.
And grant us *your* salvation,
— your mercy *and* love.
Glory to the Father, and *to* the Son, * and to the Ho*ly* Spirit.
— Lord, show *us* your mercy, * your mercy *and* love.

CANTICLE OF MARY

Ant.   Come to us, Lord, and may your presence *be* our peace; * with hearts made perfect we shall rejoice in your companionship *for* ever.

INTERCESSIONS

Jesus is Lord, born of the *Vir*gin Mary. * Let us pray to him with *joy*ful hearts:
Come, Lord, Jesus!
Son of God, you will come again as the true messenger *of* the covenant,
— help the world to recognize *and* accept you.
Born in your Father's heart, you became man in the womb of the *Vir*gin Mary,
— free us from the tyranny of change *and* decay.
In your life on earth, you came to die *as* a man,
— save us from ever*last*ing death.
When you come to judge, show us your *lov*ing mercy,
— and forgive *us* our weaknesses.
Lord Jesus, by your death you have given hope to those *who* have died,
— be merciful to those from whom *we* now pray.

Our Father . . .

Prayer

God of power and mercy,
open our hearts in welcome.
Remove the things that hinder us from receiving Christ with joy,
so that we may share his wisdom
and become one with him
when he comes in glory,
for he lives and reigns with you and the Holy Spirit,
one God, for ever and ever.

Morning Prayer

READING   Romans 13:11-12
It is now the hour for you to wake from sleep, for our salvation is closer than
when we first accepted the faith. The night is far spent; the day draws near.
Let us cast off deeds of darkness and put on the armor of light.

RESPONSORY (VI F)
Christ, Son of the *liv*ing God, * have mercy *on* us.
— Christ, Son of the *liv*ing God, * have mercy *on* us.
You are the one who is to come,
— have mercy *on* us.
Glory to the Father, and *to* the Son, * and to the Ho*ly* Spirit.
— Christ, Son of the *liv*ing God, * have mercy *on* us.

CANTICLE OF ZECHARIAH
Ant.   I am sending my an*gel* before me * to prepare the way for *my*
                  coming.

INTERCESSIONS
To the Lord Jesus Christ, judge of the living *and* the dead, * *let* us pray:
Come, Lord *Jesus!*
Lord Jesus, you came *to* save sinners,
— protect us in times *of* temptation.
You will come in glory to *be* our judge,
— show in us your pow*er* to save.
Help us to keep the precepts of your law with the strength *of* the Spirit,
— and to look forward in love *to* your coming.
You are praised throughout the ages; in your mercy help us to live devoutly and
    temperately *in* this life,
— as we wait in joyful hope for the revelation *of* your glory.

Our Father . . .

Prayer

God of power and mercy,
open our hearts in welcome.
Remove the things that hinder us from receiving Christ with joy,
so that we may share his wisdom
and become one with him
when he comes in glory,
for he lives and reigns with you and the Holy Spirit,
one God, for ever and ever.

Evening Prayer II

READING   Philippians 4:4-5

Rejoice in the Lord always! I say it again. Rejoice! Everyone should see how unselfish you are. The Lord is near.

RESPONSORY (VI F)
Lord, show *us* your mercy, * your mercy *and* love.
— Lord, show *us* your mercy, * your mercy *and* love.
And grant us *your* salvation,
— your mercy *and* love.
Glory to the Father, and *to* the Son, * and to the Ho*ly* Spirit.
— Lord, show *us* your mercy, * your mercy *and* love.

CANTICLE OF MARY
Ant.   Blessèd are you, O *Vir*gin Mary, * for your *great* faith;
                         all that the Lord *pro*mised you * will come to pass through you,
                         al*le*luia.

INTERCESSIONS
To Christ the Lord, who was born of the *Vir*gin Mary, * let us pray with *joy*ful
   hearts:
Come, Lord *Jesus!*
Lord Jesus, in the mystery of your incarnation, you revealed your glory *to* the
   world,
— give us new life *by* your coming.
You have taken our weakness up*on* yourself,
— grant *us* your mercy.
You redeemed the world from sin by your first coming *in* humility,
— free us from all guilt when you come a*gain* in glory.

You live and rule *over* all,
— in your goodness bring us to our eter*nal* inheritance.
You sit at the right hand *of* the Father,
— gladden the souls of the dead *with* your light.

Our Father . . .

Prayer

God of power and mercy,
open our hearts in welcome.
Remove the things that hinder us from receiving Christ with joy,
so that we may share his wisdom
and become one with him
when he comes in glory,
for he lives and reigns with you and the Holy Spirit,
one God, for ever and ever.

MONDAY

Morning Prayer

READING   Isaiah 2:3b

Come, let us climb the Lord's mountain,
    to the house of the God of Jacob,
That he may instruct us in his ways,
    and we may walk in his paths.
For from Zion shall go forth instruction,
    and the word of the Lord from Jerusalem.

RESPONSORY (VI F)
Your light will *come*, Jerusalem, *
the Lord will dawn on you in radi*ant* beauty.
— Your light will *come*, Jerusalem, *
the Lord will dawn on you in radi*ant* beauty.
You will see his glo*ry* within you;
— the Lord will dawn on you in radi*ant* beauty.
Glory to the Father, and *to* the Son, * and to the Ho*ly* Spirit.
— Your light will *come*, Jerusalem, *
the Lord will dawn on you in radi*ant* beauty.

CANTICLE OF ZECHARIAH
Ant.   The *Lord* proclaims: * Repent the kingdom of God is upon you,
                    al*le*luia.

INTERCESSIONS

To Christ our Redeemer, who will come again to free from the power of death all
  those who re*turn* to him, * let us *hum*bly pray:

Come, Lord *Jesus.*

As we proclaim your *com*ing, Lord,

— cleanse our hearts of every *vain* desire.

Lord, may the Church *which* you founded,

— proclaim your greatness *to* all peoples.

Your law is a light *to* our eyes,

— let it protect those who *trust* in you.

You allowed the joys of your coming to be foretold to us *by* your Church,

— may we receive you with ea*ger* devotion.

Our Father . . .

Prayer

Lord,
free us from our sins and make us whole.
Hear our prayer,
and prepare us to celebrate the incarnation of your Son, who lives and reigns
  with you and the Holy Spirit,
one God, for ever and ever.

Evening Prayer

READING Philippians 3:20b-21

  We eagerly await the coming of our Savior, the Lord Jesus Christ. He will
  give a new form to this lowly body of ours and remake it according to the
  pattern of his glorified body, by his power to subject everything to himself.

RESPONSORY (VI F)

Come and *set* us free, * Lord God of power *and* might.

— Come and *set* us free, * Lord God of power *and* might.

Let your face shine upon us and we *shall* be saved,

— Lord God of power *and* might.

Glory to the Father, and *to* the Son, * and to the Ho*ly* Spirit.

— Come and *set* us free, * Lord God of power *and* might.

CANTICLE OF MARY

Ant. See, your King comes, the master *of* the earth; * he will shatter
the yoke of *our* slavery.

INTERCESSIONS

To Christ our Lord, judge of the living *and* the dead, * let us cry *out* with faith:
Come, Lord *Jesus!*
Lord, may the world know your justice which the hea*vens* proclaim,
— may your glory *fill* the earth.
For us you took upon yourself the weak*ness* of man,
— protect us with the strength of your own *di*vine life.
Come to those imprisoned in the dark*ness* of ignorance,
— show them the radiance of your own *di*vine light.
In your humility as a man, you took a*way* our sin,
— now in your glory grant *us* true happiness.
When you come in glo*ry* to judge us,
— gather the dead in*to* your kingdom.

Our Father . . .

Prayer

Lord,
free us from our sins and make us whole.
Hear our prayer,
and prepare us to celebrate the incarnation of your Son,
who lives and reigns with you and the Holy Spirit,
one God, for ever and ever.

TUESDAY

Morning Prayer

READING   Genesis 49:10

The scepter shall never depart from Judah,
    or the mace from between his legs,
While tribute is brought to him,
    and he receives the people's homage.

RESPONSORY (VI F)
Your light will *come*, Jerusalem, *
the Lord will dawn on you in radi*ant* beauty.
— Your light will *come*, Jerusalem, *
the Lord will dawn on you in radi*ant* beauty.
You will see his glo*ry* within you;
— the Lord will dawn on you in radi*ant* beauty.

Glory to the Father, and *to* the Son, * and to the Ho*ly* Spirit.
— Your light will *come*, Jerusalem, *
the Lord will dawn on you in radi*ant* beauty.

CANTICLE OF ZECHARIAH

Ant.   Rejoice and be glad, O daugh*ter* of Zion; * I will come and make
my dwelling in you, says *the* Lord.

INTERCESSIONS

To Christ our Lord, the light *of* the world, * let us cry *out* with joy:
Come, Lord *Jesus!*
Dispel our darkness with the light *of* your presence,
— and make us worthy *of* your gifts.
Save us, *Lord* our God,
— that we may praise your holy *name* this day.
Enkindle in our hearts the flame *of* your love,
— and make us long to be uni*ted* with you.
You bore *our* infirmity,
— aid the sick and those who are to *die* this day.

Our Father . . .

Prayer

Almighty God,
help us to look forward
to the glory of the birth of Christ our Savior:
his coming is proclaimed joyfully
to the ends of the earth,
for he lives and reigns with you and the Holy Spirit,
one God, for ever and ever.

Evening Prayer

READING   See 1 Corinthians 1:7b-9
We await the revelation of our Lord Jesus Christ, who will strengthen us to
the end, so that we will be blameless on the day of our Lord Jesus Christ.
God is faithful, and it was he who called us to fellowship with his Son.

RESPONSORY (VI F)
Come and *set* us free, * Lord God of power *and* might.
— Come and *set* us free, * Lord God of power *and* might.
Let your face shine upon us and we *shall* be saved,
— Lord God of power *and* might.

Glory to the Father, and *to* the Son, * and to the Ho*ly* Spirit.
— Come and *set* us free, * Lord God of power *and* might.

CANTICLE OF MARY

Ant.   A voice is heard crying in the wilderness: † Prepare the way *of* the
                        Lord; * make straight the path of *our* God.

INTERCESSIONS

To Christ, our Lord and Redeemer, who will appear openly *on* the last day, * let us
    joy*fu*lly pray:
Come, Lord *Jesus!*
Our Redeemer and Lord, by your birth as a man you freed us from the yoke *of* the
    law,
— complete in us the works of your *loving* kindness.
From us you took whatever served *your* divinity,
— give us whatever we *need* to serve you.
Grant the desire we ask of *you* today,
— inflame our hearts with the fire *of* your love.
On earth we live with *you* by faith,
— in glory may we re*joice* with you.
Steep the souls of the faith*ful* departed,
— in the dew of your *loving* kindness.

Our Father . . .

Prayer

Almighty God,
help us to look forward
to the glory of the birth of Christ our Savior:
his coming is proclaimed joyfully
to the ends of the earth,
for he lives and reigns with you and the Holy Spirit,
one God, for ever and ever.

WEDNESDAY

Morning Prayer

READING   Isaiah 7:14b-15

The virgin shall be with child, and bear a son, and shall name him Immanuel.
He shall be living on curds and honey by the time he learns to reject the bad
and choose the good.

RESPONSORY (VI F)

Your light will *come*, Jerusalem, *
the Lord will dawn on you in radi*ant* beauty.
—Your light will *come*, Jerusalem, *
the Lord will dawn on you in radi*ant* beauty.
You will see his glo*ry* within you;
—the Lord will dawn on you in radi*ant* beauty.
Glory to the Father, and *to* the Son, * and to the Ho*ly* Spirit.
—Your light will *come*, Jerusalem, *
the Lord will dawn on you in radi*ant* beauty.

CANTICLE OF ZECHARIAH

Ant.   He will be enthroned in *Da*vid's place * to be king for ever,
                       al*le*luia.

INTERCESSIONS

To Jesus Christ our Lord, who came among us *in* his mercy, * let us constantly cry
   out with joy:
Come, Lord *Jesus!*
You came from the Father to take on our *hu*man nature,
—now set free what was harmed in *us* by sin.
One day you will come again in glory to your *cho*sen people,
—come to us today and help us sinners to recognize your mercy and *tend*er love.
We glory in praising *you*, Lord Jesus,
—come and bring us *your* salvation.
Through faith you lead us *in*to light,
—may we reveal your justice *through* our deeds.

Our Father . . .

Prayer

All-powerful Father,
we await the healing power of Christ your Son.
Let us not be discouraged by our weaknesses
as we prepare for his coming.
Keep us steadfast in your love.
We ask this through our Lord Jesus Christ, your Son,
who lives and reigns with you and the Holy Spirit,
one God, for ever and ever.

Evening Prayer

READING   1 Corinthians 4:5

Stop passing judgment before the time of the Lord's return. He will bring to
light what is hidden in the darkness and manifest the intentions of hearts. At
that time, everyone will receive his praise from God.

RESPONSORY (VI F)
Come and *set* us free, * Lord God of power *and* might.
— Come and *set* us free, * Lord God of power *and* might.
Let your face shine upon us and we *shall* be saved,
— Lord God of power *and* might.
Glory to the Father, and *to* the Son, * and to the Ho*ly* Spirit.
— Come and *set* us free, * Lord God of power *and* might.

CANTICLE OF MARY
Ant.   Zion, you will *be* renewed, * and you will see the Just One who is
                coming *to* you.

INTERCESSIONS
We humbly pray to Jesus Christ, who rescues us from the dark*ness* of sin, * and in
    faith *we* cry out:
Come, Lord Jesus!
Lord, gather together all the people *of* the earth,
— and establish with them your ever*last*ing covenant.
Lamb of God, you came of old to take away the sin *of* the world,
— purge us from the dregs *of* our guilt.
You came to recover *what* was lost,
— come once again in your mercy lest you punish what you *have* recovered.
Our faith *seeks* you out,
— let us find everlasting joy with you *when* you come.
You will judge the living *and* the dead,
— graciously gather the dead into the ranks *of* the blessèd.

Our Father . . .

Prayer

All-powerful Father,
we await the healing power of Christ your Son.
Let us not be discouraged by our weaknesses
as we prepare for his coming.
Keep us steadfast in your love.
We ask this through our Lord Jesus Christ, your Son,
who lives and reigns with you and the Holy Spirit,
one God, for ever and ever.

THURSDAY

Morning Prayer

READING Isaiah 45:8

Let justice descend, O heavens, like dew from above,
    like gentle rain let the skies drop it down.
Let the earth open and salvation bud forth;
    let justice also spring up!

RESPONSORY (VI F)
Your light will *come*, Jerusalem, *
the Lord will dawn on you in radi*ant* beauty.
— Your light will *come*, Jerusalem, *
the Lord will dawn on you in radi*ant* beauty.
You will see his glo*ry* within you;
— the Lord will dawn on you in radi*ant* beauty.
Glory to the Father, and *to* the Son, * and to the Ho*ly* Spirit.
— Your light will *come*, Jerusalem, *
the Lord will dawn on you in radi*ant* beauty.

CANTICLE OF ZECHARIAH
Ant.   I will help you, *says* the Lord. * I am your Savior, the Holy One *of* Israel.

INTERCESSIONS
Let us pray to *God* our Father * who sent his Son to *save* mankind:
*Show us your mer*cy, Lord!*
Father most merciful, we confess our faith in your Christ *with* our words,
— keep us from denying him *in* our actions.

You have sent your *Son* to rescue us,
— remove every sorrow from the face of the earth and *from* our country.
Our land looks forward with delight to the approach *of* your Son,
— let it experience the full*ness* of joy.
Through your mercy make us live holy and chaste lives *in* this world,
— eagerly awaiting the blessèd hope and coming of *Christ* in glory.

Our Father . . .

Prayer

Almighty Father,
give us the joy of your love
to prepare the way for Christ our Lord.
Help us to serve you and one another.
We ask this through our Lord Jesus Christ, your Son,
who lives and reigns with you and the Holy Spirit,
one God, for ever and ever.

Evening Prayer

READING   James 5:7-8, 9b
Be patient, my brother, until the coming of the Lord. See how the farmer
awaits the precious yield of the soil. He looks forward to it patiently while the
soil receives the winter and the spring rains. You, too, must be patient. Steady
your hearts, because the coming of the Lord is at hand. See! The judge stands
at the gate.

RESPONSORY (VI F)
Come and *set* us free, * Lord God of power *and* might.
— Come and *set* us free, * Lord God of power *and* might.
Let your face shine upon us and we *shall* be saved,
— Lord God of power *and* might.
Glory to the Father, and *to* the Son, * and to the Ho*ly* Spirit.
— Come and *set* us free, * Lord God of power *and* might.

CANTICLE OF MARY
Ant.   The one who is coming after me exist*ed* before me; * I am not
                 worthy to untie *his* sandals.

INTERCESSIONS
To Christ our Lord, who humbled himself *for* our sake, * we joy*fully* say:
Come, Lord *Jesus.*

Lord Jesus, by your coming you rescued the *world* from sin,
— cleanse our souls and bod*ies* from guilt.
By the mystery of your incarnation we are made your broth*ers* and sisters,
— do not let us become e*stranged* from you.
Do *not* judge harshly,
— those redeemed with *such* great cost.
No age, O Christ, is without your goodness and *holy* riches,
— enable us to merit the unfading *crown* of glory.
Lord, to you we commend the souls of your de*part*ed servants,
— having died to the world, may they be alive in *you* for ever.

Our Father . . .

Prayer

Almighty Father,
give us the joy of your love
to prepare the way for Christ our Lord.
Help us to serve you and one another.
We ask this through our Lord Jesus Christ, your Son,
who lives and reigns with you and the Holy Spirit,
one God, for ever and ever.

FRIDAY

Morning Prayer

READING   Jeremiah 30:21-22
        Thus says the Lord:
His leader shall be from Jacob
        and his ruler shall come from his kin.
When I summon him,
        he shall approach me.
You shall be my people,
        and I will be your God.

RESPONSORY (VI F)
Your light will *come*, Jerusalem, *
the Lord will dawn on you in radi*ant* beauty.
— Your light will *come*, Jerusalem, *
the Lord will dawn on you in radi*ant* beauty.
You will see his glo*ry* within you;
— the Lord will dawn on you in radi*ant* beauty.

Glory to the Father, and *to* the Son, * and to the Ho*ly* Spirit.
— Your light will *come*, Jerusalem, *
the Lord will dawn on you in radi*ant* beauty.

CANTICLE OF ZECHARIAH

Ant.   Say to the fainthear*ted*: Take courage! * The Lord our God is
coming *to* save us.

INTERCESSIONS

To Jesus Christ, who comes to save us *from* our sins, * let us cry *out* with joy:
Come, Lord *Jesus!*
The prophets of old foretold your *birth* among us,
— now make virtue come to *life* in us.
We proclaim your *saving* work,
— now grant us *your* salvation.
You came to *heal* the contrite,
— heal the weakness *of* your people.
You came and saw fit to recon*cile* the world,
— when you come again in judgment, free us from the tor*ments* of punishment.

Our Father . . .

Prayer

All-powerful God,
help us to look forward in hope
to the coming of our Savior.
May we live as he has taught,
ready to welcome him with burning love and faith.
We ask this through our Lord Jesus Christ, your Son,
who lives and reigns with you and the Holy Spirit,
one God, for ever and ever.

Evening Prayer

READING   2 Peter 3:8b-9
In the Lord's eyes, one day is as a thousand years and a thousand years are as
a day. The Lord does not delay in keeping his promise— though some
consider it "delay." Rather, he shows you generous patience, since he wants
none to perish but all to come to repentance.

RESPONSORY (VI F)

Come and *set* us free, * Lord God of power *and* might.

— Come and *set* us free, * Lord God of power *and* might.

Let your face shine upon us and we *shall* be saved,

— Lord God of power *and* might.

Glory to the Father, and *to* the Son, * and to the Ho*ly* Spirit.

— Come and *set* us free, * Lord God of power *and* might.

CANTICLE OF MARY

Ant. Rejoicing you *shall* draw water * from the well-springs of *the* Savior.

INTERCESSIONS

To our Redeemer who came to bring good news *to* the poor, * let us earnes*tly* pray:

Let all men see your *glory!*

Show yourself to those who have *nev*er known you,

— let them see your *saving* work.

Let your name be preached to the ends *of* the earth,

— that all may find the *way* to you.

You first came to *save* the world,

— now come again and save those who be*lieve* in you.

You brought freedom to *us* by saving us,

— continue to save us and *make* us free.

You came once as a man; you will re*turn* in judgment,

— bring eternal reward to those *who* have died.

Our Father . . .

Prayer

All-powerful God,
help us to look forward in hope
to the coming of our Savior.
May we live as he has taught,
ready to welcome him with burning love and faith.
We ask this through our Lord Jesus Christ, your Son,
who lives and reigns with you and the Holy Spirit,
one God, for ever and ever.

SATURDAY

Morning Prayer

Isaiah 11:1-3a

A shoot shall sprout from Jesse,
  and from his roots a bud shall blossom.
The spirit of the Lord shall rest upon him:
  a spirit of wisdom and of understanding,
A spirit of counsel and of strength,
  a spirit of knowledge and of fear of the Lord,
  and his delight shall be the fear of the Lord.

RESPONSORY (VI F)

Your light will *come*, Jerusalem, *
the Lord will dawn on you in radi*ant* beauty.
— Your light will *come*, Jerusalem, *
the Lord will dawn on you in radi*ant* beauty.
You will see his glo*ry* within you;
— the Lord will dawn on you in radi*ant* beauty.
Glory to the Father, and *to* the Son, * and to the Ho*ly* Spirit.
— Your light will *come*, Jerusalem, *
the Lord will dawn on you in radi*ant* beauty.

CANTICLE OF ZECHARIAH

Ant.   The Lord will set up his standard in the sight of *all* the nations, *
            and gather to himself the dispersed *of* Israel.

INTERCESSIONS

To Jesus Christ, our Redeemer, who will come again in glory *with* great power, *
  let us make our *hum*ble prayer:
Come, Lord *Jesus!*
Lord Jesus, you will come *with* great power,
— look on our lowliness and make us worthy *of* your gifts.
You came to be the good news *for* mankind,
— may we always proclaim your *saving* work.
You are worthy of praise, for you have life and *rule* all things,
— help us to wait in joyful hope for the coming *of* your glory.
We long for the grace *of* your coming,
— console us with the gift of your own *di*vine life.

Our Father . . .

Prayer

Lord,
let your glory dawn to take away our darkness.
May we be revealed as the children of light
at the coming of your Son,
who lives and reigns with you and the Holy Spirit,
one God, for ever and ever.

THIRD SUNDAY OF ADVENT

Evening Prayer I

When this Sunday occurs on December 17, the hymns are taken from those given on 1303-1304. The readings, antiphons for the canticles of Zechariah and Mary, and the intercessions, 110-112, assigned for each day, are used. Those for the Third Sunday are then omitted.

READING   1 Thessalonians 5:23-24

May the God of peace make you perfect in holiness. May he preserve you whole and entire, spirit, soul, and body, irreproachable at the coming of our Lord Jesus Christ. He who calls us is trustworthy, therefore he will do it.

RESPONSORY (VI F)

Lord, show *us* your mercy, * your mercy *and* love.
— Lord, show *us* your mercy, * your mercy *and* love.
And grant us *your* salvation,
— your mercy *and* love.
Glory to the Father, and *to* the Son, * and to the Ho*ly* Spirit.
— Lord, show *us* your mercy, * your mercy *and* love.

CANTICLE OF MARY

Ant.   There was no god before me and after me there will be none; †
every knee shall *bend* in worship, * and every tongue *shall* praise me.

INTERCESSIONS

Jesus Christ is the joy and happiness of all who look forward *to* his coming. * Let us call upon *him* and say:
*Come, Lord, and do not de*lay!*
In joy, we wait *for* your coming,
— *come*, Lord Jesus.
Before time began, you shared life *with* the Father,
— come *now* and save us.
You created the world and all who *live* in it,
— come to redeem the work *of* your hands.
You did not hesitate to become man, sub*ject* to death,
— come to free us from the pow*er* of death.
You came to give us life *to* the full,
— come and give us your un*end*ing life.
You desire all people to live in love *in* your kingdom,
— come and bring together those who long to see you *face* to face.

Our Father . . .

Prayer

Lord God,
may we, your people,
who look forward to the birthday of Christ
experience the joy of salvation
and celebrate that feast with love and thanksgiving.
We ask this through our Lord Jesus Christ, your Son,
who lives and reigns with you and the Holy Spirit,
one God, for ever and ever.

Morning Prayer

READING   Romans 13:11-12

It is now the hour for you to wake from sleep, for our salvation is closer than
when we first accepted the faith. The night is far spent; the day draws near.
Let us cast off deeds of darkness and put on the armor of light.

RESPONSORY (VI F)

Christ, Son of the *living* God, * have mercy *on* us.
— Christ, Son of the *living* God, * have mercy *on* us.
You are the one who is to come,
— have mercy *on* us.
Glory to the Father, and *to* the Son, * and to the Ho*ly* Spirit.
— Christ, Son of the *living* God, * have mercy *on* us.

CANTICLE OF ZECHARIAH

Ant.   When John, in prison, heard of the *works* of Christ, * he sent two
                        of his disciples with *this* question:
                        Are you the One whose coming *was* foretold, * or should we look
                        for *another*?

If this Sunday occurs on December 17, the ant. Believe me, and the intercessions, 110, are
said.

INTERCESSIONS

To God our Father, who has given us the grace to wait in joyful hope for the
    revelation of our Lord *Jesus* Christ, * let us *make* our prayer:
Show us your mercy, Lord.
Sanctify us, in *mind* and body,
— keep us without reproach until the coming *of* your Son.
Make us walk this *day* in holiness,
— and live upright and devout lives *in* this world.
May we be clothed in our Lord *Jesus* Christ,
— and filled with the *Holy* Spirit.

Lord, help us to stand watch*ful* and ready,
— until your Son is revealed in *all* his glory.

Our Father . . .

Prayer

Lord God,
may we, your people,
who look forward to the birthday of Christ
experience the joy of salvation
and celebrate that feast with love and thanksgiving.
We ask this through our Lord Jesus Christ, your Son,
who lives and reigns with you and the Holy Spirit,
one God, for ever and ever.

Evening Prayer II

READING   Philippians 4:4-5
Rejoice in the Lord always! I say it again. Rejoice! Everyone should see how unselfish you are. The Lord is near.

RESPONSORY (VI F)
Lord, show *us* your mercy, * your mercy *and* love.
— Lord, show *us* your mercy, * your mercy *and* love.
And grant us *your* salvation,
— your mercy *and* love.
Glory to the Father, and *to* the Son, * and to the Ho*ly* Spirit.
— Lord, show *us* your mercy, * your mercy *and* love.

CANTICLE OF MARY
Ant.   Are you the One whose coming *was* foretold, * or should we look
for *another*?
Tell John *what* you see: * the blind have their sight *re*stored,
the dead are *raised* to life, * the poor have the good news
preached to them, al*le*luia.

If this Sunday occurs on December 17, the ant. O Wisdom, and the intercessions, III, are said.

INTERCESSIONS
To Jesus Christ, our Redeemer, the way, the truth, *and* the life, * let us make our *hum*ble prayer:
Come and stay with us, Lord.

Son of the Most High, your coming was announced to the Virgin Ma*ry* by
   Gabriel,
— come and rule over your peo*ple* for ever.
Holy One of God, in your presence, John the Baptist leapt in Eli*z*abeth's womb,
— bring the joy of salvation to *all* the earth.
Jesus the Savior, the angel revealed your name to Jo*seph* the just man,
— come and save your people *from* their sins.
Light of the world, for whom Simeon and all *the* just waited,
— come and *com*fort us.
O Rising Sun that never sets, Zechariah foretold that you would visit us *from*
   above,
— come and shine on those who dwell in darkness and the shad*ow* of death.

Our Father . . .

Prayer

   Lord God,
   may we, your people,
   who look forward to the birthday of Christ
   experience the joy of salvation
   and celebrate that feast with love and thanksgiving.
   We ask this through our Lord Jesus Christ, your Son,
   who lives and reigns with you and the Holy Spirit,
   one God, for ever and ever.

On the weekdays from December 17 to December 23 inclusive, everything designated for
Week III is omitted; (hymns, readings, responsories, verses, prayers, and the intercessions
for Morning and Evening Prayer are said, 110ff.)

MONDAY

Morning Prayer

READING   Isaiah 2:3b
   Come, let us climb the Lord's mountain,
      to the house of the God of Jacob,
   That he may instruct us in his ways,
      and we may walk in his paths.
   For from Zion shall go forth instruction,
      and the word of the Lord from Jerusalem.

RESPONSORY (VI F)
Your light will *come*, Jerusalem, *
the Lord will dawn on you in radi*ant* beauty.
— Your light will *come*, Jerusalem, *
the Lord will dawn on you in radi*ant* beauty.
You will see his glo*ry* within you;
— the Lord will dawn on you in radi*ant* beauty.
Glory to the Father, and *to* the Son, * and to the Ho*ly* Spirit.
— Your light will *come*, Jerusalem, *
the Lord will dawn on you in radi*ant* beauty.

CANTICLE OF ZECHARIAH

Ant.   From heaven he comes, the *Lord* and Ruler; * in his hand are
honor and royal *au*thority.

INTERCESSIONS
Christ the Lord, Son of the living God, light from light, leads us into the light
and re*veals* his holiness. * With confidence let us *make* our prayer:
Come, Lord *Jesus*.
Light that never fades, rise to dispel the *mists* about us,
— awaken our *faith* from sleep.
Guard us from all *harm* today,
— may your glory fill *us* with joy.
Give us unfailing gentleness *at* all times,
— toward every*one* we meet.
Come to create a new *earth* for us,
— where there will be jus*tice* and peace.

Our Father . . .

Prayer
Lord hear our voices raised in prayer.
Let the light of the coming of your Son
free us from the darkness of sin.
We ask this through our Lord Jesus Christ, your Son,
who lives and reigns with you and the Holy Spirit,
one God, for ever and ever.

Evening Prayer

READING   Philippians 3:20b-21

We eagerly await the coming of our Savior, the Lord Jesus Christ. He will give a new form to this lowly body of ours and remake it according to the pattern of his glorified body, by his power to subject everything to himself.

RESPONSORY (VI F)

Come and *set* us free, * Lord God of power *and* might.
— Come and *set* us free, * Lord God of power *and* might.
Let your face shine upon us and we *shall* be saved,
— Lord God of power *and* might.
Glory to the Father, and *to* the Son, * and to the Ho*ly* Spirit.
— Come and *set* us free, * Lord God of power *and* might.

CANTICLE OF MARY

Ant.   All generations will *call* me blessèd: * the Lord has looked with favor on his low*ly* servant.

INTERCESSIONS

We cry *to* the Lord, * who will come to bring *us* salvation:
Come, Lord, and save us.
Lord Jesus Christ, our God, Sav*ior* of all,
— come swift*ly* and save us.
You came *from* the Father,
— show us the path that *leads* to him.
You were conceived by the *Ho*ly Spirit,
— by your word renew the same Spirit *in* our hearts.
You became incarnate from the *Vir*gin Mary,
— free our bodies *from* corruption.
Lord, be mindful *of* all men,
— who from the beginning of time have placed their *trust* in you.

Our Father . . .

Prayer

Lord hear our voices raised in prayer.
Let the light of the coming of your Son
free us from the darkness of sin.
We ask this through our Lord Jesus Christ, your Son,
who lives and reigns with you and the Holy Spirit,
one God, for ever and ever.

TUESDAY

If Tuesday occurs after December 16, everything is taken from the corresponding day, 110ff.

Morning Prayer

READING   Genesis 49:10

The scepter shall never depart from Judah,
    or the mace from between his legs,
While tribute is brought to him,
    and he receives the people's homage.

RESPONSORY (VI F)

Your light will *come*, **Jerusalem**, *
the Lord will dawn on you in radi*ant* beauty.
— Your light will *come*, Jerusalem, *
the Lord will dawn on you in radi*ant* beauty.
You will see his glo*ry* within you;
— the Lord will dawn on you in radi*ant* beauty.
Glory to the Father, and *to* the Son, * and to the Ho*ly* Spirit.
— Your light will *come*, Jerusalem, *
the Lord will dawn on you in radi*ant* beauty.

CANTICLE OF ZECHARIAH

Ant.   Arise, arise. † Wake from your slum*ber*, Jerusalem; * shake the
                 chain from your neck, captive daugh*ter* Zion.

INTERCESSIONS

God the almighty Father stretches forth his hand again to take possession of the
    remnant *of* his people. * Let us make our *prayer* to him:
*Lord, may your king*dom *come.*
Lord, grant that our works of pen*ance* may please you,
— and that we may be ready for your kingdom which *is* so near.
Prepare a path in our hearts for the coming *of* your Word,
— and let his glory be re*vealed* among us.
Bring low the mountains *of* our pride,
— and fill up the valleys *of* our weakness.
Break down the walls of hatred that di*vide* the nations,
— and make level for mankind the *paths* to peace.

Our Father . . .

Prayer

Father of love,
you made a new creation
through Jesus Christ your Son.
May his coming free us from sin
and renew his life within us,
for he lives and reigns with you and the Holy Spirit,
one God, for ever and ever.

Evening Prayer

READING   See 1 Corinthians 1:7b-9

We await the revelation of our Lord Jesus Christ, who will strengthen us to the end, so that we will be blameless on the day of our Lord Jesus Christ. God is faithful, and it was he who called us to fellowship with his Son.

RESPONSORY (VI F)

Come and *set* us free, * Lord God of power *and* might.
—Come and *set* us free, * Lord God of power *and* might.
Let your face shine upon us and we *shall* be saved,
—Lord God of power *and* might.
Glory to the Father, and *to* the Son, * and to the Ho*ly* Spirit.
—Come and *set* us free, * Lord God of power *and* might.

CANTICLE OF MARY

Ant.   Before Mary and Joseph had *come* together,* they learned that Mary was with child by the power of the Holy Spirit, al*le*luia.

INTERCESSIONS

To the eternal Word who became man to reveal to us the new and *living* way, * let us make our *hum*ble prayer:
Come, Lord, and save us.
God, in whom we live and move and *have* our being,
—come and teach us that you have made *us* your own.
You are not *far* from each of us,
—show yourself to all who *search* for you.
Father of the poor and consoler of *the* afflicted,
—set captives free, give joy to *those* who mourn.
You hate death *and* love life,
—free all mankind from e*ter*nal death.

Our Father . . .

Prayer

> Father of love,
> you made a new creation
> through Jesus Christ your Son.
> May his coming free us from sin
> and renew his life within us,
> for he lives and reigns with you and the Holy Spirit,
> one God, for ever and ever.

WEDNESDAY

If Wednesday occurs after December 16, everything is taken from the corresponding day,
II off.

Morning Prayer

READING   Isaiah 7:14b-15

> The virgin shall be with child, and bear a son, and shall name him Immanuel.
> He shall be living on curds and honey by the time he learns to reject the bad
> and choose the good.

RESPONSORY (VI F)

Your light will *come*, Jerusalem, *
the Lord will dawn on you in radi*ant* beauty.
— Your light will *come*, Jerusalem, *
the Lord will dawn on you in radi*ant* beauty.
You will see his glo*ry* within you;
— the Lord will dawn on you in radi*ant* beauty.
Glory to the Father, and *to* the Son, * and to the Ho*ly* Spirit.
— Your light will *come*, Jerusalem, *
the Lord will dawn on you in radi*ant* beauty.

CANTICLE OF ZECHARIAH

Ant.   Be comfort*ed*, my people; * be comforted, says the Lord *your*
                    God.

INTERCESSIONS

The Word of God humbled himself to dwell with us so that we may *see* his glory.
  * Rejoicing in hope, let us *call* upon him:
Emmanuel, be with *us.*
Ruler, *just* and righteous,
— bring justice to the poor and *the* oppressed.
King of peace, you beat swords into plowshares and spears *in*to pruning hooks,
— turn hatred into love and our grievances in*to* forgiveness.

You do not judge *by* appearances,
— recognize those who *are* your own.
When you come with power and might up*on* the clouds,
— grant that we may come before you *with*out shame.

Our Father . . .

Prayer

Father,
may the coming celebration of the birth of your Son
bring us your saving help
and prepare us for eternal life.
Grant this through our Lord Jesus Christ, your Son,
who lives and reigns with you and the Holy Spirit,
one God, for ever and ever.

Evening Prayer

READING   1 Corinthians 4:5
> Stop passing judgment before the time of the Lord's return. He will bring
> to light what is hidden in the darkness and manifest the intentions of
> hearts. At that time, everyone will receive his praise from God.

RESPONSORY (VI F)
Come and *set* us free, * Lord God of power *and* might.
— Come and *set* us free, * Lord God of power *and* might.
Let your face shine upon us and we *shall* be saved,
— Lord God of power *and* might.
Glory to the Father, and *to* the Son, * and to the Ho*ly* Spirit.
— Come and *set* us free, * Lord God of power *and* might.

CANTICLE OF MARY
Ant.   You, O Lord, are the One whose coming *was* foretold; * we long
                for you to come and set your peo*ple* free.

INTERCESSIONS
Let us pray to *God* the Father, * who sent his Son to bring us *end*less peace:
*Lord, your king*dom *come.*
Father, most holy, look kindly *on* your Church,
— come and visit this vine which your own right *hand* has planted.
Be mindful, Lord, of all the *sons* of Abraham,
— fulfill the promises you made *to* their fathers.

Merciful God, look kindly upon men and women of *every* race,
— may they honor you *for* your goodness.
Eternal Shepherd, visit the sheep *of* your flock,
— and gather them together *in* one fold.
Remember those who have gone forth from this world *in* your peace,
— lead them into glory *with* your Son.

Our Father . . .

Prayer

Father,
may the coming celebration of the birth of your Son
bring us your saving help
and prepare us for eternal life.
Grant this through our Lord Jesus Christ, your Son,
who lives and reigns with you and the Holy Spirit,
one God, for ever and ever.

THURSDAY

If Thursday occurs after December 16, everything is taken from the corresponding day, 110ff.

Morning Prayer

READING   Isaiah 45:8

Let justice descend, O heavens, like dew from above,
      like gentle rain let the skies drop it down.
Let the earth open and salvation bud forth;
      let justice also spring up!

RESPONSORY (VI F)
Your light will *come*, Jerusalem, *
the Lord will dawn on you in radi*ant* beauty.
— Your light will *come*, Jerusalem, *
the Lord will dawn on you in radi*ant* beauty.
You will see his glo*ry* within you;
— the Lord will dawn on you in radi*ant* beauty.
Glory to the Father, and *to* the Son, * and to the Ho*ly* Spirit.
— Your light will *come*, Jerusalem, *
the Lord will dawn on you in radi*ant* beauty.

CANTICLE OF ZECHARIAH
Ant.   Arise, *a*rise Lord; * show us your power *and* might.

INTERCESSIONS

Christ is the wisdom and power of God, and his delight is to be with the child*ren*
   of men. * With confidence *let* us pray:
Draw near to us, Lord.
Lord Jesus Christ, you have called us to your *glor*ious kingdom,
— make us walk worthily, pleasing God in *all* we do.
You who stand un*known* among us,
— reveal yourself to *men* and women.
You are nearer to us than we *to* ourselves,
— strengthen our faith and our hope *of* salvation.
You are the *source* of holiness,
— keep us holy and without sin now and until the day *of* your coming.

Our Father . . .

Prayer

Lord,
our sins bring us unhappiness.
Hear our prayer for courage and strength.
May the coming of your Son
bring us the joy of salvation.
We ask this through our Lord Jesus Christ, your Son,
who lives and reigns with you and the Holy Spirit,
one God, for ever and ever.

Evening Prayer

READING   James 5:7-8, 9b

Be patient, my brother, until the coming of the Lord. See how the farmer
awaits the precious yield of the soil. He looks forward to it patiently while the
soil receives the winter and the spring rains. You, too, must be patient. Steady
your hearts, because the coming of the Lord is at hand. See! The judge stands
at the gate.

RESPONSORY (VI F)

Come and *set* us free, * Lord God of power *and* might.
— Come and *set* us free, * Lord God of power *and* might.
Let your face shine upon us and we *shall* be saved,
— Lord God of power *and* might.
Glory to the Father, and *to* the Son, * and to the Ho*ly* Spirit.
— Come and *set* us free, * Lord God of power *and* might.

CANTICLE OF MARY
Ant.   All you who *love* Jerusalem, * rejoice with her *for* ever.

INTERCESSIONS
To Christ, the great light promised by the prophets to those who live in the
    shad*ow* of death, * let us raise our *voice* in prayer:
Come, Lord *Jesus.*
Word of God, in the beginning you created all things and in the fullness of time
    as*sumed* our nature,
— come and deliver *us* from death.
True light, shining *on* mankind,
— come and dis*pel* our darkness.
Only-begotten Son, dwelling in the *Father's* heart,
— come and deliver *us* from death.
Christ Jesus, you come among us as the *Son* of Man,
— transform those who know you into the *sons* of God.
You welcome all who call upon *you* in need,
— bring into your wedding feast those who beg *at* the door.

Our Father . . .

Prayer

Lord,
    our sins bring us unhappiness.
    Hear our prayer for courage and strength.
    May the coming of your Son
    bring us the joy of salvation.
    We ask this through our Lord Jesus Christ, your Son,
    who lives and reigns with you and the Holy Spirit,
    one God, for ever and ever.

FRIDAY

If Friday occurs after December 16, everything is taken from the corresponding day, 110ff.

Morning Prayer

READING   Jeremiah 30:21-22
    Thus says the Lord:
    His leader shall be from Jacob
        and his ruler shall come from his kin.
    When I summon him,
        he shall approach me.
    You shall be my people,
        and I will be your God.

RESPONSORY (VI F)
Your light will *come*, Jerusalem, *
the Lord will dawn on you in radi*ant* beauty.
—Your light will *come*, Jerusalem, *
the Lord will dawn on you in radi*ant* beauty.
You will see his glo*ry* within you;
— the Lord will dawn on you in radi*ant* beauty.
Glory to the Father, and *to* the Son, * and to the Ho*ly* Spirit.
— Your light will *come*, Jerusalem, *
the Lord will dawn on you in radi*ant* beauty.

CANTICLE OF ZECHARIAH
Ant.   Guard what is good and cherish *what* is true,* for our salvation is
                     at hand.

INTERCESSIONS
Through his Son, God the Father revealed his glory to *men* and women. * There-
    fore, let our joyful *cry* resound:
Lord, may your name be *glorified.*
Teach us, Lord, to *love* each other,
— as Christ loved us *for* God's glory.
Fill us with all joy and *peace* in faith,
— that we may walk in the hope and strength of the *Ho*ly Spirit.
Help all mankind, Lord, in your *loving* mercy,
— be near to those who seek you *with*out knowing it.
You call and sanctify *the* elect,
— though we are sinners, crown us with e*te*rnal happiness.

Our Father . . .

                          Prayer

        All-powerful Father,
        guide us with your love
        as we await the coming of your Son.
        Keep us faithful
        that we may be helped through life
        and brought to salvation.
        We ask this through our Lord Jesus Christ, your Son,
        who lives and reigns with you and the Holy Spirit,
        one God, for ever and ever.

Evening Prayer

READING   2 Peter 3:8b-9

In the Lord's eyes, one day is as a thousand years and a thousand years are as a day. The Lord does not delay in keeping his promise—though some consider it "delay." Rather, he shows you generous patience, since he wants none to perish but all to come to repentance.

RESPONSORY (VI F)

Come and *set* us free, * Lord God of power *and* might.
— Come and *set* us free, * Lord God of power *and* might.
Let your face shine upon us and we *shall* be saved,
— Lord God of power *and* might.
Glory to the Father, and *to* the Son, * and to the Ho*ly* Spirit.
— Come and *set* us free, * Lord God of power *and* might.

CANTICLE OF MARY

Ant.   This was the witness of *John* the Baptist: * The One who comes after me existed *be*fore me.

INTERCESSIONS

With confidence let us call *up*on Christ, * the shepherd and guardian *of* our souls:
Lord, have mercy on *us.*
Good shepherd *of* God's flock,
— gather all in*to* your Church.
Lord Jesus, help the shepherds of your *pil*grim people,
— until you come again may they zealously *feed* your flock.
Choose from among us heralds *of* your word,
— to proclaim your Gospel to the ends *of* the earth.
Take pity on all who struggle and fall a*long* the way,
— may they find a *friend* to help them.
Show your glo*ry* in heaven,
— to those who listen to your *voice* on earth.

Our Father . . .

Prayer

All-powerful Father,
guide us with your love
as we await the coming of your Son.
Keep us faithful
that we may be helped through life
and brought to salvation.
We ask this through our Lord Jesus Christ, your Son,
who lives and reigns with you and the Holy Spirit,
one God, for ever and ever.

On Saturday, everything is taken from the corresponding day, 110ff.

FOURTH SUNDAY OF ADVENT

PSALTER WEEK IV, 806.

Evening Prayer I

READING   1 Thessalonians 5:23-24

May the God of peace make you perfect in holiness. May he preserve you whole and entire, spirit, soul, and body, irreproachable at the coming of our Lord Jesus Christ. He who calls us is trustworthy, therefore he will do it.

RESPONSORY (VI F)

Lord, show *us* your mercy, * your mercy *and* love.
— Lord, show *us* your mercy, * your mercy *and* love.
And grant us *your* salvation,
— your mercy *and* love.
Glory to the Father, and *to* the Son, * and to the Ho*ly* Spirit.
— Lord, show *us* your mercy, * your mercy *and* love.

For the Canticle of Mary, the antiphon is taken from the office of the day, 111ff.

INTERCESSIONS

Jesus is Lord, born of the *Virg*in Mary. * Let us pray to him with *joy*ful hearts:
Come, Lord, *Jesus!*
Son of God, you will come again as the true messenger *of* the covenant,
— help the world to recognize *and* accept you.
Born in your Father's heart, you became man in the womb of the *Virg*in Mary,
— free us from the tyranny of change *and* decay.
In your life on earth, you came to die *as* a man,
— save us from ever*last*ing death.
When you come to judge, show us your *lov*ing mercy,
— and forgive *us* our weaknesses.
Lord Jesus, by your death you have given hope to those *who* have died,
— be merciful to those for whom *we* now pray.

Our Father . . .

Prayer

Lord,
fill our hearts with your love,
and as you revealed to us by an angel
the coming of your Son as man,
so lead us through his suffering and death
to the glory of his resurrection
for he lives and reigns with you and the Holy Spirit,
one God, for ever and ever.

Morning Prayer

READING   Romans 13:11-12

It is now the hour for you to wake from sleep, for our salvation is closer than when we first accepted the faith. The night is far spent; the day draws near. Let us cast off deeds of darkness and put on the armor of light.

RESPONSORY (VI F)

Christ, Son of the *living* God, * have mercy *on* us.
— Christ, Son of the *living* God, * have mercy *on* us.
You are the one who is to come,
— have mercy *on* us.
Glory to the Father, and *to* the Son, * and to the Ho*ly* Spirit.
— Christ, Son of the *living* God, * have mercy *on* us.

For the Canticle of Zechariah, the antiphon is taken from the office of the day, 110ff.

INTERCESSIONS

To the Lord Jesus Christ, judge of the living *and* the dead, * *let* us pray:
Come, Lord *Jesus!*
Lord Jesus, you came *to* save sinners,
— protect us in times *of* temptation.
You will come in glory to *be* our judge,
— show in us your pow*er* to save.
Help us to keep the precepts of your law with the strength *of* the Spirit,
— and to look forward in love *to* your coming.
You are praised throughout the ages; in your mercy help us to live devoutly and temperately *in* this life,
— as we wait in joyful hope for the revelation *of* your glory.

Our Father . . .

Prayer

Lord,
fill our hearts with your love,
and as you revealed to us by an angel
the coming of your Son as man,
so lead us through his suffering and death
to the glory of his resurrection
for he lives and reigns with you and the Holy Spirit,
one God, for ever and ever.

Evening Prayer II

READING   Philippians 4:4-5

Rejoice in the Lord always! I say it again. Rejoice! Everyone should see how unselfish you are. The Lord is near.

RESPONSORY (VI F)

Lord, show *us* your mercy, * your mercy *and* love.
— Lord, show *us* your mercy, * your mercy *and* love.
And grant us *your* salvation,
— your mercy *and* love.
Glory to the Father, and *to* the Son, * and to the Ho*ly* Spirit.
— Lord, show *us* your mercy, * your mercy *and* love.

For the Canticle of Mary, the antiphon is taken from the office of the day, 111ff.

INTERCESSIONS

To Christ the Lord, who was born of the *Vir*gin Mary, * let us pray with *joy*ful heart:
Come, Lord *Jesus!*
Lord Jesus, in the mystery of your incarnation, you revealed your glory *to* the world,
— give us new life *by* your coming.
You have taken our weakness up*on* yourself,
— grant *us* your mercy.
You redeemed the world from sin by your first coming *in* humility,
— free us from all guilt when you come a*gain* in glory.
You live and rule *over* all,
— in your goodness bring us to our eter*nal* inheritance.
You sit at the right hand *of* the Father,
— gladden the souls of the dead *with* your light.

Our Father . . .

Prayer

Lord,
fill our hearts with your love,
and as you revealed to us by an angel
the coming of your Son as man,
so lead us through his suffering and death
to the glory of his resurrection
for he lives and reigns with you and the Holy Spirit,
one God, for ever and ever.

DECEMBER 17

Morning Prayer

The antiphons are given in the proper place in the Psalter.

READING   Isaiah 11:1-3a

> A shoot shall sprout from the stump of Jesse,
>> and from his roots a bud shall blossom.
>
> The spirit of the Lord shall rest upon him:
>> a spirit of wisdom and of understanding,
>
> A spirit of counsel and of strength,
>> a spirit of knowledge and of fear of the Lord,
>> and his delight shall be the fear of the Lord.

RESPONSORY (VI F)

Your light will *come*, Jerusalem, *
the Lord will dawn on you in radi*ant* beauty.
— Your light will *come*, Jerusalem, *
the Lord will dawn on you in radi*ant* beauty.
You will see his glo*ry* within you;
— the Lord will dawn on you in radi*ant* beauty.
Glory to the Father, and *to* the Son, * and to the Ho*ly* Spirit.
— Your light will *come*, Jerusalem, *
the Lord will dawn on you in radi*ant* beauty.

CANTICLE OF ZECHARIAH

Ant.   Believe me, the kingdom of God *is* at hand; * I tell you solemnly,
                  your Savior will not delay *his* coming.

INTERCESSIONS

Let us pray to *God* our Father,* who from of old has called his people *to* salvation:
Lord, protect your *people.*
You promised to plant the seed of justice a*mong* your people,
— protect the holiness *of* your Church.
Lord, teach all men and women to listen *to* your word,
— and help believers to perse*vere* in holiness.
Keep us in the love *of* your Spirit,
— that we may know the mercy of your Son who *is* to come.
Father most merciful, strengthen us *to* the last,
— until the day of the coming of Jesus *Christ* our Lord.

Our Father . . .

Prayer

Father,
creator and redeemer of mankind,
you decreed, and your Word became man,
born of the Virgin Mary.
May we come to share the divinity of Christ,
who humbled himself to share our human nature,
for he lives and reigns with you and the Holy Spirit,
one God, for ever and ever.

Evening Prayer

The antiphons are given in the proper place in the Psalter.

READING   1 Thessalonians 5:23-24
May the God of peace make you perfect in holiness. May he preserve you
whole and entire, spirit, soul, and body, irreproachable at the coming of our
Lord Jesus Christ. He who calls us is trustworthy, therefore he will do it.

RESPONSORY (VI F)
Lord, show *us* your mercy, * your mercy *and* love.
— Lord, show *us* your mercy, * your mercy *and* love.
And grant us *your* salvation,
— your mercy *and* love.
Glory to the Father, and *to* the Son, * and to the Ho*ly* Spirit.
— Lord, show *us* your mercy, * your mercy *and* love.

CANTICLE OF MARY

Ant.   O Wisdom, O holy Word of God, † you govern all creation with
                your strong yet *ten*der care. * Come and show your people the
                way to *sal*vation.

INTERCESSIONS
Jesus Christ is the joy and happiness of all who look forward *to* his coming. * Let
    us call upon *him* and say:
*Come, Lord, and do not de*lay!*
In joy, we wait *for* your coming,
— *come*, Lord Jesus.
Before time began, you shared life *with* the Father,
— come *now* and save us.

You created the world and all who *live* in it,
— come to redeem the work *of* your hands.
You did not hesitate to become man, sub*ject* to death,
— come to free us from the pow*er* of death.
You came to give us life *to* the full,
— come and give us your un*end*ing life.
You desire all people to live in love *in* your kingdom,
— come and bring together those who long to see you *face* to face.

Prayer

Father,
creator and redeemer of mankind,
you decreed, and your Word became man,
born of the Virgin Mary.
May we come to share the divinity of Christ,
who humbled himself to share our human nature,
for he lives and reigns with you and the Holy Spirit,
one God, for ever and ever.

DECEMER 18

Morning Prayer

The antiphons are given in the proper place in the Psalter.

READING   Romans 13:11-12
It is now the hour for you to wake from sleep, for our salvation is closer than
when we first accepted the faith. The night is far spent; the day draws near.
Let us cast off deeds of darkness and put on the armor of light.

RESPONSORY (VI F)
Your light will *come*, Jerusalem, *
the Lord will dawn on you in radi*ant* beauty.
— Your light will *come*, Jerusalem, *
the Lord will dawn on you in radi*ant* beauty.
You will see his glo*ry* within you;
— the Lord will dawn on you in radi*ant* beauty.
Glory to the Father, and *to* the Son, * and to the Ho*ly* Spirit.
— Your light will *come*, Jerusalem, *
the Lord will dawn on you in radi*ant* beauty.

CANTICLE OF ZECHARIAH

Ant.   Let everything within you *watch* and wait, * for the Lord our
                 God *draws* near.

INTERCESSIONS

To the Lord Jesus Christ, judge of the living *and* the dead,* *let* us pray:
Come, Lord *Jesus!*
Lord Jesus, you came *to* save sinners,
— protect us in times *of* temptation.
You will come in glory to *be* our judge,
— show in us your pow*er* to save.
Help us to keep the precepts of your law with the strength *of* the Spirit,
— and to look forward in love *to* your coming.
You are praised throughout the ages; in your mercy help us to live devoutly and
   temperately *in* this life,
— as we wait in joyful hope for the revelation *of* your glory.

Our Father . . .

Prayer

       All-powerful God,
       renew us by the coming feast of your Son
       and free us from our slavery to sin.
       Grant this through our Lord Jesus Christ, your Son,
       who lives and reigns with you and the Holy Spirit,
       one God, for ever and ever.

Evening Prayer

The antiphons are given in the proper place in the Psalter.

READING   Philippians 4:4-5
   Rejoice in the Lord always! I say it again. Rejoice! Everyone should see how
   unselfish you are. The Lord is near.

RESPONSORY (VI F)
Lord, show *us* your mercy, * your mercy *and* love.
— Lord, show *us* your mercy, * your mercy *and* love.
And grant us *your* salvation,
— your mercy *and* love.
Glory to the Father, and *to* the Son, * and to the Ho*ly* Spirit.
— Lord, show *us* your mercy, * your mercy *and* love.

CANTICLE OF MARY

Ant.   O sacred Lord of *an*cient Israel, * who showed yourself to Moses
                     in the burn*ing* bush,
                     who gave him the holy law on *Si*nai mountain: * come, stretch
                     out your mighty hand to set *us* free.

INTERCESSIONS

To Christ the Lord, who was born of the *Vir*gin Mary, * let us pray with *joy*ful
    hearts:

Come, Lord *Jesus!*

Lord Jesus, in the mystery of your incarnation, you revealed your glory *to* the
    world,

— give us new life *by* your coming.

You have taken our weaknesses up*on* yourself,

— grant *us* your mercy.

You redeemed the world from sin by your first coming *in* humility,

— free us from all guilt when you come a*gain* in glory.

You live and rule *over* all,

— in your goodness bring us to our eter*nal* inheritance.

You sit at the right hand *of* the Father,

— gladden the souls of the dead *with* your light.

Our Father . . .

Prayer

All-powerful God,
    renew us by the coming feast of your Son
    and free us from our slavery to sin.
    Grant this through our Lord Jesus Christ, your Son,
    who lives and reigns with you and the Holy Spirit,
    one God, for ever and ever.

DECEMBER 19

Morning Prayer

The antiphons are given in the proper place in the Psalter.

READING   Isaiah 2:3b

Come, let us climb the Lord's mountain,
  to the house of the God of Jacob,
That he may instruct us in his ways,
  and we may walk in his paths.
For from Zion shall go forth instruction,
  and the word of the Lord from Jerusalem.

RESPONSORY (VI F)

Your light will *come*, Jerusalem, *
the Lord will dawn on you in radi*ant* beauty.
— Your light will *come*, Jerusalem, *
the Lord will dawn on you in radi*ant* beauty.
You will see his glo*ry* within you;
— the Lord will dawn on you in radi*ant* beauty.
Glory to the Father, and *to* the Son, * and to the Ho*ly* Spirit.
— Your light will *come*, Jerusalem, *
the Lord will dawn on you in radi*ant* beauty.

CANTICLE OF ZECHARIAH

Ant.   Like the sun in the *morn*ing sky,* the Savior of the world *will*
              dawn;
              like rain on the meadows he will descend to rest in the womb *of*
              the Virgin, * al*le*luia.

INTERCESSIONS

To Christ our Redeemer, who will come again to free from the power of death all
  those who re*turn* to him, * let us *hum*bly pray:
Come, Lord Jesus!
As we proclaim your *com*ing, Lord,
— cleanse our hearts of every *vain* desire.
Lord, may the Church *which* you founded,
— proclaim your greatness *to* all peoples.
Your law is a light *to* my eyes,
— let it protect those who *trust* in you.
You allow the joys of your coming to be foretold to us *by* your Church,
— may we receive you with ea*ger* devotion.

Our Father . . .

Prayer

Father,
you show the world the splendor of your glory
in the coming of Christ, born of the Virgin.
Give to us true faith and love
to celebrate the mystery of God made man.
We ask this through our Lord Jesus Christ, your Son,
who lives and reigns with you and the Holy Spirit,
one God, for ever and ever.

Evening Prayer

The antiphons are given in the proper place in the Psalter.

READING   Philippians 3:20b-21
We eagerly await the coming of our Savior, the Lord Jesus Christ. He will
give a new form to this lowly body of ours and remake it according to the
pattern of his glorified body, by his power to subject everything to himself.

RESPONSORY (VI F)
Come and *set* us free, * Lord God of power *and* might.
— Come and *set* us free, * Lord God of power *and* might.
Let your face shine upon us and we *shall* be saved,
— Lord God of power *and* might.
Glory to the Father, and *to* the Son, * and to the Ho*ly* Spirit.
— Come and *set* us free, * Lord God of power *and* might.

CANTICLE OF MARY
Ant.   O Flower of *Jesse*'s stem, * you have been raised up as a sign for
                  all peoples;
                  kings stand silent in your presence; † the nations bow down in
                  wor*ship* before you. * Come, let nothing keep you from coming to
                  our aid.

INTERCESSIONS
To Christ our Lord, judge of the living *and* the dead, * let us cry *out* with faith:
Come, Lord Jesus!
Lord, may the world know your justice which the heav*ens* proclaim,
— may your glory *fill* the earth.
For us you took upon yourself the weak*ness* of man,
— show them the radiance of your own *divine* light.

In your humility as a man, you took a*way* our sin,
— now in your glory grant *us* true happiness.
When you come in glo*ry* to judge us,
— gather the dead in*to* your kingdom.

Our Father . . .

Prayer

Father,
you show the world the splendor of your glory
in the coming of Christ, born of the Virgin.
Give to us true faith and love
to celebrate the mystery of God made man.
We ask this through our Lord Jesus Christ, your Son,
who lives and reigns with you and the Holy Spirit,
one God, for ever and ever.

DECEMBER 20

Morning Prayer

The antiphons are given in the proper place in the Psalter.

READING   Genesis 49:10
    The scepter shall never depart from Judah,
        or the mace from between his legs,
    While tribute is brought to him,
        and he receives the people's homage.

RESPONSORY (VI F)
Your light will *come*, Jerusalem, *
the Lord will dawn on you in radi*ant* beauty.
— Your light will *come*, Jerusalem, *
the Lord will dawn on you in radi*ant* beauty.
You will see his glo*ry* within you;
— the Lord will dawn on you in radi*ant* beauty.
Glory to the Father, and *to* the Son, * and to the Ho*ly* Spirit.
— Your light will *come*, Jerusalem, *
the Lord will dawn on you in radi*ant* beauty.

CANTICLE OF ZECHARIAH
Ant.   The angel Gabriel was sent to the *Vir*gin Mary, * who was
                 engaged to be married *to* Joseph.

INTERCESSIONS

To Christ our Lord, the light *of* the world, * let us cry *out* with joy:
Come, Lord *Jesus!*
Dispel our darkness with the light *of* your presence,
— and make us worthy *of* your gifts.
Save us, *Lord* our God,
— that we may praise your holy *name* this day.
Enkindle in our hearts the flame *of* your love,
— and make us long to be uni*ted* with you.
You bore *our* infirmity,
— aid the sick and those who are to *die* this day.

Our Father . . .

Prayer

God of love and mercy,
help us to follow the example of Mary,
· always ready to do your will.
At the message of an angel
she welcomed your eternal Son
and, filled with the light of your Spirit,
she became the temple of your Word,
who lives and reigns with you and the Holy Spirit,
one God, for ever and ever.

Evening Prayer

The antiphons are given in the proper place in the Psalter.

READING   See 1 Corinthians 1:7b-9

We await the revelation of our Lord Jesus Christ, who will stregthen us to the end, so that we will be blameless on the day of our Lord Jesus Christ. God is faithful, and it was he who called us to fellowship with his Son.

RESPONSORY (VI F)

Come and *set* us free, * Lord God of power *and* might.
— Come and *set* us free, * Lord God of power *and* might.
Let your face shine upon us and we *shall* be saved,
— Lord God of power *and* might.
Glory to the Father, and *to* the Son, * and to the Ho*ly* Spirit.
— Come and *set* us free, * Lord God of power *and* might.

CANTICLE OF MARY

Ant. O Key of David, O royal Power of Israel * controlling at your will the gate *of* heaven:
come, break down the prison walls of death † for those who dwell in darkness and the shad*ow* of death; * and lead your captive people in*to* freedom.

INTERCESSIONS

To Christ our Lord and Redeemer, who will appear openly *on* the last day, * let us joy*full*y pray:
Come, Lord *Jesus!*
Our Redeemer and Lord, by your birth as a man you freed us from the heavy yoke *of* the law,
— complete in us the works of your *loving* kindness.
From us you took whatever served *your* divinity,
— give us whatever we *need* to serve you.
Grant the desire we ask of *you* today,
— inflame our hearts with the fire *of* your love.
On earth we live with *you* by faith,
— in glory may we re*joice* with you.
Steep the souls of the faith*ful* departed,
— in the dew of your *loving* kindness.

Our Father . . .

Prayer

God of love and mercy,
help us to follow the example of Mary,
always ready to do your will.
At the message of an angel
she welcomed your eternal Son
and, filled with the light of your Spirit,
she became the temple of your Word,
who lives and reigns with you and the Holy Spirit,
one God, for ever and ever.

DECEMBER 21

Morning Prayer

The antiphons are given in the proper place in the Psalter.

READING   Isaiah 7:14b-15

The virgin shall be with child, and bear a son, and shall name him Immanuel.
He shall be living on curds and honey by the time he learns to reject the bad
and choose the good.

RESPONSORY (VI F)

Your light will *come*, Jerusalem, *
the Lord will dawn on you in radi*ant* beauty.
— Your light will *come*, Jerusalem, *
the Lord will dawn on you in radi*ant* beauty.
You will see his glo*ry* within you;
— the Lord will dawn on you in radi*ant* beauty.
Glory to the Father, and *to* the Son, * and to the Ho*ly* Spirit.
— Your light will *come*, Jerusalem, *
the Lord will dawn on you in radi*ant* beauty.

CANTICLE OF ZECHARIAH

Ant.   There is no need to *be* afraid; * in five days our Lord will
                       come *to* us.

INTERCESSIONS

To Jesus Christ our Lord, who came among us *in* his mercy, * let us constantly cry
   out with joy:
Come, Lord *Jesus!*
You came from the Father to take on our *hu*man nature,
— now set free what was harmed in *us* by sin.
One day you will come again in glory to your *chos*en people,
— come to us today and help us sinners to recognize your mercy and *ten*der love.
We glory in praising *you*, Lord Jesus,
— come and bring us *your* salvation.
Through faith you lead us *in*to light,
— may we reveal your justice *through* our deeds.

Our Father . . .

Prayer

Lord,
hear the prayers of your people.
May we who celebrate the birth of your Son as man
rejoice in the gift of eternal life when he comes in glory,
for he lives and reigns with you and the Holy Spirit,
one God, for ever and ever.

Evening Prayer

The antiphons are given in the proper place in the Psalter.

READING   1 Corinthians 4:5
Stop passing judgment before the time of the Lord's return. He will bring to
light what is hidden in the darkness and manifest the intentions of hearts. At
that time, everyone will receive his praise from God.

RESPONSORY (VI F)
Come and *set* us free, * Lord God of power *and* might.
— Come and *set* us free, * Lord God of power *and* might.
Let your face shine upon us and we *shall* be saved,
— Lord God of power *and* might.
Glory to the Father, and *to* the Son, * and to the Ho*ly* Spirit.
— Come and *set* us free, * Lord God of power *and* might.

CANTICLE OF MARY
Ant.   O Radiant Dawn, splendor of eternal light, *sun* of justice: *
                  come, shine on those who dwell in darkness and the shadow *of*
                  death.

INTERCESSIONS
We humbly pray to Jesus Christ, who rescues us from the dark*ness* of sin, * and in
    faith *we* cry out:
Come, Lord *Jesus!*
Lord, gather together all the people *of* the earth,
— and establish with them your ever*last*ing covenant.
Lamb of God, you came of old to take away the sin *of* the world,
— purge us from the dregs *of* our guilt.
You came to recover *what* was lost,
— come once again in your mercy lest you punish what you *have* recovered.
Our faith *seeks* you out,
— let us find everlasting joy with you *when* you come.

You will judge the living *and* the dead,
— graciously gather the dead into the ranks *of* the blessèd.

Our Father . . .

Prayer

Lord,
hear the prayers of your people.
May we who celebrate the birth of your Son as man
rejoice in the gift of eternal life when he comes in glory,
for he lives and reigns with you and the Holy Spirit,
one God, for ever and ever.

DECEMBER 22

Morning Prayer

The antiphons are given in the proper place in the Psalter.

READING   Isaiah 45:8

> Let justice descend, O heavens, like dew from above,
> > like gentle rain let the skies drop it down.
> Let the earth open and salvation bud forth;
> > let justice also spring up.

RESPONSORY (VI F)
Your light will *come*, Jerusalem, *
the Lord will dawn on you in radi*ant* beauty.
— Your light will *come*, Jerusalem, *
the Lord will dawn on you in radi*ant* beauty.
You will see his glo*ry* within you;
— the Lord will dawn on you in radi*ant* beauty.
Glory to the Father, and *to* the Son, * and to the Ho*ly* Spirit.
— Your light will *come*, Jerusalem, *
the Lord will dawn on you in radi*ant* beauty.

CANTICLE OF ZECHARIAH
Ant.   The moment that your greeting *reached* my ears, * the child
within my womb leapt *for* joy.

INTERCESSIONS

To Christ our Redeemer, who comes to save us *from* our sins, * let us
cry *out* with joy:
Come, Lord *Jesus!*
The prophets of old foretold your *birth* among us,
— now make virtue come to *life* in us.
We proclaim your *saving* work,
— now grant us *your* salvation.
You came to heal the con*trite* of heart,
— heal the weaknesses *of* your people.
You came and saw fit to recon*cile* the world,
— when you come again in judgment, free us from the tor*ments* of punishment.

Our Father . . .

Prayer

God our Father,
you sent your Son
to free mankind from the power of death.
May we who celebrate the coming of Christ as man
share more fully in his divine life,
for he lives and reigns with you and the Holy Spirit,
one God, for ever and ever.

Evening Prayer

The antiphons are given in the proper place in the Psalter.

READING   James 5:7-8, 9b
Be patient, my brother, until the coming of the Lord. See how the farmer
awaits the precious yield of the soil. He looks forward to it patiently while the
soil receives the winter and the spring rains. You, too, must be patient. Steady
your hearts, because the coming of the Lord is at hand. See! The judge stands
at the gate.

RESPONSORY (VI F)
Come and *set* us free, * Lord God of power *and* might.
— Come and *set* us free, * Lord God of power *and* might.
Let your face shine upon us and we *shall* be saved,
— Lord God of power *and* might.
Glory to the Father, and *to* the Son, * and to the Ho*ly* Spirit.
— Come and *set* us free, * Lord God of power *and* might.

CANTICLE OF MARY

Ant.   O King of all the nations, the only joy of every human heart; † O
                        Keystone of the mighty *arch* of man, * come and save the creature
                        you fashioned from *the* dust.

INTERCESSIONS

To Christ our Lord, who humbled himself *for* our sake, * we joy*fu*lly say:
Come, Lord *Jesus!*
Lord Jesus, by your coming you rescued the *world* from sin,
— cleanse our souls and bod*ies* from guilt.
By the mystery of your incarnation we are made your broth*ers* and sisters,
— do not let us become e*stranged* from you.
Do *not* judge harshly,
— those you redeemed with *such* great cost.
No age, O Christ, is without your goodness and *holy* riches,
— enable us to merit the enduring crown *of* your glory.
Lord, to you we commend the souls of your de*part*ed servants,
— having died to the world, may they be alive in *you* for ever.

Our Father . . .

Prayer

God our Father,
you sent your Son
to free mankind from the power of death.
May we who celebrate the coming of Christ as man
share more fully in his divine life,
for he lives and reigns with you and the Holy Spirit,
one God, for ever and ever.

DECEMBER 23

Morning Prayer

The antiphons are given in the proper place in the Psalter.

READING   Jeremiah 30:21-22

        Thus says the Lord:
    His leader shall be from Jacob
        and his ruler shall come from his kin.
    When I summon him,
        he shall approach me.
    You shall be my people,
        and I will be your God.

RESPONSORY (VI F)
Your light will *come*, Jerusalem, *
the Lord will dawn on you in radi*ant* beauty.
— Your light will *come*, Jerusalem, *
the Lord will dawn on you in radi*ant* beauty.
You will see his glo*ry* within you;
— the Lord will dawn on you in radi*ant* beauty.
Glory to the Father, and *to* the Son, * and to the Ho*ly* Spirit.
— Your light will *come*, Jerusalem, *
the Lord will dawn on you in radi*ant* beauty.

CANTICLE OF ZECHARIAH
Ant.   All that God promised to the virgin through the message *of* the
                        angel * has been *ac*complished

INTERCESSIONS
Let us pray to *God* our Father * who sent his Son to *save* mankind:
*Show us your mer*cy, Lord!*
Father most merciful, we confess our faith in your Christ *with* our words,
— keep us from denying him *in* our actions.
You have sent your *Son* to rescue us,
— remove every sorrow from the face of the earth and *from* our country.
Our land looks forward with delight to the approach *of* your Son,
— let it experience the full*ness* of joy.
Through your mercy make us live holy and chaste lives *in* this world,
— eagerly awaiting the blessèd hope and coming of *Christ* in glory.

Our Father . . .

Prayer

Father,
we contemplate the birth of your Son.
He was born of the Virgin Mary
and came to live among us.
May we receive forgiveness and mercy
through our Lord Jesus Christ, your Son,
who lives and reigns with you and the Holy Spirit,
one God, for ever and ever.

Evening Prayer

The antiphons are given in the proper place in the Psalter.

READING   2 Peter 3:8b-9

In the Lord's eyes, one day is as a thousand years and a thousand years are as a day. The Lord does not delay in keeping his promise—though some consider it "delay." Rather, he shows you generous patience, since he wants none to perish but all to come to repentance.

RESPONSORY (VI F)

Come and *set* us free, * Lord God of power *and* might.

—Come and *set* us free, * Lord God of power *and* might.

Let your face shine upon us and we *shall* be saved,

—Lord God of power *and* might.

Glory to the Father, and *to* the Son, * and to the Ho*ly* Spirit.

—Come and *set* us free, * Lord God of power *and* might.

CANTICLE OF MARY

Ant.   O Emmanuel, king and lawgiver, desire of the nations, † Savior *of* all people, * come and set us free, Lord *our* God.

INTERCESSIONS

To our Redeemer who came to bring good news *to* the poor, * let us earn*est*ly pray:

Let all men see your *glory!*

Show yourself to those who have *nev*er known you,

—let them see your *saving* work.

Let your name be preached to the ends *of* the earth,

—that all may find the *way* to you.

You first came to *save* the world,

—now come again and save those who be*lieve* in you.

You brought freedom to *us* by saving us,

—continue to save us and *make* us free.

You came once as a man; you will re*turn* in judgment,

—bring eternal reward to those *who* have died.

Our Father . . .

Prayer

Father,
we contemplate the birth of your Son.
He was born of the Virgin Mary
and came to live among us.
May we receive forgiveness and mercy
through our Lord Jesus Christ, your Son,
who lives and reigns with you and the Holy Spirit,
one God, for ever and ever.

DECEMBER 24

Morning Prayer

Ant. 1   Bethlehem in Judah's land, how glorious your *future*! * The king
                who will rule my people comes *from* you.

Psalms and canticle from the current weekday.

Ant. 2   Lift up your *heads* and see; * your redemption is now at *hand*.

Ant. 3   The day has come *at* last * when Mary will bring forth her
                *first*born Son.

READING   Isaiah 11:1-3a
    A shoot shall sprout from Jesse,
        and from his roots a bud shall blossom.
    The spirit of the Lord shall rest upon him:
        a spirit of wisdom and of understanding,
    A spirit of counsel and of strength,
        a spirit of knowledge and of fear of the Lord,
        and his delight shall be the fear of the Lord.

RESPONSORY (VI F)
Tomorrow will be the day of *your* salvation, *
the sinfulness of earth will be *de*stroyed.
— Tomorrow will be the day of *your* salvation, *
the sinfulness of earth will be *de*stroyed.
The Savior of the world will *be* our king; *
— the sinfulness of earth will be *de*stroyed.
Glory to the Father, and *to* the Son, * and to the Ho*ly* Spirit.
— Tomorrow will be the day of *your* salvation, *
the sinfulness of earth will be *de*stroyed.

CANTICLE OF ZECHARIAH

Ant.   The time has *come* for Mary * to give birth to her first*born* Son.

INTERCESSIONS

To Jesus Christ, our Redeemer, who will come again in glory *with* great power, *
   let us make our *hum*ble prayer:
Come, Lord *Jesus!*
Lord Jesus, you will come *with* great power,
— look on our lowliness and make us worthy *of* your gifts.
You came to be the good news *for* mankind,
— may we always proclaim your *saving* work.
You are worthy of praise, for you have life and *rule* all things,
— help us to wait in joyful hope for the coming *of* your glory.
We long for the grace *of* your coming,
— console us with the gift of your own *di*vine life.

Our Father . . .

Prayer

Come, Lord Jesus,
do not delay;
give new courage to your people who trust in your love.
By your coming, raise us to the joy of your kingdom,
where you live and reign with the Father and the Holy Spirit,
one God, for ever and ever.

Proper of Seasons
Christmas

December 25
CHRISTMAS

Solemnity

Evening Prayer I
HYMN
Christe, Redemptor omnium. (L.M.)

Christe, Redemptor omnium,	O Christ, Redeemer of us all,
Ex Patre, Patris unice,	Belovèd Son, the Father's Word,
Solus ante principium	Alone with him before all time,
Natus ineffabiliter,	Yet choosing to be born on earth.
Tu lumen, tu splendor Patris,	The Father's Splendor, Light from Light,
Tu spes perennis omnium,	Eternal Hope of ev'ry soul,
Intende quas fundunt preces	Hear now the prayers throughout the world
Tui per orbem servuli.	Which lovingly arise to you.
Salutis auctor, recole	O Source of all salvation true,
Quod nostri quondam corporis,	Remember that you deigned to take
Ex illibata Virgine	Our human nature's flesh and blood,
Nascendo, formam sumpseris.	Formed in a spotless virgin's womb.
His præsens testatur dies,	This is the great day of the year
Currens per anni circulum,	When Christians join to celebrate
Quod a solus sede Patris	Your coming down to save all men,
Mundi salus adveneris;	The Father's glory laid aside.
Hunc cælum, terra, hunc mare,	The earth, the sky, the very sea,
Hunc omne quod in eis est,	And all that live in them, rejoice,
Auctorem adventus tui	And praise the Father who decreed
Laudat exsultans cantico.	That you should come to us as Man.
Nos quoque, qui sancto tuo	And we who now have been redeemed
Redempti sumus sanguine,	By your divine and precious Blood
Ob diem natalis tui	Unite to sing this grateful song
Hymnum novum concinimus.	Today in honor of your birth.
Iesu, tibi sit gloria,	All glory, Jesus, be to you
Qui natus es de Virgine,	Once born of Virgin undefiled,
Cum Patre et almo Spiritu,	Who, with the Spirit of your Love
In sempiterna sæcula. Amen.	And God the Father, ever reign. Amen.

PSALMODY

Ant. 1   He comes in splendor, † the King who *is* our peace; * the whole
world *longs* to see him.

VIIIg

Psalm 113
Praise the name of the Lord
He has cast down the mighty and has lifted up the lowly (Luke 1:52).

Praise, O servants *of* the Lord, *
  praise the name *of* the Lord!
May the name of the *Lord* be blessed *
  both now and for *evermore!*
From the rising of the sun *to* its setting
  * praised be the name *of* the Lord!
High above all nations *is* the Lord, *
  above the heav*ens* his glory.
Who is like the *Lord,* our God, * who
  has risen on high *to* his throne
yet stoops from the heights *to* look
  down, * to look down upon heav*en*

and earth?
From the dust he lifts *up* the lowly, *
  from his misery he rai*ses* the poor
to set him in the company of princes, *
  yes, with the princes *of* his people.
To the childless wife he *gives* a home *
  and gladdens her *heart* with children.
Glory to the Father, and *to* the Son, *
  and to the *Holy* Spirit:
as it was in the begin*ning,* is now, * and
  will be for ev*er.* Amen.

Antiphon   He comes in splendor, † the King who *is* our peace; * the whole
world *longs* to see him.

Ant. 2   He sends forth his word *to* the earth, * and his command
spreads swiftly through *the* land.

IIA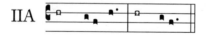

Psalm 147:12-20
The restoration of Jerusalem
Come, I will show you the bride of the Lamb (Revelation 21:9).

O praise the *Lord,* Jerusalem! *
  Zion, praise *your* God!
He has strengthened the bars *of* your
  gates, * he has blessed the children
  *with*in you.
He established peace *on* your borders, *
  he feeds you with fin*est* wheat.
He sends out his word *to* the earth *

and swiftly runs his *command.*
He showers down snow *white* as wool, *
  he scatters hoar-frost *like* ashes.
He hurls down hail*stones* like crumbs. *
  The waters are frozen at *his* touch;
he sends forth his word *and* it melts
  them: * at the breath of his mouth
  the wat*ers* flow.

He makes his word *known* to Jacob, *
to Israel his laws and *de*crees.
He has not dealt thus with *o*ther
nations; * he has not taught them his
*de*crees.

Glory to the Father, and *to* the Son, *
and to the Ho*ly* Spirit:
as it was in the begin*ning,* is now, * and
will be for ever. *A*men.

Antiphon   He sends forth his word *to* the earth, * and his command spreads
swiftly through *the* land.

Ant. 3   The eternal Word, born of the Father before time *be*gan, * today
emptied himself for our sake and be*came* man.

V a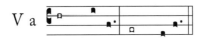

Canticle   Philippians 2:6-11
Christ, God's holy servant

Though he was in the form of
God, † Jesus did not deem
equality *with* God * something to *be*
grasped at.
Rather, he emptied himself † and took
the form of *a* slave, * being born in
the likeness *of* men.
He was known to be of human *estate,* *
and it was thus that *he* humbled
himself,
obediently accepting e*ven* death, *
death on *a* cross!
Because *of* this, * God highly e*xalted*

him
and bestowed on him *the* name * above
every *o*ther name,
So that at Jesus' name every knee must
bend † in the heavens, on *the* earth, *
and under *the* earth,
and every tongue proclaim † to the
glory of God *the* Father: * JESUS
CHRIST *IS* LORD!
Glory to the Father, and to *the* Son, *
and to the Ho*ly* Spirit:
as it was in the beginning, *is* now, * and
will be for ever. *A*men.

Antiphon   The eternal Word, born of the Father before time *be*gan, * today
emptied himself for our sake and be*came* man.

READING   Galatians 4:4-5
When the designated time had come, God sent forth his Son born of a
woman, born under the law, to deliver from the law those who were
subjected to it, so that we might receive our status as adopted sons.

RESPONSORY (VI F)
Today *you* will know * the Lord *is* coming.
— Today *you* will know * the Lord *is* coming.

And in the morning you will *see* his glory.
— The Lord *is* coming.
Glory to the Father, and *to* the Son, * and to the Ho*ly* Spirit.
— Today *you* will know * the Lord *is* coming.

CANTICLE OF MARY

Antiphon   When the sun rises in the morning sky, † you will see the King
             of kings coming forth *from* the Father * like a radiant bridegroom
             from *the* bridal chamber.

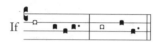

If

My soul ✠ proclaims the greatness *of* the Lord, * my spirit rejoices
in God *my* savior
for he has *looked* with favor * on his
     low*ly* servant.
From this day all *gen*erations * will call
     me blessèd:
the Almighty has done great *things* for
     me, * and holy is *his* Name.
He has mercy on *those* who fear him *
     in every gen*e*ration.
He has shown the strength *of* his arm, *
     he has scattered the proud in their
     *con*ceit.
He has cast down the mighty *from*

their thrones, * and has lifted up *the*
     lowly.
He has filled the hungry *with* good
     things, * and the rich he has sent
     a*way* empty.
He has come to the help of his *ser*vant
     Israel * for he has remembered his
     promise *of* mercy,
the promise he made *to* our fathers, * to
     Abraham and his children *for* ever.
Glory to the Father, and *to* the Son, *
     and to the Ho*ly* Spirit:
as it was in the begin*ning*, is now, * and
     will be for ever. *A*men.

Antiphon   When the sun rises in the morning sky, † you will see the King
             of kings coming forth *from* the Father * like a radiant bridegroom
             from *the* bridal chamber.

INTERCESSIONS

Christ Jesus emptied himself and took the form of a slave. He was tested like us
     in all things and *did* not sin. * Now let us worhsip him and pray to him *with*
     deep faith:
By the power of your birth, comfort those who are *saved.*
You came into the world heralding the new age foretold *by* the prophets,
— give your holy people the gift of renewal in every gen*e*ration.
You once took on the weakness of our hu*man* condition,
— be light now for those who do not see, strength for the wavering and comfort
     for the trou*bled* of heart.

You were born into pover*ty* and lowliness,
— look with favor on the poor and *com*fort them.
By your birth bring joy to all peoples with the promise of un*end*ing life,
— give joy to the dying through the hope of hea*ven*ly birth.
You came to earth to lead everyone in*to* the kingdom,
— share your life of glory with those *who* have died.

Our Father . . .

Prayer

God our Father,
every year we rejoice
as we look foward to this feast of our salvation.
May we welcome Christ as our Redeemer,
and meet him with confidence when he comes to be our judge,
who lives and reigns with you and the Holy Spirit,
one God, for ever and ever.

Morning Prayer

HYMN

A Solis ortus cardine. (L.M.)

A solis ortus cardine	From lands that see the sun arise
Adusque terræ limitem	To earth's remotest boundaries,
Christum canamus principem,	Let us proclaim the Virgin-born,
Natum Maria Virgine.	The Son of Mary, Christ the King.
Beatus auctor sæculi	Divine Creator of the world,
Servile corpus induit,	A servile form he now puts on:
Ut carne carnem liberans	The Word made flesh will free mankind
Non perderet quod condidit.	And not lose those who are his own.
Clausæ parentis viscera	Within the Mother's stainless soul
Cælestis intrat gratia;	Dwells plenitude of heav'nly grace:
Venter puellæ baiulat	Her sacred womb now bears enshrined
Secreta quæ non noverat.	A secret such as none e're told.
Domus pudici pectoris	The dwelling of that most pure heart
Templum repente fit Dei;	Becomes the temple of the Lord:
Intacta nesciens virum	Virginity remains untouched
Verbo concepit Filium.	As she conceives God's only Son.
Enixa est puerpera	That Child divine is now brought forth
Quem Gabriel prædixerat,	Whom Gabriel announced before;
Quem matris alvo gestiens	Whom, cradled in his Mother's womb,
Clausus Ioannes senserat.	The Baptist knew, and leapt for joy.
Feno iacere pertulit,	Upon mere hay Christ deigns to lie:
Præsepe non abhorruit,	He does not spurn a manger bed:
Parvoque lacte pastus est	A little milk now nourishes
Per quem nec ales esurit.	The One who feeds the very birds.
Gaudet chorus cælestium	Celestial choirs resound with song,
Et angeli canunt Deum,	And angels priase the Triune God:
Palamque fit pastoribus	To lowly shepherds they reveal
Pastor, Creator omnium.	That Shepherd kind, who made the world.
Iesu, tibi sit gloria,	All praise and glory, Lord, be yours,
Qui natus es de Virgine,	Whom Virgin bore for all mankind:
Cum Patre et almo Spiritu,	All honor to the Father too,
In sempiterna sæcula. Amen.	And Holy Spirit, Three in one. Amen.

PSALMODY

Ant. 1   Tell us, shepherds, what *have* you seen? * Who has ap*peared* on earth?   We have seen a newborn infant and a cho*ir* of angels * praising the Lord, a*l*leluia.

VIIIg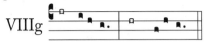

Psalm 63:2-9
A soul thirsting for God
Whoever has left the darkness of sin, yearns for God.

O God, you are my God, for *you* I long; * for you my *soul* is thirsting.
My body *pines* for you * like a dry, weary land *with*out water.
So I gaze on you *in* the sanctuary * to see your strength *and* your glory.
For your love is bet*ter* than life, * my lips will *speak* your praise.
So I will bless you *all* my life, * in your name I will lift *up* my hands.
My soul shall be filled as *with* a banquet, * my mouth shall praise *you* with joy.
On my bed I re*member* you. * On you I muse *through* the night
for you have *been* my help; * in the shadow of your wings *I* rejoice.
My soul *clings* to you; * your right hand *holds* me fast.
Glory to the Father, and *to* the Son, * and to the *Holy* Spirit:
as it was in the begin*ning*, is now, * and will be for ev*er*. Amen.

Antiphon   Tell us, shepherds, what *have* you seen? * Who has ap*peared* on earth?   We have seen a newborn infant and a cho*ir* of angels * praising the Lord, a*l*leluia.

Ant. 2   The angel said to the shepherds: † I proclaim to you *a* great joy; * today the Savior of the world is born for you, al*l*eluia.

IIA

Canticle   Daniel 3:57-88; 56
Let all creatures praise the Lord
All you servants of the Lord, sing praise to him (Revelation 19:5).

B less the Lord, all you works *of* the Lord. * Praise and exalt him above all *for*ever.
Angels of the Lord, *bless* the Lord, * You heavens, bless *the* Lord.
All you waters above the heavens, *bless* the Lord. * All you hosts of the Lord, bless *the* Lord.
Sun and moon, *bless* the Lord. * Stars of heaven, bless *the* Lord.
Every shower and dew, *bless* the Lord. * All you winds, bless *the* Lord.
Fire and heat, *bless* the Lord. * Cold and chill, bless *the* Lord.

Dew and rain, *bless* the Lord. * Frost
and chill, bless *the* Lord.

Ice and snow, *bless* the Lord. * Nights
and days, bless *the* Lord.

Light and darkness, *bless* the Lord. *
Lightnings and clouds, bless *the*
Lord.

Let the earth *bless* the Lord. * Praise
and exalt him above all *for*ever.

Mountains and hills, *bless* the Lord. *
Everything growing from the earth,
bless *the* Lord.

You springs, *bless* the Lord. * Seas and
rivers, bless *the* Lord.

You dolphins and all water creatures,
bless the Lord. * All you birds of the
air, bless *the* Lord.

All you beasts, wild and tame, *bless* the
Lord. * You sons of men, bless *the*
Lord.

O Israel, *bless* the Lord. * Praise and
exalt him above all *for*ever.

Priests of the Lord, *bless* the Lord. *
Servants of the Lord, bless *the* Lord.

Spirits and souls of the just, *bless* the
Lord. * Holy men of humble heart,
bless *the* Lord.

Hananiah, Azariah, Mishael, *bless* the
Lord. * Praise and exalt him above all
*for*ever.

Let us bless the Father, and the Son,
and the *Ho*ly Spirit. * Let us praise
and exalt him above all *for*ever.

Blessèd are you in the firma*ment* of
heaven.* Praiseworthy and glorious
and exalted above all *for*ever.

Antiphon   The angel said to the shepherds: †I proclaim to you *a* great joy; *
                  today the Savior of the world is born for you, al*le*luia.

Ant. 3   A little child is born for us *to*day; * little and yet called the
                  mighty God, al*le*luia.

Psalm 149
The joy of God's holy people
Let the sons of the Church, the children of the new people, rejoice in Christ,
their King (Hesychius).

Sing a new song to *the* Lord, *
his praise in the assembly of *the*
faithful.

Let Israel rejoice in *its* Maker, * let
Zion's sons exult in *their* king.

Let them praise his name *with* dancing
* and make music with timbrel *and*
harp.

For the Lord takes delight in *his*
people. * He crowns the poor with
sal*va*tion.

Let the faithful rejoice in *their* glory, *
shout for joy and take *their* rest.

Let the praise of God be on *their* lips *
and a two-edged sword in *their*
hand,

to deal out vengeance to *the* nations *
and punishment on all *the* peoples:

to bind their kings *in* chains * and
their nobles in fetters *of* iron;

to carry out the sentence pre-or*dained*;
* this honor is for all *his* faithful.

Glory to the Father, and to *the* Son, * and to the Ho*ly* Spirit:

as it was in the beginning, *is* now, * and will be for ever. *A*men.

Antiphon   A little child is born for us *to*day; * little and yet called the mighty God, al*le*luia.

READING   Hebrews 1:1-2

In times past, God spoke in fragmentary and varied ways to our fathers through the prophets; in this, the final age, he has spoken to us through his Son, whom he has made heir of all things and through whom he first created the universe.

RESPONSORY (VI F)

The Lord *has* made known, * alleluia, al*le*luia.
— The Lord *has* made known, * alleluia, al*le*luia.
His *saving* power,
— alleluia, al*le*luia.
Glory to the Father, and *to* the Son, * and to the Ho*ly* Spirit.
— The Lord *has* made known, * alleluia, al*le*luia.

CANTICLE OF ZECHARIAH

Antiphon   Glory to God *in* the highest, * and peace to his people on earth, al*le*luia.

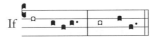

Blessèd ✠ be the Lord, the *God* of Israel; * he has come to his people and set *them* free.
He has raised up for us a *mighty* savior, * born of the house of his ser*vant* David.
Through his holy prophets he promised of old † that he would save us *from* our enemies, * from the hands of all *who* hate us.
He promised to show mercy *to* our fathers * and to remember his ho*ly* covenant.
This was the oath he swore to our *fath*er Abraham: * to set us free from the hands of *our* enemies,
free to worship him without fear, † holy and righteous *in* his sight * all

the days of *our* life.
You, my child, shall be called the prophet *of* the Most High; * for you will go before the Lord to prepare *his* way,
to give his people knowledge *of* salvation * by the forgiveness of *their* sins.
In the tender compassion *of* our God * the dawn from on high shall break *up*on us,
to shine on those who dwell in darkness and the sha*dow* of death, * and to guide our feet into the way *of* peace.
Glory to the Father, and *to* the Son, * and to the Ho*ly* Spirit:
as it was in the begin*ning*, is now, * and will be for ever. *A*men.

Antiphon   Glory to God *in* the highest, * and peace to his people on earth,
                al*le*luia.

INTERCESSIONS (VI F)

The Word of God existed before the creation of the universe yet was born
    among *us* in time. * We praise and worship him as we cry *out* in joy:
Let the earth ring out with joy for you have *come.*
You are the eternal Word of God who flooded the world with joy *at* your birth,
— fill us with joy by the continuous gift *of* your life.
You saved us and by your birth revealed to us the covenant faithfulness *of* the
    Lord,
— help us to be faithful to the promises *of* our baptism.
You are the King of heaven and earth who sent messengers to announce *peace* to
    all,
— let our lives be filled *with* your peace.
You are the true vine that brings forth the *fruit* of life,
— make us branches of the vine, bear*ing* much fruit.

Our Father . . .

                          Prayer

    Father,
    we are filled with the new light
    by the coming of your Word among us.
    May the light of faith
    shine in our words and actions.
    We ask this through our Lord Jesus Christ, your Son,
    who lives and reigns with you and the Holy Spirit,
    one God, for ever and ever.

Evening Prayer II

HYMN
Christe, Redemptor omnium. (L.M.)

Christe, Redemptor omnium,	O Christ, Redeemer of us all,
Ex Patre, Patris unice,	Belovèd Son, the Father's Word,
Solus ante principium	Alone with him before all time,
Natus ineffabiliter,	Yet choosing to be born on earth.
Tu lumen, tu splendor Patris,	The Father's Splendor, Light from Light,
Tu spes perennis omnium,	Eternal Hope of ev'ry soul,
Intende quas fundunt preces	Hear now the prayers throughout the world
Tui per orbem servuli.	Which lovingly arise to you.
Salutis auctor, recole	O Source of all salvation true,
Quod nostri quondam corporis,	Remember that you deigned to take
Ex illibata Virgine	Our human nature's flesh and blood,
Nascendo, formam sumpseris.	Formed in a spotless virgin's womb.
His præsens testatur dies,	This is the great day of the year
Currens per anni circulum,	When Christians join to celebrate
Quod a solus sede Patris	Your coming down to save all men,
Mundi salus adveneris;	The Father's glory laid aside.
Hunc cælum, terra, hunc mare,	The earth, the sky, the very sea,
Hunc omne quod in eis est,	And all that live in them, rejoice,
Auctorem adventus tui	And praise the Father who decreed
Laudat exsultans cantico.	That you should come to us as Man.
Nos quoque, qui sancto tuo	And we who now have been redeemed
Redempti sumus sanguine,	By your divine and precious Blood
Ob diem natalis tui	Unite to sing this grateful song
Hymnum novum concinimus.	Today in honor of your birth.
Iesu, tibi sit gloria,	All glory, Jesus, be to you
Aui natus es de Virgine,	Once born of Virgin undefiled,
Cum Patre et almo Spiritu,	Who, with the Spirit of your Love
In sempiterna sæcula. Amen.	And God the Father, ever reign. Amen.

Ant. 1   You have been endowed from your birth with princely gifts; † in
          *e*ter*nal* splendor, * before the dawn of light on earth, I *have*
          begotten you.

VIIIg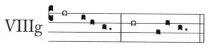

Psalm 110:1-5, 7

The Lord's revelation to my
Master: † "Sit *on* my right: * your
foes I will put be*neath* your feet."
The Lord will wield from Zion † your
scep*ter* of power: * rule in the midst
of *all* your foes.
A prince from the day of your birth †
on the *holy* mountains; * from the
womb before the dawn *I* begot you.
The Lord has sworn an oath he will
not change. † "You are a *priest* for
ever, * a priest like Melchize*dek* of

old."
The Master standing *at* your right
hand * will shatter kings in the day
of *his* great wrath.
He shall drink from the stream *by* the
wayside * and therefore he shall lift
up his head.
Glory to the Father, and *to* the Son, *
and to the *Holy* Spirit:
as it was in the begin*ning*, is now, * and
will be for ev*er*. Amen.

Antiphon You have been endowed from your birth with princely gifts; † in
          *e*ter*nal* splendor, * before the dawn of light on earth, I *have*
          begotten you.

Ant. 2   With the Lord is un*faili*ng love; * great is his power *to* save.

IIA

Psalm 130

Out of the depths I cry to *you*, O
Lord, * Lord, hear *my* voice!
O let your ears *be* attentive * to the
voice of *my* pleading.
If you, O Lord, should *mark* our guilt,
* Lord, who would *survive*?
But with you is *found* forgiveness: * for
this we *revere* you.
My soul is waiting *for* the Lord, * I
count on *his* word.
My soul is longing *for* the Lord * more

than watchman *for* daybreak.
Let the watchman *count* on daybreak *
and Israel on *the* Lord.
Because with the Lord *there* is mercy *
and fullness of *redemption*,
Israel indeed he *will* redeem * from all
its *iniquity*.
Glory to the Father, and *to* the Son, *
and to the Ho*ly* Spirit:
as it was in the begin*ning*, is now, * and
will be for ever. *A*men.

Antiphon   With the Lord is un*faili*ng love; * great is his power *to* save.

Ant. 3   In the beginning, before time began, † the Word *was* God; *
           today he is born, the Savior of *the* world.

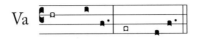

Va

Canticle   Colossians 1:12-20

Let us give thanks to the Father †
for having made *you* worthy * to
share the lot of the saints *in* light.

He rescued us from the power *of*
darkness * and brought us into the
kingdom of his belov*èd* Son.

Through him we have *re*demption, *
the forgiveness of *our* sins.

He is the image of the invisi*ble* God, *
the first-born of *all* creatures.

In him everything in heaven and on
earth was *cre*ated, * things visible and
*in*visible.

All were creat*ed* through him; * all
were creat*ed* for him.

He is before all else *that* is. * In him
everything continues *in* being.

It is he who is head of the body, the
church! † he who is the beginning,
the first-born of *the* dead, * so that
primacy may be his *in* everything.

It pleased God to make absolute
fullness reside *in* him * and, by
means of him, to reconcile everything in *his* person,

both on earth and in *the* heavens, *
making peace through the blood of
his cross.

Glory to the Father, and to *the* Son, *
and to the Ho*ly* Spirit:

as it was in the beginning, *is* now, * and
will be for ever. *A*men.

Antiphon   In the beginning, before time began, † the Word *was* God; *
             today he is born, the Savior of *the* world.

READING   1 John 1:1-3

This is what we proclaim to you:
what was from the beginning,
what we have heard,
what we have seen with our eyes,
what we have looked upon
and our hands have touched —
we speak of the word of life.
(This life became visible;
we have seen and bear witness to it,
and we proclaim to you the eternal life
that was present to the Father
and became visible to us.)
What we have seen and heard
we proclaim in turn to you
so that you may share life with us.

This fellowship of ours is with the Father
and with his Son, Jesus Christ.

RESPONSORY (VI F)

The Word *was* made man, * alleluia, al*le*luia.

— The Word *was* made man, * alleluia, al*le*luia.

He *lived* among us,

— alleluia, al*le*luia.

Glory to the Father, and *to* the Son, * and to the Ho*ly* Spirit.

— The Word *was* made man, * alleluia, al*le*luia.

CANTICLE OF MARY

Antiphon   Christ the Lord is *born* today; * today, the Savior has *ap*peared.
Earth echoes songs of *angel* choirs, * archangels' joy*ful* praise.
Today on earth his *friends* exult: * Glory to God in the highest,
al*le*luia.

If

My soul ✠ proclaims the greatness *of* the Lord, * my spirit rejoices
in God *my* savior

for he has *looked* with favor * on his low*ly* servant.

From this day all *generations* * will call *me* blessèd:

the Almighty has done great *things* for me, * and holy is *his* Name.

He has mercy on *those* who fear him * in every gen*era*tion.

He has shown the strength *of* his arm, * he has scattered the proud in their *con*ceit.

He has cast down the mighty *from* their thrones, * and has lifted up *the* lowly.

He has filled the hungry *with* good things, * and the rich he has sent a*way* empty.

He has come to the help of his *servant* Israel * for he has remembered his promise *of* mercy,

the promise he made *to* our fathers, * to Abraham and his children *for* ever.

Glory to the Father, and *to* the Son, * and to the Ho*ly* Spirit:

as it was in the begin*ning*, is now, * and will be for ever. *A*men.

Antiphon   Christ the Lord is *born* today; * today, the Savior has *ap*peared.
Earth echoes songs of *angel* choirs, * archangels' joy*ful* praise.
Today on earth his *friends* exult: * Glory to God in the highest,
al*le*luia.

INTERCESSIONS

At the birth of Jesus, angels proclaimed peace *to* the world. * We worship him
now with joy, and we pray with hearts *full* of faith:

May your birth bring peace to all.

Lord, fill your holy people with whatever *good* they need,
— let the mystery of your birth be the source *of* our peace.
You came as chief shepherd and guardian *of* our lives,
— let the pope and bishops be faithful channels of your many *gifts* of peace.
King from all eternity, you desired to be born within time and to experience the
    day-to-day life of *men* and women,
— share your gift of unending life with us, weak people, *doomed* to death.
Awaited from the beginning of the world, you came only in the full*ness* of time,
— now reveal your presence to those who are still ex*pecting* you.
You became man and gave new life to our human condition in the *grip* of death,
— now give the fullness of life to all *who* have died.

Our Father . . .

Prayer

Lord God,
    we praise you for creating man,
    and still more for restoring him in Christ.
    Your Son shared our weakness:
    may we share his glory,
    for he lives and reigns with you and the Holy Spirit,
    one God, for ever and ever.

During the octave of Christmas, with the exception of the solemnities and the Sunday
celebration in honor of the Holy Family, Evening Prayer is taken each day from within the
octave, as below, even though at the other hours the office is taken from the feast.

Each day either form of Night Prayer from Sunday, 872 or 875, is said.

Sunday in the Octave of Christmas

PSALTER WEEK I, 600.

HOLY FAMILY

Feast

When Christmas occurs on Sunday, the feast of the Holy Family is celebrated on December 30 and there is no Evening Prayer I.

Evening Prayer I

HYMN
O lux beata cælitum. (L.M.)

O lux beata cælitum	O Jesus, light of heaven's joy,
et summa spes mortalium	And highest hope of mortal man,
Iesu, o cui domestica	The purest love that home can know
arrisit orto caritas:	Surrounded your frail infancy.
Maria, dives gratia,	O Mary rich in every grace,
o sola quæ casto potes	Your privilege was quite unique,
fovere Iesum pectore,	To feed your Son and Infant God,
cum lacte donans oscula;	And softly kiss his tiny cheek.
Tuque ex vetustis partibus	Most honored patriarch of all,
delecte custos Virginis,	The Virgin Mother's strength and stay,
dulci patris quem nomine	The chosen guardian of your Lord,
divina Proles invocat:	Who called you Father day by day.
De stirpe Iesse nobili	All three from Jesse's noble stem,
nati in salutem gentium,	And born to do salvation's work,
audite nos, qui supplices	Pay heed to all the earnest prayers
ex corde vota fundimus.	We trustfully pour out to you.
Qua vestra sedes floruit	As your home flourished with the grace
virtutis omnis gratia,	Of every virtue's fairest flow'r,
hanc detur in domesticis	In love and peace may all our homes
referre posse moribus.	Reflect a little of your own.
Iesu, tuis oboediens	O Jesus, most obedient
qui factus es parentibus,	To those who held true parents' place,
cum Patre summo ac Spiritu	All praise to you who reign on high
semper tibi sit gloria. Amen.	In Godhead's perfect Trinity. Amen.

Ant. 1   Jacob was the father of Joseph, the hus*band* of Mary; * Mary gave birth to Jesus who is *called* the Christ.

Psalms and canticles from the common of the Blessed Virgin Mary, 1188.

Ant. 2   Joseph, son of David, do not be afraid to take Mary *as* your wife; * the child in her womb is conceived by the Ho*ly* Spirit.

Ant. 3   The shepherds went in haste and found Mary *and* Joseph, * with the child cradled in *a* manger.

READING   2 Corinthians 18:9

You are well acquainted with the favor shown you by our Lord Jesus Christ: how for your sake he made himself poor though he was rich, so that you might become rich by his poverty.

RESPONSORY (VI F)

The Word *was* made man, * he lived *a*mong us.
—The Word *was* made man, * he lived *a*mong us.
From his fullness we have *all* received.
—He lived *a*mong us.
Glory to the Father, and *to* the Son, * and to the Ho*ly* Spirit.
—The Word *was* made man, * he lived *a*mong us.

CANTICLE OF MARY

Ant.   The child Jesus remained *in* Jerusalem, * and his parents did *not* know it. They thought he was in the *group* of travelers * and looked for him among their relatives *and* friends.

INTERCESSIONS

Let us adore the Son of the living God who humbled himself to become a son of a *hu*man family, * and let *us* proclaim:
Lord, you are the model and Savior of all.
Christ, by the mystery of your subjection to Mar*y* and Joseph,
—teach all people reverence and obedience to law*ful* authority.
You loved your parents and were *loved* by them,
—establish our families in mutual *love* and peace.
You were eager to be about your *Fa*ther's business,
—may he be honored in *eve*ry home.
Christ, after three days your anxious parents found you in your *Fa*ther's house,
—teach all to seek first the king*dom* of God.
Christ, you have made Mary and Joseph sharers in hea*ven*ly glory,
—admit the dead into the family *of* the blessèd.

Our Father . . .

Prayer

Father,
help us to live as the holy family,
united in respect and love.
Bring us to the joy and peace of your eternal home.
Grant this through our Lord Jesus Christ, your Son,
who lives and reigns with you and the Holy Spirit,
one God, for ever and ever.

Morning Prayer

HYMN
Christe splendor Patris. (66.66)

Christe, splendor Patris,	Splendor of the Father,
Dei mater Virgo,	Jesus Christ our Savior,
Ioseph, tam sacrorum	Mary Virgin Mother,
pignorum servator,	Joseph, their protector,
Nitet vestra domus	Family most holy,
floribus virtutum,	Pattern of all virtues,
unde gratiarum	Shed those graces on us
fons promanat ipse.	Which adorned your homestead.
Angeli stupentes	Angels bow in wonder
Natum Dei cernunt	Son of God perceiving
servi forma indutum	In our human nature
servis famulantem.	Subject to his servants.
Imus praees, Ioseph,	Humble leader Joseph,
humilisque iubes;	Held a father's office,
iubes et Maria	Teacher of the Christ Child,
et utrique servis.	Serving him and Mary.
Cunctis praestant aulis	This most lowly cottage
haec egena saepta,	Court of kings surpasses,
salus unde coepit	Therein flow'red salvation,
generis humani.	For all men and nations.
Iesu, Mater, Ioseph,	Jesus, Mary, Joseph,
mansionis vestrae	Grant to us the virtues
nostras date sedes	Which make homelife happy,
donis frui sanctis.	Following your model.
Tibi laudes, Christe,	Praise to you, Christ Jesus,
spem qui nobis praebes,	Who with hope inspire us
tuos per parentes	Of attaining heaven,
caeli adire domum. Amen.	Aided by your parents. Amen.

Ant. 1   The parents of Jesus went each year *to* Jerusalem * for the
                solemn *feast* of Passover.

Psalms and canticles from Sunday, Week I, 606.

Ant. 2   The child grew in wis*dom* and strength, * and the favor of God
                was *up*on him.

Ant. 3   His father and mother were full *of* wonder * at what was said
                about *their* child.

READING   Deuteronomy 5:6
  Honor your father and your mother, as the Lord, your God, has commanded
  you, that you may have a long life and prosperity in the land which the
  Lord, your God, is giving you.

RESPONSORY (VI F)
Christ, Son of the *living* God, * have mercy *on* us.
— Christ, Son of the *living* God, * have mercy *on* us.
You were obedient to Mary and Joseph,
— have mercy *on* us.
Glory to the Father, and *to* the Son, * and to the Ho*ly* Spirit.
— Christ, Son of the *living* God, * have mercy *on* us.

CANTICLE OF ZECHARIAH
Ant.   Lord, give us light through the example *of* your family * and
                guide our feet into the way *of* peace.

INTERCESSIONS
Let us adore the Son of the living God who humbled himself to become a son of
  a *hu*man family, * and let *us* beseech him:
Jesus, you became obedient; sanctify us.
Jesus, eternal Word of the Father, you made yourself subject to Mary and Joseph,
— teach *us* humility.
You are our teacher, and your own mother pondered in her heart every one of
  your *words* and deeds,
— make us attentive to your word, and let us ponder it in hearts that are *pure* and
  good.
Christ, by your work the world was made, but you were willing to be called a
  *work*er's son,
— teach us *to* work diligently.
Jesus, in the family at Nazareth you grew in wisdom, age and grace before *God*
  and men,
— help us to grow in all things toward *you*, our Head.

Our Father . . .

Prayer

Father,
help us to live as the holy family,
united in respect and love.
Bring us to the joy and peace of your eternal home.
Grant this through our Lord Jesus Christ, your Son,
who lives and reigns with you and the Holy Spirit,
one God, for ever and ever.

Evening Prayer II

HYMN, as in Evening Prayer I, 146.

Ant. 1   After three days, Jesus was found in the temple, † seated in the midst *of* the doctors, * listening to them and ask*ing* them questions.

Psalms and canticles from the common of the Blessed Virgin Mary, 1196.

Ant. 2   Jesus returned with Mary and Jo*seph* to Nazareth; * there he lived and was obedient *to* them.

Ant. 3   Jesus grew in wisdom with *the* years * and was pleasing to God *and* men.

READING   Philippians 2:6-7
   Though he was in the form of God, Christ Jesus did not deem equality with God something to be grasped at. Rather, he emptied himself and took the form of a slave, being born in the likeness of men. He was known to be of human estate.

RESPONSORY (VI F)
He had to become like his brothers in *every* way * to show the fullness of *his* mercy.
— He had to become like his brothers in *every* way * to show the fullness of *his* mercy.
He was seen on earth and lived among *men* and women,
— to show the fullness of *his* mercy.
Glory to the Father, and *to* the Son, * and to the Ho*ly* Spirit.
-- He had to become like his brothers in *every* way * to show the fullness of *his* mercy.

CANTICLE OF MARY

Ant.   Son, why have you done *this* to us? * Think what anguish your
                        father and I have endured looking *for* you.
                        But why did you *look* for me? * Did you not know that I had to
                        be in my Fa*ther's* house?

INTERCESSIONS

Let us adore the Son of the living God who humbled himself to become a son of
    a *hu*man family, * and let *us* proclaim:
Lord, you are the model and Savior of all.
Christ, by the mystery of your subjection to Mar*y* and Joseph,
— teach all people reverence and obedience to law*ful* authority.
You loved your parents and were *loved* by them,
— establish our families in mutual *love* and peace.
You were eager to be about your *Fa*ther's business,
— may he be honored in *every* home.
Christ, after three days your anxious parents found you in your *Fa*ther's house,
— teach all to seek first the king*dom* of God.
Christ, you have made Mary and Joseph sharers in hea*ven*ly glory,
— admit the dead into the family *of* the blessèd.

Our Father . . .

Prayer

Father,
help us to live as the holy family,
united in respect and love.
Bring us to the joy and peace of your eternal home.
Grant this through our Lord Jesus Christ, your Son,
who lives and reigns with you and the Holy Spirit,
one God, for ever and ever.

DECEMBER 26

At Morning Prayer, everything is taken from the feast of Saint Stephen, First Martyr, 1162.

Evening Prayer

HYMN, antiphons, psalms, and canticle, as in Evening Prayer II of Christmas, 141.

READING   1 John 1:5b, 7

God is light;
in him there is no darkness.
If we walk in light,
as he is in the light,
we have fellowship with one another,
and the blood of his Son Jesus cleanses us from all sin.

RESPONSORY (VI F)

The Word *was* made man, * alleluia, al*le*luia.
— The Word *was* made man, * alleluia, al*le*luia.
He *lived* among us,
— alleluia, al*le*luia.
Glory to the Father, and *to* the Son, * and to the Ho*ly* Spirit.
— The Word *was* made man, * alleluia, al*le*luia.

CANTICLE OF MARY

Ant.   While earth was rapt in silence † and night only half through
its course, † your almighty *Word*, O Lord, * came down from his
royal throne, al*le*luia.

INTERCESSIONS

The Word of God, by coming to dwell with us, has opened the path to eter*nal*
   salvation. * Let us pray to him with sin*cere* humility:
Lord, deliver us from *evil.*
Through the mystery of your incarnation, through your *birth* and infancy,
— through your whole life, dedicated *to* the Father:
Lord, deliver us from *evil.*
Through your labor, your preaching *and* your journeys,
— through your continual en*count*ers with sinners:
Lord, deliver us from *evil.*
Through your agony and passion, your cross and *des*olation,
— through your sufferings, your *death* and burial:
Lord, deliver us from *evil.*
Through your resurrection and ascension, through your gift of the Holy Spirit,
   through your joys and ever*last*ing glory,
— free our departed brothers and sis*ters*, O Lord.
Lord, deliver us from *evil.*

Our Father . . .

Prayer

All-powerful God,
may the human birth of your Son
free us from our former slavery to sin
and bring us new life.
We ask this through our Lord Jesus Christ, your Son,
who lives and reigns with you and the Holy Spirit,
one God, for ever and ever.

DECEMBER 27

At Morning Prayer, everything is taken from the feast of Saint John, Apostle and
Evangelist, 1164.

Evening Prayer

HYMN, antiphons, psalms, and canticle, as in Evening Prayer II of Christmas, 141.

READING   Romans 8:3-4

God sent his Son in the likeness of sinful flesh as a sin offering, thereby
condemning sin in the flesh, so that the just demands of the law might be
fulfilled in us who live, not according to the flesh, but according to the
spirit.

RESPONSORY (VI F)

The Word *was* made man, * alleluia, al*le*luia.
— The Word *was* made man, * alleluia, al*le*luia.
He *lived* among us,
— alleluia, al*le*luia.
Glory to the Father, and *to* the Son, * and to the Ho*ly* Spirit.
— The Word *was* made man, * alleluia, al*le*luia.

CANTICLE OF MARY

Ant.   Virgin Mary, all that the prophets foretold of Christ † has been
                    fulfilled through you: † as a virgin, *you* conceived, * and after
                    you gave birth, a virgin you *re*mained.

INTERCESSIONS

Dear friends, let us humbly pray to *God* the Father * who so loved us that he sent
  us his Son:
May the favor of your Son be with us, *Lord.*
God of love, Father of our Lord Jesus Christ, you had mercy on those walk*ing* in
  darkness,
— receive the prayers we offer for the salvation *of* all people.

Lord, remember your Church spread over *all* the world,
— bless your Christian people and *give* them peace.
You are the Father of all people; graciously grant peace to all, direct the eyes of
     all *to* your Son,
— and pour forth the spirit of peace on *those* who rule them.
You announced peace on earth at the coming *of* your Son,
— give eternal peace to those *who* have died.

Our Father . . .

Prayer

Father,
we are filled with the new light
by the coming of your Word among us.
May the light of faith
shine in our words and actions.
Grant this through our Lord Jesus Christ, your Son,
who lives and reigns with you and the Holy Spirit,
one God, for ever and ever.

DECEMBER 28

At Morning Prayer, everything is taken from the feast of the Holy Innocents, 1166.

Evening Prayer

HYMN, antiphons, psalms, and canticle, as in Evening Prayer II of Christmas, 141.

READING   Ephesians 2:3b-5

By nature we deserved God's wrath like the rest. But God is rich in mercy;
because of his great love for us he brought us to life with Christ when we
were dead in sin. By this favor you were saved.

RESPONSORY (VI F)
The Word *was* made man, * alleluia, al*le*luia.
— The Word *was* made man, * alleluia, al*le*luia.
He *lived* among us,
— alleluia, al*le*luia.
Glory to the Father, and *to* the Son, * and to the Ho*ly* Spirit.
— The Word *was* made man, * alleluia, al*le*luia.

CANTICLE OF MARY
Ant.   The holy Virgin gave birth to God who became for us the frail,
             † tender baby she nursed *at* her breast. * Let us worship the
             Lord who comes *to* save us.

INTERCESSIONS

God sent his Son, fashioned from a woman, made subject to the law, to redeem
 those un*der* the law. * Trusting in this hope, let us *pray* with confidence:
May the favor of your Son be with us, O Lord.
God of love and peace, renew the faith of all Christians in the incarnation *of* your
 Son,
— that they may give thanks *at* all times.
Increase the hope of the weak, the poor *and* the aged,
— give relief to the oppressed, confidence to those who despair, consolation to
 those who mourn.
Be mindful of all *those* in prison,
— and of those driven *from* their homeland.
You let the angels be heard praising you at the birth *of* your Son,
— let the departed praise you for ever with this *heavenly* host.

Our Father . . .

Prayer

Lord God,
 we praise you for creating man,
 and still more for restoring him in Christ.
 Your Son shared our weakness:
 may we share his glory,
 for he lives and reigns with you and the Holy Spirit,
 one God, for ever and ever.

DECEMBER 29

Morning Prayer

HYMN, antiphons, psalms, and canticle, as in Morning Prayer of Christmas, 136.

READING   Hebrews 1:1-2

 In times past, God spoke in fragmentary and varied ways to our fathers
 through the prophets; in this, the final age, he has spoken to us through his
 Son, whom he has made heir of all things and through whom he first created
 the universe.

RESPONSORY (VI F)

The Lord *has* made known, * alleluia, al*le*luia.
— The Lord *has* made known, * alleluia, al*le*luia.
His *saving* power,
— alleluia, al*le*luia.
Glory to the Father, and *to* the Son, * and to the Ho*ly* Spirit.
— The Lord *has* made known, * alleluia, al*le*luia.

CANTICLE OF ZECHARIAH

Ant.   The shepherds said to one another: † Let us make our way to Bethlehem † and see *for* ourselves * this thing which the Lord has revealed *to* us.

INTERCESSIONS

Because God has been merciful to us and sent his Son, the *Prince* of peace, * let us cry *out* with confidence:

Peace to his people on *earth.*

Almighty God, Father of our Lord Jesus Christ, the Church now celebrates your *sav*ing love,

— graciously re*ceive* our praise.

From the very beginning you promised mankind your victory through *Christ* our Savior,

— let all be enlightened by *the* good news.

In praise of your Son whose coming was joyously foreseen by Abraham, hoped for by the patriarchs, announced by the prophets and yearned for *by* the Gentiles,

— save the whole peo*ple* of Israel.

You wished the birth of your Son to be proclaimed by angels and to be praised by the apostles, martyrs and faithful *of* all ages,

— grant the world that peace which the an*gels* proclaimed.

Our Father . . .

Prayer

All-powerful and unseen God,
the coming of your light into our world
has made the darkness vanish.
Teach us to proclaim the birth of your Son Jesus Christ,
who lives and reigns with you and the Holy Spirit,
one God, for ever and ever.

Evening Prayer

HYMN, antiphons, psalms, and canticle, as in Evening Prayer II of Christmas, 141.

READING   1 John 1:1-3

This is what we proclaim to you:
what was from the beginning,
what we have heard,
what we have seen with our eyes,
what we have looked upon
and our hands have touched —
we speak of the word of life.
(This life became visible; we have seen and bear witness to it,
and we proclaim to you the eternal life
that was present to the Father
and became visible to us.)
What we have seen and heard
we proclaim in turn to you
so that you may share life with us.
This fellowship of ours is with the Father
and with his Son, Jesus Christ.

RESPONSORY (VI F)

The Word *was* made man, * alleluia, al*le*luia.
— The Word *was* made man, * alleluia, al*le*luia.
He *lived* among us,
— alleluia, al*le*luia.
Glory to the Father, and *to* the Son, * and to the Ho*ly* Spirit.
— The Word *was* made man, * alleluia, al*le*luia.

CANTICLE OF MARY

Ant.   The King of heaven humbled himself to be born *of* a virgin, *
that he might restore man to the kingdom he *had* lost.

INTERCESSIONS

Let us ask the Father of mercies who anointed his Son with the *Holy* Spirit * and
sent him to preach the good news *to* the poor:
God of mercy, have mercy on *us.*
Merciful, ever-living God, you desire all to be saved and to come to the
knowledge of your truth. We thank you for giving your only-begotten Son *to*
the world,
— let the whole world rejoice *in* his birth.
You sent him to proclaim the good news to the poor, to announce release to
captives and to proclaim a *time* of favor,
— grant freedom and peace *to* mankind.

You directed the wise men to a*dore* your Son,
— receive the homage of our *faith* and prayer.
After the wisemen you called all people out of the darkness and into your
    wonderful light, so that at Jesus' name every *knee* should bend,
— make us go forth as witnesses of *the* good news.
You made Christ, born in Bethlehem, a light *to* the nations,
— reveal your glory to our brothers and sisters *who* have died.

Our Father . . .

Prayer

All-powerful and unseen God,
the coming of your light into our world
has made the darkness vanish.
Teach us to proclaim the birth of your Son Jesus Christ,
who lives and reigns with you and the Holy Spirit,
one God, for ever and ever.

DECEMBER 30

When there is no Sunday within the Octave of Christmas, the feast of the Holy Family is
celebrated today, Evening Prayer I is omitted.

Morning Prayer

HYMN, antiphons, psalms, and canticle, as in Morning Prayer of Christmas, 136.

READING   Isaiah 9:6
    A child is born to us, a son is given us;
        upon his shoulder dominion rests.
    They name him Wonder-Counselor, God-Hero,
        Father-Forever, Prince of Peace.

RESPONSORY (VI F)
The Lord *has* made known, * alleluia, al*le*luia.
— The Lord *has* made known, * alleluia, al*le*luia.
His *saving* power,
— alleluia, al*le*luia.
Glory to the Father, and *to* the Son, * and to the Ho*ly* Spirit.
— The Lord *has* made known, * alleluia, al*le*luia.

CANTICLE OF ZECHARIAH
Ant.   At the Lord's birth the choirs of *angels* sang: * Blessèd be our
                        God enthroned as King and blessèd be *the* Lamb.

INTERCESSIONS

Let us *pray* to Christ, * in whom the Father willed to make *all* things new:
Belovèd Son of God, hear us.

Son of God, you were with the Father in the beginning, and in the fullness of
time you be*came* a man,
— give us a brother's love *for* all people.

You became poor to make us rich; you emptied yourself that we might be lifted
up by your lowliness and share *in* your glory,
— make us faithful ministers *of* your Gospel.

You shone on those who dwelt in darkness and the shad*ow* of death,
— give us holiness, jus*tice* and peace.

Give us a heart that is upright and sincere, so that we may listen *to* your word,
— and bring it to perfection in ourselves and in the world for the sake *of* your
glory.

Our Father . . .

Prayer

All-powerful God,
may the human birth of your Son
free us from our former slavery to sin
and bring us new life.
We ask this through our Lord Jesus Christ, your Son,
who lives and reigns with you and the Holy Spirit,
one God, for ever and ever.

Evening Prayer

HYMN, antiphons, psalms, and canticle, as in Evening Prayer II of Christmas, 141.

READING   See 2 Peter 1:3-4

The divine power of Christ has freely bestowed on us everything necessary
for a life of genuine piety, through knowledge of him who called us by his
own glory and power. By virtue of them he has bestowed on us the great and
precious things he promised, so that through these you who have fled a
world corrupted by lust might become sharers of the divine nature.

RESPONSORY (VI F)

The Word *was* made man, * alleluia, al*le*luia.
— The Word *was* made man, * alleluia, al*le*luia.

He *lived* among us,
— alleluia, al*le*luia.

Glory to the Father, and *to* the Son, * and to the Ho*ly* Spirit.
— The Word *was* made man, * alleluia, al*le*luia.

CANTICLE OF MARY

Ant.   We sing your praises, holy Mother of God: † you gave birth to
                our Savior, *Jesus* Christ; * watch over all who hon*or* you.

INTERCESSIONS

Let us joyfully acclaim Christ, born at Bethlehem *in* Judea, * for he gives
    nourishment and guidance to his *holy* people:
Let your favor rest upon us, *Lord.*
Christ the Savior, desired of the nations, spread your Gospel to places still
    deprived of the *Word* of life,
— draw every person *to* yourself.
Christ the Lord, let your Church grow and extend the boundaries *of* its
    homeland,
— until it embraces men and women of every lang*uage* and race.
King of kings, direct the hearts and *minds* of rulers,
— to seek justice, peace and freedom *for* all nations.
Almighty ruler, strength of the weak, support those in temptation, lift up the
    fallen, protect those liv*ing* in danger,
— console those who have been deceived, comfort the incurably ill, strengthen
    the faith *of* the anxious.
Consoler of the sorrowful, com*fort* the dying,
— and lead them to the fountains of *living* water.

Our Father . . .

                        Prayer

        All-powerful God,
        may the human birth of your Son
        free us from our former slavery to sin
        and bring us new life.
        We ask this through our Lord Jesus Christ, your Son,
        who lives and reigns with you and the Holy Spirit,
        one God, for ever and ever.

DECEMBER 31

Morning Prayer

HYMN, antiphons, psalms, and canticle, as in Morning Prayer of Christmas, 136.

READING   Isaiah 4:2-3

On that day,
The branch of the Lord will be luster and glory,
and the fruit of the earth will be honor and splendor
for the survivors of Israel.
He who remains in Zion
and he that is left in Jerusalem
Will be called holy,
every one marked down for life in Jerusalem.

RESPONSORY (VI F)

The Lord *has* made known, * alleluia, al*le*luia.
—The Lord *has* made known, * alleluia, al*le*luia.
His *saving* power,
— alleluia, al*le*luia.
Glory to the Father, and *to* the Son, * and to the Ho*ly* Spirit.
—The Lord *has* made known, * alleluia, al*le*luia.

CANTICLE OF ZECHARIAH

Ant.   Suddenly there was with the angel a great company of the
heavenly host, † praising God and singing: † Glory to God *in*
the highest * and peace to his people on earth, al*le*luia.

INTERCESSIONS

Humbly yet confidently, let us invoke *Christ* the Lord * whose favor has been
shown *to* all people:
Lord, have *mercy.*
Christ, born of the Father before the ages, splendor of his glory, image of his
being, your word holds all crea*tion* in being,
— we ask you to give new life to our world *through* your Gospel.
Christ, you were born into the world at the fullness of time to save mankind and
to give freedom to *every* creature,
— we ask you to extend the liberty of our sonship in you *to* all people.
Christ, consubstantial Son of the Father, begotten before the dawn of day, and
born in Bethlehem in fulfillment *of* the Scriptures,
— we ask you to make your Church a notable example of poverty *and* simplicity.
Christ, God and man, Lord of David and Son of David, fulfillment *of* all
prophecies,
— we pray that Israel may recognize you as *its* Messiah.

Our Father . . .

Prayer

Ever-living God,
in the birth of your Son
our religion has its origin and its perfect fulfillment.
Help us to share in the life of Christ
for he is the salvation of mankind,
who lives and reigns with you and the Holy Spirit,
one God, for ever and ever.

Evening Prayer I

HYMN

Corde natus ex Parentis. (87.87.877)

Corde natus ex parentis
ante mundi exordium
Alpha et Omega vocatus,
ipse fons et clausula
Omnium quae sunt, fuerunt,
quaeque post futura sunt.

Corporis formam caduci,
membra morti obnoxia
Induit, ne gens periret
primoplasti ex germine,
Merserat quem lex profundo
noxialis tartaro.

O beatus ortus ille,
virgo cum puerpera
Edidit nostram salutem,
feta Sancto Spiritu,
Et puer redemptor orbis
os sacratum protulit.

Ecce, quem vates vetustis
concinebant sæculis,
Quem prophetarum fideles
paginae spoponderant,
Emicat promissus olim:
cuncta conlaudent eum!

Gloriam Patri melodis
personemus vocibus;
gloriam Christo canamus,
matre nato virgine,
inclitoque sempiternam
gloriam Paraclito. Amen.

Word Eternal of the Father,
Uttered long before all time,
He is Alpha and Omega,
All creation's Source and End;
Past and present and the future
Flow from his most Holy Will.
> Jesus, Lord, Emmanuel!

He assumed our human nature,
Doomed to death by Adam's fall;
God and Man, he came to save us,
Loving all that he had made,
From the law that would condemn us
To the pains of endless woe.
> Jesus, Lord, Emmanuel!

Blest indeed that birth so holy,
When the spotless Virgin pure,
Rendered fruitful by the Spirit,
Brought our great Redeemer forth,
And at last the Infant Savior
Smiled upon his treasured world.
> Jesus, Lord, Emmanuel!

He whom ancient seers promised
In their songs of long ago,
Whom the prophets' faithful pages
Oft foretold as soon to come,
Now at last he is among us,
Let us all his praises sing:
> Jesus, Lord, Emmanuel!

Let us sing to God the Father,
In sweet tones of melody,
And to God the Holy Spirit
Never ending glory be,
As we praise with grateful voices
Him whom Virgin Mother bore:
> Jesus, Lord, Emmanuel!

Ant. 1   O marvelous exchange! † Man's creator has *be*come man, * born
               of a virgin.
               We have been made sharers in the divini*ty* of Christ * who
               humbled himself to share in *our* humanity.

VIIIg

Psalm 113

Praise, O servants *of* the Lord, *
  praise the name *of* the Lord!
May the name of the *Lord* be blessed *
  both now and for *ever*more!
From the rising of the sun *to* its setting
  * praised be the name *of* the Lord!
High above all nations *is* the Lord, *
  above the heav*ens* his glory.
Who is like the *Lord*, our God, * who
  has risen on high *to* his throne
yet stoops from the heights *to* look
  down, * to look down upon heav*en*

and earth?
From the dust he lifts *up* the lowly, *
  from his misery he rai*ses* the poor
to set him in the compa*ny* of princes, *
  yes, with the princes *of* his people.
To the childless wife he *gives* a home *
  and gladdens her *heart* with children.
Glory to the Father, and *to* the Son, *
  and to the *Holy* Spirit:
as it was in the beginn*ing*, is now, * and
  will be for ev*er*. Amen.

Antiphon   O marvelous exchange! † Man's creator has *be*come man, * born
               of a virgin.
               We have been made sharers in the divini*ty* of Christ * who
               humbled himself to share in *our* humanity.

Ant. 2   By your miraculous birth *of* the Virgin * you have fulfilled *the*
               Scriptures:
               like a gentle rain falling upon the earth † you have come down
               to *save* your people. * O God *we* praise you.

IIA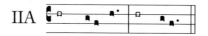

Psalm 147:12-20

O praise the *Lord*, Jerusalem! *
  Zion, praise *your* God!
He has strengthened the bars *of* your
  gates, * he has blessed the children
  *with*in you.
He established peace *on* your borders, *

he feeds you with fin*est* wheat.
He sends out his word *to* the earth *
  and swiftly runs his *com*mand.
He showers down snow *white* as wool, *
  he scatters hoar-frost *like* ashes.
He hurls down hail*stones* like crumbs. *

The waters are frozen at *his* touch;
he sends forth his word *and* it melts
  them: * at the breath of his mouth
  the wa*ters* flow.
He makes his word *known* to Jacob, *
  to Israel his laws and *de*crees.
He has not dealt thus with *o*ther

nations; * he has not taught them his
  *de*crees.
Glory to the Father, and *to* the Son, *
  and to the Ho*ly* Spirit:
as it was in the begin*ning*, is now, * and
  will be for ever. *A*men.

Antiphon   By your miraculous birth *of* the Virgin * you have fulfilled *the*
             Scriptures:
             like a gentle rain falling upon the earth † you have come down
             to *save* your people. * O God *we* praise you.

Ant. 3   Your blessèd and fruitful virginity is like the bush, † flaming yet
             unburned, which Moses saw *on* Sinai. * Pray for us, Mother *of*
             God.

Va

Canticle   Ephesians 1:3-10

Praised be the God *and* Father * of
  our Lord Je*sus* Christ,
who has bestowed on us *in* Christ *
  every spiritual blessing in *the* heavens.
God chose us in him † before the
  world *be*gan * to be holy and blameless in *his* sight.
He predestined us † to be his adopted
  sons through Je*sus* Christ, * such was
  his will *and* pleasure,
that all might praise the glor*ious* favor *
  he has bestowed on us in his *be*lovèd.
In him and through his blood, † we
  have been *re*deemed, * and our sins

forgi*ven*,
so immeasura*bly* generous * is God's
  favor *to* us.
God has given us the wisdom to
  understand fully *the* mystery, * the
  plan he was pleased to decree *in*
  Christ.
A plan to be carried out *in* Christ, * in
  the fullness *of* time,
to bring all things into one *in* him, * in
  the heavens and *on* earth.
Glory to the Father, and to *the* Son, *
  and to the Holy Spirit:
as it was in the beginning, *is* now, * and
  will be for ever. *A*men.

Antiphon   Your blessèd and fruitful virginity is like the bush, † flaming
             yet unburned, which Moses saw *on* Sinai. * Pray for us, Mother
             of God.

READING   Galatians 4:4-5

When the designated time had come, God sent forth his Son born of a woman, born under the law, to deliver from the law those who were subjected to it, so that we might receive our status as adopted sons.

RESPONSORY (VI F)

The Word *was* made man, * alleluia, al*le*luia.

— The Word *was* made man, * alleluia, al*le*luia.

He *lived* among us,

— alleluia, al*le*luia.

Glory to the Father, and *to* the Son, * and to the Ho*ly* Spirit.

— The Word *was* made man, * alleluia, al*le*luia.

CANTICLE OF MARY

Antiphon   In his great love for us, † God sent his Son in the likeness of our *sin*ful nature, * born of a woman and subject to the law, al*le*luia.

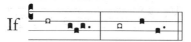

My soul ✠ proclaims the greatness *of* the Lord, * my spirit rejoices in God *my* savior

for he has *looked* with favor * on his low*ly* servant.

From this day all *gen*erations * will call *me* blessèd:

the Almighty has done great *things* for me, * and holy is *his* Name.

He has mercy on *those* who fear him * in every gen*er*ation.

He has shown the strength *of* his arm, * he has scattered the proud in their *con*ceit.

He has cast down the mighty *from* their thrones, * and has lifted up *the* lowly.

He has filled the hungry *with* good things, * and the rich he has sent a*way* empty.

He has come to the help of his *ser*vant Israel * for he has remembered his promise *of* mercy,

the promise he made *to* our fathers, * to Abraham and his children *for* ever.

Glory to the Father, and *to* the Son, * and to the Ho*ly* Spirit:

as it was in the begin*ning*, is now, * and will be for ever. *A*men.

Antiphon   In his great love for us, † God sent his Son in the likeness of our *sin*ful nature, * born of a woman and subject to the law, al*le*luia.

INTERCESSIONS

Blessèd be the Lord Jesus, our Peace, who came to unite man with God. Let us pray to him in humility:

Lord, grant your peace to all.

When you were born you showed your kindness and gentleness,
— help us always to be grateful for all your blessings.
You made Mary, your Mother, full of grace,
— give all people the fullness of grace.
You came to announce God's good news to the world,
— increase the number of preachers and hearers of your word.
You desired to become our brother by being born of the Virgin Mary,
— teach men and women to love each other in mutual brotherhood.
You came as the Sun rising over the earth,
— show the light of your countenance to those who have died.

Our Father . . .

Prayer

God our Father,
may we always profit by the prayers
of the Virgin Mother Mary,
for you bring us life and salvation
through Jesus Christ her Son,
who lives and reigns with you and the Holy Spirit,
one God, for ever and ever.

Morning Prayer

HYMN

Fit porta Christi. (L.M.)

Fit porta Christi pervia,
Omni referta gratia,
Transitque Rex, et permanet,
Clausa, ut fuit, per sæcula.

Summi Parentis Filius
Processit aula Virginis,
Sponsus, redemptor, conditor,
Suae gigas Ecclesiæ:

Honor matris et gaudium,
Immensa spes credentium,
Lapis de monte veniens,
Mundumque replens gratia.

Exsultet omnis anima,
Quod nunc salvator gentium
Advenit mundi Dominus
Redimere quos condidit.

Christo sit omnis gloria,
Quem Pater Deum genuit,
Quem Virgo mater edidit
Fecunda Sancto Spiritu. Amen.

A Virgin filled with every grace
Was chosen as Christ's holy gate,
The passing of the King preserved
Her purity for ever more.

For God the Son in course of time
Came forth from spotless Virgin's womb,
Creator, Bridegroom of the soul,
The Giant to redeem his Church.

His Mother's glory and her joy,
He is our hope which cannot fail;
The stone from mystic mountainside,
To fill the world with life and grace.

Let every soul exsult and sing,
For now the nations' Savior comes,
The Lord of all the world is here
To ransom those whom he has made.

All praise and glory be to Christ,
Begotten of the Father's love,
Whom Virgin Mother once brought forth,
Made fruitful by the Spirit's pow'r. Amen.

PSALMODY

Ant. 1   The Virgin has given birth to the Savior: † a flower has sprung
           from Jesse's stock † and a star has ris*en* from Jacob. * O *God*, we
           praise you.

VIIIg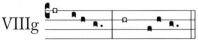

Psalm 63:2-9
A soul thirsting for God
Whoever has left the darkness of sin, yearns for God.

O God, you are my God, for
you I long; * for you my *soul is*
thirsting.
My body *pines* for you * like a dry,
weary land *with*out water.
So I gaze on you *in* the sanctuary * to
see your strength *and* your glory.
For your love is bet*ter* than life, * my
lips will *speak* your praise.
So I will bless you *all* my life, * in your
name I will lift *up* my hands.
My soul shall be filled as *with* a

banquet, * my mouth shall praise
you with joy.
On my bed I re*mem*ber you. * On you
I muse *through* the night
for you have *been* my help; * in the
shadow of your wings *I* rejoice.
My soul *clings* to you; * your right
hand *holds* me fast.
Glory to the Father, and *to* the Son, *
and to the *Holy* Spirit:
as it was in the begin*ning*, is now, *
and will be for ev*er*. Amen.

Antiphon   The Virgin has given birth to the Savior: † a flower has sprung
             from Jesse's stock † and a star has ris*en* from Jacob. * O *God*, we
             praise you.

Ant. 2   Mary has given birth *to* our Savior. * John the Baptist saw him
             and *cried* out:
             This is the Lamb of God, who takes away the sins *of* the world,
             * al*le*luia.

IIA

Canticle   Daniel 3:57-88; 56

Bless the Lord, all you works *of*
the Lord. * Praise and exalt him
above all *for*ever.
Angels of the Lord, *bless* the Lord, *
You heavens, bless *the* Lord.
All you waters above the heavens, *bless*

the Lord. * All you hosts of the
Lord, bless *the* Lord.
Sun and moon, *bless* the Lord. * Stars
of heaven, bless *the* Lord.
Every shower and dew, *bless* the Lord. *
All you winds, bless *the* Lord.

Fire and heat, *bless* the Lord. * Cold
and chill, bless *the* Lord.

Dew and rain, *bless* the Lord. * Frost
and chill, bless *the* Lord.

Ice and snow, *bless* the Lord. * Nights
and days, bless *the* Lord.

Light and darkness, *bless* the Lord. *
Lightnings and clouds, bless *the*
Lord.

Let the earth *bless* the Lord. * Praise
and exalt him above all *for*ever.

Mountains and hills, *bless* the Lord. *
Everything growing from the earth,
bless *the* Lord.

You springs, *bless* the Lord. * Seas and
rivers, bless *the* Lord.

You dolphins and all water creatures,
bless the Lord. * All you birds of the
air, bless *the* Lord.

All you beasts, wild and tame, *bless* the
Lord. * You sons of men, bless *the*
Lord.

O Israel, *bless* the Lord. * Praise and
exalt him above all *for*ever.

Priests of the Lord, *bless* the Lord. *
Servants of the Lord, bless *the* Lord.

Spirits and souls of the just, *bless* the
Lord. * Holy men of humble heart,
bless *the* Lord.

Hananiah, Azariah, Mishael, *bless* the
Lord. * Praise and exalt him above all
*for*ever.

Let us bless the Father, and the Son,
and the *Ho*ly Spirit. * Let us praise
and exalt him above all *for*ever.

Blessèd are you in the firma*ment* of
heaven.* Praiseworthy and glorious
and exalted above all *for*ever.

Antiphon   Mary has given birth *to* our Savior. * John the Baptist saw him
            and *cried* out:

            This is the Lamb of God, who takes away the sins *of* the world,
            * al*le*luia.

Ant. 3   Mary has given birth to a King whose name is ev*er*lasting; * hers
            the joy of motherhood, hers the vir*gin's* glory.

            Never was the like seen *be*fore, * never shall it be seen again,
            al*le*luia.

Va

Psalm 149

Sing a new song to *the* Lord, *
his praise in the assembly of *the*
faithful.

Let Israel rejoice in *its* Maker, * let
Zion's sons exult in *their* king.

Let them praise his name *with* dancing
* and make music with timbrel *and*
harp.

For the Lord takes delight in *his*

people. * He crowns the poor with
sal*va*tion.

Let the faithful rejoice in *their* glory, *
shout for joy and take *their* rest.

Let the praise of God be on *their* lips *
and a two-edged sword in *their*
hand,

to deal out vengeance to *the* nations *
and punishment on all *the* peoples;

to bind their kings *in* chains * and their nobles in fetters *of* iron;

to carry out the sentence pre-*or*dained: * this honor is for all *his* faithful.

Glory to the Father, and to *the* Son, * and to the Ho*ly* Spirit:

as it was in the beginning, *is* now, * and will be for ever. *A*men.

Antiphon Mary has given birth to a King whose name is ev*er*lasting; * hers the joy of motherhood, hers the vir*gin's* glory.

Never was the like seen *be*fore, * never shall it be seen again, al*le*luia.

READING   Micah 5:2, 3, 4a

The ruler in Israel will give them up, until the time
 when she who is to give birth has borne,
And the rest of his brethren shall return
 to the children of Israel.
He shall stand firm and shepherd his flock
 by the strength of the Lord,
 in the majestic name of the Lord, his God;
He shall be peace.

RESPONSORY (VI F)

The Lord *has* made known, * alleluia, al*le*luia.
— The Lord *has* made known, * alleluia, al*le*luia.
His *saving* power,
— alleluia, al*le*luia.
Glory to the Father, and *to* the Son, * and to the Ho*ly* Spirit.
— The Lord *has* made known, * alleluia, al*le*luia.

CANTICLE OF ZECHARIAH

Antiphon Marvelous is the mystery proclaimed today: man's nature is made new as God *be*comes man; * he remains what he was and becomes what he *was* not.

Yet each nature *stays* distinct * and for ever un*di*vided.

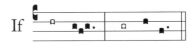

B lessèd ✠ be the Lord, the *God* of Israel; * he has come to his people and set *them* free.
He has raised up for us a *mighty* savior, * born of the house of his ser*vant* David.

Through his holy prophets he promised of old † that he would save us *from* our enemies, * from the hands of all *who* hate us.
He promised to show mercy *to* our fathers * and to remember his ho*ly*

covenant.

This was the oath he swore to our
   *fath*er Abraham: * to set us free from
   the hands of *our* enemies,

free to worship him without fear, †
   holy and righteous *in* his sight * all
   the days of *our* life.

You, my child, shall be called the
   prophet *of* the Most High; * for you
   will go before the Lord to prepare *his*
   way,

to give his people knowledge *of* salva-

tion * by the forgiveness of *their* sins.

In the tender compassion *of* our God *
   the dawn from on high shall break
   *up*on us,

to shine on those who dwell in darkness and the sha*dow* of death, * and
   to guide our feet into the way *of*
   peace.

Glory to the Father, and *to* the Son, *
   and to the Ho*ly* Spirit:

as it was in the begin*ning*, is now, * and
   will be for ever. *A*men.

Antiphon   Marvelous is the mystery proclaimed today: man's nature is
             made new as God *be*comes man; * he remains what he was and
             becomes what he *was* not.

             Yet each nature *stays* distinct * and for ever un*di*vided.

INTERCESSIONS (VI F)

Let us give glory to Christ who was born of the Virgin Mary by the power of
   the Holy Spirit, and let us pray to him in these words:

Son of the Virgin Mary, have mercy on us.

Christ, born of the Virgin Mary, you are Wonder-Counselor and Prince of
   Peace,

— give your peace to the world.

Our King and our God, you have raised us up by your coming,

— help us to honor you all the days of our lives by our faith and our deeds.

You made yourself like us,

— in your mercy grant that we may become more like you.

You made yourself a citizen of our earthly city,

— grant that we may become citizens of our true homeland, your kingdom in
   heaven.

Our Father . . .

Prayer

God our Father,
   may we always profit by the prayers
   of the Virgin Mother Mary,
   for you bring us life and salvation
   through Jesus Christ her Son,
   who lives and reigns with you and the Holy Spirit,
   one God, for ever and ever.

Evening Prayer II

HYMN, as in Evening Prayer I, 163.

PSALMODY

Ant. 1   O marvelous exchange! † Man's creator has *be*come man, * born
           of a virgin.
           We have been made sharers in the divini*ty* of Christ * who
           humbled himself to share in *our* humanity.

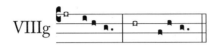

Psalm 122

I rejoiced when I *heard* them say: *
"Let us go *to* God's house."
And now our *feet* are standing * within
your gates, O Jerusalem.
Jerusalem is built *as* a city * strong*ly*
compact.
It is there that the *tribes* go up, * the
tribes *of* the Lord.
For Israel's *law* it is, * there to praise
the Lord's name.
There were set the *thrones* of judgment
* of the *house* of David.

For the peace of Jeru*sa*lem pray: *
"Peace be *to* your homes!
May peace reign *in* your walls, * in
your pal*aces*, peace!"
For love of my bre*thren* and friends * I
say: "*Peace* upon you!"
For love of the house *of* the Lord * I
will ask *for* your good.
Glory to the Father, and *to* the Son, *
and to the *Holy* Spirit:
as it was in the begin*ning*, is now, * and
will be for ev*er*. Amen.

Antiphon   O marvelous exchange! † Man's creator has *be*come man, * born
           of a virgin.
           We have been made sharers in the divini*ty* of Christ * who
           humbled himself to share in *our* humanity.

Ant. 2   By your miraculous birth *of* the Virgin * you have fulfilled *the*
           Scriptures:
           like a gentle rain falling upon the earth † you have come down
           to *save* your people. * O God *we* praise you.

Psalm 127

I f the Lord does not *build* the house,
* in vain do its buil*ders* labor;

if the Lord does not watch *over* the
city, * in vain does the watchman

keep vigil.
In vain is your ear*lier* rising, * your
  going later *to* rest,
you who toil for the *bread* you eat: *
  when he pours gifts on his belovèd
  while *they* slumber.

Truly sons are a gift *from* the Lord, * a
  blessing, the fruit of *the* womb.
Indeed the *sons* of youth * are like
  arrows in the hand of *a* warrior.
O the happiness *of* the man * who has
  filled his quiver with *these* arrows!

Antiphon   I am the handmaid *of* the Lord. * Let it be done to me as you
           have said (al*le*luia).

Ant. 3   Your blessèd and fruitful virginity is like the bush, † flaming yet
           unburned, which Moses saw *on* Sinai. * Pray for us, Mother *of*
           God.

Va

Canticle   Ephesians 1:3-10

Praised be the God *and* Father * of
  our Lord Je*sus* Christ,
who has bestowed on us *in* Christ *
  every spiritual blessing in *the* heavens.
God chose us in him before the world
  *be*gan * to be holy and blameless in
  his sight.
He predestined us † to be his adopted
  sons through Je*sus* Christ, * such was
  his will *and* pleasure,
that all might praise the glori*ous* favor *
  he has bestowed on us in his *be*lovèd.
In him and through his blood, † we
  have been *re*deemed, * and our sins

*for*given,
so immeasura*bly* generous * is God's
  favor *to* us.
God has given us the wisdom to
  understand fully *the* mystery, * the
  plan he was pleased to decree *in*
  Christ.
A plan to be carried out *in* Christ, * in
  the fullness *of* time,
to bring all things into one *in* him, * in
  the heavens and *on* earth.
Glory to the Father, and to *the* Son, *
  and to the Ho*ly* Spirit:
as it was in the beginning, *is* now, * and
  will be for ever. *A*men.

Antiphon   Your blessèd and fruitful virginity is like the bush, † flaming yet
           unburned, which Moses saw *on* Sinai. * Pray for us, Mother *of*
           God.

READING   Galatians 4:4-5

When the designated time had come, God sent forth his Son born of a woman, born under the law, to deliver from the law those who were subjected to it, so that we might receive our status as adopted sons.

RESPONSORY (VI F)

The Word *was* made man, * alleluia, al*le*luia.
— The Word *was* made man, * alleluia, al*le*luia.
He *lived* among us,
— alleluia, al*le*luia.
Glory to the Father, and *to* the Son, * and to the Ho*ly* Spirit.
— The Word *was* made man, * alleluia, al*le*luia.

CANTICLE OF MARY

Antiphon   Blessèd is the womb which bore you, O Christ, † and the *breast* that nursed you, * Lord and Savior of the world, al*le*luia.

If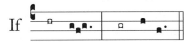

My soul ✠ proclaims the greatness *of* the Lord, * my spirit rejoices in God *my* savior
for he has *looked* with favor * on his low*ly* servant.
From this day all *gen*erations * will call *me* blessèd:
the Almighty has done great *things* for me, * and holy is *his* Name.
He has mercy on *those* who fear him * in every gen*er*ation.
He has shown the strength *of* his arm, * he has scattered the proud in their *con*ceit.
He has cast down the mighty *from* their thrones, * and has lifted up *the* lowly.
He has filled the hungry *with* good things, * and the rich he has sent a*way* empty.
He has come to the help of his *ser*vant Israel * for he has remembered his promise *of* mercy,
the promise he made *to* our fathers, * to Abraham and his children *for* ever.
Glory to the Father, and *to* the Son, * and to the Ho*ly* Spirit:
as it was in the begin*ning*, is now, * and will be for ever. *A*men.

Antiphon   Blessèd is the womb which bore you, O Christ, † and the *breast* that nursed you, * Lord and Savior of the world, al*le*luia.

INTERCESSIONS

To Christ, Emmanuel, whom the Virgin conceived and brought forth, let us give praise and pray to him:
Son of the Virgin Mary, hear us.

You gave Mary the joy of motherhood,
— give all parents true joy in their children.
King of peace, your kingdom is one of justice and peace,
— help us to seek the paths of peace.
You came to make the human race the holy people of God,
— bring all nations to acknowledge the unifying bond of your love.
By your birth you strengthened family ties,
— help families to come to a greater love for one another.
You desired to be born into the days of time,
— grant that our departed brothers and sisters may be born into the day of
   eternity.

Our Father . . .

Prayer

God our Father,
may we always profit by the prayers
of the Virgin Mother Mary,
for you bring us life and salvation
through Jesus Christ her Son,
who lives and reigns with you and the Holy Spirit,
one God, for ever and ever.

When the solemnity of the Epiphany is celebrated on the Sunday between January 2 and
January 8, the office of the Second Sunday after Christmas is not used. After the Epiphany
is celebrated, the office is as in the Psalter, with the proper parts, unless Sunday occurs on
January 7 or 8, in which case Ordinary Time begins on the following day, the feast of the
Baptism of the Lord being omitted.

SECOND SUNDAY AFTER CHRISTMAS

Sunday between January 2 and 5 when Epiphany is celebrated on January 6.

PSALTER WEEK II, 672.

Evening Prayer I

HYMN

Christe, Redemptor omnium. (L.M.)

Christe, Redemptor omnium,	O Christ, Redeemer of us all,
Ex Patre, Patris unice,	Belovèd Son, the Father's Word,
Solus ante principium	Alone with him before all time,
Natus ineffabiliter,	Yet choosing to be born on earth.
Tu lumen, tu splendor Patris,	The Father's Splendor, Light from Light,
Tu spes perennis omnium,	Eternal Hope of ev'ry soul,
Intende quas fundunt preces	Hear now the prayers throughout the world
Tui per orbem servuli.	Which lovingly arise to you.
Salutis auctor, recole	O Source of all salvation true,
Quod nostri quondam corporis,	Remember that you deigned to take
Ex illibata Virgine	Our human nature's flesh and blood,
Nascendo, formam sumpseris.	Formed in a spotless virgin's womb.
His præsens testatur dies,	This is the great day of the year
Currens per anni circulum,	When Christians join to celebrate
Quod a solus sede Patris	Your coming down to save all men,
Mundi salus adveneris;	The Father's glory laid aside.
Hunc cælum, terra, hunc mare,	The earth, the sky, the very sea,
Hunc omne quod in eis est,	And all that live in them, rejoice,
Auctorem adventus tui	And praise the Father who decreed
Laudat exsultans cantico.	That you should come to us as Man.
Nos quoque, qui sancto tuo	And we who now have been redeemed
Redempti sumus sanguine,	By your divine and precious Blood
Ob diem natalis tui	Unite to sing this grateful song
Hymnum novum concinimus.	Today in honor of your birth.
Iesu, tibi sit gloria,	All glory, Jesus, be to you
Aui natus es de Virgine,	Once born of Virgin undefiled,
Cum Patre et almo Spiritu,	Who, with the Spirit of your Love
In sempiterna sæcula. Amen.	And God the Father, ever reign. Amen.

Ant. 1   Trusting in the Lord's promise, † the Virgin Mary conceived a
                    child * and remaining a virgin, she gave birth to the King *of*
                    kings.

Psalms and canticles from Sunday, Week II, 672.

Ant. 2   Sing for joy *with* Jerusalem; * the Lord has refreshed her like a
                    river of *peace*.

Ant. 3   He who was from the beginning, God *from* God, * Light from
                    Light, is *born* for us.

READING   1 John 5:20
    We know that the Son of God has come and has given us discernment to
    recognize the One who is true, for we are in his Son Jesus Christ. He is the
    true God and eternal life.

RESPONSORY (VI F)
The Word *was* made man, * alleluia, al*le*luia.
— The Word *was* made man, * alleluia, al*le*luia.
He *lived* among us,
— alleluia, al*le*luia.
Glory to the Father, and *to* the Son, * and to the Ho*ly* Spirit.
— The Word *was* made man, * alleluia, al*le*luia.

CANTICLE OF MARY
Ant.   By the power of the Holy Spirit the Virgin Mary has con*ceived*
                   a child; * she carries in her womb this mystery which she cannot
                   com*pre*hend.

INTERCESSIONS
Christ Jesus emptied himself and took the form of a slave. He was tested like us
    in all things and *did* not sin. * Now let us worhsip him and pray to him *with*
    deep faith:
By the power of your birth, comfort those who are *saved.*
You came into the world heralding the new age foretold *by* the prophets,
— give your holy people the gift of renewal in every *gen*eration.
You once took on the weakness of our hu*man* condition,
— be light now for those who do not see, strength for the wavering and comfort
    for the trou*bled* of heart.
You were born into pover*ty* and lowliness,
— look with favor on the poor and *com*fort them.
By your birth bring joy to all peoples with the promise of un*end*ing life,
— give joy to the dying through the hope of hea*ven*ly birth.

You came to earth to lead everyone in*to* the kingdom,
— share your life of glory with those *who* have died.

Our Father . . .

Prayer

God of power and life,
glory of all who believe in you,
fill the world with your splendor and
show the nations the light of your truth.
We ask this through our Lord Jesus Christ, your Son,
who lives and reigns with you and the Holy Spirit,
one God, for ever and ever.

Morning Prayer

HYMN, as at Morning Prayer of Christmas, 136.

Ant. 1   A light has dawned for the *just* man: * the Savior of the world is born, al*le*luia.

Psalms and canticles from Sunday, Week II, 678.

Ant. 2   Let us *sing* with joy * to the Lord our *God.*

Ant. 3   The people who lived *in* darkness * have seen *a* great light.

READING   Hebrews 1:1-2

In times past, God spoke in fragmentary and varied ways to our fathers through the prophets; in this, the final age, he has spoken to us through his Son, whom he has made heir of all things and through whom he first created the universe.

RESPONSORY (VI F)

Christ, Son of the *liv*ing God, * have mercy *on* us.
— Christ, Son of the *liv*ing God, * have mercy *on* us.
Today you revealed your*self* to us.
— Have mercy *on* us.
Glory to the Father, and *to* the Son, * and to the Ho*ly* Spirit.
— Christ, Son of the *liv*ing God, * have mercy *on* us.

CANTICLE OF ZECHARIAH

Antiphon   The Virgin believed in the Lord's promise: † as a virgin she gave birth to the *Word* made man, * and yet she remained *a* virgin.

                   Let us praise *her* and say: * Blessèd are you a*mong* women.

INTERCESSIONS (VI F)

The Word of God existed before the creation of the universe yet was born
   among *us* in time. * We praise and worship him as we cry *out* in joy:
Let the earth ring out with joy for you have *come.*
You are the eternal Word of God who flooded the world with joy *at* your birth,
— fill us with joy by the continuous gift *of* your life.
You saved us and by your birth revealed to us the covenant faithfulness *of* the
   Lord,
— help us to be faithful to the promises *of* our baptism.
You are the King of heaven and earth who sent messengers to announce *peace* to
   all,
— let our lives be filled *with* your peace.
You are the true vine that brings forth the *fruit* of life,
— make us branches of the vine, bear*ing* much fruit.

Our Father . . .

Prayer

God of power and life,
glory of all who believe in you,
fill the world with your splendor and
show the nations the light of your truth.
We ask this through our Lord Jesus Christ, your Son,
who lives and reigns with you and the Holy Spirit,
one God, for ever and ever.

Evening Prayer II

HYMN, as at Evening Prayer I, 177.

Ant. 1   This pledge of new redemption and promise of eternal *joy,* *
               prepared through ages past, has dawned for us *to*day.

Psalms and canticles from Sunday, Week II, 683.

Ant. 2   The Lord *has* made manifest * his steadfast love for *us.*

Ant. 3   The Lord, the King of kings, is born for us; † the day of the
               world's salvation *has* come; * the promise of our redemption is
               fulfilled, *al*leluia.

READING   1 John 1:1-3
   This is what we proclaim to you:
   what was from the beginning,
   what we have heard,
   what we have seen with our eyes,
   what we have looked upon

and our hands have touched —
we speak of the word of life.
(This life became visible;
we have seen and bear witness to it,
and we proclaim to you the eternal life
that was present to the Father
and became visible to us.)
What we have seen and heard
we proclaim in turn to you
so that you may share life with us.
This fellowship of ours is with the Father
and with his Son, Jesus Christ.

RESPONSORY (VI F)

The Word *was* made man, * alleluia, al*le*luia.
— The Word *was* made man, * alleluia, al*le*luia.
He *lived* among us,
— alleluia, al*le*luia.
Glory to the Father, and *to* the Son, * and to the Ho*ly* Spirit.
— The Word *was* made man, * alleluia, al*le*luia.

CANTICLE OF MARY

Ant.   Blessèd is the womb that bore the Son of the E*ter*nal Father, *
                        and blessèd are the breasts that nursed Christ *the* Lord.

INTERCESSIONS

At the birth of Jesus, angels proclaimed peace *to* the world. * We worship him
    now with joy, and we pray with hearts *full* of faith:
May your birth bring peace to all.
Lord, fill your holy people with whatever *good* they need,
— let the mystery of your birth be the source *of* our peace.
You came as chief shepherd and guardian *of* our lives,
— let the pope and bishops be faithful channels of your many *gifts* of peace.
King from all eternity, you desired to be born within time and to experience the
    day-to-day life of *men* and women,
— share your gift of unending life with us, weak people, *doomed* to death.
Awaited from the beginning of the world, you came only in the full*ness* of time,
— now reveal your presence to those who are still ex*pect*ing you.
You became man and gave new life to our human condition in the *grip* of death,
— now give the fullness of life to all *who* have died.

Our Father . . .

Prayer

God of power and life,
glory of all who believe in you,
fill the world with your splendor and
show the nations the light of your truth.
We ask this through our Lord Jesus Christ, your Son,
who lives and reigns with you and the Holy Spirit,
one God, for ever and ever.

From January 2 to Epiphany
MONDAY

Morning Prayer

READING   Isaiah 49:8-9

In a time of favor I answer you,
     on the day of salvation I help you,
To restore the land
     and allot the desolate heritages,
Saying to the prisoners: Come out!
     to those in darkness: Show yourselves!

RESPONSORY (VI F)
The Lord *has* made known, * alleluia, al*le*luia.
— The Lord *has* made known, * alleluia, al*le*luia.
His *saving* power,
— alleluia, al*le*luia.
Glory to the Father, and *to* the Son, * and to the Ho*ly* Spirit.
— The Lord *has* made known, * alleluia, al*le*luia.

CANTICLE OF ZECHARIAH

Antiphon   Helpless, he lay *in* a manger; * glorious, he shone in *the* heavens.
                Humbled, he lived *among* men; * eternal, he dwelt with *the*
                Father.

INTERCESSIONS
Let us direct our prayers to Christ, the heavenly man and *the* new Adam, * who
     became a life-*giving* spirit:
Lord, have *mercy.*
Christ, Sun of Justice, you revealed your glory in our human nature in order to
     bring to perfection *the* old covenant,
— we ask you to pour out your *light* upon us.

Christ, you were glorified by the angels, announced by the shepherds, confessed and proclaimed by Sime*on* and Anna,
— let your Gospel be accepted by the people *of* the promise.
Christ, when you were born, angels sang glory to God in the highest and *peace* on earth,
— we ask you to spread your peace through*out* the world.
Christ, as the new Adam you gave new life to the old man, and prepared for us a dwelling place *in* your kingdom,
— may those overwhelmed by evil be encouraged by *hope* in you.

Our Father . . .

Prayer

Lord,
keep us true in the faith,
proclaiming that Christ your Son,
who is one with you in eternal glory,
became man and was born of a virgin mother.
Free us from all evil and lead us to the joy of eternal life.
We ask this through our Lord Jesus Christ, your Son,
who lives and reigns with you and the Holy Spirit,
one God, for ever and ever.

Evening Prayer

READING   Colossians 1:13-15

God rescued us from the power of darkness and brought us into the kingdom of his beloved Son. Through him we have redemption, the forgiveness of our sins. He is the image of the invisible God, the firstborn of all creatures.

RESPONSORY (VI F)
The Word *was* made man, * alleluia, al*le*luia.
— The Word *was* made man, * alleluia, al*le*luia.
He *lived* among us,
— alleluia, al*le*luia.
Glory to the Father, and *to* the Son, * and to the Ho*ly* Spirit.
— The Word *was* made man, * alleluia, al*le*luia.

CANTICLE OF MARY
Antiphon   O radiant child! You brought healing to human life † as you came forth from the womb of Mary, your mother, * like the bridegroom from his mar*riage* chamber.

INTERCESSIONS

God spoke to us in many different ways through his prophets and last of all he
 spoke to us *through* his Son. * Let us invoke *his* compassion:

Kyrie, eleison.

For your *holy* Church,

— that your children may profess the name of the Savior with faith *and* with
 courage:

Kyrie, eleison.

For those spreading the good news *of* salvation,

— that the workers sent by you may preach the name of the Savior *with* full
 confidence:

Kyrie, eleison.

For our sick bro*thers* and sisters,

— that they may regain their health by calling upon the name *of* the Savior:

Kyrie, eleison.

For Christians subject to *per*secution,

— that they may endure the injustice done them for the name *of* the Savior:

Kyrie, eleison.

For our brothers and sisters who have died through the *sin* of man,

— that through your compassion they *may* have life:

Kyrie, eleison.

Our Father . . .

Prayer

  Lord,
  keep us true in the faith,
  proclaiming that Christ your Son,
  who is one with you in eternal glory,
  became man and was born of a virgin mother.
  Free us from all evil and lead us to the joy of eternal life.
  We ask this through our Lord Jesus Christ, your Son,
  who lives and reigns with you and the Holy Spirit,
  one God, for ever and ever.

From January 2 to Epiphany
TUESDAY

Morning Prayer

READING   Isaiah 62:11-12

Say to daughter Zion,
   your savior comes!
Here is his reward with him,
   his recompense before him.
They shall be called the holy people,
   the redeemed of the Lord.

RESPONSORY (VI F)

The Lord *has* made known, * alleluia, al*le*luia.
— The Lord *has* made known, * alleluia, al*le*luia.
His *saving* power,
— alleluia, al*le*luia.
Glory to the Father, and *to* the Son, * and to the Ho*ly* Spirit.
— The Lord *has* made known, * alleluia, al*le*luia.

CANTICLE OF ZECHARIAH

Antiphon   The Word *was* made man; * full of grace and truth, he lived
                *a*mong us.

                From his fullness we *all* have received * gift upon gift of his
                love, al*le*luia.

INTERCESSIONS

Let us joyfully invoke the Son of God, *our* Redeemer, * who became man in
   order *to* restore man:
*Be with us, Em*manuel.
Jesus, Son of the living God, King of glory, and Son of the *Vir*gin Mary,
— brighten this day with the glory of your *in*carnation.
Jesus, Wonder-Counselor, Mighty-God, Father of the future, *Prince* of Peace,
— direct our lives according to the holiness of your *hu*man nature.
Jesus, all-powerful, patient, obedient, meek and hum*ble* of heart,
— show the power of your gentle*ness* to all.
Jesus, Father of the poor, immeasurable goodness, our way *and* our life,
— grant your Church the spir*it* of poverty.

Our Father . . .

Prayer

God our Father,
when your Son was born of the Virgin Mary
he became like us in all things but sin.
May we who have been reborn in him
be free from our sinful ways.
We ask this through our Lord Jesus Christ, your Son,
who lives and reigns with you and the Holy Spirit,
one God, for ever and ever.

Evening Prayer

READING   1 John 1:5b, 7

God is light;
in him there is no darkness.
If we walk in light,
as he is in the light,
we have fellowship with one another,
and the blood of his Son Jesus cleanses us from all sin.

RESPONSORY (VI F)

The Word *was* made man, * alleluia, al*le*luia.
— The Word *was* made man, * alleluia, al*le*luia.
He *lived* among us,
— alleluia, al*le*luia.
Glory to the Father, and *to* the Son, * and to the Ho*ly* Spirit.
— The Word *was* made man, * alleluia, al*le*luia.

CANTICLE OF MARY

Antiphon   Let us dance with delight in the Lord † and let our hearts be
              filled *with* rejoicing, * for eternal salvation has appeared on the
              earth, al*le*luia.

INTERCESSIONS

At the coming of Christ, God's holy people were made sharers *in* new life. *
   With joy and gratitude let us say *to* our Savior:
May your birth bring joy to the *world.*
Christ, our life, you came to be the head *of* your Church,
— grant your body growth root*ed* in charity.
Fully human, fully divine, you deserve our ad*o*ration,
— mold our humanity in your *di*vine image.
You became our mediator through your *in*carnation,
— unite your servants in the Church more closely to your work through the
   holiness *of* their lives.

When you came you inaugurated *a* new era,
— lead all nations to *your* salvation.
By your birth you destroyed the *chains* of death,
— free the dead from *all* their chains.

Our Father . . .

Prayer

God our Father,
when your Son was born of the Virgin Mary
he became like us in all things but sin.
May we who have been reborn in him
be free from our sinful ways.
We ask this through our Lord Jesus Christ, your Son,
who lives and reigns with you and the Holy Spirit,
one God, for ever and ever.

From January 2 to Epiphany
WEDNESDAY

Morning Prayer

READING   Isaiah 45:22-23

Turn to me and be safe,
     all you ends of the earth,
          for I am God; there is no other!
By myself I swear,
     uttering my just decree
     and my unalterable word:
To me every knee shall bend;
     by me every tongue shall swear.

RESPONSORY (VI F)
The Lord *has* made known, * alleluia, al*le*luia.
— The Lord *has* made known, * alleluia, al*le*luia.
His *saving* power,
— alleluia, al*le*luia.
Glory to the Father, and *to* the Son, * and to the Ho*ly* Spirit.
— The Lord *has* made known, * alleluia, al*le*luia.

CANTICLE OF ZECHARIAH
Antiphon   Christ our God, in whom the fullness of the Godhead dwells, †
                took upon himself our *wound*ed nature * and became the first
                new man, al*le*luia.

INTERCESSIONS

Let us glorify the Word of God who was revealed in the flesh, appeared to the
 angels, and was proclaimed *to* the nations. * Let us faithfully ac*know*ledge
 him:

We adore you, only-begotten Son of the *Father.*

Liberator of mankind, through the Virgin Mary you came *to* renew us,

— through her intercession keep us from *our* old ways.

You made your uncreated justice radiate from heav*en* to earth,

— direct our days and our nights in the brightness *of* this Sun.

Son of God, you have shown us the *Fa*ther's love,

— help us to show him to one another *by* our love.

You chose to *dwell* among us,

— make us worthy of *your* companionship.

Our Father . . .

Prayer

All-powerful Father,
you sent your Son Jesus Christ
to bring the new light of salvation to the world.
May he enlighten us with his radiance,
who lives and reigns with you and the Holy Spirit,
one God, for ever and ever.

Evening Prayer

READING   Romans 8:3-4

God sent his Son in the likeness of sinful flesh as a sin-offering, thereby
 condemning sin in the flesh, so that the just demands of the law might be
 fulfilled in us who live, not according to the flesh, but according to the
 spirit.

RESPONSORY (VI F)

The Word *was* made man, * alleluia, al*le*luia.

— The Word *was* made man, * alleluia, al*le*luia.

He *lived* among us,

— alleluia, al*le*luia.

Glory to the Father, and *to* the Son, * and to the Ho*ly* Spirit.

— The Word *was* made man, * alleluia, al*le*luia.

CANTICLE OF MARY

Antiphon   I have come forth from God in*to* the world; * I have not come of myself, but the Fath*er* sent me.

INTERCESSIONS

Christ came and gave himself up to purify his people, to make of them an acceptable offering, a band of disciples to continue *his* good work. * With fervent devotion let us *call* upon him:

Lord, have *mercy.*

For your *holy* Church,

— that all her children may be born again into *a* new life:

Lord, have *mercy.*

For the poor, for prisoners *and* for refugees,

— may they find you, the incarnate Son of God, *in* our love:

Lord, have *mercy.*

That our joy *may* be full,

— and that we may marvel at the Father's gift, which he has given *us* in you:

Lord, have *mercy.*

That your servants who have died with the knowledge of your birth may *see* your face,

— and that night may fall upon *them* no more:

Lord, have *mercy.*

Our Father . . .

Prayer

All-powerful Father,
you sent your Son Jesus Christ
to bring the new light of salvation to the world.
May he enlighten us with his radiance,
who lives and reigns with you and the Holy Spirit,
one God, for ever and ever.

From January 2 to Epiphany
THURSDAY

Morning Prayer

READING   Wisdom 7:26-27

    Wisdom is the refulgence of eternal light.
        the spotless mirror of the power of God,
        the image of his goodness,
  And she, who is one, can do all things,
        and renews everything while herself perduring;
  And passing into holy souls from age to age,
        she produces friends of God and prophets.

RESPONSORY (VI F)

The Lord *has* made known, * alleluia, al*le*luia.
— The Lord *has* made known, * alleluia, al*le*luia.
His *saving* power,
— alleluia, al*le*luia.
Glory to the Father, and *to* the Son, * and to the Ho*ly* Spirit.
— The Lord *has* made known, * alleluia, al*le*luia.

CANTICLE OF ZECHARIAH

Antiphon   The Lord God has come *to* his people * and set *them* free.

INTERCESSIONS

Christ embodied the wisdom of God, his justice, his holiness and his *saving*
    power. * Let us praise him and call up*on* him confidently:
Lord, save us by your *birth.*
King of the world, the shepherds found you wrapped in *swad*dling clothes,
  — make us willing participants in your poverty *and* simplicity.
Lord of heaven, from your royal throne you came down *to* the world,
  — teach us to respect our less fortunate broth*ers* and sisters.
Christ, light eternal, when you assumed our nature you did not take *on* its stain,
  — help your faithful people to use the good things of the earth for your hon*or*
    and glory.
You are the divine spouse of your Church; you stand in its midst as an impreg-
    nable tower,
  — help the faithful to persevere in your Church toward salvation.

Our Father . . .

Prayer

Father,
you make known the salvation of mankind
at the birth of your Son.
Make us strong in faith
and bring us to the glory you promise.
We ask this through our Lord Jesus Christ, your Son,
who lives and reigns with you and the Holy Spirit,
one God, for ever and ever.

Evening Prayer

READING   1 John 5:20
We know that the Son of God has come and has given us discernment to
recognize the One who is true, for we are in his Son Jesus Christ. He is the
true God and eternal life.

RESPONSORY (VI F)
The Word *was* made man, * alleluia, al*le*luia.
— The Word *was* made man, * alleluia, al*le*luia.
He *lived* among us,
— alleluia, al*le*luia.
Glory to the Father, and *to* the Son, * and to the Ho*ly* Spirit.
— The Word *was* made man, * alleluia, al*le*luia.

CANTICLE OF MARY
Antiphon   We have found Jesus of Nazareth, the son of Joseph. He is the
                one of whom Moses and the prophets wrote.

INTERCESSIONS
To Christ, Emmanuel, whom the Virgin conceived and brought forth, let us
     give prasie and pray to him:
Son of the Virgin Mary, hear us.
You gave Mary the joy of motherhood,
— give all parents true joy in their children.
King of peace, your kingdom is one of justice and peace,
— help us to seek the paths of peace.
You came to make the human race the holy people of God,
— bring all nations to acknowledge the unifying bond of your love.
By your birth you strengthened family ties,
— help families to come to a greater love for one another.
You desired to be born into the days of time,
— grant that our departed brothers and sisters may be born into the day of
     eternity.

Our Father . . .

Prayer

Father,
you make known the salvation of mankind
at the birth of your Son.
Make us strong in faith
and bring us to the glory you promise.
We ask this through our Lord Jesus Christ, your Son,
who lives and reigns with you and the Holy Spirit,
one God, for ever and ever.

**From January 2 to Epiphany
FRIDAY**

Morning Prayer

READING   Isaiah 61:1-2a
The spirit of the Lord God is upon me,
    because the Lord has anointed me;
He has sent me to bring glad tidings to the lowly,
    to heal the broken hearted,
To proclaim liberty to the captives
    and release to the prisoners,
To announce a year of favor from the Lord.

RESPONSORY (VI F)
The Lord *has* made known, * alleluia, al*le*luia.
— The Lord *has* made known, * alleluia, al*le*luia.
His *saving* power,
— alleluia, al*le*luia.
Glory to the Father, and *to* the Son, * and to the Ho*ly* Spirit.
— The Lord *has* made known, * alleluia, al*le*luia.

CANTICLE OF ZECHARIAH
Ant.   He came through *blood* and water, * Jesus Christ *our* Lord.

INTERCESSIONS
The Word of God existed before the creation of the universe, yet was born
    among *us* in time. * We praise and worship him as we cry *out* in joy:
Let the earth ring out with joy for you have *come.*
You are the unending Word of God who flooded the world with joy *at* your

birth,
— fill us with joy by the continuous gift *of* your life.
You saved us and by your birth revealed to us the covenant faithfulness *of* the
   Lord,
— help us to be faithful to the promises *of* our baptism.
You are King of heaven and earth who sent messengers to announce *peace* to all,
— let our lives be filled *with* your peace.
You are the true vine that brings forth the *fruit* of life,
— make us branches of the vine, bear*ing* much fruit.

Our Father . . .

Prayer

   Lord,
fill our hearts with your light.
May we always acknowledge Christ as our Savior
and be more faithful to his gospel,
   for he lives and reigns with you and the Holy Spirit,
one God, for ever and ever.

Evening Prayer

READING   Acts 10:37-38
   I take it you know what has been reported all over Judea about Jesus of
Nazareth, beginning in Galilee with the baptism John preached; of the way
God anointed him with the Holy Spirit and power. He went about doing
good works and healing all who were in the grip of the devil, and God was
with him.

RESPONSORY (VI F)
The Word *was* made man, * alleluia, al*le*luia.
— The Word *was* made man, * alleluia, al*le*luia.
He *lived* among us,
— alleluia, al*le*luia.
Glory to the Father, and *to* the Son, * and to the Ho*ly* Spirit.
— The Word *was* made man, * alleluia, al*le*luia.

CANTICLE OF MARY
Antiphon   From heaven the Father's voice proclaimed: † You are my Son,
               my belovèd, * in whom I take *de*light.

INTERCESSIONS

At the birth of Jesus, angels proclaimed peace *to* the world. * We worship him
     now with joy, and we pray with hearts *full* of faith:
May your birth bring peace to all.
Lord, fill your holy people with whatever *good* they need,
— let the mystery of your birth be the source *of* our peace.
You came as chief shepherd and guardian *of* our lives,
— let the pope and bishops be faithful channels of your many *gifts* of peace.
King from all eternity, you desired to be born within time and to experience the
     day-to-day life of *men* and women,
— share your gift of unending life with us, weak people, *doomed* to death.
Awaited from the beginning of the world, you came only in the full*ness* of time,
— now reveal your presence to those who are still ex*pect*ing you.
You became man and gave new life to our human condition in the *grip* of death,
— now give the fullness of life to all *who* have died.

Our Father . . .

Prayer

     Lord,
     fill our hearts with your light.
     May we always acknowledge Christ as our Savior
     and be more faithful to his gospel,
     for he lives and reigns with you and the Holy Spirit,
     one God, for ever and ever.

From January 2 to Epiphany
SATURDAY

Morning Prayer

READING   Isaiah 9:5

     A child is born to us, a son is given us;
         upon his shoulder dominion rests.
     They name him Wonder-Counselor, God-Hero,
         Father-Forever, Prince of Peace.

RESPONSORY (VI F)

The Lord *has* made known, * alleluia, al*le*luia.
— The Lord *has* made known, * alleluia, al*le*luia.
His *saving* power.
— Alleluia, al*le*luia.

Glory to the Father, and *to* the Son, * and to the Ho*ly* Spirit.
— The Lord *has* made known, * alleluia, al*le*luia.

CANTICLE OF ZECHARIAH
Ant.   He is the one of whom it *has* been written: * Christ is born in
                        Israel; † his kingdom will last *for* ever.

INTERCESSIONS
All the ends of the earth have seen Jesus Christ, the saving *power* of God. * Let
    us praise him and cry *out* in joy:
*Glory be to you, Lord Je*sus *Christ.*
Redeemer of all, you came to tear down the walls separating *Jew* from Gentile,
— root out the prejudices which erode the depths of *our* humanity.
Through your incarnation and your birth you established your pres*ence* among
    us,
— teach us to recognize the many forms of your presence in the Church and in
    one another.
You are the fullest revelation of God to *men* and women,
— show us how we can assent to your word with integrity of *faith* and action.
You are God-with-us, wondrously transforming *all* creation,
— let every heart, every voice, every deed throughout the universe now *be*
    transformed.

Our Father . . .

Prayer
All-powerful and ever-living God,
you give us a new vision of your glory
in the coming of Christ your Son.
He was born of the Virgin Mary
and came to share our life.
May we come to share his eternal life
in the glory of your kingdom,
where he lives and reigns with you and the Holy Spirit,
one God, for ever and ever.

EPIPHANY

Solemnity

Evening Prayer I

HYMN

Quicumque Christum. (L.M.)

Quicumque Christum quæritis,	All you who seek the gentle Christ,
oculos in altum tollite,	To heaven lift your eyes and see
illic licebit visere	The sign of glory without end,
signum perennis gloriæ.	Revealing his descent to earth.
Hæc stella, quæ solis rotam	This gleaming star outshines by far
vincit decore ac lumine,	The brightness of the sun's full glow,
venisse terris nuntiat	For it declares that God made Man
cum carne terrestri Deum.	Has come to bless and save us all.
En Persici ex orbis sinu,	Behold, three sages from the East,
sol unde sumit ianuam,	The lands of sunrise and of hope,
cernunt periti interpretes	Perceive the standard of the King,
regale vexillum magi.	And its good tidings read aright.
"Quis iste tantus— inquiunt—	"What is this marvelous thing," they say,
regnator astris imperans,	"A king who thus commands the stars,
quem sic tremunt cælestia,	Whom pow'rs above adore in fear,
cui lux et æthra inserviunt?	Whom light and heav'n's realm obey?
Illustre quiddam cernimus,	For we perceive a glory new,
quod nesciat finem pati,	Transcendent, endless and sublime,
sublime, celsum, interminum,	Far older than the skies above,
antiquius cælo et chao.	Unfathomed by the dark abyss.
Hic ille rex est gentium	He is the King of nations all,
populique rex Iudaici,	Expected by the Jews of old,
promissus Abrahae patri	The promised seed of Abraham,
eiusque in aevum semini."	Born of his race in course of time."
Iesu, tibi sit gloria,	All glory, Jesus, be to you,
qui te revelas gentibus,	Revealed to all the nations now,
cum Patre et almo Spiritu,	To God the Father glory be
in sempiterna sæcula. Amen.	And to the Spirit endlessly. Amen.

PSALMODY

Ant. 1   Begotten of the Father before the daystar shone or *time* began, *
                the Lord our Savior has appeared on *earth* today.

VIIIg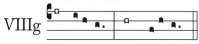

Psalm 135

I

Praise the name *of* the Lord, * praise
  him, servants *of* the Lord,
who stand in the house *of* the Lord * in
  the courts of the house *of* our God.
Praise the Lord for the *Lord* is good. *
  Sing a psalm to his name for *he* is
  loving.
For the Lord has chosen Jacob *for*
  himself * and Israel for his *own*
  possession.
For I know the *Lord* is great, * that our
  Lord is high a*bove* all gods.
The Lord does what*ever* he wills, * in
  heaven, on earth, *in* the seas.
He summons clouds from the ends of
  the earth; † makes lightning pro*duce*
  the rain; * from his treasuries he

sends *forth* the wind.
The first-born of the Egypt*ians* he
  smote, * of man and *beast* alike.
Signs and wonders he worked † in the
  midst of your *land*, O Egypt, *
  against Pharaoh and *all* his servants.
Nations in their great*ness* he struck *
  and kings in their splen*dor* he slew.
Sihon, king of the Amorites, † Og,
  the *king* of Bashan, * and all the
  king*doms* of Canaan.
He let Israel inher*it* their land; * on
  his people their land *he* bestowed.
Glory to the Father, and *to* the Son, *
  and to the *Ho*ly Spirit:
as it was in the begin*ning*, is now, *
  and will be for *ev*er. Amen.

Antiphon   Begotten of the Father before the daystar shone or *time* began, *
                the Lord our Savior has appeared on *earth* today.

Ant. 2   Great is the *Lord*, our God, * transcending all oth*er* gods.

II A

II

Lord, your name *stands* for ever, *
  unforgotten from age *to* age:
for the Lord does justice *for* his people;
  * the Lord takes pity on *his* servants.
Pagan idols are sil*ver* and gold, * the
  work of hu*man* hands.
They have mouths but they *can*not

speak; * they have eyes but they
  *can*not see.
They have ears but they *can*not hear; *
  there is never a breath on *their* lips.
Their makers will come to *be* like them
  * and so will all who trust *in* them!
Sons of Israel, *bless* the Lord! * Sons of

Aaron, bless *the* Lord!
Sons of Levi, *bless* the Lord! * You who
 fear him, bless *the* Lord!
From Zion may the *Lord* be blessed, *
 he who dwells in *Jerusalem!*

Glory to the Father, and *to* the Son, *
 and to the Ho*ly* Spirit:
as it was in the begin*ning*, is now, * and
 will be for ever. *A*men.

Ant. 2   Great is the *Lord*, our God, * transcending all oth*er* gods.

Ant. 3   The star burned like a flame, pointing the way *to* God, * the
              King *of* kings;
              the wise men saw the sign and brought *their* gifts * in homage
              to their *great* King.

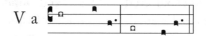

V a

Canticle   See 1 Timothy 3:16
The mystery and glory of Christ

℟ Praise *the* Lord, * all *you* nations.

Christ manifested in *the* flesh, *
Christ justified in *the* Spirit.

℟ Praise *the* Lord, * all *you* nations.

Christ contemplated by *the* angels, *
Christ proclaimed by *the* pagans.

℟ Praise *the* Lord, * all *you* nations.

Christ who is believed in *the* world, *
 Christ exalted *in* glory.

℟ Praise *the* Lord, * all *you* nations.

Glory to the Father, and to *the* Son, *
 and to the Ho*ly* Spirit:
as it was in the beginning, *is* now, * and
 will be for ever. *A*men.

Ant. 3   The star burned like a flame, pointing the way *to* God, * the
              King *of* kings;
              the wise men saw the sign and brought *their* gifts * in homage
              to their *great* King.

READING   2 Timothy 1:9-10
     God has saved us and has called us to a holy life, not because of any merit of
     ours but according to his own design—the grace held out to us in Christ
     Jesus before the world began but now made manifest through the appear-
     ance of our Savior. He has robbed death of its power and has brought life an
     immortality into clear light through the gospel.

RESPONSORY (VI F)

All peoples will be *blessed* in him, * men and women of eve*ry* race.
— All peoples will be *blessed* in him, * men and women of eve*ry* race.
All nations will ac*claim* his glory.
— Men and women of eve*ry* race.
Glory to the Father, and *to* the Son, * and to the Ho*ly* Spirit.
— All peoples will be *blessed* in him, * men and women of eve*ry* race.

CANTICLE OF MARY

Ant.   Seeing the star, the *wise* men said: * This must signify the birth
               of some *great* king.
               Let us search for him and lay our treasures *at* his feet: * gold,
               frankincense *and* myrrh.

If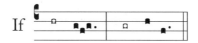

My soul ✠ proclaims the greatness *of* the Lord, * my spirit rejoices in God *my* savior
for he has *looked* with favor * on his low*ly* servant.
From this day all *gen*erations * will call *me* blessèd:
the Almighty has done great *things* for me, * and holy is *his* Name.
He has mercy on *those* who fear him * in every gen*er*ation.
He has shown the strength *of* his arm, * he has scattered the proud in their *con*ceit.

He has cast down the mighty *from* their thrones, * and has lifted up *the* lowly.
He has filled the hungry *with* good things, * and the rich he has sent a*way* empty.
He has come to the help of his *ser*vant Israel * for he has remembered his promise *of* mercy,
the promise he made *to* our fathers, * to Abraham and his children *for* ever.
Glory to the Father, and *to* the Son, * and to the Ho*ly* Spirit:
as it was in the begin*ning*, is now, * and will be for ever. *A*men.

Antiphon   Seeing the star, the *wise* men said: * This must signify the birth
              of some *great* king.
              Let us search for him and lay our treasures *at* his feet: * gold,
              frankincense *and* myrrh.

INTERCESSIONS

Today our Savior was adored *by* the Magi. * Let us also worship him with joy *as* we pray:
Save the poor, O Lord.

King of the nations, you called the Magi to adore you as the first representatives
   of the nations,
— give us a willing spirit of adora*tion* and service.
King of glory, you judge your peo*ple* with justice,
— grant mankind an abundant mea*sure* of peace.
King of ages, you endure from *age* to age,
— send your word as fresh spring rain falling *on* our hearts.
King of justice, you desire to free the poor who *have* no advocate,
— be compassionate to the suffering *and* afflicted.
Lord, your name is blessed *for* all ages,
— show the wonders of your saving power to our deceased broth*ers* and sisters.

Our Father . . .

Prayer

Father,
you revealed your Son to the nations
by the guidance of a star.
Lead us to your glory in heaven
by the light of faith.
We ask this through our Lord Jesus Christ, your Son,
who lives and reigns with you and the Holy Spirit,
one God, for ever and ever.

Morning Prayer

HYMN, as in Evening Prayer I, 196.

PSALMODY

Ant. 1   The wise men opened their treasures and offered *to* the Lord *
gifts of gold, frankincense and myrrh, *al*leluia.

VIIIg

Psalm 63:2-9

O God, you are my God, for *you* I
long; * for you my *soul* is thirsting.
My body *pines* for you * like a dry,
weary land *with*out water.
So I gaze on you *in* the sanctuary * to
see your strength *and* your glory.
For your love is bet*ter* than life, * my
lips will *speak* your praise.
So I will bless you *all* my life, * in your
name I will lift *up* my hands.
My soul shall be filled as *with* a

banquet, * my mouth shall praise *you*
with joy.
On my bed I re*mem*ber you. * On you
I muse *through* the night
for you have *been* my help; * in the
shadow of your wings *I* rejoice.
My soul *clings* to you; * your right
hand *holds* me fast.
Glory to the Father, and *to* the Son, *
and to the *Ho*ly Spirit:
as it was in the begin*ning*, is now, * and
will be for ev*er*. Amen.

Antiphon   The wise men opened their treasures and offered *to* the Lord *
gifts of gold, frankincense and myrrh, *al*leluia.

Ant. 2   Mighty seas and rivers, *bless* the Lord; * springs of water, sing his
praises, al*le*luia.

IIA

Canticle   Daniel 3:57-88; 56

B less the Lord, all you works *of* the
Lord. * Praise and exalt him above
all *for*ever.
Angels of the Lord, *bless* the Lord, *
You heavens, bless *the* Lord.
All you waters above the heavens, *bless*
the Lord. * All you hosts of the

Lord, bless *the* Lord.
Sun and moon, *bless* the Lord. * Stars
of heaven, bless *the* Lord.
Every shower and dew, *bless* the Lord. *
All you winds, bless *the* Lord.
Fire and heat, *bless* the Lord. * Cold
and chill, bless *the* Lord.

Dew and rain, *bless* the Lord. * Frost and chill, bless *the* Lord.

Ice and snow, *bless* the Lord. * Nights and days, bless *the* Lord.

Light and darkness, *bless* the Lord. * Lightnings and clouds, bless *the* Lord.

Let the earth *bless* the Lord. * Praise and exalt him above all *for*ever.

Mountains and hills, *bless* the Lord. * Everything growing from the earth, bless *the* Lord.

You springs, *bless* the Lord. * Seas and rivers, bless *the* Lord.

You dolphins and all water creatures, *bless* the Lord. * All you birds of the air, bless *the* Lord.

All you beasts, wild and tame, *bless* the Lord. * You sons of men, bless *the* Lord.

O Israel, *bless* the Lord. * Praise and exalt him above all *for*ever.

Priests of the Lord, *bless* the Lord. * Servants of the Lord, bless *the* Lord.

Spirits and souls of the just, *bless* the Lord. * Holy men of humble heart, bless *the* Lord.

Hananiah, Azariah, Mishael, *bless* the Lord. * Praise and exalt him above all *for*ever.

Let us bless the Father, and the Son, and the *Ho*ly Spirit. * Let us praise and exalt him above all *for*ever.

Blessed are you in the firma*ment* of heaven.* Praiseworthy and glorious and exalted above all *for*ever.

Antiphon   Mighty seas and rivers, *bless* the Lord; * springs of water, sing his praises, al*le*luia.

Ant. 3   Jerusalem, your light *has* come; * the glory of the Lord dawns *up*on you.
Men of every race shall walk in the splendor of *your* sunrise, * al*le*luia.

Psalm 149

Sing a new song to *the* Lord, * his praise in the assembly of *the* faithful.

Let Israel rejoice in *its* Maker, * let Zion's sons exult in *their* king.

Let them praise his name *with* dancing * and make music with timbrel *and* harp.

For the Lord takes delight in *his* people. * He crowns the poor with salvation.

Let the faithful rejoice in *their* glory, * shout for joy and take *their* rest.

Let the praise of God be on *their* lips * and a two-edged sword in *their* hand,

to deal out vengeance to *the* nations * and punishment on all *the* peoples;

to bind their kings *in* chains * and their nobles in fetters *of* iron;

to carry out the sentence pre-*or*dained:

* this honor is for all *his* faithful.
Glory to the Father, and to *the* Son, *
  and to the Ho*ly* Spirit:

as it was in the beginning, *is* now, * and
  will be for ever. *A*men.

Antiphon   Jerusalem, your light *has* come; * the glory of the Lord dawns
             *up*on you.
             Men of every race shall walk in the splendor of *your* sunrise, *
             al*le*luia.

READING   Isaiah 52:7-10

How beautiful upon the mountains
    are the feet of him who brings glad tidings,
Announcing peace, bearing good news,
    announcing salvation, and saying to Zion,
    "Your God is King!"
Hark! Your watchmen raise a cry,
    together they shout for joy,
For they see directly, before their eyes,
    the Lord restoring Zion.
Break out together in song,
    O ruins of Jerusalem!
For the Lord comforts his people,
    he redeems Jerusalem.
The Lord has bared his holy arm
    in the sight of all the nations;
All the ends of the earth will behold
    the salvation of our God.

RESPONSORY (VI F)
All the kings *of* the earth * will bow down *in* worship.
— All the kings *of* the earth * will bow down *in* worship.
Men and women of every na*tion* will serve him.
— They will bow down *in* worship.
Glory to the Father, and *to* the Son, * and to the Ho*ly* Spirit.
— All the kings *of* the earth * will bow down *in* worship.

CANTICLE OF ZECHARIAH

Ant.   Today the Bridegroom claims his *bride*, the Church, * since
              Christ has washed her sins away in Jor*dan's* waters;
              The Magi hasten with their gifts to the royal wedding; † and
              the wedding *guests* rejoice, * for Christ has changed water into
              wine, al*le*luia.

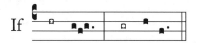

Blessèd ✠ be the Lord, the *God* of
Israel; * he has come to his people
and set *them* free.
He has raised up for us a *mighty* savior,
* born of the house of his ser*vant*
David.
Through his holy prophets he promised of old † that he would save us
from our enemies, * from the hands
of all *who* hate us.
He promised to show mercy *to* our
fathers * and to remember his ho*ly*
covenant.
This was the oath he swore to our
*fath*er Abraham: * to set us free from
the hands of *our* enemies,
free to worship him without fear, †
holy and righteous *in* his sight * all
the days of *our* life.
You, my child, shall be called the
prophet *of* the Most High; * for you
will go before the Lord to prepare *his*
way,
to give his people knowledge *of* salvation * by the forgiveness of *their* sins.
In the tender compassion *of* our God *
the dawn from on high shall break
*up*on us,
to shine on those who dwell in darkness and the sha*dow* of death, * and
to guide our feet into the way *of*
peace.
Glory to the Father, and *to* the Son, *
and to the Ho*ly* Spirit:
as it was in the begin*ning*, is now, * and
will be for ever. *A*men.

Antiphon   Today the Bridegroom claims his *bride*, the Church, * since
              Christ has washed her sins away in Jor*dan's* waters;
              The Magi hasten with their gifts to the royal wedding; † and
              the wedding *guests* rejoice, * for Christ has changed water into
              wine, al*le*luia.

INTERCESSIONS

Today our Savior was adored by *the* Magi. * Let us also worship him with joy *as*
we pray:
Light from Light, shine on us this *day.*
Christ, you revealed yourself *in* the flesh,
— sanctify us through prayer and the *word* of God.
Christ, your witness *was* the Spirit,
— free our lives from the spir*it* of doubt.

Christ, you revealed yourself *to* the angels,
— help us to feel the joy of hea*ven* on earth.
Christ, you were proclaimed *to* the nations,
— by the power of the Holy Spirit open the *hearts* of all.
Christ, you generated faith *in* the world,
— renew the faith of *all* believers.
Christ, you were taken *up* in glory,
— enkindle in us a longing *for* your kingdom.

Our Father . . .

Prayer

Father,
you revealed your Son to the nations
by the guidance of a star.
Lead us to your glory in heaven
by the light of faith.
We ask this through our Lord Jesus Christ, your Son,
who lives and reigns with you and the Holy Spirit,
one God, for ever and ever.

Evening Prayer II

HYMN

Hostis Herodes. (L.M.)

Hostis Herodes impie,	Why should the wicked Herod fear
Christum venire quid times?	The coming of the Savior, Christ?
Non eripit mortalia,	He will not plunder earthly realms,
Qui regna dat cælestia.	Who gives a Kingdom from above.
Ibant Magi, qua venerant,	The Eastern sages followed on
Stellam sequentes præviam:	As shining Star preceded them;
Lumen requirunt lumine,	By means of light, true Light they sought,
Deum fatentur munere.	And off'ring gifts, their God adored.
Lavacra puri gurgitis	The spotless Lamb from God's high throne
Cælestis Agnus attigit;	Required of John to baptize him:
Peccata, quæ non detulit,	In Jordan's waters cleasning thus
Nos abluendo sustulit.	His peoples' sin, though sinless he.
Novum genus potentiæ:	New wonder of almighty pow'r!
Aquæ rubescunt hydriæ,	The water blushed in Cana's jars;
Vinumque iussa fundere	At Christ's command the wine flowed forth,
Mutavit unda originem.	The water's very nature changed.
Iesu, tibi sit gloria,	All praise and glory, Lord, be yours,
Qui te revelas gentibus,	Who showed yourself to men this day:
Cum Patre, et almo Spiritu,	All honor to the Father too,
In sempiterna sæcula. Amen.	And Holy Spirit, Three in One. Amen.

PSALMODY

Ant. 1   He comes in splendor, the King who *is* our peace; * he is
            supreme over all the kings *of* the earth.

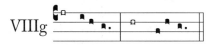

VIIIg

Psalm 110:1-5, 7

The Lord's revelation to my
    Master: † "Sit *on* my right: * your
foes I will put be*neath* your feet."
The Lord will wield from Zion † your
    scep*ter* of power: * rule in the midst
    of *all* your foes.
A prince from the day of your birth †
    on the *holy* mountains; * from the
    womb before the dawn *I* begot you.
The Lord has sworn an oath he will
    not change. † "You are a *priest* for
    ever, * a priest like Melchize*dek* of

old."
The Master standing *at* your right
    hand * will shatter kings in the day
    of *his* great wrath.
He shall drink from the stream *by* the
    wayside * and therefore he shall lift
    up his head.
Glory to the Father, and *to* the Son, *
    and to the *Holy* Spirit:
as it was in the begin*ning*, is now, * and
    will be for ev*er*. Amen.

Antiphon   He comes in splendor, the King who *is* our peace; * he is
            supreme over all the kings *of* the earth.

Ant. 2   A light has shone through the darkness for the up*right* of heart;
            * the Lord is gracious, merciful *and* just.

IIA

Psalm 112

Happy the man who *fears* the
    Lord, * who takes delight in all
his com*mands*.
His sons will be power*ful* on earth; *
    the children of the upright are
    bless*è*d.
Riches and wealth are *in* his house; *
    his justice stands firm for *ev*er.
He is a light in the darkness *for* the
    upright: * he is generous, merciful
    and *just*.

The good man takes pi*ty* and lends, *
    he conducts his affairs with *hon*or.
The just man will *nev*er waver: * he
    will be remembered for *ev*er.
He has no fear of *ev*il news; * with a
    firm heart he trusts in the *Lord*.
With a steadfast heart he *will* not fear;
    * he will see the downfall of his *foes*.
Open-handed, he gives to the poor; †
    his justice stands *firm* for ever. * His
    head will be raised in *glo*ry.

The wicked man sees and is angry, †
  grinds his teeth and *fades* away; * the
  desire of the wicked leads to *doom*.
Glory to the Father, and *to* the Son, *

and to the Holy *Spi*rit:
as it was in the begin*ning*, is now, * and
  will be for ever. *A*men.

Antiphon   A light has shone through the darkness for the up*right* of heart;
             * the Lord is gracious, merciful *and* just.

Ant. 3   All the people, whom you *have* made, * will come and worship
             before *you*, Lord.

             Canticle   Revelation 15:3-4

Mighty and wonderful are *your*
 works, * Lord God *Al*mighty!
Righteous and true are *your* ways, * O
  King of *the* nations!
Who would dare refuse *you* honor, * or
  the glory due your name, O Lord?
Since you alone *are* holy, * all nations

shall come and worship in *your*
  presence.
Your migh*ty* deeds * are clear*ly* seen.
Glory to the Father, and to *the* Son, *
  and to the Ho*ly* Spirit:
as it was in the beginning, *is* now, * and
  will be for ever. *A*men.

Antiphon   All the people, whom you *have* made, * will come and worship
             before *you*, Lord.

READING   Titus 3:4-5
  When the kindness and love of God our Savior appeared, he saved us; not
  because of any righteous deeds we had done, but because of his mercy. He
  saved us through the baptism of new birth and renewal by the Holy Spirit.

RESPONSORY (VI F)
All peoples will be *blessed* in him, * men and women of eve*ry* race.
— All peoples will be *blessed* in him, * men and women of eve*ry* race.
All nations will ac*claim* his glory.
— Men and women of eve*ry* race.
Glory to the Father, and *to* the Son, * and to the Ho*ly* Spirit.
— All peoples will be *blessed* in him, * men and women of eve*ry* race.

CANTICLE OF MARY

Antiphon   Three mysteries mark this holy day: † today the star *leads* the
               Magi * to the in*fant* Christ;
               today water is changed in*to* wine * for the wed*ding* feast;
               today Christ wills to be baptized by John in the *riv*er Jordan *
               to bring us *sal*vation.

If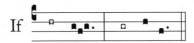

My soul ✠proclaims the greatness *of* the Lord, * my spirit rejoices
   in God *my* savior
for he has *looked* with favor * on his
   low*ly* servant.
From this day all gen*er*ations * will call
   me blessèd:
the Almighty has done great *things* for
   me, * and holy is *his* Name.
He has mercy on *those* who fear him *
   in every gen*er*ation.
He has shown the strength *of* his arm, *
   he has scattered the proud in their
   *con*ceit.

He has cast down the mighty *from* their
   thrones, * and has lifted up *the* lowly.
He has filled the hungry *with* good
   things, * and the rich he has sent
   a*way* empty.
He has come to the help of his *ser*vant
   Israel * for he has remembered his
   promise *of* mercy,
the promise he made *to* our fathers, * to
   Abraham and his children *for* ever.
Glory to the Father, and *to* the Son, *
   and to the Ho*ly* Spirit:
as it was in the begin*ning*, is now, * and
   will be for ever. *A*men.

Antiphon   Three mysteries mark this holy day: † today the star *leads* the
               Magi * to the in*fant* Christ;
               today water is changed in*to* wine * for the wed*ding* feast;
               today Christ wills to be baptized by John in the *riv*er Jordan *
               to bring us *sal*vation.

INTERCESSIONS

On this day our Savior was adored *by* the Magi. * Let us also worship him with
   joy as we *pray* to him:
Save the poor, O *Lord.*
King of the nations, you called the Magi to adore you as the first representatives
   of the nations,
— give us a willing spirit of adora*tion* and service.
King of glory, you judge your peo*ple* with justice,
— grant mankind an abundant mea*sure* of peace.
King of ages, you endure from *age* to age,
— send your word as fresh spring rain falling *on* our hearts.

King of justice, you desire to free the poor who *have* no advocate,
— be compassionate to the suffering and *the* afflicted.
Lord, your name is blessed *for* all ages,
— show the wonders of your saving power to our deceased broth*ers* and sisters.

Our Father . . .

Prayer

Father,
you revealed your Son to the nations
by the guidance of a star.
Lead us to your glory in heaven
by the light of faith.
We ask this through our Lord Jesus Christ, your Son,
who lives and reigns with you and the Holy Spirit,
one God, for ever and ever.

On the days following, until the Sunday celebration of the Baptism of the Lord, the proper
parts are taken from below. Ordinary Time begins after the Sunday celebration of the
Baptism of the Lord.
Where the solemnity of Epiphany is celebrated on the Sunday between January 2 and
January 8, on the days following the Epiphany, the proper parts are taken from below, unless
January 7 or 8 occurs on Sunday in which case Ordinary Time begins on the following day,
the feast of the Baptism of the Lord being omitted.

After Epiphany to the Baptism of the Lord
MONDAY

Morning Prayer

READING   Isaiah 9:5

A child is born to us, a son is given us;
　　upon his shoulder dominion rests.
They name him Wonder-Counselor, God-Hero,
　　Father-Forever, Prince of Peace.

RESPONSORY (VI F)

All the kings *of* the earth * will bow down *in* worship.
— All the kings *of* the earth * will bow down *in* worship.
Men and women of every na*tion* will serve him.
— They will bow down *in* worship.
Glory to the Father, and *to* the Son, * and to the Ho*ly* Spirit.
— All the kings *of* the earth * will bow down *in* worship.

CANTICLE OF ZECHARIAH

Antiphon　　　The wise men came from the East † to adore the *Lord* in
　　　　　　　Bethlehem. * Opening their treasures, the offered him three
　　　　　　　pre*cious* gifts:

　　　　　　　gold for the great King, † frankincense for the true God, † and
　　　　　　　myrrh *for* his burial, * al*le*luia.

INTERCESSIONS

All the ends of the earth have seen Jesus Christ, the saving *power* of God. * Let
　　us praise him and cry *out* in joy:
*Glory be to you, Lord Je*sus *Christ.*
Redeemer of all, you came to tear down the walls separating *Jew* from Gentile,
— root out the prejudices which erode the depths of *our* humanity.
Through your incarnation and your birth you established your pres*ence* among
　　us,
— teach us to recognize the many forms of your presence in the Church and in
　　one another.
You are the fullest revelation of God to *men* and women,
— show us how we can assent to your word with integrity of *faith* and action.
You are God-with-us, wondrously transforming *all* creation,
— let every heart, every voice, every deed throughout the universe now *be*
　　transformed.

Our Father . . .

Prayer

Lord,
let the light of your glory shine within us,
and lead us through the darkness of this world
to the radiant joy of our eternal home.
We ask this through our Lord Jesus Christ, your Son,
who lives and reigns with you and the Holy Spirit,
one God, for ever and ever.

Evening Prayer

READING   2 Peter 1:3-4

The divine power of Christ has freely bestowed on us everything necessary
for a life of genuine piety, through knowledge of him who called us by his
own glory and power. By virtue of them he has bestowed on us the great and
precious things he promised, so that through these you who have fled a
world corrupted by lust might become sharers of the divine nature.

RESPONSORY (VI F)

All peoples will be *blessed* in him, * men and women of eve*ry* race.
— All peoples will be *blessed* in him, * men and women of eve*ry* race.
All nations will ac*claim* his glory.
— Men and women of eve*ry* race.
Glory to the Father, and *to* the Son, * and to the Ho*ly* Spirit.
— All peoples will be *blessed* in him, * men and women of eve*ry* race.

CANTICLE OF MARY

Antiphon   When they saw the star the Magi were filled with great joy; †
                  entering the house, the offered their gifts *to* the Lord: * gold,
                  frankincense *and* myrrh.

INTERCESSIONS

Blessèd be Jesus Christ, the Lord, who has come to bring light to those sitting in
   darkness and in the shad*ow* of death. * With deep *faith* we beg him:
Christ, Rising Sun, give us your light.
Lord Jesus, at your coming you brought to birth your bo*dy*, the Church,
— let her be rooted in love and gift*ed* with growth.
You hold heaven and earth *in* your hands,
— let all peoples and their leaders recognize your *royal* power.
Through your incarnation you became eter*nal* high priest,
— let all priests be genuine ministers of your *saving* work.

In the womb of the Virgin Mary, you brought about a mystical union of
    divinity *and* humanity,
— bless the virgins consecrated to you, their hea*ven*ly Spouse.
You did not create the power of death but you destroyed it by be*com*ing man,
— graciously transform the mortality of our deceased brothers and sisters into
    e*ter*nal life.

Our Father . . .

Prayer

Lord,
let the light of your glory shine within us,
and lead us through the darkness of this world
to the radiant joy of our eternal home.
We ask this through our Lord Jesus Christ, your Son,
who lives and reigns with you and the Holy Spirit,
one God, for ever and ever.

After Epiphany to the Baptism of the Lord
TUESDAY

Morning Prayer

READING   Isaiah 4:2-3

On that day,
The branch of the Lord will be luster and glory,
        and the fruit of the earth will be honor and splendor
        for the survivors of Israel.
He who remains in Zion
        and he that is left in Jerusalem
Will be called holy,
        every one marked down for life in Jerusalem.

RESPONSORY (VI F)
All the kings *of* the earth * will bow down *in* worship.
— All the kings *of* the earth * will bow down *in* worship.
Men and women of every na*tion* will serve him.
— They will bow down *in* worship.
Glory to the Father, and *to* the Son, * and to the Ho*ly* Spirit.
— All the kings *of* the earth * will bow down *in* worship.

CANTICLE OF ZECHARIAH

Antiphon   The wise men offered gifts of gold, frankincense, and myrrh †
to the Lord, the *Son* of God * and King most high, al*le*luia.

INTERCESSIONS

Let us rejoice in the compassion of Christ, who came to free mankind from the
slavery of corruption and to give us the freedom of the *sons* of God. * Trusting
in this divine compas*sion*, we plead:
By your birth, deliver us from *evil.*
Lord, you existed before the ages, yet you entered into *a* new life,
— renew us continually through the mystery *of* your birth.
Without surrendering your divinity, you wondrously took on *our* humanity,
— grant that our lives may press on to a fuller participation in *your* divinity.
You came to be a light to the nations, the teach*er* of holiness,
— let your words be a light a*long* our way.
Word of God made flesh in the womb of the Virgin Mary, you en*tered* this
world,
— live in our hearts al*ways* through faith.

Our Father . . .

Prayer

Father,
your Son became like us
when he revealed himself in our nature:
help us to become more like him,
who lives and reigns with you and the Holy Spirit,
one God, for ever and ever.

Evening Prayer

READING   Ephesians 2:3b-5
By nature we deserved God's wrath like the rest. But God is rich in mercy;
because of his great love for us he brought us to life with Christ when we
were dead in sin. By this favor you were saved.

RESPONSORY (VI F)

All peoples will be *blessed* in him, * men and women of eve*ry* race.
— All peoples will be *blessed* in him, * men and women of eve*ry* race.
All nations will ac*claim* his glory.
— Men and women of eve*ry* race.

Glory to the Father, and *to* the Son, * and to the Ho*ly* Spirit.
— All peoples will be *blessed* in him, * men and women of eve*ry* race.

CANTICLE OF MARY

Antiphon   Christ, you are Light from Light; † when you appeared *on* the
               earth, * the wise men offered their gifts to you, al*le*luia.

INTERCESSIONS

United with all Christians in *prayer* and praise, * we en*treat* the Lord:
Father, hear your *children.*
Help those who do not know God but seek your presence in the shadows and
    projections of the *hu*man mind,
— make them new persons in the *light* of Christ.
Look with favor on all who adore you as the one true God and who await your
    coming in judgment on *the* last day,
— may they recognize your constant *love* for us.
Remember all those on whom you bestow life, light and *all* good things,
— let them never be *far* from you.
Watch over all travelers with angel*ic* protection,
— and keep them from sudden and un*fore*seen death.
You revealed your truth to the dead while they *were* on earth,
— lead them to contemplate the beauty *of* your countenance.

Our Father . . .

Prayer

Father,
your Son became like us
when he revealed himself in our nature:
help us to become more like him,
who lives and reigns with you and the Holy Spirit,
one God, for ever and ever.

After Epiphany to the Baptism of the Lord
WEDNESDAY

Morning Prayer

READING   Isaiah 49:8-9

In a time of favor I answer you,
    on the day of salvation I help you,
To restore the land
    and allot the desolate heritages,
Saying to the prisoners: Come out!
    to those in darkness: Show yourselves!

RESPONSORY (VI F)

All the kings *of* the earth * will bow down *in* worship.
— All the kings *of* the earth * will bow down *in* worship.
Men and women of every na*tion* will serve him.
— They will bow down *in* worship.
Glory to the Father, and *to* the Son, * and to the Ho*ly* Spirit.
— All the kings *of* the earth * will bow down *in* worship.

CANTICLE OF ZECHARIAH

Antiphon   We have seen his star *in* the East * and have come with gifts to
                worship *the* Lord.

INTERCESSIONS

In the fullness of time, the eternal Word was begotten of the Father. He is the
    child who is born for us, the son who is giv*en* to us. * To him we lift our voi*ces*
    in joy:
Praise be to you, *Lord.*
Son of the living God, you existed before the world was made and you came on
    earth *to* save all,
— enable us to be witnesses *to* your Gospel.
Sun of Justice, whose brightness shone forth from the bosom of the Father and
    flooded the en*tire* world,
— be light for all who dwell in darkness and the shad*ow* of death.
You became a little child and lay *in* a manger,
— renew in us the simplicity of *lit*tle children.
For our sake you became the living bread of e*ter*nal life,
— fill us with joy through the sacrament *of* your altar.

Our Father . . .

Prayer

God, light of all nations,
give us the joy of lasting peace,
and fill us with your radiance
as you filled the hearts of our fathers.
We ask this through our Lord Jesus Christ, your Son,
who lives and reigns with you and the Holy Spirit,
one God, for ever and ever.

Evening Prayer

READING   Colossians 1:13-15
God rescued us from the power of darkness and brought us into the kingdom of his beloved Son. Through him we have redemption, the forgiveness
of our sins. He is the image of the invisible God, the firstborn of all creatures.

RESPONSORY (VI F)
All peoples will be *blessed* in him, * men and women of eve*ry* race.
— All peoples will be *blessed* in him, * men and women of eve*ry* race.
All nations will ac*claim* his glory.
— Men and women of eve*ry* race.
Glory to the Father, and *to* the Son, * and to the Ho*ly* Spirit.
— All peoples will be *blessed* in him, * men and women of eve*ry* race.

CANTICLE OF MARY
Antiphon   Herod questioned the Magi: † What is this sign of *which* you
                  speak, * this sign of a new*born* king?
                  We saw a brilliant star *in* the heavens; * its splendor filled *the*
                  world.

INTERCESSIONS
Let us praise the Word of God, for he has come to cast our sins in*to* the sea. *
  Strengthened by this knowledge let us *pray* to him:
Lord, show us your com*passion.*
As eternal priest you entered the world and established the fullest expres*sion* of
  worship,
— though your Church let all men and women share in this *sacred* liturgy.
As physician of bodies and spirits you came to visit all *who* were sick,
— heal and strengthen those *who* are ill.

You were a source of joy for all *at* your birth,
— give hope to those in torment and to those in sin that they may be able to re*joice* in you.
Mighty King, you cut the bonds of our *form*er slavery,
— release those who are captives and show your care for *those* in prison.
You came as the door leading *in*to heaven,
— let the dead pass through that door into the hea*ven*ly kingdom.

Our Father . . .

Prayer

God, light of all nations,
give us the joy of lasting peace,
and fill us with your radiance
as you filled the hearts of our fathers.
We ask this through our Lord Jesus Christ, your Son,
who lives and reigns with you and the Holy Spirit,
one God, for ever and ever.

**After Epiphany to the Baptism of the Lord
THURSDAY**

Morning Prayer

READING   Isaiah 62:11-12

Say to daughter Zion,
    your savior comes!
Here is his reward with him,
    his recompense before him.
They shall be called the holy people,
    the redeemed of the Lord.

RESPONSORY (VI F)
All the kings *of* the earth * will bow down *in* worship.
— All the kings *of* the earth * will bow down *in* worship.
Men and women of every na*tion* will serve him.
— They will bow down *in* worship.
Glory to the Father, and *to* the Son, * and to the Ho*ly* Spirit.
— All the kings *of* the earth * will bow down *in* worship.

CANTICLE OF ZECHARIAH
Antiphon   All peoples, *bear*ing gifts, * will come from afar, al*le*luia.

INTERCESSIONS

Rejoice in the wonderful works of the Lord for he has given us hope through the
   birth *of* his Son. * Let us all cry out *with* great joy:
Glory to God in the *highest.*
With the angels and patri*archs* and prophets,
— we *praise* you, Lord.
With Mary, the Virgin Moth*er* of God,
— our whole being proclaims your *great*ness, Lord.
With the apostles *and* evangelists,
— we give you *thanks,* O Lord.
With all the *holy* martyrs,
— we offer our bodies to you as conse*crat*ed victims.
With all your holy witnesses *in* the Church,
— we dedicate our lives to you in *deep*est faith.

Our Father . . .

Prayer

God our Father,
through Christ your Son
the hope of eternal life dawned on our world.
Give to us the light of faith
that we may always acknowledge him as our Redeemer
and come to the glory of his kingdom,
where he lives and reigns with you and the Holy Spirit,
one God, for ever and ever.

Evening Prayer

READING   1 John 1:5b, 7

God is light;
in him there is no darkness.
If we walk in light,
as he is in the light,
we have fellowship with one another,
and the blood of his Son Jesus cleanses us from all sin.

RESPONSORY (VI F)

All peoples will be *blessed* in him, * men and women of eve*ry* race.
— All peoples will be *blessed* in him, * men and women of eve*ry* race.
All nations will ac*claim* his glory.
— Men and women of eve*ry* race.

Glory to the Father, and *to* the Son, * and to the Ho*ly* Spirit.
— All peoples will be *blessed* in him, * men and women of eve*ry* race.

CANTICLE OF MARY

Antiphon   The people of Saba shall come † bringing gold, frankin*cense* and
                  myrrh, * al*le*luia.

INTERCESSIONS

United in prayer with all of our broth*ers* and sisters, * we bless God and in*voke*
    his name:
Lord, show us your com*passion.*
Holy Father, we pray for those who know you only by the light of *human*
    reason,
— may they be enriched by the light of the Gos*pel* as well.
Look with favor on all who live outside the Church as they seek liberation from
    the harsh constraints of hu*man* existence,
— may they discover Christ as the way, the truth *and* the life.
Help all who practice their faith *in* sincerity,
— may they attain to the marvelous light of *your* anointed one.
Keep pure the hearts *of* believers,
— may they see you more closely at *every* moment.
Let your compassion be visible to those *who* have died,
— clothe them in the glory of your *chos*en people.

Our Father . . .

Prayer

    God our Father,
    through Christ your Son
    the hope of eternal life dawned on our world.
    Give to us the light of faith
    that we may always acknowledge him as our Redeemer
    and come to the glory of his kingdom,
    where he lives and reigns with you and the Holy Spirit,
    one God, for ever and ever.

After Epiphany to the Baptism of the Lord
FRIDAY

Morning Prayer

READING   Isaiah 45:22-23

Turn to me and be safe,
all you ends of the earth,
for I am God; there is no other!
By myself I swear,
uttering my just decree
and my unalterable word:
To me every knee shall bend;
by me every tongue shall swear.

RESPONSORY (VI F)

All the kings *of* the earth * will bow down *in* worship.
— All the kings *of* the earth * will bow down *in* worship.
Men and women of every na*tion* will serve him.
— They will bow down *in* worship.
Glory to the Father, and *to* the Son, * and to the Ho*ly* Spirit.
— All the kings *of* the earth * will bow down *in* worship.

CANTICLE OF ZECHARIAH

Antiphon   All who once reviled you will come and bow *down* in worship *
before your ver*y* footprints.

INTERCESSIONS

Give honor and glory to Jesus Christ who comes to create a new heart and a new
spir*it* in man. * We call on him *as* we say:
By the power of your birth, make us new *persons.*
You took on our life and offered us in return the mystery *of* God's life,
— help us to recognize you in the mysteries of your word and your eucharist
which you entrusted *to* your Church.
Founder of the human race, through the spotless Virgin you became a man
*a*mong men,
— through her intercession, may we touch your divinity *and* be healed.
Our Redeemer, you descended upon the earth as the rain which fell upon the
sheep*skin* of Gideon,
— now drench our lives in the living water that springs up to provide e*ter*nal
life.
As we celebrate the beginning of your *life* on this earth,
— let us imitate that perfect manhood which you revealed in your *life* among us.

Our Father . . .

Prayer

All-powerful Father,
you have made known the birth of the Savior
by the light of a star.
May he continue to guide us with his light,
for he lives and reigns with you and the Holy Spirit,
one God, for ever and ever.

Evening Prayer

READING   Romans 8:3-4

God sent his Son in the likeness of sinful flesh as a sin-offering, thereby condemning sin in the flesh, so that the just demands of the law might be fulfilled in us who live, not according to the flesh, but according to the spirit.

RESPONSORY (VI F)

All peoples will be *blessed* in him, * men and women of eve*ry* race.
— All peoples will be *blessed* in him, * men and women of eve*ry* race.
All nations will ac*claim* his glory.
— Men and women of eve*ry* race.
Glory to the Father, and *to* the Son, * and to the Ho*ly* Spirit.
— All peoples will be *blessed* in him, * men and women of eve*ry* race.

CANTICLE OF MARY

Antiphon   An angel warned the wise men *in* a dream * to return to their own country by a dif*ferent* route.

INTERCESSIONS

We pray now *to* the Father * who has appointed Christ a light *to* the nations:
Father, hear our *prayer.*
Give increase *to* your Church,
— and spread the glory *of* your Son.
Eternal Father, you led the wise men from the East *to* your Son,
— reveal him to all who *seek* the truth.
Draw all nations into your marve*l*ous light,
— so that at the name of Jesus every *knee* will bend.
Send laborers in*to* your vineyard,
— let them preach the Gospel to the poor and announce a *time* of grace.
Grant to the dead the fullness *of* redemption,
— that they may rejoice in the victory of *Christ*, your Son.

Our Father . . .

Prayer

All-powerful Father,
you have made known the birth of the Savior
by the light of a star.
May he continue to guide us with his light,
for he lives and reigns with you and the Holy Spirit,
one God, for ever and ever.

After Epiphany to the Baptism of the Lord
SATURDAY

Morning Prayer

READING   Wisdom 7:26-27

Wisdom is the refulgence of eternal light.
    the spotless mirror of the power of God,
    the image of his goodness,
And she, who is one, can do all things,
    and renews everything while herself perduring;
And passing into holy souls from age to age,
    she produces friends of God and prophets.

RESPONSORY (VI F)
All the kings *of* the earth * will bow down *in* worship.
— All the kings *of* the earth * will bow down *in* worship.
Men and women of every na*tion* will serve him.
— They will bow down *in* worship.
Glory to the Father, and *to* the Son, * and to the Ho*ly* Spirit.
— All the kings *of* the earth * will bow down *in* worship.

CANTICLE OF ZECHARIAH
Antiphon   At Cana in Galilee Jesus worked the first *of* the signs * which
            revealed *his* glory.

INTERCESSIONS
Let us give glory to Christ, the im*age* of God, * as we call upon *him* in faith:
Christ, Son of God, hear us.
Son of God, you showed us the *Fa*ther's love,
— reveal him to men and women through the love we show toward *one* another.
You revealed yourself as *Lord* of life,
— now grant us the fullness *of* your life.

Let our bodies be signs *of* your life,
— as we bear your dying *in* our flesh.
Illumin*ate* our hearts,
— with the brilliant knowledge *of* God's light.

Our Father . . .

Prayer

God our Father,
through your Son you made us a new creation.
He shared our nature and became one of us;
with his help, may we become more like him,
who lives and reigns with you and the Holy Spirit,
one God, for ever and ever.

The Sunday after January 6
BAPTISM OF THE LORD
Feast

Evening Prayer I

HYMN

A Patre Unigenite. (L.M.)

A Patre Unigenite,
Ad nos venis per Virginem,
Baptismi rore consecrans
Cunctos, fide regenerans.

De caelo celsus prodiens
Excipis formam hominis,
Facturam morte redimens,
Gaudia vitæ largiens

Hoc te, Redemptor, quæsumus:
Illabere propitius,
Clarumque nostris cordibus
Lumen præbe deificum.

Mane nobiscum, Domine,
Noctem obscuram remove,
Omne delictum ablue,
Pie medelam tribue.

O Christe, vita, ceritas,
Tibi sit omnis gloria,
Quem Patris atque Spiritus
Splendor revelat cælitus. Amen.

Or: When Jesus comes to be baptized,
He leaves the hidden years behind,
The years of safety and of peace,
To bear the sins of all mankind.

The Spirit of the Lord comes down,
Anoints the Christ to suffering,
To preach the word, to free the bound,
And to the mourner, comfort bring.

He will not quench the dying flame,
And what is bruised he will not break,
But heal the wound injustice dealt,
And out of death his triumph make.

Our everlasting Father, praise,
With Christ, his well-belovèd Son,
Who with the Spirit reigns serene,
Untroubled Trinity in One. Amen.

Ant. 1   John was in the wilder*ness* baptizing * and proclaiming a bap-
            tism of penance for the forgive*ness* of sins.

VIIIg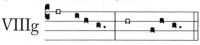

Psalm 135
I

Praise the name *of* the Lord, * praise
   him, servants *of* the Lord,
who stand in the house *of* the Lord * in
   the courts of the house *of* our God.
Praise the Lord for the *Lord* is good. *
   Sing a psalm to his name for *he* is
   loving.
For the Lord has chosen Jacob *for*
   himself * and Israel for his *own*
   possession.
For I know the *Lord* is great, * that our
   Lord is high a*bove* all gods.
The Lord does whate*ver* he wills, * in
   heaven, on earth, *in* the seas.
He summons clouds from the ends of
   the earth; † makes lightning pro*duce*
   the rain; * from his treasuries he

sends *forth* the wind.
The first-born of the Egyp*tians* he
   smote, * of man and *beast* alike.
Signs and wonders he worked † in the
   midst of your *land*, O Egypt, *
   against Pharaoh and *all* his servants.
Nations in their great*ness* he struck *
   and kings in their splen*dor* he slew.
Sihon, king of the Amorites, † Og, the
   king of Bashan, * and all the king-
   doms of Canaan.
He let Israel inher*it* their land; * on his
   people their land *he* bestowed.
Glory to the Father, and *to* the Son, *
   and to the *Holy* Spirit:
as it was in the begin*ning*, is now, * and
   will be for e*ver*. Amen.

Antiphon   John was in the wilder*ness* baptizing * and proclaiming a bap-
              tism of penance for the forgive*ness* of sins.

Ant. 2   I baptize you with water, † but the one *who* is coming * will
              baptize with the Holy Spirit and *with* fire.

II A

II

Lord, your name *stands* for ever, *
   unforgotten from age *to* age:
for the Lord does justice *for* his people;
   * the Lord takes pity on *his* servants.
Pagan idols are sil*ver* and gold, * the

work of hu*man* hands.
They have mouths but they *cannot*
   speak; * they have eyes but they
   cannot see.
They have ears but they *cannot* hear; *

there is never a breath on *their* lips.
Their makers will come to *be* like them
  * and so will all who trust *in* them!
Sons of Israel, *bless* the Lord! * Sons of
  Aaron, bless *the* Lord!
Sons of Levi, *bless* the Lord! * You who
  fear him, bless *the* Lord!

From Zion may the *Lord* be blessed, *
  he who dwells in *Je*rusalem!
Glory to the Father, and *to* the Son, *
  and to the Ho*ly* Spirit:
as it was in the begin*ning*, is now, * and
  will be for ever. *A*men.

Ant. 2   I baptize you with water, † but the one *who* is coming * will baptize with the Holy Spirit and *with* fire.

Ant. 3   As soon as Jesus was baptized, † he came out of *the* water, * and the heavens opened *be*fore him.

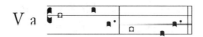

Canticle   See 1 Timothy 3:16

The mystery and glory of Christ

℞. Praise *the* Lord, * all *you* nations.

Christ manifested in *the* flesh, *
Christ justified in *the* Spirit.

℞. Praise *the* Lord, * all *you* nations.

Christ contemplated by *the* angels, *
Christ proclaimed by *the* pagans.

℞. Praise *the* Lord, * all *you* nations.

Christ who is believed in *the* world, *
  Christ exalted *in* glory.

℞. Praise *the* Lord, * all *you* nations.

Glory to the Father, and to *the* Son, *
  and to the Ho*ly* Spirit:
as it was in the beginning, *is* now, * and
  will be for ever. *A*men.

Ant. 3   As soon as Jesus was baptized, † he came out of *the* water, * and the heavens opened *be*fore him.

READING   Acts 10:37-38

I take it you know what has been reported all over Judea about Jesus of Nazareth, beginning in Galilee with the baptism John preached; of the way God anointed him with the Holy Spirit and power. He went about doing good works and healing all who were in the grip of the devil, and God was with him.

RESPONSORY (VI F)

O *Lord* our God, * hear the cry of *your* people.

— O *Lord* our God, * hear the cry of *your* people.

Open for them the spring of *living* water.
— Hear the cry of *your* people.
Glory to the Father, and *to* the Son, * and to the Ho*ly* Spirit.
— O *Lord* our God, * hear the cry of *your* people.

CANTICLE OF MARY

Ant.   Our Savior came to be baptized, † so that though the cleansing wa*ter* of baptism * he might restore the old man to *new* life, heal our *sin*ful nature, * and clothe us with unfail*ing* holiness.

If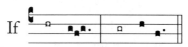

My soul ✠ proclaims the greatness *of* the Lord, * my spirit rejoices in God *my* savior
for he has *looked* with favor * on his low*ly* servant.
From this day all *gen*erations * will call *me* blessèd:
the Almighty has done great *things* for me, * and holy is *his* Name.
He has mercy on *those* who fear him * in every gen*er*ation.
He has shown the strength *of* his arm, * he has scattered the proud in their *con*ceit.

He has cast down the mighty *from* their thrones, * and has lifted up *the* lowly.
He has filled the hungry *with* good things, * and the rich he has sent a*way* empty.
He has come to the help of his *servant* Israel * for he has remembered his promise *of* mercy,
the promise he made *to* our fathers, * to Abraham and his children *for* ever.
Glory to the Father, and *to* the Son, * and to the Ho*ly* Spirit:
as it was in the begin*ning*, is now, * and will be for ever. *A*men.

Antiphon   Our Savior came to be baptized, † so that though the cleansing wa*ter* of baptism * he might restore the old man to *new* life, heal our *sin*ful nature, * and clothe us with unfail*ing* holiness.

INTERCESSIONS

Our Redeemer desired to be baptized in the Jor*dan* by John; * let us make our peti*tion* to him:
Lord, send forth your Spirit up*on* us.
Christ, Servant of God, the Father acknowleged you as his own Son with whom *he* was pleased,
— send forth your Spir*it* upon us.
Christ, Chosen One of God, you did not break the crushed reed or extinguish the *wa*vering flame,
— have mercy on all who are seeking you *in* good faith.

Christ, Son of God, the Father called you to be a light to the nations in *the* new
   covenant,
— open the eyes of the blind by the wat*ers* of baptism.
Christ, Savior of mankind, the Father anointed you with the Holy Spirit for the
   ministry *of* salvation,
— lead all to see you and to believe in you, that they may have et*er*nal life.
Christ, our hope, you lead those in darkness to the light *of* salvation,
— receive our departed brothers and sisters in*to* your kingdom.

Our Father . . .

Prayer

   Almighty, eternal God,
   when the Spirit descended upon Jesus
   at his baptism in the Jordan,
   you revealed him as your own belovèd Son.
   Keep us, your children born of water and the Spirit,
   faithful to our calling.
   We ask this through our Lord Jesus Christ, your Son,
   who lives and reigns with you and the Holy Spirit,
   one God, for ever and ever.

Morning Prayer
HYMN
Iesu refulsit omnium. (L.M.)

Iesu refulsit omnium
Pius redemptor gentium;
Totum genus fidelium
laudis celebret canticum.

Denis ter ævi circulis
iam parte vivens corporis,
lympham petit baptismatis
cunctis carens contagiis.

Felix Ioannes mergere
illum tremescit flumine,
potest suo qui sanguine
peccata mundi tergere

Vox ergo Prolem de polis
testatur excelsi Patris,
fluitque virtus Spiritus
sancti datrix charismatis.

Nos, Christe, voce supplici
precamur, omnes protege,
ac mente fac nitescere
tibique mundos vivere.

O Christe, vit, veritas,
tibi sit omnis gloria,
quem Patris atque Spiritus
splendor evelat cælitus. Amen.

Or: When Jesus comes to be baptized,
He leaves the hidden years behind,
The years of safety and of peace,
To bear the sins of all mankind.

The Spirit of the Lord comes down,
Anoints the Christ to suffering,
To preach the word, to free the bound,
And to the mourner, comfort bring.

He will not quench the dying flame,
And what is bruised he will not break,
But heal the wound injustice dealt,
And out of death his triumph make.

Our everlasting Father, praise,
With Christ, his well-belovèd Son,
Who with the Spirit reigns serene,
Untroubled Trinity in One. Amen.

PSALMODY

Ant. 1   The soldier baptiz*es* his king, * the servant his Lord, *John* his
          Savior;
          the waters of the Jordan tremble, † a dove hovers as a sign of
          witness, † and the voice of the Fath*er* is heard: * This *is* my Son.

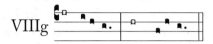

VIIIg

Psalm 63:2-9

O God, you are my God, for *you* I
    long; * for you my *soul* is thirst-
ing.
My body *pines* for you * like a dry,
    weary land *without* water.
So I gaze on you *in* the sanctuary * to
    see your strength *and* your glory.
For your love is bet*ter* than life, * my
    lips will *speak* your praise.
So I will bless you *all* my life, * in your
    name I will lift *up* my hands.
My soul shall be filled as *with* a

banquet, * my mouth shall praise *you*
    with joy.
On my bed I re*mem*ber you. * On you
    I muse *through* the night
for you have *been* my help; * in the
    shadow of your wings *I* rejoice.
My soul *clings* to you; * your right
    hand *holds* me fast.
Glory to the Father, and *to* the Son, *
    and to the *Holy* Spirit:
as it was in the begin*ning*, is now, * and
    will be for ev*er*. Amen.

Antiphon The soldier baptiz*es* his king, * the servant his Lord, *John* his
          Savior;
          the waters of the Jordan tremble, † a dove hovers as a sign of
          witness, † and the voice of the Fath*er* is heard: * This *is* my Son.

Ant. 2   Springs of water *were* made holy * as Christ revealed his glory to
          the world.
          Draw water from the fountain *of* the Savior, * for Christ our
          God has hallowed all *creation*.

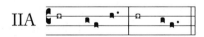

IIA

Canticle   Daniel 3:57-88; 56

B less the Lord, all you works *of* the
    Lord. * Praise and exalt him above
all *forever*.
Angels of the Lord, *bless* the Lord, *
    You heavens, bless *the* Lord.
All you waters above the heavens, *bless*

the Lord. * All you hosts of the
    Lord, bless *the* Lord.
Sun and moon, *bless* the Lord. * Stars
    of heaven, bless *the* Lord.
Every shower and dew, *bless* the Lord. *
    All you winds, bless *the* Lord.

Fire and heat, *bless* the Lord. * Cold and chill, bless *the* Lord.

Dew and rain, *bless* the Lord. * Frost and chill, bless *the* Lord.

Ice and snow, *bless* the Lord. * Nights and days, bless *the* Lord.

Light and darkness, *bless* the Lord. * Lightnings and clouds, bless *the* Lord.

Let the earth *bless* the Lord. * Praise and exalt him above all *for*ever.

Mountains and hills, *bless* the Lord. * Everything growing from the earth, bless *the* Lord.

You springs, *bless* the Lord. * Seas and rivers, bless *the* Lord.

You dolphins and all water creatures, *bless* the Lord. * All you birds of the air, bless *the* Lord.

All you beasts, wild and tame, *bless* the Lord. * You sons of men, bless *the* Lord.

O Israel, *bless* the Lord. * Praise and exalt him above all *for*ever.

Priests of the Lord, *bless* the Lord. * Servants of the Lord, bless *the* Lord.

Spirits and souls of the just, *bless* the Lord. * Holy men of humble heart, bless *the* Lord.

Hananiah, Azariah, Mishael, *bless* the Lord. * Praise and exalt him above all *for*ever.

Let us bless the Father, and the Son, and the *Ho*ly Spirit. * Let us praise and exalt him above all *for*ever.

Blessed are you in the firma*ment* of heaven. * Praiseworthy and glorious and exalted above all *for*ever.

Antiphon   Springs of water *were* made holy * as Christ revealed his glory to *the* world.
Draw water from the fountain *of* the Savior, * for Christ our God has hallowed all *cre*ation.

Ant. 3   You burned away man's guilt by fire and the Ho*ly* Spirit. * We give praise to you, our God and *Re*deemer.

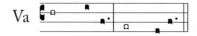

Psalm 149

Sing a new song to *the* Lord, * his praise in the assembly of *the* faithful.

Let Israel rejoice in *its* Maker, * let Zion's sons exult in *their* king.

Let them praise his name *with* dancing * and make music with timbrel *and* harp.

For the Lord takes delight in *his* people. * He crowns the poor with sal*va*tion.

Let the faithful rejoice in *their* glory, * shout for joy and take *their* rest.

Let the praise of God be on *their* lips * and a two-edged sword in *their* hand,

to deal out vengeance to *the* nations * and punishment on all *the* peoples;

to bind their kings *in* chains * and their nobles in fetters *of* iron;

to carry out the sentence pre-*or*dained:

* this honor is for all *his* faithful.
Glory to the Father, and to *the* Son, *
and to the Ho*ly* Spirit:

as it was in the beginning, *is* now, * and
will be for ever. *A*men.

Antiphon   You burned away man's guilt by fire and the Ho*ly* Spirit. * We
give praise to you, our God and *Re*deemer.

READING   Isaiah 61:1-2a

The spirit of the Lord God is upon me,
    because the Lord has anointed me;
He has sent me to bring glad tidings to the lowly,
    to heal the broken hearted,
To proclaim liberty to the captives
    and release to the prisoners,
To announce a year of favor from the Lord.

RESPONSORY (VI F)
Christ, Son of the *li*ving God, * have mercy *on* us.
— Christ, Son of the *li*ving God, * have mercy *on* us.
Today you revealed your*self* to us.
— Have mercy *on* us.
Glory to the Father, and *to* the Son, * and to the Ho*ly* Spirit.
— Christ, Son of the *li*ving God, * have mercy *on* us.

CANTICLE OF ZECHARIAH
Ant.   Christ is baptized, the world is made holy; † he has taken a*way*
our sins. * We shall be purified by water and the Ho*ly* Spirit.

If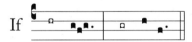

Blessèd ✠ be the Lord, the *God* of
Israel; * he has come to his people
and set *them* free.
He has raised up for us a *migh*ty savior,
* born of the house of his ser*vant*
David.
Through his holy prophets he promised of old † that he would save us
from our enemies, * from the hands
of all *who* hate us.
He promised to show mercy *to* our
fathers * and to remember his ho*ly*

covenant.
This was the oath he swore to our
*fath*er Abraham: * to set us free from
the hands of *our* enemies,
free to worship him without fear, †
holy and righteous *in* his sight * all
the days of *our* life.
You, my child, shall be called the
prophet *of* the Most High; * for you
will go before the Lord to prepare *his*
way,
to give his people knowledge *of* salva-

tion * by the forgiveness of *their* sins.
In the tender compassion *of* our God *
the dawn from on high shall break
*up*on us,
to shine on those who dwell in darkness and the sha*dow* of death, * and
to guide our feet into the way *of*
peace.
Glory to the Father, and *to* the Son, *
and to the Ho*ly* Spirit:
as it was in the begin*ning*, is now, * and
will be for ever. *A*men.

Antiphon   Christ is baptized, the world is made holy; † he has taken a*way*
our sins. * We shall be purified by water and the Ho*ly* Spirit.

INTERCESSIONS
Our Redeemer desired to be baptized in the Jor*dan* by John; * let us make this
prayer to him:
Lord, have *mercy.*
Christ, you made your light shine on us by reveal*ing* yourself,
— grant us the spirit of humble service *to* all people.
Christ, you humbled yourself and received baptism from your servant to show
us the way *of* humility,
— grant us the spirit of humble service to our *fel*low men.
Christ, through your baptism you cleansed us of every blemish and made us
children *of* your Father,
— bestow your spirit of adoption on *all* who seek you.
Christ, through baptism you have consecrated creation and opened the door of
repentance to all who pre*pared* for baptism,
— make us servants of your Gospel *in* the world.
Christ, through your baptism you revealed to us the Holy Trinity when the
Father called you his belovèd Son and the Holy Spirit came *down* upon you,
— renew the spirit of adoption among the royal priesthood *of* the baptized.

Our Father . . .

                              Prayer

          Almighty, eternal God,
          when the Spirit descended upon Jesus
          at his baptism in the Jordan,
          you revealed him as your own belovèd Son.
          Keep us, your children born of water and the Spirit,
          faithful to our calling.
          We ask this through our Lord Jesus Christ, your Son,
          who lives and reigns with you and the Holy Spirit,
          one God, for ever and ever.

Evening Prayer II

HYMN, as in Evening Prayer I, 225.

PSALMODY

Ant. 1   The Father's voice resounded from the heavens: † This is my
          Son in whom *I* delight, * listen to what he *says* to you.

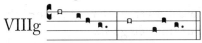

VIIIg

Psalm 110:1-5, 7

The Lord's revelation to my Master:
    † "Sit *on* my right: * your foes I
  will put be*neath* your feet."
The Lord will wield from Zion † your
    scep*ter* of power: * rule in the midst
  of *all* your foes.
A prince from the day of your birth †
  on the *holy* mountains; * from the
  womb before the dawn *I* begot you.
The Lord has sworn an oath he will
  not change. † "You are a *priest* for
  ever, * a priest like Melchize*dek* of

old."
The Master standing *at* your right
  hand * will shatter kings in the day
  of *his* great wrath.
He shall drink from the stream *by* the
  wayside * and therefore he shall lift
  up his head.
Glory to the Father, and *to* the Son, *
  and to the *Holy* Spirit:
as it was in the begin*ning*, is now, * and
  will be for ev*er*. Amen.

Antiphon   The Father's voice resounded from the heavens: † This is my
            Son in whom *I* delight, * listen to what he *says* to you.

Ant. 2   In the Jordan river our Savior crushed the *ser*pent's head * and
          wrested us from *his* grasp.

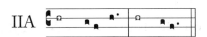

IIA

Psalm 112

Happy the man who *fears* the
    Lord, * who takes delight in all
  his *commands*.
His sons will be power*ful* on earth; *
  the children of the upright *are*
  blessèd.
Riches and wealth are *in* his house; *
  his justice stands firm *for* ever.
He is a light in the darkness *for* the
  upright: * he is generous, merciful

and just.
The good man takes pi*ty* and lends, *
  he conducts his affairs *with* honor.
The just man will nev*er* waver: * he
  will be remembered *for* ever.
He has no fear of *evil* news; * with a
  firm heart he trusts in *the* Lord.
With a steadfast heart he *will* not fear;
  * he will see the downfall of *his* foes.
Open-handed, he gives to the poor; †

his justice stands *firm* for ever. * His head will be raised *in* glory.

The wicked man sees and is angry, † grinds his teeth and *fades* away; * the desire of the wicked leads *to* doom.

Glory to the Father, and *to* the Son, * and to the Ho*ly* Spirit:

as it was in the begin*ning*, is now, * and will be for ever. *A*men.

Ant. 2   In the Jordan river our Savior crushed the *serpent*'s head * and wrested us from *his* grasp.

Ant. 3   A wondrous mystery is declared to us today: † the Creator of the universe has washed away *our* sins * in the waters of *the* Jordan.

Va

Canticle   Revelation 15:3-4

Mighty and wonderful are *your* works, * Lord God *Al*mighty!

Righteous and true are *your* ways, * O King of *the* nations!

Who would dare refuse *you* honor, * or the glory due your name, O Lord?

Since you alone *are* holy, * all nations

shall come and worship in *your* presence.

Your migh*ty* deeds * are clear*ly* seen.

Glory to the Father, and to *the* Son, * and to the Ho*ly* Spirit:

as it was in the beginning, *is* now, * and will be for ever. *A*men.

Antiphon   A wondrous mystery is declared to us today: † the Creator of the universe has washed away *our* sins * in the waters of *the* Jordan.

READING   Acts 10:37-38

I take it you know what has been reported all over Judea about Jesus of Nazareth, beginning in Galilee with the baptism John preached; of the way God anointed him with the Holy Spirit and power. He went about doing good works and healing all who were in the grip of the devil, and God was with him.

RESPONSORY (VI F)

Christ *comes* to us. * He comes in water and *in* blood.

— Christ *comes* to us. * He comes in water and *in* blood.

Jesus *Christ* our Lord.

— Comes in water and *in* blood.

Glory to the Father, and *to* the Son, * and to the Ho*ly* Spirit.

— Christ *comes* to us. * He comes in water and *in* blood.

CANTICLE OF MARY

Ant.   Christ Jesus loved us, † poured out his blood to wash away our
        sins, † and made us a kingdom and priests for *God* our Father. *
        To him be glory and honor *for* ever.

If

My soul ☩proclaims the greatness
of the Lord, * my spirit rejoices
in God *my* savior

for he has *looked* with favor * on his
lowly servant.

From this day all *generations* * will call
me blessèd:

the Almighty has done great *things* for
me, * and holy is *his* Name.

He has mercy on *those* who fear him *
in every gen*e*ration.

He has shown the strength *of* his arm,
* he has scattered the proud in their
conceit.

He has cast down the mighty *from* their
thrones, * and has lifted up *the* lowly.

He has filled the hungry *with* good
things, * and the rich he has sent
a*way* empty.

He has come to the help of his *servant*
Israel * for he has remembered his
promise *of* mercy,

the promise he made *to* our fathers, * to
Abraham and his children *for* ever.

Glory to the Father, and *to* the Son, *
and to the Ho*ly* Spirit:

as it was in the begin*ning*, is now, * and
will be for ever. *A*men.

Ant.   Christ Jesus loved us, † poured out his blood to wash away our
        sins, † and made us a kingdom and priests for *God* our Father. *
        To him be glory and honor *for* ever.

INTERCESSIONS

Our Redeemer desired to be baptized in the Jor*dan* by John; * let us make our
peti*tion* to him:
Lord, send forth your Spirit up*on us.*

Christ, Servant of God, the Father acknowleged you as his own Son with whom
he was pleased,
— send forth your Spir*it* upon us.

Christ, Chosen One of God, you did not break the crushed reed or extinguish
the wa*ver*ing flame,
— have mercy on all who are seeking you *in* good faith.

Christ, Son of God, the Father called you to be a light to the nations in *the* new
covenant,
— open the eyes of the blind by the wat*ers* of baptism.

Christ, Savior of mankind, the Father anointed you with the Holy Spirit for the
ministry *of* salvation,
— lead all to see you and to believe in you, that they may have e*ter*nal life.

Christ, our hope, you lead those in darkness to the light *of* salvation,
— receive our departed brothers and sisters in*to* your kingdom.

Our Father . . .

Prayer

Almighty, eternal God,
when the Spirit descended upon Jesus
at his baptism in the Jordan,
you revealed him as your own belovèd Son.
Keep us, your children born of water and the Spirit,
faithful to our calling.
We ask this through our Lord Jesus Christ, your Son,
who lives and reigns with you and the Holy Spirit,
one God, for ever and ever.

Proper of Seasons
Lent

Morning Prayer

Psalms and canticle, with their antiphons, may be taken from Friday, Week III, 794.

READING   Deuteronomy 7:6, 8-9

You are a people sacred to the Lord, your God; he has chosen you from all the nations on the face of the earth to be a people peculiarly his own. It was because the Lord loved you and because of his fidelity to the oath he had sworn to your fathers, that he brought you out with his strong hand from the place of slavery, and ransomed you from the hand of Pharaoh, king of Egypt. Understand, then, that the Lord, your God, is God indeed, the faithful God who keeps his merciful covenant to the thousandth generation toward those who love him and keep his commandments.

RESPONSORY (VI F)

God himself will *set* me free, * from the hun*ter's* snare.
— God himself will *set* me free, * from the hun*ter's* snare.
From those who would trap me with *ly*ing words
— and from the hun*ter's* snare.
Glory to the Father, and *to* the Son, * and to the Ho*ly* Spirit.
— God himself will *set* me free, * from the hun*ter's* snare.

CANTICLE OF ZECHARIAH

Ant.   When you fast, do not put on a *gloom*y face, * like *the* hypocrites.

INTERCESSIONS (VI F)

Today God our Father brings us to the beginning of Lent. We pray that in this time of salvation he will fill us with the Holy Spirit, purify our hearts, and strengthen *us* in love. * Let us *hum*bly ask him:
Lord, give us your Holy Spirit.
May we be *filled* and satisfied,
— by the word *which* you give us.
Teach us to be loving not only in great and excep*tion*al moments,
— but above all in the ordinary events of *dai*ly life.
May we abstain from what we do not *real*ly need,
— and help our brothers and sisters *in* distress.
May we bear the wounds *of* your Son,
— for through his body he *gave* us life.

Our Father . . .

Prayer

Lord,
protect us in our struggle against evil.
As we begin the discipline of Lent,
make this day holy by our self-denial.
Grant this through our Lord Jesus Christ, your Son,
who lives and reigns with you and the Holy Spirit,
one God, for ever and ever.

Evening Prayer

READING   Philippians 2:12b-15a
Work with anxious concern to achieve your salvation. It is God who, in his
good will toward you, begets in you any measure of desire or achievement. In
everything you do, act without grumbling or arguing; prove yourselves
innocent and straightforward, children of God without reproach.

RESPONSORY (VI F)
To *you*, O Lord,* I make my prayer *for* mercy.
— To *you*, O Lord,* I make my prayer *for* mercy.
Heal my soul, for I have *sinned* against you.
— I make my prayer *for* mercy.
Glory to the Father, and *to* the Son, * and to the Ho*ly* Spirit.
— To *you*, O Lord,* I make my prayer *for* mercy.

CANTICLE OF MARY
Ant.   When *you* give alms, * do not let your left hand know † what
                      your right hand *is* doing.

INTERCESSIONS (VI F)
All glory and honor to God, for in the blood of Christ he has ratified a new and
   everlasting covenant with his people, and renews it in the sacrament *of* the altar.
   * Let us lift our voi*ces* in prayer:
*Bless your peo*ple, *Lord.*
Lord, guide the minds and hearts of peoples and all in *pub*lic office,
— may they seek the *com*mon good.
Renew the spirit of dedication in those who have left all to *fo*llow Christ,
— may they give clear witness to the holiness *of* the Church.
You have made all men and women *in* your image,
— may they always uphold *hu*man dignity.
Lead back to your friendship and truth all who have *gone* astray,
— teach us *how* to help them.

Grant that the dead may enter in*to* your glory,
— to praise *you* for ever.

Our Father . . .

Prayer

Lord,
protect us in our struggle against evil.
As we begin the discipline of Lent,
make this day holy by our self-denial.
Grant this through our Lord Jesus Christ, your Son,
who lives and reigns with you and the Holy Spirit,
one God, for ever and ever.

THURSDAY AFTER ASH WEDNESDAY

Morning Prayer

READING   See 1 Kings 8:51-53a

We are your people and your inheritance. Thus may your eyes be open to the petition of your servant and to the petition of your people Israel. Hear us whenever we call upon you, because you have set us apart among all the peoples of the earth of your inheritance.

RESPONSORY (VI F)

God himself will *set* me free, * from the hun*ter's* snare.
— God himself will *set* me free, * from the hun*ter's* snare.
From those who would trap me with *ly*ing words
— and from the hun*ter's* snare.
Glory to the Father, and *to* the Son, * and to the Ho*ly* Spirit.
— God himself will *set* me free, * from the hun*ter's* snare.

CANTICLE OF ZECHARIAH

Ant.   If anyone wishes to be my disciple, † he must deny himself, take up his cross, and *fol*low me, * says *the* Lord.

INTERCESSIONS (VI F)

God has revealed him*self* in Christ. * Let us praise his goodness, and ask him *from* our hearts:
Remember us, Lord, for we are your *children.*
Teach us to enter more deeply into the mystery *of* the Church,
— that it may be more effective for ourselves and for the world as the sacrament *of* salvation.

Lover of mankind, inspire us to work for *hu*man progress,
— seeking to spread your kingdom in *all* we do.
May our hearts *thrist* for Christ,
— the fountain of *liv*ing water.
For*give* our sins,
— and direct our steps into the ways of justice *and* sincerity.

Our Father . . .

Prayer

> Lord,
> may everything we do
> begin with your inspiration,
> continue with your help,
> and reach perfection under your guidance.
> We ask this through our Lord Jesus Christ, your Son,
> who lives and reigns with you and the Holy Spirit,
> one God, for ever and ever.

Evening Prayer

READING   James 4:7-8, 10

Submit to God; resist the devil and he will take flight. Draw close to God, and he will draw close to you. Cleanse your hands, you sinners; purify your hearts, you backsliders. Be humbled in the sight of the Lord and he will raise you on high.

RESPONSORY (VI F)
To *you*, O Lord,* I make my prayer *for* mercy.
— To *you*, O Lord,* I make my prayer *for* mercy.
Heal my soul, for I have *sinned* against you.
— I make my prayer *for* mercy.
Glory to the Father, and *to* the Son, * and to the Ho*ly* Spirit.
— To *you*, O Lord,* I make my prayer *for* mercy.

CANTICLE OF MARY
Ant.   Whoever gives his life for my sake in this world † will find it again for ever *in* the next, * says *the* Lord.

INTERCESSIONS (VI F)
In his mercy, God sends the Holy Spirit to shine on us, so that our lives may radiate holi*ness* and faith. * Let us raise our voices in *prayer* and say:
*Lord, give life to your people, who Christ has re*deemed*.*

Lord, source of all holiness, draw bishops, priests and deacons closer to Christ
through the eucha*rist*ic mystery,
— may they grow daily in the grace of their *or*dination.
Teach Christ's faithful people to be devout and attentive at the table of his word
and *of* his body,
— so that they may bring into their daily lives the grace they receive through *faith*
and sacrament.
Grant, Lord, that we may see in each person the dignity of one redeemed by *your*
Son's blood,
— so that we may respect the freedom and the con*science* of all.
Teach us to restrain our greed for *earth*ly goods,
— and to have concern for the *needs* of others.
Be merciful to your faithful people whom you have called to your*self* today,
— grant them the gift of e*ter*nal happiness.

Our Father . . .

Prayer

Lord,
may everything we do
begin with your inspiration,
continue with your help,
and reach perfection under your guidance.
We ask this through our Lord Jesus Christ, your Son,
who lives and reigns with you and the Holy Spirit,
one God, for ever and ever.

FRIDAY AFTER ASH WEDNESDAY

Morning Prayer

READING   Isaiah 53:11B-12

Through his suffering, my servant shall justify many,
    and their guilt he shall bear.
Therefore I will give him his portion among the great,
    and he shall divide the spoils with the mighty,
Because he surrendered himself to death
    and was counted among the wicked;
And he shall take away the sins of many
    and win pardon for their offenses.

RESPONSORY (VI F)

God himself will *set* me free, * from the hun*ter's* snare.
— God himself will *set* me free, * from the hun*ter's* snare.
From those who would trap me with *ly*ing words
— and from the hun*ter's* snare.
Glory to the Father, and *to* the Son, * and to the Ho*ly* Spirit.
— God himself will *set* me free, * from the hun*ter's* snare.

CANTICLE OF ZECHARIAH

Ant.   When you meet those who are in need of clothing, † do not turn
                  a*way* from them, * for they are *your* brothers. Then your light
                  shall break forth *like* the dawn, * and your good deeds shall go
                  *be*fore you.

INTERCESSIONS (VI F)

Let us pray to *Christ* our Savior, * who redeemed us by his death and *re*surrection:
Lord, have mercy on *us.*
You went up to Jerusalem to suffer and so enter in*to* your glory,
— bring your Church to the Passover *feast* of heaven.
You were lifted high on the cross and pierced by the *sol*dier's lance,
— *heal* our wounds.
You made the cross the *tree* of life,
— give its fruit to those re*born* in baptism.
On the cross you forgave the re*pent*ant thief,
— forgive *us* our sins.

Our Father . . .

Prayer

Lord,
with your loving care
guide the penance we have begun.
Help us to persevere with love and sincerity.
Grant this through our Lord Jesus Christ, your Son,
who lives and reigns with you and the Holy Spirit,
one God, for ever and ever.

Evening Prayer

READING   James 5:16, 19-20
Declare your sins to one another, and pray for one another, that you may find
healing. The fervent petition of a holy man is powerful indeed. My brothers,
the case may arise among you of someone straying from the truth, and of
another bringing him back. Remember this: the person who brings a sinner
back from his way will save his soul from death and cancel a multitude of
sins.

RESPONSORY (VI F)
To *you*, O Lord,* I make my prayer *for* mercy.
— To *you*, O Lord,* I make my prayer *for* mercy.
Heal my soul, for I have *sinned* against you.
— I make my prayer *for* mercy.
Glory to the Father, and *to* the Son, * and to the Ho*ly* Spirit.
— To *you*, O Lord,* I make my prayer *for* mercy.

CANTICLE OF MARY
Ant.   When the bridegroom is taken a*way* from them, * then will be
                    the time for the wedding guests *to* fast.

INTERCESSIONS (VI F)
The Savior of mankind by dying destroyed death and by rising again *re*stored life.
    * Let us *hum*bly ask him:
Sanctify your people, redeemed by your *blood.*
Redeemer of the world, give us a greater share of your passion through a deeper
    spirit *of* repentance,
— so that we may share the glory of your *re*surrection.
May your Mother, comfort of the afflic*ted*, protect us,
— may we console others as you *con*sole us.
In their trials enable your faithful people to share *in* your passion,
— and so reveal in their lives your *sav*ing power.
You humbled yourself by being obedient even to accepting death, death *on* a cross,
— give all who serve you the gifts of obedience and pa*tient* endurance.
Transform the bodies of the dead to be like your *own* in glory,
— and bring us at last in*to* their fellowship.

Our Father . . .

Prayer

Lord,
with your loving care
guide the penance we have begun.
Help us to persevere with love and sincerity.
Grant this through our Lord Jesus Christ, your Son,
who lives and reigns with you and the Holy Spirit,
one God, for ever and ever.

SATURDAY AFTER ASH WEDNESDAY

Morning Prayer

READING   Isaiah 1:16-18

    Wash yourselves clean!
Put away your misdeeds from before my eyes;
    cease doing evil; learn to do good.
Make justice your aim; redress the wronged,
    hear the orphan's plea, defend the widow.
Come now, let us set things right,
    says the Lord:
Though your sins be like scarlet,
    they may become white as snow;
Though they be crimson red,
    they may become white as wool.

RESPONSORY (VI F)

God himself will *set* me free, * from the hunt*er's* snare.
— God himself will *set* me free, * from the hunt*er's* snare.
From those who would trap me with *ly*ing words
— and from the hunt*er's* snare.
Glory to the Father, and *to* the Son, * and to the Ho*ly* Spirit.
— God himself will *set* me free, * from the hunt*er's* snare.

CANTICLE OF ZECHARIAH

Ant.   Store up for yourselves treas*ures* in heaven * where neither rust
              nor moth can *de*stroy.

INTERCESSIONS (VI F)

Let us always and everywhere give thanks to *Christ* our Savior, * and ask *him* with
   confidence:
Lord, help us with your *grace.*

May we keep our *bodies* pure,
— as temples of the *Holy* Spirit.
May we offer ourselves this morning to the ser*vice* of others,
— and do your will in all things through*out* the day.
Teach us to seek the bread of ever*last*ing life,
— the bread that *is* your gift.
May your Mother, the refuge of sinners, *pray* for us,
— and gain for us your lov*ing* forgiveness.

Our Father . . .

Prayer

Father,
look upon our weakness
and reach out to help us with your loving power.
We ask this through our Lord Jesus Christ, your Son,
who lives and reigns with you and the Holy Spirit,
one God, for ever and ever.

FIRST SUNDAY OF LENT

PSALTER, WEEK I, 600.

Evening Prayer I

READING   2 Corinthians 6:1-4a

We beg you not to receive the grace of God in vain. For he says, "In an acceptable time I have heard you; on a day of salvation I have helped you." Now is the acceptable time! Now is the day of salvation! We avoid giving anyone offense, so that our ministry may not be blamed. On the contrary, in all that we do we strive to present ourselves as ministers of God.

RESPONSORY (VI F)

Listen to us, O Lord, *and* have mercy, * for we have sinned *a*gainst you.
— Listen to us, O Lord, *and* have mercy, * for we have sinned *a*gainst you.
Christ Jesus, hear our hum*ble* petitions,
— for we have sinned *a*gainst you.
Glory to the Father, and *to* the Son, * and to the Ho*ly* Spirit.
— Listen to us, O Lord, *and* have mercy, * for we have sinned *a*gainst you.

CANTICLE OF MARY

Ant.   Man cannot live on *bread* alone * but by every word that comes
                  from the mouth *of* God.

INTERCESSIONS (VI F)

Let us give glory to Christ the Lord, who became our teacher and example *and*
   our brother. * Let us pray *to* him, saying:
Lord, fill your people with your *life.*
Lord Jesus, you became like us in all things but sin; teach us how to share with
   others their *joy* and sorrow,
— that our love may grow deeper *every* day.
Help us to feed you in feed*ing* the hungry,
— and to give you drink in giving drink *to* the thirsty.
You raised Lazarus from the *sleep* of death,
— grant that those who have died the death of sin may rise again through faith
   and repentance.
Inspire many to follow you with greater zeal *and* perfection,
— through the example of the Blessèd Virgin Mary *and* the saints.
Let the dead rise *in* your glory,
— to enjoy your *love* for ever.

Our Father . . .

Prayer

Father,
through our observance of Lent,
help us to understand the meaning
of your Son's death and resurrection,
and teach us to reflect it in our lives.
Grant this through our Lord Jesus Christ, your Son,
who lives and reigns with you and the Holy Spirit,
one God, for ever and ever.

Morning Prayer

READING   See Nehemiah 8:9, 10
Today is holy to the Lord your God. Do not be sad, and do not weep; for
today is holy to our Lord. Do not be saddened this day, for rejoicing in the
Lord must be your strength!

RESPONSORY (VI F)
Christ, Son of the *living* God, * have mercy *on* us.
— Christ, Son of the *living* God, * have mercy *on* us.
You were wounded for *our* offenses,
— have mercy *on* us.
Glory to the Father, and *to* the Son, * and to the Ho*ly* Spirit.
— Christ, Son of the *living* God, * have mercy *on* us.

CANTICLE OF ZECHARIAH
Ant.   Jesus was led by the Spirit into the desert † to be tempted *by* the
                devil; * and when he had fasted for forty days and forty nights, †
                he *was* hungry.

INTERCESSIONS (VI F)
Let us praise our loving Redeemer, who gained for us this sea*son* of grace, * and
  pray *to* him, saying:
Lord, create a new spirit in us.
Christ, our life, through baptism we were buried with you and rose to *life* with
  you,
— may we walk today in new*ness* of life.
Lord, you have brought blessings to *all* mankind,
— bring us to share your concern for the *good* of all.
May we work together to build up the *earth*ly city,
— with our eyes fixed on the city that *lasts* for ever.
Healer of body and soul, cure the sickness *of* our spirit,
— so that we may grow in holiness through your *con*stant care.

Our Father . . .

Prayer

Father,
through our observance of Lent,
help us to understand the meaning
of your Son's death and resurrection,
and teach us to reflect it in our lives.
Grant this through our Lord Jesus Christ, your Son,
who lives and reigns with you and the Holy Spirit,
one God, for ever and ever.

Evening Prayer II

READING   1 Corinthians 9:24-25
While all the runners in the stadium take part in the race, the award goes to
one man. In that case, run so as to win! Athletes deny themselves all sorts of
things. They do this to win a crown of leaves that withers, but we a crown
that is imperishable.

RESPONSORY (VI F)
Listen to us, O Lord, *and* have mercy, * for we have sinned *a*gainst you.
— Listen to us, O Lord, *and* have mercy, * for we have sinned *a*gainst you.
Christ Jesus, hear our hum*ble* petitions,
— for we have sinned *a*gainst you.
Glory to the Father, and *to* the Son, * and to the Ho*ly* Spirit.
— Listen to us, O Lord, *and* have mercy, * for we have sinned *a*gainst you.

CANTICLE OF MARY
Ant.   Watch over us, eternal Savior; † do not let the cunning *tempt*er
                       seize us. * We place all our trust in your unfail*ing* help.

INTERCESSIONS (VI F)
All praise to God the Father who brought his chosen people to rebirth from
    imperishable seed through his e*ter*nal Word. * Let us ask him *as* his children:
Lord, be gracious to your *people.*
God of mercy , hear the prayers we offer for *all* your people,
— may they hunger for your word more than for bod*i*ly food.
Give us a sincere and active love for our own nation and for *all* mankind,
— may we work always to build a world of *peace* and goodness.
Look with love on all to be re*born* in baptism,
— that they may be living stones in your temple *of* the Spirit.

You moved Nineveh to repentance by the *preach*ing of Jonah,
— in your mercy touch the hearts of sinners by the preaching *of* your word.
May the dying go in hope to meet *Christ* their judge,
— may they rejoice for ever in the vision *of* your glory.

Our Father . . .

Prayer

Father,
through our observance of Lent,
help us to understand the meaning
of your Son's death and resurrection,
and teach us to reflect it in our lives.
Grant this through our Lord Jesus Christ, your Son,
who lives and reigns with you and the Holy Spirit,
one God, for ever and ever.

MONDAY

Morning Prayer

READING   Exodus 19:4-6a
You have seen for yourselves how I bore you up on eagle wings and brought
you here to myself. Therefore, if you harken to my voice and keep my covenant, you shall be my special possession, dearer to me than all other people,
though all the earth is mine. You shall be to me a kingdom of priests, a holy
nation.

RESPONSORY (VI F)
God himself will *set* me free, * from the hun*ter's* snare.
— God himself will *set* me free, * from the hun*ter's* snare.
From those who would trap me with *ly*ing words
— and from the hun*ter's* snare.
Glory to the Father, and *to* the Son, * and to the Ho*ly* Spirit.
— God himself will *set* me free, * from the hun*ter's* snare.

CANTICLE OF ZECHARIAH
Ant.   You have been blessed *by* my Father; * come and receive the
                  kingdom prepared for you † from the foundation of *the* world.

INTERCESSIONS (VI F)

Praise to Jesus, our Savior; by his death he has opened for us the way *of* salvation.
 * *Let* us ask him:
Lord, guide your people to walk in your *ways.*

God of mercy, you gave us new *life* through baptism,
— make us grow day by day *in* your likeness.

May our generosity today bring joy to *those* in need,
— in helping them *may* we find you.

Help us to do what is good, right and true *in* your sight,
— and to seek you always with undi*vid*ed hearts.

Forgive our sins against the unity *of* your family,
— make us one in *heart* and spirit.

Our Father . . .

Prayer

God our savior,
bring us back to you
and fill our minds with your wisdom.
May we be enriched by our observance of Lent.
Grant this through our Lord Jesus Christ, your Son,
who lives and reigns with you and the Holy Spirit,
one God, for ever and ever.

Evening Prayer

READING Romans 12:1-2

Brothers, I beg you through the mercy of God to offer your bodies as a living
sacrifice holy and acceptable to God, your spiritual worship. Do not conform
yourselves to this age but be transformed by the renewal of your mind, so that
you may judge what is God's will, what is good, pleasing and perfect.

RESPONSORY (VI F)

To *you*, O Lord,* I make my prayer *for* mercy.
— To *you*, O Lord,* I make my prayer *for* mercy.
Heal my soul, for I have *sinned* against you.
— I make my prayer *for* mercy.
Glory to the Father, and *to* the Son, * and to the Ho*ly* Spirit.
— To *you*, O Lord,* I make my prayer *for* mercy.

CANTICLE OF MARY

Ant. Whatever you do for the least *of* my brothers, * you do *for* me.

INTERCESSIONS (VI F)

Our Lord Jesus Christ has saved us *from* our sins. * As his people, let us call *out* to
  him:

Jesus, Son of David, have mercy on *us.*

Lord Christ, we pray for your holy Church; you gave yourself up to make it holy,
  cleansing it with water and the life-*giving* word,

— renew it constantly, and purify *it* by penance.

Good Master, show young people the way you have chosen for *each* of them,

— may they walk in it, and *find* fulfillment.

In your compassion you healed all forms of sickness; bring hope to the sick and
  raise them up,

— teach us to love and *care* for them.

Make us mindful of the dignity you gave *us* in baptism,

— may we live for you at *every* moment.

May the dead rise to glory *in* your peace,

— grant us with them a share *in* your kingdom.

Our Father . . .

Prayer

God our savior,
bring us back to you
and fill our minds with your wisdom.
May we be enriched by our observance of Lent.
Grant this through our Lord Jesus Christ, your Son,
who lives and reigns with you and the Holy Spirit,
one God, for ever and ever.

TUESDAY

Morning Prayer

READING   Joel 2:12-13

Return to me with your whole heart,
    with fasting, and weeping, and mourning;
Rend your hearts, not your garments,
    and return to the Lord, your God.
For gracious and merciful is he,
    slow to anger, rich in kindness,
    and relenting in punishment.

RESPONSORY (VI F)

God himself will *set* me free, * from the hunt*er's* snare.

— God himself will *set* me free, * from the hunt*er's* snare.

From those who would trap me with *ly*ing words

— and from the hunt*er's* snare.

Glory to the Father, and *to* the Son, * and to the Ho*ly* Spirit.

— God himself will *set* me free, * from the hunt*er's* snare.

CANTICLE OF ZECHARIAH

Ant.   Lord, teach *us* to pray * as John taught his *dis*ciples.

INTERCESSIONS (VI F)

Praise to Christ, who has given us himself as the *bread* from heaven. * Let us pray
    to him saying:

*Jesus, you feed and heal our souls; come to strength*en *us.*

Lord, feed us at the banquet *of* the eucharist,

— with all the gifts of your *pas*chal sacrifice.

Give us a perfect heart to re*ceive* your word,

— that we may bring forth *fruit* in patience.

Make us eager to work with you in building a *bet*ter world,

— so that it may listen to your Church and its gos*pel* of peace.

We confess, Lord, that *we* have sinned,

— wash us clean by your gift *of* salvation.

Our Father . . .

Prayer

    Father,
    look on us, your children.
    Through the discipline of Lent
    help us to grow in our desire for you.
    We ask this through our Lord Jesus Christ, your Son,
    who lives and reigns with you and the Holy Spirit,
    one God, for ever and ever.

Evening Prayer

READING   James 2:14, 17, 18b

My brothers, what good is it to profess faith without practicing it? Such faith
has no power to save one, has it? So it is with the faith that does nothing in
practice. It is thoroughly lifeless. Show me faith without works, and I will
show you the faith that underlies my works!

RESPONSORY (VI F)

To *you*, O Lord,* I make my prayer *for* mercy.
— To *you*, O Lord,* I make my prayer *for* mercy.
Heal my soul, for I have *sinned* against you.
— I make my prayer *for* mercy.
Glory to the Father, and *to* the Son, * and to the Ho*ly* Spirit.
— To *you*, O Lord,* I make my prayer *for* mercy.

CANTICLE OF MARY

Ant.   When you wish to pray, † go to your room, *shut* the door, * and
            pray to your Father *in* secret.

INTERCESSIONS (VI F)

Christ our Lord has warned us to watch and pray to a*void* temptation. * With our
    whole heart let us *pray to him:*
Turn to us, Lord, and have *mercy.*
Jesus, our Christ, you promised to be with those who pray *in* your name,
— help us always to pray with you to the Father in the *Ho*ly Spirit.
Bridegroom of the Church, cleanse her from *every* stain,
— teach her to walk in hope and in the power of the *Ho*ly Spirit.
Friend of the human race, teach us concern for our neighbor as you *have*
    commanded,
— that all may see you more clearly as the light *of* the world.
King of peace, give your peace *to* the world,
— that your presence may reveal your saving power in *every* place.
Open the door of eternal happiness to *all* the dead,
— welcome them into the glory of un*end*ing life.

Our Father . . .

Prayer

Father,
look on us, your children.
Through the discipline of Lent
help us to grow in our desire for you.
We ask this through our Lord Jesus Christ, your Son,
who lives and reigns with you and the Holy Spirit,
one God, for ever and ever.

WEDNESDAY

Morning Prayer

READING Deuteronomy 7:6, 8-9

The Lord, your God, has chosen you from all the nations on the face of the earth to be a people peculiarly his own. It was because the Lord loved you and because of his fidelity to the oath he had sworn to your fathers, that he brought you out with his strong hand from the place of slavery, and ransomed you from the hand of Pharaoh, king of Egypt. Understand, then, that the Lord, your God, is God indeed, the faithful God who keeps his merciful covenant to the thousandth generation toward those who love him and keep his commandments.

RESPONSORY (VI F)

God himself will *set* me free, * from the hun*ter's* snare.
— God himself will *set* me free, * from the hun*ter's* snare.
From those who would trap me with *ly*ing words
— and from the hun*ter's* snare.
Glory to the Father, and *to* the Son, * and to the Ho*ly* Spirit.
— God himself will *set* me free, * from the hun*ter's* snare.

CANTICLE OF ZECHARIAH

Ant.   This evil and faithless generation asks *for* a sign, * but no sign will be given it except the sign of the pro*phet* Jonah.

INTERCESSIONS (VI F)

Blessèd be God, the giver of salvation, who decreed that mankind should become a new creation in himself, when all would *be* made new. * With great confidence *let* us ask him:
Lord, renew us in your Spirit.
Lord, you promised a new heaven and a new earth; renew us daily *through* your Spirit,
— that we may enjoy your presence for ever in the heaven*ly* Jerusalem.
Help us to work with you to make this world alive *with* your Spirit,
— and to build on earth a city of justice, *love* and peace.
Free us from all negli*gence* and sloth,
— and give us joy in your *gifts* of grace.
Deliver *us* from evil,
— and from slavery to the senses, which blinds *us* to goodness.

Our Father . . .

Prayer

Lord,
look upon us and hear our prayer.
By the good works you inspire,
help us to discipline our bodies
and to be renewed in spirit.
Grant this through our Lord Jesus Christ, your Son,
who lives and reigns with you and the Holy Spirit,
one God, for ever and ever.

Evening Prayer

READING   Philippians 2:12b-15a
Work with anxious concern to achieve your salvation. It is God who, in his
good will toward you, begets in you any measure of desire or achievement. In
everything you do, act without grumbling or arguing; prove yourselves
innocent and straightforward, children of God without reproach.

RESPONSORY (VI F)
To *you*, O Lord,* I make my prayer *for* mercy.
— To *you*, O Lord,* I make my prayer *for* mercy.
Heal my soul, for I have *sinned* against you.
— I make my prayer *for* mercy.
Glory to the Father, and *to* the Son, * and to the Ho*ly* Spirit.
— To *you*, O Lord,* I make my prayer *for* mercy.

CANTICLE OF MARY
Ant.   As Jonah was three days and three nights in the belly *of* the
                        whale, * so will the Son of Man spend three days and three nights
                        in the heart of *the* earth.

INTERCESSIONS (VI F)
Blessèd be almighty God, who watches over us as a Father; he knows all our
    needs but wants us to seek *first* his kingdom. * Let us cry out to him *as* his
    people:
May your kingdom come, that justice may reign.
Father of all holiness, you gave us Christ as the shepherd of our souls; stay with
    your shepherds and the flock entrusted to them, do not leave this flock without
    the loving care *of* its shepherd,
— do not leave your shepherds without an obedient flock to *fo*llow them.
Teach Christians to help the weak with *loving* care,
— and in serving them to *serve* your Son.

Gather into your Church those who do not *yet* believe,
—and help them to build it up by good deeds done for *love* of you.
Help us to turn to you *for* forgiveness,
—and, as you forgive us, reconcile us also *with* your Church.
May the dead pass from this world to e*ter*nal life,
—to be with *you* for ever.

Our Father . . .

Prayer

Lord,
look upon us and hear our prayer.
By the good works you inspire,
help us to discipline our bodies
and to be renewed in spirit.
Grant this through our Lord Jesus Christ, your Son,
who lives and reigns with you and the Holy Spirit,
one God, for ever and ever.

THURSDAY

Morning Prayer

READING   See 1 Kings 8:51-53a

We are your people and your inheritance. Thus may your eyes be open to the petition of your servant and to the petition of your people Israel. Hear us whenever we call upon you, because you have set us apart among all the peoples of the earth of your inheritance.

RESPONSORY (VI F)
God himself will *set* me free, * from the hunt*er's* snare.
—God himself will *set* me free, * from the hunt*er's* snare.
From those who would trap me with *ly*ing words
—and from the hunt*er's* snare.
Glory to the Father, and *to* the Son, * and to the Ho*ly* Spirit.
—God himself will *set* me free, * from the hunt*er's* snare.

CANTICLE OF ZECHARIAH
Ant.   If you, evil as you are, † know how to give your children *what* is good, * how much more will your Father in heaven † pour out his gifts on all who pray *to* him.

INTERCESSIONS (VI F)

Christ our Lord came among us as the light of the world, that we might walk in his light, and not in the dark*ness* of death. * Let us praise him and cry *out* to him:

Let your word be a lamp to *guide us.*

God of mercy, help us today to grow *in* your likeness,
—that we who sinned in Adam may rise a*gain* in Christ.

Let your word be a *lamp* to guide us,
—that we may live the truth and grow always *in* your love.

Teach us to be faithful in seeking the common good *for* your sake,
—that your light may shine on the whole human family by *means* of your Church.

Touch our hearts to seek your friendship *more* and more,
—and to make amends for our sins against your wis*dom* and goodness.

Our Father . . .

Prayer

Father,
without you we can do nothing.
By your Spirit help us to know what is right
and to be eager in doing your will.
We ask this through our Lord Jesus Christ, your Son,
who lives and reigns with you and the Holy Spirit,
one God, for ever and ever.

Evening Prayer

READING   James 4:7-8, 10

Submit to God; resist the devil and he will take flight. Draw close to God, and he will draw close to you. Cleanse your hands, you sinners; purify your hearts, you backsliders. Be humbled in the sight of the Lord and he will raise you on high.

RESPONSORY (VI F)

To *you*, O Lord,* I make my prayer *for* mercy.
—To *you*, O Lord,* I make my prayer *for* mercy.
Heal my soul, for I have *sinned* against you.
—I make my prayer *for* mercy.
Glory to the Father, and *to* the Son, * and to the Ho*ly* Spirit.
—To *you*, O Lord,* I make my prayer *for* mercy.

CANTICLE OF MARY

Ant.   Ask and you shall receive, † seek and *you* shall find, * knock and the door shall be opened *to* you.

INTERCESSIONS (VI F)

Christ the Lord gave us a new commandment, of love *for* each other. * Let us *pray* to him:

Lord, build up your people in *love.*

Good Master, teach us to love you *in* our neighbor,

— and in serving them *to* serve you.

On the cross you asked pardon for your *ex*ecutioners,

— give us strength to love our enemies and pray for *those* who persecute us.

Through the mystery of your body and blood, deepen our love, our perseverance *and* our trust,

— strengthen the weak, console the sorrowful, and give *hope* to the dying.

Light of the world, you gave light to the man born blind when he had washed in the *pool* of Siloam,

— enlighten catechumens through the water of baptism and the *word* of life.

Give to the dead the perfect joy of your e*ter*nal love,

— and number us also a*mong* your chosen ones.

Our Father . . .

Prayer

Father,
without you we can do nothing.
By your Spirit help us to know what is right
and to be eager in doing your will.
We ask this through our Lord Jesus Christ, your Son,
who lives and reigns with you and the Holy Spirit,
one God, for ever and ever.

FRIDAY

Morning Prayer

READING   Isaiah 53:11b-12

Through his suffering, my servant shall justify many,
    and their guilt he shall bear.
Therefore I will give him his portion among the great,
    and he shall divide the spoils with the mighty,
Because he surrendered himself to death
    and was counted among the wicked;
And he shall take away the sins of many
    and win pardon for their offenses.

RESPONSORY (VI F)

God himself will *set* me free, * from the hunt*er's* snare.
— God himself will *set* me free, * from the hunt*er's* snare.
From those who would trap me with *ly*ing words
— and from the hunt*er's* snare.
Glory to the Father, and *to* the Son, * and to the Ho*ly* Spirit.
— God himself will *set* me free, * from the hunt*er's* snare.

CANTICLE OF ZECHARIAH

Ant.   If your virtue does not surpass that of the *scribes* and Pharisees, *
          you will never enter the kingdom *of* heaven.

INTERCESSIONS (VI F)

Thanks be to Christ the Lord, who brought us life by his death *on* the cross. *
    With our whole heart *let* us ask him:
By your death raise us to life.
Teacher and Savior, you have shown us your fidelity and made us a new creation
    by your passion,
— keep us from falling again *in*to sin.
Help us to deny our*selves* today,
— and not deny *those* in need.
May we receive this day of penance *as* your gift,
— and give it back to you through *works* of mercy.
Master our re*bel*lious hearts,
— and teach us *gen*erosity.

Our Father . . .

Prayer

Lord,
may our observance of Lent
help to renew us and prepare us
to celebrate the death and resurrection of Christ,
who lives and reigns with you and the Holy Spirit,
one God, for ever and ever.

Evening Prayer

READING   James 5:16, 19-20
Declare your sins to one another, and pray for one another, that you may find
healing. The fervent petition of a holy man is powerful indeed. My brothers,
the case may arise among you of someone straying from the truth, and of
another bringing him back. Remember this: the person who brings a sinner
back from his way will save his soul from death and cancel a multitude of
sins.

RESPONSORY (VI F)
To *you*, O Lord,* I make my prayer *for* mercy.
—To *you*, O Lord,* I make my prayer *for* mercy.
Heal my soul, for I have *sinned* against you.
—I make my prayer *for* mercy.
Glory to the Father, and *to* the Son, * and to the Ho*ly* Spirit.
—To *you*, O Lord,* I make my prayer *for* mercy.

CANTICLE OF MARY
Ant.   If you are bringing your gift to the altar, † and there you remem-
              ber that your brother has something against you, † leave your
              gift in front *of* the altar; * go at once and make peace with your
              brother, † and then come back and offer *your* gift.

INTERCESSIONS (VI F)
The Lord Jesus sanctified his people *with* his blood. * Let us cry *out* to him:
Lord, have mercy on your *people.*
Loving Redeemer, through your passion teach us self-denial, strengthen us
    against evil and adversity, and in*crease* our hope,
—and so make us ready to celebrate your *res*urrection.
Grant that Christians, as your prophets, may make you known in *eve*ry place,
—and bear witness to you with living faith and *hope* and love.
Give your strength to all *in* distress,
—and help us to raise them up through our lov*ing* concern.

Teach the faithful to see your passion *in* their sufferings,
— and to show to others your pow*er* to save.
Author of life, remember those who have passed *from* this world,
— grant them the glory of your *ris*en life.

Our Father . . .

Prayer

Lord,
may our observance of Lent
help to renew us and prepare us
to celebrate the death and resurrection of Christ,
who lives and reigns with you and the Holy Spirit,
one God, for ever and ever.

SATURDAY

Morning Prayer

READING   Isaiah 1:16-18

> Wash yourselves clean!
> Put away your misdeeds from before my eyes;
>   cease doing evil; learn to do good.
> Make justice your aim; redress the wronged,
>   hear the orphan's plea, defend the widow.
> Come now, let us set things right,
>   says the Lord:
> Though your sins be like scarlet,
>   they may become white as snow;
> Though they be crimson red,
>   they may become white as wool.

RESPONSORY (VI F)
God himself will *set* me free, * from the hun*ter's* snare.
— God himself will *set* me free, * from the hun*ter's* snare.
From those who would trap me with *ly*ing words
— and from the hun*ter's* snare.
Glory to the Father, and *to* the Son, * and to the Ho*ly* Spirit.
— God himself will *set* me free, * from the hun*ter's* snare.

CANTICLE OF ZECHARIAH

Ant.   If you want to be true children of your heavenly Father, † then you must pray for those who persecute you † and speak all kinds of e*vil* against you, * says *the* Lord.

INTERCESSIONS (VI F)

To make us his new creation, Christ the Lord gave us the waters of rebirth and spread the table of his body *and* his word. * Let us call upon *him* and say:

Lord, renew us in your *grace.*

Jesus, meek and humble of heart, clothe us with compassion, kindness *and* humility,

— make us want to be pa*tient* with everyone.

Teach us to be true neighbors to all in trouble *and* distress,

— and so imitate you, the *Good* Samaritan.

May the Blessèd Virgin, your Mother, pray for all those vowed to a life *of* virginity,

— that they may deepen their dedication to you and *to* the Church.

Grant us the gift *of* your mercy,

— forgive our sins and re*mit* their punishment.

Our Father . . .

Prayer

Eternal Father,
turn our hearts to you.
By seeking your kingdom
and loving one another,
may we become a people who worship you
in spirit and truth.
Grant this through our Lord Jesus Christ, your Son,
who lives and reigns with you and the Holy Spirit,
one God, for ever and ever.

SECOND SUNDAY OF LENT

Evening Prayer I

READING   2 Corinthians 6:1–4a

We beg you not to receive the grace of God in vain. For he says, "In an acceptable time I have heard you; on a day of salvation I have helped you." Now is the acceptable time! Now is the day of salvation! We avoid giving anyone offense, so that our ministry may not be blamed. On the contrary, in all that we do we strive to present ourselves as ministers of God.

RESPONSORY (VI F)

Listen to us, O Lord, *and* have mercy, * for we have sinned *a*gainst you.
— Listen to us, O Lord, *and* have mercy, * for we have sinned *a*gainst you.
Christ Jesus, hear our hum*ble* petitions,
— for we have sinned *a*gainst you.
Glory to the Father, and *to* the Son, * and to the Ho*ly* Spirit.
— Listen to us, O Lord, *and* have mercy, * for we have sinned *a*gainst you.

CANTICLE OF MARY

Ant.   A voice spoke from the cloud: † This is my belovèd Son in whom
                I *am* well pleased; * listen *to* him.

INTERCESSIONS (VI F)

Let us give glory to God, who has concern *for* us all. * Let us call upon *him* and
    say:
Lord, save the people you have re*deemed.*
Giver of all gifts and source of all truth, give the fullness of your blessing to the
    col*lege* of bishops,
— and keep all those entrusted to their care faithful to the teaching of *the*
    apostles.
Pour your love into the hearts of all who share the one *bread* of life,
— that they may grow in unity in the body *of* your Son.
Help us to strip off our *sin*ful selves,
— and to be clothed with Christ, your Son, *the* new Adam.
Grant that all may do penance and *find* forgiveness,
— and so share in the fruits of Christ's re*deem*ing death.
May those who have died in your peace give you everlasting glo*ry* in heaven,
— where we, too, hope to praise *you* for ever.

Our Father . . .

Prayer

God our Father,
help us to hear your Son.
Enlighten us with your word,
that we may find the way to your glory.
We ask this through our Lord Jesus Christ, your Son,
who lives and reigns with you and the Holy Spirit,
one God, for ever and ever.

Morning Prayer

READING   See Nehemiah 8:9, 10

Today is holy to the Lord your God. Do not be sad, and do not weep; for today is holy to our Lord. Do not be saddened this day, for rejoicing in the Lord must be your strength!

RESPONSORY (VI F)

Christ, Son of the *living* God, * have mercy *on* us.
— Christ, Son of the *living* God, * have mercy *on* us.
You were wounded for *our* offenses,
— have mercy *on* us.
Glory to the Father, and *to* the Son, * and to the Ho*ly* Spirit.
— Christ, Son of the *living* God, * have mercy *on* us.

CANTICLE OF ZECHARIAH

Ant.   Our Lord Jesus Christ a*bol*ished death, * and through the Gospel
he revealed eter*nal* life.

INTERCESSIONS (VI F)

Let us give glory to God, whose kindness *knows* no limit. * Through Jesus Christ,
who lives for ever to intercede for us, *let* us pray:
Kindle in our hearts the fire of your love.
God of mercy, let today be a day rich *in* good works,
— a day of generosity to *all* we meet.
From the waters of the flood you saved Noah *through* the ark,
— from the waters of baptism raise up to new life those un*der* instruction.
May we live not *by* bread only,
— but by every word falling *from* your lips.
Help us to do away with *all* dissension,
— so that we may rejoice in your gifts of *peace* and love.

Our Father . . .

Prayer

God our Father,
help us to hear your Son.
Enlighten us with your word,
that we may find the way to your glory.
We ask this through our Lord Jesus Christ, your Son,
who lives and reigns with you and the Holy Spirit,
one God, for ever and ever.

Evening Prayer II

READING   1 Corinthians 9:24-25
While all the runners in the stadium take part in the race, the award goes to
one man. In that case, run so as to win! Athletes deny themselves all sorts of
things. They do this to win a crown of leaves that withers, but we a crown
that is imperishable.

RESPONSORY (VI f)
Listen to us, O Lord, *and* have mercy, * for we have sinned *a*gainst you.
— Listen to us, O Lord, *and* have mercy, * for we have sinned *a*gainst you.
Christ Jesus, hear our hum*ble* petitions,
— for we have sinned *a*gainst you.
Glory to the Father, and *to* the Son, * and to the Ho*ly* Spirit.
— Listen to us, O Lord, *and* have mercy, * for we have sinned *a*gainst you.

CANTICLE OF MARY
Ant.   Tell no one about the vision *you* have seen * until the Son of Man
                has risen from *the* dead.

INTERCESSIONS (VI f)
Let us give thanks continually to Christ, our teacher and our head, who came to
    serve and to do *good* to all. * In humility and confidence *let* us ask him:
Come, Lord, to visit your family.
Lord, be present to the bishops and priests of your Church, who share your role as
    head and shepherd,
— may they lead your people to the Father un*der* your guidance.
May your angel be with *all* who travel,
— to keep them safe in *soul* and body.
Teach us to serve the *needs* of others,
— and to be like you, who came to serve, not *to* be served.
Grant that in the human family, brother may al*ways* help brother,
— so that, with your assistance, it may be a city com*pact* and strong.

Have mercy on *all* the dead,
— bring them to the vision *of* your glory.

Our Father . . .

Prayer

God our Father,
help us to hear your Son.
Enlighten us with your word,
that we may find the way to your glory.
We ask this through our Lord Jesus Christ, your Son,
who lives and reigns with you and the Holy Spirit,
one God, for ever and ever.

MONDAY

Morning Prayer

READING   Exodus 19:4-6a
You have seen for yourselves how I bore you up on eagle wings and brought
you here to myself. Therefore, if you harken to my voice and keep my covenant, you shall be my special possession, dearer to me than all other people,
though all the earth is mine. You shall be to me a kingdom of priests, a holy
nation.

RESPONSORY (VI F)
God himself will *set* me free, * from the hun*ter's* snare.
— God himself will *set* me free, * from the hun*ter's* snare.
From those who would trap me with *ly*ing words
— and from the hun*ter's* snare.
Glory to the Father, and *to* the Son, * and to the Ho*ly* Spirit.
— God himself will *set* me free, * from the hun*ter's* snare.

CANTICLE OF ZECHARIAH
Ant.   Be compassionate *and* forgiving * as your Father is, says *the* Lord.

INTERCESSIONS (VI F)
Blessèd be God the Father for his gift of this sacri*fice* of praise. * In the spirit of
   this Lenten season, *let* us pray:
Instruct us, Lord, in the ways of your *kingdom.*
God of power and mercy, give us the spirit of prayer *and* repentance,
— with burning love for you and for *all* mankind.

Help us to work with you in making all things *new* in Christ,
— and in spreading justice and peace through*out* the world.
Teach us the meaning and value *of* creation,
— so that we may join its voice to ours as we *sing* your praise.
Forgive us for failing to see Christ in the poor, the distressed *and* the troublesome,
— and for our failure to reverence your Son *in* their persons.

Our Father . . .

Prayer

God our Father,
teach us to find new life through penance.
Keep us from sin,
and help us live by your commandment of love.
We ask this through our Lord Jesus Christ, your Son,
who lives and reigns with you and the Holy Spirit,
one God, for ever and ever.

Evening Prayer

READING   Romans 12:1-2
Brothers, I beg you through the mercy of God to offer your bodies as a living
sacrifice holy and acceptable to God, your spiritual worship. Do not conform
yourselves to this age but be transformed by the renewal of your mind, so that
you may judge what is God's will, what is good, pleasing and perfect.

RESPONSORY (VI F)
To *you*, O Lord,* I make my prayer *for* mercy.
— To *you*, O Lord,* I make my prayer *for* mercy.
Heal my soul, for I have *sinned* against you.
— I make my prayer *for* mercy.
Glory to the Father, and *to* the Son, * and to the Ho*ly* Spirit.
— To *you*, O Lord,* I make my prayer *for* mercy.

CANTICLE OF MARY
Ant.   Do not judge others, and you will *not* be judged, * for as you have
                        judged them, so God will *judge* you.

INTERCESSIONS (VI F)
Glory to God the Father, who has promised through his Son to grant what is
    asked by those who *pray* together. * With confidence in this promise, *let* us pray:
Lord, look with favor on your *people.*

Lord, you gave the Law to Moses on Mount Sinai, and brought it to perfection in
  your Anointed One,
— may all recognize the Law written in their hearts, and keep it faithfully *as* a
  covenant.
Give those in authority a true concern for their brothers and sisters entrusted *to*
  their care,
— and inspire the hearts of the people to sup*port* their leaders.
Strengthen with your Spirit the minds and *hearts* of missionaries,
— and raise up a great company to help them from *every* nation.
Give your grace to children, that they may grow *in* your favor,
— and to young people, that they may reach their full stature by loving you and
  keeping *your* commandments.
Remember our brothers and sisters, who have fallen asleep *in* your peace,
— bring them at last to e*ter*nal life.

Our Father . . .

Prayer

God our Father,
teach us to find new life through penance.
Keep us from sin,
and help us live by your commandment of love.
We ask this through our Lord Jesus Christ, your Son,
who lives and reigns with you and the Holy Spirit,
one God, for ever and ever.

TUESDAY

Morning Prayer

READING   Joel 2:12-13
  Return to me with your whole heart,
      with fasting, and weeping, and mourning;
  Rend your hearts, not your garments,
      and return to the Lord, your God.
  For gracious and merciful is he,
      slow to anger, rich in kindness,
      and relenting in punishment.

RESPONSORY (VI F)
God himself will *set* me free, * from the hunt*er's* snare.
— God himself will *set* me free, * from the hunt*er's* snare.

From those who would trap me with *ly*ing words
— and from the hunt*er's* snare.
Glory to the Father, and *to* the Son, * and to the Ho*ly* Spirit.
— God himself will *set* me free, * from the hunt*er's* snare.

CANTICLE OF ZECHARIAH
Ant.   You have one teacher, and he *is* in heaven: * Christ *your* Lord.

INTERCESSIONS (VI F)
God the Father has given us his only Son, the Word made man, to be our food
   and our life. * Let us thank *him* and pray:
May the word of Christ dwell among us in all its richness.
Help us in this Lenten season to listen more frequently *to* your word,
— that we may celebrate the solemnity of Easter with greater love for Christ, our
   *pas*chal sacrifice.
May your Holy Spirit *be* our teacher,
— that we may encourage those in doubt and error to follow what is *true* and
   good.
Enable us to enter more deeply into the mystery of *your* Anointed One,
— that our lives may reveal him *more* effectively.
Purify and renew your Church in this time *of* salvation,
— that it may give an ever greater wit*ness* to you.

Our Father . . .

                               Prayer
      Lord,
      watch over your Church,
      and guide it with your unfailing love.
      Protect us from what could harm us
      and lead us to what will save us.
      Help us always,
      for without you we are bound to fail.
      Grant this through our Lord Jesus Christ, your Son,
      who lives and reigns with you and the Holy Spirit,
      one God, for ever and ever.

Evening Prayer

READING   James 2:14, 17, 18b

My brothers, what good it is to profess faith without practicing it? Such faith
has no power to save one, has it? So it is with the faith that does nothing in
practice. It is thoroughly lifeless. Show me faith without works, and I will
show you the faith that underlies my works!

RESPONSORY (VI F)

To *you*, O Lord,* I make my prayer *for* mercy.
— To *you*, O Lord,* I make my prayer *for* mercy.
Heal my soul, for I have *sinned* against you.
— I make my prayer *for* mercy.
Glory to the Father, and *to* the Son, * and to the Ho*ly* Spirit.
— To *you*, O Lord,* I make my prayer *for* mercy.

CANTICLE OF MARY

Ant.   You are all brothers, sons of one Father who *is* in heaven. * Do
                  not call anyone on earth *your* father.
                  Nor must any of you be *called* a teacher, * for your only teacher *is*
                  Christ.

INTERCESSIONS (VI F)

Let us praise the Lord Jesus, who, lifted high on the cross, drew all things *to*
    himself. * With loving hearts *let* us pray:
Draw all things to yourself, O Lord.
Lord, may the mystery of your cross shine on *all* mankind,
— that all may see you as the way, the truth *and* the life.
May all who thirst for you, the li*v*ing water,
— drink their *fill* for ever.
Inspire all teach*ers* and artists,
— to prepare mankind *for* your kingdom.
Guide all estranged from you by *sin* or scandal,
— that they may come back to you, and remain always *in* your love.
Welcome all our deceased brothers and sisters to your *home* in heaven,
— to share the joy of the blessèd Virgin Mary and *all* the saints.

Our Father . . .

Prayer

Lord,
watch over your Church,
and guide it with your unfailing love.
Protect us from what could harm us
and lead us to what will save us.
Help us always,
for without you we are bound to fail.
Grant this through our Lord Jesus Christ, your Son,
who lives and reigns with you and the Holy Spirit,
one God, for ever and ever.

WEDNESDAY

Morning Prayer

READING   Deuteronomy 7:6, 8-9

The Lord, your God, has chosen you from all the nations on the face of the
earth to be a people peculiarly his own. It was because the Lord loved you
and because of his fidelity to the oath he had sworn to your fathers, that he
brought you out with his strong hand from the place of slavery, and ransomed
you from the hand of Pharaoh, king of Egypt. Understand, then, that the
Lord, your God, is God indeed, the faithful God who keeps his merciful
covenant to the thousandth generation toward those who love him and keep
his commandments.

RESPONSORY (VI F)

God himself will *set* me free, * from the hun*ter's* snare.
— God himself will *set* me free, * from the hun*ter's* snare.
From those who would trap me with *ly*ing words
— and from the hun*ter's* snare.
Glory to the Father, and *to* the Son, * and to the Ho*ly* Spirit.
— God himself will *set* me free, * from the hun*ter's* snare.

CANTICLE OF ZECHARIAH

Ant.   The Son of Man did not come to be served *but* to serve, * and to
             give his life as a ransom *for* many.

INTERCESSIONS (VI F)

Let us give thanks to God our Father; through the power of the Spirit he purifies
our hearts and strengthens *us* in love. * Let us *hum*bly ask him:
Lord, give us your Holy Spirit.

Help us to receive good things from your bounty with a deep *sense* of gratitude,
— and to accept with patience the evil that *comes* to us.
Teach us to be loving not only in great and excep*tio*nal moments,
— but above all in the ordinary events of *dai*ly life.
May we abstain from what we do not *real*ly need,
— and help our brothers and sisters *in* distress.
May we bear the wounds *of* your Son,
— for through his body he *gave* us life.

Our Father . . .

Prayer

Father,
teach us to live good lives,
encourage us with your support
and bring us to eternal life.
We ask this through our Lord Jesus Christ, your Son,
who lives and reigns with you and the Holy Spirit,
one God, for ever and ever.

Evening Prayer

READING   Philippians 2:12b-15a

Work with anxious concern to achieve your salvation. It is God who, in his good will toward you, begets in you any measure of desire or achievement. In everything you do, act without grumbling or arguing; prove yourselves innocent and straightforward, children of God without reproach.

RESPONSORY (VI F)
To *you*, O Lord,* I make my prayer *for* mercy.
— To *you*, O Lord,* I make my prayer *for* mercy.
Heal my soul, for I have *sinned* against you.
— I make my prayer *for* mercy.
Glory to the Father, and *to* the Son, * and to the Ho*ly* Spirit.
— To *you*, O Lord,* I make my prayer *for* mercy.

CANTICLE OF MARY
Ant.   The Son of Man will be handed over to the Gentiles † to be mocked, *scourged* and crucified; * and on the third day he will rise *a*gain.

INTERCESSIONS (VI F)

All glory and honor to God, for in the blood of Christ he has ratified a new and everlasting covenant with his people, and renews it in the sacrament *of* the altar.
   * Let us lift our voic*es* in prayer:

*Bless your peo*ple, *Lord.*

Lord, guide the minds and hearts of peoples and all in *pub*lic office,
— may they always seek the *com*mon good.

Renew the spirit of dedication in those who have left all to *fol*low Christ,
— may they give clear witness to the holiness *of* the Church.

You have made all men and women *in* your image,
— may they always uphold *hu*man dignity.

Lead back to your friendship and truth all who have *gone* astray,
— teach us *how* to help them.

Grant that the dead may enter in*to* your glory,
— to praise *you* for ever.

Our Father . . .

Prayer

Father,
teach us to live good lives,
encourage us with your support
and bring us to eternal life.
We ask this through our Lord Jesus Christ, your Son,
who lives and reigns with you and the Holy Spirit,
one God, for ever and ever.

THURSDAY

Morning Prayer

READING   See 1 Kings 8:51-53a

We are your people, O Lord, and your inheritance. Thus may your eyes be open to the petition of your servant and to the petition of your people Israel. Hear us whenever we call upon you, because you have set us apart among all the peoples of the earth of your inheritance.

RESPONSORY (VI F)

God himself will *set* me free, * from the hun*ter's* snare.
— God himself will *set* me free, * from the hun*ter's* snare.
From those who would trap me with *ly*ing words
— and from the hun*ter's* snare.

Glory to the Father, and *to* the Son, * and to the Ho*ly* Spirit.
— God himself will *set* me free, * from the hun*ter's* snare.

CANTICLE OF ZECHARIAH

Ant.   Son, remember the good things you received *in* your lifetime *
                        and the bad things Lazarus received *in* his.

INTERCESSIONS (VI F)

God has revealed him*self* in Christ. * Let us praise his goodness, and ask him *from*
    our hearts:
Remember us, Lord, for we are your *children.*
Teach us to enter more deeply into the mystery *of* the Church,
— that it may be more effective for ourselves and for the world as the sacrament
    of salvation.
Lover of mankind, inspire us to work for *hu*man progress,
— seeking to spread your kingdom in *all* we do.
May our hearts *thirst* for Christ,
— the fountain of *living* water.
Forgive *us* our sins,
— and direct our steps into the ways of justice *and* sincerity.

Our Father . . .

Prayer

God of love,
bring us back to you.
Send your Spirit to make us strong in faith
and active in good works.
Grant this through our Lord Jesus Christ, your Son,
who lives and reigns with you and the Holy Spirit,
one God, for ever and ever.

Evening Prayer

READING   James 4:7-8, 10
    Submit to God; resist the devil and he will take flight. Draw close to God,
    and he will draw close to you. Cleanse your hands, you sinners; purify your
    hearts, you backsliders. Be humbled in the sight of the Lord and he will raise
    you on high.

RESPONSORY (VI F)

To *you*, O Lord,* I make my prayer *for* mercy.
— To *you*, O Lord,* I make my prayer *for* mercy.

Heal my soul, for I have *sinned* against you.
— I make my prayer *for* mercy.
Glory to the Father, and *to* the Son, * and to the Ho*ly* Spirit.
— To *you*, O Lord,* I make my prayer *for* mercy.

CANTICLE OF MARY
Ant.   The rich man, who had refused Lazarus a *crust* of bread, *
                        pleaded for a drop *of* water.

INTERCESSIONS (VI F)
In his mercy, God sends the Holy Spirit to shine on us, so that our lives may
    radiate holi*ness* and faith. * Let us raise our voices in *prayer* and say:
Lord, give life to your people, who Christ has redeemed.
Lord, source of all holiness, draw bishops, priests and deacons closer to Christ
    through the eucha*ris*tic mystery,
— may they grow daily in the grace of their *or*dination.
Teach Christ's faithful people to be devout and attentive at the table of his word
    and *of* his body,
— so that they may bring into their daily lives the grace they receive through *faith*
    and sacrament.
Grant, Lord, that we may see in each person the dignity of one redeemed by *your*
    Son's blood,
— so that we may respect the freedom and the con*science* of all.
Teach us to restrain our greed for *earth*ly goods,
— and to have concern for the *needs* of others.
Be merciful to your faithful people whom you have called to your*self* today,
— grant them the gift of e*ter*nal happiness.

Our Father . . .

                                Prayer

        God of love,
        bring us back to you.
        Send your Spirit to make us strong in faith
        and active in good works.
        Grant this through our Lord Jesus Christ, your Son,
        who lives and reigns with you and the Holy Spirit,
        one God, for ever and ever.

FRIDAY

Morning Prayer

READING   Isaiah 53:11b-12

Through his suffering, my servant shall justify many,
    and their guilt he shall bear.
Therefore I will give him his portion among the great,
    and he shall divide the spoils with the mighty,
Because he surrendered himself to death
    and was counted among the wicked;
And he shall take away the sins of many
    and win pardon for their offenses.

RESPONSORY (VI F)

God himself will *set* me free, * from the hunt*er's* snare.
— God himself will *set* me free, * from the hunt*er's* snare.
From those who would trap me with *ly*ing words
— and from the hunt*er's* snare.
Glory to the Father, and *to* the Son, * and to the Ho*ly* Spirit.
— God himself will *set* me free, * from the hunt*er's* snare.

CANTICLE OF ZECHARIAH

Ant.   He will bring those evil men to an evil end † and entrust his
                vineyard to *o*ther tenants * who will give him the harvest at the
                pro*per* season.

INTERCESSIONS (VI F)

Let us pray to *Christ* our Savior, * who redeemed us by his death and *re*surrection:
Lord, have mercy on *us.*
You went up to Jerusalem to suffer and so enter in*to* your glory,
— bring your Church to the Passover *feast* of heaven.
You were lifted high on the cross and pierced by the *sol*dier's lance,
— *heal* our wounds.
You made the cross the *tree* of life,
— give its fruit to those re*born* in baptism.
On the cross you forgave the re*pent*ant thief,
— forgive *us* our sins.

Our Father . . .

Prayer

Merciful Father,
may our acts of penance bring us your forgiveness,
open our hearts to your love,
and prepare us for the coming feast of the resurrection.
We ask this through our Lord Jesus Christ, your Son,
who lives and reigns with you and the Holy Spirit,
one God, for ever and ever.

Evening Prayer

READING   James 5:16, 19-20

Declare your sins to one another, and pray for one another, that you may find healing. The fervent petition of a holy man is powerful indeed. My brothers, the case may arise among you of someone straying from the truth, and of another bringing him back. Remember this: the person who brings a sinner back from his way will save his soul from death and cancel a multitude of sins.

RESPONSORY (VI F)

To *you*, O Lord,* I make my prayer *for* mercy.
—To *you*, O Lord,* I make my prayer *for* mercy.
Heal my soul, for I have *sinned* against you.
—I make my prayer *for* mercy.
Glory to the Father, and *to* the Son, * and to the Ho*ly* Spirit.
—To *you*, O Lord,* I make my prayer *for* mercy.

CANTICLE OF MARY

Ant.   They would have arrested Jesus but they *feared* the people * who
              regarded him as *a* prophet.

INTERCESSIONS (VI F)

The Savior of mankind by dying destroyed death and by rising again *re*stored life.
    * Let us *hum*bly ask him:
Sanctify your people, redeemed by your *blood.*
Redeemer of the world, give us a greater share of your passion through a deeper
    spirit *of* repentance,
—so that we may share the glory of your *re*surrection.
May your Mother, comfort of the afflict*ed*, protect us,
—may we console others as you *con*sole us.
In their trials enable your faithful people to share *in* your passion,
—and so reveal in their lives your *sav*ing power.

You humbled yourself by being obedient even to accepting death, death *on* a cross,
— give all who serve you the gifts of obedience and pa*tient* endurance.
Transform the bodies of the dead to be like your *own* in glory,
— and bring us at last in*to* their fellowship.

Our Father . . .

Prayer

Merciful Father,
may our acts of penance bring us your forgiveness,
open our hearts to your love,
and prepare us for the coming feast of the resurrection.
We ask this through our Lord Jesus Christ, your Son,
who lives and reigns with you and the Holy Spirit,
one God, for ever and ever.

SATURDAY

Morning Prayer

READING   Isaiah 1:16-18

    Wash yourselves clean!
Put away your misdeeds from before my eyes;
    cease doing evil; learn to do good.
Make justice your aim; redress the wronged,
    hear the orphan's plea, defend the widow.
Come now, let us set things right,
    says the Lord:
Though your sins be like scarlet,
    they may become white as snow;
Though they be crimson red,
    they may become white as wool.

RESPONSORY (VI F)
God himself will *set* me free, * from the hun*ter's* snare.
— God himself will *set* me free, * from the hun*ter's* snare.
From those who would trap me with *ly*ing words
— and from the hun*ter's* snare.
Glory to the Father, and *to* the Son, * and to the Ho*ly* Spirit.
— God himself will *set* me free, * from the hun*ter's* snare.

CANTICLE OF ZECHARIAH

Ant.　　　　Father, I have sinned against heaven and against you; † I no longer deserve to be *called* your son; * treat me as one of *your* servants.

INTERCESSIONS (VI F)

Let us always and everywhere give thanks to *Christ* our Savior, * and ask *him* with confidence:

Lord, help us with your *grace.*

May we keep our *bod*ies pure,

— as temples of the *Ho*ly Spirit.

May we offer ourselves this morning to the ser*vice* of others,

— and do your will in all things through*out* the day.

Teach us to seek the bread of ever*last*ing life,

— the bread that *is* your gift.

May your Mother, the refuge of sinners, *pray* for us,

— and gain for us your lov*ing* forgiveness.

Our Father . . .

Prayer

God our Father,
by your gifts to us on earth
we already share in your life.
In all we do,
guide us to the light of your kingdom.
Grant this through our Lord Jesus Christ, your Son,
who lives and reigns with you and the Holy Spirit,
one God, for ever and ever.

THIRD SUNDAY OF LENT

Evening Prayer I

READING   2 Corinthians 6:1-4a

We beg you not to receive the grace of God in vain. For he says, "In an acceptable time I have heard you; on a day of salvation I have helped you." Now is the acceptable time! Now is the day of salvation! We avoid giving anyone offense, so that our ministry may not be blamed. On the contrary, in all that we do we strive to present ourselves as ministers of God.

RESPONSORY (VI F)

Listen to us, O Lord, *and* have mercy, * for we have sinned *a*gainst you.
—Listen to us, O Lord, *and* have mercy, * for we have sinned *a*gainst you.
Christ Jesus, hear our hum*ble* petitions,
—for we have sinned *a*gainst you.
Glory to the Father, and *to* the Son, * and to the Ho*ly* Spirit.
—Listen to us, O Lord, *and* have mercy, * for we have sinned *a*gainst you.

CANTICLE OF MARY

Ant.   Now that we have been justi*fied* by faith, * let us be at peace with God through our Lord Je*sus* Christ.

INTERCESSIONS (VI F)

Let us give glory to Christ the Lord, who became our teacher, our example *and* our brother. * Let us pray *to* him, saying:
Lord, fill your people with your *life.*
Lord Jesus, you became like us in all things but sin; teach us how to share with others their *joy* and sorrow,
—that our love may grow deeper *eve*ry day.
Help us to feed you in feed*ing* the hungry,
—and to give you drink in giving *drink* to the thirsty.
You raised Lazarus from the *sleep* of death,
—grant that those who have died the death of sin may rise again through faith *and* repentance.
Through the example of the Blessèd Virgin Mary *and* the saints,
—inspire many to follow you with greater zeal *and* perfection.
Let the dead rise *in* your glory,
—to enjoy your *love* for ever.

Our Father . . .

Prayer

Father,
you have taught us to overcome our sins
by prayer, fasting and works of mercy.
When we are discouraged by our weakness,
give us confidence in your love.
We ask this through our Lord Jesus Christ, your Son,
who lives and reigns with you and the Holy Spirit,
one God, for ever and ever.

Morning Prayer

READING   See Nehemiah 8:9, 10

Today is holy to the Lord your God. Do not be sad, and do not weep; for
today is holy to our Lord. Do not be saddened this day, for rejoicing in the
Lord must be your strength!

RESPONSORY (VI F)

Christ, Son of the *living* God, * have mercy *on* us.
—Christ, Son of the *living* God, * have mercy *on* us.
You were wounded for *our* offenses,
—have mercy *on* us.
Glory to the Father, and *to* the Son, * and to the Ho*ly* Spirit.
—Christ, Son of the *living* God, * have mercy *on* us.

CANTICLE OF ZECHARIAH

Ant.   Destroy this temple, says the Lord, † and in three days I *will*
                rebuild it. * He was speaking of the temple of *his* body.

INTERCESSIONS (VI F)

Let us praise our loving Redeemer, who gained for us this sea*son* of grace, * and
    pray *to* him, saying:
Lord, create a new spirit in us.
Christ, our life, through baptism we were buried with you and rose to *life* with
    you,
—may we walk today in new*ness* of life.
Lord, you have brought blessings to *all* mankind,
—bring us to share your concern for the *good* of all.
May we work together to build up the *earth*ly city,
—with our eyes fixed on the city that *lasts* for ever.
Healer of body and soul, cure the sickness *of* our spirit,
—so that we may grow in holiness through your *con*stant care.

Our Father . . .

Prayer

Father,
you have taught us to overcome our sins
by prayer, fasting and works of mercy.
When we are discouraged by our weakness,
give us confidence in your love.
We ask this through our Lord Jesus Christ, your Son,
who lives and reigns with you and the Holy Spirit,
one God, for ever and ever.

Evening Prayer II

READING   1 Corinthians 9:24-25

While all the runners in the stadium take part in the race, the award goes to
one man. In that case, run so as to win! Athletes deny themselves all sorts of
things. They do this to win a crown of leaves that withers, but we a crown
that is imperishable.

RESPONSORY (VI F)
Listen to us, O Lord, *and* have mercy, * for we have sinned *a*gainst you.
— Listen to us, O Lord, *and* have mercy, * for we have sinned *a*gainst you.
Christ Jesus, hear our hum*ble* petitions,
— for we have sinned *a*gainst you.
Glory to the Father, and *to* the Son, * and to the Ho*ly* Spirit.
— Listen to us, O Lord, *and* have mercy, * for we have sinned *a*gainst you.

CANTICLE OF MARY
Ant.   Whoever drinks the water that *I* shall give * will never be thirsty
                     again, says *the* Lord.

INTERCESSIONS (VI F)
All praise to God the Father who brought his chosen people to rebirth from
    imperishable seed through his e*ter*nal Word. * Let us ask him *as* his children:
Lord, be gracious to your *people.*
God of mercy, hear the prayers we offer for *all* your people,
— may they hunger for your word more than for bod*i*ly food.
Give us a sincere and active love for our own nation and for *all* mankind,
— may we work always to build a world of *peace* and goodness.
Look with love on all to be re*born* in baptism,
— that they may be living stones in your temple *of* the Spirit.

You moved Nineveh to repentance by the preach*ing* of Jonah,
— in your mercy touch the hearts of sinners by the preaching *of* your word.
May the dying go in hope to meet *Christ* their judge,
— may they rejoice for ever in the vision *of* your glory.

Our Father . . .

Prayer

Father,
you have taught us to overcome our sins
by prayer, fasting and works of mercy.
When we are discouraged by our weakness,
give us confidence in your love.
We ask this through our Lord Jesus Christ, your Son,
who lives and reigns with you and the Holy Spirit,
one God, for ever and ever.

MONDAY

Morning Prayer

READING   Exodus 19:4-6a
You have seen for yourselves how I bore you up on eagle wings and brought
you here to myself. Therefore, if you harken to my voice and keep my covenant, you shall be my special possession, dearer to me than all other people,
though all the earth is mine. You shall be to me a kingdom of priests, a holy
nation.

RESPONSORY (VI F)
God himself will *set* me free, * from the hun*ter's* snare.
— God himself will *set* me free, * from the hun*ter's* snare.
From those who would trap me with *ly*ing words
— and from the hun*ter's* snare.
Glory to the Father, and *to* the Son, * and to the Ho*ly* Spirit.
— God himself will *set* me free, * from the hun*ter's* snare.

CANTICLE OF ZECHARIAH
Ant.   I tell *you* assuredly, * no prophet is accepted in his *own* country.

INTERCESSIONS (VI F)
Praise to Jesus, our Savior; by his death he has opened for us the way *of* salvation.
   * *Let* us ask him:
Lord, guide your people to walk in your *ways.*

God of mercy, you gave us new *life* through baptism,
— make us grow day by day *in* your likeness.
May our generosity today bring joy to *those* in need,
— in helping them may *we* find you.
Help us to do what is good, right and true *in* your sight,
— and to seek you always with undi*vid*ed hearts.
Forgive our sins against the unity *of* your family,
— make us one in heart *and* spirit.

Our Father . . .

Prayer

God of mercy
free your Church from sin
and protect it from evil.
Guide us, for we cannot be saved without you.
We ask this through our Lord Jesus Christ, your Son,
who lives and reigns with you and the Holy Spirit,
one God, for ever and ever.

Evening Prayer

READING   Romans 12:1-2
Brothers, I beg you through the mercy of God to offer your bodies as a living
sacrifice holy and acceptable to God, your spiritual worship. Do not conform
yourselves to this age but be transformed by the renewal of your mind, so that
you may judge what is God's will, what is good, pleasing and perfect.

RESPONSORY (VI F)
To *you*, O Lord,* I make my prayer *for* mercy.
— To *you*, O Lord,* I make my prayer *for* mercy.
Heal my soul, for I have *sinned* against you.
— I make my prayer *for* mercy.
Glory to the Father, and *to* the Son, * and to the Ho*ly* Spirit.
— To *you*, O Lord,* I make my prayer *for* mercy.

CANTICLE OF MARY
Ant.   Jesus walked *through* the crowd * and went *away*.

INTERCESSIONS (VI F)
Our Lord Jesus Christ has saved us *from* our sins. * As his people, let us call *out* to
    him:
Jesus, Son of David, have mercy on *us*.

Lord Christ, we pray for your holy Church; you gave yourself up to make it holy, cleansing it with water and the life-*giving* word,
— renew it constantly, and purify *it* by penance.
Good Master, show young people the way you have chosen for *each* of them,
— may they walk in it, and *find* fulfillment.
In your compassion you healed all forms of sickness; bring hope to the sick and *raise* them up,
— teach us to love and *care* for them.
Make us mindful of the dignity you gave *us* in baptism,
— may we live for you at *every* moment.
May the dead rise to glory *in* your peace,
— grant us with them a share *in* your kingdom.

Our Father . . .

Prayer

God of mercy
free your Church from sin
and protect it from evil.
Guide us, for we cannot be saved without you.
We ask this through our Lord Jesus Christ, your Son,
who lives and reigns with you and the Holy Spirit,
one God, for ever and ever.

TUESDAY

Morning Prayer

READING Joel 2:12-13
Return to me with your whole heart,
with fasting, and weeping, and mourning;
Rend your hearts, not your garments,
and return to the Lord, your God.
For gracious and merciful is he,
slow to anger, rich in kindness,
and relenting in punishment.

RESPONSORY (VI F)
God himself will *set* me free, * from the hunt*er's* snare.
— God himself will *set* me free, * from the hunt*er's* snare.
From those who would trap me with *lying* words
— and from the hunt*er's* snare.

Glory to the Father, and *to* the Son, * and to the Ho*ly* Spirit.
— God himself will *set* me free, * from the hun*ter's* snare.

CANTICLE OF ZECHARIAH
Ant.   The Lord said: † Peter, I do not tell you to forgive only *seven* times, * but seventy *times* seven.

INTERCESSIONS (VI F)
Praise to Christ, who has given us himself as the *bread* from heaven. * Let us pray *to* him saying:
*Jesus, you feed and heal our souls; come to strength*en *us.*
Lord, feed us at the banquet *of* the eucharist,
— with all the gifts of your *pasch*al sacrifice.
Give us a perfect heart to re*ceive* your word,
— that we may bring forth *fruit* in patience.
Make us eager to work with you in building a *bet*ter world,
— so that it may listen to your Church and its gos*pel* of peace.
We confess, Lord, that *we* have sinned,
— wash us clean by your gift *of* salvation.

Our Father . . .

Prayer

Lord,
you call us to your service
and continue your saving work among us.
May your love never abandon us.
We ask this through our Lord Jesus Christ, your Son,
who lives and reigns with you and the Holy Spirit,
one God, for ever and ever.

Evening Prayer

READING   James 2:14, 17, 18b
My brothers, what good it is to profess faith without practicing it? Such faith has no power to save one, has it? So it is with the faith that does nothing in practice. It is thoroughly lifeless. Show me faith without works, and I will show you the faith that underlies my works!

RESPONSORY (VI F)
To *you*, O Lord,* I make my prayer *for* mercy.
— To *you*, O Lord,* I make my prayer *for* mercy.

Heal my soul, for I have *sinned* against you.
— I make my prayer *for* mercy.
Glory to the Father, and *to* the Son, * and to the Ho*ly* Spirit.
— To *you*, O Lord,* I make my prayer *for* mercy.

CANTICLE OF MARY

Ant.   This is how my heavenly Father will treat each *one* of you, *
              unless you forgive your brothers and sisters from *your* heart.

INTERCESSIONS (VI F)

Christ our Lord has warned us to watch and pray to a*void* temptation. * With our
  whole heart let us *pray* to him:
*Turn to us, Lord, and have *mercy.*
Jesus, our Christ, you promised to be with those who pray *in* your name,
— help us always to pray with you to the Father in the *Ho*ly Spirit.
Bridegroom of the Church, cleanse her from *every* stain,
— teach her to walk in hope and in the power of the *Ho*ly Spirit.
Friend of the human race, teach us concern for our neighbor as you *have*
  commanded,
— that all may see you more clearly as the light *of* the world.
King of peace, give your peace *to* the world,
— that your presence may reveal your saving power in *every* place.
Open the door of eternal happiness to *all* the dead,
— welcome them into the glory of un*end*ing life.

Our Father . . .

Prayer

Lord,
  you call us to your service
  and continue your saving work among us.
May your love never abandon us.
We ask this through our Lord Jesus Christ, your Son,
  who lives and reigns with you and the Holy Spirit,
  one God, for ever and ever.

WEDNESDAY

Morning Prayer

READING Deuteronomy 7:6, 8-9

The Lord, your God, has chosen you from all the nations on the face of the earth to be a people peculiarly his own. It was because the Lord loved you and because of his fidelity to the oath he had sworn to your fathers, that he brought you out with his strong hand from the place of slavery, and ransomed you from the hand of Pharaoh, king of Egypt. Understand, then, that the Lord, your God, is God indeed, the faithful God who keeps his merciful covenant to the thousandth generation toward those who love him and keep his commandments.

RESPONSORY (VI F)

God himself will *set* me free, * from the hun*ter's* snare.
— God himself will *set* me free, * from the hun*ter's* snare.
From those who would trap me with *ly*ing words
— and from the hun*ter's* snare.
Glory to the Father, and *to* the Son, * and to the Ho*ly* Spirit.
— God himself will *set* me free, * from the hun*ter's* snare.

CANTICLE OF ZECHARIAH

Ant. The Lord said: † Do not think that I have come to abolish the law *and* the prophets; * I have come not to abolish but to *ful*fill them.

INTERCESSIONS (VI F)

Blessèd be God, the giver of salvation, who decreed that mankind should become a new creation in himself, when all would *be* made new. * With great confidence let *us* ask him:
Lord, renew us in your *Spirit.*
Lord, you promised a new heaven and a new earth; renew us daily *through* your Spirit,
— that we may enjoy your presence for ever in the heaven*ly* Jerusalem.
Help us to work with you to make this world alive *with* your Spirit,
— and to build on earth a city of justice, *love* and peace.
Free us from all negli*gence* and sloth,
— and give us joy in your *gifts* of grace.
Deliver *us* from evil,
— and from slavery to the senses, which blinds *us* to goodness.

Our Father . . .

Prayer

Lord,
during this lenten season
nourish us with your word of life
and make us one in love and prayer.
Grant this through our Lord Jesus Christ, your Son,
who lives and reigns with you and the Holy Spirit,
one God, for ever and ever.

Evening Prayer

READING Philippians 2:12b-15a

Work with anxious concern to achieve your salvation. It is God who, in his good will toward you, begets in you any measure of desire or achievement. In everything you do, act without grumbling or arguing; prove yourselves innocent and straightforward, children of God without reproach.

RESPONSORY (VI F)

To *you*, O Lord,* I make my prayer *for* mercy.
— To *you*, O Lord,* I make my prayer *for* mercy.
Heal my soul, for I have *sinned* against you.
— I make my prayer *for* mercy.
Glory to the Father, and *to* the Son, * and to the Ho*ly* Spirit.
— To *you*, O Lord,* I make my prayer *for* mercy.

CANTICLE OF MARY

Ant. The one who obeys God's law and teaches o*thers* to do so * will be great in the kingdom *of* heaven.

INTERCESSIONS (VI F)

Blessèd be almighty God, who watches over us as a Father; he knows all our needs but wants us to seek *first* his kingdom. * Let us cry out to him as *his* people:
May your kingdom come, that justice may *reign.*
Father of all holiness, you gave us Christ as the shepherd of our souls; stay with your shepherds and the flock entrusted to them, do not leave this flock without the loving care *of* its shepherd,
— do not leave your shepherds without an obedient flock to *fo*llow them.
Teach Christians to help the weak with *lov*ing care,
— and in serving them to *serve* your Son.
Gather into your Church those who do not *yet* believe,
— and help them to build it up by good deeds done for *love* of you.

Help us to turn to you *for* forgiveness,
— and, as you forgive us, reconcile us also *with* your Church.
May the dead pass from this world to e*ter*nal life,
— to be with *you* for ever.

Our Father . . .

Prayer

Lord,
during this lenten season
nourish us with your word of life
and make us one in love and prayer.
Grant this through our Lord Jesus Christ, your Son,
who lives and reigns with you and the Holy Spirit,
one God, for ever and ever.

THURSDAY

Morning Prayer

READING   See 1 Kings 8:51-53a

We are your people and your inheritance. Thus may your eyes be open to the petition of your servant and to the petition of your people Israel. Hear us whenever we call upon you, because you have set us apart among all the peoples of the earth of your inheritance.

RESPONSORY (VI F)

God himself will *set* me free, * from the hun*ter's* snare.
— God himself will *set* me free, * from the hun*ter's* snare.
From those who would trap me with *ly*ing words
— and from the hun*ter's* snare.
Glory to the Father, and *to* the Son, * and to the Ho*ly* Spirit.
— God himself will *set* me free, * from the hun*ter's* snare.

CANTICLE OF ZECHARIAH

Ant.   If it is by the power of God that I cast our devils, *says* the Lord, *
                then the kingdom of God has come to you *al*ready.

INTERCESSIONS (VI F)

Christ our Lord came among us as the light of the world, that we might walk in his light, and not in the dark*ness* of death. * Let us praise him and cry *out* to him:
Let your word be a lamp to *guide us.*

God of mercy, help us today to grow *in* your likeness,
— that we who sinned in Adam may rise a*gain* in Christ.
Let your word be a *lamp* to guide us,
— that we may live the truth and grow always *in* your love.
Teach us to be faithful in seeking the common good *for* your sake,
— that your light may shine on the whole human family by means *of* your Church.
Touch our hearts to seek your friendship *more* and more,
— and to make amends for our sins against your wis*dom* and goodness.

Our Father . . .

Prayer

Father,
help us to be ready to celebrate the great paschal mystery.
Make our love grow each day
as we approach the feast of our salvation.
We ask this through our Lord Jesus Christ, your Son,
who lives and reigns with you and the Holy Spirit,
one God, for ever and ever.

Evening Prayer

READING   James 4:7-8, 10
Submit to God; resist the devil and he will take flight. Draw close to God, and he will draw close to you. Cleanse your hands, you sinners; purify your hearts, you backsliders. Be humbled in the sight of the Lord and he will raise you on high.

RESPONSORY (VI F)
To *you*, O Lord,* I make my prayer *for* mercy.
— To *you*, O Lord,* I make my prayer *for* mercy.
Heal my soul, for I have *sinned* against you.
— I make my prayer *for* mercy.
Glory to the Father, and *to* the Son, * and to the Ho*ly* Spirit.
— To *you*, O Lord,* I make my prayer *for* mercy.

CANTICLE OF MARY
Ant.   A woman in the crowd called out: † How happy your mo*ther* must be, * she bore you and fed you at *her* breast. But *Jesus* answered: * Happier still those who hear the word of God and live *by* it.

INTERCESSIONS (VI F)

Christ the Lord gave us a new commandment, of love *for* each other. * Let us
    pray to him:
Lord, build up your people in *love.*
Good Master, teach us to love you *in* our neighbor,
— and in serving them *to* serve you.
On the cross you asked pardon for your *ex*ecutioners,
— give us strength to love our enemies and pray for *those* who persecute us.
Through the mystery of your body and blood, deepen our love, our perseverance
    and our trust,
— strengthen the weak, console the sorrowful, and give hope *to* the dying.
Light of the world, you gave light to the man born blind when he had washed in
    the *pool* of Siloam,
— enlighten catechumens through the water of baptism and the *word* of life.
Give to the dead the perfect joy of your e*ter*nal love,
— and number us also among your *cho*sen ones.

Our Father . . .

Prayer

Father,
help us to be ready to celebrate the great paschal mystery.
Make our love grow each day
as we approach the feast of our salvation.
We ask this through our Lord Jesus Christ, your Son,
who lives and reigns with you and the Holy Spirit,
one God, for ever and ever.

FRIDAY

Morning Prayer

READING   Isaiah 53:11b-12

Through his suffering, my servant shall justify many,
    and their guilt he shall bear.
Therefore I will give him his portion among the great,
    and he shall divide the spoils with the mighty,
Because he surrendered himself to death
    and was counted among the wicked;
And he shall take away the sins of many
    and win pardon for their offenses.

RESPONSORY (VI F)

God himself will *set* me free, * from the hunt*er's* snare.
— God himself will *set* me free, * from the hunt*er's* snare.
From those who would trap me with *ly*ing words
— and from the hunt*er's* snare.
Glory to the Father, and *to* the Son, * and to the Ho*ly* Spirit.
— God himself will *set* me free, * from the hunt*er's* snare.

CANTICLE OF ZECHARIAH

Ant.   Teacher, what is the greatest commandment *in* the law? * Jesus
              said to him: † You shall love the Lord your God with your *whole*
              heart.

INTERCESSIONS (VI F)

Thanks be to Christ the Lord, who brought us life by his death *on* the cross. *
    With our whole heart *let* us ask him:
By your death raise us to *life.*
Teacher and Savior, you have shown us your fidelity and made us a new creation
    by your passion,
— keep us from falling again *in*to sin.
Help us to deny our*selves* today,
— and not deny *those* in need.
May we receive this day of penance *as* your gift,
— and give it back to you through *works* of mercy.
Master our re*bel*lious hearts,
— and teach us *gen*erosity.

Our Father . . .

Prayer

Merciful Father,
fill our hearts with your love
and keep us faithful to the gospel of Christ.
Give us the grace to rise above our human weakness.
who lives and reigns with you and the Holy Spirit,
one God, for ever and ever.

Evening Prayer

READING   James 5:16, 19-20

Declare your sins to one another, and pray for one another, that you may find
healing. The fervent petition of a holy man is powerful indeed. My brothers,
the case may arise among you of someone straying from the truth, and of

another bringing him back. Remember this: the person who brings a sinner back from his way will save his soul from death and cancel a multitude of sins.

RESPONSORY (VI F)
To *you*, O Lord,* I make my prayer *for* mercy.
— To *you*, O Lord,* I make my prayer *for* mercy.
Heal my soul, for I have *sinned* against you.
— I make my prayer *for* mercy.
Glory to the Father, and *to* the Son, * and to the Ho*ly* Spirit.
— To *you*, O Lord,* I make my prayer *for* mercy.

CANTICLE OF MARY
Ant.   It is far more important to love your neighbor *as* yourself * than
                    to of*fer* sacrifice.

INTERCESSIONS (VI F)
The Lord Jesus sanctified his people *with* his blood. * Let us cry *out* to him:
Lord, have mercy on your *people.*
Loving Redeemer, through your passion teach us self-denial, strengthen us
    against evil and adversity, and in*crease* our hope,
— and so make us ready to celebrate your *res*urrection.
Grant that Christians, as your prophets, may make you known in *every* place,
— and bear witness to you with living faith and *hope* and love.
Give your strength to all *in* distress,
— and help us to raise them up through our lov*ing* concern.
Teach the faithful to see your passion *in* their sufferings,
— and to show to others your pow*er* to save.
Author of life, remember those who have passed *from* this world,
— grant them the glory of your *ris*en life.

Our Father . . .

Prayer
Merciful Father,
fill our hearts with your love
and keep us faithful to the gospel of Christ.
Give us the grace to rise above our human weakness.
who lives and reigns with you and the Holy Spirit,
one God, for ever and ever.

SATURDAY

Morning Prayer

Wash yourselves clean!
Put away your misdeeds from before my eyes;
    cease doing evil; learn to do good.
Make justice your aim; redress the wronged,
    hear the orphan's plea, defend the widow.
Come now, let us set things right,
    says the Lord:
Though your sins be like scarlet,
    they may become white as snow;
Though they be crimson red,
    they may become white as wool.

RESPONSORY (VI F)
God himself will *set* me free, * from the hun*ter's* snare.
— God himself will *set* me free, * from the hun*ter's* snare.
From those who would trap me with *ly*ing words
— and from the hun*ter's* snare.
Glory to the Father, and *to* the Son, * and to the Ho*ly* Spirit.
— God himself will *set* me free, * from the hun*ter's* snare.

CANTICLE OF ZECHARIAH
Ant.   The tax collector stood *far* away * and would not even raise his
            eyes *to* heaven. He struck his *breast* and prayed: * God, have
            mercy on me, *a* sinner.

INTERCESSIONS (VI F)
To make us his new creation, Christ the Lord gave us the waters of rebirth and
    spread the table of his body *and* his word. * Let us call upon *him* and say:
Lord, renew us in your *grace.*
Jesus, meek and humble of heart, clothe us with compassion, kindness *and*
    humility,
— make us want to be pa*tient* with everyone.
Teach us to be true neighbors to all in trouble *and* distress,
— and so imitate you, the *Good* Samaritan.
May the Blessèd Virgin, your Mother, pray for all those vowed to a life *of*
    virginity,
— that they may deepen their dedication to you and *to* the Church.

Grant us the gift *of* your mercy,
— forgive our sins and re*mit* their punishment.

Our Father ...

Prayer

Lord,
make this lenten observance
of the suffering, death and resurrection of Christ
bring us to the full joy of Easter.
We ask this through our Lord Jesus Christ, your Son,
who lives and reigns with you and the Holy Spirit,
one God, for ever and ever.

FOURTH SUNDAY OF LENT

Evening Prayer I

READING   2 Corinthians 6:1-4a

We beg you not to receive the grace of God in vain. For he says, "In an
acceptable time I have heard you; on a day of salvation I have helped you."
Now is the acceptable time! Now is the day of salvation! We avoid giving
anyone offense, so that our ministry may not be blamed. On the contrary, in
all that we do we strive to present ourselves as ministers of God.

RESPONSORY (VI F)

Listen to us, O Lord, *and* have mercy, * for we have sinned *a*gainst you.
— Listen to us, O Lord, *and* have mercy, * for we have sinned *a*gainst you.
Christ Jesus, hear our hum*ble* petitions,
— for we have sinned *a*gainst you.
Glory to the Father, and *to* the Son, * and to the Ho*ly* Spirit.
— Listen to us, O Lord, *and* have mercy, * for we have sinned *a*gainst you.

CANTICLE OF MARY

Ant.   God loved the world so much that he gave his *only* Son * to save
                        all who have faith in him † and to give them eter*nal* life.

INTERCESSIONS (VI F)

Let us give glory to God, who has concern *for* us all. * Let us call upon *him* and
      say:
*Lord, save the people you have re*deemed.
Giver of all gifts and source of all truth, give the fullness of your blessing to the
      col*lege* of bishops,
— and keep all those entrusted to their care faithful to the teaching of *the*
      apostles.
Pour your love into the hearts of all who share the one *bread* of life,
— that they may grow in unity in the body *of* your Son.
Help us to strip off our *sin*ful selves,
— and to be clothed with Christ, your Son, *the* new Adam.
Grant that all may do penance and *find* forgiveness,
— and so share in the fruits of Christ's re*deem*ing death.
May those who have died in your peace give you everlasting glo*ry* in heaven,
— where we, too, hope to praise *you* for ever.

Our Father . . .

Prayer

Father of peace,
we are joyful in your Word,
your Son Jesus Christ,
who reconciles us to you.
Let us hasten toward Easter
with the eagerness of faith and love.
We ask this through our Lord Jesus Christ, your Son,
who lives and reigns with you and the Holy Spirit,
one God, for ever and ever.

Morning Prayer

READING   See Nehemiah 8:9, 10
   Today is holy to the Lord your God. Do not be sad, and do not weep; for
   today is holy to our Lord. Do not be saddened this day, for rejoicing in the
   Lord must be your strength!

RESPONSORY (VI F)
Christ, Son of the *living* God, * have mercy *on* us.
— Christ, Son of the *living* God, * have mercy *on* us.
You were wounded for *our* offenses,
— have mercy *on* us.
Glory to the Father, and *to* the Son, * and to the Ho*ly* Spirit.
— Christ, Son of the *living* God, * have mercy *on* us.

CANTICLE OF ZECHARIAH
Ant.   It was unheard of for anyone † to open the eyes of a *man* born
                    blind * until the coming of Christ, the Son *of* God.

INTERCESSIONS (VI F)
Let us give glory to God, whose kindness *knows* no limit. * Through Jesus Christ,
   who lives for ever to intercede for us, *let* us pray:
Kindle in our hearts the fire of your *love.*
God of mercy, let today be a day rich *in* good works,
— a day of generosity to *all* we meet.
From the waters of the flood you saved Noah *through* the ark,
— from the waters of baptism raise up to new life those un*der* instruction.
May we live not *by* bread only,
— but by every word falling *from* your lips.
Help us to do away with *all* dissension,
— so that we may rejoice in your gifts of *peace* and love.

Our Father . . .

Prayer

Father of peace,
we are joyful in your Word,
your Son Jesus Christ,
who reconciles us to you.
Let us hasten toward Easter
with the eagerness of faith and love.
We ask this through our Lord Jesus Christ, your Son,
who lives and reigns with you and the Holy Spirit,
one God, for ever and ever.

Evening Prayer II

READING   1 Corinthians 9:24-25

While all the runners in the stadium take part in the race, the award goes to
one man. In that case, run so as to win! Athletes deny themselves all sorts of
things. They do this to win a crown of leaves that withers, but we a crown
that is imperishable.

RESPONSORY (VI F)

Listen to us, O Lord, *and* have mercy, * for we have sinned *a*gainst you.
— Listen to us, O Lord, *and* have mercy, * for we have sinned *a*gainst you.
Christ Jesus, hear our hum*ble* petitions,
— for we have sinned *a*gainst you.
Glory to the Father, and *to* the Son, * and to the Ho*ly* Spirit.
— Listen to us, O Lord, *and* have mercy, * for we have sinned *a*gainst you.

CANTICLE OF MARY

Ant.   My son, you have been with me *all* the time * and everything I
                 have *is* yours.
                 But we had to feast and rejoice, † because your brother was dead
                 and has come to *life* again; * he was lost to us and now has *been*
                 found.

INTERCESSIONS (VI F)

Let us give thanks continually to Christ, our teacher and our head, who came to
    serve and to do *good* to all. * In humility and confidence *let* us ask him:
Come, Lord, *to visit* your *family.*
Lord, be present to the bishops and priests of your Church, who share your role as
    head and shepherd,
— may they lead your people to the Father un*der* your guidance.

May your angel be with *all* who travel,
— to keep them safe in *soul* and body.
Teach us to serve the *needs* of others,
— and to be like you, who came to serve, not *to* be served.
Grant that in the human family, brother may al*ways* help brother,
— so that, with your assistance, it may be a city com*pact* and strong.
Have mercy on *all* the dead,
— bring them to the vision *of* your glory.

Our Father . . .

Prayer

Father of peace,
we are joyful in your Word,
your Son Jesus Christ,
who reconciles us to you.
Let us hasten toward Easter
with the eagerness of faith and love.
We ask this through our Lord Jesus Christ, your Son,
who lives and reigns with you and the Holy Spirit,
one God, for ever and ever.

MONDAY

Morning Prayer

READING   Exodus 19:4-6a
You have seen for yourselves how I bore you up on eagle wings and brought
you here to myself. Therefore, if you harken to my voice and keep my covenant, you shall be my special possession, dearer to me than all other people,
though all the earth is mine. You shall be to me a kingdom of priests, a holy
nation.

RESPONSORY (VI F)
God himself will *set* me free, * from the hunt*er's* snare.
— God himself will *set* me free, * from the hunt*er's* snare.
From those who would trap me with *lying* words
— and from the hunt*er's* snare.
Glory to the Father, and *to* the Son, * and to the Ho*ly* Spirit.
— God himself will *set* me free, * from the hunt*er's* snare.

CANTICLE OF ZECHARIAH
Ant.   A royal official, hearing that Jesus had *come* to Galilee, * begged
him to heal his son who lay ill in *Ca*pernaum.

INTERCESSIONS (VI F)
Blessèd be God the Father for his gift of this sacri*fice* of praise. * In the spirit of
this Lenten season, *let* us pray:
Instruct us, Lord, in the ways of your kingdom.
God of power and mercy, give us the spirit of prayer *and* repentance,
— with burning love for you and for *all* mankind.
Help us to work with you in making all things *new* in Christ,
— and in spreading justice and peace through*out* the world.
Teach us the meaning and value *of* creation,
— so that we may join its voice to ours as we *sing* your praise.
Forgive us for failing to see Christ in the poor, the distressed *and* the troublesome,
— and for our failure to reverence your Son *in* their persons.

Our Father . . .

Prayer
Father, creator,
you give the world new life by your scraments.
May we, your Church, grow in your life
and continue to receive your help on earth.
Grant this through our Lord Jesus Christ, your Son,
who lives and reigns with you and the Holy Spirit,
one God, for ever and ever.

Evening Prayer

READING   Romans 12:1-2
Brothers, I beg you through the mercy of God to offer your bodies as a living
sacrifice holy and acceptable to God, your spiritual worship. Do not conform
yourselves to this age but be transformed by the renewal of your mind, so that
you may judge what is God's will, what is good, pleasing and perfect.

RESPONSORY (VI F)
To *you*, O Lord,* I make my prayer *for* mercy.
— To *you*, O Lord,* I make my prayer *for* mercy.
Heal my soul, for I have *sinned* against you.
— I make my prayer *for* mercy.
Glory to the Father, and *to* the Son, * and to the Ho*ly* Spirit.
— To *you*, O Lord,* I make my prayer *for* mercy.

CANTICLE OF MARY

Ant.   The father realized that it was at that very hour when Jesus had
                  told him: † Your *son* will live; * and he and his household became
                  *be*lievers.

INTERCESSIONS (VI F)

Glory to God the Father, who has promised through his Son to grant what is
    asked by those who *pray* together. * With confidence in this promise, *let* us pray:
Lord, look with favor on your *people.*

Lord, you gave the Law to Moses on Mount Sinai, and brought it to perfection in
    your Anointed One,
— may all recognize the Law written in their hearts, and keep it faithfully *as* a
    covenant.
Give those in authority a true concern for their brothers and sisters entrusted *to*
    their care,
— and inspire the hearts of the people to sup*port* their leaders.
Strengthen with your Spirit the minds and *hearts* of missionaries,
— and raise up a great company to help them from *every* nation.
Give your grace to children, that they may grow *in* your favor,
— and to young people, that they may reach their full stature by loving you and
    keeping *your* commandments.
Remember our brothers and sisters, who have fallen asleep *in* your peace,
— bring them at last to e*ter*nal life.

Our Father ...

Prayer

Father, creator,
you give the world new life by your scraments.
May we, your Church, grow in your life
and continue to receive your help on earth.
Grant this through our Lord Jesus Christ, your Son,
who lives and reigns with you and the Holy Spirit,
one God, for ever and ever.

TUESDAY

Morning Prayer

READING   Joel 2:12-13

    Return to me with your whole heart,
        with fasting, and weeping, and mourning;
    Rend your hearts, not your garments,
        and return to the Lord, your God.
    For gracious and merciful is he,
        slow to anger, rich in kindness,
        and relenting in punishment.

RESPONSORY (VI F)

God himself will *set* me free, * from the hunt*er's* snare.
— God himself will *set* me free, * from the hunt*er's* snare.
From those who would trap me with *ly*ing words
— and from the hunt*er's* snare.
Glory to the Father, and *to* the Son, * and to the Ho*ly* Spirit.
— God himself will *set* me free, * from the hunt*er's* snare.

CANTICLE OF ZECHARIAH

Ant.   The man who cured me told me to pick *up* my sleeping mat * and
          go *in* peace.

INTERCESSIONS (VI F)

God the Father has given us his only Son, the Word made man, to be our food
    and our life. * Let us thank *him* and pray:
May the word of Christ dwell among us in all its *richness.*
Help us in this Lenten season to listen more frequently *to* your word,
— that we may celebrate the solemnity of Easter with greater love for Christ, our
    *pas*chal sacrifice.
May your Holy Spirit *be* our teacher,
— that we may encourage those in doubt and error to follow what is *true* and
    good.
Enable us to enter more deeply into the mystery of *your* Anointed One,
— that our lives may reveal him *more* effectively.
Purify and renew your Church in this time *of* salvation,
— that it may give an ever greater wit*ness* to you.

Our Father . . .

Prayer

Father,
may our lenten observance
prepare us to embrace the paschal mystery
and to proclaim your salvation with joyful praise.
We ask this through our Lord Jesus Christ, your Son,
who lives and reigns with you and the Holy Spirit,
one God, for ever and ever.

Evening Prayer

READING   James 2:14, 17, 18b

My brothers, what good it is to profess faith without practicing it? Such faith has no power to save one, has it? So it is with the faith that does nothing in practice. It is thoroughly lifeless. Show me faith without works, and I will show you the faith that underlies my works!

RESPONSORY (VI F)

To *you*, O Lord,* I make my prayer *for* mercy.
— To *you*, O Lord,* I make my prayer *for* mercy.
Heal my soul, for I have *sinned* against you.
— I make my prayer *for* mercy.
Glory to the Father, and *to* the Son, * and to the Ho*ly* Spirit.
— To *you*, O Lord,* I make my prayer *for* mercy.

CANTICLE OF MARY

Ant.   Now that you are well again, do not sin *any* more, * or something worse may happen *to* you.

INTERCESSIONS (VI F)

Let us praise the Lord Jesus, who, lifted high on the cross, drew all things *to* himself. * With loving hearts *let* us pray:
Draw all things to yourself, O Lord.
Lord, may the mystery of your cross shine on *all* mankind,
— that all may see you as the way, the truth *and* the life.
May all who thirst for you, the *li*ving water,
— drink their *fill* for ever.
Inspire all teach*ers* and artists,
— to prepare mankind *for* your kingdom.
Guide all estranged from you by *sin* or scandal,
— that they may come back to you, and remain always *in* your love.
Welcome all our deceased brothers and sisters to your *home* in heaven,
— to share the joy of the blessèd Virgin Mary and *all* the saints.

Our Father . . .

Prayer

Father,
may our lenten observance
prepare us to embrace the paschal mystery
and to proclaim your salvation with joyful praise.
We ask this through our Lord Jesus Christ, your Son,
who lives and reigns with you and the Holy Spirit,
one God, for ever and ever.

WEDNESDAY

Morning Prayer

READING					Deuteronomy 7:6, 8-9

The Lord, your God, has chosen you from all the nations on the face of the
earth to be a people peculiarly his own. It was because the Lord loved you
and because of his fidelity to the oath he had sworn to your fathers, that he
brought you out with his strong hand from the place of slavery, and ransomed
you from the hand of Pharaoh, king of Egypt. Understand, then, that the
Lord, your God, is God indeed, the faithful God who keeps his merciful
covenant to the thousandth generation toward those who love him and keep
his commandments.

RESPONSORY (VI F)

God himself will *set* me free, * from the hun*ter's* snare.
— God himself will *set* me free, * from the hun*ter's* snare.
From those who would trap me with *ly*ing words
— and from the hun*ter's* snare.
Glory to the Father, and *to* the Son, * and to the Ho*ly* Spirit.
— God himself will *set* me free, * from the hun*ter's* snare.

CANTICLE OF ZECHARIAH

Ant.			Whoever hears my words, *says* the Lord, * and believes in him
			who sent me, has eter*nal* life.

INTERCESSIONS (VI F)

Let us give thanks to God our Father; through the power of the Spirit he purifies
	our hearts and strengthens *us* in love. * Let us *hum*bly ask him:
*Lord, give us your Ho*ly* Spirit.*
Help us to receive good things from your bounty with a deep *sense* of gratitude,
— and to accept with patience the evil that *comes* to us.

Teach us to be loving not only in great and excep*tion*al moments,
— but above all in the ordinary events of *dai*ly life.
May we abstain from what we do not *real*ly need,
— and help our brothers and sisters *in* distress.
May we bear the wounds *of* your Son,
— for through his body he *gave* us life.

Our Father . . .

Prayer

Lord,
you reward virtue
and forgive the repentant sinner.
Grant us your forgiveness
as we come before you confessing our guilt.
We ask this through our Lord Jesus Christ, your Son,
who lives and reigns with you and the Holy Spirit,
one God, for ever and ever.

Evening Prayer

READING   Philippians 2:12b-15a

Work with anxious concern to achieve your salvation. It is God who, in his good will toward you, begets in you any measure of desire or achievement. In everything you do, act without grumbling or arguing; prove yourselves innocent and straightforward, children of God without reproach.

RESPONSORY (VI F)
To *you*, O Lord,* I make my prayer *for* mercy.
— To *you*, O Lord,* I make my prayer *for* mercy.
Heal my soul, for I have *sinned* against you.
— I make my prayer *for* mercy.
Glory to the Father, and *to* the Son, * and to the Ho*ly* Spirit.
— To *you*, O Lord,* I make my prayer *for* mercy.

CANTICLE OF MARY
Ant.   By myself, says the Lord, I *can* do nothing. * I judge as I am told to judge, and my sentence *is* just.

INTERCESSIONS (VI F)

All glory and honor to God, for in the blood of Christ he has ratified a new and
    everlasting covenant with his people, and renews it in the sacrament *of* the altar.
      * Let us lift our voi*ces* in prayer:

*Bless your peo*ple, *Lord.*

Lord, guide the minds and hearts of peoples and all in *pub*lic office,
— may they always seek the *com*mon good.

Renew the spirit of dedication in those who have left all to *fo*llow Christ,
— may they give clear witness to the holiness *of* the Church.

You have made all men and women *in* your image,
— may they always uphold *hu*man dignity.

Lead back to your friendship and truth all who have *gone* astray,
— teach us *how* to help them.

Grant that the dead may enter in*to* your glory,
— to praise *you* for ever.

Our Father . . .

Prayer

    Lord,
    you reward virtue
    and forgive the repentant sinner.
    Grant us your forgiveness
    as we come before you confessing our guilt.
    We ask this through our Lord Jesus Christ, your Son,
    who lives and reigns with you and the Holy Spirit,
    one God, for ever and ever.

THURSDAY

Morning Prayer

READING   See 1 Kings 8:51-53a

    We are your people, O Lord, and your inheritance. Thus may your eyes be
    open to the petition of your servant and to the petition of your people Israel.
    Hear us whenever we call upon you, because you have set us apart among all
    the peoples of the earth of your inheritance.

RESPONSORY (VI F)

God himself will *set* me free, * from the hunt*er's* snare.
— God himself will *set* me free, * from the hunt*er's* snare.
From those who would trap me with *ly*ing words
— and from the hunt*er's* snare.

Glory to the Father, and *to* the Son, * and to the Ho*ly* Spirit.
— God himself will *set* me free, * from the hun*ter's* snare.

CANTICLE OF ZECHARIAH

Ant.   John bore testimony to the truth, † and although I have no need
of human testimony, *says* the Lord, * I remind you of this for your
own *sal*vation.

INTERCESSIONS (VI F)

God has revealed him*self* in Christ. * Let us praise his goodness, and ask him *from*
 our hearts:
Remember us, Lord, for we are your *children.*
Teach us to enter more deeply into the mystery *of* the Church,
— that it may be more effective for ourselves and for the world as the sacrament
 of salvation.
Lover of mankind, inspire us to work for *hu*man progress,
— seeking to spread your kingdom in *all* we do.
May our hearts *thirst* for Christ,
— the fountain of *liv*ing water.
Forgive *us* our sins,
— and direct our steps into the ways of justice *and* sincerity.

Our Father . . .

Prayer

Merciful Father,
may the penance of our lenten observance
make us your obedient people.
May the love within us be seen in what we do
and lead us to the joy of Easter.
Grant this through our Lord Jesus Christ, your Son,
who lives and reigns with you and the Holy Spirit,
one God, for ever and ever.

Evening Prayer

READING   James 4:7-8, 10

Submit to God; resist the devil and he will take flight. Draw close to God,
and he will draw close to you. Cleanse your hands, you sinners; purify your
hearts, you backsliders. Be humbled in the sight of the Lord and he will raise
you on high.

RESPONSORY (VI F)

To *you*, O Lord,* I make my prayer *for* mercy.
— To *you*, O Lord,* I make my prayer *for* mercy.
Heal my soul, for I have *sinned* against you.
— I make my prayer *for* mercy.
Glory to the Father, and *to* the Son, * and to the Ho*ly* Spirit.
— To *you*, O Lord,* I make my prayer *for* mercy.

CANTICLE OF MARY

Ant.   The works that I do speak on my behalf, *says* the Lord. * They
                        prove that the Father *has* sent me.

INTERCESSIONS (VI F)

In his mercy, God sends the Holy Spirit to shine on us, so that our lives may radiate
    holi*ness* and faith. * Let us raise our voices in *prayer* and say:
*Lord, give life to your people, who Christ has re*deemed.*
Lord, source of all holiness, draw bishops, priests and deacons closer to Christ
    through the eucha*ris*tic mystery,
— may they grow daily in the grace of their *ordi*nation.
Teach Christ's faithful people to be devout and attentive at the table of his word
    and *of* his body,
— so that they may bring into their daily lives the grace they receive through *faith*
    and sacrament.
Grant, Lord, that we may see in each person the dignity of one redeemed by *your*
    Son's blood,
— so that we may respect the freedom and the con*science* of all.
Teach us to restrain our greed for *earth*ly goods,
— and to have concern for the *needs* of others.
Be merciful to your faithful people whom you have called to your*self* today,
— grant them the gift of e*ter*nal happiness.

Our Father . . .

Prayer

Merciful Father,
may the penance of our lenten observance
make us your obedient people.
May the love within us be seen in what we do
and lead us to the joy of Easter.
Grant this through our Lord Jesus Christ, your Son,
who lives and reigns with you and the Holy Spirit,
one God, for ever and ever.

FRIDAY

Morning Prayer

Through his suffering, my servant shall justify many,
    and their guilt he shall bear.
Therefore I will give him his portion among the great,
    and he shall divide the spoils with the mighty,
Because he surrendered himself to death
    and was counted among the wicked;
And he shall take away the sins of many
    and win pardon for their offenses.

RESPONSORY (VI F)

God himself will *set* me free, * from the hun*ter's* snare.
— God himself will *set* me free, * from the hun*ter's* snare.
From those who would trap me with *ly*ing words
— and from the hun*ter's* snare.
Glory to the Father, and *to* the Son, * and to the Ho*ly* Spirit.
— God himself will *set* me free, * from the hun*ter's* snare.

CANTICLE OF ZECHARIAH

Ant.   Indeed you know me, *says* the Lord, * and you know where *I*
                  come from.
                  Yet I have not come of my *own* accord; * it was my Father *who*
                  sent me.

INTERCESSIONS (VI F)

Let us pray to *Christ* our Savior, * who redeemed us by his death and *res*urrection:
Lord, have mercy on *us.*
You went up to Jerusalem to suffer and so enter in*to* your glory,
— bring your Church to the Passover *feast* of heaven.
You were lifted high on the cross and pierced by the *sol*dier's lance,
— *heal* our wounds.
You made the cross the *tree* of life,
— give its fruit to those re*born* in baptism.
On the cross you forgave the re*pent*ant thief,
— forgive *us* our sins.

Our Father . . .

Prayer

Father, our source of life,
you know our weakness.
May we reach out with joy to grasp your hand
and walk more readily in your ways.
We ask this through our Lord Jesus Christ, your Son,
who lives and reigns with you and the Holy Spirit,
one God, for ever and ever.

Evening Prayer

READING   James 5:16, 19-20
Declare your sins to one another, and pray for one another, that you may find
healing. The fervent petition of a holy man is powerful indeed. My brothers,
the case may arise among you of someone straying from the truth, and of
another bringing him back. Remember this: the person who brings a sinner
back from his way will save his soul from death and cancel a multitude of
sins.

RESPONSORY (VI F)
To *you*, O Lord,* I make my prayer *for* mercy.
— To *you*, O Lord,* I make my prayer *for* mercy.
Heal my soul, for I have *sinned* against you.
— I make my prayer *for* mercy.
Glory to the Father, and *to* the Son, * and to the Ho*ly* Spirit.
— To *you*, O Lord,* I make my prayer *for* mercy.

CANTICLE OF MARY
Ant.   No one could lay a *hand* on Jesus, * because his time had not *yet*
come.

INTERCESSIONS (VI F)
The Savior of mankind by dying destroyed death and by rising again *re*stored life.
    * Let us *hum*bly ask him:
Sanctify your people, redeemed by your *blood.*
Redeemer of the world, give us a greater share of your passion through a deeper
    spirit *of* repentance,
— so that we may share the glory of your *re*surrection.
May your Mother, comfort of the afflic*ted*, protect us,
— may we console others as you *con*sole us.
In their trials enable your faithful people to share *in* your passion,
— and so reveal in their lives your *saving* power.

You humbled yourself by being obedient even to accepting death, death *on* a cross,
— give all who serve you the gifts of obedience and pa*tient* endurance.
Transform the bodies of the dead to be like your *own* in glory,
— and bring us at last in*to* their fellowship.

Our Father . . .

Prayer

Father, our source of life,
you know our weakness.
May we reach out with joy to grasp your hand
and walk more readily in your ways.
We ask this through our Lord Jesus Christ, your Son,
who lives and reigns with you and the Holy Spirit,
one God, for ever and ever.

SATURDAY

Morning Prayer

READING   Isaiah 1:16-18

     Wash yourselves clean!
Put away your misdeeds from before my eyes;
    cease doing evil; learn to do good.
Make justice your aim; redress the wronged,
    hear the orphan's plea, defend the widow.
Come now, let us set things right,
    says the Lord:
Though your sins be like scarlet,
    they may become white as snow;
Though they be crimson red,
    they may become white as wool.

RESPONSORY (VI F)
God himself will *set* me free, * from the hun*ter's* snare.
— God himself will *set* me free, * from the hun*ter's* snare.
From those who would trap me with *ly*ing words
— and from the hun*ter's* snare.
Glory to the Father, and *to* the Son, * and to the Ho*ly* Spirit.
— God himself will *set* me free, * from the hun*ter's* snare.

CANTICLE OF ZECHARIAH
Ant.   Nev*er* before * has anyone spoken like *this* man.

INTERCESSIONS (VI F)

Let us always and everywhere give thanks to *Christ* our Savior, * and ask *him* will
  confidence:
Lord, help us with your *grace.*

May we keep our *bod*ies pure,
— as temples of the *Ho*ly Spirit.

May we offer ourselves this morning to the ser*vice* of others,
— and do your will in all things through*out* the day.

Teach us to seek the bread of ever*last*ing life,
— the bread that *is* your gift.

May your Mother, the refuge of sinners, *pray* for us,
— and gain for us your lov*ing* forgiveness.

Our Father . . .

Prayer

> Lord,
> guide us in your gentle mercy,
> for left to ourselves
> we cannot do your will.
> Grant this through our Lord Jesus Christ, your Son,
> who lives and reigns with you and the Holy Spirit,
> one God, for ever and ever.

FIFTH SUNDAY OF LENT

PSALTER, WEEK I, 600.

Evening Prayer I

READING   1 Peter 1:18-21

Realize that you were delivered from the futile way of life your fathers handed on to you, not by any diminishable sum of silver or gold, but by Christ's blood beyond all price: the blood of a spotless, unblemished lamb chosen before the world's foundation and revealed for your sake in these last days. It is through him that you are believers in God, the God who raised him from the dead and gave him glory. You faith and hope, then, are centered in God.

RESPONSORY (VI F)

Listen to us, O Lord, *and* have mercy, * for we have sinned *a*gainst you.
— Listen to us, O Lord, *and* have mercy, * for we have sinned *a*gainst you.
Christ Jesus, hear our hum*ble* petitions,
— for we have sinned *a*gainst you.
Glory to the Father, and *to* the Son, * and to the Ho*ly* Spirit.
— Listen to us, O Lord, *and* have mercy, * for we have sinned *a*gainst you.

CANTICLE OF MARY

Ant.   Unless a grain of wheat falls into the ground and dies, † it remains only a *sing*le grain; * but if it dies, it produces a *rich* harvest.

INTERCESSIONS (VI F)

Let us give glory to Christ the Lord, who became our teacher, our example *and* our brother. * Let us pray *to* him, saying:
Lord, fill your people with your *life.*
Lord Jesus, you became like us in all things but sin; teach us how to share with others their *joy* and sorrow,
— that our love may grow deeper *every* day.
Help us to feed you in feed*ing* the hungry,
— and to give you drink in giving *drink* to the thirsty.
You raised Lazarus from the *sleep* of death,
— grant that those who have died the death of sin may rise again through faith *and* repentance.
Through the example of the Blessèd Virgin Mary *and* the saints,
— inspire many to follow you with greater zeal *and* perfection.
Let the dead rise *in* your glory,
— to enjoy your *love* for ever.

Our Father . . .

Prayer

Father,
help us to be like Christ your Son,
who loved the world and died for salvation.
Inspire us by his love,
guide us by his example,
who lives and reigns with you and the Holy Spirit,
one God, for ever and ever.

Morning Prayer

READING   Leviticus 23:4-7

These are the festivals of the Lord which you shall celebrate at their proper
time with a sacred assembly. The Passover of the Lord falls on the fourteenth
day of the first month, at the evening twilight. The fifteenth day of this
month is the Lord's feast of Unleavened Bread. For seven days you shall eat
unleavened bread. On the first of these days you shall hold a sacred assembly
and do no sort of work.

RESPONSORY (VI F)
Christ, Son of the *living* God, * have mercy *on* us.
— Christ, Son of the *living* God, * have mercy *on* us.
You were wounded for *our* offenses,
— have mercy *on* us.
Glory to the Father, and *to* the Son, * and to the Ho*ly* Spirit.
— Christ, Son of the *living* God, * have mercy *on* us.

CANTICLE OF ZECHARIAH
Ant.   Our friend Lazarus has fall*en* asleep; * let us go *and* wake him.

INTERCESSIONS (VI F)
Let us praise our loving Redeemer, who gained for us this sea*son* of grace, * and
    pray *to* him, saying:
Lord, create a new spirit in us.
Christ, our life, through baptism we were buried with you and rose to *life* with
    you,
— may we walk today in new*ness* of life.
Lord, you have brought blessings to *all* mankind,
— bring us to share your concern for the *good* of all.
May we work together to build up the *earth*ly city,
— with our eyes fixed on the city that *lasts* for ever.
Healer of body and soul, cure the sickness *of* our spirit,
— so that we may grow in holiness through your *con*stant care.

Our Father . . .

Prayer

Father,
help us to be like Christ your Son,
who loved the world and died for salvation.
Inspire us by his love,
guide us by his example,
who lives and reigns with you and the Holy Spirit,
one God, for ever and ever.

Evening Prayer II

READING   Acts 13:26-30

My brothers, it was to us that this message of salvation was sent forth. The
inhabitants of Jerusalem and their rulers failed to recognize him, and in
condemning him they fulfilled the words of the prophets which we read
sabbath after sabbath. Even though they found no charge against him which
deserved death, they begged Pilate to have him executed. Once they had
brought about all that had been written of him, they took him down from the
tree and laid him in a tomb. Yet God raised him from the dead.

RESPONSORY (VI F)

Listen to us, O Lord, *and* have mercy, * for we have sinned *a*gainst you.
— Listen to us, O Lord, *and* have mercy, * for we have sinned *a*gainst you.
Christ Jesus, hear our hum*ble* petitions,
— for we have sinned *a*gainst you.
Glory to the Father, and *to* the Son, * and to the Ho*ly* Spirit.
— Listen to us, O Lord, *and* have mercy, * for we have sinned *a*gainst you.

CANTICLE OF MARY

Ant.   When I am lifted up *from* the earth, * I will draw all people to
                  *my*self.

INTERCESSIONS (VI F)

All praise to God the Father who brought his chosen people to rebirth from
   imperishable seed through his e*ter*nal Word. * Let us ask him *as* his children:
Lord, be gracious to your *people.*
God of mercy, hear the prayers we offer for *all* your people,
— may they hunger for your word more than for bod*i*ly food.
Give us a sincere and active love for our own nation and for *all* mankind,
— may we work always to build a world of *peace* and goodness.

Look with love on all to be re*born* in baptism,
— that they may be living stones in your temple *of* the Spirit.
You moved Nineveh to repentance by the preach*ing* of Jonah,
— in your mercy touch the hearts of sinners by the preaching *of* your word.
May the dying go in hope to meet *Christ* their judge,
— may they rejoice for ever in the vision *of* your glory.

Our Father . . .

Prayer

Father,
help us to be like Christ your Son,
who loved the world and died for salvation.
Inspire us by his love,
guide us by his example,
who lives and reigns with you and the Holy Spirit,
one God, for ever and ever.

MONDAY

Morning Prayer

READING   Jeremiah 11:19-20
Yet I, like a trusting lamb led to slaughter, had not realized that they were
hatching plots against me: "Let us destroy the tree in its vigor; let us cut him
off from the land of the living, so that his name will be spoken no more."
But, you, O Lord of hosts, O just Judge,
searcher of mind and heart,
Let me witness the vengeance you take on them,
for to you I have entrusted my cause!

RESPONSORY (VI F)
God himself will *set* me free, * from the hun*ter's* snare.
— God himself will *set* me free, * from the hun*ter's* snare.
From those who would trap me with *ly*ing words
— and from the hun*ter's* snare.
Glory to the Father, and *to* the Son, * and to the Ho*ly* Spirit.
— God himself will *set* me free, * from the hun*ter's* snare.

CANTICLE OF ZECHARIAH
Ant.   Whoever follows me does not walk *in* the dark; * he will have the
               light *of* life.

INTERCESSIONS (VI F)

Praise to Jesus, our Savior; by his death he has opened for us the way *of* salvation.
* *Let* us ask him:
Lord, guide your people to walk in your *ways.*
God of mercy, you gave us new *life* through baptism,
— make us grow day by day *in* your likeness.
May our generosity today bring joy to *those* in need,
— in helping them may *we* find you.
Help us to do what is good, right and true *in* your sight,
— and to seek you always with undi*vid*ed hearts.
Forgive our sins against the unity *of* your family,
— make us one in heart *and* spirit.

Our Father . . .

Prayer

Father of love, source of all blessings,
help us to pass from our old life of sin
to the new life of grace.
Prepare us for the glory of your kingdom.
We ask this through our Lord Jesus Christ, your Son,
who lives and reigns with you and the Holy Spirit,
one God, for ever and ever.

Evening Prayer

READING Romans 5:8-9

It is precisely in this that God proves his love for us: that while we were still sinners, Christ died for us. Now that we have been justified by his blood, it is all the more certain that we shall be saved by him from God's wrath.

RESPONSORY (VI F)

To *you*, O Lord,* I make my prayer *for* mercy.
— To *you*, O Lord,* I make my prayer *for* mercy.
Heal my soul, for I have *sinned* against you.
— I make my prayer *for* mercy.
Glory to the Father, and *to* the Son, * and to the Ho*ly* Spirit.
— To *you*, O Lord,* I make my prayer *for* mercy.

CANTICLE OF MARY

Ant. I am my own testimony, *says* the Lord, * and my Father who sent me also testifies on my *be*half.

INTERCESSIONS (VI F)

Our Lord Jesus Christ has saved us *from* our sins. * As his people, let us call *out* to him:

Jesus, Son of David, have mercy on us.

Lord Christ, we pray for your holy Church; you gave yourself up to make it holy, cleansing it with water and the life-*giving* word,

— renew it constantly, and purify *it* by penance.

Good Master, show young people the way you have chosen for *each* of them,

— may they walk in it, and *find* fulfillment.

In your compassion you healed all forms of sickness; bring hope to the sick and *raise* them up,

— teach us to love and *care* for them.

Make us mindful of the dignity you gave *us* in baptism,

— may we live for you at *every* moment.

May the dead rise to glory *in* your peace,

— grant us with them a share *in* your kingdom.

Our Father . . .

Prayer

Father of love, source of all blessings,
help us to pass from our old life of sin
to the new life of grace.
Prepare us for the glory of your kingdom.
We ask this through our Lord Jesus Christ, your Son,
who lives and reigns with you and the Holy Spirit,
one God, for ever and ever.

TUESDAY

Morning Prayer

READING   Zechariah 12:10-11a

I will pour out on the house of David and on the inhabitants of Jerusalem a spirit of grace and petition; and they shall look on him whom they have thrust through, and they shall mourn for him as one mourns for an only son, that they shall grieve over him as one grieves over a first-born. On that day the mourning in Jerusalem shall be great.

RESPONSORY (VI F)

God himself will *set* me free, * from the hun*ter's* snare.

— God himself will *set* me free, * from the hun*ter's* snare.

From those who would trap me with *ly*ing words
— and from the hun*ter's* snare.
Glory to the Father, and *to* the Son, * and to the Ho*ly* Spirit.
— God himself will *set* me free, * from the hun*ter's* snare.

CANTICLE OF ZECHARIAH
Ant.   When you have lifted up the Son of Man, *says* the Lord, * you
                    will know that I *am* he.

INTERCESSIONS (VI F)
Praise to Christ, who has given us himself as the *bread* from heaven. * Let us pray
   to him saying:
Jesus, you feed and heal our souls; come to strengthen us.
Lord, feed us at the banquet *of* the eucharist,
— with all the gifts of your *pas*chal sacrifice.
Give us a perfect heart to re*ceive* your word,
— that we may bring forth *fruit* in patience.
Make us eager to work with you in building a *bet*ter world,
— so that it may listen to your Church and its gos*pel* of peace.
We confess, Lord, that *we* have sinned,
— wash us clean by your gift *of* salvation.

Our Father . . .

                                    Prayer
   Lord,
   help us to do your will
   that your Church may grow
   and become more faithful in your service.
   Grant this through our Lord Jesus Christ, your Son,
   who lives and reigns with you and the Holy Spirit,
   one God, for ever and ever.

Evening Prayer

READING   1 Corinthians 1:27b-30
   God singled out the weak of this world to shame the strong. He chose the
   world's lowborn and despised, those who count for nothing, to reduce to
   nothing those who were something; so that mankind can do no boasting
   before God. God it is who has given you life in Christ Jesus. He has made
   him our wisdom and also our justice, our sanctification, and our redemption.

RESPONSORY (VI F)

To *you*, O Lord,* I make my prayer *for* mercy.
— To *you*, O Lord,* I make my prayer *for* mercy.
Heal my soul, for I have *sinned* against you.
— I make my prayer *for* mercy.
Glory to the Father, and *to* the Son, * and to the Ho*ly* Spirit.
— To *you*, O Lord,* I make my prayer *for* mercy.

CANTICLE OF MARY

Ant.   The One who sent me is with me; † he has not left *me* alone, *
because I always do *what* pleases him.

INTERCESSIONS (VI f)

Christ our Lord has warned us to watch and pray to a*void* temptation. * With our
whole heart let us *pray* to him:
Turn to us, Lord, and have *mercy.*
Jesus, our Christ, you promised to be with those who pray *in* your name,
— help us always to pray with you to the Father in the *Ho*ly Spirit.
Bridegroom of the Church, cleanse her from *every* stain,
— teach her to walk in hope and in the power of the *Ho*ly Spirit.
Friend of the human race, teach us concern for our neighbor as you *have*
commanded,
— that all may see you more clearly as the light *of* the world.
King of peace, give your peace *to* the world,
— that your presence may reveal your saving power in *every* place.
Open the door of eternal happiness to *all* the dead,
— welcome them into the glory of un*ending* life.

Our Father . . .

Prayer

Lord,
help us to do your will
that your Church may grow
and become more faithful in your service.
Grant this through our Lord Jesus Christ, your Son,
who lives and reigns with you and the Holy Spirit,
one God, for ever and ever.

WEDNESDAY

Morning Prayer

READING   Isaiah 50:4b-7
> The Lord God opens my ear that I may hear;
> And I have not rebelled,
>> have not turned back.
> I gave my back to those who beat me,
>> my cheeks to those who plucked my beard:
> My face I did not shield
>> from buffets and spitting.
> The Lord God is my help,
>> therefore I am not disgraced;
> I have set my face like flint,
>> knowing that I shall not be put to shame.

RESPONSORY (VI F)

God himself will *set* me free, * from the hun*ter's* snare.
— God himself will *set* me free, * from the hun*ter's* snare.
From those who would trap me with *ly*ing words
— and from the hun*ter's* snare.
Glory to the Father, and *to* the Son, * and to the Ho*ly* Spirit.
— God himself will *set* me free, * from the hun*ter's* snare.

CANTICLE OF ZECHARIAH

Ant.   If you are faithful to my teaching, says the Lord, † you will
              indeed be *my* disciples. * You will know the truth and the truth
              will make *you* free.

INTERCESSIONS (VI F)

Blessèd be God, the giver of salvation, who decreed that mankind should become
   a new creation in himself, when all would *be* made new. * With great confidence
   let *us* ask him:
Lord, renew us in your Spirit.
Lord, you promised a new heaven and a new earth; renew us daily *through* your
   Spirit,
— that we may enjoy your presence for ever in the heaven*ly* Jerusalem.
Help us to work with you to make this world alive *with* your Spirit,
— and to build on earth a city of justice, *love* and peace.
Free us from all negli*gence* and sloth,
— and give us joy in your *gifts* of grace.

Deliver *us* from evil,
— and from slavery to the senses, which blinds *us* to goodness.

Our Father . . .

Prayer

Father of mercy,
hear the prayers of your repentant children
who call on you in love.
Enlighten our minds and sanctify our hearts.
We ask this through our Lord Jesus Christ, your Son,
who lives and reigns with you and the Holy Spirit,
one God, for ever and ever.

Evening Prayer

READING   Ephesians 4:32-5:2
Be kind to one another, compassionate, and mutually forgiving, just as God
has forgiven you in Christ. Be imitators of God as his dear children. Follow
the way of love, even as Christ loved you. He gave himself for us as an
offering to God, a gift of pleasing fragrance.

RESPONSORY (VI F)
To *you*, O Lord,* I make my prayer *for* mercy.
— To *you*, O Lord,* I make my prayer *for* mercy.
Heal my soul, for I have *sinned* against you.
— I make my prayer *for* mercy.
Glory to the Father, and *to* the Son, * and to the Ho*ly* Spirit.
— To *you*, O Lord,* I make my prayer *for* mercy.

CANTICLE OF MARY
Ant.   Why are you *bent* on killing me, * when I have told you *the* truth?

INTERCESSIONS (VI F)
Blessèd be almighty God, who watches over us as a Father; he knows all our
   needs but wants us to seek *first* his kingdom. * Let us cry out to him as *his*
   people:
May your kingdom come, that justice may *reign.*
Father of all holiness, you gave us Christ as the shepherd of our souls; stay with
   your shepherds and the flock entrusted to them, do not leave this flock without
   the loving care *of* its shepherd,
— do not leave your shepherds without an obedient flock to *fo*llow them.

Teach Christians to help the weak with *lov*ing care,
— and in serving them to *serve* your Son.
Gather into your Church those who do not *yet* believe,
— and help them to build it up by good deeds done for *love* of you.
Help us to turn to you *for* forgiveness,
— and, as you forgive us, reconcile us also *with* your Church.
May the dead pass from this world to e*ter*nal life,
— to be with *you* for ever.

Our Father . . .

Prayer

Father of mercy,
hear the prayers of your repentant children
who call on you in love.
Enlighten our minds and sanctify our hearts.
We ask this through our Lord Jesus Christ, your Son,
who lives and reigns with you and the Holy Spirit,
one God, for ever and ever.

THURSDAY

Morning Prayer

READING   Hebrews 2:9-10
We see Jesus crowned with glory and honor because he suffered death, that
through God's gracious will he might taste death for the sake of all men.
Indeed, it was fitting that when bringing many sons to glory God, for whom
and through whom all things exist, should make their leader in the work of
salvation perfect through suffering.

RESPONSORY (VI F)
God himself will *set* me free, * from the hunt*er's* snare.
— God himself will *set* me free, * from the hunt*er's* snare.
From those who would trap me with *ly*ing words
— and from the hunt*er's* snare.
Glory to the Father, and *to* the Son, * and to the Ho*ly* Spirit.
— God himself will *set* me free, * from the hunt*er's* snare.

CANTICLE OF ZECHARIAH
Ant.   Jesus said to the chief priests and the crowds of the Jews: †
                        Whoever comes from God hears the *word* of God. * You will not
                        listen because you do not come *from* God.

INTERCESSIONS (VI F)

Christ our Lord came among us as the light of the world, that we might walk in his light, and not in the dark*ness* of death. * Let us praise him and cry *out* to him:

Let your word be a lamp to guide us.

God of mercy, help us today to grow *in* your likeness,

— that we who sinned in Adam may rise a*gain* in Christ.

Let your word be a *lamp* to guide us,

— that we may live the truth and grow always *in* your love.

Teach us to be faithful in seeking the common good *for* your sake,

— that your light may shine on the whole human family by means *of* your Church.

Touch our hearts to seek your friendship *more* and more,

— and to make amends for our sins against your wis*dom* and goodness.

Our Father . . .

Prayer

Lord,
come to us:
free us from the stain of our sins.
Help us to remain faithful to a holy way of life,
and guide us to the inheritance you have promised.
Grant this through our Lord Jesus Christ, your Son,
who lives and reigns with you and the Holy Spirit,
one God, for ever and ever.

Evening Prayer

READING   Hebrews 13:12-15

Jesus died outside the gate, to sanctify the people by his own blood. Let us go to him outside the camp, bearing the insult which he bore. For here we have no lasting city; we are seeking one which is to come. Through him let us continually offer God a sacrifice of praise, that is, the fruit of lips which acknowledge his name.

RESPONSORY (VI F)

To *you*, O Lord,* I make my prayer *for* mercy.

— To *you*, O Lord,* I make my prayer *for* mercy.

Heal my soul, for I have *sinned* against you.

— I make my prayer *for* mercy.

Glory to the Father, and *to* the Son, * and to the Ho*ly* Spirit.

— To *you*, O Lord,* I make my prayer *for* mercy.

CANTICLE OF MARY
Ant.   You are not yet fifty years old; † how can you *have* seen
                 Abraham? * In very truth I tell you, † before Abraham was, *I*
                 AM.

INTERCESSIONS (VI F)
Christ the Lord gave us a new commandment, of love *for* each other. * Let us
    pray to him:
Lord, build up your people in *love.*
Good Master, teach us to love you *in* our neighbor,
— and in serving them *to* serve you.
On the cross you asked pardon for your *ex*ecutioners,
— give us strength to love our enemies and pray for *those* who persecute us.
Through the mystery of your body and blood, deepen our love, our perseverance
    and our trust,
— strengthen the weak, console the sorrowful, and give hope *to* the dying.
Light of the world, you gave light to the man born blind when he had washed in
    the *pool* of Siloam,
— enlighten catechumens through the water of baptism and the *word* of life.
Give to the dead the perfect joy of your e*ter*nal love,
— and number us also among your *chos*en ones.

Our Father . . .

Prayer

Lord, come to us:
free us from the stain of our sins.
Help us to remain faithful to a holy way of life,
and guide us to the inheritance you have promised.
Grant this through our Lord Jesus Christ, your Son,
who lives and reigns with you and the Holy Spirit,
one God, for ever and ever.

FRIDAY

Morning Prayer

READING   Isaiah 53:13-15
See, my servant shall prosper,
    he shall be raised high and greatly exalted.
Even as many were amazed at him—
    so marred was his look beyond that of man,
    and his appearance beyond that of mortals—
So shall he startle many nations,
    because of him kings shall stand speechless;
For those who have not been told shall see,
    those who have not heard shall ponder it.

RESPONSORY (VI F)

God himself will *set* me free, * from the hunt*er's* snare.

— God himself will *set* me free, * from the hunt*er's* snare.

From those who would trap me with *ly*ing words

— and from the hunt*er's* snare.

Glory to the Father, and *to* the Son, * and to the Ho*ly* Spirit.

— God himself will *set* me free, * from the hunt*er's* snare.

CANTICLE OF ZECHARIAH

Ant.   The Lord said: † I have done you many *acts* of kindness; * for
                 which of them do you want *to* kill me?

INTERCESSIONS (VI F)

Thanks be to Christ the Lord, who brought us life by his death *on* the cross. *
    With our whole heart *let* us ask him:

By your death raise us to life.

Teacher and Savior, you have shown us your fidelity and made us a new creation
    by your passion,

— keep us from falling again *in*to sin.

Help us to deny our*selves* today,

— and not deny *those* in need.

May we receive this day of penance *as* your gift,

— and give it back to you through *works* of mercy.

Master our re*bel*lious hearts,

— and teach us *gen*erosity.

Our Father . . .

Prayer

Lord,
grant us your forgiveness,
and set us free from our enslavement to sin.
We ask this through our Lord Jesus Christ, your Son,
who lives and reigns with you and the Holy Spirit,
one God, for ever and ever.

Evening Prayer

READING   1 Peter 2:21-24

Christ suffered for you and left you an example, to have you follow in his
footsteps. He did no wrong; no deceit was found in his mouth. When he was
insulted, he returned no insult. When he was made to suffer, he did not
counter with threats. Instead, he delivered himself up to the One who judges
justly. In his own body he brought your sins to the cross, so that all of us, dead
to sin, could live in accord with God's will. By his wounds you were healed.

RESPONSORY (VI F)

To *you*, O Lord,* I make my prayer *for* mercy.
—To *you*, O Lord,* I make my prayer *for* mercy.
Heal my soul, for I have *sinned* against you.
— I make my prayer *for* mercy.
Glory to the Father, and *to* the Son, * and to the Ho*ly* Spirit.
—To *you*, O Lord,* I make my prayer *for* mercy.

CANTICLE OF MARY

Ant.   Even if you have no faith *in* my words, * you should at least
                        believe the evidence † of the works I do in *God's* name.

INTERCESSIONS (VI F)

The Lord Jesus sanctified his people *with* his blood. * Let us cry *out* to him:
Lord, have mercy on your *people.*
Loving Redeemer, through your passion teach us self-denial, strengthen us
    against evil and adversity, and in*crease* our hope,
— and so make us ready to celebrate your *re*surrection.
Grant that Christians, as your prophets, may make you known in *every* place,
— and bear witness to you with living faith and *hope* and love.
Give your strength to all *in* distress,
— and help us to raise them up through our lov*ing* concern.
Teach the faithful to see your passion *in* their sufferings,
— and to show to others your pow*er* to save.
Author of life, remember those who have passed *from* this world,
— grant them the glory of your *ris*en life.

Our Father . . .

Prayer

Lord,
grant us your forgiveness,
and set us free from our enslavement to sin.
We ask this through our Lord Jesus Christ, your Son,
who lives and reigns with you and the Holy Spirit,
one God, for ever and ever.

SATURDAY

Morning Prayer

READING   Isaiah 65:1B-3a

        I said: Here I am! Here I am!
                To a nation that did not call upon my name.
        I have stretched out my hands all the day
                to a rebellious people,

Who walk in evil paths
and follow their own thoughts,
People who provoke me
continually, to my face.

RESPONSORY (VI F)

God himself will *set* me free, * from the hun*ter's* snare.
— God himself will *set* me free, * from the hun*ter's* snare.
From those who would trap me with *ly*ing words
— and from the hun*ter's* snare.
Glory to the Father, and *to* the Son, * and to the Ho*ly* Spirit.
— God himself will *set* me free, * from the hun*ter's* snare.

CANTICLE OF ZECHARIAH

Ant.   Jesus died to gather into one family * all the scattered children *of* God.

INTERCESSIONS (VI F)

To make us his new creation, Christ the Lord gave us the waters of rebirth and spread the table of his body *and* his word. * Let us call upon *him* and say:
Lord, renew us in your *grace.*
Jesus, meek and humble of heart, clothe us with compassion, kindness *and* humility,
— make us want to be pa*tient* with everyone.
Teach us to be true neighbors to all in trouble *and* distress,
— and so imitate you, the *Good* Samaritan.
May the Blessèd Virgin, your Mother, pray for all those vowed to a life *of* virginity,
— that they may deepen their dedication to you and *to* the Church.
Grant us the gift *of* your mercy,
— forgive our sins and re*mit* their punishment.

Our Father . . .

Prayer

God our Father,
you always work to save us,
and now we rejoice in the great love
you give to your chosen people.
Protect all who are about to become your children,
and continue to bless those who are already baptized.
Grant this through our Lord Jesus Christ, your Son,
who lives and reigns with you and the Holy Spirit,
one God, for ever and ever.

PASSION SUNDAY
(PALM SUNDAY)

PSALTER, WEEK II, 672.

Evening Prayer I

HYMN

Vexilla Regis. Mode I (L.M.)

Vexilla regis prodeunt,	Behold the standard of the King,
fulget crucis mysterium,	The Cross gleams forth its mystery;
quo carne carnis conditor	On it the Son of God as Man
suspensus est patibulo;	Atoned on earth for sinners all.
Quo, vulneratus insuper	His side was pierced by cruel lance
mucrone diro lanceæ,	That drew out water with his Blood,
ut nos lavaret crimine,	To cleanse our souls from ev'ry stain,
manavit unda et sanguine.	And nourish them with its pure stream.
Arbor decora et fulgida,	O Tree that shines with beauty rare,
ornata regis purpura,	Ennobled by Christ's precious Blood,
electa digno stipite	He chose you as the royal bed
tam sancta membra tangere!	To rest his sacred limbs in death.
Beata, cuius bracchiis	O blessèd were your rugged arms,
sæcli pependit pretium;	From which the whole world's ransom hung,
statera facta est corporis	You bore the weight of sacrifice
prædam tulitque tartari.	That snatched from greedy hell its prey.
Salve, ara, salve, victima,	Hail, holy altar, Victim hail,
de passionis gloria,	For all the glory of that Cross,
que Vita mortem pertulit	By which Life chose and welcomed death,
et morte vitam reddidit!	And dying gave us life once more.
O crux, ave, spes unica!	Hail, holy Cross, our only hope,
in hac triumphi gloria	Wash all our guilt and crimes away,
piis adauge gratiam	Increase our grace while we adore
reisque dele crimina.	In honor of your victory.
Te, fons salutis, Trinitas,	Let ev'ry soul sing in your praise,
collaudet omnis spiritus;	Salvation's Fount, O Trinity,
quos per crucis mysterium	For ever cherish those redeemed
salvas, fove per sæcula. Amen.	Through that great mystery, the Cross. Amen.

READING $\qquad$ 1 Peter 1:18-21

Realize that you were delivered from the futile way of life your fathers handed on to you, not by any diminishable sum of silver or gold, but by Christ's blood beyond all price: the blood of a spotless, unblemished lamb chosen before the world's foundation and revealed for your sake in these last days. It is through him that you are believers in God, the God who raised him from the dead and gave him glory. Your faith and hope, then, are centered in God.

RESPONSORY (VI F)

We worship *you*, O Christ, * and *we* praise you.
— We worship *you*, O Christ, * and *we* praise you.
Because by your cross you have re*deemed* the world.
— *We* praise you.
Glory to the Father, and *to* the Son, * and to the Ho*ly* Spirit.
— We worship *you*, O Christ, * and *we* praise you.

CANTICLE OF MARY

Ant.   Praise to our King, the Son of David, † the Redeemer *of* the world; * praise to the Savior † whose coming had been foretold by *the* prophets.

INTERCESSIONS (VI F)

Before his passion, Christ looked out over Jerusalem and wept for it, because it had not recognized the hour of God's *visi*tation. * With sorrow for our sins, let us adore *him*, and say:
Lord, have mercy on your *people.*
You longed to gather to yourself the people of Jerusalem, as the hen ga*thers* her young,
— teach all peoples to recognize the hour of your *visi*tation.
Do not forsake those who have for*sak*en you,
— turn our hearts to you, and we will return to *you*, our God.
Through your passion you gave grace *to* the world,
— help us to live always by your Spirit, given to *us* in baptism.
By your passion, help us to de*ny* ourselves,
— and so prepare to celebrate your *res*urrection.
You reign in the glory *of* the Father,
— remember those who have *died* today.

Our Father . . .

Prayer

Almighty, ever-living God,
you have given the human race Jesus Christ our Savior
as a model of humility.
He fulfilled your will
by becoming man and giving his life on the cross.
Help us to bear witness to you
by following his example of suffering
and make us worthy to share in his resurrection.
We ask this through our Lord Jesus Christ, your Son,
who lives and reigns with you and the Holy Spirit,
one God, for ever and ever.

Passion Sunday

Morning Prayer
HYMN

En, acetum. Mode I (87.87.87)

En acétum, fel, arundo,	See the reed, the gall so bitter,
sputa, clavi, lancea;	See the nails and cruel spear,
mite corpus perforatur,	As they pierce Christ's sacred Body,
sanguis, unda, profluit;	Blood and water flowed in streams,
terra, pontus, astra, mundus	Which would cleanse the whole creation,
quo lavantur flumine!	Giving life to all and each.
Crux fidélis, inter omnes	Faithful Cross beyond all others,
arbor una nobilis!	Noble tree of priceless worth,
Nulla talem silva profert	Never forest was productive
flore, fronde, gérmine.	Of such blossom, leaf or seed.
Dulce lignum, dulci clavo	Honored wood, and nails more honored
dulce pondus sustinens!	Christ as burden to sustain.
Flecte ramos, arbor alta,	Bend your branches, tree exalted,
tensa laxa viscera,	Make your trunk a gentle bed,
et rigor lentescat ille	Change the hard and rigid nature
quem dedit nativitas,	Of the strength you raise on high,
ut superni membra regis	To receive the holy members
miti tendas stipite.	Of your dying Lord and King.
Sola digna tu fuisti	You alone were chosen worthy
ferre sæculi pretium,	Love's oblation to uphold,
atque portum præparare	For the Lamb bedewed your fibers
nauta mundo naufrago,	With the Blood divine he shed.
quem sacer cruor perunixt	You revealed the sinner's haven
fusus Agni corpore.	In a world condemned to die.
Æqua Patri Filioque,	Equal glory be for ever
inclito Paraclito,	To the Father and the Son,
sempiterna sit beatæ	To the Holy Spirit also,
Trinitati gloria,	Blessèd Trinity in One;
cuius alma nos redémit	Love and Mercy, Grace together,
atque servat gratia. Amen.	Ransom and preserve us all. Amen.

READING   Zechariah 9:9

Rejoice heartily, O daughter Zion,
      shout for joy, O daughter Jerusalem!
See, your king shall come to you;
      a just savior is he,
Meek, and riding on an ass,
      on a colt, the foal of an ass.

RESPONSORY (VI F)

By your *own* blood, Lord, * you brought us back *to* God.
— By your *own* blood, Lord, * you brought us back *to* God.
From every tribe, and tongue, and peo*ple* and nation,
— you brought us back *to* God.
Glory to the Father, and *to* the Son, * and to the Ho*ly* Spirit.
— By your *own* blood, Lord, * you brought us back *to* God.

CANTICLE OF ZECHARIAH

Ant.   With palms let us welcome the Lord *as* he comes, * with songs
             and hymns let us run *to* meet him,
             as we offer him our wor*ship* and sing: * Blessèd be *the* Lord!

INTERCESSIONS (VI F)

As Christ entered Jerusalem he was greeted as King *and* Messiah. * Let us adore
   him, and joy*fu*lly praise him:
Blessèd is he who comes in the name of the Lord.
Hosanna to you, Son of David, King *of* the ages,
— hosanna to you, victor over death and the pow*ers* of darkness.
You went up to Jerusalem to suffer and so enter in*to* your glory,
— lead your Church into the paschal *feast* of heaven.
You made your cross the *tree* of life,
— grant its fruit to those re*born* in baptism.
Savior of mankind, you came *to* save sinners,
— bring into your kingdom all who have faith, *hope* and love.

Our Father . . .

Prayer

    Almighty, ever-living God,
    you have given the human race Jesus Christ our Savior
    as a model of humility.
    He fulfilled your will
    by becoming man and giving his life on the cross.
    Help us to bear witness to you
    by following his example of suffering
    and make us worthy to share in his resurrection.
    We ask this through our Lord Jesus Christ, your Son,
    who lives and reigns with you and the Holy Spirit,
    one God, for ever and ever.

Evening Prayer II

HYMN, 334.

READING   Acts 13:26-30

    My brothers, it was to us that this message of salvation was sent forth. The
    inhabitants of Jerusalem and their rulers failed to recognize him, and in

condemning him they fulfilled the words of the prophets which we read sabbath after sabbath. Even though they found no charge against him which deserved death, they begged Pilate to have him executed. Once they had brought about all that had been written of him, they took him down from the tree and laid him in a tomb. Yet God raised him from the dead.

RESPONSORY (VI F)
We worship *you*, O Christ, * and *we* praise you.
— We worship *you*, O Christ, * and *we* praise you.
Because by your cross you have re*deemed* the world.
— *We* praise you.
Glory to the Father, and *to* the Son, * and to the Ho*ly* Spirit.
— We worship *you*, O Christ, * and *we* praise you.

CANTICLE OF MARY
Ant.   It is written: I will *strike* the shepherd * and his flock shall *be* scattered.
              But when I have risen, † I will go before you *into* Galilee. * There you shall see me, says *the* Lord.

INTERCESSIONS (VI F)
The Savior of mankind by dying destroyed death and by rising again re*stored* life.
    * Let us *hum*bly ask him:
Sanctify your people, redeemed by your blood.
Redeemer of the world, give us a greater share of your passion through a deeper spirit *of* repentance,
— so that we may share the glory of your re*sur*rection.
May your Mother, comfort of the afflict*ed*, protect us,
— may we console others as you *con*sole us.
Look with love on those who suffer because of *our* indifference,
— come to their aid, and turn our uncaring hearts to works of jus*tice* and charity.
You humbled yourself by being obedient even to accepting death, death *on* a cross,
— give all who serve you the gifts of obedience and pa*tient* endurance.
Transform the bodies of the dead to be like your *own* in glory,
— and bring us at last in*to* their friendship.

Our Father . . .

Prayer, as in Morning Prayer, 337.

MONDAY

Morning Prayer
HYMN, 336.

Ant. 1   Jesus said: My heart is nearly broken with *sorrow*; * stay here and keep watch *with* me.

Psalms and canticle from Monday, Week II, 689.

Ant. 2   Now the time has come for this world to re*ceive* its sentence; * now the prince of this world will be driven *out*.

Ant. 3   Jesus, the beginning and end of our faith, † endured the cross, heedless of *the* shame, * and is seated now at the right hand of the *throne* of God.

READING   Jeremiah 11:19-20

I, like a trusting lamb led to the slaughter, had not realized that they were hatching plots against me: "Let us destroy the tree in its vigor; let us cut him off from the land of the living, so that his name will be spoken no more."

But you, O Lord of hosts, O just Judge,
         searcher of mind and heart,
Let me witness the vengeance you take on them,
         for to you I have entrusted my cause, O Lord my God!

RESPONSORY (VI F)
By your *own* blood, Lord, * you brought us back *to* God.
— By your *own* blood, Lord, * you brought us back *to* God.
From every tribe, and tongue, and peo*ple* and nation,
— you brought us back *to* God.
Glory to the Father, and *to* the Son, * and to the Ho*ly* Spirit.
— By your *own* blood, Lord, * you brought us back *to* God.

CANTICLE OF ZECHARIAH
Ant.   Father, righteous One, † the world *does* not know you, * but I know you, † because you are the One *who* sent me.

INTERCESSIONS (VI F)
Let us pray to *Christ* our Savior, * who redeemed us by his death and re*sur*rection:
Lord, have mercy on *us.*
You went up to Jerusalem to suffer and so enter in*to* your glory,
— bring your Church to the Passover *feast* of heaven.
You were lifted high on the cross and pierced by the *sol*dier's lance,
— *heal* our wounds.

You made the cross the *tree* of life,
— give its fruit to those re*born* in baptism.
On the cross you forgave the re*pent*ant thief,
— forgive *us* our sins.

Our Father . . .

Prayer

All-powerful God,
by the suffering and death of your Son,
strengthen and protect us in our weakness.
We ask this through our Lord Jesus Christ, your Son,
who lives and reigns with you and the Holy Spirit,
one God, for ever and ever.

Evening Prayer

HYMN, 334.

Ant. 1 He had neither beauty, nor *majesty,* * nothing to attract *our* eyes.

Psalms and canticle from Monday, Week II, 693.

Ant. 2 I will entrust all people *to* his care, * for he has given himself up to death for *all.*

Ant. 3 God has blessed us in Christ. † Through him, at the cost of *his* blood, * we have *been* redeemed.

READING   Romans 5:8-9

It is precisely in this that God proves his love for us: that while we were still sinners, Christ died for us. Now that we have been justified by his blood, it is all the more certain that we shall be saved by him from God's wrath.

RESPONSORY (VI F)

We worship *you,* O Christ, * and *we* praise you.
— We worship *you,* O Christ, * and *we* praise you.
Because by your cross you have re*deemed* the world.
— *We* praise you.
Glory to the Father, and *to* the Son, * and to the Ho*ly* Spirit.
— We worship *you,* O Christ, * and *we* praise you.

CANTICLE OF MARY

Ant. As Moses lifted up the serpent in the desert, † so must the Son of Man *be* raised up, * so that all who believe in him may have eter*nal* life.

INTERCESSIONS (VI F)

The Savior of mankind by dying destroyed death and by rising again *re*stored life.
   * Let us *hum*bly ask him:
Sanctify your people, redeemed by your blood.
Redeemer of the world, give us a greater share of your passion through a deeper
   spirit *of* repentance,
— so that we may share the glory of your *re*surrection.
May your Mother, comfort of the afflic*ted*, protect us,
— may we console others as you *con*sole us.
Look with love on those who suffer because of *our* indifference,
— come to their aid, and turn our uncaring hearts to works of jus*tice* and charity.
You humbled yourself by being obedient even to accepting death, death *on* a cross,
— give all who serve you the gifts of obedience and pa*tient* endurance.
Transform the bodies of the dead to be like your *own* in glory,
— and bring us at last in*to* their friendship.

Our Father . . .

Prayer

   All-powerful God,
   by the suffering and death of your Son,
   strengthen and protect us in our weakness.
   We ask this through our Lord Jesus Christ, your Son,
   who lives and reigns with you and the Holy Spirit,
   one God, for ever and ever.

TUESDAY

Morning Prayer
HYMN, 336.

Ant. 1   O Lord, defend my *cause*; * rescue me from deceitful and imp*ious*
                men.

Psalms and canticle from Tuesday, Week II, 698.

Ant. 2   Lord, my God, you defend*ed* my cause; * you ransomed my *life.*

Ant. 3   My servant, the Just One, will justi*fy* many * by taking their sins
                on himself.

READING   Zechariah 12:10-11a
   I will pour out on the house of David and on the inhabitants of Jerusalem a
   spirit of grace and petition; and they shall look on him whom they have
   thrust through, and they shall mourn for him as one mourns for an only son,
   that they shall grieve over him as one grieves over a first-born. On that day
   the mourning in Jerusalem shall be great.

RESPONSORY (VI F)

By your *own* blood, Lord, * you brought us back *to* God.
— By your *own* blood, Lord, * you brought us back *to* God.
From every tribe, and tongue, and peo*ple* and nation,
— you brought us back *to* God.
Glory to the Father, and *to* the Son, * and to the Ho*ly* Spirit.
— By your *own* blood, Lord, * you brought us back *to* God.

CANTICLE OF ZECHARIAH

Ant.   Father, give me the glory that I *had* with you * before the world *was* made.

INTERCESSIONS (VI F)

Let us pray to *Christ* our Savior, * who redeemed us by his death and *resurrection*:
Lord, have mercy on *us*.
You went up to Jerusalem to suffer and so enter in*to* your glory,
— bring your Church to the Passover *feast* of heaven.
You were lifted high on the cross and pierced by the *soldier's* lance,
— *heal* our wounds.
You made the cross the *tree* of life,
— give its fruit to those re*born* in baptism.
On the cross you forgave the re*pentant* thief,
— forgive *us* our sins.

Our Father . . .

Prayer

Father,
may we receive your forgiveness and mercy
as we celebrate the passion and death of the Lord,
who lives and reigns with you and the Holy Spirit,
one God, for ever and ever.

Evening Prayer

HYMN, 334.

Ant. 1   They insulted me and filled me with *dread*, * but the Lord was at my side, like a mighty warrior.

Psalms and canticle from Tuesday, Week II, 702.

Ant. 2   Deliver me, Lord, and place me *at* your side, * then let whoever will, lift his hand to *strike* me.

Ant. 3   You were slain, Lord, † and by *your* blood * you have ransomed *us* for God.

READING   1 Corinthians 1:27b-30
God singled out the weak of this world to shame the strong. He chose the
world's lowborn and despised, those who count for nothing, to reduce to
nothing those who were something; so that mankind can do no boasting
before God. God it is who has given you life in Christ Jesus. He has made
him our wisdom and also our justice, our sanctification, and our redemption.

RESPONSORY (VI F)
We worship *you*, O Christ, * and *we* praise you.
— We worship *you*, O Christ, * and *we* praise you.
Because by your cross you have re*deemed* the world.
— *We* praise you.
Glory to the Father, and *to* the Son, * and to the Ho*ly* Spirit.
— We worship *you*, O Christ, * and *we* praise you.

CANTICLE OF MARY
Ant.   I have power to lay *down* my life, * and I have power to take it up
                  *a*gain.

INTERCESSIONS (VI F)
The Savior of mankind by dying destroyed death and by rising again *re*stored life.
  * Let us *hum*bly ask him:
Sanctify your people, redeemed by your blood.
Redeemer of the world, give us a greater share of your passion through a deeper
  spirit *of* repentance,
— so that we may share the glory of your *re*surrection.
May your Mother, comfort of the afflict*ed*, protect us,
— may we console others as you *con*sole us.
Look with love on those who suffer because of *our* indifference,
— come to their aid, and turn our uncaring hearts to works of jus*tice* and charity.
You humbled yourself by being obedient even to accepting death, death *on* a cross,
— give all who serve you the gifts of obedience and pa*tient* endurance.
Transform the bodies of the dead to be like your *own* in glory,
— and bring us at last in*to* their friendship.

Our Father . . .

                           Prayer
   Father,
   may we receive your forgiveness and mercy
   as we celebrate the passion and death of the Lord,
   who lives and reigns with you and the Holy Spirit,
   one God, for ever and ever.

WEDNESDAY

Morning Prayer
HYMN, 336.

Ant. 1   In the day of my dis*tress*, * I reached out with my hands to seek
              the *Lord's* help.

Psalms and canticle from Wednesday, Week II, 707.

Ant. 2   If we have *died* with Christ, * we believe that we shall also live
              with *Christ*.

Ant. 3   God has made Christ Jesus our wisdom and *our* holiness. * By
              him we have been sanctified *and* redeemed.

READING   Isaiah 50:4b-7

  The Lord God opens my ear that I may hear;
And I have not rebelled,
  have not turned back.
I gave my back to those who beat me,
  my cheeks to those who plucked my beard:
My face I did not shield
  from buffets and spitting.
The Lord God is my help,
  therefore I am not disgraced;
I have set my face like flint,
  knowing that I shall not be put to shame.

RESPONSORY (VI F)

By your *own* blood, Lord, * you brought us back *to* God.
— By your *own* blood, Lord, * you brought us back *to* God.
From every tribe, and tongue, and peo*ple* and nation,
— you brought us back *to* God.
Glory to the Father, and *to* the Son, * and to the Ho*ly* Spirit.
— By your *own* blood, Lord, * you brought us back *to* God.

CANTICLE OF ZECHARIAH

Ant.   Through the eternal Spirit, † Christ offered himself to God as
              the *per*fect sacrifice. * His blood purifies us from sin † and makes
              us fit servants of the liv*ing* God.

INTERCESSIONS (VI F)

Let us pray to *Christ* our Savior, * who redeemed us by his death and *re*surrection:
Lord, have mercy on *us.*

You went up to Jerusalem to suffer and so enter in*to* your glory,
— bring your Church to the Passover *feast* of heaven.
You were lifted high on the cross and pierced by the *sold*ier's lance,
— *heal* our wounds.
You made the cross the *tree* of life,
— give its fruit to those re*born* in baptism.
On the cross you forgave the re*pent*ant thief,
— forgive *us* our sins.

Our Father . . .

Prayer

Father,
in your plan of salvation
your Son Jesus Christ accepted the cross
and freed us from the power of the enemy.
May we come to share the glory of his resurrection,
for he lives and reigns with you and the Holy Spirit,
one God, for ever and ever.

Evening Prayer

HYMN, 334.

Ant. 1   Evil men said: Let us make the just man *suf*fer; * he sets himself
against our way *of* life.

Psalms and canticle from Wednesday, Week II, 712.

Ant. 2   He took all our sins up*on* himself * and asked forgiveness for our
of*fen*ses.

Ant. 3   In Christ we have found *de*liverance; * through his blood, the
forgiveness *of* our sins.

READING   Ephesians 4:32-5:2
Be kind to one another, compassionate, and mutually forgiving, just as God
has forgiven you in Christ. Be imitators of God as his dear children. Follow
the way of love, even as Christ loved you. He gave himself for us as an
offering to God, a gift of pleasing fragrance.

RESPONSORY (VI F)
We worship *you*, O Christ, * and *we* praise you.
— We worship *you*, O Christ, * and *we* praise you.
Because by your cross you have re*deemed* the world.
— *We* praise you.

Glory to the Father, and *to* the Son, * and to the Ho*ly* Spirit.
— We worship *you*, O Christ, * and *we* praise you.

CANTICLE OF MARY

Ant.   The Master says: † My hour is *close* at hand; * I and my disciples
                   shall celebrate the Passover in *your* house.

INTERCESSIONS (VI F)

The Savior of mankind by dying destroyed death and by rising again *re*stored life.
   * Let us *hum*bly ask him:
Sanctify your people, redeemed by your blood.
Redeemer of the world, give us a greater share of your passion through a deeper
   spirit *of* repentance,
— so that we may share the glory of your *re*surrection.
May your Mother, comfort of the afflict*ed*, protect us,
— may we console others as you *con*sole us.
Look with love on those who suffer because of *our* indifference,
— come to their aid, and turn our uncaring hearts to works of jus*tice* and charity.
You humbled yourself by being obedient even to accepting death, death *on* a cross,
— give all who serve you the gifts of obedience and pa*tient* endurance.
Transform the bodies of the dead to be like your *own* in glory,
— and bring us at last in*to* their friendship.

Our Father . . .

Prayer

   Father,
   in your plan of salvation
   your Son Jesus Christ accepted the cross
   and freed us from the power of the enemy.
   May we come to share the glory of his resurrection,
   for he lives and reigns with you and the Holy Spirit,
   one God, for ever and ever.

THURSDAY

Morning Prayer
HYMN, 336.

Ant. 1   Look, O Lord, and see my *suffering*. * Come quickly to *my* aid.

Psalms and canticle from Thursday, Week II, 716.

Ant. 2   God *is* my savior; * I trust in him and shall not *fear*.

Ant. 3   The Lord has fed us with the fin*est* wheat; * he has filled us with honey *from* the rock.

READING   Hebrews 2:9-10

We see Jesus crowned with glory and honor because he suffered death, that through God's gracious will he might taste death for the sake of all men. Indeed, it was fitting that when bringing many sons to glory God, for whom and through whom all things exist, should make their leader in the work of salvation perfect through suffering.

RESPONSORY (VI F)

By your *own* blood, Lord, * you brought us back *to* God.
— By your *own* blood, Lord, * you brought us back *to* God.
From every tribe, and tongue, and peo*ple* and nation,
— you brought us back *to* God.
Glory to the Father, and *to* the Son, * and to the Ho*ly* Spirit.
— By your *own* blood, Lord, * you brought us back *to* God.

CANTICLE OF ZECHARIAH

Ant.   I have longed to *eat* this meal * with you before *I* suffer.

INTERCESSIONS (VI F)

The Father anointed Christ with the Holy Spirit to proclaim forgiveness to *those* in bondage. * Let us humbly call upon the e*ter*nal priest:
Lord, have mercy on us.
You went up to Jerusalem to suffer and so enter in*to* your glory,
— bring your Church to the Passover *feast* of heaven.
You were lifted high on the cross and pierced by the *sol*dier's lance,
— *heal* our wounds.
You made the cross the *tree* of life,
— give its fruit to those re*born* in baptism.
On the cross you forgave the re*pent*ant thief,
— forgive *us* our sins.

Our Father . . .

Prayer

God of infinite compassion,
to love you is to be made holy;
fill our hearts with your love.
By the death of your Son
you have given us hope, born of faith;
by his rising again
fulfill this hope
in the perfect love of heaven,
where he lives and reigns with you and the Holy Spirit,
one God, for ever and ever.

Proper of Seasons
Easter Triduum
of the Passion and Resurrection
of the Lord

HOLY THURSDAY

Evening Prayer

Evening Prayer is said only by those who do not participate in the evening Mass of the Lord's Supper.

HYMN
O memoriale. Mode V (11.11.11.11)

O memoriale mortis Domini,	Memory undying of Christ's sacrifice,
panis vivus vitam præstans homini,	Bread of life eternal for humanity,
præsta meæ menti de te vivere	May my soul draw always life and strength from you.
et te illi semper dulce sapere.	Growing yet more grateful for this mystery.
Pie pelicane, Iesu Domine,	Jesus, loving Victim on the Cross for me,
me immundum munda tuo sanguine,	May I, guilty sinner, by your Blood win grace;
cuius una stilla salvum facere	But one drop so sacred could atonement make
totum mundum quit ab omni scelere.	For all crimes committed by our fallen race.
Te cum revelata cernam facie	When at last I see you, Jesus Christ my Lord,
visu tandem lætus tuæ gloriæ,	Ever in your presence may I find reward;
Patri, tibi laudes et Spiritui	There to praise the glory of the Trinity,
dicam beatorum iunctus cœtui. Amen.	Father, Son and Spirit, for eternity. Amen.

Ant. 1   Jesus Christ, the firstborn from the dead † and ruler of the kings of the *earth*, * has made us a royal people to serve his God *and* Father.

Psalms and canticle from Thursday, Week II, 721.

Ant. 2   The Lord will be the champion *of* the helpless; * he will free the poor from the grip of the *powerful.*

Ant. 3   The saints won their victory over death † through the blood of *the* Lamb * and the truth to which *they* bore witness.

READING   Hebrews 13:12-15

Jesus died outside the gate, to sanctify the people by his own blood. Let us go to him outside the camp, bearing the insult which he bore. For here we have no lasting city; we are seeking one which is to come. Through him let us continually offer God a sacrifice of praise, that is, the fruit of lips which acknowledge his name.

In place of the responsory the following is said:

Antiphon   For our sake Christ *was* obedient, * accepting ev*en* death.

CANTICLE OF MARY

Antiphon   While they were at supper, † Jesus took bread, *said* the blessing,
                * broke the bread and gave it to his *dis*ciples.

INTERCESSIONS (VI F)

At the Last Supper, on the night he was betrayed, our Savior entrusted to his
    Church the memorial of his death and resurrection, to be cele*brat*ed for ever. *
    Let us adore *him*, and say:
Sanctify your people, redeemed by your blood.
Redeemer of the world, give us a greater share of your passion through a deeper
    spirit *of* repentance,
— so that we may share the glory of your *re*surrection.
May your Mother, comfort of the afflic*ted*, protect us,
— may we console others as you *con*sole us.
In their trials enable your faithful people to share *in* your passion,
— and so reveal in their lives your *sav*ing power.
You humbled yourself by being obedient even to accepting death, death *on* a
    cross,
— give all who serve you the gifts of obedience and pa*tient* endurance.
Transform the bodies of the dead to be like your *own* in glory,
— and bring us at last in*to* their fellowship.

Our Father . . .

Prayer

Father,
for your glory and our salvation
you appointed Jesus Christ eternal High Priest.
May the people he gained for you by his blood
come to share in the power of his cross and resurrection
by celebrating his memorial in this eucharist,
for he lives and reigns with you and the Holy Spirit,
one God, for ever and ever.

GOOD FRIDAY

Morning Prayer

HYMN, 336.

HYMN, 336.

PSALMODY

Ant. 1   God did not spare *his* own Son, * but gave him up to suffer *for* our sake.

VIIIg

Psalm 51

Have mercy on me, God, *in* your kindness. * In your compassion blot out *my* offense.

O wash me more and more *from* my guilt * and cleanse me *from* my sin.

My offenses tru*ly* I know them; * my sin is al*ways* before me.

Against you, you alone, *have* I sinned; * what is evil in your sight *I* have done.

That you may be justified when *you* give sentence * and be without reproach *when* you judge.

O see, in guilt *I* was born, * a sinner was *I* conceived.

Indeed you love truth *in* the heart; * then in the secret of my heart *teach* me wisdom.

O purify me, then I *shall* be clean; * O wash me, I shall be whi*ter* than snow.

Make me hear rejoi*cing* and gladness, * that the bones you have crushed *may* revive.

From my sins turn a*way* your face * and blot out *all* my guilt.

A pure heart create for *me*, O God, * put a steadfast spir*it* within me.

Do not cast me away *from* your presence, * nor deprive me of your *holy* spirit.

Give me again the joy *of* your help; * with a spirit of fer*vor* sustain me,

that I may teach transgres*sors* your ways * and sinners may re*turn* to you.

O rescue me, *God*, my helper, * and my tongue shall ring *out* your goodness.

O Lord, *open* my lips * and my mouth shall de*clare* your praise.

For in sacrifice you take *no* delight, * burnt offering from me you *would* refuse,

my sacrifice, a *con*trite spirit. * A humbled, contrite heart you *will* not spurn.

In your goodness, show fa*vor* to Zion; * rebuild the walls *of* Jerusalem.

Then you will be pleased with *lawful* sacrifice, * holocausts offered *on* your altar.

Glory to the Father, and *to* the Son, * and to the *Holy* Spirit:

as it was in the begin*ning*, is now, * and will be for ev*er*. Amen.

Antiphon   God did not spare *his* own Son, * but gave him up to suffer *for* our sake.

Ant. 2   Jesus Christ loved us, † and poured out his own *blood* for us * to wash away our *sins.*

IID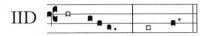

Canticle   Habakkuk 3:2-4, 13a, 15-19

O Lord, I have heard *your* renown, * and feared, O Lord, your *work.*

In the course of the years revive it, † in the course of the years *make* it known; * in your wrath remember com*pass*ion!

God *comes* from Teman, * the Holy One from Mount *Par*an.

Covered are the heavens *with* his glory, * and with his praise the earth is *filled.*

His splendor spreads like the light; † rays shine forth *from* beside him, * where his power is con*cealed.*

You come forth to *save* your people, * to save your a*noint*ed one.

You tread the sea *with* your steeds * amid the churning of the deep *wat*ers.

I hear, and my *body* trembles; * at the sound, my lips *quiv*er.

Decay in*vades* my bones, * my legs tremble be*neath* me.

I await the day *of* distress * that will come upon the people who at*tack* us.

For though the fig tree *blos*som not * nor fruit be on the *vines,*

though the yield of the *ol*ive fail * and the terraces produce no *nour*ishment,

Though the flocks disappear *from* the fold * and there be no herd in the *stalls,*

yet will I rejoice *in* the Lord * and exult in my saving *God.*

God, my Lord, is my strength; † he makes my feet swift as *those* of hinds * and enables me to go upon the *heights.*

Glory to the Father, and *to* the Son, * and to the Holy *Spir*it:

as it was in the begin*ning,* is now, * and will be for ever. A*men.*

Antiphon   Jesus Christ loved us, † and poured out his own *blood* for us * to wash away our *sins.*

Ant. 3   We worship your cross, O Lord, † and we praise and glorify your holy res*ur*rection, * for the wood of the cross has brought joy *to* the world.

Vc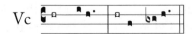

Psalm 147:12-20

O praise the Lord, *Jeru*salem! * Zion, *praise* your God!

He has strengthened the bars of *your* gates, * he has blessed the child*ren* within you.

He established peace on *your* borders, *
  he feeds you with *fin*est wheat.

He sends out his word to *the* earth *
  and swiftly runs *his* command.

He showers down snow white *as* wool,
  * he scatters hoar-*frost* like ashes.

He hurls down hailstones *like* crumbs.
  * The waters are frozen *at* his touch;

he sends forth his word and *it* melts
  them: * at the breath of his mouth

the *wa*ters flow.

He makes his word known *to* Jacob, *
  to Israel his laws *and* decrees.

He has not dealt thus with *o*ther
  nations; * he has not taught them *his*
  decrees.

Glory to the Father, and to *the* Son, *
  and to the *Holy* Spirit:

as it was in the beginning, *is* now, * and
  will be for *e*ver. Amen.

Antiphon   We worship your cross, O Lord, † and we praise and glorify
               your holy res*ur*rection, * for the wood of the cross has brought
               joy *to* the world

READING   Isaiah 53:13-15

See, my servant shall prosper,
    he shall be raised high and greatly exalted.
Even as many were amazed at him—
    so marred was his look beyond that of man,
    and his appearance beyond that of mortals—
So shall he startle many nations,
    because of him kings shall stand speechless;
For those who have not been told shall see,
    those who have not heard shall ponder it.

In place of the responsory the following is said:

Antiphon   For our sake Christ was obedient, † accepting *e*ven death; *
               death on *a* cross.

CANTICLE OF ZECHARIAH

Antiphon   Over his head they hung their *ac*cusation: * Jesus of Nazareth,
               King of *the* Jews.

INTERCESSIONS (VI F)

For our sake our Redeemer suffered death and was buried, and *rose* again. * With
    heartfelt love let us adore *him*, and pray:

Lord, have mercy on us.

Christ our teacher, for our sake you were obedient even to ac*cep*ting death,
— teach us to obey the Father's will *in* all things.

Christ our life, by your death on the cross you destroyed the power of e*vil* and death,

— may we die with you, to rise with *you* in glory.

Christ our King, you became an outcast among us, a worm *and* no man,

— teach us the humility by which you *saved* the world.

Christ our salvation, you gave yourself up to death out of *love* for us,

— help us to show your love to *one* another.

Christ our Savior, on the cross you embraced all time with your *out*stretched arms,

— unite God's scattered children in your kingdom *of* salvation.

Our Father . . .

Prayer

Father,
look with love upon your people,
the love which our Lord Jesus Christ showed us
when he delivered himself to evil men
and suffered the agony of the cross,
for he lives and reigns with you and the Holy Spirit,
one God, for ever and ever.

Evening Prayer

HYMN, 334.

Evening Prayer is said only by those who do not participate in the celebration of the Lord's passion.

PSALMODY

Ant. 1   Look well, *all* you peoples, * and see *my* suffering.

IIA

Psalm 116: 10-19

I trusted, even *when* I said: * "I am sorely *afflicted*,"

and when I said in *my* alarm: * "No man can *be* trusted."

How can I re*pay* the Lord * for his goodness *to* me?

This cup of salvation *I* will raise; * I will call on *the* Lord's name.

My vows to the Lord I *will* fulfill * before all *his* people.

O precious in the eyes *of* the Lord * is the death of *his* faithful.

Your servant, Lord, your ser*vant* am I; * you have loosened *my* bonds.

A thanksgiving sacri*fice* I make: * I will call on *the* Lord's name.

My vows to the Lord I *will* fulfill *
  before all *his* people,
in the courts of the house *of* the Lord, *
  in your midst, O *Jerusalem.*

Glory to the Father, and *to* the Son, *
  and to the Ho*ly* Spirit:
as it was in the beginn*ing*, is now, * and
  will be for ever. *Amen.*

Antiphon   Look well, *all* you peoples, * and see *my* suffering.

Ant. 2   My soul is in *anguish*, * my heart is *in* torment.

VIIIa

Psalm 143:1-11

Lord, listen to my *prayer.* * turn
  your ear to my *ap*peal.
You are faithful, you are just; give
  answer. † Do not call your servant to
  *judg*ment * for no one is just in *your*
  sight.
The enemy pursues my *soul*; * he has
  crushed my life to *the* ground;
he has made me dwell in the *dark*ness *
  like the dead, long *forgotten.*
Therefore my spirit *fails*; * my heart is
  numb *with*in me.
I remember the days that are *past*: * I
  ponder all *your* works.
I muse on what your hand has
  wrought † and to you I stretch out
  my *hands.* * Like a parched land my
  soul thirsts *for* you.
Lord, make haste and *answer*; * for my
  spirit fails *with*in me.

Do not hide your *face* * lest I become
  like those in *the* grave.
In the morning let me know your *love*
  * for I put my trust *in* you.
Make me know the way I should *walk*:
  * to you I lift up *my* soul.
Rescue me, Lord, from my *enemies*; * I
  have fled to you *for* refuge.
Teach me to do your *will* * for you, O
  Lord, are *my* God.
Let your good spirit *guide* me * in ways
  that are level *and* smooth.
For your name's sake, Lord, save my
  life; * in your justice save my soul
  from *dis*tress.
Glory to the Father, and to the *Son*, *
  and to the Ho*ly* Spirit:
as it was in the beginning, is *now*, * and
  will be for ever. *Amen.*

Antiphon   My soul is in *anguish*, * my heart is *in* torment.

Ant. 3   When Jesus had taken the vinegar, † he said: "It is *accom*-
            plished." * Then he bowed his head *and* died.

Va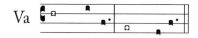

Canticle   Philippians 2:6-11

Though he was in the form *of* God, * Jesus did not deem equality with God something to *be* grasped at.

Rather, he emptied himself and took the form of *a* slave, * being born in the likeness *of* men.

He was known to be of human *estate*, * and it was thus that *he* humbled himself,

obediently accepting *even* death, * death on *a* cross!

Because of this, God highly *exalted* him * and bestowed on him the name above every oth*er* name,

So that at Jesus' name every knee *must* bend * in the heavens, on the earth, and under *the* earth,

and every tongue proclaim to the glory of God *the* Father: * JESUS CHRIST *IS* LORD!

Glory to the Father, and to *the* Son, * and to the Ho*ly* Spirit:

as it was in the beginning, *is* now, * and will be for ever. *A*men.

Antiphon   When Jesus had taken the vinegar, † he said: "It is *accom*plished." * Then he bowed his head *and* died.

READING   1 Peter 2:21-24

Christ suffered for you and left you an example, to have you follow in his footsteps. He did no wrong; no deceit was found in his mouth. When he was insulted, he returned no insult. When he was made to suffer, he did not counter with threats. Instead, he delivered himself up to the One who judges justly. In his own body he brought your sins to the cross, so that all of us, dead to sin, could live in accord with God's will. By his wounds you were healed.

In place of the responsory the following is said:

Antiphon   For our sake Christ was obedient, † accepting *even* death; * death on *a* cross.

CANTICLE OF MARY

Antiphon   When we were his enemies, † God reconciled us *to* himself * by the death of *his* Son.

INTERCESSIONS (VI F)

As intercessions the General Intercessions found in the Sacramentary for this day may be used. The prayers suggested here may be used as an alternative, or silent prayer may be offered for these intentions.

Today we lovingly remember the death of our Lord Jesus Christ, from which was born new life for the whole world. Let us turn to God the Father, and say:
By the merits of your Son's death, hear us, Lord.

Give unity to your Church.
Protect N., our Pope.
Sanctify your people, both clergy and faithful, by your Spirit.
Increase faith and understanding in those under instruction.
Gather all Christians in unity.
Lead the Jewish people to the fullness of redemption.
Enlighten with your glory those who do not yet believe in Christ.
Show the marks of your love in creation to those who deny them.
Guide the minds and hearts of those who govern us.
Console all who are troubled.
Have pity on those who have died.

Our Father . . .

Prayer

Father,
look with love upon your people,
the love which our Lord Jesus Christ showed us
when he delivered himself to evil men
and suffered the agony of the cross,
for he lives and reigns with you and the Holy Spirit,
one God, for ever and ever.

Night Prayer from Sunday, after Evening Prayer II, 875.

In place of the responsory the following is said:

Antiphon   For our sake Christ was obedient, † accepting *even* death; *
             death on *a* cross.

HOLY SATURDAY

Morning Prayer

HYMN
Tibi Redemptor. (L.M.)

Tibi, Redemptor omnium,	Redeemer of our fallen race
hymnum deflentes canimus;	With contrite hearts we sing to you;
ignosce nobis, Domine,	Forgive us, Lord, we humbly pray,
ignosce confitentibus.	Forgive us who confess your Name.
Qui vires hostis veteris	The pow'r of Satan and his hordes
per crucem mortis conteris,	You broke by death upon the Cross;
qua nos vexillum fidei,	Singed on the forehead with this seal
fronte signati, ferimus,	We bear the banner of our faith.
Illum a nobis iugiter	His grim dominion over us
repellere dignaveris,	You deigned to shatter and dispel,
ne possit umquam lædere	Lest he for ever should do harm
redemptos tuo sanguine.	To souls once ransomed by your Blood.
Qui propter nos ad inferos	You visited the gloom of hell
descendere dignatus es,	To lead to everlasting joy
ut mortis debitoribus	The faithful of the ancient Law,
vitæ donares munera,	Awaiting you in silent hope.
Tu es qui certo tempore	Alone you know the certain time
daturus finem sæculo,	When this our world must pass away,
iustus cunctorum merita	And when as Judge of every soul
remunerator statues.	You will award what justice claims.
Te ergo, Christe, quæsumus,	So heal our wounds we beg this day,
ut nostra cures vulnera,	O Savior Jesus Christ, our Lord,
qui es cum Patre et Spiritu	Who with the Father will be praised
laudandus in perpetuum. Amen.	For ever with your Spirit's Love. Amen.

PSALMODY

Ant. 1   Though sinless, the Lord has been *put* to death. * The world is
in mourning as for an *only* son.

VIIIg

Psalm 64

Hear my voice, O God, as *I* complain, * guard my life from	dread *of* the foe. Hide me from the band *of* the wicked,

* from the throng of those *who* do evil.
They sharpen their *tongues* like swords; * they aim bitter *words* like arrows
to shoot at the inno*cent* from ambush, * shooting sudden*ly* and recklessly.
They scheme their *evil* course; * they conspire to lay *secret* snares.
They say: "*Who* will see us, * Who can search *out* our crimes?"
He will search who search*es* the mind * and knows the depth *of* the heart.
God has shot them *with* his arrow *

and dealt them *sud*den wounds.
Their own tongue has brought *them* to ruin * and all who *see* them mock.
Then will *all* men fear; * they will tell what *God* has done.
They will under*stand* God's deeds. * The just will rejoice *in* the Lord
and fly to *him* for refuge. * All the upright *hearts* will glory.
Glory to the Father, and *to* the Son, * and to the *Holy* Spirit,
as it was in the begin*ning* is now, * and will be for ev*er.* Amen.

Antiphon   Though sinless, the Lord has been *put* to death. * The world is in mourning as for an *only* son.

Ant. 2   From the *jaws* of hell, * Lord, rescue my *soul.*

IID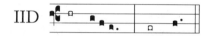

Canticle   Isaiah 38:10-14, 17-20

Once I said, "In the noon*time* of life * I must de*part*!
To the gates of the nether world I shall *be* consigned * for the rest of my *years.*"
I said, "I shall see the *Lord* no more * in the land of the *living.*
No longer shall I behold my *fellow* men * among those who dwell in the *world.*"
My dwelling, like a *shep*herd's tent, * is struck down and borne away from *me*;
you have folded up my life, *like* a weaver * who severs the last *thread.*
Day and night you give me ov*er* to torment; * I cry out until the *dawn.*
Like a lion he breaks *all* my bones; * day and night you give me over to

torment.
Like a swallow I ut*ter* shrill cries; * I moan like a *dove.*
My eyes grow weak, *gazing* heavenward: * O Lord, I am in straits; be my *sure*ty!
You have pre*served* my life * from the pit of des*truc*tion,
when you cast be*hind* your back * all my *sins.*
For it is not the nether world that *gives* you thanks, * nor death that praises *you*;
neither do those who go down in*to* the pit * await your *kind*ness.
The living, the living *give* you thanks, * as I do to*day.*
Fathers declare *to* their sons, * O God, your *faith*fulness.

The Lord *is* our savior; * we shall sing to stringed *in*struments
in the house *of* the Lord * all the days of our *life*.

Glory to the Father, and *to* the Son, * and to the Holy *Spi*rit:
as it was in the begin*ning*, is now, * and will be for ever. A*men*.

Antiphon   From the *jaws* of hell, * Lord, rescue my *soul*.

Ant. 3   I was dead, but now I live *for* ever, * and I hold the keys of death *and* of hell.

Vc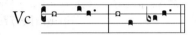

Psalm 150

Praise God in his ho*ly* place, * praise him in his *migh*ty heavens.
Praise him for his power*ful* deeds, * praise his sur*pas*sing greatness.
O praise him with sound *of* trumpet, * praise him with *lute* and harp.
Praise him with timbrel *and* dance, * praise him with *strings* and pipes.
O praise him with resound*ing* cymbals,

* praise him with cla*shing* of cymbals.
Let everything that lives and *that* breathes * give praise *to* the Lord.
Glory to the Father, and to *the* Son, * and to the *Ho*ly Spirit,
as it was in the beginning, *is* now, * and will be for e*ver*. Amen.

Antiphon   I was dead, but now I live *for* ever, * and I hold the keys of death *and* of hell.

READING   Hosea 5:15b-6:2

Thus says the Lord:
In their affliction, they shall look for me:
"Come, let us return to the Lord,
For it is he who has rent, but he will heal us;
he has struck us, but he will bind our wounds.
He will revive us after two days;
on the third day he will raise us up,
to live in his presence."

In place of the responsory the following is said:
Antiphon   For our sake Christ was obedient, † accepting *even* death; * death on *a* cross.
                       Therefore God raised *him* on high * and gave him the name above all oth*er* names.

CANTICLE OF ZECHARIAH

Antiphon   Save us, O Savior of the world. † On the cross you redeemed us
by the shedding *of* your blood; * we cry out for your help, O
God.

INTERCESSIONS (VI F)

Our Redeemer suffered and was buried for us in order to *rise* again. * With
sincere love we adore him, and aware of our needs *we* cry out:

Lord, have mercy on *us.*

Christ our Savior, your sorrowing Mother stood by you at your *death* and burial,
— in our sorrows may we *share* your suffering.

Christ our Lord, like the seed buried in the ground, you brought forth for us
the har*vest* of grace,
— may we die to sin and *live* for God.

Christ the Good Shepherd, in death you lay hidden *from* the world,
— teach us to love a life hidden with you *in* the Father.

Christ, the New Adam, you entered the kingdom of death to release all the just
since the beginning *of* the world,
— may all who lie dead in sin hear your voice and *rise* to life.

Christ, Son of the living God, through baptism we were bur*ied* with you,
— risen also with you in baptism, may we walk in new*ness* of life.

Our Father . . .

Prayer

All-powerful and ever-living God,
your only Son went down among the dead
and rose again in glory.
In your goodness
raise up your faithful people,
buried with him in baptism,
to be one with him
in the eternal life of heaven,
where he lives and reigns with you and the Holy Spirit,
one God, for ever and ever.

Evening Prayer

HYMN

Auctor salutis unice. Mode VIII (L.M.)

Auctor salutis unice,	Salvation's only King and Lord,
mundi redemptor inclite,	The world's Redeemer, as foretold,
rex, Christe, nobis annue	Christ Jesus, now bestow on us
crucis fecundæ gloriam.	The grace and glory of the Cross.
Tu morte mortem diruens	By dying you have conquered death,
vitamque vita largiens,	True Life Itself, you give us life,
mortis ministrum subdolum	No longer Satan can exult,
deviceras diabolum.	As crafty minister of doom.
Piis amoris artibus	By mourning love and tender hands,
somno seulcri traditus,	Your limbs within the tomb were laid,
sedes recludis inferi	While you descended to the shades
patresque dicis liberos.	And set the Old Law's servants free.
Nunc in Parentis dextera	At God the Father's side enthroned,
sacrata fulgens victima,	Resplendent with those sacred wounds,
audi, precamur, vivido	Hear now the prayer of those redeemed
tuo redemptos sanguine,	By your life-giving precious Blood.
Quo te diebus omnibus	That as we strive to follow you
puris sequentes moribus,	By blameless lives from day to day,
adversus omnes impetus	We may raise high the holy Cross
crucis feramus labarum.	Against the evil one's assaults.
Patri, tibi, Paraclito	With Father and the Spirit One,
sit æqua, Iesu, floria,	All glory, Jesus, be to you,
qui nos crucis victoria	Who by the triumph of the Cross
concedis usque perfrui. Amen.	Will lead us to eternal life. Amen.

PSALMODY

Ant. 1　　　Death, you shall *die* in me; * hell, you shall be destroyed *by* me.

Psalm 116: 10-19

I trusted, even *when* I said: * "I am sorely *afflicted*,"　　and when I said in *my* alarm: * "No man can *be* trusted."

How can I re*pay* the Lord * for his goodness *to* me?

The cup of salvation *I* will raise; * I will call on *the* Lord's name.

My vows to the Lord I *will* fulfill * before all *his* people.

O precious in the eyes *of* the Lord * is the death of *his* faithful.

Your servant, Lord, your ser*vant* am I; * you have loosened *my* bonds.

A thanksgiving sacri*fice* I make: * I will call on *the* Lord's name.

My vows to the Lord I *will* fulfill * before all *his* people,

in the courts of the house *of* the Lord, * in your midst, O *Jerusalem.*

Glory to the Father, and *to* the Son, * and to the Ho*ly* Spirit:

as it was in the beginn*ing*, is now, * and will be for ever. *A*men.

Antiphon   Death, you shall *die* in me; * hell, you shall be destroyed *by* me.

Ant. 2   As Jonah was three days and three *nights* * in the belly of *the* whale,
so will the Son of Man be three days and three *nights* * in the heart of *the* earth.

VIIIa

Psalm 143:1-11

Lord, listen to my *prayer*: * turn your ear to my *ap*peal.

You are faithful, you are just; give answer. † Do not call your servant to *judg*ment * for no one is just in *your* sight.

The enemy pursues my *soul*; * he has crushed my life to *the* ground;

he has made me dwell in *dark*ness * like the dead, long *for*gotten.

Therefore my spirit *fails*; * my heart is numb *with*in me.

I remember the days that are *past*: * I ponder all *your* works.

I muse on what your hand has wrought † and to you I stretch out my *hands*. * Like a parched land my soul thirsts *for* you.

Lord, make haste and *an*swer; * for my spirit fails *with*in me.

Do not hide your *face* * lest I become like those in *the* grave.

In the morning let me know your *love* * for I put my trust *in* you.

Make me know the way I should *walk*: * to you I lift up *my* soul.

Rescue me, Lord, from my *ene*mies; * I have fled to you *for* refuge.

Teach me to do your *will* * for you, O Lord, are *my* God.

Let your good spirit *guide* me * in ways that are level *and* smooth.

For your name's sake, Lord, save my *life*; * in your justice save my soul from *dis*tress.

Glory to the Father, and to the *Son*, * and to the Ho*ly* Spirit:

as it was in the beginning, is *now*, * and will be for ever. *A*men.

Antiphon	As Jonah was three days and three *nights* * in the belly of *the* whale, so will the Son of Man be three days and three *nights* * in the heart of *the* earth.

Ant. 3	Destroy this temple, says the Lord, † and in three days I will *re*build it. * He was speaking of the temple of *his* body.

Va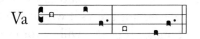

Canticle   Philippians 2:6-11
Christ, God's holy servant

Though he was in the form *of* God, * Jesus did not deem equality with God something to *be* grasped at.

Rather, he emptied himself and took the form of *a* slave, * being born in the likeness *of* men.

He was known to be of human *es*tate, * and it was thus that *he* humbled himself,

obediently accepting e*ven* death, * death on *a* cross!

Because of this, God highly *ex*alted him * and bestowed on him the name above every oth*er* name,

So that at Jesus' name every knee *must* bend * in the heavens, on the earth, and under *the* earth,

and every tongue proclaim to the glory of God *the* Father: * JESUS CHRIST *IS* LORD!

Glory to the Father, and to *the* Son, * and to the Ho*ly* Spirit:

as it was in the beginning, *is* now, * and will be for ever. *A*men.

Antiphon	Destroy this temple, says the Lord, † and in three days I will *re*build it. * He was speaking of the temple of *his* body.

READING   1 *Peter* 1:18-21

Realize that you were delivered from the futile way of life your fathers handed on to you, not by any diminishable sum of silver or gold, but by Christ's blood beyond all price: the blood of a spotless, unblemished lamb chosen before the world's foundation and revealed for your sake in these last days. It is through him that you are believers in God, the God who raised him from the dead and gave him glory. You faith and hope, then, are centered in God.

In place of the responsory the following is said:

Antiphon	For our sake Christ was obedient, † accepting e*ven* death; * death on *a* cross. Therefore God raised *him* on high * and gave him the name above all oth*er* names.

CANTICLE OF MARY

Antiphon　　Now the Son of Man *has* been glorified * and God has been glorified *in* him.

INTERCESSIONS (VI F)

For our sake our Redeemer suffered death and was buried, and *rose* again. * With heartfelt love let us adore *him*, and pray:

Lord, have mercy on *us.*

Lord Jesus, when your side was pierced, there flowed out blood and water, the marvelous symbol of *the* whole Church,

— through your death, burial and resurrection, bring life to your *bride*, the Church.

Lord Jesus, you remembered those who did not remember your promise of *re*surrection,

　remember those without hope, who do not know that *you* have risen.

Lamb of God, you were offered for all as our *pas*chal sacrifice,

— draw all mankind *to* yourself.

God of all the world, you encompass the universe but were pleased to be laid *in* a tomb,

— free the human race from the powers of darkness, and grant it the gift of im*mor*tal glory.

Christ, Son of the living God, you opened the gates of paradise to the re*pent*ant thief,

— gather all who have shared your death and burial into the glory of your *re*surrection.

Our Father . . .

Prayer

All-powerful and ever-living God,
your only Son went down among the dead
and rose again in glory.
In your goodness
raise up your faithful people,
buried with him in baptism,
to be one with him
in the eternal life of heaven,
where he lives and reigns with you and the Holy Spirit,
one God, for ever and ever.

Night Prayer from Sunday, after Evening Prayer II, 875. It is said only by those who do not participate in the Easter Vigil.

In place of the responsory the following is said:

Antiphon   For our sake Christ was obedient, † accepting *even* death; *
death on *a* cross.
Therefore God raised *him* on high * and gave him the name
above all oth*er* names.

Proper of Seasons
Easter

On Easter Sunday the Invitatory is always said at the beginning of Morning Prayer.

Lord, ✝ open my lips.   And my mouth will proclaim your praise.

Antiphon   The Lord is *ri*sen, * al*le*luia.

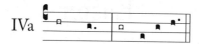

IVa

Psalm 95
A call to praise God
Encourage each other daily while it is still today (Hebrews 13:13).
(The antiphon is recited and then repeated)

Come, let us sing to the *Lord* * and shout with joy to the *Rock* who saves us.

Let us approach him with praise and thanks*giving* * and sing joyful songs *to* the Lord.

(Antiphon repeated)

The Lord is God, the mighty *God,* * the great king over *all* the gods.

He holds in his hands the depths of the *earth* * and the highest moun*tains* as well.

He made the sea; it belongs to *him,* * the dry land, too, for it was formed *by* his hands.

(Antiphon repeated)

Come, then, let us bow down and *worship,* * bending the knee before the *Lord,* our maker.

For he is our God and we are his *people,* * the *flock* he shepherds.

(Antiphon repeated)

Today, listen to the voice of the Lord: †
Do not grow *stub*born, * as your fathers did *in* the wilderness,

when at Meriba and Massah they challenged me and pro*voked* me, * Although they had seen all *of* my works.

(Antiphon repeated)

Forty years I endured that generation. †
I said, "They are a people whose hearts go a*stray* * and they do not *know* my ways."

So I swore in my *ang*er, * "They shall not enter in*to* my rest."

(Antiphon repeated)

Glory to the Father, and to the *Son,* * and to the *Holy* Spirit:

as it was in the beginning, is *now,* * and will be for *ev*er. Amen.

(Antiphon repeated)

EASTER SUNDAY

The beginning of the Easter Season.

Morning Prayer

EASTER HYMN
Aurora lucis rutilat. Mode VIII (L.M.)

Aurora lucis rutilat, Cælum resultat laudibus, Mundus exsultans iubilat, Gemens infernus ululat.	The morn had spread her crimson rays, When rang the skies with shouts of praise; Earth joined the joyful hymn to swell, That brought despair to vanquished hell.
Cum rex ille fortissimus, Mortis confractis viribus, Pede conculcans tartara Solvit catena miseros.	He comes victorious from the grave, The Lord omnipotent to save, And brings with him to light of day The Saints who long imprisoned lay.
Ille, quem clausum lapide Miles custodit acriter, Triumphans pompa nobili Victor surgit de funere.	Vain is the cavern's threefold ward— The stone, the seal, the armèd guard; O death, no more thine arm we fear, The Victor's tomb is now thy bier.
Inferni iam gemitibus solutis et doloribus, Quia surrexit Dominus Resplendens clamat angelus.	Enough of death, enough of tears, Enough of sorrows and of fears! O hear yon white-robed angel cry, Death's Conqueror lives, no more to die.
Esto perenne mentibus Paschale, Iesu, gaudium, Et nos renatos gratiæ Tuis triumphis aggrega.	Grant, Lord, in thee each faithful mind Unceasing Paschal joy may find; And from the death of sin set free Souls newly born to life by thee.
Iesu, tibi sit gloria, Qui morte victa prænites, Cum Patre et almo Spiritu, In sempiterna sæcula. Amen.	To thee, once dead, who now dost live, All glory, Lord, thy people give, Whom, with the Father we adore, And Holy Ghost for evermore. Amen.

PSALMODY

Ant. 1   The splendor of Christ risen *from* the dead * has shone on the people redeemed by his blood, *a*lleluia.

VIIIg

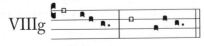

Psalm 63:2-9
A soul thirsting for God
Whoever has left the darkness of sin, yearns for God.

O God, you are my God, for *you* I long; * for you my *soul* is thirsting.
My body *pines* for you * like a dry, weary land *with*out water.
So I gaze on you *in* the sanctuary * to see your strength *and* your glory.
For your love is bet*ter* than life, * my lips will *speak* your praise.
So I will bless you *all* my life, * in your name I will lift *up* my hands.
My soul shall be filled as *with* a banquet, * my mouth shall praise *you*

with joy.
On my bed I re*mem*ber you. * On you I muse *through* the night
for you have *been* my help; * in the shadow of your wings *I* rejoice.
My soul *clings* to you; * your right hand *holds* me fast.
Glory to the Father, and *to* the Son, * and to the *Holy* Spirit:
as it was in the begin*ning*, is now, * and will be for *ever*. Amen.

Antiphon   The splendor of Christ risen *from* the dead * has shone on the people redeemed by his blood, *al*leluia.

Ant. 2   Our Redeemer has risen *from* the tomb; * let us sing a hymn of praise to the Lord our God, al*le*luia.

IIA

Canticle   Daniel 3:57-88; 56
Let all creatures praise the Lord
All you servants of the Lord, sing praise to him (Revelation 19:5).

B less the Lord, all you works *of* the Lord. * Praise and exalt him above all *for*ever.
Angels of the Lord, *bless* the Lord, * You heavens, bless *the* Lord.
All you waters above the heavens, *bless* the Lord. * All you hosts of the Lord, bless *the* Lord.
Sun and moon, *bless* the Lord. * Stars of heaven, bless *the* Lord.
Every shower and dew, *bless* the Lord. * All you winds, bless *the* Lord.
Fire and heat, *bless* the Lord. * Cold and chill, bless *the* Lord.
Dew and rain, *bless* the Lord. * Frost and chill, bless *the* Lord.
Ice and snow, *bless* the Lord. * Nights and days, bless *the* Lord.

Light and darkness, *bless* the Lord. * Lightnings and clouds, bless *the* Lord.
Let the earth *bless* the Lord. * Praise and exalt him above all *for*ever.
Mountains and hills, *bless* the Lord. * Everything growing from the earth, bless *the* Lord.
You springs, *bless* the Lord. * Seas and rivers, bless *the* Lord.
You dolphins and all water creatures, *bless* the Lord. * All you birds of the air, bless *the* Lord.
All you beasts, wild and tame, *bless* the Lord. * You sons of men, bless *the* Lord.
O Israel, *bless* the Lord. * Praise and exalt him above all *for*ever.

Priests of the Lord, *bless* the Lord. *
    Servants of the Lord, bless *the* Lord.
Spirits and souls of the just, *bless* the
    Lord. * Holy men of humble heart,
    bless *the* Lord.
Hananiah, Azariah, Mishael, *bless* the
    Lord. * Praise and exalt him above all

*fo*rever.
Let us bless the Father, and the Son,
    and the *Ho*ly Spirit. * Let us praise
    and exalt him above all *fo*rever.
Bless̀ed are you in the firma*ment* of
    heaven.* Praiseworthy and glorious
    and exalted above all *fo*rever.

Antiphon   Our Redeemer has risen *from* the tomb; * let us sing a hymn of
               praise to the Lord our God, al*le*luia.

Ant. 3   Alleluia, the Lord is risen as *he* promised, * al*le*luia.

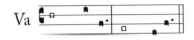

Psalm 149
The joy of God's holy people
Let the sons of the Church, the children of the new people, rejoice in Christ,
their King (Hesychius).

Sing a new song to *the* Lord, * his
praise in the assembly of *the*
faithful.
Let Israel rejoice in *its* Maker, * let
    Zion's sons exult in *their* king.
Let them praise his name *with* dancing
    * and make music with timbrel *and*
    harp.
For the Lord takes delight in *his* people.
    * He crowns the poor with *sal*vation.
Let the faithful rejoice in *their* glory, *
    shout for joy and take *their* rest.

Let the praise of God be on *their* lips *
    and a two-edged sword in *their* hand,
to deal out vengeance to *the* nations *
    and punishment on all *the* peoples;
to bind their kings *in* chains * and their
    nobles in fetters *of* iron;
to carry out the sentence pre-*or*dained:
    * this honor is for all *his* faithful.
Glory to the Father, and to *the* Son, *
    and to the *Ho*ly Spirit:
as it was in the beginning, *is* now, * and
    will be for ever. *A*men.

Antiphon   Alleluia, the Lord is risen as *he* promised, * al*le*luia.

READING   Acts 10:40-43

    God raised up Jesus on the third day and granted that he be seen, not by all,
but only by such witnesses as had been chosen beforehand by God— by us
who ate and drank with him after he rose from the dead. He commissioned
us to preach to the people and to bear witness that he is the one set apart by
God as judge of the living and the dead. To him all the prophets testify,
saying that everyone who believes in him has forgiveness of sins through his
name.

374 Easter Sunday

In place of the responsory the following is said:

Ant.   This is the day the *Lord* has made; * let us rejoice and be glad, al*le*luia. (VI F)

CANTICLE OF ZECHARIAH

Ant.   Very early on the morning after the Sabbath, † when the sun *had* just risen, * they came to the tomb, al*le*luia.

If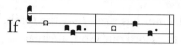

Blessèd ✠ be the Lord, the *God* of Israel; * he has come to his people and set *them* free.

He has raised up for us a *mighty* savior, * born of the house of his ser*vant* David.

Through his holy prophets he promised of old † that he would save us *from* our enemies, * from the hands of all *who* hate us.

He promised to show mercy *to* our fathers * and to remember his ho*ly* covenant.

This was the oath he swore to our *father* Abraham: * to set us free from the hands of *our* enemies,

free to worship him without fear, † holy and righteous *in* his sight * all the days of *our* life.

You, my child, shall be called the prophet *of* the Most High; * for you will go before the Lord to prepare *his* way,

to give his people knowledge *of* salvation * by the forgiveness of *their* sins.

In the tender compassion *of* our God * the dawn from on high shall break *up*on us,

to shine on those who dwell in darkness and the sha*dow* of death, * and to guide our feet into the way *of* peace.

Glory to the Father, and *to* the Son, * and to the Ho*ly* Spirit:

as it was in the begin*ning*, is now, * and will be for ever. *A*men.

Ant.   Very early on the morning after the Sabbath, † when the sun *had* just risen, * they came to the tomb, al*le*luia.

INTERCESSIONS (VI F)

Christ is the Lord of life, raised up by the Father; in his turn he will raise us up *by* his power. * Let us pray *to* him, saying:

Christ our life, *save us.*

Lord Jesus, light shining in the darkness, you lead you people into life, and give our mortal nature the *gift* of holiness,

— may we spend this day in praise *of* your glory.

Lord, you walked the way of suffering and *cru*cifixion,

— may we suffer and die with you, and rise again to *share* your glory.

Son of the Father, our master and our brother, you have made us a kingdom of
   priests *for* our God,
— may we offer you our joyful sacri*fice* of praise.
King of glory, we look forward to the great day of your com*ing* in splendor,
— that we may see you face to face, and be transformed *in* your likeness.

Our Father . . .

Prayer

God our Father,
by raising Christ your Son
you conquered the power of death
and opened for us the way to eternal life.
Let our celebration today
raise us up and renew our lives
by the Spirit that is within us.
Grant this through our Lord Jesus Christ, your Son,
who lives and reigns with you and the Holy Spirit,
one God, for ever and ever.

The following dismissal is said:

Go in the peace of Christ, al- le- lu- ia, al- le- lu- ia.
Thanks be to God, al- le- lu- ia, al- le- lu- ia.

Easter Sunday

Evening Prayer

HYMN

Ad coenam Agni providi. Mode VIII (L.M.)

Mode 8

Ad cenam Agni providi,
Stolis salutis candidi,
Post transitum maris Rubri
Christo canamus principi.

The Lamb's high banquet we await
In snow-white robes of royal state;
And now, the Red Sea's channel past,
To Christ, our Prince, we sing at last.

Cuius corpus sanctissimum
In ara crucis torridum,
Sed et cruorem roseum
Gustando, Dei vivimus.

Upon the altar of the Cross
His body hath redeemed our loss;
And tasting of his life-red Blood
Our life is hid with him in God.

Protecti paschae vespero
A devastante angelo,
De Pharaonis aspero
Sumus erepti imperio.

That Paschal eve God's arm was bared;
The devastating Angel spared:
By strength of hand our hosts went free
From Pharoah's ruthless tyranny.

Iam pascha nostrum Christus est,
Agnus occisus innocens;
Sinceritatis azyma
Qui carnem suam obtulit.

Now Christ, our Paschal Lamb, is slain,
The Lamb of God that knows no stain;
The true Oblation offered here,
Our own unleavened Bread sincere.

O vera, digna hostia,
Per quam franguntur tartara,
Captiva plebs redimitur,
Redduntur vitae præmia!

O thou from whom hell's monarch flies,
O great, O very Sacrifice,
Thy captive people are set free,
And endless life restored in thee.

Consurgit Christus tumulo,
Victor redit de barathro,
Tyrannum trudens vinculo
Et paradisum reserans.

For Christ arising from the dead,
From conquered hell victorious sped;
He thrusts the tyrant down to chains,
And Paradise for man regains.

Esto perenne mentibus
Paschale, Iesu, gaudium
Et nos renatos gratiæ
Tuis triumphis aggrega.

Maker of all, to thee we pray,
Fulfill in us thy joy today;
When death assails, grant, Lord, that we
May share the Paschal victory.

Iesu, tibi sit gloria,
Qui morte victa prænites,
Cum Patre et almo Spiritu,
In sempiterna sæcula. Amen.

To thee, who dead, again dost live,
All glory, Lord, thy people give;
All glory as is ever meet,
To Father and to Paraclete. Amen.

PSALMODY

Ant. 1   Mary Magdalene and the other Mary came to *see* the Lord's tomb,* *al*leluia.

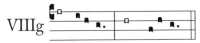

VIIIg

Psalm 110:1-5, 7
The Messiah, king and priest
Christ's reign will last until all his enemies are made subject to him
(1 Corinthians 15:25).

The Lord's revelation to my Master:
† "Sit *on* my right: * your foes I will put be*neath* your feet."
The Lord will wield from Zion † your scep*ter* of power: * rule in the midst of *all* your foes.
A prince from the day of your birth † on the *holy* mountains; * from the womb before the dawn *I* begot you.
The Lord has sworn an oath he will not change. † "You are a *priest* for ever, *

a priest like Melchize*dek* of old."
The Master standing *at* your right hand * will shatter kings in the day of *his* great wrath.
He shall drink from the stream *by* the wayside * and therefore he shall lift *up* his head.
Glory to the Father, and *to* the Son, * and to the *Holy* Spirit:
as it was in the begin*ning*, is now, * and will be for ev*er*. Amen.

Antiphon   Mary Magdalene and the other Mary came to *see* the Lord's tomb,* *al*leluia.

Ant. 2   Come and see the place where the *Lord* was buried, * al*le*luia.

IIA

Psalm 114
The Israelites are delivered from the bondage of Egypt
You too left Egypt when, at baptism, you renounced that world which is at enmity with God
(St. Augustine).

When Israel came *forth* from Egypt, * Jacob's sons from an ali*en* people,
Judah became *the* Lord's temple, * Israel became *his* kingdom.
The sea fled *at* the sight: * the Jordan turned back on *its* course,
the mountains *leapt* like rams * and the

hills like year*ling* sheep.
Why was it, sea, *that* you fled, * that you turned back, Jordan, on *your* course?
Mountains, that you *leapt* like rams, * hills, like year*ling* sheep?
Tremble, O earth, be*fore* the Lord, * in the presence of the God *of* Jacob,

who turns the rock in*to* a pool * and
   flint into a spring *of* water.
Glory to the Father, and *to* the Son, *

and to the Ho*ly* Spirit:
   as it was in the begin*ning*, is now, * and
   will be for ever. *A*men.

Antiphon   Come and see the place where the *Lord* was buried, * al*le*luia.

Ant. 3   Jesus said: Do not be afraid. † Go and tell my brothers to set out
                  for Galilee; † there they *will* see me, * alleluia, alleluia.

                              ** al- le- lu- ia, al- le- lu- ia.

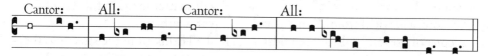

      *Al- le- lu- ia.   ** al- le- lu- ia,   al- le - lu- ia.

                          Canticle   See Revelation 19:1-7

Salvation, glory, and power to *our* God:
   * Alleluia.
his judgments are hon*est* and true.
** Alleluia, alleluia.
Sing praise to our God, all you *his* servants,
* Alleluia.
all who worship him reverently, *great* and small.
** Alleluia, alleluia.

The Lord our all-powerful God *is* King;
* Alleluia.
let us rejoice, sing praise, and *give* him glory.
** Alleluia, alleluia.

The wedding feast of the Lamb has *begun*,
* Alleluia.
and his bride is pre*pared* to welcome him.
** Alleluia, alleluia.

Glory to the Father, and to the Son, †
and to the Ho*ly* Spirit.
* Alleluia.
As it was in the beginning, is now, †
and will be for ev*er*. Amen.
** Alleluia, alleluia.

Antiphon   Jesus said: Do not be afraid. † Go and tell my brothers to set out for Galilee; † there they *will* see me, * alleluia, alleluia.

READING   Hebrews 10:12-14

Jesus offered one sacrifice for sins and took his seat forever at the right hand of God; now he waits until his enemies are placed beneath his feet. By one offering he has forever perfected those who are being sanctified.

In place of the responsory the following is said:

Ant.   This is the day the *Lord* has made; * let us rejoice and be glad, al*le*luia. (VI F)

CANTICLE OF MARY

Ant.   On the evening of the first day *of* the week, * the disciples were gathered together behind *locked* doors;
suddenly, Jesus stood among *them* and said: * Peace be with you, al*le*luia.

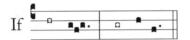

My soul ✠ proclaims the greatness *of* the Lord, * my spirit rejoices in God *my* savior

for he has *looked* with favor * on his low*ly* servant.

From this day all *gen*erations * will call *me* blessèd:

the Almighty has done great *things* for me, * and holy is *his* Name.

He has mercy on *those* who fear him * in every gen*er*ation.

He has shown the strength *of* his arm, * he has scattered the proud in their *con*ceit.

He has cast down the mighty *from* their thrones, * and has lifted up *the* lowly.

He has filled the hungry *with* good things, * and the rich he has sent a*way* empty.

He has come to the help of his *serv*ant Israel * for he has remembered his promise *of* mercy,

the promise he made *to* our fathers, * to Abraham and his children *for* ever.

Glory to the Father, and *to* the Son, * and to the Ho*ly* Spirit:

as it was in the begin*ning*, is now, * and will be for ever. *A*men.

Antiphon   On the evening of the first day *of* the week, * the disciples were gathered together behind *locked* doors;
suddenly, Jesus stood among *them* and said: * Peace be with you, al*le*luia.

INTERCESSIONS (VI F)

With joy in our hearts, let us call upon *Christ* the Lord, * who died and rose again,
   and lives always to inter*cede* for us:
Victorious King, hear our *prayer.*

Light and salvation *of* all peoples,
— send into our hearts the fire of your Spirit, as we proclaim your *re*surrection.

Let Israel recognize in you her longed-*for* Messiah,
— and the whole earth be filled with the knowledge *of* your glory.

Keep us in the communion *of* your saints,
— and grant us rest from our labors *in* their company.

You have triumphed over death, your enemy; destroy in us the pow*er* of death,
— that we may live only for you, victorious and im*mor*tal Lord.

Savior Christ, you were obedient even to accepting death, and were raised up to
   the right hand *of* the Father,
— in your goodness welcome your brothers and sisters into the kingdom *of* your
   glory.

Our Father . . .

Prayer

   God our Father,
   by raising Christ your Son
   you conquered the power of death
   and opened for us the way to eternal life.
   Let our celebration today
   raise us up and renew our lives
   by the Spirit that is within us.
   Grant this through our Lord Jesus Christ, your Son,
   who lives and reigns with you and the Holy Spirit,
   one God, for ever and ever.

The following dismissal is said:

Go in the peace of Christ, al- le- lu- ia, al- le-   lu-   ia.

   Thanks be to God,   al- le- lu- ia, al- le-   lu-   ia.

OCTAVE OF EASTER

Morning Prayer

EASTER HYMN
Aurora lucis rutilat. Mode VIII (L.M.)

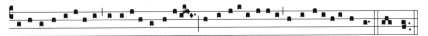

Aurora lucis rutilat,	The morn had spread her crimson rays,
Cælum resultat laudibus,	When rang the skies with shouts of praise;
Mundus exsultans iubilat,	Earth joined the joyful hymn to swell,
Gemens infernus ululat.	That brought despair to vanquished hell.
Cum rex ille fortissimus,	He comes victorious from the grave,
Mortis contractis viribus,	The Lord omnipotent to save,
Pede conculcans tartara	And brings with him to light of day
Solvit catena miseros.	The Saints who long imprisoned lay.
Ille, quem clausum lapide	Vain is the cavern's threefold ward—
Miles custodit acriter,	The stone, the seal, the armèd guard;
Triumphans pompa nobili	O death, no more thine arm we fear,
Victor surgit de funere.	The Victor's tomb is now thy bier.
Inferni iam gemitibus	Enough of death, enough of tears,
solutis et doloribus,	Enough of sorrows and of fears!
Quia surrexit Dominus	O hear yon white-robed angel cry,
Resplendens clamat angelus.	Death's Conqueror lives, no more to die.
Esto perenne mentibus	Grant, Lord, in thee each faithful mind
Paschale, Iesu, gaudium,	Unceasing Paschal joy may find;
Et nos renatos gratiæ	And from the death of sin set free
Tuis triumphis aggrega.	Souls newly born to life by thee.
Iesu, tibi sit gloria,	To thee, once dead, who now dost live,
Qui morte victa prænites,	All glory, Lord, thy people give,
Cum Patre et almo Spiritu,	Whom, with the Father we adore,
In sempiterna sæcula. Amen.	And Holy Ghost for evermore. Amen.

Ant. 1   The splendor of Christ risen *from* the dead * has shone on the
people redeemed by his blood, *al*leluia.

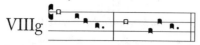

VIIIg

Psalm 63:2-9
A soul thirsting for God
Whoever has left the darkness of sin, yearns for God.

O God, you are my God, for *you* I
long; * for you my *soul* is thirsting.
My body *pines* for you * like a dry,
weary land *with*out water.
So I gaze on you *in* the sanctuary * to
see your strength *and* your glory.
For your love is bet*ter* than life, * my
lips will *speak* your praise.
So I will bless you *all* my life, * in your
name I will lift *up* my hands.
My soul shall be filled as *with* a banquet, * my mouth shall praise *you*

with joy.
On my bed I re*mem*ber you. * On you I
muse *through* the night
for you have *been* my help; * in the
shadow of your wings *I* rejoice.
My soul *clings* to you; * your right hand
holds me fast.
Glory to the Father, and *to* the Son, *
and to the *Holy* Spirit:
as it was in the begin*ning*, is now, * and
will be for ev*er*. Amen.

Antiphon   The splendor of Christ risen *from* the dead * has shone on the
people redeemed by his blood, *al*leluia.

Ant. 2   Our Redeemer has risen *from* the tomb; * let us sing a hymn of
praise to the Lord our God, al*le*luia.

IIA

Canticle   Daniel 3:57-88; 56
Let all creatures praise the Lord
All you servants of the Lord, sing praise to him (Revelation 19:5).

Bless the Lord, all you works *of* the
Lord. * Praise and exalt him above
all *for*ever.
Angels of the Lord, *bless* the Lord, *
You heavens, bless *the* Lord.
All you waters above the heavens, *bless*
the Lord. * All you hosts of the Lord,

bless *the* Lord.
Sun and moon, *bless* the Lord. * Stars of
heaven, bless *the* Lord.
Every shower and dew, *bless* the Lord. *
All you winds, bless *the* Lord.
Fire and heat, *bless* the Lord. * Cold
and chill, bless *the* Lord.

Dew and rain, *bless* the Lord. * Frost and chill, bless *the* Lord.

Ice and snow, *bless* the Lord. * Nights and days, bless *the* Lord.

Light and darkness, *bless* the Lord. * Lightnings and clouds, bless *the* Lord.

Let the earth *bless* the Lord. * Praise and exalt him above all *for*ever.

Mountains and hills, *bless* the Lord. * Everything growing from the earth, bless *the* Lord.

You springs, *bless* the Lord. * Seas and rivers, bless *the* Lord.

You dolphins and all water creatures, *bless* the Lord. * All you birds of the air, bless *the* Lord.

All you beasts, wild and tame, *bless* the Lord. * You sons of men, bless *the* Lord.

O Israel, *bless* the Lord. * Praise and exalt him above all *for*ever.

Priests of the Lord, *bless* the Lord. * Servants of the Lord, bless *the* Lord.

Spirits and souls of the just, *bless* the Lord. * Holy men of humble heart, bless *the* Lord.

Hananiah, Azariah, Mishael, *bless* the Lord. * Praise and exalt him above all *for*ever.

Let us bless the Father, and the Son, and the *Ho*ly Spirit. * Let us praise and exalt him above all *for*ever.

Blessèd are you in the firma*ment* of heaven.* Praiseworthy and glorious and exalted above all *for*ever.

Antiphon   Our Redeemer has risen *from* the tomb; * let us sing a hymn of praise to the Lord our God, al*le*luia.

Ant. 3   Alleluia, the Lord is risen as *he* promised, * al*le*luia.

Va

Psalm 149
The joy of God's holy people
Let the sons of the Church, the children of the new people, rejoice in Christ, their King (Hesychius).

Sing a new song to *the* Lord, * his praise in the assembly of *the* faithful.

Let Israel rejoice in *its* Maker, * let Zion's sons exult in *their* king.

Let them praise his name *with* dancing * and make music with timbrel *and* harp.

For the Lord takes delight in *his* people. * He crowns the poor with sal*va*tion.

Let the faithful rejoice in *their* glory, * shout for joy and take *their* rest.

Let the praise of God be on *their* lips * and a two-edged sword in *their* hand,

to deal out vengeance to *the* nations * and punishment on all *the* peoples;

to bind their kings *in* chains * and their nobles in fetters *of* iron;

to carry out the sentence pre-or*dained*: * this honor is for all *his* faithful.

Glory to the Father, and to *the* Son, * and to the *Ho*ly Spirit:

as it was in the beginning, *is* now, * and will be for ever. *A*men.

Antiphon   Alleluia, the Lord is risen as *he* promised, * all*e*luia.

READING

MONDAY   Romans 10:8b-10
   The word is near you, on your lips and in your heart (that is , the word of
faith which we preach). For if you confess with your lips that Jesus is Lord,
and believe in your heart that God raised him from the dead, you will be
saved. Faith in the heart leads to justification, confession on the lips to
salvation.

TUESDAY   Acts 13:30-33
   God raised Jesus from the dead, and for many days thereafter Jesus appeared
to those who had come up with him from Galilee to Jerusalem. These are his
witnesses now before the people. We ourselves announce to you the good
news that what God promised our fathers he has fulfilled for us, their children, in raising up Jesus, according to what is written in the second psalm,
"You are my son; this day I have begotten you."

WEDNESDAY   Romans 6:8-11
   If we have died with Christ, we believe that we are also to live with him. We
know that Christ, once raised from the dead, will never die again; death has
no more power over him. His death was death to sin, once for all; his life is
life for God. In the same way, you must consider yourselves dead to sin but
alive for God in Christ Jesus.

THURSDAY   Romans 8:10-11
   If Christ is in you the body is dead because of sin, while the spirit lives
because of justice. If the Spirit of him who raised Jesus from the dead dwells
in you, then he who raised Christ from the dead will bring your mortal bodies
to life also, through his Spirit dwelling in you.

FRIDAY   Acts 5:30-32
   The God of our fathers has raised up Jesus whom you put to death, hanging
him on a tree. He whom God has exalted at his right hand as ruler and savior
is to bring repentance to Israel and forgiveness of sins. We testify to this. So
too does the Holy Spirit whom God has given to those that obey him.

SATURDAY   Romans 14:7-9
   None of us lives as his own master and none of us dies as his own master.
While we live we are responsible to the Lord, and when we die we die as his
servants. Both in life and in death we are the Lord's. That is why Christ died
and came to life again, that he might be Lord of both the dead and the living.

In place of the responsory the following is said: (VI F)

Ant.   This is the day the *Lord* has made; * let us rejoice and be glad, al*le*luia.

CANTICLE OF ZECHARIAH

MONDAY   Go quickly and tell *his* disciples: * the Lord is risen, al*le*luia.

TUESDAY   Jesus called her by name: Mary. † She turned to him and *said*: Rabboni. * Then he said to her: Do *not* touch me; I have not yet ascended *to* my Father, * al*le*luia.

WEDNESDAY   Beginning with Moses and the prophets, † Jesus interpret*ed* for them * all that had been written of him in the Scriptures, al*le*luia.

THURSDAY   Jesus stood in the midst of his disci*ples* and said: * Peace be with you, al*le*luia.

FRIDAY   This was the third time Jesus had shown himself to *his* disciples * after he had risen from the dead, al*le*luia.

SATURDAY   When Jesus had risen from the dead on the morning after the sabbath, † he appeared first to *Mary* Magdalene, * from whom he had cast out seven devils, al*le*luia.

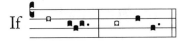

B lessèd ✠ be the Lord, the *God* of Israel; * he has come to his people and set *them* free.
He has raised up for us a *mighty* savior, * born of the house of his ser*vant* David.
Through his holy prophets he promised of old † that he would save us *from* our enemies, * from the hands of all *who* hate us.
He promised to show mercy *to* our fathers * and to remember his ho*ly* covenant.
This was the oath he swore to our *fath*er Abraham: * to set us free from the hands of *our* enemies,
free to worship him without fear, † holy and righteous *in* his sight * all the days of *our* life.
You, my child, shall be called the prophet *of* the Most High; * for you will go before the Lord to prepare *his* way,
to give his people knowledge *of* salvation * by the forgiveness of *their* sins.
In the tender compassion *of* our God * the dawn from on high shall break *up*on us,
to shine on those who dwell in darkness and the sha*dow* of death, * and to guide our feet into the way *of* peace.
Glory to the Father, and *to* the Son, * and to the Ho*ly* Spirit:
as it was in the begin*ning*, is now, * and will be for ever. *A*men.

Antiphon repeated.

INTERCESSIONS (VI F)

MONDAY

The Father glorified Jesus and appointed him heir *to* all nations. * Let us *praise* him, saying:

Save us, Lord, through your *victory.*

Lord Christ, by your victory you broke the power of evil and destroyed *sin* and death,

— make us victorious over *sin* today.

You laid death low, and brought *us* new life,

— grant that we may walk today in *this* new life.

You gave life to the dead, and led mankind from *death* to life,

— give eternal life to all those we shall *meet* today.

You brought confusion on the guards at your tomb, but joy to *your* disciples,

— grant the fullness of joy to *all* who serve you.

TUESDAY

By his own power Christ raised up the temple of his body when it had been des*troyed* in death. * With joy *let* us ask him:

Lord, share with us the fruits of your *victory.*

Christ our Savior, when you rose again you brought to the holy women and the apostles the joyful news of a *world* redeemed,

— make us witnesses to your *risen* life.

You promised to all people that we would rise up again to new*ness* of life,

— make us heralds *of* your Gospel.

You showed yourself to your apostles and breathed the Holy Spir*it* on them,

— renew in us the presence of the same crea*tor* Spirit.

You promised to be with your disciples to the end *of* the world,

— stay with us today, and remain *with* us always.

WEDNESDAY

Christ was given up for our sins and rose again to *make* us righteous. * Let us cry out *to* him, saying:

Save us, Lord, by your *victory.*

Christ our Savior, in conquering death you brought us joy, in rising again you raised us up and filled us with the abundance *of* your gifts,

— stir up our hearts, and sanctify this day through the gift of your *Holy* Spirit.

You are glorified by the angels in heaven and adored by mankind on earth; as we celebrate your *resurrection,*

— accept our worship in spirit *and* in truth.

Lord Jesus, save us; show your great mercy to your people, as we look forward to our own *resurrection,*

— have mercy on us, and protect us today from *every* evil.

King of glory, source of our life, grant that, when you *come* again,
— we may be one with *you* in glory.

THURSDAY

Christ rose from the dead and is always present *in* his Church. * Let us adore *him*,
    and say:
Stay with us, Lord.
Lord Jesus, victor over sin and death, glorious *and* immortal,
— be always *in* our midst.
Come to us in the power *of* your victory,
— and show our hearts the loving kindness *of* your Father.
Come to heal a world wounded *by* division,
— for you alone can transform our hearts and *make* them one.
Strengthen our faith in *final* victory,
— and renew our hope in your *second* coming.

FRIDAY

Let us pray to *God* the Father, * who gave us new life through the *risen* Christ:
Give us the glory of your Son.
Lord our God, your mighty works have revealed your eternal plan: you created
    the earth, and you are faithful in every *generation*,
— hear us, Fa*ther* of mercy.
Purify our hearts with your truth, and guide them in the *way* of holiness,
— so that we may do what is pleasing *in* your sight.
Let your face *shine* upon us,
— that we may be freed from sin and filled *with* your plenty.
You gave the apostles the *peace* of Christ,
— grant peace to your people, and to *the* whole world.

SATURDAY

Christ is the bread of life; he will raise up on the last day all who share the table
    of his word *and* his body. * In our joy *let* us pray:
Lord, give us peace and joy.
Son of God, you were raised from the dead to lead us *into* life,
— bless and sanctify all the children *of* your Father.
You give peace and joy to all who be*lieve* in you,
— grant that we may walk as children of the light, rejoicing *in* your victory.
Build up the faith of your pilgrim *Church* on earth,
— that it may bear witness to your resurrection before *the* whole world.
You suffered and so entered into the glory *of* the Father,
— change the tears of the sorrowful *into* joy.

Our Father . . .

Prayer

Father,
you give your Church constant growth
by adding new members to your family.
Help us to put into action in our lives
the baptism we have received with faith.
We ask this through our Lord Jesus Christ, your Son,
who lives and reigns with you and the Holy Spirit,
one God, for ever and ever.

TUESDAY

Father,
by this Easter mystery you touch our lives
with the healing power of your love.
You have given us the freedom of the sons of God.
May we who now celebrate your gift
find joy in it for ever in heaven.
Grant this through our Lord Jesus Christ, your Son,
who lives and reigns with you and the Holy Spirit,
one God, for ever and ever.

WEDNESDAY

God our Father,
on this solemn feast you give us the joy of recalling
the rising of Christ to new life.
May the joy of our annual celebration
bring us to the joy of eternal life.
We ask this through our Lord Jesus Christ, your Son,
who lives and reigns with you and the Holy Spirit,
one God, for ever and ever.

THURSDAY

Father,
you gather the nations to praise your name.
May all who are reborn in baptism
be one in faith and love.
Grant this through our Lord Jesus Christ, your Son,
who lives and reigns with you and the Holy Spirit,
one God, for ever and ever.

FRIDAY

Eternal Father,
you gave us the Easter mystery
as our covenant of reconciliation.
May the new birth we celebrate
show its effects in the way we live.
We ask this through our Lord Jesus Christ, your Son,
who lives and reigns with you and the Holy Spirit,
one God, for ever and ever.

SATURDAY

Father of love,
by the outpouring of your grace
you increase the number of those who believe in you.
Watch over your chosen family.
Give undying life to all
who have been born again in baptism.
Grant this through our Lord Jesus Christ, your Son,
who lives and reigns with you and the Holy Spirit,
one God, for ever and ever.

The following dismissal is said:

Go in the peace of Christ, al- le- lu- ia, al- le- lu- ia.

Thanks be to God, al- le- lu- ia, al- le- lu- ia.

Evening Prayer

HYMN

Ad coenam Agni providi. Mode VIII (L.M.)

Mode 8

Ad cenam Agni providi,	The Lamb's high banquet we await
Stolis salutis candidi,	In snow-white robes of royal state;
Post transitum maris Rubri	And now, the Red Sea's channel past,
Christo canamus principi.	To Christ, our Prince, we sing at last.
Cuius corpus sanctissimum	Upon the altar of the Cross
In ara crucis torridum,	His body hath redeemed our loss;
Sed et cruorem roseum	And tasting of his life-red Blood
Gustando, Dei vivimus.	Our life is hid with him in God.
Protecti paschae vespero	That Paschal eve God's arm was bared;
A devastante angelo,	The devastating Angel spared:
De Pharaonis aspero	By strength of hand our hosts went free
Sumus erept*i* imperio.	From Pharoah's ruthless tyranny.
Iam pascha nostrum Christus est,	Now Christ, our Paschal Lamb, is slain,
Agnus occisus innocens;	The Lamb of God that knows no stain;
Sinceritatis azyma	The true Oblation offered here,
Qui carnem suam obtulit.	Our own unleavened Bread sincere.
O vera, digna hostia,	O thou from whom hell's monarch flies,
Per quam franguntur tartara,	O great, O very Sacrifice,
Captiva plebs redimitur,	Thy captive people are set free,
Redduntur vitae præmia!	And endless life restored in thee.
Consurgit Christus tumulo,	For Christ arising from the dead,
Victor redit de barathro,	From conquered hell victorious sped;
Tyrannum trudens vinculo	He thrusts the tyrant down to chains,
Et paradisum reserans.	And Paradise for man regains.
Esto perenne mentibus	Maker of all, to thee we pray,
Paschale, Iesu, gaudium	Fulfill in us thy joy today;
Et nos renatos gratiæ	When death assails, grant, Lord, that we
Tuis triumphis aggrega.	May share the Paschal victory.
Iesu, tibi sit gloria,	To thee, who dead, again dost live,
Qui morte victa prænites,	All glory, Lord, thy people give;
Cum Patre et almo Spiritu,	All glory as is ever meet,
In sempiterna sæcula. Amen.	To Father and to Paraclete. Amen.

PSALMODY

Ant. 1   Mary Magdalene and the other Mary came to *see* the Lord's
              tomb,* *al*leluia.

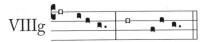

VIIIg

Psalm 110:1-5, 7
The Messiah, king and priest
Christ's reign will last until all his enemies are made subject to him
(1 Corinthians 15:25).

The Lord's revelation to my Master:
† "Sit *on* my right: * your foes I
will put be*neath* your feet."
The Lord will wield from Zion † your
scep*ter* of power: * rule in the midst
of *all* your foes.
A prince from the day of your birth †
on the *holy* mountains; * from the
womb before the dawn *I* begot you.
The Lord has sworn an oath he will not
change. † "You are a *priest* for ever, *

a priest like Melchize*dek* of old."
The Master standing *at* your right hand
* will shatter kings in the day of *his*
great wrath.
He shall drink from the stream *by* the
wayside * and therefore he shall lift
up his head.
Glory to the Father, and *to* the Son, *
and to the *Holy* Spirit:
as it was in the begin*ning*, is now, * and
will be for ev*er*. Amen.

Antiphon   Mary Magdalene and the other Mary came to *see* the Lord's
              tomb,* *al*leluia.

Ant. 2   Come and see the place where the *Lord* was buried, * al*le*luia.

IIA

Psalm 114
The Israelites are delivered from the bondage of Egypt
You too left Egypt when, at baptism, you renounced that world which is at enmity with God
(St. Augustine).

When Israel came *forth* from
Egypt, * Jacob's sons from an
ali*en* people,
Judah became *the* Lord's temple, * Israel
became *his* kingdom.
The sea fled *at* the sight: * the Jordan
turned back on *its* course,
the mountains *leapt* like rams * and the

hills like year*ling* sheep.
Why was it, sea, *that* you fled, * that
you turned back, Jordan, on *your*
course?
Mountains, that you *leapt* like rams, *
hills, like year*ling* sheep?
Tremble, O earth, be*fore* the Lord, * in
the presence of the God *of* Jacob,

who turns the rock in*to* a pool * and
  flint into a spring *of* water.
Glory to the Father, and *to* the Son, *

and to the Ho*ly* Spirit:
as it was in the begin*ning*, is now, * and
  will be for ever. *A*men.

Antiphon   Come and see the place where the *Lord* was buried, * al*le*luia.

Ant. 3   Jesus said: Do not be afraid. † Go and tell my brothers to set out
             for Galilee; † there they *will* see me, * alleluia, alleluia.

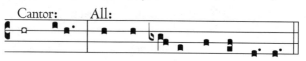

        ** al- le- lu- ia, al- le- lu- ia.

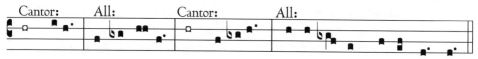

  *Al- le- lu- ia.   ** al- le- lu- ia, al- le - lu- ia.

Canticle
See Revelation 19:1-7

Salvation, glory, and power to *our* God:
 * Alleluia.
his judgments are hon*est* and true.
** Alleluia, alleluia.
Sing praise to our God, all you *his* servants,
* Alleluia.
all who worship him reverently, *great* and small.
** Alleluia, alleluia.

The Lord our all-powerful God *is* King;
* Alleluia.
let us rejoice, sing praise, and *give* him glory.
** Alleluia, alleluia.

The wedding feast of the Lamb has *be*gun,
* Alleluia.
and his bride is pre*pared* to welcome him.
** Alleluia, alleluia.

Glory to the Father, and to the Son, †
and to the Ho*ly* Spirit.
* Alleluia.
As it was in the beginning, is now, †
and will be for *ev*er. Amen.
** Alleluia, alleluia.

Antiphon   Jesus said: Do not be afraid. † Go and tell my brothers to set out
              for Galilee; † there they *will* see me, * alleluia, alleluia.

READING

MONDAY   Hebrews 8:1b-3a
We have such a high priest, who has taken his seat at the right hand of the
throne of the Majesty in heaven, minister of the sanctuary and of that true
tabernacle set up, not by man, but by the Lord. Now every high priest is
appointed to offer gifts and sacrifices.

TUESDAY   1 Peter 2:4-5
Come to the Lord, a living stone, rejected by men but approved, nonetheless,
and precious in God's eyes. You too are living stones, built as an edifice of
spirit into a holy priesthood, offering spiritual sacrifices acceptable to God
through Jesus Christ.

WEDNESDAY   Hebrews 7:24-27
Jesus, because he remains forever, has a priesthood that does not pass away.
Therefore he is always able to save those who approach God through him,
since he forever lives to make intercession for them. It was fitting that we
should have such a high priest: holy, innocent, undefiled, separated from
sinners, higher than the heavens. Unlike the other high priests, he has no
need to offer sacrifice day after day, first for his own sins and then for those of
the people; he did that once for all when he offered himself.

THURSDAY   1 Peter 3:18, 22
The reason why Christ died for sins once for all, the just man for the sake of
the unjust, was that he might lead you to God. He was put to death insofar as
fleshly existence goes, but was given life in the realm of the spirit. He went to
heaven and is at God's right hand, with angelic rulers and power subjected to
him.

FRIDAY   Hebrews 5:8-10
Son though he was, Christ learned obedience from what he suffered; and
when perfected, he became the source of eternal salvation for all who obey
him, designated by God as high priest according to the order of Melchizedek.

In place of the responsory the following is said:
Ant.   This is the day the *Lord* has made; * let us rejoice and be glad,
              al*le*luia. (VI F)

CANTICLE OF MARY

MONDAY   Jesus met the women and greeted them. † They came up to him and knelt *at* his feet, * al*le*luia.

TUESDAY   While I was weeping at the tomb, I *saw* my Lord, * al*le*luia.

WEDNESDAY   Jesus went in with them, † and while they were at table he took bread and said the blessing; † he broke the bread and gave *it* to them, * al*le*luia.

THURSDAY   See my hands and my feet and know that I am *here* among you, * al*le*luia.

FRIDAY   The disciple whom Jesus loved said: † It *is* the Lord, * al*le*luia.

If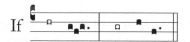

My soul ✠ proclaims the greatness *of* the Lord, * my spirit rejoices in God *my* savior

for he has *looked* with favor * on his low*ly* servant.

From this day all gen*er*ations * will call *me* blessèd:

the Almighty has done great *things* for me, * and holy is *his* Name.

He has mercy on *those* who fear him * in every gen*er*ation.

He has shown the strength *of* his arm, * he has scattered the proud in their *con*ceit.

He has cast down the mighty *from* their thrones, * and has lifted up *the* lowly.

He has filled the hungry *with* good things, * and the rich he has sent a*way* empty.

He has come to the help of his *ser*vant Israel * for he has remembered his promise *of* mercy,

the promise he made *to* our fathers, * to Abraham and his children *for* ever.

Glory to the Father, and *to* the Son, * and to the Ho*ly* Spirit:

as it was in the begin*ning*, is now, * and will be for ever. *A*men.

Antiphon repeated.

INTERCESSIONS (VI F)

MONDAY

The Holy Spirit raised the body of Christ to life and made it the *source* of life. * With joy in our hearts let us call upon the ris*en* Christ, saying:
Lord, make all things new and fill them with *life.*
Savior of the world and King of the new creation, raise our minds and hearts *to* your kingdom,
— where you sit at the right hand *of* the Father.
Lord, you are always present *in* your Church,
— through your Holy Spirit guide it in*to* all truth.

Show your mercy to the sick, the overburdened *and* the dying,
— that all may receive strength and courage *from* your love.
Light that never fails, as the day draws to its close we offer you our sacri*fice* of praise,
— and pray that the glory of your resurrection may shine on our deceased broth*ers* and sisters.

TUESDAY

As Christ lay in the darkness of the earth he saw the light of *a* new glory. * Let us cry out to *him* in joy:
King of glory, hear us.
We pray for all bishops, priests and deacons, that they may be zealous *in* their ministry,
— and prepare for you a people devoted to eve*ry* good work.
We pray for all who teach in the serv*ice of* your Church,
— that they may seek your truth with a *sin*cere heart.
We pray for your faithful people, that they may be victorious in the con*test* of faith,
— and win the prize of victory *in* your kingdom.
You cancelled our condemnation by nailing it *to* the cross,
— free us from our chains, and lead us *out* of darkness.
You went down among the dead and opened for them the *gates* to life,
— welcome our dead brothers and sisters in*to* your kingdom.

WEDNESDAY

Christ rose from the dead and is seated at the right hand *of* the Father. * Let us pray *to* him, saying:
Lord Jesus, you live for ever; hear our *prayer.*
Lord, remember all who minister *in* your service,
— may their holy lives be an example *to* your people.
Give to those who govern us a spirit of jus*tice* and peace,
— so that the human family may *live* in harmony.
Guide our days in the way *of* salvation,
— and fill the earth with your plenty for the sake *of* the needy.
Christ our savior, light of the world, you have called creation from *death* to life,
— may your light shine for ever on our departed broth*ers* and sisters.

THURSDAY

Christ rose from the dead as the first fruits of *those* who sleep. * In our joy let us praise *him*, and say:
Firstborn from the dead, hear our *prayer.*

Lord Jesus, remember your holy Church, built on the apostles and reaching to
the ends *of* the earth,
— and let your blessing rest on all who be*lieve* in you.
You are the healer of *soul* and body,
— come to our aid, and save us *in* your love.
Raise up the sick and *give* them strength,
— free them from *their* infirmities.
Help those in distress of *mind* or body,
— and in your compassion lift up *those* in need.
Through your cross and resurrection you opened for all the way to *im*mortality,
— grant to our deceased brothers and sisters the joys *of* your kingdom.

FRIDAY

Christ is the way, the truth *and* the life. * Let us praise *him*, and say:
Son of the living God, bless your *people.*
We pray to you, Lord Jesus, for all ministers *of* your Church,
— as they break for us the bread of life, may they themselves receive nourish*ment*
and strength.
We pray for the whole Christian people, that all may be worthy *of* their calling,
— and safeguard their unity in the Spirit by the *bond* of peace.
We pray for those who govern us, that they may temper jus*tice* with mercy,
— and promote harmony and peace through*out* the world.
We pray for ourselves, that our hearts may be purified to sing your praises in the
commun*ion* of saints,
— that we be reunited with our deceased brothers and sisters, whom we
commend to your *lov*ing kindness.

Our Father . . .

Prayer
MONDAY

Father,
you give your Church constant growth
by adding new members to your family.
Help us to put into action in our lives
the baptism we have received with faith.
We ask this through our Lord Jesus Christ, your Son,
who lives and reigns with you and the Holy Spirit,
one God, for ever and ever.

TUESDAY

Father,
by this Easter mystery you touch our lives
with the healing power of your love.
You have given us the freedom of the sons of God.
May we who now celebrate your gift
find joy in it for ever in heaven.
Grant this through our Lord Jesus Christ, your Son,
who lives and reigns with you and the Holy Spirit,
one God, for ever and ever.

WEDNESDAY

God our Father,
on this solemn feast you give us the joy of recalling
the rising of Christ to new life.
May the joy of our annual celebration
bring us to the joy of eternal life.
We ask this through our Lord Jesus Christ, your Son,
who lives and reigns with you and the Holy Spirit,
one God, for ever and ever.

THURSDAY

Father,
you gather the nations to praise your name.
May all who are reborn in baptism
be one in faith and love.
Grant this through our Lord Jesus Christ, your Son,
who lives and reigns with you and the Holy Spirit,
one God, for ever and ever.

FRIDAY

Eternal Father,
you gave us the Easter mystery
as our covenant of reconciliation.
May the new birth we celebrate
show its effects in the way we live.
We ask this through our Lord Jesus Christ, your Son,
who lives and reigns with you and the Holy Spirit,
one God, for ever and ever.

The following dismissal is said:

Go in the peace of Christ, al- le- lu- ia, al- le- lu- ia.

Thanks be to God, al- le- lu- ia, al- le- lu- ia.

During the octave of Easter, Night Prayer is said each day from either of the Night Prayers for Sunday, 873 or 875.

SUNDAY WITHIN THE OCTAVE OF EASTER
(Second Sunday of Easter)

Evening Prayer I

Hymn, antiphons, psalms and canticle, as on Easter Sunday, 376.

READING   1 Peter 2:9-10

You are "a chosen race, a royal priesthood, a holy nation, a people he claims for his own to proclaim the glorious works" of the One who called you from darkness into his marvelous light. Once you were no people, but now you are God's people; once there was no mercy for you, but now you have found mercy.

In place of the responsory the following is said: (VI F)

Ant.   This is the day the *Lord* has made, * let us rejoice and be glad, al*le*luia.

CANTICLE OF MARY

Ant.   After eight days, although the doors were locked, † the Lord came among *them* and said: * Peace be with you, al*le*luia.

INTERCESSIONS (VI F)

In rising from the dead, Christ destroyed death and *re*stored life. * Let us cry out *to* him, saying:
Lord Jesus, you live for ever; hear our *prayer.*
You are the stone rejected by the builders which became the chief *cor*nerstone,
— make us living stones in the temple *of* your Church.
You are the faithful and true witness, the firstborn *from* the dead,
— make your Church bear constant witness *to* yourself.
You alone are the Bridegroom of the Church, born from your *wound*ed side,
— make us reveal to the world the love of Bride*groom* and Bride.
You are the first and the last, you were dead and *are* alive,
— keep those who have been baptized faithful until death, that they may receive the *crown* of victory.
Light and lamp of God's *holy* city,
— shine on our friends who have died, that they may *reign* for ever.

Our Father . . .

Prayer

God of mercy,
you wash away our sins in water,
you give us new birth in the Spirit,
and redeem us in the blood of Christ.
As we celebrate Christ's resurrection
increase our awareness of these blessings,
and renew your gift of life within us.
We ask this through our Lord Jesus Christ, your Son,
who lives and reigns with you and the Holy Spirit,
one God, for ever and ever.

Morning Prayer

HYMN, antiphons, psalms and canticle as on Easter Sunday, 371.

READING   Acts 10:40-43

God raised up Jesus on the third day and granted that he be seen, not by all, but only by such witnesses as had been chosen beforehand by God— by us who ate and drank with him after he rose from the dead. He commissioned us to preach to the people and to bear witness that he is the one set apart by God as judge of the living and the dead. To him all the prophets testify, saying that everyone who believes in him has forgiveness of sins through his name.

In place of the responsory the following is said:

Ant.   This is the day the *Lord* has made; * let us rejoice and be glad, al*le*luia. (VI F)

CANTICLE OF ZECHARIAH
Ant.   With your hand, touch the mark *of* the nails; * doubt no longer, but believe, al*le*luia.

INTERCESSIONS (VI F)
God the almighty Father raised Jesus as the firstborn from the dead, and made
    him our savior. * Let us call up*on* him, saying:
Give us, Lord, the glory of your *Son.*
All-holy Father, you brought your belovèd Son Jesus from the darkness of death
    into the splendor *of* your glory,
— bring us also into your mar*ve*lous light.
You have given us *faith* to save us,
— may we live today by the faith *of* our baptism.
You command us to seek the things that are above, where Christ is seated at *your*
    right hand,
— do not let us be deceived by the allure*ments* of sin.

May our life, hidden with Christ in you, our Father, shine be*fore* the world,
— foreshadowing a new heaven and *a* new earth.

Our Father . . .

Prayer

God of mercy,
you wash away our sins in water,
you give us new birth in the Spirit,
and redeem us in the blood of Christ.
As we celebrate Christ's resurrection
increase our awareness of these blessings,
and renew your gift of life within us.
We ask this through our Lord Jesus Christ, your Son,
who lives and reigns with you and the Holy Spirit,
one God, for ever and ever.

Evening Prayer II

HYMN, antiphons, psalms and canticle, as on Easter Sunday, 376.

READING   Hebrews 10:12-14
Jesus offered one sacrifice for sins and took his seat forever at the right hand
of God; now he waits until his enemies are placed beneath his feet. By one
offering he has forever perfected those who are being sanctified.

In place of the responsory the following is said:
Ant.   This is the day the *Lord* has made; * let us rejoice and be glad,
                    al*le*luia. (VI F)

CANTICLE OF MARY
Ant.   Because you have seen me, Thomas, you have believed; † bless*è*d
                    are they who have not seen me and *yet* believe, * al*le*luia.

INTERCESSIONS (VI F)
God the Father raised Christ from the dead and exalted him at *his* right hand. *
    Let us pray to the *Fa*ther, saying:
*Through Christ in glory, watch over your peo*ple, Lord.
Righteous Father, you lifted Jesus above the earth through the triumph *of* the
    cross,
— may all things be lifted *up* in him.
Through your Son in glory send the Holy Spirit up*on* the Church,
— that it may be the sacrament of unity for the whole *hu*man race.

You have brought a new family into being through water and the *Ho*ly Spirit,
— keep them faithful to their baptism, and bring them to ever*last*ing life.
Through your exalted Son help those in distress, free those in captivity, *heal* the
   sick,
— and by your blessings give joy *to* the world.
You nourished our deceased brothers and sisters with the body and blood of the
   *ri*sen Christ,
— raise them up at *the* last day.

Our Father . . .

Prayer

God of mercy,
   you wash away our sins in water,
   you give us new birth in the Spirit,
   and redeem us in the blood of Christ.
   As we celebrate Christ's resurrection
   increase our awareness of these blessings,
   and renew your gift of life within us.
   We ask this through our Lord Jesus Christ, your Son,
   who lives and reigns with you and the Holy Spirit,
   one God, for ever and ever.

MONDAY
PSALTER, WEEK II
Morning Prayer

READING   Romans 10:8b-10
   The word is near you, on your lips and in your heart (that is, the word of faith
   which we preach). For if you confess with your lips that Jesus is Lord, and
   believe in your heart that God raised him from the dead, you will be saved.
   Faith in the heart leads to justification, confession on the lips to salvation.

RESPONSORY (VI F)
The Lord is risen *from* the tomb, * alleluia, al*le*luia.
— The Lord is risen *from* the tomb, * alleluia, al*le*luia.
He hung upon the *cross* for us,
— alleluia, al*le*luia.
Glory to the Father, and *to* the Son, * and to the Ho*ly* Spirit.
— The Lord is risen *from* the tomb, * alleluia, al*le*luia.

CANTICLE OF ZECHARIAH
Ant.   Truly I tell you, unless you are *born* again * you cannot see the
                         kingdom of God, al*le*luia.

INTERCESSIONS (VI F)

God the Father was glorified in the death and resurrection *of* his Son. * Let us
    pray to him with con*fi*dence, saying:
Lord, enlighten our *minds.*
Father of lights, you bathed the world in splendor when Christ rose a*gain* in
    glory,
— fill our minds today with the *light* of faith.
Through the resurrection of your Son you opened for us the way to e*ter*nal life,
— as we work today sustain us with the *hope* of glory.
Through your risen Son you sent the Holy Spirit in*to* the world,
— set our hearts on fire with spir*itual* love.
May Jesus Christ, who was crucified to *set* us free,
— be today our salvation *and* redemption.

Our Father . . .

Prayer

    Almighty and ever-living God,
    your Spirit made us your children,
    confident to call you Father.
    Increase your Spirit of love within us
    and bring us to our promised inheritance.
    Grant this through our Lord Jesus Christ, your Son,
    who lives and reigns with you and the Holy Spirit,
    one God, for ever and ever.

Evening Prayer

READING   Hebrews 8:1b-3a

    We have such a high priest, who has taken his seat at the right hand of the
    throne of the Majesty in heaven, minister of the sanctuary and of that true
    tabernacle set up, not by man, but by the Lord. Now every high priest is
    appointed to offer gifts and sacrifices.

RESPONSORY (VI F)

The dis*ci*ples rejoiced, * alleluia, al*le*luia.
— The dis*ci*ples rejoiced, * alleluia, al*le*luia.
When they saw the *ris*en Lord,
— alleluia, al*le*luia.
Glory to the Father, and *to* the Son, * and to the Ho*ly* Spirit.
— The dis*ci*ples rejoiced, * alleluia, al*le*luia.

CANTICLE OF MARY

Ant.   What is born of the *flesh* is flesh, * and what is born of the spirit
                        is spirit, al*le*luia.

INTERCESSIONS (VI F)

Let us pray to Christ the Lord, who bathed the world in glory through his
    re*surrection. * With joyful hearts *let* us say:
Christ, our life, hear our *prayer.*
Lord Jesus Christ, you walked with your disciples *on* the way,
— be with your Church on its pilgrim*age* through life.
Do not let us be slow *to* believe,
— but ready to proclaim you as victor *over* death.
Look with kindness on those who do not recog*nize* your presence,
— reveal yourself to them, so that they may welcome *you* as Savior.
Through the cross you have brought reconciliation to mankind *in* your body,
— grant unity and peace *to* all nations.
Judge of the living *and* the dead,
— forgive the sins of the faith*ful* departed.

Our Father . . .

Prayer

Almighty and ever-living God,
your Spirit made us your children,
confident to call you Father.
Increase your Spirit of love within us
and bring us to our promised inheritance.
Grant this through our Lord Jesus Christ, your Son,
who lives and reigns with you and the Holy Spirit,
one God, for ever and ever.

TUESDAY

Morning Prayer

READING   Acts 13:30-33

God raised Jesus from the dead, and for many days thereafter Jesus appeared
to those who had come up with him from Galilee to Jerusalem. These are his
witnesses now before the people. We ourselves announce to you the good
news that what God has promised our fathers he has fulfilled for us, his
children, in raising up Jesus, according to what is written in the second psalm,
"You are my son; this day I have begotten you."

RESPONSORY (VI F)

The Lord is risen *from* the tomb, * alleluia, al*le*luia.

— The Lord is risen *from* the tomb, * alleluia, al*le*luia.

He hung upon the *cross* for us,

— alleluia, al*le*luia.

Glory to the Father, and *to* the Son, * and to the Ho*ly* Spirit.

— The Lord is risen *from* the tomb, * alleluia, al*le*luia.

CANTICLE OF ZECHARIAH

Ant.   I am the Alpha and the Omega, † the first *and* the last, * the
               beginning and *the* end;
               I am the root and offspring of David's race; † I am the splendor
               of the *morn*ing star, * alle*lu*ia.

INTERCESSIONS (VI F)

The spotless Lamb of God takes away the sins *of* the world. * Let us give thanks
   to the Fath*er,* and say:

Source of all life, raise us to life.

Source of all life, remember the death and resurrection of the Lamb slain *on* the
   cross,

— listen to his voice as he lives for ever, making interces*sion* for us.

Now that the old leaven of wickedness and evil *is* destroyed,

— may we always feed on the unleavened bread of sinceri*ty* and truth.

Grant that today we may put aside all fric*tion* and jealousy,

— and show greater concern for the *needs* of others.

Send into our hearts the spirit *of* the Gospel,

— that we may walk in the way of your commandments, today *and* for ever.

Our Father . . .

Prayer

   All-powerful God,
   help us to proclaim the power of the Lord's resurrection.
   May we who accept this sign of the love of Christ
   come to share the eternal life he reveals,
   for he lives and reigns with you and the Holy Spirit,
   one God, for ever and ever.

Evening Prayer

READING   1 Peter 2:4-5

   Come to the Lord, a living stone, rejected by men but approved, nonetheless,
   and precious in God's eyes. You too are living stones, built as an edifice of

spirit, into a holy priesthood, offering spiritual sacrifices acceptable to God through Jesus Christ.

RESPONSORY (VI F)

The disciples rejoiced, * alleluia, alleluia.
— The disciples rejoiced, * alleluia, alleluia.
When they saw the risen Lord,
— alleluia, alleluia.
Glory to the Father, and to the Son, * and to the Holy Spirit.
— The disciples rejoiced, * alleluia, alleluia.

CANTICLE OF MARY

Ant.   Did not our hearts burn within us † as Jesus talked to us on the road? * alleluia.

INTERCESSIONS (VI F)

By his resurrection Christ has given sure hope to his people. * Let us ask him with our whole hearts:
Lord Jesus, you live for ever; hear our prayer.
Lord Jesus, from your wounded side flowed blood and water,
— make the Church your spotless bride.
Chief shepherd, after your resurrection you made Peter shepherd of your flock when he professed his love for you,
— increase from day to day the love and devotion of N., our Pope.
You showed your disciples how to make a great catch of fish,
— send others to continue their work as fishers of men.
At the lakeside you prepared bread and fish for your disciples,
— grant that we may never allow others to die of hunger.
Jesus, the new Adam and life-giving spirit, transform the dead into your own likeness,
— that the fullness of your joy may be theirs.

Our Father . . .

Prayer

All-powerful God,
help us to proclaim the power of the Lord's resurrection.
May we who accept this sign of the love of Christ
come to share the eternal life he reveals,
for he lives and reigns with you and the Holy Spirit,
one God, for ever and ever.

WEDNESDAY

Morning Prayer

READING   Romans 6:8-11
If we have died with Christ, we believe that we are also to live with him. We know that Christ, once raised from the dead, will never die again; death has no more power over him. His death was death to sin, once for all; his life is life for God. In the same way, you must consider yourselves dead to sin but alive for God in Christ Jesus.

RESPONSORY (VI F)
The Lord is risen *from* the tomb, * alleluia, al*le*luia.
— The Lord is risen *from* the tomb, * alleluia, al*le*luia.
He hung upon the *cross* for us,
— alleluia, al*le*luia.
Glory to the Father, and *to* the Son, * and to the Ho*ly* Spirit.
— The Lord is risen *from* the tomb, * alleluia, al*le*luia.

CANTICLE OF ZECHARIAH
Ant.   God loved the world so much that he gave his only Son † to save all who have *faith* in him, * and to give them eternal life, al*le*luia.

INTERCESSIONS (VI F)
By the gift of the Father, the risen Christ was seen by *the* apostles. * Let us pray to the Fath*er*, and say:
Give us, Lord, the glory of your Son.
Father of lights, today we offer you our thanks and praise for calling us into your marve*lo*us light,
— to re*ceive* your mercy.
May the efforts of mankind to make the *world* more human,
— be purified and strengthened by the power *of* your Spirit.
May we be so dedicated to the ser*vice* of others,
— that the whole human family may become a pleasing sacrifice *in* your honor.
At the dawn of a new day, fill us *with* your mercy,
— that the whole day may be a day of *joy* and praise.

Our Father . . .

Prayer

God of mercy,
you have filled us with the hope of resurrection
by restoring man to his original dignity.

May we who relive this mystery each year
come to share it in perpetual love.
Grant this through our Lord Jesus Christ, your Son,
who lives and reigns with you and the Holy Spirit,
one God, for ever and ever.

Evening Prayer

READING   Hebrews 7:24-27

Jesus, because he remains forever, has a priesthood that does not pass away.
Therefore he is always able to save those who approach God through him,
since he forever lives to make intercession for them. It was fitting that we
should have such a high priest: holy, innocent, undefiled, separated from
sinners, higher than the heavens. Unlike the other high priests, he has no
need to offer sacrifice day after day, first for his own sins and then for those of
the people; he did that once for all when he offered himself.

RESPONSORY (VI F)

The disciples rejoiced, * alleluia, alleluia.
— The disciples rejoiced, * alleluia, alleluia.
When they saw the risen Lord,
— alleluia, alleluia.
Glory to the Father, and to the Son, * and to the Holy Spirit.
— The disciples rejoiced, * alleluia, alleluia.

CANTICLE OF MARY

Ant.   The man of God welcomes the light that searches his deeds * and
finds them true, alleluia.

INTERCESSIONS (VI F)

In his Son, risen from the dead, God has opened for us the way to everlasting life.
  * Let us ask the Father:
Through the victory of Christ, save the people he has redeemed.
God of our fathers, you raised your Son Jesus from the dead and clothed him in
glory; move our hearts to complete repentance,
— that we may walk in newness of life.
You have led us back to the shepherd and bishop of our souls,
— keep us faithful under the guidance of the shepherds of the Church.
You chose the firstfruits of Christ's disciples from the Jewish people,
— reveal to the children of Israel the fulfillment of the promise made to their
forefathers.

Remember the lonely, the orphaned *and* the widowed,
— and do not abandon those who have been reconciled with you by the death *of* your Son.
You called Stephen to your presence when he bore witness to Jesus, standing at *your* right hand,
— welcome our deceased brothers and sisters who in faith and love hoped for the vision *of* your glory.

Our Father . . .

Prayer

God of mercy,
you have filled us with the hope of resurrection
by restoring man to his original dignity.
May we who relive this mystery each year
come to share it in perpetual love.
Grant this through our Lord Jesus Christ, your Son,
who lives and reigns with you and the Holy Spirit,
one God, for ever and ever.

THURSDAY

Morning Prayer

READING   Romans 8:10-11

If Christ is in you the body is dead because of sin, while the spirit lives because of justice. If the Spirit of him who raised Jesus from the dead dwells in you, then he who raised Jesus from the dead will bring your mortal bodies to life also, through his Spirit dwelling in you.

RESPONSORY (VI F)
The Lord is risen *from* the tomb, * alleluia, al*le*luia.
— The Lord is risen *from* the tomb, * alleluia, al*le*luia.
He hung upon the *cross* for us,
— alleluia, al*le*luia.
Glory to the Father, and *to* the Son, * and to the Ho*ly* Spirit.
— The Lord is risen *from* the tomb, * alleluia, al*le*luia.

CANTICLE OF ZECHARIAH
Ant.   The Father *loves* the Son * and has entrusted everything to him, al*le*luia.

INTERCESSIONS (VI F)

God the Father has given us his Son for the resurrection *of* his people. * Let us
   turn with confidence to the Fath*er*, and say:
May the Lord Jesus be our very life.
As a pillar of fire, you lighted the way for your people *in* the desert,
— through his resurrection may Christ be today the light *of* our life.
Through the voice of Moses you taught your people *from* the mountain,
— through his resurrection may Christ be today the light *of* our life.
You fed your pilgrim people with your *gift* of manna,
— through his resurrection may Christ be today the light *of* our life.
You gave your people water *from* the rock,
— through his resurrection may Christ be today the light *of* our life.

Our Father . . .

Prayer

   God of mercy,
   may the Easter mystery we celebrate
   be effective throughout our lives.
   Grant this through our Lord Jesus Christ, your Son,
   who lives and reigns with you and the Holy Spirit,
   one God, for ever and ever.

Evening Prayer

READING   1 Peter 3:18, 22

   The reason why Christ died for sins once for all, the just man for the sake of
   the unjust, was that he might lead you to God. He was put to death insofar as
   fleshly existence goes, but was given life in the realm of the spirit. He went to
   heaven and is at God's right hand, with angelic rulers and power subjected to
   him.

RESPONSORY (VI F)

The dis*ci*ples rejoiced, * alleluia, al*le*luia.
— The dis*ci*ples rejoiced, * alleluia, al*le*luia.
When they saw the *ris*en Lord,
— alleluia, al*le*luia.
Glory to the Father, and *to* the Son, * and to the Ho*ly* Spirit.
— The dis*ci*ples rejoiced, * alleluia, al*le*luia.

CANTICLE OF MARY

Ant.   Whoever believes in the Son possesses e*ter*nal life, * al*le*luia.

INTERCESSIONS (VI F)

The Father has established in Christ the foundation of all our hope and the
principle of our *re*surrection. * Let us rejoice in Christ, and cry out *to* him,
saying:

King of glory, hear our *prayer.*

Lord Jesus, through your resurrection you entered the sanctuary of heaven to offer
the blood of *your* own sacrifice,

— lead us with you into the glory *of* the Father.

Through your resurrection you confirmed the faith of your dsciples and sent them
out in*to* the world,

— make all bishops and priests faithful preach*ers* of the Gospel.

Through your resurrection you became our peace and recon*ci*/iation,

— united the baptized in perfect communion of *faith* and love.

Through your resurrection the crippled man was healed at the gate *of* the temple,

— look on the sick and reveal in them the power *of* your glory.

You became the firstborn from the dead, the firstfruits of the *re*surrection,

— grant to the dead who hoped in you a share *in* your glory.

Our Father . . .

Prayer

God of mercy,
may the Easter mystery we celebrate
be effective throughout our lives.
Grant this through our Lord Jesus Christ, your Son,
who lives and reigns with you and the Holy Spirit,
one God, for ever and ever.

FRIDAY

Morning Prayer

READING   Acts 5:30-32

The God of our fathers has raised up Jesus whom you put to death, hanging
him on a tree. He whom God has exalted at his right hand as ruler and savior
is to bring repentance to Israel and forgiveness of sins. We testify to this. So
too does the Holy Spirit, whom God has given to those that obey him.

RESPONSORY (VI F)

The Lord is risen *from* the tomb, * alleluia, al/eluia.

— The Lord is risen *from* the tomb, * alleluia, al/eluia.

He hung upon the *cross* for us,

— alleluia, al/eluia.

Glory to the Father, and *to* the Son, * and to the Ho*ly* Spirit.
— The Lord is risen *from* the tomb, * alleluia, al*le*luia.

CANTICLE OF ZECHARIAH
Ant.   Jesus took bread, † and when he had *giv*en thanks, * he gave it to
                            those who were at table with him, al*le*luia.

INTERCESSIONS (VI F)
God the Father raised up Christ through the Spirit, and will also raise up our
     *mor*tal bodies. * Let us cry *out* to him:
Lord, raise us to life through your Holy Spirit.
All-holy Father, you accepted the holocaust of your Son in raising him *from* the
     dead,
— accept the offering we make today, and lead us to e*ter*nal life.
Look with favor on all we *do* today,
— that it may be for your glory and the sanctification *of* the world.
May our work today not be in vain but for the good of *the* whole world,
— and through it lead us *to* your kingdom.
Open our eyes today to recognize our brothers and sisters, and our *hearts* to love
     them,
— so that we may love and *serve* each other.

Our Father . . .

Prayer

       Father,
       in your plan of salvation
       your Son Jesus Christ accepted the cross
       and freed us from the power of the enemy.
       May we come to share the glory of his resurrection
       for he lives and reigns with you and the Holy Spirit,
       one God, for ever and ever.

Evening Prayer

READING   Hebrews 5:8-10
       Son though he was, Christ learned obedience from what he suffered; and
       when perfected, he became the source of eternal salvation for all who obey
       him, designated by God as high priest according to the order of Melchizedek.

RESPONSORY (VI F)
The dis*ci*ples rejoiced, * alleluia, al*le*luia.
— The dis*ci*ples rejoiced, * alleluia, al*le*luia.

When they saw the *ris*en Lord,
—alleluia, al*le*luia.
Glory to the Father, and *to* the Son, * and to the Ho*ly* Spirit.
—The dis*ci*ples rejoiced, * alleluia, al*le*luia.

CANTICLE OF MARY

Ant.   To destroy the power of hell Christ died upon the cross; †
         clothed in strength and glory, † he triumphed over death on *the*
         third day, * al*le*luia.

INTERCESSIONS (VI F)

Let us praise Christ, the source *of* all life * and the foundation *of* all virtue:
Lord, establish your kingdom in the *world.*
Jesus our Savior, you died in your human nature but were restored to life *by* the
    Spirit,
—make us die to sin, and live *by* the Spirit.
You sent your disciples into the whole world to preach the Gospel to *every*
    creature,
—inspire those who preach the Gospel to live *by* your Spirit.
All power in heaven and on earth has been given to you, to bear witness *to* the
    truth,
—keep the hearts of those who govern us faithful *to* the truth.
You make all things new, and command us to wait and watch *for* your kingdom,
—grant that the more we look forward to a new heaven and a new earth, the
    more we may seek to better this *pres*ent world.
You went down among the dead to bring them the good news *of* the Gospel,
—be the great joy and hope of *all* the dead.

Our Father . . .

Prayer

Father,
in your plan of salvation
your Son Jesus Christ accepted the cross
and freed us from the power of the enemy.
May we come to share the glory of his resurrection
for he lives and reigns with you and the Holy Spirit,
one God, for ever and ever.

SATURDAY

Morning Prayer

READING   Romans 14:7-9

None of us lives as his own master and none of us dies as his own master. While we live we are responsible to the Lord, and when we die we die as his servants. Both in life and death we are the Lord's. That is why Christ died and came to life again, that he might be Lord of both the dead and the living.

RESPONSORY (VI F)

The Lord is risen *from* the tomb, * alleluia, al*le*luia.
— The Lord is risen *from* the tomb, * alleluia, al*le*luia.
He hung upon the *cross* for us,
— alleluia, al*le*luia.
Glory to the Father, and *to* the Son, * and to the Ho*ly* Spirit.
— The Lord is risen *from* the tomb, * alleluia, al*le*luia.

CANTICLE OF ZECHARIAH

Ant.   Peace be with you; † it is I, *al*leluia; * do not be afraid, al*le*luia.

INTERCESSIONS (VI F)

Christ has made known to us the life that *lasts* for ever. * With faith and joy let us cry out *to* him, saying:
Lord, may your resurrection bring us the riches of your *grace.*
Eternal shepherd, look on your flock as it ris*es* from sleep,
— feed us with the word of life and the *bread* from heaven.
Keep us safe from *wolf* and hireling,
— and make us faithful in listening *to* your voice.
You are present to all who preach your Gospel, and give power *to* their words,
— make us today preachers of your resurrection by our holi*ness* of life.
Be our great joy that no one can *take* from us,
— so that we may reject sin with its sadness, and reach out to e*ter*nal life.

Our Father . . .

Prayer

God our Father,
look upon us with love.
You redeem us and make us your children in Christ.
Give us true freedom
and bring us to the inheritance you promised.
We ask this through our Lord Jesus Christ, your Son,
who lives and reigns with you and the Holy Spirit,
one God, for ever and ever.

THIRD SUNDAY OF EASTER

Evening Prayer I

READING   1 Peter 2:9-10

You are "a chosen race, a royal priesthood, a holy nation, a people he claims for his own to proclaim the glorious works" of the One who called you from darkness into his marvelous light. Once you were no people, but now you are God's people; once there was no mercy for you, but now you have found mercy.

RESPONSORY (VI F)

The disciples rejoiced, * alleluia, alleluia.
— The disciples rejoiced, * alleluia, alleluia.
When they saw the risen Lord,
— alleluia, alleluia.
Glory to the Father, and to the Son, * and to the Holy Spirit.
— The disciples rejoiced, * alleluia, alleluia.

CANTICLE OF MARY

Ant.   Stay with us, Lord, † for evening draws near and daylight is fading, * alleluia.

INTERCESSIONS (VI F)

Christ is our life and resurrection. * Let us cry out to him with faith:
Son of the living God, protect your people.
Lord Jesus, we pray for your Catholic Church,
— make it holy, so that your kingdom may be established among all nations.
We pray for the sick and the sorrowful, for those in bondage and in exile,
— that they may receive consolation and help.
We pray for those who have turned away from your paths,
— that they may experience the grace of your forgiveness and the joy of rising to new life.
Crucified and risen Savior, you will come to judge the world,
— have mercy on us sinners.
We pray for all the living,
— and for all who have gone from us in the hope of resurrection.

Our Father . . .

Prayer

God our Father,
may we look forward with hope to our resurrection,

for you have made us your sons and daughters,
and restored the joy of our youth.
We ask this through our Lord Jesus Christ, your Son,
who lives and reigns with you and the Holy Spirit,
one God, for ever and ever.

Morning Prayer

READING   Acts 10:40-43

God raised up Jesus on the third day and granted that he be seen, not by all,
but only by such witnesses as had been chosen beforehand by God—by us
who ate and drank with him after he rose from the dead. He commissioned
us to preach to the people and to bear witness that he is the one set apart by
God as judge of the living and the dead. To him all the prophets testify,
saying that everyone who believes in him has forgiveness of sins through his
name.

RESPONSORY (VI F)
Christ, Son of the living God, have mer*cy* on us, * alleluia, al*le*luia.
— Christ, Son of the living God, have mer*cy* on us, * alleluia, al*le*luia.
You have risen *from* the dead,
— alleluia, al*le*luia.
Glory to the Father, and *to* the Son, * and to the Ho*ly* Spirit.
— Christ, Son of the living God, have mer*cy* on us, * alleluia, al*le*luia.

CANTICLE OF ZECHARIAH
Ant.   It was ordained that *Christ* should suffer, * and on the third day
                      rise from the dead, al*le*luia.

INTERCESSIONS (VI F)
Christ is the Lord of life, raised up by the Father; in his turn he will raise us up *by*
    his power. * Let us pray *to* him, saying:
Christ our life, *save us.*
Lord Jesus, light shining in the darkness, you lead your people into life, and give
    our mortal nature the *gift* of holiness,
— may we spend this day in praise *of* your glory.
Lord, you walked the way of suffering and *cru*cifixion,
— may we suffer and die with you, and rise again to *share* your glory.
Son of the Father, our master and our brother, you have made us a kingdom of
    priests *for* our God,
— may we offer you our joyful sacri*fice* of praise.
King of glory, we look forward to the great day of your com*ing* in splendor,
— that we may see you face to face, and be transformed *in* your likeness.

Our Father . . .

Prayer

God our Father,
may we look forward with hope to our resurrection,
for you have made us your sons and daughters,
and restored the joy of our youth.
We ask this through our Lord Jesus Christ, your Son,
who lives and reigns with you and the Holy Spirit,
one God, for ever and ever.

Evening Prayer II

READING   Hebrews 10:12-14

Jesus offered one sacrifice for sins and took his seat forever at the right hand of God; now he waits until his enemies are placed beneath his feet. By one offering he has forever perfected those who are being sanctified.

RESPONSORY (VI F)

The *Lord* is risen, * alleluia, al*le*luia.
— The *Lord* is risen, * alleluia, al*le*luia.
He has ap*peared* to Simon,
— alleluia, al*le*luia.
Glory to the Father, and *to* the Son, * and to the Ho*ly* Spirit.
— The *Lord* is risen, * alleluia, al*le*luia.

CANTICLE OF MARY

Ant.   Jesus said to *his* disciples: * Bring me some of the fish you have
                 just caught.
                 Simon Peter went aboard and hauled a*shore* the net, * full of large
                 fish, al*le*luia.

INTERCESSIONS (VI F)

With joy in our hearts, let us call upon *Christ* the Lord, * who died and rose again,
   and lives always to inter*cede* for us:
Victorious King, hear our *prayer.*
Light and salvation *of* all peoples,
— send into our hearts the fire of your Spirit, as we proclaim your *re*surrection.
Let Israel recognize in you her longed-*for* Messiah,
— and the whole earth be filled with the knowledge *of* your glory.
Keep us in the communion *of* your saints,
— and grant us rest from our labors *in* their company.

You have triumphed over death, your enemy; destroy in us the pow*er* of death,
— that we may live only for you, victorious and im*mor*tal Lord.
Savior Christ, you were obedient even to accepting death, and were raised up to
the right hand *of* the Father,
— in your goodness welcome your brothers and sisters into the kingdom *of* your
glory.

Our Father . . .

Prayer

God our Father,
may we look forward with hope to our resurrection,
for you have made us your sons and daughters,
and restored the joy of our youth.
We ask this through our Lord Jesus Christ, your Son,
who lives and reigns with you and the Holy Spirit,
one God, for ever and ever.

MONDAY

Morning Prayer

READING   Romans 10:8b-10
The word is near you, on your lips and in your heart (that is , the word of
faith which we preach). For if you confess with your lips that Jesus is Lord,
and believe in your heart that God raised him from the dead, you will be
saved. Faith in the heart leads to justification, confession on the lips to
salvation.

RESPONSORY (VI F)
The Lord is risen *from* the tomb, * alleluia, al*le*luia.
— The Lord is risen *from* the tomb, * alleluia, al*le*luia.
He hung upon the *cross* for us,
— alleluia, al*le*luia.
Glory to the Father, and *to* the Son, * and to the Ho*ly* Spirit.
— The Lord is risen *from* the tomb, * alleluia, al*le*luia.

CANTICLE OF ZECHARIAH
Ant.   Do not work for food *that* will perish, * but for food that lasts to
                eternal life, al*le*luia.

INTERCESSIONS (VI F)

The Father glorified Jesus and appointed him heir *to* all nations. * Let us *praise* him, saying:

Save us, Lord, through your *victory.*

Lord Christ, by your victory you broke the power of evil and destroyed *sin* and death,

— make us victorious over *sin* today.

You laid death low, and brought *us* new life,

— grant that we may walk today in *this* new life.

You gave life to the dead, and led mankind from *death* to life,

— give eternal life to all those we shall *meet* today.

You brought confusion on the guards at your tomb, but joy to *your* disciples,

— grant the fullness of joy to *all* who serve you.

Our Father . . .

Prayer

God our Father,
your light of truth
guides us to the way of Christ.
May all who follow him
reject what is contrary to the gospel.
We ask this through our Lord Jesus Christ, your Son,
who lives and reigns with you and the Holy Spirit,
one God, for ever and ever.

Evening Prayer

READING   Hebrews 8:1b-3a

We have such a high priest, who has taken his seat at the right hand of the throne of the Majesty in heaven, minister of the sanctuary and of that true tabernacle set up, not by man, but by the Lord. Now every high priest is appointed to offer gifts and sacrifices.

RESPONSORY (VI F)

The dis*ci*ples rejoiced, * alleluia, al*le*luia.

— The dis*ci*ples rejoiced, * alleluia, al*le*luia.

When they saw the *ris*en Lord,

— alleluia, al*le*luia.

Glory to the Father, and *to* the Son, * and to the Ho*ly* Spirit.

— The dis*ci*ples rejoiced, * alleluia, al*le*luia.

CANTICLE OF MARY

Ant.   This is what God *asks* of you: * trust in the one whom he has sent, al*le*luia.

INTERCESSIONS (VI F)

The Holy Spirit raised the body of Christ to life and made it the *source* of life. *
   With joy in our hearts let us call upon the ris*en* Christ, saying:
Lord, make all things new and fill them with *life.*
Savior of the world and King of the new creation, raise our minds and hearts *to*
   your kingdom,
— where you sit at the right hand *of* the Father.
Lord, you are always present *in* your Church,
— through your Holy Spirit guide it in*to* all truth.
Show your mercy to the sick, the overburdened *and* the dying,
— that all may receive strength and courage *from* your love.
Light that never fails, as the day draws to its close we offer you our sacri*fice* of
   praise,
— and pray that the glory of your resurrection may shine on our deceased
   broth*ers* and sisters.

Our Father . . .

Prayer

God our Father,
your light of truth
guides us to the way of Christ.
May all who follow him
reject what is contrary to the gospel.
We ask this through our Lord Jesus Christ, your Son,
who lives and reigns with you and the Holy Spirit,
one God, for ever and ever.

TUESDAY

Morning Prayer

READING Acts 13:30-33

READING   Acts 13:30-33
God raised Jesus from the dead, and for many days thereafter Jesus appeared to those who had come up with him from Galilee to Jerusalem. These are his witnesses now before the people. We ourselves announce to you the good news that what God promised our fathers he has fulfilled for us, their children, in raising up Jesus, according to what is written in the second psalm, "You are my son; this day I have begotten you."

RESPONSORY (VI F)
The Lord is risen *from* the tomb, * alleluia, al*le*luia.
— The Lord is risen *from* the tomb, * alleluia, al*le*luia.
He hung upon the *cross* for us,
— alleluia, al*le*luia.
Glory to the Father, and *to* the Son, * and to the Ho*ly* Spirit.
— The Lord is risen *from* the tomb, * alleluia, al*le*luia.

CANTICLE OF ZECHARIAH
Ant.   Truly I say to you: † Moses did not give you the *bread* of heaven; my Father gives you the true bread from heaven, al*le*luia.

INTERCESSIONS (VI F)
By his own power Christ raised up the temple of his body when it had been des*troyed* in death. * With joy *let* us ask him:
Lord, share with us the fruits of your *victory.*
Christ our Savior, when you rose again you brought to the holy women and the apostles the joyful news of a *world* redeemed,
— make us witnesses to your *ris*en life.
You promised to all people that we would rise up again to new*ness* of life,
— make us heralds *of* your Gospel.
You showed yourself to your apostles and breathed the Holy Spir*it* on them,
— renew in us the presence of the same crea*tor* Spirit.
You promised to be with your disciples to the end *of* the world,
— stay with us today, and remain *with* us always.

Our Father . . .

Prayer

Father,
you open the kingdom of heaven

to those born again by water and the Spirit.
Increase your gift of love in us.
May all who have been freed from sins in baptism
receive all that you have promised.
We ask this through our Lord Jesus Christ, your Son,
who lives and reigns with you and the Holy Spirit,
one God, for ever and ever.

Evening Prayer

READING 1 Peter 2:4-5

Come to the Lord, a living stone, rejected by men but approved, nonetheless, and precious in God's eyes. You too are living stones, built as an edifice of spirit into a holy priesthood, offering spiritual sacrifices acceptable to God through Jesus Christ.

RESPONSORY (VI F)

The disciples rejoiced, * alleluia, alleluia.
— The disciples rejoiced, * alleluia, alleluia.
When they saw the risen Lord,
— alleluia, alleluia.
Glory to the Father, and to the Son, * and to the Holy Spirit.
— The disciples rejoiced, * alleluia, alleluia.

CANTICLE OF MARY

Ant. The bread of God that comes *down* from heaven * gives life to the world, alleluia.

INTERCESSIONS (VI F)

As Christ lay in the darkness of the earth he saw the light of *a* new glory. * Let us cry out to *him* in joy:
King of glory, hear us.
We pray for all bishops, priests and deacons, that they may be zealous *in* their ministry,
— and prepare for you a people devoted to eve*ry* good work.
We pray for all who teach in the service *of* your Church,
— that they may seek your truth with a *sin*cere heart.
We pray for your faithful people, that they may be victorious in the con*test* of faith,
— and win the prize of victory *in* your kingdom.
You cancelled our condemnation by nailing it *to* the cross,
— free us from our chains, and lead us *out* of darkness.

You went down among the dead and opened for them the *gates* to life,
— welcome our dead brothers and sisters in*to* your kingdom.

Our Father . . .

Prayer

Father,
you open the kingdom of heaven
to those born again by water and the Spirit.
Increase your gift of love in us.
May all who have been freed from sins in baptism
receive all that you have promised.
We ask this through our Lord Jesus Christ, your Son,
who lives and reigns with you and the Holy Spirit,
one God, for ever and ever.

WEDNESDAY

Morning Prayer

READING   Romans 6:8-11
If we have died with Christ, we believe that we are also to live with him. We know that Christ, once raised from the dead, will never die again; death has no more power over him. His death was death to sin, once for all; his life is life for God. In the same way, you must consider yourselves dead to sin but alive for God in Christ Jesus.

RESPONSORY (VI F)
The Lord is risen *from* the tomb, * alleluia, al*le*luia.
— The Lord is risen *from* the tomb, * alleluia, al*le*luia.
He hung upon the *cross* for us,
— alleluia, al*le*luia.
Glory to the Father, and *to* the Son, * and to the Ho*ly* Spirit.
— The Lord is risen *from* the tomb, * alleluia, al*le*luia.

CANTICLE OF ZECHARIAH
Ant.   Whoever sees the Son and believes in him † will *live* for ever, *
              and I shall raise him up on the last day, al*le*luia.

INTERCESSIONS (VI F)
Christ was given up for our sins and rose again to *make* us righteous. * Let us cry
   out *to* him, saying:
Save us, Lord, by your *victory.*

Christ our Savior, in conquering death you brought us joy, in rising again you
raised us up and filled us with the abundance *of* your gifts,
— stir up our hearts, and sanctify this day through the gift of your *Ho*ly Spirit.

You are glorified by the angels in heaven and adored by mankind on earth; as we
celebrate your *re*surrection,
— accept our worship in spirit *and* in truth.

Lord Jesus, save us; show your great mercy to your people, as we look forward to
our own *re*surrection,
— have mercy on us, and protect us today from *eve*ry evil.

King of glory, source of our life, grant that, when you *come* again,
— we may be one with *you* in glory.

Our Father . . .

Prayer

Merciful Lord,
hear the prayers of your people.
May we who have received your gift of faith
share for ever in the new life of Christ.
Grant this through our Lord Jesus Christ, your Son,
who lives and reigns with you and the Holy Spirit,
one God, for ever and ever.

Evening Prayer

READING   Hebrews 7:24-27

Jesus, because he remains forever, has a priesthood that does not pass away.
Therefore he is always able to save those who approach God through him,
since he forever lives to make intercession for them. It was fitting that we
should have such a high priest: holy, innocent, undefiled, separated from
sinners, higher than the heavens. Unlike the other high priests, he has no
need to offer sacrifice day after day, first for his own sins and then for those of
the people; he did that once for all when he offered himself.

RESPONSORY (VI F)
The dis*ci*ples rejoiced, * alleluia, al*le*luia.
— The dis*ci*ples rejoiced, * alleluia, al*le*luia.
When they saw the *ris*en Lord,
— alleluia, al*le*luia.
Glory to the Father, and *to* the Son, * and to the Ho*ly* Spirit.
— The dis*ci*ples rejoiced, * alleluia, al*le*luia.

CANTICLE OF MARY

Ant.   All that the Father gives me will come to me, † and whoever
                        comes to me I shall not *turn* away, * al*le*luia.

INTERCESSIONS (VI F)

Christ rose from the dead and is seated at the right hand *of* the Father. * Let us
   pray *to* him, saying:
Lord Jesus, you live for ever; hear our prayer.
Lord, remember all who minister *in* your service,
— may their holy lives be an example *to* your people.
Give to those who govern us a spirit of jus*tice* and peace,
— so that the human family may *live* in harmony.
Guide our days in the way *of* salvation,
— and fill the earth with your plenty for the sake *of* the needy.
Christ our savior, light of the world, you have called creation from *death* to life,
— may your light shine for ever on our departed broth*ers* and sisters.

Our Father . . .

Prayer

   Merciful Lord,
   hear the prayers of your people.
   May we who have received your gift of faith
   share for ever in the new life of Christ.
   Grant this through our Lord Jesus Christ, your Son,
   who lives and reigns with you and the Holy Spirit,
   one God, for ever and ever.

THURSDAY

Morning Prayer

READING   Romans 8:10-11
   If Christ is in you the body is dead because of sin, while the spirit lives
   because of justice. If the Spirit of him who raised Jesus from the dead dwells
   in you, then he who raised Christ from the dead will bring your mortal bodies
   to life also, through his Spirit dwelling in you.

RESPONSORY (VI F)
The Lord is risen *from* the tomb, * alleluia, al*le*luia.
— The Lord is risen *from* the tomb, * alleluia, al*le*luia.

He hung upon the *cross* for us,
— alleluia, al*le*luia.
Glory to the Father, and *to* the Son, * and to the Ho*ly* Spirit.
— The Lord is risen *from* the tomb, * alleluia, al*le*luia.

CANTICLE OF ZECHARIAH
Ant. Amen, amen, I say to you: † Whoever believes in me will *live* for
ever, * al*le*luia.

INTERCESSIONS (VI F)
Christ rose from the dead and is always present *in* his Church. * Let us adore
him, and say:
Stay with us, *Lord.*
Lord Jesus, victor over sin and death, glorious *and* immortal,
— be always *in* our midst.
Come to us in the power *of* your victory,
— and show our hearts the loving kindness *of* your Father.
Come to heal a world wounded *by* division,
— for you alone can transform our hearts and *make* them one.
Strengthen our faith in *fin*al victory,
— and renew our hope in your *sec*ond coming.

Our Father . . .

Prayer

Father,
in this holy season
we come to know the full depth of your love.
You have freed us from the darkness of error and sin.
Help us to cling to your truths with fidelity.
We ask this through our Lord Jesus Christ, your Son,
who lives and reigns with you and the Holy Spirit,
one God, for ever and ever.

Evening Prayer

READING 1 Peter 3:18, 22
The reason why Christ died for sins once for all, the just man for the sake of
the unjust, was that he might lead you to God. He was put to death insofar as
fleshly existence goes, but was given life in the realm of the spirit. He went to
heaven and is at God's right hand, with angelic rulers and power subjected to
him.

RESPONSORY (VI F)

The disciples rejoiced, * alleluia, alleluia.
— The disciples rejoiced, * alleluia, alleluia.
When they saw the risen Lord,
— alleluia, alleluia.
Glory to the Father, and to the Son, * and to the Holy Spirit.
— The disciples rejoiced, * alleluia, alleluia.

CANTICLE OF MARY

Ant.   I am the living bread come down from heaven; * anyone who eats
                    this bread will live for ever; .
                    the bread that I will give is my flesh, * for the life of the world,
                    alleluia.

INTERCESSIONS (VI F)

Christ rose from the dead as the firstfruits of those who sleep. * In our joy let us
    praise him, and say:
Firstborn from the dead, hear our prayer.
Lord Jesus, remember your holy Church, built on the apostles and reaching to
    the ends of the earth,
— and let your blessing rest on all who believe in you.
You are the healer of soul and body,
— come to our aid, and save us in your love.
Raise up the sick and give them strength,
— free them from their infirmities.
Help those in distress of mind or body,
— and in your compassion lift up those in need.
Through your cross and resurrection you opened for all the way to immortality,
— grant to our deceased brothers and sisters the joys of your kingdom.

Our Father . . .

                              Prayer

        Father,
        in this holy season
        we come to know the full depth of your love.
        You have freed us from the darkness of error and sin.
        Help us to cling to your truths with fidelity.
        We ask this through our Lord Jesus Christ, your Son,
        who lives and reigns with you and the Holy Spirit,
        one God, for ever and ever.

FRIDAY

Morning Prayer

READING Acts 5:30-32

READING Acts 5:30-32

The God of our fathers has raised up Jesus whom you put to death, hanging him on a tree. He whom God has exalted at his right hand as ruler and savior is to bring repentance to Israel and forgiveness of sins. We testify to this. So too does the Holy Spirit whom God has given to those that obey him.

RESPONSORY (VI F)

The Lord is risen *from* the tomb, * alleluia, al*le*luia.
—The Lord is risen *from* the tomb, * alleluia, al*le*luia.
He hung upon the *cross* for us,
—alleluia, al*le*luia.
Glory to the Father, and *to* the Son, * and to the Ho*ly* Spirit.
—The Lord is risen *from* the tomb, * alleluia, al*le*luia.

CANTICLE OF ZECHARIAH

Ant.   Whoever eats my flesh and *drinks* my blood * shall live in me and I in him, al*le*luia.

INTERCESSIONS (VI F)

Let us pray to *God* the Father, * who gave us new life through the *ris*en Christ:
Give us the glory of your Son.
Lord our God, your mighty works have revealed your eternal plan: you created the earth, and you are faithful in every *gen*eration,
—hear us, Fa*ther* of mercy.
Purify our hearts with your truth, and guide them in the *way* of holiness,
—so that we may do what is pleasing *in* your sight.
Let your face *shine* upon us,
—that we may be freed from sin and filled *with* your plenty.
You gave the apostles the *peace* of Christ,
—grant peace to your people, and to *the* whole world.

Our Father . . .

Prayer

Father,
by the love of your Spirit,
may we who have experienced
the grace of the Lord's resurrection
rise to the newness of life in joy.

Grant this through our Lord Jesus Christ, your Son,
who lives and reigns with you and the Holy Spirit,
one God, for ever and ever.

Evening Prayer

READING   Hebrews 5:8-10
Son though he was, Christ learned obedience from what he suffered; and
when perfected, he became the source of eternal salvation for all who obey
him, designated by God as high priest according to the order of Melchizedek.

RESPONSORY (VI F)
The disciples rejoiced, * alleluia, al/eluia.
— The disciples rejoiced, * alleluia, al/eluia.
When they saw the risen Lord,
— alleluia, al/eluia.
Glory to the Father, and to the Son, * and to the Holy Spirit.
— The disciples rejoiced, * alleluia, al/eluia.

CANTICLE OF MARY
Ant.   Our crucified and risen Lord has redeemed us, * al/eluia.

INTERCESSIONS (VI F)
Christ is the way, the truth and the life. * Let us praise him, and say:
Son of the living God, bless your people.
We pray to you, Lord Jesus, for all ministers of your Church,
— as they break for us the bread of life, may they themselves receive nourishment
and strength.
We pray for the whole Christian people, that all may be worthy of their calling,
— and safeguard their unity in the Spirit by the bond of peace.
We pray for those who govern us, that they may temper justice with mercy,
— and promote harmony and peace throughout the world.
We pray for ourselves, that our hearts may be purified to sing your praises in the
communion of saints,
— that we be reunited with our deceased brothers and sisters, whom we
commend to your loving kindness.

Our Father . . .

Prayer

Father,
by the love of your Spirit,
may we who have experienced

the grace of the Lord's resurrection
rise to the newness of life in joy.
Grant this through our Lord Jesus Christ, your Son,
who lives and reigns with you and the Holy Spirit,
one God, for ever and ever.

SATURDAY

Morning Prayer

READING   Romans 14:7-9

None of us lives as his own master and none of us dies as his own master.
While we live we are responsible to the Lord, and when we die we die as his
servants. Both in life and death we are the Lord's. That is why Christ died
and came to life again, that he might be Lord of both the dead and the living.

RESPONSORY (VI F)
The Lord is risen *from* the tomb, * alleluia, al*le*luia.
— The Lord is risen *from* the tomb, * alleluia, al*le*luia.
He hung upon the *cross* for us,
— alleluia, al*le*luia.
Glory to the Father, and *to* the Son, * and to the Ho*ly* Spirit.
— The Lord is risen *from* the tomb, * alleluia, al*le*luia.

CANTICLE OF ZECHARIAH
Ant.   Simon Peter said: Lord, to whom *shall* we go? * You have the
                words of eter*nal* life;
                and we believe and we are convinced † that you *are* the Christ, *
                the Son of God, al*le*luia.

INTERCESSIONS (VI F)
Christ is the bread of life; he will raise up on the last day all who share the table
    of his word *and* his body. * In our joy *let* us pray:
Lord, give us peace and *joy.*
Son of God, you were raised from the dead to lead us *in*to life,
— bless and sanctify all the children *of* your Father.
You give peace and joy to all who be*lieve* in you,
— grant that we may walk as children of the light, rejoicing *in* your victory.
Build up the faith of your pilgrim *Church* on earth,
— that it may bear witness to your resurrection before *the* whole world.
You suffered and so entered into the glory *of* the Father,
— change the tears of the sorrowful *into* joy.

Our Father . . .

Prayer

God our Father,
by the waters of baptism
you give new life to the faithful.
May we not succumb to the influence of evil
but remain true to your gift of life.
We ask this through our Lord Jesus Christ, your Son,
who lives and reigns with you and the Holy Spirit,
one God, for ever and ever.

FOURTH SUNDAY OF EASTER

PSALTER, WEEK IV, 806.

Evening Prayer I

READING

1 Peter 2:9-10

You are "a chosen race, a royal priesthood, a holy nation, a people he claims for his own to proclaim the glorious works" of the One who called you from darkness into his marvelous light. Once you were no people, but now you are God's people; once there was no mercy for you, but now you have found mercy.

RESPONSORY (VI F)

The disciples rejoiced, * alleluia, alleluia.

— The disciples rejoiced, * alleluia, alleluia.

When they saw the risen Lord,

— alleluia, alleluia.

Glory to the Father, and to the Son, * and to the Holy Spirit.

— The disciples rejoiced, * alleluia, alleluia.

CANTICLE OF MARY

Ant.   I am the gate, says the Lord; † whoever enters through me *shall* be saved * and find pasture, alleluia.

INTERCESSIONS (VI F)

In rising from the dead, Christ destroyed death and *restored* life. * Let us cry out *to* him, saying:

Lord Jesus, you live for ever; hear our prayer.

You are the stone rejected by the builders which became the chief *corner*stone,

— make us living stones in the temple *of* your Church.

You are the faithful and true witness, the firstborn *from* the dead,

— make your Church bear constant witness *to* yourself.

You alone are the Bridegroom of the Church, born from your *wound*ed side,

— make us reveal to the world the love of Bride*groom* and Bride.

You are the first and the last, you were dead and *are* alive,

— keep those who have been baptized faithful until death, that they may receive the *crown* of victory.

Light and lamp of God's *holy* city,

— shine on our friends who have died, that they may *reign* for ever.

Our Father . . .

Prayer

Almighty and ever-living God,
give us new strength
from the courage of Christ our shepherd,
and lead us to join the saints in heaven,
where he lives and reigns with you and the Holy Spirit,
one God, for ever and ever.

Morning Prayer

READING   Acts 10:40-43

God raised up Jesus on the third day and granted that he be seen, not by all,
but only by such witnesses as had been chosen beforehand by God— by us
who ate and drank with him after he rose from the dead. He commissioned
us to preach to the people and to bear witness that he is the one set apart by
God as judge of the living and the dead. To him all the prophets testify,
saying that everyone who believes in him has forgiveness of sins through his
name.

RESPONSORY (VI F)

Christ, Son of the living God, have mer*cy* on us, * alleluia, al*le*luia.
— Christ, Son of the living God, have mer*cy* on us, * alleluia, al*le*luia.
You have risen *from* the dead,
— alleluia, al*le*luia.
Glory to the Father, and *to* the Son, * and to the Ho*ly* Spirit.
— Christ, Son of the living God, have mer*cy* on us, * alleluia, al*le*luia.

CANTICLE OF ZECHARIAH

Ant.   I am the shepherd *of* the sheep; * I am the way, the truth and *the*
life:
I know my sheep, and my *sheep* know me, * a*l*leluia.

INTERCESSIONS (VI F)

God the almighty Father raised Jesus as the firstborn from the dead, and made
him our savior. * Let us call up*on* him, saying:
Give us, Lord, the glory of your Son.
All-holy Father, you brought your belovèd Son Jesus from the darkness of death
into the splendor *of* your glory,
— bring us also into your marve*lo*us light.
You have given us *faith* to save us,
— may we live today by the faith *of* our baptism.
You command us to seek the things that are above, where Christ is seated at *your*
right hand,
— do not let us be deceived by the allure*ments* of sin.

May our life, hidden with Christ in you, our Father, shine be*fore* the world,
— foreshadowing a new heaven and *a* new earth.

Our Father . . .

Prayer

Almighty and ever-living God,
give us new strength
from the courage of Christ our shepherd,
and lead us to join the saints in heaven,
where he lives and reigns with you and the Holy Spirit,
one God, for ever and ever.

Evening Prayer II

READING   Hebrews 10:12-14
Jesus offered one sacrifice for sins and took his seat forever at the right hand
of God; now he waits until his enemies are placed beneath his feet. By one
offering he has forever perfected those who are being sanctified.

RESPONSORY (VI F)
The *Lord* is risen, * alleluia, al*le*luia.
— The *Lord* is risen, * alleluia, al*le*luia.
He has ap*peared* to Simon,
— alleluia, al*le*luia.
Glory to the Father, and *to* the Son, * and to the Ho*ly* Spirit.
— The *Lord* is risen, * alleluia, al*le*luia.

CANTICLE OF MARY
Ant.   My sheep will *hear* my voice. * I, their *Lord*, know them.

INTERCESSIONS (VI F)
God the Father raised Christ from the dead and exalted him at *his* right hand. *
    Let us pray to the *Fa*ther, saying:
*Through Christ in glory, watch over your peo*ple, Lord.
Righteous Father, you lifted Jesus above the earth through the triumph *of* the
    cross,
— may all things be lifted *up* in him.
Through your Son in glory send the Holy Spirit up*on* the Church,
— that it may be the sacrament of unity for the whole *hu*man race.
You have brought a new family into being through water and the *Ho*ly Spirit,
— keep them faithful to their baptism, and bring them to ever*last*ing life.

Through your exalted Son help those in distress, free those in captivity, *heal* the
  sick,
—and by your blessings give joy *to* the world.
You nourished our deceased brothers and sisters with the body and blood of the
  *ris*en Christ,
—raise them up at *the* last day.

Our Father . . .

Prayer

Almighty and ever-living God,
  give us new strength
  from the courage of Christ our shepherd,
  and lead us to join the saints in heaven,
  where he lives and reigns with you and the Holy Spirit,
  one God, for ever and ever.

MONDAY

Morning Prayer

READING   Romans 10:8b-10
  The word is near you, on your lips and in your heart (that is, the word of faith
  which we preach). For if you confess with your lips that Jesus is Lord, and
  believe in your heart that God raised him from the dead, you will be saved.
  Faith in the heart leads to justification, confession on the lips to salvation.

RESPONSORY (VI F)
The Lord is risen *from* the tomb, * alleluia, al*le*luia.
—The Lord is risen *from* the tomb, * alleluia, al*le*luia.
He hung upon the *cross* for us,
—alleluia, al*le*luia.
Glory to the Father, and *to* the Son, * and to the Ho*ly* Spirit.
—The Lord is risen *from* the tomb, * alleluia, al*le*luia.

CANTICLE OF ZECHARIAH
Ant.   I am the Good Shepherd; † I pas*ture* my sheep * and I lay down
             my life for them, al*le*luia.

INTERCESSIONS (VI F)
God the Father was glorified in the death and resurrection *of* his Son. * Let us
  pray to him with con*fi*dence, saying:
Lord, enlighten our minds.

Father of lights, you bathed the world in splendor when Christ rose a*gain* in
   glory,
— fill our minds today with the *light* of faith.
Through the resurrection of your Son you opened for us the way to e*ter*nal life,
— as we work today sustain us with the *hope* of glory.
Through your risen Son you sent the Holy Spirit in*to* the world,
— set our hearts on fire with spir*itual* love.
May Jesus Christ, who was crucified to *set* us free,
— be today our salvation *and* redemption.

Our Father . . .

Prayer

Father,
through the obedience of Jesus,
your servant and your Son,
you raised a fallen world.
Free us from sin
and bring us the joy that lasts for ever.
We ask this through our Lord Jesus Christ, your Son,
who lives and reigns with you and the Holy Spirit,
one God, for ever and ever.

Evening Prayer

READING   Hebrews 8:1b-3a
   We have such a high priest, who has taken his seat at the right hand of the
   throne of the Majesty in heaven, minister of the sanctuary and of that true
   tabernacle set up, not by man, but by the Lord. Now every high priest is
   appointed to offer gifts and sacrifices.

RESPONSORY (VI F)
The dis*ci*ples rejoiced, * alleluia, al*le*luia.
— The dis*ci*ples rejoiced, * alleluia, al*le*luia.
When they saw the *ris*en Lord,
— alleluia, al*le*luia.
Glory to the Father, and *to* the Son, * and to the Ho*ly* Spirit.
— The dis*ci*ples rejoiced, * alleluia, al*le*luia.

CANTICLE OF MARY
Ant.   I have other sheep that do not belong *to* this flock; * these also I
                     must lead.
                     They will hear my voice, † and there will be one fold *and* one
                     shepherd, * al*le*luia.

INTERCESSIONS (VI F)

Let us pray to Christ the Lord, who bathed the world in glory through his
   re*surrection.* * With joyful hearts *let* us say:

Christ, our life, hear our *prayer.*

Lord Jesus Christ, you walked with your disciples *on* the way,

— be with your Church on its pilgrim*age* through life.

Do not let us be slow *to* believe,

— but ready to proclaim you as victor *over* death.

Look with kindness on those who do not recog*nize* your presence,

— reveal yourself to them, so that they may welcome *you* as Savior.

Through the cross you have brought reconciliation to mankind *in* your body,

— grant unity and peace *to* all nations.

Judge of the living *and* the dead,

— forgive the sins of the faith*ful* departed.

Our Father . . .

Prayer

Father,
through the obedience of Jesus,
your servant and your Son,
you raised a fallen world.
Free us from sin
and bring us the joy that lasts for ever.
We ask this through our Lord Jesus Christ, your Son,
who lives and reigns with you and the Holy Spirit,
one God, for ever and ever.

TUESDAY

Morning Prayer

READING   Acts 13:30-33

God raised Jesus from the dead, and for many days thereafter Jesus appeared
to those who had come up with him from Galilee to Jerusalem. These are his
witnesses now before the people. We ourselves announce to you the good
news that what God has promised our fathers he has fulfilled for us, his
children, in raising up Jesus, according to what is written in the second psalm,
"You are my son; this day I have begotten you."

RESPONSORY (VI F)

The Lord is risen *from* the tomb, * alleluia, al*le*luia.

— The Lord is risen *from* the tomb, * alleluia, al*le*luia.

He hung upon the *cross* for us,
— alleluia, al*le*luia.
Glory to the Father, and *to* the Son, * and to the Ho*ly* Spirit.
— The Lord is risen *from* the tomb, * alleluia, al*le*luia.

CANTICLE OF ZECHARIAH

Ant. The works that I do in the name *of* my Father * speak on my behalf, al*le*luia.

INTERCESSIONS (VI F)

The spotless Lamb of God takes away the sins *of* the world. * Let us give thanks to the Fath*er,* and say:
Source of all life, raise us to life.
Source of all life, remember the death and resurrection of the Lamb slain *on* the cross,
— listen to his voice as he lives for ever, making interces*sion* for us.
Now that the old leaven of wickedness and evil *is* destroyed,
— may we always feed on the unleavened bread of sinceri*ty* and truth.
Grant that today we may put aside all fric*tion* and jealousy,
— and show greater concern for the *needs* of others.
Send into our hearts the spirit *of* the Gospel,
— that we may walk in the way of your commandments, today *and* for ever.

Our Father . . .

Prayer

Almighty God,
as we celebrate the resurrection,
may we share with each other
the joy the risen Christ has won for us.
We ask this through our Lord Jesus Christ, your Son,
who lives and reigns with you and the Holy Spirit,
one God, for ever and ever.

Evening Prayer

READING 1 Peter 2:4-5
Come to the Lord, a living stone, rejected by men but approved, nonetheless, and precious in God's eyes. You too are living stones, built as an edifice of spirit, into a holy priesthood, offering spiritual sacrifices acceptable to God through Jesus Christ.

RESPONSORY (VI F)

The disciples rejoiced, * alleluia, alleluia.
— The disciples rejoiced, * alleluia, alleluia.
When they saw the risen Lord,
— alleluia, alleluia.
Glory to the Father, and to the Son, * and to the Holy Spirit.
— The disciples rejoiced, * alleluia, alleluia.

CANTICLE OF MARY

Ant.   I know my sheep and they follow me; * I give them eternal life,
              alleluia.

INTERCESSIONS (VI F)

By his resurrection Christ has given sure hope to his people. * Let us ask him
   with our whole hearts:
Lord Jesus, you live for ever; hear our prayer.
Lord Jesus, from your wounded side flowed blood and water,
— make the Church your spotless bride.
Chief shepherd, after your resurrection you made Peter shepherd of your flock
   when he professed his love for you,
— increase from day to day the love and devotion of N., our Pope.
You showed your disciples how to make a great catch of fish,
— send others to continue their work as fishers of men.
At the lakeside you prepared bread and fish for your disciples,
— grant that we may never allow others to die of hunger.
Jesus, the new Adam and life-giving spirit, transform the dead into your own
   likeness,
— that the fullness of your joy may be theirs.

Our Father . . .

Prayer

    Almighty God,
    as we celebrate the resurrection,
    may we share with each other
    the joy the risen Christ has won for us.
    We ask this through our Lord Jesus Christ, your Son,
    who lives and reigns with you and the Holy Spirit,
    one God, for ever and ever.

WEDNESDAY

Morning Prayer

READING   Romans 6:8-11

If we have died with Christ, we believe that we are also to live with him. We know that Christ, once raised from the dead, will never die again; death has no more power over him. His death was death to sin, once for all; his life is life for God. In the same way, you must consider yourselves dead to sin but alive for God in Christ Jesus.

RESPONSORY (VI F)

The Lord is risen *from* the tomb, * alleluia, al*le*luia.
— The Lord is risen *from* the tomb, * alleluia, al*le*luia.
He hung upon the *cross* for us,
— alleluia, al*le*luia.
Glory to the Father, and *to* the Son, * and to the Ho*ly* Spirit.
— The Lord is risen *from* the tomb, * alleluia, al*le*luia.

CANTICLE OF ZECHARIAH

Ant.   I *am* the light; * I have come into *the* world,
              that those who be*lieve* in me * may not remain in darkness,
              al*le*luia.

INTERCESSIONS (VI F)

By the gift of the Father, the risen Christ was seen by *the* apostles. * Let us pray to the Fath*er*, and say:
Give us, Lord, the glory of your *Son.*
Father of lights, today we offer you our thanks and praise for calling us into your mar*vel*ous light,
— to re*ceive* your mercy.
May the efforts of mankind to make the *world* more human,
— be purified and strengthened by the power *of* your Spirit.
May we be so dedicated to the ser*vice* of others,
— that the whole human family may become a pleasing sacrifice *in* your honor.
At the dawn of a new day, fill us *with* your mercy,
— that the whole day may be a day of *joy* and praise.

Our Father . . .

                              Prayer

God our Father,
life of the faithful, glory of the humble,
happiness of the just, hear our prayer.

Fill our emptiness
with the blessing of the eucharist,
the foretaste of eternal joy.
We ask this through our Lord Jesus Christ, your Son,
who lives and reigns with you and the Holy Spirit,
one God, for ever and ever.

Evening Prayer

READING   Hebrews 7:24-27
Jesus, because he remains forever, has a priesthood that does not pass away.
Therefore he is always able to save those who approach God through him,
since he forever lives to make intercession for them. It was fitting that we
should have such a high priest: holy, innocent, undefiled, separated from
sinners, higher than the heavens. Unlike the other high priests, he has no
need to offer sacrifice day after day, first for his own sins and then for those of
the people; he did that once for all when he offered himself.

RESPONSORY (VI F)
The disciples rejoiced, * alleluia, alleluia.
— The disciples rejoiced, * alleluia, alleluia.
When they saw the risen Lord,
— alleluia, alleluia.
Glory to the Father, and to the Son, * and to the Holy Spirit.
— The disciples rejoiced, * alleluia, alleluia.

CANTICLE OF MARY
Ant.   God sent his Son into the world * not as its judge but as its savior,
              alleluia.

INTERCESSIONS (VI F)
In his Son, risen from the dead, God has opened for us the way to everlasting life.
    * Let us ask the Father:
Through the victory of Christ, save the people he has redeemed.
God of our fathers, you raised your Son Jesus from the dead and clothed him in
    glory; move our hearts to complete repentance,
— that we may walk in newness of life.
You have led us back to the shepherd and bishop of our souls,
— keep us faithful under the guidance of the shepherds of the Church.
You chose the firstfruits of Christ's disciples from the Jewish people,
— reveal to the children of Israel the fulfillment of the promise made to their
    forefathers.

Remember the lonely, the orphaned *and* the widowed,
— and do not abandon those who have been reconciled with you by the death *of* your Son.
You called Stephen to your presence when he bore witness to Jesus, standing at *your* right hand,
— welcome our deceased brothers and sisters who in faith and love hoped for the vision *of* your glory.

Our Father . . .

Prayer

God our Father,
life of the faithful, glory of the humble,
happiness of the just, hear our prayer.
Fill our emptiness
with the blessing of the eucharist,
the foretaste of eternal joy.
We ask this through our Lord Jesus Christ, your Son,
who lives and reigns with you and the Holy Spirit,
one God, for ever and ever.

THURSDAY

Morning Prayer

READING   Romans 8:10-11

If Christ is in you the body is dead because of sin, while the spirit lives because of justice. If the Spirit of him who raised Jesus from the dead dwells in you, then he who raised Jesus from the dead will bring your mortal bodies to life also, through his Spirit dwelling in you.

RESPONSORY (VI F)
The Lord is risen *from* the tomb, * alleluia, al*le*luia.
— The Lord is risen *from* the tomb, * alleluia, al*le*luia.
He hung upon the *cross* for us,
— alleluia, al*le*luia.
Glory to the Father, and *to* the Son, * and to the Ho*ly* Spirit.
— The Lord is risen *from* the tomb, * alleluia, al*le*luia.

CANTICLE OF ZECHARIAH
Ant.   No disciple is greater than his teacher; † he should be glad to become *like* his master, * al*le*luia.

INTERCESSIONS (VI F)

God the Father has given us his Son for the resurrection *of* his people. * Let us
    turn with confidence to the Fath*er*, and say:
May the Lord Jesus be our very life.
As a pillar of fire, you lighted the way for your people *in* the desert,
— through his resurrection may Christ be today the light *of* our life.
Through the voice of Moses you taught your people *from* the mountain,
— through his resurrection may Christ be today the light *of* our life.
You fed your pilgrim people with your *gift* of manna,
— through his resurrection may Christ be today the light *of* our life.
You gave your people water *from* the rock,
— through his resurrection may Christ be today the light *of* our life.

Our Father . . .

Prayer

Father,
in restoring human nature
you have given us a greater dignity
than we had in the beginning.
Keep us in your love
and continue to sustain those
who have received new life in baptism.
We ask this through our Lord Jesus Christ, your Son,
who lives and reigns with you and the Holy Spirit,
one God, for ever and ever.

Evening Prayer

READING   1 Peter 3:18, 22

The reason why Christ died for sins once for all, the just man for the sake of
the unjust, was that he might lead you to God. He was put to death insofar as
fleshly existence goes, but was given life in the realm of the spirit. He went to
heaven and is at God's right hand, with angelic rulers and power subjected to
him.

RESPONSORY (VI F)

The dis*c*iples rejoiced, * alleluia, al*l*eluia.
— The dis*c*iples rejoiced, * alleluia, al*l*eluia.
When they saw the *ris*en Lord,
— alleluia, al*l*eluia.
Glory to the Father, and *to* the Son, * and to the Ho*ly* Spirit.
— The dis*c*iples rejoiced, * alleluia, al*l*eluia.

CANTICLE OF MARY

Ant.   I am the shepherd of my sheep. † I have come that they *may* have life, * and have it more abundantly, al*le*luia.

INTERCESSIONS (VI F)

The Father has established in Christ the foundation of all our hope and the principle of our *re*surrection. * Let us rejoice in Christ, and cry out *to* him, saying:

King of glory, hear our *prayer.*

Lord Jesus, through your resurrection you entered the sanctuary of heaven to offer the blood of *your* own sacrifice,

— lead us with you into the glory *of* the Father.

Through your resurrection you confirmed the faith of your dsciples and sent them out in*to* the world,

— make all bishops and priests faithful preach*ers* of the Gospel.

Through your resurrection you became our peace and recon*ci*liation,

— united the baptized in perfect communion of *faith* and love.

Through your resurrection the crippled man was healed at the gate *of* the temple,

— look on the sick and reveal in them the power *of* your glory.

You became the firstborn from the dead, the firstfruits of the *re*surrection,

— grant to the dead who hoped in you a share *in* your glory.

Our Father . . .

Prayer

Father,
in restoring human nature
you have given us a greater dignity
than we had in the beginning.
Keep us in your love
and continue to sustain those
who have received new life in baptism.
We ask this through our Lord Jesus Christ, your Son,
who lives and reigns with you and the Holy Spirit,
one God, for ever and ever.

FRIDAY

Morning Prayer

READING   Acts 5:30-32

The God of our fathers has raised up Jesus whom you put to death, hanging him on a tree. He whom God has exalted at his right hand as ruler and savior is to bring repentance to Israel and forgiveness of sins. We testify to this. So too does the Holy Spirit, whom God has given to those that obey him.

RESPONSORY (VI F)

The Lord is risen *from* the tomb, * alleluia, al*le*luia.
— The Lord is risen *from* the tomb, * alleluia, al*le*luia.
He hung upon the *cross* for us,
— alleluia, al*le*luia.
Glory to the Father, and *to* the Son, * and to the Ho*ly* Spirit.
— The Lord is risen *from* the tomb, * alleluia, al*le*luia.

CANTICLE OF ZECHARIAH

Ant.   I go now to prepare a *place* for you, * but I shall return to take *you* with me,
              so that where I am you al*so* may be, * al*le*luia.

INTERCESSIONS (VI F)

God the Father raised up Christ through the Spirit, and will also raise up our *mor*tal bodies. * Let us cry *out* to him:
*Lord, raise us to life through your Ho*ly* Spirit.*
All-holy Father, you accepted the holocaust of your Son in raising him *from* the dead,
— accept the offering we make today, and lead us to e*ter*nal life.
Look with favor on all we *do* today,
— that it may be for your glory and the sanctification *of* the world.
May our work today not be in vain but for the good of *the* whole world,
— and through it lead us *to* your kingdom.
Open our eyes today to recognize our brothers and sisters, and our *hearts* to love them,
— so that we may love and *serve* each other.

Our Father . . .

Prayer

Father of our freedom and salvation,
hear the prayers of those redeemed by your Son's suffering.

Through you may we have life;
with you may we have eternal joy.
We ask this through our Lord Jesus Christ, your Son,
who lives and reigns with you and the Holy Spirit,
one God, for ever and ever.

Evening Prayer

READING   Hebrews 5:8-10

Son though he was, Christ learned obedience from what he suffered; and
when perfected, he became the source of eternal salvation for all who obey
him, designated by God as high priest according to the order of Melchizedek.

RESPONSORY (VI F)

The disciples rejoiced, * alleluia, alleluia.
— The disciples rejoiced, * alleluia, alleluia.
When they saw the risen Lord,
— alleluia, alleluia.
Glory to the Father, and to the Son, * and to the Holy Spirit.
— The disciples rejoiced, * alleluia, alleluia.

CANTICLE OF MARY

Ant.   The Good Shepherd laid down his life for his sheep, * alleluia.

INTERCESSIONS (VI F)

Let us praise Christ, the source of all life * and the foundation of all virtue:
Lord, establish your kingdom in the world.
Jesus our Savior, you died in your human nature but were restored to life by the
    Spirit,
— make us die to sin, and live by the Spirit.
You sent your disciples into the whole world to preach the Gospel to every
    creature,
— inspire those who preach the Gospel to live by your Spirit.
All power in heaven and on earth has been given to you, to bear witness to the
    truth,
— keep the hearts of those who govern us faithful to the truth.
You make all things new, and command us to wait and watch for your kingdom,
— grant that the more we look forward to a new heaven and a new earth, the
    more we may seek to better this present world.
You went down among the dead to bring them the good news of the Gospel,
— be the great joy and hope of all the dead.

Our Father . . .

Prayer

Father of our freedom and salvation,
hear the prayers of those redeemed by your Son's suffering.
Through you may we have life;
with you may we have eternal joy.
We ask this through our Lord Jesus Christ, your Son,
who lives and reigns with you and the Holy Spirit,
one God, for ever and ever.

SATURDAY

Morning Prayer

READING   Romans 14:7-9

None of us lives as his own master and none of us dies as his own master.
While we live we are responsible to the Lord, and when we die we die as his
servants. Both in life and death we are the Lord's. That is why Christ died
and came to life again, that he might be Lord of both the dead and the living.

RESPONSORY (VI F)

The Lord is risen *from* the tomb, * alleluia, al*le*luia.
— The Lord is risen *from* the tomb, * alleluia, al*le*luia.
He hung upon the *cross* for us,
— alleluia, al*le*luia.
Glory to the Father, and *to* the Son, * and to the Ho*ly* Spirit.
— The Lord is risen *from* the tomb, * alleluia, al*le*luia.

CANTICLE OF ZECHARIAH

Ant.   When the prince of pastors comes again, † you will receive from
                him an unfading *crown* of glory, * al*le*luia.

INTERCESSIONS (VI F)

Christ has made known to us the life that *lasts* for ever. * With faith and joy let us
    cry out *to* him, saying:
Lord, may your resurrection bring us the riches of your *grace.*
Eternal shepherd, look on your flock as it ris*es* from sleep,
— feed us with the word of life and the *bread* from heaven.
Keep us safe from *wolf* and hireling,
— and make us faithful in listening *to* your voice.
You are present to all who preach your Gospel, and give power *to* their words,
— make us today preachers of your resurrection by our holi*ness* of life.
Be our great joy that no one can *take* from us,
— so that we may reject sin with its sadness, and reach out to e*ter*nal life.

Our Father . . .

Prayer

Father,
may we whom you renew in baptism
bear witness to our faith by the way we live.
By the suffering, death, and resurrection of your Son
may we come to eternal joy.
We ask this through our Lord Jesus Christ, your Son,
who lives and reigns with you and the Holy Spirit,
one God, for ever and ever.

Evening Prayer I

READING   1 Peter 2:9-10

You are "a chosen race, a royal priesthood, a holy nation, a people he claims for his own to proclaim the glorious works" of the One who called you from darkness into his marvelous light. Once you were no people, but now you are God's people; once there was no mercy for you, but now you have found mercy.

RESPONSORY (VI F)

The disciples rejoiced, * alleluia, alleluia.

— The disciples rejoiced, * alleluia, alleluia.

When they saw the risen Lord,

— alleluia, alleluia.

Glory to the Father, and to the Son, * and to the Holy Spirit.

— The disciples rejoiced, * alleluia, alleluia.

CANTICLE OF MARY

Ant.   I am the way, the truth and the life; † no one comes to the Father except through me, * alleluia.

INTERCESSIONS (VI F)

Christ is our life and resurrection. * Let us cry out to him with faith:

Son of the living God, protect your people.

Lord Jesus, we pray for your Catholic Church,

— make it holy, so that your kingdom may be established among all nations.

We pray for the sick and the sorrowful, for those in bondage and in exile,

— that they may receive consolation and help.

We pray for those who have turned away from your paths,

— that they may experience the grace of your forgiveness and the joy of rising to new life.

Crucified and risen Savior, you will come to judge the world,

— have mercy on us sinners.

We pray for all the living,

— and for all who have gone from us in the hope of resurrection.

Our Father . . .

Prayer

God our Father,

look upon us with love.

You redeem us and make us your children in Christ.

Give us true freedom
and bring us to the inheritance you promised.
We ask this through our Lord Jesus Christ, your Son,
who lives and reigns with you and the Holy Spirit,
one God, for ever and ever.

Morning Prayer

READING   Acts 10:40-43

God raised up Jesus on the third day and granted that he be seen, not by all,
but only by such witnesses as had been chosen beforehand by God—by us
who ate and drank with him after he rose from the dead. He commissioned
us to preach to the people and to bear witness that he is the one set apart by
God as judge of the living and the dead. To him all the prophets testify,
saying that everyone who believes in him has forgiveness of sins through his
name.

RESPONSORY (VI F)

Christ, Son of the living God, have mer*cy* on us, * alleluia, al*le*luia.
— Christ, Son of the living God, have mer*cy* on us, * alleluia, al*le*luia.
You have risen *from* the dead,
— alleluia, al*le*luia.
Glory to the Father, and *to* the Son, * and to the Ho*ly* Spirit.
— Christ, Son of the living God, have mer*cy* on us, * alleluia, al*le*luia.

CANTICLE OF ZECHARIAH

Ant.   Whoever lives in me and I in him will *yield* much fruit, * says the
Lord, al*le*luia.

INTERCESSIONS (VI F)

Christ is the Lord of life, raised up by the Father; in his turn he will raise us up *by*
his power. * Let us pray *to* him, saying:
Christ our life, *save us.*
Lord Jesus, light shining in the darkness, you lead you people into life, and give
our mortal nature the *gift* of holiness,
— may we spend this day in praise *of* your glory.
Lord, you walked the way of suffering and *cruci*fixion,
— may we suffer and die with you, and rise again to *share* your glory.
Son of the Father, our master and our brother, you have made us a kingdom of
priests *for* our God,
— may we offer you our joyful sacri*fice* of praise.
King of glory, we look forward to the great day of your com*ing* in splendor,
— that we may see you face to face, and be transformed *in* your likeness.

Our Father . . .

Prayer

God our Father,
look upon us with love.
You redeem us and make us your children in Christ.
Give us true freedom
and bring us to the inheritance you promised.
We ask this through our Lord Jesus Christ, your Son,
who lives and reigns with you and the Holy Spirit,
one God, for ever and ever.

Evening Prayer II

READING   Hebrews 10:12-14

Jesus offered one sacrifice for sins and took his seat forever at the right hand of God; now he waits until his enemies are placed beneath his feet. By one offering he has forever perfected those who are being sanctified.

RESPONSORY (VI F)

The *Lord* is risen, * alleluia, al*le*luia.
— The *Lord* is risen, * alleluia, al*le*luia.
He has ap*peared* to Simon,
— alleluia, al*le*luia.
Glory to the Father, and *to* the Son, * and to the Ho*ly* Spirit.
—The *Lord* is risen, * alleluia, al*le*luia.

CANTICLE OF MARY

Ant.   I give you a new commandment: † love one another as I *have* loved you, * says the Lord, al*le*luia.

INTERCESSIONS (VI F)

With joy in our hearts, let us call upon *Christ* the Lord, * who died and rose again, and lives always to inter*cede* for us:
Victorious King, hear our *prayer.*
Light and salvation *of* all peoples,
— send into our hearts the fire of your Spirit, as we proclaim your *res*urrection.
Let Israel recognize in you her longed-*for* Messiah,
— and the whole earth be filled with the knowledge *of* your glory.
Keep us in the communion *of* your saints,
— and grant us rest from our labors *in* their company.
You have triumphed over death, your enemy; destroy in us the pow*er* of death,
— that we may live only for you, victorious and im*mor*tal Lord.

Savior Christ, you were obedient even to accepting death, and were raised up to
   the right hand *of* the Father,
— in your goodness welcome your brothers and sisters into the kingdom *of* your
   glory.

Our Father . . .

Prayer

God our Father,
look upon us with love.
You redeem us and make us your children in Christ.
Give us true freedom
and bring us to the inheritance you promised.
We ask this through our Lord Jesus Christ, your Son,
who lives and reigns with you and the Holy Spirit,
one God, for ever and ever.

MONDAY

Morning Prayer

READING   Romans 10:8b-10
   The word is near you, on your lips and in your heart (that is , the word of
   faith which we preach). For if you confess with your lips that Jesus is Lord,
   and believe in your heart that God raised him from the dead, you will be
   saved. Faith in the heart leads to justification, confession on the lips to
   salvation.

RESPONSORY (VI F)
The Lord is risen *from* the tomb, * alleluia, al*le*luia.
— The Lord is risen *from* the tomb, * alleluia, al*le*luia.
He hung upon the *cross* for us,
— alleluia, al*le*luia.
Glory to the Father, and *to* the Son, * and to the Ho*ly* Spirit.
— The Lord is risen *from* the tomb, * alleluia, al*le*luia.

CANTICLE OF ZECHARIAH
Ant.   Whoever loves me will be loved by my Father, † and I will love
                  him and show my*self* to him, * al*le*luia.

INTERCESSIONS (VI F)
The Father glorified Jesus and appointed him heir *to* all nations. * Let us *praise*
   him, saying:
Save us, Lord, through your *victory.*

Lord Christ, by your victory you broke the power of evil and destroyed *sin* and death,
— make us victorious over *sin* today.
You laid death low, and brought *us* new life,
— grant that we may walk today in *this* new life.
You gave life to the dead, and led mankind from *death* to life,
— give eternal life to all those we shall *meet* today.
You brought confusion on the guards at your tomb, but joy to *your* disciples,
— grant the fullness of joy to *all* who serve you.

Our Father . . .

Prayer

Father,
help us to seek the values
that will bring us eternal joy in this changing world.
In our desire for what you promise
make us one in mind and heart.
Grant this through our Lord Jesus Christ, your Son,
who lives and reigns with you and the Holy Spirit,
one God, for ever and ever.

Evening Prayer

READING   Hebrews 8:1b-3a
We have such a high priest, who has taken his seat at the right hand of the throne of the Majesty in heaven, minister of the sanctuary and of that true tabernacle set up, not by man, but by the Lord. Now every high priest is appointed to offer gifts and sacrifices.

RESPONSORY (VI F)
The dis*ci*ples rejoiced, * alleluia, al*le*luia.
— The dis*ci*ples rejoiced, * alleluia, al*le*luia.
When they saw the *ris*en Lord,
— alleluia, al*le*luia.
Glory to the Father, and *to* the Son, * and to the Ho*ly* Spirit.
— The dis*ci*ples rejoiced, * alleluia, al*le*luia.

CANTICLE OF MARY
Ant.   The Holy Spirit, the Paraclete, † whom the Father will send in my name, † will teach you, *and* remind you * of all that I told you, al*le*luia.

INTERCESSIONS (VI F)

The Holy Spirit raised the body of Christ to life and made it the *source* of life. *
 With joy in our hearts let us call upon the ris*en* Christ, saying:
Lord, make all things new and fill them with *life.*

Savior of the world and King of the new creation, raise our minds and hearts *to*
 your kingdom,
— where you sit at the right hand *of* the Father.

Lord, you are always present *in* your Church,
— through your Holy Spirit guide it in*to* all truth.

Show your mercy to the sick, the overburdened *and* the dying,
— that all may receive strength and courage *from* your love.

Light that never fails, as the day draws to its close we offer you our sacri*fice* of
 praise,
— and pray that the glory of your resurrection may shine on our deceased
 broth*ers* and sisters.

Our Father . . .

Prayer

Father,
help us to seek the values
that will bring us eternal joy in this changing world.
In our desire for what you promise
make us one in mind and heart.
Grant this through our Lord Jesus Christ, your Son,
who lives and reigns with you and the Holy Spirit,
one God, for ever and ever.

TUESDAY

Morning Prayer

READING   Acts 13:30-33

 God raised Jesus from the dead, and for many days thereafter Jesus appeared
 to those who had come up with him from Galilee to Jerusalem. These are his
 witnesses now before the people. We ourselves announce to you the good
 news that what God promised our fathers he has fulfilled for us, their children, in raising up Jesus, according to what is written in the second psalm,
 "You are my son; this day I have begotten you."

RESPONSORY (VI F)

The Lord is risen *from* the tomb, * alleluia, al*le*luia.
— The Lord is risen *from* the tomb, * alleluia, al*le*luia.

He hung upon the *cross* for us,
— alleluia, al*l*eluia.
Glory to the Father, and *to* the Son, * and to the Ho*ly* Spirit.
— The Lord is risen *from* the tomb, * alleluia, al*l*eluia.

CANTICLE OF ZECHARIAH
Ant.　　　　　Peace I leave with you, *a*lleluia; * peace is my gift to you, al*l*eluia.

INTERCESSIONS (VI F)
By his own power Christ raised up the temple of his body when it had been des*troyed* in death. * With joy *let* us ask him:
Lord, share with us the fruits of your *victory.*
Christ our Savior, when you rose again you brought to the holy women and the apostles the joyful news of a *world* redeemed,
— make us witnesses to your *ris*en life.
You promised to all people that we would rise up again to new*ness* of life,
— make us heralds *of* your Gospel.
You showed yourself to your apostles and breathed the Holy Spi*rit* on them,
— renew in us the presence of the same crea*tor* Spirit.
You promised to be with your disciples to the end *of* the world,
— stay with us today, and remain *with* us always.

Our Father . . .

Prayer
Father,
you restored your people to eternal life
by raising Christ your Son from death.
Make our faith strong and our hope sure.
May we never doubt that you will fulfill
the promises you have made.
Grant this through our Lord Jesus Christ, your Son,
who lives and reigns with you and the Holy Spirit,
one God, for ever and ever.

Evening Prayer

READING　　　　　　　　　　　　　　　　　　　　　1 Peter 2:4-5
Come to the Lord, a living stone, rejected by men but approved, nonetheless, and precious in God's eyes. You too are living stones, built as an edifice of spirit into a holy priesthood, offering spiritual sacrifices acceptable to God through Jesus Christ.

RESPONSORY (VI F)

The disciples rejoiced, * alleluia, alleluia.
— The disciples rejoiced, * alleluia, alleluia.
When they saw the risen Lord,
— alleluia, alleluia.
Glory to the Father, and to the Son, * and to the Holy Spirit.
— The disciples rejoiced, * alleluia, alleluia.

CANTICLE OF MARY

Ant.   If you loved me, † you would surely be glad that I am going to
                    the Father, * alleluia.

INTERCESSIONS (VI F)

As Christ lay in the darkness of the earth he saw the light of a new glory. * Let
    us cry out to him in joy:
King of glory, hear us.
We pray for all bishops, priests and deacons, that they may be zealous in their
    ministry,
— and prepare for you a people devoted to every good work.
We pray for all who teach in the service of your Church,
— that they may seek your truth with a sincere heart.
We pray for your faithful people, that they may be victorious in the contest of
    faith,
— and win the prize of victory in your kingdom.
You cancelled our condemnation by nailing it to the cross,
— free us from our chains, and lead us out of darkness.
You went down among the dead and opened for them the gates to life,
— welcome our dead brothers and sisters into your kingdom.

Our Father . . .

Prayer

Father,
    you restored your people to eternal life
    by raising Christ your Son from death.
    Make our faith strong and our hope sure.
    May we never doubt that you will fulfill
    the promises you have made.
    Grant this through our Lord Jesus Christ, your Son,
    who lives and reigns with you and the Holy Spirit,
    one God, for ever and ever.

WEDNESDAY

Morning Prayer

READING   Romans 6:8-11

If we have died with Christ, we believe that we are also to live with him. We know that Christ, once raised from the dead, will never die again; death has no more power over him. His death was death to sin, once for all; his life is life for God. In the same way, you must consider yourselves dead to sin but alive for God in Christ Jesus.

RESPONSORY (VI F)

The Lord is risen *from* the tomb, * alleluia, al*le*luia.
— The Lord is risen *from* the tomb, * alleluia, al*le*luia.
He hung upon the *cross* for us,
— alleluia, al*le*luia.
Glory to the Father, and *to* the Son, * and to the Ho*ly* Spirit.
— The Lord is risen *from* the tomb, * alleluia, al*le*luia.

CANTICLE OF ZECHARIAH

Ant.   I am the true vine, a*ll*eluia; * you are the branches, al*le*luia.

INTERCESSIONS (VI F)

Christ was given up for our sins and rose again to *make* us righteous. * Let us cry out *to* him, saying:
Save us, Lord, by your victory.
Christ our Savior, in conquering death you brought us joy, in rising again you raised us up and filled us with the abundance *of* your gifts,
— stir up our hearts, and sanctify this day through the gift of your *Holy* Spirit.
You are glorified by the angels in heaven and adored by mankind on earth; as we celebrate your *res*urrection,
— accept our worship in spirit *and* in truth.
Lord Jesus, save us; show your great mercy to your people, as we look forward to our own *res*urrection,
— have mercy on us, and protect us today from *every* evil.
King of glory, source of our life, grant that, when you *come* again,
— we may be one with *you* in glory.

Our Father . . .

Prayer

Father of all holiness,
guide our hearts to you.

Keep in the light of your truth
all those you have freed from the darkness of unbelief.
We ask this through our Lord Jesus Christ, your Son,
who lives and reigns with you and the Holy Spirit,
one God, for ever and ever.

Evening Prayer

READING   Hebrews 7:24-27

Jesus, because he remains forever, has a priesthood that does not pass away.
Therefore he is always able to save those who approach God through him,
since he forever lives to make intercession for them. It was fitting that we
should have such a high priest: holy, innocent, undefiled, separated from
sinners, higher than the heavens. Unlike the other high priests, he has no
need to offer sacrifice day after day, first for his own sins and then for those of
the people; he did that once for all when he offered himself.

RESPONSORY (VI F)
The disciples rejoiced, * alleluia, alleluia.
— The disciples rejoiced, * alleluia, alleluia.
When they saw the risen Lord,
— alleluia, alleluia.
Glory to the Father, and to the Son, * and to the Holy Spirit.
— The disciples rejoiced, * alleluia, alleluia.

CANTICLE OF MARY
Ant.   If you live in me and my words live in you, * all you ask for will
                    be yours, alleluia.

INTERCESSIONS (VI F)
Christ rose from the dead and is seated at the right hand of the Father. * Let us
    pray to him, saying:
Lord Jesus, you live for ever; hear our prayer.
Lord, remember all who minister in your service,
— may their holy lives be an example to your people.
Give to those who govern us a spirit of justice and peace,
— so that the human family may live in harmony.
Guide our days in the way of salvation,
— and fill the earth with your plenty for the sake of the needy.
Christ our savior, light of the world, you have called creation from death to life,
— may your light shine for ever on our departed brothers and sisters.

Our Father . . .

Prayer

Father of all holiness,
guide our hearts to you.
Keep in the light of your truth
all those you have freed from the darkness of unbelief.
We ask this through our Lord Jesus Christ, your Son,
who lives and reigns with you and the Holy Spirit,
one God, for ever and ever.

THURSDAY

Morning Prayer

READING   Romans 8:10-11

If Christ is in you the body is dead because of sin, while the spirit lives because of justice. If the Spirit of him who raised Jesus from the dead dwells in you, then he who raised Christ from the dead will bring your mortal bodies to life also, through his Spirit dwelling in you.

RESPONSORY (VI F)

The Lord is risen *from* the tomb, * alleluia, al*le*luia.
— The Lord is risen *from* the tomb, * alleluia, al*le*luia.
He hung upon the *cross* for us,
— alleluia, al*le*luia.
Glory to the Father, and *to* the Son, * and to the Ho*ly* Spirit.
— The Lord is risen *from* the tomb, * alleluia, al*le*luia.

CANTICLE OF ZECHARIAH

Ant.   If you keep *my* commandments, * you will live in my love, al*le*luia.

INTERCESSIONS (VI F)

Christ rose from the dead and is always present *in* his Church. * Let us adore
    him, and say:
Stay with us, Lord.
Lord Jesus, victor over sin and death, glorious *and* immortal,
— be always *in* our midst.
Come to us in the power *of* your victory,
— and show our hearts the loving kindness *of* your Father.
Come to heal a world wounded *by* division,
— for you alone can transform our hearts and *make* them one.
Strengthen our faith in *fi*nal victory,
— and renew our hope in your *se*cond coming.

Our Father . . .

Prayer

Father,
in your love you have brought us
from evil to good and from misery to happiness.
Through your blessings
give the courage of perseverance
to those you have called and justified by faith.
Grant this through our Lord Jesus Christ, your Son,
who lives and reigns with you and the Holy Spirit,
one God, for ever and ever.

Evening Prayer

READING   1 Peter 3:18, 22

The reason why Christ died for sins once for all, the just man for the sake of
the unjust, was that he might lead you to God. He was put to death insofar as
fleshly existence goes, but was given life in the realm of the spirit. He went to
heaven and is at God's right hand, with angelic rulers and power subjected to
him.

RESPONSORY(VI F)

The disciples rejoiced, * alleluia, alleluia.
— The disciples rejoiced, * alleluia, alleluia.
When they saw the risen Lord,
— alleluia, alleluia.
Glory to the Father, and to the Son, * and to the Holy Spirit.
— The disciples rejoiced, * alleluia, alleluia.

CANTICLE OF MARY

Ant.   I have said these things to you † so that my joy may be in you *
                  and your joy may be complete, alleluia.

INTERCESSIONS (VI F)

Christ rose from the dead as the firstfruits of those who sleep. * In our joy let us
   praise him, and say:
Firstborn from the dead, hear our prayer.
Lord Jesus, remember your holy Church, built on the apostles and reaching to
   the ends of the earth,
— and let your blessing rest on all who believe in you.
You are the healer of soul and body,
— come to our aid, and save us in your love.

Raise up the sick and *give* them strength,
— free them from *their* infirmities.
Help those in distress of *mind* or body,
— and in your compassion lift up *those* in need.
Through your cross and resurrection you opened for all the way to *im*mortality,
— grant to our deceased brothers and sisters the joys *of* your kingdom.

Our Father . . .

Prayer

Father,
in your love you have brought us
from evil to good and from misery to happiness.
Through your blessings
give the courage of perseverance
to those you have called and justified by faith.
Grant this through our Lord Jesus Christ, your Son,
who lives and reigns with you and the Holy Spirit,
one God, for ever and ever.

FRIDAY

Morning Prayer

READING   Acts 5:30-32
The God of our fathers has raised up Jesus whom you put to death, hanging him on a tree. He whom God has exalted at his right hand as ruler and savior is to bring repentance to Israel and forgiveness of sins. We testify to this. So too does the Holy Spirit whom God has given to those that obey him.

RESPONSORY (VI F)
The Lord is risen *from* the tomb, * alleluia, al*le*luia.
— The Lord is risen *from* the tomb, * alleluia, al*le*luia.
He hung upon the *cross* for us,
— alleluia, al*le*luia.
Glory to the Father, and *to* the Son, * and to the Ho*ly* Spirit.
— The Lord is risen *from* the tomb, * alleluia, al*le*luia.

CANTICLE OF ZECHARIAH
Ant.   My commandment is this: † love one another as I *have* loved you, * al*le*luia.

INTERCESSIONS (VI F)

Let us pray to *God* the Father, * who gave us new life through the *risen* Christ:
Give us the glory of your Son.
Lord our God, your mighty works have revealed your eternal plan: you created
the earth, and you are faithful in every *gen*eration,
— hear us, Fa*ther* of mercy.
Purify our hearts with your truth, and guide them in the *way* of holiness,
— so that we may do what is pleasing *in* your sight.
Let your face *shine* upon us,
— that we may be freed from sin and filled *with* your plenty.
You gave the apostles the *peace* of Christ,
— grant peace to your people, and to *the* whole world.

Our Father . . .

Prayer

Lord,
by this Easter mystery
prepare us for eternal life.
May our celebration of Christ's death and resurrection
guide us to salvation.
We ask this through our Lord Jesus Christ, your Son,
who lives and reigns with you and the Holy Spirit,
one God, for ever and ever.

Evening Prayer

READING   Hebrews 5:8-10

Son though he was, Christ learned obedience from what he suffered; and
when perfected, he became the source of eternal salvation for all who obey
him, designated by God as high priest according to the order of Melchizedek.

RESPONSORY (VI F)

The dis*ci*ples rejoiced, * alleluia, al*le*luia.
— The dis*ci*ples rejoiced, * alleluia, al*le*luia.
When they saw the *ris*en Lord,
— alleluia, al*le*luia.
Glory to the Father, and *to* the Son, * and to the Ho*ly* Spirit.
— The dis*ci*ples rejoiced, * alleluia, al*le*luia.

CANTICLE OF MARY

Ant.   There is no greater love † than to lay down your life *for* your
                        friends, * al*le*luia.

INTERCESSIONS (VI F)

Christ is the way, the truth *and* the life. * Let us praise *him*, and say:
Son of the living God, bless your *people.*

We pray to you, Lord Jesus, for all ministers *of* your Church,
— as they break for us the bread of life, may they themselves receive nourish*ment* and strength.

We pray for the whole Christian people, that all may be worthy *of* their calling,
— and safeguard their unity in the Spirit by the *bond* of peace.

We pray for those who govern us, that they may temper jus*tice* with mercy,
— and promote harmony and peace through*out* the world.

We pray for ourselves, that our hearts may be purified to sing your praises in the commun*ion* of saints,
— that we be reunited with our deceased brothers and sisters, whom we commend to your *loving* kindness.

Our Father . . .

Prayer

Lord,
by this Easter mystery
prepare us for eternal life.
May our celebration of Christ's death and resurrection
guide us to salvation.
We ask this through our Lord Jesus Christ, your Son,
who lives and reigns with you and the Holy Spirit,
one God, for ever and ever.

SATURDAY

Morning Prayer

READING   Romans 14:7-9

None of us lives as his own master and none of us dies as his own master. While we live we are responsible to the Lord, and when we die we die as his servants. Both in life and death we are the Lord's. That is why Christ died and came to life again, that he might be Lord of both the dead and the living.

RESPONSORY (VI F)

The Lord is risen *from* the tomb, * alleluia, al*le*luia.
— The Lord is risen *from* the tomb, * alleluia, al*le*luia.
He hung upon the *cross* for us,
— alleluia, al*le*luia.

Glory to the Father, and *to* the Son, * and to the Ho*ly* Spirit.
— The Lord is risen *from* the tomb, * alleluia, al*le*luia.

CANTICLE OF ZECHARIAH
Ant.   Christ died and rose from the dead, † that he might be the Lord
                 of the living *and* the dead, * al*le*luia.

INTERCESSIONS (VI F)
Christ is the bread of life; he will raise up on the last day all who share the table
   of his word *and* his body. * In our joy *let* us pray:
Lord, give us peace and *joy.*
Son of God, you were raised from the dead to lead us *in*to life,
— bless and sanctify all the children *of* your Father.
You give peace and joy to all who be*lieve* in you,
— grant that we may walk as children of the light, rejoicing *in* your victory.
Build up the faith of your pilgrim *Church* on earth,
— that it may bear witness to your resurrection before *the* whole world.
You suffered and so entered into the glory *of* the Father,
— change the tears of the sorrowful *into* joy.

Our Father . . .

                              Prayer
      Loving Father,
      through our rebirth in baptism
      you give us your life and promise immortality.
      By your unceasing care,
      guide our steps toward the life of glory.
      Grant this through our Lord Jesus Christ, your Son,
      who lives and reigns with you and the Holy Spirit,
      one God, for ever and ever.

SIXTH SUNDAY OF EASTER
PSALTER, WEEK II, 672.

Evening Prayer I

READING   1 Peter 2:9-10

You are "a chosen race, a royal priesthood, a holy nation, a people he claims for his own to proclaim the glorious works" of the One who called you from darkness into his marvelous light. Once you were no people, but now you are God's people; once there was no mercy for you, but now you have found mercy.

RESPONSORY (VI F)

The disciples rejoiced, * alleluia, alleluia.
— The disciples rejoiced, * alleluia, alleluia.
When they saw the risen Lord,
— alleluia, alleluia.
Glory to the Father, and to the Son, * and to the Holy Spirit.
— The disciples rejoiced, * alleluia, alleluia.

CANTICLE OF MARY

Ant.   I will ask the Father and he will give you another Parclete * to remain with you for ever, alleluia.

INTERCESSIONS (VI F)

In rising from the dead, Christ destroyed death and restored life. * Let us cry out to him, saying:
Lord Jesus, you live for ever; hear our prayer.
You are the stone rejected by the builders which became the chief cornerstone,
— make us living stones in the temple of your Church.
You are the faithful and true witness, the firstborn from the dead,
— make your Church bear constant witness to yourself.
You alone are the Bridegroom of the Church, born from your wounded side,
— make us reveal to the world the love of Bridegroom and Bride.
You are the first and the last, you were dead and are alive,
— keep those who have been baptized faithful until death, that they may receive the crown of victory.
Light and lamp of God's holy city,
— shine on our friends who have died, that they may reign for ever.

Our Father . . .

Prayer

Ever-living God,
help us to celebrate our joy
in the resurrection of the Lord
and to express in our lives
the love we celebrate.
Grant this through our Lord Jesus Christ, your Son,
who lives and reigns with you and the Holy Spirit,
one God, for ever and ever.

Morning Prayer

READING   Acts 10:40-43

God raised up Jesus on the third day and granted that he be seen, not by all, but only by such witnesses as had been chosen beforehand by God— by us who ate and drank with him after he rose from the dead. He commissioned us to preach to the people and to bear witness that he is the one set apart by God as judge of the living and the dead. To him all the prophets testify, saying that everyone who believes in him has forgiveness of sins through his name.

RESPONSORY (VI F)

Christ, Son of the living God, have mer*cy* on us, * alleluia, al*le*luia.
— Christ, Son of the living God, have mer*cy* on us, * alleluia, al*le*luia.
You have risen *from* the dead,
— alleluia, al*le*luia.
Glory to the Father, and *to* the Son, * and to the Ho*ly* Spirit.
— Christ, Son of the living God, have mer*cy* on us, * alleluia, al*le*luia.

CANTICLE OF ZECHARIAH

Ant.   As the Father has loved me, † so I *have* loved you; * live on in my love, al*le*luia.

INTERCESSIONS (VI F)

God the almighty Father raised Jesus as the firstborn from the dead, and made *him* our savior. * Let us call up*on* him, saying:
Give us, Lord, the glory of your Son.
All-holy Father, you brought your belovèd Son Jesus from the darkness of death into the splendor *of* your glory,
— bring us also into your marve*lo*us light.
You have given us *faith* to save us,
— may we live today by the faith *of* our baptism.

You command us to seek the things that are above, where Christ is seated at *your* right hand,

— do not let us be deceived by the allure*ments* of sin.

May our life, hidden with Christ in you, our Father, shine be*fore* the world,

— foreshadowing a new heaven and *a* new earth.

Our Father . . .

Prayer

Ever-living God,
help us to celebrate our joy
in the resurrection of the Lord
and to express in our lives
the love we celebrate.
Grant this through our Lord Jesus Christ, your Son,
who lives and reigns with you and the Holy Spirit,
one God, for ever and ever.

Evening Prayer II

READING   Hebrews 10:12-14

Jesus offered one sacrifice for sins and took his seat forever at the right hand of God; now he waits until his enemies are placed beneath his feet. By one offering he has forever perfected those who are being sanctified.

RESPONSORY (VI F)

The *Lord* is risen, * alleluia, al*le*luia.

— The *Lord* is risen, * alleluia, al*le*luia.

He has ap*peared* to Simon,

— alleluia, al*le*luia.

Glory to the Father, and *to* the Son, * and to the Ho*ly* Spirit.

— The *Lord* is risen, * alleluia, al*le*luia.

CANTICLE OF MARY

Ant.   If anyone loves me he will *keep* my word, * and my Father *will* love him.
We will come to him and make our *home* with him, * al*le*luia.

INTERCESSIONS (VI F)

God the Father raised Christ from the dead and exalted him at *his* right hand. *

Let us pray to the *Fa*ther, saying:

*Through Christ in glory, watch over your peo*ple, Lord.*

Righteous Father, you lifted Jesus above the earth through the triumph *of* the cross,
— may all things be lifted *up* in him.
Through your Son in glory send the Holy Spirit up*on* the Church,
— that it may be the sacrament of unity for the whole *hu*man race.
You have brought a new family into being through water and the *Ho*ly Spirit,
— keep them faithful to their baptism, and bring them to ever*last*ing life.
Through your exalted Son help those in distress, free those in captivity, *heal* the sick,
— any by your blessings give joy *to* the world.
You nourished our deceased brothers and sisters with the body and blood of the *ris*en Christ,
— raise them up at *the* last day.

Our Father . . .

Prayer

Ever-living God,
help us to celebrate our joy
in the resurrection of the Lord
and to express in our lives
the love we celebrate.
Grant this through our Lord Jesus Christ, your Son,
who lives and reigns with you and the Holy Spirit,
one God, for ever and ever.

MONDAY

Morning Prayer

READING   Romans 10:8b-10

The word is near you, on your lips and in your heart (that is , the word of faith which we preach). For if you confess with your lips that Jesus is Lord, and believe in your heart that God raised him from the dead, you will be saved. Faith in the heart leads to justification, confession on the lips to salvation.

RESPONSORY (VI F)
The Lord is risen *from* the tomb, * alleluia, al*le*luia.
— The Lord is risen *from* the tomb, * alleluia, al*le*luia.
He hung upon the *cross* for us,
— alleluia, al*le*luia.
Glory to the Father, and *to* the Son, * and to the Ho*ly* Spirit.
— The Lord is risen *from* the tomb, * alleluia, al*le*luia.

CANTICLE OF ZECHARIAH

Ant.   By raising Jesus Christ *from* the dead, * God has given us a new
                       birth to a liv*ing* hope
                       in the promise of an inheritance that will *last* for ever, * al*le*luia.

INTERCESSIONS (VI F)

God the Father was glorified in the death and resurrection *of* his Son. * Let us
    pray to him with con*fi*dence, saying:
Lord, enlighten our *minds.*
Father of lights, you bathed the world in splendor when Christ rose a*gain* in
    glory,
— fill our minds today with the *light* of faith.
Through the resurrection of your Son you opened for us the way to e*ter*nal life,
— as we work today sustain us with the *hope* of glory.
Through your risen Son you sent the Hol y Spirit in*to* the world,
— set our hearts on fire with spir*itual* love.
May Jesus Christ, who was crucified to *set* us free,
— be today our salvation *and* redemption.

Our Father . . .

Prayer

God of mercy,
    may our celebration of your Son's resurrection
    help us to experience its effect in our lives.
    We ask this through our Lord Jesus Christ, your Son,
    who lives and reigns with you and the Holy Spirit,
    one God, for ever and ever.

Evening Prayer

READING   Hebrews 8:1b-3a
    We have such a high priest, who has taken his seat at the right hand of the
    throne of the Majesty in heaven, minister of the sanctuary and of that true
    tabernacle set up, not by man, but by the Lord. Now every high priest is
    appointed to offer gifts and sacrifices.

RESPONSORY (VI F)

The dis*ci*ples rejoiced, * alleluia, al*le*luia.
— The dis*ci*ples rejoiced, * alleluia, al*le*luia.
When they saw the *ris*en Lord,
— alleluia, al*le*luia.

Glory to the Father, and *to* the Son, * and to the Ho*ly* Spirit.
— The dis*ci*ples rejoiced, * alleluia, al*le*luia.

CANTICLE OF MARY
Ant.   The Spirit of truth who proceeds from the Father † will *be* my
               witness, * and you will also bear witness to me, al*le*luia.

INTERCESSIONS (VI F)
Let us pray to Christ the Lord, who bathed the world in glory through his
    *re*surrection. * With joyful hearts *let* us say:
Christ, our life, hear our *prayer.*
Lord Jesus Christ, you walked with your disciples *on* the way,
— be with your Church on its pilgrim*age* through life.
Do not let us be slow *to* believe,
— but ready to proclaim you as victor *over* death.
Look with kindness on those who do not recog*nize* your presence,
— reveal yourself to them, so that they may welcome *you* as Savior.
Through the cross you have brought reconciliation to mankind *in* your body,
— grant unity and peace *to* all nations.
Judge of the living *and* the dead,
— forgive the sins of the faith*ful* departed.

Our Father . . .

Prayer

God of mercy,
may our celebration of your Son's resurrection
help us to experience its effect in our lives.
We ask this through our Lord Jesus Christ, your Son,
who lives and reigns with you and the Holy Spirit,
one God, for ever and ever.

TUESDAY

Morning Prayer

READING   Acts 13:30-33
    God raised Jesus from the dead, and for many days thereafter Jesus appeared
    to those who had come up with him from Galilee to Jerusalem. These are his
    witnesses now before the people. We ourselves announce to you the good
    news that what God has promised our fathers he has fulfilled for us, his
    children, in raising up Jesus, according to what is written in the second psalm,
    "You are my son; this day I have begotten you."

RESPONSORY (VI F)

The Lord is risen *from* the tomb, * alleluia, al*le*luia.
— The Lord is risen *from* the tomb, * alleluia, al*le*luia.
He hung upon the *cross* for us,
— alleluia, al*le*luia.
Glory to the Father, and *to* the Son, * and to the Ho*ly* Spirit.
— The Lord is risen *from* the tomb, * alleluia, al*le*luia.

CANTICLE OF ZECHARIAH

Ant.   In a little while the world will no longer see me, † but *you* will see me, * for I live and you will live, al*le*luia.

INTERCESSIONS (VI F)

The spotless Lamb of God takes away the sins *of* the world. * Let us give thanks to the Fath*er*, and say:
Source of all life, raise us to life.
Source of all life, remember the death and resurrection of the Lamb slain *on* the cross,
— listen to his voice as he lives for ever, making interces*sion* for us.
Now that the old leaven of wickedness and evil *is* destroyed,
— may we always feed on the unleavened bread of sinceri*ty* and truth.
Grant that today we may put aside all fric*tion* and jealousy,
— and show greater concern for the *needs* of others.
Send into our hearts the spirit *of* the Gospel,
— that we may walk in the way of your commandments, today *and* for ever.

Our Father . . .

Prayer

God our Father,
may we look forward with hope to our resurrection,
for you have made us your sons and daughters,
and restored the joy of our youth.
We ask this through our Lord Jesus Christ, your Son,
who lives and reigns with you and the Holy Spirit,
one God, for ever and ever.

Evening Prayer

READING   1 Peter 2:4-5

Come to the Lord, a living stone, rejected by men but approved, nonetheless, and precious in God's eyes. You too are living stones, built as an edifice of spirit, into a holy priesthood, offering spiritual sacrifices acceptable to God through Jesus Christ.

RESPONSORY (VI F)

The dis*ci*ples rejoiced, * alleluia, al*le*luia.
— The dis*ci*ples rejoiced, * alleluia, al*le*luia.
When they saw the *ri*sen Lord,
— alleluia, al*le*luia.
Glory to the Father, and *to* the Son, * and to the Ho*ly* Spirit.
— The dis*ci*ples rejoiced, * alleluia, al*le*luia.

CANTICLE OF MARY

Ant. Believe me, it is for your own good that *I* am going. * If I do not go, the Paraclete will not come, al*le*luia.

INTERCESSIONS (VI F)

By his resurrection Christ has given sure hope *to* his people. * Let us ask him with *our* whole hearts:
Lord Jesus, you live for ever; hear our *prayer.*
Lord Jesus, from your wounded side flowed *blood* and water,
— make the Church your *spot*less bride.
Chief shepherd, after your resurrection you made Peter shepherd of your flock when he professed his *love* for you,
— increase from day to day the love and devotion of *N.,* our Pope.
You showed your disciples how to make a great *catch* of fish,
— send others to continue their work as fish*ers* of men.
At the lakeside you prepared bread and fish for *your* disciples,
— grant that we may never allow others to *die* of hunger.
Jesus, the new Adam and life-giving spirit, transform the dead into *your* own likeness,
— that the fullness of your joy *may* be theirs.

Our Father . . .

Prayer

God our Father,
may we look forward with hope to our resurrection,
for you have made us your sons and daughters,
and restored the joy of our youth.
We ask this through our Lord Jesus Christ, your Son,
who lives and reigns with you and the Holy Spirit,
one God, for ever and ever.

WEDNESDAY

Morning Prayer

READING Romans 6:8-11

If we have died with Christ, we believe that we are also to live with him. We know that Christ, once raised from the dead, will never die again; death has no more power over him. His death was death to sin, once for all; his life is life for God. In the same way, you must consider yourselves dead to sin but alive for God in Christ Jesus.

RESPONSORY (VI F)

The Lord is risen *from* the tomb, * alleluia, al*le*luia.
—The Lord is risen *from* the tomb, * alleluia, al*le*luia.
He hung upon the *cross* for us,
— alleluia, al*le*luia.
Glory to the Father, and *to* the Son, * and to the Ho*ly* Spirit.
—The Lord is risen *from* the tomb, * alleluia, al*le*luia.

CANTICLE OF ZECHARIAH

Ant.   I have many more things to tell you, † but they would be too much *for* you now. * When the Spirit of truth comes he will guide you to all truth, al*le*luia.

INTERCESSIONS (VI F)

By the gift of the Father, the risen Christ was seen by *the* apostles. * Let us pray to the Fath*er*, and say:
Give us, Lord, the glory of your Son.
Father of lights, today we offer you our thanks and praise for calling us into your mar*ve*lous light,
— to re*ceive* your mercy.
May the efforts of mankind to make the *world* more human,
— be purified and strengthened by the power *of* your Spirit.
May we be so dedicated to the ser*vice* of others,
— that the whole human family may become a pleasing sacrifice *in* your honor.
At the dawn of a new day, fill us *with* your mercy,
— that the whole day may be a day of *joy* and praise.

Our Father . . .

Prayer

Lord,
as we celebrate your Son's resurrection,
so may we rejoice with all the saints

when he returns in glory,
who lives and reigns with you and the Holy Spirit,
one God, for ever and ever.

Evening Prayer

Where the solemnity of the Ascension is transferred to Sunday, the following is said:

READING   Hebrews 7:24-27
Jesus, because he remains forever, has a priesthood that does not pass away.
Therefore he is always able to save those who approach God through him,
since he forever lives to make intercession for them. It was fitting that we
should have such a high priest: holy, innocent, undefiled, separated from
sinners, higher than the heavens. Unlike the other high priests, he has no
need to offer sacrifice day after day, first for his own sins and then for those of
the people; he did that once for all when he offered himself.

RESPONSORY (VI F)
The dis*ci*ples rejoiced, * alleluia, al*le*luia.
— The dis*ci*ples rejoiced, * alleluia, al*le*luia.
When they saw the *ris*en Lord,
—alleluia, al*le*luia.
Glory to the Father, and *to* the Son, * and to the Ho*ly* Spirit.
—The dis*ci*ples rejoiced, * alleluia, al*le*luia.

CANTICLE OF MARY
Ant.   The Spirit will glorify me † for he will pro*claim* to you all * that
                he has received from me, al*le*luia.

INTERCESSIONS (VI F)
In his Son, risen from the dead, God has opened for us the way to ever*last*ing life.
    * Let us *ask* the Father:
*Through the victory of Christ, save the people he has re*deemed.*
God of our fathers, you raised your Son Jesus from the dead and clothed him in
    glory; move our hearts to com*plete* repentance,
— that we may walk in new*ness* of life.
You have led us back to the shepherd and bishop *of* our souls,
— keep us faithful under the guidance of the shepherds *of* the Church.
You chose the firstfruits of Christ's disciples from the *Jew*ish people,
— reveal to the children of Israel the fulfillment of the promise made *to* their
    forefathers.
Remember the lonely, the orphaned *and* the widowed,
— and do not abandon those who have been reconciled with you by the death *of*
    your Son.

You called Stephen to your presence when he bore witness to Jesus, standing at
   your right hand,
—welcome our deceased brothers and sisters who in faith and love hoped for the
   vision *of* your glory.

Our Father . . .

Prayer

    Lord,
      as we celebrate your Son's resurrection,
      so may we rejoice with all the saints
      when he returns in glory,
      who lives and reigns with you and the Holy Spirit,
      one God, for ever and ever.

THURSDAY

Morning Prayer

READING   Romans 8:10-11

   If Christ is in you the body is dead because of sin, while the spirit lives
   because of justice. If the Spirit of him who raised Jesus from the dead dwells
   in you, then he who raised Jesus from the dead will bring your mortal bodies
   to life also, through his Spirit dwelling in you.

RESPONSORY (VI F)
The Lord is risen *from* the tomb, * alleluia, al*le*luia.
—The Lord is risen *from* the tomb, * alleluia, al*le*luia.
He hung upon the *cross* for us,
—alleluia, al*le*luia.
Glory to the Father, and *to* the Son, * and to the Ho*ly* Spirit.
—The Lord is risen *from* the tomb, * alleluia, al*le*luia.

CANTICLE OF ZECHARIAH
Ant.   In a little while you will no longer see me, says the Lord; † then a
             little while later you will see *me* again, * since I am going to the
             Father, al*le*luia.

INTERCESSIONS (VI F)
God the Father has given us his Son for the resurrection *of* his people. * Let us
   turn with confidence to the Fath*er*, and say:
May the Lord Jesus be our very life.
As a pillar of fire, you lighted the way for your people *in* the desert,
— through his resurrection may Christ be today the light *of* our life.

Through the voice of Moses you taught your people *from* the mountain,
—through his resurrection may Christ be today the light *of* our life.
You fed your pilgrim people with your *gift* of manna,
—through his resurrection may Christ be today the light *of* our life.
You gave your people water *from* the rock,
—through his resurrection may Christ be today the light *of* our life.

Our Father . . .

Prayer

Father,
may we always give you thanks
for raising Christ our Lord to glory,
because we are his people
and share the salvation he won,
for he lives and reigns with you and the Holy Spirit,
one God, for ever and ever.

Evening Prayer

READING   1 Peter 3:18, 22

The reason why Christ died for sins once for all, the just man for the sake of
the unjust, was that he might lead you to God. He was put to death insofar as
fleshly existence goes, but was given life in the realm of the spirit. He went to
heaven and is at God's right hand, with angelic rulers and power subjected to
him.

RESPONSORY (VI F)
The dis*ci*ples rejoiced, * alleluia, al*le*luia.
— The dis*ci*ples rejoiced, * alleluia, al*le*luia.
When they saw the *ris*en Lord,
—alleluia, al*le*luia.
Glory to the Father, and *to* the Son, * and to the Ho*ly* Spirit.
—The dis*ci*ples rejoiced, * alleluia, al*le*luia.

CANTICLE OF MARY
Ant.   Your sorrow will be turned *in*to joy, * and that joy no one will
              take from you, al*le*luia.

INTERCESSIONS (VI F)
The Father has established in Christ the foundation of all our hope and the
principle of our *res*urrection. * Let us rejoice in Christ, and cry out *to* him,
saying:
King of glory, hear our *prayer.*

Lord Jesus, through your resurrection you entered the sanctuary of heaven to offer
  the blood of *your* own sacrifice,
— lead us with you into the glory *of* the Father.
Through your resurrection you confirmed the faith of your dsciples and sent them
  out in*to* the world,
— make all bishops and priests faithful preach*ers* of the Gospel.
Through your resurrection you became our peace and reconci*li*ation,
— united the baptized in perfect communion of *faith* and love.
Through your resurrection the crippled man was healed at the gate *of* the temple,
— look on the sick and reveal in them the power *of* your glory.
You became the firstborn from the dead, the firstfruits of the *re*surrection,
— grant *to* the dead who hoped in you a share *in* your glory.

Our Father . . .

Prayer

Father,
may we always give you thanks
for raising Christ our Lord to glory,
because we are his people
and share the salvation he won,
for he lives and reigns with you and the Holy Spirit,
one God, for ever and ever.

ASCENSION OF THE LORD
Solemnity

Evening Prayer I

HYMN, as in Evening Prayer II, 486.

PSALMODY

Ant. 1   I came forth from the Father and have come in*to* the world; *
now I leave the world to return to the Father, a*l*leluia.

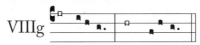

VIIIg

Psalm 113

Praise, O servants *of* the Lord, *
  praise the name *of* the Lord!
May the name of the *Lord* be blessed *
  both now and for *ev*ermore!
From the rising of the sun *to* its setting
  * praised be the name *of* the Lord!
High above all nations *is* the Lord, *
  above the heav*ens* his glory.
Who is like the *Lord*, our God, * who
  has risen on high *to* his throne
yet stoops from the heights *to* look
  down, * to look down upon heav*en*

and earth?
From the dust he lifts *up* the lowly, *
  from his misery he rais*es* the poor
to set him in the compan*y* of princes, *
  yes, with the princes *of* his people.
To the childless wife he *gives* a home *
  and gladdens her *heart* with children.
Glory to the Father, and *to* the Son, *
  and to the *Ho*ly Spirit:
as it was in the beginn*ing*, is now, * and
  will be for ev*er*. Amen.

Antiphon   I came forth from the Father and have come in*to* the world; *
now I leave the world to return to the Father, a*l*leluia.

Ant. 2   After he spoke to his disciples, † the Lord Jesus ascended *into*
heaven * where he is seated at the right hand of the Father,
al*le*luia.

IIA

Psalm 117

O praise the Lord, all *you*
  nations, * acclaim him all *you*
  peoples!
Strong is his love *for* us; * he is faithful
  for ever.

Glory to the Father, and to *the* Son, *
  and to the Ho*ly* Spirit:
as it was in the beginning, *is* now, * and
  will be for ever. *A*men.

Antiphon   After he spoke to his disciples, † the Lord Jesus ascended *into* heaven * where he is seated at the right hand of the Father, al*le*luia.

Ant. 3   No one has ascended into heaven † except the one who descended *from* heaven, * the Son of Man, who is in heaven, al*le*luia.

Va

Canticle   Revelation 11:17-18; 12:10b-12a

We praise you, the Lord God *Al*mighty, * who is *and* who was.
You have assumed your *great* power, * you have be*gun* your reign.
The nations have raged in anger, † but then came your day *of* wrath * and the moment to *judge* the dead:
the time to reward your servants the prophets † and the holy ones who *re*vere you, * the great and the *small* alike.
Now have salvation and po*wer* come, * the reign of our God and the authori-ty of *his* Anointed One.

For the accuser of our brothers is *cast* out, * who night and day accused them *be*fore God.
They defeated him by the blood of the Lamb † and by the word of *their* testimony; * love for life did not deter *them* from death.
So rejoice, *you* heavens, * and you that *dwell* therein!
Glory to the Father, and to *the* Son, * and to the *Ho*ly Spirit:
as it was in the beginning, *is* now, * and will be for *ev*er. Amen.

Antiphon   No one has ascended into heaven † except the one who descended *from* heaven, * the Son of Man, who is in heaven, al*le*luia.

READING   Ephesians 2:4-6
 God is rich in mercy; because of his great love for us he brought us to life with Christ Jesus when we were dead in sin. By this favor you are saved. Both with and in Christ Jesus he raised us up and gave us a place in the heavens.

RESPONSORY (VI F)
God ascends to *shouts* of joy, * alleluia, al*le*luia.
— God ascends to *shouts* of joy, * alleluia, al*le*luia.
The Lord to the *blast* of trumpets,
— alleluia, al*le*luia.
Glory to the Father, and *to* the Son, * and to the Ho*ly* Spirit.
— God ascends to *shouts* of joy, * alleluia, al*le*luia.

CANTICLE OF MARY

Ant.   Father, I have made known your name to the men you have given
                  me; † now I am praying for them and not *for* the world, * because
                  I am coming to you, al*le*luia.

If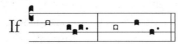

My soul ✠ proclaims the greatness
of the Lord, * my spirit rejoices
in God *my* savior

for he has *looked* with favor * on his
low*ly* servant.

From this day all *gene*rations * will call
me blessèd:

the Almighty has done great *things* for
me, * and holy is *his* Name.

He has mercy on *those* who fear him *
in every gen*era*tion.

He has shown the strength *of* his arm, *
he has scattered the proud in their
*con*ceit.

He has cast down the mighty *from* their
thrones, * and has lifted up *the* lowly.

He has filled the hungry *with* good
things, * and the rich he has sent
a*way* empty.

He has come to the help of his *ser*vant
Israel * for he has remembered his
promise *of* mercy,

the promise he made *to* our fathers, * to
Abraham and his children *for* ever.

Glory to the Father, and *to* the Son, *
and to the Ho*ly* Spirit:

as it was in the begin*ning*, is now, * and
will be for ever. *A*men.

Antiphon   Father, I have made known your name to the men you have given
                  me; † now I am praying for them and not *for* the world, * because
                  I am coming to you, al*le*luia.

INTERCESSIONS (VI F)

In joy of spirit let us ac*claim* Christ, * who sits at the right hand *of* the Father:
Lord Jesus, you are the King of *glory.*

King of glory, you took with you our frail humanity to be glorified in heaven;
    remove the sins *of* the world,

— and restore us to the innocence which was ours be*fore* the Fall.

You came down from heaven on a pilgrim*age* of love,

— grant that we may take the same path *to* your presence.

You promised to draw all things *to* yourself,

— do not allow any one of us to be separated *from* your body.

Where you have gone before *us* in glory,

— may we follow you in *mind* and heart.

True God, we await your coming *as* our judge,

— may we see the vision of your glory and your mercy in company with *all* the
    dead.

Our Father . . .

Prayer

God our Father,
make us joyful in the ascension of your Son Jesus Christ.
May we follow him into the new creation,
for his ascension is our glory and our hope.
Grant this through our Lord Jesus Christ, your Son,
who lives and reigns with you and the Holy Spirit,
one God, for ever and ever.

Morning Prayer

HYMN

Optatus votis omnium. Mode VIII (L.M.)

Optatus votis omnium
sacratus illuxit dies,
quo Christus, mundi spes, Deus,
conscendit cælos arduos.

Greeting the dawn of this great feast
Our hearts are filled with joy today,
When we recall how Christ our God
Ascended to his realms of light.

Magni triumphum prœlii,
mundi perempto principe,
Patris præsentans vultibus
victicis carnis gloriam,

Winner for ever in the strife
Against the prince of death and sin,
Glory of all creation's hope,
Before the Father's face he stands.

In nube fertur lucida
et spem facit credentiubus,
iam paradisum reserans
quem protoplasti clauserant.

Brightest of clouds hid him from sight,
But pledge remained of life to come,
Since Paradise can now be ours
Which our first parents lost by sin.

O grande cunctis gaudium,
quod pqrtus nostræ Virginis,
post sputa, flagra, post crucem
pasternæ sedi iungitur.

Greatest of joys mankind can claim,
That he whom holy Mary bore,
Reigns at his Father's side in pow'r,
His Cross and bitter Passion past.

Agamus ergo gratias
nostræ salutis vindici,
nostrum quod corpus vexerit
sublime ad cæli regiam.

Saving Avenger of our race,
To him our grateful hearts we raise;
In his immortal deity
Our mortal nature dwells on high.

Sit nobis cum cælestibus
commune manens gaudium:
illis, quod semet obtulit,
nobis, quod se non abstulit.

We have a lasting cause for joy,
Which all the saints and angels share;
Theirs is the bliss of seeing him,
And we still know that he is near.

Nunc, Christe, scandens æthera
ad te cor nosturm subleva,
tuum Patrisque Spiritum
emittens nobis cælitus. Amen.

Jesus, in splendor bright enthroned,
Keep all our hearts at rest in you,
Sending your Spirit down to us,
To teach the Father's love for all. Amen.

PSALMODY

Ant. 1   Men of Galilee, why are you looking up into the sky? † This
              Jesus who has been taken up *in*to heaven * will return in the
              same way, a*l*leluia.

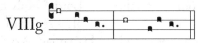

VIIIg

Psalm 63:2-9

O God, you are my God, for
  you I long; * for you my *soul* is
thirsting.
My body *pines* for you * like a dry,
  weary land *with*out water.
So I gaze on you *in* the sanctuary * to
  see your strength *and* your glory.
For your love is bet*ter* than life, * my
  lips will *speak* your praise.
So I will bless you *all* my life, * in your
  name I will lift *up* my hands.
My soul shall be filled as *with* a ban-

quet, * my mouth shall praise *you*
  with joy.
On my bed I re*mem*ber you. * On you I
  muse *through* the night
for you have *been* my help; * in the
  shadow of your wings *I* rejoice.
My soul *clings* to you; * your right hand
  holds me fast.
Glory to the Father, and *to* the Son, *
  and to the *Ho*ly Spirit:
as it was in the begin*ning*, is now, * and
  will be for ev*er*. Amen.

Antiphon   Men of Galilee, why are you looking up into the sky? † This
              Jesus who has been taken up *in*to heaven * will return in the
              same way, a*l*leluia.

Ant. 2   Give glory to the *King* of kings, * sing praise to God, al*l*eluia.

IIA

Canticle   Daniel 3:57-88; 56

B less the Lord, all you works *of*
  the Lord. * Praise and exalt him
above all *for*ever.
Angels of the Lord, *bless* the Lord, *
  You heavens, bless *the* Lord.
All you waters above the heavens, *bless*
  the Lord. * All you hosts of the Lord,
  bless *the* Lord.
Sun and moon, *bless* the Lord. * Stars of
  heaven, bless *the* Lord.

Every shower and dew, *bless* the Lord. *
  All you winds, bless *the* Lord.
Fire and heat, *bless* the Lord. * Cold
  and chill, bless *the* Lord.
Dew and rain, *bless* the Lord. * Frost
  and chill, bless *the* Lord.
Ice and snow, *bless* the Lord. * Nights
  and days, bless *the* Lord.
Light and darkness, *bless* the Lord. *
  Lightnings and clouds, bless *the*

Lord.

Let the earth *bless* the Lord. * Praise and exalt him above all *for*ever.

Mountains and hills, *bless* the Lord. * Everything growing from the earth, bless *the* Lord.

You springs, *bless* the Lord. * Seas and rivers, bless *the* Lord.

You dolphins and all water creatures, *bless* the Lord. * All you birds of the air, bless *the* Lord.

All you beasts, wild and tame, *bless* the Lord. * You sons of men, bless *the* Lord.

O Israel, *bless* the Lord. * Praise and exalt him above all *for*ever.

Priests of the Lord, *bless* the Lord. * Servants of the Lord, bless *the* Lord.

Spirits and souls of the just, *bless* the Lord. * Holy men of humble heart, bless *the* Lord.

Hananiah, Azariah, Mishael, *bless* the Lord. * Praise and exalt him above all *for*ever.

Let us bless the Father, and the Son, and the *Ho*ly Spirit. * Let us praise and exalt him above all *for*ever.

Blessèd are you in the firma*ment* of heaven.* Praiseworthy and glorious and exalted above all *for*ever.

Antiphon   Give glory to the *King* of kings, * sing praise to God, al*le*luia.

Ant. 3   As they watched, he was lift*ed* up, * and a cloud took him from their sight, al*le*luia.

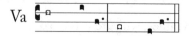

Psalm 149

Sing a new song to *the* Lord, * his praise in the assembly of *the* faithful.

Let Israel rejoice in *its* Maker, * let Zion's sons exult in *their* king.

Let them praise his name *with* dancing * and make music with timbrel *and* harp.

For the Lord takes delight in *his* people. * He crowns the poor with sal*va*tion.

Let the faithful rejoice in *their* glory, * shout for joy and take *their* rest.

Let the praise of God be on *their* lips * and a two-edged sword in *their* hand,

to deal out vengeance to *the* nations * and punishment on all *the* peoples;

to bind their kings *in* chains * and their nobles in fetters *of* iron;

to carry out the sentence pre-*or*dained: * this honor is for all *his* faithful.

Glory to the Father, and to *the* Son, * and to the Ho*ly* Spirit:

as it was in the beginning, *is* now, * and will be for ever. *A*men.

Antiphon   As they watched, he was lift*ed* up, * and a cloud took him from their sight, al*le*luia.

READING   Hebrews 10:12-14

Jesus offered one sacrifice for sins and took his seat forever at the right hand
of God; now he waits until his enemies are placed beneath his feet. By one
offering he has forever perfected those who are being sanctified.

RESPONSORY (VI F)

Christ ascended *into* heaven, * alleluia, al*le*luia.
— Christ ascended *into* heaven, * alleluia, al*le*luia.
He led capti*vity* captive,
— alleluia, al*le*luia.
Glory to the Father, and *to* the Son, * and to the Ho*ly* Spirit.
— Christ ascended *into* heaven, * alleluia, al*le*luia.

CANTICLE OF ZECHARIAH

Ant.   I am ascending to my Father *and* your Father, * to my God and
               your God, al*le*luia.

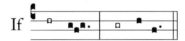
If

B lessèd ✠ be the Lord, the *God* of
Israel; * he has come to his people
and set *them* free.
He has raised up for us a *mighty* savior,
* born of the house of his ser*vant*
David.
Through his holy prophets he promised
of old † that he would save us *from*
our enemies, * from the hands of all
who hate us.
He promised to show mercy *to* our
fathers * and to remember his ho*ly*
covenant.
This was the oath he swore to our
*fath*er Abraham: * to set us free from
the hands of *our* enemies,
free to worship him without fear, † holy
and righteous *in* his sight * all the

days of *our* life.
You, my child, shall be called the
prophet *of* the Most High; * for you
will go before the Lord to prepare *his*
way,
to give his people knowledge *of* salvation * by the forgiveness of *their* sins.
In the tender compassion *of* our God *
the dawn from on high shall break
*up*on us,
to shine on those who dwell in darkness
and the sha*dow* of death, * and to
guide our feet into the way *of* peace.
Glory to the Father, and *to* the Son, *
and to the Ho*ly* Spirit:
as it was in the begin*ning*, is now, * and
will be for ever. *A*men.

Antiphon   I am ascending to my Father *and* your Father, * to my God and
               your God, al*le*luia.

INTERCESSIONS (VI F)

The Lord has been lifted high above the earth and draws all things *to* himself. *
   Let us cry out to him *in* our joy:

Lord Jesus, you are the King of *glory.*

Lord Jesus, King of glory, you were offered once as the victim for sins, and
   ascended to the right hand *of* the Father,

— make perfect for all time those *whom* you sanctify.

Eternal Priest and minister of the new Covenant, you live for ever to make
   interces*sion* for us,

— save the people that *prays* to you.

You showed yourself alive after your passion and appeared to the disciples for
   *for*ty days,

— confirm our *faith* today.

Today you promised the Spirit to your apostles, to make them your witnesses to
   the ends *of* the earth,

— by the power of the Spirit strengthen *our* own witness.

Our Father . . .

Prayer

God our Father,
make us joyful in the ascension of your Son Jesus Christ.
May we follow him into the new creation,
for his ascension is our glory and our hope.
Grant this through our Lord Jesus Christ, your Son,
who lives and reigns with you and the Holy Spirit,
one God, for ever and ever.

Evening Prayer II

HYMN

Iesu, nostra redemptio. Mode IV (L.M.)

Iesu, nostra redemptio	Lord Jesus, our redemption's Price,
amor et desiderium,	Our love and deepening desire,
Deus creator omnium,	Creator, God before all time,
homo in fine temporum,	You deigned to come to earth as Man.
Quæ te vicit clementia,	What clemency has prompted you
ut ferres nostra crimina,	To bear the weight of all our sins,
crudelem mortem patiens,	To undergo a cruel death
ut nos a morte tolleres;	To save us from eternal woe!

Inferni claustra penetrans,	You penetrated Death's abode
tuos captivos redimens;	And set its hapless captives free;
victor triumpho nobili	Your triumph won, you take your place
ad dextram Patris residens?	In splendor at the Father's side.
Ipsa te cogat pietas,	Your tender love and nothing else
ut mala nostra superes	Impelled you to endure our fate,
parcendo, et voti compotes	That sparing, you might raise us up,
nos tuo vultu saties.	To see the glory of your Face.
Tu esto nostrum gaudium,	You are our joy on earth below,
qui es futurus præmium;	And later will be our reward;
sit nostra in te gloria	May all our glory be in you
per cuncta semper sæcula.	When earth and time have passed away.
Amen.	Amen.

PSALMODY

Ant. 1   He ascended *into* heaven * and is seated at the right hand of the
              Father, *al*leluia.

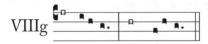

VIIIg

Psalm 110:1-5, 7

The Lord's revelation to my
   Master: † "Sit *on* my right: * your
foes I will put be*neath* your feet."
The Lord will wield from Zion † your
   scep*ter* of power: * rule in the midst
   of *all* your foes.
A prince from the day of your birth †
   on the *holy* mountains; * from the
   womb before the dawn *I* begot you.
The Lord has sworn an oath he will not
   change. † "You are a *priest* for ever, *

a priest like Melchize*dek* of old."
The Master standing *at* your right hand
   * will shatter kings in the day of *his*
   great wrath.
He shall drink from the stream *by* the
   wayside * and therefore he shall lift
   up his head.
Glory to the Father, and *to* the Son, *
   and to the *Holy* Spirit:
as it was in the begin*ning*, is now, * and
   will be for ev*er*. Amen.

Antiphon   He ascended *into* heaven * and is seated at the right hand of the
              Father, *al*leluia.

Ant. 2   God ascends to *shouts* of joy, * the Lord to the blast of trumpets,
              al*le*luia.

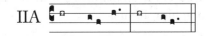

IIA

Psalm 47

All peoples, *clap* your hands, *
cry to God with shouts *of* joy!
For the Lord, the Most High, *we* must
fear, * great king over all *the* earth.
He subdues peoples *un*der us * and
nations under *our* feet.
Our inheritance, our glory, *is* from him,
* given to Jacob out *of* love.
God goes up with *shouts* of joy; * the
Lord goes up with trump*et* blast.
Sing praise for *God*, sing praise, * sing
praise to our king, *sing* praise.
God is king of *all* the earth. * Sing

praise with all *your* skill.
God is king ov*er* the nations; * God
reigns on his ho*ly* throne.
The princes of the peoples *are* assembled * with the people of Abra*ham's*
God.
The rulers of the earth be*long* to God, *
to God who reigns ov*er* all.
Glory to the Father, and *to* the Son, *
and to the Ho*ly* Spirit:
as it was in the begin*ning*, is now, * and
will be for ever. *A*men.

Antiphon God ascends to *shouts* of joy, * the Lord to the blast of trumpets,
al*le*luia.

Ant. 3 Now the Son of Man has *been* glorified * and God has been
glorified in him, al*le*luia.

V a

Canticle   Revelation 11:17-18; 12:10b-12a

We praise you, the Lord God
Almighty, * who is and *who* was.
You have assumed your *great* power, *
you have begun *your* reign.
The nations have raged in anger, † but
then came your day *of* wrath * and the
moment to judge *the* dead:
the time to reward your servants the
prophets † and the holy ones who
re*vere* you, * the great and the small
*a*like.
Now have salvation and po*wer* come, *
the reign of our God and the authority of his *A*nointed One.

For the accuser of our brothers is *cast*
out, * who night and day accused
them be*fore* God.
They defeated him by the blood of the
Lamb † and by the word of *their*
testimony; * love for life did not deter
them *from* death.
So rejoice, *you* heavens, * and you that
dwell *there*in!
Glory to the Father, and to *the* Son, *
and to the Ho*ly* Spirit:
as it was in the beginning, *is* now, * and
will be for ever. *A*men.

Antiphon Now the Son of Man has *been* glorified * and God has been
glorified in him, al*le*luia.

READING   1 Peter 3:18, 22

The reason why Christ died for sins once for all, the just man for the sake of
the unjust, was that he might lead you to God. He was put to death insofar as
fleshly existence goes, but was given life in the realm of the spirit. He went to
heaven and is at God's right hand, with angelic rulers and power subjected to
him.

RESPONSORY (VI F)

I am ascending to my Father *and* your Father, * alleluia, al*le*luia.
— I am ascending to my Father *and* your Father, * alleluia, al*le*luia.
To my God *and* your God,
—alleluia, al*le*luia.
Glory to the Father, and *to* the Son, * and to the Ho*ly* Spirit.
—I am ascending to my Father *and* your Father, * alleluia, al*le*luia.

CANTICLE OF MARY

Ant.   O Victor King, Lord of pow*er* and might, * today you have
                ascended in glory above *the* heavens.
                Do not leave us orphans, † but send us the Father's *pro*mised gift,
                * the Spirit of truth, al*le*luia.

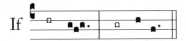

My soul ✠ proclaims the greatness *of* the Lord, * my spirit rejoices in God *my* savior
for he has *looked* with favor * on his low*ly* servant.
From this day all *gen*erations * will call *me* blessèd:
the Almighty has done great *things* for me, * and holy is *his* Name.
He has mercy on *those* who fear him * in every gen*er*ation.
He has shown the strength *of* his arm, * he has scattered the proud in their *con*ceit.

He has cast down the mighty *from* their thrones, * and has lifted up *the* lowly.
He has filled the hungry *with* good things, * and the rich he has sent a*way* empty.
He has come to the help of his *ser*vant Israel * for he has remembered his promise *of* mercy,
the promise he made *to* our fathers, * to Abraham and his children *for* ever.
Glory to the Father, and *to* the Son, * and to the Ho*ly* Spirit:
as it was in the begin*ning*, is now, * and will be for ever. *A*men.

Antiphon   O Victor King, Lord of pow*er* and might, * today you have
                ascended in glory above *the* heavens.
                Do not leave us orphans, † but send us the Father's *pro*mised gift,
                * the Spirit of truth, al*le*luia.

INTERCESSIONS (VI F)

In joy of spirit let us *ac*claim Christ, * who sits at the right hand *of* the Father:
Lord Jesus, you are the King of glory.

King of glory, you took with you our frail humanity to be glorified in heaven;
   remove the sins *of* the world,

— and restore us to the innocence which was ours be*fore* the Fall.

You came down from heaven on a pilgrim*age* of love,

— grant that we may take the same path *to* your presence.

You promised to draw all things *to* yourself,

— do not allow any one of us to be separated *from* your body.

Where you have gone before *us* in glory,

— may we follow you in *mind* and heart.

True God, we await your coming *as* our judge,

— may we see the vision of your glory and your mercy in company with *all* the
   dead.

Our Father . . .

Prayer

   God our Father,
   make us joyful in the ascension of your Son Jesus Christ.
   May we follow him into the new creation,
   for his ascension is our glory and our hope.
   Grant this through our Lord Jesus Christ, your Son,
   who lives and reigns with you and the Holy Spirit,
   one God, for ever and ever.

FRIDAY

Morning Prayer

READING Acts 5:30-32

The God of our fathers has raised up Jesus whom you put to death, hanging him on a tree. He whom God has exalted at his right hand as ruler and savior is to bring repentance to Israel and forgiveness of sins. We testify to this. So too does the Holy Spirit, whom God has given to those that obey him.

RESPONSORY (VI F)

The Lord is risen *from* the tomb, * alleluia, al*le*luia.
—The Lord is risen *from* the tomb, * alleluia, al*le*luia.
He hung upon the *cross* for us,
      alleluia, al*le*luia.
Glory to the Father, and *to* the Son, * and to the Ho*ly* Spirit.
—The Lord is risen *from* the tomb, * alleluia, al*le*luia.

CANTICLE OF ZECHARIAH

Ant.   Because he suffered death, † we see Jesus crowned with glo*ry* and honor, * al*le*luia.

INTERCESSIONS (VI F)

Before the Ascension:
God the Father raised up Christ through the Spirit, and will also raise up our *mor*tal bodies. * Let us cry *out* to him:
*Lord, raise us to life through your Ho*ly *Spirit.*
All-holy Father, you accepted the holocaust of your Son in raising him *from* the dead,
—accept the offering we make today, and lead us to e*ter*nal life.
Look with favor on all we *do* today,
—that it may be for your glory and the sanctification *of* the world.
May our work today not be in vain but for the good of *the* whole world,
—and through it lead us *to* your kingdom.
Open our eyes today to recognize our brothers and sisters, and our *hearts* to love them,
—so that we may love and *serve* each other.

Our Father . . .

Prayer

Lord,
hear our prayer

that your gospel may reach all men
and that we who receive salvation through your Word
may be your children in deed as well as in name.
We ask this through our Lord Jesus Christ, your Son,
who lives and reigns with you and the Holy Spirit,
one God, for ever and ever.

After the Ascension:
Christ ascended into heaven to send the Holy Spirit on *the* apostles. * Let us join
   with one voice in praising *him*, and say:
Send us your *Spirit.*
Lord Jesus, you ascended into heaven; send us the promise *of* the Father,
— that we may be clothed with power *from* on high.
Your disciples were to be as wise as serpents and as sim*ple* as doves,
— through your Spirit teach us prudence *and* simplicity.
You are seated at the right hand of the Father; pray for us *as* our Priest,
— and pray in us *as* our Head.
Grant that in every trial we may suf*fer* with you,
— and so be glori*fied* with you.

Our Father . . .

Prayer

Father,
   you have given us eternal life
through Christ your Son who rose from the dead
and now sits at your right hand.
When he comes again in glory,
may he clothe with immortality
all who have been born again in baptism.
We ask this through our Lord Jesus Christ, your Son,
who lives and reigns with you and the Holy Spirit,
one God, for ever and ever.

Evening Prayer

READING   Hebrews 5:8-10
   Son though he was, Christ learned obedience from what he suffered; and
   when perfected, he became the source of eternal salvation for all who obey
   him, designated by God as high priest according to the order of Melchizedek.

RESPONSORY (VI F)
Before the Ascension:
The disciples rejoiced, * alleluia, alleluia.
— The disciples rejoiced, * alleluia, alleluia.
When they saw the *risen* Lord,
— alleluia, alleluia.
Glory to the Father, and *to* the Son, * and to the Ho*ly* Spirit.
— The disciples rejoiced, * alleluia, alleluia.

After the Ascension:
The Holy Spirit *is* the Paraclete, * alleluia, alleluia.
— The Holy Spirit *is* the Paraclete, * alleluia, alleluia.
He will teach *you* all things,
— alleluia, alleluia.
Glory to the Father, and *to* the Son, * and to the Ho*ly* Spirit.
— The Holy Spirit *is* the Paraclete, * alleluia, alleluia.

CANTICLE OF MARY
Ant.   To those who ask him, † the Father will send the *Holy* Spirit, *
             al*le*luia.

INTERCESSIONS (VI F)
Before the Ascension:
Let us praise Christ, the source *of* all life * and the foundation *of* all virtue:
Lord, establish your kingdom in the *world.*
Jesus our Savior, you died in your human nature but were restored to life *by* the
   Spirit,
— make us die to sin, and live *by* the Spirit.
You sent your disciples into the whole world to preach the Gospel to *every*
   creature,
— inspire those who preach the Gospel to live *by* your Spirit.
All power in heaven and on earth has been given to you, to bear witness *to* the
   truth,
— keep the hearts of those who govern us faithful *to* the truth.
You make all things new, and command us to wait and watch *for* your kingdom,
— grant that the more we look forward to a new heaven and a new earth, the
   more we may seek to better this *pres*ent world.
You went down among the dead to bring them the good news *of* the Gospel,
— be the great joy and hope of *all* the dead.

Our Father . . .

Prayer

Lord,
hear our prayer
that your gospel may reach all men
and that we who receive salvation through your Word
may be your children in deed as well as in name.
We ask this through our Lord Jesus Christ, your Son,
who lives and reigns with you and the Holy Spirit,
one God, for ever and ever.

After the Ascension:

All praise and glory to Christ, who promised that the power of the Holy Spirit
 would come down on *the* apostles. * Let *us* cry out:
Send forth your light and your *truth.*

Jesus, word of truth, wisdom and splendor of the Father, send forth your light *and*
 your truth,
— that our words and deeds today may bear witness to you before our broth*ers*
 and sisters.
May we always understand and savor the things *of* the Spirit,
— so as not to fall into sin but enter into *life* and peace.
May your Spirit help us *in* our weakness,
— that we may know how to pray *as* we ought.
Fill us with love *and* all knowledge,
— that we may instruct and correct *one* another.

Our Father . . .

Prayer

Father,
you have given us eternal life
through Christ your Son who rose from the dead
and now sits at your right hand.
When he comes again in glory,
may he clothe with immortality
all who have been born again in baptism.
We ask this through our Lord Jesus Christ, your Son,
who lives and reigns with you and the Holy Spirit,
one God, for ever and ever.

SATURDAY

Morning Prayer

READING Romans 14:7-9
None of us lives as his own master and none of us dies as his own master.
While we live we are responsible to the Lord, and when we die we die as his
servants. Both in life and death we are the Lord's. That is why Christ died
and came to life again, that he might be Lord of both the dead and the living.

RESPONSORY (VI F)
The Lord is risen *from* the tomb, * alleluia, al*le*luia.
—The Lord is risen *from* the tomb, * alleluia, al*le*luia.
He hung upon the *cross* for us,
—allcluia, al*le*luia.
Glory to the Father, and *to* the Son, * and to the Ho*ly* Spirit.
—The Lord is risen *from* the tomb, * alleluia, al*le*luia.

CANTICLE OF ZECHARIAH
Ant.   I promise that the Fa*ther* will give you * anything you ask for in
my name, al*le*luia.

INTERCESSIONS (VI F)
Before the Ascension:
Christ has made known to us the life that *lasts* for ever. * With faith and joy let us
cry out *to* him, saying:
Lord, may your resurrection bring us the riches of your *grace.*
Eternal shepherd, look on your flock as it ris*es* from sleep,
—feed us with the word of life and the *bread* from heaven.
Keep us safe from *wolf* and hireling,
—and make us faithful in listening *to* your voice.
You are present to all who preach your Gospel, and give power *to* their words,
—make us today preachers of your resurrection by our holi*ness* of life.
Be our great joy that no one can *take* from us,
—so that we may reject sin with its sadness, and reach out to e*ter*nal life.

Our Father . . .

Prayer
Lord,
teach us to know you better
by doing good to others.
Help us to grow in your love

and come to understand the eternal mystery
of Christ's death and resurrection.
We ask this through our Lord Jesus Christ, your Son,
who lives and reigns with you and the Holy Spirit,
one God, for ever and ever.

After the Ascension:
Let us praise the Lord Jesus, anointed *by* the Holy Spirit, * and *let* us pray:
You are seated at the right hand of the Father; † *make intercession* for *us.*
Christ our Lord, look with favor on all who are called *by* your name,
— and gather them in unity by the power of the *Ho*ly Spirit.
Give light to those who suffer *for* your sake,
— that they may know what to say when faced *with* their persecutors.
You are the true vine; may all ac*know*ledge you,
— and become your branches, bearing fruit *in* the Spirit.
King of all the world, you ascended to heav*en* in triumph,
— rule o*ver* all peoples.
May those who in baptism were made one with you in ris*ing* again,
— pass with you from *death* to life.

Our Father . . .

Prayer

Father,
at your Son's ascension into heaven
you promised to send the Holy Spirit on your apostles.
You filled them with heavenly wisdom:
fill us also with the gift of your Spirit.
Grant this through our Lord Jesus Christ, your Son,
who lives and reigns with you and the Holy Spirit,
one God, for ever and ever.

SEVENTH SUNDAY OF EASTER

PSALTER, WEEK III, 740.

Evening Prayer I

READING   1 Peter 2:9-10

You are "a chosen race, a royal priesthood, a holy nation, a people he claims for his own to proclaim the glorious works" of the One who called you from darkness into his marvelous light. Once you were no people, but now you are God's people; once there was no mercy for you, but now you have found mercy.

RESPONSORY (VI F)

The Holy Spirit *is* the Paraclete, * alleluia, al*le*luia.
— The Holy Spirit *is* the Paraclete, * alleluia, al*le*luia.
He will teach *you* all things,
— alleluia, al*le*luia.
Glory to the Father, and *to* the Son, * and to the Ho*ly* Spirit.
—The Holy Spirit *is* the Paraclete, * alleluia, al*le*luia.

CANTICLE OF MARY

Ant.   I will not leave you orphans; † I am going now but I will come *back* to you * and your hearts will rejoice, al*le*luia.

INTERCESSIONS (VI F)

Let us bless Christ, on whom the Holy Spirit came down in the form *of* a dove. *
    Let us pray to him, and seal our *prayer* by saying:
Amen. Amen.
Lord, send the Spirit *of* your promise,
— that your Church may be continually renewed in *life* and vigor.
May all peoples acclaim you as *king* and God,
— may Israel become your *prized* possession.
You *cast* out devils,
— cast out from us all scandal and *stub*born pride.
At Pentecost you undid the disuni*ty* of Babel,
— by your Spirit gather all in unity, and spread the one faith through*out* the world.
May your Spirit *dwell* within us,
— and raise to life our *mor*tal bodies.

Our Father . . .

Prayer

Father,
help us keep in mind that Christ our Savior
lives with you in glory
and promised to remain with us until the end of time.
We ask this through our Lord Jesus Christ, your Son,
who lives and reigns with you and the Holy Spirit,
one God, for ever and ever.

Morning Prayer

READING   Acts 10:40-43

God raised up Jesus on the third day and granted that he be seen, not by all, but only by such witnesses as had been chosen beforehand by God— by us who ate and drank with him after he rose from the dead. He commissioned us to preach to the people and to bear witness that he is the one set apart by God as judge of the living and the dead. To him all the prophets testify, saying that everyone who believes in him has forgiveness of sins through his name.

RESPONSORY (VI F)

Christ, Son of the living God, have mercy on us, * alleluia, alleluia.
—Christ, Son of the living God, have mercy on us, * alleluia, alleluia.
You have risen *from* the dead,
—alleluia, alleluia.
Glory to the Father, and *to* the Son, * and to the Holy Spirit.
—Christ, Son of the living God, have mercy on us, * alleluia, alleluia.

CANTICLE OF ZECHARIAH

Ant.   Father, I have glorified you up*on* the earth, * I have accomplished the work you gave me to do, alleluia.

INTERCESSIONS (VI F)

In company with all who have been reconciled with the Father by the power of the *Holy* Spirit, * let us join in prayer *and* praise, saying:
May your Spirit come to our *aid.*
Lord Jesus, may we be guided today *by* God's Spirit,
—and walk always as children *of* your Father.
Through your Spirit intercede for us *with* the Father,
—that we may be made worthy to receive *what* you promise.
Give us a generous heart, that we may not seek our *self*ish interests,
—but be concerned for the *good* of others.

Teach us *to* know God,
— that we may advance in knowledge of you and the Father through the *Ho*ly
  Spirit.

Our Father . . .

Prayer

Father,
help us keep in mind that Christ our Savior
lives with you in glory
and promised to remain with us until the end of time.
We ask this through our Lord Jesus Christ, your Son,
who lives and reigns with you and the Holy Spirit,
one God, for ever and ever.

Evening Prayer II

READING   Hebrews 10:12-14
  Jesus offered one sacrifice for sins and took his seat forever at the right hand
  of God; now he waits until his enemies are placed beneath his feet. By one
  offering he has forever perfected those who are being sanctified.

RESPONSORY (VI F)
The Holy Spirit *is* the Paraclete, * alleluia, al*le*luia.
— The Holy Spirit *is* the Paraclete, * alleluia, al*le*luia.
He will teach *you* all things,
— alleluia, al*le*luia.
Glory to the Father, and *to* the Son, * and to the Ho*ly* Spirit.
— The Holy Spirit *is* the Paraclete, * alleluia, al*le*luia.

CANTICLE OF MARY
Ant.   I will send you the Spirit of truth who comes *from* the Father. *
                When the Paraclete comes he will bear witness to me, al*le*luia.

INTERCESSIONS (VI F)
We do not know how to pray as we ought, but the Spirit himself intercedes for us
  with inexpress*i*ble longing. * Let *us* then say:
May the Holy Spirit intercede for us.
Lord Jesus, shepherd in glory, give wisdom and counsel *to* our shepherds,
— to lead your flock more surely *to* salvation.
You are exalted in heaven, and are *rich* in mercy,
— look with compassion on the poor and need*y* on earth.

You were conceived by the Virgin Mary by the over-shadowing of the *Holy* Spirit,
— sustain those vowed to virginity in the spirit of *their* self-offering.
You are our priest, offering praise to the Father in the *Ho*ly Spirit,
— unite all mankind in your sacri*fice* of praise.
May all the dead enter into the glorious freedom *of* God's children,
— and the fullness of redemption *for* their bodies.

Our Father . . .

Prayer

Father,
help us keep in mind that Christ our Savior
lives with you in glory
and promised to remain with us until the end of time.
We ask this through our Lord Jesus Christ, your Son,
who lives and reigns with you and the Holy Spirit,
one God, for ever and ever.

MONDAY

Morning Prayer

READING   Romans 10:8b-10
The word is near you, on your lips and in your heart (that is , the word of
faith which we preach). For if you confess with your lips that Jesus is Lord,
and believe in your heart that God raised him from the dead, you will be
saved. Faith in the heart leads to justification, confession on the lips to
salvation.

RESPONSORY (VI F)
The Lord is risen *from* the tomb, * alleluia, al*le*luia.
— The Lord is risen *from* the tomb, * alleluia, al*le*luia.
He hung upon the *cross* for us,
— alleluia, al*le*luia.
Glory to the Father, and *to* the Son, * and to the Ho*ly* Spirit.
— The Lord is risen *from* the tomb, * alleluia, al*le*luia.

CANTICLE OF ZECHARIAH
Ant.   The world will persecute you, but *have* courage, * I have over-
                 come the world, al*le*luia.

INTERCESSIONS (VI F)

Christ promised to send the Holy Spirit from the Father in his name, to be our
   help*er* and guide. * Let us bless *him* and ask him:

Lord Jesus, give us your *Spirit.*

Lord Jesus, we thank you, and through you the Father also, in the unity of the
   *Ho*ly Spirit,

— may everything we say and do today be *in* your name.

Give us the Holy Spirit to *dwell* within us,

— that we may be living members *in* your body.

Grant that we may never condemn or *de*spise others,

— for we shall all one day face you *as* our judge.

Fill us with the fullness of joy and peace *in* believing,

— that we may be rich in hope and in the power of the *Ho*ly Spirit.

Our Father . . .

Prayer

Lord,
send the power of your Holy Spirit upon us
that we may remain faithful
and do your will in our daily lives.
We ask this through our Lord Jesus Christ, your Son,
who lives and reigns with you and the Holy Spirit,
one God, for ever and ever.

Evening Prayer

READING   Romans 8:14-17

All who are led by the Spirit of God are sons of God. You did not receive a
spirit of slavery leading you back into fear, but a spirit of adoption through
whom we cry our, "Abba!" (that is, "Father"). The Spirit himself gives witness
with our spirit that we are children of God. But if we are children, we are
heirs as well: heirs of God, heirs with Christ, if only we suffer with him so as
to be glorified with him.

RESPONSORY (VI F)

The Holy Spirit *is* the Paraclete, * alleluia, al*le*luia.

— The Holy Spirit *is* the Paraclete, * alleluia, al*le*luia.

He will teach *you* all things,

— alleluia, al*le*luia.

Glory to the Father, and *to* the Son, * and to the Ho*ly* Spirit.

— The Holy Spirit *is* the Paraclete, * alleluia, al*le*luia.

CANTICLE OF MARY

Ant.   The Spirit, the Advocate, will re*main* with you* and live in you, al*le*luia.

INTERCESSIONS (VI F)

Let us give thanks to Christ, who filled the apostles and the whole Church with the consolation of the *Ho*ly Spirit. * In union with all the faithful, let *us* cry out:
Lord, send your consoling Spirit into your *Church.*

Lord Jesus, mediator between God and men, you chose priests to *share* your work,
— through them may all rise with you *to* the Father.

Grant that rich and poor may meet in friendship, for you are the *God* of both,
— do not let the rich make rich*es* their god.

Make your Gospel known *to* all peoples,
— that all may come to obey *you* in faith.

Send forth your Spirit, gentlest *of* consolers,
— to wipe away the tears of *all* who mourn.

Purify the souls of *the* departed,
— and receive them into the company of your saints and chosen *ones* in heaven.

Our Father . . .

Prayer

Lord,
send the power of your Holy Spirit upon us
that we may remain faithful
and do your will in our daily lives.
We ask this through our Lord Jesus Christ, your Son,
who lives and reigns with you and the Holy Spirit,
one God, for ever and ever.

TUESDAY

Morning Prayer

READING   Acts 13:30-33

God raised Jesus from the dead, and for many days thereafter Jesus appeared to those who had come up with him from Galilee to Jerusalem. These are his witnesses now before the people. We ourselves announce to you the good news that what God promised our fathers he has fulfilled for us, their children, in raising up Jesus, according to what is written in the second psalm, "You are my son; this day I have begotten you."

RESPONSORY (VI F)

The Lord is risen *from* the tomb, * alleluia, al*le*luia.

— The Lord is risen *from* the tomb, * alleluia, al*le*luia.

He hung upon the *cross* for us,

— alleluia, al*le*luia.

Glory to the Father, and *to* the Son, * and to the Ho*ly* Spirit.

— The Lord is risen *from* the tomb, * alleluia, al*le*luia.

CANTICLE OF ZECHARIAH

Ant.   The Lord has risen from the dead as he promised; † let all the
                    earth rejoice *and* be glad, * for he shall reign for ever, al*le*luia.

INTERCESSIONS (VI F)

Christ the Lord promised to send us from the Father their Holy Spirit. Let us
   give Christ glory and ask him:

Lord Jesus, give us your Spirit.

Lord Jesus, may your word dwell in us in all its richness,

— that we may thank you in psalms, hymns and spiritual canticles.

Through the Spirit you have made us children of God,

— grant that through the Spirit we may join with you in always calling on God as
   Father.

Give us wisdom in our daily lives,

— that we may do everything for God's glory.

You are patient and full of compassion,

— make us live at peace with all mankind.

Our Father . . .

Prayer

   God of power and mercy,
   send your Holy Spirit
   to live in our hearts
   and make us temples of his glory.
   We ask this through our Lord Jesus Christ, your Son,
   who lives and reigns with you and the Holy Spirit,
   one God, for ever and ever.

Evening Prayer

READING   Romans 8:26-27

   The Spirit helps us in our weakness, for we do not know how to pray as we
   ought; but the Spirit himself makes intercession for us with groanings that

cannot be expressed in speech. He who searches hearts knows what the Spirit means, for the Spirit intercedes for the saints as God himself wills.

RESPONSORY (VI F)

The Holy Spirit *is* the Paraclete, * alleluia, al*le*luia.
— The Holy Spirit *is* the Paraclete, * alleluia, al*le*luia.
He will teach *you* all things,
— alleluia, al*le*luia.
Glory to the Father, and *to* the Son, * and to the Ho*ly* Spirit.
— The Holy Spirit *is* the Paraclete, * alleluia, al*le*luia.

CANTICLE OF MARY

Ant.   You will receive the power of the *Holy* Spirit. * You will be my witnesses to the ends of the earth, al*le*luia.

INTERCESSIONS (VI F)

All honor and glory to Christ, who has given the faithful a share in the *Holy* Spirit. * Let us cry out *to* him, saying:
O Christ, *hear us.*
Send forth the Holy Spirit *from* the Father,
— to cleanse and strengthen the Church and spread it through*out* the world.
Lord, by your Spirit, guide *those* who govern us,
— that they may be servants of the common good *in* your name.
Pour out your Spirit, the protector *of* the poor,
— to help and lift up all *those* in need.
We pray for all stewards *of* your mysteries,
— that they may always *be* found faithful.
By your suffering, resurrection and ascension you accomplished *our* redemption,
— bring it to completion in the souls and bodies *of* the dead.

Our Father . . .

Prayer

God of power and mercy,
send your Holy Spirit
to live in our hearts
and make us temples of his glory.
We ask this through our Lord Jesus Christ, your Son,
who lives and reigns with you and the Holy Spirit,
one God, for ever and ever.

WEDNESDAY

Morning Prayer

READING   Romans 6:8-11

If we have died with Christ, we believe that we are also to live with him. We know that Christ, once raised from the dead, will never die again; death has no more power over him. His death was death to sin, once for all; his life is life for God. In the same way, you must consider yourselves dead to sin but alive for God in Christ Jesus.

RESPONSORY (VI F)

The Lord is risen *from* the tomb, * alleluia, al*l*eluia.
— The Lord is risen *from* the tomb, * alleluia, al*l*eluia.
He hung upon the *cross* for us,
— alleluia, al*l*eluia.
Glory to the Father, and *to* the Son, * and to the Ho*ly* Spirit.
— The Lord is risen *from* the tomb, * alleluia, al*l*eluia.

CANTICLE OF ZECHARIAH

Ant.   Thanks be to God who has given *us* the victory * through our Lord Jesus Christ, al*l*eluia.

INTERCESSIONS (VI F)

The Holy Spirit gives witness to our spirit that we are chil*dren* of God. * Let us give thanks to God the Father *as* we pray:
Father, hear your *children.*
God of patience and consolation, teach us to be one in mind and heart, following the exam*ple* of Jesus,
— so that we may praise you with one voice *and* one spirit.
Grant that we may all seek to *serve* our neighbor,
— by doing good and building up a communi*ty* of love.
Do not let us be led by the spirit of the world, root*ed* in evil,
— but guide us by the Spirit that *comes* from you.
You search the *hearts* of all,
— lead us always along the way of sinceri*ty* and truth.

Our Father . . .

Prayer

God of mercy,
unite your Church in the Holy Spirit
that we may serve you with all our hearts
and work together with unselfish love.

Grant this through our Lord Jesus Christ, your Son,
who lives and reigns with you and the Holy Spirit,
one God, for ever and ever.

Evening Prayer

READING   1 Corinthians 2:9b-10

Eye has not seen, ear has not heard,
      nor has it so much as dawned on man
      what God has prepared for those who love him.
Yet God has revealed this wisdom to us through the Spirit. The Spirit
scrutinizes all matters, even the deep things of God.

RESPONSORY (VI F)

The Holy Spirit *is* the Paraclete, * alleluia, al*le*luia.
— The Holy Spirit *is* the Paraclete, * alleluia, al*le*luia.
He will teach *you* all things,
— alleluia, al*le*luia.
Glory to the Father, and *to* the Son, * and to the Ho*ly* Spirit.
— The Holy Spirit *is* the Paraclete, * alleluia, al*le*luia.

CANTICLE OF MARY

Ant.   Christ will baptize *you* with fire * and the Holy Spirit, al*le*luia.

INTERCESSIONS (VI F)

In company with the apostles and all who have the firstfruits of the *Ho*ly Spirit, *
      let us praise *God* and say:
Lord, hear our *prayer.*
Almighty God, you raised Christ to glo*ry* in heaven,
— may all mankind recognize his presence *in* the Church.
All-holy Father, you said of Christ: This is my belov*èd* Son, hear him,
— grant that all may hear his voice *and* be saved.
Send your Spirit into the hearts of your *faith*ful people,
— as cleansing water and re*fresh*ing rain.
Send your Spirit to guide the *course* of nature,
— and renew life over the face *of* the earth.
We commend to your care all *who* have died,
— and ask you to strengthen our hope in the resurrec*tion* to come.

Our Father . . .

Prayer

God of mercy,
unite your Church in the Holy Spirit

that we may serve you with all our hearts
and work together with unselfish love.
Grant this through our Lord Jesus Christ, your Son,
who lives and reigns with you and the Holy Spirit,
one God, for ever and ever.

THURSDAY

Morning Prayer

READING   Romans 8:10-11

If Christ is in you the body is dead because of sin, while the spirit lives
because of justice. If the Spirit of him who raised Jesus from the dead dwells
in you, then he who raised Jesus from the dead will bring your mortal bodies
to life also, through his Spirit dwelling in you.

RESPONSORY (VI F)

The Lord is risen *from* the tomb, * alleluia, al*le*luia.
— The Lord is risen *from* the tomb, * alleluia, al*le*luia.
He hung upon the *cross* for us,
— alleluia, al*le*luia.
Glory to the Father, and *to* the Son, * and to the Ho*ly* Spirit.
— The Lord is risen *from* the tomb, * alleluia, al*le*luia.

CANTICLE OF ZECHARIAH

Ant.   Go into the world and *teach* all nations. * Baptize them in the
               name of the Father † and of the Son † and of the Holy Spirit,
               al*le*luia.

INTERCESSIONS (VI F)

Blessèd be Christ the Lord: through him we all have access to the Father in the
    *Ho*ly Spirit. * Now *let* us pray:
O Christ, *hear us.*
Send your Spirit, the longed-for guest *of* our hearts,
— and grant that we may nev*er* offend him.
You rose from the dead and are seated at the right *hand* of God,
— make intercession for us always *with* the Father.
Through your Spirit unite us *with* yourself,
— so that trial or persecution or danger may never separate us *from* your love.
May we wel*come* each other,
— in the way you have welcomed us, to the glo*ry* of God.

Our Father . . .

Prayer

Father,
let your Spirit come upon us with power
to fill us with your gifts.
May he make our hearts pleasing to you,
and ready to do your will.
We ask this through our Lord Jesus Christ, your Son,
who lives and reigns with you and the Holy Spirit,
one God, for ever and ever.

Evening Prayer

READING   1 Corinthians 6:19-20
> You must know that your body is a temple of the Holy Spirit, who is with-
> in— the Spirit you have received from God. You are not your own. You have
> been purchased, and at a price. So glorify God in your body.

RESPONSORY (VI F)
The Holy Spirit *is* the Paraclete, * alleluia, al*le*luia.
— The Holy Spirit *is* the Paraclete, * alleluia, al*le*luia.
He will teach *you* all things,
— alleluia, al*le*luia.
Glory to the Father, and *to* the Son, * and to the Ho*ly* Spirit.
— The Holy Spirit *is* the Paraclete, * alleluia, al*le*luia.

CANTICLE OF MARY
Ant.   When the Spirit of truth comes, † he will teach *you* all truth *
                     and will proclaim to you the things to come, al*le*luia.

INTERCESSIONS (VI F)
Christ is God, bless*èd* for ever. * Let us ask him to send the Holy Spirit on all
   redeemed by his blood, *as* we say:
Lord, look with favor on those you have re*deemed.*
Send into the Church the Spir*it* of unity,
— to remove all dissension, hatred *and* division.
You freed those pos*sessed* by devils,
— free the world from the evils *that* afflict it.
You prayed, and were led by the Spirit to be*gin* your ministry,
— may priests find in prayer the guidance of the Spirit to per*form* their duties.
May your Spirit guide all *in* authority,
— to seek the *common* good.
You live in the glory *of* the Father,
— summon into your glory all *the* departed.

Our Father . . .

Prayer

Father,
let your Spirit come upon us with power
to fill us with your gifts.
May he make our hearts pleasing to you,
and ready to do your will.
We ask this through our Lord Jesus Christ, your Son,
who lives and reigns with you and the Holy Spirit,
one God, for ever and ever.

FRIDAY

Morning Prayer

READING   Acts 5:30-32

The God of our fathers has raised up Jesus whom you put to death, hanging
him on a tree. He whom God has exalted at his right hand as ruler and savior
is to bring repentance to Israel and forgiveness of sins. We testify to this. So
too does the Holy Spirit whom God has given to those that obey him.

RESPONSORY (VI F)

The Lord is risen *from* the tomb, * alleluia, al*le*luia.
— The Lord is risen *from* the tomb, * alleluia, al*le*luia.
He hung upon the *cross* for us,
— alleluia, al*le*luia.
Glory to the Father, and *to* the Son, * and to the Ho*ly* Spirit.
— The Lord is risen *from* the tomb, * alleluia, al*le*luia.

CANTICLE OF ZECHARIAH

Ant.   Jesus Christ died and is risen from the dead. † Now he lives for
                        ever at the right hand *of* the Father * where he intercedes for us,
                        al*le*luia.

INTERCESSIONS (VI F)

Honor and glory to God for ever and ever. May he make us rich in hope and in
the power of the *Holy* Spirit. * In peace, *let* us pray:
Lord, come to our aid and *save us.*
Almighty Father, you know that we are weak, even *when* we pray,
— give us your Spirit to *be* our advocate.
Send forth your Spirit, light of ra*di*ant joy,
— to take possession *of* our hearts.
Lord, we are the work *of* your hands,
— do not leave us in capitivity *to* our sins.

Help us to show reverence for those who are *weak* in faith,
— may we never be hard or impatient with them, but always treat *them* with love.

Our Father . . .

Prayer

Father,
in glorifying Christ and sending us your Spirit,
you open the way to eternal life.
May our sharing in this gift increase our love
and make our faith grow stronger.
Grant this through our Lord Jesus Christ, your Son,
who lives and reigns with you and the Holy Spirit,
one God, for ever and ever.

Evening Prayer

READING   Galatians 5:16, 22-23a, 25
Live in accord with the spirit and you will not yield to the cravings of the
flesh. The fruit of the spirit is love, joy, peace, patient endurance, kindness,
generosity, faith, mildness and chastity. Since we live by the spirit, let us
follow the spirit's lead.

RESPONSORY (VI F)
The Holy Spirit *is* the Paraclete, * alleluia, al*le*luia.
— The Holy Spirit *is* the Paraclete, * alleluia, al*le*luia.
He will teach *you* all things,
— alleluia, al*le*luia.
Glory to the Father, and *to* the Son, * and to the Ho*ly* Spirit.
— The Holy Spirit *is* the Paraclete, * alleluia, al*le*luia.

CANTICLE OF MARY
Ant.   Together they perse*vered* in prayer * with Mary, the mother of
              Jesus, al*le*luia.

INTERCESSIONS (VI F)
Let us praise and thank the Father, who has poured out the grace of the Spirit *on*
   all peoples. * Let us ask him for an ever greater share in his *Spi*rit, saying:
Lord, pour out the grace of the Holy Spirit throughout the *world.*
Lord, you gave us your chosen One as the light *of* all peoples,
— open the eyes of the blind, and lead from captivity those who *sit* in darkness.
You anointed Christ by the power of the Holy Spirit for the ministry *of* salvation,
— may he once more go about the world, doing good and *heal*ing all.
Send your Spirit, the light *of* all hearts,

— to strengthen the faith of *those* in doubt.
Send your Spirit, our *rest* in labor,
— to support the weary and the *brok*en-hearted.
Fulfill the hope of those *who* have died,
— so that they may rise again at the com*ing* of Christ.

Our Father . . .

Prayer

Father,
in glorifying Christ and sending us your Spirit,
you open the way to eternal life.
May our sharing in this gift increase our love
and make our faith grow stronger.
Grant this through our Lord Jesus Christ, your Son,
who lives and reigns with you and the Holy Spirit,
one God, for ever and ever.

SATURDAY

Morning Prayer

READING   Romans 14:7-9

None of us lives as his own master and none of us dies as his own master.
While we live we are responsible to the Lord, and when we die we die as his
servants. Both in life and death we are the Lord's. That is why Christ died
and came to life again, that he might be Lord of both the dead and the living.

RESPONSORY (VI F)
The Lord is risen *from* the tomb, * alleluia, al*le*luia.
— The Lord is risen *from* the tomb, * alleluia, al*le*luia.
He hung upon the *cross* for us,
— alleluia, al*le*luia.
Glory to the Father, and *to* the Son, * and to the Ho*ly* Spirit.
— The Lord is risen *from* the tomb, * alleluia, al*le*luia.

CANTICLE OF ZECHARIAH
Ant.   Know that I am *with* you always, * even until the end of the
                  world, al*le*luia.

INTERCESSIONS (VI F)

We have been baptized in the *Ho*ly Spirit. * With all who are baptized, let us give
   glory to the *Lord*, and ask him:

Lord Jesus, give us your Spirit to make us *holy.*

Send us your *Ho*ly Spirit,

— that we may acclaim you before the world as *Lord* and king.

Give us *a* sincere love,

— that the Church may be a *lov*ing family.

Give your life-giving grace to *all* the faithful,

— that they may receive with joy the gifts *of* the Spirit.

Give us the power of your *Ho*ly Spirit,

— to heal our wounds and *make* us strong.

Our Father . . .

Prayer

Almighty Father,
let the love we have celebrated in this Easter season
be put into practice in our daily lives.
We ask this through our Lord Jesus Christ, your Son,
who lives and reigns with you and the Holy Spirit,
one God, for ever and ever.

PENTECOST
Solemnity

Evening Prayer I

HYMN
Veni Creator Spiritus. Mode VIII (L.M.)

Veni Creator Spiritus,	Most Holy Spirit come this day
mentes tuorum visita;	And fill the hearts which you have made;
imple superna gratia	With your abundant gifts of grace
quæ tu creasti pectora.	Increase your presence in our souls.
Qui diceris Paraclitus,	For you are called our Advocate,
donum Dei altissimi,	Consoling Gift from God Most High,
fons vivus, ignis caritas,	True living Fount and Fire of Love,
et spiritalis unctio.	Eternal Source of happiness.
Tu septiformis munere,	You lavish graces sevenfold,
dextræ Dei tu digitus,	Like finger of Right Hand divine;
tu rite promissum Patris,	You are the Father's promised Gift
sermone ditans guttura.	To help us witness to the truth.
Accende lumen sensibus,	Instill your light into our minds
infunde amorem cordibus,	And flood our hearts with joy and love;
infirma nostri corporis	And with your strength which cannot fail,
virtute firmans perpeti.	Repair the weakness of our state.
Hostem repellas longius,	Our deadly foe keep far away,
pacemque dones protinus;	Bestow on us your wondrous peace;
Ductore sic te prævio,	Be with us ev'rywhere we go
Vitemus omne noxium.	To guard us from all sin and harm.
Per te sciamus da Patrem,	May we the Father know through you
Noscamus atque Filium,	And grow in knowledge of the Son,
Te utriusque Spiritum	And love you, Spirit of them both
Credamus omni tempore. Amen.	In time and in eternity. Amen.

PSALMODY

Ant. 1   On the *day* of Pentecost * they had all gathered together in one
place, *al*leluia.

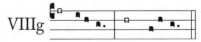

VIIIg

Psalm 113

Praise, O servants *of* the Lord, *	both now and for *ever*more!
praise the name *of* the Lord!	From the rising of the sun *to* its setting
May the name of the *Lord* be blessed *	* praised be the name *of* the Lord!

High above all nations *is* the Lord, *
  above the heav*ens* his glory.
Who is like the *Lord*, our God, * who
  has risen on high *to* his throne
yet stoops from the heights *to* look
  down, * to look down upon heav*en*
  and earth?
From the dust he lifts *up* the lowly, *
  from his misery he rais*es* the poor

to set him in the compan*y* of princes, *
  yes, with the princes *of* his people.
To the childless wife he *gives* a home *
  and gladdens her *heart* with children.
Glory to the Father, and *to* the Son, *
  and to the *Holy* Spirit:
as it was in the beginn*ing*, is now, * and
  will be for ev*er*. Amen.

Antiphon   On the *day* of Pentecost * they had all gathered together in one
             place, a*l*leluia.

Ant. 2   Tongues as of fire appeared before the apostles, † and the Holy
             Spirit came upon *each* of them, * al*le*luia.

IIA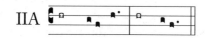

Psalm 147:1-11

Praise the Lord for he is good; †
  sing to our God for *he* is loving: * to
him our praise *is* due.
The Lord builds *up* Jerusalem * and
  brings back Isra*el's* exiles,
he heals the *bro*ken-hearted, * he binds
  up all *their* wounds.
He fixes the number *of* the stars; * he
  calls each one by *its* name.
Our Lord is great *and* almighty; * his
  wisdom can never *be* measured.
The Lord rais*es* the lowly; * he humbles
  the wicked to *the* dust.
O sing to the Lord, *giving* thanks; *
  sing psalms to our God with *the* harp.

He covers the heav*ens* with clouds; * he
  prepares the rain for *the* earth,
making mountains *sprout* with grass *
  and with plants to serve *man's* needs.
He provides the beasts *with* their food *
  and young ravens that call *up*on him.
His delight is *not* in horses * nor his
  pleasure in warri*ors'* strength.
The Lord delights in those *who* revere
  him, * in those who wait for *his* love.
Glory to the Father, and *to* the Son, *
  and to the Ho*ly* Spirit:
as it was in the beginn*ing*, is now, * and
  will be for ever. *A*men.

Antiphon   Tongues as of fire appeared before the apostles, † and the Holy
             Spirit came upon *each* of them, * al*le*luia.

Ant. 3   The Spirit who comes from *the* Father * will glorify me, al*le*luia.

Va

Canticle   Revelation 15:3-4

Mighty and wonderful are *your* works, * Lord God *Al*mighty!
Righteous and true are *your* ways, * O King of *the* nations!
Who would dare refuse *you* honor, * or the glory due your name, O Lord?
Since you alone *are* holy, * all nations

shall come and worship in *your* presence.
Your mighty deeds * are clear*ly* seen.
Glory to the Father, and to *the* Son, * and to the Ho*ly* Spirit:
as it was in the beginning, *is* now, * and will be for ever. *A*men.

Antiphon   The Spirit who comes from *the* Father * will glorify me, al*le*luia.

READING   Romans 8:11

If the Spirit of God who raised Jesus from the dead dwells in you, then he who raised Christ from the dead will bring your mortal bodies to life also, through his Spirit dwelling in you.

RESPONSORY (VI F)

The Holy Spirit *is* the Paraclete, * alleluia, al*le*luia.
— The Holy Spirit *is* the Paraclete, * alleluia, al*le*luia.
He will teach *you* all things,
—alleluia, al*le*luia.
Glory to the Father, and *to* the Son, * and to the Ho*ly* Spirit.
—The Holy Spirit *is* the Paraclete, * alleluia, al*le*luia.

CANTICLE OF MARY

Ant.   Come, Holy Spirit, † fill the hearts of *all* believers * and set them on fire with *your* love.
             Though they spoke many differnt languages, † you unit*ed* the nations * in professing the same faith, al*le*luia.

If

My soul ☩proclaims the greatness *of* the Lord, * my spirit rejoices in God *my* savior
for he has *looked* with favor * on his low*ly* servant.
From this day all *gen*erations * will call

me blessèd:
the Almighty has done great *things* for me, * and holy is *his* Name.
He has mercy on *those* who fear him * in every gen*er*ation.
He has shown the strength *of* his arm, *

he has scattered the proud in their *con*ceit.

He has cast down the mighty *from* their thrones, * and has lifted up *the* lowly.

He has filled the hungry *with* good things, * and the rich he has sent a*way* empty.

He has come to the help of his *ser*vant

Israel * for he has remembered his promise *of* mercy,

the promise he made *to* our fathers, * to Abraham and his children *for* ever.

Glory to the Father, and *to* the Son, * and to the Ho*ly* Spirit:

as it was in the begin*ning*, is now, * and will be for ever. *A*men.

Antiphon   Come, Holy Spirit, † fill the hearts of *all* believers * and set them on fire with *your* love.
Though they spoke many differnt languages, † you unit*ed* the nations * in professing the same faith, al*le*luia.

INTERCESSIONS (VI F)

When the days of Pentecost were complete, God sent the Holy Spirit upon *the* apostles. * As we celebrate this great feast with joy and faith, let *us* cry out:
Send forth your Spirit and make the whole world *new.*

In the beginning you created heaven and earth, and in the fullness of time you renewed all *things* in Christ,

— through your Spirit go on renewing the world with the gift *of* salvation.

You breathed the breath of life *into* Adam,

— send your Spirit into your Church to be its life and vigor, that it may bring new life to *the* whole world.

By the light of your Spirit, enlighten the world and dispel the darkness *of* our times,

— turn hatred into love, sorrow into joy and war into the peace we *so* desire.

Water flowed from the side of Christ as the fountain *of* your Spirit,

— may it flow over all the earth and *bring* forth goodness.

You bring life and glory to mankind through the *Ho*ly Spirit,

— through the Spirit lead the departed into the love and *joy* of heaven.

Our Father . . .

Prayer

Almighty and ever-living God,
you fulfilled the Easter promise
by sending us your Holy Spirit.
May that Spirit unite the races and nations on earth
to proclaim your glory.
Grant this through our Lord Jesus Christ, your Son,
who lives and reigns with you and the Holy Spirit,
one God, for ever and ever.

Morning Prayer

HYMN

Beata nobis gaudia. Mode I (L.M.)

Beata nobis gaudia
anni reduxit orbita,
cum Spiritus Paraclitus
effulsit in discipulos.

The cycle of the Christian year
Completes our happiness today,
As we recall with joy the morn
The Spirit came upon the Church.

Ignis vibrante lumine
linguæ figuram detulit,
verbis ut essent proflui,
et caritate fervidi.

The parted tongues of flaming fire
Enkindled each disciple's zeal,
And now would prompt his eager lips
In spreading far and wide the faith.

Linguis loquuntur omnium,
turbæ pavent gentilium:
musto madere deputant,
quos Spiritus repleverat.

Surprised, dumb-founded, willed with awe,
The Gentile crowd first lends an ear,
Then brands the speakers with rough scorn
As men unsteady with new wine.

Parata sunt hæc mystice,
Paschæ peracto tempore,
sacro dierum circulo,
quo lege fit remissio.

Just like the Old Law's Jubilee,
Remitting debts the fiftieth year,
So fifty days from Easter morn
The plenitute of grace descends.

Te nunc, Deus piissime,
vultu precamur cernuo:
illapsa nobis cælitus
largire dona Spiritus.

Most loving Father, hear our prayer,
As low before your throne we bow :
Send down your Holy Spirit's gifts
To fill our souls with strength and light.

Dudum sacrata pectora
tua replesti gratia:
dimitte nunc peccamina
et da quieta tempora.

As you once flooded loving hearts
With all the favors of your grace,
So now forgive us all our sins,
Bestow on us your gifts of peace.

Per te sciamus da Patrem
noscamus atque Filium,
te utriusque Spiritum
credamus omni tempore. Amen.

All glory to our Father, God,
And to our risen Lord, the Son,
Who with the Holy Spirit, reign,
Eternal pow'r beyond all time. Amen.

PSALMODY

Ant. 1   O Lord, how *good* and gentle * is your Spirit in us, *a*lleluia.

VIIIg

Psalm 63:2-9

O God, you are my God, for *you* I
long; * for you my *soul* is thirsting.

My body *pines* for you * like a dry,
weary land *with*out water.

So I gaze on you *in* the sanctuary * to
  see your strength *and* your glory.
For your love is bet*ter* than life, * my
  lips will *speak* your praise.
So I will bless you *all* my life, * in your
  name I will lift *up* my hands.
My soul shall be filled as *with* a banquet, * my mouth shall praise *you*
  with joy.
On my bed I re*mem*ber you. * On you I

muse *through* the night
for you have *been* my help; * in the
  shadow of your wings *I* rejoice.
My soul *clings* to you; * your right hand
  holds me fast.
Glory to the Father, and *to* the Son, *
  and to the *Ho*ly Spirit:
as it was in the begin*ning*, is now, * and
  will be for ev*er*. Amen.

Antiphon   O Lord, how *good* and gentle * is your Spirit in us, a*l*leluia.

Ant. 2   Let streams and rivers and all creatures that live *in* the waters *
           sing praise to God, al*le*luia.

IIA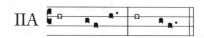

Canticle   Daniel 3:57-88; 56

Bless the Lord, all you works *of*
the Lord. * Praise and exalt him
above all *for*ever.
Angels of the Lord, *bless* the Lord, *
  You heavens, bless *the* Lord.
All you waters above the heavens, *bless*
  the Lord. * All you hosts of the Lord,
  bless *the* Lord.
Sun and moon, *bless* the Lord. * Stars of
  heaven, bless *the* Lord.
Every shower and dew, *bless* the Lord. *
  All you winds, bless *the* Lord.
Fire and heat, *bless* the Lord. * Cold
  and chill, bless *the* Lord.
Dew and rain, *bless* the Lord. * Frost
  and chill, bless *the* Lord.
Ice and snow, *bless* the Lord. * Nights
  and days, bless *the* Lord.
Light and darkness, *bless* the Lord. *
  Lightnings and clouds, bless *the*
  Lord.
Let the earth *bless* the Lord. * Praise
  and exalt him above all *for*ever.

Mountains and hills, *bless* the Lord. *
  Everything growing from the earth,
  bless *the* Lord.
You springs, *bless* the Lord. * Seas and
  rivers, bless *the* Lord.
You dolphins and all water creatures,
  bless the Lord. * All you birds of the
  air, bless *the* Lord.
All you beasts, wild and tame, *bless* the
  Lord. * You sons of men, bless *the*
  Lord.
O Israel, *bless* the Lord. * Praise and
  exalt him above all *for*ever.
Priests of the Lord, *bless* the Lord. *
  Servants of the Lord, bless *the* Lord.
Spirits and souls of the just, *bless* the
  Lord. * Holy men of humble heart,
  bless *the* Lord.
Hananiah, Azariah, Mishael, *bless* the
  Lord. * Praise and exalt him above all
  *for*ever.
Let us bless the Father, and the Son,
  and the *Ho*ly Spirit. * Let us praise

and exalt him above all *for*ever.
Bless*èd* are you in the firma*ment* of

heaven.* Praiseworthy and glorious
and exalted above all *for*ever.

Antiphon   Let streams and rivers and all creatures that live *in* the waters *
sing praise to God, al*le*luia.

Ant. 3   The apostles preached in differ*ent* tongues * and proclaimed the
great works of God, al*le*luia.

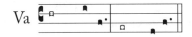

Psalm 149

Sing a new song to *the* Lord, *
his praise in the assembly of *the*
faithful.
Let Israel rejoice in *its* Maker, * let
Zion's sons exult in *their* king.
Let them praise his name *with* dancing
* and make music with timbrel *and*
harp.
For the Lord takes delight in *his*
people. * He crowns the poor with
sal*va*tion.
Let the faithful rejoice in *their* glory, *
shout for joy and take *their* rest.

Let the praise of God be on *their* lips *
and a two-edged sword in *their* hand,
to deal out vengeance to *the* nations *
and punishment on all *the* peoples;
to bind their kings *in* chains * and their
nobles in fetters *of* iron;
to carry out the sentence pre-*or*dained: *
this honor is for all *his* faithful.
Glory to the Father, and to *the* Son, *
and to the Ho*ly* Spirit:
as it was in the beginning, *is* now, * and
will be for ever. *A*men.

Antiphon   The apostles preached in differ*ent* tongues * and proclaimed the
great works of God, al*le*luia.

READING   Acts 5:30-32
The God of our fathers has raised up Jesus whom you put to death, hanging
him on a tree. He whom God has exalted at his right hand as ruler and savior
is to bring repentance to Israel and forgiveness of sins. We testify to this. So
too does the Holy Spirit whom God has given to those that obey him.

RESPONSORY (VI F)
All were filled with the *Ho*ly Spirit, * alleluia, al*le*luia.
—All were filled with the *Ho*ly Spirit, * alleluia, al*le*luia.
They be*gan* to speak,
—alleluia, al*le*luia.
Glory to the Father, and *to* the Son, * and to the Ho*ly* Spirit.
—All were filled with the *Ho*ly Spirit, * alleluia, al*le*luia.

CANTICLE OF ZECHARIAH

Ant.   Receive the Holy Spirit; † the sins of those *you* forgive * shall be
                        forgiven, al*le*luia.

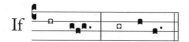

B lessèd ✠ be the Lord, the *God* of
   Israel; * he has come to his people
and set *them* free.
He has raised up for us a *mighty* savior,
   * born of the house of his ser*vant*
   David.
Through his holy prophets he promised
   of old † that he would save us *from*
   our enemies, * from the hands of all
   who hate us.
He promised to show mercy *to* our
   fathers * and to remember his ho*ly*
   covenant.
This was the oath he swore to our
   *fath*er Abraham: * to set us free from
   the hands of *our* enemies,
free to worship him without fear, † holy
   and righteous *in* his sight * all the

days of *our* life.
You, my child, shall be called the
   prophet *of* the Most High; * for you
   will go before the Lord to prepare *his*
   way,
to give his people knowledge *of* salvation * by the forgiveness of *their* sins.
In the tender compassion *of* our God *
   the dawn from on high shall break
   *up*on us,
to shine on those who dwell in darkness
   and the sha*dow* of death, * and to
   guide our feet into the way *of* peace.
Glory to the Father, and *to* the Son, *
   and to the Ho*ly* Spirit:
as it was in the begin*ning*, is now, * and
   will be for ever. *A*men.

Antiphon   Receive the Holy Spirit; † the sins of those *you* forgive * shall be
                  forgiven, al*le*luia.

INTERCESSIONS (VI F)

Christ the Lord has gathered his Church in unity *through* the Spirit. * With sure
   hope *let* us ask him:
Lord, make the whole world *new.*
Lord Jesus, when you were raised high upon the cross, streams of living water
   flowed from your *pierc*èd side,
— pour out on us your life-*giving* Spirit.
In glory at the right hand of God, you gave the Gift of the Father to *your*
   disciples,
— send forth your Spirit to re*new* the world.
You gave your Spirit to the apostles, with the power *to* forgive sins,
— destroy all sin *in* the world.
You promised us the Holy Spirit, to teach us all things and remind us of all *you*
   had said,
— send us your Spirit to enlighten our *minds* in faith.

You promised to send the Spirit of truth, to bear witness *to* yourself,
— send forth your Spirit to make us your *faith*ful witnesses.

Our Father . . .

Prayer

God our Father,
let the Spirit you sent on your church
to begin the teaching of the gospel
continue to work in the world
through the hearts of all who believe.
We ask this through our Lord Jesus Christ, your Son,
who lives and reigns with you and the Holy Spirit,
one God, for ever and ever.

Evening Prayer II

HYMN, as in Evening Prayer I, 513.

PSALMODY

Ant. 1   The Spirit *of* the Lord * has filled the whole world, *a*lleluia.

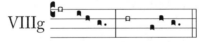

VIIIg

Psalm 110:1-5, 7

The Lord's revelation to my
Master: † "Sit *on* my right: * your
foes I will put be*neath* your feet."
The Lord will wield from Zion † your
scep*ter* of power: * rule in the midst
of *all* your foes.
A prince from the day of your birth †
on the *ho*ly mountains; * from the
womb before the dawn *I* begot you.
The Lord has sworn an oath he will not
change. † "You are a *priest* for ever, *

a priest like Melchize*dek* of old."
The Master standing *at* your right hand
* will shatter kings in the day of *his*
great wrath.
He shall drink from the stream *by* the
wayside * and therefore he shall lift
up his head.
Glory to the Father, and *to* the Son, *
and to the *Ho*ly Spirit:
as it was in the begin*ning*, is now, * and
will be for ev*er*. Amen.

Antiphon   The Spirit *of* the Lord * has filled the whole world, *a*lleluia.

Ant. 2   Send us your strength, O God, † from your holy temple *in*
              Jerusalem, * and perfect your work in us, al*le*luia.

IIA

Psalm 114

When Israel came *forth* from
    Egypt, * Jacob's sons from an
ali*en* people,
Judah became *the* Lord's temple, * Israel
    became *his* kingdom.
The sea fled *at* the sight: * the Jordan
    turned back on *its* course,
the mountains *leapt* like rams * and the
    hills like year*ling* sheep.
Why was it, sea, *that* you fled, * that
    you turned back, Jordan, on *your*

course?
Mountains, that you *leapt* like rams, *
    hills, like year*ling* sheep?
Tremble, O earth, be*fore* the Lord, * in
    the presence of the God *of* Jacob,
who turns the rock in*to* a pool * and
    flint into a spring *of* water.
Glory to the Father, and *to* the Son, *
    and to the Ho*ly* Spirit:
as it was in the begin*ning*, is now, * and
    will be for ever. *A*men.

Antiphon   Send us your strength, O God, † from your holy temple *in*
             Jerusalem, * and perfect your work in us, al*le*luia.

Ant. 3   All were filled with the Holy Spirit, † and they began *to* speak, *
             alleluia, alleluia.

** al- le- lu- ia, al- le- lu- ia.

*Al- le- lu- ia.   ** al- le- lu- ia, al- le - lu- ia.

Canticle   See Revelation 19:1-7

Salvation, glory, and power to *our* God:
    * Alleluia.
his judgments are hon*est* and true.
** Alleluia, alleluia.

Sing praise to our God, all you *his* servants,
* Alleluia.
all who worship him reverently, *great* and small.
** Alleluia, alleluia.

The Lord our all-powerful God *is* King;
* Alleluia.
let us rejoice, sing praise, and *give* him glory.
** Alleluia, alleluia.

The wedding feast of the Lamb has *be*gun,
* Alleluia.
and his bride is pre*pared* to welcome him.
** Alleluia, alleluia.

Glory to the Father, and to the Son, †
and to the Ho*ly* Spirit.
* Alleluia.
As it was in the beginning, is now, †
and will be for ev*er*. Amen.
** Alleluia, alleluia.

Antiphon   All were filled with the Holy Spirit, † and they began *to* speak, *
                alleluia, alleluia.

READING   Ephesians 4:3-6
   Make every effort to preserve the unity which has the Spirit as its origin and
   peace as its binding force. There is but one body and one Spirit, just as there
   is but one hope given all of you by your call. There is one Lord, one faith, one
   baptism; one God and Father of all, who is over all, and works through all,
   and is in all.

RESPONSORY (VI F)
The Spirit of the Lord has filled *the* whole world, * alleluia, al*le*luia.
— The Spirit of the Lord has filled *the* whole world, * alleluia, al*le*luia.
He sustains all creation and knows every word *that* is spoken,
— alleluia, al*le*luia.
Glory to the Father, and *to* the Son, * and to the Ho*ly* Spirit.
— The Spirit of the Lord has filled *the* whole world, * alleluia, al*le*luia.

CANTICLE OF MARY

Ant.   Today we celebrate the feast of Pentecost, alleluia; † on this day the Holy Spirit appeared before the apostles in *ton*gues of fire * and gave them his spirit*ual* gifts.

He sent them out to preach to the whole world, † and to proclaim that all *who* believe * and are baptized shall be saved, al*le*luia.

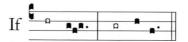

My soul ✠ proclaims the greatness *of* the Lord, * my spirit rejoices in God *my* savior

for he has *looked* with favor * on his low*ly* servant.

From this day all *gen*erations * will call *me* blessèd:

the Almighty has done great *things* for me, * and holy is *his* Name.

He has mercy on *those* who fear him * in every gen*er*ation.

He has shown the strength *of* his arm, * he has scattered the proud in their *con*ceit.

He has cast down the mighty *from* their thrones, * and has lifted up *the* lowly.

He has filled the hungry *with* good things, * and the rich he has sent a*way* empty.

He has come to the help of his *ser*vant Israel * for he has remembered his promise *of* mercy,

the promise he made *to* our fathers, * to Abraham and his children *for* ever.

Glory to the Father, and *to* the Son, * and to the Ho*ly* Spirit:

as it was in the begin*ning*, is now, * and will be for ever. *A*men.

Antiphon   Today we celebrate the feast of Pentecost, alleluia; † on this day the Holy Spirit appeared before the apostles in *ton*gues of fire * and gave them his spirit*ual* gifts.

He sent them out to preach to the whole world, † and to proclaim that all *who* believe * and are baptized shall be saved, al*le*luia.

INTERCESSIONS (VI F)

God the Father has gathered his Church in uni*ty* through Christ. * With joy in our hearts *let* us ask him:

Send your Holy Spirit into the *Church.*

You desire the unity of all Christians through one baptism *in* the Spirit,

— make all who believe one in *heart* and soul.

You desire the whole world to be filled *with* the Spirit,

— help all mankind to build a world of jus*tice* and peace.

Lord God, Father of all mankind, you desire to gather together your scattered children in uni*ty* of faith,

— enlighten the world by the grace of the *Ho*ly Spirit.

Through the Spirit you make *all* things new,
— heal the sick, comfort the distressed, give salva*tion* to all.
Through the Spirit you raised your Son *from* the dead,
— raise up the bodies of the dead into ever*last*ing life.

Our Father . . .

Prayer

God our Father,
let the Spirit you sent on your church
to begin the teaching of the gospel
continue to work in the world
through the hearts of all who believe.
We ask this through our Lord Jesus Christ, your Son,
who lives and reigns with you and the Holy Spirit,
one God, for ever and ever.

The following dismissal is said:

Go in the peace of Christ, al- le- lu- ia, al- le- lu- ia.

Thanks be to God, al- le- lu- ia, al- le- lu- ia.

The Easter Season ends with the conclusion of Evening Prayer.

Proper of Seasons
Ordinary Time

First Week in Ordinary Time   Psalter, Week I

The feast of the Baptism of the Lord takes the place of the First Sunday in Ordinary Time.

Gospel Canticle Antiphon (I f)

Year A   The Kingdom of heaven is like a merchant in search *of* fine pearls; * when he found one of great value, he sold everything he had *and* bought it.

Year B   When those men saw the signs Jesus per*formed*, they said: * Surely this is the Prophet who is to come into *the* world.

Year C   Ask and you will receive, seek and *you* will find, * knock and the door will be opened *to* you.

Prayer   God our Father and protector,
without you nothing is holy,
nothing has value.
Guide us to everlasting life
by helping us to use wisely
the blessings you have given to the world.
We ask this through our Lord Jesus Christ, your Son,
who lives and reigns with you and the Holy Spirit,
one God, for ever and ever.

2.   Second Week in Ordinary Time   Psalter, Week II

Gospel Canticle Antiphon (VII d)

Year A   Behold the *Lamb* of God, * behold him who takes away the sins of *the* world.

Year B   The disciples came to see where *Je*sus lived, * and all that day they stayed *with* him.

Year C   There was a wedding in Ca*na* of Galilee, * and Jesus was there with Mary *his* mother.

Prayer   Father of heaven and earth,
hear our prayers,
and show us the way to peace in the world.
Grant this through our Lord Jesus Christ, your Son,
who lives and reigns with you and the Holy Spirit,
one God, for ever and ever.

3.   Third Week in Ordinary Time   Psalter, Week III

Gospel Canticle Antiphon (I f)

Year A   Jesus preached the Gospel *of* the kingdom * and cured those who were in need *of* healing.

Year B   Come, follow me, *says* the Lord; * I will make you fishers *of* men.

Year C   The Spirit of the Lord *rests* upon me; * he has sent me to preach the good news to *the* poor.

Prayer   All-powerful and ever-living God,
direct your love that is within us,
that our efforts in the name of your Son
may bring mankind to unity and peace.
We ask this through our Lord Jesus Christ, your Son,
who lives and reigns with you and the Holy Spirit,
one God, for ever and ever.

4.   Fourth Week in Ordinary Time   Psalter, Week IV

Gospel Canticle Antiphon (VII d)

Year A   When Jesus saw the crowds, he went up the mountain; † his disciples came and gath*ered* around him, * and he opened his mouth and began *to* teach them.

Year B   Everyone heard with amazement what *Jesus* taught,* for he spoke with such *authority.*

Year C   They all marveled *at* the words * that came forth from the mouth *of* God.

Prayer   Lord our God,
help us to love you with all our hearts
and to love all men as you love them.
Grant this through our Lord Jesus Christ, your Son,
who lives and reigns with you and the Holy Spirit,
one God, for ever and ever.

Fifth Week in Ordinary Time   Psalter, Week I

Gospel Canticle Antiphon (I f)

Year A   You are the light of the world. † Let your light shine *be*fore men,
          * that they may see your good works and give glory to your
          heaven*ly* Father.

Year B   Jesus rose early in the morning and went out to a *place* of soli-
          tude, * and there *he* prayed.

Year C   Master, we have worked all night and *have* caught nothing; * but
          if you say so, I will lower the nets *a*gain.

Prayer   Father,
          watch over your family
          and keep us safe in your care,
          for all our hope is in you.
          Grant this through our Lord Jesus Christ, your Son,
          who lives and reigns with you and the Holy Spirit,
          one God, for ever and ever.

6.   Sixth Week in Ordinary Time   Psalter, Week II

Gospel Canticle Antiphon (VII d)

Year A   If you are bringing your gift to the altar, † and there you remem-
          ber that your brother has some*thing* against you, * leave your gift
          in front of *the* altar;
          go at once and make peace *with* your brother, * and then come
          back and offer *your* gift.

Year B   Lord, if you will, you can *make* me clean. * And Jesus said: I do
          will it; you are *made* clean.

Year C   Blessèd are you who are poor, for the kingdom of *God* is yours. *
          And blessèd are you who hunger now; you shall *be* satisfied.

Prayer   God our Father,
          you have promised to remain for ever
          with those who do what is just and right.
          Help us to live in your presence.
          We ask this through our Lord Jesus Christ, your Son,
          who lives and reigns with you and the Holy Spirit,
          one God, for ever and ever.

Seventh Week in Ordinary Time   Psalter, Week III

Gospel Canticle Antiphon (I f)

Year A   If you want to be true children of your heavenly Father, † then you must pray for *those* who persecute you * and speak all kinds of evil against you, says *the* Lord.

Year B   The paralyzed man picked up the bed on which he was lying, † and gave *praise* to God; * all who saw it gave glory *to* God.

Year C   Do not judge others, and you will *not* be judged, * for as you have judged them, so God will *judge* you.

Prayer   Father,
keep before us the wisdom and love
you have revealed in your Son.
Help us to be like him
in word and deed,
for he lives and reigns with you and the Holy Spirit,
one God, for ever and ever.

Eighth Week in Ordinary Time   Psalter, Week IV

Gospel Canticle Antiphon (VII d)

Year A   Seek first the kingdom of God *and* his justice, * and all the rest will be given to you as well, al*le*luia.

Year B   No one pours new wine in*to* old wineskins; * new wine should be put in *new* wineskins.

Year C   A good tree cannot *bear* bad fruit, * nor a bad tree *good* fruit.

Prayer   Lord,
guide the course of world events
and give your Church the joy and peace
of serving you in freedom.
We ask this through our Lord Jesus Christ, your Son,
who lives and reigns with you and the Holy Spirit,
one God, for ever and ever.

Ninth Week in Ordinary Time   Psalter, Week I

Gospel Canticle Antiphon (I f)

Year A   Not everyone who says: "Lord, Lord," will enter the kingdom of heaven, † but the one who does the will of my heave*n*ly Father * will certainly en*ter* it.

Year B   The sabbath was *made* for man, * not man for *the* sabbath.

Year C   Lord, I am not worthy to have you en*ter* my house; * just say the word and my servant will *be* healed.

Prayer   Father,
your love never fails.
Hear our call.
Keep us from danger
and provide for all our needs.
Grant this through our Lord Jesus Christ, your Son,
who lives and reigns with you and the Holy Spirit,
one God, for ever and ever.

10.   Tenth Week in Ordinary Time   Psalter, Week II

Gospel Canticle Antiphon (VII d)

Year A   I desire mercy *and* not sacrifice. * I did not come to call the virtuous *but* sinners.

Year B   Whoever does the *will* of God, * he is my brother, and my sister, and *my* mother.

Year C   A great prophet has risen *up* among us * and God has visited *his* people.

Prayer   God of wisdom and love,
source of all good,
send your Spirit to teach us your truth
and guide our actions
in your way of peace.
We ask this through our Lord Jesus Christ, your Son,
who lives and reigns with you and the Holy Spirit,
one God, for ever and ever.

11.	Eleventh Week in Ordinary Time	Psalter, Week III

Gospel Canticle Antiphon (I f)

Year A
Go, preach the good news *of* the kingdom; * freely you have received, freely give, al*le*luia.

Year B
The kingdom of heaven is like a mustard seed, † the smallest *of* all seeds; * yet when full-grown it is the largest *of* shrubs.

Year C
Jesus said *to* the woman: * Your faith has saved you, go *in* peace.

Prayer
Almighty God,
our hope and our strength,
without you we falter.
Help us to follow Christ
and to live according to your will.
We ask this through our Lord Jesus Christ, your Son,
who lives and reigns with you and the Holy Spirit,
one God, for ever and ever.

12.	Twelfth Week in Ordinary Time	Psalter, Week IV

Gospel Canticle Antiphon (VII d)

Year A
If anyone bears witness to me *be*fore men, * I will praise him in the presence of *my* Father.

Year B
Help us, O Lord, for *we* are troubled; * give the command, O God, and bring *us* peace.

Year C
Whoever wishes to come after me must de*ny* himself, * take up his cross and fol*low* me.

Prayer
Father,
guide and protector of your people,
grant us an unfailing respect for your name,
and keep us always in your love.
Grant this through our Lord Jesus Christ, your Son,
who lives and reigns with you and the Holy Spirit,
one God, for ever and ever.

13.	Thirteenth Week in Ordinary Time	Psalter, Week I

Gospel Canticle Antiphon (I f)

Year A   Those who welcome you are wel*com*ing me, * and those who welcome me are welcoming him *who* sent me.

Year B   Jesus, turning, saw the wo*man* and said: * Take courage, daughter; your faith has saved you, al*le*luia.

Year C   The Son of Man did not come *to* condemn men * but *to* save them.

Prayer   Father,
you call your children
to walk in the light of Christ.
Free us from darkness
and keep us in the radiance of your truth.
We ask this through our Lord Jesus Christ, your Son,
who lives and reigns with you and the Holy Spirit,
one God, for ever and ever.

14.	Fourteenth Week in Ordinary Time	Psalter, Week II

Gospel Canticle Antiphon (VII d)

Year A   My yoke is easy and my bur*den* is light, * says *the* Lord.

Year B   Many who heard the teaching of Jesus were astonished and said: † where did he *get* all this? * Is he not the carpenter, the son *of* Mary?

Year C   So great a harvest, and so few to gather it in; † pray to the Lord *of* the harvest; * beg him to send out laborers for *his* harvest.

Prayer   Father,
through the obedience of Jesus,
your servant and your Son,
you raised a fallen world.
Free us from sin
and bring us the joy that lasts for ever.
We ask this through our Lord Jesus Christ, your Son,
who lives and reigns with you and the Holy Spirit,
one God, for ever and ever.

15.	Fifteenth Week in Ordinary Time	Psalter, Week III

Gospel Canticle Antiphon (I f)

Year A The seed is the word of God; the sow*er* is Christ; *
all who listen to his words will live *for* ever.

Year B The disciples went out and *preached* repentance. * They anointed
many sick people with oil *and* healed them.

Year C Teacher, what is the greatest commandment *in* the law? * Jesus
said to him: You shall love the Lord your God with your *whole*
heart.

Prayer God our Father,
your light of truth
guides us to the way of Christ.
May all who follow him
reject what is contrary to the Gospel.
We ask this through our Lord Jesus Christ, your Son,
who lives and reigns with you and the Holy Spirit,
one God, for ever and ever.

16.	Sixteenth Week in Ordinary Time	Psalter, Week IV

Gospel Canticle Antiphon (VII d)

Year A The kingdom of heaven is like yeast † which a woman took and
kneaded into three mea*sures* of flour * until all the dough *had*
risen.

Year B He saw the great crowd and had pi*ty* on them, * for they were
like sheep without *a* shepherd.

Year C Mary has chosen the *bet*ter part, * and it shall not be taken *from*
her.

Prayer Lord, be merciful to your people.
Fill us with your gifts
and make us always eager to serve you
in faith, hope, and love.
Grant this through our Lord Jesus Christ, your Son,
who lives and reigns with you and the Holy Spirit,
one God, for ever and ever.

Gospel Canticle Antiphon (I f)

Year A   The Kingdom of heaven is like a merchant in search of fine
pearls; † when he found one *of* great value, * he sold everything
he had *and* bought it.

Year B   When those men saw the signs Jesus per*formed*, they said: *
Surely this is the Prophet who is to come into *the* world.

Year C   Ask and you will receive, seek and *you* will find, * knock and the
door will be opened *to* you.

Prayer   God our Father and protector,
without you nothing is holy,
nothing has value.
Guide us to everlasting life
by helping us to use wisely
the blessings you have given to the world.
We ask this through our Lord Jesus Christ, your Son,
who lives and reigns with you and the Holy Spirit,
one God, for ever and ever.

18.   Eighteenth Week in Ordinary Time   Psalter, Week II

Gospel Canticle Antiphon (VII d)

Year A   A crowd gathered around Jesus, and they had nothing to eat. †
He called his disci*ples* and said: * I have compassion on all *these*
people.

Year B   Do not work for food *that* will perish, * but for food that lasts to
eter*nal* life.

Year C   Brothers, if you desire to be *tru*ly rich, * set your heart on *true*
riches.

Prayer   Father of everlasting goodness,
our origin and guide,
be close to us
and hear the prayers of all who praise you.
Forgive our sins and restore us to life.
Keep us safe in your love.
Grant this through our Lord Jesus Christ, your Son,
who lives and reigns with you and the Holy Spirit,
one God, for ever and ever.

19

Nineteenth Week in Ordinary Time   Psalter, Week III

Gospel Canticle Antiphon (I f)

Year A   Lord, bid me walk across the waters. † Jesus reached out to take hold of Pet*er*, and said: * O man of little faith, why did *you* falter?

Year B   Amen, amen I *say* to you: * Whoever believes in me will live for ever, al*le*luia.

Year C   Where your treasure is, there *is* your heart, * says *the* Lord.

Prayer   Almighty and ever-living God,
your Spirit made us your children,
confident to call you Father.
Increase your Spirit within us
and bring us to our promised inheritance.
Grant this through our Lord Jesus Christ, your Son,
who lives and reigns with you and the Holy Spirit,
one God, for ever and ever.

Twentieth Week in Ordinary Time   Psalter, Week IV

Gospel Canticle Antiphon (VII d)

Year A   Woman, great *is* your faith; * what you ask, I give *to* you.

Year B   I am the living bread come *down* from heaven. * Anyone who eats this bread will live for ever, al*le*luia.

Year C   I have come to cast fire up*on* the earth; * how I long to see the flame *leap* up!

Prayer   God our Father,
may we love you in all things and above all things
and reach the joy you have prepared for us
beyond all our imagining.
We ask this through our Lord Jesus Christ, your Son,
who lives and reigns with you and the Holy Spirit,
one God, for ever and ever.

Twenty-First Week in Ordinary Time   Psalter, Week I

Gospel Canticle Antiphon (I f)

Year A You are Christ, the Son of the *living* God. * Blessèd are you, Simon, son *of* John.

Year B Lord, to whom *shall* we go? * You have the words of eter*nal* life. We believe and we *are* convinced * that you are Christ, the Son of God, al*le*luia.

Year C Many shall come from the east and the west, † and they shall sit down with Abraham and I*saac* and Jacob * in the kingdom *of* heaven.

Prayer Father,
help us to seek the values
that will bring us lasting joy in this changing world.
In our desire for what you promise
make us one in mind and heart.
Grant this through our Lord Jesus Christ, your Son,
who lives and reigns with you and the Holy Spirit,
one God, for ever and ever.

22. Twenty-Second Week in Ordinary Time   Psalter, Week II

Gospel Canticle Antiphon (VII d)

Year A Of what use is it to a man to gain *the* whole world, * if he pays for it by losing *his* soul?

Year B Listen and *un*derstand * the instructions the Lord has given *to* you.

Year C When you are invited to a wedding, † go to the lowest place, † so that the one who invited you can say: † Friend, *go* up higher. * Then you will be honored in the eyes of all who are at table *with* you.

Prayer Almighty God,
every good thing comes from you.
Fill our hearts with love for you,
increase our faith,
and by your constant care
protect the good you have given us.
We ask this through our Lord Jesus Christ, your Son,
who lives and reigns with you and the Holy Spirit,
one God, for ever and ever.

23

Twenty-Third Week in Ordinary Time   Psalter, Week III

Gospel Canticle Antiphon (I f)

Year A   Where two or three are gathered together *in* my name, * I am there among them, says *the* Lord.

Year B   He has done *all* things well: * he has made the deaf hear and the mute speak, al*le*luia.

Year C   Whoever refuses to take up his cross and *fo*llow me * cannot be my disciple, says *the* Lord.

Prayer   God our Father,
you redeem us
and make us your children in Christ.
Look upon us,
give us true freedom
and bring us to the inheritance you promised.
Grant this through our Lord Jesus Christ, your Son,
who lives and reigns with you and the Holy Spirit,
one God, for ever and ever.

Twenty-Fourth Week in Ordinary Time   Psalter, Week IV

Gospel Canticle Antiphon (VII d)

Year A   Jesus said to Peter: † I do not tell you to forgive only *seven* times, * but seventy *times* seven.

Year B   He who loses his life because of me and for the sake *of* the Gospel * shall save it, says *the* Lord.

Year C   I say to you: there is great rejoicing among the an*gels* of God * over one repent*ant* sinner.

Prayer   Almighty God,
our creator and guide,
may we serve you with all our heart
and know your forgiveness in our lives.
We ask this through our Lord Jesus Christ, your Son,
who lives and reigns with you and the Holy Spirit,
one God, for ever and ever.

Twenty-Fifth Week in Ordinary Time   Psalter, Week I

Gospel Canticle Antiphon (I f)

Year A   Go in*to* my vineyard, * and I will pay you a *just* wage.

Year B   The greatest among you will be your servant, *says* the Lord; * for
            I will lift up in glory the man who humbles *him*self.

Year C   No servant can o*bey* two masters: * you cannot serve God and the
            love of money at the *same* time.

Prayer   Father,
            guide us, as you guide creation
            according to your law of love.
            May we love one another
            and come to perfection
            in the eternal life prepared for us.
            Grant this through our Lord Jesus Christ, your Son,
            who lives and reigns with you and the Holy Spirit,
            one God, for ever and ever.

26.   Twenty-Sixth Week in Ordinary Time   Psalter, Week II

Gospel Canticle Antiphon (VII d)

Year A   Not everyone who says: "Lord, Lord," † will enter the king*dom* of
            heaven, * but the one who does the will of my heavenly Father,
            al*le*luia.

Year B   Whoever gives you a cup of water in my name † because you are
            a follow*er* of Christ, * shall not go unrewarded, says *the* Lord.

Year C   Son, remember the good things you received *in* your lifetime *
            and the bad things Lazarus received *in* his.

Prayer   Father,
            you show your almighty power
            in your mercy and forgiveness.
            Continue to fill us with your gifts of love.
            Help us to hurry toward the eternal life you promise
            and come to share in the joys of your kingdom.
            Grant this through our Lord Jesus Christ, your Son,
            who lives and reigns with you and the Holy Spirit,
            one God, for ever and ever.

Twenty-Seventh Week in Ordinary Time   Psalter, Week III

Gospel Canticle Antiphon (I f)

Year A   He will bring those evil men to an *evil* end * and entrust his vineyard to other tenants who will give him the harvest at the pro*per* season.

Year B   Let the little children *come* to me, * for they are at home in my Fath*er's* kingdom.

Year C   Tell yourselves: We are *use*less servants, * for we did only what we should *have* done.

Prayer   Father,
your love for us
surpasses all our hopes and desires.
Forgive our failings,
keep us in your peace
and lead us in the way of salvation.
We ask this through our Lord Jesus Christ, your Son,
who lives and reigns with you and the Holy Spirit,
one God, for ever and ever.

28.   Twenty-Eighth Week in Ordinary Time   Psalter, Week IV

Gospel Canticle Antiphon (VII d)

Year A   A certain man held a banquet and in*vit*ed many; * when it was time for the banquet to *be*gin,
he sent his servant to *call* his guests, * for now the feast was ready, al*le*luia.

Year B   You have left everything to *fo*llow me; * you will have it all returned a hundredfold and will inherit eter*nal* life.

Year C   One of them, realizing that he *had* been cured, * returned praising God in a loud voice, al*le*luia.

Prayer   Lord,
our help and guide,
make your love the foundation of our lives.
May our love for you express itself
in our eagerness to do good for others.
Grant this through our Lord Jesus Christ, your Son,
who lives and reigns with you and the Holy Spirit,
one God, for ever and ever.

Twenty-Ninth Week in Ordinary Time

Gospel Canticle Antiphon (I f)

Year A | Give to Caesar what be*longs* to Caesar, * but to God what belongs to God, al*l*eluia.

Year B | The Son of Man did not come to be served *but* to serve, * and to give his life as a ransom *for* many.

Year C | When the Son of Man *comes* to earth, * do you think he will find faith in *men's* hearts?

Prayer | Almighty and ever-living God,
our source of power and inspiration,
give us strength and joy
in serving you as followers of Christ,
who lives and reigns with you and the Holy Spirit,
one God, for ever and ever.

30. | Thirtieth Week in Ordinary Time | Psalter, Week II

Gospel Canticle Antiphon (VII d)

Year A | Teacher, what is the greatest commandment in the law? † Jesus *said* to him: * You shall love the Lord your God with your whole heart, al*l*eluia.

Year B | Son of David, have pity on me. † What do you want me to *do* for you? * Lord, restore *my* sight.

Year C | The publican went home at peace with God, † for everyone who exalts himself *shall* be humbled, * and whoever humbles himself shall be *ex*alted.

Prayer | Almighty and ever-living God,
strengthen our faith, hope, and love.
May we do with loving hearts
what you ask of us
and come to share the life you promise.
We ask this through our Lord Jesus Christ, your Son,
who lives and reigns with you and the Holy Spirit,
one God, for ever and ever.

31

Thirty-First Week in Ordinary Time   Psalter, Week III

Gospel Canticle Antiphon (I f)

Year A   You have one teacher, and he *is* in heaven: * Christ *your* Lord.

Year B   Love the Lord your God with all your heart † and love your
          neighbor *as* yourself. * There is no greater commandment *than*
          these.

Year C   The Son of Man came to seek out *and* to save * those who *were*
          lost.

Prayer   God of power and mercy,
          only with your help
          can we offer you fitting service and praise.
          May we live the faith we profess
          and trust your promise of eternal life.
          Grant this through our Lord Jesus Christ, your Son,
          who lives and reigns with you and the Holy Spirit,
          one God, for ever and ever.

32

Thirty-second Week in Ordinary Time   Psalter, Week IV

Gospel Canticle Antiphon (VII d)

Year A   At midnight a cry was heard: † Behold, the *Bride*groom comes, *
          go out *to* meet him.

Year B   That poor widow gave *more* than everyone,* because in her
          poverty she gave all *she* had.

Year C   He is not a God of the dead, but *of* the living: * for to him all
          things are alive, all*e*luia.

Prayer   God of power and mercy,
          protect us from all harm.
          Give us freedom of spirit
          and health in mind and body
          to do your work on earth.
          We ask this through our Lord Jesus Christ, your Son,
          who lives and reigns with you and the Holy Spirit,
          one God, for ever and ever.

Gospel Canticle Antiphon (I f)

Year A   Well done, my good and faithful servant, † you have been trustworthy *in* small things. * Now share your mas*ter's* joy.

Year B   They will see the *Son* of Man * coming in the clouds with great glory *and* majesty.

Year C   By your trusting accept*ance* of trials, * you will gain your life, says *the* Lord.

Prayer   Father of all that is good,
keep us faithful in serving you,
for to serve you is our lasting joy.
We ask this through our Lord Jesus Christ, your Son,
who lives and reigns with you and the Holy Spirit,
one God, for ever and ever.

TRINITY SUNDAY

Evening Prayer I

HYMN
Imménsa et una Trinitas. Mode I (L.M.)

Imménsa et una Trinitas,	Almighty Trinity in One,
cuius potéstas omnia facit	Whose sov'reign pow'r all things has made,
regitque tempora	You rule the ages and the world,
et exstat ante sæcula	Before all time You reigned supreme.
Tu sola pleno sufficis tibi	Full plenitude of joy is yours,
beata gaudio;	Alone and perfect, needing naught,
tu pure, simplex,	Unsullied, Simple, Purity,
povida cælos et orbem contines.	All things are held within your sway.
Omnis, Pater, fons gratiæ,	O Father, fount of every grace,
Lumen paternae gloriæ,	O Father's glory, God the Son,
Sancte utriusque Spiritus	O Holy Spirit of them both,
interminata caritas,	Unending source of love divine.
Ex te suprema origine,	To you, the Origin serene,
Trias benigna, profluit creata	The Godhead one in Persons three,
quicquid sustinet,	All things created owe their form
quicquid decore perficit.	And every beauty they contain.
Quos et corona muneras	Your children whom you have endowed
adoptionis intimae,	With sonship and adoption's gift,
nos templa fac nitentia	Beg you to make them temples fair
tibi placere iugiter.	For your indwelling Spirit's joy.
O viva lux, nos angelis	O living Light, grant us the grace
da iungi in aula cælicia,	To join the angels round your throne,
ut grati amoris laudibus	That praising your with grateful love,
te concinamus perpetim. Amen.	Creation's hymn may never end. Amen.

PSALMODY

Ant. 1   Glory to you, O Trinity, † one God in three *equal* Persons, * as in
the beginning, so now, *and* for ever.

VIIIg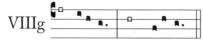

Psalm 113

Praise, O servants *of* the Lord, *	both now and for *evermore!*
praise the name *of* the Lord!	From the rising of the sun *to* its setting
May the name of the *Lord* be blessed *	* praised be the name *of* the Lord!

High above all nations *is* the Lord, *
above the heav*ens* his glory.
Who is like the *Lord*, our God, * who
has risen on high *to* his throne
yet stoops from the heights *to* look
down, * to look down upon heav*en*
and earth?
From the dust he lifts *up* the lowly, *
from his misery he rais*es* the poor

to set him in the compan*y* of princes, *
yes, with the princes *of* his people.
To the childless wife he *gives* a home *
and gladdens her *heart* with children.
Glory to the Father, and *to* the Son, *
and to the *Ho*ly Spirit:
as it was in the begin*ning*, is now, * and
will be for ev*er*. Amen.

Antiphon   Glory to you, O Trinity, † one God in three *equal* Persons, * as
               in the beginning, so now, *and* for ever.

Ant. 2   Praise to the Holy Trinity and undi*vid*ed Unity. * Let us praise
               God for he has shown us *his* mercy.

IIA

Psalm 147:12-20

O praise the *Lord*, Jerusalem! * Zion,
praise *your* God!
He has strengthened the bars *of* your
gates, * he has blessed the children
*with*in you.
He established peace *on* your borders, *
he feeds you with fin*est* wheat.
He sends out his word *to* the earth * and
swiftly runs his *com*mand.
He showers down snow *white* as wool, *
he scatters hoar-frost *like* ashes.
He hurls down hail*stones* like crumbs. *

The waters are frozen at *his* touch;
he sends forth his word *and* it melts them:
* at the breath of his mouth the wa*ters*
flow.
He makes his word *known* to Jacob, * to
Israel his laws and *de*crees.
He has not dealt thus with *other* nations;
* he has not taught them his *de*crees.
Glory to the Father, and *to* the Son, *
and to the Ho*ly* Spirit:
as it was in the begin*ning*, is now, * and
will be for ever. *A*men.

Antiphon   Praise to the Holy Trinity and undi*vid*ed Unity. * Let us praise
               God for he has shown us *his* mercy.

Ant. 3   Glory and honor to God in three Persons: † Father, Son, and
               Ho*ly* Spirit; * glory and praise to him for *end*less ages.

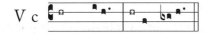

V c

Canticle   Ephesians 1:3-10

Praised be the God *and* Father * of
 our Lord *Jesus* Christ,
who has bestowed on us *in* Christ *
 every spiritual blessing *in* the
 heavens.
God chose us in him before the world
 began * to be holy and blameless *in*
 his sight.
He predestined us to be his adopted
 sons through Je*sus* Christ, * such was
 his *will* and pleasure,
that all might praise the glori*ous* favor *
 he has bestowed on us in *his* belovèd.
In him and through his blood, we have
 been *redeemed*, * and our *sins*

forgiven,
so immeasura*bly* generous * is God's
 fa*vor* to us.
God has given us the wisdom to
 understand fully *the* mystery, * the
 plan he was pleased to de*cree* in
 Christ.
A plan to be carried out *in* Christ, * in
 the full*ness* of time,
to bring all things into one *in* him, * in
 the heavens *and* on earth.
Glory to the Father, and to *the* Son, *
 and to the *Holy* Spirit:
as it was in the beginning, *is* now, * and
 will be for e*ver*. Amen.

Antiphon   Glory and honor to God in three Persons: † Father, Son, and
 Ho*ly* Spirit; * glory and praise to him for *end*less ages.

READING   Romans 11:33-36

How deep are the riches and the wisdom and the knowledge of God! How
inscrutable his judgments, how unsearchable his ways! For "who has known
the mind of the Lord? Or who has been his counselor? Who has given him
anything so as to deserve return?" For from him and through him and for
him all things are. To him be glory forever. Amen.

RESPONSORY (VI F)

Let us worship the Father, the Son and the *Holy* Spirit; * let us praise God *for*
 ever.
— Let us worship the Father, the Son and the *Holy* Spirit; * let us praise God *for*
 ever.
To God alone be hon*or* and glory;
— let us praise God *for* ever.
Glory to the Father, and *to* the Son, * and to the Ho*ly* Spirit.
— Let us worship the Father, the Son and the *Holy* Spirit; * let us praise God *for*
 ever.

CANTICLE OF MARY

Antiphon   We give you *thanks*, O God; * we give you thanks, Trinity one
 and true,
 Divinity one *and* most high, * Unity one *and* holy.

My soul ✠ proclaims the greatness
of the Lord, * my spirit rejoices
in God *my* savior

for he has *looked* with favor * on his
low*ly* servant.

From this day all *gen*erations * will call
me blessèd:

the Almighty has done great *things* for
me, * and holy is *his* Name.

He has mercy on *those* who fear him *
in every gen*er*ation.

He has shown the strength *of* his arm, *
he has scattered the proud in their
*con*ceit.

He has cast down the mighty *from*

their thrones, * and has lifted up *the*
lowly.

He has filled the hungry *with* good
things, * and the rich he has sent
a*way* empty.

He has come to the help of his *ser*vant
Israel * for he has remembered his
promise *of* mercy,

the promise he made *to* our fathers, * to
Abraham and his children *for* ever.

Glory to the Father, and *to* the Son, *
and to the Ho*ly* Spirit:

as it was in the begin*ning*, is now, * and
will be for ever. *A*men.

Antiphon   We give you *thanks*, O God; * we give you thanks, Trinity one
and true,
Divinity one *and* most high, * Unity one *and* holy.

INTERCESSIONS (VI F)

The Father through the Holy Spirit has given life to the humanity of Christ his
Son, and has made him a source of *life* for us; * let us raise our voices in praise
to the *tri*une God:

*Glory to the Father, and to the Son and to the Ho*ly *Spirit.*

Father, almighty and eternal God, send the Holy Spirit upon your Church in
your Son's name,

— preserve it in the unity of charity and in the full*ness* of truth.

Send laborers into your harvest, Lord, to teach the truth to all nations, and to
baptize them in the name of the Father, and of the Son and of the *Ho*ly Spirit,

— and to con*firm* their faith.

Father, send help to all who suffer persecution in the name *of* your Son,

— for he promised to send the Spirit of Truth to an*swer* for them.

Father omnipotent, may all men come to acknowledge you, together with the
Word and the Holy Spirit, as the *one* true God,

— may they believe in you, hope *in* you, love you.

Father of all the living, bring the dead to share *in* your glory,

— the glory of your eternal reign with your Son and the *Ho*ly Spirit.

Our Father . . .

Prayer

Father,
you sent your Word to bring us truth
and your Spirit to make us holy.
Through them we come to know the mystery of your life.
Help us to worship you, one God in three Persons,
by proclaiming and living our faith in you.
Grant this through our Lord Jesus Christ, your Son,
who lives and reigns with you and the Holy Spirit,
one God, for ever and ever.

Morning Prayer

HYMN

Trinitas, summo solio coruscans. Mode VIII (L.M.)

Trinitas, summo solio coruscans,	Most holy Trinity, One God,
gloriae carmen tibi sit perenne,	Enthroned in splendour and in light,
quae tenes nostri vehementi amore	Your love holds every human heart,
pectoris ima.	Unending praise is but your due.
Conditor rerum, Pater, alma virtus,	O Father, Essence of all life,
quos tuae vitae facis atque formae	Bestowing it upon mankind,
esse consortes, fidei fac usque	Help us by faith your gifts to win,
dona mereri.	Your image meriting to bear.
Candor aeternae speculumque lucis,	Clear brightness of Eternal Light,
Nate, quos dicis sociasque fratres,	O God the Son, who shared our state,
palimites viti tibi nos inesse	Make us true branches of your Vine
da viridantes.	That strive to yield abundant fruit.
Caritas, ignis, pietas, potenti	O Holy Spirit, Fire of Love,
lumine ac blando moderans creata,	Whose gentle force directs the world,
Spiritus, mentem renova, foveto	Renew our minds at dawn of day,
intima cordis.	And prompt our wills to do your work.
Hospes o dulcis, Trias obsecranda,	O Trinity, delightful Guest,
nos tibi iugi fac amore nexos,	Abide with us in closest bond,
perpetes donec modulemur hymnos	Until we sing to you above,
teque fruamur. Amen.	In gratitude and joy untold. Amen.

PSALMODY

Ant. 1   To you, O *bless*èd Trinity, * be worship and honor, glo*ry* and
power,
praise and joyful *ado*ration * through e*ter*nal ages.

VIIIg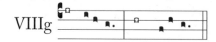

Psalm 63:2-9

O God, you are my God, for *you* I long; * for you my *soul* is thirsting.

My body *pines* for you * like a dry, weary land *with*out water.

So I gaze on you *in* the sanctuary * to see your strength *and* your glory.

For your love is bet*ter* than life, * my lips will speak *your* praise.

So I will bless you *all* my life, * in your name I will lift *up* my hands.

My soul shall be filled as *with* a banquet, * my mouth shall praise *you* with joy.

On my bed I re*member* you. * On you I muse *through* the night

for you have *been* my help; * in the shadow of your wings *I* rejoice.

My soul *clings* to you; * your right hand *holds* me fast.

Glory to the Father, and *to* the Son, * and to the *Ho*ly Spirit:

as it was in the begin*ning*, is now, * and will be for *ev*er. Amen.

Antiphon   To you, O *bless*èd Trinity, * be worship and honor, glo*ry* and power,

praise and joyful *ado*ration * through e*ter*nal ages.

Ant. 2   May all your creatures give you fitting praise, † adora*tion* and glory, * O bless*èd* Trinity.

IIA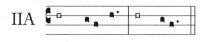

Canticle   Daniel 3:57-88; 56

Bless the Lord, all you works *of* the Lord. * Praise and exalt him above all *for*ever.

Angels of the Lord, *bless* the Lord, * You heavens, bless *the* Lord.

All you waters above the heavens, *bless* the Lord. * All you hosts of the Lord, bless *the* Lord.

Sun and moon, *bless* the Lord. * Stars of heaven, bless *the* Lord.

Every shower and dew, *bless* the Lord. * All you winds, bless *the* Lord.

Fire and heat, *bless* the Lord. * Cold and chill, bless *the* Lord.

Dew and rain, *bless* the Lord. * Frost and chill, bless *the* Lord.

Ice and snow, *bless* the Lord. * Nights and days, bless *the* Lord.

Light and darkness, *bless* the Lord. *

Lightnings and clouds, bless *the* Lord.

Let the earth *bless* the Lord. * Praise and exalt him above all *for*ever.

Mountains and hills, *bless* the Lord. * Everything growing from the earth, bless *the* Lord.

You springs, *bless* the Lord. * Seas and rivers, bless *the* Lord.

You dolphins and all water creatures, *bless* the Lord. * All you birds of the air, bless *the* Lord.

All you beasts, wild and tame, *bless* the Lord. * You sons of men, bless *the* Lord.

O Israel, *bless* the Lord. * Praise and exalt him above all *for*ever.

Priests of the Lord, *bless* the Lord. * Servants of the Lord, bless *the* Lord.

Spirits and souls of the just, *bless* the Lord. * Holy men of humble heart, bless *the* Lord.

Hananiah, Azariah, Mishael, *bless* the Lord. * Praise and exalt him above all *fore*ver.

Let us bless the Father, and the Son, and the *Ho*ly Spirit. * Let us praise and exalt him above all *fore*ver.

Blessèd are you in the firma*ment* of heaven.* Praiseworthy and glorious and exalted above all *fore*ver.

Antiphon   May all your creatures give you fitting praise, † adora*tion* and glory, * O blessèd *Trinity*.

Ant. 3   All things are from him, † through him, *and* in him; * to him be glory *for* ever.

Psalm 149

Sing a new song to *the* Lord, * his praise in the assembly of *the* faithful.

Let Israel rejoice in *its* Maker, * let Zion's sons exult in *their* king.

Let them praise his name *with* dancing * and make music with timbrel *and* harp.

For the Lord takes delight in *his* people. * He crowns the poor with sal*va*tion.

Let the faithful rejoice in *their* glory, * shout for joy and take *their* rest.

Let the praise of God be on *their* lips * and a two-edged sword in *their* hand,

to deal out vengeance to *the* nations * and punishment on all *the* peoples;

to bind their kings *in* chains * and their nobles in fetters *of* iron;

to carry out the sentence pre-*or*dained: * this honor is for all *his* faithful.

Glory to the Father, and to *the* Son, * and to the *Ho*ly Spirit:

as it was in the beginning, *is* now, * and will be for ever. *A*men.

Antiphon   All things are from him, † through him, *and* in him; * to him be glory *for* ever.

READING   1 Corinthians 12:4-6

There are different gifts but the same Spirit; there are different ministries but the same Lord; there are different works but the same God who accomplishes all of them in everyone.

RESPONSORY (VI F)

All praise, all glo*ry* to you, * O Ho*ly* Trinity.

— All praise, all glo*ry* to you, * O Ho*ly* Trinity.

May we give thanks to *you* for ever,

— O Ho*ly* Trinity.

Glory to the Father, and *to* the Son, * and to the Ho*ly* Spirit.
— All praise, all glo*ry* to you, * O Ho*ly* Trinity.

CANTICLE OF ZECHARIAH

Antiphon   O holy, undi*vid*ed Trinity, * Creator and Ruler of all that *ex*ists,
                  may all *praise* be yours * now, for ever, and for ages *un*ending.

If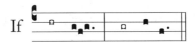

B lessèd ✠ be the Lord, the *God* of
Israel; * he has come to his people
and set *them* free.
He has raised up for us a *mighty* savior,
* born of the house of his ser*vant*
David.
Through his holy prophets he promised of old † that he would save us
from our enemies, * from the hands
of all *who* hate us.
He promised to show mercy *to* our
fathers * and to remember his ho*ly*
covenant.
This was the oath he swore to our
*fath*er Abraham: * to set us free from
the hands of *our* enemies,
free to worship him without fear, †
holy and righteous *in* his sight * all

the days of *our* life.
You, my child, shall be called the
prophet *of* the Most High; * for you
will go before the Lord to prepare *his*
way,
to give his people knowledge *of* salvation * by the forgiveness of *their* sins.
In the tender compassion *of* our God *
the dawn from on high shall break
*up*on us,
to shine on those who dwell in darkness and the sha*dow* of death, * and
to guide our feet into the way *of*
peace.
Glory to the Father, and *to* the Son, *
and to the Ho*ly* Spirit:
as it was in the begin*ning*, is now, * and
will be for ever. *Amen.*

Antiphon   O holy, undi*vid*ed Trinity, * Creator and Ruler of all that *ex*ists,
                  may all *praise* be yours * now, for ever, and for ages *un*ending.

INTERCESSIONS (VI F)

Let us give all honor and glory to the Father, Son, and *Holy* Spirit, * as we cry *out*
with joy:
Glory to the Father, and to the Son, and to the Holy Spirit.
Holy Father send your Spirit to us who know not how to pray *as* we ought,
— that he may help us in our frailty, and ask for us those gifts which will make
us pleas*ing* to you.
Christ, Son of the living God, you asked the Father to send the Holy Spirit up*on*
your Church,
— make us worthy to have this Spirit of Truth *with* us always.

Come, Holy Spirit, that we may show your fruit in our lives, charity, joy, peace, equanimity, kindness, *gen*erosity,

—long-suffering, patience, faithfulness, modesty, self-con*trol*, and chastity.

Father all powerful, you have sent the Spirit of your Son into our hearts, so that we cry: *Ab*ba, Father,

—make us submissive to your Spirit that we may be your heirs, and co*heirs* with Christ.

Christ Jesus, you sent the Paraclete who proceeds from the Father to bear wit*ness* to you,

—enable us also to be your witnesses *bef*ore men.

Our Father . . .

Prayer

Father,
you sent your Word to bring us truth
and your Spirit to make us holy.
Through them we come to know the mystery of your life.
Help us to worship you, one God in three Persons,
by proclaiming and living our faith in you.
Grant this through our Lord Jesus Christ, your Son,
who lives and reigns with you and the Holy Spirit,
one God, for ever and ever.

Evening Prayer II

HYMN, as in Evening Prayer I, 546.

PSALMODY

Ant. 1   O Trinity most high, eter*nal* and true: * Father, Son and *Holy* Spirit.

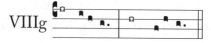

VIIIg

Psalm 110:1-5, 7

The Lord's revelation to my Master:
† "Sit *on* my right: * your foes I
will put be*neath* your feet."
The Lord will wield from Zion † your
scep*ter* of power: * rule in the midst
of *all* your foes.
A prince from the day of your birth
on the *holy* mountains; * from the
womb before the dawn *I* begot you.
The Lord has sworn an oath he will not
change. † "You are a *priest* for ever, * a
priest like Melchize*dek* of old."
The Master standing at *your* right
hand * will shatter kings in the day

of *his* great wrath.

He shall drink from the stream *by the* wayside * and therefore he shall lift *up* his head.

Glory to the Father, and *to* the Son, * and to the *Ho*ly Spirit:

as it was in the begin*ning*, is now, * and will be for e*ver*. Amen.

Antiphon   O Trinity most high, eter*nal* and true: * Father, Son and *Ho*ly Spirit.

Ant. 2   Save us, set us free and *give* us life, * O bless*èd* Trinity.

IIA

Psalm 114

When Israel came *forth* from Egypt, * Jacob's sons from an ali*en* people,

Judah became *the* Lord's temple, * Israel became *his* kingdom.

The sea fled *at* the sight: * the Jordan turned back on *its* course,

the mountains *leapt* like rams * and the hills like year*ling* sheep.

Why was it, sea, *that* you fled, * that you turned back, Jordan, on *your*

course?

Mountains, that you *leapt* like rams, * hills, like year*ling* sheep?

Tremble, O earth, be*fore* the Lord, * in the presence of the God *of* Jacob,

who turns the rock in*to* a pool * and flint into a spring *of* water.

Glory to the Father, and *to* the Son, * and to the Ho*ly* Spirit:

as it was in the begin*ning*, is now, * and will be for ever. *A*men.

Antiphon   Save us, set us free and *give* us life, * O bless*èd* Trinity.

Ant. 3   Holy, holy, holy Lord, God of power and might, † the God who is, who was, and who is *to* come, * alleluia, alleluia.

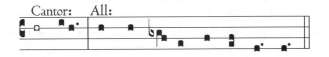

** al- le- lu- ia, al- le- lu- ia.

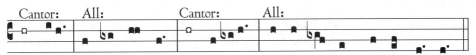

*Al- le- lu- ia.   ** al- le- lu- ia, al- le - lu- ia.

Canticle   See Revelation 19:1-7

Salvation, glory, and power to *our* God:
* Alleluia.
his judgments are hon*est* and true.
** Alleluia, alleluia.

Sing praise to our God, all you *his* servants,
* Alleluia.
all who worship him reverently, *great* and small.
** Alleluia, alleluia.

The Lord our all-powerful God *is* King;
* Alleluia.
let us rejoice, sing praise, and *give* him glory.
** Alleluia, alleluia.

The wedding feast of the Lamb has *be*gun,
* Alleluia.
and his bride is pre*pared* to welcome him.
** Alleluia, alleluia.

Glory to the Father, and to the Son, †
and to the Ho*ly* Spirit.
* Alleluia.
As it was in the beginning, is now, †
and will be for ev*er*. Amen.
** Alleluia, alleluia.

Antiphon   Holy, holy, holy Lord, God of power and might, † the God
                  who is, who was, and who is *to* come, * alleluia, alleluia.

READING   Ephesians 4:3-6
  Make every effort to preserve the unity which has the Spirit as its origin and
  peace as its binding force. There is but one body and one Spirit, just as there
  is but one hope given all of you by your call. There is one Lord, one faith,
  one baptism; one God and Father of all, who is over all, and works through
  all, and is in all.

RESPONSORY (VI F)
Let us worship the Father, the Son and the *Ho*ly Spirit; * let us praise God *for* ever.
— Let us worship the Father, the Son and the *Ho*ly Spirit; * let us praise God *for* ever.
To God alone be hon*or* and glory;
— let us praise God *for* ever.
Glory to the Father, and *to* the Son, * and to the Ho*ly* Spirit.
— Let us worship the Father, the Son and the *Ho*ly Spirit; * let us praise God *for* ever.

CANTICLE OF MARY

Antiphon   With our whole heart and voice we acclaim *you*, O God; * we
                offer you our praise *and* worship,
                unbegotten Father, † only-be*got*ten Son, * Holy Spirit, constant
                friend *and* guide;
                most holy and undi*vid*ed Trinity, * to you be glory *for* ever.

If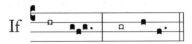

My soul ✠proclaims the greatness *of* the Lord, * my spirit rejoices in God *my* savior

for he has *looked* with favor * on his low*ly* servant.

From this day all *gen*erations * will call *me* blessèd:

the Almighty has done great *things* for me, * and holy is *his* Name.

He has mercy on *those* who fear him * in every gen*er*ation.

He has shown the strength *of* his arm, * he has scattered the proud in their *con*ceit.

He has cast down the mighty *from* their thrones, * and has lifted up *the* lowly.

He has filled the hungry *with* good things, * and the rich he has sent a*way* empty.

He has come to the help of his *ser*vant Israel * for he has remembered his promise *of* mercy,

the promise he made *to* our fathers, * to Abraham and his children *for* ever.

Glory to the Father, and *to* the Son, * and to the Ho*ly* Spirit:

as it was in the begin*ning*, is now, * and will be for ever. *A*men.

Antiphon   With our whole heart and voice we acclaim *you*, O God; * we
                offer you our praise *and* worship,
                unbegotten Father, † only-be*got*ten Son, * Holy Spirit, constant
                friend *and* guide;
                most holy and undi*vid*ed Trinity, * to you be glory *for* ever.

INTERCESSIONS (VI F)

The Father through the Holy Spirit has given life to the humanity of Christ his Son, and has made him a source of *life* for us; * let us raise our voices in praise to the *tri*une God:

Glory to the Father, and to the Son and to the Holy Spirit.

Father, almighty and eternal God, send the Holy Spirit upon your Church in *your* Son's name,

—preserve it in the unity of charity and in the full*ness* of truth.

Send laborers into your harvest, Lord, to teach the truth to all nations, and to baptize them in the name of the Father, and of the Son and of the *Ho*ly Spirit,

—and to con*firm* their faith.

Father, send help to all who suffer persecution in the name *of* your Son,
— for he promised to send the Spirit of Truth to an*swer* for them.
Father omnipotent, may all men come to acknowledge you, together with the
  Word and the Holy Spirit, as the *one* true God,
— may they believe in you, hope *in* you, love you.
Father of all the living, bring the dead to share *in* your glory,
— the glory of your eternal reign with your Son and the *Holy* Spirit.

Our Father . . .

Prayer

Father,
you sent your Word to bring us truth
and your Spirit to make us holy.
Through them we come to know the mystery of your life.
Help us to worship you, one God in three Persons,
by proclaiming and living our faith in you.
Grant this through our Lord Jesus Christ, your Son,
who lives and reigns with you and the Holy Spirit,
one God, for ever and ever.

Thursday after Trinity Sunday
CORPUS CHRISTI

Solemnity

Where the solemnity of Corpus Christi is not observed as a holy day, it is assigned to the Sunday after Trinity Sunday, which is then considered its proper day in the calendar.

Evening Prayer I

HYMN

Pange, lingua, gloriosi. (87.87.87)

Pange, lingua, gloriosi	Sing, my tongue, the Savior's glory,
Corporis mysterium,	of His flesh the mystery sing;
Sanguinisque pretiosi,	of the Blood, all price exceeding,
quem in mundi pretium	shed by our immortal King,
fructus ventris generosi	destined, for the world's redemption,
Rex effudit Gentium.	from a noble womb to spring.
Nobis datus, nobis natus	Of a pure and spotless Virgin
ex intacta Virgine,	born for us on earth below,
et in mundo conversatus,	He, as Man, with man conversing,
sparso verbi semine,	stayed, the seeds of truth to sow;
sui moras incolatus	then He closed in solemn order
miro clausit ordine.	wondrously His life of woe.
In supremae nocte coenae	On the night of that Last Supper,
recumbens cum fratribus	seated with His chosen band,
observata lege plene	He the Pascal victim eating,
cibis in legalibus,	first fulfills the Law's command;
cibum turbae duodenae	then as Food to His Apostles
se dat suis manibus.	gives Himself with His own hand.
Verbum caro, panem verum	Word-made-Flesh, the bread of nature
verbo carnem efficit:	by His word to Flesh He turns;
fitque sanguis Christi merum,	wine into His Blood He changes;
et si sensus deficit,	what though sense no change discerns?
ad firmandum cor sincerum	Only be the heart in earnest,
sola fides sufficit.	faith her lesson quickly learns.
Tantum ergo Sacramentum	Down in adoration falling,
veneremur cernui:	Lo! the sacred Host we hail;
et antiquum documentum	Lo! o'er ancient forms departing,
novo cedat ritui:	newer rites of grace prevail;
praestet fides supplementum	faith for all defects supplying,
sensuum defectui.	where the feeble senses fail.
Genitori, Genitoque	To the everlasting Father,
laus et jubilatio,	and the Son who reigns on high,
salus, honor, virtus quoque	with the Holy Ghost proceeding
sit et benedictio:	forth from Each eternally,
procedenti ab utroque	be salvation, honor, blessing,
compar sit laudatio. Amen.	might and endless majesty. Amen.

Ant. 1   The Lord is compassionate; † he gives food to *those* who fear
                him * as a remembrance of *his* great deeds.

VIIIg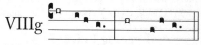

Psalm 111

I will thank the Lord with *all* my
heart * in the meeting of the just
and *their* assembly.

Great are the works *of* the Lord; * to be
pondered by *all* who love them.

Majestic and glor*ious* his work, * his
justice stands *firm* for ever.

He makes us remem*ber* his wonders. *
The Lord is compas*sion* and love.

He gives food to *those* who fear him; *
keeps his covenant ev*er* in mind.

He has shown his might *to* his people *
by giving them the lands *of* the
nations.

His works are jus*tice* and truth: * his

precepts are all *of* them sure,
standing firm for ev*er* and ever: * they
are made in upright*ness* and truth.

He has sent deliverance to his people †
and established his cove*nant* for ever.
* Holy his name, *to* be feared.

To fear the Lord is the first stage of
wisdom; † all who do so prove
*them*selves wise. * His praise shall *last*
for ever!

Glory to the Father, and *to* the Son, *
and to the *Holy* Spirit:

as it was in the begin*ning*, is now, * and
will be for ev*er*. Amen.

Antiphon   The Lord is compassionate; † he gives food to *those* who fear
                him * as a remembrance of *his* great deeds.

Ant. 2   The Lord brings peace *to* his Church, * and fills us with the
                fin*est* wheat.

IIA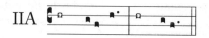

Psalm 147:12-20

O praise the *Lord*, Jerusalem! *
Zion, praise *your* God!

He has strengthened the bars *of* your
gates, * he has blessed the children
*with*in you.

He established peace *on* your borders, *
he feeds you with fin*est* wheat.

He sends out his word *to* the earth *
and swiftly runs his *com*mand.

He showers down snow *white* as wool, *
he scatters hoar-frost *like* ashes.

He hurls down hail*stones* like crumbs. *
The waters are frozen at *his* touch;

he sends forth his word *and* it melts
them: * at the breath of his mouth
the wa*ters* flow.

He makes his word *known* to Jacob, *
to Israel his laws and *de*crees.

He has not dealt thus with *other*
nations; * he has not taught them his
*de*crees.
Glory to the Father, and *to* the Son, *

and to the Ho*ly* Spirit:
as it was in the begin*ning*, is now, * and
will be for ever. *A*men.

Antiphon   The Lord brings peace *to* his Church, * and fills us with the
              fin*est* wheat.

Ant. 3   Truly I say *to* you: * Moses did not give you the bread *from*
              heaven;
              my Father gives you the true bread *from* heaven, * al*le*luia.

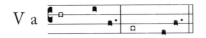

Canticle   Revelation 11:17-18; 12:10b-12a

We praise you, the Lord God
Almighty, * who is and *who*
was.
You have assumed your *great* power, *
you have begun *your* reign.
The nations have raged *in* anger, * but
then came your day *of* wrath
and the moment to judge *the* dead: *
the time to reward your servants *the*
prophets
and the holy ones who *re*vere you, * the
great and the small *a*like.
Now have salvation and po*wer* come, *
the reign of our God and the author-

ity of his *A*nointed One.
For the accuser of our brothers is *cast*
out, * who night and day accused
them be*fore* God.
They defeated him by the blood of *the*
Lamb * and by the word of *their*
testimony;
love for life did not deter them *from*
death. * So rejoice, you heavens, and
you that dwell *there*in!
Glory to the Father, and to *the* Son, *
and to the Ho*ly* Spirit:
as it was in the beginning, *is* now, * and
will be for ever. *A*men.

Antiphon   Truly I say *to* you: * Moses did not give you the bread *from*
              heaven;
              my Father gives you the true bread *from* heaven, * al*le*luia.

READING   1 Corinthians 10:16-17
    Is not the cup of blessing we bless a sharing in the blood of Christ? And is
    not the bread we break a sharing in the body of Christ? Because the loaf of
    bread is one, we, many though we are, are one body, for we all partake of the
    one loaf.

RESPONSORY (VI F)
He gave them *bread* from heaven, * alleluia, al*le*luia.
— He gave them *bread* from heaven, * alleluia, al*le*luia.

Man has eaten the bread of angels,
—alleluia, al*le*luia.
Glory to the Father, and *to* the Son, * and to the Ho*ly* Spirit.
—He gave them *bread* from heaven, * alleluia, al*le*luia.

CANTICLE OF MARY

Antiphon   How kind and gentle you are, O Lord. † You showed your
goodness *to* your sons * by giving them bread *from* heaven.
You filled the hungry *with* good things, * and the rich you sent
a*way* empty.

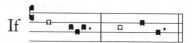

My soul ✠proclaims the greatness
of the Lord, * my spirit rejoices
in God *my* savior
for he has *looked* with favor * on his
low*ly* servant.
From this day all *gen*erations * will call
me blessèd:
the Almighty has done great *things* for
me, * and holy is *his* Name.
He has mercy on *those* who fear him *
in every gen*er*ation.
He has shown the strength *of* his arm, *
he has scattered the proud in their
*con*ceit.
He has cast down the mighty *from*

their thrones, * and has lifted up *the*
lowly.
He has filled the hungry *with* good
things, * and the rich he has sent
a*way* empty.
He has come to the help of his *ser*vant
Israel * for he has remembered his
promise *of* mercy,
the promise he made *to* our fathers, * to
Abraham and his children *for* ever.
Glory to the Father, and *to* the Son, *
and to the Ho*ly* Spirit:
as it was in the begin*ning*, is now, * and
will be for ever. *A*men.

Antiphon   How kind and gentle you are, O Lord. † You showed your
goodness *to* your sons * by giving them bread *from* heaven.
You filled the hungry *with* good things, * and the rich you sent
a*way* empty.

INTERCESSIONS (VI F)

Christ invites all to the supper in which he gives his body and blood for the life
of the world. * *Let* us ask him:
*Christ, the bread of heaven, grant us everlast*ing *life.*
Christ, Son of the living God, you commanded that this thanksgiving meal be
done in memo*ry* of you,
—enrich your Church through the faithful celebration *of* these mysteries.

Christ, eternal priest of the Most High, you have commanded your priests to *offer* your sacraments,
— may they help them to exemplify in their lives the meaning of the sacred mysteries *which* they celebrate.
Christ, bread from heaven, you form one body out of all who partake of *the* one bread,
— refresh all who believe in you with harmo*ny* and peace.
Christ, through your bread you offer the remedy for immortality and the pledge of future *re*surrection,
— restore health to the sick and living *hope* to sinners.
Christ, our king who is to come, you commanded that the mysteries which proclaim your death be celebrated until *you* return,
— grant that all who die in you may share in your *re*surrection.

Our Father . . .

Prayer

Lord Jesus Christ,
you gave us the eucharist
as the memorial of your suffering and death.
May our worship of this sacrament of your body and blood
help us to experience the salvation you won for us
and the peace of the kingdom
where you live and reign with the Father and the Holy Spirit,
one God, for ever and ever.

Morning Prayer

HYMN

Verbum supernum. Mode VIII (L.M.)

Verbum supernum prodiens,	Remaining at the Father's side,
Nec Patris linquens dexteram,	The Word Incarnate came to earth;
Ad opus suum exiens,	Fulfilling his redemptive work,
Venit ad vitæ vesperam.	The Hour he longed for came at last.
In mortem a discipulo	He knew full well he was betrayed
Suis tradendus æmulis,	By one whom he had called his own;
Prius in vitæ ferculo	And yet before his death he gave
Se tradidit discipulis.	Himself as living food for all.
Quibus sub bina specie	As bread he gave his sacred Flesh,
Carnem dedit et sanguinem;	Transforming wine into his Blood:
Ut duplicis substantiæ	That man, who needs both food and drink,
Totum cibaret hominem.	Should have his whole desire supplied.
Se nascens dedit socium,	By birth our fellowman was He,
Convescens in edulium,	our Food while seated at the board;
Se moriens in pretium,	He died, our ransomer to be;
Se regnans dat in præmium.	He ever reigns, our great reward.

O salutaris hostia,	O saving Victim, open wide
Quæ cæli pandis ostium,	The gate of Heaven to man below;
Bella premunt hostilia;	Our foes press on from every side;
Da robur, fer auxilium.	Your aid supply; Your strength bestow.
Uni trinoque Domino	To your great Name be endless praise;
Sit sempiterna gloria:	Immortal Godhead, One in Three;
Qui vitam sine termino	Grant us, for endless length of days,
Nobis donet in patria. Amen.	In our true native land to be. Amen.

PSALMODY

Ant. 1   You fed your people with the *food* of angels; * you gave them bread from heaven, *a*lleluia.

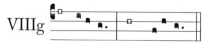

Psalm 63:2-9

O God, you are my God, for *you* I long; * for you my *soul* is thirsting.
My body *pines* for you * like a dry, weary land *with*out water.
So I gaze on you *in* the sanctuary * to see your strength *and* your glory.
For your love is bet*ter* than life, * my lips will speak *your* praise.
So I will bless you *all* my life, * in your name I will lift *up* my hands.
My soul shall be filled as *with* a

banquet, * my mouth shall praise *you* with joy.
On my bed I re*mem*ber you. * On you I muse *through* the night
for you have *been* my help; * in the shadow of your wings *I* rejoice.
My soul *clings* to you; * your right hand *holds* me fast.
Glory to the Father, and *to* the Son, * and to the *Ho*ly Spirit:
as it was in the begin*ning*, is now, * and will be for e*ver*. Amen.

Antiphon   You fed your people with the *food* of angels; * you gave them bread from heaven, *a*lleluia.

Ant. 2   Holy priests will offer incense and *bread* to God, * al*le*luia.

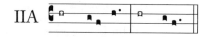

Canticle   Daniel 3:57-88; 56

Bless the Lord, all you works *of* the Lord. * Praise and exalt him above all *for*ever.
Angels of the Lord, *bless* the Lord, *

You heavens, bless *the* Lord.
All you waters above the heavens, *bless* the Lord. * All you hosts of the Lord, bless *the* Lord.

Sun and moon, *bless* the Lord. * Stars
of heaven, bless *the* Lord.

Every shower and dew, *bless* the Lord. *
All you winds, bless *the* Lord.

Fire and heat, *bless* the Lord. * Cold
and chill, bless *the* Lord.

Dew and rain, *bless* the Lord. * Frost
and chill, bless *the* Lord.

Ice and snow, *bless* the Lord. * Nights
and days, bless *the* Lord.

Light and darkness, *bless* the Lord. *
Lightnings and clouds, bless *the*
Lord.

Let the earth *bless* the Lord. * Praise
and exalt him above all *for*ever.

Mountains and hills, *bless* the Lord. *
Everything growing from the earth,
bless *the* Lord.

You springs, *bless* the Lord. * Seas and
rivers, bless *the* Lord.

You dolphins and all water creatures,
bless the Lord. * All you birds of the
air, bless *the* Lord.

All you beasts, wild and tame, *bless* the
Lord. * You sons of men, bless *the*
Lord.

O Israel, *bless* the Lord. * Praise and
exalt him above all *for*ever.

Priests of the Lord, *bless* the Lord. *
Servants of the Lord, bless *the* Lord.

Spirits and souls of the just, *bless* the
Lord. * Holy men of humble heart,
bless *the* Lord.

Hananiah, Azariah, Mishael, *bless* the
Lord. * Praise and exalt him above all
*for*ever.

Let us bless the Father, and the Son,
and the *Ho*ly Spirit. * Let us praise
and exalt him above all *for*ever.

Blessèd are you in the firma*ment* of
heaven.* Praiseworthy and glorious and
exalted above all *for*ever.

Antiphon   Holy priests will offer incense and *bread* to God, * al*le*luia.

Ant. 3   I will give to the one who is victorious † the hidden bread and a
new name, * al*le*luia.

Psalm 149

Sing a new song to *the* Lord, * his
praise in the assembly of *the*
faithful.

Let Israel rejoice in *its* Maker, * let
Zion's sons exult in *their* king.

Let them praise his name *with* dancing
* and make music with timbrel *and*
harp.

For the Lord takes delight in *his*
people. * He crowns the poor with
sal*va*tion.

Let the faithful rejoice in *their* glory, *
shout for joy and take *their* rest.

Let the praise of God be on *their* lips *
and a two-edged sword in *their*
hand,

to deal out vengeance to *the* nations *
and punishment on all *the* peoples;

to bind their kings *in* chains * and
their nobles in fetters *of* iron;

to carry out the sentence pre-*ordained:* * this honor is for all *his* faithful.

Glory to the Father, and to *the* Son, *

and to the Ho*ly* Spirit:
as it was in the beginning, *is* now, * and
will be for ever. *A*men.

Antiphon   I will give to the one who is victorious † the hidden bread and a *new* name, * al*le*luia.

READING   Malachi 1:11

From the rising of the sun, even to its setting,
    my name is great among the nations;
And everywhere they bring sacrifice to my name,
    and a pure offering;
For great is my name among the nation,
    says the Lord of hosts.

RESPONSORY (VI F)

You will bring forth bread *from* the earth, * alleluia, al*le*luia.

—You will bring forth bread *from* the earth, * alleluia, al*le*luia.

And wine which gives warmth *to* men's hearts,

—alleluia, al*le*luia.

Glory to the Father, and *to* the Son, * and to the Ho*ly* Spirit.

—You will bring forth bread *from* the earth, * alleluia, al*le*luia.

CANTICLE OF ZECHARIAH

Antiphon   I am the living bread come down from heaven; † anyone who eats this bread will *live* for ever, * al*le*luia.

If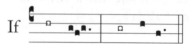

Blessèd ✠ be the Lord, the *God* of Israel; * he has come to his people and set *them* free.

He has raised up for us a *mighty* savior, * born of the house of his ser*vant* David.

Through his holy prophets he promised of old † that he would save us *from* our enemies, * from the hands of all *who* hate us.

He promised to show mercy *to* our fathers * and to remember his ho*ly* covenant.

This was the oath he swore to our *fath*er Abraham: * to set us free from

the hands of *our* enemies,

free to worship him without fear, †
holy and righteous *in* his sight * all
the days of *our* life.

You, my child, shall be called the prophet *of* the Most High; * for you will go before the Lord to prepare *his* way,

to give his people knowledge *of* salvation * by the forgiveness of *their* sins.

In the tender compassion *of* our God * the dawn from on high shall break *u*pon us,

to shine on those who dwell in darkness and the sha*dow* of death, * and to guide our feet into the way *of* peace.

Glory to the Father, and *to* the Son, *

and to the Ho*ly* Spirit: as it was in the begin*ning*, is now, * and will be for ever. *A*men.

Antiphon   I am the living bread come down from heaven; † anyone who eats this bread will *live* for ever, * all*e*luia.

INTERCESSIONS (VI F)

Brethren, let us pray to Jesus Christ, the *bread* of life, * as we joy*fu*lly say:

*Happy are those who are called to your heaven*ly banquet.

Priest of the new and eternal covenant, you offered perfect sacrifice to the Father on the altar *of* the cross,

—teach us to offer our*selves* with you.

King of justice and peace, you consecrated bread and wine as the sign *of* your offering,

—unite us as vic*tims* with you.

True worshiper of the Father, your perfect offering is celebrated by the Church from the rising to the setting *of* the sun,

—unite in your body those who partake of *the* one bread.

Manna from heaven, you nourish the Church with your bo*dy* and blood,

—grant that we may walk strengthened *by* this food.

Unseen host of our banquet, you stand at the *door* and knock,

—come to us, stay and share the evening *meal* with us.

Our Father . . .

Prayer

Lord Jesus Christ,
you gave us the eucharist
as the memorial of your suffering and death.
May our worship of this sacrament of your body and blood
help us to experience the salvation you won for us
and the peace of the kingdom
where you live and reign with the Father and the Holy Spirit,
one God, for ever and ever.

Evening Prayer II

<small>HYMN,</small> as in Evening Prayer I, 559.

<small>PSALMODY</small>

Ant. 1　　Christ the Lord is a priest for ever † in the line *of* Melchizedek; * he offered up *bread* and wine.

VIIIg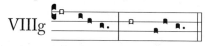

Psalm 110:1-5, 7

The Lord's revelation to my Master:
† "Sit *on* my right: * your foes I
will put be*neath* your feet."
The Lord will wield from Zion † your
scep*ter* of power: * rule in the midst
of *all* your foes.
A prince from the day of your birth
on the *holy* mountains; * from the
womb before the dawn *I* begot you.
The Lord has sworn an oath he will
not change. † "You are a *priest* for

ever, * a priest like Melchize*dek* of
old."
The Master standing at *your* right
hand * will shatter kings in the day
of *his* great wrath.
He shall drink from the stream *by* the
wayside * and therefore he shall lift
up his head.
Glory to the Father, and *to* the Son, *
and to the *Holy* Spirit:
as it was in the begin*ning*, is now, * and
will be for e*ver*. Amen.

Antiphon　　Christ the Lord is a priest for ever † in the line *of* Melchizedek; * he offered up *bread* and wine.

Ant. 2　　I will take up the cup *of* salvation, * and I will offer a sacrifice *of* praise.

IIA

Psalm 116:10-19

I trusted, even *when* I said: * "I am
sorely *afflicted*,"
and when I said in *my* alarm: * "No
man can *be* trusted."
How can I re*pay* the Lord * for his
goodness *to* me?
The cup of salvation *I* will raise; * I
will call on *the* Lord's name.
My vows to the Lord I *will* fulfill *

before all *his* people.
O precious in the eyes *of* the Lord * is
the death of *his* faithful.
Your servant, Lord, your ser*vant* am I;
* you have loosened *my* bonds.
A thanksgiving sacri*fice* I make: * I will
call on *the* Lord's name.
My vows to the Lord I *will* fulfill *
before all *his* people,

in the courts of the house *of* the Lord, *	and to the Ho*ly* Spirit:
in your midst, O *Je*rusalem.	as it was in the beginn*ing*, is now, * and
Glory to the Father, and *to* the Son, *	will be for ever. *A*men.

Antiphon   I will take up the cup *of* salvation, * and I will offer a sacrifice *of* praise.

Ant. 3   You are the way, the truth and the life of the world, O Lord, * alleluia, alleluia.

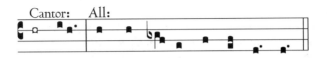

** al- le- lu- ia, al- le- lu- ia.

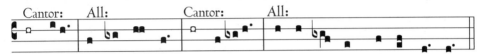

*Al- le- lu- ia.   ** al- le- lu- ia,   al- le - lu- ia.

Canticle   See Revelation 19:1-7

Salvation, glory, and power to *our* God:
* Alleluia.
his judgments are hon*est* and true.
** Alleluia, alleluia.

Sing praise to our God, all you *his* servants,
* Alleluia.
all who worship him reverently, *great* and small.
** Alleluia, alleluia.

The Lord our all-powerful God *is* King;
* Alleluia.
let us rejoice, sing praise, and *give* him glory.
** Alleluia, alleluia.

The wedding feast of the Lamb has *be*gun,
* Alleluia.
and his bride is pre*pared* to welcome him.
** Alleluia, alleluia.

Glory to the Father, and to the Son, †
and to the Ho*ly* Spirit.
* Alleluia.
As it was in the beginning, is now, †
and will be for ev*er*. Amen.
** Alleluia, alleluia.

Antiphon   You are the way, the truth and the life of the world, O Lord, *
alleluia, alleluia.

READING   1 Corinthians 11:23-25

I received from the Lord what I handed on to you, namely, that the Lord
Jesus on the night in which he was betrayed took bread, and after he had
given thanks, broke it and said, "This is my body, which is for you. Do this
in remembrance of me." In the same way, after the supper, he took the cup,
saying, "This cup is the new covenant in my blood. Do this, whenever you
drink it, in remembrance of me."

RESPONSORY (VI F)

He gave them *bread* from heaven, * alleluia, al*le*luia.
— He gave them *bread* from heaven, * alleluia, al*le*luia.
Man has eaten the bread of angels,
— alleluia, al*le*luia.
Glory to the Father, and *to* the Son, * and to the Ho*ly* Spirit.
— He gave them *bread* from heaven, * alleluia, al*le*luia.

CANTICLE OF MARY

Antiphon   How holy this feast in which Christ *is* our food; * his passion is
re*called;
grace fills our hearts; † and we receive the pledge of the glo*ry* to
come, * al*le*luia.

If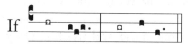

My soul ✠ proclaims the greatness
of the Lord, * my spirit rejoices
in God *my* savior
for he has *looked* with favor * on his
low*ly* servant.
From this day all *generations* * will call
me blessèd:
the Almighty has done great *things* for
me, * and holy is *his* Name.
He has mercy on *those* who fear him *

in every gen*er*ation.
He has shown the strength *of* his arm, *
he has scattered the proud in their
con*ceit.
He has cast down the mighty *from*
their thrones, * and has lifted up *the*
lowly.
He has filled the hungry *with* good
things, * and the rich he has sent
a*way* empty.

He has come to the help of his *servant*
 Israel * for he has remembered his
 promise *of* mercy,
the promise he made *to* our fathers, * to
 Abraham and his children *for* ever.

Glory to the Father, and *to* the Son, *
 and to the Ho*ly* Spirit:
as it was in the begin*ning*, is now, * and
 will be for ever. *A*men.

Antiphon How holy this feast in which Christ *is* our food; * his passion is
 *re*called;
 grace fills our hearts; † and we receive the pledge of the glo*ry* to
 come, * al*le*luia.

INTERCESSIONS (VI F)
Christ invites all to the supper in which he gives his body and blood for the life
 of the world. * *Let* us ask him:
*Christ, the bread of heaven, grant us everlast*ing *life.*
Christ, Son of the living God, you commanded that this thanksgiving meal be
 done in memo*ry* of you,
— enrich your Church through the faithful celebration *of* these mysteries.
Christ, eternal priest of the Most High, you have commanded your priests to
 of*fer* your sacraments,
— may they help them to exemplify in their lives the meaning of the sacred
 mysteries *which* they celebrate.
Christ, bread from heaven, you form one body out of all who partake of *the* one
 bread,
— refresh all who believe in you with harmo*ny* and peace.
Christ, through your bread you offer the remedy for immortality and the pledge
 of future *re*surrection,
— restore health to the sick and living *hope* to sinners.
Christ, our king who is to come, you commanded that the mysteries which
 proclaim your death be celebrated until *you* return,
— grant that all who die in you may share in your *re*surrection.

Our Father . . .

Prayer

Lord Jesus Christ,
 you gave us the eucharist
 as the memorial of your suffering and death.
 May our worship of this sacrament of your body and blood
 help us to experience the salvation you won for us
 and the peace of the kingdom
 where you live and reign with the Father and the Holy Spirit,
 one God, for ever and ever.

Friday after the Second Sunday After Pentecost
SACRED HEART
Evening Prayer I

HYMN

Auctor beate saeculi. (L.M.)

Auctor beate saeculi,	Jesus, Creator of the world!
Christe, Redemptor omnium,	Of all mankind Redeemer blest!
Lumen Patris de lumine	True God of God in whom we see
Deusque verus de Deo:	The Father's image clear expressed!
Amor coégit te tuus	You, Savior, love alone constrained
Mortale corpus sumere,	To make our mortal flesh your own;
ut, novus Adam, rédderes	And as a second Adam come,
quod vetus ille abstulerat:	For the first Adam to atone.
Ille amor, almus artifex	That self-same love that made the sky,
terrae marisque et siderum,	Which made the sea, and stars, and earth;
errata patrum miserans	Took pity on our misery,
et nostra rumpens vincula.	And broke the bondage of our birth.
Non corde discedat tuo	O Jesus! in your Heart divine
vis illa amoris incliti:	May that same love for ever flow,
hoc fonte gentes hauriant	Mercy for ever to mankind
remissionis gratium.	From that unending fountain flow.
Ad hoc acerbam lanceam	For this your Sacred Heart was pierced,
passumque ad hoc est vulnera,	And both with blood and water ran
ut nos lavaret sordibus	To cleanse us from the stains of guilt
unda fluente et sanguine.	And be the hope and strength of man.
Iesu, tibi sit gloria,	Jesus, to thee be glory giv'n,
qui corde fundis gratiam,	Who from your Heart dost grace outpour,
cum Patre et almo Spiritu	With Father and with Holy Ghost,
in sempiterna saecula. Amen.	Through endless ages evermore. Amen.

PSALMODY

Ant. 1   God has loved us with an everlasting love; † therefore, when he was lifted up *from* the earth, * in his mercy he drew us *to* his heart.

VIIIg

Psalm 113

Praise, O servants *of* the Lord, *
   praise the name *of* the Lord!
May the name of the *Lord* be blessed *
   both now and for *ever*more!

From the rising of the sun *to* its setting
   * praised be the name *of* the Lord!
High above all nations *is* the Lord, *
   above the heav*ens* his glory.

Who is like the *Lord*, our God, * who
 has risen on high *to* his throne
yet stoops from the heights *to* look
 down, * to look down upon heav*en*
 and earth?
From the dust he lifts *up* the lowly, *
 from his misery he rais*es* the poor
to set him in the compan*y* of princes, *
yes, with the princes *of* his people.
To the childless wife he *gives* a home *
 and gladdens her *heart* with children.
Glory to the Father, and *to* the Son, *
 and to the *Ho*ly Spirit:
as it was in the begin*ning*, is now, * and
 will be for ev*er.* Amen.

Antiphon   God has loved us with an everlasting love; † therefore, when he
            was lifted up *from* the earth, * in his mercy he drew us *to* his
            heart.

Ant. 2   Learn from *me*, * for I am gentle and humble *of* heart.

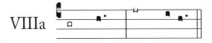

Psalm 146

My soul, give praise to the Lord;
† I will praise the Lord all my
days, * make music to my God
while *I* live.
Put no trust in *princ*es, * in mortal
men in whom there is *no* help.
Take their breath, they return to *clay*
 * and their plans that day come *to*
nothing.
He is happy who is helped by Jacob's
 God, * whose hope is in the Lord
 his God,
who alone made heaven and *earth*, *
 the seas and all they *con*tain.
It is he who keeps faith for *ev*er, *
 who is just to those who are
*op*pressed.
It is he who gives bread to the *hun*gry,
 * the Lord, who sets prison*ers* free,
the Lord who gives sight to the *blind*, *
 who raises up those who are *bowed*
down,
the Lord, who protects the *strang*er *
 and upholds the widow *and* orphan.
It is the Lord who loves the *just* * but
 thwarts the path of *the* wicked.
The Lord will reign for *ev*er, * Zion's
 God, from age *to* age.
Glory to the Father, and *to* the Son, *
 and to the *Ho*ly Spirit:
as it was in the beginning, is *now*, * and
 will be for ever. *A*men.

Antiphon   Learn from *me*, * for I am gentle and humble *of* heart.

Ant. 3   I am the *Good* Shepherd; * I pasture my sheep and I lay down my
          life *for* them.

Canticle   Revelation 4:11; 5:9, 10, 12

O Lord our God, you *are* worthy *
to receive glory and honor *and*
power.

For you have created *all* things; * by
your will they came to be and *were*
made.

Worthy are you, *O* Lord, * to receive
the scroll and break open *its* seals.

For you *were* slain; * with your blood
you purchased *for* God

men of every race *and* tongue, * of
every people *and* nation.

You made of them a kingdom, and
priests to serve *our* God, * and they
shall reign on *the* earth.

Worthy is the Lamb that *was* slain * to
receive power *and* riches,

wisdom *and* strength, * honor and
glory *and* praise.

Glory to the Father, and to *the* Son, *
and to the Ho*ly* Spirit:

as it was in the beginning, *is* now, * and
will be for ever. *A*men.

Antiphon   I am the *Good* Shepherd; * I pasture my sheep and I lay down
my life *for* them.

READING   Ephesians 5:25b-27

Christ loved the church. He gave himself up for her to make her holy,
purifying her in the bath of water by the power of the word, to present to
himself a glorious church, holy and immaculate, without stain or wrinkle or
anything of that sort.

RESPONSORY (VI F)

Christ *has* loved us, * and in his blood he has washed away *our* sins.

— Christ *has* loved us, * and in his blood he has washed away *our* sins.

He has made us a kingdom and priests to serve *God* our Father.

— And in his blood he has washed away *our* sins.

Glory to the Father, and *to* the Son, * and to the Ho*ly* Spirit.

— Christ *has* loved us, * and in his blood he has washed away *our* sins.

CANTICLE OF MARY

Antiphon   I have come to cast fire up*on* the earth; * how I long to see the
flame *leap* up.

If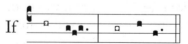

M y soul ✠ proclaims the greatness
of the Lord, * my spirit rejoices
in God *my* savior

for he has *looked* with favor * on his
low*ly* servant.

From this day all *gen*erations * will call
me blessèd:

the Almighty has done great *things* for
me, * and holy is *his* Name.

He has mercy on *those* who fear him *
in every gen*er*ation.

He has shown the strength *of* his arm, *
he has scattered the proud in their
con*ceit.*

He has cast down the mighty *from* their thrones, * and has lifted up *the* lowly.

He has filled the hungry *with* good things, * and the rich he has sent a*way* empty.

He has come to the help of his *servant* Israel * for he has remembered his promise *of* mercy,

the promise he made *to* our fathers, * to Abraham and his children *for* ever.

Glory to the Father, and *to* the Son, * and to the Ho*ly* Spirit:

as it was in the begin*ning*, is now, * and will be for ever. *A*men.

Antiphon   I have come to cast fire up*on* the earth; * how I long to see the flame *leap* up.

INTERCESSIONS (VI F)

Brethren, let us pray to the Lord Jesus, the refuge *of* our souls; * let *us* ask him:
Most loving Lord, have mercy on us.

Jesus, whose heart when pierced by a lance poured forth blood and water and gave birth to your *spouse* the Church,
— cleanse and sanc*tify* us.

Jesus, holy temple of God, slain by men and raised up again *by* the Father,
— make your Church the dwelling place *of* the Most High.

Jesus, King and center of all hearts, you love us and lead us to yourself with unending *love* and mercy,
— renew your covenant *with* all men.

Jesus, our peace and reconciliation, you unite all in the peace of the new creation and put enmity to death *through* the cross,
— show us the path *to* the Father.

Jesus, our life and resurrection, you refresh the burdened and give rest *to* the weary,
— draw all sinners *to* yourself.

Jesus, because you loved us with so great a love, you were obedient even to death *on* the cross,
— raise up again all who sleep *in* your peace.

Our Father . . .

Prayer

Father,
we rejoice in the gifts of love
we have received from the heart of Jesus your Son.
Open our hearts to share his life
and continue to bless us with his love.
We ask this through our Lord Jesus Christ, your Son,
who lives and reigns with you and the Holy Spirit,
one God, for ever and ever.

Morning Prayer

HYMN

Cor Jesu, Cor purissimum. (L.M.)

Iesu, auctor clementiæ,	O Jesus, source of pardon sure,
totius spes lætitiæ,	And hope of all our deepest joy,
dulcoris fons et gratiæ,	You are the fountain of all grace,
veræ cordis deliciæ:	And true delight of every heart.
Iesu, spes pænitentibus,	O Jesus, hope of sinners all,
quam pius es petentibus,	How kind you are to those who ask,
quam bonus te quærentibus;	How good to those who search for you,
sed quid invenientibus?	And what indeed to those who find!
Tua, Iesu, dilectio,	Your love it is that feeds our souls,
grata mentis refectio,	As gratefully we turn to you,
replet sine fastidio,	Repast that pleases every taste,
dans famem desiderio.	And makes us long to love you more.
O Iesus dilectissime,	O Jesus, loved above all else,
spes suspirantis animæ,	True hope of eager hearts' desire;
te quærunt piæ lacrimæ,	The soul's most ardent search for good
te clamor mentis intimæ.	Is satisfied by you alone.
Mane nobiscum, Domine,	Remain with us, belovèd Lord,
Mane novum cum lumine,	Be with us like the dawning day,
pulsa noctis caligine	The shades of night are now dispelled,
mundum replens dulcedine.	Your sweetness fills the world with light.
Iesu, summa benignitas,	O Jesus, perfect tenderness,
mira cordis iucunditas,	Surpassing joy of every heart,
incomprehensa bonitas,	Your goodness is beyond our grasp,
tua nos stringit caritas.	Your love surrounds and hold us fast.
Iesu, flos Matris virginis,	O Jesus, Flow'r of Virgin birth,
amor nostræ dulcedinis,	And sweetest love that man can know,
laus tibi sine terminis,	Praise be to you for evermore,
regnum beatitudinis. Amen.	In your eternal sovereignty. Amen.

PSALMODY

Ant. 1   Jesus stood and cried out: † If anyone thirsts, * let him come to *me* and drink.

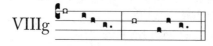

Psalm 63:2-9

O God, you are my God, for *you* I long; * for you my *soul* is thirsting.

My body *pines* for you * like a dry, weary land *with*out water.

So I gaze on you *in* the sanctuary * to see your strength *and* your glory.

For your love is bet*ter* than life, * my lips will speak *your* praise.

So I will bless you *all* my life, * in your name I will lift *up* my hands.

My soul shall be filled as *with* a banquet, * my mouth shall praise *you* with joy.

On my bed I re*mem*ber you. * On you I muse *through* the night

for you have *been* my help; * in the shadow of your wings *I* rejoice.

My soul *clings* to you; * your right hand *holds* me fast.

Glory to the Father, and *to* the Son, * and to the *Holy* Spirit:

as it was in the begin*ning*, is now, * and will be for e*ver*. Amen.

Antiphon   Jesus stood and cried out: † If anyone thirsts, * let him come to *me* and drink.

Ant. 2   Come to me, † all you who labor *and* are burdened, * and I will give *you* rest.

Canticle   Daniel 3:57-88; 56

B less the Lord, all you works *of* the Lord. * Praise and exalt him above all *for*ever.

Angels of the Lord, *bless* the Lord, * You heavens, bless *the* Lord.

All you waters above the heavens, *bless* the Lord. * All you hosts of the Lord, bless *the* Lord.

Sun and moon, *bless* the Lord. * Stars of heaven, bless *the* Lord.

Every shower and dew, *bless* the Lord. * All you winds, bless *the* Lord.

Fire and heat, *bless* the Lord. * Cold and chill, bless *the* Lord.

Dew and rain, *bless* the Lord. * Frost and chill, bless *the* Lord.

Ice and snow, *bless* the Lord. * Nights and days, bless *the* Lord.

Light and darkness, *bless* the Lord. * Lightnings and clouds, bless *the* Lord.

Let the earth *bless* the Lord. * Praise and exalt him above all *for*ever.

Mountains and hills, *bless* the Lord. * Everything growing from the earth, bless *the* Lord.

You springs, *bless* the Lord. * Seas and rivers, bless *the* Lord.

You dolphins and all water creatures, *bless* the Lord. * All you birds of the air, bless *the* Lord.

All you beasts, wild and tame, *bless* the Lord. * You sons of men, bless *the* Lord.

O Israel, *bless* the Lord. * Praise and exalt him above all *for*ever.

Priests of the Lord, *bless* the Lord. * Servants of the Lord, bless *the* Lord.

Spirits and souls of the just, *bless* the Lord. * Holy men of humble heart,

bless *the* Lord.
Hananiah, Azariah, Mishael, *bless* the
    Lord. * Praise and exalt him above all
    *for*ever.
Let us bless the Father, and the Son,

and the *Ho*ly Spirit. * Let us praise
    and exalt him above all *for*ever.
Blessèd are you in the firma*ment* of
    heaven.* Praiseworthy and glorious and
    exalted above all *for*ever.

Antiphon   Come to me, † all you who labor *and* are burdened, * and I will
                   give *you* rest.

Ant. 3   My son, give me *your* heart; * note carefully the way I point out
                   to you.

V a

Psalm 149

Sing a new song to *the* Lord, * his
   praise in the assembly of *the*
   faithful.
Let Israel rejoice in *its* Maker, * let
   Zion's sons exult in *their* king.
Let them praise his name *with* dancing
   * and make music with timbrel *and*
   harp.
For the Lord takes delight in *his*
   people. * He crowns the poor with
   sal*va*tion.
Let the faithful rejoice in *their* glory, *
   shout for joy and take *their* rest.

Let the praise of God be on *their* lips *
   and a two-edged sword in *their*
   hand,
to deal out vengeance to *the* nations *
   and punishment on all *the* peoples;
to bind their kings *in* chains * and
   their nobles in fetters *of* iron;
to carry out the sentence pre-*or*dained:
   * this honor is for all *his* faithful.
Glory to the Father, and to *the* Son, *
   and to the Ho*ly* Spirit:
as it was in the beginning, *is* now, * and
   will be for ever. *A*men.

Antiphon   My son, give me *your* heart; * note carefully the way I point out
                   to you.

READING   Jeremiah 31:33
     This is the covenant which I will make with the house of Israel after those
     days, says the Lord. I will place my law within them, and write it upon their
     hearts; I will be their God, and they shall be my people.

RESPONSORY (VI F)
Take my *yoke* upon you * and learn *from* me.
—Take my *yoke* upon you * and learn *from* me.
For I am gentle and hum*ble* of heart.
—Learn *from* me.

Glory to the Father, and *to* the Son, * and to the Ho*ly* Spirit.
— Take my *yoke* upon you * and learn *from* me.

CANTICLE OF ZECHARIAH

Antiphon   With tender compassion, † our God has come *to* his people * and
                  set *them* free.

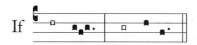

Bless*èd* ✠ be the Lord, the *God* of
Israel; * he has come to his people
and set *them* free.
He has raised up for us a *mighty* savior,
* born of the house of his serv*ant*
David.
Through his holy prophets he promised of old † that he would save us
from our enemies, * from the hands
of all *who* hate us.
He promised to show mercy *to* our
fathers * and to remember his ho*ly*
covenant.
This was the oath he swore to our
*fath*er Abraham: * to set us free from
the hands of *our* enemies,
free to worship him without fear, †
holy and righteous *in* his sight * all

the days of *our* life.
You, my child, shall be called the
prophet *of* the Most High; * for you
will go before the Lord to prepare *his*
way,
to give his people knowledge *of* salvation * by the forgiveness of *their* sins.
In the tender compassion *of* our God *
the dawn from on high shall break
*up*on us,
to shine on those who dwell in darkness and the sha*dow* of death, * and
to guide our feet into the way *of*
peace.
Glory to the Father, and *to* the Son, *
and to the Ho*ly* Spirit:
as it was in the begin*ning*, is now, * and
will be for ever. *A*men.

Antiphon   With tender compassion, † our God has come *to* his people *
                  and set *them* free.

INTERCESSIONS (VI F)

Brethren, let us pray to the Lord Jesus, who is meek and hum*ble* of heart. * *Let* us
ask him:
Most loving Lord, have mercy on us.
Jesus, the fullness of divinity *dwells* in you,
— give us a share in your *di*vine life.
Jesus, in you are all the treasures of wis*dom* and knowledge,
— make known to us through your Church the manifold wis*dom* of God.
Jesus, the Father was well *pleased* in you,
— help us to hear your *word* and keep it.
Jesus, of your fullness we have *all* received,
— pour out upon us in abundance the Father's fa*vor* and truth.

Jesus, you are the source of *life* and holiness,
—make us holy and blame*less* in love.

Our Father . . .

Prayer

Father,
we rejoice in the gifts of love
we have received from the heart of Jesus your Son.
Open our hearts to share his life
and continue to bless us with his love.
We ask this through our Lord Jesus Christ, your Son,
who lives and reigns with you and the Holy Spirit,
one God, for ever and ever.

Evening Prayer II

HYMN, as in Evening Prayer I, 572.

PSALMODY

Ant. 1   Lord, rule in the midst *of* your enemies * with your *gen*tle yoke.

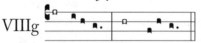

VIIIg

Psalm 110:1-5, 7

The Lord's revelation to my Master:
  † "Sit *on* my right: * your foes I
will put be*neath* your feet."
The Lord will wield from Zion † your
  scep*ter* of power: * rule in the midst
  of *all* your foes.
A prince from the day of your birth
  on the *holy* mountains; * from the
  womb before the dawn *I* begot you.
The Lord has sworn an oath he will
  not change. † "You are a *priest* for
  ever, * a priest like Melchize*dek* of

old."
The Master standing at *your* right
  hand * will shatter kings in the day
  of *his* great wrath.
He shall drink from the stream *by* the
  wayside * and therefore he shall lift
  up his head.
Glory to the Father, and *to* the Son, *
  and to the *Holy* Spirit:
as it was in the begin*ning*, is now, * and
  will be for e*ver*. Amen.

Antiphon   Lord, rule in the midst *of* your enemies * with your *gen*tle yoke.

Ant. 2   The Lord is lov*ing* and merciful; * he gives food to those *who* fear him.

IIA

Psalm 111

I will thank the Lord with *all* my heart * in the meeting of the just and their *as*sembly.

Great are the works *of* the Lord; * to be pondered by all *who* love them.

Majestic and glori*ous* his work, * his justice stands firm *for* ever.

He makes us remem*ber* his wonders. * The Lord is compassion *and* love.

He gives food to *those* who fear him; * keeps his covenant ever *in* mind.

He has shown his might *to* his people * by giving them the lands of *the* nations.

His works are jus*tice* and truth: * his

precepts are all of *them* sure, standing firm for ev*er* and ever: * they are made in uprightness *and* truth.

He has sent deliverance to his people † and established his cove*nant* for ever. * Holy his name, to *be* feared.

To fear the Lord is the first stage of wisdom; † all who do so prove *them*selves wise. * His praise shall last *for* ever!

Glory to the Father, and *to* the Son, * and to the Ho*ly* Spirit:

as it was in the begin*ning*, is now, * and will be for ever. *A*men.

Antiphon   The Lord is lov*ing* and merciful; * he gives food to those *who* fear him.

Ant. 3   This is the Lamb *of* God * who takes away the sins *of* the world.

V c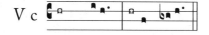

Canticle   Philippians 2:6-11

Though he was in the form *of* God, * Jesus did not deem equality with God something *to* be grasped at.

Rather, he emptied himself and took the form of *a* slave, * being born in the like*ness* of men.

He was known to be of human *estate*, * and it was thus that he hum*bled* himself,

obediently accepting ev*en* death, * death *on* a cross!

Because *of* this, * God high*ly* exalted him

and bestowed on him *the* name * above every *other* name,

So that at Jesus' name every knee *must* bend * in the heavens, on the earth, and un*der* the earth,

and every tongue proclaim to the glory

of God *the* Father: * JESUS *CHRIST* IS LORD!

Glory to the Father, and to *the* Son, *

and to the *Holy* Spirit:
as it was in the beginning, *is* now, * and will be for ev*er*. Amen.

Antiphon   This is the Lamb *of* God * who takes away the sins *of* the world.

READING   Ephesians 2:4-7

God is rich in mercy; because of his great love for us he brought us to life with Christ when we were dead in sin. By this favor you were saved. Both with and in Christ Jesus he raised us up and gave us a place in the heavens, that in the ages to come he might display the great wealth of his favor, manifested by his kindness to us in Christ Jesus.

RESPONSORY (VI F)

Christ *has* loved us, * and in his blood he has washed away *our* sins.
— Christ *has* loved us, * and in his blood he has washed away *our* sins.
He has made us a kingdom and priests to serve *God* our Father.
— And in his blood he has washed away *our* sins.
Glory to the Father, and *to* the Son, * and to the Ho*ly* Spirit.
— Christ *has* loved us, * and in his blood he has washed away *our* sins.

CANTICLE OF MARY

Antiphon   The Lord has lifted us up and drawn us to his heart, † for he has remembered his pro*mise* of mercy, * Al*le*luia.

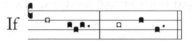

If

My soul ✠ proclaims the greatness *of* the Lord, * my spirit rejoices in God *my* savior

for he has *looked* with favor * on his low*ly* servant.

From this day all *generations* * will call *me* blessèd:

the Almighty has done great *things* for me, * and holy is *his* Name.

He has mercy on *those* who fear him * in every gen*er*ation.

He has shown the strength *of* his arm, * he has scattered the proud in their *con*ceit.

He has cast down the mighty *from* their thrones, * and has lifted up *the* lowly.

He has filled the hungry *with* good things, * and the rich he has sent a*way* empty.

He has come to the help of his *servant* Israel * for he has remembered his promise *of* mercy,

the promise he made *to* our fathers, * to Abraham and his children *for* ever.

Glory to the Father, and *to* the Son, * and to the Ho*ly* Spirit:

as it was in the begin*ning*, is now, * and will be for ever. *A*men.

Antiphon   The Lord has lifted us up and drawn us to his heart, † for he has remembered his pro*mise* of mercy, * Al*le*luia.

INTERCESSIONS (VI F)

Brethren, let us pray to the Lord Jesus, the refuge *of* our souls; * let *us* ask him:
Most loving Lord, have mercy on *us.*

Jesus, whose heart when pierced by a lance poured forth blood and water and
gave birth to your *spouse* the Church,
— cleanse and sanc*tif*y us.

Jesus, holy temple of God, slain by men and raised up again *by* the Father,
— make your Church the dwelling place *of* the Most High.

Jesus, King and center of all hearts, you love us and lead us to yourself with
unending *love* and mercy,
— renew your covenant *with* all men.

Jesus, our peace and reconciliation, you unite all in the peace of the new creation
and put enmity to death *through* the cross,
— show us the path *to* the Father.

Jesus, our life and resurrection, you refresh the burdened and give rest *to* the
weary,
— draw all sinners *to* yourself.

Jesus, because you loved us with so great a love, you were obedient even to death
on the cross,
— raise up again all who sleep *in* your peace.

Our Father . . .

Prayer

Father,
we rejoice in the gifts of love
we have received from the heart of Jesus your Son.
Open our hearts to share his life
and continue to bless us with his love.
We ask this through our Lord Jesus Christ, your Son,
who lives and reigns with you and the Holy Spirit,
one God, for ever and ever.

Last Sunday in Ordinary Time
CHRIST THE KING
Solemnity

Evening Prayer I

HYMN

Te saeculorum. Mode I (L.M.)

Te sæculórum príncipem,	O Christ, the Ruler of all time,
te, Christe, regem géntium,	You hold the world beneath your sway,
te méntium, te córdium	As Judge supreme of every soul
unum fatémur árbitrum.	We offer you our hearts this day.
Quem prona adórant ágmina	Before your throne the angels sing
hymnísque laudant cælitum,	And down in adoration fall,
te nos ovántes ómnium	We praise you with our heart's delight,
regem suprémum dícimus.	Proclaiming you the King of all.
O Christe, princeps pácifer,	O Christ, our Shepherd, Prince of Peace,
mentes rebélles súbice,	Our rebel hearts and minds subdue,
tuóque amóre dévios	And draw the sheep that roam astray,
ovíle in unum cóngrega.	Within the fold, at one with you.
Ad hoc cruénta ab árbore	For this you hung upon the Tree,
pendes apértis brácchiis,	With saving arms extended wide;
diráque fossum cúspide	To prove the measure of your love
cor igne flagrans éxhibes.	The cruel lance would pierce your side.
Ad hoc in aris ábderis	Upon our altars you descend,
vini dapísque imágine,	Beneath the forms of bread and wine,
fundens salútem fíliis	That we may our salvation win,
transverberáto péctore.	And even share your life divine.
Iesu, tibi sit glória,	All glory, Jesus, be to you,
qui cuncta amóre témperas,	Who with the Father reign above,
cum Patre et almo Spíritu	Who with the Spirit rule all things
in sempitérna sæcula. Amen.	With infinite and wondrous love. Amen.

PSALMODY

Ant. 1   We will call *him* the peacemaker, * and his throne shall stand *firm* for ever.

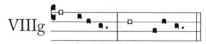

VIIIg

Psalm 113

P raise, O servants *of* the Lord, * | May the name of the *Lord* be blessed *
praise the name *of* the Lord! | both now and for *ev*ermore!

From the rising of the sun *to* its setting
  * praised be the name *of* the Lord!
High above all nations *is* the Lord, *
  above the heav*ens* his glory.
Who is like the *Lord*, our God, * who
  has risen on high *to* his throne
yet stoops from the heights *to* look
  down, * to look down upon heav*en*
  and earth?
From the dust he lifts *up* the lowly, *

from his misery he rais*es* the poor
to set him in the compan*y* of princes, *
  yes, with the princes *of* his people.
To the childless wife he *gives* a home *
  and gladdens her *heart* with children.
Glory to the Father, and *to* the Son, *
  and to the *Holy* Spirit:
as it was in the begin*ning*, is now, * and
  will be for ev*er*. Amen.

Antiphon   We will call *him* the peacemaker, * and his throne shall stand
              firm for ever.

Ant. 2   His kingdom will en*dure* for ever, * and all the kings of the earth
              will serve and *obey* him.

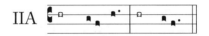

IIA

Psalm 117

O praise the Lord, *all* you
  nations, * acclaim him all *you*
  peoples!
Strong is his *love* for us; * he is
  faithful *for* ever.

Glory to the Father, and *to* the Son, *
  and to the Ho*ly* Spirit:
as it was in the begin*ning*, is now, * and
  will be for ever. *A*men.

Antiphon   His kingdom will en*dure* for ever, * and all the kings of the earth
              will serve and *obey* him.

Ant. 3   The authority and honor of a king have been given *to* Christ; *
              all peoples, tribes and nations will serve him *for* ever.

V a

Canticle   Revelation 4:11; 5:9, 10, 12

O Lord our God, you *are* worthy *
  to receive glory and honor *and*
  power.
For you have created *all* things; * by
  your will they came to be and *were*
  made.
Worthy are you, O Lord, * to receive

the scroll and break open *its* seals.
For you *were* slain; * with your blood
  you purchased *for* God
men of every race *and* tongue, * of
  every people *and* nation.
You made of them a kingdom, and
  priests to serve *our* God, * and they

shall reign on *the* earth.
Worthy is the Lamb that *was* slain * to
    receive power *and* riches,
wisdom *and* strength, * honor and
    glory *and* praise.

Glory to the Father, and to *the* Son, *
    and to the Ho*ly* Spirit:
as it was in the beginning, *is* now, * and
    will be for ever. *A*men.

Antiphon   The authority and honor of a king have been given *to* Christ; *
                  all peoples, tribes and nations will serve him *for* ever.

READING   See Ephesians 1:20-23
    God raised Christ from the dead and seated him at his right hand in heaven,
    high above every principality, power, virtue, and domination, and every name
    that can be given in this age or in the age to come. He has put all things
    under Christ's feet and has made him, thus exalted, head of the church,
    which is his body: the fullness of him who fills the universe in all its parts.

RESPONSORY (VI F)
Yours is the splendor *and* the power; * yours is the kingdom, O Lord.
— Yours is the splendor *and* the power; * yours is the kingdom, O Lord.
You will rule *over* all,
— yours is the kingdom, O Lord.
Glory to the Father, and *to* the Son, * and to the Ho*ly* Spirit.
— Yours is the splendor *and* the power; * yours is the kingdom, O Lord.

CANTICLE OF MARY
Antiphon   The Lord God will give him the throne of David, his ancestor; †
                  he will rule in the house of Ja*cob* for ever * and his kingdom will
                  have no end, al*le*luia.

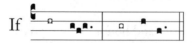

M*y* soul ✠ proclaims the greatness
of the Lord, * my spirit rejoices
    in God *my* savior
for he has *looked* with favor * on his
    low*ly* servant.
From this day all *gen*erations * will call
    me blessèd:
the Almighty has done great *things* for
    me, * and holy is *his* Name.
He has mercy on *those* who fear him *
    in every gen*er*ation.
He has shown the strength *of* his arm, *

he has scattered the proud in their
    *con*ceit.
He has cast down the mighty *from* their
    thrones, * and has lifted up *the* lowly.
He has filled the hungry *with* good
    things, * and the rich he has sent
    a*way* empty.
He has come to the help of his *ser*vant
    Israel * for he has remembered his
    promise *of* mercy,
the promise he made *to* our fathers, * to
    Abraham and his children *for* ever.

Glory to the Father, and *to* the Son, * | as it was in the begin*ning*, is now, *
and to the Ho*ly* Spirit: | and will be for ever. *A*men.

Antiphon   The Lord God will give him the throne of David, his ancestor;
            † he will rule in the house of Jac*ob* for ever * and his kingdom
            will have no end, al*le*luia.

INTERCESSIONS (VI F)

Let us pray to Christ the King. He is the firstborn of *all* creation; * all things ex*ist*
in him.
May your kingdom come, O Lord.
Christ, our king and shepherd, gather your sheep from *eve*ry land,
— give them pasture in green and fer*tile* meadows.
Christ, our leader and savior, form all men into your own people, heal the sick,
seek out the lost, *guard* the strong,
— call back those who have wandered far away, strengthen those who waver,
gather all your sheep in*to* one flock.
Judge of all ages, when you hand over your kingdom to the Father, place us at
your right hand,
— so that we may inherit the kingdom prepared for us from the beginning *of* the
world.
Prince of peace, break the wea*pons* of war,
— and inspire the nations *with* your peace.
Christ, heir of all nations, gather humanity and all the good things of your
creation into the kingdom of your Church which your Father be*stowed* on you,
— so that the whole body of your people, united in the Holy Spirit, may
acknowledge you *as* their head.
Christ, firstborn of the dead and firstfruits of those who have fallen a*sleep* in
death,
— bring all who have died to the glory of the *re*surrection.

Our Father . . .

Prayer

Almighty and merciful God,
you break the power of evil
and make all things new
in your Son Jesus Christ, the King of the universe.
May all in heaven and earth acclaim your glory
and never cease to praise you.
We ask this through our Lord Jesus Christ, your Son,
who lives and reigns with you and the Holy Spirit,
one God, for ever and ever.

Morning Prayer

HYMN

Ætérna imágo Altíssimi. Mode I (L.M.)

Ætérna imágo Altíssimi,	The Father's image, Jesus Lord,
Lumen, Deus, de Lúmine,	Eternal God, True Light's pure Beam,
tibi, Redémptor, glória,	To you, Redeemer of all men,
honor, potéstas régia.	All glory, honor, pow'r supreme.
Tu solus ante sæcula	Before all time you ruled alone,
spes atque centrum témporum;	Then Hope of ages you became,
tibi voléntes súbdimur,	To your sweet yoke we gladly bow
qui iure cunctis ímperas.	And your supremacy proclaim.
Tu flos pudícæ Vírginis,	The Second Adam of our race,
nostræ caput propáginis,	You are the Flower of Virgin-birth,
lapis cadúcus vértice	The Stone that crushed the Kingdom's might
ac mole terras óccupans.	And grew until it filled the earth.
Diro tyránno súbdita,	Ensnared by evil demon's wiles,
damnáta stirps mortálium	Man lost the grace he had before,
per te refrégit víncula	But you have conquered sin and death
sibíque cælum víndicat.	And heaven is our hope once more.
Doctor, sacérdos, légifer,	Our Teacher, Priest, Law-giver too,
præfers notátum sánguine	New life to all your Triumph brings;
in veste « Princeps príncipum	Your blood-stained robe reveals your name:
regúmque rex altíssimus ».	The Lord of lords and King of kings.
Patri, tibi, Paráclito	Unending glory be to Christ,
sit, Christe, perpes glória,	Who by his Blood our ransom paid;
qui nos redémptos sánguine	The Spirit's Love, the Father's will,
ad regna cæli pértrahis. Amen.	Decreed the plan which he obeyed. Amen.

PSALMODY

Ant. 1   A man will come whose name is the Dayspring; † from his
             throne he will rule *over* all; * he will speak of peace *to* the
             nations.

VIIIg

Psalm 63:2-9

O God, you are my God, for *you* I long; * for you my *soul* is thirsting.	weary land *without* water. So I gaze on you *in* the sanctuary * to see your strength *and* your glory.
My body *pines* for you * like a dry,	For your love is bet*ter* than life, * my

lips will speak *your* praise.
So I will bless you *all* my life, * in your
name I will lift *up* my hands.
My soul shall be filled as *with* a
banquet, * my mouth shall praise *you*
with joy.
On my bed I re*mem*ber you. * On you
I muse *through* the night

for you have *been* my help; * in the
shadow of your wings *I* rejoice.
My soul *clings* to you; * your right
hand *holds* me fast.
Glory to the Father, and *to* the Son, *
and to the *Holy* Spirit:
as it was in the begin*ning*, is now, * and
will be for e*ver*. Amen.

Antiphon   A man will come whose name is the Dayspring; † from his
throne he will rule *over* all; * he will speak of peace *to* the
nations.

Ant. 2   They will sing his praises to the ends *of* the earth, * and he will
be *their* peace.

IIA

Canticle   Daniel 3:57-88; 56

Bless the Lord, all you works *of* the
Lord. * Praise and exalt him above
all *for*ever.
Angels of the Lord, *bless* the Lord, *
You heavens, bless *the* Lord.
All you waters above the heavens, *bless*
the Lord. * All you hosts of the
Lord, bless *the* Lord.
Sun and moon, *bless* the Lord. * Stars
of heaven, bless *the* Lord.
Every shower and dew, *bless* the Lord. *
All you winds, bless *the* Lord.
Fire and heat, *bless* the Lord. * Cold
and chill, bless *the* Lord.
Dew and rain, *bless* the Lord. * Frost
and chill, bless *the* Lord.
Ice and snow, *bless* the Lord. * Nights
and days, bless *the* Lord.
Light and darkness, *bless* the Lord. *
Lightnings and clouds, bless *the*
Lord.
Let the earth *bless* the Lord. * Praise
and exalt him above all *for*ever.

Mountains and hills, *bless* the Lord. *
Everything growing from the earth,
bless *the* Lord.
You springs, *bless* the Lord. * Seas and
rivers, bless *the* Lord.
You dolphins and all water creatures,
bless the Lord. * All you birds of the
air, bless *the* Lord.
All you beasts, wild and tame, *bless* the
Lord. * You sons of men, bless *the*
Lord.
O Israel, *bless* the Lord. * Praise and
exalt him above all *for*ever.
Priests of the Lord, *bless* the Lord. *
Servants of the Lord, bless *the* Lord.
Spirits and souls of the just, *bless* the
Lord. * Holy men of humble heart,
bless *the* Lord.
Hananiah, Azariah, Mishael, *bless* the
Lord. * Praise and exalt him above all
*for*ever.
Let us bless the Father, and the Son,
and the *Holy* Spirit. * Let us praise

and exalt him above all *for*ever.   heaven.* Praiseworthy and glorious and
Blessèd are you in the firma*ment* of   exalted above all *for*ever.

Antiphon   They will sing his praises to the ends *of* the earth, * and he will
                  be *their* peace.

Ant. 3   The Lord will give him power and honor *and* kingship; * all
                  peoples, tribes and nations *will* serve him.

Psalm 149

Sing a new song to *the* Lord, * his
praise in the assembly of *the*
faithful.
Let Israel rejoice in *its* Maker, * let
Zion's sons exult in *their* king.
Let them praise his name *with* dancing
* and make music with timbrel *and*
harp.
For the Lord takes delight in *his*
people. * He crowns the poor with
sal*va*tion.
Let the faithful rejoice in *their* glory, *
shout for joy and take *their* rest.

Let the praise of God be on *their* lips *
and a two-edged sword in *their*
hand,
to deal out vengeance to *the* nations *
and punishment on all *the* peoples;
to bind their kings *in* chains * and
their nobles in fetters *of* iron;
to carry out the sentence pre-*or*dained:
* this honor is for all *his* faithful.
Glory to the Father, and to *the* Son, *
and to the Ho*ly* Spirit:
as it was in the beginning, *is* now, * and
will be for ever. *A*men.

Antiphon   The Lord will give him power and honor *and* kingship; * all
                  peoples, tribes and nations *will* serve him.

READING   Ephesians 4:15-16
    Let us profess the truth in love and grow to the full maturity of Christ the
    head. Through him the whole body grows, and with the proper functioning
    of the members joined firmly together by each supporting ligament, builds
    itself up in love.

RESPONSORY (VI F)
Your *saints*, O Lord, * will tell of the glory of *your* kingdom.
— Your *saints*, O Lord, * will tell of the glory of *your* kingdom.
They will pro*claim* your power.
— They will tell of the glory of *your* kingdom.
Glory to the Father, and *to* the Son, * and to the Ho*ly* Spirit.
— Your *saints*, O Lord, * will tell of the glory of *your* kingdom.

CANTICLE OF ZECHARIAH

Antiphon   He fashioned us into a kingdom for the glory of his God and
            Father; † he is the firstborn *of* the dead * and the leader of all the
            kings of the earth, al*le*luia.

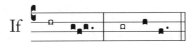

Blessèd ✠ be the Lord, the *God* of
Israel; * he has come to his people
and set *them* free.
He has raised up for us a *might*y savior,
* born of the house of his ser*vant*
David.
Through his holy prophets he promised of old † that he would save us
from our enemies, * from the hands
of all *who* hate us.
He promised to show mercy *to* our
fathers * and to remember his ho*ly*
covenant.
This was the oath he swore to our
*fath*er Abraham: * to set us free from
the hands of *our* enemies,
free to worship him without fear, †
holy and righteous *in* his sight * all

the days of *our* life.
You, my child, shall be called the
prophet *of* the Most High; * for you
will go before the Lord to prepare *his*
way,
to give his people knowledge *of* salvation * by the forgiveness of *their* sins.
In the tender compassion *of* our God *
the dawn from on high shall break
*up*on us,
to shine on those who dwell in darkness and the sha*dow* of death, * and
to guide our feet into the way *of*
peace.
Glory to the Father, and *to* the Son, *
and to the Ho*ly* Spirit:
as it was in the begin*ning*, is now, * and
will be for ever. *A*men.

Antiphon   He fashioned us into a kingdom for the glory of his God and
            Father; † he is the firstborn *of* the dead * and the leader of all the
            kings of the earth, al*le*luia.

INTERCESSIONS (VI F)

Let us pray to Christ the King. He is the firstborn of *all* creation; * all things ex*ist*
in him.
May your kingdom come, O Lord.
Christ, you are our savior and our God, our shepherd *and* our king,
— lead your people to life-*giv*ing pastures.
Good Shepherd, you laid down your life *for* your sheep,
— rule over us, and in your care we shall *want* for nothing.
Christ, our redeemer, you have been made king over *all* the earth,
— restore all creation *in* yourself.
King of all creation, you came into the world to bear witness *to* the truth,
— may all men come to acknowledge your primacy *in* all things.

Christ, our model and master, you have brought us in*to* your kingdom,
— grant that we may be holy and blameless before *you* this day.

Our Father . . .

Prayer

Almighty and merciful God,
you break the power of evil
and make all things new
in your Son Jesus Christ, the King of the universe.
May all in heaven and earth acclaim your glory
and never cease to praise you.
We ask this through our Lord Jesus Christ, your Son,
who lives and reigns with you and the Holy Spirit,
one God, for ever and ever.

Evening Prayer II

HYMN, as in Evening Prayer I, 584.

PSALMODY

Ant. 1   He shall sit upon the *throne* of David * and rule over his
kingdom for ever, al*le*luia.

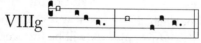

VIIIg

Psalm 110:1-5, 7

The Lord's revelation to my Master:
† "Sit *on* my right: * your foes I
will put be*neath* your feet."
The Lord will wield from Zion † your
scep*ter* of power: * rule in the midst
of *all* your foes.
A prince from the day of your birth
on the *holy* mountains; * from the
womb before the dawn *I* begot you.
The Lord has sworn an oath he will
not change. † "You are a *priest* for
ever, * a priest like Melchize*dek* of

old."
The Master standing at *your* right
hand * will shatter kings in the day
of *his* great wrath.
He shall drink from the stream *by* the
wayside * and therefore he shall lift
up his head.
Glory to the Father, and *to* the Son, *
and to the *Holy* Spirit:
as it was in the begin*ning*, is now, * and
will be for e*ver*. Amen.

Antiphon   He shall sit upon the *throne* of David * and rule over his
kingdom for ever, al*le*luia.

Ant. 2   Your kingdom shall be an everlasting *king*dom, * and you shall
          rule from generation to gen*er*ation.

VIII a

Psalm 145:1-13

I will give you glory, O God my
King, * I will bless your name *for*
ever.
I will bless you day after *day* * and
praise your name *for* ever.
The Lord is great, highly to be *praised*,
* his greatness cannot *be* measured.
Age to age shall proclaim your *works*, *
shall declare your mighty deeds,
shall speak of your splendor and *glo*ry,
* tell the tale of your wonder*ful*
works.
They will speak of your terrible *deeds*, *
recount your greatness *and* might.
They will recall your abundant *good*-
ness; * age to age shall ring out *your*
justice.
The Lord is kind and full of com*pas*-
sion, * slow to anger, abounding *in*

love.
How good is the Lord to *all*, * compassionate to all *his* creatures.
All your creatures shall thank you, O
Lord, * and your friends shall repeat
their blessing.
They shall speak of the glory of your
reign * and declare your might, O
God,
to make known to men your mighty
deeds * and the glorious splendor of
your reign.
Yours is an everlasting *king*dom; * your
rule lasts from age *to* age.
Glory to the Father, and to the *Son*, *
and to the Ho*ly* Spirit:
as it was in the beginning, is *now*, * and
will be for ever. *A*men.

Antiphon   Your kingdom shall be an everlasting *king*dom, * and you shall
            rule from generation to gen*er*ation.

Ant. 3   On his cloak and on his thigh a name was written: † King of
          kings, and Lord of lords. † To him be glory and power *for* ever, *
          alleluia, alleluia.

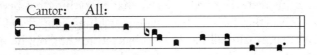

** al- le- lu- ia, al- le- lu- ia.

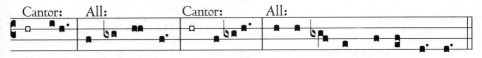

*Al- le- lu- ia.   ** al- le- lu- ia, al- le - lu- ia.

Canticle   See Revelation 19:1-7

S alvation, glory, and power to *our* God:
* Alleluia.
his judgments are hon*est* and true.
** Alleluia, alleluia.

Sing praise to our God, all you *his* servants,
* Alleluia.
all who worship him reverently, *great* and small.
** Alleluia, alleluia.

The Lord our all-powerful God *is* King;
* Alleluia.
let us rejoice, sing praise, and *give* him glory.
** Alleluia, alleluia.

The wedding feast of the Lamb has *be*gun,
* Alleluia.
and his bride is pre*pared* to welcome him.
** Alleluia, alleluia.

Glory to the Father, and to the Son, †
and to the Ho*ly* Spirit.
* Alleluia.
As it was in the beginning, is now, †
and will be for ev*er*. Amen.
** Alleluia, alleluia.

Antiphon   On his cloak and on his thigh a name was written: † King of
                  kings, and Lord of lords. † To him be glory and power *for* ever, *
                  alleluia, alleluia.

READING   1 Corinthians 15:25-28
Christ must reign until God has put all enemies under his feet, and the last
enemy to be destroyed is death. Scripture reads that God "has placed all
things under his feet." But when it says that everything has been made
subject, it is clear that he who has made everything subject to Christ is
excluded. When, finally, all has been subjected to the Son, he will then
subject himself to the One who made all things subject to him, so that God
may be all in all.

RESPONSORY (VI F)
Your *throne*, O God, * shall stand *for* ever.
— Your *throne*, O God, * shall stand *for* ever.
The scepter of your kingdom is a scep*ter* of justice.
— It shall stand *for* ever.

Glory to the Father, and *to* the Son, * and to the Ho*ly* Spirit.
— Your *throne*, O God, * shall stand *for* ever.

CANTICLE OF MARY

Antiphon   All authority in heaven and on earth has been giv*en* to me, * says
                  the Lord.

If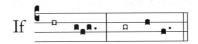

M y soul ✠ proclaims the greatness
     of the Lord, * my spirit rejoices
in God *my* savior
for he has *looked* with favor * on his
    low*ly* servant.
From this day all *gen*erations * will call
    me blessèd:
the Almighty has done great *things* for
    me, * and holy is *his* Name.
He has mercy on *those* who fear him *
    in every gen*er*ation.
He has shown the strength *of* his arm, *
    he has scattered the proud in their
    *con*ceit.

He has cast down the mighty *from* their
    thrones, * and has lifted up *the* lowly.
He has filled the hungry *with* good
    things, * and the rich he has sent
    a*way* empty.
He has come to the help of his *servant*
    Israel * for he has remembered his
    promise *of* mercy,
the promise he made *to* our fathers, * to
    Abraham and his children *for* ever.
Glory to the Father, and *to* the Son, *
    and to the Ho*ly* Spirit:
as it was in the begin*ning*, is now, * and
    will be for ever. *A*men.

Antiphon   All authority in heaven and on earth has been giv*en* to me, *
                  says *the* Lord.

INTERCESSIONS (VI F)

Let us pray to Christ the King. He is the firstborn of *all* creation; * all things
    ex*ist* in him.
May your kingdom come, O Lord.
Christ, our king and shepherd, gather your sheep from *every* land,
— give them pasture in green and fer*tile* meadows.
Christ, our leader and savior, form all men into your own people, heal the sick,
    seek out the lost, *guard* the strong,
— call back those who have wandered far away, strengthen those who waver,
    gather all your sheep in*to* one flock.
Judge of all ages, when you hand over your kingdom to the Father, place us at
    your right hand,
— so that we may inherit the kingdom prepared for us from the beginning *of* the
    world.
Prince of peace, break the wea*pons* of war,
— and inspire the nations *with* your peace.

Christ, heir of all nations, gather humanity and all the good things of your
    creation into the kingdom of your Church which your Father be*stowed* on you,
— so that the whole body of your people, united in the Holy Spirit, may
    acknowledge you *as* their head.
Christ, firstborn of the dead and firstfruits of those who have fallen a*sleep* in
    death,
— bring all who have died to the glory of the *res*urrection.

Our Father . . .

Prayer

Almighty and merciful God,
you break the power of evil
and make all things new
in your Son Jesus Christ, the King of the universe.
May all in heaven and earth acclaim your glory
and never cease to praise you.
We ask this through our Lord Jesus Christ, your Son,
who lives and reigns with you and the Holy Spirit,
one God, for ever and ever.

The Four-week Psalter

SUNDAY, WEEK I

Evening Prayer I

HYMN, 1311.
Deus, creátor ómnium. (L.M.)

Deus, creátor ómnium
políque rector, véstiens
diem decóro lúmine,
noctem sopóris grátia,

Artus solútos ut quies
reddat labóris úsui
mentésque fessas állevet
luctúsque solvat ánxios,

Grates perácto iam die
et noctis exórtu preces,
voti reos ut ádiuves,
hymnum canéntes sólvimus.

Te cordis ima cóncinant,
te vox canóra cóncrepet,
te díligat castus amor,
te mens adóret sóbria,

Ut cum profúnda cláuserit
diem calígo nóctium,
fides tenébras nésciat
et nox fide relúceat.

Christum rogámus et Patrem,
Christi Patrísque Spíritum;
unum potens per ómnia,
fove precántes, Trínitas. Amen.

Creator of the earth and sky,
Ruling the firmament on high,
Clothing the day with robes of light,
Blessing with gracious sleep the night,

That rest may comfort weary men,
And brace to useful toil again,
And soothe awhile the troubled mind,
And sorrow's heavy load unbind:

Day sinks; we thank thee for thy gift;
Night comes; and once again we lift
Our prayer and vows and hymns that we
Against all ills may shieldèd be.

Thee let the secret heart acclaim,
Thee let our tuneful voices name,
Round thee our chaste affections cling,
Thee sober reason own as King.

That when black darkness closes day,
And shadows thicken 'round our way,
Faith may no darkness know and night
From faith's clear beam may borrow light.

Pray we the Father and the Son,
And Holy Ghost: O Three in One,
Blest Trinity, whom all obey,
Guard thou thy sheep by night and day. Amen.

Ant. 1   Like burning *in*cense, Lord, * let my prayer rise *up* to you.

Advent: Proclaim the good news a*mong* the nations: * Our God will *come* to save us.

Lent, 1ˢᵗ Sunday: Lord God, we ask you to receive us † and be pleased *with* the sacrifice * we offer you this day with humble and *con*trite hearts.

Lent, 5ᵗʰ Sunday: I shall place my law *in* their hearts; * I shall be their God, and they will *be* my people.

Easter, 5ᵗʰ Sunday: Like the *e*vening offering * my hands rise up in prayer to you, O Lord, a*l*leluia.

VIIIg

Psalm 141:1-9

A prayer when in danger

An angel stood before the face of God, thurible in hand. The fragrant incense soaring aloft was the prayer of God's people on earth (Revelation 8:4).

I have called to you, Lord; has*ten* to help me! * Hear my voice when I *cry* to you.

Let my prayer arise before *you* like incense, * the raising of my hands like an even*ing* oblation.

Set, O Lord, a guard ov*er* my mouth; * keep watch at the door *of* my lips!

Do not turn my heart to things *that* are wrong, * to evil deeds with men *who* are sinners.

Never allow me to share *in* their feasting. * If a good man strikes or reproves me *it* is kindness;

but let the oil of the wicked not a*noint* my head. * Let my prayer be ever

a*gainst* their malice.

Their princes were thrown down by the side *of* the rock: * then they understood that my *words* were kind.

As a millstone is shattered to pieces *on* the ground, * so their bones were strewn at the mouth *of* the grave.

To you, Lord God, my *eyes* are turned: * in you I take refuge; *spare* my soul!

From the trap they have laid for me *keep* me safe: * keep me from the snares of those *who* do evil.

Glory to the Father, and *to* the Son, * and to the *Ho*ly Spirit:

as it was in the begin*ning*, is now, * and will be for ev*er*. Amen.

Antiphon   Like burning *in*cense, Lord, * let my prayer rise *up* to you.

Advent: Proclaim the good news a*mong* the nations: * Our God will *come* to save us.

Lent, 1ˢᵗ Sunday: Lord God, we ask you to receive us † and be pleased *with* the sacrifice * we offer you this day with humble and *con*trite hearts.

Lent, 5ᵗʰ Sunday: I shall place my law *in* their hearts; * I shall be their God, and they will *be* my people.

Easter, 5ᵗʰ Sunday: Like the *e*vening offering * my hands rise up in prayer to you, O Lord, a*l*leluia.

Ant. 2   You are my *re*fuge, Lord; * you are all that I desire *in* life.
Advent: Know that the Lord is coming and with him *all* his saints; * that day will
              dawn with a wonderful light, al*le*luia.
Lent, 1ˢᵗ Sunday: Call upon the Lord and *he* will hear you; * cry out and he will answer: Here *I*
              am.
Lent, 5ᵗʰ Sunday: I count everything as *loss* but this: * the surpassing worth of knowing Christ
              Jesus *my* Lord.
Easter, 5ᵗʰ Sunday: You have led me forth from my prison, † that I may give priase *to* your name,
              * al*le*luia.

Psalm 142

You, Lord, are my refuge

What is written in this psalm was fulfilled in our Lord's passion (Saint Hilary).

With all my voice I cry *to* the
  Lord, * with all my voice I
entreat *the* Lord.
I pour out my trou*bles* before him; * I
  tell him all my *dis*tress
while my spirit *faints* within me. * But
  you, O Lord, know *my* path.
On the way where *I* shall walk * they
  have hidden a snare to *en*trap me.
Look on my *right* and see: * there is not
  one who takes *my* part.
I have no means *of* escape, * not one
  who cares for *my* soul.
I cry to you, O Lord. † I have said:

"You *are* my refuge, * all I have left in
  the land of *the* living."
Listen then *to* my cry * for I am in the
  depths of *dis*tress.
Rescue me from those *who* pursue me *
  for they are stronger *than* I.
Bring my soul out *of* this prison * and
  then I shall praise *your* name.
Around me the just *will* assemble *
  because of your goodness *to* me.
Glory to the Father, and *to* the Son, *
  and to the Ho*ly* Spirit:
as it was in the begin*ning*, is now, * and
  will be for ever. *A*men.

Antiphon   You are my *re*fuge, Lord; * you are all that I desire *in* life.
Advent: Know that the Lord is coming and with him *all* his saints; * that day will
              dawn with a wonderful light, al*le*luia.
Lent, 1ˢᵗ Sunday: Call upon the Lord and *he* will hear you; * cry out and he will answer: Here *I*
              am.
Lent, 5ᵗʰ Sunday: I count everything as *loss* but this: * the surpassing worth of knowing Christ
              Jesus *my* Lord.
Easter, 5ᵗʰ Sunday: You have led me forth from my prison, † that I may give priase *to* your name,
              * al*le*luia.

Ant. 3   The Lord Jesus humbled *him*self * and God exalted him *for*
                  ever.

Advent: The Lord will come with mighty power; * all mortal eyes *shall* see him.

Lent, 1ˢᵗ Sunday: Christ died for our sins, † the innocent for *the* guilty, * to bring us back *to* God.
                  In the body he was put *to* death, * but in the spirit he was raised *to* life.

Lent, 5ᵗʰ Sunday: Although he was the Son *of* God, * Christ learned obedience *through* suffering.

Easter, 5ᵗʰ Sunday: The Son of God learned obedience through suffering † and became for all who
                  obey him the source of eternal *sal*vation, * al*le*luia.

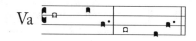

Canticle

Philippians 2:6-11

Christ, God's holy servant

Though he was in the form *of*
God, * Jesus did not deem equality
with God something to *be* grasped
at.
Rather, he emptied himself and took
the form of *a* slave, * being born in
the likeness *of* men.
He was known to be of human *estate*, *
and it was thus that *he* humbled
himself,
obediently accepting e*ven* death, *
death on *a* cross!
Because of this, God highly e*xal*ted

him * and bestowed on him the name
above every oth*er* name,
So that at Jesus' name every knee *must*
bend * in the heavens, on the earth,
and under *the* earth,
and every tongue proclaim to the glory
of God *the* Father: * JESUS
CHRIST *IS* LORD!
Glory to the Father, and to *the* Son, *
and to the Ho*ly* Spirit:
as it was in the beginning, *is* now, * and
will be for ever. *A*men.

Antiphon   The Lord Jesus humbled *him*self * and God exalted him *for* ever.
Advent: The Lord will come with mighty power; * all mortal eyes *shall* see him.

Lent, 1ˢᵗ Sunday: Christ died for our sins, † the innocent for *the* guilty, * to bring us back *to* God.
                  In the body he was put *to* death, * but in the spirit he was raised *to* life.

Lent, 5ᵗʰ Sunday: Although he was the Son *of* God, * Christ learned obedience *through* suffering.

Easter, 5ᵗʰ Sunday: The Son of God learned obedience through suffering † and became for all who
                  obey him the source of eternal *sal*vation, * al*le*luia.

READING   Romans 11:33-36

How deep are the riches and the wisdom and the knowledge of God! How
inscrutable his judgments, how unsearchable his ways! For "who has known
the mind of the Lord? Or who has been his counselor? Who has given him
anything so as to deserve return?" For from him and through him and for
him all things are. To him be glory forever. Amen.

RESPONSORY (VI F)

Our hearts are *filled* with wonder * as we contemplate your works, O Lord.
— Our hearts are *filled* with wonder * as we contemplate your works, O Lord.
We praise the wisdom which *wrought* them all,
— as we contemplate your works, O Lord.
Glory to the Father, and *to* the Son, * and to the Ho*ly* Spirit.
— Our hearts are *filled* with wonder * as we contemplate your works, O Lord.

CANTICLE OF MARY, antiphon as in the Proper of Seasons.

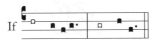

If

My soul ✠ proclaims the greatness *of* the Lord, * my spirit rejoices in God *my* savior

for he has *looked* with favor * on his low*ly* servant.

From this day all *gen*erations * will call *me* blessèd:

the Almighty has done great *things* for me, * and holy is *his* Name.

He has mercy on *those* who fear him * in every gen*er*ation.

He has shown the strength *of* his arm, * he has scattered the proud in their *con*ceit.

He has cast down the mighty *from* their thrones, * and has lifted up *the* lowly.

He has filled the hungry *with* good things, * and the rich he has sent a*way* empty.

He has come to the help of his *ser*vant Israel * for he has remembered his promise *of* mercy,

the promise he made *to* our fathers, * to Abraham and his children *for* ever.

Glory to the Father, and *to* the Son, * and to the Ho*ly* Spirit:

as it was in the begin*ning*, is now, * and will be for ever. *A*men.

Antiphon repeated.

INTERCESSIONS

We give glory to the one God— Father, Son and *Holy* Spirit— * and in our weak*ness* we pray:
Lord, be with your *people.*
Holy Lord, Father all-powerful, let justice spring up *on* the earth,
— then your people will dwell in the beau*ty* of peace.
Let every nation come in*to* your kingdom,
— so that all peoples *will* be saved.
Let married couples live *in* your peace,
— and grow in mu*tual* love.
Reward all who have done good to *us*, O Lord,
— and grant them e*ter*nal life.

Look with compassion on victims of ha*tred* and war,
— grant them hea*ven*ly peace.

Our Father . . .

Prayer, as in the Proper of Seasons.

SUNDAY, WEEK I

Morning Prayer

HYMN, 1312.
Ætérne rerum cónditor. (L.M.)

Ætérne rérum cónditor,
noctem diémque qui regis,
et témporum das témpora
ut álleves fastídium,

Præco diéi iam sonat,
noctis profúndæ pervigil,
noctúrna lux viántibus
a nocte noctem ségregans.

Hoc excitátus Lúcifer
solvit polum calígine;
hoc omnis errónum chorus
vias nocéndi déserit.

Hoc nauta vires cólligit
pontíque mitéscunt freta;
hoc, ipse Petra Ecclésiæ,
canénte, culpam díluit.

Iesu, labántes réspice
et nos vidéndo córrige;
si réspicis, lapsus cadunt
fletúque culpa sólvitur.

Tu, lux, refúlge sénsibus
mentísque somnum díscute;
te nostra vox primus sonet
et vota solvámus tibi.

Sit Christe, rex piíssime,
tibi Patríque glória
cum Spíritu Paráclito,
in sempitérna sæcula. Amen.

Eternal Maker of the world,
The sov'reign Lord of night and day:
You give the seasons of the year
To take time's heaviness away.

In deepest night you never sleep,
A Lamp for trav'lers on the way;
A Light dividing night from night,
The rooster crows announcing day.

See, at the sound, the daystar wakes
And drives the darkness from the sky;
All those who strayed on deadly roads
Now take the path to life on high.

The ocean hears; the waves die down;
The sailor overcomes his fears.
Saint Peter hears; the Church's Rock
Removes denial's stain with tears.

O Jesus, save us, for we fall;
Look down and set us right, we pray,
For at your glance our failings fail,
And sorrow washes sins away.

O Light, upon our senses shine,
Dispel the sleepiness within;
Let our first words be words of you;
With faithful praise our day begin.

To you, O Christ, most kindly King,
And to the Father, glory be;
Praise to the Spirit Paraclete,
In ev'ry age, eternally. Amen.

PSALMODY

Ant. 1	As morning breaks I look to *you*, O God, * to be my strength this day, *a*lleluia.
Advent:	On that day sweet wine will flow *from* the mountains, * milk and honey from the hills, *a*lleluia.
Lent, 1ˢᵗ Sunday:	I will praise you all my *life*, O Lord; * in your name I will lift *up* my hands.
Lent, 5ᵗʰ Sunday:	O *Lord* my God, * you have be*come* my help.
Easter, 5ᵗʰ Sunday:	Who*ev*er thirsts * will drink freely of life-giving water, *a*lleluia.

VIIIg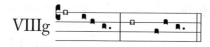

Psalm 63:2-9
A soul thirsting for God
Whoever has left the darkness of sin, yearns for God.

O God, you are my God, for *you* I long; * for you my *soul* is thirsting.
My body *pines* for you * like a dry, weary land *with*out water.
So I gaze on you *in* the sanctuary * to see your strength *and* your glory.
For your love is bet*ter* than life, * my lips will *speak* your praise.
So I will bless you *all* my life, * in your name I will lift *up* my hands.
My soul shall be filled as *with* a ban-

quet, * my mouth shall praise *you* with joy.
On my bed I re*mem*ber you. * On you I muse *through* the night
for you have *been* my help; * in the shadow of your wings *I* rejoice.
My soul *clings* to you; * your right hand *holds* me fast.
Glory to the Father, and *to* the Son, * and to the *Ho*ly Spirit:
as it was in the begin*ning*, is now, * and will be for ev*er*. Amen.

Antiphon	As morning breaks I look to *you*, O God, * to be my strength this day, *a*lleluia.
Advent:	On that day sweet wine will flow *from* the mountains, * milk and honey from the hills, *a*lleluia.
Lent, 1ˢᵗ Sunday:	I will praise you all my *life*, O Lord; * in your name I will lift *up* my hands.
Lent, 5ᵗʰ Sunday:	O *Lord* my God, * you have be*come* my help.
Easter, 5ᵗʰ Sunday:	Who*ev*er thirsts * will drink freely of life-giving water, *a*lleluia.

Ant. 2 From the midst of the flames † the three young men cried out *with* one voice: * Bless*è*d be God, al*le*luia.

Advent: The mountains and hills will sing *praise* to God; * all the trees of the forest will clap *their* hands,
for he is coming, † the Lord of a kingdom that *lasts* for ever, * al*le*luia.

Lent, 1st Sunday: Sing a hymn of praise *to* our God; * praise him above all *for* ever.

Lent, 5th Sunday: Free us by your won*der*ful works; * deliver us from the power *of* death.

Easter, 5th Sunday: Worship the Lord who made the heavens *and* the earth, * springs of water and the mighty sea, al*le*luia.

IIA

Canticle

Daniel 3:57-88; 56

Let all creatures praise the Lord

All you servants of the Lord, sing praise to him (Revelation 19:5).

Bless the Lord, all you works *of* the Lord. * Praise and exalt him above all *fore*ver.

Angels of the Lord, *bless* the Lord, * You heavens, bless *the* Lord.

All you waters above the heavens, *bless* the Lord. * All you hosts of the Lord, bless *the* Lord.

Sun and moon, *bless* the Lord. * Stars of heaven, bless *the* Lord.

Every shower and dew, *bless* the Lord. * All you winds, bless *the* Lord.

Fire and heat, *bless* the Lord. * Cold and chill, bless *the* Lord.

Dew and rain, *bless* the Lord. * Frost and chill, bless *the* Lord.

Ice and snow, *bless* the Lord. * Nights and days, bless *the* Lord.

Light and darkness, *bless* the Lord. * Lightnings and clouds, bless *the* Lord.

Let the earth *bless* the Lord. * Praise and exalt him above all *fore*ver.

Mountains and hills, *bless* the Lord. * Everything growing from the earth, bless *the* Lord.

You springs, *bless* the Lord. * Seas and rivers, bless *the* Lord.

You dolphins and all water creatures, *bless* the Lord. * All you birds of the air, bless *the* Lord.

All you beasts, wild and tame, *bless* the Lord. * You sons of men, bless *the* Lord.

O Israel, *bless* the Lord. * Praise and exalt him above all *fore*ver.

Priests of the Lord, *bless* the Lord. * Servants of the Lord, bless *the* Lord.

Spirits and souls of the just, *bless* the Lord. * Holy men of humble heart, bless *the* Lord.

Hananiah, Azariah, Mishael, *bless* the Lord. * Praise and exalt him above all *fore*ver.

Let us bless the Father, and the Son, and the *Holy* Spirit. * Let us praise and exalt him above all *fore*ver.

Bless*è*d are you in the firma*ment* of heaven.* Praiseworthy and glorious and exalted above all *fore*ver.

Antiphon   From the midst of the flames † the three young men cried out *with* one voice: * Blessèd be God, al*le*luia.

Advent: The mountains and hills will sing *praise* to God; * all the trees of the forest will clap *their* hands,

for he is coming, † the Lord of a kingdom that *lasts* for ever, * al*le*luia.

Lent, 1ˢᵗ Sunday: Sing a hymn of praise *to* our God; * praise him above all *for* ever.

Lent, 5ᵗʰ Sunday: Free us by your won*der*ful works; * deliver us from the power *of* death.

Easter, 5ᵗʰ Sunday: Worship the Lord who made the heavens *and* the earth, * springs of water and the mighty sea, al*le*luia.

Ant. 3   Let the people of Zion rejoice in *their* King, * al*le*luia.

Advent: A great prophet will come to *Je*rusalem; * of that people he will make a new *cre*ation.

Lent, 1ˢᵗ Sunday: The Lord delights in *his* people; * he honors the humble *with* victory.

Lent, 5ᵗʰ Sunday: The hour *has* come * for the Son of Man to *be* glorified.

Easter, 5ᵗʰ Sunday: The saints will rejoice *in* glory, * al*le*luia.

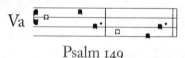

Va

Psalm 149
The joy of God's holy people
Let the sons of the Church, the children of the new people, rejoice in Christ,
their King (Hesychius).

Sing a new song to *the* Lord, *
his praise in the assembly of *the*
faithful.
Let Israel rejoice in *its* maker, * let
Zion's sons exult in *their* king.
Let them praise his name *with* dancing
* and make music with timbrel *and*
harp.
For the Lord takes delight in *his*
people. * He crowns the poor with
sal*va*tion.
Let the faithful rejoice in *their* glory, *
shout for joy and take *their* rest.

Let the praise of God be on *their* lips *
and a two-edged sword in *their* hand,
to deal out vengeance to *the* nations *
and punishment on all *the* peoples;
to bind their kings *in* chains * and their
nobles in fetters *of* iron;
to carry out the sentence pre-*or*dained; *
this honor is for all *his* faithful.
Glory to the Father, and to *the* Son, *
and to the Ho*ly* Spirit:
as it was in the beginning, *is* now, * and
will be for ever. *A*men.

Antiphon   Let the people of Zion rejoice in *their* King, * al*le*luia.

Advent: A great prophet will come to *Je*rusalem; * of that people he will make a new *cre*ation.

Lent, 1ˢᵗ Sunday: The Lord delights in *his* people; * he honors the humble *with* victory.

Lent, 5ᵗʰ Sunday: The hour *has* come * for the Son of Man to *be* glorified.

Easter, 5ᵗʰ Sunday: The saints will rejoice *in* glory, * al*le*luia.

READING   Revelation 7:10, 12

Salvation is from our God, who is seated on the throne, and from the Lamb! Praise and glory, wisdom and thanksgiving and honor, power and might, to our God forever and ever. Amen!

RESPONSORY (VI F)

Christ, Son of the *living* God, * have mercy *on* us.
— Christ, Son of the *living* God, * have mercy *on* us.
You are seated at the right hand *of* the Father,
— have mercy *on* us.
Glory to the Father, and *to* the Son, * and to the Ho*ly* Spirit.
— Christ, Son of the *living* God, * have mercy *on* us.

CANTICLE OF ZECHARIAH, antiphon as in the Proper of Seasons.

B<small>LESSÈD</small> ✠ be the Lord, the *God of* Israel; * he has come to his people and set *them* free.
He has raised up for us a *mighty* savior, * born of the house of his ser*vant* David.
Through his holy prophets he promised of old † that he would save us *from* our enemies, * from the hands of all *who* hate us.
He promised to show mercy *to* our fathers * and to remember his ho*ly* covenant.
This was the oath he swore to our *father* Abraham: * to set us free from the hands of *our* enemies,
free to worship him without fear, † holy and righteous *in* his sight * all the

days of *our* life.
You, my child, shall be called the prophet *of* the Most High; * for you will go before the Lord to prepare *his* way,
to give his people knowledge *of* salvation * by the forgiveness of *their* sins.
In the tender compassion *of* our God * the dawn from on high shall break *up*on us,
to shine on those who dwell in darkness and the sha*dow* of death, * and to guide our feet into the way *of* peace.
Glory to the Father, and *to* the Son, * and to the Ho*ly* Spirit:
as it was in the begin*ning*, is now, * and will be for ever. *A*men.

Antiphon repeated.

INTERCESSIONS (VI F)

Christ is the sun that never sets, the true light that shines on *every* man. * Let us call out to *him* in praise:
*Lord, you are our life and our sal*vation.*

Creator of the stars, we thank you for your gift, the first rays *of* the dawn,
— and we commemorate your *re*surrection.
May your Holy Spirit teach us to do your *will* today,
— and may your Wisdom *guide* us always.
Each Sunday give us the joy of gathering *as* your people,
— around the table of your Word *and* your Body.
From our *hearts* we thank you,
— for your *count*less blessings.

Our Father . . .

Prayer, as in the Proper of Seasons.

SUNDAY, WEEK I

Evening Prayer II

HYMN, 1314.

Lucis creátor óptime. (L.M.)

Lucis creátor óptime,
lucem diérum próferens,
primórdiis lucis novæ
mundi parans oríginem;

Qui mane iunctum vésperi
diem vocari præcipis:
tætrum chaos illábitur;
audi preces cum flétibus.

Ne mens graváta crimine
vitæ sit exsul múnere,
dum nil perénne cógitat
seséque culpis ílligat.

Cælorum pulset íntimum,
vitale tollat præmium;
vitémus omne nóxium,
purgémus omne péssimum.

Præsta, Pater piíssime,
Patríque compar Únice,
cum Spíritu Paráclito
regnans per omne sæculum. Amen.

O blest Creator of the light,
Who mak'st the day with radiance bright,
And o'er the forming world didst call
The light from chaos first of all;

Whose wisdom joined in meet array
The morn and eve, and named them Day:
Night comes with all its darkling fears;
Regard thy people's prayers and tears,

Lest, sunk in sin, and whelm'd with strife,
They lose the gift of endless life;
While thinking but the thoughts of time,
They weave new chains of woe and crime.

But grant them grace that they may strain
The heav'nly gate and prize to gain:
Each harmful lure aside to cast,
And purge away each error past.

O Father, that we ask be done,
Through Jesus Christ, thine only Son;
Who, with the Holy Ghost and thee,
Doth live and reign eternally. Amen.

PSALMODY

Ant. 1   The Lord will stretch forth his mighty scep*ter* from Zion, * and he will reign for ever, a*l*leluia.

Advent: Rejoice, daugh*ter* of Zion; * shout for joy, daughter of Jerusalem, a*l*leluia.

Lent, 1ˢᵗ Sunday: Worship your *Lord* and God; * serve *him* alone.

Lent, 5ᵗʰ Sunday: As the serpent was lifted up *in* the desert, * so the Son of Man must be *lift*ed up.

Easter, 5ᵗʰ Sunday: The *Lord* has risen * and is seated at the right hand of God, a*l*leluia.

VIIIg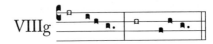

Psalm 110:1-5, 7
The Messiah, king and priest
Christ's reign will last until all his enemies are made subject to him
(1 Corinthians 15:25).

The Lord's revelation to my Master: † "Sit *on* my right: * your foes I will put be*neath* your feet."
The Lord will wield from Zion † your scep*ter* of power: * rule in the midst of *all* your foes.
A prince from the day of your birth † on the *holy* mountains; * from the womb before the dawn *I* begot you.
The Lord has sworn an oath he will not change. † "You are a *priest* for ever, *

a priest like Melchize*dek* of old."
The Master standing *at* your right hand * will shatter kings in the day of *his* great wrath.
He shall drink from the stream *by* the wayside * and therefore he shall lift *up* his head.
Glory to the Father, and *to* the Son, * and to the *Holy* Spirit:
as it was in the begin*ning*, is now, * and will be for ev*er*. Amen.

Antiphon   The Lord will stretch forth his mighty scep*ter* from Zion, * and he will reign for ever, a*l*leluia.

Advent: Rejoice, daugh*ter* of Zion; * shout for joy, daughter of Jerusalem, a*l*leluia.

Lent, 1ˢᵗ Sunday: Worship your *Lord* and God; * serve *him* alone.

Lent, 5ᵗʰ Sunday: As the serpent was lifted up *in* the desert, * so the Son of Man must be *lift*ed up.

Easter, 5ᵗʰ Sunday: The *Lord* has risen * and is seated at the right hand of God, a*l*leluia.

Ant. 2   The earth is shaken *to* its depths * before the glory of *your* face.

Advent: Christ our King will *come* to us: * the Lamb of God foretold *by* John.

Lent, 1ˢᵗ Sunday: This is the time when you can *win* God's favor, * the day when you can *be* saved.

Lent, 5ᵗʰ Sunday: The Lord of hosts protects us and *sets* us free; * he guides and saves *his* people.

Easter, 5ᵗʰ Sunday: He has rescued us from the power of darkness † and has brought us into the kingdom *of* his Son, * al*le*luia.

IIA

Psalm 114
The Israelites are delivered from the bondage of Egypt
You too left Egypt when, at baptism, you renounced that world which is at enmity with God
(St. Augustine)

When Israel came *forth* from Egypt, * Jacob's sons from an ali*en* people,

Judah became *the* Lord's temple, * Israel became *his* kingdom.

The sea fled *at* the sight: * the Jordan turned back on *its* course,

the mountains *leapt* like rams * and the hills like year*ling* sheep.

Why was it, sea, *that* you fled, * that you turned back, Jordan, on *your* course?

Mountains, that you *leapt* like rams, * hills, like year*ling* sheep?

Tremble, O earth, be*fore* the Lord, * in the presence of the God *of* Jacob,

who turns the rock in*to* a pool * and flint into a spring *of* water.

Glory to the Father, and *to* the Son, * and to the Ho*ly* Spirit:

as it was in the begin*ning*, is now, * and will be for ever. *A*men.

Antiphon   The earth is shaken *to* its depths * before the glory of *your* face.

Advent: Christ our King will *come* to us: * the Lamb of God foretold *by* John.

Lent, 1ˢᵗ Sunday: This is the time when you can *win* God's favor, * the day when you can *be* saved.

Lent, 5ᵗʰ Sunday: The Lord of hosts protects us and *sets* us free; * he guides and saves *his* people.

Easter, 5ᵗʰ Sunday: He has rescued us from the power of darkness † and has brought us into the kingdom *of* his Son, * al*le*luia.

Ant. 3   All power is yours, Lord God, our mighty King, * alleluia, alleluia.

Advent: I am coming soon, says the Lord; † I will give to everyone the reward his deeds *de*serve, * alleluia, alleluia.

Easter, 5ᵗʰ Sunday: Alleluia, our God is king; glory and praise *to* him, * alleluia, alleluia.

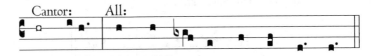

** al- le- lu- ia, al- le- lu- ia.

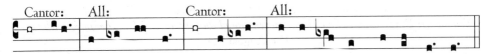

*Al- le- lu- ia.   ** al- le- lu- ia, al- le - lu- ia.

Canticle   See Revelation 19:1-7
The wedding of the Lamb

Salvation, glory, and power to *our* God:
* Alleluia.
his judgments are hon*est* and true.
** Alleluia, alleluia.

Sing praise to our God, all you *his* servants,
* Alleluia.
all who worship him reverently, *great* and small.
** Alleluia, alleluia.

The Lord our all-powerful God *is* King;
* Alleluia.
let us rejoice, sing praise, and *give* him glory.
** Alleluia, alleluia.

The wedding feast of the Lamb has *be*gun,
* Alleluia.
and his bride is pre*pared* to welcome him.
** Alleluia, alleluia.

Glory to the Father, and to the Son, †
and to the Ho*ly* Spirit.
* Alleluia.
As it was in the beginning, is now, †
and will be for *ever.* Amen.
** Alleluia, alleluia.

Antiphon   All power is yours, Lord God, our mighty King, * alleluia, alleluia.

Advent: I am coming soon, says the Lord; † I will give to everyone the reward his deeds *de*serve, * alleluia, alleluia.

Easter, 5th Sunday: Alleluia, our God is king; glory and praise *to* him, * alleluia, alleluia.

Lent: Antiphon 3

Lent, 1st Sunday: Now we must go up to *Je*rusalem * where all that has been written about the Son of Man will be *ful*filled.

Lent, 5th Sunday: He was pierced for our offenses and burdened with *our* sins. * By his wounds we *are* healed.

Va

Canticle   1 Peter 2:21-24
The willing acceptance of his passion by Christ, the servant of God

Christ suffered for you, † and left you an *example* * to have you follow in *his* footsteps.

He did *no* wrong; * no deceit was found in *his* mouth.

When he was *in*sulted * he returned *no* insult.

When he was made *to* suffer, * he did not counter *with* threats.

Instead he delivered him*self* up * to the One who judg*es* justly.

In his *own* body * he brought his sins to *the* cross,

so that all of us, dead *to* sin, * could live in accord with *God's* will.

By *his* wounds * you *were* healed.

Glory to the Father, and to *the* Son, * and to the Ho*ly* Spirit:

as it was in the beginning, *is* now, * and will be for ever. *A*men.

Lent, 1st Sunday: Now we must go up to *Je*rusalem * where all that has been written about the Son of Man will be *ful*filled.

Lent, 5th Sunday: He was pierced for our offenses and burdened with *our* sins. * By his wounds we *are* healed.

READING   2 Corinthians 1:3-4

Praised be God, the Father of our Lord Jesus Christ, the Father of mercies and the God of all consolation! He comforts us in all our afflictions and thus enables us to comfort those who are in trouble, with the same consolation we have received from him.

RESPONSORY (VI F)

The whole crea*tion* proclaims * the greatness of *your* glory.

— The whole crea*tion* proclaims * the greatness of *your* glory.

Eternal *age*s praise

— the greatness of *your* glory.

Glory to the Father, and *to* the Son, * and to the Ho*ly* Spirit.

— The whole crea*tion* proclaims * the greatness of *your* glory.

CANTICLE OF MARY, antiphon as in the Proper of Seasons.

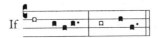

M y soul ✠ proclaims the greatness of the Lord, * my spirit rejoices in God *my* savior

for he has *looked* with favor * on his low*ly* servant.

From this day all *gen*erations * will call *me* blessèd:

the Almighty has done great *things* for me, * and holy is *his* Name.

He has mercy on *those* who fear him * in every gen*er*ation.

He has shown the strength *of* his arm, * he has scattered the proud in their *con*ceit.

He has cast down the mighty *from* their thrones, * and has lifted up *the* lowly.

He has filled the hungry *with* good things, * and the rich he has sent a*way* empty.

He has come to the help of his *ser*vant Israel * for he has remembered his promise *of* mercy,

the promise he made *to* our fathers, * to Abraham and his children *for* ever.

Glory to the Father, and *to* the Son, * and to the Ho*ly* Spirit:

as it was in the begin*ning*, is now, * and will be for ever. *A*men.

Antiphon repeated.

INTERCESSIONS   (VI F)

Christ the Lord is our head; we *are* his members. * In joy let us call *out* to him:

*Lord, may your king*dom *come.*

Christ our Savior, make your Church a more vivid symbol of the unity of *all* mankind,

— make it more effectively the sacrament of salvation *for* all peoples.

Through your presence, guide the college of bishops in union *with* the Pope,

— give them the gifts of unity, *love* and peace.

Bind all Christians more closely to yourself, *their* divine Head,

— lead them to proclaim your kingdom by the witness *of* their lives.

Grant peace *to* the world,

— let every land flourish in justice *and* security.

Grant to the dead the glory of *res*urrection,
— and give us a share *in* their happiness.

Our Father . . .

Prayer, as in the Proper of Seasons.

MONDAY, WEEK I

Morning Prayer

HYMN, 1315.
Splendor patérnæ glóriæ. (L.M.)

Splendor patérnæ glóriæ,
de luce lucem próferens,
lux lucis et fons lúminis,
diem dies illúminans,

Verúsque sol, illábere
micans nitóre pérpeti,
iubárque Sancti Spíritus
infúnde nostris sénsibus.

Votis vocémus et Patrem,
Patrem perénnis glóriæ,
Patrem poténtis grátiæ,
culpam reléget lúbricam.

Infórmet actus sténuos,
dentem retúndat ínvidi,
casus secúndet ásperos,
donet geréndi grátiam.

Mentem gubérnet et regat
casto, fidéli córpore;
fides calóre férveat,
fraudis cenéna nésciat.

Christúsque nobis sit cibus,
potúsque noster sit fides;
læti bibámus sóbriam
ebrietátem Spíritus.

Lætus dies hic tránseat;
pudor sit ut dilúculum,
fides velut merídies,
crepúsculum mens nésciat.

Auróra cursus próvehit;
Auróra totus pródeat,
in Patre totus Fílius
et totus in Verbo Pater. Amen.

O splendor of God's glory bright,
O Thou that bringest light from Light;
O Light of Light, light's living spring;
O Day, all days illumining:

O Thou, true Sun, on us thy glance
Let fall in royal radiance,
The Spirit's sanctifying beam
Upon our earthly senses stream.

The Father too our prayers implore,
Father of glory evermore,
The Father of all grace and might,
To banish sin from our delight.

To guide what e'er we nobly do;
With love all envy to subdue;
To make ill fortune turn to fair;
And give us grace our wrongs to bear.

Our mind be in his keeping placed,
Our body true to him and chaste,
Where only faith her fire shall feed
To burn the tares of Satan's seed.

And Christ to us for food shall be,
From him our drink that welleth free,
The Spirit's wine, that maketh whole,
And mocking not, exalts the soul.

Now let the day in joy pass on:
Our modesty like early dawn,
Our faith like noontide splendor glow,
Our souls the twilight never know.

See! morn pursues her shining way:
True Morning, all thy beams display!
Son with the mighty Father one,
The Father wholly in the Son.

All laud to God the Father be;
All praise, eternal Son, to thee;
All glory, as is ever meet,
To God the Holy Paraclete. Amen.

PSALMODY

Ant. 1   I lift up my heart to *you*, O Lord, * and you will hear my *morn*ing prayer.

Easter: All those who *love* your name * will rejoice in you, *a*lleluia.

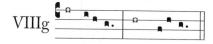

VIIIg

Psalm 5: 2-10, 12-13
A morning prayer asking for help
Those who welcome the Word as the guest of their hearts will have abiding joy.

To my words give *ear*, O Lord, *
give heed *to* my groaning.
Attend to the sound *of* my cries, * my
King *and* my God.
It is you whom I in*voke*, O Lord. * In
the morn*ing* you hear me;
in the morning I offer *you* my prayer, *
watch*ing* and waiting.
You are no God *who* loves evil; * no
sinner *is* your guest.
The boastful shall not *stand* their
ground * be*fore* your face.
You hate all *who* do evil: * you destroy
all who lie.
The deceitful and blood*thirs*ty man *
the *Lord* detests.
But I through the greatness of your
love † have access *to* your house. * I
bow down before your holy temple,

filled with awe.
Lead, me, Lord, in your justice, †
because of those who *lie* in wait; *
make clear your *way* before me.
No truth can be found *in* their mouths,
* their heart *is* all mischief,
their throat a wide-*o*pen grave, * all
hon*ey* their speech.
All those you protect *shall* be glad * and
ring *out* their joy.
You shelter them, in you *they* rejoice, *
those who *love* your name.
It is you who bless the *just* man, Lord: *
you surround him with favor as *with*
a shield.
Glory to the Father, and *to* the Son, *
and to the *Holy* Spirit:
as it was in the begin*ning*, is now, * and
will be for ev*er*. Amen.

Antiphon   I lift up my heart to *you*, O Lord, * and you will hear my *morn*ing prayer.

Easter: All those who *love* your name * will rejoice in you, *a*lleluia.

Ant. 2   We praise your glor*ious* name, * O Lord, *our* God.

Easter: Yours is the kingdom, Lord, † and yours the primacy over all the rulers *of* the earth, * al*le*luia.

Canticle   1 Chronicles 29: 10-13

Glory and honor are due to God alone

Blessed be the God and Father of our Lord Jesus Christ (Ephesians 1:3).

Blessèd may you be, O Lord, †
God of Isra*el* our father, * from
eternity to *e*ternity.

Yours, O Lord, are gran*deur* and power,
* majesty, splendor, *and* glory.

For all in heaven and on earth is yours;
† yours, O Lord, *is* the sovereignty: *
you are exalted as head o*ver* all.

Riches and honor *are* from you, * and
you have dominion o*ver* all.

In your hand are po*wer* and might; * it
is yours to give grandeur and strength
to all.

Therefore, our God, we *give* you thanks
* and we praise the majesty of *your*
name.

Glory to the Father, and *to* the Son, *
and to the Ho*ly* Spirit:

as it was in the begin*ning*, is now, * and
will be for ever. *A*men.

Antiphon   We praise your glor*ious* name, * O Lord, *our* God.

Easter: Yours is the kingdom, Lord, † and yours the primacy over all the rulers *of* the earth, * al*le*luia.

Ant. 3   Adore *the* Lord * in his ho*ly* court.

Easter: The Lord is enthroned as king *for* ever, * al*le*luia.

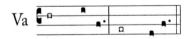

Psalm 29

A tribute of praise to the Word of God

The Father's voice proclaimed: "This is my beloved Son" (Matthew 3:17).

O give the Lord, you sons *of*
God, * give the Lord glory *and*
power;

give the Lord the glory of *his* name. *
Adore the Lord in his ho*ly* court.

The Lord's voice resounding on *the*
waters, * the Lord on the immensity
of waters;

the voice of the Lord, full *of* power, *

the voice of the Lord, full *of* splendor.

The Lord's voice shattering *the* cedars, *
the Lord shatters the cedars *of*
Lebanon;

he makes Lebanon leap like *a* calf * and
Sirion like a young *wild*-ox.

The *Lord's* voice * flashes flames *of* fire.

The Lord's voice shaking *the* wilderness, * the Lord shakes the wilderness

of *Ka*desh;
the Lord's voice rending *the* oak tree *
  and stripping the for*est* bare.
The God of glo*ry* thunders. * In his
  temple they all *cry*: "Glory!"
The Lord sat enthroned over *the* flood;
  * the Lord sits as king *for* ever.

The Lord will give strength to *his*
  people, * the Lord will bless his
  people *with* peace.
Glory to the Father, and to *the* Son, * and
  to the Ho*ly* Spirit:
as it was in the beginning, *is* now, * and
  will be for ever. *A*men.

Antiphon   Adore *the* Lord * in his ho*ly* court.
Easter: The Lord is enthroned as king *for* ever, * al*le*luia.

READING   2 Thessalonians 3:10b-13

Anyone who would not work should not eat. We hear that some of you are
unruly, not keeping busy but acting like busy-bodies. We enjoin all such, and
we urge them strongly in the Lord Jesus Christ, to earn the food they eat by
working quietly. You must never grow weary of doing what is right, brothers.

RESPONSORY (VI F)

Blessèd be the *Lord* our God, * blessèd from age *to* age.
— Blessèd be the *Lord* our God, * blessèd from age *to* age.
His marvelous works are be*yond* compare,
— blessèd from age *to* age.
Glory to the Father, and *to* the Son, * and to the Ho*ly* Spirit.
— Blessèd be the *Lord* our God, * blessèd from age *to* age.

CANTICLE OF ZECHARIAH
Antiphon   Blessèd *be* the Lord, * the Lord *our* God.

INTERCESSIONS (VI F)

We esteem Christ above all men, for he was filled with grace and the *Ho*ly Spirit.
  * In faith let *us* implore him:
Give us your Spirit, O Lord.
  Grant us a *peace*ful day,
— when evening comes we will praise you with joy and puri*ty* of heart.
Let your splendor rest upon *us* today,
— direct the work *of* our hands.
May your face shine upon us and keep *us* in peace,
— may your strong *arm* protect us.
Look kindly on all who put their trust *in* our prayers,
— fill them with every bodily and spi*rit*ual grace.

Our Father . . .

Week I

Prayer

Father,
may everything we do
begin with your inspiration
and continue with your saving help.
Let our work always find its origin in you
and through you reach completion.
We ask this through our Lord Jesus Christ, your Son,
who lives and reigns with you and the Holy Spirit,
one God, for ever and ever.

MONDAY, WEEK I

Evening Prayer

HYMN, 1317.

Imménse cæli cónditor. (L.M.)

Imménse cæli cónditor,	O boundless Wisdom, God most high,
qui, mixta ne confúnderent,	O Maker of the earth and sky,
aquæ fluénta dívidens,	Who bid'st the parted waters flow
cælum dedísti límitem,	In heav'n above, on earth below:
Firmans locum cæléstibus	The streams on earth, the clouds in heav'n,
simúlque terræ rívulis,	By thee their ordered bounds were giv'n,
ut unda flammas témperet,	Lest 'neath th'untempered fires of day
terræ solum ne díssipet:	The parched soil should waste away.
Infúnde nunc, piíssime,	E'en so on us who seek thy face
donum perénnis grátiæ,	Pour forth the waters of thy grace;
fraudis novæ ne cásibus	Renew the fount of life within,
nos error átterat vetus.	And quench the wasting fires of sin.
Lucem fides inveniat,	Let faith discern th'eternal Light
sic lúminis iubar ferat;	Beyond the darkness of the night,
hæc vana cuncta térreat,	And through the mists of falsehood see
hanc falsa nulla cómprimant.	The path of truth revealed by thee.
Præsta, Pater piíssime,	O Father, that we ask be done,
Patríque compare Únice,	Through Jesus Christ, thine only Son;
cum Spíritu Paráclito	Who, with the Holy Ghost and thee,
regnans per omne sæculum. Amen.	Doth live and reign eternally. Amen.

PSALMODY

Ant. 1   The *Lord* looks tenderly * on those *who* are poor.

Easter: Have courage; I have over*come* the world, * al*le*luia.

VIIIg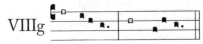

Psalm 11
God is the unfailing support of the just

Blessed are those who hunger and thirst for justice; they shall be satisfied
(Matthew 5:6).

In the Lord I have taken my
refuge. † How can you say *to* my
soul: * "Fly like a bird *to* its mountain.
See the wicked bracing their bow; †
they are fixing their arrows *on* the
string * to shoot upright men *in* the
dark.
Foundations *once* destroyed, * what *can*
the just do?"
The Lord is in his *ho*ly temple, * the
Lord, whose throne *is* in heaven.
His eyes look down *on* the world; * his

gaze tests *mor*tal men.
The Lord tests the just *and* the wicked:
* the lover of vio*lence* he hates.
He sends fire and brimstone *on* the
wicked; * he sends a scorching wind
as their lot.
The Lord is just *and* loves justice: * the
upright shall *see* his face.
Glory to the Father, and *to* the Son, *
and to the *Ho*ly Spirit:
as it was in the begin*ning*, is now, * and
will be for ev*er*. Amen.

Antiphon   The *Lord* looks tenderly * on those *who* are poor.

Easter: Have courage; I have over*come* the world, * al*le*luia.

Ant. 2   Blessèd are the *pure* of heart, * for they shall *see* God.

Easter: He shall sojourn *in* your tent; * he shall dwell on your holy mountain, al*le*luia.

IIA

Psalm 15
Who is worthy to stand in God's presence?

You have come to Mount Zion, to the city of the living God (Hebrews 12:22).

Lord, who shall be admitted *to*
your tent * and dwell on your ho*ly*
mountain?
He who walks *with*out fault; * he who
acts *with* justice
and speaks the truth *from* his heart; * he

who does not slander with *his* tongue;
he who does no wrong *to* his brother, *
who casts no slur on *his* neighbor,
who holds the godless *in* disdain, * but
honors those who fear *the* Lord;
he who keeps his pledge, *come* what

may; * who takes no interest on *a* loan
and accepts no bribes *against* the
   innocent. * Such a man will stand
firm *for* ever.

Glory to the Father, and *to* the Son, *
   and to the Ho*ly* Spirit:
as it was in the begin*ning*, is now, * and
   will be for ever. *A*men.

Antiphon   Bless*èd* are the *pure* of heart, * for they shall *see* God.

Easter: He shall sojourn *in* your tent; * he shall dwell on your holy mountain, al*le*luia.

Ant. 3   God chose us in *his* Son * to be his adopt*ed* children.

Easter: When I am lifted up from the earth † I shall draw all people to *my*self, *
   al*le*luia.

Va

Canticle

God our Savior

Ephesians 1:3-10

Praised be the God *and* Father * of
   our Lord Je*sus* Christ,
who has bestowed on us *in* Christ *
   every spiritual blessing in *the* heavens.
God chose us in him before the world
   *be*gan * to be holy and blameless in
   his sight.
He predestined us † to be his adopted
   sons through Je*sus* Christ, * such was
   his will *and* pleasure,
that all might praise the glori*ous* favor *
   he has bestowed on us in his *be*lovèd.
In him and through his blood, † we
   have been *re*deemed, * and our sins
   *for*given,

so immeasura*bly* generous * is God's
   favor *to* us.
God has given us the wisdom † to
   understand fully *the* mystery, * the
   plan he was pleased to decree *in*
   Christ.
A plan to be carried out *in* Christ, * in
   the fullness *of* time,
to bring all things into one *in* him, * in
   the heavens and *on* earth.
Glory to the Father, and to *the* Son, *
   and to the Ho*ly* Spirit:
as it was in the beginning, *is* now, * and
   will be for ever. *A*men.

Antiphon   God chose us in *his* Son * to be his adopt*ed* children.

Easter: When I am lifted up from the earth † I shall draw all people to *my*self, *
   al*le*luia.

READING   Colossians 1:9b-11

May you attain full knowledge of God's will through perfect wisdom and
spiritual insight. Then you will lead a life worthy of the Lord and pleasing to
him in every way. You will multiply good works of every sort and grow in the
knowledge of God. By the might of his glory you will be endowed with the
strength needed to stand fast, even to endure joyfully whatever may come.

RESPONSORY (VI F)

Lord, you a*lone* can heal me, * for I have grieved you by *my* sins.
— Lord, you a*lone* can heal me, * for I have grieved you by *my* sins.
Once more I say: O Lord, have mer*cy* on me,
— for I have grieved you by *my* sins.
Glory to the Father, and *to* the Son, * and to the Ho*ly* Spirit.
— Lord, you a*lone* can heal me, * for I have grieved you by *my* sins.

CANTICLE OF MARY

Antiphon   My soul proclaims the greatness *of* the Lord * for he has looked
                with favor on his low*ly* servant.

INTERCESSIONS (VI F)

God has made an everlasting covenant with his people, and he never ceas*es* to
    bless them. * Grateful for these gifts, we confidently direct our *prayer* to him:
Lord, bless your *people.*
Save your *people*, Lord,
— and bless *your* inheritance.
Gather into one body all who bear the *name* of Christian,
— that the world may believe in Christ whom *you* have sent.
Give our friends and our loved ones a share *in* divine life,
— let them be symbols of Christ *be*fore men.
Show your love to those *who* are suffering,
— open their eyes to the vision of your *re*velation.
Be compassionate to those *who* have died,
— welcome them into the company of the faith*ful* departed.

Our Father . . .

Prayer

    Father,
    may this evening pledge of our service to you
    bring you glory and praise.
    For our salvation you looked with favor
    on the lowliness of the Virgin Mary;
    lead us to the fullness of the salvation
    you have prepared for us.
    We ask this through our Lord Jesus Christ, your Son,
    who lives and reigns with you and the Holy Spirit,
    one God, for ever and ever.

TUESDAY, WEEK I

Morning Prayer

HYMN, 1318.
Pergráta mundo núntiat. (L.M.)

Pergráta mundo núntiat
auróra solis spicula,
res et colóre véstiens
iam cuncta dat nitéscere.

Qui sol per ævum prænites,
o Christe, nobis vívidus,
ad te canéntes vértimur,
te géstientes pérfrui.

Tu Patris es scientia
Verbúmque per quod ómnia
miro refulgent órdine
mentésque nostras áttrahunt.

Da lucis ut nos fílii
sic ambulémus ímpigri,
ut Patris usque grátiam
mores et actus éxprimant.

Sincéra pasta ut prófluant
ex ore nostro iúgiter,
et véritatis dúlcius
ut excitémur gáudiis.

Sit, Christe, rex piíssime,
tibi Patríque Glória
cum spíritu Paráclito,
in sempitérna sæcula. Amen.

The beauty of the rising sun
Begins to tint the world with light,
Awakened nature glows with life
As form and color reappear.

Lord Jesus Christ, you far surpass
The sun that shines since time began;
We turn to you with joyous song
That you may bless us with your smile.

You are God's knowledge infinite,
His Word, through whom all things were made;
their wondrous order speaks to us
And draws our hearts and minds to you.

Give us your light that like true sons
Intrepid we may tread life's path.
May all our ways and actions show
The gift of God the Father's grace.

Let ev'ry word our lips may say
Prove our sincerity and truth,
That our serenity of soul
May radiate our inward joy.

To you, O Christ, most kindly King,
And to the Father, glory be;
Praise to the Spirit Paraclete,
In ev'ry age, eternally. Amen.

Ant. 1   The man whose deeds are blameless and whose *heart* is pure *
will climb the mountain *of* the Lord.

Easter: The one who came *down* from heaven * has ascended above all the heavens,
*al*leluia.

VIIIg

Psalm 24
The Lord's entry into his temple
Christ opened heaven for us in the manhood he assumed (Saint Irenaeus).

The Lord's is the earth *and* its
fullness, * the world and *all* its
peoples.
It is he who set it *on* the seas; * on the
waters he *made* it firm.
Who shall climb the mountain *of* the
Lord? * Who shall stand in his *holy*
place?
The man with clean hands and pure
heart, † who desires not *worth*less
things, * who has not sworn so as to
de*ceive* his neighbor.
He shall receive blessings *from* the
Lord * and reward from the *God* who
saves him.
Such are the *men* who seek him, * seek
the face of the *God* of Jacob.

O gates, lift high your heads; † grow
higher, *ancient* doors. * Let him
enter, the *king* of glory!
Who is the king of glory? † The Lord,
the migh*ty*, the valiant, * the Lord,
the val*iant* in war.
O gates, lift high your heads; † grow
higher, *ancient* doors. * Let him
enter, the *king* of glory!
Who is he, the king of glory? † He,
the *Lord* of armies,* he is the *king* of
glory.
Glory to the Father, and *to* the Son, *
and to the *Holy* Spirit:
as it was in the begin*ning*, is now, * and
will be for eve*r*. Amen.

Antiphon   The man whose deeds are blameless and whose *heart* is pure *
will climb the mountain *of* the Lord.

Easter: The one who came *down* from heaven * has ascended above all the heavens,
*al*leluia.

Ant. 2   Praise the e*ter*nal King * in all *your* deeds.

Easter: Keep this day as a fes*ti*val day * and give praise to the Lord, al*le*luia.

IIA

Canticle   Tobit 13:1-8
God afflicts but only to heal
*Blessed be the God and Father of our Lord Jesus Christ, who in his great love for us has brought
us to a new birth* (1 Peter 1:3).

Blessèd be God who *lives* forever, * because his kingdom lasts for *all* ages.
For he scourges and *then* has mercy; * he casts down to the depths of *the* nether world,
and he brings up from the *great* abyss. * No one can escape *his* hand.
Praise him, you Israelites, be*fore* the Gentiles, * for though he has scattered you *among* them,
he has shown you his greatness e*ven* there. * Exalt him before every liv*ing* being,
because he is the *Lord* our God, * our Father and God *forever*.
He scourged you for *your* iniquities, * but will again have mercy on *you* all.
He will gather you *from* the Gentiles * among whom you have *been* scattered.
When you turn back to him with *all* your heart, * to do what is right before him,
then he will turn *back* to you, * and no longer hide his face *from* you.
So now consider what he has *done* for you, * and praise him with *full* voice.
Bless the *Lord* of righteousness, * and exalt the King of *the* ages.
In the land of my ex*ile* I praise him, * and show his power and majesty to a sin*ful* nation.
"Turn back, you sinners! do the right before him: † perhaps he may look with fa*vor* upon you * and show *you* mercy.
"As for me, I ex*alt* my God, * and my spirit rejoices in the King *of* heaven.
Let all men speak *of* his majesty, * and sing his praises in *Jerusalem*."
Glory to the Father, and *to* the Son, * and to the Ho*ly* Spirit:
as it was in the begin*ning*, is now, * and will be for ever. *Amen.*

Antiphon   Praise the e*ter*nal King * in all *your* deeds.

Easter: Keep this day as a fes*ti*val day * and give praise to the Lord, al*le*luia.

Ant. 3   The loy*al* heart * must praise *the* Lord.

Easter: The mercy of the Lord fills *the* earth, * al*le*luia.

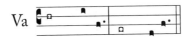

Psalm 33
Song of praise for God's continual care
Through the Word all things were made (John 1:3).

Ring out your joy to the Lord, O *you* just; * for praise is fitting for loy*al* hearts.
Give thanks to the Lord upon *the* harp, * with a ten-stringed lute sing *him* songs.
O sing him a song that *is* new, * play loudly, with all *your* skill.
For the word of the Lord *is* faithful * and all his works to *be* trusted.
The Lord loves justice *and* right * and fills the earth with *his* love.
By his word the heavens *were* made, * by the breath of his mouth all *the* stars.
He collects the waves of *the* ocean; * he

stores up the depths of *the* sea.
Let all the earth fear *the* Lord, * all who
live in the world *re*vere him.
He spoke; and it came *to* be. * He
commanded; it sprang in*to* being.
He frustrates the designs of *the* nations,
* he defeats the plans of *the* peoples.
His own designs shall stand *for* ever, *
the plans of his heart from age *to* age.
They are happy, whose God is *the* Lord,
* the people he has chosen as *his* own.
From the heavens the Lord *looks* forth,
* he sees all the children *of* men.
From the place where he dwells *he*
gazes * on all the dwellers on *the*
earth,
he who shapes the hearts of *them* all *
and considers all *their* deeds.

A king is not saved by *his* army, * nor a
warrior preserved by *his* strength.
A vain hope for safety is *the* horse; *
despite its power it can*not* save.
The Lord looks on those who *re*vere
him, * on those who hope in *his* love,
to rescue their souls *from* death, * to
keep them alive *in* famine.
Our soul is waiting for *the* Lord. * The
Lord is our help and *our* shield.
In him do our hearts *find* joy. * We trust
in his ho*ly* name.
May your love be upon us, O Lord, * as
we place all our hope *in* you.
Glory to the Father, and to *the* Son, *
and to the Ho*ly* Spirit:
as it was in the beginning, *is* now, * and
will be for ever. *A*men.

Antiphon   The loy*al* heart * must praise *the* Lord.
Easter: The mercy of the Lord fills *the* earth, * al*le*luia.

READING   Romans 13:11b, 12-13a
It is now the hour for you to wake from sleep. The night is far spent; the day
draws near. Let us cast off deeds of darkness and put on the armor of light.
Let us live honorably as in daylight.

RESPONSORY (VI F)
My God *stands* by me, * all my trust is *in* him.
— My God *stands* by me, * all my trust is *in* him.
I find refuge in him, and I am *truly* free;
— all my trust is *in* him.
Glory to the Father, and *to* the Son, * and to the Ho*ly* Spirit.
— My God *stands* by me, * all my trust is *in* him.

CANTICLE OF ZECHARIAH
Antiphon   God has raised up for us a *mighty* Savior, * as he promised of old
through his ho*ly* prophets.

INTERCESSIONS (VI F)
Beloved brothers and sisters, we share a heavenly calling under Christ, *our* high
priest. * Let us praise him with *shouts* of joy:
Lord, our God and our *Savior.*

Almighty King, through baptism you conferred on us a *royal* priesthood,
— inspire us to offer you a continual sacri*fice* of praise.
Help us to keep *your* commandments,
— that through the power of the Holy Spirit we may live in you and *you* in us.
Give us your e*ter*nal wisdom,
— to be with us today *and* to guide us.
May our companions today be *free* of sorrow,
— and *filled* with joy.

Our Father . . .

Prayer

God our Father,
hear our morning prayer
and let the radiance of your love
scatter the gloom of our hearts.
The light of heaven's love has restored us to love:
free us from the desires that belong to darkness.
We ask this through our Lord Jesus Christ, your Son,
who lives and reigns with you and the Holy Spirit,
one God, for ever and ever.

TUESDAY, WEEK I

Evening Prayer

HYMN, 1320.

Tellúris ingens cónditor. (L.M.)

Tellúris ingens cónditor,	Earth's mighty Maker, whose command
mundi solum qui éruens,	Raised from the sea the solid land,
pulsis aquæ moléstiis,	And drove each billowy heap away,
terram dedist*i* immóbilem,	And bade the earth stand firm for aye:
Ut germen aptum próferens,	That so, with flowers of golden hue,
fulvis decóra flóribus,	The seeds of each it might renew;
fecúnda fructu sísteret	And fruit-trees bearing fruit might yield—
pastúmque gratum rédderet:	And pleasant pasture of the field;
Mentis perústae vúlnera	Our spirit's rankling wounds efface
munda viróre grátiæ,	With dewy freshness of thy grace:
ut facta fletu díluat	That grief might cleanse each deed of ill,
motúsque pravos átterat,	And o'er each lust may triumph still.
Iussis tuis obtemperet,	Let every soul thy law obey,
nullis malis approximet,	And keep from every evil way;
bonis repleri gáudeat	Rejoice each promised good to win
et mortis actum nésciat.	And flee from every mortal sin.
Præsta, Pater piissime,	O Father, that we ask be done,
Patrique compare Unice,	Through Jesus Christ, thine only Son;
cum Spiritu Paraclito	Who, with the Holy Ghost and thee,
regnans per omne sæculum Amen.	Doth live and reign eternally. Amen.

PSALMODY

Ant. 1   God has *crowned* his Christ * with *vic*tory.

Easter: Now the reign of our God has begun † and power is given to Christ, *his* anointed, * al*le*luia.

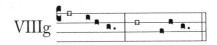

VIIIg

Psalm 20

A prayer for the king's victory

Whoever calls upon the name of the Lord will be saved (Acts 2:21).

May the Lord answer in *time* of trial; * may the name of Jacob's *God* protect you.
May he send you help *from* his shrine * and give you sup*port* from Zion.
May he remember *all* your offerings * and receive your sacri*fice* with favor.
May he give you your *heart's* desire * and fulfill every one *of* your plans.
May we ring out our joy at your victory † and rejoice in the name *of* our God.
* May the Lord grant *all* your prayers.
I am sure now *that* the Lord * will give

victory to *his* anointed,
will reply from his *ho*ly heaven * with the mighty victory *of* his hand.
Some trust in chari*ots* or horses, * but we in the name *of* the Lord.
They will col*lapse* and fall, * but we shall hold *and* stand firm.
Give victory to the *king*, O Lord, * give answer on the *day* we call.
Glory to the Father, and *to* the Son, * and to the *Ho*ly Spirit:
as it was in the begin*ning*, is now, * and will be for ev*er*. Amen.

Antiphon   God has *crowned* his Christ * with *vic*tory.

Easter: Now the reign of our God has begun † and power is given to Christ, *his* anointed, * al*le*luia.

Ant. 2   We celebrate your *migh*ty works * with songs of praise, *O* Lord.

Easter: You have assumed the authority *that* is yours; * you have established your kingdom, al*le*luia.

IIA

Psalm 21:2-8, 14

Thanksgiving for the king's victory

He accepted life that he might rise and live for ever (Saint Hilary).

O Lord, your strength gives joy *to* the king; * how your saving help makes *him* glad!
You have granted him his *heart's* desire;

* you have not refused the prayer of *his* lips.
You came to meet him with the bless-ings *of* success, * you have set on his

head a crown of *pure* gold.
He asked you for life and this *you* have given, * days that will last from age *to* age.
Your saving help has giv*en* him glory. * You have laid upon him majesty *and* splendor,
you have granted your blessings to *him* for ever. * You have made him rejoice with the joy of *your* presence.

The king has put his trust *in* the Lord: * through the mercy of the Most High he shall *stand* firm.
O Lord, arise *in* your strength; * we shall sing and praise *your* power.
Glory to the Father, and *to* the Son, * and to the Ho*ly* Spirit:
as it was in the begin*ning*, is now, * and will be for ever. *A*men.

Antiphon We celebrate your *mighty* works * with songs of praise, O Lord.

Easter: You have assumed the authority *that* is yours; * you have established your kingdom, al*le*luia.

Ant. 3   Lord, you have made us *a* kingdom * and priests for God *our* Father.

Easter: Let all creation serve you, † for all things came into being at *your* word, * al*le*luia.

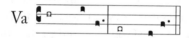

Va

Canticle   Revelation 4:11; 5:9, 10, 12
Redemption hymn

O Lord our God, you *are* worthy * to receive glory and honor *and* power.
For you have created *all* things; * by your will they came to be and *were* made.
Worthy are you, O Lord, * to receive the scroll and break open *its* seals.
For you *were* slain; * with your blood you purchased *for* God
men of every race *and* tongue, * of every people *and* nation.

You made of them a kingdom, † and priests to serve *our* God, * and they shall reign on *the* earth.
Worthy is the Lamb that *was* slain * to receive power *and* riches,
wisdom *and* strength, * honor and glory *and* praise.
Glory to the Father, and to *the* Son, * and to the Ho*ly* Spirit:
as it was in the beginning, *is* now, * and will be for ever. *A*men.

Antiphon Lord, you have made us *a* kingdom * and priests for God *our* Father.

Easter: Let all creation serve you, † for all things came into being at *your* word, * al*le*luia.

READING   1 John 3:1a, 2

> See what love the Father has bestowed on us
> in letting us be called children of God!
> Yet that is what we are.
> Dearly beloved,
> we are God's children now;
> what we shall later be has not yet come to light.
> We know that when it comes to light
> we shall be like him
> for we shall see him as he is.

RESPONSORY (VI F)

Through all eterni*ty*, O Lord, * your promise stands *un*shaken.
— Through all eterni*ty*, O Lord, * your promise stands *un*shaken.
Your faithfulness will *nev*er fail;
— your promise stands *un*shaken.
Glory to the Father, and *to* the Son, * and to the Ho*ly* Spirit.
— Through all eterni*ty*, O Lord, * your promise stands *un*shaken.

CANTICLE OF MARY

Antiphon   My spir*it* rejoices * in God *my* Savior.

INTERCESSIONS (VI F)

Let us praise Christ the Lord, who lives among us, the people *he* redeemed, * and
    let us say:
Lord, hear our *prayer.*
Lord, king and ruler of nations, be with all your people *and* their governments,
— inspire them to pursue the good of all according *to* your law.
You made captive *our* captivity,
— to our brothers who are enduring bodily or spiritual chains, grant the freedom
    of the *sons* of God.
May our young people be concerned with remaining blameless *in* your sight,
— and may they generously fol*low* your call.
May our children imitate *your* example,
— and grow in wis*dom* and peace.
Accept our dead brothers and sisters into your e*ter*nal kingdom,
— where we hope to *reign* with you.

Our Father . . .

Prayer

Almighty God,
we give you thanks
for bringing us safely
to this evening hour.
May this lifting up of our hands in prayer
be a sacrifice pleasing in your sight.
We ask this through our Lord Jesus Christ, your Son,
who lives and reigns with you and the Holy Spirit,
one God, for ever and ever.

WEDNESDAY, WEEK I

Morning Prayer

HYMN, 1321.
Nox et tenébræ et núblia. (L.M.)

Nox et tenebræ et núbila,
confúsa mundi et túrbida,
lux intrat, albéscit polus:
Christus venit; discédite.

Calígo terræ scínditur
percússa solis spículo,
rebúsque iam color redit
vultu niténtis síderis.

Sic nostra mox obscúritas
fraudísque pectus cónscium,
ruptis retéctum núbibus,
regnánte palléscet Deo.

Te, Christe, solum nóvimus,
te mente pura et símplici
rogáre curváto genu
flendo et canéndo díscimus.

Inténde nostris sénsibus
vitámque totam díspice:
sunt multa fucis íllita
quæ luce purgéntur tua.

Sit, Christe, rex piíssime,
tibi Patríque glória
cum Spíritu Paráclito,
in sempitérna sæcula. Amen.

When breaks the day, and dawn grows bright,
Christ nearer seems, the Light of Light:
From us, like shades that nighttime brings,
Drive forth, O Lord, all darksome things.

Earth's dusky veil is torn away,
Pierced by the sparkling beams of day;
Our life resumes its hues apace,
Soon as the Daystar shows his face.

So thee, O Christ, alone we seek,
With conscience pure and temper meek:
With tears and chants we humbly pray
That thou wouldst guide us through each day.

For many'a shade obscures each sense
Which needs thy beams to purge it thence;
Light of the Morning Star, thy grace
Shed on us from thy cloudless face.

All laud to God the Father be,
All praise, eternal Son, to thee;
All glory, as is ever meet,
To God the Holy Paraclete. Amen.

PSALMODY

Ant. 1   O Lord, *in* your light * we see *light* itself.

Easter: You, O Lord, are the *source* of life, * al*le*luia.

VIIIg

Psalm 36
The malice of sinners and God's goodness
No follower of mine wanders in the dark; he shall have the light of life (John 8:12).

Sin speaks *to* the sinner * in the
  depths *of* his heart.
There is no *fear* of God * be*fore* his
  eyes.
He so flatters himself *in* his mind * that
  he knows *not* his guilt.
In his mouth are mischief *and* deceit. *
  All wis*dom* is gone.
He plots the de*feat* of goodness * as he
  lies *on* his bed.
He has set his foot on e*vil* ways, * he
  clings to *what* is evil.
Your love, Lord, reach*es* to heaven; *
  your truth *to* the skies.
Your justice is *like* God's mountain, *
  your judgments *like* the deep.
To both man and beast you *give*
  protection. * O Lord, how precious *is*
  your love.

My God, the *sons* of men * find refuge
  in the shelter *of* your wings.
They feast on the riches *of* your house; *
  they drink from the stream of *your*
  delight.
In you is the *source* of life * and in your
  light *we* see light.
Keep on loving *those* who know you, *
  doing justice for *up*right hearts.
Let the foot of the *proud* not crush me *
  nor the hand of the wicked *cast* me
  out.
See how the evil-*do*ers fall! * Flung
  down, they shall nev*er* arise.
Glory to the Father, and *to* the Son, *
  and to the *Holy* Spirit:
as it was in the begin*ning*, is now, * and
  will be for ev*er*. Amen.

Antiphon   O Lord, *in* your light * we see *light* itself.

Easter: You, O Lord, are the *source* of life, * al*le*luia.

Ant. 2   O God, you are *great* and glorious; * we marvel at *your* power.

Easter: You sent forth your Spirit, O Lord, † and all things *were* created, * al*le*luia.

II A

Canticle   Judith 16:2-3a, 13-15
God who created the world takes care of his people
They were singing a new song (Revelation 5:9).

Strike up the instruments, † a song to my *God* with timbrels, * chant to the Lord *with* cymbals.

Sing to him *a* new song, * exalt and acclaim *his* name.

A new hymn I will sing to my God. † O Lord, great are *you* and glorious, * wonderful in power and un*sur*pass-able.

Let your every *crea*ture serve you; * for you spoke, and they *were* made,

you sent forth your spirit, and they *were* created; * no one can resist *your* word.

The mountains to their bases, and the *seas*, are shaken; * the rocks, like wax, melt before *your* glance.

But to *those* who fear you, * you are ve*ry* merciful.

Glory to the Father, and *to* the Son, * and to the Ho*ly* Spirit:

as it was in the begin*ning*, is now, * and will be for ever. *A*men.

Antiphon   O God, you are *great* and glorious; * we marvel at *your* power.

Easter: You sent forth your Spirit, O Lord, † and all things *were* created, * al*le*luia.

Ant. 3   Exult in *God's* presence * with hymns *of* praise.

Easter: God is King over all the earth; † make music for him with all *your* skill, * al*le*luia.

Psalm 47
The Lord Jesus is King of all
He is seated at the right hand of the Father, and his kingdom will have no end.

All peoples, clap *your* hands, * cry to God with shouts *of* joy!

For the Lord, the Most High, we *must* fear, * great king over all *the* earth.

He subdues peoples un*der* us * and nations under *our* feet.

Our inheritance, our glory, is *from* him, * given to Jacob out *of* love.

God goes up with shouts *of* joy; * the Lord goes up with trum*pet* blast.

Sing praise for God, *sing* praise, * sing praise to our king, *sing* praise.

God is king of all *the* earth. * Sing

praise with all *your* skill.

God is king over *the* nations; * God reigns on his ho*ly* throne.

The princes of the peoples are *assem*-bled * with the people of Abra*ham's* God.

The rulers of the earth belong *to* God, * to God who reigns o*ver* all.

Glory to the Father, and to *the* Son, * and to the Ho*ly* Spirit:

as it was in the beginning, *is* now, * and will be for ever. *A*men.

Antiphon   Exult in *God's* presence * with hymns *of* praise.

Easter: God is King over all the earth; † make music for him with all *your* skill, * al*le*luia.

READING   Tobit 4:15a, 16a, 18a, 19
Do to no one what you yourself dislike. Give to the hungry some of your
bread, and to the naked some of your clothing. Seek counsel from every wise
man. At all times bless the Lord God, and ask him to make all your paths
straight and to grant success to all your endeavors and plans.

RESPONSORY (VI F)
In*cline* my heart * according to your will, O God.
— In*cline* my heart * according to your will, O God.
Speed my steps a*long* your path,
— according to your will, O God.
Glory to the Father, and *to* the Son, * and to the Ho*ly* Spirit.
— In*cline* my heart * according to your will, O God.

CANTICLE OF ZECHARIAH
Antiphon   Show us your *mercy*, Lord; * remember your ho*ly* covenant.

INTERCESSIONS
Let us give thanks to Christ and offer him contin*ual* praise, * for he sanctifies us
and calls *us* his brothers:
Lord, help your brothers to grow in holiness.
With single-minded devotion we dedicate the beginnings of this day to the
    honor of your *re*surrection,
— may we make the whole day pleasing to you by our *works* of holiness.
As a sign of your love, you renew each day for the sake of our well-be*ing* and
    happiness,
— renew us daily for the sake *of* your glory.
Teach us today to recognize your presence *in* all men,
— especially in the poor and in *those* who mourn.
Grant that we may live today in peace *with* all men,
— never rendering e*vil* for evil.

Our Father . . .

Prayer

God our Savior,
hear our morning prayer:
help us to follow the light
and live the truth.
In you we have been born again
as sons and daughters of light:
may we be your witnesses before all the world.
We ask this through our Lord Jesus Christ, your Son,
who lives and reigns with you and the Holy Spirit,
one God, for ever and ever.

WEDNESDAY, WEEK I

Evening Prayer

HYMN, 1322.
Cæli Deus sanctíssime. (L.M.)

Cæli Deus sanctíssime,	O God, whose hand hath spread the sky
Qui lúcidum centrum poli	And all its shining hosts on high,
candóre pingis ígneo	And painting it with fiery light,
augens decóri lúmina,	Made it so beauteous and so bright:
Quarto die qui flámmeam	Who, on the fourth day, didst reveal
solis rotam constítuens,	The sun's enkindled flaming wheel,
lunæ minístras órdini	Didst set the moon her ordered ways,
vagos recúrsus síderum,	And stars their ever-winding maze;
Ut nóctibus vel lúmini	That each in its appointed way
diremptiónis términum,	Might separate the night from day,
primórdiis et ménsium	And of the seasons through the year
signum dares notíssimum:	The well-remembered signs declare:
Illúmina cor hóminum,	Illuminate our hearts within,
abstérge sordes méntium,	And cleanse our minds from stain of sin;
resólve culpæ vínculum,	Unburdened of our guilty load
evérte moles críminum.	May we unfettered serve our God.
Præsta, Pater piíssime,	O Father, that we ask be done,
Patríque compare Únice,	Through Jesus Christ, thine only Son;
cum Spíritu Paráclito	Who, with the Holy Ghost and thee,
regnans per omne sæculum Amen.	Doth live and reign eternally. Amen.

PSALMODY

Ant. 1   The Lord is my light *and* my help; * whom *shall* I fear?

Easter: With his right hand † God has raised him up as *king* and savior, * al*le*luia.

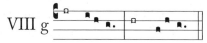

Psalm 27
God stands by us in dangers
God now truly dwells with men (Revelation 21:3).

I

The Lord is my light *and* my help; * whom *shall* I fear?
The Lord is the stronghold *of* my life; * before whom *shall* I shrink?
When evil-do*ers* draw near * to de*vour* my flesh,
it is they, my ene*mies* and foes, * who stum*ble* and fall.
Though an army en*camp* against me * my heart *would* not fear.
Though war break *out* against me * even then *would* I trust.
There is one thing I ask *of* the Lord, * for *this* I long,
to live in the house *of* the Lord, * all the days *of* my life,

to savor the sweetness *of* the Lord, * to be*hold* his temple.
For there he keeps me safe *in* his tent * in the *day* of evil.
He hides me in the shelter *of* his tent, * on a rock he *sets* me safe.
And now my head *shall* be raised * above my foes *who* surround me
and I shall offer within his tent † a sacri*fice* of joy. * I will sing and make music *for* the Lord.
Glory to the Father, and *to* the Son, * and to the Ho*ly* Spirit:
as it was in the begin*ning*, is now, * and will be for ev*er*. Amen.

Antiphon   The Lord is my light *and* my help; * whom *shall* I fear?

Easter: With his right hand † God has raised him up as *king* and savior, * al*le*luia.

Ant. 2   I long to look on *you*, O Lord; * do not turn your face *from* me.

Easter: I believe that I shall see the goodness *of* the Lord * in the land of the living, al*le*luia.

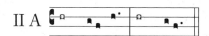

II
Some rose to present lies and false evidence against Jesus (Mark 14:57).

O Lord, hear my voice *when* I call; * have mercy *and* answer.

Of you my *heart* has spoken: * "Seek *his* face."

It is your face, O Lord, *that* I seek; * hide not *your* face.
Dismiss not your ser*vant* in anger; * you have been *my* help.
Do not abandon *or* forsake me, * O God *my* help!
Though father and moth*er* forsake me, * the Lord will *receive* me.
Instruct me, Lord, *in* your way; * on an even *path* lead me.
When they lie in am*bush* protect me *

from my ene*my's* greed.
False witnesses *rise* against me, * breathing *out* fury.
I am sure I shall see *the* Lord's goodness * in the land of *the* living.
Hope in him, hold firm *and* take heart. * Hope in *the* Lord!
Glory to the Father, and *to* the Son, * and to the Ho*ly* Spirit:
as it was in the begin*ning*, is now, * and will be for ever. *A*men.

Antiphon   I long to look on *you*, O Lord; * do not turn your face *from* me.
Easter: I believe that I shall see the goodness *of* the Lord * in the land of the living, al*le*luia.

Ant. 3   He is the first-born of all *creation*; * in every way the primacy *is* his.
Easter: From him, through him, and in him all things *exist*: * glory to him for ever, al*le*luia.

Canticle   Colossians 1:12-20
Christ, the first-born of all creation and the first-born from the dead

Let us give thanks to the Father †
for having made *you* worthy * to share the lot of the saints *in* light.
He rescued us from the power *of* darkness * and brought us into the kingdom of his belov*èd* Son.
Through him we have *redemption*, * the forgiveness of *our* sins.
He is the image of the invisi*ble* God, * the first-born of *all* creatures.
In him everything in heaven and on earth was *created*, * things visible and *invisible*.
All were creat*ed* through him; * all were creat*ed* for him.
He is before all else *that* is. * In him

everything continues *in* being.
It is he who is head of the body, the church! † he who is the beginning, the first-born of *the* dead, * so that primacy may be his *in* everything.
It pleased God to make absolute fullness reside *in* him * and, by means of him, to reconcile everything in *his* person,
both on earth and in *the* heavens, * making peace through the blood of *his* cross.
Glory to the Father, and to *the* Son, * and to the Ho*ly* Spirit:
as it was in the beginning, *is* now, * and will be for ever. *A*men.

Antiphon He is the first-born of all *creation;* * in every way the primacy *is* his.

Easter: From him, through him, and in him all things *exist:* * glory to him for ever, al*le*luia.

READING James 1:22, 25

Act on this word. If all you do is listen to it, you are deceiving yourselves. There is, on the other hand, the man who peers into freedom's ideal law and abides by it. He is no forgetful listener, but one who carries out the law in practice. Blest will this man be in whatever he does.

RESPONSORY (VI F)

Claim me once more *as* your own, Lord, * and have mercy *on* me.
— Claim me once more *as* your own, Lord, * and have mercy *on* me.
Do not abandon me *with* the wicked;
— have mercy *on* me.
Glory to the Father, and *to* the Son, * and to the Ho*ly* Spirit.
— Claim me once more *as* your own, Lord, * and have mercy *on* me.

CANTICLE OF MARY

Antiphon The Almighty has done great *things* for me, * and holy is *his* Name.

INTERCESSIONS

In all that we do, let the name of the Lord be praised, for he surrounds his chosen people with *bound*less love. * Let our prayer rise *up* to him:
Lord, show us your love.
Remem*ber* your Church, Lord,
— keep her from every evil and let her grow to the fullness *of* your love.
Let the nations recognize you as the *one* true God,
— and Jesus your Son, as the Messiah *whom* you sent.
Grant prosperity *to* our neighbors,
— give them life and happi*ness* for ever.
Console those who are burdened with oppressive work and *dai*ly hardships,
— preserve the digni*ty* of workers.
Open wide the doors of your compassion to those who have *died* today,
— and in your mercy receive them in*to* your kingdom.

Our Father . . .

Prayer

Lord,
watch over us by day and by night.
In the midst of life's countless changes
strengthen us with your never-changing love.
We ask this through our Lord Jesus Christ, your Son,
who lives and reigns with you and the Holy Spirit,
one God, for ever and ever.

THURSDAY, WEEK I

Morning Prayer

HYMN, 1323.
Sol ecce surgit aurea. (L.M.)

Sol ecce surgit ígneus: piget, pudéscit, pænitet, nec teste quisquam lúmine peccáre constánter potest.	Behold, the golden dawn arise; The paling night forsakes the skies: Those shades that hid the world from view, And us to dangerous error drew.
Tandem facéssat cæcitas, quae nosmet in præceps diu lapsos sinístris gréssibus erróre traxit dévio.	May this new day be calmly passed, May we keep pure while it shall last: Nor let our lips from truth depart, Nor dark designs engage the heart.
Hæc lux serénum cónferat purósque nos præstet sibi; nihil loquámur súbdolum, volvámus obscúrum nihil.	So may the day speed on; the tongue No falsehood know, the hands no wrong: Our eyes from wonton gaze refrain, No guilt our guarded bodies stain.
Sic tota decúrrat dies, ne lingua mendax, ne manus ocu*lí*ve peccent lúbrici, ne noxa corpus ínquinet.	For God all-seeing from on high Surveys us with a watchful eye: Each day our every act he knows From early dawn to evening's close.
Specu*lá*tor astat désuper, qui nos diébus ómnibus actúsque nostros próspicit a luce prim*a* in vésperum.	All laud to God the Father be; All praise, eternal Son, to thee; All glory, as is ever meet, To God the Holy Paraclete. Amen.
Deo Patri sit glória eiúsque soli Fílio cum Spíritu Paráclito, in sempitérna sæcula. Amen.	

PSALMODY

Ant. 1   Awake, *lyre* and harp, * with praise let us a*wake* the dawn.

Easter: Be exalt*ed*, O God, * high above the heavens, a*l*leluia.

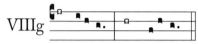

VIIIg

Psalm 57
Morning prayer in affliction
This psalm tells of our Lord's passion (St. Augustine).

Have mercy on me, *God*, have mercy * for in you my soul has *tak*en refuge.
In the shadow of your wings *I* take refuge * till the storms of destruc*tion* pass by.
I call to God *the* Most High, * to God who has always *been* my help.
May he send from heaven and save me † and shame those *who* assail me. * May God send his truth *and* his love.
My soul lies down *a*mong lions, * who would devour the *sons* of men.
Their teeth are *spears* and arrows, * their tongue a *sharp*ened sword.
O God, arise a*bove* the heavens; * may your glory *shine* on earth!
They laid a snare *for* my steps, * my soul *was* bowed down.

They dug a pit *in* my path * but fell in *it* themselves.
My heart is ready, O God, † my *heart* is ready. * I will sing, I will *sing* your praise.
Awake, my soul, † awake, *lyre* and harp, * I will a*wake* the dawn.
I will thank you, Lord, a*mong* the peoples, * among the nations *I* will praise you
for your love reaches *to* the heavens * and your truth *to* the skies.
O God, arise a*bove* the heavens; * may your glory *shine* on earth!
Glory to the Father, and *to* the Son, * and to the *Ho*ly Spirit:
as it was in the begin*ning*, is now, * and will be for e*ver*. Amen.

Antiphon   Awake, *lyre* and harp, * with praise let us a*wake* the dawn.

Easter: Be exalt*ed*, O God, * high above the heavens, a*l*leluia.

Ant. 2   My people, *says* the Lord, * will be filled with *my* blessings.

Easter: The Lord has ran*somed* his people, * al*le*luia.

II A

Canticle   Jeremiah 31: 10-14
The happiness of a people who have been redeemed
Jesus was to die…to gather God's scattered children into one fold (John 11:51, 52).

Hear the word of the *Lord*, O nations, * proclaim it on distant coasts, *and* say:

He who scattered Israel, now gathers *them* together, * he guards them as a shepherd *his* flock.

The Lord shall *ran*som Jacob, * he shall redeem him from the hand of *his* conqueror.

Shouting, they shall mount the *heights* of Zion, * they shall come streaming to the *Lord's* blessings:

the grain, the wine, *and* the oil, * the sheep and *the* oxen;

they themselves shall be like *wat*ered gardens, * never again shall *they*

languish.

Then the virgins shall make mer*ry* and dance, * and young men and old *as* well.

I will turn their mourning *into* joy, * I will console and gladden them after *their* sorrows.

I will lavish choice portions upon the priests, † and my people shall be filled *with* my blessings, * says *the* Lord.

Glory to the Father, and *to* the Son, * and to the Ho*ly* Spirit:

as it was in the begin*ning*, is now, * and will be for ever. *A*men.

Antiphon My people, *says* the Lord, * will be filled with *my* blessings.
Easter: The Lord has ran*somed* his people, * al*le*luia.

Ant. 3 The Lord is great and worthy to *be* praised * in the city of *our* God.
Easter: Such is our God, he will be our guide *for* ever, * al*le*luia.

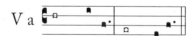

Psalm 48
Thanksgiving for the people's deliverance
He took me up a high mountain and showed me Jerusalem, God's holy city (Revelation 21:10).

The Lord is great and worthy to *be* praised * in the city of *our* God.

His holy mountain rises *in* beauty, * the joy of all *the* earth.

Mount Zion, true pole of *the* earth, * the Great *King's* city!

God, in the midst of *its* citadels, * has shown himself *its* stronghold.

For the kings assembled *together*, * together they ad*vanced*.

They saw; at once they were *a*stounded; * dismayed, they fled *in* fear.

A trembling seized *them* there, * like the pangs *of* birth.

By the east wind you have *destroyed* * the ships *of* Tarshish.

As we have heard, so we *have* seen * in the city of *our* God,

in the city of the Lord *of* hosts * which God upholds *for* ever.

O God, we ponder *your* love * within *your* temple.

Your praise, O God, like *your* name * reaches to the ends of *the* earth.

With justice your right hand *is* filled. *
  Mount Zion *re*joices;
the people of Judah *re*joice * at the sight
  of *your* judgments.
Walk through Zion, walk all *a*round it;
  * count the number of *its* towers.
Review all *its* ramparts, * examine *its*
  castles,

that you may tell the next gen*e*ration *
  that such is *our* God,
our God for ever *and* always. * It is he
  who leads us.
Glory to the Father, and to *the* Son, *
  and to the Ho*ly* Spirit:
as it was in the beginning, *is* now, * and
  will be for ever. *A*men.

Antiphon   The Lord is great and worthy to *be* praised * in the city of *our*
               God.

Easter: Such is our God, he will be our guide *for* ever, * al*le*luia.

READING   Isaiah 66:1-2
        Thus says the Lord:
    The heavens are my throne,
        and the earth is my footstool.
    What kind of house can you build for me;
        what is to be my resting place?
    My hand made all these things
        when all of them came to be, says the Lord.
    This is the one whom I approve:
        the lowly and afflicted man who trembles at my word.

RESPONSORY (VI F)
From the depths of my heart I *cry* to you; * hear me, O Lord.
— From the depths of my heart I *cry* to you; * hear me, O Lord.
I will do what *you* desire;
— hear me, O Lord.
Glory to the Father, and *to* the Son, * and to the Ho*ly* Spirit.
— From the depths of my heart I *cry* to you; * hear me, O Lord.

CANTICLE OF ZECHARIAH
Antiphon   Let us serve the *Lord* in holiness, * and he will save us from *our*
               enemies.

INTERCESSIONS
The Lord Jesus Christ has given us the light of a*n*other day. * In return we thank
  him as *we* cry out:
Lord, bless us and bring us close to *you.*
You offered yourself in sacrifice *for* our sins,
— accept our intentions and our *work* today.
You bring us joy by the light of an*oth*er day,
— let the morning star rise *in* our hearts.

Give us strength to be patient with those we *meet* today,
— and so im*i*tate you.
Make us aware of your mercy this *morn*ing, Lord,
— and let your strength be *our* delight.

Our Father . . .

Prayer

All-powerful and ever-living God,
at morning, noon, and evening we pray:
cast out from our hearts the darkness of sin
and bring us to the light of your truth,
 Jesus Christ, who lives and reigns with you and the Holy Spirit,
one God, for ever and ever.

THURSDAY, WEEK I

Evening Prayer

HYMN, 1324.
Magnæ Deus poténtiæ. (L.M.)

Magnæ Deus poténtiæ,
Qui ex aquis ortum genus
partim remíttis gúrgiti,
partim levas in áera,

Almighty God, whose will supreme
Made ocean's flood with life to teem;
Part in the firmament to fly,
And part in ocean depth to lie:

Demérsa lymphis imprimens,
subvécta cælis írrogans,
ut, stirpe una pródita,
divérsa répleant loca:

Appointing fishes in the sea,
And fowls in open air to be;
That each, by origin the same,
Its separate dwelling place might claim:

Largire cunctis sérvulis,
quos mundat unda sánguinis,
nescire lapsus críminum
nec ferre mortis tædium,

Grant that thy servants by the tide
Of Blood and Water purified
No guilty fall from thee may know,
Nor death eternal undergo.

Ut culpa nullum déprimat,
nullum levet iactántia,
elisa mens ne cóncidat,
elata mens ne córruat.

Let none despair through sin's distress,
Be none puffed up with boastfulness;
That contrite hearts be not dismayed,
Nor haughty souls in ruin laid.

Præsta, Pater piíssime,
Patrique compare Únice,
cum Spíritu Paráclito
regnans per omne sæculum Amen.

O Father, that we ask be done,
Through Jesus Christ, thine only Son;
Who, with the Holy Ghost and thee,
Doth live and reign eternally. Amen.

PSALMODY

Ant. 1   I cried to you, Lord, *and* you healed me; * I will praise *you* for
             ever.

Easter: You have turned my mourning *in*to joy, * al*le*luia.

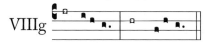

Psalm 30
Thanksgiving for deliverance from death
Christ risen in glory, gives continual thanks to his Father (Cassian).

I will praise you, Lord, *you* have
rescued me * and have not let my
enemies rejoice *over* me.
O Lord, I cried to *you* for help * and
you, my *God*, have healed me.
O Lord, you have raised my soul *from*
the dead, * restored me to life from
those who sink in*to* the grave.
Sing psalms to the Lord, *you* who love
him, * give thanks to his *holy* name.
His anger lasts a moment; his fa*vor*
through life. * At night there are
tears, but joy *comes* with dawn.
I said to myself in *my* good fortune: *
"Nothing will ev*er* disturb me."
Your favor had set me on a *moun*tain
fastness, * then you hid your face and
I was put *to* confusion.

To you, *Lord*, I cried, * to my God I
made appeal:
"What profit would my death be, † my
going *to* the grave? * Can dust give
you praise or pro*claim* your truth?"
The Lord listened *and* had pity. * The
Lord came *to* my help.
For me you have changed my mourning
*in*to dancing, * you removed my
sackcloth and clothed *me* with joy.
So my soul sings psalms to *you* unceasingly. * O Lord my God, I will thank
you for ever.
Glory to the Father, and *to* the Son, *
and to the *Holy* Spirit:
as it was in the begin*ning*, is now, * and
will be for ev*er*. Amen.

Antiphon   I cried to you, Lord, *and* you healed me; * I will praise *you* for
             ever.

Easter: You have turned my mourning *in*to joy, * al*le*luia.

Ant. 2   The one who is sinless in the *eyes* of God * is blessed *in*deed.

Easter: We have been reconciled to God by the death *of* his Son, * al*le*luia.

Psalm 32
They are happy whose sins are forgiven
*David speaks of the happiness of the man who is holy in God's eyes not because of his own
worth, but because God has justified him* (Romans 4:6)

Happy the man whose offense *is*
forgiven, * whose sin is *re*mitted.
O happy the man to whom the Lord
im*putes* no guilt, * in whose spirit is
no guile.
I kept it secret and my *frame* was
wasted. * I groaned all the *day* long
for night and *day* your hand * was heavy
*up*on me.
Indeed, my strength *was* dried up * as
by the sum*mer's* heat.
But now I have acknow*ledged* my sins; *
my guilt I did *not* hide.
I said: "I *will* confess * my offense to *the*
Lord."
And you, Lord, *have* forgiven * the guilt
of *my* sin.
So let every good man *pray* to you * in
the time *of* need.
The floods of water *may* reach high *
but him they shall *not* reach.

You are my hiding *place*, O Lord; * you
save me from *dis*tress.
You surround me with cries of deliverance. † I will instruct *you* and teach
you * the way you *should* go;
I will *give* you counsel * with my eye
*up*on you.
Be not like horse and mule, unintelli-
gent, † needling bri*dle* and bit, * else
they will not *ap*proach you.
Many sorrows has the wicked † but he
who trusts *in* the Lord, * loving
mercy *sur*rounds him.
Rejoice, rejoice *in* the Lord, * exult, *you*
just!
O come, ring *out* your joy, * all you
upright *of* heart.
Glory to the Father, and *to* the Son, *
and to the Ho*ly* Spirit:
as it was in the begin*ning*, is now, * and
will be for ever. *A*men.

Antiphon   The one who is sinless in the *eyes* of God * is blessed *in*deed.

Easter: We have been reconciled to God by the death *of* his Son, * al*le*luia.

Ant. 3   The Father has given Christ all power, honor *and* kingship; * all
people will *o*bey him.

Easter: Lord, who is your equal in power? † Who is like you, majestic *in* holiness? *
al*le*luia.

V a

Canticle   Revelation 11:17-18; 12:10b-12a
The judgment of God

We praise you, the Lord God
*Al*mighty, * who is and *who* was.
You have assumed your *great* power, *
you have begun *your* reign.
The nations have raged in anger, † but
then came your day *of* wrath * and
the moment to judge *the* dead:

the time to reward your servants the
prophets † and the holy ones who
*re*vere you, * the great and the small
*a*like.
Now have salvation and po*wer* come, *
the reign of our God and the authority of his *A*nointed One.

For the accuser of our brothers is *cast* out, * who night and day accused them be*fore* God.
They defeated him by the blood of the Lamb † and by the word of *their* testimony; * love for life did not deter them *from* death.

So rejoice, *you* heavens, * and you that dwell *there*in!
Glory to the Father, and to *the* Son, * and to the Ho*ly* Spirit:
as it was in the beginning, *is* now, * and will be for ever. *A*men.

Antiphon   The Father has given Christ all power, honor *and* kingship; * all people will *o*bey him.

Easter: Lord, who is your equal in power? † Who is like you, majestic *in* holiness? * al*le*luia.

READING   1 Peter 1:6-9

There is cause for rejoicing here. You may for a time have to suffer the distress of many trials; but this is so that your faith, which is more precious than the passing splendor of fire-tried gold, may by its genuineness lead to praise, glory, and honor when Jesus Christ appears. Although you have never seen him, you love him and without seeing you now believe in him, and rejoice with inexpressible joy touched with glory because you are achieving faith's goal, your salvation.

RESPONSORY (VI F)
The Lord has giv*en* us food, * bread of the fin*est* wheat.
— The Lord has giv*en* us food, * bread of the fin*est* wheat.
Honey from the rock to our *heart's* content,
— bread of the fin*est* wheat.
Glory to the Father, and *to* the Son, * and to the Ho*ly* Spirit.
— The Lord has giv*en* us food, * bread of the fin*est* wheat.

CANTICLE OF MARY
Antiphon   God has cast down the mighty *from* their thrones, * and has lifted up *the* lowly.

INTERCESSIONS
Our hope is in God, who *gives* us help. * Let us call upon *him*, and say:
*Look kindly on your child*ren, *Lord.*
 Lord, our God, you made an eternal covenant *with* your people,
— keep us ever mindful of your *mighty* deeds.
Let your ordained ministers grow toward *per*fect love,
— and preserve your faithful people in unity by the *bond* of peace.
Be with us in our work of building the *earthly* city,
— that in building we may not la*bor* in vain.

Send workers in*to* your vineyard,
— and glorify your name a*mong* the nations.
Welcome into the company of your saints our relatives and benefactors *who* have
    died,
— may we share their happi*ness* one day.

Our Father . . .

Prayer

Father,
you illumine the night
and bring the dawn to scatter darkness.
Let us pass this night in safety,
free from Satan's power,
and rise when morning comes
to give you thanks and praise.
We ask this through our Lord Jesus Christ, your Son,
who lives and reigns with you and the Holy Spirit,
one God, for ever and ever.

Morning Prayer

HYMN, 1325.
Ætérna cæli glória. (L.M.)

Ætérna cæli glória,
beáta spes mortálium,
celsi Paréntis Únice
castæque proles Vírginis,

Da déxteram surgéntibus,
exsúrgat et mens sóbria
flagrans et in laudem Dei
grates repéndat débitas.

Ortus refúlget Lúcifer
ipsámque lucem núntiat,
cadit calígo nóctium,
lux sancta nos illúminet,

Manénsque nostris sénsibus
noctem repéllat sæculi
omníque fine témporis
purgáta servet péctora.

Quæsíta iam primum fides
radícet altis sénsibus,
secúnda spes congáudeat;
tunc maior exstat cáritas.

Sit, Christe, rex piíssime,
tibi Patríque glória
cum Spíritu Paráclito,
in sempitérna sæcula. Amen.

Eternal glory of the sky,
Blest hope of frail humanity,
The Father's sole-begotten One,
Yet born a spotless Virgin's Son!

Uplift us with thine arm of might,
And let our hearts rise pure and bright,
And, ardent in God's praises, pay
The thanks we owe him every day.

The day-star's rays are glittering clear,
And tell that day itself is near:
The shadows of the night depart;
Thou, holy Light, illume the heart!

Within our senses ever dwell,
And worldly darkness thence expel;
Long as the days of life endure,
Preserve our souls devout and pure.

The faith that first must be possest,
Root deep within our inmost breast;
And joyous hope in second place,
Then charity, thy greatest grace.

All laud to God the Father be;
All praise, eternal Son, to thee;
All glory, as is ever meet,
To God the Holy Paraclete. Amen.

PSALMODY

Ant. I   Lord, you will accept *the* true sacrifice * offered *on* your altar.

Easter: Remember *me*, Lord God, * when you come into your kingdom, *al*leluia.

VIIIg

Psalm 51
O God, have mercy on me
Your inmost being must be renewed, and you must put on the new man (Ephesians 4:23-24).

Have mercy on me, God, *in* your
kindness. * In your compassion
blot out *my* offense.
O wash me more and more *from* my
guilt * and cleanse me *from* my sin.
My offenses tru*ly* I know them; * my
sin is al*ways* before me.
Against you, you alone, *have* I sinned; *
what is evil in your sight *I* have done.
That you may be justified when *you*
give sentence * and be without
reproach *when* you judge.
O see, in guilt *I* was born, * a sinner was
I conceived.
Indeed you love truth *in* the heart; *
then in the secret of my heart *teach*
me wisdom.
O purify me, then I *shall* be clean; * O
wash me, I shall be whi*ter* than snow.
Make me hear rejoi*cing* and gladness, *
that the bones you have crushed *may*
revive.
From my sins turn a*way* your face * and
blot out *all* my guilt.
A pure heart create for *me*, O God, *
put a steadfast spir*it* within me.

Do not cast me away *from* your presence, * nor deprive me of your *holy*
spirit.
Give me again the joy *of* your help; *
with a spirit of fer*vor* sustain me,
that I may teach transgres*sors* your ways
* and sinners may re*turn* to you.
O rescue me, *God*, my helper, * and my
tongue shall ring *out* your goodness.
O Lord, o*pen* my lips * and my mouth
shall de*clare* your praise.
For in sacrifice you take *no* delight, *
burnt offering from me you *would*
refuse,
my sacrifice, a *con*trite spirit. * A
humbled, contrite heart you *will* not
spurn.
In your goodness, show fa*vor* to Zion: *
rebuild the walls *of* Jerusalem.
Then you will be pleased with *lawful*
sacrifice, * holocausts offered *on* your
altar.
Glory to the Father, and *to* the Son, *
and to the *Holy* Spirit:
as it was in the begin*ning*, is now, * and
will be for ev*er*. Amen.

Antiphon   Lord, you will accept *the* true sacrifice * offered *on* your altar.

Easter: Remember *me*, Lord God, * when you come into your kingdom, *al*leluia.

Ant. 2   All the descendants of Isra*el* will glory * in the Lord's gift *of* victory.

Easter: Truly you are a *hid*den God, * the God of Israel, the Savior, al*le*luia.

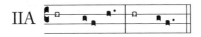

Canticle   Isaiah 45:15-25

People of all nations will become disciples of the Lord
Every knee shall bend at the name of Jesus (Philippians 2:10).

Truly with you *God* is hidden, *
the God of Israel, *the* savior!

Those are put to shame *and* disgrace *
who vent their anger *against* him.

Those go *in* disgrace * who *carve*
images.

Israel, you are saved *by* the Lord, *
saved *for*ever!

You shall never be put to shame *or*
disgrace * in fu*ture* ages.

For thus *says* the Lord, * the creator of
the heavens, who *is* God,

the designer and maker *of* the earth *
who *es*tablished it,

not creating it to *be* a waste, * but
designing it to *be* lived in:

I am the Lord, and there is no other. †
I have not spo*ken* from hiding * nor
from some dark place of *the* earth.

And I have not said to the descend*ants*
of Jacob, * "Look for me in an emp*ty*
waste."

I, the Lord, *promise* justice, * I foretell
what *is* right.

Come and assemble, gath*er* together, *
you fugitives from among *the*
Gentiles!

They are without knowledge who bear

wood*en* idols * and pray to gods that
can*not* save.

Come here *and* declare * in counsel
*to*gether:

Who announced this from *the* beginning * and foretold it from *of* old?

Was it not I, the Lord, † besides whom
there is no *o*ther God? * There is no
just and saving God *but* me.

Turn to me and be safe, † all you ends
of the earth, * for I am God; there is
no other!

By myself I swear, † uttering my *just*
decree * and my unaltera*ble* word:

To me every *knee* shall bend; * by me
every tongue *shall* swear,

saying, "Only *in* the Lord * are just
deeds *and* power.

Before him in *shame* shall come * all
who vent their anger *against* him.

In the Lord shall be the vindication *and*
the glory * of all the descendants *of*
Israel."

Glory to the Father, and *to* the Son, *
and to the Ho*ly* Spirit:

as it was in the begin*ning*, is now, * and
will be for ever. *A*men.

Antiphon   All the descendants of Isra*el* will glory * in the Lord's gift *of*
victory.

Easter: Truly you are a *hid*den God, * the God of Israel, the Savior, al*le*luia.

Ant. 3   Let us go into *God's* presence * singing *for* joy.

Easter: Serve the Lord *with* gladness, * al*le*luia.

Psalm 100
The joyful song of those entering God's Temple
The Lord calls his ransomed people to sing songs of victory (St. Athanasius).

Cry out with joy to the Lord, all the earth. † Serve the Lord *with* gladness. * Come before him, singing *for* joy.
Know that he, the Lord, is God. † He made us, we belong *to* him, * we are his people, the sheep of *his* flock.
Go within his gates, giving thanks. † Enter his courts with songs *of* praise.

* Give thanks to him and bless *his* name.
Indeed, how good is the Lord, † eternal his merci*ful* love. * He is faithful from age *to* age.
Glory to the Father, and to *the* Son, * and to the Ho*ly* Spirit:
as it was in the beginning, *is* now, * and will be for ever. *A*men.

Antiphon   Let us go into *God's* presence * singing *for* joy.

Easter: Serve the Lord *with* gladness, * al*le*luia.

READING   Ephesians 4:29-32

Never let evil talk pass your lips; say only the good things men need to hear, things that will really help them. Do nothing that will sadden the Holy Spirit with whom you were sealed against the day of redemption. Get rid of all bitterness, all passion and anger, harsh words, slander, and malice of every kind. In place of these, be kind to one another, compassionate, and mutually forgiving, just as God has forgiven you in Christ.

RESPONSORY (VI F)

At day*break*, O Lord, * be merciful *to* me.
— At day*break*, O Lord, * be merciful *to* me.
Make known to me the path that *I* must walk
— Be merciful *to* me.
Glory to the Father, and *to* the Son, * and to the Ho*ly* Spirit.
— At day*break*, O Lord, * be merciful *to* me.

CANTICLE OF ZECHARIAH

Antiphon   The Lord has come *to* his people * and set *them* free.

INTERCESSIONS

Through his cross the Lord Jesus brought salvation to the *hu*man race. * We
   adore him and in faith we call *out* to him:
*Lord, pour out your mercy up*on us.*
Christ, Rising Sun, warm us *with* your rays,
— and restrain us from every *e*vil impulse.
Keep guard over our thoughts, *words* and actions,
— and make us pleasing in your *sight* this day.
Turn your gaze *from* our sinfulness,
— and cleanse us from *our* iniquities.
Through your cross and *re*surrection,
— fill us with the consolation *of* the Spirit.

Our Father . . .

Prayer

   God our Father,
   you conquer the darkness of ignorance
   by the light of your Word.
   Strengthen within our hearts
   the faith you have given us;
   let not temptation ever quench the fire
   that your love has kindled within us.
   We ask this through our Lord Jesus Christ, your Son,
   who lives and reigns with you and the Holy Spirit,
   one God, for ever and ever.

FRIDAY, WEEK I

Evening Prayer

HYMN, 1327.

Plasmátor hóminis, Deus. (L.M.)

Plasmátor hóminis, Deus,
qui, cuncta solus órdinans,
humum iubes prodúcere
reptántis et feræ genus;

Qui magna rerum córpora,
dictum iubéntis vívida,
ut sérviant per órdinem
subdens dedísti hómini:

Repélle a servis tuis
quicquid per immundítiam
aut moribus se sí súggerit,
aut actibus *se* intérserit.

Da gaudiórum præmia,
da grátiarum múnera;
dissólve litis víncula,
astrínge pacis foedera.

Præsta, Pater piíssime,
Patríque compare Únice,
cum Spíritu Paráclito
regnans per omne sæculum Amen.

Maker of men, who from thy throne
Dost order all things, God alone;
By whose decree the teeming earth
To reptile and to beast gave birth:

The mighty forms that fill the land,
Instinct with life at thy command,
Are giv'n subdued to humankind
For service in their rank assigned.

From all thy servants drive away
Whate'er of thought impure today
Hath been with open action blent,
Or mingled with the heart's intent.

In heav'n thine endless joys bestow,
And grant thy gifts of grace below;
From chains of strife our souls release,
Bind fast the gentle bands of peace.

O Father, that we ask be done,
Through Jesus Christ, thine only Son;
Who, with the Holy Ghost and thee,
Doth live and reign eternally. Amen.

PSALMODY

Ant. 1   Lord, lay your healing *hand* upon me, * for *I* have sinned.

Easter: Christ became poor *for* our sake, * that we might become rich, *a*lleluia.

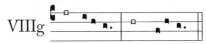

VIIIg

Psalm 41
Prayer of a sick person
One of you will betray me, yes, one who eats with me (Mark 14:18).

Happy the man who considers
the poor *and* the weak. * The
Lord will save him in the *day* of evil,
will guard him, give him life, make him
happy *in* the land * and will not give
him up to the will *of* his foes.
The Lord will help him on his *bed* of
pain, * he will bring him back from
sick*ness* to health.
As for me, I said: "Lord, have *mer*cy on
me, * heal my soul for I have *sinned*
against you."
My foes are speaking e*vil* against me. *
"How long before he dies and his
name *be* forgotten?"
They come to visit me and speak *empty*
words, * their hearts full of malice,
they spread *it* abroad.
My enemies whisper to*gether* against
me. * They all weigh up the evil *which*
is on me:

"Some deadly thing has fast*ened* upon
him, * he will not rise again from
where he lies."
Thus even my friend, in *whom* I
trusted, * who ate my bread, has
turned against me.
But you, O Lord, have mer*cy* on me. *
Let me rise once more and I *will*
repay them.
By this I shall know that you *are* my
friend, * if my foes do not shout in
*tri*umph over me.
If you uphold me I shall *be* unharmed *
and set in your pre*sence* for evermore.
Blessèd be the Lord, the *God* of Israel *
from age to age. A*men*. Amen.
Glory to the Father, and *to* the Son, *
and to the *Holy* Spirit:
as it was in the begin*ning*, is now, * and
will be for ev*er*. Amen.

Antiphon   Lord, lay your healing *hand* upon me, * for *I* have sinned.

Easter: Christ became poor *for* our sake, * that we might become rich, *a*lleluia.

Ant. 2   The mighty *Lord* is with us; * the God of Jacob is *our* stronghold.

Easter: The streams *of* the river * gladden the city of God, all*e*luia.

Psalm 46
God our refuge and strength
He shall be called Emmanuel, which means: God-with-us (Matthew 1:23)

G od is for us a re*fuge* and
    strength, * a helper close at hand,
in time of *di*stress:
so we shall not fear though the *earth*
    should rock, * though the mountains
    fall into the depths of *the* sea,
even though its waters *rage* and foam, *
    even though the mountains be
    shaken by *its* waves.
The Lord of *hosts* is with us: * the God
    of Jacob is *our* stronghold.
The waters of a river give joy *to* God's
    city, * the holy place where the Most
    High dwells.
God is within, it can*not* be shaken; *
    God will help it at the dawning of *the*
    day.
Nations are in tumult, king*doms* are
    shaken: * he lifts his voice, the earth

shrinks *a*way.
The Lord of *hosts* is with us: * the God
    of Jacob is *our* stronghold.
Come, consider the works *of* the Lord, *
    the redoubtable deeds he has done on
    the earth.
He puts an end to wars over all the
    earth; † the bow he breaks, the *spear*
    he snaps. * He burns the shields *with*
    fire.
"Be still and know that *I* am God, *
    supreme among the nations, supreme
    on *the* earth!"
The Lord of *hosts* is with us: * the God
    of Jacob is *our* stronghold.
Glory to the Father, and *to* the Son, *
    and to the Ho*ly* Spirit:
as it was in the begin*ning*, is now, * and
    will be for ever. *A*men.

Antiphon   The mighty *Lord* is with us; * the God of Jacob is *our* stronghold.

Easter: The streams *of* the river * gladden the city of God, all*e*luia.

Ant. 3   All nations *will* come * and worship before you, *O* Lord.

Easter: Let us sing to the Lord, glorious in *his* triumph, * al*le*luia.

Canticle   Revelation 15:3-4
Hymn of adoration

Mighty and wonderful are *your* works, * Lord God *Al*mighty!
Righteous and true are *your* ways, * O King of *the* nations!
Who would dare refuse *you* honor, * or the glory due your name, *O* Lord?
Since you alone *are* holy, * all nations shall come and worship in *your* presence.
Your mighty deeds * are clear*ly* seen.
Glory to the Father, and to *the* Son, * and to the Ho*ly* Spirit:
as it was in the beginning, *is* now, * and will be for ever. *A*men.

Antiphon   All nations *will* come * and worship before you, *Ó* Lord.

Easter: Let us sing to the Lord, glorious in *his* triumph, * al*le*luia.

READING   Romans 15:1-3

We who are strong in faith should be patient with the scruples of those whose faith is weak; we must not be selfish. Each should please his neighbor so as to do him good by building up his spirit. Thus, in accord with Scripture, Christ did not please himself: "The reproaches they uttered against you fell on me."

RESPONSORY (VI F)

Christ loved us and washed a*way* our sins, * in his *own* blood.
— Christ loved us and washed a*way* our sins, * in his *own* blood.
He made us a nation of *kings* and priests,
— in his *own* blood.
Glory to the Father, and *to* the Son, * and to the Ho*ly* Spirit.
— Christ loved us and washed a*way* our sins, * in his *own* blood.

CANTICLE OF MARY

Antiphon   The Lord has come to the help *of* his servants, * for he has remembered his promise *of* mercy.

INTERCESSIONS

Bless*èd* be God, who hears the prayers of the needy, and fills the hungry *with* good things. * Let us pray to *him* in confidence:
Lord, show us your *mercy.*
Merciful Father, upon the cross Jesus offered you the perfect *even*ing sacrifice,
— we pray now for all the suffering members *of* his Church.

Release those in bondage, give sight *to* the blind,
— shelter the widow *and* the orphan.
Clothe your faithful people in the armor *of* salvation,
— and shield them from the deceptions *of* the devil.
Let your merciful presence be with us, Lord, at the hour *of* our death,
— may we be found faithful and leave this world *in* your peace.
Lead the departed into the light of your *dwell*ing-place,
— that they may gaze upon you for *all* eternity.

Our Father…

Prayer

God our Father,
help us to follow the example
of your Son's patience in suffering.
By sharing the burden he carries,
may we come to share his glory
in the kingdom where he lives and reigns
with you and the Holy Spirit,
one God, for ever and ever.

SATURDAY, WEEK I

Morning Prayer

HYMN, 1328.

Aurora iam spargit polum. (L.M.)

Aurora iam spargit polum,	The dawn is sprinkling in the east
terris dies illábitur,	Its golden shower, as day flows in;
lucis resúltat spéculum:	Fast mount the pointed shafts of light:
discédat omne lúbricum.	Farewell to darkness and to sin!
Iam vana noctis décidant,	Away, ye midnight phantoms all!
mentis reátus súbruat,	Away, despondence and despair!
quicquid tenébris hórridum	Whatever guilt the night has brought
nox áttulit culpæ, cadat,	Now let it vanish into air.
Ut mane illud últimum,	So, that last morning, dread and great,
quod præstolámur cérnui,	Which we with trembling hope await,
in lucem nobis éffluat,	With blessèd light for us shall glow
dum hoc canóre cóncrepat.	Who chant the song we sang below:
Deo Patri sit glória	All laud to God the Father be;
eiúsque soli Fílio	All praise, eternal Son, to thee;
cum Spíritu Paráclito,	All glory, as is ever meet,
in sempitérna sæcula. Amen.	To God the Holy Paraclete. Amen.

PSALMODY

Ant. 1   Dawn *finds* me ready * to welcome *you*, my God.

Easter: Lord, *in* your love, * give me life, *al*leluia.

VIIIg

Psalm 119:145-152
XIX (Koph)

I call with all my *heart*, Lord, hear me, * I will keep *your* commands.
I call up*on* you, save me * and I will *do* your will.
I rise before dawn and *cry* for help, * I hope *in* your word.
My eyes watch *through* the night * to pon*der* your promise.
In your love hear my *voice*, O Lord; * give me life by *your* decrees.

Those who harm me unjust*ly* draw near: * they are far *from* your law.
But you, O *Lord*, are close: * your com*mands* are truth.
Long have I known *that* your will * is estab*lished* for ever.
Glory to the Father, and *to* the Son, * and to the *Holy* Spirit:
as it was in the begin*ning*, is now, * and will be for ev*er*. Amen.

Antiphon   Dawn *finds* me ready * to welcome *you*, my God.

Easter: Lord, *in* your love, * give me life, *al*leluia.

Ant. 2   The Lord is my strength, and I shall *sing* his praise, * for he has become *my* Savior.

Easter: Those who were victorious sang the hymn of Moses, † the ser*vant* of God, * and the hymn of the Lamb, al*le*luia.

IIA

Canticle   Exodus 15:1-4a, 8-13, 17-18
Hymn of victory after the crossing of the Red Sea
Those who had conquered the beast were singing the song of Moses, God's servant
(See Revelation 15:2-3).

I will sing to the Lord, for he is glorious*ly* triumphant; * horse and chariot he has cast into *the* sea.
My strength and my courage *is* the Lord, * and he has been *my* savior.
He is my *God*, I praise him; * the God of my father, I ex*tol* him.
The Lord *is* a warrior, * Lord is *his*

name!
Pharaoh's chariots and army he hurled in*to* the sea. * At a breath of your anger the waters *piled* up,
the flowing waters stood *like* a mound, * the flood waters congealed in the midst of *the* sea.
The enemy boasted, "I will pursue and

overtake them; † I will divide the spoils and *have* my fill of them; * I will draw my sword; my hand shall *de*spoil them!"

When your wind blew, *the* sea covered them; * like lead they sank in the migh*ty* waters.

Who is like to you among the *gods*, O Lord? * Who is like to you, magnificent *in* holiness?

O terrible in renown, work*er* of wonders, * when you stretched out your right hand, the *earth* swallowed them!

In your mercy you led the people *you*

redeemed; * in your strength you guided them to your ho*ly* dwelling.

And you brought them in and planted them on the mountain of *your* inheritance— * the place where you made your seat, O Lord,

the sanctuary, O Lord, which your *hands* established. * The Lord shall reign forever *and* ever.

Glory to the Father, and *to* the Son, * and to the Ho*ly* Spirit:

as it was in the begin*ning*, is now, * and will be for ever. *A*men.

| Antiphon | The Lord is my strength, and I shall *sing* his praise, * for he has become *my* Savior. |
| Easter: | Those who were victorious sang the hymn of Moses, † the ser*vant* of God, * and the hymn of the Lamb, al*le*luia. |

| Ant. 3 | O praise *the* Lord, * all *you* nations. |
| Easter: | Strong and steadfast is his love *for* us, * al*le*luia. |

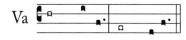

Psalm 117
Praise for God's loving compassion

I affirm that…the Gentile peoples are to praise God because of his mercy (Romans 15:8-9).

O praise the Lord, all *you* nations, * acclaim him, all *you* peoples!

Strong is his love *for* us; * he is faithful *for* ever.

Glory to the Father, and to *the* Son, * and to the Ho*ly* Spirit:

as it was in the beginning, *is* now, * and will be for ever. *A*men.

| Antiphon | O praise *the* Lord, * all *you* nations. |
| Easter: | Strong and steadfast is his love *for* us, * al*le*luia. |

READING 2 Peter 1:10-11

Be solicitous to make your call and election permanent, brothers; surely those who do so will never be lost. On the contrary, your entry into the everlasting kingdom of our Lord and Savior Jesus Christ will be richly provided for.

RESPONSORY (VI F)

I cry to *you*, O Lord, * for you are *my* refuge.
— I cry to *you*, O Lord, * for you are *my* refuge.
You are all I desire in the land *of* the living,
— for you are *my* refuge.
Glory to the Father, and *to* the Son, * and to the Ho*ly* Spirit.
— I cry to *you*, O Lord, * for you are *my* refuge.

CANTICLE OF ZECHARIAH

Antiphon   Lord, shine on those who *dwell* in darkness * and the shadow *of* death.

INTERCESSIONS

Let us all praise Christ. In order to become our faithful and merciful high priest before the Father's throne, he chose to become one of us, a brother *in* all things. * In prayer we *ask* of him:
Lord, share with us the treasure of your love.
Sun of Justice, you filled us with light *at* our baptism,
— we dedicate this *day* to you.
At every hour of the day, we *give* you glory,
— in all our deeds, we of*fer* you praise.
Mary, your mother, was obedient *to* your word,
— direct our lives in accordance *with* that word.
Our lives are surrounded with passing things; set our hearts on *things* of heaven,
— so that through faith, hope and charity we may come to enjoy the vision *of* your glory.

Our Father . . .

Prayer

Lord,
free us from the dark night of death.
Let the light of resurrection
dawn within our hearts
to bring us to the radiance of eternal life.
We ask this through our Lord Jesus Christ, your Son,
who lives and reigns with you and the Holy Spirit,
one God, for ever and ever.

SUNDAY, WEEK II

Evening Prayer I

Rerum, Deus, fons omnium. (L.M.)

Rerum, Deus, fons ómnium,
qui, rebus actis ómnibus,
totíus orbis ámbitum
censu replésti múnerum,

Ac, mole tanta cóndita,
tandem quiétem díceris
sumpsísse, dans labóribus
ut nos levémur grátius.

Concéde nunc morálibus
deflére vitæ crímina,
instáre iam virtútibus
et munerári prósperis,

Ut cum treméndi iúdicis
horror suprémus cœperit,
lætémur omnes ínvicem
pacis repléti múnere.

Præsta, Pater piíssime,
Patríque compar Unice,
cum Spíritu Paráclito
regnans per omne sæculum. Amen.

O God, the Source and Fount of life,
Creating all things by your will,
To give us joy you never cease
The earth with wondrous gifts to fill.

And when creation was complete,
Repose for man you also blest
By resting on the seventh day,
That he might toil again refreshed.

To fallen mortals grant the grace
Of sorrow for each sin's offence,
And courage to begin anew
And strive for virtue's recompense.

When Christ the Judge supreme appears
To sift the present and the past,
May we his servants thrill with joy
And peace to gaze on him at last.

O God of mercy, hear our prayer,
With Christ your Son, and Spirit blest,
Transcedent Trinity in whom
Created things all come to rest. Amen.

671

PSALMODY

Ant. 1	Your word, O *Lord*, * is the lantern to light our way, al*le*luia.
Advent:	New city of Zion, † let your heart sing for *joy*; * see how humbly your King comes *to* save you.
Lent, 2ⁿᵈ Sunday:	Jesus took Peter, James and his brother John † and led them up a high *moun*tain. * There he was transfigured *be*fore them.
Passion Sunday:	Day after day I sat teaching you in the temple † and you did not lay hands on *me*. * Now you come to scourge me and lead me to *the* cross.
Easter, 6ᵗʰ Sunday:	The man of truth welcomes the *light*, * al*le*luia.

VIII a

Psalm 119:105-112
XIV (Nun)
A meditation on God's law
This is my commandment: that you should love one another (John 15:12).

Your word is a lamp for my *steps* *
and a light for *my* path.
I have sworn and have made up my
mind * to obey your *de*crees.
Lord, I am deeply af*flict*ed: * by your
word give *me* life.
Accept, Lord, the homage of my *lips* *
and teach me your *de*crees.
Though I carry my life in my *hands*, * I
remember *your* law.

Though the wicked try to en*snare* me *
I do not stray from *your* precepts.
Your will is my heritage for *ever*, * the
joy of *my* heart.
I set myself to carry out your *will* * in
fullness, *for* ever.
Glory to the Father, and to the *Son*, *
and to the Ho*ly* Spirit:
as it was in the beginning, is *now*, * and
will be for ever. *A*men.

Antiphon	Your word, O *Lord*, * is the lantern to light our way, al*le*luia.
Advent:	New city of Zion, † let your heart sing for *joy*; * see how humbly your King comes *to* save you.
Lent, 2ⁿᵈ Sunday:	Jesus took Peter, James and his brother John † and led them up a high *moun*tain. * There he was transfigured *be*fore them.
Passion Sunday:	Day after day I sat teaching you in the temple † and you did not lay hands on *me*. * Now you come to scourge me and lead me to *the* cross.
Easter, 6ᵗʰ Sunday:	The man of truth welcomes the *light*, * al*le*luia.

Ant. 2   When I see your *face*, O Lord, * I shall know the fullness of joy,
alle*lu*ia.

Advent: Have courage, all of you, lost and fearful; † take *heart* and say: * Our God will
come to save us, alle*lu*ia.

Lent, 2nd Sunday: His face was radiant *as* the sun, * and his clothing white as *snow.*

Passion Sunday: The Lord God *is* my help; * no shame can *harm* me.

Easter, 6th Sunday: God freed Jesus from the *pangs* of death, * and raised him up to life, alle*lu*ia.

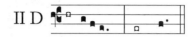

Psalm 16
The Lord himself is my heritage
The Father raised up Jesus, freeing him from the grip of death (Acts 2:24).

Preserve me, God, I take refuge
in you. † I say to the Lord: "You *are*
my God. * My happiness lies in you
a*lone.*"

He has put into my heart a mar*ve*lous
love * for the faithful ones who dwell
in his *land.*

Those who choose other gods increase
their sorrows. † Never will I offer
their offer*ings* of blood. * Never will I
take their name upon my *lips.*

O Lord, it is you who are my por*tion*
and cup; * it is you yourself who are
my *prize.*

The lot marked out for me is *my*
delight: * welcome indeed the heritage that falls to *me!*

I will bless the Lord who *gives* me

counsel, * who even at night directs
my *heart.*

I keep the Lord ever *in* my sight: *
since he is at my right hand, I shall
stand *firm.*

And so my heart rejoices, my *soul* is
glad; * even my body shall rest in
*safe*ty.

For you will not leave my soul a*mong*
the dead, * nor let your beloved know
de*cay.*

You will show me the path of life, † the
fullness of joy *in* your presence, * at
your right hand happiness for *ev*er.

Glory to the Father, and *to* the Son, *
and to the Holy *Spir*it:

as it was in the begin*ning*, is now, * and
will be for ever. A*men.*

Antiphon   When I see your *face*, O Lord, * I shall know the fullness of joy,
alle*lu*ia.

Advent: Have courage, all of you, lost and fearful; † take *heart* and say: * Our God will
come to save us, alle*lu*ia.

Lent, 2nd Sunday: His face was radiant *as* the sun, * and his clothing white as *snow.*

Passion Sunday: The Lord God *is* my help; * no shame can *harm* me.

Easter, 6th Sunday: God freed Jesus from the *pangs* of death, * and raised him up to life, alle*lu*ia.

Ant. 3   Let everything in heaven and *on* earth * bend the knee at the name of Jesus, *al*leluia.

Advent: The law was given *to* Moses, * but grace and truth come through *Jesus* Christ.

Lent, 2ⁿᵈ Sunday: Moses and Elijah were speaking *to* him * of the death he would endure *in* Jerusalem.

Passion Sunday: The Lord Jesus humbled himself † by showing obedience even when this *meant* death, * death *on* a cross.

Easter, 6ᵗʰ Sunday: Was it not necessary for Christ *to* suffer * and so enter into his glory? *al*leluia.

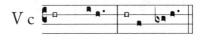

Canticle   Philippians 2:6-11
Christ, God's holy servant

Though he was in the form *of* God, * Jesus did not deem equality with God something *to* be grasped at.

Rather, he emptied himself and took the form of *a* slave, * being born in the like*ness* of men.

He was known to be of human *estate*, * and it was thus that he hum*bled* himself,

obediently accepting *even* death, * death *on* a cross!

Because *of* this, * God high*ly* exalted him

and bestowed on him *the* name * above every *other* name,

So that at Jesus' name every knee *must* bend * in the heavens, on the earth, and un*der* the earth,

and every tongue proclaim to the glory of God *the* Father: * JESUS *CHRIST* IS LORD!

Glory to the Father, and to *the* Son, * and to the *Ho*ly Spirit:

as it was in the beginning, *is* now, * and will be for *ev*er. Amen.

Antiphon   Let everything in heaven and *on* earth * bend the knee at the name of Jesus, *al*leluia.

Advent: The law was given *to* Moses, * but grace and truth come through *Jesus* Christ.

Lent, 2ⁿᵈ Sunday: Moses and Elijah were speaking *to* him * of the death he would endure *in* Jerusalem.

Passion Sunday: The Lord Jesus humbled himself † by showing obedience even when this *meant* death, * death *on* a cross.

Easter, 6ᵗʰ Sunday: Was it not necessary for Christ *to* suffer * and so enter into his glory? *al*leluia.

READING   Colossians 1:2b-6a

May God our Father give you grace and peace. We always give thanks to
God, the Father of our Lord Jesus Christ, in our prayers for you because we
have heard of your faith in Christ Jesus and the love you bear toward all the
saints—moved as you are by the hope held in store for you in heaven. You
heard of this hope through the message of truth, the gospel, which has come
to you, has borne fruit, and has continued to grow in your midst, as it has
everywhere in the world.

RESPONSORY (VI F)

From the rising of the sun *to* its setting, * may the name of the Lord *be* praised.
— From the rising of the sun *to* its setting, * may the name of the Lord *be* praised.
His splendor reaches far be*yond* the heavens;
— may the name of the Lord *be* praised.
Glory to the Father, and *to* the Son, * and to the Ho*ly* Spirit.
— From the rising of the sun *to* its setting, * may the name of the Lord *be* praised.

CANTICLE OF MARY, antiphon as in the Proper of Seasons.

VII d

My soul ✠ proclaims the greatness
of the Lord, * my spirit rejoices
in God *my* savior
for he has *looked* with favor * on his
low*ly* servant.
From this day all *gen*erations * will call
me blessèd:
the Almighty has done great *things* for
me, * and holy is *his* Name.
He has mercy on *those* who fear him *
in every gen*er*ation.
He has shown the strength *of* his arm, *
he has scattered the proud in their
*con*ceit.

He has cast down the mighty *from* their
thrones, * and has lifted up *the* lowly.
He has filled the hungry *with* good
things, * and the rich he has sent
a*way* empty.
He has come to the help of his *ser*vant
Israel * for he has remembered his
promise *of* mercy,
the promise he made *to* our fathers, * to
Abraham and his children *for* ever.
Glory to the Father, and *to* the Son, *
and to the Ho*ly* Spirit:
as it was in the begin*ning*, is now, * and
will be for ever. *A*men.

Antiphon repeated.

INTERCESSIONS (VI F)

God aids and protects the people he has chosen for *his* inheritance. * Let us give thanks to him and pro*claim* his goodness:

Lord, we trust in you.

We pray for N., our Pope, and *N.*, our bishop,

— protect them and in your goodness *make* them holy.

May the sick feel their companionship with the *suffering* Christ,

— and know that they will enjoy his eternal *con*solation.

In your goodness have compassion *on* the homeless,

— help them to find *proper* housing.

In your goodness give and preserve the fruits *of* the earth,

— so that each day there may be bread e*nough* for all.

(*or:* Graciously protect our na*tion* from evil,

— that it may prosper *in* your peace.)

Lord, you attend the dying *with* great mercy,

— grant them an e*ter*nal dwelling.

Our Father . . .

Prayer, as in the Proper of Seasons.

SUNDAY, WEEK II

Morning Prayer

HYMN, 1330.
Ecce iam noctis. (11.11.11.5)

Ecce iam noctis tenuátur umbra,
lucis auróra rútilans corúscat;
nísibus totis rogitémus omnes
cunctipoténtem,

Ut Deus, nostri miserátus, omnem
pellat angórem, tríbuat salútem,
donet et nobis pietáte patris
regna polórum.

Præstet hoc nobis Déitas beáta
Patris ac Nati, paritérque Sancti
Spíritus, cuius résonat per omnem
glória mundum. Amen.

Lo! the dim shadows of the night are waning;
Radiantly glowing, dawn of day returneth;
Fervent in spirit, to the mighty Father
Pray we devoutly.

So shall our Maker of his great compassion,
Banish all sickness, kindly health bestowing;
And may he grant us, of a Father's goodness,
Mansions in heaven.

This he vouchsafe us, God for ever blessèd
Father eternal, Son, and Holy Spirit,
Whose is the glory which through all creation
Ever resoundeth. Amen.

PSALMODY

Ant. 1	Blessèd is he who comes in the name of the *Lord*, * al*le*luia.
Advent:	Zion is our mighty citadel, † our saving Lord its wall and its defense; † throw open the *gates*, * for our God is here among us, al*le*luia.
Lent, 2nd Sunday:	The right hand of the Lord has shown its *pow*er; * the right hand of the Lord has raised *me* up.
Passion Sunday:	The great crowd that had gathered for the *feast* * cried out to *the* Lord: Blessèd is he who comes in the name of the *Lord*. * Hosanna in *the* highest.
Easter, 6th Sunday:	This is the day which the Lord has *made*, * al*le*luia.

VIII a

Psalm 118
Song of joy for salvation
This Jesus is the stone which, rejected by you builders, has become the chief stone
supporting all the rest (Acts 4:11).

Give thanks to the Lord for he
is *good*, * for his love endures *for*
ever.
Let the sons of Israel *say*: * "His love
endures *for* ever."
Let the sons of Aaron *say*: * "His love
endures *for* ever."
Let those who fear the Lord *say*: * "His
love endures *for* ever."
I called to the Lord in my dis*tress*; * he
answered *and* freed me.
The Lord is at my side; I do not *fear*. *
What can man do *a*gainst me?
The Lord is at my side as my *help*er: * I
shall look down on *my* foes.
It is better to take refuge in the *Lord* *
than to trust *in* men:
it is better to take refuge in the *Lord* *
than to trust *in* princes.
The nations all en*com*passed me; * in
the Lord's name *I* crushed them.
They compassed me, compassed me
a*bout*; * in the Lord's name *I* crushed
them.
They compassed me about like bees; †

they blazed like a fire among *thorns*. *
In the Lord's name *I* crushed them.
I was hard-pressed and was *fall*ing * but
the Lord came *to* help me.
The Lord is my strength and my *song*; *
he is *my* savior.
There are shouts of joy and *vic*tory * in
the tents of *the* just.
The Lord's right hand has *tri*umphed; *
his right *hand* raised me.
The Lord's right hand has *tri*umphed; *
I shall not die, I shall live and recount
his deeds.
I was punished, I was punishèd by the
Lord, * but not doomed *to* die.
Open to me the gates of *ho*liness: * I
will enter and *give* thanks.
This is the Lord's own *gate* * where the
just *may* enter.
I will thank you for you have *an*swered
* and you are *my* savior.
The stone which the builders re*ject*ed *
has become *the* corner stone.
This is the work of the *Lord*, * a marvel
in *our* eyes.

This day was made by the *Lord*; * we rejoice and *are* glad.

O Lord, grant us sal*va*tion; * O Lord, grant *success*.

Blessèd in the name of the *Lord* * is he *who* comes.

We bless you from the house of the *Lord*; * the Lord God is *our* light.

Go forward in procession with *branch*es * even to *the* altar.

You are my God, I *thank* you. * My God, *I* praise you.

Give thanks to the Lord for he is *good*; * for his love endures *for* ever.

Glory to the Father, and to the *Son*, * and to the Ho*ly* Spirit:

as it was in the beginning, is *now*, * and will be for ever. *A*men.

Antiphon	Blessèd is he who comes in the name of the *Lord*, * al*le*luia.
Advent:	Zion is our mighty citadel, † our saving Lord its wall and its defense; † throw open the *gates*, * for our God is here among us, al*le*luia.
Lent, 2nd Sunday:	The right hand of the Lord has shown its *pow*er; * the right hand of the Lord has raised *me* up.
Passion Sunday:	The great crowd that had gathered for the *feast* * cried out to *the* Lord: Blessèd is he who comes in the name of the *Lord*. * Hosanna in *the* highest.
Easter, 6th Sunday:	This is the day which the Lord has *made*, * al*le*luia.

Ant. 2	Let us sing a hymn of praise *to* our God, * alle*lu*ia.
Advent:	Come to the waters, all you who thirst; † seek the Lord while he *can* be found, * alle*lu*ia.
Lent, 2nd Sunday:	Let us sing the hymn of the three young men † which they sang in the *fi*ery furnace, * giving praise to *God*.
Passion Sunday:	God grant that with the angels and the children we may be faithful, † and sing with them to the conquer*or* of death: * Hosanna in the *high*est.
Easter, 6th Sunday:	Blessèd are you, Lord our God, in the firmament of heaven. † You are worthy of *praise* for ever, * alle*lu*ia.

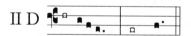

Canticle
Daniel 3:52-57

Let all creatures praise the Lord
The Creator…is blessed for ever (Romans 1:25).

Blessèd are you, O Lord, the God *of* our fathers, * praiseworthy and exalted above all for*ev*er.

And blessèd is your holy and glo*ri*ous name, * praiseworthy and exalted above all for all *ages*.

Blessèd are you in the temple of your *ho*ly glory, * praiseworthy and glorious above all for*ev*er.

Blessèd are you on the throne *of* your kingdom, * praiseworthy and exalted above all for*ev*er.

Blessèd are you who look into the depths from your throne up*on* the cherubim, * praiseworthy and exalted above all for*ev*er.

Blessèd are you in the firma*ment* of heaven, * praiseworthy and glorious forever.

Bless the Lord, all you works *of* the Lord, * praise and exalt him above all for*e*ver.

Glory to the Father, and *to* the Son, * and to the Holy *Spirit:*

as it was in the begin*ning,* is now, * and will be for ever. A*men.*

Antiphon	Let us sing a hymn of praise *to* our God, * alle*lu*ia.
Advent:	Come to the waters, all you who thirst; † seek the Lord while he *can* be found, * alle*lu*ia.
Lent, 2nd Sunday:	Let us sing the hymn of the three young men † which they sang in the *fie*ry furnace, * giving praise to *God.*
Passion Sunday:	God grant that with the angels and the children we may be faithful, † and sing with them to the conquer*or* of death: * Hosanna in the *high*est.
Easter, 6th Sunday:	Blessèd are you, Lord our God, in the firmament of heaven. † You are worthy of *praise* for ever, * alle*lu*ia.

Ant. 3	Praise the Lord for his infin*ite* greatness, * a*l*leluia.
Advent:	Our God will come with great power † to enlighten the eyes of *his* servants, * a*l*leluia.
Lent, 2nd Sunday:	Praise *the* Lord * in his heav*en*ly power.
Passion Sunday:	Blessèd is he who comes in the name of *the* Lord; * peace in heaven and glory *in* the highest.
Easter, 6th Sunday:	Worship God who is seated upon the throne; † sing to him *in* praise: * Amen, a*l*leluia.

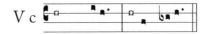

Psalm 150
Praise the Lord

Let mind and heart be in your song: this is to glorify God with your whole self (Hesychius).

Praise God in his ho*ly* place, * praise him in his *migh*ty heavens.

Praise him for his power*ful* deeds, * praise his sur*pass*ing greatness.

O praise him with sound *of* trumpet, * praise him with *lute* and harp.

Praise him with timbrel *and* dance, * praise him with *strings* and pipes.

O praise him with resound*ing* cymbals, * praise him with cla*shing* of cymbals.

Let everything that lives and *that* breathes * give praise *to* the Lord.

Glory to the Father, and to *the* Son, * and to the *Holy* Spirit:

as it was in the beginning, *is* now, * and will be for ev*er.* Amen.

Antiphon	Praise the Lord for his infin*ite* greatness, * a*l*leluia.
Advent:	Our God will come with great power † to enlighten the eyes of *his* servants, * a*l*leluia.
Lent, 2nd Sunday:	Praise *the* Lord * in his heav*en*ly power.
Passion Sunday:	Blessèd is he who comes in the name of *the* Lord; * peace in heaven and glory *in* the highest.
Easter, 6th Sunday:	Worship God who is seated upon the throne; † sing to him *in* praise: * Amen, a*l*leluia.

READING   Ezekiel 36:25-27

I will sprinkle clean water upon you to cleanse you from all your impurities, and from all your idols I will cleanse you. I will give you a new heart and place a new spirit within you, taking from your bodies your stony hearts and giving you natural hearts. I will put my spirit within you and make you live by my statutes, careful to observe my decrees.

RESPONSORY (VI F)

We give thanks to *you*, O God, * as we call upon *your* name.
—We give thanks to *you*, O God, * as we call upon *your* name.
We cry aloud how marve*lous* you are,
— as we call upon *your* name.
Glory to the Father, and *to* the Son, * and to the Ho*ly* Spirit.
—We give thanks to *you*, O God, * as we call upon *your* name.

CANTICLE OF ZECHARIAH, antiphon, as in the Proper of Seasons.

VII d

Blessèd ✠ be the Lord, the *God* of Israel; * he has come to his people and set *them* free.
He has raised up for us a *mighty* savior, * born of the house of his ser*vant* David.
Through his holy prophets he promised of old † that he would save us *from* our enemies, * from the hands of all *who* hate us.
He promised to show mercy *to* our fathers * and to remember his ho*ly* covenant.
This was the oath he swore to our *fath*er Abraham: * to set us free from the hands of *our* enemies,
free to worship him without fear, † holy and righteous *in* his sight * all the

days of *our* life.
You, my child, shall be called the prophet *of* the Most High; * for you will go before the Lord to prepare *his* way,
to give his people knowledge *of* salvation * by the forgiveness of *their* sins.
In the tender compassion *of* our God * the dawn from on high shall break *up*on us,
to shine on those who dwell in darkness and the sha*dow* of death, * and to guide our feet into the way *of* peace.
Glory to the Father, and *to* the Son, * and to the Ho*ly* Spirit:
as it was in the begin*ning*, is now, * and will be for ever. *A*men.

Antiphon is repeated.

INTERCESSIONS (VI F)

Let us give thanks to our Savior who came into this world as God's pre*sence*
     among us. * Let us *call* upon him:

Christ, King of Glory, be our light and our joy.

Lord Jesus, you are the rising Sun, the firstfruits of the future *re*surrection,

— grant that we may not sit in the shadow of death but walk in the *light* of life.

Show us your goodness, present in *eve*ry creature,

— that we may contemplate your *glo*ry everywhere.

Do not allow us to be overcome by e*vil* today,

— but grant that we may overcome evil through the po*wer* of good.

You were baptized in the Jordan and anointed by the *Ho*ly Spirit,

— grant that we may this day give thanks to your *Ho*ly Spirit.

Our Father . . .

Prayer, as in the Proper of Seasons.

SUNDAY, WEEK II

Evening Prayer II

HYMN, 1331.

O lux, beata Trinitas. (L.M.)

O lux, beáta Trínitas	O Trinity of blessèd light,
et principális Unitas,	O Unity of princely might,
iam sol recédit ígneus:	The fiery sun now goes his way;
infúnde lumen córdibus.	Shed thou within our hearts thy ray.
Te mane laudum cármine,	To thee our morning song of praise,
te deprecémur véspere;	To thee our evening prayer we raise;
te nostra supplex glória	Thy glory suppliant we adore
per cuncta laudet sæcula.	For ever and for evermore.
Christum rogámus et Patrem,	All laud to God the Father be;
Christi Patrísque Spíritum;	All praise eternal Son, to thee;
unum potens per ómnia,	All glory, as is ever meet,
fove precántes, Trínitas. Amen.	To God the Holy Paraclete. Amen.

PSALMODY

Ant. 1   Christ our Lord is a priest for *ever*, * like Melchizedek of old, al*le*luia.

Advent: The Lord will come on the clouds of heaven † with great power and *might*, * al*le*luia.

Lent, 2nd Sunday: In holy spendor the Lord will send *forth* * your mighty scepter *from* Zion.

Passion Sunday: Christ was scourged and treated with con*tempt*, * but God's right hand has raised *him* up.

Easter, 6th Sunday: God raised up Christ from the dead † and gave him a place at his right hand in *heav*en, * al*le*luia.

VIII a

Psalm 110:1-5, 7
The Messiah, king and priest
Christ's reign will last until all his enemies are made subject to him
(1 Corinthians 15:25).

The Lord's revelation to my Master: † "Sit on my *right*: * your foes I will put beneath *your* feet."
The Lord will wield from Zion † your scepter of *pow*er: * rule in the midst of all *your* foes.
A prince from the day of your birth on the holy *mount*ains; * from the womb before the dawn I *beg*ot you.
The Lord has sworn an oath he will not change. † "You are a priest for *ever*, * a priest like Melchizedek *of* old."
The Master standing at your *right* hand * will shatter kings in the day of his

great wrath.

He shall drink from the stream by the *way*side * and therefore he shall lift up *his* head.

Glory to the Father, and to the *Son*, *
and to the Ho*ly* Spirit:

as it was in the beginning, is *now*, * and will be for ever. *A*men.

Antiphon	Christ our Lord is a priest for *ev*er, * like Melchizedek of old, al*le*luia.
Advent:	The Lord will come on the clouds of heaven † with great power and *might*, * al*le*luia.
Lent, 2nd Sunday:	In holy spendor the Lord will send *forth* * your mighty scepter *from* Zion.
Passion Sunday:	Christ was scourged and treated with con*tempt*, * but God's right hand has raised *him* up.
Easter, 6th Sunday:	God raised up Christ from the dead † and gave him a place at his right hand in *hea*ven, * al*le*luia.

Ant. 2	God dwells in *high*est heaven; * he has power to do all he wills, alle*lu*ia.
Advent:	The Lord will come; he is true to his word. † If he seems to delay, keep *watch* for him, * for he will surely come, alle*lu*ia.
Lent, 2nd Sunday:	We worship the *one* true God * who made heaven and *earth*.
Passion Sunday:	The blood of Christ washes a*way* our sins * and makes us worthy to serve the living *God*.
Easter, 6th Sunday:	You have been turned from faith in idols † to the *liv*ing God, * alle*lu*ia.

II D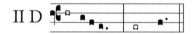

Psalm 115
Praise of the true God
You have renounced idol worship to serve the living and true God (1 Thessalonians 1:9).

Not to us, Lord, *not* to us, * but to your name give the *glo*ry

for the sake of your love *and* your truth, * lest the heathen say: "Where is their *God?*"

But our God is *in* the heavens; * he does whatever he *wills*.

Their idols are sil*ver* and gold, * the work of human *hands*.

They have mouths but they *can*not speak; * they have eyes but they cannot *see*;

they have ears but they *can*not hear; * they have nostrils but they cannot *smell*.

With their hands they *can*not feel; * with their feet they cannot *walk*.

No sound comes from their throats. † Their makers will come to *be* like them * and so will all who trust in *them*.

Sons of Israel, trust *in* the Lord; * he is their help and their *shield*.

Sons of Aaron, trust *in* the Lord; * he is their help and their *shield*.

You who fear him, trust *in* the Lord; * he is their help and their *shield*.

He remembers us, and he will bless us; † he will bless the *sons* of Israel. * He will bless the sons of *Aa*ron.

The Lord will bless *those* who fear him,
* the little no less than the *great*:

to you may the *Lord* grant increase, * to you and all your *child*ren.

May you be blessed *by* the Lord, * the maker of heaven and *earth*.

The heavens belong *to* the Lord * but the earth he has given to *men*.

The dead shall not *praise* the Lord, *

nor those who go down into the silence.

But we who live *bless* the Lord * now and for ever. A*men*.

Glory to the Father, and *to* the Son, * and to the Holy *Spi*rit:

as it was in the begin*ning*, is now, * and will be for ever. A*men*.

Antiphon	God dwells in *high*est heaven; * he has power to do all he wills, alle*lu*ia.
Advent:	The Lord will come; he is true to his word. † If he seems to delay, keep *watch* for him, * for he will surely come, alle*lu*ia.
Lent, 2nd Sunday:	We worship the *one* true God * who made heaven and *earth*.
Passion Sunday:	The blood of Christ washes a*way* our sins * and makes us worthy to serve the living *God*.
Easter, 6th Sunday:	You have been turned from faith in idols † to the *liv*ing God, * alle*lu*ia.

Ant. 3	Praise God, all you who serve him, both great *and* small, * alleluia, alleluia.
Advent:	The Lord our king and lawgiver will come *to* save us * alleluia, alleluia.
Easter, 6th Sunday:	Alleluia, salvation, glory and power to *our* God, * alleluia, alleluia.

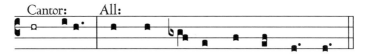

** al- le- lu- ia, al- le- lu- ia.

*Al- le- lu- ia.   ** al- le- lu- ia, al- le - lu- ia.

Canticle   See Revelation 19:1-7
The wedding of the Lamb

Salvation, glory, and power to *our* God:
* Alleluia.

his judgments are hon*est* and true.
** Alleluia, alleluia.

Sing praise to our God, all you *his* servants,
* Alleluia.

all who worship him reverently, *great* and small.
** Alleluia, alleluia.

The Lord our all-powerful God *is* King;
* Alleluia.
let us rejoice, sing praise, and *give* him glory.
** Alleluia, alleluia.

The wedding feast of the Lamb has *be*gun,
* Alleluia.
and his bride is pre*pared* to welcome him.
** Alleluia, alleluia.

Glory to the Father, and to the Son, †
and to the Ho*ly* Spirit.
* Alleluia.
As it was in the beginning, is now, †
and will be for ev*er.* Amen.
** Alleluia, alleluia.

Antiphon   Praise God, all you who serve him, both great *and* small, *
alleluia, alleluia.

Advent: The Lord our king and lawgiver will come *to* save us * alleluia, alleluia.

Easter, 6th Sunday: Alleluia, salvation, glory and power to *our* God, * alleluia, alleluia.

Lent: Antiphon 3

Lent, 2nd Sunday: God did not spare his *own* Son * but gave him up *for* us all.

Passion Sunday: Christ bore our sins in his own body on the cross † so that we might die *to* sin *
and be alive to all that *is* good.

Canticle   1 Peter 2:21-24
The willing acceptance of his passion by Christ, the servant of God

Christ suffered for you, † and left
you an *ex*ample * to have you
follow in *his* footsteps.
He did *no* wrong; * no deceit was found
in *his* mouth.
When he was *in*sulted * he returned *no*
insult.
When he was made *to* suffer, * he did

not counter *with* threats.
Instead he delivered him*self* up * to the
One who judg*es* justly.
In his *own* body * he brought his sins to
the cross,
so that all of us, dead *to* sin, * could live
in accord with *God's* will.
By *his* wounds * you *were* healed.

Glory to the Father, and to *the* Son, * and to the Ho*ly* Spirit: | as it was in the beginning, *is* now, * and will be for ever. *A*men.

Lent, 2nd Sunday: God did not spare his *own* Son * but gave him up *for* us all.

Passion Sunday: Christ bore our sins in his own body on the cross † so that we might die *to* sin * and be alive to all that *is* good.

READING   2 Thessalonians 2: 13-14

We are bound to thank God for you always, beloved brothers in the Lord, because you are the first fruits of those whom God has chosen for salvation, in holiness of spirit and fidelity to truth. He called you through our preaching of the good news so that you might achieve the glory of our Lord Jesus Christ.

RESPONSORY (VI F)

Our *Lord* is great, * mighty is *his* power.

— Our *Lord* is great, * mighty is *his* power.

His wisdom is be*yond* compare,

— mighty is *his* power.

Glory to the Father, and *to* the Son, * and to the Ho*ly* Spirit.

— Our *Lord* is great, * mighty is *his* power.

CANTICLE OF MARY, antiphon, as in the Proper of Seasons.

VII d

My soul ✠ proclaims the greatness *of* the Lord, * my spirit rejoices in God *my* savior

for he has *looked* with favor * on his low*ly* servant.

From this day all *gen*erations * will call *me* blessèd:

the Almighty has done great *things* for me, * and holy is *his* Name.

He has mercy on *those* who fear him * in every gen*er*ation.

He has shown the strength *of* his arm, * he has scattered the proud in their *con*ceit.

He has cast down the mighty *from* their thrones, * and has lifted up *the* lowly.

He has filled the hungry *with* good things, * and the rich he has sent a*way* empty.

He has come to the help of his *servant* Israel * for he has remembered his promise *of* mercy,

the promise he made *to* our fathers, * to Abraham and his children *for* ever.

Glory to the Father, and *to* the Son, * and to the Ho*ly* Spirit:

as it was in the begin*ning*, is now, * and will be for ever. *A*men.

Antiphon repeated.

INTERCESSIONS (VI F)

All praise and honor to Christ! He lives for ever to intercede for us, and he is
   able to save those who approach the Father *in* his name. * Sustained by our
   faith, let us *call* upon him:

Remember your people, O *Lord.*

As the day draws to a close, Sun of Justice, we invoke your name upon the whole
   *hu*man race,
— so that all men may enjoy your never *fai*ling light.

Preserve the covenant which you have ratified *in* your blood,
— cleanse and sanct*ify* your Church.

Remember your as*sem*bly, Lord,
— your *dwel*ling place.

Guide travelers along the path of peace *and* prosperity,
— so that they may reach their destinations in safe*ty* and joy.

Receive the souls of the *dead*, O Lord,
— grant them your favor and the gift of e*ter*nal glory.

Our Father . . .

Prayer, as in the Proper of Seasons.

MONDAY, WEEK II

Morning Prayer

HYMN, 1332.
Lucis largítor spléndide. (L.M.)

Lucis largítor spléndide,	O lavish Giver of the light
cuius seréno lúmine	That bathes the world in dawning glow;
post lapsa noctis témpora	The daylight cheers our hearts again
dies refúsus pánditur,	When sombre hours of night are past.
Tu verus mundi lúcifer	You are the world's true Morning Star,
non is qui parvi síderis	Compared with whom the eager gleam
ventúræ lucis núntius	That heralds in the dawning light
angústo fulget lúmine,	Is but a timid, narrow ray.
Sed toto sole clárıor,	True Light itself, Eternal Day,
lux ipse totus et dies,	You are far brighter than the sun,
intérna nostri péctoris	Illuminating with your grace
illúminans præcórdia.	The deep recesses of each heart.
Evíncat mentis cástitas	And may our purity of mind
quæ caro cupit árrogans,	Suppress what lower nature claims,
sanctúmque puri córporis	So that our bodies too may be
delúbrum servet Spíritus.	The Holy Spirit's spotless shrine.
Sit, Christe, rex piíssime,	Jesus, to you, beneath whose sway
tibi Patríque glória	All earth shall bow, all praise we pay;
cum Spíritu Paráclito	With Father and with Spirit be
in sempitérna sæcula. Amen.	All glory yours eternally. Amen.

PSALMODY

Ant. 1   When will I come to the end of my *pil*grimage * and enter the presence *of* God?

Easter: As a deer longs for flowing streams, † so my soul longs for you, my *God,* * al*le*luia.

VIIIa

Psalm 42
Longing for the Lord's presence in his Temple
Let all who thirst come; let all who desire it drink from the life-giving water
(Revelation 22:17).

Like the deer that *yearns* * for
run*ning* streams,
so my soul is *yearn*ing * for you, *my*

God.
My soul is thirsting for *God,* * the God
of *my* life;

when can I enter and *see* * the face *of*
  God?
My tears have become my *bread,* * by
  night, *by* day,
as I hear it said all the day *long:* *
  "Where is *your* God?"
These things will I re*member* * as I pour
  out *my* soul:
how I would lead the rejoicing *crowd* *
  into the house *of* God,
amid cries of gladness and thanks*giv*–
  ing, * the throng wild *with* joy.
Why are you cast down, my *soul,* * why
  groan *with*in me?
Hope in God; I will praise him *still,* *
  my savior and *my* God.
My soul is cast down with*in* me * as I
  think *of* you,
from the country of Jordan and Mount
  *Her*mon, * from the Hill *of* Mizar.
Deep is calling on *deep,* * in the roar *of*
  waters:

your torrents and all your *waves* * swept
  over me.
By day the Lord will *send* * his lov*ing*
  kindness;
by night I will sing to *him,* * praise the
  God of *my* life.
I will say to God, my *rock:* * "Why have
  you *for*gotten me?
Why do I go *mourn*ing, * oppressed by
  the foe?"
With cries that pierce me to the *heart,* *
  my enemies *re*vile me,
saying to me all the day *long:* * "Where
  is *your* God?"
Why are you cast down, my *soul,* * why
  groan *with*in me?
Hope in God; I will praise him *still,* *
  my savior and *my* God.
Glory to the Father, and to the *Son,* *
  and to the Ho*ly* Spirit:
as it was in the beginning, is *now,* * and
  will be for ever. *A*men.

Antiphon   When will I come to the end of my *pil*grimage * and enter the
             presence *of* God?

Easter: As a deer longs for flowing streams, † so my soul longs for you, my *God,* *
            al*le*luia.

Ant. 2   Lord, show *us* the radiance * of your *mercy.*
Easter: Fill Zion with your praises, Lord, † and let your wonders *be* proclaimed, *
            alle*lu*ia.

IID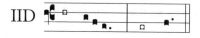

Canticle   Sirach 36:1-2, 10-13
Prayer of entreaty for the holy city, Jerusalem
This is eternal life: to know you, the one true God, and Jesus Christ whom you have sent
(John 17:3).

Come to our aid, O God *of* the
  universe, * and put all the nations
in dread *of* you!
Raise your hand a*gainst* the heathen, *
  that they may realize your *pow*er.

As you have used us to show *them* your
  holiness, * so now use them to show
  us your *glory.*
Thus they will know, *as* we know, * that
  there is no God but *you.*

Give new signs and *work* new wonders;
  * show forth the splendor of your
  right hand and *arm.*
Gather all the *tribes* of Jacob, * that they
  may inherit the land as of *old.*
Show mercy to the people called *by*
  your name; * Israel, whom you named
  your *first*-born.

Take pity on your *holy* city, * Jerusalem,
  your *dwelling* place.
Fill Zion *with* your majesty, * your
  temple with your *glory.*
Glory to the Father, and *to* the Son, *
  and to the Holy *Spirit:*
as it was in the begin*ning*, is now, * and
  will be for ever. A*men.*

Antiphon   Lord, show *us* the radiance * of your *mercy.*

Easter: Fill Zion with your praises, Lord, † and let your wonders *be* proclaimed, *
                alle*lu*ia.

Ant. 3   The vaults *of* heaven * ring with your *praise*, O Lord.

Easter: The glory of God illumines *the* city; * the Lamb of God is its light, a*l*leluia.

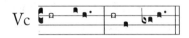

Psalm 19A
Praise of the Lord, Creator of all
The dawn from on high shall break on us...to guide our feet into the way of peace
(Luke 1:78, 79).

The heavens proclaim the glory *of*
  God * and the firmament shows
  forth the work *of* his hands.
Day unto day takes up *the* story * and
  night unto night makes *known* the
  message.
No speech, no word, no voice is heard †
  yet their span extends through all *the*
  earth, * their words to the utmost
  bounds *of* the world.
There he has placed a tent for the sun;

† it comes forth like a bridegroom
  coming from *his* tent, * rejoices like a
  champion to *run* its course.
At the end of the sky is the rising of the
  sun; † to the furthest end of the sky is
  its course. * There is nothing concealed from its *burn*ing heat.
Glory to the Father, and to *the* Son, *
  and to the *Holy* Spirit:
as it was in the beginning, *is* now, * and
  will be for e*ver.* Amen.

Antiphon   The vaults *of* heaven * ring with your *praise*, O Lord.
Easter: The glory of God illumines *the* city; * the Lamb of God is its light, a*l*leluia.

READING   Jeremiah 15:16

  When I found your words, I devoured them;
      they became my joy and the happiness of my heart,
  Because I bore your name,
      O Lord, God of hosts.

RESPONSORY (VI F)

Sing for *joy*, God's chosen ones, * give him the praise that *is* due.
— Sing for *joy*, God's chosen ones, * give him the praise that *is* due.
Sing a new song *to* the Lord, *
— give him the praise that *is* due.
Glory to the Father, and *to* the Son, * and to the Ho*ly* Spirit.
— Sing for *joy*, God's chosen ones, * give him the praise that *is* due.

CANTICLE OF ZECHARIAH

Antiphon   Blessèd *be* the Lord, * for he has come to his people and set *them*
                  free.

INTERCESSIONS (VI F)

Our Savior has made us a nation of priests to offer acceptable sacrifice *to* the
  Father. * Let us call upon *him* in gratitude:
Preserve us in your ministry, O Lord.
Christ, eternal priest, you conferred the holy priesthood *on* your people,
— grant that we may offer spiritual sacrifices acceptable *to* the Father.
In your goodness pour out on us the fruits *of* your Spirit,
— patience, kind*ness* and gentleness.
May we love you and possess you, for *you* are love,
— and may every action of *our* lives praise you.
May we seek those things which are beneficial to our brothers, without count*ing*
  the cost,
— to help them on the way *to* salvation.

Our Father . . .

Prayer

  Almighty Father,
  you have brought us to the light of a new day:
  keep us safe the whole day through
  from every sinful inclination.
  May all our thoughts, words and actions
  aim at doing what is pleasing in your sight.
  We ask this through our Lord Jesus Christ, your Son,
  who lives and reigns with you and the Holy Spirit,
  one God, for ever and ever.

MONDAY, WEEK II

Evening Prayer

HYMN, 1333.
Luminous fons, lux et origo lucis. (L.M.)

Lúminis fons, lux et orígo lucis,	O fount of light, True Light itself,
tu pius nostris précibus favéto,	Smile down on us as here we pray.
luxque, peccáti ténebris fugátis,	May your bright splendor shine on us,
nos tua adórnet.	When shades of sin are cast away.
Ecce transáctus labor est diéi,	We thank you for your loving care
teque nos tuti sumus adnuénte ;	While work and toil have been our lot,
en tibi grates ágimus libéntes	And now the day is near its close,
tempus in omne.	Dear Lord, we pray, forsake us not.
Solis abscéssus ténebras reduxit :	Though sun declines and shadows fall,
ille sol nobis rádiet corúscus	Our souls draw light from those fair rays
luce qui fulva fovet angelórum	The Sun of Justice n'er withholds,
ágmina sancta.	On whom the hosts of angels gaze.
Quas dies culpas hodiérna texit,	May all the faults which we deplore,
Christus deléto pius atque mitis,	Be washed away by Christ our Light,
pectus et puro rútilet nitóre	And may he purify our hearts
témpore noctis.	Throughout the hours of coming night.
Laus tibi Patri, decus atque Nato,	All glory, Father, be to you,
Flámini Sancto párilis potéstas,	Praise to the Spirit and the Son,
cuncta qui sceptro régitis suprémo	Who rule all things with pow'r supreme
omne per ævum. Amen.	Till all created time is done. Amen.

PSALMODY

Ant. 1   Yours is more than mortal *beau*ty; * every word you speak is
full *of* grace.

Easter: Bless*è*d is he who comes in the name of the *Lord*, * al*le*luia.

VIIIa

Psalm 45
The marriage of the king
The bridegroom is here; go out and welcome him (Matthew 25:6).

I

My heart overflows with noble words. † To the king I must speak the song I have *made*; * my tongue as nimble as the pen of *a* scribe.
You are the fairest of the children of

men † and graciousness is poured upon your *lips*: * because God has blessed you for eve*r*more.

O mighty one, gird your sword upon your thigh; † in splendor and state, ride on in *tri*umph * for the cause of truth and goodness *and* right.

Take aim with your bow in your dread right hand. † Your arrows are sharp: peoples fall be*neath* you. * The foes of the king fall down and *lose* heart.

Your throne, O God, shall endure for ever. † A scepter of justice is the scepter of your *king*dom. * Your love

is for justice; your hatred *for* evil.

Therefore God, your God, has anointed you † with the oil of gladness above other *kings*: * your robes are fragrant with aloes *and* myrrh.

From the ivory palace you are greeted with music. † The daughters of kings are among your *loved* ones. * On your right stands the queen in gold *of* Ophir.

Glory to the Father, and to the *Son*, * and to the Ho*ly* Spirit,

As it was in the beginning, is *now*, * and will be for ever. *A*men.

Antiphon   Yours is more than mortal *beau*ty; * every word you speak is full *of* grace.

Easter: Bless*è*d is he who comes in the name of the *Lord*, * all*e*luia.

Ant. 2   The Bride*groom* is here; * go out and *wel*come him.

Easter: Bless*è*d are those who are called to the wedding feast *of* the Lamb, * alle*lu*ia.

IID
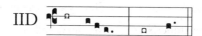

II

Listen, O daughter, give ear *to* my words: * forget your own people and your father's *house*.

So will the king de*sire* your beauty: * he is your lord, pay homage to *him*.

And the people of Tyre shall *come* with gifts, * the richest of the people shall seek your *favor*.

The daughter of the king is *clothed* with splendor, * her robes embroidered with pearls set in *gold*.

She is led to the king with her maiden companions. † They are escorted

amid glad*ness* and joy; * they pass within the palace of the *king*.

Sons shall be yours in place *of* your fathers: * you will make them princes over all the *earth*.

May this song make your name for ev*er* remembered. * May the peoples praise you from age to *age*.

Glory to the Father, and *to* the Son, * and to the Holy *Spi*rit:

as it was in the begin*ning*, is now, * and will be for ever. *A*men.

Antiphon   The Bride*groom* is here; * go out and *wel*come him.

Easter: Bless*è*d are those who are called to the wedding feast *of* the Lamb, * alle*lu*ia.

Ant. 3   God planned in the fullness *of* time * to restore all *things* in
          Christ.

Easter: From his fullness we have all *received*, * grace upon grace, *a*lleluia.

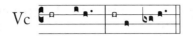

Vc

Canticle   Ephesians 1:3-10
God our Savior

Praised be the God *and* Father * of
    our Lord *Je*sus Christ,
who has bestowed on us *in* Christ *
    every spiritual blessing *in* the
    heavens.
God chose us in him before the world
    *be*gan * to be holy and blameless *in*
    his sight.
He predestined us to be his adopted
    sons through Je*sus* Christ, * such was
    his *will* and pleasure,
that all might praise the glori*ous* favor *
    he has bestowed on us in *his* belovèd.
In him and through his blood, we have
    been *re*deemed, * and our *sins*

forgiven,
    so immeasura*bly* generous * is God's
    favor to us.
God has given us the wisdom to
    understand fully *the* mystery, * the
    plan he was pleased to de*cree* in
    Christ.
A plan to be carried out *in* Christ, * in
    the full*ness* of time,
to bring all things into one *in* him, * in
    the heavens *and* on earth.
Glory to the Father, and to *the* Son, *
    and to the *Ho*ly Spirit:
as it was in the beginning, *is* now, * and
    will be for *ever*. Amen.

Antiphon God planned in the fullness *of* time * to restore all *things* in
          Christ.

Easter: From his fullness we have all *received*, * grace upon grace, *a*lleluia.

READING   1 Thessalonians 2:13
    We thank God constantly that in receiving his message from us you took it,
    not as the word of men, but as it truly is, the word of God at work within you
    who believe.

RESPONSORY (VI F)
Accept my *prayer*, O Lord, * which rises up *to* you.
— Accept my *prayer*, O Lord, * which rises up *to* you.
Like burning incense *in* your sight,
— which rises up *to* you.
Glory to the Father, and *to* the Son, * and to the Ho*ly* Spirit.
— Accept my *prayer*, O Lord, * which rises up *to* you.

CANTICLE OF MARY
Antiphon   For ever will my *soul* proclaim * the greatness of *the* Lord.

INTERCESSIONS (VI F)
Let us praise Christ, who loves, nourishes and sup*ports* his Church. * With faith
    let us cry *out* to him:
*Answer the prayers of your peo*ple, *Lord.*
Lord Jesus, grant that all *men* be saved,
— and come to the know*ledge* of truth.
Preserve our holy father, Pope N., and *N.,* our bishop,
— come with your po*wer* to help them.
Remember those who long for *hon*est work,
— so that they may lead a life of peace*ful* security.
Lord, be the refuge *of* the poor,
— their help *in* distress.
We commend to your care all bishops, priests and deacons *who* have died,
— may they sing your praises for ever around your hea*ven*ly throne.

Our Father . . .

                                Prayer
    Almighty Father,
    you have given us the strength
    to work throughout this day.
    Receive our evening sacrifice of praise
    in thanksgiving for your countless gifts.
    We ask this through our Lord Jesus Christ, your Son,
    who lives and reigns with you and the Holy Spirit,
    one God, for ever and ever.

TUESDAY, WEEK II

Morning Prayer

HYMN, 1334.
Æterne lucis conditor. (L.M.)

Ætérne lucis cónditor,
lux ipse totus et dies,
noctem nec ullam séntiens
natúra lucis pérpeti,

Iam cedit pallens próximo
diéi nox advéntui,
obtúndens lumen síderum
adest et clarus lúcifer.

Iam stratis læti súrgimus
grates canéntes et tuas,
quod cæcam noctem vícerit
revéctans rursus sol diem.

Te nunc, ne carnis gáudia
blandis subrépant æstibus,
dolis ne cedat sæculi
mens nostra, sancte, quæsumus.

Ira ne rixas próvocet,
gulam ne venter íncitet,
opum pervértat ne famis,
turpis ne luxus óccupet,

Sed firma mente sóbrii,
casto manéntes córpore
totum fidéli spíritu
Christo ducámus hunc diem.

Præsta, Pater piíssime,
Patríque compar Unice,
cum Spíritu Paráclito
regnans per omne sæculum. Amen.

Eternal Maker of the light,
True Light itself, surpassing day,
No gloom or darkness can you know,
In your own light which has no end.

Pale shades of night are yielding fast,
Before the bold advance of day;
Resplendent shines the morning star
While other constellations fade.

We gladly rise to sing your praise,
And thank you with renewed delight,
That rising sun brings back the day,
To conquer night's obscurity.

Most Holy One, we beg of you
Let not our souls be led astray,
By nature's pleasures and desires
Or by the world's deceiving glare.

Let no contention raise disputes,
Nor greed disgrace a Christian's name,
Nor greed for riches be a snare,
Nor evil thoughts corrupt our minds.

But let us show well-governed souls,
Within a body chaste and pure,
To spend this day in work and prayer,
For Christ our Leader and our Lord.

O Father, this we ask be done
Through Jesus Christ your only Son,
Whom in the Spirit we adore:
One God who reigns for evermore. Amen.

PSALMODY

Ant. 1   Lord, send forth your *light* * and *your* truth.

Easter: You have come to Mount Zion and to the city of the living *God*, * al*le*luia.

VIIIa

Psalm 43
Longing for the temple
I have come into the world to be its light (John 12:46).

Defend me, O God, and plead my *cause* * against a god*less* nation.

From deceitful and cunning *men* * rescue me, O God.

Since you, O God, are my *strong*hold, * why have you *re*jected me?

Why do I go *mourn*ing * oppressed by *the* foe?

O send forth your light and your *truth*; * let these be *my* guide.

Let them bring me to your holy *mount*ain * to the place where *you* dwell.

And I will come to the altar of *God*, * the God of *my* joy.

My redeemer, I will thank you on the *harp*, * O God, *my* God.

Why are you cast down, my *soul*, * why groan *with*in me?

Hope in God; I will praise him *still*, * my savior and *my* God.

Glory to the Father, and to the *Son*, * and to the Ho*ly* Spirit:

as it was in the beginning, is *now*, * and will be for ever. *A*men.

Antiphon   Lord, send forth your *light* * and *your* truth.

Easter: You have come to Mount Zion and to the city of the living *God*, * al*le*luia.

Ant. 2   Lord, *keep* us safe * all the days of our *life*.

Easter: Lord, you have preserved my life *from* destruction, * alle*lu*ia.

IID

Canticle   Isaiah 38:10-14, 17-20
Anguish of a dying man and joy in his restoration
I am living, I was dead…and I hold the keys of death (Revelation 1:17-18).

Once I said, "In the noon*time* of life * I must de*part*!

To the gates of the nether world I shall *be* consigned * for the rest of my *years*."

I said, "I shall see the *Lord* no more * in the land of the *living*.

No longer shall I behold my *fel*low men * among those who dwell in the *world*."

My dwelling, like a *shep*herd's tent, * is struck down and borne away from *me*;

you have folded up my life, *like* a

weaver * who severs the last *thread*.
Day and night you give me ov*er* to
  torment; * I cry out until the *dawn*.
Like a lion he breaks *all* my bones; *
  day and night you give me over to
  *tor*ment.
Like a swallow I ut*ter* shrill cries; * I
  moan like a *dove*.
My eyes grow weak, *gazing* heavenward: * O Lord, I am in straits; be my
  sur*e*ty!
You have pre*served* my life * from the
  pit of des*truc*tion,
when you cast be*hind* your back * all my
  sins.
For it is not the nether world that *gives*

you thanks, * nor death that praises
  you;
neither do those who go down in*to* the
  pit * await your *kind*ness.
The living, the living *give* you thanks, *
  as I do to*day*.
Fathers declare *to* their sons, * O God,
  your *faith*fulness.
The Lord *is* our savior; * we shall sing
  to stringed *in*struments
in the house *of* the Lord * all the days
  of our *life*.
Glory to the Father, and *to* the Son, *
  and to the Holy *Spir*it:
as it was in the begin*ning*, is now, * and
  will be for ever. A*men*.

Antiphon   Lord, *keep* us safe * all the days of our *life*.
Easter: Lord, you have preserved my life *from* destruction, * alle*lu*ia.

Ant. 3   To you, O God, * our praise is *due* in Zion.
Easter: You have visited the earth and brought life-giv*ing* rain * to fill it with plenty,
                *al*leluia.

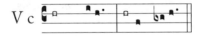

Psalm 65
Solemn thanksgiving
Zion represents heaven (Origen).

To you our praise *is* due * in Zi*on*, O
  God.
To you we pay *our* vows, * you who *hear*
  our prayer.
To you all flesh *will* come * with its
  bur*den* of sin.
Too heavy for us, our *of*fenses, * but you
  wipe *them* away.
Blessèd is he whom you choose *and* call
  * to dwell *in* your courts.
We are filled with the blessings of *your*
  house, * of your *ho*ly temple.
You keep your pledge *with* wonders, *
  O *God* our savior,

the hope of all *the* earth * and of far
  *dis*tant isles.
You uphold the mountains with *your*
  strength, * you are gird*ed* with power.
You still the roaring of the seas, † the
  roaring of *their* waves * and the
  tumult *of* the peoples.
The ends of the earth stand *in* awe * at
  the sight *of* your wonders.
The lands of sunrise *and* sunset * you
  fill *with* your joy.
You care for the earth, give *it* water, *
  you fill *it* with riches.
Your river in heaven *brims* over * to

pro*vide* its grain.
And thus you provide for *the* earth; * you *drench* its furrows,
you level it, soften it *with* showers, * you *bless* its growth.
You crown the year with your goodness.
† Abundance flows in *your* steps, * in the pastures of the wilder*ness* it flows.

The hills are girded *with* joy, * the meadows cov*ered* with flocks,
the valleys are decked *with* wheat. * They shout for joy, *yes*, they sing.
Glory to the Father, and to *the* Son, * and to the *Ho*ly Spirit:
as it was in the beginning, *is* now, * and will be for e*ver*. Amen.

Antiphon   To you, *O* God, * our praise is *due* in Zion.
Easter: You have visited the earth and brought life-giv*ing* rain * to fill it with plenty, a*l*leluia.

READING   1 Thessalonians 5:4-5
You are not in the dark, brothers, that the day should catch you off guard, like a thief. No, all of you are children of light and of the day. We belong neither to darkness nor to night.

RESPONSORY (VI F)
Lord, listen *to* my cry; * all my trust is in *your* promise.
— Lord, listen *to* my cry; * all my trust is in *your* promise.
Dawn finds me watching, crying *out* for you.
— all my trust is in *your* promise.
Glory to the Father, and *to* the Son, * and to the Ho*ly* Spirit.
— Lord, listen *to* my cry; * all my trust is in *your* promise.

CANTICLE OF ZECHARIAH
Antiphon   Lord, save us *from* the hands * of all *who* hate us.

INTERCESSIONS (VI F)
Let us bless our Savior who enlightens the world by his *res*urrection. * Let us *hum*bly beg him:
Keep us, Lord, on your *path.*
Lord Jesus, we honor your resurrection in our *morn*ing prayer,
— the hope of your glory enligh*tens* our day.
Accept, Lord, our prayers *and* petitions,
— as the first fruits *of* our day.
Grant that we may progress today *in* your love,
— and that all things may work together for our good and the *good* of all.
Make our light shine so brightly *be*fore men,
— that seeing our good works they may give glory *to* the Father.

Our Father . . .

Prayer

Lord Jesus Christ,
true light of the world,
you guide all mankind to salvation.
Give us the courage, strength and grace
to build a world of justice and peace,
ready for the coming of that kingdom.
You live and reign for ever and ever.

TUESDAY, WEEK II

Evening Prayer

HYMN, 1336.
Sator princepsque temporum. (L.M.)

Sator princépsque témporum,	Great Ruler of all space and time,
clarum diem labóribus	You give us daylight to employ
noctémque qui sopóribus	In work for you, that with the night
fixo distínguis órdine,	Refreshing sleep we may enjoy.
Mentem tu castam dírige,	While silence and the darkness reign
obscúra ne siléntia	Preserve our souls from sin and harm,
ad dira cordis vúlnera	Let nothing evil venture near
telis patéscant ínvidi.	To cause us panic or alarm.
Vacent ardóre péctora,	And while we thus renew our strength,
faces nec ullas pérferant,	Untouched by taint of sinful fire
quæ nostro hæréntes sénsui	Let hearts and minds find rest in you,
mentis vigórem sáucient.	The Source of every good desire.
Præsta, Pater piíssime,	O Father, this we ask be done
Patríque compar Unice,	Through Jesus Christ, your only Son,
cum Spíritu Paráclito	Whom in the Spirit we adore:
regnans per omne sæculum. Amen.	One God who reigns for evermore. Amen.

PSALMODY

Ant. 1   You cannot *serve* * both God *and* mammon.
Easter: Seek the things of heaven, † not those that are on the *earth*, * al*le*luia.

VIIIa

Psalm 49
Emptiness of riches
It is difficult for a rich man to enter the kingdom of heaven (Matthew 19:23).

I

Hear this, all you *peo*ples, * give
  heed, all who dwell in *the* world,
men both low and *high*, * rich and poor
  a*like*!
My lips will speak words of *wis*dom. *
  My heart is full *of* insight.
I will turn my mind to a *pa*rable, * with

the harp I will solve *my* problem.
Why should I fear in evil *days* * the
  malice of the foes who sur*round* me,
men who trust in their *wealth*, * and
  boast of the vastness of *their* riches?
For no man can buy his own *ran*som, *
  or pay a price to God for *his* life.

The ransom of his soul is beyond him.
  † He cannot buy life without *end*, *
  nor avoid coming to *the* grave.
He knows that wise men and fools
  must both *per*ish * and leave their
  wealth *to* others.
Their graves are their homes for ever, †
  their dwelling place from age to *age*, *
though their names spread wide
  through *the* land.
In his riches, man lacks *wis*dom: * he is
  like the beasts that are *des*troyed.
Glory to the Father, and to the *Son*, *
  and to the Ho*ly* Spirit:
as it was in the beginning, is *now*, * and
  will be for ever. *A*men.

Antiphon   You cannot *serve* * both God *and* mammon.
Easter: Seek the things of heaven, † not those that are on the *earth*, * al*le*luia.

Ant. 2   Store up for yourselves trea*sure* in heaven, * says the *Lord*.
Easter: The Lord has rescued my life from the pow*er* of hell, * alle*lu*ia.

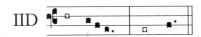

II

This is the lot of those who trust *in*
  themselves, * who have others at
  their beck and *call*.
Like sheep they are driven to the grave,
  † where death shall *be* their shepherd
  * and the just shall become their
  rulers.
With the morning their out*ward* show
  vanishes * and the grave becomes
  their *home*.
But God will ransom *me* from death *
  and take my soul to him*self*.
Then do not fear when a *man* grows
  rich, * when the glory of his house
  in*creas*es.
He takes nothing with him *when* he
  dies, * his glory does not follow him
  be*low*.
Though he flattered himself *while* he
  lived: * "Men will praise me for all my
  suc*cess*,"
yet he will go to *join* his fathers, * who
  will never see the light any *more*.
In his riches, *man* lacks wisdom: * he is
  like the beasts that are *des*troyed.
Glory to the Father, and *to* the Son, *
  and to the Holy *Spir*it:
as it was in the beginn*ing*, is now, * and
  will be for ever. *A*men.

Antiphon   Store up for yourselves trea*sure* in heaven, * says the *Lord*.
Easter: The Lord has rescued my life from the pow*er* of hell, * alle*lu*ia.

Ant. 3   Adoration and glory belong *by* right * to the Lamb *who* was slain.
Easter: Yours, O Lord, is majesty *and* power, * glory and triumph, *a*lleluia.

Vc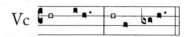

Canticle   Revelation 4:11; 5:9, 10, 12
Redemption hymn

O Lord our God, you *are* worthy *
  to receive glory and hon*or* and
power.
For you have created *all* things; * by
  your will they came to be *and* were
  made.
Worthy are you, *O* Lord, * to receive
  the scroll and break o*pen* its seals.
For you *were* slain; * with your blood
  you pur*chased* for God
men of every race *and* tongue, * of every
  peo*ple* and nation.

You made of them a kingdom, † and
  priests to serve *our* God, * and they
  shall reign *on* the earth.
Worthy is the Lamb that *was* slain * to
  receive pow*er* and riches,
wisdom *and* strength, * honor and glo*ry*
  and praise.
Glory to the Father, and to *the* Son, *
  and to the *Ho*ly Spirit:
as it was in the beginning, *is* now, * and
  will be for e*ver*. Amen.

Antiphon   Adoration and glory belong *by* right * to the Lamb *who* was slain.
Easter: Yours, O Lord, is majesty *and* power, * glory and triumph, *a*lleluia.

READING   Romans 3:23-25a
  All men have sinned and are deprived of the glory of God. All men are now
  undeservedly justified by the gift of God, through the redemption wrought in
  Christ Jesus. Through his blood, God made him the means of expiation for
  all who believe. He did so to manifest his own justice.

RESPONSORY (VI F)
I shall know the full*ness* of joy, * when I see your face, O Lord.
— I shall know the full*ness* of joy, * when I see your face, O Lord.
Fulfillment and endless peace *in* your presence,
— when I see your face, O Lord.
Glory to the Father, and *to* the Son, * and to the Ho*ly* Spirit.
— I shall know the full*ness* of joy, * when I see your face, O Lord.

CANTICLE OF MARY
Antiphon   Do great things for *us*, O Lord, * for you are mighty, and holy is
                your name.

INTERCESSIONS (VI F)

Let us praise Christ, the shepherd and guardian of our souls, who loves and
    pro*tects* his people. * Placing our hope in him, *we* cry out:
Protect your people, Lord.
 Eternal shepherd, protect our *bish*op N.,
— and all the shepherds *of* your Church.
Look kindly on those who suffer *per*secution,
— hasten to free them from *all* adversity.
Have mercy on the *needy*, Lord,
— provide food *for* the hungry.
Enlight*en* all legislators,
— to enact laws in the spirit of wis*dom* and justice.
Come to the aid of our departed brothers and sisters, whom you have redeemed
    with your blood,
— make them worthy to enter your *wed*ding feast.

Our Father . . .

Prayer

Father,
yours is the morning
and yours is the evening.
Let the Sun of Justice, Jesus Christ,
shine for ever in our hearts
and draw us to that light
where you live in radiant glory.
We ask this through our Lord Jesus Christ, your Son,
who lives and reigns with you and the Holy Spirit,
one God, for ever and ever.

WEDNESDAY, WEEK II

Morning Prayer

HYMN, 1337.
Fulgentis auctor aetheris. (L.M.)

Fulgéntis auctor ætheris,
qui lunam lumen nóctibus,
solem diérum cúrsibus
certo fundásti trámite,

Nox atra iam depéllitur,
mundi nitor renáscitur,
novúsque iam mentis vigor
dulces in actus érigit.

Laudes sonáre iam tuas
dies relátus ádmonet,
vultúsque cæli blándior
nostra serénat péctora.

Vitémus omne lúbricam,
declínet prava spíritus,
vitam facta non ínquinent,
linguam culpa non ímplicet;

Sed, sol diem dum cónficit,
fides profúnda férveat,
spes ad promíssa próvocet,
Christo coniúngat cáritas.

Præsta, Pater piíssime,
Patríque compar Unice,
cum Spíritu Paráclito
regnans per omne sæculum. Amen.

Creator of the skies above,
The wisdom of your plan decreed
That sun should give us light by day,
And moon should rule the hours of night.

The darkness is dispelled at last,
The world's great beauty is revealed;
Our strength of soul is now renewed
To spur us on to kindly deeds.

Returning day call us to prayer,
And bids us sing your praise anew;
The bright'ning aspect of the sky
Gives courage and serenity.

May we avoid all stain of sin,
No evil mar our thoughts this day,
No sinful action spoil our lives,
No wrong or idle words offend.

But while the sun draws on the day,
May our weak faith grow strong and sure
With hope that presses to the goal,
And love unites us all to Christ.

O Father, this we ask be done
Through Jesus Christ, your only Son,
Whom in the Spirit we adore:
One God who reigns for evermore. Amen.

PSALMODY

Ant. 1　　　　O God, all your ways are *holy*; * what god can compare with *our* God?

Easter:　　　The waters saw you, O God; † you led your people through the *sea,* * al*le*luia.

VIIIa

Psalm 77
Recalling God's works
We suffer all kinds of afflictions and yet are not overcome (2 Corinthians 4:8).

I cry aloud to God, † cry aloud to God that he may *hear* me. * In the day of my distress I sought *the* Lord.

My hands were raised at night without *ceas*ing; * my soul refused to be *con*soled.

I remembered my God and I *groaned.* * I pondered and my spir*it* fainted.

You withheld sleep from my *eyes.* * I was troubled, I could *not* speak.

I thought of the days of long a*go* * and remembered the years *long* past.

At night I mused within my *heart.* * I pondered and my spir*it* questioned.

"Will the Lord reject us for *ever?* * Will he show us his favor *no* more?

Has his love vanished for *ever?* * Has his promise come to *an* end?

Does God forget his *mer*cy * or in anger withhold his com*pas*sion?"

I said: "This is what causes my *grief;* * that the way of the Most High *has* changed."

I remember the deeds of the *Lord,* * I remember your wonders *of* old,

I muse on all your *works* * and ponder your mighty deeds.

Your ways, O God, are *holy.* * What god is great as *our* God?

You are the God who works *wonders.* * You showed your power among *the* peoples.

Your strong arm redeemed your *peo*ple, * the sons of Jacob *and* Joseph.

The waters saw you, O *God,* * the waters saw you *and* trembled;

the depths were moved with *ter*ror. * The clouds poured *down* rain,

the skies sent forth their *voice;* * your arrows flashed to *and* fro.

Your thunder rolled around the *sky,* * your flashes lighted up *the* world.

The earth was moved and *trem*bled * when your way led through *the* sea,

your path through the mighty *wa*ters, * and no one saw *your* footprints.

You guided your people like a *flock* * by the hand of Moses *and* Aaron.

Glory to the Father, and to the *Son,* * and to the Ho*ly* Spirit:

as it was in the beginning, is *now,* * and will be for ever. *A*men.

Antiphon　　O God, all your ways are *holy*; * what god can compare with *our* God?

Easter:　　　The waters saw you, O God; † you led your people through the *sea,* * al*le*luia.

Ant. 2   My heart leaps up with joy *to* the Lord, * for he humbles only to
                    ex*alt* us.

Easter: The Lord puts to death and rai*ses* to life, * alle*lu*ia.

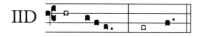

Canticle   1 Samuel 2:1-10
The humble find joy in God
He has cast down the mighty from their thrones and has lifted up the lowly.
He has filled the hungry with good things. (Luke 1:52-53).

My heart exults *in* the Lord, * my
  horn is exalted in my *God.*
I have swallowed *up* my enemies; * I
  rejoice in my *vic*tory.
There is no Holy One *like* the Lord; *
  there is no Rock like our *God.*
Speak boastful*ly* no longer, * nor let
  arrogance issue from your *mouths.*
For an all-knowing God *is* the Lord, * a
  God who judges *deeds.*
The bows of the mighty are broken, *
  while the tottering gird on *strength.*
The well-fed hire themselves *out* for
  bread, * while the hungry batten on
  spoil.
The barren wife bears *se*ven sons, *
  while the mother of many *lan*guishes.
The Lord puts to death and gives life; †
  he casts down *to* the nether world; *
  he raises up a*gain.*
The Lord makes poor *and* makes rich, *

he humbles, he also ex*alts.*
He raises the needy *from* the dust; *
  from the ash heap he lifts up the *poor,*
  to seat *them* with nobles * and make a
  glorious throne their *he*ritage.
For the pillars of the earth *are* the
  Lord's, * and he has set the world
  up*on* them.
He will guard the footsteps *of* his
  faithful ones, * but the wicked shall
  perish in the *dark*ness.
For not by strength does *man* prevail; *
  the Lord's foes shall be *shat*tered.
The Most High in *hea*ven thunders; *
  the Lord judges the ends of the *earth.*
Now may he give strength *to* his king *
  and exalt the horn of his a*noin*ted!
Glory to the Father, and *to* the Son, *
  and to the Holy *Spi*rit:
as it was in the begin*ning*, is now, * and
  will be for ever. A*men.*

Antiphon   My heart leaps up with joy *to* the Lord, * for he humbles only to
                    ex*alt* us.

Easter: The Lord puts to death and rai*ses* to life, * alle*lu*ia.

Ant. 3 The Lord *is* king, * let the *earth* rejoice.

Easter: A light has dawned for *the* just; * joy has come to the upright of heart, *a*lleluia.

Psalm 97
The glory of the Lord in his decrees for the world
*This psalm foretells a world-wide salvation and that peoples of all nations
will believe in Christ* (St. Athanasius).

The Lord is king, let earth *re*joice, *
let all the coast*lands* be glad.
Cloud and darkness are *his* raiment; *
his throne, just*ice* and right.
A fire prepares *his* path; * it burns up
his foes on *every* side.
His lightnings light up *the* world, * the
earth trembles *at* the sight.
The mountains melt *like* wax * before
the Lord of *all* the earth.
The skies proclaim *his* justice; * all
peoples *see* his glory.
Let those who serve idols be ashamed,
† those who boast of their worth*less*
gods. * All you spirits, *wor*ship him.
Zion hears and is glad; † the people of

Judah *re*joice * because of your
judg*ments*, O Lord.
For you indeed are the Lord, † most
high above all *the* earth, * exalted far
a*bove* all spirits.
The Lord loves those who hate evil: †
he guards the souls of *his* saints; * he
sets them free *from* the wicked.
Light shines forth for *the* just * and joy
for the up*right* of heart.
Rejoice, you just, in *the* Lord; * give
glory to his *ho*ly name.
Glory to the Father, and to *the* Son, *
and to the *Ho*ly Spirit:
as it was in the beginning, *is* now, * and
will be for e*ver*. Amen.

Antiphon The Lord *is* king, * let the *earth* rejoice.

Easter: A light has dawned for *the* just; * joy has come to the upright of heart, *a*lleluia.

READING Romans 8:35, 37

Who will separate us from the love of Christ? Trial or distress, or persecution,
or hunger, or nakedness, or danger, or the sword? Yet in all this we are more
than conquerors because of him who has loved us.

RESPONSORY (VI F)

I will *bless* the Lord * all my *life* long.
— I will *bless* the Lord * all my *life* long.
With a song of praise ever *on* my lips,
— all my *life* long.
Glory to the Father, and *to* the Son, * and to the Ho*ly* Spirit.
— I will *bless* the Lord * all my *life* long.

CANTICLE OF ZECHARIAH
Antiphon   Let us serve the *Lord* in holiness * all the days of *our* life.

INTERCESSIONS (VI F)
Blessèd be God our savior, who promised to remain with his Church all days,
 until the end *of* the world. * Let us give him thanks *and* call out:
Remain with us, *Lord.*
Remain with us the *whole* day, Lord,
— let your grace be a sun that *never* sets.
We dedicate this day to you *as* an offering,
— do not let us offer anything *that* is evil.
May your gift of light pervade *this* whole day,
— that we may be the salt of the earth and the light *of* the world.
May the love of your Holy Spirit direct our hearts *and* our lips,
— and may we always act in accordance *with* your will.

Our Father...

Prayer

 Lord,
 as a new day dawns
 send the radiance of your light
 to shine in our hearts.
 Make us true to your teaching;
 keep us free from error and sin.
 We ask this through our Lord Jesus Christ, your Son,
 who lives and reigns with you and the Holy Spirit,
 one God, for ever and ever.

WEDNESDAY, WEEK II

Evening Prayer

HYMN, 1338.
Sol, ecce, lentus occidens. (L.M.)

Sol, ecce, lentus óccidens
montes et arva et æquora
mæstus relínquit, ínnovat
sed lucis omen crástinæ,

Mirántibus mortálibus
sic te, Creátor próvide,
leges vicésque témporum
umbris dedísse et lúmini.

Ac dum, tenébris æthera
siléntio preméntibus,
vigor labórum déficit,
quies cupíta quæritur,

Spe nos fidéque dívites
tui beámur lúmine
Verbi, quod est a sæculis
splendor patérnæ glóriæ.

Est ille sol qui nésciat
ortum vel umquam vésperum;
quo terra gestit cóntegi,
quo cæli in ævum iúbilant.

Hac nos seréna pérpetim
da luce tandem pérfrui,
cum Nato et almo Spíritu
tibi novántes cántica. Amen.

As sun declines and shadows fall,
The sea and hills will fade from sight;
Its fiery orb bids us farewell
But promises tomorrow's light.

And thus, O God, creator wise,
You regulate in wondrous way
The laws of this great universe
At which we marvel night and day.

While darkness rides across the sky,
And stars their silent watches keep,
Your children leave their constant toil,
Regaining strength by peaceful sleep.

Made rich in hope, kept strong in faith,
May we be blest throughout the night,
By Christ, the Word, who timeless reigns,
True splendor of the Father's light.

He is the sun that never sets,
No dusk can make his lustre die,
The kind Protector of the earth,
The joy of all the saints on high.

O Father, Son, and Spirit blest
Grant us at last that light to see,
And full of joy your praises sing,
Bathed in your love eternally. Amen.

PSALMODY

Ant. 1   Eagerly we await the fulfillment of our *hope*, * the glorious
              coming of *our* Savior.

Easter: Do not let your hearts be troubled; † have faith in *me*, * al*le*luia.

VIIIa

Psalm 62
Peace in God
May God, the source of our hope, fill your hearts with peace as you believe in him
(Romans 15:13).

In God alone is my soul at *rest*; * my
   help comes *from* him.
He alone is my rock, my *strong*hold, *
   my fortress: I *stand* firm.
How long will you all attack one *man* *
   to break *him* down,
as though he were a tottering *wall*, * or
   a tumb*ling* fence?
Their plan is only to de*stroy*: * they take
   pleasure *in* lies.
With their mouth they utter *bless*ing *
   but in their heart *they* curse.
In God alone be at rest, my *soul*; * for
   my hope comes *from* him.
He alone is my rock, my *strong*hold, *
   my fortress: I *stand* firm.
In God is my safety and *glo*ry, * the
   rock of *my* strength.
Take refuge in God, all you *peo*ple. *
   Trust him at *all* times.

Pour out your hearts be*fore* him * for
   God is *our* refuge.
Common folk are only a *breath*, * great
   men an i*llu*sion.
Placed in the scales, they *rise*; * they
   weigh less than *a* breath.
Do not put your trust in op*pres*sion *
   nor vain hopes *on* plunder.
Do not set your heart on *rich*es * even
   when they *in*crease.
For God has said only *one* thing: * only
   two do *I* know:
that to God alone belongs *pow*er * and
   to you, *Lord*, love;
and that you repay each *man* * according to *his* deeds.
Glory to the Father, and to the *Son*, *
   and to the Ho*ly* Spirit:
as it was in the beginning, is *now*, * and
   will be for ever. *A*men.

Antiphon   Eagerly we await the fulfillment of our *hope*, * the glorious
              coming of *our* Savior.

Easter: Do not let your hearts be troubled; † have faith in *me*, * al*le*luia.

Ant. 2 May God turn his radiant *face* toward us, * and fill us with his *bless*ings.

Easter: Let the peoples praise you, Lord God; † let them rejoice in *your* salvation, * alle*lu*ia.

IID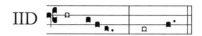

Psalm 67
People of all nations will worship the Lord
You must know that God is offering his salvation to all the world (Acts 28:28).

O God, be gra*cious* and bless us *
and let your face shed its light
up*on* us.
So will your ways be known *up*on earth
* and all nations learn your saving
help.
Let the peoples praise *you*, O God; * let
all the peoples *praise* you.
Let the nations be glad *and* exult * for
you rule the world with *jus*tice.
With fairness you *rule* the peoples, *

you guide the nations on *earth*.
Let the peoples praise *you*, O God; * let
all the peoples *praise* you.
The earth has yiel*ded* its fruit * for
God, our God, has *bless*ed us.
May God still give *us* his blessing * till
the ends of the earth re*vere* him.
Glory to the Father, and *to* the Son, *
and to the Holy *Spir*it:
as it was in the begin*ning*, is now, * and
will be for ever. A*men*.

Antiphon May God turn his radiant *face* toward us, * and fill us with his *bless*ings.

Easter: Let the peoples praise you, Lord God; † let them rejoice in *your* salvation, * alle*lu*ia.

Ant. 3 Through him all things *were* made; * he holds all creation together *in* himself.

Easter: His glory covers *the* heavens * and his praise fills the earth, *a*lleluia.

Vc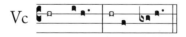

Canticle   Colossians 1:12-20
Christ, the first-born of all creation and the first-born from the dead

L et us give thanks to the Father †
for having made *you* worthy * to
share the lot of the *saints* in light.
He rescued us from the power *of*
darkness * and brought us into the
kingdom of his be*lov*èd Son.
Through him we have re*demp*tion, *

the forgiveness *of* our sins.
He is the image of the invisi*ble* God, *
the first-born *of* all creatures.
In him everything in heaven and on
earth was *cre*ated, * things visible *and*
invisible.
All were created *through* him; * all were

created *for* him.

He is before all else *that* is. * In him everything contin*ues* in being.

It is he who is head of the body, the church! † he who is the beginning, the first-born of *the* dead, * so that primacy may be *his* in everything.

It pleased God to make absolute fullness reside *in* him * and, by means of him, to reconcile everything *in* his person,

both on earth and in *the* heavens, * making peace through the blood *of* his cross.

Glory to the Father, and to *the* Son, * and to the *Ho*ly Spirit:

as it was in the beginning, *is* now, * and will be for e*ver.* Amen.

Antiphon	Through him all things *were* made; * he holds all creation together *in* himself.
Easter:	His glory covers *the* heavens * and his praise fills the earth, a*l*leluia.

READING   1 Peter 5:5b-7

In your relations with one another, clothe yourselves with humility, because God "is stern with the arrogant but to the humble he shows kindness." Bow humbly under God's mighty hand, so that in due time he may lift you high. Cast all your cares on him because he cares for you.

RESPONSORY (VI F)

Keep *us*, O Lord, * as the apple of *your* eye.

— Keep *us*, O Lord, * as the apple of *your* eye.

Gather us under the shadow of your *wings*, and keep us,

— as the apple of *your* eye.

Glory to the Father, and *to* the Son, * and to the Ho*ly* Spirit.

— Keep *us*, O Lord, * as the apple of *your* eye.

CANTICLE OF MARY

Antiphon	Lord, with the strength *of* your arm * scatter the proud and lift up *the* lowly.

INTERCESSIONS (VI F)

Bless*èd* brothers and sisters, let us rejoice in our God, for he takes great delight in bestowing benefits *on* his people. * Let us fer*vent*ly pray:

Increase your grace and your peace, O Lord.

Eternal God, for whom a thousand years are like the *pass*ing day,

— help us to remember that life is like a flower which blossoms in the morning, but withers *in* the evening.

Give your people manna to satis*fy* their hunger,

— and living water to quench their thirst for *all* eternity.

Let your faithful ones seek and taste the things that *are* above,

— and let them direct their work and their leisure *to* your glory.

Grant us good *wea*ther, Lord,
— that we may reap the copious fruits *of* the earth.
(or: Deliver us from *all* harm, Lord,
— and pour out your abundant blessings *on* our homes.)
Show the faithful departed the vision *of* your face,
— let them rejoice in the contemplation *of* your presence.

Our Father . . .

Prayer

Lord God,
holy is your name,
and renowned your compassion,
cherished by every generation.
Hear our evening prayer
and let us sing your praise,
and proclaim your greatness for ever.
We ask this through our Lord Jesus Christ, your Son,
who lives and reigns with you and the Holy Spirit,
one God, for ever and ever.

THURSDAY, WEEK II

Morning Prayer

HYMN, 1339.
Iam lucis orto sídere. (L.M.)

Iam lucis orto sídere	Now that the daylight fills the sky,
Deum precémur súpplices,	We lift our hearts to God on high,
ut in diúrnis áctibus	That he, in all we do or say,
nos servet a nocéntibus.	Would keep us free from harm today:
Linguam refrénans témperet,	Would guard our hearts and tongues from strife;
ne litis horror ínsonet;	From anger's din would hide our life;
visum fovéndo cóntegat,	From all ill sights would turn our eyes;
ne vanitátes háuriat.	Would close our ears from vanities:
Sint pura cordis íntima,	Would keep our inmost conscience pure;
absístat et vecórdia;	Our souls from folly would secure;
carnis terat supérbiam	Would bid us check the pride of sense
potus cibíque párcitas;	With due and holy abstinence.
Ut, cum dies abscésserit	So we, when this new day is gone,
noctémque sor redúxerit,	And night in turn is drawing on,
mundi per abstinéntiam	With conscience by the world unstained
ipsi canámus glóriam.	Shall praise his name for vict'ry gained.
Deo Patri sit glória	All laud to God the Father be;
eiúsque soli Fílio	All praise, eternal Son, to thee;
cum Spíritu Paráclito,	All glory, as is ever meet,
in sempitérna sæcula. Amen.	To God the Holy Paraclete. Amen.

PSALMODY

Ant. 1   Stir up your mighty power, *Lord*; * come to *our* aid.

Easter: I am the vine; you are the *branch*es, * al*le*luia.

VIIIa

Psalm 80
Lord, come, take care of your vineyard
Come, Lord Jesus (Revelation 22:20).

O shepherd of Israel, *hear* us, * you who lead Jo*seph's* flock, shine forth from your cherubim *throne* * upon Ephraim, Benjamin, Man*as*seh.	O Lord, rouse up your *might*, * O Lord, come to *our* help. God of hosts, bring us *back*; * let your face shine on us and we shall *be* saved.

Lord God of hosts, how *long* * will you
frown on your peo*ple's* plea?
You have fed them with tears for their
bread, * an abundance of tears for
their drink.
You have made us the taunt of our
*neigh*bors, * our enemies laugh us *to*
scorn.
God of hosts, bring us *back*; * let your
face shine on us, and we shall *be*
saved.
You brought a vine out of *Egypt*; * to
plant it you drove out *the* nations.
Before it you cleared the *ground*; * it
took root and spread through *the*
land.
The mountains were covered with its
*shad*ow, * the cedars of God with *its*
boughs.
It stretched out its branches to the *sea*, *
to the Great River it stretched out *its*
shoots.
Then why have you broken down its
walls? * It is plucked by all who *pass*

by.
It is ravaged by the boar of the *for*est, *
devoured by the beasts of *the* field.
God of hosts, turn again, we im*plore*, *
look down from heaven *and* see.
Visit this vine and pro*tect* it, * the vine
your right hand *has* planted.
Men have burnt it with fire and de-
stroyed it. * May they perish at the
frown of *your* face.
May your hand be on the man you have
*chos*en, * the man you have given *your*
strength.
And we shall never forsake you a*gain*: *
give us life that we may call upon
your name.
God of hosts, bring us *back*; * let your
face shine on us and we shall *be*
saved.
Glory to the Father, and to the *Son*, *
and to the Ho*ly* Spirit:
as it was in the beginning, is *now*, * and
will be for ever. *A*men.

Antiphon   Stir up your mighty power, *Lord*; * come to *our* aid.
Easter: I am the vine; you are the *branch*es, * al*le*luia.

Ant. 2   The Lord has worked mar*vels* for us; * make it known to the ends
of the *world*.
Easter: Rejoicing, you will draw water from the well-springs *of* the Savior, * alle*lu*ia.

IID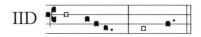

Canticle   Isaiah 12:1-6
Joy of God's ransomed people
If anyone thirsts, let him come to me and drink (John 7:37).

I give you *thanks*, O Lord; * though
you have been angry with *me*,
your anger *has* abated, * and you have
con*soled* me.
God indeed *is* my savior; * I am confi-

dent and una*fraid*.
My strength and my courage *is* the
Lord, * and he has been my *sav*ior.
With joy you *will* draw water * at the
fountain of sal*va*tion,

and say *on* that day: * Give thanks to
the Lord, acclaim his *name*;
among the nations make *known* his
deeds, * proclaim how exalted is his
name.
Sing praise to the Lord for his glori*ous*
achievement; * let this be known
throughout all the *earth*.

Shout with exultation, O city of Zion, †
for great *in* your midst * is the Holy
One of *I*srael.
Glory to the Father, and *to* the Son, *
and to the Holy *Spi*rit:
as it was in the begin*ning*, is now, * and
will be for ever. A*men*.

Antiphon   The Lord has worked mar*vels* for us; * make it known to the ends
of the *world*.

Easter: Rejoicing, you will draw water from the well-springs *of* the Savior, * alle*lu*ia.

Ant. 3   Ring out *your* joy * to *God* our strength.

Easter: The Lord *has* fed us * with the finest wheat, *a*lleluia.

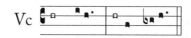

Psalm 81
Solemn renewal of the Covenant
See that no one among you has a faithless heart (Hebrews 3:12).

Ring out your joy to God *our*
strength, * shout in triumph to
the *God* of Jacob.
Raise a song and sound *the* timbrel, *
the sweet-sounding harp *and* the lute,
blow the trumpet at the *new* moon, *
when the moon is full, *on* our feast.
For this is Isra*el's* law, * a command of
the *God* of Jacob.
He imposed it as a rule *on* Joseph, *
when he went out against the *land* of
Egypt.
A voice I did not know said *to* me: * "I
freed your shoulder *from* the burden;
your hands were freed from *the* load. *
You called in distress *and* I saved you.
I answered, concealed in *the* storm
cloud, * at the waters of Meri*bah* I
tested you.
Listen, my people, to *my* warning, * O

Israel, if only *you* would heed!
Let there be no foreign god *a*mong you,
* no worship of an a*li*en god.
I am the Lord your God, † who
brought you from the land *of* Egypt. *
Open wide your mouth and *I* will fill
it.
But my people did not heed *my* voice *
and Israel would *not* obey,
so I left them in their stubbornness *of*
heart * to follow their *own* designs.
O that my people *would* heed me, * that
Israel would walk *in* my ways!
At once I would subdue *their* foes, *
turn my hand a*gainst* their enemies.
The Lord's enemies would cringe at
their feet * and their subjection would
last for ever.
But Israel I would feed with fin*est*
wheat * and fill them with honey *from*

the rock."
Glory to the Father, and to *the* Son, *
and to the *Ho*ly Spirit:

as it was in the beginning, *is* now, * and
will be for e*ver.* Amen.

Antiphon Ring out *your* joy * to *God* our strength.
Easter: The Lord *has* fed us * with the finest wheat, *a*lleluia.

READING Romans 14:17

The kingdom of God is not a matter of eating or drinking, but of justice,
peace, and the joy that is given by the Holy Spirit. Whoever serves Christ in
this way pleases God and wins the esteem of men. Let us, then, make it our
aim to work for peace and to strengthen one another.

RESPONSORY (VI F)
In the early hours *of* the morning, * I think of you, O Lord.
— In the early hours *of* the morning, * I think of you, O Lord.
Always you are *there* to help me,
— I think of you, O Lord.
Glory to the Father, and *to* the Son, * and to the Ho*ly* Spirit.
— In the early hours *of* the morning, * I think of you, O Lord.

CANTICLE OF ZECHARIAH
Antiphon Give your people knowledge of sal*va*tion, Lord, * and forgive us
our sins.

INTERCESSIONS (VI F)
Blessèd be God, our Father, who protects his children and never *spurns* their
prayers. * Let us hum*bly* implore him:
Enlighten us, O Lord.
We thank you, Lord, for enlightening us *through* your Son,
— fill us with his light through*out* the day.
Let your wisdom lead us to*day,* O Lord,
— that we may walk in the new*ness* of life.
May we bear hardships with courage *for* your name's sake,
— and be generous in *serv*ing you.
Direct our thoughts, feelings and act*ions* this day,
— help us to follow your provi*den*tial guidance.

Our Father . . .

Prayer

Lord,
true light and source of light,
listen to our morning prayer.
Turn our thoughts to what is holy
and may we ever live in the light of your love.
We ask this through our Lord Jesus Christ, your Son,
who lives and reigns with you and the Holy Spirit,
one God, for ever and ever.

THURSDAY, WEEK II

Evening Prayer

HYMN, 1340.

Deus, qui claro lumine. (L.M.)

Deus, qui claro lúmine diem fecísti, Dómine, tuam rogámus glóriam dum pronus dies vólvitur	O Lord our God, who made the day To gladden us with its fair light, We praise your name, imploring aid, For day will soon give place to night.
Iam sol urgénte véspero occásum suum gráditur, mundum conclúdens ténebris, suum obsérvans órdinem.	The evening shadows grow apace, Advancing, they will hide the sun, As darkness creeps upon the earth When day-light hours their course have run.
Tu vero, excélse Dómine, precántes tuos fámulos diúrno lassos ópere ne sinas umbris ópprimi,	We beg you, Lord and God Most High, Protect us with your presence blessed, Though weary, keep our souls in peace And not by gloom of night oppressed.
Ut non fuscátis méntibus dies abscédat sæculi, sed tua tecti grátia cernámus lucem prósperam.	Let not the setting sun go down On hearts distressed with sin, and sore, But sheltered by your gentle grace, May we behold the day once more.
Præsta, Pater piíssime, Patríque compar Unice, cum Spíritu Paráclito regnans per omne sæculum. Amen.	To you, O Christ, most kindly King, And to the Father, glory be, Praise to the Spirit Paraclete, In ev'ry age eternally. Amen.

PSALMODY

Ant. 1   I have made you the light of all *na*tions * to carry my salvation to the ends of *the* earth.

Easter: God has appointed him to judge the living and the *dead*, * al*le*luia.

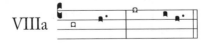

VIIIa

Psalm 72
The Messiah's royal power
Opening their treasures, they offered him gifts: gold, frankincense and myrrh
(Matthew 2:11).

I

O God, give your judgment to the king, * to a king's son *your* justice, that he may judge your people in *justice* * and your poor in *right* judgment.

May the mountains bring forth peace for the *people* * and the *hills*, justice.

May he defend the poor of the people † and save the children of the *needy* * and crush the *oppressor*.

He shall endure like the sun and the *moon* * from age *to* age.

He shall descend like rain on the *meadow*, * like raindrops on *the* earth.

In his days justice shall *flourish* * and peace till the *moon* fails.

He shall rule from sea to *sea*, * from the Great River to *earth's* bounds.

Before him his enemies shall *fall*, * his foes lick *the* dust.

The kings of Tarshish and the *sea* coasts * shall pay *him* tribute.

The kings of Sheba and *Seba* * shall bring *him* gifts.

Before him all kings shall fall *prostrate*, * all nations *shall* serve him.

Glory to the Father, and to the *Son*, * and to the Ho*ly* Spirit:

as it was in the beginning, is *now*, * and will be for ever. *Amen*.

Antiphon   I have made you the light of all *nations* * to carry my salvation to the ends of *the* earth.

Easter: God has appointed him to judge the living and the *dead*, * al*le*luia.

Ant. 2   The Lord will save the children *of* the poor * and rescue them from *sla*very.

Easter: All the peoples of the earth will be *blessed* in him, * alle*lui*a.

IID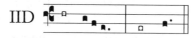

II

F or he shall save the poor *when* they cry * and the needy who are *help*less.

He will have pity *on* the weak * and save the lives of the *poor*.

From oppression he will res*cue* their lives, * to him their blood is *dear*.

Long *may* he live, * may the gold of Sheba be given *him*.

They shall pray for him *with*out ceasing * and bless him all the *day*.

May corn be abundant *in* the land * to the peaks of the *mount*ains.

May its fruit rustle like Lebanon; † may men flourish *in* the cities * like grass

on the *earth*.

May his name be *blessed* for ever * and endure like the *sun*.

Every tribe shall be *blessed* in him, * all nations bless his *name*.

Bless*èd* be the Lord, God of Israel, † who a*lone* works wonders, * ever bless*èd* his glorious *name*.

Let his glory *fill* the earth. * Amen! A*men*!

Glory to the Father, and *to* the Son, * and to the Holy *Spir*it:

as it was in the begin*ning*, is now, * and will be for ever. A*men*.

| Antiphon | The Lord will save the children *of* the poor * and rescue them from *slav*ery. |
| Easter: | All the peoples of the earth will be *blessed* in him, * alle*lu*ia. |

| Ant. 3 | Now the victor*ious* reign * of our God *has* begun. |
| Easter: | Christ yesterday and *to*day: * he is the same for ever, *al*leluia. |

Vc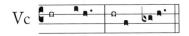

Canticle Revelation 11:17-18; 12:10b-12a

The judgment of God

We praise you, the Lord God *Al*mighty, * who is *and* who was.
You have assumed your *great* power, * you have be*gun* your reign.
The nations have raged in anger, † but then came your day *of* wrath * and the moment to *judge* the dead:
the time to reward your servants the prophets † and the holy ones who *re*vere you, * the great and the *small* alike.
Now have salvation and po*wer* come, * the reign of our God and the authority of *his* Anointed One.

For the accuser of our brothers is *cast* out, * who night and day accused them *be*fore God.
They defeated him by the blood of the Lamb † and by the word of *their* testimony; * love for life did not deter *them* from death.
So rejoice, *you* heavens, * and you that *dwell* therein!
Glory to the Father, and to *the* Son, * and to the *Ho*ly Spirit:
as it was in the beginning, *is* now, * and will be for e*ver*. Amen.

| Antiphon | Now the victor*ious* reign * of our God *has* begun. |
| Easter: | Christ yesterday and *to*day: * he is the same for ever, *al*leluia. |

READING 1 Peter 1:22-23

By obedience to the truth you have purified yourselves for a genuine love of your brothers; therefore, love one another constantly from the heart. Your rebirth has come, not from a destructible but from an indestructible seed, through the living and enduring word of God.

RESPONSORY (VI F)
The Lord *is* my shepherd, * I shall want *for* nothing.
— The Lord *is* my shepherd, * I shall want *for* nothing.
He has brought me *to* green pastures.
— I shall want *for* nothing.
Glory to the Father, and *to* the Son, * and to the *Ho*ly Spirit.
— The Lord *is* my shepherd, * I shall want *for* nothing.

CANTICLE OF MARY

Antiphon   If you hun*ger* for holiness, * God will satisfy your longing, good
                  measure, and flow*ing* over.

INTERCESSIONS (VI F)

Lift up your hearts to our Lord and Savior who gives his people every spi*ri*tual
   blessing. * In the spirit of devotion, *let* us ask him:
Bless your people, O Lord.
 Merciful God, strengthen N., our Pope, and N., our bishop,
— keep them *free* from harm.
Look favorably on our *coun*try, Lord,
— free us *from* all evil.
Call men to serve *at* your altar,
— and to follow you more closely in chastity, poverty *and* obedience.
Take care of your handmaidens vowed *to* virginity,
— that they may follow you, the divine Lamb, wherev*er* you go.
May the dead rest in e*ter*nal peace,
— may their union with us be strengthened through the sharing of spi*ri*tual
   goods.

Our Father . . .

Prayer

      Father of mercy
      hear our evening prayer of praise,
      and let our hearts never waver
      from the love of your law.
      Lead us on through night's darkness
      to the dawning of eternal life.
      We ask this through our Lord Jesus Christ, your Son,
      who lives and reigns with you and the Holy Spirit,
      one God, for ever and ever.

FRIDAY, WEEK II

Morning Prayer

HYMN, 1341.

Deus, qui caeli lumen es. (L.M.)

Deus, qui cæli lumen es
satórque lucis, qui polum
patérno fultum brácchio
præclára pandis déxtera,

Auróra stellas iam tegit
rubrum sustóllens gúrgitem,
uméctis atque flátibus
terram baptízans róribus.

Iam noctis umbra línquitur,
polum calígo déserit,
typúsque Christi, lúcifer
diem sopítum súscitat.

Dies diérum tu, Deus,
lucísque lumen ipse es,
Unum potens per ómnia,
potens in unum Trínitas.

Te nunc, Salvátor, quæsumus
tibíque genu fléctimus,
Patrem cum Sancto Spíritu
totis laudántes vócibus. Amen.

O God, the lamp of heaven high
And source of light: your shining hand
Unrolls the banner of the sky,
Upholding it above the land.

Dawn, casting up a crimson tide,
Has veiled the stars that saw its rise;
The morning breezes, far and wide,
With dewy breath the earth baptize.

The darkness from the sky has gone
As nightly shadows pass away;
The morning star, sign of the Son,
Arising, wakes the sleepy day.

O God, O radiance wonderful,
Most glorious day and fairest light:
One God, in all things powerful,
Three Persons, matchless in one might!

To you, Our Savior, brightest, best,
On bended knee our prayer we raise;
To Father and to Spirit blest,
With all our power, we offer praise. Amen.

PSALMODY

Ant. 1   A humble, contrite *heart,* * O God, you will *not* spurn.

Easter: Have courage, my son; your sins are for*gi*ven, * al*le*luia.

VIIIa

Psalm 51
O God, have mercy on me
Your inmost being must be renewed, and you must put on the new man (Ephesians 4:23-24).

Have mercy on me, God, in your
*kind*ness. * In your compassion
blot out my *of*fense.
O wash me more and more from my

guilt * and cleanse me from *my* sin.
My offenses truly I *know* them; * my
sin is always *be*fore me.
Against you, you alone, have I *sinned;* *

what is evil in your sight I *have* done.
That you may be justified when you
  give *sen*tence * and be without
  reproach when *you* judge.
O see, in guilt I was *born*, * a sinner was
  I *con*ceived.
Indeed you love truth in the *heart;* *
  then in the secret of my heart teach
  me wisdom.
O purify me, then I shall be *clean*; * O
  wash me, I shall be whiter *than* snow.
Make me hear rejoicing and *glad*ness, *
  that the bones you have crushed may
  re*vive.*
From my sins turn away your *face* * and
  blot out all *my* guilt.
A pure heart create for me, O *God,* *
  put a steadfast spirit *with*in me.
Do not cast me away from your *pres-*
  ence, * nor deprive me of your ho*ly*
  spirit.
Give me again the joy of your *help;* *

with a spirit of fervor *sus*tain me,
  that I may teach transgressors your
  ways * and sinners may return *to* you.
O rescue me, God, my *help*er, * and my
  tongue shall ring out *your* goodness.
O Lord, open my *lips* * and my mouth
  shall declare *your* praise.
For in sacrifice you take no de*light,* *
  burnt offering from me you would
  re*fuse,*
my sacrifice, a contrite *spir*it. * A
  humbled, contrite heart you will *not*
  spurn.
In your goodness, show favor to *Zion:* *
  rebuild the walls of *Je*rusalem.
Then you will be pleased with lawful
  *sac*rifice, * holocausts offered on *your*
  altar.
Glory to the Father, and to the *Son,* *
  and to the Ho*ly* Spirit:
as it was in the beginning, is *now,* * and
  will be for ever. *A*men.

Antiphon   A humble, contrite *heart,* * O God, you will *not* spurn.
Easter: Have courage, my son; your sins are for*gi*ven, * al*le*luia.

Ant. 2   Even in your *an*ger, Lord, * you will remember com*pas*sion.
Easter: You go forth to save your people, † to save *your* anointed one, * alle*lu*ia.

IID

Canticle   Habakkuk 3:2-4, 13a, 15-19
                  God comes to judge
     Lift up your heads for your redemption is at hand (Luke 21:28).

O Lord, I have heard *your* renown, *
  and feared, O Lord, your *work.*
In the course of the years revive it, † in
  the course of the years *make* it known;
  * in your wrath remember com*pas*-
  sion!
God *comes* from Teman, * the Holy One
  from Mount *Par*an.

Covered are the heavens *with* his glory,
  * and with his praise the earth is
  filled.
His splendor spreads like the light; †
  rays shine forth *from* beside him, *
  where his power is con*cealed.*
You come forth to *save* your people, * to
  save your a*noint*ed one.

You tread the sea *with* your steeds *
amid the churning of the deep
*wat*ers.
I hear, and my *bo*dy trembles; * at the
sound, my lips *qui*ver.
Decay in*vades* my bones, * my legs
tremble be*neath* me.
I await the day *of* distress * that will
come upon the people who at*tack* us.
For though the fig tree *blos*som not *
nor fruit be on the *vines*,
though the yield of the *o/ive* fail * and
the terraces produce no *nou*rishment,

Though the flocks disappear *from* the
fold * and there be no herd in the
stalls,
yet will I rejoice *in* the Lord * and exult
in my saving *God.*
God, my Lord, is my strength; † he
makes my feet swift as *those* of hinds *
and enables me to go upon the
heights.
Glory to the Father, and *to* the Son, *
and to the Holy *Spi*rit:
as it was in the begin*ning*, is now, * and
will be for ever. A*men.*

Antiphon   Even in your *anger,* Lord, * you will remember com*pas*sion.
Easter: You go forth to save your people, † to save *your* anointed one, * alle*lu*ia.

Ant. 3   O praise *the* Lord, * Je*ru*salem!
Easter: Zion, give praise to *your* God; * he has brought peace to your borders, a/leluia.

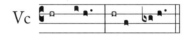

Psalm 147:12-20
The restoration of Jerusalem
Come, I will show you the bride of the Lamb (Revelation 21:9).

O praise the Lord, *Jeru*salem! *
Zion, *praise* your God!
He has strengthened the bars of *your*
gates, * he has blessed the child*ren*
within you.
He established peace on *your* borders, *
he feeds you with *fin*est wheat.
He sends out his word to *the* earth *
and swiftly runs *his* command.
He showers down snow white *as* wool, *
he scatters hoar-*frost* like ashes.
He hurls down hailstones *like* crumbs. *
The waters are frozen *at* his touch;

he sends forth his word and *it* melts
them: * at the breath of his mouth the
*wat*ers flow.
He makes his word known *to* Jacob, *
to Israel his laws *and* decrees.
He has not dealt thus with *o*ther
nations; * he has not taught them *his*
decrees.
Glory to the Father, and to *the* Son, *
and to the *Holy* Spirit:
as it was in the beginning, *is* now, * and
will be for *e*ver. Amen.

Antiphon   O praise *the* Lord, * Je*ru*salem!
Easter: Zion, give praise to *your* God; * he has brought peace to your borders, a/leluia.

READING   Ephesians 2:13-16

Now in Christ Jesus you who once were far off have been brought near through the blood of Christ. It is he who is our peace, and who made the two of us one by breaking down the barrier of hostility that kept us apart. In his own flesh he abolished the law with its commands and precepts, to create in himself one new man from us who had been two and to make peace, reconciling both of us to God in one body through his cross, which put that enmity to death.

RESPONSORY (VI F)

The Lord, the Most High, has done good *things* for me. * In need I shall cry out *to* him.
— The Lord, the Most High, has done good *things* for me. * In need I shall cry out *to* him.
May he send his *strength* to rescue me.
— In need I shall cry out *to* him.
Glory to the Father, and *to* the Son, * and to the Ho*ly* Spirit.
— The Lord, the Most High, has done good *things* for me. * In need I shall cry out *to* him.

CANTICLE OF ZECHARIAH

Antiphon   Through the tender compassion *of* our God * the dawn from on high shall break *upo*n us.

INTERCESSIONS (VI F)

Let us adore Christ who offered himself to the Father through the Holy Spirit to cleanse us from the *works* of death. * Let us adore him and call upon him *with* sincere hearts:
In your will is our peace, O Lord.
From your generosity we have received the beginning *of* this day,
— grant us also the beginning *of* new life.
You created all things, and now you provide *for* their growth,
— may we always perceive your handiwork *in* creation.
With your own blood, you ratified the new and e*ter*nal covenant,
— may we remain faithful to that covenant by follow*ing* your precepts.
On the cross, blood and water flowed *from* your side,
— may this saving stream wash away our sins and gladden the Ci*ty* of God.

Our Father . . .

Prayer

All-powerful Father,
as now we bring you our songs of praise,
so may we sing your goodness
in the company of your saints for ever.
We ask this through our Lord Jesus Christ, your Son,
who lives and reigns with you and the Holy Spirit,
one God, for ever and ever.

FRIDAY, WEEK II

Evening Prayer

HYMN, 1342.
Horis peractis undecim. (L.M.)

Horis peráctis úndecim	The hours are passing swiftly by,
ruit dies in vésperum;	And into night the shades will flow,
solvámus omnes débitum	So let us sing to God with joy
mentis libénter cánticum.	The grateful hymn of praise we owe.
Labor diúrnus tránsiit	The burden and the heat of day
quo, Christe, nos condúxeras;	Have passed in working for our Lord,
da iam colónis víneæ	So may his vineyard workers all
promíssa dona glóriæ.	Receive from him the great reward.
Mercéde quos nunc ádvocas,	Lord Jesus Christ, you call us now
quos ad futúrum múneras,	To labor for our recompense,
nos in labóre ádiuva	Assist our work, then grant us rest,
et post labórem récrea.	Until your love shall call us hence.
Sit, Christe, rex piíssime,	All glory, Lord, to you we bring,
tibi Patríque glória	Creation's true and only King,
cum Spíritu Paráclito,	Whom with the Father we adore
in sempitérna sæcula. Amen.	And Holy Ghost, for evermore. Amen.

PSALMODY

Ant. 1   Lord, keep my soul from *death*, * never let *me* stumble.

Easter: The Lord has rescued my life from the grasp of *hell*, * al*le*luia.

VIIIa

Psalm 116:1-9
Thanksgiving
We must endure many trials before entering God's kingdom (Acts 14:21).

I love the Lord for he has *heard* * the
cry of my *ap*peal;
for he turned his ear to *me* * in the day
when *I* called him.
They surrounded me, the snares of
death, * with the anguish of *the* tomb;
they caught me, sorrow and dis*tress*. * I
called on *the* Lord's name.

O Lord my *God*, * deliv*er* me!
How gracious is the Lord, and *just*; *
our God has *com*passion.
The Lord protects the simple *hearts*; * I
was helpless so *he* saved me.
Turn back, my soul, to your *rest* * for the
Lord has *been* good;
he has kept my soul from death, † my

eyes from *tears* * and my feet *from* stumbling.
I will walk in the presence of the *Lord* * in the land of *the* living.

Glory to the Father, and to the *Son,* * and to the Ho*ly* Spirit:
as it was in the beginning, is *now,* * and will be for ever. *A*men.

Antiphon   Lord, keep my soul from *death,* * never let *me* stumble.
Easter: The Lord has rescued my life from the grasp of *hell,* * al*le*luia.

Ant. 2   My help comes *from* the Lord, * who made heaven and *earth*.
Easter: The Lord watches over his people, † and protects them as the apple *of* his eye, * alle*lu*ia.

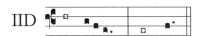

Psalm 121
Guardian of his people
Never again will they hunger and thrist, never again know scorching heat (Revelation 7:16).

I lift up my eyes *to* the mountains; * from where shall come my *help*?
My help shall come *from* the Lord * who made heaven and *earth*.
May he never allow *you* to stumble! * Let him sleep not, your *guard*.
No, he sleeps *not* nor slumbers, * Israel's *guard*.
The Lord is your guard *and* your shade; * at your right side he *stands*.

By day the sun *shall* not smite you * nor the moon in the *night*.
The Lord will guard *you* from evil, * he will guard your *soul*.
The Lord will guard your go*ing* and coming * both now and for *ever*.
Glory to the Father, and *to* the Son, * and to the Holy *Spi*rit:
as it was in the begin*ning*, is now, * and will be for ever. *A*men.

Antiphon   My help comes *from* the Lord, * who made heaven and *earth*.
Easter: The Lord watches over his people, † and protects them as the apple *of* his eye, * alle*lu*ia.

Ant. 3   King of all *the* ages, * your ways are per*fect* and true.
Easter: The Lord is my strength, I shall al*ways* praise him, * for he has become my Savior, a*lle*luia.

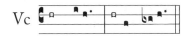

Canticle   Revelation 15:3-4
Hymn of adoration

Mighty and wonderful are *your* works, * Lord *God* Almighty!
Righteous and true are *your* ways, * O King *of* the nations!
Who would dare refuse *you* honor, * or the glory due your *name*, O Lord?
Since you alone *are* holy, * all nations shall come and worship *in* your presence.
Your mighty deeds * are *clearly* seen.
Glory to the Father, and to *the* Son, * and to the *Holy* Spirit:
as it was in the beginning, *is* now, * and will be for *ever*. Amen.

Antiphon   King of all *the* ages, * your ways are per*fect* and true.
Easter: The Lord is my strength, I shall al*ways* praise him, * for he has become my
                  Savior, al*le*luia.

READING   1 Corinthians 2:7-10a

What we utter is God's wisdom: a mysterious, a hidden wisdom. God planned it before all ages for our glory. None of the rulers of this age knew the mystery; if they had known it, they would never have crucified the Lord of glory. Of this wisdom it is written:
>   "Eye has not see, ear has not heard,
>   nor has it so much as dawned on man
>   what God has prepared for those who love him."
Yet God has revealed this wisdom to us through the Spirit.

RESPONSORY (VI F)
Christ died *for* our sins * to make of us an offering *to* God.
— Christ died *for* our sins * to make of us an offering *to* God.
He died to this world of sin, and rose in the power *of* the Spirit,
— to make of us an offering *to* God.
Glory to the Father, and *to* the Son, * and to the Ho*ly* Spirit.
— Christ died *for* our sins * to make of us an offering *to* God.

CANTICLE OF MARY
Antiphon   Remember your *mercy*, Lord, * the promise of mercy you made
                  to *our* fathers.

INTERCESSIONS (VI F)
Let us bless Christ, the compassionate and merciful Lord, who wipes away the tears of *those* who weep. * Let us cry out to him in *love* and ask:
*Have mercy on your peo*ple, *Lord.*
Lord Jesus, you con*sole* the humble,
— be attentive to the tears *of* the poor.
Merciful God, hear the cries *of* the dying,
— comfort them *with* your presence.

Make exiles aware of your provi*dent*ial care,
— may they return to their home on earth and finally enter their *home* in heaven.
Be merciful to sinners who have fallen away *from* your love,
— reconcile them to yourself and *to* your Church.
Save our brothers *who* have died,
— let them share in the fullness *of* redemption.

Our Father…

Prayer

God our Father,
the contradiction of the cross
proclaims your infinite wisdom.
Help us to see that the glory of your Son
is revealed in the suffering he freely accepted.
Give us faith to claim as our only glory
the cross of our Lord Jesus Christ,
who lives and reigns with you and the Holy Spirit,
one God, for ever and ever.

SATURDAY, WEEK II

Morning Prayer

HYMN, 1343.
Diéi luce réddita. (L.M.)

Diéi luce réddita,	As light of day returns once more,
lætis gratísque vocíbus	With joyful voices let us sing
Dei canámus glóriam,	To God of glory infinite,
Christi faténtes grátiam,	To Christ our Lord for all his grace.
Per quem creátor ómnium	Through whom the great Creator's will
diem noctémque cóndidit,	Called day and night from nothingness,
ætérna lege sánciens	Appointing them successive law,
ut semper succédant sibi.	Till time itself shall pass away.
Tu vera lux fidélium,	True light of every faithful soul
quem lex vetérna non tenet,	Unfettered by the law of old;
noctis nec ortu súccidens,	No shades of night can fall that dim
ætérno fulgens lúmine.	Your dazzling and undying light.
Præsta, Pater ingénite,	O Father, uncreated Light,
totum ducámus iúgiter	Be with us as the hours go by,
Christo placéntes hunc diem	That we may please your Son this day,
Sancto repléti Spíritu. Amen.	Filled with the Holy Spirit's pow'r. Amen.

PSALMODY

Ant. 1   As morning breaks we sing of your mercy, *Lord*, * and night will
find us proclaiming your *fi*delity.

Easter: You have filled me with gladness, Lord; † I will sing for joy at the works of your
hands, * al*le*luia.

VIIIa

Psalm 92
Praise of God the creator
Sing in praise of Christ's redeeming work (Saint Athanasius).

I t is good to give thanks to the *Lord*,
    * to make music to your name, O
Most High,
to proclaim your love in the *morn*ing *
    and your truth in the watches of *the*
    night,

on the ten-stringed lyre and the *lute*, *
    with the murmuring sound of *the*
    harp.
Your deeds, O Lord, have made me
    glad; * for the work of your hands I
    shout *with* joy.

O Lord, how great are your *works*! *
　How deep are your *de*signs!
The foolish man cannot *know* this * and
　the fool cannot un*der*stand.
Though the wicked spring up like *grass*
　* and all who do e*vil* thrive:
they are doomed to be eternally de-
　stroyed. * But you, Lord, are eternally
　on high.
See how your enemies *pe*rish; * all doers
　of evil *are* scattered.
To me you give the wild-ox's *strength;* *
　you anoint me with the pur*est* oil.
My eyes looked in triumph on my *foes*;

* my ears heard gladly of *their* fall.
The just will flourish like the *palm*-tree
　* and grow like a Leba*non* cedar.
Planted in the house of the *Lord* * they
　will flourish in the courts of *our* God,
still bearing fruit when they are *old*, *
　still full of sap, *still* green,
to proclaim that the Lord is *just*; * in
　him, my rock, there is *no* wrong.
Glory to the Father, and to the *Son*, *
　and to the Ho*ly* Spirit:
as it was in the beginning, is *now*, * and
　will be for ever. *A*men.

Antiphon　　As morning breaks we sing of your mercy, *Lord*, * and night will
　　　　　　find us proclaiming your *fi*delity.

Easter:　　　You have filled me with gladness, Lord; † I will sing for joy at the works of your
　　　　　　hands, * al*le*luia.

Ant. 2　　　Ex*tol* the greatness * of our *God*.

Easter:　　　It is I who bring death and I who give life; † I inflict injury and *I* bring healing,
　　　　　　* alle*lu*ia.

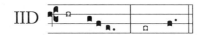

IID

Canticle　　　　　　　　　Deuteronomy 32:1-12
God's kindness to his people
How often I have longed to gather your children as a hen gathers her brood under her wing
(Matthew 23:37).

Give ear, O heavens, *while* I speak; *
　let the earth hearken to the words
of my *mouth*!
May my instruction soak in *like* the
　rain, * and my discourse permeate like
　the *dew*,
like a downpour up*on* the grass, * like a
　shower upon the *crops*:
For I will sing the *Lord's* renown. * Oh,
　proclaim the greatness of our *God*!
The Rock—how faultless *are* his deeds,
　* how right all his *ways*!

A faithful God, with*out* deceit, * how
　just and upright he *is*!
Yet basely has he been treated by his
　degene*rate* children, * a perverse and
　crooked *race*!
Is the Lord to be thus re*paid* by you, *
　O stupid and foolish *peo*ple?
Is he not your father *who* created you? *
　Has he not made you and e*stab*lished
　you?
Think back on the *days* of old, * reflect
　on the years of age upon *age*.

Ask your father and he *will* inform you,
  * ask your elders and they will *tell*
  you:
When the Most High assigned the
  na*tions* their heritage, * when he
  parceled out the descendants of
  *A*dam,
he set up the boundaries *of* the peoples
  * after the number of the sons of *God*;
while the Lord's own por*tion* was Jacob,
  * his hereditary share was *I*srael.
He found them *in* a wilderness, * a
  wasteland of howling *des*ert.

He shielded them and *cared* for them, *
  guarding them as the apple of his *eye*.
As an eagle incites its *nestl*ings forth *
  by hovering over its *brood*,
so he spread his wings *to* receive them *
  and bore them up on his *pin*ions.
The Lord alone *was* their leader, * no
  strange god was *with* him.
Glory to the Father, and *to* the Son, *
  and to the Holy *Spir*it:
as it was in the begin*ning*, is now, * and
  will be for ever. A*men*.

Antiphon   Ex*tol* the greatness * of our *God*.

Easter: It is I who bring death and I who give life; † I inflict injury and *I* bring healing,
           * alle*lu*ia.

Ant. 3   How wonderful is your name, O Lord, * in *all* creation.

Easter: You have crowned your *A*nointed One * with glory and honor, a*l*leluia.

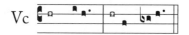

Psalm 8
The majesty of the Lord and man's dignity
The Father gave Christ lordship of creation and made him head of the Church
(Ephesians 1:22).

How great is your name, O Lord
  our God, * through *all* the earth!
Your majesty is praised above *the*
  heavens; * on the lips of children *and*
  of babes
you have found praise to foil *your*
  enemy, * to silence the foe *and* the
  rebel.
When I see the heavens, the work of
  your hands, * the moon and the stars
  which *you* arranged,
what is man that you should keep him
  in mind, * mortal man that you *care*
  for him?
Yet you have made him little less than *a*

god; * with glory and hon*or* you
  crowned him,
gave him power over the works of *your*
  hand, * put all things un*der* his feet.
All of them, sheep *and* cattle, * yes, even
  the *sav*age beasts,
birds of the air, *and* fish * that make
  their way *through* the waters.
How great is your name, O Lord *our*
  God, * through *all* the earth!
Glory to the Father, and to *the* Son, *
  and to the *Ho*ly Spirit:
as it was in the beginning, *is* now, * and
  will be for *ev*er. Amen.

Antiphon How wonderful is your name, *O* Lord, * in *all* creation.
Easter: You have crowned your *A*nointed One * with glory and honor, *a*lleluia.

READING Romans 12:14-16a

Bless your persecutors; bless and do not curse them. Rejoice with those who rejoice, weep with those who weep. Have the same attitude toward all. Put away ambitious thoughts and associate with those who are lowly.

RESPONSORY (VI F)

It is my *joy,* O God, * to praise you *with* song.
— It is my *joy,* O God, * to praise you *with* song.
To sing as I pon*der* your goodness,
— to praise you *with* song.
Glory to the Father, and *to* the Son, * and to the Ho*ly* Spirit.
— It is my *joy,* O God, * to praise you *with* song.

CANTICLE OF ZECHARIAH

Antiphon Lord, *guide* our feet * into the way *of* peace.

INTERCESSIONS (VI F)

Let us celebrate the kindness and wisdom of Christ. He offers his love and understanding to all men, especially *to* the suffering. * Let us earnestly *pray* to him:
Perfect us in love, O Lord.
This morning we recall your *re*surrection,
— and we long for the benefits of *your* redemption.
Grant that we bear witness to you to*day,* O Lord,
— and offer an acceptable gift to the Fa*ther* through you.
Enable us to see your image *in* all men,
— and to serve *you* in them.
Lord Jesus, you are the true vine and we *are* the branches,
— allow us to remain in you, to bear much fruit, and to give glory *to* the Father.

Our Father . . .

Prayer

Lord,
we praise you
with our lips,
and with our lives and hearts.
Our very existence is a gift from you;
to you we offer all that we have and are.
We ask this through our Lord Jesus Christ, your Son,
who lives and reigns with you and the Holy Spirit,
one God, for ever and ever.

SUNDAY, WEEK III

Evening Prayer I

HYMN, 1311.
Deus, creátor ómnium. (L.M.)

Deus, creátor ómnium	Creator of the earth and sky,
políque rector, véstiens	Ruling the firmament on high,
diem decóro lúmine,	Clothing the day with robes of light,
noctem sopóris grátia,	Blessing with gracious sleep the night,
Artus solútos ut quies	That rest may comfort weary men,
reddat labóris úsui	And brace to useful toil again,
mentésque fessas állevet	And soothe awhile the troubled mind,
luctúsque solvat ánxios,	And sorrow's heavy load unbind:
Grates perácto iam die	Day sinks; we thank thee for thy gift;
et noctis exórtu preces,	Night comes; and once again we lift
voti reos ut ádiuves,	Our prayer and vows and hymns that we
hymnum canéntes sólvimus.	Against all ills may shielded be.
Te cordis ima cóncinant,	Thee let the secret heart acclaim,
te vox canóra cóncrepet,	Thee let our tuneful voices name,
te díligat castus amor,	Round thee our chaste affections cling,
te mens adóret sóbria,	Thee sober reason own as King.
Ut cum profúnda cláuserit	That when black darkness closes day,
diem calígo nóctium,	And shadows thicken 'round our way,
fides tenébras nésciat	Faith may no darkness know and night
et nox fide relúceat.	From faith's clear beam may borrow light.
Christum rogámus et Patrem,	Pray we the Father and the Son,
Christi Patrísque Spíritum;	And Holy Ghost: O Three in One,
unum potens per ómnia,	Blest Trinity, whom all obey,
fove precántes, Trínitas. Amen.	Guard thou thy sheep by night and day. Amen.

PSALMODY

Ant. 1	From the rising of the sun *to* its setting, * may the name of the *Lord* be praised.
Advent:	Rejoice, Jerusalem, let your joy *overflow*; * your Savior will come to you, *a*lleluia.
Lent, 3rd Sunday:	The Lord says: Turn a*way* from sin * and open your hearts *to* the Gospel.
Easter, 3rd, 7th:	The Lord our God is high a*bove* the heavens; * he raises up the lowly from the dust, *a*lleluia.

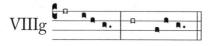

VIIIg

Psalm 113
Praise the name of the Lord

He has cast down the mighty and has lifted up the lowly (Luke 1:52).

Praise, O servants *of* the Lord, *
   praise the name *of* the Lord!
May the name of the *Lord* be blessed *
   both now and for *ev*ermore!
From the rising of the sun *to* its setting
   * praised be the name *of* the Lord!
High above all nations *is* the Lord, *
   above the heav*ens* his glory.
Who is like the *Lord*, our God, * who
   has risen on high *to* his throne
yet stoops from the heights *to* look
   down, * to look down upon heav*en*

and earth?
From the dust he lifts *up* the lowly, *
   from his misery he rais*es* the poor
to set him in the compa*ny* of princes, *
   yes, with the princes *of* his people.
To the childless wife he *gives* a home *
   and gladdens her *heart* with children.
Glory to the Father, and *to* the Son, *
   and to the *Ho*ly Spirit:
as it was in the beginn*ing*, is now, * and
   will be for ev*er*. Amen.

Antiphon	From the rising of the sun *to* its setting, * may the name of the *Lord* be praised.
Advent:	Rejoice, Jerusalem, let your joy *over*flow; * your Savior will come to you, *a*lleluia.
Lent, 3rd Sunday:	The Lord says: Turn a*way* from sin * and open your hearts *to* the Gospel.
Easter, 3rd, 7th:	The Lord our God is high a*bove* the heavens; * he raises up the lowly from the dust, *a*lleluia.

Ant. 2   I shall take into my hand the *saving* chalice * and invoke the
                name of *the* Lord.

Advent: I, the Lord, am coming to save you; † already *I* am near; * soon I will free you
                from *your* sins.

Lent, 3rd Sunday: I will offer a sacri*fice* of praise * and call upon the name of *the* Lord.

Easter, 3rd, 7th: Lord, you have broken the chains that *held* me bound; * I will offer you a
                sacrifice of praise, al*le*luia.

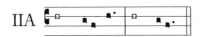

Psalm 116: 10-19
Thanksgiving in the Temple

I trusted, even *when* I said, * "I am
   sorely *afflicted*,"
and when I said in *my* alarm: * "No
   man can *be* trusted."
How can I re*pay* the Lord * for his
   goodness *to* me?
The cup of salvation *I* will raise; * I will
   call on *the* Lord's name.
My vows to the Lord I *will* fulfill *
   before all *his* people.
O precious in the eyes *of* the Lord * is
   the death of *his* faithful.

Your servant, Lord, your ser*vant* am I; *
   you have loosened *my* bonds.
A thanksgiving sacri*fice* I make: * I will
   call on *the* Lord's name.
My vows to the Lord I *will* fulfill *
   before all *his* people,
in the courts of the house *of* the Lord, *
   in your midst, O *Je*rusalem.
Glory to the Father, and *to* the Son, *
   and to the Ho*ly* Spirit:
as it was in the begin*ning*, is now, * and
   will be for ever. *A*men.

Antiphon   I shall take into my hand the *saving* chalice * and invoke the
                name of *the* Lord.

Advent: I, the Lord, am coming to save you; † already *I* am near; * soon I will free you
                from *your* sins.

Lent, 3rd Sunday: I will offer a sacri*fice* of praise * and call upon the name of *the* Lord.

Easter, 3rd, 7th: Lord, you have broken the chains that *held* me bound; * I will offer you a
                sacrifice of praise, al*le*luia.

Ant. 3   The Lord Jesus humbled *himself* * and God exalted him *for* ever.

Advent: Lord, send the Lamb, the ruler of *the* earth, * from the rock in the desert to the
                 mountain of the daughter *of* Zion.

Lent, 3ʳᵈ Sunday: No one takes my life away *from* me; * I lay it down freely and I shall take it up
                    *a*gain.

Easter, 3ʳᵈ, 7ᵗʰ: Though he was the Son *of* God, * Christ learned obedience *through* suffering;
                    and for all who *o*bey him, * he has become the source of life, al*le*luia.

Va

Canticle
Christ, God's holy servant

Philippians 2:6-11

Though he was in the form *of* God,
   * Jesus did not deem equality with
   God something to *be* grasped at.
Rather, he emptied himself and took
   the form of *a* slave, * being born in
   the likeness *of* men.
He was known to be of human *e*state, *
   and it was thus that *he* humbled
   himself,
obediently accepting *e*ven death, *
   death on *a* cross!
Because of this, God highly *e*xalted

him * and bestowed on him the name
   above every oth*er* name,
So that at Jesus' name every knee *must*
   bend * in the heavens, on the earth,
   and under *the* earth,
and every tongue proclaim to the glory
   of God *the* Father: * JESUS
   CHRIST *IS* LORD!
Glory to the Father, and to *the* Son, *
   and to the Ho*ly* Spirit:
as it was in the beginning, *is* now, * and
   will be for ever. *A*men.

Antiphon   The Lord Jesus humbled *himself* * and God exalted him *for* ever.

Advent: Lord, send the Lamb, the ruler of *the* earth, * from the rock in the desert to the
                 mountain of the daughter *of* Zion.

Lent, 3ʳᵈ Sunday: No one takes my life away *from* me; * I lay it down freely and I shall take it up
                    *a*gain.

Easter, 3ʳᵈ, 7ᵗʰ: Though he was the Son *of* God, * Christ learned obedience *through* suffering;
                    and for all who *o*bey him, * he has become the source of life, al*le*luia.

READING   Hebrews 13:20-21

May the God of peace, who brought up from the dead the great Shepherd of
the sheep by the blood of the eternal covenant, Jesus our Lord, furnish you
with all that is good, that you may do his will. Through Jesus Christ may he
carry out in you all that is pleasing to him. To Christ be glory forever! Amen.

RESPONSORY (VI F)

Our hearts are *filled* with wonder * as we contemplate your works, O Lord.
— Our hearts are *filled* with wonder * as we contemplate your works, O Lord.
We praise the wisdom which *wrought* them all,
— as we contemplate your works, O Lord.
Glory to the Father, and *to* the Son, * and to the Ho*ly* Spirit.
— Our hearts are *filled* with wonder * as we contemplate your works, O Lord.

CANTICLE OF MARY, antiphon as in the Proper of Seasons.

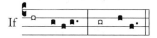

My soul ✠ proclaims the greatness *of* the Lord, * my spirit rejoices in God *my* savior
for he has *looked* with favor * on his low*ly* servant.
From this day all gen*er*ations * will call *me* blessèd:
the Almighty has done great *things* for me, * and holy is *his* Name.
He has mercy on *those* who fear him * in every gen*er*ation.
He has shown the strength *of* his arm, * he has scattered the proud in their con*ceit*.

He has cast down the mighty *from* their thrones, * and has lifted up *the* lowly.
He has filled the hungry *with* good things, * and the rich he has sent a*way* empty.
He has come to the help of his *servant* Israel * for he has remembered his promise *of* mercy,
the promise he made *to* our fathers, * to Abraham and his children *for* ever.
Glory to the Father, and *to* the Son, * and to the Ho*ly* Spirit:
as it was in the begin*ning*, is now, * and will be for ever. *A*men.

Antiphon repeated.

INTERCESSIONS
Christ had compassion on the hungry and performed a miracle of *love* for them. * Mindful of this, *let* us pray:
Show us your love, O Lord.
Lord, we recognize that all the favors we have received today come through your gen*er*osity,
— do not let them return to you empty, but let *them* bear fruit.
Light and salvation of all nations, protect the missionaries you have sent in*to* the world,
— enkindle in them the fire *of* your Spirit.
Grant that man may shape the world in keeping with *hu*man dignity,
— and respond generously to the needs *of* our time.
Healer of body and spirit, comfort the sick and be present *to* the dying,
— in your mercy visit *and* refresh us.
May the faithful departed be numbered a*mong* the saints,
— whose names are in the *Book* of Life.

Our Father . . .

Prayer, as in the Proper of Seasons.

SUNDAY, WEEK III

Morning Prayer

HYMN, 1312.
Ætérne rerum cónditor. (L.M.)

Ætérne rérum cónditor,
noctem diémque qui regis,
et témporum das témpora
ut álleves fastídium,

Præco diéi iam sonat,
noctis profúndæ pervigil,
noctúrna lux viántibus
a nocte noctem ségregans.

Hoc excitátus Lúcifer
solvit polum calígine;
hoc omnis errónum chorus
vias nocéndi déserit.

Hoc nauta vires cólligit
pontíque mitéscunt freta;
hoc, ipse Petra Ecclésiæ,
canénte, culpam díluit.

Iesu, labántes réspice
et nos vidéndo córrige;
si réspicis, lapsus cadunt
fletúque culpa sólvitur.

Tu, lux, refúlge sénsibus
mentísque somnum díscute;
te nostra vox primus sonet
et vota solvámus tibi.

Sit Christe, rex piíssime,
tibi Patríque glória
cum Spíritu Paráclito,
in sempitérna sæcula. Amen.

Eternal Maker of the world,
The sov'reign Lord of night and day:
You give the seasons of the year
To take time's heaviness away.

In deepest night you never sleep,
A Lamp for trav'lers on the way;
A Light dividing night from night,
The rooster crows announcing day.

See, at the sound, the daystar wakes
And drives the darkness from the sky;
All those who strayed on deadly roads
Now take the path to life on high.

The ocean hears; the waves die down;
The sailor overcomes his fears.
Saint Peter hears; the Church's Rock
Removes denial's stain with tears.

O Jesus, save us, for we fall;
Look down and set us right, we pray,
For at your glance our failings fail,
And sorrow washes sins away.

O Light, upon our senses shine,
Dispel the sleepiness within;
Let our first words be words of you;
With faithful praise our day begin.

To you, O Christ, most kindly King,
And to the Father, glory be;
Praise to the Spirit Paraclete,
In ev'ry age, eternally. Amen.

PSALMODY

Ant. 1   Glorious is the *Lord* on high, * al*le*luia.

Advent: The Lord is coming without delay. † He will reveal *things* kept hidden * and show himself to all mankind, *al*leluia.

Lent, 3ʳᵈ Sunday: Your decrees, O Lord, are *to* be trusted; * your truth is more powerful than the roaring *of* the seas.

Easter, 3ʳᵈ, 7ᵗʰ: The *Lord* is king, * robed in splendor, *al*leluia.

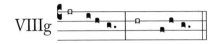

VIIIg

Psalm 93

Splendor of God the Creator

The Lord our mighty God now reigns supreme; let us rejoice and be glad and give him praise
(Revelation 19:6-7).

The Lord is king, with majesty enrobed; † the Lord has robed him*self* with might, * he has girded him*self* with power.

The world you made firm, not to be moved; † your throne has stood firm *from* of old. * From all eternity, O *Lord*, you are.

The waters have lifted up, O Lord, † the waters have lifted *up* their voice, * the waters have lifted *up* their

thunder.

Greater than the roar of mighty waters, † more glorious than the surgings *of* the sea, * the Lord is glori*ous* on high.

Truly your decrees are to be trusted. † Holiness is fitting *to* your house, * O Lord, until the *end* of time.

Glory to the Father, and *to* the Son, * and to the *Ho*ly Spirit:

as it was in the beginn*ing*, is now, * and will be for ev*er*. Amen.

Antiphon   Glorious is the *Lord* on high, * al*le*luia.

Advent: The Lord is coming without delay. † He will reveal *things* kept hidden * and show himself to all mankind, *al*leluia.

Lent, 3ʳᵈ Sunday: Your decrees, O Lord, are *to* be trusted; * your truth is more powerful than the roaring *of* the seas.

Easter, 3ʳᵈ, 7ᵗʰ: The *Lord* is king, * robed in splendor, *al*leluia.

Ant. 2   To you, Lord, be highest glory and *praise* for ever, * al*le*luia.

Advent: Mountains and hills shall be level, † crooked paths straight, *rough* ways smooth.
                * Come, Lord, do not delay, al*le*luia.

Lent, 3ʳᵈ Sunday: Springs of water, *bless* the Lord; * praise and exalt him above all *for* ever.

Easter, 3ʳᵈ, 7ᵗʰ: All creation will be freed; † all peoples will know the glory and freedom *of*
                God's children, * al*le*luia.

IIA

Canticle   Daniel 3:57-88, 56

Let all creatures praise the Lord

All you servants of the Lord, sing praise to him (Revelation 19:5).

Bless the Lord, all you works *of*
the Lord. * Praise and exalt him
above all *for*ever.

Angels of the Lord, *bless* the Lord, *
You heavens, bless *the* Lord.

All you waters above the heavens, *bless*
the Lord. * All you hosts of the Lord,
bless *the* Lord.

Sun and moon, *bless* the Lord. * Stars of
heaven, bless *the* Lord.

Every shower and dew, *bless* the Lord. *
All you winds, bless *the* Lord.

Fire and heat, *bless* the Lord. * Cold
and chill, bless *the* Lord.

Dew and rain, *bless* the Lord. * Frost
and chill, bless *the* Lord.

Ice and snow, *bless* the Lord. * Nights
and days, bless *the* Lord.

Light and darkness, *bless* the Lord. *
Lightnings and clouds, bless *the*
Lord.

Let the earth *bless* the Lord. * Praise
and exalt him above all *for*ever.

Mountains and hills, *bless* the Lord. *
Everything growing from the earth,

bless *the* Lord.

You springs, *bless* the Lord. * Seas and
rivers, bless *the* Lord.

You dolphins and all water creatures,
bless the Lord. * All you birds of the
air, bless *the* Lord.

All you beasts, wild and tame, *bless* the
Lord. * You sons of men, bless *the*
Lord.

O Israel, *bless* the Lord. * Praise and
exalt him above all *for*ever.

Priests of the Lord, *bless* the Lord. *
Servants of the Lord, bless *the* Lord.

Spirits and souls of the just, *bless* the
Lord. * Holy men of humble heart,
bless *the* Lord.

Hananiah, Azariah, Mishael, *bless* the
Lord. * Praise and exalt him above all
*for*ever.

Let us bless the Father, and the Son,
and the *Ho*ly Spirit. * Let us praise
and exalt him above all *for*ever.

Bless*èd* are you in the firma*ment* of
heaven. * Praiseworthy and glorious
and exalted above all *for*ever.

Antiphon   To you, Lord, be highest glory and *praise* for ever, * al*le*luia.

Advent: Mountains and hills shall be level, † crooked paths straight, *rough* ways smooth.
                * Come, Lord, do not delay, al*le*luia.

Lent, 3ʳᵈ Sunday: Springs of water, *bless* the Lord; * praise and exalt him above all *for* ever.

Easter, 3ʳᵈ, 7ᵗʰ: All creation will be freed; † all peoples will know the glory and freedom *of*
                God's children, * al*le*luia.

Ant. 3	Praise the Lord from *the* heavens, * al*le*luia.
Advent:	I shall enfold Zion with my sa*l*vation * and shed my glory around Jerusalem, al*le*luia.
Lent, 3rd Sunday:	All kings and peoples of *the* earth, * give praise *to* God.
Easter, 3rd, 7th:	The name of *the* Lord * is praised in heaven and on earth, al*le*luia.

Psalm 148
Praise to the Lord, the Creator
Praise and honor, glory and power for ever to him who sits upon the throne and to the Lamb (Revelation 5:13).

Praise the Lord from *the* heavens, *
   praise him in *the* heights.
Praise him, all *his* angels, * praise him,
   all *his* host.
Praise him, sun *and* moon, * praise him,
   shin*ing* stars.
Praise him, high*est* heavens * and the
   waters above *the* heavens.
Let them praise the name of *the* Lord. *
   He commanded: they *were* made.
He fixed them *for* ever, * gave a law
   which shall not pass *a*way.
Praise the Lord from *the* earth, * sea
   creatures and *all* oceans,
fire and hail, snow *and* mist, * stormy
   winds that obey *his* word;
all mountains *and* hills, * all fruit trees
   and cedars,

beasts, wild *and* tame, * reptiles and
   birds on *the* wing;
all earth's kings *and* peoples, * earth's
   princes *and* rulers;
young men *and* maidens, * old men
   together *with* children.
Let them praise the name of *the* Lord *
   for he alone is *e*xalted.
The splendor of *his* name * reaches
   beyond heaven *and* earth.
He exalts the strength of *his* people. *
   He is the praise of all *his* saints,
of the sons *of* Israel, * of the people to
   whom he *comes* close.
Glory to the Father, and to *the* Son, *
   and to the Ho*ly* Spirit:
as it was in the beginning, *is* now, * and
   will be for ever. *A*men.

Antiphon	Praise the Lord from *the* heavens, * al*le*luia.
Advent:	I shall enfold Zion with my salvation and shed my glory around Jerusalem, alleluia.
Lent, 3rd Sunday:	All kings and peoples of *the* earth, * give praise *to* God.
Easter, 3rd, 7th:	The name of *the* Lord * is praised in heaven and on earth, al*le*luia.

READING   Ezekiel 37:12b-14

Thus says the Lord God: O my people, I will open your graves and have you rise from them, and bring you back to the land of Israel. Then you shall know that I am the Lord, when I open your graves and have you rise from them, O my people! I will put my spirit in you that you may live, and I will settle you upon your land; thus you shall know that I am the Lord. I have promised, and I will do it, says the Lord.

RESPONSORY (VI F)

Christ, Son of the *living* God, * have mercy *on* us.
— Christ, Son of the *living* God, * have mercy *on* us.
You are seated at the right hand *of* the Father,
— have mercy *on* us.
Glory to the Father, and *to* the Son, * and to the Ho*ly* Spirit.
— Christ, Son of the *living* God, * have mercy *on* us.

CANTICLE OF ZECHARIAH, antiphon as in the Proper of Seasons.

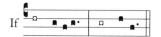

B lessèd ✠ be the Lord, the *God* of Israel; * he has come to his people and set *them* free.

He has raised up for us a *mighty* savior, * born of the house of his ser*vant* David.

Through his holy prophets he promised of old † that he would save us *from* our enemies, * from the hands of all *who* hate us.

He promised to show mercy *to* our fathers * and to remember his ho*ly* covenant.

This was the oath he swore to our *fath*er Abraham: * to set us free from the hands of *our* enemies,

free to worship him without fear, † holy and righteous *in* his sight * all the days *of our* life.

You, my child, shall be called the prophet *of* the Most High; * for you will go before the Lord to prepare *his* way,

to give his people knowledge *of* salvation * by the forgiveness of *their* sins.

In the tender compassion *of* our God * the dawn from on high shall break *up*on us,

to shine on those who dwell in darkness and the sha*dow* of death, * and to guide our feet into the way *of* peace.

Glory to the Father, and *to* the Son, * and to the Ho*ly* Spirit:

as it was in the begin*ning*, is now, * and will be for ever. *A*men.

Antiphon repeated.

INTERCESSIONS

Father, you sent the Holy Spirit to enlighten the *hearts* of men; * hear us *as* we
   pray:

*Enlighten your peo*ple, *Lord.*

 Blessèd are you, O *God*, our light,

— you have given us a new day resplendent *with* your glory.

You enlightened the world through the resurrection *of* your Son,

— through your Church shed this light *on* all men.

You gave the disciples of your only-begotten Son the Spirit's gift of
   *un*derstanding,

— through the same Spirit keep the Church faith*ful* to you.

Light of nations, remember those who re*main* in darkness,

— open their eyes and let them recognize you, the on*ly* true God.

Our Father . . .

Prayer, as in the Proper of Seasons.

SUNDAY, WEEK III

Evening Prayer II

HYMN, 1314.

Lucis creátor óptime. (L.M.)

Lucis creátor óptime,	O blest Creator of the light,
lucem diérum próferens,	Who mak'st the day with radiance bright,
primórdiis lucis novæ	And o'er the forming world didst call
mundi parans oríginem;	The light from chaos first of all;
Qui mane iunctum vésperi	Whose wisdom joined in meet array
diem vocari præcipis:	The morn and eve, and named them Day:
tætrum chaos illábitur;	Night comes with all its darkling fears;
audi preces cum flétibus.	Regard thy people's prayers and tears,
Ne mens graváta crimine	Lest, sunk in sin, and whelm'd with strife,
vitæ sit exsul múnere,	They lose the gift of endless life;
dum nil perénne cógitat	While thinking but the thoughts of time,
seséque culpis ílligat.	They weave new chains of woe and crime.
Cælorum pulset íntimum,	But grant them grace that they may strain
vitale tollat præmium;	The heav'nly gate and prize to gain:
vitémus omne nóxium,	Each harmful lure aside to cast,
purgémus omne péssimum.	And purge away each error past.
Præsta, Pater piíssime,	O Father, that we ask be done,
Patríque compar Únice,	Through Jesus Christ, thine only Son;
cum Spíritu Paráclito	Who, with the Holy Ghost and thee,
regnans per omne sæculum. Amen.	Doth live and reign eternally. Amen.

PSALMODY

Ant. 1 The Lord said *to* my Master: * Sit at my right hand, *a*lleluia.

Advent: Our Lord will come to claim his *glor*ious throne * in the assembly *of* the princes.

Lent, 3rd Sunday: Lord, all-powerful King, † free us for the sake *of* your name. * Give us time to turn *from* our sins.

Easter, 3rd, 7th: He purified us *from* our sins, * and is seated on high at God's right hand, *a*lleluia.

VIIIg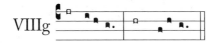

Psalm 110:1-5, 7
The Messiah, king and priest
Christ's reign will last until all his enemies are made subject to him
(1 Corinthians 15:25).

The Lord's revelation to my Master: † "Sit *on* my right: * your foes I will put be*neath* your feet."

The Lord will wield from Zion † your scep*ter* of power: * rule in the midst of *all* your foes.

A prince from the day of your birth † on the *holy* mountains; * from the womb before the dawn *I* begot you.

The Lord has sworn an oath he will not change. † "You are a *priest* for ever, * a priest like Melchize*dek* of

old."

The Master standing *at* your right hand * will shatter kings in the day of *his* great wrath.

He shall drink from the stream *by* the wayside * and therefore he shall lift *up* his head.

Glory to the Father, and *to* the Son, * and to the *Holy* Spirit:

As it was in the begin*ning*, is now, * and will be for ever. Amen.

Antiphon The Lord said *to* my Master: * Sit at my right hand, *a*lleluia.

Advent: Our Lord will come to claim his *glor*ious throne * in the assembly *of* the princes.

Lent, 3rd Sunday: Lord, all-powerful King, † free us for the sake *of* your name. * Give us time to turn *from* our sins.

Easter, 3rd, 7th: He purified us *from* our sins, * and is seated on high at God's right hand, *a*lleluia.

Ant. 2	Our compas*sio*nate Lord * has left us a memorial of his wonderful work, al*le*luia.
Advent:	Let the mountains break out with joy and the hills with answering gladness, † for the world's true *light*, the Lord, * comes with power *and* might.
Lent, 3rd Sunday:	We have been redeemed by the precious *blood* of Christ, * the lamb with*out* blemish.
Easter, 3rd, 7th:	The Lord has re*deemed* his people, * al*le*luia

IIA

Psalm 111
God's marvelous works
We are lost in wonder at all that you have done for us, our Lord and mighty God
(Revelation 15:3).

I will thank the Lord with *all* my heart * in the meeting of the just and their *a*ssembly.

Great are the works *of* the Lord; * to be pondered by all *who* love them.

Majestic and glori*ous* his work, * his justice stands firm *for* ever.

He makes us remem*ber* his wonders. * The Lord is compassion *and* love.

He gives food to *those* who fear him; * keeps his covenant ever *in* mind.

He has shown his might *to* his people * by giving them the lands of *the* nations.

His works are jus*tice* and truth: * his

precepts are all of *them* sure, standing firm for ev*er* and ever: * they are made in uprightness *and* truth.

He has sent deliverance to his people † and established his cove*nant* for ever. * Holy his name, to *be* feared.

To fear the Lord is the first stage of wisdom; † all who do so prove *them*selves wise. * His praise shall last *for* ever!

Glory to the Father, and *to* the Son, * and to the Ho*ly* Spirit:

as it was in the begin*ning*, is now, * and will be for ever. *A*men.

Antiphon	Our compas*sio*nate Lord * has left us a memorial of his wonderful work, al*le*luia.
Advent:	Let the mountains break out with joy and the hills with answering gladness, † for the world's true *light*, the Lord, * comes with power *and* might.
Lent, 3rd Sunday:	We have been redeemed by the precious *blood* of Christ, * the lamb with*out* blemish.
Easter, 3rd, 7th:	The Lord has re*deemed* his people, * al*le*luia

Ant. 3	All power is yours, Lord God, our mighty King, * alleluia, alleluia.
Advent:	Let us live in holiness and love † as we patiently await our blessèd hope, † the coming of *our* Savior, * alleluia, alleluia.
Easter, 3rd, 7th:	Alleluia, our Lord is king; † let us rejoice and give glory *to* him, * alleluia, alleluia.

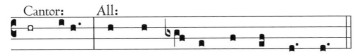

** al- le- lu- ia, al- le- lu- ia.

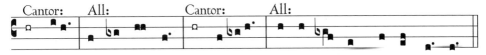

*Al- le- lu- ia.   ** al- le - lu- ia, al- le - lu- ia.

Canticle   See Revelation 19:1-7
The wedding of the Lamb

Salvation, glory, and power to *our* God:
* Alleluia.
his judgments are hon*est* and true.
** Alleluia, alleluia.

Sing praise to our God, all you *his* servants,
* Alleluia.
all who worship him reverently, *great* and small.
** Alleluia, alleluia.

The Lord our all-powerful God *is* King;
* Alleluia.
let us rejoice, sing praise, and *give* him glory.
** Alleluia, alleluia.

The wedding feast of the Lamb has *be*gun,
* Alleluia.
and his bride is pre*pared* to welcome him.
** Alleluia, alleluia.

Glory to the Father, and to the Son, †
and to the Ho*ly* Spirit.
* Alleluia.
As it was in the beginning, is now, †
and will be for ev*er*. Amen.
** Alleluia, alleluia.

Antiphon   All power is yours, Lord God, our mighty King, * alleluia,
                  alleluia.

Advent: Let us live in holiness and love † as we patiently await our blessèd hope, † the
                  coming of *our* Savior, * alleluia, alleluia.

Easter, 3ʳᵈ, 7ᵗʰ: Alleluia, our Lord is king; † let us rejoice and give glory *to* him, * alleluia,
                  alleluia.

Lent

Lent, 3rd Sunday: Ours were the sufferings *he* bore; * ours the torments he *endured.*

Va

Canticle   1 Peter 2:21-24
The willing acceptance of his passion by Christ, the servant of God

Christ suffered for you, † and
left you an *example* * to have you
follow in *his* footsteps.

He did *no* wrong; * no deceit was found
in *his* mouth.

When he was *insulted* * he returned *no*
insult.

When he was made *to* suffer, * he did
not counter *with* threats.

Instead he delivered him*self* up * to the

One who judg*es* justly.

In his *own* body * he brought our sins
to *the* cross,

so that all of us, dead *to* sin, * could live
in accord with *God's* will.

By *his* wounds * you *were* healed.

Glory to the Father, and to *the* Son, *
and to the Ho*ly* Spirit:

as it was in the beginning, *is* now, * and
will be for ever. *A*men.

Lent, 3ʳᵈ Sunday: Ours were the sufferings *he* bore; * ours the torments he *endured.*

READING   1 Peter 1:3-5
    Praised be the God and Father
    of our Lord Jesus Christ,
    he who in his great mercy
    gave us new birth;
    a birth unto hope which draws its life
    from the resurrection of Jesus Christ from the dead;
    a birth to an imperishable inheritance,
    incapable of fading or defilement,
    which is kept in heaven for you
    who are guarded with God's power through faith;

a birth to a salvation which stands ready
to be revealed in the last days.

RESPONSORY (VI F)
The whole crea*tion* proclaims * the greatness of *your* glory.
— The whole crea*tion* proclaims * the greatness of *your* glory.
Eternal *a*ges praise
— the greatness of *your* glory.
Glory to the Father, and *to* the Son, * and to the Ho*ly* Spirit.
— The whole crea*tion* proclaims * the greatness of *your* glory.

CANTICLE OF MARY, antiphon as in the Proper of Seasons.

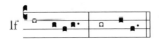

My soul ✠ proclaims the greatness *of* the Lord, * my spirit rejoices in God *my* savior
for he has *looked* with favor * on his low*ly* servant.
From this day all *gen*erations * will call *me* blessèd:
the Almighty has done great *things* for me, * and holy is *his* Name.
He has mercy on *those* who fear him * in every gen*er*ation.
He has shown the strength *of* his arm, * he has scattered the proud in their *con*ceit.

He has cast down the mighty *from* their thrones, * and has lifted up *the* lowly.
He has filled the hungry *with* good things, * and the rich he has sent a*way* empty.
He has come to the help of his *servant* Israel * for he has remembered his promise *of* mercy,
the promise he made *to* our fathers, * to Abraham and his children *for* ever.
Glory to the Father, and *to* the Son, * and to the Ho*ly* Spirit:
as it was in the begin*ning*, is now, * and will be for ever. *A*men.

Antiphon repeated.

INTERCESSIONS
Christ the Lord is our head; we *are* his members. * In joy let us call *out* to him:
*Lord, may your king*dom *come.*
Christ our Savior, make your Church a more vivid symbol of the unity of *all* mankind,
— make it more effectively the sacrament of salvation *for* all peoples.
Through your presence, guide the college of bishops in union *with* the Pope,
— give them the gifts of unity, *love* and peace.
Bind all Christians more closely to yourself, *their* divine Head,
— lead them to proclaim your kingdom by the witness *of* their lives.

Grant peace *to* the world,
— let every land flourish in justice *and* security.
Grant to the dead the glory of *re*surrection,
— and give us a share *in* their happiness.

Our Father . . .

Prayer, as in the Proper of Seasons.

MONDAY, WEEK III

Morning Prayer

HYMN, 1315.
Splendor patérnæ glóriæ. (L.M.)

Splendor patérnæ glóriæ,
de luce lucem próferens,
lux lucis et fons lúminis,
diem dies illúminans,

Verúsque sol, illábere
micans nitóre pérpeti,
iubárque Sancti Spíritus
infúnde nostris sénsibus.

Votis vocémus et Patrem,
Patrem perénnis glóriæ,
Patrem poténtis grátiæ,
culpam reléget lúbricam.

Infórmet actus sténuos,
dentem retúndat ínvidi,
casus secúndet ásperos,
donet geréndi grátiam.

Mentem gubérnet et regat
casto, fidéli córpore;
fides calóre férveat,
fraudis cenéna nésciat.

Christúsque nobis sit cibus,
potúsque noster sit fides;
læti bibámus sóbriam
ebrietátem Spíritus.

Lætus dies hic tránseat;
pudor sit ut dilúculum,
fides velut merídies,
crepúsculum mens nésciat.

Auróra cursus próvehit;
Auróra totus pródeat,
in Patre totus Fílius
et totus in Verbo Pater. Amen.

O splendor of God's glory bright,
O Thou that bringest light from Light;
O Light of Light, light's living spring;
O Day, all days illumining:

O Thou, true Sun, on us thy glance
Let fall in royal radiance,
The Spirit's sanctifying beam
Upon our earthly senses stream.

The Father too our prayers implore,
Father of glory evermore,
The Father of all grace and might,
To banish sin from our delight.

To guide what e'er we nobly do;
With love all envy to subdue;
To make ill fortune turn to fair;
And give us grace our wrongs to bear.

Our mind be in his keeping placed,
Our body true to him and chaste,
Where only faith her fire shall feed
To burn the tares of Satan's seed.

And Christ to us for food shall be,
From him our drink that welleth free,
The Spirit's wine, that maketh whole,
And mocking not, exalts the soul.

Now let the day in joy pass on:
Our modesty like early dawn,
Our faith like noontide splendor glow,
Our souls the twilight never know.

See! morn pursues her shining way:
True Morning, all thy beams display!
Son with the mighty Father one,
The Father wholly in the Son.

All laud to God the Father be;
All praise, eternal Son, to thee;
All glory, as is ever meet,
To God the Holy Paraclete. Amen.

Ant. 1   Blessèd are they * who dwell in your *house*, O Lord.

December 17-23:   The Lord, the ruler over the kings of the *earth*, will come; * blessèd are they
                    who are ready to go and *wel*come him.

Easter: My heart and my *flesh* rejoice * in the living God, a*l*leluia.

VIIIg

Psalm 84
Longing for God's Temple
Here we do not have a lasting city; we seek a home that is yet to come
(Hebrews 13:14).

How lovely *is* your dwelling place, *
Lord, *God* of hosts.
My soul is long*ing* and yearning, * is
yearning for the courts *of* the Lord.
My heart and my soul ring *out* their joy
* to God, the *liv*ing God.
The sparrow herself *finds* a home * and
the swallow a nest *for* her brood;
she lays her young *by* your altars, *
Lord of hosts, my king *and* my God.
They are happy, who dwell *in* your
house, * for ever sing*ing* your praise.
They are happy, whose strength *is* in
you, * in whose hearts are the *roads*
to Zion.
As they go through the Bitter Valley †
they make it a *place* of springs, * the
autumn rain covers *it* with blessings.
They walk with ever *grow*ing strength,
* they will see the God of *gods* in

Zion.
O Lord God of hosts, *hear* my prayer, *
give ear, O *God* of Jacob.
Turn your eyes, O *God*, our shield, *
look on the face of *your* anointed.
One day with*in* your courts * is better
than a *thou*sand elsewhere.
The threshold of the *house* of God * I
prefer to the dwellings *of* the wicked.
For the Lord God is a ram*part*, a shield;
* he will give us his fa*vor* and glory.
The Lord will not refuse *any* good * to
those who walk *with*out blame.
Lord, *God* of hosts, * happy the man
who *trusts* in you!
Glory to the Father, and *to* the Son, *
and to the *Ho*ly Spirit:
as it was in the begin*ning*, is now, * and
will be for ev*er*. Amen.

Antiphon   Blessèd are they * who dwell in your *house*, O Lord.

December 17-23:   The Lord, the ruler over the kings of the *earth*, will come; * blessèd are they
                    who are ready to go and *wel*come him.

Easter: My heart and my *flesh* rejoice * in the living God, a*l*leluia.

Ant. 2   Come, *let* us climb * the mountain of *the* Lord.

December 17-23:   Sing a new song *to* the Lord; * proclaim his praises to the ends of *the* earth.

Easter: The house of the Lord has been *raised* on high, * and all the nations will go up
to it, al*le*luia.

IIA

Canticle   Isaiah 2:2-5

The mountain of the Lord's dwelling towers above every mountain

All peoples shall come and worship in your presence (Revelation 15:4).

In *days* to come, * the mountain of *the* Lord's house
shall be established as the *high*est mountain * and raised above *the* hills.
All nations *shall* stream toward it; * many peoples shall come *and* say:
"Come, let us climb *the* Lord's mountain, * to the house of the God *of* Jacob,
that he may instruct us *in* his ways, * and we may walk in *his* paths."
For from Zion shall go *forth* instruction, * and the word of the Lord from *Je*rusalem.

He shall judge be*tween* the nations, * and impose terms on man*y* peoples.
They shall beat their swords *in*to plowshares * and their spears in*to* pruning hooks;
one nation shall not raise the sword a*gainst* another, * nor shall they train for war a*gain*.
O house of *Ja*cob, come, * let us walk in the light of *the* Lord!
Glory to the Father, and *to* the Son, * and to the Ho*ly* Spirit:
as it was in the begin*ning*, is now, * and will be for ever. *A*men.

Antiphon   Come, *let* us climb * the mountain of *the* Lord.

December 17-23:   Sing a new song *to* the Lord; * proclaim his praises to the ends of *the* earth.

Easter: The house of the Lord has been *raised* on high, * and all the nations will go up
to it, al*le*luia.

Ant. 3   Sing to *the* Lord * and bless *his* name.

December 17-23:   When the Son of Man comes *to* earth, * do you think he will find faith in *men's* hearts?

Easter: Proclaim this among *the* nations: * the Lord is king, al*le*luia.

Va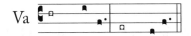

Psalm 96

The Lord, king and judge of the world

A new theme now inspires their praise of God; they belong to the Lamb
(Revelation 14:3).

O sing a new song to the Lord,
† sing to the Lord, all *the* earth. *

O sing to the Lord, bless *his* name.
Proclaim his help day by day, † tell

among the nations *his* glory * and his
wonders among all *the* peoples.
The Lord is great and worthy of praise,
 † to be feared above *all* gods; * the
gods of the heathens *are* naught.
It was the Lord who made the heavens,
 † his are majesty and state *and* power
 * and splendor in his ho*ly* place.
Give the Lord, you families of peoples,
 † give the Lord glory *and* power, *
give the Lord the glory of *his* name.
Bring an offering and enter his courts,
 † worship the Lord in *his* temple. * O
earth, tremble *before* him.
Proclaim to the nations: "God is king."
 † The world he made firm in *its*

place; * he will judge the peoples *in*
fairness.
Let the heavens rejoice and earth *be*
glad, * let the sea and all within it
thun*der* praise,
let the land and all it bears re*joice*, * all
the trees of the wood shout *for* joy
at the presence of the Lord for *he*
comes, * he comes to rule *the* earth.
With justice he will rule *the* world, * he
will judge the peoples with *his* truth.
Glory to the Father, and to *the* Son, *
and to the Ho*ly* Spirit:
as it was in the beginning, *is* now, * and
will be for ever. *A*men.

Antiphon   Sing to *the* Lord * and bless *his* name.
December 17-23:   When the Son of Man comes *to* earth, * do you think he will find faith in *men's* hearts?
Easter: Proclaim this among *the* nations: * the Lord is king, al*le*luia.

READING   James 2:12-13
Always speak and act as men destined for judgment under the law of freedom. Merciless is the judgment on the man who has not shown mercy; but mercy triumphs over judgment.

RESPONSORY (VI F)
Blessèd be the *Lord* our God, * blessèd from age *to* age.
— Blessèd be the *Lord* our God, * blessèd from age *to* age.
His marvelous works are be*yond* compare,
— blessèd from age *to* age.
Glory to the Father, and *to* the Son, * and to the Ho*ly* Spirit.
— Blessèd be the *Lord* our God, * blessèd from age *to* age.

CANTICLE OF ZECHARIAH
Antiphon   Blessèd *be* the Lord, * the Lord *our* God.

INTERCESSIONS (VI F)
Man was created to glorify God *through* his deeds. * Let us earne*st*ly pray:
May we give glory to your name, O Lord.
We bless you, Creator *of* all things,
— for you have given us the goods of the earth and brought us *to* this day.

Look with favor on us as we begin our *daily* work,
— let us be fellow work*ers* with you.
Make our work today benefit our broth*ers* and sisters,
— that with them and for them we may build an earthly city, pleas*ing* to you.
Grant joy and *peace* to us,
— and to all we *meet* this day.

Our Father . . .

Prayer

    Lord God,
    king of heaven and earth,
    direct our minds and bodies throughout this day,
    and make us holy.
    Keep us faithful to your law in thought, word and deed.
    Be our helper now and always,
    free us from sin,
    and bring us to salvation in that kingdom
    where you live and reign with the Father and the Holy Spirit,
    one God, for ever and ever.

MONDAY, WEEK III

Evening Prayer

HYMN, 1317.

Imménse cæli cónditor. (L.M.)

Imménse cæli cónditor,	O boundless Wisdom, God most high,
qui, mixta ne confúnderent,	O Maker of the earth and sky,
aquæ fluénta dívidens,	Who bid'st the parted waters flow
cælum dedísti límitem,	In heav'n above, on earth below:
Firmans locum cæléstibus	The streams on earth, the clouds in heav'n,
simúlque terræ rívulis,	By thee their ordered bounds were giv'n,
ut unda flammas témperet,	Lest 'neath th'untempered fires of day
terræ solum ne díssipet:	The parchèd soil should waste away.
Infúnde nunc, piíssime,	E'en so on us who seek thy face
donum perénnis grátiæ,	Pour forth the waters of thy grace;
fraudis novæ ne cásibus	Renew the fount of life within,
nos error átterat vetus.	And quench the wasting fires of sin.
Lucem fides inveniat,	Let faith discern th'eternal Light
sic lúminis iubar ferat;	Beyond the darkness of the night,
hæc vana cuncta térreat,	And through the mists of falsehood see
hanc falsa nulla cómprimant.	The path of truth revealed by thee.
Præsta, Pater piíssime,	O Father, that we ask be done,
Patríque compare Únice,	Through Jesus Christ, thine only Son;
cum Spíritu Paráclito	Who, with the Holy Ghost and thee,
regnans per omne sæculum. Amen.	Doth live and reign eternally. Amen.

PSALMODY

Ant. 1   Our eyes are fixed intently *on* the Lord, * waiting for his mer*ci*ful help.

December 17-23:   The Lord, the ruler over the kings of the *earth*, will come; * blessèd are they who are ready to go and *wel*come him.

Easter: The Lord will be your *light* for ever; * your God will be your glory, a*l*leluia.

VIII g

Psalm 123
The Lord, unfailing hope of his people
Two blind men cried out: "Have pity on us, Lord, Son of David" (Matthew 20:30).

To you I have lifted *up* my eyes, *   my eyes, like the *eyes* of slaves * on the
you who dwell *in* the heavens: hand *of* their lords.

Like the eyes *of* a servant * on the hand
  of her mistress,
so our eyes are on the *Lord* our God *
  till he show *us* his mercy.
Have mercy on us, *Lord*, have mercy. *
  We are filled *with* contempt.
Indeed all too full is our soul † with the

scorn *of* the rich, * with the proud
  man's disdain.
Glory to the Father, and *to* the Son, *
  and to the *Holy* Spirit.
as it was in the begin*ning*, is now, * and
  will be for ev*er*. Amen.

Antiphon   Our eyes are fixed intently *on* the Lord, * waiting for his mer*ciful* help.

December 17-23:   The Lord, the ruler over the kings of the *earth*, will come; * blessèd are they who are ready to go and *wel*come him.

Easter: The Lord will be your *light* for ever; * your God will be your glory, a*l*leluia.

Ant. 2   Our help is in the name *of* the Lord * who made heaven *and* earth.

December 17-23:   Sing a new song *to* the Lord; * proclaim his praises to the ends of *the* earth.

Easter: The snare was broken and we *were* set free, * al*l*eluia.

IIA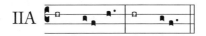

Psalm 124
Our help is in the name of the Lord
The Lord said to Paul: "Fear not... I am with you" (Acts 18:9-10).

" **I**f the Lord had not been *on* our side,"
  * this is Isra*el's* song.
"If the Lord had not *been* on our side *
  when men rose *against* us,
then would they have swallowed *us*
  alive * when their anger *was* kindled.
Then would the waters *have* engulfed
  us, * the torrent *gone* over us;
over our head *would* have swept * the
  rag*ing* waters."
Blessèd be the Lord who *did* not give

us * a prey to *their* teeth!
Our life, like a bird, *has* escaped * from
  the snare of *the* fowler.
Indeed the snare *has* been broken * and
  we have *escaped*.
Our help is in the name *of* the Lord, *
  who made heaven *and* earth.
Glory to the Father, and *to* the Son, *
  and to the Ho*ly* Spirit:
as it was in the begin*ning*, is now, * and
  will be for ever. *A*men.

Antiphon   Our help is in the name *of* the Lord * who made heaven *and* earth.

December 17-23:   Sing a new song *to* the Lord; * proclaim his praises to the ends of *the* earth.

Easter: The snare was broken and we *were* set free, * al*l*eluia.

Ant. 3   God chose us in *his* Son * to be his adopt*ed* children.

December 17-23:   When the Son of Man comes *to* earth, * do you think he will find faith in *men's* hearts?

Easter: When I am lifted up from *the* earth, * I shall draw all people to myself, al*le*luia.

Va

Canticle   Ephesians 1:3-10
God our Savior

Praised be the God *and* Father * of our Lord Je*sus* Christ,

who has bestowed on us *in* Christ * every spiritual blessing in *the* heavens.

God chose us in him † before the world be*gan* * to be holy and blameless in *his* sight.

He predestined us † to be his adopted sons through Je*sus* Christ, * such was his will *and* pleasure,

that all might praise the glori*ous* favor * he has bestowed on us in his *beloved*.

In him and through his blood, † we have been *re*deemed, * and our sins *for*given,

so immeasura*bly* generous * is God's favor *to* us.

God has given us the wisdom † to understand fully *the* mystery, * the plan he was pleased to decree *in* Christ.

A plan to be carried out *in* Christ, * in the fullness *of* time,

to bring all things into one *in* him, * in the heavens and *on* earth.

Glory to the Father, and to *the* Son, * and to the Ho*ly* Spirit:

as it was in the beginning, *is* now, * and will be for ever. *A*men.

Antiphon   God chose us in *his* Son * to be his adopt*ed* children.

December 17-23:   When the Son of Man comes *to* earth, * do you think he will find faith in *men's* hearts?

Easter: When I am lifted up from *the* earth, * I shall draw all people to myself, al*le*luia

READING   James 4:11-12

Do not, my brothers, speak ill of one another. The one who speaks ill of his brother or judges his brother is speaking against the law. It is the law he judges. If, however, you judge the law you are no observer of the law, you are its judge. There is but one Lawgiver and Judge, one who can save and destroy. Who then are you to judge your neighbor?

RESPONSORY (VI F)

Lord, you a*lone* can heal me, * for I have grieved you by *my* sins.

— Lord, you a*lone* can heal me, * for I have grieved you by *my* sins.

Once more I say: O Lord, have mer*cy* on me,

— for I have grieved you by *my* sins.

Glory to the Father, and *to* the Son, * and to the Ho*ly* Spirit.

— Lord, you a*lone* can heal me, * for I have grieved you by *my* sins.

CANTICLE OF MARY

Antiphon   My soul proclaims the greatness *of* the Lord *
                for he has looked with favor on his low*ly* servant.

INTERCESSIONS (VI F)

Christ desires to lead all men *to* salvation. * Let us implore him with *all* our heart:
Draw all things to yourself, O Lord.
Through your precious blood, Lord, you redeemed us from the slave*ry* of sin,
— grant us the freedom of the *sons* of God.
Bestow your grace upon our bishop N., and up*on* all bishops,
— may they administer your sacraments with *fer*vent joy.
Grant that all who seek the *truth* may find it,
— and in finding it may they desire it *all* the more.
Be present to comfort widows, orphans and all the a*ban*doned, Lord,
— may they feel close to you and *cling* to you.
Receive our departed brethren into the hea*ven*ly kingdom,
— where with the Father and the Holy Spirit you will be *all* in all.

Our Father . . .

Prayer

God our Father,
at the close of day we come to you,
the light that never fades.
Shine in the darkness of our night
and forgive our sins and failings.
We ask this through our Lord Jesus Christ, your Son,
who lives and reigns with you and the Holy Spirit,
one God, for ever and ever.

Morning Prayer

HYMN, 1318.

Pergráta mundo núntiat. (L.M.)

Pergráta mundo núntiat	The beauty of the rising sun
auróra solis spicula,	Begins to tint the world with light,
res et colóre véstiens	Awakened nature glows with life
iam cuncta dat nitéscere.	As form and color reappear.
Qui sol per ævum prænites,	Lord Jesus Christ, you far surpass
o Christe, nobis vívidus,	The sun that shines since time began;
ad te canéntes vértimur,	We turn to you with joyous song
te géstientes pérfrui.	That you may bless us with your smile.
Tu Patris es scientia	You are God's knowledge infinite,
Verbúmque per quod ómnia	His Word, through whom all things were made;
miro refulgent órdine	Their wondrous order speaks to us
mentésque nostras áttrahunt.	And draws our hearts and minds to you.
Da lucis ut nos fílii	Give us your light that like true sons
sic ambulémus ímpigri,	Intrepid we may tread life's path.
ut Patris usque grátiam	May all our ways and actions show
mores et actus éxprimant.	The gift of God the Father's grace.
Sincéra past*a* ut prófluant	Let ev'ry word our lips may say
ex ore nostro iúgiter,	Prove our sincerity and truth,
et véritatis dúlcius	That our serenity of soul
ut excitémur gáudiis.	May radiate our inward joy.
Sit, Christe, rex piíssime,	To you, O Christ, most kindly King,
tibi Patríque Glória	And to the Father, glory be;
cum spíritu Paráclito,	Praise to the Spirit Paraclete,
in sempitérna sæcula. Amen.	In ev'ry age, eternally. Amen.

PSALMODY

Ant. 1	Lord, you have *blessed* your land; * you have forgiven the sins *of* your people.
December 17-23:	The Lord will come from his *holy* place * to *save* his people.
Easter:	You will turn back, O God, and bring *us* to life, * and your people will rejoice in you, *a*lleluia.

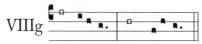

VIIIg

Psalm 85
Our salvation is near
God blessed the land when our Savior came to earth (Origen).

O Lord, you once fa*vored* your land
* and revived the for*tunes* of
Jacob,
you forgave the guilt *of* your people *
and covered *all* their sins.
You averted *all* your rage, * you calmed
the heat *of* your anger.
Revive us now, *God*, our helper! * Put
an end to your grie*vance* against us.
Will you be angry with *us* for ever, *
will your anger *nev*er cease?
Will you not restore a*gain* our life * that
your people may re*joice* in you?
Let us see, O *Lord*, your mercy * and
give us your *saving* help.
I will hear what the Lord God *has* to
say, * a voice that *speaks* of peace,

peace for his people *and* his friends *
and those who turn to him *in* their
hearts.
His help is near for *those* who fear him *
and his glory will dwell *in* our land.
Mercy and faithful*ness* have met; *
justice and peace *have* embraced.
Faithfulness shall spring *from* the earth
* and justice look *down* from heaven.
The Lord will *make* us prosper * and
our earth shall *yield* its fruit.
Justice shall *march* before him * and
peace shall fol*low* his steps.
Glory to the Father, and *to* the Son, *
and to the *Holy* Spirit:
as it was in the begin*ning*, is now, * and
will be for ev*er*. Amen.

Antiphon	Lord, you have *blessed* your land; * you have forgiven the sins *of* your people.
December 17-23:	The Lord will come from his *holy* place * to *save* his people.
Easter:	You will turn back, O God, and bring *us* to life, * and your people will rejoice in you, *a*lleluia.

Ant. 2   My soul has yearned for you *in* the night, * and as morning breaks I watch for *your* coming.

December 17-23:   Zion is our mighty citadel, † our saving Lord its wall and its defense; † throw op*en* the gates, * for our God is here among us, al*le*luia.

Easter: We have placed all our hope *in* the Lord, * and he has given us his peace, al*le*luia.

Canticle   Isaiah 26:1-4, 7-9, 12

Hymn after the defeat of the enemy

The city wall had twelve foundation stones (See Revelation 21:14).

A strong ci*ty* have we; * he sets up walls and ramparts to *protect* us.

Open up the gates to let in a nation *that* is just, * one that *keeps* faith.

A nation of firm purpose you *keep* in peace; * in peace, for its trust *in* you.

Trust in the *Lord* forever! * For the Lord is an eter*nal* Rock.

The way of the *just* is smooth; * the path of the just you *make* level.

Yes, for your way and your judg*ments*, O Lord, * we look *to* you;

your name *and* your title * are the desire of *our* souls.

My soul yearns for you *in* the night, * yes, my spirit within me keeps vigil *for* you;

when your judgment dawns up*on* the earth, * the world's inhabitants *learn* justice.

O Lord, you mete out *peace* to us, * for it is you who have accomplished all we *have* done.

Glory to the Father, and *to* the Son, * and to the Ho*ly* Spirit:

as it was in the begin*ning*, is now, * and will be for ever. *A*men.

Antiphon   My soul has yearned for you *in* the night, * and as morning breaks I watch for *your* coming.

December 17-23:   Zion is our mighty citadel, † our saving Lord its wall and its defense; † throw op*en* the gates, * for our God is here among us, al*le*luia.

Easter: We have placed all our hope *in* the Lord, * and he has given us his peace, al*le*luia.

Ant. 3   Lord, let the light of *your* face * shine up*on* us.

December 17-23:   Lord, make known your will throughout *the* earth; * proclaim your salvation to eve*ry* nation.

Easter: The earth has yielded its fruit; † let the nations be glad and sing *for* joy, * al*le*luia.

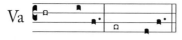

Psalm 67

People of all nations will worship the Lord

You must know that God is offering his salvation to all the world (Acts 28:28).

O God, be gracious *and* bless us *
and let your face shed its light
*up*on us.
So will your ways be known up*on* earth
* and all nations learn your sav*ing*
help.
Let the peoples praise you, O God; * let
all the peo*ples* praise you.
Let the nations be glad and *ex*ult * for
you rule the world *with* justice.
With fairness you rule *the* peoples, *
you guide the nations *on* earth.

Let the peoples praise you, O God; * let
all the peo*ples* praise you.
The earth has yielded *its* fruit * for
God, our God, *has* blessed us.
May God still give us *his* blessing * till
the ends of the earth *re*vere him.
Let the peoples praise you, O God; * let
all the peo*ples* praise you.
Glory to the Father, and to *the* Son, *
and to the Ho*ly* Spirit:
as it was in the beginning, *is* now, * and
will be for ever. *A*men.

Antiphon   Lord, let the light of *your* face * shine up*on* us.

December 17-23:   Lord, make known your will throughout *the* earth, * proclaim your salvation to
every nation.

Easter: The earth has yielded its fruit; † let the nations be glad and sing *for* joy, * al*le*luia.

READING   1 John 4:14-15

We have seen for ourselves, and can testify,
that the Father has sent the Son as savior of the world.
When anyone acknowledges that Jesus is the Son of God,
God dwells in him
and he in God.

RESPONSORY (VI F)
My God *stands* by me, * all my trust is *in* him.
— My God *stands* by me, * all my trust is *in* him.
I find refuge in him, and I am *tru*ly free;
— all my trust is *in* him.
Glory to the Father, and *to* the Son, * and to the Ho*ly* Spirit.
— My God *stands* by me, * all my trust is *in* him.

CANTICLE OF ZECHARIAH
Antiphon   God has raised up for us a *mighty* Savior, * as he promised of old
through his ho*ly* prophets.

INTERCESSIONS (VI F)

Lord Jesus, by your blood you have purchased for yourself *a* new people. * We
adore you *and* beseech you:
Remember your people, Lord.
Our King and our Redeemer, hear the praises of your Church at the beginning *of*
this day,
— teach her to glorify your majesty *with*out ceasing.

You are our hope and our strength, in *you* we trust,
— may we nev*er* despair.
Look kindly upon our weakness and hasten *to* our aid,
— for without you we *can* do nothing.
Remember the poor and the afflicted, do not let this day be a bur*den* to them,
— but a consolation *and* a joy.

Our Father . . .

Prayer

God our Father,
yours is the beauty of creation
and the good things you have given us.
Help us to begin this day joyfully in your name
and to spend it in loving service
of you and our fellow man.
We ask this through our Lord Jesus Christ, your Son,
who lives and reigns with you and the Holy Spirit,
one God, for ever and ever.

TUESDAY, WEEK III

Evening Prayer

HYMN, 1320.

Tellúris ingens cónditor. (L.M.)

Tellúris ingens cónditor,	Earth's mighty Maker, whose command
mundi solum qui éruens,	Raised from the sea the solid land,
pulsis aquæ moléstiis,	And drove each billowy heap away,
terram dedist*i* immóbilem,	And bade the earth stand firm for aye:
Ut germen aptum próferens,	That so, with flowers of golden hue,
fulvis decóra flóribus,	The seeds of each it might renew;
fecúnda fructu sísteret	And fruit-trees bearing fruit might yield—
pastúmque gratum rédderet:	And pleasant pasture of the field;
Mentis perústae vúlnera	Our spirit's rankling wounds efface
munda viróre grátiæ,	With dewy freshness of thy grace:
ut facta fletu díluat	That grief might cleanse each deed of ill,
motúsque pravos átterat,	And o'er each lust may triumph still.
Iussis tuis obtemperet,	Let every soul thy law obey,
nullis malis approximet,	And keep from every evil way;
bonis repleri gáudeat	Rejoice each promised good to win
et mortis actum nésciat.	And flee from every mortal sin.
Præsta, Pater piissime,	O Father, that we ask be done,
Patrique compare Unice,	Through Jesus Christ, thine only Son;
cum Spiritu Paraclito	Who, with the Holy Ghost and thee,
regnans per omne sæculum Amen.	Doth live and reign eternally. Amen.

PSALMODY

Ant. 1	The *Lord* surrounds * his people *with* his strength.
December 17-23:	The Lord will come from his *ho*ly place * to *save* his people.
Easter:	Peace be with you; *it* is I, * do not be afraid, *al*leluia.

VIIIg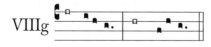

Psalm 125
The Lord, guardian of his people
Peace to God's true Israel (Galatians 6:16).

Those who put their trust in the
Lord † are *like* Mount Zion, * that
cannot be shaken, that *stands* for ever.
Jerusalem! The mountains surround
her, † so the Lord sur*rounds* his
people * both now *and* for ever.
For the scepter of the wicked *shall* not
rest * over the land *of* the just
for fear that the hands *of* the just *

should *turn* to evil.
Do good, Lord, to those *who* are good,
* to the up*right* of heart;
but the crooked and those who do evil, †
drive *them* away! * On Is*ra*el, peace!
Glory to the Father, and *to* the Son, *
and to the *Holy* Spirit:
as it was in the begin*ning*, is now, * and
will be for e*ver*. Amen.

Antiphon   The *Lord* surrounds * his people *with* his strength.

December 17-23: The Lord will come from his *holy* place * to *save* his people.

Easter: Peace be with you; *it* is I, * do not be afraid, al*l*eluia.

Ant. 2   Unless you acquire the heart *of* a child, * you cannot enter the
                 kingdom *of* God.

December 17-23: Zion is our mighty citadel, † our saving Lord its wall and its defense; † throw
                 op*en* the gates, * for our God is here among us, al*l*eluia.

Easter: Let Israel hope *in* the Lord, * al*l*eluia.

IIA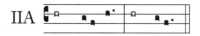

Psalm 131
Childlike trust in God
Learn from me, for I am gentle and humble of heart (Matthew 11:29).

O Lord, my heart *is* not proud * nor
haughty *my* eyes.
I have not gone after *things* too great *
nor marvels *be*yond me.
Truly I have *set* my soul * in silence *and*
peace.
As a child has rest in its *moth*er's arms, *

even so *my* soul.
O Israel, hope *in* the Lord * both now
and *for* ever.
Glory to the Father, and *to* the Son, *
and to the Ho*ly* Spirit:
as it was in the begin*ning*, is now, * and
will be for ever. *A*men.

Antiphon   Unless you acquire the heart *of* a child, * you cannot enter the
                 kingdom *of* God.

December 17-23: Zion is our mighty citadel, † our saving Lord its wall and its defense; † throw
                 op*en* the gates, * for our God is here among us, al*l*eluia.

Easter: Let Israel hope *in* the Lord, * al*l*eluia.

Ant. 3   Lord, you have made us *a* kingdom * and priests for God *our* Father.

December 17-23:   Lord, make known your will throughout *the* earth; * proclaim your salvation to *eve*ry nation.

Easter: Let all creation serve you, † for all things came into being at *your* word, * al*le*luia.

Canticle   Revelation 4:11; 5:9, 10, 12
Redemption Hymn

O Lord our God, you *are* worthy *
to receive glory and honor *and* power.

For you have created *all* things; * by your will they came to be and *were* made.

Worthy are you, O Lord, * to receive the scroll and break open *its* seals.

For you *were* slain; * with your blood you purchased *for* God

men of every race *and* tongue, * of every people *and* nation.

You made of them a kingdom, † and priests to serve *our* God, * and they shall reign on *the* earth.

Worthy is the Lamb that *was* slain * to receive power *and* riches,

wisdom *and* strength, * honor and glory *and* praise.

Glory to the Father, and to *the* Son, * and to the Ho*ly* Spirit:

as it was in the beginning, *is* now, * and will be for ever. *A*men.

Antiphon   Lord, you have made us *a* kingdom * and priests for God *our* Father.

December 17-23:   Lord, make known your will throughout *the* earth; * proclaim your salvation to *eve*ry nation.

Easter: Let all creation serve you, † for all things came into being at *your* word, * al*le*luia.

READING   Romans 12:9-12
Your love must be sincere. Detest what is evil, cling to what is good. Love one another with the affection of brothers. Anticipate each other in showing respect. Do not grow slack but be fervent in spirit; he whom you serve is the Lord. Rejoice in hope, be patient under trial, persevere in prayer.

RESPONSORY (VI F)
Through all eterni*ty*, O Lord, * your promise stands *un*shaken.
—Through all eterni*ty*, O Lord, * your promise stands *un*shaken.
Your faithfulness will *never* fail;
—your promise stands *un*shaken.
Glory to the Father, and *to* the Son, * and to the Ho*ly* Spirit.
—Through all eterni*ty*, O Lord, * your promise stands *un*shaken.

CANTICLE OF MARY
Antiphon   My spir*it* rejoices * in God *my* Savior.

INTERCESSIONS (VI F)
God establishes his peo*ple* in hope. * Let us cry out to *him* with joy:
*You are the hope of your peo*ple, *Lord.*
We *thank* you, Lord,
— because in Christ you have given us all the treasures of wis*dom* and knowledge.
O God, in your hands are the hearts of the powerful; bestow your wisdom upon
   go*vern*ment leaders,
— may they draw from the fountain of your counsel and please you in *thought* and
   deed.
The talents of artists re*flect* your splendor,
— may their work give the world *hope* and joy.
You do not allow us to be tested beyond *our* ability,
— strengthen the weak and raise *up* the fallen.
Through your Son you promised to raise men up *on* the Last Day.
— do not forget those *who* have died.

Our Father . . .

Prayer

   Lord,
      may our evening prayer rise up to you,
      and your blessing come down upon us.
      May your help and salvation be ours
      now and through all eternity.
      We ask this through our Lord Jesus Christ, your Son,
      who lives and reigns with you and the Holy Spirit,
      one God, for ever and ever.

WEDNESDAY, WEEK III

Morning Prayer

HYMN, 1321.
Nox et tenébræ et núbila. (L.M.)

Nox et tenebræ et núbila,
confúsa mundi et túrbida,
lux intrat, albéscit polus:
Christus venit; discédite.

When breaks the day, and dawn grows bright,
Christ nearer seems, the Light of Light:
From us, like shades that nighttime brings,
Drive forth, O Lord, all darksome things.

Calígo terræ scínditur
percússa solis spículo,
rebúsque iam color redit
vultu niténtis síderis.

Earth's dusky veil is torn away,
Pierced by the sparkling beams of day;
Our life resumes its hues apace,
Soon as the Daystar shows his face.

Sic nostra mox obscúritas
fraudísque pectus cónscium,
ruptis retéctum núbibus,
regnánte palléscet Deo.

So thee, O Christ, alone we seek,
With conscience pure and temper meek:
With tears and chants we humbly pray
That thou wouldst guide us through each day.

Te, Christe, solum nóvimus,
te mente pura et símplici
rogáre curváto genu
flendo et canéndo díscimus.

For many'a shade obscures each sense
Which needs thy beams to purge it thence;
Light of the Morning Star, thy grace
Shed on us from thy cloudless face.

Inténde nostris sénsibus
vitámque totam díspice:
sunt multa fucis íllita
quæ luce purgéntur tua.

All laud to God the Father be,
All praise, eternal Son, to thee;
All glory, as is ever meet,
To God the Holy Paraclete. Amen.

Sit, Christe, rex piíssime,
tibi Patríque glória
cum Spíritu Paráclito,
in sempitérna sæcula. Amen.

PSALMODY

Ant. 1   Give joy to your *servant*, Lord; * to you I lift *up* my heart.

December 17-23:   The Lord, the *migh*ty God, * will come forth from Zion to set his *peo*ple free.

Easter: People of every na*tion* shall come * and worship you, O Lord, a*l*leluia.

VIIIg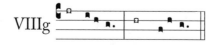

Psalm 86
The prayer of the poor man in distress
Blessed be God who comforts us in all our trials (2 Corinthians 1:3, 4).

Turn your ear, O Lord, *and* give answer * for I am *poor* and needy.

Preserve my life, for *I* am faithful: * save the servant who *trusts* in you.

You are my God, have mercy *on* me, Lord, * for I cry to you all *the* day long.

Give joy to your ser*vant*, O Lord, * for to you I lift *up* my soul.

O Lord, you are good *and* forgiving, * full of love to *all* who call.

Give heed, O Lord, *to* my prayer * and attend to the sound *of* my voice.

In the day of distress *I* will call * and surely you *will* reply.

Among the gods there is none like *you*, O Lord; * nor work to com*pare* with yours.

All the nations shall come *to* adore you * and glorify your *name*, O Lord:

for you are great and do mar*vel*lous deeds, * you who a*lone* are God.

Show me, Lord, your way † so that I may walk *in* your truth. * Guide my heart to *fear* your name.

I will praise you, Lord my God, with *all* my heart * and glorify your *name* for ever;

for your love to me *has* been great: * you have saved me from the depths *of* the grave.

The proud have risen against me; † ruthless men *seek* my life: * to you they *pay* no heed.

But you, God of mercy *and* compassion, * slow to an*ger*, O Lord,

abounding in *love* and truth, * turn and take pi*ty* on me.

O give your strength *to* your servant * and save your *hand*maid's son.

Show me a sign of your favor † that my foes may see *to* their shame * that you console me and give *me* your help.

Glory to the Father, and *to* the Son, * and to the *Holy* Spirit:

as it was in the begin*ning*, is now, * and will be for e*ver*. Amen.

Antiphon   Give joy to your ser*vant*, Lord; * to you I lift *up* my heart.

December 17-23:   The Lord, the *migh*ty God, * will come forth from Zion to set his *peo*ple free.

Easter: People of every na*tion* shall come * and worship you, O Lord, al*le*luia.

Ant. 2   Blessèd is the *up*right man, * who speaks *the* truth.

December 17-23:   I shall not cease to plead with *God* for Zion * until he sends his Holy One in all his ra*diant* beauty.

Easter: Our eyes will see the King in all his *ra*diant beauty, * al*le*luia.

IIA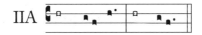

Canticle   Isaiah 33:13-16
God's flawless judgment
What God has promised is for you, for your children, and for those still far away
(Acts 2:39).

Hear, you who *are* far off, * what I *have* done;

you *who* are near, * acknowledge *my* might.

On Zion sinners *are* in dread, * trembling grips *the* impious;

"Who of us can live with the con*sum*-ing fire? * Who of us can live with the everlast*ing* flames?"
He who practices virtue *and* speaks honestly, * who spurns what is gained by *op*pression,
brush*ing* his hands * free of contact with *a* bribe,
stopping his ears lest he *hear* of blood-shed, * closing his eyes lest he look *on* evil.
He shall dwell *on* the heights, * his stronghold shall be the rock*y* fastness,
his *food* and drink * in steady *sup*ply.
Glory to the Father, and *to* the Son, * and to the Ho*ly* Spirit:
as it was in the begin*ning*, is now, * and will be for ever. *A*men.

Antiphon	Blessèd is the *up*right man, * who speaks *the* truth.
December 17-23:	I shall not cease to plead with *God* for Zion * until he sends his Holy One in all his ra*diant* beauty.
Easter:	Our eyes will see the King in all his *ra*diant beauty, * al*le*luia.

Ant. 3	Let us celebrate *with* joy * in the presence of our Lord *and* King.
December 17-23:	The Spirit of the Lord rests *up*on me; * he has sent me to preach his joyful message to *the* poor.
Easter:	All people will see the saving power *of* God, * al*le*luia.

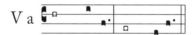

Psalm 98
The Lord triumphs in his judgment
This psalm tells of the Lord's first coming and that people of all nations will believe in him
(St. Athanasius).

Sing a new song to *the* Lord * for he has *worked* wonders.
His right hand and his ho*ly* arm * have brought sal*va*tion.
The Lord has made known his sal*va*tion; * has shown his justice to *the* nations.
He has remembered his truth *and* love * for the house *of* Israel.
All the ends of the earth *have* seen * the salvation of *our* God.
Shout to the Lord, all *the* earth, * ring out *your* joy.
Sing psalms to the Lord with *the* harp * with the sound *of* music.

With trumpets and the sound of *the* horn * acclaim the King, *the* Lord.
Let the sea and all within *it* thunder; * the world, and all *its* peoples.
Let the rivers clap *their* hands * and the hills ring out *their* joy.
Rejoice at the presence of *the* Lord, * for he comes to rule *the* earth.
He will rule the world *with* justice * and the peoples *with* fairness.
Glory to the Father, and to *the* Son, * and to the Ho*ly* Spirit:
as it was in the beginning, *is* now, * and will be for ever. *A*men.

Antiphon   Let us celebrate *with* joy * in the presence of our Lord *and* King.

December 17-23:   The Spirit of the Lord rests *upon* me; * he has sent me to preach his joyful message to *the* poor.

Easter: All people will see the saving power *of* God, * al*le*luia.

READING   Job 1:21; 2:10b

Naked I came forth from my mother's womb,
     and naked I shall go back again.
The Lord gave and the Lord has taken away;
     blessed be the name of the Lord!
We accept good things from God;
     and should we not accept evil?

RESPONSORY (VI F)

In*cline* my heart * according to your will, O God.
— In*cline* my heart * according to your will, O God.
Speed my steps a*long* your path,
— according to your will, O God.
Glory to the Father, and *to* the Son, * and to the Ho*ly* Spirit.
— In*cline* my heart * according to your will, O God.

CANTICLE OF ZECHARIAH

Antiphon   Show us your *mer*cy, Lord; * remember your ho*ly* covenant.

INTERCESSIONS (VI F)

Christ nourishes and supports the Church for which he gave himself *up* to death.
* In peace *let* us ask him:
Remember your Church, O Lord.
You are the Good Shepherd who has given life and *light* today,
— make us grateful *for* these gifts.
Look with mercy on the flock you have gathered together *in* your name,
— let no one whom the Father has giv*en* you perish.
Lead your Church in the way of *your* commandments,
— may your Holy Spirit *keep* her faithful.
Nourish the Church at the banquet of your *Word* and Bread,
— strengthened by this food may she follow *you* in joy.

Our Father . . .

Prayer

Lord,
as daylight fills the sky,
fill us with your holy light.
May our lives mirror our love for you
whose wisdom has brought us into being,
and whose care guides us on our way.
We ask this through our Lord Jesus Christ, your Son,
who lives and reigns with you and the Holy Spirit,
one God, for ever and ever.

WEDNESDAY, WEEK III

Evening Prayer

HYMN, 1322.
Cæli Deus sanctíssime. (L.M.)

Cæli Deus sanctíssime, Qui lúcidum centrum poli candóre pingis ígneo augens decóri lúmina,	O God, whose hand hath spread the sky And all its shining hosts on high, And painting it with fiery light, Made it so beauteous and so bright:
Quarto die qui flámmeam solis rotam constítuens, lunæ minístras órdini vagos recúrsus síderum,	Who, on the fourth day, didst reveal The sun's enkindled flaming wheel, Didst set the moon her ordered ways, And stars their ever-winding maze;
Ut nóctibus vel lúmini diremptiónis términum, primórdiis et ménsium signum dares notíssimum:	That each in its appointed way Might separate the night from day, And of the seasons through the year The well-remembered signs declare:
Illúmina cor hóminum, abstérge sordes méntium, resólve culpæ vínculum, evérte moles críminum.	Illuminate our hearts within, And cleanse our minds from stain of sin; Unburdened of our guilty load May we unfettered serve our God.
Præsta, Pater piíssime, Patríque compare Única, cum Spíritu Paráclito regnans per omne sæculum Amen.	O Father, that we ask be done, Through Jesus Christ, thine only Son; Who, with the Holy Ghost and thee, Doth live and reign eternally. Amen.

PSALMODY

Ant. 1   Those who *sow* in tears * will *reap* in joy.

December 17-23:   The Lord, the *migh*ty God, * will come forth from Zion to set his *peo*ple free.

Easter: Your sorrow *will* be turned * into joy, a*l*leluia.

VIIIg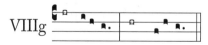

Psalm 126
Joyful hope in God
Just as you share in sufferings so you will share in the divine glory (2 Corinthians 1:7).

When the Lord delivered *Zion* from bondage, * it seemed *like a* dream.	Then was our mouth *filled* with laughter, * on our lips *there* were songs.

The heathens *them*selves said: * "What marvels the Lord *worked* for them!"
What marvels the Lord *worked* for us! * Indeed *we* were glad.
Deliver us, O Lord, *from* our bondage * as streams *in* dry land.
Those who are sow*ing* in tears * will sing *when* they reap.

They go out, they go out, *full* of tears, * carrying seed *for* the sowing:
they come back, they come back, *full* of song, * carry*ing* their sheaves.
Glory to the Father, and *to* the Son, * and to the *Ho*ly Spirit:
as it was in the begin*ning*, is now, * and will be for e*ver*. Amen.

Antiphon	Those who *sow* in tears * will *reap* in joy.
December 17-23:	The Lord, the *migh*ty God, * will come forth from Zion to set his *peo*ple free.
Easter:	Your sorrow *will* be turned * into joy, *al*leluia.

Ant. 2	May the Lord *build* our house * and guard *our* city.
December 17-23:	I shall not cease to plead with *God* for Zion * until he sends his Holy One in all his radi*ant* beauty.
Easter:	Whether we *live* or die, * we are the Lord's, al*le*luia.

II A

Psalm 127
Apart from God our labors are worthless
You are God's building (1 Corinthians 3:9).

If the Lord does not *build* the house, * in vain do its build*ers* labor;
if the Lord does not watch o*ver* the city, * in vain does the watchman *keep* vigil.
In vain is your ear*li*er rising, * your going later *to* rest,
you who toil for the *bread* you eat: * when he pours gifts on his belovèd while *they* slumber.
Truly sons are a gift *from* the Lord, * a blessing, the fruit of *the* womb.

Indeed the *sons* of youth * are like arrows in the hand of *a* warrior.
O the happiness *of* the man * who has filled his quiver with *these* arrows!
He will have no *cause* for shame * when he disputes with his foes in *the* gateways.
Glory to the Father, and *to* the Son, * and to the Ho*ly* Spirit:
as it was in the begin*ning*, is now, * and will be for ever. *A*men.

Antiphon	May the Lord *build* our house * and guard *our* city.
December 17-23:	I shall not cease to plead with *God* for Zion * until he sends his Holy One in all his radi*ant* beauty.
Easter:	Whether we *live* or die, * we are the Lord's, al*le*luia.

Ant. 3   He is the first-born of all *crea*tion; * in every way the primacy *is* his.

December 17-23:   The Spirit of the Lord rests *up*on me; * he has sent me to preach his joyful message to *the* poor.

Easter: From him, through him, and in him all things *ex*ist; * glory to him for ever, al*le*luia.

Va

Canticle   Colossians 1:12-20
Christ, the first-born of all creation and the first-born from the dead

Let us give thanks to the Father †
for having made *you* worthy * to
share the lot of the saints *in* light.

He rescued us from the power *of*
darkness * and brought us into the
kingdom of his belov*èd* Son.

Through him we have *re*demption, *
the forgiveness of *our* sins.

He is the image of the invisi*ble* God, *
the first-born of *all* creatures.

In him everything in heaven and on
earth † was *cre*ated, * things visible
and *in*visible.

All were created *through* him; * all were
created *for* him.

He is before all else *that* is. * In him

everything continues *in* being.

It is he who is head of the body, *the*
church! * he who is the *be*ginning,
the first-born of *the* dead, * so that
primacy may be his *in* everything.

It pleased God to make absolute
fullness reside in him † and, by means
of him, * to reconcile everything in *his*
person,
both on earth and in *the* heavens, *
making peace through the blood of
his cross.

Glory to the Father, and to *the* Son, *
and to the Ho*ly* Spirit,
as it was in the beginning, *is* now, * and
will be for ever. *A*men.

Antiphon   He is the first-born of all *crea*tion; * in every way the primacy *is* his.

December 17-23:   The Spirit of the Lord rests *up*on me; * he has sent me to preach his joyful message to *the* poor.

Easter: From him, through him, and in him all things *ex*ist; * glory to him for ever, al*le*luia.

READING   Ephesians 3:20-21

To God whose power now at work in us can do immeasurably more than we ask or imagine—to him be glory in the church and in Christ Jesus through all generations, world without end. Amen.

RESPONSORY (VI F)

Claim me once more *as* your own, Lord, * and have mercy *on* me.
— Claim me once more *as* your own, Lord, * and have mercy *on* me.
Do not abandon me *with* the wicked;
— have mercy *on* me.
Glory to the Father, and *to* the Son, * and to the Ho*ly* Spirit.
— Claim me once more *as* your own, Lord, * and have mercy *on* me.

CANTICLE OF MARY

Antiphon   The Almighty has done great *things* for me, * and holy is *his*
              Name.

INTERCESSIONS (VI F)

Let us humbly pray to God who *sent* his Son * as the Savior and exemplar *of* his
    people:
May your people praise you, Lord.
Let us give thanks to God who chose us as the first-fruits *of* salvation,
— and who called us to share in the glory of our Lord *Je*sus Christ.
May those who confess your holy name be united *in* your truth,
— and fervent *in* your love.
Creator of all things, your Son desired to work among men *with* his own hands,
— be mindful of all who earn their living by the sweat *of* their brow.
Be mindful of those who devote themselves to the service *of* their brothers,
— do not let them be deterred from their goals by discouraging results or lack *of*
    support.
Be merciful to the faith*ful* departed,
— keep them from the power *of* the Evil One.

Our Father . . .

Prayer

Merciful Lord,
let the evening prayer of your Church
come before you.
May we do your work faithfully;
free us from sin
and make us secure in your love.
We ask this through our Lord Jesus Christ, your Son,
who lives and reigns with you and the Holy Spirit,
one God, for ever and ever.

THURSDAY, WEEK III

Morning Prayer

HYMN, 1323.

Sol ecce surgit aurea. (L.M.)

Sol ecce surgit ígneus:
piget, pudéscit, pænitet,
nec teste quisquam lúmine
peccáre constánter potest.

Tandem facéssat cæcitas,
quae nosmet in præceps diu
lapsos sinístris gréssibus
erróre traxit dévio.

Hæc lux serénum cónferat
purósque nos præstet sibi;
nihil loquámur súbdolum,
volvámus obscúrum nihil.

Sic tota decúrrat dies,
ne lingua mendax, ne manus
oculíve peccent lúbrici,
ne noxa corpus ínquinet.

Speculátor astat désuper,
qui nos diébus ómnibus
actúsque nostros próspicit
a luce prima in vésperum.

Deo Patri sit glória
eiúsque soli Fílio
cum Spíritu Paráclito,
in sempitérna sǽcula. Amen.

Behold, the golden dawn arise;
The paling night forsakes the skies:
Those shades that hid the world from view,
And us to dangerous error drew.

May this new day be calmly passed,
May we keep pure while it shall last:
Nor let our lips from truth depart,
Nor dark designs engage the heart.

So may the day speed on; the tongue
No falsehood know, the hands no wrong:
Our eyes from wonton gaze refrain,
No guilt our guarded bodies stain.

For God all-seeing from on high
Surveys us with a watchful eye:
Each day our every act he knows
From early dawn to evening's close.

All laud to God the Father be;
All praise, eternal Son, to thee;
All glory, as is ever meet,
To God the Holy Paraclete. Amen.

PSALMODY

Ant. 1	Glorious things are *said* of you, * O ci*ty* of God.
December 17-23:	To you, O Lord, I lift up my soul; † come and *res*cue me, * for you are my refuge *and* my strength.
Easter:	City of God, you are the source *of* our life; * with music and dance we shall rejoice in you, *al*leluia.

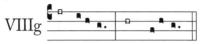

Psalm 87
Jerusalem is mother of us all
The heavenly Jerusalem is a free woman; she is our mother (Galatians 4:26).

On the holy mountain *is* his city *
cherished *by* the Lord.
The Lord prefers the *gates* of Zion * to
all *Jacob's* dwellings.
Of you are told glo*rious* things, * O ci*ty*
of God!
"Babylon and Egypt *I* will count *
among *those* who know me;
Philistia, Tyre, *E*thiopia, * these will *be*
her children
and Zion shall *be* called 'Mother' * for

all shall *be* her children."
It is he, the *Lord* Most High, * who
gives *each* his place.
In his register of peo*ples* he writes: *
"These *are* her children,"
and while they dance *they* will sing: *
"In you all *find* their home."
Glory to the Father, and *to* the Son, *
and to the *Ho*ly Spirit:
as it was in the begin*ning*, is now, * and
will be for e*ver*. Amen.

Antiphon	Glorious things are *said* of you, * O ci*ty* of God.
December 17-23:	To you, O Lord, I lift up my soul; † come and *res*cue me, * for you are my refuge *and* my strength.
Easter:	City of God, you are the source *of* our life; * with music and dance we shall rejoice in you, *al*leluia.

Ant. 2	The Lord, the mighty conquer*or*, will come; * he will bring with him the prize *of* victory.
December 17-23:	Bless those, O Lord, who have waited *for* your coming; * let your prophets be *proved* true.
Easter:	Like a shepherd he will gather the lambs *in* his arms * and carry them close to his heart, al*le*luia.

Canticle   Isaiah 40:10-17
The Good Shepherd: God most high and most wise
See, I come quickly; I have my reward in hand (Revelation 22:12).

Here comes with power *the*
Lord God, * who rules by his
strong arm;
here is his re*ward* with him, * his
recompense *be*fore him.
Like a shepherd he *feeds* his flock; * in
his arms he gathers *the* lambs,
carrying them *in* his bosom, * and
leading the ewes *with* care.
Who has cupped in his hand the
waters *of* the sea, * and marked off
the heavens with *a* span?
Who has held in a measure the dust of
the earth, † weighed the moun*tains*
in scales * and the hills in *a* balance?
Who has directed the spirit of the
Lord, † or has instructed him *as* his
counselor? * Whom did he consult to

gain knowledge?
Who taught him the *path* of judgment,
* or showed him the way of un*der*-
standing?
Behold, the nations count as a drop of
the bucket, † as dust *on* the scales; *
the coastlands weigh no more *than*
powder.
Lebanon would not suf*fice* for fuel, *
nor its animals be enough *for* holocausts.
Before him all the nations *are* as
nought, * as nothing and void he
*ac*counts them.
Glory to the Father, and *to* the Son, *
and to the Ho*ly* Spirit:
as it was in the begin*ning*, is now, * and
will be for ever. *A*men.

Antiphon   The Lord, the mighty conquer*or*, will come; * he will bring with
him the prize *of* victory.

December 17-23: Bless those, O Lord, who have waited *for* your coming; * let your prophets be
proved true.

Easter: Like a shepherd he will gather the lambs *in* his arms * and carry them close to
his heart, al*le*luia.

Ant. 3   Give praise to the Lord *our* God, * bow down before his ho*ly*
mountain.

December 17-23: Turn to us, O Lord, * make haste to help *your* people.

Easter: Great is the Lord *in* Zion; * he is exalted above all the peoples, al*le*luia.

V a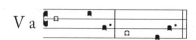

Psalm 99
Holy is the Lord our God
*Christ, higher than the Cherubim, when you took our lowly nature you transformed
our sinful world* (St. Athanasius).

The Lord is king; the peoples
tremble. † He is throned on the
cherubim; the *earth* quakes. * The
Lord is great *in* Zion.
He is supreme over all the peoples. †
Let them praise his name, so terrible

and great. * He is holy, full *of* power.
You are a king who loves what is right;
† you have established equity, justice
and right; * you have established
them *in* Jacob.
Exalt the Lord our God; † bow down

before Zion, *his* footstool. * He the Lord *is* holy.
Among his priests were Aaron and Moses, † among those who invoked his name *was* Samuel. * They invoked the Lord and *he* answered.
To them he spoke in the pillar of cloud. † They did his will; they kept *the* law, * which he, the Lord, *had* given.
O Lord our God, you answered them. †

For them you were a God who *for*gives; * yet you punished all their *off*enses.
Exalt the Lord our God; † bow down before his ho*ly* mountain * for the Lord our God *is* holy.
Glory to the Father, and to *the* Son, * and to the Ho*ly* Spirit:
as it was in the beginning, *is* now, * and will be for ever. *A*men.

Antiphon Give praise to the Lord *our* God, * bow down before his ho*ly* mountain.

December 17-23: Turn to us, O Lord, * make haste to help *your* people.

Easter: Great is the Lord *in* Zion; * he is exalted above all the peoples, al*le*luia.

READING   1 Peter 4:10-11a

As generous distributors of God's manifold grace, put your gifts at the service of one another, each in the measure he has received. The one who speaks is to deliver God's message. The one who serves is to do it with the strength provided by God. Thus, in all of you God is to be glorified through Jesus Christ.

RESPONSORY (VI F)
From the depths of my heart I *cry* to you; * hear me, O Lord.
— From the depths of my heart I *cry* to you; * hear me, O Lord.
I will do what *you* desire;
— hear me, O Lord.
Glory to the Father, and *to* the Son, * and to the Ho*ly* Spirit.
— From the depths of my heart I *cry* to you; * hear me, O Lord.

CANTICLE OF ZECHARIAH
Antiphon Let us serve the *Lord* in holiness, * and he will save us from *our* enemies.

INTERCESSIONS (VI F)
Let us joyfully cry out in thanks to *God* the Father * whose love guides and nourish*es* his people:
May you be glorified, Lord, for all ages.
Most merciful Father, we praise you *for* your love,
— for you wondrously created us and even more wondrously restored *us* to grace.
At the beginning of this day fill our hearts with *zeal* for serving you,
— so that our thoughts and actions may redound *to* your glory.

Purify our hearts of every e*vil* desire,
— make us intent on do*ing* your will.
Open our hearts to the needs *of* all men,
— fill us with bro*ther*ly love.

Our Father . . .

Prayer

All-powerful and ever-living God,
shine with the light of your radiance
on a people who live in the shadow of death.
Let the dawn from on high break upon us:
your Son our Lord Jesus Christ,
who lives and reigns with you and the Holy Spirit,
one God, for ever and ever.

THURSDAY, WEEK III

Evening Prayer

HYMN, 1324.
Magnæ Deus poténtiæ. (L.M.)

Magnæ Deus poténtiæ,	Almighty God, whose will supreme
Qui ex aquis ortum genus	Made ocean's flood with life to teem;
partim remíttis gúrgiti,	Part in the firmament to fly,
partim levas in áera,	And part in ocean depth to lie:
Demérsa lymphis imprimens,	Appointing fishes in the sea,
subvécta cælis írrogans,	And fowls in open air to be;
ut, stirpe una pródita,	That each, by origin the same,
divérsa répleant loca:	Its separate dwelling place might claim:
Largire cunctis sérvulis,	Grant that thy servants by the tide
quos mundat unda sánguinis,	Of Blood and Water purified
nescire lapsus críminum	No guilty fall from thee may know,
nec ferre mortis tædium,	Nor death eternal undergo.
Ut culpa nullum déprimat,	Let none despair through sin's distress,
nullum levet iactántia,	Be none puffed up with boastfulness;
elisa mens ne cóncidat,	That contrite hearts be not dismayed,
elata mens ne córruat.	Nor haughty souls in ruin laid.
Præsta, Pater piíssime,	O Father, that we ask be done,
Patrique compare Únice,	Through Jesus Christ, thine only Son;
cum Spíritu Paráclito	Who, with the Holy Ghost and thee,
regnans per omne sæculum Amen.	Doth live and reign eternally. Amen.

PSALMODY

Ant. 1   Let your holy people re*joice*, O Lord, * as they enter your *dwell*ing place.

December 17-23:   To you, O Lord, I lift up my soul; † come and *rescue* me, * for you are my refuge *and* my strength.

Easter: The Lord God has given *him* the throne * of David his father, *al*leluia.

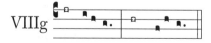

Psalm 132
God's promises to the house of David
The Lord God will give him the throne of his ancestor David (Luke 1:32).

789

I

O Lord, remember David * and all
the many hardships he endured,
the oath he swore to the Lord, * his
vow to the Strong One of Jacob.
"I will not enter the house where I live *
nor go to the bed where I rest.
I will give no sleep to my eyes, * to my
eyelids I will give no slumber
till I find a place for the Lord, * a
dwelling for the Strong One of
Jacob."
At Ephrathah we heard of the ark; * we
found it in the plains of Yearìm.

"Let us go to the place of his dwelling; *
let us go to kneel at his footstool."
Go up, Lord, to the place of your rest, *
you and the ark of your strength.
Your priests shall be clothed with
holiness: * your faithful shall ring out
their joy.
For the sake of David your servant * do
not reject your anointed.
Glory to the Father, and to the Son, *
and to the Holy Spirit:
as it was in the beginning, is now, * and
will be for ever. Amen.

Antiphon   Let your holy people rejoice, O Lord, * as they enter your
                  dwelling place.
December 17-23:   To you, O Lord, I lift up my soul; † come and rescue me, * for you are my
                  refuge and my strength.
Easter: The Lord God has given him the throne * of David his father, alleluia.

Ant. 2   The Lord has chosen Zion * as his sanctuary.
December 17-23:   Bless those, O Lord, who have waited for your coming; * let your prophets be
                   proved true.
Easter: Jesus Christ is supreme in his power. * He is King of kings and Lord of lords,
                   alleluia.

IIA

II

The Lord swore an oath to David; *
he will not go back on his word:
"A son, the fruit of your body, * will I set
upon your throne.
If they keep my covenant in truth * and
my laws that I have taught them,
their sons also shall rule * on your
throne from age to age."
For the Lord has chosen Zion; * he has
desired it for his dwelling:
"This is my resting-place for ever, * here
have I chosen to live.
I will greatly bless her produce, * I will

fill her poor with bread.
I will clothe her priests with salvation *
and her faithful shall ring out their
joy.
There David's stock will flower: * I will
prepare a lamp for my anointed.
I will cover his enemies with shame *
but on him my crown shall shine."
Glory to the Father, and to the Son, *
and to the Holy Spirit:
as it was in the beginning, is now, * and
will be for ever. Amen.

Antiphon	The Lord has *cho*sen Zion * as *his* sanctuary.
December 17-23:	Bless those, O Lord, who have waited *for* your coming; * let your prophets be *proved* true.
Easter:	Jesus Christ is supreme *in* his power. * He is King of kings and Lord of lords, al*le*luia.

Ant. 3	The Father has given Christ all power, honor *and* kingship; * all people will *o*bey him.
December 17-23:	Turn to us, O Lord, * make haste to help *your* people.
Easter:	Lord, who is your equal *in* power? * Who is like you, majestic in holiness? al*le*luia.

V a

Canticle Revelation 11:17-18; 12:10b-12a

The judgment of God

We praise you, the Lord God *Al*mighty, * who is and *who* was.
You have assumed your *great* power, *
  you have begun *your* reign.
The nations have raged *in* anger, * but
  then came your day *of* wrath
and the moment to judge *the* dead: * the
  time to reward your servants *the*
  prophets
and the holy ones who *re*vere you, * the
  great and the small *a*like.
Now have salvation and po*wer* come, *
  the reign of our God and the authority of his *A*nointed One.

For the accuser of our brothers is *cast*
  out, * who night and day accused
  them be*fore* God.
They defeated him by the blood of *the*
  Lamb * and by the word of *their*
  testimony;
love for life did not deter them from
  death. † So rejoice, *you* heavens, *
  and you that dwell *there*in!
Glory to the Father, and to *the* Son, *
  and to the Ho*ly* Spirit:
as it was in the beginning, *is* now, * and
  will be for ever. *A*men.

Antiphon	The Father has given Christ all power, honor *and* kingship; * all people will *o*bey him.
December 17-23:	Turn to us, O Lord, * make haste to help *your* people.
Easter:	Lord, who is your equal *in* power? * Who is like you, majestic in holiness? al*le*luia.

READING 1 Peter 3:8-9

All of you should be like-minded, sympathetic, loving toward one another, kindly disposed, and humble. Do not return evil for evil or insult for insult. Return a blessing instead. This you have been called to do, that you may receive a blessing as your inheritance.

RESPONSORY (VI F)

The Lord has giv*en* us food, * bread of the fin*est* wheat.
— The Lord has giv*en* us food, * bread of the fin*est* wheat.
Honey from the rock to our *heart's* content,
— bread of the fin*est* wheat.
Glory to the Father, and *to* the Son, * and to the Ho*ly* Spirit.
— The Lord has giv*en* us food, * bread of the fin*est* wheat.

CANTICLE OF MARY

Antiphon   God has cast down the mighty *from* their thrones, *
                and has lifted up *the* lowly.

INTERCESSIONS (VI F)

Let us call upon Christ, *the* good Shepherd * who comes to the aid *of* his people:
Hear us, O God our *refuge.*
Blessèd are you, Lord, for you graciously called us into your *holy* Church,
— keep us within the Church *un*til death.
You have given the care of all the churches to *N.,* our Pope,
— give him unfailing faith, lively hope and lov*ing* concern.
Grant the grace of conversion *to* all sinners,
— and the grace of true repentance *to* all men.
You were willing to live as a stranger *in* our world,
— be mindful of those who are separated from fami*ly* and homeland.
To all the departed who have *hoped* in you,
— grant e*ter*nal peace.

Our Father . . .

Prayer

Lord,
we thank you for guiding us
through the course of this day's work.
In your compassion forgive the sins
we have committed through human weakness.
We ask this through our Lord Jesus Christ, your Son,
who lives and reigns with you and the Holy Spirit,
one God, for ever and ever.

FRIDAY, WEEK III

Morning Prayer

HYMN, 1325.

Ætérna cæli glória. (L.M.)

Ætérna cæli glória,	Eternal glory of the sky,
beáta spes mortálium,	Blest hope of frail humanity,
celsi Paréntis Únice	The Father's sole-begotten One,
castæque proles Vírginis,	Yet born a spotless Virgin's Son!
Da déxteram surgéntibus,	Uplift us with thine arm of might,
exsúrgat et mens sóbria	And let our hearts rise pure and bright,
flagrans et in laudem Dei	And, ardent in God's praises, pay
grates repéndat débitas.	The thanks we owe him every day.
Ortus refúlget Lúcifer	The day-star's rays are glittering clear,
ipsámque lucem núntiat,	And tell that day itself is near:
cadit calígo nóctium,	The shadows of the night depart;
lux sancta nos illúminet,	Thou, holy Light, illume the heart!
Manénsque nostris sénsibus	Within our senses ever dwell,
noctem repéllat sæculi	And worldly darkness thence expel;
omníque fine témporis	Long as the days of life endure,
purgáta servet péctora.	Preserve our souls devout and pure.
Quæsíta iam primum fides	The faith that first must be possest,
radícet altis sénsibus,	Root deep within our inmost breast;
secúnda spes congáudeat;	And joyous hope in second place,
tunc maior exstat cáritas.	Then charity, thy greatest grace.
Sit, Christe, rex piíssime,	All laud to God the Father be;
tibi Patríque glória	All praise, eternal Son, to thee;
cum Spíritu Paráclito,	All glory, as is ever meet,
in sempitérna sæcula. Amen.	To God the Holy Paraclete. Amen.

PSALMODY

Ant. 1	You alone I have grieved *by* my sin; * have pity on *me*, O Lord.
December 17-23:	Our King will *come* from Zion; * the Lord, God-is-with-us, is his *migh*ty name.
Easter:	Lord, *wash* away * my guilt, a*l*leluia.

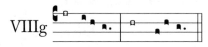

VIIIg

Psalm 51
O God, have mercy on me
Your inmost being must be renewed, and you must put on the new man
(Ephesians 4:23-24).

Have mercy on me, God, *in* your kindness. * In your compassion blot out *my* offense.

O wash me more and more *from* my guilt * and cleanse me *from* my sin.

My offenses tru*ly* I know them; * my sin is al*ways* before me.

Against you, you alone, *have* I sinned; * what is evil in your sight *I* have done.

That you may be justified when *you* give sentence * and be without reproach *when* you judge.

O see, in guilt *I* was born, * a sinner was *I* conceived.

Indeed you love truth *in* the heart; * then in the secret of my heart *teach* me wisdom.

O purify me, then I *shall* be clean; * O wash me, I shall be whi*ter* than snow.

Make me hear rejoic*ing* and gladness, * that the bones you have crushed *may* revive.

From my sins turn a*way* your face * and blot out *all* my guilt.

A pure heart create for *me*, O God, * put a steadfast spi*rit* within me.

Do not cast me away *from* your presence, * nor deprive me of your *holy* spirit.

Give me again the joy *of* your help; * with a spirit of fer*vor* sustain me,

that I may teach transgres*sors* your ways * and sinners may re*turn* to you.

O rescue me, *God*, my helper, * and my tongue shall ring *out* your goodness.

O Lord, o*pen* my lips * and my mouth shall de*clare* your praise.

For in sacrifice you take *no* delight, * burnt offering from me you *would* refuse,

my sacrifice, a *con*trite spirit. * A humbled, contrite heart you *will* not spurn.

In your goodness, show fa*vor* to Zion: * rebuild the walls *of* Jerusalem.

Then you will be pleased with *lawful* sacrifice, * holocausts offered *on* your altar.

Glory to the Father, and *to* the Son, * and to the *Holy* Spirit:

as it was in the begin*ning*, is now, * and will be for e*ver*. Amen.

Antiphon	You alone I have grieved *by* my sin; * have pity on *me*, O Lord.
December 17-23:	Our King will *come* from Zion; * the Lord, God-is-with-us, is his *migh*ty name.
Easter:	Lord, *wash* away * my guilt, a*l*leluia.

Ant. 2   Truly we know our *offen*ses, Lord, * for we have sinned *a*gainst
                you.

December 17-23: Wait for the Lord and he will *come* to you * with his sav*ing* power.

Easter: Christ bore our sins in *his* own body * as he hung upon the cross, al*le*luia.

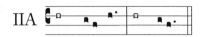

Canticle   Jeremiah 14:17-21
The lament of the people in war and famine
The kingdom of God is at hand (Mark 1:15).

Let my eyes *stream* with tears * day
and night, with*out* rest,
over the great destruction which
overwhelms † the virgin daughter *of*
my people, * over her incura*ble*
wound.
If I walk out in*to* the field, * look! those
slain by *the* sword;
if I en*ter* the city, * look! those con-
sumed *by* hunger.
Even the prophet *and* the priest *
forage in a land they *know* not.
Have you cast Judah *off* completely? * Is
Zion loathsome *to* you?
Why have you struck *us* a blow * that

cannot *be* healed?
We wait for peace, to *no* avail; * for a
time of healing, but *terror* comes
in*stead*.
We recognize, O Lord, our wickedness,
† the guilt *of* our fathers; * that we
have sinned *a*gainst you.
For your name's sake spurn us not, †
disgrace not the throne *of* your glory;
* remember your covenant with us,
and break *it* not.
Glory to the Father, and *to* the Son, *
and to the Ho*ly* Spirit:
as it was in the begin*ning*, is now, * and
will be for ever. *A*men.

Antiphon   Truly we know our *offen*ses, Lord, * for we have sinned *a*gainst
               you.

December 17-23: Wait for the Lord and he will *come* to you * with his sav*ing* power.

Easter: Christ bore our sins in *his* own body * as he hung upon the cross, al*le*luia.

Ant. 3   The Lord is God; we are *his* people, * the flock *he* shepherds.

December 17-23: Eagerly I watch for the Lord; † I wait in joy*ful* hope * for the coming of God
                my Savior.

Easter: Come into the *Lord's* presence * singing for joy, al*le*luia.

Psalm 100
The joyful song of those entering God's Temple
The Lord calls his ransomed people to sing songs of victory (St. Athanasius).

Cry out with joy to the Lord, all the earth. † Serve the Lord *with* gladness. * Come before him, singing *for* joy.
Know that he, the Lord, is God. † He made us, we belong *to* him, * we are his people, the sheep of *his* flock.
Go within his gates, giving thanks. † Enter his courts with songs *of* praise.

* Give thanks to him and bless *his* name.
Indeed, how good is the Lord, † eternal his merci*ful* love. * He is faithful from age *to* age.
Glory to the Father, and to *the* Son, * and to the Ho*ly* Spirit:
as it was in the beginning, *is* now, * and will be for ever. *A*men.

Antiphon   The Lord is God; we are *his* people, * the flock *he* shepherds.
December 17-23:   Eagerly I watch for the Lord; † I wait in joy*ful* hope * for the coming of God *my* Savior.
Easter: Come into the *Lord's* presence * singing for joy, al*le*luia.

READING   2 Corinthians 12:9b-10
I willingly boast of my weakness, that the power of Christ may rest upon me. Therefore I am content with weakness, with mistreatment, with distress, with persecutions and difficulties for the sake of Christ; for when I am powerless, it is then that I am strong.

RESPONSORY (VI F)
At day*break*, O Lord, * be merciful *to* me.
— At day*break*, O Lord, * be merciful *to* me.
Make known to me the path that *I* must walk.
— Be merciful *to* me.
Glory to the Father, and *to* the Son, * and to the Ho*ly* Spirit.
— At day*break*, O Lord, * be merciful *to* me.

CANTICLE OF ZECHARIAH
Antiphon   The Lord has come *to* his people * and set *them* free.

INTERCESSIONS (VI F)
Raising our eyes to Christ, who was born and died and rose again *for* his people, * let *us* cry out:
Save those you have redeemed by your blood, O Lord.
Blessèd are you, Jesus, redeemer of mankind; you did not hesitate to undergo your pas*sion* and death,
— to redeem us by your *precious* blood.
You promised that you would provide living water, the fountain of e*ter*nal life,
— pour forth your Spirit up*on* all men.
You send disciples to preach the Gospel *to* all nations,
— help them to extend the victory *of* your cross.

You have given the sick and the suffering a share *in* your cross,
—give them pa*tience* and strength.

Our Father . . .

Prayer

Father all-powerful,
let your radiance dawn in our lives,
that we may walk in the light of your law
with you as our leader.
We ask this through our Lord Jesus Christ, your Son,
who lives and reigns with you and the Holy Spirit,
one God, for ever and ever.

FRIDAY, WEEK III

Evening Prayer

HYMN, 1327.
Plasmátor hóminis, Deus. (L.M.)

Plasmátor hóminis, Deus, qui, cuncta solus órdinans, humum iubes prodúcere reptántis et feræ genus;	Maker of men, who from thy throne Dost order all things, God alone; By whose decree the teeming earth To reptile and to beast gave birth:
Qui magna rerum córpora, dictum iubéntis vívida, ut sérviant per órdinem subdens dedísti hómini:	The mighty forms that fill the land, Instinct with life at thy command, Are giv'n subdued to humankind For service in their rank assigned.
Repélle a servis tuis quicquid per immundítiam aut moribus se sí súggerit, aut actibus *se* intérserit.	From all thy servants drive away Whate'er of thought impure today Hath been with open action blent, Or mingled with the heart's intent.
Da gaudiórum præmia, da grátiarum múnera; dissólve litis víncula, astrínge pacis foedera.	In heav'n thine endless joys bestow, And grant thy gifts of grace below; From chains of strife our souls release, Bind fast the gentle bands of peace.
Præsta, Pater piíssime, Patríque compare Únice, cum Spíritu Paráclito regnans per omne sæculum Amen.	O Father, that we ask be done, Through Jesus Christ, thine only Son; Who, with the Holy Ghost and thee, Doth live and reign eternally. Amen.

PSALMODY

Ant. 1   Great is the *Lord*, our God, * transcending all *o*ther gods.

December 17-23:   Our King will *come* from Zion; * the Lord, God-is-with-us, is his *migh*ty name.

Easter: I, the Lord, *am* your savior * and redeemer, *al*leluia.

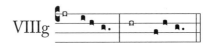

VIIIg

Psalm 135
Praise for the wonderful things God does for us
*He has won us for himself…and you must proclaim what he has done for you. He has called you
out of darkness into his own wonderful light* (see 1 Peter 2:9).

I

Praise the name *of* the Lord, *
 praise him, servants *of* the Lord,
who stand in the house *of* the Lord * in
 the courts of the house *of* our God.
Praise the Lord for the *Lord* is good. *
 Sing a psalm to his name for *he* is
 loving.
For the Lord has chosen Jacob *for*
 himself * and Israel for his *own*
 possession.
For I know the *Lord* is great, * that our
 Lord is high a*bove* all gods.
The Lord does what*ever* he wills, * in
 heaven, on earth, *in* the seas.
He summons clouds from the ends of
 the earth; † makes lightning pro*duce*
 the rain; * from his treasuries he

sends *forth* the wind.
The first-born of the Egypt*ians* he
 smote, * of man and *beast* alike.
Signs and wonders he worked † in the
 midst of your *land*, O Egypt, * against
 Pharaoh and *all* his servants.
Nations in their great*ness* he struck *
 and kings in their splend*or* he slew.
Sihon, king of the Amorites, † Og, the
 king of Bashan, * and all the king*doms*
 of Canaan.
He let Israel inher*it* their land; * on his
 people their land *he* bestowed.
Glory to the Father, and *to* the Son, *
 and to the *Holy* Spirit:
as it was in the begin*ning*, is now, * and
 will be for e*ver*. Amen.

Antiphon   Great is the *Lord*, our God, * transcending all *other* gods.

December 17-23:   Our King will *come* from Zion; * the Lord, God-is-with-us, is his *migh*ty name.

Easter: I, the Lord, *am* your savior * and redeemer, a*lle*luia.

Ant. 2   House of Israel, *bless* the Lord! * Sing psalms to him, for he *is*
 merciful.

December 17-23:   Wait for the Lord and he will *come* to you * with his sav*ing* power.

Easter: Bless*èd* is the kingdom of Dav*id* our father * which has come among us,
 al*le*luia.

IIA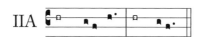

II

Lord, your name *stands* for ever, *
 unforgotten from age *to* age:
for the Lord does justice *for* his people;
 * the Lord takes pity on *his* servants.
Pagan idols are sil*ver* and gold, * the
 work of hu*man* hands.
They have mouths but they *can*not
 speak; * they have eyes but they
 *can*not see.
They have ears but they *can*not hear; *
 there is never a breath on *their* lips.
Their makers will come to *be* like them

* and so will all who trust *in* them!
Sons of Israel, *bless* the Lord! * Sons of
 Aaron, bless *the* Lord!
Sons of Levi, *bless* the Lord! * You who
 fear him, bless *the* Lord!
From Zion may the *Lord* be blessed, *
 he who dwells in *Jerusalem!*
Glory to the Father, and *to* the Son, *
 and to the Ho*ly* Spirit:
as it was in the begin*ning*, is now, * and
 will be for ever. *A*men.

Antiphon	House of Israel, *bless* the Lord! * Sing psalms to him, for he *is* merciful.
December 17-23:	Wait for the Lord and he will *come* to you * with his sav*ing* power.
Easter:	Blessèd is the kingdom of Dav*id* our father * which has come among us, al*le*luia.

Ant. 3	All nations will come *and* worship * before you, O Lord.
December 17-23:	Eagerly I watch for the Lord; † I wait in joy*ful* hope * for the coming of God *my* Savior.
Easter:	Let us sing to the Lord, glorious in *his* triumph, * al*le*luia.

Va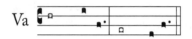

Canticle   Revelation 15:3-4
Hymn of adoration

Mighty and wonderful are *your* works, * Lord God *Al*mighty!
Righteous and true are *your* ways, * O King of *the* nations!
Who would dare refuse *you* honor, * or the glory due your name, O Lord?
Since you alone *are* holy, * all nations shall come and worship in *your* presence.
Your mighty deeds * are clear*ly* seen.
Glory to the Father, and to *the* Son, * and to the Ho*ly* Spirit:
as it was in the beginning, *is* now, * and will be for ever. *A*men.

Antiphon	All nations will come *and* worship * before you, O Lord.
December 17-23:	Eagerly I watch for the Lord; † I wait in joy*ful* hope * for the coming of God *my* Savior.
Easter:	Let us sing to the Lord, glorious in *his* triumph, * al*le*luia.

READING   James 1:2-4

My brothers, count it pure joy when you are involved in every sort of trial. Realize that when your faith is tested this makes for endurance. Let endurance come to its perfection so that you may be fully mature and lacking in nothing.

RESPONSORY (VI F)
Christ loved us and washed a*way* our sins, * in his *own* blood.
— Christ loved us and washed a*way* our sins, * in his *own* blood.
He made us a nation of *kings* and priests,
— in his *own* blood.
Glory to the Father, and *to* the Son, * and to the Ho*ly* Spirit.
— Christ loved us and washed a*way* our sins, * in his *own* blood.

CANTICLE OF MARY

Antiphon   The Lord has come to the help *of* his servants, * for he has
             remembered his promise *of* mercy.

INTERCESSIONS (VI F)

Because of our sins the Father gave the Lord Jesus up to death, and for our
    justification he raised him *up* again. * In peace *let* us pray:
*Have mercy on your peo*ple, *Lord.*
Hear our prayers and spare us as we con*fess* our sins,
— grant us forgive*ness* and peace.
Your Apostle, said: "Where sin abounds, grace abounds *all* the more,"
— forgive us *our* transgressions.
Lord, we have sinned, yet we have also acknowledged your in*fi*nite mercy,
— bring us *to* conversion.
Save your people from their *sins*, O Lord,
— make them pleas*ing* to you.
You opened Paradise to the thief who be*lieved* in you,
— do not close the gates of heaven to the faith*ful* departed.

Our Father ...

                                 Prayer

       Father,
       in your loving plan
       Christ your Son became the price of our salvation.
       May we be united with him in his suffering
       so that we may experience
       the power of his resurrection
       in the kingdom
       where he lives and reigns with you and the Holy Spirit,
       one God, for ever and ever.

SATURDAY, WEEK III

Morning Prayer

HYMN, 1328.

Aurora iam spargit polum. (L.M.)

Aurora iam spargit polum,	The dawn is sprinkling in the east
terris dies illábitur,	Its golden shower, as day flows in;
lucis resúltat spéculum:	Fast mount the pointed shafts of light:
discédat omne lúbricum.	Farewell to darkness and to sin!
Iam vana noctis décidant,	Away, ye midnight phantoms all!
mentis reátus súbruat,	Away, despondence and despair!
quicquid tenébris hórridum	Whatever guilt the night has brought
nox áttulit culpæ, cadat,	Now let it vanish into air.
Ut mane illud últimum,	So, that last morning, dread and great,
quod præstolámur cérnui,	Which we with trembling hope await,
in lucem nobis éffluat,	With blessèd light for us shall glow
dum hoc canóre cóncrepat.	Who chant the song we sang below:
Deo Patri sit glória	All laud to God the Father be;
eiúsque soli Fílio	All praise, eternal Son, to thee;
cum Spíritu Paráclito,	All glory, as is ever meet,
in sempitérna sæcula. Amen.	To God the Holy Paraclete. Amen.

PSALMODY

Ant. 1   Lord, *you* are near to us, * and all your *ways* are true.

December 17-23:   Our God will *come* from Lebanon; * he shall be as brilliant *as* the sun.

Easter: The words I have spok*en* to you * are spirit and life, *al*leluia.

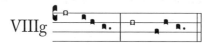

VIIIg

Psalm 119:145-152
XIX (Koph)

I call with all my *heart*; Lord, hear me, * I will keep *your* commands.	pon*der* your promise.
	In your love hear my *voice*, O Lord; * give me life by *your* decrees.
I call up*on* you, save me * and I will *do* your will.	Those who harm me unjust*ly* draw near: * they are far *from* your law.
I rise before dawn and *cry* for help, * I hope *in* your word.	But you, O *Lord*, are close: * your com*mands* are truth.
My eyes watch *through* the night * to	

Long have I known *that* your will * is
  esta*blished* for ever.
Glory to the Father, and *to* the Son, *

and to the *Holy* Spirit:
  as it was in the begin*ning*, is now, * and
  will be for *ever*. Amen.

Antiphon   Lord, *you* are near to us, * and all your *ways* are true.
December 17-23:   Our God will *come* from Lebanon; * he shall be as brilliant *as* the sun.

Easter: The words I have spok*en* to you * are spirit and life, a*l*leluia.

Ant. 2   Wisdom of *God*, be with me, * always at work *in* me.
December 17-23:   May the Holy One from heaven come down like gentle rain; † may the earth
                burst *into* blossom * and bear the ten*der* Savior.

Easter: Lord, you have built your temple and altar on your *holy* mountain, * al*l*eluia.

IIA

Canticle   Wisdom 9:1-6, 9-11
Lord, give me wisdom
I will inspire you with wisdom which your adversaries will be unable to resist (Luke 21:15).

God of my fathers, *Lord* of mercy,
  * you who have made all things
by *your* word
and in your wisdom have e*stab*lished
  man * to rule the creatures produced
  by you,
to govern the world in holi*ness* and
  justice, * and to render judgment in
  integrity *of* heart:
Give me Wisdom, the attendant *at*
  your throne, * and reject me not from
  among *your* children;
for I am your servant, the son of your
  handmaid, † a man weak *and* short-
  lived * and lacking in comprehension
  of judgment and *of* laws.
Indeed, though one be perfect among
  the sons of men, † if Wisdom, who
  comes from you, *be* not with him, * he
  shall be held in no *es*teem.

Now with you is Wisdom, who *knows*
  your works * and was present when
  you made *the* world;
who understands what is pleasing *in*
  your eyes * and what is conformable
  with your *com*mands.
Send her forth from your *holy* heavens *
  and from your glorious throne
  *dis*patch her
that she may be with *me* and work with
  me, * that I may know what is *your*
  pleasure.
For she knows and understands all
  things, † and will guide me discreetly
  in *my* affairs * and safeguard me by
  her glory.
Glory to the Father, and *to* the Son, *
  and to the Ho*ly* Spirit:
as it was in the begin*ning*, is now, * and
  will be for ever. *A*men.

Antiphon   Wisdom of *God*, be with me, * always at work *in* me.
December 17-23:   May the Holy One from heaven come down like gentle rain; † may the earth
                burst *into* blossom * and bear the ten*der* Savior.

Easter: Lord, you have built your temple and altar on your *holy* mountain, * al*l*eluia.

Ant. 3   The Lord re*mains* faithful * to his promise *for* ever.
December 17-23:   Israel, prepare yourself to meet *the* Lord, * for he *is* coming.
Easter: I am the way, the truth and *the* life, * al*le*luia.

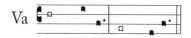

Psalm 117
Praise for God's loving compassion
I affirm that…the Gentile peoples are to praise God because of his mercy (Romans 15:8-9).

O praise the Lord, all *you* nations, *
acclaim him, all *you* peoples!
Strong is his love *for* us; * he is faithful
for ever.

Glory to the Father, and to *the* Son, *
and to the Ho*ly* Spirit:
as it was in the beginning, *is* now, * and
will be for ever. *A*men.

Antiphon   The Lord re*mains* faithful * to his promise *for* ever.
December 17-23:   Israel, prepare yourself to meet *the* Lord, * for he *is* coming.
Easter: I am the way, the truth and *the* life, * al*le*luia.

READING   Philippians 2:14-15
In everything you do, act without grumbling or arguing; prove yourselves
innocent and straightforward, children of God beyond reproach in the midst
of a twisted and depraved generation – among whom you shine like the stars
in the sky.

RESPONSORY (VI F)
I cry to *you*, O Lord, * for you are *my* refuge.
— I cry to *you*, O Lord, * for you are *my* refuge.
You are all I desire in the land *of* the living,
— for you are *my* refuge.
Glory to the Father, and *to* the Son, * and to the Ho*ly* Spirit.
— I cry to *you*, O Lord, * for you are *my* refuge.

CANTICLE OF ZECHARIAH
Antiphon   Lord, shine on those who *dwell* in darkness * and the shadow *of*
                   death.

INTERCESSIONS (VI F)
With confidence let us pray *to* the Father * who willed that the Virgin Mary
should surpass all creatures in heav*en* and earth:
Look upon the Mother of your Son and hear our *prayer.*

We are grateful to you, Father of mercy, for you gave us Mary to be our mother
  and our model,
— through her intercession *cleanse* our hearts.
You inspired Mary to be attentive to your word and faithful *in* your service,
— through her intercession give us the gifts of the *Holy* Spirit.
You strengthened Mary at the foot of the cross and filled her with joy at the
  resurrection *of* your Son,
— through her intercession relieve our distress and strength*en* our hope.

Our Father . . .

Prayer

God our Father,
fountain and source of our salvation,
may we proclaim your glory every day of our lives,
that we may sing your praise for ever in heaven.
We ask this through our Lord Jesus Christ, your Son,
who lives and reigns with you and the Holy Spirit,
one God, for ever and ever.

SUNDAY, WEEK IV

Evening Prayer I

HYMN, 1329.
Rerum, Deus, fons omnium.(L.M.)

Rerum, Deus, fons ómnium,	O God, the Source and Fount of life,
qui, rebus actis ómnibus,	Creating all things by your will,
totíus orbis ámbitum	To give us joy you never cease
censu replésti múnerum,	The earth with wondrous gifts to fill.
Ac, mole tanta cóndita,	And when creation was complete,
tandem quiétem díceris	Repose for man you also blest
sumpsísse, dans labóribus	By resting on the seventh day,
ut nos levémur grátius:	That he might toil again refreshed.
Concéde nunc morálibus	To fallen mortals grant the grace
deflére vitæ crímina,	Of sorrow for each sin's offence,
instáre iam virtútibus	And courage to begin anew
et munerári prósperis,	And strive for virtue's recompense.
Ut cum treméndi iúdicis	When Christ the Judge supreme appears
horror suprémus cœperit,	To sift the present and the past,
lætémur omnes ínvicem	May we his servants thrill with joy
pacis repléti múnere.	And peace to gaze on him at last.
Præsta, Pater piíssime,	O God of mercy, hear our prayer,
Patríque compar Unice,	With Christ your Son, and Spirit blest,
cum Spíritu Paráclito	Transcedent Trinity in whom
regnans per omne sæculum. Amen.	Created things all come to rest. Amen.

PSALMODY

Ant. 1   Pray for the *peace* * of *Je*rusalem.

Advent: He comes, the desire of all human hearts; † his dwelling place shall be resplendent with *glo*ry, * al*le*luia.

Lent, 4th Sunday: Let us go to God's *house* * with *re*joicing.

Easter, 4th Sunday: May the peace of Christ fill your hearts with *joy*, * al*le*luia.

VIIIa

Psalm 122
Holy city Jerusalem
You have come to Mount Zion, to the city of the living God, heavenly Jerusalem
(Hebrews 12:22).

I rejoiced when I heard them *say*: *
  "Let us go to *God's* house."
And now our feet are *stand*ing * within
  your gates, O *Je*rusalem.
Jerusalem is built as a *city* * strongly
  *com*pact.
It is there that the tribes go *up*, * the
  tribes of *the* Lord.
For Israel's law it *is*, * there to praise *the*
  Lord's name.
There were set the thrones of *judg*ment
  * of the house *of* David.

For the peace of Jerusalem *pray*: *
  "Peace be to *your* homes!
May peace reign in your *walls*, * in your
  pa*lac*es, peace!"
For love of my brethren and *friends* * I
  say: "Peace up*on* you!"
For love of the house of the *Lord* * I will
  ask for *your* good.
Glory to the Father, and to the *Son*, *
  and to the Ho*ly* Spirit:
as it was in the beginning, is *now*, * and
  will be for ever. *A*men.

Antiphon   Pray for the *peace* * of *Je*rusalem.

Advent: He comes, the desire of all human hearts; † his dwelling place shall be
                resplendent with *glo*ry, * al*le*luia.

Lent, 4th Sunday: Let us go to God's *house* * with re*joic*ing.

Easter, 4th Sunday: May the peace of Christ fill your hearts with *joy*, * al*le*luia.

Ant. 2   From the morning watch *un*til night, * I have waited trustingly
                for the *Lord*.

Advent: Come, Lord, do *not* delay; * free your people from their *sin*fulness.

Lent, 4th Sunday: Awake from your sleep, † rise *from* the dead, * and Christ will give you *light*.

Easter, 4th Sunday: With your own blood, you have redeemed *us* for God, * alle*lu*ia.

IID

Psalm 130
A cry from the depths
He himself will save his people from their sins (Matthew 1:21).

O ut of the depths I cry to *you*, O
  Lord, * Lord, hear my *voice*!
O let your ears *be* attentive * to the
  voice of my *plead*ing.
If you, O Lord, should *mark* our guilt, *
  Lord, who would sur*vive*?
But with you is *found* forgiveness: * for
  this we re*vere* you.
My soul is waiting *for* the Lord, * I
  count on his *word*.
My soul is longing *for* the Lord * more

than watchman for *day*break.
Let the watchman *count* on daybreak *
  and Israel on the *Lord*.
Because with the Lord *there* is mercy *
  and fullness of re*demp*tion,
Israel indeed he *will* redeem * from all
  its in*iq*uity.
Glory to the Father, and *to* the Son, *
  and to the Holy *Spir*it:
as it was in the begin*ning*, is now, * and
  will be for ever. *A*men.

Antiphon	From the morning watch *un*til night, * I have waited trustingly for the *Lord.*
Advent:	Come, Lord, do *not* delay; * free your people from their *sin*fulness.
Lent, 4th Sunday:	Awake from your sleep, † rise *from* the dead, * and Christ will give you *light.*
Easter, 4h Sunday:	With your own blood, you have redeemed *us* for God, * alle*lu*ia.

Ant. 3	Let everything in heaven and *on* earth * bend the knee at the *name* of Jesus.
Advent:	The fullness of time has come upon us *at* last; * God sends his Son in*to* the world.
Lent, 4th Sunday:	So great was God's love for us † that when we were dead because of *our* sins, * he brought us to life *in* Christ Jesus.
Easter, 4th Sunday:	Was it not necessary for Christ *to* suffer * and so enter into his glory? *Al*leluia.

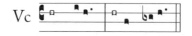

Canticle   Philippians 2:6-11
Christ, God's holy servant

Though he was in the form *of* God, * Jesus did not deem equality with God something *to* be grasped at.

Rather, he emptied himself and took the form of *a* slave, * being born in the like*ness* of men.

He was known to be of human *e*state, * and it was thus that he hum*bled* himself,

obediently accepting *e*ven death, * death *on* a cross!

Because *of* this, * God high*ly* exalted him

and bestowed on him *the* name * above every *o*ther name,

So that at Jesus' name every knee *must* bend * in the heavens, on the earth, and un*der* the earth,

and every tongue proclaim to the glory of God *the* Father: * JESUS *CHRIST* IS LORD!

Glory to the Father, and to *the* Son, * and to the *Holy* Spirit:

as it was in the beginning, *is* now, * and will be for ev*er.* Amen.

Antiphon	Let everything in heaven and *on* earth * bend the knee at the *name* of Jesus.
Advent:	The fullness of time has come upon us *at* last; * God sends his Son in*to* the world.
Lent, 4th Sunday:	So great was God's love for us † that when we were dead because of *our* sins, * he brought us to life *in* Christ Jesus.
Easter, 4th Sunday:	Was it not necessary for Christ *to* suffer * and so enter into his glory? *Al*leluia.

READING   2 Peter 1:19-21

We possess the prophetic message as something altogether reliable. Keep
your attention closely fixed on it, as you would on a lamp shining in a dark
place until the first streaks of dawn appear and the morning star rises in your
hearts. First you must understand this: there is no prophecy contained in
Scripture which is a personal interpretation. Prophecy has never been put
forward by man's willing it. It is rather that men impelled by the Holy Spirit
have spoken under God's influence.

RESPONSORY (VI F)

From the rising of the sun *to* its setting, * may the name of the Lord *be* praised.
— From the rising of the sun *to* its setting, * may the name of the Lord *be*
     praised.
His splendor reaches far be*yond* the heavens;
— may the name of the Lord *be* praised.
Glory to the Father, and *to* the Son, * and to the Ho*ly* Spirit.
— From the rising of the sun *to* its setting, * may the name of the Lord *be*
     praised.

CANTICLE OF MARY

Antiphon, as in the Proper of Seasons.

VII d

M y soul ✠ proclaims the greatness
of the Lord, * my spirit rejoices
     in God *my* savior
for he has *looked* with favor * on his
     low*ly* servant.
From this day all *gen*erations * will call
     me blessèd:
the Almighty has done great *things* for
     me, * and holy is *his* Name.
He has mercy on *those* who fear him *
     in every gen*er*ation.
He has shown the strength *of* his arm, *
     he has scattered the proud in their
     *con*ceit.

He has cast down the mighty *from* their
     thrones, * and has lifted up *the* lowly.
He has filled the hungry *with* good
     things, * and the rich he has sent
     a*way* empty.
He has come to the help of his *ser*vant
     Israel * for he has remembered his
     promise *of* mercy,
the promise he made *to* our fathers, * to
     Abraham and his children *for* ever.
Glory to the Father, and *to* the Son, *
     and to the Ho*ly* Spirit:
as it was in the begin*ning*, is now, * and
     will be for ever. *A*men.

Antiphon repeated.

INTERCESSIONS (VI F)

Everyone who waits for the *Lord* finds joy. * Now we *pray* to him:
Look on us with favor, Lord, and *hear us.*

Faithful witness, first-born of the dead, you washed away our sins *in* your blood,
— make us always remember your won*der*ful works.

You called men to be heralds *of* your good news,
— make them strong and faithful messengers *of* your kingdom.

King of peace, send your Spirit on the leaders *of* the world,
— turn their eyes toward the poor *and* the suffering.

Protect and defend those who are discriminated against because of race, color,
   class, language *or* religion,
— that they may be accorded the rights and dignity *which* are theirs.

May all who died in your love share *in* your happiness,
— with Mary, our mother, and *all* your holy ones.

Our Father . . .

Prayer, as in the Proper of Seasons.

SUNDAY, WEEK IV

Morning Prayer

HYMN, 1330.
Ecce iam noctis. (11.11.11.5)

Ecce iam noctis tenuátur umbra,
lucis auróra rútilans corúscat;
nísibus totis rogitémus omnes
cunctipoténtem,

Ut Deus, nostri miserátus, omnem
pellat angórem, tríbuat salútem,
donet et nobis pietáte patris
regna polórum.

Præstet hoc nobis Déitas beáta
Patris ac Nati, paritérque Sancti
Spíritus, cuius résonat per omnem
glória mundum. Amen.

Lo! the dim shadows of the night are waning;
Radiantly glowing, dawn of day returneth;
Fervent in spirit, to the mighty Father
Pray we devoutly.

So shall our Maker of his great compassion,
Banish all sickness, kindly health bestowing;
And may he grant us, of a Father's goodness,
Mansions in heaven.

This he vouchsafe us, God for ever blessèd
Father eternal, Son, and Holy Spirit,
Whose is the glory which through all creation
Ever resoundeth. Amen.

PSALMODY

If this Sunday occurs on December 24, everything is taken from the corresponding day. Otherwise:

Ant. 1   Praise the Lord, for his loving kindness will never *fail*, * al*le*luia.

Advent: Sound the trumpet in Zion, † the day of the Lord is *near*; * he comes to save us, al*le*luia.

Lent, 4th Sunday: O God, my God, I give you *thanks*; * you are my God, I shall proclaim *your* glory.

Easter, 4th Sunday: I shall not die but live † and proclaim the works of the *Lord*, * al*le*luia.

VIIIa

Psalm 118

Song of joy for salvation

This Jesus is the stone which, rejected by you builders, has become the chief stone supporting all the rest (Acts 4:11).

Give thanks to the Lord for he is *good*, * for his love endures *for* ever.

Let the sons of Israel *say*: * "His love endures *for* ever."

Let the sons of Aaron *say*: * "His love endures *for* ever."

Let those who fear the Lord *say*: * "His love endures *for* ever."

I called to the Lord in my dis*tress*; * he answered *and* freed me.

The Lord is at my side; I do not *fear*. * What can man do *against* me?

The Lord is at my side as my *hel*per: * I shall look down on *my* foes.

It is better to take refuge in the *Lord* * than to trust *in* men:

it is better to take refuge in the *Lord* * than to trust *in* princes.

The nations all en*com*passed me; * in the Lord's name *I* crushed them.

They compassed me, compassed me *about*; * in the Lord's name *I* crushed them.

They compassed me about like bees; †

they blazed like a fire among *thorns*. * In the Lord's name *I* crushed them.

I was hard-pressed and was *fall*ing * but the Lord came *to* help me.

The Lord is my strength and my *song*; * he is *my* savior.

There are shouts of joy and *victory* * in the tents of *the* just.

The Lord's right hand has *tri*umphed; * his right *hand* raised me.

The Lord's right hand has *tri*umphed; * I shall not die, I shall live and recount *his* deeds.

I was punished, I was punished by the *Lord*, * but not doomed *to* die.

Open to me the gates of *holiness*: * I will enter and *give* thanks.

This is the Lord's own *gate* * where the just *may* enter.

I will thank you for you have *an*swered * and you are *my* savior.

The stone which the builders re*ject*ed * has become *the* corner stone.

This is the work of the *Lord*, * a marvel in *our* eyes.

This day was made by the *Lord*; * we rejoice and *are* glad.

O Lord, grant us sal*va*tion; * O Lord, grant *suc*cess.

Blessèd in the name of the *Lord* * is he *who* comes.

We bless you from the house of the *Lord*; * the Lord God is *our* light.

Go forward in procession with *branch*es

* even to *the* altar.

You are my God, I *thank* you.* My God, *I* praise you.

Give thanks to the Lord for he is *good*; * for his love endures *for* ever.

Glory to the Father, and to the *Son*, * and to the Ho*ly* Spirit,

as it was in the begin*ning*, is *now*, * and will be for ever. *A*men.

Antiphon	Praise the Lord, for his loving kindness will never *fail*, * al*le*luia.
Advent:	Sound the trumpet in Zion, † the day of the Lord is *near*, * he comes to save us, al*le*luia.
Lent, 4ᵗʰ Sunday:	O God, my God, I give you *thanks*; * you are my God, I shall proclaim *your* glory.
Easter, 4ᵗʰ Sunday:	I shall not die but live † and proclaim the works of the *Lord*, * al*le*luia.

Ant. 2	Alleluia! Bless the Lord, all you works *of* the Lord, * alle*lu*ia!
Advent:	The Lord is here; go out to meet him, saying: † Great his birth, eter*nal* his kingdom, * strong God, Ruler of all, Prince of peace, alle*lu*ia.
Lent, 4ᵗʰ Sunday:	God of might, de*liv*er us; * free us from the power of the *en*emy.
Easter, 4ᵗʰ Sunday:	Blessèd be your holy and glorious *name*, O Lord, * alle*lu*ia.

IID

Canticle
Daniel 3:52-27
Let all creatures praise the Lord

The Creator…is blessed for ever (Romans 1:25).

Blessèd are you, O Lord, the God *of* our fathers, * praiseworthy and exalted above all for*ev*er.

And blessèd is your holy and glo*ri*ous name, * praiseworthy and exalted above all for all *ages*.

Blessèd are you in the temple of your *ho*ly glory, * praiseworthy and glorious above all for*ev*er.

Blessèd are you on the throne *of* your kingdom, * praiseworthy and exalted above all for*ev*er.

Blessèd are you who look into the

depths from your throne up*on* the cherubim, * praiseworthy and exalted above all for*ev*er.

Blessèd are you in the firma*ment* of heaven, * praiseworthy and glorious for*ev*er.

Bless the Lord, all you works *of* the Lord, * praise and exalt him above all for*ev*er.

Glory to the Father, and *to* the Son, * and to the Holy *Spi*rit,

as it was in the begin*ning*, is now, * and will be for ever. *A*men.

Antiphon	Alleluia! Bless the Lord, all you works *of* the Lord, * alle*lui*a!
Advent:	The Lord is here; go out to meet him, saying: † Great his birth, eter*nal* his kingdom, * strong God, Ruler of all, Prince of peace, alle*lui*a.
Lent, 4th Sunday:	God of might, de*liv*er us; * free us from the power of the *en*emy.
Easter, 4th Sunday:	Blessèd be your holy and glorious *name*, O Lord, * alle*lui*a.

Ant. 3	Let everything *that* breathes * give praise to the Lord, *al*leluia.
Advent:	Your all-powerful Word, O Lord, * will come to earth from his throne of glory, *al*leluia.
Lent, 4th Sunday:	O *praise* God * for his *might*y deeds.
Easter, 4th Sunday:	Give honor and praise to our God; † all that he does *is* perfect * and all his ways are true, *al*leluia.

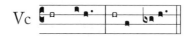

Psalm 150
Praise the Lord

Let mind and heart be in your song: this is to glorify God with your whole self (Hesychius).

Praise God in his ho*ly* place, *
 praise him in his *migh*ty heavens.
Praise him for his power*ful* deeds, *
 praise his sur*pass*ing greatness.
O praise him with sound *of* trumpet, *
 praise him with *lute* and harp.
Praise him with timbrel *and* dance, *
 praise him with *strings* and pipes.

O praise him with resound*ing* cymbals, *
 praise him with cla*shing* of cymbals.
Let everything that lives and *that*
 breathes * give praise *to* the Lord.
Glory to the Father, and to *the* Son, *
 and to the *Ho*ly Spirit,
as it was in the beginning, *is* now, * and
 will be for *ev*er. Amen.

Antiphon	Let everything *that* breathes * give praise to the Lord, *al*leluia.
Advent:	Your all-powerful Word, O Lord, * will come to earth from his throne of glory, *al*leluia.
Lent, 4th Sunday:	O *praise* God * for his *might*y deeds.
Easter, 4th Sunday:	Give honor and praise to our God; † all that he does *is* perfect * and all his ways are true, *al*leluia.

READING   2 Timothy 2:8, 11-13

Remember that Jesus Christ, a descendant of David, was raised from the dead. You can depend on this:
 If we have died with him
  we shall also live with him;
 If we hold out to the end
  we shall also reign with him.
But if we deny him he will deny us. If we are unfaithful he will still remain faithful, for he cannot deny himself.

RESPONSORY (VI F)

We give thanks to *you*, O God, * as we call upon *your* name.

— We give thanks to *you*, O God, * as we call upon *your* name.

We cry aloud how marvel*ous* you are,

— as we call upon *your* name.

Glory to the Father, and *to* the Son, * and to the Ho*ly* Spirit.

— We give thanks to *you*, O God, * as we call upon *your* name.

CANTICLE OF ZECHARIAH, antiphon, as in the Proper of Seasons.

Blessèd ✠ be the Lord, the *God* of Is*rael*; * he has come to his people and set *them* free.

He has raised up for us a *mighty* savior, * born of the house of his ser*vant* David.

Through his holy prophets he promised of old † that he would save us *from* our enemies, * from the hands of all *who* hate us.

He promised to show mercy *to* our fathers * and to remember his ho*ly* covenant.

This was the oath he swore to our *fath*er Abraham: * to set us free from the hands of *our* enemies,

free to worship him without fear, † holy and righteous *in* his sight * all the days of *our* life

You, my child, shall be called the prophet *of* the Most High; * for you will go before the Lord to prepare *his* way,

to give his people knowledge *of* salvation * by the forgiveness of *their* sins.

In the tender compassion *of* our God * the dawn from on high shall break *up*on us,

to shine on those who dwell in darkness and the sha*dow* of death, * and to guide our feet into the way *of* peace.

Glory to the Father, and *to* the Son, * and to the Ho*ly* Spirit:

as it was in the begin*ning*, is now, * and will be for ever. *A*men.

Antiphon is repeated.

INTERCESSIONS (VI F)

Open your hearts to praise the God of po*wer* and goodness, * for he loves us and *knows* our needs:

We praise you, Lord, and trust in *you.*

We bless you, almighty God, King of the universe, because you called us while we *were* yet sinners,

— to acknowledge your truth and to *serve* your majesty.

O God, you opened the gates of mer*cy* for us,
— let us never turn aside from the *path* of life.
As we celebrate the resurrection of your be*lov*èd Son,
— help us to spend this day in the spir*it* of joy.
Give to your faithful, O Lord, a prayerful spir*it* of gratitude,
— that we may thank you for *all* your gifts.

Our Father . . .

Prayer, as in the Proper of Seasons.

SUNDAY, WEEK IV

Evening Prayer II

HYMN, 1331.

O lux, beata Trinitas. (L.M.)

O lux, beáta Trínitas et principális Unitas, iam sol recédit ígneus: infúnde lumen córdibus.	O Trinity of blessèd light, O Unity of princely might, The fiery sun now goes his way; Shed thou within our hearts thy ray.
Te mane laudum cármine, te deprecémur véspere; te nostra supplex glória per cuncta laudet sæcula.	To thee our morning song of praise, To thee our evening prayer we raise; Thy glory suppliant we adore For ever and for evermore.
Christum rogámus et Patrem, Christi Patrísque Spíritum; unum potens per ómnia, fove precántes, Trínitas. Amen.	All laud to God the Father be; All praise eternal Son, to thee; All glory, as is ever meet, To God the Holy Paraclete. Amen.

PSALMODY

Ant. 1   In eternal splendor, before the dawn of light on *earth*, * I have begotten you, al*le*luia.

Advent: See how glorious he *is*, * coming forth as a Savior of *all* peoples!

Lent, 4ᵗʰ Sunday: God has appointed *Christ* * to be the judge of the living and *the* dead.

Easter, 4ᵗʰ Sunday: Seek the things that are above † where Christ is seated at God's right *hand*, * al*le*luia.

VIIIa

Psalm 110:1-5, 7
The Messiah, king and priest
Christ's reign will last until all his enemies are made subject to him
(1 Corinthians 15:25).

The Lord's revelation to my Master:
† "Sit on my *right*: * your foes I
will put beneath *your* feet."
The Lord will wield from Zion † your
scepter of *power*: * rule in the midst
of all *your* foes.
A prince from the day of your birth on

the holy *mount*ains; * from the womb
before the dawn I *be*got you.
The Lord has sworn an oath he will not
change. † "You are a priest for *ever*, *
a priest like Melchizedek *of* old."
The Master standing at your *right* hand
* will shatter kings in the day of his

817

great wrath.
He shall drink from the stream by the *way*side * and therefore he shall lift up *his* head.

Glory to the Father, and to the *Son*, * and to the Ho*ly* Spirit:
as it was in the beginning, is *now*, * and will be for ever. *A*men.

Antiphon	In eternal splendor, before the dawn of light on *earth*, * I have begotten you, al*le*luia.
Advent:	See how glorious he *is*, * coming forth as a Savior of *all* peoples!
Lent, 4ᵗʰ Sunday:	God has appointed *Christ* * to be the judge of the living and *the* dead.
Easter, 4ᵗʰ Sunday:	Seek the things that are above † where Christ is seated at God's right *hand*, * al*le*luia.
Ant. 2	Blessèd are they who hunger and *thirst* for holiness; * they will be sa*tis*fied.
Advent:	Crooked paths will be straightened, † and rough *ways* made smooth. * Come, O Lord, do not delay, alle*lu*ia.
Lent, 4ᵗʰ Sunday:	Happy the man who shows mercy *for* the Lord's sake; * he will stand firm for *ev*er.
Easter, 4ᵗʰ Sunday:	In the darkness he dawns: † a light for *up*right hearts, * alle*lu*ia.

IID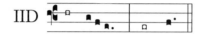

Psalm 112
The happiness of the just man
Live as children born of the light. Light produces every kind of goodness and justice and truth
(Ephesians 5:8-9).

Happy the man who *fears* the Lord, * who takes delight in all his com*mands*.
His sons will be power*ful* on earth; * the children of the upright are *bless*èd.
Riches and wealth are *in* his house; * his justice stands firm for *ev*er.
He is a light in the darkness *for* the upright: * he is generous, merciful and *just*.
The good man takes pi*ty* and lends, * he conducts his affairs with *hon*or.
The just man will *nev*er waver: * he will be remembered for *ev*er.

He has no fear of *ev*il news; * with a firm heart he trusts in the *Lord*.
With a steadfast heart he *will* not fear; * he will see the downfall of his *foes*.
Open-handed, he gives to the poor; † his justice stands *firm* for ever. * His head will be raised in *glo*ry.
The wicked man sees and is angry, † grinds his teeth and *fades* away; * the desire of the wicked leads to *doom*.
Glory to the Father, and *to* the Son, * and to the Holy *Spir*it:
as it was in the begin*ning*, is now, * and will be for ever. *A*men.

Antiphon	Blessèd are they who hunger and *thirst* for holiness; * they will be *sat*isfied.
Advent:	Crooked paths will be straightened, † and rough *ways* made smooth. * Come, O Lord, do not delay, alle*lu*ia.
Lent, 4th Sunday:	Happy the man who shows mercy *for* the Lord's sake; * he will stand firm for *ev*er.
Easter, 4th Sunday:	In the darkness he dawns: † a light for *up*right hearts, * alle*lu*ia.

Ant. 3	Praise God, all you who serve him, both great *and* small, * alleluia, alleluia.
Advent:	Ever wider will his kingdom spread, eternally *at* peace, * alleluia, alleluia.
Easter, 4th Sunday:	Alleluia, salvation, glory and power to *our* God, * alleluia, alleluia.

** al- le- lu- ia, al- le- lu- ia.

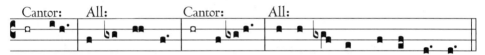

*Al- le- lu- ia.   ** al- le- lu- ia, al- le - lu- ia.

Canticle   See Revelation 19:1-7

The wedding of the Lamb

Salvation, glory, and power to *our* God:
* Alleluia.
his judgments are hon*est* and true.
** Alleluia, alleluia.

Sing praise to our God, all you *his* servants,
* Alleluia.
all who worship him reverently, *great* and small.
** Alleluia, alleluia.

The Lord our all-powerful God *is* King;
* Alleluia.
let us rejoice, sing praise, and *give* him glory.
** Alleluia, alleluia.

The wedding feast of the Lamb has *be*gun,
* Alleluia.
and his bride is pre*pared* to welcome him.
** Alleluia, alleluia.

Glory to the Father, and to the Son, †
and to the Ho*ly* Spirit.
* Alleluia.
As it was in the beginning, is now, †
and will be for ev*er*. Amen.
** Alleluia, alleluia.

Antiphon   Praise God, all you who serve him, both great *and* small, *
alleluia, alleluia.

Advent: Ever wider will his kingdom spread, eternally *at* peace, * alleluia, alleluia.

Easter, 4th Sunday: Alleluia, salvation, glory and power to *our* God, * alleluia, alleluia.

Lent: Antiphon 3

Lent, 4th Sunday: Those things, which God foretold through his prophets † concerning the
sufferings that Christ would *endure*, * have *been* fulfilled.

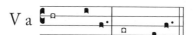

Canticle   1 Peter 2:21-24
The willing acceptance of his passion by Christ, the servant of God

Christ suffered for you, † and
left you an *example* * to have you
follow in *his* footsteps.
He did *no* wrong; * no deceit was found
in *his* mouth.
When he was *in*sulted * he returned *no*
insult.
When he was made *to* suffer, * he did
not counter *with* threats.
Instead he delivered him*self* up * to the

One who judg*es* justly.
In his *own* body * he brought his sins to
the cross,
so that all of us, dead *to* sin, * could live
in accord with *God's* will.
By *his* wounds * you *were* healed.
Glory to the Father, and to *the* Son, *
and to the Ho*ly* Spirit:
as it was in the beginning, *is* now, * and
will be for ever. *A*men.

Lent, 4th Sunday: Those things, which God foretold through his prophets † concerning the
sufferings that Christ would *endure*, * have *been* fulfilled.

READING   Hebrews 12:22-24
You have drawn near to Mount Zion and the city of the living God, the
heavenly Jerusalem, to myriads of angels in festal gathering, to the assembly
of the first-born enrolled in heaven, to God the judge of all, to the spirits of
just men made perfect, to Jesus, the mediator of a new covenant, and to the
sprinkled blood which speaks more eloquently than that of Abel.

RESPONSORY (VI F)

Our *Lord* is great, * mighty is *his* power.

— Our *Lord* is great, * mighty is *his* power.

His wisdom is be*yond* compare,

— mighty is *his* power.

Glory to the Father, and *to* the Son, * and to the Ho*ly* Spirit.

— Our *Lord* is great, * mighty is *his* power.

CANTICLE OF MARY

Antiphon, as in the Proper of Seasons.

VII d

My soul ✛ proclaims the greatness *of* the Lord, * my spirit rejoices in God *my* savior

for he has *looked* with favor * on his low*ly* servant.

From this day all *gen*erations * will call *me* blessèd:

the Almighty has done great *things* for me, * and holy is *his* Name.

He has mercy on *those* who fear him * in every gen*er*ation.

He has shown the strength *of* his arm, * he has scattered the proud in their *con*ceit.

He has cast down the mighty *from* their thrones, * and has lifted up *the* lowly.

He has filled the hungry *with* good things, * and the rich he has sent a*way* empty.

He has come to the help of his *servant* Israel * for he has remembered his promise *of* mercy,

the promise he made *to* our fathers, * to Abraham and his children *for* ever.

Glory to the Father, and *to* the Son, * and to the Ho*ly* Spirit:

as it was in the begin*ning*, is now, * and will be for ever. *A*men.

Antiphon repeated.

INTERCESSIONS (VI F)

Rejoicing in the Lord, from whom all *good* things come, * *let* us pray:

Lord, hear our *prayer.*

Father and Lord of all, you sent your Son into the world, that your name might be glorified in *every* place,

— strengthen the witness of your Church a*mong* the nations.

Make us obedient to the teachings of *your* apostles,

— and bound to the truth *of* our faith.

As you *love* the innocent,

— render justice to those *who* are wronged.

Free those in bondage and give sight *to* the blind,
— raise up the fallen and pro*tect* the stranger.
Fulfill your promise to those who already sleep *in* your peace,
— through your Son grant them a blessèd *re*surrection.

Our Father . . .

Prayer, as in the Proper of Seasons.

MONDAY, WEEK IV

Morning Prayer

HYMN, 1332.
Lucis largítor spléndide. (L.M.)

Lucis largítor spléndide,	O lavish Giver of the light
cuius seréno lúmine	That bathes the world in dawning glow;
post lapsa noctis témpora	The daylight cheers our hearts again
dies refúsus pánditur,	When sombre hours of night are past.
Tu verus mundi lúcifer	You are the world's true Morning Star,
non is qui parvi síderis	Compared with whom the eager gleam
ventúræ lucis núntius	That heralds in the dawning light
angústo fulget lúmine,	Is but a timid, narrow ray.
Sed toto sole clárior,	True Light itself, Eternal Day,
lux ipse totus et dies,	You are far brighter than the sun,
intérna nostri péctoris	Illuminating with your grace
illúminans præcórdia.	The deep recesses of each heart.
Evíncat mentis cástitas	And may our purity of mind
quæ caro cupit árrogans,	Suppress what lower nature claims,
sanctúmque puri córporis	So that our bodies too may be
delúbrum servet Spíritus.	The Holy Spirit's spotless shrine.
Sit, Christe, rex piíssime,	Jesus, to you, beneath whose sway
tibi Patríque glória	All earth shall bow, all praise we pay;
cum Spíritu Paráclito	With Father and with Spirit be
in sempitérna sæcula. Amen.	All glory yours eternally. Amen.

PSALMODY

Ant. 1   Each morning, *Lord,* * you fill us with *your* kindness.

December 17-23:   The Lord, the ruler over the kings of the earth, will *come*; * blessèd are they who are ready to go and wel*come* him.

Easter: Let the splendor of the Lord our God be up*on* us, * al*le*luia.

VIIIa

Psalm 90
May we live in the radiance of God
There is no time with God: a thousand years, a single day: it is all one (2 Peter 3:8).

O Lord, you have been our *refuge* *
from one generation to *the* next.

Before the mountains were born † or
the earth or the world brought *forth*, *
you are God, without beginning *or*
end.

You turn men back to dust and *say*: *
"Go back, sons *of* men."

To your eyes a thousand years † are like
yesterday, come and *gone*, * no more
than a watch in *the* night.

You sweep men away like a *dream*, * like
grass which springs up in *the* morning.

In the morning it springs up and
flowers: * by evening it withers *and*
fades.

So we are destroyed in your *anger*, *
struck with terror in *your* fury.

Our guilt lies open be*fore* you; * our
secrets in the light of *your* face.

All our days pass away in your *anger*. *
Our life is over like *a* sigh.

Our span is seventy *years* * or eighty for
those who *are* strong.

And most of these are emptiness and
pain. * They pass swiftly and we *are*
gone.

Who understands the power of your
anger * and fears the strength of *your*
fury?

Make us know the shortness of our *life*
* that we may gain wisdom *of* heart.

Lord, relent! Is your anger for *ever*? *
Show pity to *your* servants.

In the morning, fill us with your *love*; *
we shall exult and rejoice all *our* days.

Give us joy to balance our *affliction* *
for the years when we knew *misfor-*
tune.

Show forth your work to your *servants*;
* let your glory shine on *their*
children.

Let the favor of the Lord be upon us: †
give success to the work of our *hands*,
* give success to the work of *our*
hands.

Glory to the Father, and to the *Son*, *
and to the Ho*ly* Spirit,

as it was in the beginning, is *now*, * and
will be for ever. *A*men.

Antiphon   Each morning, *Lord*, * you fill us with *your* kindness.
December 17-23:   The Lord, the ruler over the kings of the earth, will *come*; * blessèd are they who
are ready to go and wel*come* him.
Easter: Let the splendor of the Lord our God be up*on* us, * al*le*luia.

Ant. 2   From the farthest *bounds* of earth, * may God be *praised*!
December 17-23:   Sing a new song *to* the Lord; * proclaim his praises to the ends of the *earth*.
Easter: I will turn darkness into *light* before them, * alle*lu*ia.

IID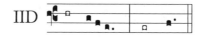

Canticle   Isaiah 42:10-16
God victor and savior
They were singing a new hymn before the throne of God (Revelation 14:3).

Sing to the Lord *a* new song, * his
praise from the end of the *earth*:
Let the sea and what fills *it* resound, *
   the coastlands, and those who dwell
   in *them.*
Let the steppe and its cit*ies* cry out, *
   the villages where Kedar *dwells*;
Let the inhabitants of Se*la* exult, * and
   shout from the top of the *moun*tains.
let them give glory *to* the Lord, * and
   utter his praise in the *coast*lands.
The Lord goes forth *like* a hero, * like a
   warrior he stirs up his *ardor*;
he shouts *out* his battle cry, * against his
   enemies he shows his *might*:
I have looked away, *and* kept silence, * I

have said nothing, holding myself *in*;
but now, I cry out as a wo*man* in labor, *
   gasping and *pant*ing.
I will lay waste moun*tains* and hills, * all
   their herbage I will dry *up*;
I will turn the rivers *in*to marshes, * and
   the marshes I will dry *up.*
I will lead the blind *on* their journey; *
   by paths unknown I will *guide* them.
I will turn darkness into *light* before
   them,* and make crooked ways
   straight.
Glory to the Father, and *to* the Son, *
   and to the H*o*ly *Spirit,*
as it was in the begin*ning*, is now, * and
   will be for ever. A*men.*

Antiphon   From the farthest *bounds* of earth, * may God be *praised*!
December 17-23:   Sing a new song *to* the Lord; * proclaim his praises to the ends of the *earth*.
Easter: I will turn darkness into *light* before them, * alle*lu*ia.

Ant. 3   You who stand in *his* sanctuary, * praise the name *of* the Lord.
December 17-23:   When the Son of Man comes *to* earth, * do you think he will find faith *in* men's
                hearts?
Easter: The Lord does whatever *he* wills, * a*l*leluia.

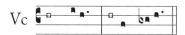

Psalm 135:1-12
Praise for the wonderful things God does for us
*He has won you for himself…and you must proclaim what he has done for you: he has called
you out of darkness into his own wonderful light* (1 Peter 2:9).

Praise the name of *the* Lord, * praise
him, servants *of* the Lord,
who stand in the house of *the* Lord, * in
   the courts of the house *of* our God.
Praise the Lord for the Lord *is* good. *
   Sing a psalm to his name for *he* is
   loving.
For the Lord has chosen Jacob for
   *him*self * and Israel for his *own*
   possession.

For I know the Lord *is* great, * that our
   Lord is high a*bove* all gods.
The Lord does whatever *he* wills, * in
   heaven, on earth, *in* the seas.
He summons clouds from the ends of
   the earth; † makes lightning produce
   the rain; * from his treasuries he sends
   forth the wind.
The first-born of the Egyptians *he*
   smote,* of man and *beast* alike.

Signs and wonders he worked † in the midst of your land, *O* Egypt, * against Pharaoh and *all* his servants.	of Canaan.
	He let Israel inherit *their* land; * on his people their land *he* bestowed.
Nations in their greatness *he* struck * and kings in their splen*dor* he slew.	Glory to the Father, and to *the* Son, * and to the *Ho*ly Spirit:
Sihon, king of the Amorites, † Og, the king *of* Bashan, * and all the king*doms*	as it was in the beginning, *is* now, * and will be for e*ver.* Amen.

Antiphon	You who stand in *his* sanctuary, * praise the name *of* the Lord.
December 17-23:	When the Son of Man comes *to* earth, * do you think he will find faith *in* men's hearts?
Easter:	The Lord does whatever *he* wills, * a*l*leluia.

READING   Judith 8:25-27

> We should be grateful to the Lord our God, for putting us to the test, as he did our forefathers. Recall how he dealt with Abraham, and how he tried Isaac, and all that happened to Jacob in Syrian Mesopotamia while he was tending the flocks of Laban, his mother's brother. Not for vengeance did the Lord put them in the crucible to try their hearts, nor has he done so with us. It is by way of admonition that he chastises those who are close to him.

RESPONSORY (VI F)

Sing for *joy*, God's chosen ones, * give him the praise that *is* due.
— Sing for *joy*, God's chosen ones, * give him the praise that *is* due.
Sing a new song *to* the Lord, *
— give him the praise that *is* due.
Glory to the Father, and *to* the Son, * and to the Ho*ly* Spirit.
— Sing for *joy*, God's chosen ones, * give him the praise that *is* due.

CANTICLE OF ZECHARIAH

Antiphon	Blessèd *be* the Lord, * for he has come to his people and set *them* free.

INTERCESSIONS (VI F)

Because Christ hears and saves those who *hope* in him, * *let* us pray:
We praise you, Lord, we hope in you.
We thank you because you are *rich* in mercy,
— and for the abundant love with which *you* have loved us.
With the Father you are always at work *in* the world,
— make all things new through the power of your *Holy* Spirit.
Open our eyes and the eyes *of* our brothers,
— to see your won*ders* this day.
You call us today *to* your service,
— make us stewards of your *many* gifts.

Our Father . . .

Prayer

God our creator,
you gave us the earth to cultivate
and the sun to serve our needs.
Help us to spend this day
for your glory and our neighbor's good.
We ask this through our Lord Jesus Christ, your Son,
who lives and reigns with you and the Holy Spirit,
one God, for ever and ever.

MONDAY, WEEK IV

Evening Prayer

HYMN, 1333.
Luminous fons, lux et origo lucis. (L.M.)

Lúminis fons, lux et orígo lucis,
tu pius nostris précibus favéto,
luxque, peccáti ténebris fugátis,
    nos tua adórnet.

O fount of light, True Light itself,
Smile down on us as here we pray.
May your bright splendor shine on us,
When shades of sin are cast away.

Ecce transáctus labor est diéi,
teque nos tuti sumus adnuénte ;
en tibi grates ágimus libéntes
    tempus in omne.

We thank you for your loving care
While work and toil have been our lot,
And now the day is near its close,
Dear Lord, we pray, forsake us not.

Solis abscéssus ténebras redúxit :
ille sol nobis rádiet corúscus
luce qui fulva fovet angelórum
    ágmina sancta.

Though sun declines and shadows fall,
Our souls draw light from those fair rays
The Sun of Justice n'er withholds,
On whom the hosts of angels gaze.

Quas dies culpas hodiérna texit,
Christus deléto pius atque mitis,
pectus et puro rútilet nitóre
    témpore noctis.

May all the faults which we deplore,
Be washed away by Christ our Light,
And may he purify our hearts
Throughout the hours of coming night.

Laus tibi Patri, decus atque Nato,
Flámini Sancto párilis potéstas,
cuncta qui sceptro régitis suprémo
    omne per ævum. Amen.

All glory, Father, be to you,
Praise to the Spirit and the Son,
Who rule all things with pow'r supreme
Till all created time is done. Amen.

PSALMODY

Ant. 1   Give thanks to the *Lord*, * for his great love is with*out* end.

December 17-23:   The Lord, the ruler over the kings of the earth, will *come*; * blessèd are they who are ready to go and wel*come* him.

Easter: Whoever is in Christ is a new *crea*ture, * al*le*luia.

VIIIa

Psalm 136
Easter hymn
We praise God by recalling his marvelous deeds (Cassiodorus).

I

O give thanks to the Lord for he is good, * for his love endures for ever.

Give thanks to the God of gods, * for his love endures for ever.

Give thanks to the Lord of lords, * for his love endures for ever;

who alone has wrought marvelous works, * for his love endures for ever;

whose wisdom it was made the skies, * for his love endures for ever;

who fixed the earth firmly on the seas, *

for his love endures for ever.

It was he who made the great lights, * for his love endures for ever,

the sun to rule in the day, * for his love endures for ever,

the moon and the stars in the night, * for his love endures for ever.

Glory to the Father, and to the Son, * and to the Holy Spirit,

as it was in the beginning, is now, * and will be for ever. Amen.

Antiphon	Give thanks to the Lord, * for his great love is without end.
December 17-23:	The Lord, the ruler over the kings of the earth, will come; * blessèd are they who are ready to go and welcome him.
Easter:	Whoever is in Christ is a new creature, * alleluia.

Ant. 2	Great and wonderful are your deeds, * Lord God the Almighty.
December 17-23:	Sing a new song to the Lord; * proclaim his praises to the ends of the earth.
Easter:	Let us love God, † for he has first loved us, * alleluia.

IID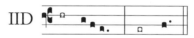

II

The first-born of the Egyptians he smote, * for his love endures for ever.

He brought Israel out from their midst, * for his love endures for ever;

arm outstretched, with power in his hand, * for his love endures for ever.

He divided the Red Sea in two, * for his love endures for ever;

he made Israel pass through the midst, * for his love endures for ever;

he flung Pharaoh and his force in the sea, * for his love endures for ever.

Through the desert his people he led, * for his love endures for ever.

Nations in their greatness he struck, * for his love endures for ever.

Kings in their splendor he slew, * for his love endures for ever.

Sihon, king of the Amorites, * for his love endures for ever;

and Og, the king of Bashan, * for his love endures for ever.

He let Israel inherit their land, * for his love endures for ever.

On his servant their land he bestowed, * for his love endures for ever.

He remembered us in our distress, * for his love endures for ever.

And he snatched us away from our foes, * for his love endures for ever.

He gives food to all living things, * for his love endures for ever.

To the God of heaven give thanks, * for

his love endures for *ever*.
Glory to the Father, and *to* the Son, *
and to the Holy *Spir*it,

as it was in the begin*ning*, is now, * and
will be for ever. A*men*.

Antiphon	Great and wonderful *are* your deeds, * Lord God the Al*mighty*.
December 17-23:	Sing a new song *to* the Lord; * proclaim his praises to the ends of the *earth*.
Easter:	Let us love God, † for he has *first* loved us, * alle*lu*ia.

Ant. 3	God planned in the fullness *of* time * to restore all *things* in Christ.
December 17-23:	When the Son of Man comes *to* earth, * do you think he will find faith *in* men's hearts?
Easter:	From his fullness we have all *received*, * grace upon grace, a*ll*eluia.

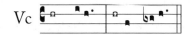

Vc

Canticle   Ephesians 1:3-10
God our Savior

Praised be the God *and* Father * of
our Lord *Je*sus Christ,
who has bestowed on us *in* Christ *
every spiritual blessing *in* the
heavens.
God chose us in him before the world
*be*gan * to be holy and blameless *in*
his sight.
He predestined us † to be his adopted
sons through Je*sus* Christ, * such was
his *will* and pleasure,
that all might praise the glori*ous* favor *
he has bestowed on us in *his* belovèd.
In him and through his blood, † we
have been *re*deemed, * and our *sins*

forgiven,
so immeasura*bly* generous * is God's
fa*vor* to us.
God has given us the wisdom to
understand fully *the* mystery, * the
plan he was pleased to de*cree* in
Christ.
A plan to be carried out *in* Christ, * in
the full*ness* of time,
to bring all things into one *in* him, * in
the heavens *and* on earth.
Glory to the Father, and to *the* Son, *
and to the *Ho*ly Spirit:
as it was in the beginning, *is* now, * and
will be for *ev*er. Amen.

Antiphon	God planned in the fullness *of* time * to restore all *things* in Christ.
December 17-23:	When the Son of Man comes *to* earth, * do you think he will find faith *in* men's hearts?
Easter:	From his fullness we have all *received*, * grace upon grace, a*ll*eluia.

READING 1 Thessalonians 3:12-13

May the Lord increase you and make you overflow with love for one another and for all, even as our love does for you. May he strengthen your hearts, making them blameless and holy before our God and Father at the coming of our Lord Jesus Christ with all his holy ones.

RESPONSORY (VI F)

Accept my *prayer*, O Lord, * which rises up *to* you.
— Accept my *prayer*, O Lord, * which rises up *to* you.
Like burning incense *in* your sight,
— which rises up *to* you.
Glory to the Father, and *to* the Son, * and to the Ho*ly* Spirit.
— Accept my *prayer*, O Lord, * which rises up *to* you.

CANTICLE OF MARY

Antiphon   For ever will my *soul* proclaim * the greatness of *the* Lord.

INTERCESSIONS (VI F)

Jesus does not abandon those who *hope* in him; * therefore, let us *hum*bly ask him:
Our Lord and our God, *hear us.*
Christ our light, brighten your Church *with* your splendor,
— so that it may be for the nations the great sacrament *of* your love.
Watch over the priests and ministers *of* your Church,
— so that after they have preached to others, they themselves may remain
    faithful *in* your service.
Through your blood you gave peace *to* the world,
— turn away the sin of strife, the *scourge* of war.
O Lord, help married couples with an abundance *of* your grace,
— so that they may better symbolize the mystery *of* your Church.
In your mercy forgive the sins of *all* the dead,
— that they may live *with* your saints.

Our Father . . .

Prayer

Stay with us, Lord Jesus,
for evening draws near,
and be our companion on our way
to set our hearts on fire with new hope.
Help us to recognize your presence among us
in the Scriptures we read,
and in the breaking of bread,
for you live and reign with the Father and the Holy Spirit,
one God, for ever and ever.

TUESDAY, WEEK IV

Morning Prayer

HYMN, 1334.
Æterne lucis conditor. (L.M.)

Ætérne lucis cónditor,
lux ipse totus et dies,
noctem nec ullam séntiens
natúra lucis pérpeti,

Iam cedit pallens próximo
diéi nox advéntui,
obtúndens lumen síderum
adest et clarus lúcifer.

Iam stratis læti súrgimus
grates canéntes et tuas,
quod cæcam noctem vícerit
revéctans rursus sol diem.

Te nunc, ne carnis gáudia
blandis subrépant æstibus,
dolis ne cedat sæculi
mens nostra, sancte, quæsumus.

Ira ne rixas próvocet,
gulam ne venter íncitet,
opum pervértat ne famis,
turpis ne luxus óccupet,

Sed firma mente sóbrii,
casto manéntes córpore
totum fidéli spíritu
Christo ducámus hunc diem.

Præsta, Pater piíssime,
Patríque compar Unice,
cum Spíritu Paráclito
regnans per omne sæculum. Amen.

Eternal Maker of the light,
True Light itself, surpassing day,
No gloom or darkness can you know,
In your own light which has no end.

Pale shades of night are yielding fast,
Before the bold advance of day;
Resplendent shines the morning star
While other constellations fade.

We gladly rise to sing your praise,
And thank you with renewed delight,
That rising sun brings back the day,
To conquer night's obscurity.

Most Holy One, we beg of you
Let not our souls be led astray,
By nature's pleasures and desires
Or by the world's deceiving glare.

Let no contention raise disputes,
Nor greed disgrace a Christian's name,
Nor greed for riches be a snare,
Nor evil thoughts corrupt our minds.

But let us show well-governed souls,
Within a body chaste and pure,
To spend this day in work and prayer,
For Christ our Leader and our Lord.

O Father, this we ask be done
Through Jesus Christ your only Son,
Whom in the Spirit we adore:
One God who reigns for evermore. Amen.

PSALMODY

Ant. 1	I will sing to you, O *Lord*; * I will learn from you the way of *per*fection.
December 17-23:	The Lord will come from his holy *place* * to save *his* people.
Easter:	Whoever does the will of my *Fa*ther * will enter the kingdom of heaven, al*le*luia.

VIIIa

Psalm 101
Avowal of a good ruler
If you love me, keep my commandments (John 14:15)

My song is of mercy and *jus*tice; * I
sing to you, O Lord.
I will walk in the way of per*fec*tion. * O
when, Lord, will *you* come?
I will walk with blameless *heart* * within
my house;
I will not set before my *eyes* * whatever
is base.
I will hate the ways of the *crooked*; *
they shall not be *my* friends.
The false-hearted must keep far a*way*; *
the wicked I *dis*own.
The man who slanders his neighbor in
*se*cret * I will bring *to* silence.
The man of proud looks and haughty
heart * I will never *en*dure.

I look to the faithful in the *land* * that
they may dwell *with* me.
He who walks in the way of per*fec*tion *
shall be *my* friend.
No man who practices de*ceit* * shall live
within *my* house.
No man who utters lies shall *stand* *
before *my* eyes.
Morning by morning I will *si*lence * all
the wicked in *the* land,
uprooting from the city of the *Lord* * all
who *do* evil.

Glory to the Father, and to the *Son*, *
and to the Ho*ly* Spirit:
as it was in the beginning, is *now*, * and
will be for ever. *A*men.

Antiphon	I will sing to you, O *Lord*; * I will learn from you the way of *per*fection.
December 17-23:	The Lord will come from his holy *place* * to save *his* people.
Easter:	Whoever does the will of my *Fa*ther * will enter the kingdom of heaven, al*le*luia.

Ant. 2   **Lord, do *not* withhold * your compassion from *us*.**

December 17-23:   Zion is our mighty citadel, † our saving Lord its wall and its defense; † throw op*en* the gates, * for our God is here among us, alle*lu*ia.

Easter: Let all the na*tions*, O Lord, * know the depths of your loving mercy for us, alle*lu*ia.

IID

Canticle   Daniel 3:26, 27, 29, 34-41
Azariah's prayer in the furnace
With your whole hearts turn to God and he will blot out all your sins (Acts 3:19).

Blessèd are you, and praiseworthy, †
O Lord, the God *of* our fathers, *
and glorious forever is your *name*.

For you are just in all *you* have done; *
all your deeds are *fault*less,

all *your* ways right, * and all your
judgments *prop*er.

For we have sinned and transgressed †
by depart*ing* from you, * and we have
done every kind of *e*vil.

For your name's sake,† do not deliver us
up forever, * or make void your
*co*venant.

Do not take away your mercy from us,
† for the sake of Abraham, *your*
belovèd, * Isaac, your servant, and
Israel your *ho*ly one,

To whom you promised to multiply
their offspring † like the *stars* of
heaven, * or the sand on the shore of
the *sea*.

For we are re*duced*, O Lord, * beyond
any other *na*tion,

brought low everywhere in the *world*

this day * because of our *sins*.

We have in our day no prince, pro*phet*,
or leader, * no holocaust, sacrifice,
oblation, or *in*cense,

no place to of*fer* first fruits, * to find
favor with *you*.

But with contrite heart and *hum*ble
spirit * let us be re*ceived*;

as though it were holocausts of *rams*
and bullocks, * or thousands of fat
lambs,

so let our sacrifice be in your pre*sence*
today * as we follow you unre*serv*èd-
ly;

for those who *trust* in you * cannot be
put to *shame*.

And now we follow you with *our* whole
heart,* we fear you and we pray to
you.

Glory to the Father, and *to* the Son, *
and to the Holy *Spi*rit:

as it was in the begin*ning*, is now, * and
will be for ever. A*men*.

Antiphon   **Lord, do *not* withhold * your compassion from *us*.**

December 17-23:   Zion is our mighty citadel, † our saving Lord its wall and its defense; † throw op*en* the gates, * for our God is here among us, alle*lu*ia.

Easter: Let all the na*tions*, O Lord, * know the depths of your loving mercy for us, alle*lu*ia.

Ant. 3   O God, I *will* sing * to you *a* new song.

December 17-23:   Lord, make known your will throughout *the* earth; * proclaim your salvation to *eve*ry nation.

Easter: The Lord is *my* refuge * and my savior, *a*lleluia.

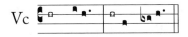

Psalm 144:1-10
Prayer for victory and peace
I can do all things in him who strengthens me (Phillippians 4:13).

Blessèd be the Lord, my rock, † who trains my arms *for* battle, * who prepares my *hands* for war

He is my love, *my* fortress; * he is my strong*hold*, my savior,

my shield, my place *of* refuge. * He brings peoples un*der* my rule.

Lord, what is man that you care *for* him, * mortal man, that you keep *him* in mind;

man, who is merely *a* breath, * whose life fades like a *pass*ing shadow?

Lower your heavens and *come* down; * touch the mountains, wreathe *them* in smoke.

Flash your lightnings; rout *the* foe, *

shoot your arrows and put *them* to flight.

Reach down from heaven *and* save me; * draw me out from the *migh*ty waters,

from the hands of alien foes † whose mouths are filled *with* lies, * whose hands are *raised* in perjury.

To you, O God, will I sing a *new* song; * I will play on the *ten*-stringed harp

to you who give kings *their* victory, * who set David your *ser*vant free.

Glory to the Father, and to *the* Son, * and to the *Ho*ly Spirit:

as it was in the beginning, *is* now, * and will be for e*ver*. Amen.

Antiphon   O God, I *will* sing * to you *a* new song.

December 17-23:   Lord, make known your will throughout *the* earth; * proclaim your salvation to *eve*ry nation.

Easter: The Lord is *my* refuge * and my savior, *a*lleluia.

READING   Isaiah 55:1

All you who are thirsty,
    come to the water!
You who have no money,
    come, receive grain and eat;
Come, without paying and without cost,
    drink wine and milk!

RESPONSORY (VI F)

Lord, listen *to* my cry; * all my trust is in *your* promise.

— Lord, listen *to* my cry; * all my trust is in *your* promise.

Dawn finds me watching, crying *out* for you.

— All my trust is in *your* promise.

Glory to the Father, and *to* the Son, * and to the Ho*ly* Spirit.

— Lord, listen *to* my cry; * all my trust is in *your* promise.

CANTICLE OF ZECHARIAH

Antiphon   Lord, save us *from* the hands * of all *who* hate us.

INTERCESSIONS (VI F)

To the God who gives us the joy of praising him this morning, and who
    strength*ens* our hope, * *let* us pray:

Hear us, O Lord, for the glory of your name.

We thank you, God and Father of Je*sus* our Savior,

— for the knowledge and immortality you have given *us* through him.

Make us hum*ble* of heart,

— help us to serve one another out of rever*ence* for Christ.

Pour out your Spirit upon *us*, your servants,

— make us sincere in our love *for* each other.

You instructed man to labor and to exercise dominion o*ver* the earth,

— may our work honor you and sanctify our broth*ers* and sisters.

Our Father . . .

Prayer

Increase in us, Lord,
the faith you have given us,
and bring to a harvest worthy of heaven
the praise we offer you at the beginning of this new day.
We ask this through our Lord Jesus Christ, your Son,
who lives and reigns with you and the Holy Spirit,
one God, for ever and ever.

TUESDAY, WEEK IV

Evening Prayer

HYMN, 1336.
Sator principesque temporum. (L.M.)

Sator princépsque témporum,	Great Ruler of all space and time,
clarum diem labóribus	You give us daylight to employ
noctémque qui sopóribus	In work for you, that with the night
fixo distínguis órdine,	Refreshing sleep we may enjoy.
Mentem tu castam dírige,	While silence and the darkness reign
obscúra ne siléntia	Preserve our souls from sin and harm,
ad dira cordis vúlnera	Let nothing evil venture near
telis patéscant ínvidi.	To cause us panic or alarm.
Vacent ardóre péctora,	And while we thus renew our strength,
faces nec ullas pérferant,	Untouched by taint of sinful fire
quæ nostro hæréntes sénsui	Let hearts and minds find rest in you,
mentis vigórem sáucient.	The Source of every good desire.
Præsta, Pater piíssime,	O Father, this we ask be done
Patríque compar Unice,	Through Jesus Christ, your only Son,
cum Spíritu Paráclito	Whom in the Spirit we adore:
regnans per omne sæculum. Amen.	One God who reigns for evermore. Amen.

PSALMODY

Ant. 1 — If I forget you, Je*ru*salem, * let my right *hand* wither.

December 17-23: — The Lord will come from his holy *place* * to save *his* people.

Easter: — Sing for us one of Zion's *songs,* * al*le*luia.

VIIIa

Psalm 137:1-6
By the rivers of Babylon
The Babylonian captivity is a type of our spiritual captivity (Saint Hilary).

By the rivers of Babylon there we sat
and *wept,* * remember*ing* Zion;
on the poplars that *grew* there * we
  hung up *our* harps.
For it was there that they asked us, our
  captors, for *songs,* * our oppressors, *for*

joy.
"Sing to us," they *said,* * "one of Zion's
  songs."
O how could we sing the song of the
  Lord * on ali*en* soil?
If I forget you, Je*ru*salem, * let my right

hand wither!

O let my tongue cleave to my *mouth* * if
  I remember *you* not,

if I prize not Je*ru*salem * above all *my*
  joys!

Glory to the Father, and to the *Son*, *
  and to the Ho*ly* Spirit:

as it was in the beginning, is *now*, * and
  will be for ever. *A*men.

Antiphon	If I forget you, Je*ru*salem, * let my right *hand* wither.
December 17-23:	The Lord will come from his holy *place* * to save *his* people.
Easter:	Sing for us one of Zion's *songs*, * al*le*luia.

Ant. 2	In the presence *of* the angels * I will sing to you, my *God*.
December 17-23:	Zion is our mighty citadel, † our saving Lord its wall and its defense; † throw o*pen* the gates, * for our God is here among us, alle*lu*ia.
Easter:	Though I am surrounded *by* affliction, * you preserve my life, alle*lu*ia.

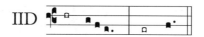

IID

Psalm 138
Thanksgiving
The kings of the earth will bring his glory and honor into the holy city (see Revelation 21:24).

I thank you, Lord, with *all* my heart, *
  you have heard the words of my
  mouth.

In the presence of the angels *I* will bless
  you. * I will adore before your holy
  temple.

I thank you for your faithful*ness* and
  love * which excel all we ever knew of
  you.

On the day I *called*, you answered; * you
  increased the strength of my *soul*.

All earth's *kings* shall thank you * when
  they hear the words of your *mouth*.

They shall sing *of* the Lord's ways: *
  "How great is the glory of the *Lord*!"

The Lord is high yet he looks *on* the
  lowly * and the haughty he knows
  from a*far*.

Though I walk in the midst *of* affliction
  * you give me life and frustrate my
  foes.

You stretch out your *hand* and save me,
  * your hand will do all things for *me*.

Your love, O Lord, *is* eternal, * discard
  not the work of your *hands*.

Glory to the Father, and *to* the Son, *
  and to the Holy *Spirit*:

as it was in the begin*ning*, is now, * and
  will be for ever. *A*men.

Antiphon	In the presence *of* the angels * I will sing to you, my *God*.
December 17-23:	Zion is our mighty citadel, † our saving Lord its wall and its defense; † throw o*pen* the gates, * for our God is here among us, alle*lu*ia.
Easter:	Though I am surrounded *by* affliction, * you preserve my life, alle*lu*ia.

Ant. 3   Adoration and glory belong *by* right * to the Lamb *who* was slain.

December 17-23:   Lord, make known your will throughout *the* earth; * proclaim your salvation to *eve*ry nation.

Easter: Yours, O Lord, is majesty *and* power, * glory and triumph, a*l*leluia.

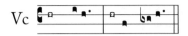

Canticle   Revelation 4:11; 5:9, 10, 12
Redemption hymn

O Lord our God, you *are* worthy *
   to receive glory and hon*or* and
power.
For you have created *all* things; * by
   your will they came to be *and* were
   made.
Worthy are you, O Lord, * to receive
   the scroll and break *open* its seals.
For you *were* slain; * with your blood
   you pur*chased* for God
men of every race *and* tongue, * of every
   peo*ple* and nation.

You made of them a kingdom, † and
   priests to serve *our* God, * and they
   shall reign *on* the earth.
Worthy is the Lamb that *was* slain * to
   receive po*wer* and riches,
wisdom *and* strength, * honor and glo*ry*
   and praise.
Glory to the Father, and to *the* Son, *
   and to the *Ho*ly Spirit:
as it was in the beginning, *is* now, * and
   will be for e*ver.* Amen.

Antiphon   Adoration and glory belong *by* right * to the Lamb *who* was slain.

December 17-23:   Lord, make known your will throughout *the* earth; * proclaim your salvation to *eve*ry nation.

Easter: Yours, O Lord, is majesty *and* power, * glory and triumph, a*l*leluia.

READING   Colossians 3:16

Let the word of Christ, rich as it is, dwell in you. In wisdom made perfect,
instruct and admonish one another. Sing gratefully to God from your hearts
in psalms, hymns, and inspired songs.

RESPONSORY (VI F)

I shall know the full*ness* of joy, * when I see your face, O Lord.
— I shall know the full*ness* of joy, * when I see your face, O Lord.
Fulfillment and endless peace *in* your presence,
— when I see your face, O Lord.
Glory to the Father, and *to* the Son, * and to the Ho*ly* Spirit.
— I shall know the full*ness* of joy, * when I see your face, O Lord.

CANTICLE OF MARY

Antiphon   Do great things for *us*, O Lord, * for you are mighty, and holy is *your* name.

INTERCESSIONS (VI F)

Let us praise Christ who gives power and strength *to* his people, * and let us
   entreat him with *sin*cere hearts:
Hear us, O Lord, and we shall praise you for *ever.*
Christ, our strength, you called your faithful ones *to* your truth,
— mercifully grant them faith and *per*severance.
Direct our leaders according *to* your will,
— and help them to keep *us* in peace.
You provided bread for the *hun*gry crowd,
— teach us to share our resources *with* the needy.
Do not direct world leaders to give attention only to the needs of *their* own
   nations,
— but give them, above all, a respect and deep concern *for* all peoples.
Grant blessèd life and resurrrection to our brothers who have fall*en* asleep,
— and may those who have believed in you share *in* your glory.

Our Father . . .

Prayer

    Lord,
      may our evening prayer come before you
      and let the faith our lips profess
      live in the prayerful thoughts of our hearts.
      We ask this through our Lord Jesus Christ, your Son,
      who lives and reigns with you and the Holy Spirit,
      one God, for ever and ever.

Morning Prayer

HYMN, 1337.
Fulgentis auctor aetheris. (L.M.)

Fulgéntis auctor ætheris,	Creator of the skies above,
qui lunam lumen nóctibus,	The wisdom of your plan decreed
solem diérum cúrsibus	That sun should give us light by day,
certo fundásti trámite,	And moon should rule the hours of night.
Nox atra iam depéllitur,	The darkness is dispelled at last,
mundi nitor renáscitur,	The world's great beauty is revealed;
novúsque iam mentis vigor	Our strength of soul is now renewed
dulces in actus érigit.	To spur us on to kindly deeds.
Laudes sonáre iam tuas	Returning day call us to prayer,
dies relátus ádmonet,	And bids us sing your praise anew;
vultúsque cæli blándior	The bright'ning aspect of the sky
nostra serénat péctora.	Gives courage and serenity.
Vitémus omne lúbricam,	May we avoid all stain of sin,
declínet prava spíritus,	No evil mar our thoughts this day,
vitam facta non ínquinent,	No sinful action spoil our lives,
linguam culpa non ímplicet;	No wrong or idle words offend.
Sed, sol diem dum cónficit,	But while the sun draws on the day,
fides profúnda férveat,	May our weak faith grow strong and sure
spes ad promíssa próvocet,	With hope that presses to the goal,
Christo coniúngat cáritas.	And love unites us all to Christ.
Præsta, Pater piíssime,	O Father, this we ask be done
Patríque compar Unice,	Through Jesus Christ, your only Son,
cum Spíritu Paráclito	Whom in the Spirit we adore:
regnans per omne sæculum. Amen.	One God who reigns for evermore. Amen.

PSALMODY

Ant. 1   My heart is ready, O *God*, * my heart *is* ready.
December 17-23:   The Lord, the mighty *God*, * will come forth from Zion to set his peo*ple* free.
Easter: O God, arise above the *hea*vens, * al*le*luia.

VIIIa

Psalm 108
Praise of God and a plea for help
Since the Son of God has been exalted above the heavens, his glory is proclaimed
through all the earth (Arnobius).

My heart is ready, O *God*; * I will
  sing, sing *your* praise.
Awake, my soul; awake, lyre and *harp*. *
  I will awake *the* dawn.
I will thank you, Lord, among the
  *peo*ples, * among the nations I *will*
  praise you,
for your love reaches to the *hea*vens *
  and your truth to *the* skies.
O God, arise above the *hea*vens; * may
  your glory shine *on* earth!
O come and deliver your *friends*; * help
  with your right hand and *re*ply.
From his holy place God has made this
  promise: † "I will triumph and divide
  the land of *Shech*em; * I will measure
  out the valley *of* Succoth.
Gilead is mine and Ma*nas*seh. *
  Ephraim I take for *my* helmet,

Judah for my commander's *staff*. *
  Moab I will use for *my* washbowl,
on Edom I will plant my *shoe*. * Over
  the Philistines I will shout *in* triumph."
But who will lead me to conquer the
  *fort*ress? * Who will bring me face to
  face *with* Edom?
Will you utterly reject us, O *God*, * and
  no longer march with *our* armies?
Give us help against the *foe*: * for the
  help of man *is* vain.
With God we shall do *bravely* * and he
  will trample down *our* foes.
Glory to the Father, and to the *Son*, *
  and to the Ho*ly* Spirit:
as it was in the beginning, is *now*, * and
  will be for ever. *A*men.

Antiphon   My heart is ready, O *God*, * my heart *is* ready.
December 17-23:   The Lord, the mighty *God*, * will come forth from Zion to set his peo*ple* free.
Easter: O God, arise above the *hea*vens, * al*le*luia.

Ant. 2   The Lord has robed *me* with grace * and sal*va*tion.

December 17-23:   I shall not cease to plead with *God* for Zion * until he sends his Holy One in all
                   his radiant *beau*ty.

Easter: The Lord will make praise and justice blossom before *all* the nations, * alle*lu*ia.

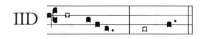

IID

Canticle   Isaiah 61:10-62:5
The prophet's joy in the vision of a new Jerusalem
I saw the holy city, new Jerusalem, with the beauty of a bride adorned for her husband
(Revelation 21:2).

I rejoice heartily *in* the Lord, * in my
God is the joy of my *soul*;

for he has clothed me with a robe *of*
salvation, * and wrapped me in a
mantle of *jus*tice,

like a bridegroom adorned *with* a
diadem, * like a bride bedecked with
her *jew*els.

As the earth brings *forth* its plants, *
and a garden makes its growth spring
up,

so will the Lord God make jus*tice* and
praise * spring up before all the
*na*tions.

For Zion's sake I will *not* be silent, * for
Jerusalem's sake I will not be *qui*et,

until her vindication shines forth *like*
the dawn * and her victory like a
burning *torch*.

Nations shall behold your *vin*dication, *
and all kings your *glo*ry;

you shall be called *by* a new name *
pronounced by the mouth of the
Lord.

You shall be a glorious crown in the
hand *of* the Lord, * a royal diadem
held by your *God*.

No more shall men call *you* "Forsaken,"
* or your land "*De*solate,"

but you shall be called "*My* delight," *
and your land "E*spoused*."

For the Lord de*lights* in you, * and
makes your land his *spouse*.

As a young man mar*ries* a virgin, * your
Builder shall marry *you*;

and as a bridegroom rejoices *in* his
bride * so shall your God rejoice in
you.

Glory to the Father, and *to* the Son, *
and to the Holy *Spir*it:

as it was in the begin*ning*, is now, * and
will be for ever. A*men*.

Antiphon   The Lord has robed *me* with grace * and sal*va*tion.

December 17-23:   I shall not cease to plead with *God* for Zion * until he sends his Holy One in all
                   his radiant *beau*ty.

Easter: The Lord will make praise and justice blossom before *all* the nations, * alle*lu*ia.

Ant. 3   I will praise *my* God * all the days *of* my life.

December 17-23:   The Spirit of the Lord rests *upon* me; * he has sent me to preach his joyful message *to* the poor.

Easter: Zion, the Lord, *your* God, * will reign for ever, a*l*leluia.

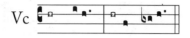

Vc

Psalm 146

Those who trust in God know what it is to be happy

To praise God in our lives means all we do must be for his glory (Arnobius).

My soul, give praise to the Lord; †
I will praise the Lord all *my*
days, * make music to my God *while*
I live.

Put no trust *in* princes, * in mortal men
in whom there *is* no help.

Take their breath, they return *to* clay *
and their plans that day *come* to
nothing.

He is happy who is helped by Ja*cob's*
God, * whose hope is in the *Lord* his
God,

who alone made heaven *and* earth, * the
seas and all *they* contain.

It is he who keeps faith *for* ever, * who
is just to those who *are* oppressed.

It is he who gives bread to *the* hungry, *
the Lord, who sets pris*o*ners free,

the Lord who gives sight to *the* blind, *
who raises up those who *are* bowed
down,

the Lord, who protects *the* stranger *
and upholds the wi*dow* and orphan.

It is the Lord who loves *the* just * but
thwarts the path *of* the wicked.

The Lord will reign *for* ever, * Zion's
God, from *age* to age.

Glory to the Father, and to *the* Son, *
and to the *Holy* Spirit:

as it was in the beginning, *is* now, * and
will be for e*ver.* Amen.

Antiphon   I will praise *my* God * all the days *of* my life.

December 17-23:   The Spirit of the Lord rests *upon* me; * he has sent me to preach his joyful message *to* the poor.

Easter: Zion, the Lord, *your* God, * will reign for ever, a*l*leluia.

READING   Deuteronomy 4:39-40a

Know, and fix in your heart, that the Lord is God in the heavens above and on earth below, and that there is no other. You must keep his statutes and commandments which I enjoin on you today.

RESPONSORY (VI F)

I will *bless* the Lord * all my *life* long.
— I will *bless* the Lord * all my *life* long.
With a song of praise ever *on* my lips,
— all my *life* long.
Glory to the Father, and *to* the Son, * and to the Ho*ly* Spirit.
— I will *bless* the Lord * all my *life* long.

CANTICLE OF ZECHARIAH

Antiphon   Let us serve the *Lord* in holiness * all the days of *our* life.

INTERCESSIONS (VI F)

Christ, the splendor of the Father's glory, enlightens us *with* his word. * With
    deep love we *call* upon him:
*Hear us, King of eter*nal *glory.*
 Blessèd are you, the alpha and the omega *of* our faith,
— for you called us out of darkness into your mar*ve*lous light.
You enabled the blind to see, the *deaf* to hear,
— help our *un*belief.
Lord, keep us in your love, preserve *our* community,
— do not let us become separated from *one* another.
Give us strength in temptation, endur*ance* in trial,
— and gratitude *in* prosperity.

Our Father…

Prayer

     Father,
     keep in mind your holy covenant,
     sealed with the blood of the Lamb.
     Forgive the sins of your people
     and let this new day bring us closer to salvation.
     We ask this through our Lord Jesus Christ, your Son,
     who lives and reigns with you and the Holy Spirit,
     one God, for ever and ever.

WEDNESDAY, WEEK IV

Evening Prayer

HYMN, 1338.
Sol, ecce, lentus occidens. (L.M.)

Sol, ecce, lentus óccidens	As sun declines and shadows fall,
montes et arva et æquora	The sea and hills will fade from sight;
mæstus relínquit, ínnovat	Its fiery orb bids us farewell
sed lucis omen crástinæ,	But promises tomorrow's light.
Mirántibus mortálibus	And thus, O God, creator wise,
sic te, Creátor próvide,	You regulate in wondrous way
leges vicésque témporum	The laws of this great universe
umbris dedísse et lúmini.	At which we marvel night and day.
Ac dum, tenébris æthera	While darkness rides across the sky,
siléntio preméntibus,	And stars their silent watches keep,
vigor labórum déficit,	Your children leave their constant toil,
quies cupíta quæritur,	Regaining strength by peaceful sleep.
Spe nos fidéque dívites	Made rich in hope, kept strong in faith,
tui beámur lúmine	May we be blest throughout the night,
Verbi, quod est a sæculis	By Christ, the Word, who timeless reigns,
splendor patérnæ glóriæ.	True splendor of the Father's light.
Est ille sol qui nésciat	He is the sun that never sets,
ortum vel umquam vésperum ;	No dusk can make his lustre die,
quo terra gestit cóntegi,	The kind Protector of the earth,
quo cæli in ævum iúbilant.	The joy of all the saints on high.
Hac nos seréna pérpetim	O Father, Son, and Spirit blest
da luce tandem pérfrui,	Grant us at last that light to see,
cum Nato et almo Spíritu	And full of joy your praises sing,
tibi novántes cántica. Amen.	Bathed in your love eternally. Amen.

PSALMODY

Ant. 1	Lord, how wonderful is your *wis*dom, * so far beyond my un*der*standing.
December 17-23:	The Lord, the mighty *God*, * will come forth from Zion to set his peo*ple* free.
Easter:	The night will be as clear as *day*, * al*le*luia.

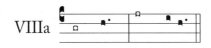

VIIIa

Psalm 139:1-18, 23-24
God sees all that is
Who has known the mind of God, who has been his counselor? (Romans 11:34).

O Lord, you search me and you
know me, † you know my resting
and my *ris*ing, * you discern my
purpose from *a*far.
You mark when I walk or lie *down*, * all
my ways lie open *to* you.
Before ever a word is on my *tongue* *
you know it, O Lord, through *and*
through.
Behind and before you be*siege* me, *
your hand ever laid *up*on me.
Too wonderful for me, this *knowl*edge, *
too high, beyond *my* reach.
O where can I go from your *spir*it, * or
where can I flee from *your* face?

If I climb the heavens, you are *there*. * If
I lie in the grave, you *are* there.
If I take the wings of the *dawn* * and
dwell at the sea's furth*est* end,
even there your hand would *lead* me, *
your right hand would hold *me* fast.
If I say: "Let the darkness *hide* me * and
the light around me *be* night,"
even darkness is not dark for *you* * and
the night is as clear as *the* day.
Glory to the Father, and to the *Son*, *
and to the Ho*ly* Spirit:
as it was in the beginning, is *now*, * and
will be for ever. *A*men.

Antiphon	Lord, how wonderful is your *wis*dom, * so far beyond my un*der*standing.
December 17-23:	The Lord, the mighty *God*, * will come forth from Zion to set his peo*ple* free.
Easter:	The night will be as clear as *day*, * al*le*luia.

Ant. 2	I am the Lord: † I search the mind and *probe* the heart; * I give to each one as his deeds de*serve*.
December 17-23:	I shall not cease to plead with *God* for Zion * until he sends his Holy One in all his radiant *beau*ty.
Easter:	I know my sheep and *mine* know me, * alle*lu*ia.

IID

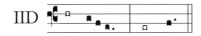

II

For it was you who creat*ed* my being,
  * knit me together in my mother's
womb.
I thank you for the wonder *of* my being,
  * for the wonders of all your cre*a*tion.
Already you *knew* my soul, * my body
  held no secret from *you*
when I was being fa*shi*oned in secret *
  and molded in the depths of the
earth.
Your eyes saw *all* my actions, * they
  were all of them written in your *book*;
every one of my days *was* decreed *
  before one of them came into *be*ing.

To me, how mysteri*ous* your thoughts, *
  the sum of them not to be *num*bered!
If I count them, they are more *than* the
  sand; * to finish, I must be eternal,
like *you*.
O search me, God, and *know* my heart.
  * O test me and know my *thoughts*.
See that I follow *not* the wrong path *
  and lead me in the path of life
e*ter*nal.
Glory to the Father, and *to* the Son, *
  and to the Holy *Spi*rit:
as it was in the begin*ning*, is now, * and
  will be for ever. A*men*.

Antiphon   I am the Lord: † I search the mind and *probe* the heart; * I give to
             each one as his deeds de*serve*.

December 17-23:   I shall not cease to plead with *God* for Zion * until he sends his Holy One in all
                  his radiant *beau*ty.

Easter: I know my sheep and *mine* know me, * alle*lu*ia.

Ant. 3   Through him all things *were* made; * he holds all creation
             together *in* himself.

December 17-23:   The Spirit of the Lord rests u*po*n me; * he has sent me to preach his joyful
                  message *to* the poor.

Easter: His glory covers *the* heavens * and his praise fills the earth, a*l*leluia.

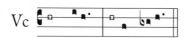

Canticle   Colossians 1:12-20

Christ, the first-born of all creation and the first-born from the dead

Let us give thanks to the Father †
  for having made *you* worthy * to
share the lot of the *saints* in light.
He rescued us from the power *of*
  darkness * and brought us into the
  kingdom of his be*lov*èd Son.
Through him we *have* redemption, *
  the forgiveness *of* our sins.
He is the image of the invisi*ble* God, *
  the first-born *of* all creatures.
In him everything in heaven and on

earth was *cre*ated, * things visible *and*
  invisible.
All were created *through* him; * all were
  creat*ed* for him.
He is before all else *that* is. * In him
  everything contin*ues* in being.
It is he who is head of the body, the
  church! † he who is the beginning,
  the first-born of *the* dead, * so that
  primacy may be *his* in everything.
It pleased God to make absolute

fullness reside *in* him * and, by means of him, to reconcile everything *in* his person,

both on earth and in *the* heavens, * making peace through the blood *of*

his cross.

Glory to the Father, and to *the* Son, * and to the *Holy* Spirit:

as it was in the beginning, *is* now, * and will be for e*ver.* Amen.

Antiphon	Through him all things *were* made; * he holds all creation together *in* himself.
December 17-23:	The Spirit of the Lord rests *up*on me; * he has sent me to preach his joyful message *to* the poor.
Easter:	His glory covers *the* heavens * and his praise fills the earth, *al*leluia.

READING   1 John 2:3-6

The way we can be sure of our knowledge of Christ
is to keep his commandments.
The man who claims, "I have known him,"
without keeping his commandments,
is a liar; in such a one there is no truth.
But whoever keeps his word,
truly has the love of God been made perfect in him.
The way we can be sure we are in union with him
is for the man who claims to abide in him
to conduct himself just as he did.

RESPONSORY (VI F)
Keep *us*, O Lord, * as the apple of *your* eye.
— Keep *us*, O Lord, * as the apple of *your* eye.
Gather us under the shadow of your *wings*, and keep us,
— as the apple of *your* eye.
Glory to the Father, and *to* the Son, * and to the Ho*ly* Spirit.
— Keep *us*, O Lord, * as the apple of *your* eye.

CANTICLE OF MARY
Antiphon   Lord, with the strength *of* your arm * scatter the proud and lift up *the* lowly.

INTERCESSIONS (VI F)
With joyful hearts, let us praise the E*ter*nal Father * whose mercy toward his people is exalted *to* the heavens:
Let all who hope in you rejoice, O Lord.
Remember, Lord, that you sent your Son into the world to be its savior, *not* its judge,
— let his glorious death bring *us* salvation.

You ordained your priests to be ministers of Christ and stewards of your
    marvelous gifts,
— fill them with fidelity, wisdom and love.
You have called men and women to chastity for the sake of the kingdom,
— let them faithfully follow your Son.
From the beginning you intended husband and wife to be one,
— keep all families united in sincere love.
You sent Christ Jesus into the world to absolve the sins of men,
— free all the dead from their sins.

Our Father . . .

Prayer

God our Father,
you have filled the hungry with the good things of heaven.
Keep in mind your infinite compassion.
Look upon our poverty:
and let us share the riches of your life and love.
We ask this through our Lord Jesus Christ, your Son,
who lives and reigns with you and the Holy Spirit,
one God, for ever and ever.

THURSDAY, WEEK IV

Morning Prayer

HYMN, 1339.
Iam lucis orto sídere. (L.M.)

Iam lucis orto sídere	Now that the daylight fills the sky,
Deum precémur súpplices,	We lift our hearts to God on high,
ut in diúrnis áctibus	That he, in all we do or say,
nos servet a nocéntibus.	Would keep us free from harm today:
Linguam refrénans témperet,	Would guard our hearts and tongues from strife;
ne litis horror ínsonet;	From anger's din would hide our life;
visum fovéndo cóntegat,	From all ill sights would turn our eyes;
ne vanitátes háuriat.	Would close our ears from vanities:
Sint pura cordis íntima,	Would keep our inmost conscience pure;
absístat et vecórdia;	Our souls from folly would secure;
carnis terat supérbiam	Would bid us check the pride of sense
potus cibíque párcitas;	With due and holy abstinence.
Ut, cum dies abscésserit	So we, when this new day is gone,
noctémque sor redúxerit,	And night in turn is drawing on,
mundi per abstinéntiam	With conscience by the world unstained
ipsi canámus glóriam.	Shall praise his name for vict'ry gained.
Deo Patri sit glória	All laud to God the Father be;
eiúsque soli Fílio	All praise, eternal Son, to thee;
cum Spíritu Paráclito,	All glory, as is ever meet,
in sempitérna sæcula. Amen.	To God the Holy Paraclete. Amen.

PSALMODY

Ant. 1   At daybreak, be merciful to *me*, * O Lord, *my* God.

December 17-23:   To you, O Lord, I lift up my soul; † come and rescue *me*, * for you are my refuge and *my* strength.

Easter: Be true to your name, O *Lord*, * and preserve my life, al*le*luia.

VIIIa

Psalm 143:1-11
Prayer in distress
A man is not justified by observance of the law but only through faith in Jesus Christ
(Galatians 2:16).

Lord, listen to my *prayer*: * turn your ear to my *ap*peal.

You are faithful, you are just; give answer. † Do not call your servant to *judg*ment * for no one is just in *your* sight.

The enemy pursues my *soul*; * he has crushed my life to *the* ground;

he has made me dwell in *dark*ness * like the dead, long *for*gotten.

Therefore my spirit *fails*; * my heart is numb *with*in me.

I remember the days that are *past*: * I ponder all *your* works.

I muse on what your hand has wrought † and to you I stretch out my *hands*. * Like a parched land my soul thirsts *for* you.

Lord, make haste and *an*swer; * for my spirit fails *with*in me.

Do not hide your *face* * lest I become like those in *the* grave.

In the morning let me know your *love* * for I put my trust *in* you.

Make me know the way I should *walk*: * to you I lift up *my* soul.

Rescue me, Lord, from my *en*emies; * I have fled to you *for* refuge.

Teach me to do your *will* * for you, O Lord, are *my* God.

Let your good spirit *guide* me * in ways that are level *and* smooth.

For your name's sake, Lord, save my *life*; * in your justice save my soul from *dis*tress.

Glory to the Father, and to the *Son*, * and to the Ho*ly* Spirit:

as it was in the beginning, is *now*, * and will be for ever. *A*men.

Antiphon	At daybreak, be merciful to *me*, * O Lord, *my* God.
December 17-23:	To you, O Lord, I lift up my soul; † come and rescue *me*, * for you are my refuge and *my* strength.
Easter:	Be true to your name, O *Lord*, * and preserve my life, al*le*luia.

Ant. 2	The Lord will make a ri*ver* of peace * flow through Jer*u*salem.
December 17-23:	Bless those, O Lord, who have waited *for* your coming; * let your prophets be proved *true*.
Easter:	I will see you again and your hearts *will* rejoice, * alle*lu*ia.

IID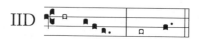

Canticle   Isaiah 66:10-14a

Joys of heaven

The heavenly Jerusalem is a free woman and our mother (Galatians 4:26).

Rejoice with Jerusalem and be glad be*cause* of her, * all you who *love* her;

exult, ex*ult* with her, * all you who were mourning *over* her!

Oh, that you *may* suck fully * of the

milk of her *comfort*,

that you may nurse *with* delight * at her abundant *breasts*!

For thus says the Lord: † Lo, I will spread prosperity over her *like* a river, * and the wealth of the nations like an

overflowing *torrent.*
As nurslings, you shall be carried *in* her arms, * and fondled in her *lap;*
as a mother comforts her son, † so will I *com*fort you; * in Jerusalem you shall find your *com*fort.
When you see this, your heart *shall*

rejoice, * and your bodies flourish like the *grass.*
Glory to the Father, and *to* the Son, * and to the Holy *Spir*it:
as it was in the begin*ning,* is now, * and will be for ever. A*men.*

Antiphon   The Lord will make a ri*ver* of peace * flow through Je*ru*salem.
December 17-23:   Bless those, O Lord, who have waited *for* your coming; * let your prophets be proved *true.*
Easter: I will see you again and your hearts *will* rejoice, * alle*lui*a.

Ant. 3   Let us joyful*ly* praise * the *Lord* our God.
December 17-23:   Turn to us, O Lord, * make haste to *help* your people.
Easter: The Lord rebuilds *Je*rusalem * and heals the brokenhearted, a*lle*luia.

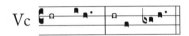

Psalm 147:1-11
The loving kindness of God who can do all he wills
You are God: we praise you; you are the Lord: we acclaim you.

Praise the Lord for he is good; †
sing to our God for he *is* loving: *
to him our *praise* is due.
The Lord builds up *Je*rusalem * and brings back Isr*ae*l's exiles,
he heals the bro*ken*-hearted, * he binds up *all* their wounds.
He fixes the number of *the* stars; * he calls each one *by* its name.
Our Lord is great and al*migh*ty; * his wisdom can ne*ver* be measured.
The Lord raises *the* lowly; * he humbles the wicked *to* the dust.
O sing to the Lord, giv*ing* thanks; * sing psalms to our God *with* the

harp.
He covers the heavens *with* clouds; * he prepares the rain *for* the earth,
making mountains sprout *with* grass * and with plants to *serve* man's needs.
He provides the beasts with *their* food * and young ravens that *call* upon him.
His delight is not *in* horses * nor his pleasure in warriors' strength.
The Lord delights in those who re*vere* him, * in those who wait *for* his love.
Glory to the Father, and to *the* Son, * and to the *Ho*ly Spirit:
as it was in the beginning, *is* now, * and will be for e*ver.* Amen.

Antiphon   Let us joyful*ly* praise * the *Lord* our God.
December 17-23:   Turn to us, O Lord, * make haste to *help* your people.
Easter: The Lord rebuilds *Je*rusalem * and heals the brokenhearted, a*lle*luia.

READING   Romans 8:18-21

The sufferings of the present are as nothing compared with the glory to be
revealed in us. Indeed, the whole created world eagerly awaits the revelation
of the sons of God. Creation was made subject to futility, not of its own
accord but by him who once subjected it; yet not without hope, because the
world itself will be freed from its slavery to corruption and share in the
glorious freedom of the children of God.

RESPONSORY (VI F)

In the early hours *of* the morning, * I think of you, O Lord.
— In the early hours *of* the morning, * I think of you, O Lord.
Always you are *there* to help me,
— I think of you, O Lord.
Glory to the Father, and *to* the Son, * and to the Ho*ly* Spirit.
— In the early hours *of* the morning, * I think of you, O Lord.

CANTICLE OF ZECHARIAH

Antiphon   Give your people knowledge of sal*va*tion, Lord, * and forgive us
                  our sins.

INTERCESSIONS (VI F)

Let us *pray* to God, * who gives salvation *to* his people:
You are our life, O Lord.
Bless*èd* are you, Father of our Lord Jesus Christ, for by your mercy we have been
   reborn to a *living* hope,
— through the resurrection of Jesus Christ *from* the dead.
You made man in your image and renewed *him* in Christ,
— mold us into the likeness *of* your Son.
Pour out your love through the *Holy* Spirit,
— heal our hearts, wounded by ha*tred* and jealousy.
Today grant work to laborers, bread to the hungry, joy *to* the sorrowful,
— grace and redemption *to* all men.

Our Father . . .

Prayer

Lord,
let the knowledge of salvation
enlighten our hearts,
so that, freed from fear and from the power of our enemies,
we may serve you faithfully all the days of our life.
We ask this through our Lord Jesus Christ, your Son,
who lives and reigns with you and the Holy Spirit,
one God, for ever and ever.

THURSDAY, WEEK IV

Evening Prayer

HYMN, 1340.
Deus, qui claro lumine. (L.M.)

Deus, qui claro lúmine diem fecísti, Dómine, tuam rogámus glóriam dum pronus dies vólvitur	O Lord our God, who made the day To gladden us with its fair light, We praise your name, imploring aid, For day will soon give place to night.
Iam sol urgénte véspero occásum suum gráditur, mundum conclúdens ténebris, suum obsérvans órdinem.	The evening shadows grow apace, Advancing, they will hide the sun, As darkness creeps upon the earth When day-light hours their course have run.
Tu vero, excélse Dómine, precántes tuos fámulos diúrno lassos ópere ne sinas umbris ópprimi,	We beg you, Lord and God Most High, Protect us with your presence blessed, Though weary, keep our souls in peace And not by gloom of night oppressed.
Ut non fuscátis méntibus dies abscédat sæculi, sed tua tecti grátia cernámus lucem prósperam.	Let not the setting sun go down On hearts distressed with sin, and sore, But sheltered by your gentle grace, May we behold the day once more.
Præsta, Pater piíssime, Patríque compar Unice, cum Spíritu Paráclito regnans per omne sæculum. Amen.	To you, O Christ, most kindly King, And to the Father, glory be, Praise to the Spirit Paraclete, In ev'ry age eternally. Amen.

PSALMODY

Ant. 1   He is my comfort and my *re*fuge. * In him I put *my* trust.

December 17-23:   To you, O Lord, I lift up my soul; † come and rescue *me*, * for you are my refuge and *my* strength.

Easter: The Lord is my stronghold and my *savi*or, * al*le*luia.

Psalm 144
Prayer for victory and peace
Christ learned the art of warfare when he overcame the world, as he said: "I have overcome the world" (Saint Hilary).

I

Blessèd be the Lord, my rock †
    who trains my arms for *bat*tle, *
    who prepares my hands *for* war.
He is my love, my *for*tress; * he is my
    stronghold, *my* savior,
my shield, my place of *refuge*. * He
    brings peoples under *my* rule.
Lord, what is man that you care for
    him, * mortal man, that you keep him
    in mind;
man, who is merely a *breath*, * whose
    life fades like *a* shadow?
Lower your heavens and come *down*; *
    touch the mountains; wreathe them

in smoke.
Flash your lightnings; rout the *foe*, *
    shoot your arrows and put them *to*
    flight.
Reach down from heaven and *save* me;
    * draw me out from the migh*ty*
    waters,
from the hands of alien foes † whose
    mouths are filled with *lies*, * whose
    hands are raised *in* perjury.
Glory to the Father, and to the *Son*, *
    and to the Ho*ly* Spirit:
as it was in the beginning, is *now*, * and
    will be for ever. *A*men.

Antiphon	He is my comfort and my *refuge*. * In him I put *my* trust.
December 17-23:	To you, O Lord, I lift up my soul; † come and rescue *me*, * for you are my refuge and *my* strength.
Easter:	The Lord is my stronghold and my *savior*, * al*le*luia.

Ant. 2	Blessèd *are* the people * whose God is the *Lord*.
December 17-23:	Bless those, O Lord, who have waited *for* your coming; * let your prophets be proved *true*.
Easter:	Thanks be to God who has given *us* the victory * through our Lord Jesus Christ, alle*lu*ia.

IID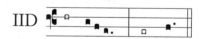

II

To you, O God, will I sing *a*
    new song; * I will play on the ten-
    stringed *harp*
to you who give *kings* their victory, *
    who set David your servant *free*.
You set him free from the *evil* sword; *
    you rescued him from alien *foes*
whose mouths were *filled* with lies, *
    whose hands were raised in *per*jury.
Let our sons then flour*ish* like saplings
    * grown tall and strong from their
    youth:
our daughters grace*ful* as columns, *
    adorned as though for a *pal*ace.

Let our barns be filled to overflowing †
    with crops of *every* kind; * our sheep
    increasing by *thou*sands,
myriads of sheep *in* our fields, * our
    cattle heavy with *young*,
no ruined *wall*, no exile, * no sound of
    weeping in our *streets*.
Happy the people *with* such blessings; *
    happy the people whose God is the
    Lord.
Glory to the Father, and *to* the Son, *
    and to the Holy *Spir*it:
as it was in the begin*ning*, is now, * and
    will be for ever. *A*men.

Antiphon   Blessèd *are* the people * whose God is the *Lord*.

December 17-23:   Bless those, O Lord, who have waited *for* your coming; * let your prophets be
                  proved *true*.

Easter: Thanks be to God who has given *us* the victory * through our Lord Jesus
                  Christ, alle*lu*ia.

Ant. 3   Now the victor*ious* reign * of our God *has* begun.

December 17-23:   Turn to us, O Lord, * make haste to *help* your people.

Easter: Christ yesterday and *to*day: * he is the same for ever, a*l*leluia.

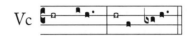

Canticle   Revelation 11:17-18; 12:10b-12a
The judgment of God

We praise you, the Lord God
  *Al*mighty, * who is *and* who was.
You have assumed your *great* power, *
  you have be*gun* your reign.
The nations have raged in anger, † but
  then came your day *of* wrath * and the
  moment to *judge* the dead:
the time to reward your servants the
  prophets † and the holy ones who
  *re*vere you, * the great and the *small*
  alike.
Now have salvation and po*wer* come, *
  the reign of our God and the authority of *his* Anointed One.

For the accuser of our brothers is *cast*
  out, * who night and day accused
  them *be*fore God.
They defeated him by the blood of the
  Lamb † and by the word of *their*
  testimony; * love for life did not deter
  them from death.
so rejoice, *you* heavens, * and you that
  dwell therein!
Glory to the Father, and to *the* Son, *
  and to the *Ho*ly Spirit:
as it was in the beginning, *is* now, * and
  will be for e*ver*. Amen.

Antiphon   Now the victor*ious* reign * of our God *has* begun.

December 17-23:   Turn to us, O Lord, * make haste to *help* your people.

Easter: Christ yesterday and *to*day: * he is the same for ever, a*l*leluia.

READING   See Colossians 1:23

You must hold fast to faith, be firmly grounded and steadfast in it, unshaken
in the hope promised you by the gospel you have heard. It is the gospel which
has been announced to every creature under heaven.

RESPONSORY (VI F)

The Lord *is* my shepherd, * I shall want *for* nothing.

— The Lord *is* my shepherd, * I shall want *for* nothing.

He has brought me *to* green pastures.

— I shall want *for* nothing.

Glory to the Father, and *to* the Son, * and to the Ho*ly* Spirit.

— The Lord *is* my shepherd, * I shall want *for* nothing.

CANTICLE OF MARY

Antiphon   If you hun*ger* for holiness, * God will satisfy your longing, † good measure, and flow*ing* over.

INTERCESSIONS (VI F)

Let us *pray* to Christ, * the light of the nations and the joy of every *living* creature:

*Give us light, peace and securi*ty, Lord.

Brilliant Light, Word of the Father, you came to *save* all men,

— lead the catechumens of your Church into your marve*lo*us light.

Overlook our *sins*, O Lord,

— for you are the source *of* forgiveness.

Lord, it is your will that men use their minds to unlock nature's secrets and mas*ter* the world,

— may the arts and sciences advance your glory and the happiness *of* all peoples.

Look kindly on those who have dedicated themselves to the service of their *fe*llow men,

— may they fulfill their work freely *and* completely.

Lord, you open the way and no *one* can close it,

— lead into your light those who have fallen asleep in the hope of *re*surrection.

Our Father . . .

Prayer

Lord,
hear the evening prayers we bring before you:
help us to follow in the footsteps of your Son
so that we may produce an abundant harvest of goodness
in patience and in faith.
We ask this through our Lord Jesus Christ, your Son,
who lives and reigns with you and the Holy Spirit,
one God, for ever and ever.

FRIDAY, WEEK IV

Morning Prayer

HYMN, 1341.
Deus, qui caeli lumen es. (L.M.)

Deus, qui cæli lumen es	O God, the lamp of heaven high
satórque lucis, qui polum	And source of light: your shining hand
patérno fultum brácchio	Unrolls the banner of the sky,
præclára pandis déxtera,	Upholding it above the land.
Auróra stellas iam tegit	Dawn, casting up a crimson tide,
rubrum sustóllens gúrgitem,	Has veiled the stars that saw its rise;
uméctis atque flátibus	The morning breezes, far and wide,
terram baptízans róribus.	With dewy breath the earth baptize.
Iam noctis umbra línquitur,	The darkness from the sky has gone
polum calígo déserit,	As nightly shadows pass away;
typúsque Christi, lúcifer	The morning star, sign of the Son,
diem sopítum súscitat.	Arising, wakes the sleepy day.
Dies diérum tu, Deus,	O God, O radiance wonderful,
lucísque lumen ipse es,	Most glorious day and fairest light:
Unum potens per ómnia,	One God, in all things powerful,
potens in unum Trínitas.	Three Persons, matchless in one might!
Te nunc, Salvátor, quæsumus	To you, Our Savior, brightest, best,
tibíque genu fléctimus,	On bended knee our prayer we raise;
Patrem cum Sancto Spíritu	To Father and to Spirit blest,
totis laudántes vócibus. Amen.	With all our power, we offer praise. Amen.

PSALMODY

Ant. 1	Create a clean heart in me, O *God*; * renew in me a stead*fast* spirit.
December 17-23:	Our King will come from *Zion*; * the Lord, God-is-with-us, is his migh*ty* name.
Easter:	Christ gave himself up for *us* * as a sacrificial offering to God, al*le*luia.

VIIIa

Psalm 51
O God, have mercy on me
Your inmost being must be renewed, and you must put on the new man (Ephesians 4:23-24).

Have mercy on me, God, in your *kind*ness. * In your compassion blot out my *off*ense.

O wash me more and more from my *guilt* * and cleanse me from *my* sin.

My offenses truly I *know* them; * my sin is always *be*fore me.

Against you, you alone, have I *sinned*; * what is evil in your sight I *have* done.

That you may be justified when you give *sent*ence * and be without reproach when *you* judge,

O see, in guilt I was *born*, * a sinner was I *con*ceived.

Indeed you love truth in the *heart*; * then in the secret of my heart teach *me* wisdom.

O purify me, then I shall be *clean*; * O wash me, I shall be whiter *than* snow.

Make me hear rejoicing and *glad*ness, * that the bones you have crushed may *re*vive.

From my sins turn away your *face* * and blot out all *my* guilt.

A pure heart create for me, O *God*, * put a steadfast spirit *with*in me.

Do not cast me away from your *presence*, * nor deprive me of your ho*ly* spirit.

Give me again the joy of your *help*; * with a spirit of fervor *sus*tain me,

that I may teach transgressors your *ways* * and sinners may return *to* you.

O rescue me, God, my *help*er, * and my tongue shall ring out *your* goodness.

O Lord, open my *lips* * and my mouth shall declare *your* praise.

For in sacrifice you take no de*light*, * burnt offering from me you would *re*fuse,

my sacrifice, a contrite *spir*it. * A humbled, contrite heart you will *not* spurn.

In your goodness, show favor to *Zion*: * rebuild the walls of *Je*rusalem.

Then you will be pleased with lawful *sac*rifice, * holocausts offered on *your* altar.

Glory to the Father, and to the *Son*, * and to the Ho*ly* Spirit:

as it was in the beginning, is *now*, * and will be for ever. *A*men.

Antiphon	Create a clean heart in me, O *God*; * renew in me a stead*fast* spirit.
December 17-23:	Our King will come from *Zion*; * the Lord, God-is-with-us, is his migh*ty* name.
Easter:	Christ gave himself up for *us* * as a sacrificial offering to God, al*le*luia.

Ant. 2   Re*joice*, Jerusalem, * for through you all men will be gathered to the *Lord*.

December 17-23:   Wait for the Lord and he will *come* to you * with his saving *pow*er.

Easter: Jerusalem, city of God, † you will shine with a *ra*diant light, * alle*lu*ia.

Canticle   Tobit 13:8-11, 13-15

Thanksgiving for the people's deliverance

He showed me the holy city Jerusalem which shone with the glory of God
(Revelation 21:10-11).

Let all men speak of *the* Lord's majesty, * and sing his praises in Je*ru*salem.

O Jerusalem, holy city, † he scourged you for the works *of* your hands, * but will again pity the children of the *right*eous.

Praise the Lord for his goodness † and bless the King *of* the ages, * so that his tent may be rebuilt in you with *joy*.

May he gladden within you all who were captives; † all who were ravaged may he cher*ish* within you * for all generations to *come*.

A bright light will shine to all parts *of* the earth; * many nations shall come to you from a*far*,

and the inhabitants of all the limits of the earth, † drawn to you by the name of *the* Lord God, * bearing in their hands their gifts for the King of *heav*en.

Every generation shall give joyful praise in you, † and shall call you the *cho*sen one, * through all ages for*ev*er.

Go, then, rejoice over the children of the righteous, † who shall all be *gath*ered together * and shall bless the Lord of the *ages*.

Happy are *those* who love you, * and happy those who rejoice in your pros*per*ity.

Happy are all the men who shall grieve *o*ver you, * over all your chas*tise*ments, for they shall re*joice* in you * as they behold all your joy for*ev*er.

My spirit bless*es* the Lord, * the great *King*.

Glory to the Father, and *to* the Son, * and to the Holy *Spir*it:

as it was in the begin*ning*, is now, * and will be for ever. A*men*.

Antiphon   Re*joice*, Jerusalem, * for through you all men will be gathered to the *Lord*.

December 17-23:   Wait for the Lord and he will *come* to you * with his saving *pow*er.

Easter: Jerusalem, city of God, † you will shine with a *ra*diant light, * alle*lu*ia.

Ant. 3   Zion, praise *your* God, * who sent his Word to re*new* the earth.

December 17-23:   Eagerly I watch for the Lord; † I wait in joy*ful* hope * for the coming of *God*
                  my Savior.

Easter: I saw the new *Jer*usalem, * coming down from heaven, a*l*leluia.

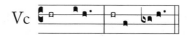

Psalm 147:12-20
The restoration of Jerusalem
Come, I will show you the bride of the Lamb (Revelation 21:9).

O praise the Lord, *Jerusalem!* *
　Zion, *praise* your God!
He has strengthened the bars of *your*
　gates, * he has blessed the child*ren*
　within you.
He established peace on *your* borders, *
　he feeds you with *fin*est wheat.
He sends out his word to *the* earth *
　and swiftly runs *his* command.
He showers down snow white *as* wool, *
　he scatters hoar-*frost* like ashes.
He hurls down hailstones *like* crumbs. *
　The waters are frozen *at* his touch;

he sends forth his word and *it* melts
　them: * at the breath of his mouth the
　*wat*ers flow.
He makes his work known *to* Jacob, *
　to Israel his laws *and* decrees.
He has not dealt thus with o*ther*
　nations; * he has not taught them *his*
　decrees.
Glory to the Father, and to *the* Son, *
　and to the *Ho*ly Spirit:
as it was in the beginning, *is* now, * and
　will be for e*ver*. Amen.

Antiphon   Zion, praise *your* God, * who sent his Word to re*new* the earth.

December 17-23:   Eagerly I watch for the Lord; † I wait in joy*ful* hope * for the coming of *God*
                  my Savior.

Easter: I saw the new *Jer*usalem, * coming down from heaven, a*l*leluia.

READING   Galatians 2:19b-20

I have been crucified with Christ, and the life I live now is not my own;
Christ is living in me. I still live my human life, but it is a life of faith in the
Son of God, who loved me and gave himself for me.

RESPONSORY (VI F)

The Lord, the Most High, has done good *things* for me. * In need I shall cry out *to* him.

— The Lord, the Most High, has done good *things* for me. * In need I shall cry out *to* him.

May he send his *strength* to rescue me.

— In need I shall cry out *to* him.

Glory to the Father, and *to* the Son, * and to the Ho*ly* Spirit.

— The Lord, the Most High, has done good *things* for me. * In need I shall cry out *to* him.

CANTICLE OF ZECHARIAH

Antiphon   Through the tender compassion *of* our God * the dawn from on high shall break *upo*n us.

INTERCESSIONS (VI F)

We trust in God's concern for every person he has created and redeemed *through* his Son. * Let us, therefore, renew our *prayer* to him:

Fulfill the good work you have begun in us, Lord.

O God of mercy, guide us toward spi*ri*tual growth,

— fill our minds with thoughts of truth, jus*tice* and love.

For your name's sake, do not abandon *us* for ever,

— and do not an*nul* your covenant.

Accept us, for our hearts are humble and our spir*its* contrite,

— and those who trust in you shall not be *put* to shame.

You have called us to a prophetic voca*tion* in Christ,

— help us proclaim your *migh*ty deeds.

Our Father . . .

Prayer

Lord,
fill our hearts with your love
as morning fills the sky.
By living your law may we have
your peace in this life
and endless joy in the life to come.
We ask this through our Lord Jesus Christ, your Son,
who lives and reigns with you and the Holy Spirit,
one God, for ever and ever.

FRIDAY, WEEK IV

Evening Prayer

HYMN, 1342.
Horis peractis undecim. (L.M.)

Horis peráctis úndecim	The hours are passing swiftly by,
ruit dies in vésperum;	And into night the shades will flow,
solvámus omnes débitum	So let us sing to God with joy
mentis libénter cánticum.	The grateful hymn of praise we owe.
Labor diúrnus tránsiit	The burden and the heat of day
quo, Christe, nos condúxeras;	Have passed in working for our Lord,
da iam colónis víneæ	So may his vineyard workers all
promíssa dona glóriæ.	Receive from him the great reward.
Mercéde quos nunc ádvocas,	Lord Jesus Christ, you call us now
quos ad futúrum múneras,	To labor for our recompense,
nos in labóre ádiuva	Assist our work, then grant us rest,
et post labórem récrea.	Until your love shall call us hence.
Sit, Christe, rex piíssime,	All glory, Lord, to you we bring,
tibi Patríque glória	Creation's true and only King,
cum Spíritu Paráclito,	Whom with the Father we adore
in sempitérna sæcula. Amen.	And Holy Ghost, for evermore. Amen.

PSALMODY

Ant. 1   Day after day I will bless you, *Lord*; * I will tell of your marve*lous* deeds.

December 17-23:   Our King will come from *Zion*; * the Lord, God-is-with-us, is his migh*ty* name.

Easter: God so loved the world that he gave us his only *Son*, * al*le*luia.

VIIIa

Psalm 145
Praise of God's majesty
Lord, you are the Just One, who was and who is (Revelation 16:5).

I

I will give you glory, O God my
King, * I will bless your name *for*
ever.
I will bless you day after *day* * and

praise your name *for* ever.
The Lord is great, highly to be *praised*,
    * his greatness cannot *be* measured.
Age to age shall proclaim your *works*, *

shall declare your migh*ty* deeds,
shall speak of your splendor and *glo*ry, *
   tell the tale of your wonder*ful* works.
They will speak of your terrible *deeds*, *
   recount your greatness *and* might.
They will recall your abundant *good*-
   ness; * age to age shall ring out *your*
   justice.
The Lord is kind and full of com*pas*-
   sion, * slow to anger, abounding *in*
   love.
How good is the Lord to *all*, * compassionate to all *his* creatures.
All your creatures shall thank you, O

Lord, * and your friends shall repeat
   their blessing.
They shall speak of the glory of your
   reign * and declare your might, *O*
   God,
to make known to men your mighty
   deeds * and the glorious splendor of
   your reign.
Yours is an everlasting *king*dom; * your
   rule lasts from age *to* age.
Glory to the Father, and to the *Son*, *
   and to the Ho*ly* Spirit:
as it was in the beginning, is *now*, * and
   will be for ever. *Amen.*

Antiphon	Day after day I will bless you, *Lord*; * I will tell of your marve*lous* deeds.
December 17-23:	Our King will come from *Zion*; * the Lord, God-is-with-us, is his migh*ty* name.
Easter:	God so loved the world that he gave us his only *Son*, * al*le*luia.

Ant. 2	To you alone, Lord, we *look* with confidence; * you are ever close to those who call up*on* you.
December 17-23:	Wait for the Lord and he will *come* to you * with his saving *pow*er.
Easter:	To the King of ages, immortal *and* invisible, * be all honor and glory, alle*lu*ia.

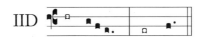

II

The Lord is faithful in *all* his words
   * and loving in all his *deeds.*
The Lord supports *all* who fall * and
   raises all who are bowed *down.*
The eyes of all creatures *look* to you *
   and you give them their food in due
   time.
You open *wide* your hand, * grant the
   desires of all who *live.*
The Lord is just in *all* his ways * and
   loving in all his *deeds.*
He is close to *all* who call him, * who
   call on him from their *hearts.*

He grants the desires of *those* who fear
   him, * he hears their cry and he *saves*
   them.
The Lord protects *all* who love him; *
   but the wicked he will utterly de*stroy.*
Let me speak the praise of the Lord, †
   let all mankind bless his *holy* name *
   for ever, for ages un*end*ing.
Glory to the Father, and *to* the Son, *
   and to the Holy *Spir*it:
as it was in the begin*ning*, is now, * and
   will be for ever. A*men.*

Antiphon	To you alone, Lord, we *look* with confidence; * you are ever close to those who call up*on* you.
December 17-23:	Wait for the Lord and he will *come* to you * with his saving *pow*er.
Easter:	To the King of ages, immortal *and* invisible, * be all honor and glory, alle*lu*ia.

Ant. 3	King of all *the* ages, * your ways are per*fect* and true.
December 17-23:	Eagerly I watch for the Lord; † I wait in joy*ful* hope * for the coming of *God* my Savior.
Easter:	The Lord is my strength, † I shall al*ways* praise him, * for he has become my savior, *al*leluia.

Canticle   Revelation 15:3-4
Hymn of adoration

Mighty and wonderful are *your* works, * Lord *God* Almighty!
Righteous and true are *your* ways, * O King *of* the nations!
Who would dare refuse *you* honor, * or the glory due your *name*, O Lord?
Since you alone *are* holy, * all nations shall come and worship in *your* presence.
Your migh*ty* deeds * are *clear*ly seen.
Glory to the Father, and to *the* Son, * and to the *Ho*ly Spirit:
as it was in the beginning, *is* now, * and will be for ev*er*. Amen.

Antiphon	King of all *the* ages, * your ways are per*fect* and true.
December 17-23:	Eagerly I watch for the Lord; † I wait in joy*ful* hope * for the coming of *God* my Savior.
Easter:	The Lord is my strength, † I shall al*ways* praise him, * for he has become my savior, *al*leluia.

READING   Romans 8:1-2

There is no condemnation now for those who are in Christ Jesus. The law of the spirit, the spirit of life is Christ Jesus, has freed you from the law of sin and death.

RESPONSORY (VI F)

Christ died *for* our sins * to make of us an offering *to* God.
— Christ died *for* our sins * to make of us an offering *to* God.
He died to this world of sin, and rose in the power *of* the Spirit,
— to make of us an offering *to* God.
Glory to the Father, and *to* the Son, * and to the Ho*ly* Spirit.
— Christ died *for* our sins * to make of us an offering *to* God.

CANTICLE OF MARY

Antiphon   Remember your *mercy*, Lord, * the promise of mercy you made to *our* fathers.

INTERCESSIONS (VI F)

Let us *pray* to Christ, * the source of hope for all who *know* his name:
Lord, have *mercy.*
Christ, our frail humanity is *prone* to fall,
— strengthen us *through* your help.
Left to itself, our nature is in*clined* to sin,
— let your love always restore *it* to grace.
Lord, sin offends you, re*pent*ance pleases you,
— do not punish us in your wrath even when *we* have sinned.
You forgave the penitent woman, and placed the wandering sheep *on* your shoulders,
— do not deprive us *of* your mercy.
By your death on the cross you opened the *gates* of heaven,
— admit into your kingdom all who *hoped* in you.

Our Father...

Prayer

God our Father,
you brought salvation to all mankind
through the suffering of Christ your Son.
May your people strive to offer themselves to you as a living sacrifice
and be filled with the abundance of your love.
We ask this through our Lord Jesus Christ, your Son,
who lives and reigns with you and the Holy Spirit,
one God, for ever and ever.

SATURDAY, WEEK IV

Morning Prayer

HYMN, 1343.
Diéi luce réddita. (L.M.)

Diéi luce réddita,	As light of day returns once more,
lætis gratísque vocíbus	With joyful voices let us sing
Dei canámus glóriam,	To God of glory infinite,
Christi faténtes grátiam,	To Christ our Lord for all his grace.
Per quem creátor ómnium	Through whom the great Creator's will
diem noctémque cóndidit,	Called day and night from nothingness,
ætérna lege sánciens	Appointing them successive law,
ut semper succédant sibi.	Till time itself shall pass away.
Tu vera lux fidélium,	True light of every faithful soul
quem lex vetérna non tenet,	Unfettered by the law of old;
noctis nec ortu súccidens,	No shades of night can fall that dim
ætérno fulgens lúmine.	Your dazzling and undying light.
Præsta, Pater ingénite,	O Father, uncreated Light,
totum ducámus iúgiter	Be with us as the hours go by,
Christo placéntes hunc diem	That we may please your Son this day,
Sancto repléti Spíritu. Amen.	Filled with the Holy Spirit's pow'r. Amen.

PSALMODY

Ant. 1   We do well to sing to your name, Most *High,* * and proclaim
your mercy *at* daybreak.

December 24:   Bethlehem in Judah's land, † how glorious your *future!* * The king who will rule
my people comes *from* you.

Easter: How wonderful are your works, O *Lord,* * al*le*luia.

VIIIa

Psalm 92
Praise of God the creator
Sing in praise of Christ's redeeming work (Saint Athanasius).

It is good to give thanks to the *Lord,*
  * to make music to your name, O
Most High,
to proclaim your love in the *morning* *
  and your truth in the watches of *the*

night,
on the ten-stringed lyre and the *lute,* *
  with the murmuring sound of *the*
harp.
Your deeds, O Lord, have made me

glad; * for the work of your hands I
shout *with* joy.
O Lord, how great are your *works*! *
How deep are your *de*signs!
The foolish man cannot *know* this * and
the fool cannot un*der*stand.
Though the wicked spring up like *grass*
* and all who do e*vil* thrive:
they are doomed to be eternally de-
stroyed. * But you, Lord, are eternally
on high.
See how your enemies *perish*; * all doers
of evil *are* scattered.
To me you give the wild-ox's *strength,* *
you anoint me with the pur*est* oil.

My eyes looked in triumph on my *foes*;
* my ears heard gladly of *their* fall.
The just will flourish like the *palm*-tree
* and grow like a Leba*non* cedar.
Planted in the house of the *Lord,* * they
will flourish in the courts of *our* God,
still bearing fruit when they are *old,* *
still full of sap, *still* green,
to proclaim that the Lord is *just.* * In
him, my rock, there is *no* wrong.
Glory to the Father, and to the *Son,* *
and to the Ho*ly* Spirit:
as it was in the beginning, is *now,* * and
will be for ever. *A*men.

Antiphon	We do well to sing to your name, Most *High,* * and proclaim your mercy *at* daybreak.
December 24:	Bethlehem in Judah's land, † how glorious your *fu*ture! * The king who will rule my people comes *from* you.
Easter:	How wonderful are your works, O *Lord,* * al*le*luia.

Ant. 2	I will create a new *heart* in you, * and breathe into you a new *spi*rit.
December 24:	Lift up your *heads* and see; * your redemption is now at *hand.*
Easter:	I will pour cleansing wa*ter* upon you, * alle*lu*ia.

IID

Canticle

Ezekiel 36:24-28

The Lord will renew his people

They will be his own people and God himself will be with them, their own God

(Revelation 21:3).

I will take you away from among the
nations, † gather you from all the
*fo*reign lands, * and bring you back to
your *own* land.
I will sprinkle clean water upon you †
to cleanse you from all *your* impurities, * and from all your idols I will
cleanse you.

I will give *you* a new heart * and place a
new spirit with*in* you,
taking from your bodies your *sto*ny
hearts * and giving you natural *hearts.*
I will put my spirit within you † and
make you live *by* my statutes, * careful
to observe my de*crees.*
You shall live in the land I gave your

fathers; † you shall *be* my people, *
and I will be your *God*.
Glory to the Father, and *to* the Son, *

and to the Holy *Spir*it:
as it was in the begin*ning*, is now, * and
will be for ever. A*men*.

Antiphon	I will create a new *heart* in you, * and breathe into you a new *spir*it.
December 24:	Lift up your *heads* and see; * your redemption is now at *hand*.
Easter:	I will pour cleansing wa*ter* upon you, * alle*lui*a.

Ant. 3	On the lips of children *and* infants * you have found *per*fect praise.
December 24:	The day has come *at* last * when Mary will bring forth her *first*born Son.
Easter:	All things are yours, and you *are* Christ's, * and Christ is God's, *al*leluia

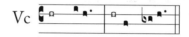

Psalm 8
The majesty of the Lord and man's dignity
The Father gave Christ lordship of creation and made him head of the Church
(Ephesians 1:22).

How great is your name, O Lord
our God, * through *all* the earth!
Your majesty is praised above *the*
heavens; * on the lips of children *and*
of babes
you have found praise to foil *your*
enemy, * to silence the foe *and* the
rebel.
When I see the heavens, the work of
your hands, * the moon and the stars
which *you* arranged,
what is man that you should keep him
in mind, * mortal man that you *care*
for him?
Yet you have made him little less than *a*

god; * with glory and ho*nor* you
crowned him,
gave him power over the works of *your*
hand, * put all things un*der* his feet.
All of them, sheep *and* cattle, * yes, even
the *sav*age beasts,
birds of the air, *and* fish * that make
their way *through* the waters.
How great is your name, O Lord *our*
God, * through *all* the earth!
Glory to the Father, and to *the* Son, *
and to the *Holy* Spirit:
as it was in the beginning, *is* now, * and
will be for *ever*. Amen.

Antiphon	On the lips of children *and* infants * you have found *per*fect praise.
December 24:	The day has come *at* last * when Mary will bring forth her *first*born Son.
Easter:	All things are yours, and you *are* Christ's, * and Christ is God's, *al*leluia

READING 2 Peter 3:13-15a

What we await are new heavens and a new earth where, according to his promise, the justice of God will reside. So, beloved, while waiting for this, make every effort to be found without stain or defilement, and at peace in his sight. Consider that our Lord's patience is directed toward salvation.

RESPONSORY (VI F)

It is my *joy,* O God, * to praise you *with* song.
— It is my *joy,* O God, * to praise you *with* song.
To sing as I pon*der* your goodness,
— to praise you *with* song.
Glory to the Father, and *to* the Son, * and to the Ho*ly* Spirit.
— It is my *joy,* O God, * to praise you *with* song.

CANTICLE OF ZECHARIAH

Antiphon   Lord, *guide* our feet * into the way *of* peace.

INTERCESSIONS (VI F)

Let us adore God, who has given hope and life to the world *through* his Son, * and
    let us *hum*bly ask him:
Hear us, O Lord.
Lord, Father of all, you have brought us to the dawn *of* this day,
— make us live with Christ and *praise* your glory.
You have poured out faith, hope and *love* upon us,
— keep them firmly rooted *in* our hearts.
Lord, let our eyes be always raised *up* to you,
— so that we may swiftly an*swer* your call.
Protect us from the snares and entice*ments* of evil,
— keep our *feet* from stumbling.

Our Father . . .

Prayer

All-powerful and ever-living God,
splendor of true light, and never ending day:
let the radiance of your coming
banish from our minds
the darkness of sin.
We ask this through our Lord Jesus Christ, your Son,
who lives and reigns with you and the Holy Spirit,
one God, for ever and ever.

Night Prayer

AFTER EVENING PRAYER I
ON SUNDAYS AND SOLEMNITIES

HYMN

Te lucis ante terminum. Mode I (L.M.)

Te lucis ante terminum,
rerum creator, poscimus,
ut solita clementia
sis præsul ad custodiam.

Te corda nostra somnient,
te per soporem sentiant,
tuamque semper gloriam
vicina luce concinant.

Vitam salubrem tribue,
nostrum calorem refice,
tætram noctis caliginem
tua collustret claritas.

Præsta, Pater omnipotens,
per Iesum Christum Dominum,
qui tecum in perpetuum
regnat cum Sancto Spiritu. Amen.

Before the ending of the day,
Creator of the world, we pray
That with thy wonted favor thou
Wouldst be our guard and keeper now.

From all ill dreams defend our eyes,
From nightly fears and fantasies,
Tread under foot our ghostly foe,
That no pollution we may know.

O Father, that we ask be done,
Through Jesus Christ, thine only Son,
Who, with the Holy Ghost and thee,
Doth live and reign eternally. Amen.

Or:

All praise to you, O God, this night,
For all the blessings of the light;
Keep us, we pray, O King of kings,
Beneath your own almighty wings.

Enlighten us, O blessèd Light,
And give us rest throughout this night.
O strengthen us, that for your sake,
We all may serve you when we wake.

To you, O Christ, all glory be,
Whose advent sets your people free,
Whom, with the Father we adore,
And Holy Spirit, evermore. Amen.

Ant. 1   Have *mer*cy, Lord, * and *hear* my prayer.

Easter: Al*le*luia, * alleluia, *al*leluia.

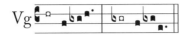

Psalm 4
Thanksgiving
The resurrection of Christ was God's supreme and wholly marvelous work (Saint Augustine).

When I call, answer me, O God of justice; † from anguish *you* released me; * have mer*cy* and hear me!

O men, how long will your *hearts* be closed, * will you love what is futile and seek *what* is false?

It is the Lord who grants favors to those *whom* he loves; * the Lord hears me whenev*er* I call him.

Fear him; do not sin: † ponder on your bed *and* be still. * Make justice your sacrifice and trust *in* the Lord.

"What can bring us happiness?" *many* say. * Let the light of your face shine on *us*, O Lord.

You have put into my heart a *great*er joy * than they have from abundance of corn *and* new wine.

I will lie down in peace and sleep *comes* at once * for you alone, Lord, make me *dwell* in safety.

Glory to the Father, and *to* the Son, * and to the *Ho*ly Spirit,

as it was in the begin*ning* is now, * and will be for ev*er*. Amen.

Antiphon   Have *mer*cy, Lord, * and *hear* my prayer.

Easter: Al*le*luia, * alleluia, *al*leluia.

Ant. 2   In the *si*lent hours * of the night, *bless* the Lord.

Psalm 134
Evening Prayer in the Temple
Praise our God, all you his servants, you who fear him, small and great (Revelation 19:5).

O come, *bless* the Lord, * all you who *serve* the Lord,

who stand in the house *of* the Lord, * in the courts of the house *of* our God.

Lift up your hands to the *ho*ly place * and bless the Lord *through* the night.

May the Lord bless *you* from Zion, * he who made both heav*en* and earth.

Glory to the Father, and *to* the Son, * and to the *Ho*ly Spirit,

as it was in the begin*ning* is now, * and will be for ev*er*. Amen.

Antiphon   In the *si*lent hours * of the night, *bless* the Lord.

READING   Deuteronomy 6:4-7

Hear, O Israel! The Lord is our God, the Lord alone! Therefore, you shall love the Lord, your God, with all your heart, and with all your soul, and with all your strength. Take to heart these words which I enjoin on you today. Drill them into your children. Speak of them at home and abroad, whether you are busy or at rest.

RESPONSORY (IV a)

Into your hands, *Lord,* * I com*mend* my spirit.
— Into your hands, *Lord,* * I com*mend* my spirit.
You have redeemed us, Lord God of *truth*.
— I com*mend* my spirit.
Glory to the Father, and to the *Son*, * and to the *Holy* Spirit.
— Into your hands, *Lord,* * I com*mend* my spirit.

During the octave of Easter in place of the responsory, the antiphon *This is the day*, as given in the Proper of Seasons, is said.

Easter:
Into your hands, Lord, I commend my *spir*it. * alleluia, *a*lleluia.
— Into your hands, Lord, I commend my *spir*it. * alleluia, *a*lleluia.
You have redeemed us, Lord God of *truth*,
— alleluia, *a*lleluia.
Glory to the Father, and to the *Son*, * and to the *Holy* Spirit,
— Into your hands, Lord, I commend my *spir*it. * alleluia, *a*lleluia.

CANTICLE OF SIMEON (VII d)

Antiphon   Protect us, Lord, as we *stay* awake; * watch over us as *we* sleep, that awake, we may keep *watch* with Christ, * and asleep, rest in *his* peace, (al*le*luia).

L ORD, ✠ now you let your servant *go* in peace; * your word has been *ful*filled:
my own eyes have seen *the* salvation * which you have prepared in the sight of eve*ry* people:

a light to reveal you *to* the nations * and the glory of your peo*ple* Israel.
Glory to the Father, and *to* the Son, *and to the Ho*ly* Spirit,
As it was in the begin*ning* is now, * and will be for ever. *A*men.

Antiphon   Protect us, Lord, as we *stay* awake; * watch over us as *we* sleep, that awake, we may keep *watch* with Christ, * and asleep, rest in *his* peace, (al*le*luia).

Prayer

On Sundays and during the octave of Easter:
> Lord,
> be with us throughout this night.
> When day comes may we rise from sleep

to rejoice in the resurrection of your Christ,
who lives and reigns for ever and ever.

Or: on solemnities that do not occur on Sunday:

Lord,
we beg you visit this house
and banish from it
all the deadly power of the enemy.
May your holy angels dwell here
to keep us in peace,
and may your blessing be upon us always.
We ask this through Christ our Lord.

CONCLUSION

The blessing is said, even in individual recitation:

May the all powerful Lord grant us a restful night and a peaceful death.
Amen.

Antiphon of the Blessed Virgin Mary, 1344.

AFTER EVENING PRAYER II
ON SUNDAYS AND SOLEMNITIES

PSALMODY

Ant.   Night holds no terrors for me * sleeping under God's wings.

Easter: Alleluia, * alleluia, alleluia.

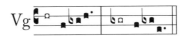

Psalm 91
Safe in God's sheltering care
I have given you the power to tread upon serpents and scorpions (Luke 10:19).

He who dwells in the shelter *of* the
Most High * and abides in the
shade of *the* Almighty
says to the *Lord*: "My refuge, * my
stronghold, my God in *whom* I
trust!"
It is he who will free you *from* the
snare * of the fowler who seeks *to*
destroy you;
he will conceal you *with* his pinions *

and under his wings you *will* find
refuge.
You will not fear the terror *of* the night
* nor the arrow that *flies* by day,
nor the plague that prowls *in* the
darkness * nor the scourge that lays
waste at noon.
A thousand may fall *at* your side, * ten
thousand fall *at* your right,
you, it will nev*er* approach; * his

faithfulness is buck*ler* and shield.
Your eyes have on*ly* to look * to see
  how the wicked *are* repaid,
you who have said: "*Lord*, my refuge!" *
  and have made the Most *High* your
  dwelling.
Upon you no e*vil* shall fall, * no plague
  approach *where* you dwell.
For you has he command*ed* his angels,
  * to keep you in *all* your ways.
They shall bear you up*on* their hands *
  lest you strike your foot a*gainst* a
  stone.
On the lion and the viper *you* will tread

* and trample the young lion *and* the
  dragon.
Since he clings to me in love, *I* will free
  him; * protect him for he *knows* my
  name.
When he calls I shall answer: "*I* am
  with you." * I will save him in
  distress and *give* him glory.
With length of life I *will* content him;
  * I shall let him see my *saving* power.
Glory to the Father, and *to* the Son, *
  and to the *Holy* Spirit:
as it was in the begin*ning*, is now, * and
  will be for ev*er*. Amen.

Antiphon   Night holds no ter*rors* for me * sleeping un*der* God's wings.
Easter: Al*leluia, * alleluia, a*lleluia.

READING   Revelation 22:4-5
  They shall see the Lord face to face and bear his name on their foreheads.
  The night shall be no more. They will need no light from lamps or the sun,
  for the Lord God shall give them light, and they shall reign forever.

RESPONSORY (IV a)

Into your hands, *Lord*, * I com*mend* my spirit.
— Into your hands, *Lord*, * I com*mend* my spirit.
You have redeemed us, Lord God of *truth*.
— I com*mend* my spirit.
Glory to the Father, and to the *Son*, * and to the *Holy* Spirit.
— Into your hands, *Lord*, * I com*mend* my spirit.

During the Easter Triduum and the octave of Easter in place of the responsory, the antiphon
For our sake Christ or This is the day, as given in the Proper of Seasons, is said.

Easter:
Into your hands, Lord, I commend my *spir*it. * alleluia, a*lleluia.
— Into your hands, Lord, I commend my *spir*it. * alleluia, a*lleluia.
You have redeemed us, Lord God of *truth*,
— alleluia, a*lleluia.
Glory to the Father, and to the *Son*, * and to the *Holy* Spirit,
— Into your hands, Lord, I commend my *spir*it. * alleluia, a*lleluia.

CANTICLE OF SIMEON (VII d)

Antiphon   Protect us, Lord, as we *stay* awake; * watch over us as *we* sleep, that awake, we may keep *watch* with Christ, * and asleep, rest in *his* peace, (al*le*luia).

L ORD, ✠ now you let your servant *go* in peace; * your word has been *ful*filled:

my own eyes have seen *the* salvation *
    which you have prepared in the sight
of eve*ry* people:

a light to reveal you *to* the nations *
    and the glory of your peo*ple* Israel.
Glory to the Father, and *to* the Son,
    *and to the Ho*ly* Spirit,
As it was in the begin*ning* is now, * and
    will be for ever. *A*men.

Antiphon   Protect us, Lord, as we *stay* awake; * watch over us as *we* sleep, that awake, we may keep *watch* with Christ, * and asleep, rest in *his* peace, (al*le*luia).

Prayer

On Sundays and during the octave of Easter:
> Lord,
> we have celebrated today
> the mystery of the rising of Christ to new life.
> May we now rest in your peace,
> safe from all that could harm us,
> and rise again refreshed and joyful,
> to praise you throughout another day.
> We ask this through Christ our Lord.

During the Easter Triduum and on solemnities that do not occur on Sunday:
> Lord,
> we beg you visit this house
> and banish from it
> all the deadly power of the enemy.
> May your holy angels dwell here
> to keep us in peace,
> and may your blessing be upon us always.
> We ask this through Christ our Lord.

CONCLUSION

The blessing is said, even in individual recitation:
> May the all powerful Lord grant us a restful night and a peaceful death.
> Amen.

Antiphon of the Blessed Virgin Mary, 1344.

MONDAY

Antiphon   O *Lord*, our God, * unwearied is your *love* for us.

Easter: Al*le*luia, * alleluia, *a*lleluia.

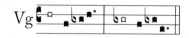

Psalm 86
Poor man's prayer in trouble
Blessed be God who comforts us in all our trials (2 Corinthians 1:3, 4).

Turn your ear, O Lord, *and* give
answer * for I am *poor* and needy.
Preserve my life, for *I* am faithful: *
save the servant who *trusts* in you.
You are my God; have mercy *on* me,
Lord, * for I cry to you *all* day long.
Give joy to your ser*vant*, O Lord, * for
to you I lift *up* my soul.
O Lord, you are good *and* forgiving, *
full of love to *all* who call.
Give heed, O Lord, *to* my prayer * and
attend to the sound *of* my voice.
In the day of distress *I* will call * and
surely you *will* reply.
Among the gods there is none like *you*,
O Lord; * nor work to com*pare* with
yours.
All the nations shall come *to* adore you
* and glorify your *name*, O Lord:
for you are great and do mar*vel*lous
deeds, * you who a*lone* are God.
Show me, Lord, you way † so that I
may walk *in* your truth. * Guide my
heart to *fear* your name.

I will praise you, Lord my God, † with
all my heart * and glorify your *name*
for ever;
for your love to me *has* been great: *
you have saved me from the depths
of the grave.
The proud have risen against me; †
ruthless men *seek* my life: * to you
they *pay* no heed.
But you, God of mercy *and* compassion, * slow to an*ger*, O Lord,
abounding in *love* and truth, * turn
and take pi*ty* on me.
O give your strength *to* your servant *
and save your *hand*maid's son.
Show me a sign of your favor † that
my foes may see *to* their shame * that
you console me and give *me* your
help.
Glory to the Father, and *to* the Son, *
and to the *Ho*ly Spirit:
as it was in the begin*ning*, is now, * and
will be for ev*er*. Amen.

Antiphon   O *Lord*, our God, * unwearied is your *love* for us.
Easter: Al*le*luia, * alleluia, *a*lleluia.

READING   1 Thessalonians 5:9-10

God has destined us for acquiring salvation through our Lord Jesus Christ.
He died for us, that all of us, whether awake or asleep, together might live
with him.

RESPONSORY (IV a)

Into your hands, *Lord,* * I com*mend* my spirit.
— Into your hands, *Lord,* * I com*mend* my spirit.
You have redeemed us, Lord God of *truth.*
— I com*mend* my spirit.
Glory to the Father, and to the *Son,* * and to the *Ho*ly Spirit.
— Into your hands, *Lord,* * I com*mend* my spirit.

Easter:
Into your hands, Lord, I commend my *spir*it. * alleluia, a*l*leluia.
— Into your hands, Lord, I commend my *spir*it. * alleluia, a*l*leluia.
You have redeemed us, Lord God of *truth,*
— alleluia, a*l*leluia.
Glory to the Father, and to the *Son,* * and to the *Ho*ly Spirit,
— Into your hands, Lord, I commend my *spir*it. * alleluia, a*l*leluia.

CANTICLE OF SIMEON (VII d)

Antiphon   Protect us, Lord, as we *stay* awake; * watch over us as *we* sleep,
                  that awake, we may keep *watch* with Christ, * and asleep, rest in
                  his peace, (al*l*eluia).

LORD, ✠ now you let your servant *go*
in peace; * your word has been
*ful*filled:
my own eyes have seen *the* salvation *
  which you have prepared in the sight
  of eve*ry* people:

a light to reveal you *to* the nations *
    and the glory of your peo*ple* Israel.
Glory to the Father, and *to* the Son,
   *and to the Ho*ly* Spirit,
As it was in the begin*ning* is now, * and
    will be for ever. *A*men.

Antiphon   Protect us, Lord, as we *stay* awake; * watch over us as *we* sleep,
                  that awake, we may keep *watch* with Christ, * and asleep, rest in
                  his peace, (al*l*eluia).

Prayer

Lord,
give our bodies restful sleep
and let the work we have done today
bear fruit in eternal life.
We ask this through Christ our Lord.

CONCLUSION

The blessing is said, even in individual recitation:

May the all powerful Lord grant us a restful night and a peaceful death. Amen.

Antiphon of the Blessed Virgin Mary, 1344.

TUESDAY

PSALMODY

Antiphon   Do not hide your *face* from me; * in you I *put* my trust.

Easter: Al*le*luia, * alleluia, *al*leluia.

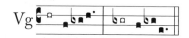

Psalm 143: 1-11
Prayer in distress

Only by faith in Jesus Christ is a man made holy in God's sight. No observance of the law can achieve this (Galatians 2:16).

Lord, listen *to* my prayer: * turn your ear to *my* appeal.

You are faithful, you are just; give answer. † Do not call your ser*vant* to judgment * for no one is just *in* your sight.

The enemy pur*sues* my soul; * he has crushed my life *to* the ground;

he has made me *dwell* in darkness * like the dead, *long* forgotten.

Therefore my *spir*it fails; * my heart is *numb* within me.

I remember the days *that* are past: * I ponder *all* your works.

I muse on what your hand has wrought † and to you I stretch *out* my hands. * Like a parched land my soul *thirsts* for you.

Lord, make *haste* and answer; * for my spirit *fails* within me.

Do not *hide* your face * lest I become like those *in* the grave.

In the morning let me *know* your love * for I put my *trust* in you.

Make me know the way *I* should walk: * to you I lift *up* my soul.

Rescue me, Lord, *from* my enemies; * I have fled to *you* for refuge.

Teach me to *do* your will * for you, O Lord, *are* my God.

Let your good *spir*it guide me * in ways that are le*vel* and smooth.

For your name's sake, Lord, *save* my life; * in your justice save my soul *from* distress.

Glory to the Father, and *to* the Son, * and to the *Ho*ly Spirit:

as it was in the begin*ning*, is now, * and will be for ev*er*. Amen.

Antiphon   Do not hide your *face* from me; * in you I *put* my trust.
Easter: Al*l*eluia, * alleluia, *a*leluia.

READING   1 Peter 5:8-9a

Stay sober and alert. Your opponent the devil is prowling like a roaring lion looking for someone to devour. Resist him, solid in your faith.

RESPONSORY (IV a)

Into your hands, *Lord,* * I com*mend* my spirit.
— Into your hands, *Lord,* * I com*mend* my spirit.
You have redeemed us, Lord God of *truth.*
— I com*mend* my spirit.
Glory to the Father, and to the *Son,* * and to the *Holy* Spirit.
— Into your hands, *Lord,* * I com*mend* my spirit.

Easter:

Into your hands, Lord, I commend my *spir*it. * alleluia, *a*leluia.
— Into your hands, Lord, I commend my *spir*it. * alleluia, *a*leluia.
You have redeemed us, Lord God of *truth,*
— alleluia, *a*leluia.
Glory to the Father, and to the *Son,* * and to the *Holy* Spirit,
— Into your hands, Lord, I commend my *spir*it. * alleluia, *a*leluia.

CANTICLE OF SIMEON (VII d)
Antiphon   Protect us, Lord, as we *stay* awake; * watch over us as *we* sleep,
            that awake, we may keep *watch* with Christ, * and asleep, rest in
            his peace, (al*l*eluia).

L ORD, ✠ now you let your servant *go* in peace; * your word has been *ful*filled:
my own eyes have seen *the* salvation *
which you have prepared in the sight of eve*ry* people:

a light to reveal you *to* the nations *
and the glory of your peo*ple* Israel.
Glory to the Father, and *to* the Son,
*and to the Ho*ly* Spirit,
As it was in the begin*ning* is now, * and will be for ever. *A*men.

Antiphon   Protect us, Lord, as we *stay* awake; * watch over us as *we* sleep,
            that awake, we may keep *watch* with Christ, * and asleep, rest in
            his peace, (al*l*eluia).

Prayer

Lord,
fill this night with your radiance.
May we sleep in peace and rise with joy
to welcome the light of a new day in your name.
We ask this through Christ our Lord.

CONCLUSION

The blessing is said, even in individual recitation:

> May the all powerful Lord grant us a restful night and a peaceful death.
> Amen.

Antiphon of the Blessed Virgin Mary, 1344.

WEDNESDAY

PSALMODY

Ant. 1   Lord God, *be* my refuge; * Lord God, *be* my strength.

Easter: Al*le*luia, * alleluia, *a*leluia.

Psalm 31: 1-6
Trustful prayer in adversity
Father, into your hands I commend my spirit (Luke 23:46).

In you, O Lord, *I* take refuge. * Let
me never be *put* to shame.
In your justice, *set* me free, * hear me
and speed*i*ly rescue me.
Be a rock of re*fuge* for me, * a mighty
strong*hold* to save me,
for you are my *rock*, my stronghold. *
For your name's sake, lead *me* and
guide me.

Release me from the snares *they* have
hidden * for you are my *re*fuge,
Lord.
Into your hands I com*mend* my spirit.
* It is you who will re*deem* me, Lord.
Glory to the Father, and *to* the Son, *
and to the *Ho*ly Spirit:
as it was in the begin*ning*, is now, * and
will be for *ev*er. Amen.

Antiphon   Lord God, *be* my refuge; * Lord God, *be* my strength.
Easter: Al*le*luia, * alleluia, *a*leluia.

Ant. 2   Out *of* the depths * I cry to *you*, O Lord.

Psalm 130

A cry from the depths

He will save his people from their sins (Matthew 1:21).

Out of the depths I cry to *you*, O
Lord, * Lord, *hear* my voice!
O let your ears *be* attentive * to the
voice *of* my pleading.
If you, O Lord, should *mark* our guilt,
* Lord, who *would* survive?
But with you is *found* forgiveness: * for
this *we* revere you.
My soul is waiting *for* the Lord, * I
count *on* his word.
My soul is longing *for* the Lord * more

than watch*man* for daybreak.
Let the watchman *count* on daybreak *
and Israel *on* the Lord.
Because with the Lord *there* is mercy *
and fullness *of* redemption,
Israel indeed he *will* redeem * from all
its iniquity.
Glory to the Father, and *to* the Son, *
and to the *Holy* Spirit:
as it was in the begin*ning*, is now, * and
will be for ev*er*. Amen.

Antiphon   Out *of* the depths * I cry to *you*, O Lord.

READING   Ephesians 4:26-27

If you are angry, let it be without sin. The sun must not go down on your
wrath; do not give the devil a chance to work on you.

RESPONSORY (IV a)

Into your hands, *Lord,* * I com*mend* my spirit.
— Into your hands, *Lord,* * I com*mend* my spirit.
You have redeemed us, Lord God of *truth.*
— I com*mend* my spirit.
Glory to the Father, and to the *Son,* * and to the *Holy* Spirit.
— Into your hands, *Lord,* * I com*mend* my spirit.

Easter:
Into your hands, Lord, I commend my *spir*it. * alleluia, *a*lleluia.
— Into your hands, Lord, I commend my *spir*it. * alleluia, *a*lleluia.
You have redeemed us, Lord God of *truth,*
— alleluia, *a*lleluia.
Glory to the Father, and to the *Son,* * and to the *Holy* Spirit,
— Into your hands, Lord, I commend my *spir*it. * alleluia, *a*lleluia.

CANTICLE OF SIMEON (VII d)

Ant.   Protect us, Lord, as we *stay* awake; * watch over us as *we* sleep, that awake, we may keep *watch* with Christ, * and asleep, rest in *his* peace, (al*le*luia).

LORD, ✠ now you let your servant *go* in peace; * your word has been *ful*filled:

my own eyes have seen *the* salvation *
which you have prepared in the sight
of eve*ry* people:

a light to reveal you *to* the nations *
and the glory of your peo*ple* Israel.

Glory to the Father, and *to* the Son,
*and to the Ho*ly* Spirit,

As it was in the begin*ning* is now, * and
will be for ever. *A*men.

Ant.   Protect us, Lord, as we *stay* awake; * watch over us as *we* sleep, that awake, we may keep *watch* with Christ, * and asleep, rest in *his* peace, (al*le*luia).

Prayer

Lord Jesus Christ,
you have given your followers
an example of gentleness and humility,
a task that is easy, a burden that is light.
Accept the prayers and work of this day,
and give us the rest that will strengthen us
to render more faithful service to you
who live and reign for ever and ever.

CONCLUSION

The blessing is said, even in individual recitation:

    May the all powerful Lord grant us a restful night and a peaceful death.
    Amen.

Antiphon of the Blessed Virgin Mary, 1344.

THURSDAY

PSALMODY

Antiphon   In *you*, my God, * my body will *rest* in hope.

Easter: Al*le*luia, * alleluia, *a*lleluia.

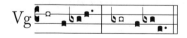

Psalm 16
God is my portion, my inheritance
The Father raised Jesus from the dead and broke the bonds of death (Acts 2:24).

reserve me, God, I take refuge in you. † I say to the Lord: "You *are* my God. * My happiness lies in *you* alone."

He has put into my heart a mar*ve*/lous love * for the faithful ones who dwell *in* his land.

Those who choose other gods increase their sorrows. † Never will I offer their offer*ings* of blood. * Never will I take their name up*on* my lips.

O Lord, it is you who are my por*tion* and cup; * it is you yourself who *are* my prize.

The lot marked out for me is *my* delight: * welcome indeed the heritage that *falls* to me!

I will bless the Lord who *gives* me counsel, * who even at night di*rects* my heart.

I keep the Lord ever *in* my sight: * since he is at my right hand, I *shall* stand firm.

And so my heart rejoices, † my *soul* is glad; * even my body shall *rest* in safety.

For you will not leave my soul a*mong* the dead, * nor let your belovèd *know* decay.

You will show me the path of life, † the fullness of joy *in* your presence, * at your right hand happi*ness* for ever.

Glory to the Father, and *to* the Son, * and to the *Ho*ly Spirit:

as it was in the begin*ning*, is now, * and will be for ev*er*. Amen.

Antiphon   In *you*, my God, * my body will *rest* in hope.
Easter: Al*le*luia, * alleluia, a*l*leluia.

READING   1 Thessalonians 5:23

May the God of peace make you perfect in holiness. May he preserve you whole and entire, spirit, soul, and body, irreproachable at the coming of our Lord Jesus Christ.

RESPONSORY (IV a)

Into your hands, *Lord,* * I com*mend* my spirit.
— Into your hands, *Lord,* * I com*mend* my spirit.
You have redeemed us, Lord God of *truth.*
— I com*mend* my spirit.
Glory to the Father, and to the *Son,* * and to the *Ho*ly Spirit.
— Into your hands, *Lord,* * I com*mend* my spirit.

Easter:
Into your hands, Lord, I commend my *spir*it. * alleluia, a*l*leluia.
— Into your hands, Lord, I commend my *spir*it. * alleluia, a*l*leluia.
You have redeemed us, Lord God of *truth,*
— alleluia, a*l*leluia.
Glory to the Father, and to the *Son,* * and to the *Ho*ly Spirit,
— Into your hands, Lord, I commend my *spir*it. * alleluia, a*l*leluia.

CANTICLE OF SIMEON (VII d)

Antiphon   Protect us, Lord, as we *stay* awake; * watch over us as *we* sleep,
                that awake, we may keep *watch* with Christ, * and asleep, rest in
                his peace, (al*le*luia).

LORD, ✠ now you let your servant *go* | a light to reveal you *to* the nations *
in peace; * your word has been | and the glory of your peo*ple* Israel.
*ful*filled: | Glory to the Father, and *to* the Son,
my own eyes have seen *the* salvation * | *and to the Ho*ly* Spirit,
which you have prepared in the sight | As it was in the begin*ning* is now, * and
of eve*ry* people: | will be for ever. *A*men.

Antiphon   Protect us, Lord, as we *stay* awake; * watch over us as *we* sleep,
                that awake, we may keep *watch* with Christ, * and asleep, rest in
                his peace, (al*le*luia).

Prayer

Lord God,
send peaceful sleep
to refresh our tired bodies.
May your help always renew us
and keep us strong in your service.
We ask this through Christ our Lord.

CONCLUSION
The blessing is said, even in individual recitation:
    May the all powerful Lord grant us a restful night and a peaceful death.
    Amen.

Antiphon of the Blessed Virgin Mary, 1344.

FRIDAY

PSALMODY

Antiphon   Day and *night* I cry to you, * I cry to *you*, my God
Easter: Al*le*luia, * alleluia, a*lle*luia.

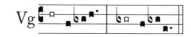

Psalm 88
Prayer of a sick person
This is your hour when darkness reigns (Luke 22:53).

Lord my God, I call for *help* by day; * I cry at *night* before you.

Let my prayer come in*to* your presence. * O turn your ear *to* my cry.

For my soul is *filled* with evils; * my life is on the brink *of* the grave.

I am reckoned as one *in* the tomb: * I have reached the end *of* my strength,

like one alone a*mong* the dead; * like the slain lying *in* their graves;

like those you remem*ber* no more, * cut off, as they are, *from* your hand.

You have laid me in the depths *of* the tomb, " in places that are dark, *in* the depths.

Your anger weighs *down* upon me: * I am drowned be*neath* your waves.

You have taken a*way* my friends * and made me hateful *in* their sight.

Imprisoned, I can*not* escape; * my eyes are sunk*en* with grief.

I call to you, Lord, all *the* day long; * to you I stretch *out* my hands.

Will you work your wonders *for* the dead? * Will the shades *stand* and praise you?

Will your love be told *in* the grave * or your faithfulness a*mong* the dead?

Will your wonders be known *in* the dark * or your justice in the land *of* oblivion?

As for me, Lord, I call to *you* for help: * in the morning my prayer *comes* before you.

Lord, why do *you* reject me? * Why do your *hide* your face?

Wretched, close to death *from* my youth, * I have borne your trials; *I* am numb.

Your fury has swept *down* upon me; * your terrors have utter*ly* destroyed me.

They surround me all the day *like* a flood, * they assail me *all* together.

Friend and neighbor you have tak*en* away: * my one compan*ion* is darkness.

Glory to the Father, and *to* the Son, * and to the *Holy* Spirit:

as it was in the begin*ning*, is now, * and will be for ev*er*. Amen.

Antiphon Day and *night* I cry to you, * I cry to *you*, my God
Easter: All*e*luia, * alleluia, a*l*leluia.

READING   Jeremiah 5:14, 9a

You are in our midst, O Lord,
    your name we bear:
    do not forsake us, O Lord, our God!

RESPONSORY (IV a)

Into your hands, *Lord,* * I com*mend* my spirit.
— Into your hands, *Lord,* * I com*mend* my spirit.
You have redeemed us, Lord God of *truth.*
— I com*mend* my spirit.
Glory to the Father, and to the *Son,* * and to the *Holy* Spirit.
— Into your hands, *Lord,* * I com*mend* my spirit.

Easter:

Into your hands, Lord, I commend my *spir*it. * alleluia, *a*lleluia.

— Into your hands, Lord, I commend my *spir*it. * alleluia, *a*lleluia.

You have redeemed us, Lord God of *truth*,

— alleluia, *a*lleluia.

Glory to the Father, and to the *Son*, * and to the *Ho*ly Spirit,

— Into your hands, Lord, I commend my *spir*it. * alleluia, *a*lleluia.

CANTICLE OF SIMEON (VII d)

Antiphon   Protect us, Lord, as we *stay* awake; * watch over us as *we* sleep, that awake, we may keep *watch* with Christ, * and asleep, rest in *his* peace, (al*le*luia).

L ORD, ✠ now you let your servant *go* in peace; * your word has been *ful*filled: my own eyes have seen *the* salvation * which you have prepared in the sight of eve*ry* people:

a light to reveal you *to* the nations * and the glory of your peo*ple* Israel. Glory to the Father, and *to* the Son, *and to the Ho*ly* Spirit, As it was in the begin*ning* is now, * and will be for ever. *A*men.

Antiphon   Protect us, Lord, as we *stay* awake; * watch over us as *we* sleep, that awake, we may keep *watch* with Christ, * and asleep, rest in *his* peace, (al*le*luia).

Prayer

All-powerful God,
keep us united with your Son
in his death and burial
so that we may rise to new life with him,
who lives and reigns for ever and ever.

CONCLUSION

The blessing is said, even in individual recitation:

May the all powerful Lord grant us a restful night and a peaceful death. Amen.

Antiphon of the Blessed Virgin Mary, 1344.

Proper of Saints

BASIL THE GREAT AND GREGORY NAZIANZEN, BISHOPS AND DOCTORS

Memorial

From the common of pastors: for several pastors, 1238, or from the common of doctors, 1246.

Morning Prayer

CANTICLE OF ZECHARIAH

Ant.   Those *who* are learnèd * will be as radiant as the sky in all *its* beauty;
those who instruct the peo*ple* in goodness * will shine like the stars for all *e*ternity.

Prayer

God our Father,
you inspired the Church
with the example and teaching of your saints Basil and Gregory.
In humility may we come to know your truth
and put it into action with faith and love.
Grant this through our Lord Jesus Christ, your Son,
who lives and reigns with you and the Holy Spirit,
one God, for ever and ever.

Evening Prayer

CANTICLE OF MARY

Ant.   The man who not only teaches but does *what* is right * will be counted great in the kingdom *of* God.

January 3
THE MOST HOLY NAME OF JESUS

Prayer

Lord,
may we who honor the holy name of Jesus
enjoy his friendship in this life
and be filled with eternal joy in his kingdom,
where he lives and reigns with you and the Holy Spirit,
one God, for ever and ever.

January 4

[In the dioceses of the United States]
January 4
ELIZABETH ANN SETON, RELIGIOUS
Memorial

From the common of holy women: religious, 1274.

Prayer

Lord God,
you blessed Elizabeth Seton with gifts of grace
as wife and mother, educator and foundress,
so that she might spend her life in service to your people.
Through her example and prayers
may we learn to express our love for you
in love for our fellow men and women.
We ask this through our Lord Jesus Christ, your Son
who lives and reigns with you and the Holy Spirit,
one God, for ever and ever.

[In the dioceses of the United States]
January 5
BLESSED JOHN NEUMANN, BISHOP
Memorial

From the common of pastors, 1238.

Prayer

Father, you called blessèd John Neumann to labor for the gospel
among the people of the new world.
His ministry strengthened many others in the Christian faith:
through his prayers may faith grow strong in this land.
Grant this through our Lord Jesus Christ, your Son
who lives and reigns with you and the Holy Spirit,
one God, for ever and ever.

January 6
BLESSED ANDRE BESSETTE, RELIGIOUS

From the common of holy men, 1263.

Prayer

Lord our God, friend of the lowly,
you gave your servant, Brother André,
a great devotion to Saint Joseph
and a special commitment to the poor and afflicted.

Through his intercession
help us to follow his example of prayer and love
and so come to share with him in your glory.
We ask this through our Lord Jesus Christ, your Son
who lives and reigns with you and the Holy Spirit,
one God, for ever and ever.

January 7
RAYMOND OF PENYAFORT, PRIEST

From the common of pastors, 1238.

Prayer

Lord,
you gave Saint Raymond the gift of compassion
in his ministry to sinners.
May his prayers free us from the slavery of sin
and help us to love and serve you in liberty.
We ask this through our Lord Jesus Christ, your Son
who lives and reigns with you and the Holy Spirit,
one God, for ever and ever.

January 13
HILARY, BISHOP AND DOCTOR

From the common of pastors, 1238, or doctors, 1246.

Prayer

All powerful God,
as Saint Hilary defended the divinity of Christ your Son,
give us a deeper understanding of this mystery
and help us to profess it in all truth.
Grant this through our Lord Jesus Christ, your Son
who lives and reigns with you and the Holy Spirit,
one God, for ever and ever.

January 17
ANTHONY, ABBOT
Memorial

From the common of holy men: religious, 1263.

Prayer

Father,
you called Saint Anthony
to renounce the world
and serve you in the solitude of the desert.

By his prayers and example,
may we learn to deny ourselves
and to love you above all things.
We ask this through our Lord Jesus Christ, your Son
who lives and reigns with you and the Holy Spirit,
one God, for ever and ever.

January 20
FABIAN, POPE AND MARTYR

From the common of one martyr, 1228, or of pastors, 1238.

Prayer

God our Father, glory of your priests,
may the prayers of your martyr Fabian
help us to share his faith
and offer you loving service.
Grant this through our Lord Jesus Christ, your Son
who lives and reigns with you and the Holy Spirit,
one God, for ever and ever.

On the same day, January 20
SEBASTIAN, MARTYR

From the common of one martyr, 1228.

Prayer

Lord, fill us with that spirit of courage
which gave your martyr Sebastian
strength to offer his life in faithful witness.
Help us to learn from him to cherish your law
and to obey you rather than men.
We ask this through our Lord Jesus Christ, your Son
who lives and reigns with you and the Holy Spirit,
one God, for ever and ever.

January 21
AGNES, VIRGIN AND MARTYR
Memorial

From the common of one martyr, 1228, or of virgins, 1253.

Morning Prayer
HYMN
Agnes beatæ. (L.M.)

Agnes beatæ virginis	Saint Agnes, model of the pure,
natalis est, quo spiritum	And of the brave who shed their blood,
cælo refudit debitum,	Was born to heaven on this day,
pio sacrata sanguine.	Where her desires already dwelt.
Matura martyrio fuit	Mature for dauntless martyr's crown,
matura nondum nuptiis;	If not for human bridal joys,
prodire quis nyptum putet,	Her childish features seemed to shine
sic læta vultu ducitur.	With happiness of marriage feast.
Aras nefandi numinis	When urged to set a lighted torch
adolere tædis cogitur;	Upon an altar of false god,
respondet: "Haud tales faces	"The faithful brides of Christ," she said,
sumpsere Christi virgines.	"Have never touched such evil flame.
Hic ignis extinguit fidem,	"That fire extinguishes all faith,
hæc flamma lumen eripit;	"That flame destroys its fervent light.
hic, hic ferite, ut profluo	"Strike here, pray strike, that my young blood
cruore restinguam focos."	"May swiftly quench its evil glare."
Percussa quam pompam tulit!	What glory she obtained by death!
Nam veste se totam tegens,	Like fairest robe it wrapped her round,
terram genu flexo petit	As sinking to her knees in prayer
lapsu verecundo cadens.	Her tender body fell to earth.
Iesu, tibi sit gloria,	All glory, Jesus, be to you,
qui natus es de Virgine,	Once born of Virgin undefiled,
cum Patre et almo Spiritu,	Who, with the Spirit of your Love
in sempiterna sæcula. Amen.	And God the Father, ever reign. Amen.

Ant. 1   My Lord Jesus Christ has espoused me *with* his ring; * he has crowned me *like* a bride.

Psalms and canticles from Sunday, Week I, 606.

Ant. 2   I am espoused to him whom the *an*gels serve; * sun and moon stand in wonder at *his* beauty.

Ant. 3   Rejoice with me, and be glad, † for I have taken *my* place * with all the saints in the kingdom *of* light.

READING   2 Corinthians 1:3-5

Praised be God, the Father of our Lord Jesus Christ, the Father of mercies, and the God of all consolation! He comforts us in all our afflictions and thus enables us to comfort those who are in trouble, with the same consolation we have received from him. As we have shared much in the sufferings of Christ, so through Christ do we share abundantly in his consolation.

RESPONSORY (VI F)

The *Lord* will help her; * his loving presence will *be* with her.
— The *Lord* will help her; * his loving presence will *be* with her.
He dwells in her; she *will* not falter.
— His loving presence will *be* with her.
Glory to the Father, and *to* the Son, * and to the Ho*ly* Spirit.
— The *Lord* will help her; * his loving presence will *be* with her.

CANTICLE OF ZECHARIAH

Ant.   What I longed for, *I* now see; * what I hoped for, I now *pos*sess; in heaven I am es*poused* to him * whom on earth I loved with all *my* heart.

Prayer

Almighty, eternal God,
you choose what the world considers weak
to put the worldly power to shame.
May we who celebrate the birth of Saint Agnes into eternal joy
be loyal to the faith she professed.
Grant this through our Lord Jesus Christ, your Son
who lives and reigns with you and the Holy Spirit,
one God, for ever and ever.

Evening Prayer

HYMN, as in Morning Prayer, 895.

Ant. 1   Christ's virgin could not be broken by *any* terror, * nor won over by *false* allurements.

Psalms and canticles from the common of one martyr, 1232.

Ant. 2   To him alone I *pledge* my trust; * to him alone I give my undi*ded* love.

Ant. 3   I give thanks to you, the Father of my Lord Je*sus* Christ, * for through him you have made your servant *vic*torious.

READING 1 Peter 4:13-14

Rejoice, beloved, in the measure that you share Christ's sufferings. When his glory is revealed, you will rejoice exultantly. Happy are you when you are insulted for the sake of Christ, for then God's Spirit in its glory has come to rest on you.

RESPONSORY (VI F)

The *Lord* chose her, * his loved one from the *be*ginning.
— The *Lord* chose her, * his loved one from the *be*ginning.
He has taken her to *live* with him,
— his loved one from the *be*ginning.
Glory to the Father, and *to* the Son, * and to the Ho*ly* Spirit.
— The *Lord* chose her, * his loved one from the *be*ginning.

CANTICLE OF MARY

Ant. Saint Agnes raised her *hands* and prayed: * Holy Fa*ther*, hear me.
I am coming to you whom *I* have loved, * whom I have sought and always *de*sired.

Prayer, as in Morning Prayer.

January 22
VINCENT, DEACON AND MARTYR

From the common of one martyr, 1228.

Prayer

Eternal Father,
you gave Saint Vincent
the courage to endure torture and death for the gospel:
fill us with your Spirit
and strengthen us in your love.
We ask this through our Lord Jesus Christ, your Son
who lives and reigns with you and the Holy Spirit,
one God, for ever and ever.

January 24
FRANCIS DE SALES, BISHOP AND DOCTOR
Memorial

From the common of pastors, 1238, or of doctors, 1246.

Prayer

Father,
you gave Francis de Sales the spirit of compassion
to befriend all men on the way to salvation.

By his example, lead us to show your gentle love
in the service of our fellow men.
Grant this through our Lord Jesus Christ, your Son
who lives and reigns with you and the Holy Spirit,
one God, for ever and ever.

January 25
CONVERSION OF SAINT PAUL, APOSTLE
Feast

Morning Prayer
HYMN
Doctor egregie. (L.M.)

Doctor egregie, Paule, mores instrue	Great convert Teacher of the Faith,
et mente polum nos transferre satage,	Who never ceased from preaching Christ,
donec perfectum largiatur plenius,	Saint Paul impart to us your zeal,
evacuato quod ex parte gerimus.	That we may reach the joys unseen.
Sit Trinitati sempiterna gloria,	All glory to the Trinity,
honor, potestas atque iubilatio,	For ever honor, sov'reignty;
in unitate, cui manet imperium	To God Almighty be all praise,
ex tunc et modo per æternal sæcula.	Beginning and the End of all. Amen.

Ant. 1   I know the one whom I have trusted † and I am certain that he,
the just judge, † has power to keep safe what he has entrust*ed* to
me * un*til* that Day.

Psalms and canticles from Sunday, Week I, 606.

Ant. 2   Paul, my grace is suffi*cient* for you; * my power is made perfect
in weakness.

Ant. 3   God's grace in me has not been with*out* fruit; * it is always at
work *in* me.

READING   Acts 26:16b-18
I have appeared to you to designate you as my servant and as a witness to
what you have seen of me and what you will see of me. I have delivered you
from this people and from the nations, to open the eyes of those to whom I
am sending you, to turn them from darkness to light and from the dominion of Satan to God; that through their faith in me they may obtain the
forgiveness of their sins and a portion among God's people.

RESPONSORY (VI F)
You are a *chos*en instrument, * holy apos*tle* Paul.
— You are a *chos*en instrument, * holy apos*tle* Paul.

Preacher of truth to *the* whole world,
— holy apos*tle* Paul.
Glory to the Father, and *to* the Son, * and to the Ho*ly* Spirit.
— You are a *chos*en instrument, * holy apos*tle* Paul.

CANTICLE OF ZECHARIAH

Ant.   Let us celebrate the conversion of Saint Paul the apostle. † He was transformed from being a persecu*tor* of Christ * into a vessel of *his* grace.

INTERCESSIONS

Belovèd friends, we have inherited heaven along with *the* apostles. * Let us give thanks to the Father for *all* his gifts:
The company of apostles praises you, O Lord.
Praise be to you, Lord, for the banquet of Christ's body and blood given us through *the* apostles,
— which refreshes us and *gives* us life.
The company of apostles praises you, O Lord.
Praise be to you, Lord, for the feast of your word prepared for us by *the* apostles,
— giving us *light* and joy.
The company of apostles praises you, O Lord.
Praise be to you, Lord, for your holy Church, founded on *the* apostles,
— where we are gathered together into *your* community.
The company of apostles praises you, O Lord.
Praise be to you, Lord, for the cleansing power of baptism and penance that you have entrusted to *your* apostles,
— through which we are cleansed *of* our sins.
The company of apostles praises you, O Lord.

Our Father . . .

Prayer

God our Father,
you taught the gospel to all the world
through the preaching of Paul your apostle.
May we who celebrate his conversion to the faith
follow him in bearing witness to your truth.
We ask this through our Lord Jesus Christ, your Son
who lives and reigns with you and the Holy Spirit,
one God, for ever and ever.

Evening Prayer

HYMN

Excelsam Pauli. (L.M.)

Excelsam Pauli gloriam	The Church concelebrates today
concelebret Ecclesia,	The great Saint Paul who was her foe,
quem mire sibi apostolum	Becoming an Apostle true
ex hoste fecit Dominus.	When once his Lord he came to know.
Quibus succensus æstibus	The fire and heat with which he fought
in Christi nomen sæviit,	The name of Christ when he was young,
exarsit his impensius	Were turned to overflowing love
amorem Christi prædicans.	For him who on the cross had hung.
O magnum Pauli meritum!	O wondrous merit of Saint Paul
Cælum conscendit tertium,	Enraptured to third heaven's height,
audit verba mysterii	To hear such mysteries sublime
quae nullus audet eloqui.	That words could not convey aright.
Dum verbi spargit semina,	His sowing of the seeds of truth
seges surgit uberrima;	Brought forth a harvest rich and sound,
sic cæli replent horreum	That heaven's granaries above
bonorum fruges operum.	With fruit of good works should abound.
Micantis more lampadis	As shining lamp that can dispel
perfundit orbem radiis;	The darkest shadows of the night,
fugat errorum tenebras,	He strove to spread the reign of truth
ut sola regnet veritas.	While forcing error to take flight.
Christo sit omnis gloria,	All glory be to Jesus Christ,
cum Patre et almo Spiritu,	The Father and the Spirit too,
qui dedit vas tam fugidum	Who chose Saint Paul as instrument
electionis gentibus. Amen.	Of light to many nations new. Amen.

Ant. 1   Willingly I glory in *my* infirmities, * that the healing power of Christ may *dwell* in me.

Psalms and canticles from the common of apostles, 1208.

Ant. 2   I planted the seed; A*pollo*s watered it, * but it was God who gave *the* increase.

Ant. 3   For me life is Christ, and death is gain. † God forbid that I *should* boast * except in the cross of our Lord Je*sus* Christ.

READING   1 Corinthians 15:9-10
I am the least of the apostles; in fact, because I persecuted the church of God, I do not even deserve the name. But by God's favor I am what I am.

This favor of his to me has not proved fruitless. Indeed, I have worked harder than all the others, not on my own but through the favor of God.

RESPONSORY (VI F)

I will sing your *praise*, O Lord, * with all *my* heart.
— I will sing your *praise*, O Lord, * with all *my* heart.
I will glorify your name a*mong* the nations,
— with all *my* heart.
Glory to the Father, and *to* the Son, * and to the Ho*ly* Spirit.
— I will sing your *praise*, O Lord, * with all *my* heart.

CANTICLE OF MARY

Ant. Holy apostle Paul, † preacher of truth and teacher *of* the Gentiles, * intercede for us with God, *who* chose you.

INTERCESSIONS

My brothers, we build on the foundation of *the* apostles. * Let us pray to our almighty Father for his holy peo*ple* and say:
Be mindful of your Church, O Lord.
Father, you wanted your Son to be seen first by the apostles after the resurrection *from* the dead,
— we ask you to make us his witnesses to the farthest corners *of* the world.
You sent your Son to preach the good news *to* the poor,
— help us to preach the Gospel to *every* creature.
You sent your Son to sow the seed of un*end*ing life,
— grant that we who work at sowing the seed may share the joy *of* the harvest.
You sent your Son to reconcile all men to you *through* his blood,
— help us all to work toward achieving this recon*ci*liation.
Your Son sits at your right *hand* in heaven,
— let the dead enter your king*dom* of joy.

Our Father . . .

Prayer

God our Father,
you taught the gospel to all the world
through the preaching of Paul your apostle.
May we who celebrate his conversion to the faith
follow him in bearing witness to your truth.
We ask this through our Lord Jesus Christ, your Son
who lives and reigns with you and the Holy Spirit,
one God, for ever and ever.

January 26
TIMOTHY AND TITUS, BISHOPS
Memorial

From the common of pastors, 1238.

Morning Prayer

CANTICLE OF ZECHARIAH

Ant.   Pro*claim* the message, * insist on it in season and out *of* season, refute falsehood, correct error, † call *to* obedience, * but do all with patience and *sound* doctrine.

Prayer

God our Father,
you gave your saints Timothy and Titus
the courage and wisdom of the apostles:
may their prayers help us to live holy lives
and lead us to heaven, our true home.
Grant this through our Lord Jesus Christ, your Son,
who lives and reigns with you and the Holy Spirit,
one God, for ever and ever.

Evening Prayer

CANTICLE OF MARY

Ant.   Let us live holy and upright lives, † as we wait in *joy*ful hope * for the coming of our Savior Je*sus* Christ.

January 27
ANGELA MERICI, VIRGIN

From the common of virgins, 1253, or of holy women: teachers, 1274.

Prayer

Lord,
may Saint Angela commend us to your mercy;
may her charity and wisdom help us
to be faithful to your teaching
and to follow it in our lives.
We ask this through our Lord Jesus Christ, your Son
who lives and reigns with you and the Holy Spirit,
one God, for ever and ever.

January 28
THOMAS AQUINAS, PRIEST AND DOCTOR
Memorial
From the common of doctors, 1246.

Morning Prayer

CANTICLE OF ZECHARIAH
Ant.   Blessèd be the Lord; † for love of him Saint Thomas Aquinas *
spent long hours in prayer, study *and* writing.

Prayer
God our Father,
you made Thomas Aquinas known for his holiness and learning.
Help us to grow in wisdom by his teaching,
and in holiness by imitating his faith.
Grant this through our Lord Jesus Christ, your Son,
who lives and reigns with you and the Holy Spirit,
one God, for ever and ever.

Evening Prayer

CANTICLE OF MARY
Ant.   God gave him surpassing wisdom † which he taught with*out*
deceit, * and shared freely *with* others.

January 31
JOHN BOSCO, PRIEST
Memorial
From the common of pastors, 1238, or of holy men: teachers, 1263.

Prayer
Lord,
you called John Bosco
to be a teacher and father to the young.
Fill us with love like his:
may we give ourselves completely to your service
and to the salvation of mankind.
We ask this through our Lord Jesus Christ, your Son,
who lives and reigns with you and the Holy Spirit,
one God, for ever and ever.

February 2
PRESENTATION OF THE LORD
Feast

If this feast falls on Sunday, Evening Prayer I is said.

Evening Prayer I
HYMN

Quod chorus. (11.11.11.5)

Quod chorus vatum venerandus olim	God's plan of mercy promised by the prophets
spiritu sancto cecinit repletus,	Touched by the Spirit, has attained fulfillment,
in dei factum genitrice constat	Christ our Redeemer comes to us through Mary,
esse maria.	Chosen as Mother.
Haec Deum caeli Dominumque terrae	Virgin's conception welcomes Heaven's Ruler,
virgo concepit peperitque virgo,	Virgin and Mother bore the world's Creator,
atque post partum meruit manere	Ever remaining, after that great honor,
inviolata.	Purest of Virgins.
Quem senex iustus Simeon in ulnas	Simeon's yearning to behold the Savior
in domo sumpsit domini gavisus	So long expected, brought him to the Temple,
ob quod optavit proprio videre	Where he received him from the arms of Mary,
lumine Christum.	With exultation.
Tu libens votis petimus precantum	Hear our petitions, Mary, Queen of heaven,
regis aeterni genitrix, faveto,	Tender and gracious, you will not refuse us,
clara quae fundis Geniti benigni	But as a mother, send us many graces
munera lucis.	From your Divine Son.
Christe, qui lumen Patris es superni,	Light of the Father, Jesus Christ our Savior,
qui Patris nobis reseras profunda,	Light of our creatures, showing us the Father,
nos fac aeternae tibi ferre laudes	May we be with you in the light of heaven
lucis in aula. Amen.	Singing your praises. Amen.

PSALMODY

Ant. 1   The parents of Jesus brought him *to* Jerusalem * to present him *to* the Lord.

VIIIg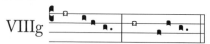

Psalm 113

Praise, O servants *of* the Lord, *	above the heav*ens* his glory.
praise the name *of* the Lord!	Who is like the *Lord*, our God, * who
May the name of the *Lord* be blessed *	has risen on high *to* his throne
both now and for *evermore*!	yet stoops from the heights *to* look
From the rising of the sun *to* its setting	down, * to look down upon heav*en*
* praised be the name *of* the Lord!	and earth?
High above all nations *is* the Lord, *	From the dust he lifts *up* the lowly, *

from his misery he rai*se*s the poor
to set him in the compan*y* of princes, *
  yes, with the princes *of* his people.
To the childless wife he *gives* a home *
  and gladdens her *heart* with children.

Glory to the Father, and *to* the Son, *
  and to the *Ho*ly Spirit:
as it was in the begin*ning*, is now, * and
  will be for ev*er*. Amen.

Antiphon   The parents of Jesus brought him *to* Jerusalem * to present him
                to the Lord.

Ant. 2   Zion, prepare your *wed*ding chamber * to receive Christ *the*
                King.

IIA

Psalm 147:12-20

O praise the *Lord*, Jerusalem! *
  Zion, praise *your* God!
He has strengthened the bars *of* your
  gates, * he has blessed the children
  *with*in you.
He established peace *on* your borders, *
  he feeds you with fin*est* wheat.
He sends out his word *to* the earth *
  and swiftly runs his *com*mand.
He showers down snow *white* as wool, *
  he scatters hoar-frost *like* ashes.
He hurls down hail*stones* like crumbs. *
  The waters are frozen at *his* touch;

he sends forth his word *and* it melts
  them: * at the breath of his mouth
  the wa*ters* flow.
He makes his word *known* to Jacob, *
  to Israel his laws and *de*crees.
He has not dealt thus with *o*ther
  nations; * he has not taught them his
  *de*crees.
Glory to the Father, and *to* the Son, *
  and to the Ho*ly* Spirit:
as it was in the begin*ning*, is now, * and
  will be for ever. *A*men.

Antiphon   Zion, prepare your *wed*ding chamber * to receive Christ *the*
                King.

Ant. 3   Blessèd are you, good Simeon; † you held in your arms Christ
                the Lord, * the Savior of *his* people.

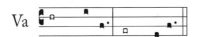

Va

Canticle   Philippians 2:6-11

Though he was in the form *of* God,
  * Jesus did not deem equality
  with God something to *be* grasped

at.
Rather, he emptied himself and took
  the form of *a* slave, * being born in

the likeness *of* men.
He was known to be of human *estate,* *
   and it was thus that *he* humbled
   himself,
obediently accepting e*ven* death, *
   death on *a* cross!
Because of this, God highly e*x*alted
   him * and bestowed on him the
   name above every oth*er* name,
So that at Jesus' name every knee *must*

bend * in the heavens, on the earth,
   and under *the* earth,
and every tongue proclaim to the glory
   of God *the* Father: * JESUS
   CHRIST *IS* LORD!
Glory to the Father, and to *the* Son, *
   and to the Ho*ly* Spirit:
as it was in the beginning, *is* now, * and
   will be for ever. *A*men.

Antiphon   Bless*è*d are you, good Simeon; † you held in your arms Christ
                the Lord, * the Savior of *his* people.

READING   Hebrews 10:5-7
      On coming into the world, Jesus said:
   "Sacrifice and offering you did not desire,
      but a body you have prepared for me;
   Holocausts and sin offerings you took no delight in.
   Then I said, 'As is written of me in the book,
      I have come to do your will, O God.'"

RESPONSORY (VI F)
The Lord *has* made known * his sav*ing* power.
— The Lord *has* made known * his sav*ing* power.
Which he has prepared in the sight of *ev*ery people.
— His sav*ing* power.
Glory to the Father, and *to* the Son, * and to the Ho*ly* Spirit.
— The Lord *has* made known * his sav*ing* power.

CANTICLE OF MARY
Ant.   The old man car*ried* the child, * but the child was the old *man's*
                Lord.
                The Virgin gave birth to the child † yet remained a vir*gin* for
                ever. * She knelt in worship before *her* child.

INTERCESSIONS
Today our Savior was presented *in* the temple. * Let us adore him *as* we say:
Lord, may our eyes see your saving power.
Christ Jesus, you are the light that enlight*ens* all nations,
— shine upon those who do not know you, that they may come to believe in
   you, the *one* true God.
You are the redeemer and the glory of your *peo*ple Israel,
— may your Church proclaim your salvation to the ends *of* the earth.

Jesus, desire of the nation, Simeon, the just man, rejoiced *at* your coming,
— lead all men to recognize that you still *come* to them.
Lord, when you were presented in the temple, Simeon foretold that a sword of
sorrow would pierce your *moth*er's heart,
— strengthen us to accept the sufferings we endure for the sake *of* your name.
Christ Jesus, joy of all the saints, Simeon longed to see you before he died, and
his *prayer* was answered,
— hear our plea for all the dead who still yearn to see you *face* to face.

Our Father . . .

Prayer

All-powerful Father,
Christ your Son became man for us
and was presented in the temple.
May he free our hearts from sin
and bring us into your presence.
We ask this through our Lord Jesus Christ, your Son,
who lives and reigns with you and the Holy Spirit,
one God, for ever and ever.

Morning Prayer

HYMN
Adorna Sion. (L.M.)

Adorna, Sion, thalamum,
quæ præstolaris Dominum;
sponsum et sponsam suscipe
vigil fidei lumine.

Adorn your fairest bridal room,
Keep watch, O Zion, with delight,
For Christ our Light now comes to you,
Encradled in his Mother's arms.

Beate senes, propers,
promissa comple gaudia
et revelandum gentibus
revela lumen omnibus.

Come, Prophet far advanced in years,
Make known to all your joy fulfilled,
Show unto us the Infant Christ,
The Light for all the world to see.

Parentes Christum deferunt,
in templo templum offerunt;
legi parere voluit
qui legi nihil debuit.

The Temple gates admit the Babe,
The truest Temple of the Lord,
His happy parents gladly come
To keep the Law that he transcends.

Offer, beata, parvulum,
tuum et Patris unicum;
offer per quem offerimur,
pretium quo redimimur.

O Mary, to the Father bring
His only Son, your little One,
And offer him the Victim pure,
The price with which we are redeemed.

Procede, virgo regia,	Come forward, royal Virgin, come,
profer Natum cum hostia;	As Love's oblation bring your Son;
monet omnes ad gaudium	And he who comes to save us all,
qui venit salus omnium.	With gentle smile bids us rejoice.
Iesu, tibi sit gloria,	All glory, Jesus, be to you,
qui te revelas gentibus,	Revealed to all the nations now;
cum Patre et almo Spiritu,	To God the Father glory be,
in sempiterna sæcula. Amen.	And to the Spirit endlessly. Amen.

Ant. 1   Simeon was a holy and devout man † who looked for the redemp*tion* of Israel, * and the Holy Spir*it* was with him.

Psalms and canticles from Sunday, Week I, 606.

Ant. 2   Simeon took the child *in* his arms * and gave thanks *to* God.

Ant. 3   He is a light to reveal you to *the* nations, * and the glory of your peo*ple* Israel.

READING   Malachi 3:1

Lo, I am sending my messenger
    to prepare the way before me;
And suddenly there will come to the temple
    the Lord whom you seek,
And the messenger of the covenant whom you desire.

RESPONSORY (VIF)
Wor*ship* the Lord * in his ho*ly* court.
— Wor*ship* the Lord * in his ho*ly* court.
Bring him your hom*age* and praise,
— in his ho*ly* court.
Glory to the Father, and *to* the Son, * and to the Ho*ly* Spirit.
— Wor*ship* the Lord * in his ho*ly* court.

CANTICLE OF ZECHARIAH
Ant.   When the parents of Jesus brought him in*to* the temple, *
             Simeon took him in his arms and gave thanks *to* God.

INTERCESSIONS (VI F)
Today our Savior was presented *in* the temple. * Let us adore him *as* we say:
*Lord, may our eyes see your sav*ing *power.*
Christ Jesus, in obedience to the law, you desired to be presented to your Father
    in the temple,
— teach us to offer ourselves to the Father with you in your *Church*'s sacrifice.

Jesus, comforter of Israel, Simeon, the just man, took you into his arms when
　　you came *to* the temple,
— help us to welcome you in our broth*ers* and sisters.
Jesus, desire of nations, Anna the prophetess spoke of you to all who were
　　awaiting Isra*el's* redemption,
— help us to proclaim you in our words and actions to all who yet yearn for
　　your salvation.
Lord Jesus, cornerstone of God's kingdom, you were destined to be a sign that *is*
　　rejected,
— be for those who acknowledge you the source of rising *to* new life.

Our Father . . .

Prayer

All-powerful Father,
Christ your Son became man for us
and was presented in the temple.
May he free our hearts from sin
and bring us into your presence.
We ask this through our Lord Jesus Christ, your Son,
who lives and reigns with you and the Holy Spirit,
one God, for ever and ever.

<h2 style="text-align:center">Evening Prayer II</h2>

HYMN, as in Morning Prayer, 907.

PSALMODY

Ant. 1　　　　　The Holy Spirit had re*vealed* to Simeon * that he would not see
　　　　　　　death until he had *seen* the Lord.

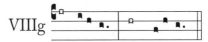

VIIIg

Psalm 110:1-5, 7

The Lord's revelation to my Master:
† "Sit *on* my right: * your foes I
will put be*neath* your feet."
The Lord will wield from Zion † your
scep*ter* of power: * rule in the midst
of *all* your foes.
A prince from the day of your birth †
on the *holy* mountains; * from the
womb before the dawn *I* begot you.
The Lord has sworn an oath he will
not change. † "You are a *priest* for
ever, * a priest like Melchize*dek* of
old."
The Master standing at *your* right
hand * will shatter kings in the day
of *his* great wrath.

He shall drink from the stream *by* the wayside * and therefore he shall lift *up* his head.
Glory to the Father, and *to* the Son, *

and to the *Holy* Spirit:
as it was in the begin*ning*, is now, * and will be for ev*er*. Amen.

Antiphon   The Holy Spirit had re*vealed* to Simeon * that he would not see death until he had *seen* the Lord.

Ant. 2   As the law prescribed, † they offered *to* the Lord * a pair of turtle doves or two *young* pigeons.

IIA

Psalm 130

Out of the depths I cry to *you*, O Lord, * Lord, hear *my* voice!
O let your ears *be* attentive * to the voice of *my* pleading.
If you, O Lord, should *mark* our guilt, * Lord, who would *sur*vive?
But with you is *found* forgiveness: * for this we re*vere* you.
My soul is waiting *for* the Lord, * I count on *his* word.
My soul is longing *for* the Lord * more

than watchman *for* daybreak.
Let the watchman *count* on daybreak * and Israel on *the* Lord.
Because with the Lord *there* is mercy * and fullness of re*demption*,
Israel indeed he *will* redeem * from all its *in*iquity.
Glory to the Father, and *to* the Son, *
and to the Ho*ly* Spirit:
as it was in the begin*ning*, is now, * and will be for ever. *A*men.

Antiphon   As the law prescribed, † they offered *to* the Lord * a pair of turtle doves or two *young* pigeons.

Ant. 3   My own eyes have seen the sal*va*tion * which you have prepared in the sight of eve*ry* people.

Va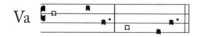

Canticle   Colossians 1:12-20

Let us give thanks to the Father † for having made *you* worthy * to share the lot of the saints *in* light.
He rescued us from the power *of* darkness * and brought us into the kingdom of his belov*èd* Son.

Through him we have re*demption*, * the forgiveness of *our* sins.
He is the image of the invisi*ble* God, * the first-born of *all* creatures.
In him everything in heaven and on earth was *created*, * things visible and

*in*visible.

All were created *through* him; * all were created *for* him.

He is before all else *that* is. * In him everything continues *in* being.

It is he who is head of the body, *the* church! * he who is the *be*ginning,

the first-born of *the* dead, * so that primacy may be his *in* everything.

It pleased God to make absolute

fullness reside in him † and, by means *of* him, * to reconcile everything in *his* person,

both on earth and in *the* heavens, * making peace through the blood of *his* cross.

Glory to the Father, and to *the* Son, * and to the Ho*ly* Spirit:

as it was in the beginning, *is* now, * and will be for ever. *A*men.

Antiphon   My own eyes have seen the *sal*vation * which you have prepared in the sight of eve*ry* people.

READING   Hebrews 4:15-16

We do not have a high priest who is unable to sympathize with our weakness, but one who was tempted in every way we are, yet never sinned. So let us confidently approach the throne of grace to receive mercy and favor and to find help in time of need.

RESPONSORY (VI F)

The Lord *has* made known * his sav*ing* power.

— The Lord *has* made known * his sav*ing* power.

Which he has prepared in the sight of *eve*ry people.

— His sav*ing* power.

Glory to the Father, and *to* the Son, * and to the Ho*ly* Spirit.

— The Lord *has* made known * his sav*ing* power.

CANTICLE OF MARY

Ant.   Today the Bless*èd Vir*gin Mary * presented the Child Jesus in *the* temple;

and Simeon, inspired by the Holy Spirit, † took him *in* his arms, * and gave thanks *to* God.

INTERCESSIONS

Today our Savior was presented *in* the temple. * Let us adore him *as* we say:

*Lord, may our eyes see your sav*ing *power.*

Christ Jesus, you are the light that enligh*tens* all nations,

— shine upon those who do not know you, that they may come to believe in you, the *one* true God.

You are the redeemer and the glory of your *peo*ple Israel,

— may your Church proclaim your salvation to the ends *of* the earth.

Jesus, desire of the nation, Simeon, the just man, rejoiced *at* your coming,

— lead all men to recognize that you still *come* to them.

Lord, when you were presented in the temple, Simeon foretold that a sword of sorrow would pierce your *moth*er's heart,

— strengthen us to accept the sufferings we endure for the sake *of* your name.

Christ Jesus, joy of all the saints, Simeon longed to see you before he died, and his *prayer* was answered,

— hear our plea for all the dead who still yearn to see you *face* to face.

Our Father . . .

Prayer

All-powerful Father,
Christ your Son became man for us
and was presented in the temple.
May he free our hearts from sin
and bring us into your presence.
We ask this through our Lord Jesus Christ, your Son,
who lives and reigns with you and the Holy Spirit,
one God, for ever and ever.

February 3
BLAISE, BISHOP AND MARTYR

From the common of one martyr, 1228, or of pastors, 1238.

Prayer

Lord,
hear the prayers of your martyr Blase.
Give us the joy of your peace in this life
and help us to gain the happiness that will never end.
Grant this through our Lord Jesus Christ, your Son,
who lives and reigns with you and the Holy Spirit,
one God, for ever and ever.

On the same day, February 3
ANSGAR, BISHOP

From the common of pastors, 1238.

Prayer

Father,
you sent Saint Ansgar
to bring the light of Christ to many nations.
May his prayers help us
to walk in the light of your truth.

We ask this through our Lord Jesus Christ, your Son,
who lives and reigns with you and the Holy Spirit,
one God, for ever and ever.

February 5
AGATHA, VIRGIN AND MARTYR
Memorial
Lent: Commemoration

From the common of one martyr, 1228, or of virgins, 1253.

Morning Prayer

CANTICLE OF ZECHARIAH

Ant.   With a festal spirit as though to a wedding banquet, † Agatha *went* to prison; * in prayer she offered her bitter suffering *to* God.

Prayer

Lord,
let your forgiveness be won for us
by the pleading of Saint Agatha,
who found favor with you by her chastity
and by her courage in suffering death for the gospel.
Grant this through our Lord Jesus Christ, your Son,
who lives and reigns with you and the Holy Spirit,
one God, for ever and ever.

Evening Prayer

CANTICLE OF MARY

Ant.   Lord Jesus Christ, my belovèd Master, † it is you who have given me victory in the *midst* of torments. * Call me, Lord, to undying happiness *with* you.

February 6
PAUL MIKI AND COMPANIONS, MARTYRS
Memorial
Lent: Commemoration

From the common of several martyrs, 1214.

Prayer

God our Father,
source of strength for all your saints,
you led Paul Miki and his companions

through the suffering of the cross
to the joy of eternal life.
May their prayers give us the courage
to be loyal until death in professing our faith.
We ask this through our Lord Jesus Christ, your Son,
who lives and reigns with you and the Holy Spirit,
one God, for ever and ever.

February 8
JEROME EMILIANI, PRIEST
Lent: Commemoration
From the common of holy men: teachers, 1263.

Prayer

God of mercy,
you chose Jerome Emiliani
to be a father and friend of orphans.
May his prayers keep us faithful
to the Spirit we have received,
who makes us your children.
Grant this through our Lord Jesus Christ, your Son,
who lives and reigns with you and the Holy Spirit,
one God, for ever and ever.

On the same day, February 8
JOSEPHINE BAKHITA, VIRGIN
Lent: Commemoration
From the common of virgins, 1253.

Prayer

God our Savior,
we celebrate with joy the memory of the virgin Josephine,
may we learn from her example of faithfulness and love.
We ask this through our Lord Jesus Christ, your Son,
who lives and reigns with you and the Holy Spirit,
one God, for ever and ever.

February 10
SCHOLASTICA, VIRGIN
Memorial
Lent: Commemoration
From the common of virgins, 1253.

Morning Prayer

CANTICLE OF ZECHARIAH

Ant.   Now this wise virgin has gone to Christ. † Among the *choirs* of virgins, * she is radiant as the sun in *the* heavens.

Prayer

Lord,
as we recall the memory of Saint Scholastica,
we ask that by her example
we may serve you with love and obtain perfect joy.
Grant this through our Lord Jesus Christ, your Son,
who lives and reigns with you and the Holy Spirit,
one God, for ever and ever.

Evening Prayer

CANTICLE OF MARY

Ant.   Come, spouse of Christ, re*ceive* the crown * the Lord has prepared for you from all *e*ternity.

February 11
OUR LADY OF LOURDES
Lent: Commemoration

From the common of the Blessed Virgin Mary, 1192.

Morning Prayer

CANTICLE OF ZECHARIAH

Ant.   Virgin Mary, radiant dawn of *our* salvation, * the Sun of Justice, the light from on high, rose *from* you.

Prayer

God of mercy,
we celebrate the feast of Mary,
the sinless mother of God.
May her prayers help us
to rise above our human weakness.
We ask this through our Lord Jesus Christ, your Son,
who lives and reigns with you and the Holy Spirit,
one God, for ever and ever.

February 14

Evening Prayer

CANTICLE OF MARY

Ant.   Hail, Mary, full of grace, the Lord is with you; † blessèd are you among women, * and blessèd is the fruit of *your* womb.

February 14
CYRIL, MONK, AND METHODIUS, BISHOP
Memorial
Lent: Commemoration
From the common of pastors, 1238.

Morning Prayer

CANTICLE OF ZECHARIAH

Ant.   Holy and righteous *in* his sight, * they served the Lord all the days of *their* lives.

Prayer
Father,
you brought the light of the gospel to the Slavic nations
through Saint Cyril and his brother Saint Methodius.
Open our hearts to understand your teaching
and help us to become one in faith and praise.
Grant this through our Lord Jesus Christ, your Son,
who lives and reigns with you and the Holy Spirit,
one God, for ever and ever.

Evening Prayer

CANTICLE OF MARY

Ant.   Because these holy men pro*claimed* his truth, * God made them glorious and gave them *his* friendship.

February 17
SEVEN FOUNDERS OF THE ORDER OF SERVITES, RELIGIOUS
Lent: Commemoration
From the common of holy men: religious, 1263.

Morning Prayer

CANTICLE OF ZECHARIAH

Ant.   See how good and delight*ful* it is * for brothers to live *in* unity.

Prayer

Lord,
fill us with the love
which inspired the seven holy brothers
to honor the mother of God with special devotion
and to lead your people to you.
We ask this through our Lord Jesus Christ, your Son,
who lives and reigns with you and the Holy Spirit,
one God, for ever and ever.

Evening Prayer

CANTICLE OF MARY

Ant.　　　　Where brothers praise *God* together, * there the Lord will
shower *his* graces.

February 21
PETER DAMIAN, BISHOP AND DOCTOR
Lent: Commemoration
From the common of pastors, 1238, or of doctors, 1246.

Morning Prayer

CANTICLE OF ZECHARIAH

Ant.　　　　Those who are learnèd will be as radiant *as* the sky * in all *its*
beauty;
those who instruct the peo*ple* in goodness * will shine like the
stars for all *e*ternity.

Prayer

All-powerful God,
help us to follow the teachings and example of Peter Damian.
By making Christ and the service of his Church
the first love of our lives,
may we come to the joys of eternal light
where he lives and reigns with you and the Holy Spirit,
one God, for ever and ever.

Evening Prayer

CANTICLE OF MA RY

Ant.　　　　O blessèd doctor, Saint Peter, † light of holy Church and lover
of God's law, * pray to the Son of God *for* us.

February 22
CHAIR OF PETER, APOSTLE
Feast

Morning Prayer
HYMN

Petrus beatus.

Petrus beatus catenarum laqueos
Christo iubente rupit mirabiliter;
custos ovilis et doctor Ecclesiæ,
pastorque gregis, conservator ovium
arcet luporum truculentam rabiem.

Quodcumque vinclis super terram strinxerit,
erit in astris religatum fortier,
et quod resolvit in terris arbitrio,
erit solutum super cæli radium;
in fine mundi iudex erit sæculi.

Gloria Patri per immensa sæcula,
sit tibi, Nate, decus et imperium,
honor, potestas Sanctoque Spiritui;
sit Trinitati salus individua
per infinita sæculorum sæcula. Amen.

Or: (L.M.)

O Peter, who were named by Christ
The guardian-shepherd of his flock,
Protect the Church he built on you
To stand unyielding, firm on rock.

Your weakness Christ exchanged for strength,
You faltered, but he made you true;
He knew the greatness of your love
And gave the keys of heav'n to you.

Unseen, eternal Trinity,
We give you glory, praise your name,
Your love keeps faith with faithless men:
Through change and stress you are the same.
Amen.

Ant. 1   The Lord said to Simon: † There is no need to *be* afraid; * from now on you will be a fish*er* of men.

Psalms and canticle from Sunday, Week I, 606.

Ant. 2   You are the Christ, the Son of the *living* God. * How bless*èd* are you, Simon Peter, for *that* witness.

Ant. 3   The Lord said to Peter: † I will give you *the* keys * of the kingdom *of* heaven.

READING   Acts 15:7b-9
God selected me to be the one from whose lips the Gentiles would hear the message of the gospel and believe. God, who reads the hearts of men, showed his approval by granting the Holy Spirit to them just as he did to us. He made no distinction between them and us, but purified their hearts by means of faith also.

RESPONSORY (VI f)
You have *made* them rulers * over all *the* earth.
— You have *made* them rulers * over all *the* earth.

They will always remember your *name*, O Lord,
— over all *the* earth.
Glory to the Father, and *to* the Son, * and to the Ho*ly* Spirit.
— You have *made* them rulers * over all *the* earth.

CANTICLE OF ZECHARIAH
Ant.   The Lord said to Simon Peter: † I have prayed *for* you, Peter, *
          that your faith may *not* fail;
          and when you have *turned* to me, * you must strengthen the
          faith of *your* brothers.

INTERCESSIONS
Belovèd friends, we have inherited heaven along with *the* apostles. * Let us give
    thanks to the Father for *all* his gifts:
The company of apostles praises you, O Lord.
Praise be to you, Lord, for the banquet of Christ's body and blood given us
    through *the* apostles,
— which refreshes us and *gives* us life.
The company of apostles praises you, O Lord.
Praise be to you, Lord, for the feast of your word prepared for us by *the* apostles,
— giving us *light* and joy.
The company of apostles praises you, O Lord.
Praise be to you, Lord, for your holy Church, founded on *the* apostles,
— where we are gathered together into *your* community.
The company of apostles praises you, O Lord.
Praise be to you, Lord, for the cleansing power of baptism and penance that you
    have entrusted to *your* apostles,
— through which we are cleansed *of* our sins.
The company of apostles praises you, O Lord.

Our Father . . .

Prayer

All-powerful Father,
you have built your Church
on the rock of Saint Peter's confession of faith.
May nothing divide or weaken
our unity in faith and love.
Grant this through our Lord Jesus Christ, your Son,
who lives and reigns with you and the Holy Spirit,
one God, for ever and ever.

Evening Prayer

HYMN, from the Common of Apostles, 1203.

Ant. 1   Do you love me, Peter? † Lord, you know *that* I love you. *
                   Peter, *feed* my sheep.

Psalms and canticle from the common of apostles, 1208.

Ant. 2   Peter was *kept* in prison, * and the Church prayed unceasingly to
                   God *for* him.

Ant. 3   You *are* Peter, * and upon this rock I will build *my* Church.

READING   1 Peter 1:3-5
Praised be the God and Father
of our Lord Jesus Christ,
he who in his great mercy
gave us new birth;
a birth unto hope which draws its life
from the resurrection of Jesus Christ from the dead;
a birth to an imperishable inheritance,
incapable of fading or defilement,
which is kept in heaven for you
who are guarded with God's power through faith;
a birth to a salvation which stands ready
to be revealed in the last days.

RESPONSORY (VI F)
Tell *all* the nations * how glorious *God* is.
— Tell *all* the nations * how glorious *God* is.
Make known his wonders to *every* people.
— How glorious *God* is.
Glory to the Father, and *to* the Son, * and to the Ho*ly* Spirit.
— Tell *all* the nations * how glorious *God* is.

CANTICLE OF MARY
Ant.   You are the shepherd of Christ's flock † and the prince of *the*
                 apostles; * to you Christ has entrusted the keys of the kingdom
                 of heaven.

INTERCESSIONS
My brothers, we build on the foundation of *the* apostles. * Let us pray to our
    almighty Father for his holy peo*ple* and say:
Be mindful of your Church, O Lord.

Father, you wanted your Son to be seen first by the apostles after the
resurrection *from* the dead,
— we ask you to make us his witnesses to the farthest corners *of* the world.
You sent your Son to preach the good news *to* the poor,
— help us to preach the Gospel to *every* creature.
You sent your Son to sow the seed of un*end*ing life,
— grant that we who work at sowing the seed may share the joy *of* the harvest.
You sent your Son to reconcile all men to you *through* his blood,
— help us all to work toward achieving this reconci*li*ation.
Your Son sits at your right *hand* in heaven,
— let the dead enter your king*dom* of joy.

Our Father . . .

Prayer

All-powerful Father,
you have built your Church
on the rock of Saint Peter's confession of faith.
May nothing divide or weaken
our unity in faith and love.
Grant this through our Lord Jesus Christ, your Son,
who lives and reigns with you and the Holy Spirit,
one God, for ever and ever.

February 23
POLYCARP, BISHOP AND MARTYR
Lent: Commemoration

From the common of one martyr, 1228, or of pastors, 1238.

Morning Prayer

CANTICLE OF ZECHARIAH

Ant.   For eighty-six years I have served Jesus Christ † and he has
never a*band*oned me. * How could I curse my blessèd King *and*
Savior?

Prayer

God of all creation,
you gave your bishop Polycarp
the privilege of being counted among the saints
who gave their lives in faithful witness to the gospel.
May his prayers give us the courage

to share with him the cup of suffering
and to rise to eternal glory.
We ask this through our Lord Jesus Christ, your Son,
who lives and reigns with you and the Holy Spirit,
one God, for ever and ever.

Evening Prayer

Ant.   Lord, mighty God, I give you praise, † for you have counted me
worthy to be a*mong* your martyrs, * who drink of the cup of
Christ's sufferings.

March 3
KATHARINE DREXEL, VIRGIN

From the common of virgins, 1253.

Prayer

Ever-loving God,
you called Blessèd Katharine Drexel
to teach the message of the Gospel
and to bring the life of the Eucharist
to the African-American and Native American peoples.
By her prayers and example,
enable us to work for justice
among the poor and the oppressed,
and keep us undivided in love
in the eucharistic community of your Church.
Grant this through our Lord Jesus Christ, your Son,
who lives and reigns with you and the Holy Spirit,
one God, for ever and ever.

March 4
CASIMIR
Lent: Commemoration

From the common of holy men, 1263.

Prayer

All-powerful God,
to serve you is to reign:
by the prayers of Saint Casimir,
help us to serve you in holiness and justice.

Grant this through our Lord Jesus Christ, your Son,
who lives and reigns with you and the Holy Spirit,
one God, for ever and ever.

March 7
PERPETUA AND FELICITY, MARTYRS
Lent: Commemoration
From the common of several martyrs, 1214.

Prayer
Father,
your love gave the Saints Perpetua and Felicity
courage to suffer a cruel martyrdom.
By their prayers, help us to grow in love of you.
We ask this through our Lord Jesus Christ, your Son,
who lives and reigns with you and the Holy Spirit,
one God, for ever and ever.

March 8
JOHN OF GOD, RELIGIOUS
Lent: Commemoration
From the common of holy men: religious, or those who worked for the underprivileged, 1284.

Prayer
Father,
you gave John of God
love and compassion for others.
Grant that by doing good for others
we may be counted among the saints in your kingdom.
We ask this through our Lord Jesus Christ, your Son,
who lives and reigns with you and the Holy Spirit,
one God, for ever and ever.

March 9
FRANCES OF ROME, RELIGIOUS
Lent: Commemoration
From the common of holy women: religious, 1282.

Prayer
Merciful Father,
in Frances of Rome
you have given us a unique example of love in marriage
as well as in religious life.
Keep us faithful in your service,

and help us to see and follow you
in all the aspects of life.
We ask this through our Lord Jesus Christ, your Son,
who lives and reigns with you and the Holy Spirit,
one God, for ever and ever.

March 17
PATRICK, BISHOP
Commemoration
Morning Prayer

CANTICLE OF ZECHARIAH

Ant.   Go, and teach all nations, † baptizing them in the name *of* the
Father, * and of the Son, and of the Ho*ly* Spirit.

Prayer

God our Father,
you sent Saint Patrick
to preach your glory to the people of Ireland.
By the help of his prayers,
may all Christians proclaim your love to all men.
Grant this through our Lord Jesus Christ, your Son,
who lives and reigns with you and the Holy Spirit,
one God, for ever and ever.

Evening Prayer

CANTICLE OF MARY

Ant.   Many shall come from the east and the west, † and they shall sit
down with Abraham and Is*aac* and Jacob * in the kingdom *of*
heaven.

March 18
CYRIL OF JERUSALEM, BISHOP AND DOCTOR
Commemoration

Morning Prayer

CANTICLE OF ZECHARIAH

Ant.   Those who are learnèd will be as radiant *as* the sky * in all *its*
beauty;
those who instruct the peo*ple* in goodness * will shine like the
stars for all *e*ternity.

Prayer

Father,
through Cyril of Jerusalem
you led your Church to a deeper understanding
of the mysteries of salvation.
Let his prayers help us to know your Son better
and to have eternal life in all its fullness.
We ask this through our Lord Jesus Christ, your Son,
who lives and reigns with you and the Holy Spirit,
one God, for ever and ever.

March 19
JOSEPH, HUSBAND OF MARY
Solemnity

Evening Prayer I
HYMN

*Te, Ioseph, celebrent agmina cælitum.*Mode I (12.12.12.8)

Te, Ioseph, celebrent agmina cælitum,
te cuncti resonent christiadum chori,
qui, clarus meritis, iunctus es inclitæ
 casto fœdere Virgini.

Almo cum tumidam germine coniugem
admirans dubio tangeris anxius,
afflatu superi Flaminis angelus
 conceptum puerum docet.

Tu natum Dominum stringis, ad exteras
Ægypti profugum tu sequeris plagas;
amissum Solymis quæris et invenis,
 miscens gaudia fletibus.

Electos reliquos mors pia consecrat
palmamque emeritos gloria susciptit;
tu vivens, superis par, frueris Deo,
 mira sorte beatior.

Nobis, summa Trias, parce precantibus;
da Ioseph meritis sidera scandere,
ut tandem liceat nos tibi perpetim
 gratum promere canticum. Amen.

O Joseph, heav'nly hosts thy worthiness proclaim,
And Christendom conspires to celebrate thy fame,
Thou who in purest bonds were to the Virgin bound;
 How glorious is thy name renowned.

Thou, when thou didst behold thy Spouse about to bear,
Were sore oppressed with doubt, were filled with wond'ring care;
At length the Angel's word thy anxious heart relieved:
 She by the Spirit hath conceived.

Thou with thy newborn Lord didst seek far Egypt's land,
As wand'ring pilgrims, ye fled o'er the desert sand;
That Lord, when lost, by thee is in the temple found,
 While tears are shed, and joys abound.

Not till death's hour is past do other men obtain
The meed of holiness, and glorious rest attain;
Thou, like to Angels made, in life completely blest,
     Dost clasp thy God unto they breast.

O Holy Trinity, thy suppliant servants spare;
Grant us to rise to heav'n for Joseph's sake and prayer,
And so our grateful hearts to thee shall ever raise
     Exulting canticles of praise. Amen.

PSALMODY

Ant. 1   Jacob became the father of Joseph, † the hus*band* of Mary. * She gave birth to Jesus who *is* called Christ (*a*lleluia).

VIIIg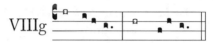

Psalm 113

Praise, O servants *of* the Lord, *
    praise the name *of* the Lord!
May the name of the *Lord* be blessed *
    both now and for *ever*more!
From the rising of the sun *to* its
    setting * praised be the name *of* the
    Lord!
High above all nations *is* the Lord, *
    above the heav*ens* his glory.
Who is like the *Lord*, our God, * who
    has risen on high *to* his throne
yet stoops from the heights *to* look

down, * to look down upon heav*en*
    and earth?
From the dust he lifts *up* the lowly, *
    from his misery he rais*es* the poor
to set him in the compan*y* of princes, *
    yes, with the princes *of* his people.
To the childless wife he *gives* a home *
    and gladdens her *heart* with children.
Glory to the Father, and *to* the Son, *
    and to the *Holy* Spirit:
as it was in the begin*ning*, is now, * and
    will be for ev*er*. Amen.

Antiphon   Jacob became the father of Joseph, † the hus*band* of Mary. * She gave birth to Jesus who *is* called Christ (*a*lleluia).

Ant. 2   The angel Gabriel was sent by God † to a town of Gali*lee* called Nazareth, * to a virgin betrothed to a man *named* Joseph (al*le*luia).

IIA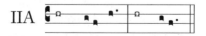

Psalm 146

My soul, give praise to the Lord; †
    I will praise the Lord *all* my
days, * make music to my God while

I live.
Put no *trust* in princes, * in mortal men
    in whom there is *no* help.

Take their breath, they re*turn* to clay *
and their plans that day come *to*
nothing.
He is happy who is helped by *Jacob's*
God, * whose hope is in the Lord *his*
God,
who alone made heav*en* and earth, * the
seas and all they *con*tain.
It is he who keeps *faith* for ever, * who
is just to those who are *op*pressed.
It is he who gives bread *to* the hungry,
* the Lord, who sets prison*ers* free,
the Lord who gives sight *to* the blind, *

who raises up those who are *bowed*
down,
the Lord, who pro*tects* the stranger *
and upholds the widow *and* orphan.
It is the Lord who *loves* the just * but
thwarts the path of *the* wicked.
The Lord will *reign* for ever, * Zion's
God, from age *to* age.
Glory to the Father, and *to* the Son, *
and to the Ho*ly* Spirit:
as it was in the begin*ning*, is now, * and
will be for ever. *A*men.

Antiphon   The angel Gabriel was sent by God † to a town of Gali*lee* called
Nazareth, * to a virgin betrothed to a man *named* Joseph
(al*le*luia).

Ant. 3   Mary the mother of Jesus was betrothed to Joseph, † but before
they came together, † she was found to be *with* child * through
the power of the Ho*ly* Spirit (al*le*luia).

Va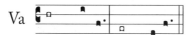

Canticle   Ephesians 1:3-10

Praised be the God *and* Father * of
our Lord Je*sus* Christ,
who has bestowed on us *in* Christ *
every spiritual blessing in *the* heavens.
God chose us in him † before the
world *be*gan * to be holy and blameless in *his* sight.
He predestined us † to be his adopted
sons through Je*sus* Christ, * such was
his will *and* pleasure,
that all might praise the glori*ous* favor *
he has bestowed on us in his *be*lovèd.
In him and through his blood, † we
have been *re*deemed, * and our sins

*for*given,
so immeasura*bly* generous * is God's
favor *to* us.
God has given us the wisdom † to
understand fully *the* mystery, * the
plan he was pleased to decree *in*
Christ.
A plan to be carried out *in* Christ, * in
the fullness *of* time,
to bring all things into one *in* him, * in
the heavens and *on* earth.
Glory to the Father, and to *the* Son, *
and to the Ho*ly* Spirit:
as it was in the beginning, *is* now, * and
will be for ever. *A*men.

Antiphon Mary the mother of Jesus was betrothed to Joseph, † but before they came together, † she was found to be *with* child * through the power of the Ho*ly* Spirit (al*le*luia).

READING   Colossians 3:23-24

Whatever you do, work at it with your whole being. Do it for the Lord rather than for men, since you know full well that you will receive an inheritance from him as your reward. Be slaves of Christ the Lord.

RESPONSORY (VI F)

Lent:

The just *man* shall blossom * like *the* lily.

— The just *man* shall blossom * like *the* lily.

He shall flourish for ever in the courts *of* our God,

— like *the* lily.

Glory to the Father, and *to* the Son, * and to the Ho*ly* Spirit.

— The just *man* shall blossom * like *the* lily.

Easter:

The just man shall blossom *like* the lily, * alleluia, al*le*luia.

— The just man shall blossom *like* the lily, * alleluia, al*le*luia.

He shall flourish for ever in the courts *of* our God,

— alleluia, al*le*luia

Glory to the Father, and *to* the Son, * and to the Ho*ly* Spirit.

— The just man shall blossom *like* the lily, * alleluia, al*le*luia.

CANTICLE OF MARY

Antiphon This is the faithful and *pru*dent steward * whom the Lord has set over *his* household (al*le*luia).

If

My soul ✠ proclaims the greatness *of* the Lord, * my spirit rejoices in God *my* savior

for he has *looked* with favor * on his low*ly* servant.

From this day all *gen*erations * will call *me* bless*èd*:

the Almighty has done great *things* for me, * and holy is *his* Name.

He has mercy on *those* who fear him * in every gen*er*ation.

He has shown the strength *of* his arm, * he has scattered the proud in their *con*ceit.

He has cast down the mighty *from* their thrones, * and has lifted up *the* lowly.

He has filled the hungry *with* good things, * and the rich he has sent a*way* empty.

He has come to the help of his *servant* Israel * for he has remembered his

promise *of* mercy,
the promise he made *to* our fathers, * to
  Abraham and his children *for* ever.
Glory to the Father, and *to* the Son, *

and to the Ho*ly* Spirit:
as it was in the begin*ning*, is now, * and
  will be for ever. *A*men.

Antiphon   This is the faithful and *pru*dent steward * whom the Lord has
                set over *his* household (al*le*luia).

INTERCESSIONS (VI F)

All fatherhood in heaven and on earth has its ori*gin* in God. * Let us turn to *him*
  and pray:
Our Father in heaven, hear our *prayer.*
All-holy Father, you revealed to Saint Joseph your eternal plan of salva*tion* in
  Christ,
— deepen our understanding of your Son, true God *and* true man.
Father in heaven, you feed the birds of the air, and clothe the fields with the
  fruit *of* the earth,
— give all your children their daily bread, to sustain *soul* and body.
Maker of the universe, you have entrusted your creation to *our* safekeeping,
— may all who work receive a just reward *for* their labors.
God of all righteousness, you want us all to *be* like you,
— may Saint Joseph inspire us to walk always in your *way* of holiness.
Look kindly on the dying and the dead, and grant *them* your mercy,
— through the intercession of Jesus, Ma*ry* and Joseph.

Our Father . . .

Prayer

    Father,
    you entrusted our Savior to the care of Saint Joseph.
    By the help of his prayers
    may your Church continue to serve its Lord, Jesus Christ,
    who lives and reigns with you and the Holy Spirit,
    one God, for ever and ever.

Morning Prayer

HYMN

Cælitum, Ioseph, decus atque nostræ. (11.11.11.5)

Cælitum, Ioseph, decus atque nostræ	Joseph the glory and the joy of heaven,
certa spes vitæ columenque mundi,	Hope of salvation for the world you cherish,
quas tibi læti canimus, benignus	Graciously listen to our humble praises
suscipe laudes.	Joyfully offered.

Te, satum David, statuit Creator
Virginis sponsum, voluitque Verbi
te patrem dici, dedit et ministrum
    esse salutis.
	David's descendant, God's decree ordained you
	Spouse of the Virgin Mother of Christ Jesus,
	Who called you father, sharing in his life work
	    For our salvation.

Tu Redemptorem stabulo iacentem,
quem chorus vatum cecinit futurum,
aspicis gaudens, sociusque matris
    primus adoras.
	One whom the prophets sang as coming Savior
	You contemplated lying in a manger;
	Gazing in wonder at the Infant Jesus,
	    Godhead you worshiped.

Rex Deus regum, dominator orbis,
cuius ad nutum tremit inferorum
turba, cui pronus famulatur æther,
    se tibi subdit.
	Word of the Father, King of kings and Ruler,
	At whose displeasure hordes of hell must tremble,
	Whom all the angels worship without ceasing,
	    Chose to obey you.

Laus sit excelsæ Triadi perennis, quæ, tibi insignes tribuens honores, det tuis nobis meritis beatæ gaudia vitæ. Amen.	Praise to the Father, Son, and Holy Spirit, Who deigned to raise you to the highest honors, May they reward us with the joys of heaven, Through your great merits. Amen.

PSALMODY

Ant. 1   The shepherds went in haste and found Jo*seph* and Mary, * and
the infant lying *in* the manger (*a*lleluia).

VIIIg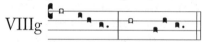

Psalm 63:2-9

O God, you are my God, for
you I long; * for you my *soul* is
thirsting.
My body *pines* for you * like a dry,
weary land *with*out water.
So I gaze on you *in* the sanctuary * to
see your strength *and* your glory.
For your love is bet*ter* than life, * my
lips will *speak* your praise.
So I will bless you *all* my life, * in your
name I will lift *up* my hands.
My soul shall be filled as *with* a

banquet, * my mouth shall praise *you*
with joy.
On my bed I re*mem*ber you. * On you
I muse *through* the night
for you have *been* my help; * in the
shadow of your wings *I* rejoice.
My soul *clings* to you; * your right
hand *holds* me fast.
Glory to the Father, and *to* the Son, *
and to the *Holy* Spirit:
as it was in the begin*ning*, is now, * and
will be for ev*er*. Amen.

Antiphon   The shepherds went in haste and found Jo*seph* and Mary, * and
the infant lying *in* the manger (*a*lleluia).

Ant. 2   Joseph and Mary, the mother of Jesus, † marveled at what was said *of* their child, * and Sime*on* blessed them (al*le*luia).

IIA

Canticle   Daniel 3:57-88, 56

Bless the Lord, all you works *of* the Lord. * Praise and exalt him above all *for*ever.

Angels of the Lord, *bless* the Lord, * You heavens, bless *the* Lord.

All you waters above the heavens, *bless* the Lord. * All you hosts of the Lord, bless *the* Lord.

Sun and moon, *bless* the Lord. * Stars of heaven, bless *the* Lord.

Every shower and dew, *bless* the Lord. * All you winds, bless *the* Lord.

Fire and heat, *bless* the Lord. * Cold and chill, bless *the* Lord.

Dew and rain, *bless* the Lord. * Frost and chill, bless *the* Lord.

Ice and snow, *bless* the Lord. * Nights and days, bless *the* Lord.

Light and darkness, *bless* the Lord. * Lightnings and clouds, bless *the* Lord.

Let the earth *bless* the Lord. * Praise and exalt him above all *for*ever.

Mountains and hills, *bless* the Lord. * Everything growing from the earth, bless *the* Lord.

You springs, *bless* the Lord. * Seas and rivers, bless *the* Lord.

You dolphins and all water creatures, *bless* the Lord. * All you birds of the air, bless *the* Lord.

All you beasts, wild and tame, *bless* the Lord. * You sons of men, bless *the* Lord.

O Israel, *bless* the Lord. * Praise and exalt him above all *for*ever.

Priests of the Lord, *bless* the Lord. * Servants of the Lord, bless *the* Lord.

Spirits and souls of the just, *bless* the Lord. * Holy men of humble heart, bless *the* Lord.

Hananiah, Azariah, Mishael, *bless* the Lord. * Praise and exalt him above all *for*ever.

Let us bless the Father, and the Son, and the *Ho*ly Spirit. * Let us praise and exalt him above all *for*ever.

Bless̀ed are you in the firma*ment* of heaven. * Praiseworthy and glorious and exalted above all *for*ever.

Antiphon   Joseph and Mary, the mother of Jesus, † marveled at what was said *of* their child, * and Sime*on* blessed them (al*le*luia).

Ant. 3   Joseph rose in the night and took the child † and his mother in*to* Egypt. * There they stayed until the death *of* Herod (al*le*luia).

Va

Psalm 149

Sing a new song to *the* Lord, * his praise in the assembly of *the* faithful.

Let Israel rejoice in *its* Maker, * let Zion's sons exult in *their* king.

Let them praise his name *with* dancing * and make music with timbrel *and* harp.

For the Lord takes delight in *his* people. * He crowns the poor with *sal*vation.

Let the faithful rejoice in *their* glory, * shout for joy and take *their* rest.

Let the praise of God be on *their* lips * and a two-edged sword in *their* hand,

to deal out vengeance to *the* nations * and punishment on all *the* peoples;

to bind their kings *in* chains * and their nobles in fetters *of* iron;

to carry out the sentence pre-*or*dained: * this honor is for all *his* faithful.

Glory to the Father, and to *the* Son, * and to the Ho*ly* Spirit:

as it was in the beginning, *is* now, * and will be for ever. *A*men.

Antiphon   Joseph rose in the night and took the child † and his mother in*to* Egypt. * There they stayed until the death *of* Herod (al*le*-luia).

READING   2 Samuel 7:28-29

Lord God, you are God and your words are truth; you have made this generous promise to your servant. Do, then, bless the house of your servant that it may be before you forever; for you, Lord God, have promised, and by your blessing the house of your servant shall be blessed forever.

RESPONSORY (VI F)
Lent:
God made *him* the master * of *his* household.
— God made *him* the master * of *his* household.
He gave him charge over all *his* possessions,
— and made the master of *his* household.
Glory to the Father, and *to* the Son, * and to the Ho*ly* Spirit.
— God made *him* the master * of *his* household.

Easter:
God made him the master *of* his household, * alleluia, al*le*luia.
— God made him the master *of* his household, * alleluia, al*le*luia.
He gave him charge over all *his* possessions,
— alleluia, al*le*luia
Glory to the Father, and *to* the Son, * and to the Ho*ly* Spirit.
— God made him the master *of* his household, * alleluia, al*le*luia.

CANTICLE OF ZECHARIAH

Antiphon   Joseph lived in the town of Nazareth † to fulfill what the
             prophets had fore*told* of Christ: * He will be called a Na*za*rean
             (al*le*luia).

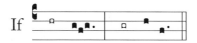

B lessèd ✠ be the Lord, the *God* of
    Israel; * he has come to his people
and set *them* free.
He has raised up for us a *migh*ty savior,
    * born of the house of his ser*vant*
    David.
Through his holy prophets he prom-
    ised of old † that he would save us
    from our enemies, * from the hands
    of all *who* hate us.
He promised to show mercy *to* our
    fathers * and to remember his ho*ly*
    covenant.
This was the oath he swore to our
    *fath*er Abraham: * to set us free from
    the hands of *our* enemies,
free to worship him without fear, †
    holy and righteous *in* his sight * all

the days of *our* life.
You, my child, shall be called the
    prophet *of* the Most High; * for you
    will go before the Lord to prepare *his*
    way,
to give his people knowledge *of* salva-
    tion * by the forgiveness of *their* sins.
In the tender compassion *of* our God *
    the dawn from on high shall break
    *up*on us,
to shine on those who dwell in dark-
    ness and the sha*dow* of death, * and
    to guide our feet into the way *of*
    peace.
Glory to the Father, and *to* the Son, *
    and to the Ho*ly* Spirit:
as it was in the begin*ning*, is now, * and
    will be for ever. *A*men.

Antiphon   Joseph lived in the town of Nazareth † to fulfill what the
             prophets had fore*told* of Christ: * He will be called a Na*za*rean
             (al*le*luia).

INTERCESSIONS (VI F)

The Lord is the giv*er* of holiness. * Let us turn to *him* and pray:
Holy God, raise us up to new life in holiness.
Lord our God, you called our fathers in faith to walk before you in holi*ness* of
    heart,
— may we follow in their footsteps, and obey your command *to* be perfect.
You chose Joseph the righteous to care for your Son in child*hood* and youth,
— teach us to care for Christ's body by caring for our broth*ers* and sisters.
You entrusted the earth to mankind, to people it and *make* it prosper,
— inspire us to work wholeheartedly in this world, seeking always to *give* you
    glory.

Father of all mankind, do not forget what your *hands* have made,
— grant that all who work may have secure employment and a fitting stan*dard*
    of living.

Our Father . . .

Prayer

Father,
you entrusted our Savior to the care of Saint Joseph.
By the help of his prayers
may your Church continue to serve its Lord, Jesus Christ,
who lives and reigns with you and the Holy Spirit,
one God, for ever and ever.

Evening Prayer II

HYMN, as in Evening Prayer I, 925.

PSALMODY

Ant. 1   His parents found Jesus in the temple † sitting in the midst *of*
              the doctors, * listening to them and ask*ing* them questions
              (*a*lleluia).

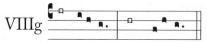

VIIIg

Psalm 15

Lord, who shall be admitted *to* your
tent * and dwell on your *holy*
mountain?
He who walks *with*out fault; * he who
acts with justice
and speaks the truth *from* his heart; *
he who does not slander *with* his
tongue;
he who does no wrong *to* his brother, *
who casts no slur *on* his neighbor,
who holds the godless *in* disdain, * but

honors those who *fear* the Lord;
he who keeps his pledge, *come* what
may; * who takes no interest *on* a
loan
and accepts no bribes a*gainst* the
innocent. * Such a man will stand
firm for ever.
Glory to the Father, and *to* the Son, *
and to the *Ho*ly Spirit:
as it was in the begin*ning*, is now, * and
will be for ev*er*. Amen.

Antiphon   His parents found Jesus in the temple † sitting in the midst *of*
              the doctors, * listening to them and ask*ing* them questions
              (*a*lleluia).

Ant. 2   The mother of Jesus *said* to him: * Son, why have you done this *to us?*

See how your fath*er* and I * have been anxiously searching *for* you (al*le*luia).

IIA

Psalm 112

Happy the man who *fears* the Lord, * who takes delight in all his *com*mands.

His sons will be power*ful* on earth; * the children of the upright *are* blessèd.

Riches and wealth are *in* his house; * his justice stands firm *for* ever.

He is a light in the darkness *for* the upright: * he is generous, merciful *and* just.

The good man takes pi*ty* and lends, * he conducts his affairs *with* honor.

The just man will *never* waver: * he will be remembered *for* ever.

He has no fear of *evil* news; * with a firm heart he trusts in *the* Lord.

With a steadfast heart he *will* not fear; * he will see the downfall of *his* foes.

Open-handed, he gives to the poor; † his justice stands *firm* for ever. * His head will be raised *in* glory.

The wicked man sees and is angry, † grinds his teeth and *fades* away; * the desire of the wicked leads *to* doom.

Glory to the Father, and *to* the Son, * and to the Ho*ly* Spirit:

as it was in the begin*ning*, is now, * and will be for ever. *A*men.

Antiphon   The mother of Jesus *said* to him: * Son, why have you done this *to us?*

See how your fath*er* and I * have been anxiously searching *for* you (al*le*luia).

Ant. 3   Jesus returned with Mary and Joseph *to* Nazareth; * there he lived and was obedient *to* them (al*le*luia).

Va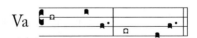

Canticle   Revelation 15:3-4

Mighty and wonderful are *your* works, * Lord God *Al*mighty!

Righteous and true are *your* ways, * O King of *the* nations!

Who would dare refuse *you* honor, * or the glory due your name, O Lord?

Since you alone *are* holy, * all nations

shall come and worship in *your* presence.

Your migh*ty* deeds * are clear*ly* seen.

Glory to the Father, and to *the* Son, * and to the Ho*ly* Spirit:

as it was in the beginning, *is* now, * and will be for ever. *A*men.

Antiphon   Jesus returned with Mary and Joseph *to* Nazareth; * there he lived and was obedient *to* them (al*le*luia).

Whatever you do, work at it with your whole being. Do it for the Lord rather than for men, since you know full well that you will receive an inheritance from him as your reward. Be slaves of Christ the Lord.

RESPONSORY (VI F)

Lent:

The just *man* shall blossom * like *the* lily.
— The just *man* shall blossom * like *the* lily.
He shall flourish for ever in the courts *of* our God,
— like *the* lily.
Glory to the Father, and *to* the Son, * and to the Ho*ly* Spirit.
— The just *man* shall blossom * like *the* lily.

Easter:

The just man shall blossom *like* the lily, * alleluia, al*le*luia.
— The just man shall blossom *like* the lily, * alleluia, al*le*luia.
He shall flourish for ever in the courts *of* our God,
— alleluia, al*le*luia
Glory to the Father, and *to* the Son, * and to the Ho*ly* Spirit.
— The just man shall blossom *like* the lily, * alleluia, al*le*luia.

CANTICLE OF MARY

Antiphon   When Jesus began his ministry, † he was about thir*ty* years old, * and was thought to be the son *of* Joseph (al*le*luia).

Ify

My soul ✠ proclaims the greatness
of the Lord, * my spirit rejoices
   in God *my* savior
for he has *looked* with favor * on his
   low*ly* servant.
From this day all *gen*erations * will call
   me blessèd:
the Almighty has done great *things* for
   me, * and holy is *his* Name.
He has mercy on *those* who fear him *
   in every gen*er*ation.
He has shown the strength *of* his arm, *

he has scattered the proud in their
   con*ceit.*
He has cast down the mighty *from*
   their thrones, * and has lifted up *the*
   lowly.
He has filled the hungry *with* good
   things, * and the rich he has sent
   a*way* empty.
He has come to the help of his *servant*
   Israel * for he has remembered his
   promise *of* mercy,
the promise he made *to* our fathers, * to

Abraham and his children *for* ever.
Glory to the Father, and *to* the Son, *
  and to the Ho*ly* Spirit:

as it was in the begin*ning*, is now, * and
  will be for ever. *A*men.

Antiphon   When Jesus began his ministry, † he was about thir*ty* years old,
          * and was thought to be the son *of* Joseph (al*le*luia).

INTERCESSIONS (VI F)

All fatherhood in heaven and on earth has its ori*gin* in God. * Let us turn to *him*
  and pray:
Our Father in heaven, hear our *prayer.*
All-holy Father, you revealed to Saint Joseph your eternal plan of salva*tion* in
  Christ,
— deepen our understanding of your Son, true God *and* true man.
Father in heaven, you feed the birds of the air, and clothe the fields with the
  fruit *of* the earth,
— give all your children their daily bread, to sustain *soul* and body.
Maker of the universe, you have entrusted your creation to *our* safekeeping,
— may all who work receive a just reward *for* their labors.
God of all righteousness, you want us all to *be* like you,
— may Saint Joseph inspire us to walk always in your *way* of holiness.
Look kindly on the dying and the dead, and grant *them* your mercy,
— through the intercession of Jesus, Ma*ry* and Joseph.

Our Father . . .

Prayer

Father,
you entrusted our Savior to the care of Saint Joseph.
By the help of his prayers
may your Church continue to serve its Lord, Jesus Christ,
who lives and reigns with you and the Holy Spirit,
one God, for ever and ever.

March 23
TORIBIO DE MONGROVEJO, BISHOP
Commemoration

Morning Prayer

CANTICLE OF ZECHARIAH

Ant.   It is not *you* who speak * but the Spirit of your Father who
           speaks *in* you.

Prayer

Lord,
through the apostolic work of Saint Turibius
and his unwavering love of truth,
you helped your Church to grow.
May your chosen people continue to grow
in faith and holiness.
Grant this through our Lord Jesus Christ, your Son,
who lives and reigns with you and the Holy Spirit,
one God, for ever and ever.

Evening Prayer

CANTICLE OF MARY

Ant.   This is a faithful and wise steward: † the Lord entrusted the
                care of his house*hold* to him, * so that he might give them their
                portion of food at the prop*er* season.

March 25
ANNUNCIATION
Solemnity

Evening Prayer I

HYMN

Agnoscat omne sæculum. (L.M.)

Agnoscat omne sæculum	Let all proclaim that Life has come
venisse vitæ præmium;	To this sad world oppressed by sin;
post hostis asperi iugum	Redemption is the wondrous gift
apparuit redemptio.	Bestowed on us by Virgin's Son.
Isaias quæ præcinit	The mystery Isaiah sang
completa sunt in Virgine;	fulfillment found in Mary's faith,
annuntiavit Angelus,	The angel greeted her in hope,
Sanctus replevit Spiritus.	The Spirit flooded her with love.
Maria ventre concipit	By her belief in angel's word,
verbi fidelis semine;	A mother's joy Our Lady knew,
quem totus orbis non capit,	Her virgin womb became the shrine
portant puellæ viscera.	Of him whom earth could not contain.
Adam vetus quod polluit,	The guilt that Adam had incurred
Adam novus hoc abluit;	The Second Adam washed away;
tumens quod ille deicit,	What Adam's pride has head-long hurled
humillimus hic erigit.	The humble Christ raised up once more.

Christo sit omnis gloria,	All glory be to Christ our Lord,
Dei Parentis Filio,	Whom God the Father gave to us,
quem Virgo felix concipit	Whom happy Virgin once conceived,
Sancti sub umbra Spiritus. Amen.	A mother by the Spirit's grace. Amen.

PSALMODY

Ant. 1   A shoot will spring forth from the stock of Jesse, † and a flower
              will blossom *from* his root. * The Spirit of the Lord will *rest*
              upon him (*a*lleluia).

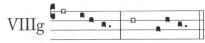

VIIIg

Psalm 113

Praise, O servants *of* the Lord, *
    praise the name *of* the Lord!
May the name of the *Lord* be blessed *
    both now and for *ever*more!
From the rising of the sun *to* its setting
    * praised be the name *of* the Lord!
High above all nations *is* the Lord, *
    above the heav*ens* his glory.
Who is like the *Lord*, our God, * who
    has risen on high *to* his throne
yet stoops from the heights *to* look
    down, * to look down upon heav*en*

and earth?
From the dust he lifts *up* the lowly, *
    from his misery he rai*ses* the poor
to set him in the compa*ny* of princes, *
    yes, with the princes *of* his people.
To the childless wife he *gives* a home *
    and gladdens her *heart* with children.
Glory to the Father, and *to* the Son, *
    and to the *Ho*ly Spirit:
as it was in the begin*ning*, is now, * and
    will be for *ever*. Amen.

Antiphon   A shoot will spring forth from the stock of Jesse, † and a flower
              will blossom *from* his root. * The Spirit of the Lord will *rest*
              upon him (*a*lleluia).

Ant. 2   The Lord God will give him the throne of Da*vid* his father, *
              and he will reign *for* ever (al*le*luia).

IIA

Psalm 147:12-20

O praise the *Lord*, Jerusalem! *
    Zion, praise *your* God!
He has strengthened the bars *of* your
    gates, * he has blessed the children
    *with*in you.
He established peace *on* your borders, *

he feeds you with fin*est* wheat.
He sends out his word *to* the earth *
    and swiftly runs his com*mand*.
He showers down snow *white* as wool, *
    he scatters hoar-frost *like* ashes.
He hurls down hail*stones* like crumbs. *

The waters are frozen at *his* touch;
he sends forth his word *and* it melts
  them: * at the breath of his mouth
  the wa*ters* flow.
He makes his word *known* to Jacob, *
  to Israel his laws and *decrees.*
He has not dealt thus with *other*
nations; * he has not taught them his
  *de*crees.
Glory to the Father, and *to* the Son, *
  and to the Ho*ly* Spirit:
as it was in the begin*ning,* is now, * and
  will be for ever. *A*men.

Antiphon   The Lord God will give him the throne of Da*vid* his father, *
and he will reign *for* ever (al*le*luia).

Ant. 3   The eternal Word, born of the Father before time *began,* * today
emptied himself for our sake and be*came* man (al*le*luia).

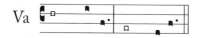

Canticle   Philippians 2:6-11

Though he was in the form of God,
  † Jesus did not deem equality
with God * something to *be* grasped
  at.
Rather, he emptied himself † and took
  the form of *a* slave, * being born in
  the likeness *of* men.
He was known to be of human *estate,* *
  and it was thus that *he* humbled
  himself,
obediently accepting e*ven* death, *
  death on *a* cross!
Because of this, God highly *exalted*
him * and bestowed on him the
  name above every oth*er* name,
So that at Jesus' name every knee *must*
  bend * in the heavens, on the earth,
  and under *the* earth,
and every tongue proclaim to the glory
  of God *the* Father: * JESUS
  CHRIST *IS* LORD!
Glory to the Father, and to *the* Son, *
  and to the Ho*ly* Spirit:
as it was in the beginning, *is* now, * and
  will be for ever. *A*men.

Antiphon   The eternal Word, born of the Father before time *began,* * today
emptied himself for our sake and be*came* man (al*le*luia).

READING   1 John 1:1-2
    This is what we proclaim to you:
    what was from the beginning,
    what we have heard,
    what we have seen with our eyes,
    what we have looked upon
    and our hands have touched—
    we speak of the word of life.

This life became visible;
we have seen and bear witness to it,
and we proclaim to you the eternal life
that was present to the Father
and became visible to us.

RESPONSORY (VI F)
Lent:
A flower has sprung from *Jesse's* stock * and a star has risen *from* Jacob.
— A flower has sprung from *Jesse's* stock * and a star has risen *from* Jacob.
The Virgin has given birth *to* the Savior,
— and a star has risen *from* Jacob.
Glory to the Father, and *to* the Son, * and to the Ho*ly* Spirit.
—A flower has sprung from *Jesse's* stock * and a star has risen *from* Jacob.

Easter:
A flower has sprung from Jesse's stock † and a star has ris*en* from Jacob, * alleluia, al*le*luia.
— A flower has sprung from Jesse's stock † and a star has ris*en* from Jacob, * alleluia, al*le*luia.
The Virgin has given birth *to* the Savior,
— alleluia, al*le*luia.
Glory to the Father, and *to* the Son, * and to the Ho*ly* Spirit.
— A flower has sprung from Jesse's stock † and a star has ris*en* from Jacob, * alleluia, al*le*luia.

CANTICLE OF MARY
Antiphon   The Holy Spirit will come up*on* you, Mary; * and the power of
             the Most High will overshad*ow* you (al*le*luia).

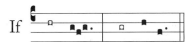

My soul ✠ proclaims the greatness *of* the Lord, * my spirit rejoices in God *my* savior
for he has *looked* with favor * on his low*ly* servant.
From this day all *generations* * will call *me* blessèd:
the Almighty has done great *things* for me, * and holy is *his* Name.
He has mercy on *those* who fear him * in every gen*er*ation.
He has shown the strength *of* his arm, *
he has scattered the proud in their *con*ceit.
He has cast down the mighty *from* their thrones, * and has lifted up *the* lowly.
He has filled the hungry *with* good things, * and the rich he has sent *away* empty.
He has come to the help of his *servant* Israel * for he has remembered his promise *of* mercy,
the promise he made *to* our fathers, * to

Abraham and his children *for* ever. | as it was in the begin*ning*, is now, * and
Glory to the Father, and *to* the Son, * | will be for ever. *A*men.
and to the Ho*ly* Spirit:

Antiphon   The Holy Spirit will come up*on* you, Mary; * and the power of
the Most High will overshad*ow* you (al*le*luia).

INTERCESSIONS (VI F)

On this day the eternal Father sent his angel to bring Mary the good news of
our salvation. * Let us turn to God and *pray* with confidence:
Lord, fill our hearts with your *love.*
You chose the Virgin Mary as the mother *of* your Son,
— have mercy on all who look for your gift *of* salvation.
You sent Gabriel to give Mary your message of *peace* and joy,
— give to the whole world the joy of salvation and your gift *of* true peace.
Mary gave her consent, the Holy Spirit overshadowed her, and your Word came
to *dwell* among us,
— touch our hearts that we may welcome Christ as *Mary* did.
You look with love on the humble, and fill the hungry *with* your gifts,
— raise up the downcast, help all in need, comfort and strength*en* the dying.
Lord our God, you alone work wonders and with you all *things* are possible,
— give us the fullness of salvation when you raise up the dead on *the* last day.

Our Father . . .

Prayer

God our Father,
your Word became man and was born of the Virgin Mary.
May we become more like Jesus Christ,
whom we acknowledge as our redeemer, God and man.
We ask this through our Lord Jesus Christ, your Son,
who lives and reigns with you and the Holy Spirit,
one God, for ever and ever.

Morning Prayer

HYMN

O lux, salutis nuntia. (L.M.)

O lux, salutis nuntia, | O day on which salvation dawned,
qua Virgini fert Angelus | You saw an angel visit earth,
complenda mox oracula | When prophecies would be fulfilled,
et cara terris gaudia. | Rejoicing over virgin birth.

Qui Patris æterno sinu æterna Proles nascitur, obnoxius fit tempori matremqu*e* in orbe seligit.	For he who with the Father dwells Comes down to earth, Eternal Son, Who at his will would enter time And choose a human mother's love.
Nobis piandis victima nostros *se* in artus colligit, ut innocenti sanguine scelus nocentum diluat.	He deigned to take the form of man To reconcile our race with God, By shedding Blood so innocent That guilty man it could redeem.
Concepta carne Veritas, umbrata velo Virginis, puris videnda mentibus, imple tuo nos lumine.	O Truth, that once assumed our flesh, And lay concealed by Virgin's veil Before you walked on earth as Man, Enrich us with your light divine.
Et quæ modesto pectore te dicis ancillam Dei, regina nunc cælestium, patrona sis fidelium.	Fair Virgin, who declared yourself The lowly handmaid of the Lord, From your bright throne in heaven's height Be now the Queen of Faithful souls.
Iesu, tibi sit gloria, qui natus es de Virgine, cum Patr*e* et almo Spiritu, in sempiterna sæcula. Amen.	All glory, Jesus, be to you, Once born of Virgin undefiled, Who with the Spirit of your Love And God the Father, ever reign. Amen.

PSALMODY

Ant. 1   The angel Gabriel was sent to the *Vir*gin Mary, * who was
              engaged to be mar*ried* to Joseph (*al*leluia).

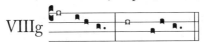

VIIIg

Psalm 63:2-9

O God, you are my God, for *you* I long; * for you my *soul* is thirsting.
My body *pines* for you * like a dry, weary land *with*out water.
So I gaze on you *in* the sanctuary * to see your strength *and* your glory.
For your love is bet*ter* than life, * my lips will *speak* your praise.
So I will bless you *all* my life, * in your name I will lift *up* my hands.
My soul shall be filled as *with* a banquet, * my mouth shall praise *you* with joy.
On my bed I re*mem*ber you. * On you I muse *through* the night
for you have *been* my help; * in the shadow of your wings *I* rejoice.
My soul *clings* to you; * your right hand *holds* me fast.
Glory to the Father, and *to* the Son, * and to the *Holy* Spirit:
as it was in the begin*ning*, is now, * and will be for ev*er*. Amen.

Antiphon   The angel Gabriel was sent to the *Virgin* Mary, * who was engaged to be mar*ried* to Joseph (*al*leluia).

Ant. 2   Bless*èd* are you *a*mong women, * and bless*èd* is the fruit of *your* womb (al*le*luia).

IIA

Canticle   Daniel 3:57-88; 56

Bless the Lord, all you works *of* the Lord. * Praise and exalt him above all *for*ever.
Angels of the Lord, *bless* the Lord, * You heavens, bless *the* Lord.
All you waters above the heavens, *bless* the Lord. * All you hosts of the Lord, bless *the* Lord.
Sun and moon, *bless* the Lord. * Stars of heaven, bless *the* Lord.
Every shower and dew, *bless* the Lord. * All you winds, bless *the* Lord.
Fire and heat, *bless* the Lord. * Cold and chill, bless *the* Lord.
Dew and rain, *bless* the Lord. * Frost and chill, bless *the* Lord.
Ice and snow, *bless* the Lord. * Nights and days, bless *the* Lord.
Light and darkness, *bless* the Lord. * Lightnings and clouds, bless *the* Lord.
Let the earth *bless* the Lord. * Praise and exalt him above all *for*ever.
Mountains and hills, *bless* the Lord. * Everything growing from the earth,

bless *the* Lord.
You springs, *bless* the Lord. * Seas and rivers, bless *the* Lord.
You dolphins and all water creatures, *bless* the Lord. * All you birds of the air, bless *the* Lord.
All you beasts, wild and tame, *bless* the Lord. * You sons of men, bless *the* Lord.
O Israel, *bless* the Lord. * Praise and exalt him above all *for*ever.
Priests of the Lord, *bless* the Lord. * Servants of the Lord, bless *the* Lord.
Spirits and souls of the just, *bless* the Lord. * Holy men of humble heart, bless *the* Lord.
Hananiah, Azariah, Mishael, *bless* the Lord. * Praise and exalt him above all *for*ever.
Let us bless the Father, and the Son, and the *Ho*ly Spirit. * Let us praise and exalt him above all *for*ever.
Bless*èd* are you in the firma*ment* of heaven. * Praiseworthy and glorious and exalted above all *for*ever.

Antiphon   Bless*èd* are you *a*mong women, * and bless*èd* is the fruit of *your* womb (al*le*luia).

Ant. 3   Trusting in the Lord's promise, † the Virgin Mary conceived a
          child, † and remaining *a* virgin, * she gave birth to *the* Savior
          (al*le*luia).

Va

Psalm 149

Sing a new song to *the* Lord, * his
praise in the assembly of *the*
faithful.
Let Israel rejoice in *its* Maker, * let
Zion's sons exult in *their* king.
Let them praise his name *with* dancing
* and make music with timbrel *and*
harp.
For the Lord takes delight in *his*
people. * He crowns the poor with
sa*l*vation.
Let the faithful rejoice in *their* glory, *
shout for joy and take *their* rest.

Let the praise of God be on *their* lips *
and a two-edged sword in *their* hand,
to deal out vengeance to *the* nations *
and punishment on all *the* peoples;
to bind their kings *in* chains * and their
nobles in fetters *of* iron;
to carry out the sentence pre-*or*dained:
* this honor is for all *his* faithful.
Glory to the Father, and to *the* Son, *
and to the Ho*ly* Spirit:
as it was in the beginning, *is* now, * and
will be for ever. *A*men.

Antiphon   Trusting in the Lord's promise, † the Virgin Mary conceived a
           child, † and remaining *a* virgin, * she gave birth to *the* Savior
           (al*le*luia).

READING   Philippians 2:6-7
    Though he was in the form of God,
        Jesus did not deem equality with God
        something to be grasped at.
    Rather, he emptied himself
        and took the form of a slave,
        being born in the likeness of men.
    He was known to be of human estate.

RESPONSORY (VI F)
Lent:
Hail Mary, *full* of grace, * the Lord is *with* you.
— Hail Mary, *full* of grace, * the Lord is *with* you.
Blessèd are you among women, † and blessèd is the fruit *of* your womb.
— The Lord is *with* you.
Glory to the Father, and *to* the Son, * and to the Ho*ly* Spirit.
— Hail Mary, *full* of grace, * the Lord is *with* you.

Easter:

Hail Mary, full of grace, † the Lord *is* with you, * alleluia, al*le*luia.

— Hail Mary, full of grace, † the Lord *is* with you, * alleluia, al*le*luia.

Blessèd are you among women, † and blessèd is the fruit *of* your womb.

— Alleluia, al*le*luia.

Glory to the Father, and *to* the Son, * and to the Ho*ly* Spirit.

— Hail Mary, full of grace, † the Lord *is* with you, * alleluia, al*le*luia.

CANTICLE OF ZECHARIAH

Antiphon   In his great *love* for us, * God sent his Son in the likeness of our
                  sin*ful* nature (al*le*luia).

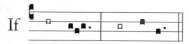

Blessèd ✠ be the Lord, the *God* of Israel; * he has come to his people and set *them* free.

He has raised up for us a *mighty* savior, * born of the house of his ser*vant* David.

Through his holy prophets he promised of old † that he would save us *from* our enemies, * from the hands of all *who* hate us.

He promised to show mercy *to* our fathers * and to remember his ho*ly* covenant.

This was the oath he swore to our *fath*er Abraham: * to set us free from the hands of *our* enemies,

free to worship him without fear, † holy and righteous *in* his sight * all the days of *our* life.

You, my child, shall be called the prophet *of* the Most High; * for you will go before the Lord to prepare *his* way,

to give his people knowledge *of* salvation * by the forgiveness of *their* sins.

In the tender compassion *of* our God * the dawn from on high shall break *up*on us,

to shine on those who dwell in darkness and the sha*dow* of death, * and to guide our feet into the way *of* peace.

Glory to the Father, and *to* the Son, * and to the Ho*ly* Spirit:

as it was in the begin*ning*, is now, * and will be for ever. *Amen.*

Antiphon   In his great *love* for us, * God sent his Son in the likeness of our
                  sin*ful* nature (al*le*luia).

INTERCESSIONS (VI F)

Today we celebrate the beginning of our salvation when the coming of the Lord was announced *by* the angel. * Let us pray with joy in *our* hearts, saying:

May God's holy Mother intercede for us.

Mary received God's *word* with joy,

— may joy fill our hearts as we wel*come* our Savior.

You looked with love on your *lowly* servant,

— in your mercy, Father, remember us and *all* your children.

Mary, the new Eve, was obedient *to* your word,
— may we echo her lov*ing* obedience.
May God's holy Mother help all in distress, encourage the fainthearted, con*sole*
   the sorrowful,
— may she pray for your holy people, for the clergy, and for all women dedicated *to* your service.

Our Father . . .

<h2 style="text-align:center">Prayer</h2>

God our Father,
   your Word became man and was born of the Virgin Mary.
May we become more like Jesus Christ,
   whom we acknowledge as our redeemer, God and man.
We ask this through our Lord Jesus Christ, your Son,
   who lives and reigns with you and the Holy Spirit,
   one God, for ever and ever.

<h2 style="text-align:center">Evening Prayer II</h2>

HYMN, as in Evening Prayer I, 938.

PSALMODY

Ant. 1   The angel of the Lord brought God's mes*sage* to Mary. * And
                 she conceived by the power of the *Holy* Spirit (*alleluia*).

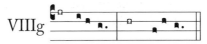

VIIIg

Psalm 110:1-5, 7

The Lord's revelation to my
   Master: † "Sit *on* my right: * your
foes I will put be*neath* your feet."
The Lord will wield from Zion † your
   scep*ter* of power: * rule in the midst
   of *all* your foes.
A prince from the day of your birth †
   on the *holy* mountains; * from the
   womb before the dawn *I* begot you.
The Lord has sworn an oath he will
   not change. † "You are a *priest* for
   ever, * a priest like Melchize*dek* of

old."
The Master standing at *your* right
   hand * will shatter kings in the day
   of *his* great wrath.
He shall drink from the stream *by* the
   wayside * and therefore he shall lift
   up his head.
Glory to the Father, and *to* the Son, *
   and to the *Holy* Spirit:
as it was in the begin*ning*, is now, * and
   will be for ev*er*. Amen.

Antiphon The angel of the Lord brought God's message to Mary. * And she conceived by the power of the *Ho*ly Spirit (*al*leluia).

Ant. 2 Do not be afraid, Mary; you have found favor with God. †
Behold you shall conceive and *bear* a son, * and he will be called the Son of the *Most* High (al*le*luia).

IIA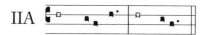

Psalm 130

Out of the depths I cry to *you*, O Lord, * Lord, hear *my* voice!
O let your ears *be* attentive * to the voice of *my* pleading.
If you, O Lord, should *mark* our guilt, * Lord, who would *survive?*
But with you is *found* forgiveness: * for this we *revere* you.
My soul is waiting *for* the Lord, * I count on *his* word.
My soul is longing *for* the Lord * more

than watchman *for* daybreak.
Let the watchman *count* on daybreak * and Israel on *the* Lord.
Because with the Lord *there* is mercy * and fullness of *re*demption,
Israel indeed he *will* redeem * from all its *in*iquity.
Glory to the Father, and *to* the Son, * and to the *Ho*ly Spirit:
as it was in the begin*ning*, is now, * and will be for ever. *A*men.

Antiphon Do not be afraid, Mary; you have found favor with God. †
Behold you shall conceive and *bear* a son, * and he will be called the Son of the *Most* High (al*le*luia).

Ant. 3 I am the handmaid of *the* Lord. * Let it be done to me as you *have* said (al*le*luia).

Va

Canticle Colossians 1:12-20

Let us give thanks to the Father †
for having made *you* worthy * to share the lot of the saints *in* light.
He rescued us from the power *of* darkness * and brought us into the kingdom of his belov*èd* Son.
Through him we have *re*demption, * the forgiveness of *our* sins.

He is the image of the invisi*ble* God, * the first-born of *all* creatures.
In him everything in heaven and on earth was *cre*ated, * things visible and *in*visible.
All were cre*at*ed through him; * all were creat*ed* for him.
He is before all else *that* is. * In him

everything continues *in* being.
It is he who is head of the body, the
church! † he who is the beginning,
the first-born of *the* dead, * so that
primacy may be his *in* everything.
It pleased God to make absolute
fullness reside *in* him * and, by
means of him, to reconcile every-

thing in *his* person,
both on earth and in *the* heavens, *
making peace through the blood of
his cross.
Glory to the Father, and to *the* Son, *
and to the Ho*ly* Spirit:
as it was in the beginning, *is* now, * and
will be for ever. *A*men.

Antiphon   I am the handmaid of *the* Lord. * Let it be done to me as you
have said (al*le*luia).

READING   1 John 1:1-2

This is what we proclaim to you:
what was from the beginning,
what we have heard,
what we have seen with our eyes,
what we have looked upon
and our hands have touched—
we speak of the word of life.
This life became visible;
we have seen and bear witness to it,
and we proclaim to you the eternal life
that was present to the Father
and became visible to us.

RESPONSORY (VI F)
Lent:
The Word *was* made man * and he lived *a*mong us.
— The Word *was* made man * and he lived *a*mong us.
He was in the begin*ning* with God,
— and he lived *a*mong us.
Glory to the Father, and *to* the Son, * and to the Ho*ly* Spirit.
— The Word *was* made man * and he lived *a*mong us.

Easter:
The Word was made man and he *lived* among us, * alleluia, al*le*luia.
— The Word was made man and he *lived* among us, * alleluia, al*le*luia.
He was in the begin*ning* with God,
— alleluia, al*le*luia.
Glory to the Father, and *to* the Son, * and to the Ho*ly* Spirit.
— The Word was made man and he *lived* among us, * alleluia, al*le*luia.

CANTICLE OF MARY

Antiphon   The angel Gabriel said to Mary in greeting: † Hail, full of
             grace, the Lord *is* with you; * blessèd are you a*mong* women
             (al*le*luia).

If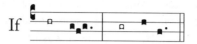

My soul ✠ proclaims the greatness *of* the Lord, * my spirit rejoices in God *my* savior

for he has *looked* with favor * on his low*ly* servant.

From this day all *gen*erations * will call *me* blessèd:

the Almighty has done great *things* for me, * and holy is *his* Name.

He has mercy on *those* who fear him * in every gen*er*ation.

He has shown the strength *of* his arm, * he has scattered the proud in their *con*ceit.

He has cast down the mighty *from* their thrones, * and has lifted up *the* lowly.

He has filled the hungry *with* good things, * and the rich he has sent a*way* empty.

He has come to the help of his *servant* Israel * for he has remembered his promise *of* mercy,

the promise he made *to* our fathers, * to Abraham and his children *for* ever.

Glory to the Father, and *to* the Son, * and to the Ho*ly* Spirit:

as it was in the begin*ning*, is now, * and will be for ever. *A*men.

Antiphon   The angel Gabriel said to Mary in greeting: † Hail, full of
             grace, the Lord *is* with you; * blessèd are you a*mong* women
             (al*le*luia).

INTERCESSIONS (VI F)

On this day the eternal Father sent his angel to bring Mary the good news of *our* salvation. * Let us turn to God and *pray* with confidence:

Lord, fill our hearts with your *love.*

You chose the Virgin Mary as the mother *of* your Son,

— have mercy on all who look for your gift *of* salvation.

You sent Gabriel to give Mary your message of *peace* and joy,

— give to the whole world the joy of salvation and your gift *of* true peace.

Mary gave her consent, the Holy Spirit overshadowed her, and your Word came to *dwell* among us,

— touch our hearts that we may welcome Christ as *Mary* did.

You look with love on the humble, and fill the hungry *with* your gifts,

— raise up the downcast, help all in need, comfort and strength*en* the dying.

Lord our God, you alone work wonders and with you all *things* are possible,

— give us the fullness of salvation when you raise up the dead on *the* last day.

Our Father . . .

Prayer

God our Father,
your Word became man and was born of the Virgin Mary.
May we become more like Jesus Christ,
whom we acknowledge as our redeemer, God and man.
We ask this through our Lord Jesus Christ, your Son,
who lives and reigns with you and the Holy Spirit,
one God, for ever and ever.

April 2
FRANCIS OF PAOLA, HERMIT

From the common of holy men: religious, 1282.

Morning Prayer

CANTICLE OF ZECHARIAH

Ant.   Behold I stand at the door and knock. † If anyone hears my
        voice and opens the door, † I will come into his house and *share*
        his supper, * he and I *to*gether, (al*le*luia).

Prayer

Father of the lowly,
you raised Saint Francis of Paola
to the glory of your saints.
By his example and prayers,
may we come to the rewards
you have promised to the humble.
We ask this through our Lord Jesus Christ, your Son,
who lives and reigns with you and the Holy Spirit,
one God, for ever and ever.

Evening Prayer

CANTICLE OF MARY

Ant.   If a man should give away all his possessions *out* of love, * he
        would feel that he has lost nothing *at* all, (al*le*luia).

April 4
ISIDORE, BISHOP AND DOCTOR

From the common of pastors, 1238, or of doctors, 1246.

Morning Prayer

For a commemoration during Lent:

CANTICLE OF ZECHARIAH

Ant.   Those *who* are learnèd * will be as radiant as the sky in all *its* beauty;
those who instruct the peo*ple* in goodness * will shine like the stars for all *e*ternity.

Prayer

Lord,
hear the prayers we offer in commemoration of Saint Isidore.
May your Church learn from his teaching
and benefit from his intercession.
Grant this through our Lord Jesus Christ, your Son,
who lives and reigns with you and the Holy Spirit,
one God, for ever and ever.

Evening Prayer

For a commemoration during Lent:

CANTICLE OF MARY

Ant.   O blessèd doctor, Saint Isidore, † light of holy Church and lover *of* God's law, * pray to the Son of God *for* us.

April 5
VINCENT FERRER, PRIEST

From the common of pastors, 1238.

Morning Prayer

For a commemoration during Lent:

CANTICLE OF ZECHARIAH

Ant.   It is not *you* who speak * but the Spirit of your Father who speaks *in* you.

Prayer

Father,
you called Saint Vincent Ferrer
to preach the gospel of the last judgment.
Through his prayers may we come with joy
to meet your Son in the kingdom of heaven,
where he lives and reigns with you and the Holy Spirit,
one God, for ever and ever.

Evening Prayer

For a commemoration during Lent:
CANTICLE OF MARY
Ant. I became all things *to* all men, * that all might find *sal*vation.

April 7
JOHN BAPTIST DE LA SALLE, PRIEST
Memorial
From the common of pastors, 1238, or of holy men: teachers, 1285.

Morning Prayer

For a commemoration during Lent:
CANTICLE OF ZECHARIAH
Ant. The man of compassion guides and teaches his brothers * with the gentle care of the good shepherd for *his* sheep.

Prayer

Father,
you chose Saint John Baptist de la Salle
to give young people a Christian education.
Give your Church teachers who will devote themselves
to helping your children grow
as Christian men and women.
We ask this through our Lord Jesus Christ, your Son,
who lives and reigns with you and the Holy Spirit,
one God, for ever and ever.

Evening Prayer

For a commemoration during Lent:
CANTICLE OF MARY
Ant. Let the little children *come* to me, * for they are at home in my Fa*ther's* kingdom.

April 11
STANISLAUS, BISHOP AND MARTYR
Memorial
From the common of one martyr, 1228, or of pastors, 1238.

Morning Prayer

For a commemoration during Lent:
CANTICLE OF ZECHARIAH
Ant. Whoever hates his life *in* this world * keeps it safe for life ever*lasting.*

Prayer

Father,
to honor you, Saint Stanislaus faced martyrdom with courage.
Keep us strong and loyal in our faith until death.
Grant this through our Lord Jesus Christ, your Son,
who lives and reigns with you and the Holy Spirit,
one God, for ever and ever.

Evening Prayer

For a commemoration during Lent:

CANTICLE OF MARY

Ant.   The saints find their home in the king*dom* of heaven; * their life
is eter*nal* peace.

April 13
MARTIN I, POPE AND MARTYR

From the common of one martyr, 1228, or of pastors, 1238.

Morning Prayer

For a commemoration during Lent:

CANTICLE OF ZECHARIAH

Ant.   Whoever hates his life *in* this world * keeps it safe for life
ev*er*lasting.

Prayer

Merciful God, our Father,
neither hardship, pain, nor the threat of death
could weaken the faith of Saint Martin.
Through our faith, give us courage
to endure whatever sufferings the world may inflict upon us.
We ask this through our Lord Jesus Christ, your Son,
who lives and reigns with you and the Holy Spirit,
one God, for ever and ever.

Evening Prayer

For a commemoration during Lent:

CANTICLE OF MARY

Ant.   The saints find their home in the king*dom* of heaven; * their life
is eter*nal* peace.

April 21
ANSELM, BISHOP AND DOCTOR
From the common of pastors, 1238, or of doctors, 1246.

Prayer
Father,
you called Saint Anslem
to study and teach the sublime truths you have revealed.
Let your gift of faith come to the aid of our understanding
and open our hearts to your truth.
Grant this through our Lord Jesus Christ, your Son,
who lives and reigns with you and the Holy Spirit,
one God, for ever and ever.

April 23
GEORGE, MARTYR
From the common of one martyr during the Easter Season, 1228.

Prayer
Lord,
hear the prayers of those who praise your mighty power.
As Saint George was ready to follow Christ in suffering and death,
so may he be ready to help us in our weakness.
We ask this through our Lord Jesus Christ, your Son,
who lives and reigns with you and the Holy Spirit,
one God, for ever and ever.

On the same day, April 23
ADALBERT, BISHOP AND MARTYR
From the common of one martyr during the Easter Season, 1228, or of pastors, 1238.

Prayer
God our Father,
you have honored the Church with the victorious witness of St. Adalbert,
who died for his faith.
As he imitated the sufferings and death of the Lord,
may we follow in his footsteps and come to eternal joy.
Grant this through our Lord Jesus Christ, your Son,
who lives and reigns with you and the Holy Spirit,
one God, for ever and ever.

April 24
FIDELIS OF SIGMARINGEN, PRIEST AND MARTYR

From the common of one martyr during the Easter Season, 1228, or of pastors, 1238.

Prayer

Father,
you filled Saint Fidelis with the fire of your love
and gave him the privilege of dying
that the faith might live.
Let his prayers keep us firmly grounded in your love,
and help us to come to know the power of Christ's resurrection.
We ask this through our Lord Jesus Christ, your Son,
who lives and reigns with you and the Holy Spirit,
one God, for ever and ever.

April 25
MARK, EVANGELIST
Feast

Morning Prayer
HYMN
Mentibus lætis. (11.11.11.5)

Mentibus lætis tua festa, Marce,	Grateful rejoicing prompts us all to greet you,
atque pergratis celebramus omnes,	Mark, the disciple of the great Saint Peter,
magna qui Christi tribuisse plebi	As we remember what God's People owe you
te memoramus.	Right through the ages.
Matris exemplis, venerans amore	Mary your mother, harbored the Apostles,
fervido Petrum, sequeris fidelis,	You served Saint Peter as a son belovèd,
verba de Christi labiis ab ipso	Learning the details of the life of Jesus
hausta recondis.	From his sure knowledge.
Spiritu accensus, modico libello	Moved by the Spirit you set down in writing
mira tu summi reseras Magistri	Brief but most vivid stories of the Master,
gesta, tu narras quibus et loquelis	Teaching for all time ev'ry generation,
instruat orbem.	Christ's words and actions.
Carus et Paulo, studiosus eius	Dear to Saint Paul too, his companion later,
cordis ardores imitans, laboras,	Sharing his labors with his zeal unbounded;
multa pro Iesu pateris, cruorem	After much hardship for the name of Jesus,
fundis amanter.	Life you surrendered.
Laus, honor Christo, decus atque virtus,	Praise be to Jesus, glory and all honor,
cuius et testes valeamus esse,	May we bear witness to his holy Gospel,
ac,tuis escis recreati, in ævum	Fed by Mark's teaching, may we duly merit
cernere vultum. Amen.	Life in Christ's Kingdom. Amen.

Ant. 1   The holy evangelists searched the wisdom *of* past ages. *
                Through their gospels they confirmed the words of the proph-
                ets, *a*lleluia.

Psalms and canticles from Sunday, Week I, 606.

Ant. 2   Through the Gospel † God called us to believe *in* the truth *
                and to share the glory of our Lord Jesus Christ, al*le*luia.

Ant. 3   Many will praise *their* wisdom; * it shall be remembered for ever,
                al*le*luia.

READING   1 Corinthians 15:1-2a, 3-4
Brothers, I want to remind you of the gospel I preached to you, which you
received and in which you stand firm. You are being saved by it at this very
moment. I handed on to you first of all what I myself received, that Christ
died for our sins in accordance with the Scriptures; that he was buried and,
in accordance with the Scriptures, rose on the third day.

RESPONSORY (VI F)
They proclaimed the Lord's praises, † told of his pow*er* to save, * alleluia, al*le*luia.
— They proclaimed the Lord's praises, † told of his pow*er* to save, * alleluia, al*le*luia.
And of the wonders *he* had worked,
— alleluia, al*le*luia.
Glory to the Father, and *to* the Son, * and to the Ho*ly* Spirit.
— They proclaimed the Lord's praises, † told of his pow*er* to save, * alleluia, al*le*luia.

CANTICLE OF ZECHARIAH
Ant.   Through the grace of Jesus Christ, † preachers and teachers were
                sent out to be ministers *of* the faith * for all who believe, al*le*luia.

INTERCESSIONS
Let us sing a song of praise to our Savior, who destroyed the power of death and
    made clear the path to life and immortality *through* the Gospel; * and let us
    petition him in humble *sup*plication:
Strengthen your Church in faith and *love.*
You gave wonderful guidance to your Church through her holy and dis*tin*-
    guished teachers,
— may Christians rejoice always in the splendid legacy given *to* your Church.
When their holy pastors prayed to you, as Moses had done, you forgave the sins
    of the people,
— through the intercession of these holy pastors continue to sanctify and puri*fy*
    your Church.
You anointed your holy ones in the midst of their brothers and called the Holy
    Spirit *down* upon them,
— fill all the leaders of your people with the *Ho*ly Spirit.

You yourself are the sole possession of your *holy* pastors,
— grant that those you have redeemed with your blood may remain al*ways* in you.

Our Father . . .

Prayer

Father,
you gave Saint Mark
the privilege of proclaiming your gospel.
May we profit by his wisdom
and follow Christ more faithfully.
Grant this through our Lord Jesus Christ, your Son
who lives and reigns with you and the Holy Spirit,
one God, for ever and ever.

Evening Prayer

HYMN, as in Morning Prayer, 956.

Ant. 1   My life is at the service *of* the Gospel; * God has given me this gift of his grace, *a*lleluia.

Psalms and canticles from the common of apostles, 1208.

Ant. 2   I do all this for the sake *of* the Gospel, * in order to share in its rewards, al*l*eluia.

Ant. 3   This grace has been given to me: † to proclaim to *the* nations * the infinite riches of Christ, al*l*eluia.

READING   Colossians 11:3-6a
We always give thanks to God, the Father of our Lord Jesus Christ, in our prayers for you because we have heard of your faith in Christ Jesus and the love you bear toward all the saints— moved as you are by the hope held in store for you in heaven. You heard of this hope through the message of truth, the gospel, which has come to you, has borne fruit, and has continued to grow in your midst, as it has everywhere in the world.

RESPONSORY (VI F)
Tell all the nations how glor*ious* God is, * alleluia, al*l*eluia.
— Tell all the nations how glor*ious* God is, * alleluia, al*l*eluia.
Make known his wonders to *eve*ry people,
— alleluia, al*l*eluia.
Glory to the Father, and *to* the Son, * and to the Ho*ly* Spirit.
— Tell all the nations how glor*ious* God is, * alleluia, al*l*eluia.

CANTICLE OF MARY

Ant. The word of the Lord shall en*dure* for ever: * this is the message which has been proclaimed, al*le*luia.

INTERCESSIONS

Our God is Father of light. Through the good news of his Son he has called us to believe *in* the truth. * We pray now for his chosen people *as* we say:
*Remember your holy peo*ple, *Lord.*
Father, you raised your Son, our Good Shepherd, *from* the dead,
— make us his witnesses to the very ends *of* the earth.
You sent your Son to bring good news *to* the poor,
— give us courage to bring that good news to *eve*ry creature.
You sent your Son to sow the *word* of life,
— help us to sow his word and to reap its har*vest* with joy.
You sent your Son to make the world one *through* his blood,
— may all of us work together *for* this unity.
You set your Son at your right hand *in* the heavens,
— open the gates of your kingdom to those *who* have died.

Our Father . . .

Prayer

Father,
you gave Saint Mark
the privilege of proclaiming your gospel.
May we profit by his wisdom
and follow Christ more faithfully.
Grant this through our Lord Jesus Christ, your Son,
who lives and reigns with you and the Holy Spirit,
one God, for ever and ever.

April 28
PETER CHANEL, PRIEST AND MARTYR
From the common of one martyr during the Easter Season, 1228.

Prayer

Father,
you called Saint Peter Chanel to work for your Church
and gave him the crown of martyrdom.
May our celebration of Christ's death and resurrection
make us faithful witnesses to the new life he brings,
for he lives and reigns with you and the Holy Spirit,
one God, for ever and ever.

On the same day, April 28
LOUIS MARY DE MONTFORT, PRIEST

From the common of pastors, 1238.

Prayer

God our Father,
in St. Louis Mary de Montfort you gave
a light to your faithful people.
You made him a pastor of the Church
to feed your sheep with his word
and to teach them by his example.
Help us by his prayers to keep the faith he taught
and follow the way of life he showed us.
Grant this through our Lord Jesus Christ, your Son,
who lives and reigns with you and the Holy Spirit,
one God, for ever and ever.

April 29
CATHERINE OF SIENA, VIRGIN AND DOCTOR
Memorial

From the common of virgins, 1253, except for the following:

Morning Prayer
HYMN
Te Catharina. (L.M.)

Te, Catharina, maximis
nunc veneramur laudibus,
cunctæ lumen Ecclesiæ,
sertis ornata plurimis.

Magnis aucta virtutibus
et vita florens inclita,
humili mente ac strenua
per crucis pergis tramitem.

Stella videris populis
salubris pacis nuntia;
mores restauras optimos,
feroces mulces animos.

Sancto compulsa Spiritu,
ignita verba loqueris,
quæ lucem sapientiæ,
æstus amoris ingerunt.

We praise you, Cath'rine, joyfully
And glory in your great renown;
As shining light within the Church,
Full many jewels deck your crown.

Your virtues and your purity
Allowed your eyes to see but God;
The courage of the humble soul
Sustained you in the path you trod.

In troubled times you were a star
Annoucing true salvation's peace,
Restoring Christian ways of life,
And causing angry strife to cease.

The Holy Spirit prompted you
To utter words of burning zeal
And shed his Wisdom's light abroad
With charity as sacred seal.

Tuis confisos precibus,	Belovèd spouse of Christ our Lord,

Tuis confisos precibus,
virgo dilecta Domino,
nos caritate concitos
fac Sponsi regna quærere.

Iesus, tibi sit gloria,
qui natus es de Virgine,
cum Patre et almo Spiritu
in sempiterna sæcula. Amen.

Belovèd spouse of Christ our Lord,
Set our cold hearts aglow with love,
That by your prayers we too may seek
His Kingdom and the things above.

All glory, Jesus, be to you,
Once born of Virgin undefiled,
Who, with the Spirit of your Love,
And God the Father, ever reign. Amen.

CANTICLE OF ZECHARIAH

Ant. The holy virgin Catherine steadfastly *begged* the Lord * to restore peace to his holy Church, al/eluia.

Prayer

Father,
in meditating on the sufferings of your Son
and in serving your Church,
Saint Catherine was filled with the fervor of your love.
By her prayers,
may we share in the mystery of Christ's death
and rejoice in the revelation of his glory,
for he lives and reigns with you and the Holy Spirit,
one God, for ever and ever.

Evening Prayer

CANTICLE OF MARY

Ant. Always and everywhere Catherine sought *and* found God. * Through the strength of her love she entered into union with him, al/eluia.

April 30
PIUS V, POPE

From the common of pastors, 1238.

Prayer

Father,
you chose Saint Pius V as pope of your Church
to protect the faith and give you more fitting worship.
By his prayers, help us to celebrate your holy mysteries
with a living faith and an effective love.
We ask this through our Lord Jesus Christ, your Son,
who lives and reigns with you and the Holy Spirit,
one God, for ever and ever.

May 1
JOSEPH THE WORKER

When this memorial is celebrated with greater solemnity, the parts not found below are taken from March 19, 925.

Morning Prayer

HYMN

Aurora solis. (L.M.)

Aurora solis nuntia, mundi labores excitans, fabri sonoram malleo domum salutat Nazaræ.	At tip of dawn, before the sun, Earth's toilers to their work had stirred, Within the home at Nazareth The hammer's ringing sound was heard.
Salve, caput domesticum, sub quo supernus Artifex, sudore salso roridus, exercet artem patriam.	Hail, Joseph, head of perfect home, For he by whom the world was made, From your instruction learned to toil, And ply a hard and humble trade.
Altis locatus sedibus celsæque Sponsæ proximus, adesto nunc clientibus, quos vexat indigentia.	Now from your lofty throne above, In honor close to heaven's Queen, Assist all those who cry to you In need, or want, or anguish keen.
Absintque vis et iurgia, fraus omnis a mercedibus, victus cibique copiam mensuret una parcitas.	Far from us be all words of strife, All violence and greed for gain; When taking sustenance we need May Christian moderation reign.
Sit Trinitati gloria, quæ, te precante, iugiter in pace nostros omnium gressus viamque dirigat. Amen.	All glory to the Trinity Who at Saint Joseph's faithful prayer, Will guard us in the way of peace Till heaven's joy we too may share. Amen.

READING   2 Samuel 7:28-29

Lord God, you are God and your words are truth; you have made this generous promise to your servant. Do, then, bless the house of your servant that it may be before you forever; for you, Lord God, have promised, and by your blessing the house of your servant shall be blessed forever.

RESPONSORY (VI F)

God made him the master *of* his household, * alleluia, al*le*luia.
— God made him the master *of* his household, * alleluia, al*le*luia.
He gave him charge over all *his* possessions,
— alleluia, al*le*luia.
Glory to the Father, and *to* the Son, * and to the Ho*ly* Spirit.
— God made him the master *of* his household, * alleluia, al*le*luia.

CANTICLE OF ZECHARIAH

Ant.   Saint Joseph faithfully practiced the car*pent*er's trade. * He is a shining example for all workers, al*le*luia.

INTERCESSIONS (VI F)

The Lord is the giv*er* of holiness. * Let us turn to *him* and pray:

Holy God, raise us up to new life in *holiness.*

Lord our God, you called our fathers in faith to walk before you in holi*ness* of heart,

— may we follow in their footsteps, and obey your command *to* be perfect.

You chose Joseph the righteous to care for your Son in child*hood* and youth,

— teach us to care for Christ's body by caring for our broth*ers* and sisters.

You entrusted the earth to mankind, to people it and *make* it prosper,

— inspire us to work wholeheartedly in this world, seeking always to *give* you glory.

Father of all mankind, do not forget what your *hands* have made,

— grant that all who work may have secure employment and a fitting stan*dard* of living.

Our Father . . .

Prayer

God our Father,
creator and ruler of the universe,
in every age you call man
to develop and use his gifts for the good of others.
With Saint Joseph as our example and guide,
help us to do the work you have asked
and come to the rewards you have promised.
We ask this through our Lord Jesus Christ, your Son,
who lives and reigns with you and the Holy Spirit,
one God, for ever and ever.

Evening Prayer

HYMN, as in Morning Prayer, 962.

READING   Colossians 3:23-24

Whatever you do, work at it with your whole being. Do it for the Lord rather than for men, since you know full well that you will receive an inheritance from him as your reward. Be slaves of Christ the Lord.

RESPONSORY (VI F)

The just man shall blossom *like* the lily, * alleluia, al*le*luia.
— The just man shall blossom *like* the lily, * alleluia, al*le*luia.
He shall flourish for ever in the courts *of* our God,
— alleluia, al*le*luia.
Glory to the Father, and *to* the Son, * and to the Ho*ly* Spirit.
— The just man shall blossom *like* the lily, * alleluia, al*le*luia.

CANTICLE OF MARY

Ant.   Christ the *Lord* felt honored * to be known as the son of a
                        carpenter, al*le*luia.

INTERCESSIONS (VI F)

All fatherhood in heaven and on earth has its ori*gin* in God. * Let us turn to *him*
    and pray:
Our Father in heaven, hear our *prayer.*
All-holy Father, you revealed to Saint Joseph your eternal plan of salva*tion* in
    Christ,
— deepen our understanding of your Son, true God *and* true man.
Father in heaven, you feed the birds of the air, and clothe the fields with the
    fruit *of* the earth,
— give all your children their daily bread, to sustain *soul* and body.
Maker of the universe, you have entrusted your creation to *our* safekeeping,
— may all who work receive a just reward *for* their labors.
God of all righteousness, you want us all to *be* like you,
— may Saint Joseph inspire us to walk always in your *way* of holiness.
Look kindly on the dying and the dead, and grant *them* your mercy,
— through the intercession of Jesus, Ma*ry* and Joseph.

Our Father . . .

Prayer

    God our Father,
    creator and ruler of the universe,
    in every age you call man
    to develop and use his gifts for the good of others.
    With Saint Joseph as our example and guide,
    help us to do the work you have asked
    and come to the rewards you have promised.
    We ask this through our Lord Jesus Christ, your Son,
    who lives and reigns with you and the Holy Spirit,
    one God, for ever and ever.

May 2
ATHANASIUS, BISHOP AND DOCTOR
Memorial
From the common of pastors: bishops, 1238, or of doctors, 1246.

Prayer

Father,
you raised up Saint Athanasius
to be an outstanding defender
of the truth of Christ's divinity.
By his teaching and protection
may we grow in your knowledge and love.
Grant this through our Lord Jesus Christ, your Son,
who lives and reigns with you and the Holy Spirit,
one God, for ever and ever.

May 3
PHILIP AND JAMES, APOSTLES
Feast
From the common of apostles during the Easter Season, 1206, except for the following:

Morning Prayer

Ant. 1   Lord, show *us* the Father, * and we shall be satisfied, al*l*eluia.

Psalms and canticle from Sunday, Week I, 606.

Ant. 2   Have I been with you all this time and still you do not know
              me? † Philip, whoever sees me, sees my *Fa*ther also, * al*l*eluia.

Ant. 3   Do not let your hearts be troubled or afraid; † trust in God and
              trust also *in* me; * there are many rooms in my Father's house,
              al*l*eluia.

READING   Ephesians 2:19-20
You are strangers and aliens no longer. No, you are fellow citizens of the
saints and members of the household of God. You form a building which
rises on the foundation of the apostles and prophets, with Christ Jesus
himself as the capstone. Through him the whole structure is fitted together
and takes shape as a holy temple in the Lord; in him you are being built
into this temple, to become a dwelling place for God in the Spirit.

RESPONSORY (VI F)
You have made them rulers over *all* the earth, * alleluia, al*l*eluia.
— You have made them rulers over *all* the earth, * alleluia, al*l*eluia.

They will always remember your *name*, O Lord,
— alleluia, al*le*luia.
Glory to the Father, and *to* the Son, * and to the Ho*ly* Spirit.
— You have made them rulers over *all* the earth, * alleluia, al*le*luia.

CANTICLE OF ZECHARIAH

Ant.   Philip found Nathanael and said to him: † We have found the
                man Moses wrote of *in* the law, * the one of whom the pro*phets*
                spoke.
                He is Jesus, *son* of Joseph, * from Nazareth, al*le*luia.

INTERCESSIONS (VI F)

Belovèd friends, we have inherited heaven along with *the* apostles. * Let us give
  thanks to the Father for *all* his gifts:
The company of apostles praises you, O Lord.
Praise be to you, Lord, for the banquet of Christ's body and blood given us
  through *the* apostles,
— which refreshes us and *gives* us life.
The company of apostles praises you, O Lord.
Praise be to you, Lord, for the feast of your word prepared for us by *the*
  apostles,
— giving us *light* and joy.
The company of apostles praises you, O Lord.
Praise be to you, Lord, for your holy Church, founded on *the* apostles,
— where we are gathered together into *your* community.
The company of apostles praises you, O Lord.
Praise be to you, Lord, for the cleansing power of baptism and penance that
  you have entrusted to *your* apostles,
— through which we are cleansed *of* our sins.
The company of apostles praises you, O Lord.

Our Father . . .

Prayer

            God our Father,
            every year you give us joy
            on the festival of the apostles Philip and James.
            By the help of their prayers
            may we share in the suffering, death, and resurrection
            of your only Son
            and come to the eternal vision of your glory.
            We ask this through our Lord Jesus Christ, your Son,
            who lives and reigns with you and the Holy Spirit,
            one God, for ever and ever.

Evening Prayer

Ant. 1   Philip, who*ever* sees me * sees my Father also, *al*leluia.

Psalms and canticle from the common of apostles, 1206.

Ant. 2   If you had known me you would have known my Father also. †
                 Now you both know *him* and see him, * al*le*luia.

Ant. 3   If you love me, says the Lord, keep my *com*mandments, *
                 al*le*luia.

READING   Ephesians 4:11-13
    Christ gave apostles, prophets, evangelists, pastors and teachers in roles of
    service for the faithful to build up the body of Christ, till we become one in
    faith and in the knowledge of God's Son, and form that perfect man who is
    Christ come to full stature.

RESPONSORY (VI F)
Tell all the nations how glor*ious* God is, * alleluia, al*le*luia.
— Tell all the nations how glor*ious* God is, * alleluia, al*le*luia.
Make known his wonders to *eve*ry people,
— alleluia, al*le*luia.
Glory to the Father, and *to* the Son, * and to the Ho*ly* Spirit.
— Tell all the nations how glor*ious* God is, * alleluia, al*le*luia.

CANTICLE OF MARY
Ant.   If you live in me and my words *live* in you, * all you ask for will
                 be yours, al*le*luia.

INTERCESSIONS (VI F)
My brothers, we build on the foundation of *the* apostles. * Let us pray to our
    almighty Father for his holy peo*ple* and say:
Be mindful of your Church, O Lord.
Father, you wanted your Son to be seen first by the apostles after the
    resurrection *from* the dead,
— we ask you to make us his witnesses to the farthest corners *of* the world.
You sent your Son to preach the good news *to* the poor,
— help us to preach the Gospel to *eve*ry creature.
You sent your Son to sow the seed of un*end*ing life,
— grant that we who work at sowing the seed may share the joy *of* the harvest.
You sent your Son to reconcile all men to you *through* his blood,
— help us all to work toward achieving this reconci*li*ation.
Your Son sits at your right *hand* in heaven,
— let the dead enter your king*dom* of joy.

Our Father . . .

Prayer

God our Father,
every year you give us joy
on the festival of the apostles Philip and James.
By the help of their prayers
may we share in the suffering, death, and resurrection
of your only Son
and come to the eternal vision of your glory.
We ask this through our Lord Jesus Christ, your Son,
who lives and reigns with you and the Holy Spirit,
one God, for ever and ever.

May 10
DAMIEN JOSPEH DE VEUSTER OF MOLOKA'I, PRIEST

From the common of pastors, 1238.

Prayer

Father of mercy,
in Blessed Damien you have given
a shining witness of love
for the poorest and most abandoned.
Grant that, by his intercession,
as faithful witness of the heart of your Son, Jesus,
we too may be servants of the most needy and rejected.
We ask this through our Lord Jesus Christ, your Son,
who lives and reigns with you and the Holy Spirit,
one God, for ever and ever.

May 12
NEREUS AND ACHILLEUS, MARTYRS

From the common of several martyrs during the Easter Season, 1214.

Prayer

Father,
we honor Saints Nereus and Achilleus for their courage
in dying to profess their faith in Christ.
May we experience the help of their prayers
at the throne of your mercy.
Grant this through our Lord Jesus Christ, your Son,
who lives and reigns with you and the Holy Spirit,
one God, for ever and ever.

On the same day, May 12
PANCRAS, MARTYR

From the common of one martyr during the Easter Season, 1228.

Prayer

God of mercy,
give your Church joy and confidence
through the prayers of Saint Pancras.
Keep us faithful to you
and steadfast in your service.
We ask this through our Lord Jesus Christ, your Son,
who lives and reigns with you and the Holy Spirit,
one God, for ever and ever.

May 13
OUR LADY OF FATIMA

From the common of the Blessed Virgin Mary, 1192.

Prayer

Lord God,
give to your people the joy
of continual health in mind and body.
With the prayers of the Virgin Mary to help us,
guide us through the sorrows of this life
to eternal happiness in the life to come.
Grant this through our Lord Jesus Christ, your Son,
who lives and reigns with you and the Holy Spirit,
one God, for ever and ever.

May 14
MATTHIAS, APOSTLE
Feast

From the common of apostles during the Easter Season, 1206, except for the following:

Morning Prayer

CANTICLE OF ZECHARIAH

Ant. We must choose someone *who* was with us * all the time that
the Lord Jesus lived *a*mong us;
he will take his place with us in *giv*ing witness * to the Lord's
resurrection, al*le*luia.

Prayer

Father,
you called Saint Matthias to share in the mission of the apostles.
By the help of his prayers
may we receive with joy the love you share with us
and be counted among those you have chosen.
We ask this through our Lord Jesus Christ, your Son,
who lives and reigns with you and the Holy Spirit,
one God, for ever and ever.

Evening Prayer

CANTICLE OF MARY

Ant.   You have not chosen me but I have chosen you † and have appointed you to go forth *and* bear fruit, * and your fruit will remain, al*e*luia.

[In the dioceses of the United States]
May 15
ISIDORE

From the common of holy men, 1263.

Prayer

Lord God,
all creation is yours, and you call us to serve you
by caring for the gifts that surround us.
May the example of Saint Isidore urge us
to share our food with the hungry
and to work for the salvation of mankind.
We ask this through our Lord Jesus Christ, your Son,
who lives and reigns with you and the Holy Spirit,
one God, for ever and ever.

May 18
JOHN I, POPE AND MARTYR

From the common of one martyr during the Easter Season, 1228, or of pastors: popes, 1238.

Prayer

God our Father,
rewarder of all who believe,
hear our prayers
as we celebrate the martyrdom of Pope John.
Help us to follow him in loyalty to the faith.
Grant this through our Lord Jesus Christ, your Son,
who lives and reigns with you and the Holy Spirit,
one God, for ever and ever.

May 20
BERNARDINE OF SIENA, PRIEST

From the common of pastors, 1238.

Prayer

Father,
you gave Saint Bernardine a special love
for the holy name of Jesus.
By the help of his prayers,
may we always be alive with the spirit of your love.
We ask this through our Lord Jesus Christ, your Son,
who lives and reigns with you and the Holy Spirit,
one God, for ever and ever.

May 21
CHRISTOPHER MAGALLANES, PRIEST
AND COMPANIONS, MARTYRS

From the common of martyrs outside the Easter Season, 1214, or the common of martyrs
during the Easter Season, 1214.

Prayer

God our Father,
your generous gift of love
brought St. Christopher and his companions to unending glory.
Through the prayers of your martyrs
forgive our sins and free us from every danger.
We ask this through our Lord Jesus Christ, your Son,
who lives and reigns with you and the Holy Spirit,
one God, for ever and ever.

May 22
RITA OF CASCIA, RELIGIOUS

From the common of holy women: religious, 1282.

Prayer

Lord God,
you kept Saint Rita faithful to Christ's pattern of poverty and humility.
May her prayers help us to live in fidelity to our calling
and bring us to the perfection you have shown us in your Son,
who lives and reigns with you and the Holy Spirit,
one God, for ever and ever.

May 25
BEDE THE VENERABLE, PRIEST AND DOCTOR

From the common of doctors, 1246, or of holy men: religious, 1282.

Prayer

Lord,
you have enlightened your Church
with the learning of Saint Bede.
In your love
may your people learn from his wisdom
and benefit from his prayers.
Grant this through our Lord Jesus Christ, your Son,
who lives and reigns with you and the Holy Spirit,
one God, for ever and ever.

On the same day, May 25
GREGORY VII, POPE

From the common of pastors, 1238.

Prayer

Lord,
give your Church
the spirit of courage and love for justice
which distinguished Pope Gregory.
Make us courageous in condemning evil
and free us to pursue justice with love.
We ask this through our Lord Jesus Christ, your Son,
who lives and reigns with you and the Holy Spirit,
one God, for ever and ever.

On the same day, May 25
MARY MAGDALENE DE PAZZI, VIRGIN

From the common of virgins, 1253, or of holy women: religious, 1282.

Prayer

Father,
you love those who give themselves completely to your service,
and you filled Saint Mary Magdalene de Pazzi
with heavenly gifts and the fire of your love.
As we honor her today
may we follow her example of purity and charity.
Grant this through our Lord Jesus Christ, your Son,
who lives and reigns with you and the Holy Spirit,
one God, for ever and ever.

May 26
PHILIP NERI, PRIEST
Memorial

From the common of pastors, 1238, or of holy men: religious, 1282.

Prayer

Father,
you continually raise up your faithful
to the glory of holiness.
In your love
kindle in us the fire of the Holy Spirit
who so filled the heart of Philip Neri.
We ask this through our Lord Jesus Christ, your Son,
who lives and reigns with you and the Holy Spirit,
one God, for ever and ever.

May 27
AUGUSTINE OF CANTERBURY, BISHOP

From the common of pastors, 1238.

Prayer

Father,
by the preaching of Saint Augustine of Canterbury,
you led the people of England to the gospel.
May the fruits of his work continue in the Church.
Grant this through our Lord Jesus Christ, your Son,
who lives and reigns with you and the Holy Spirit,
one God, for ever and ever.

May 31
VISITATION
Feast

From the common of the Blessed Virgin Mary, 1192, except for the following:

Morning Prayer
HYMN

Veniens, Mater. (L.M.)

Veniens, mater inclita,	Enriched by Holy Spirit's gift,
cum Sancti dono Spiritus,	Come, Mother of the hidden Christ,
nos ut Ioannem visita	And visit us as once you came
in huius carnis sedibus.	And gladdened John who lept for joy.
Procede, portans parvulum,	Come forward with your little Son,
ut mundus possit credere	That all the world may grow in faith,
et tuæ laudis titulum	And call you blessèd for all time,
omnes sciant extollere.	As lowly handmaid of the Lord.

Saluta nunc Ecclesiam,	Now greet the Church that it may hear
ut tuam vocem audiens	Your gentle voice so sweet and low,
exurgat in lætitia,	That hearing, it may thrill with joy
adventum Christi sentiens.	And feel the presence of its Lord.
Maria, levans oculos,	O Mary, raise your eyes and see
vide credentes populos:	The multitudes who trust in you;
te quærunt piis mentibus,	They seek you with most loving hearts,
his opem feres omnibus.	It is to you for help they turn.
O veræ spes lætitiæ,	O Hope of all true happiness,
nostræ portus miseriæ,	And Haven of our wretchedness,
nos iunge cæli curiæ	In robes of glory and of grace
ornatos stola gloriæ.	Join us to heaven's holy court.
Tecum, Virgo, magnificat	With you, O Virgin highly blest,
anima nostra Dominum,	Our souls now magnify the Lord,
qui laude te nobilitat	Who did such wondrous things in you
et hominum et cælitum. Amen.	That men and angels praise your name. Amen.

Ant. 1   Mary arose and went with haste in*to* the hill country, * to a *town* of Judah, (*al*leluia.)

Psalms and canticles from Sunday, Week I, 606.

Ant. 2   When Elizabeth heard Mary's greeting, † the infant in her womb *leaped* for joy, * and she was filled with the Ho*ly* Spirit, (al*le*luia.)

Ant. 3   Blessèd are you, Mary, † because you believed that the Lord's words *to* you * would be *ful*filled, (al*le*luia.)

READING   Joel 2:27-3:1a

You shall know that I am in the midst of Israel;
    I am the Lord, your God, and there is no other;
    my people shall nevermore be put to shame.
Then afterward I will pour out
    my spirit upon all mankind.
Your sons and daughters shall prophesy.

RESPONSORY (VI F)

The Lord has *chos*en her, * his loved one from the *begin*ning.
— The Lord has *chos*en her, * his loved one from the *begin*ning.
He has taken her to *live* with him,
— his loved one from the *begin*ning.
Glory to the Father, and *to* the Son, * and to the Ho*ly* Spirit.
— The Lord has *chos*en her, * his loved one from the *begin*ning.

Easter:

The Lord has chosen her, † his loved one from *the* beginning, * alleluia, al*le*luia.

— The Lord has chosen her, † his loved one from *the* beginning, * alleluia, al*le*luia.

He has taken her to *live* with him,

— alleluia, al*le*luia.

Glory to the Father, and *to* the Son, * and to the Ho*ly* Spirit.

— The Lord has chosen her, † his loved one from *the* beginning, * alleluia, al*le*luia.

CANTICLE OF ZECHARIAH

Ant.　　　　When Elizabeth heard Mary's greeting, † she cried *out* and said: * Who am I that the mother of my Lord should come *to* me? (Al*le*luia.)

INTERCESSIONS (VI F)

Let us glorify our Savior, who chose the Virgin Mary *for* his mother. * *Let* us ask him:

May your mother intercede for us, Lord.

Sun of Justice, the Immaculate Virgin was the white dawn announc*ing* your rising,

— grant that we may always live in the light *of* your coming.

Lord, help us imitate Mary, your mother, who chose *the* best part,

— may we seek the food that will sustain *us* for ever.

Savior of the world, by your redeeming might you preserved your mother beforehand from all *stain* of sin,

— keep watch over us, *lest* we sin.

You are our redeemer, who made the immaculate Virgin Mary your purest home and the sanctuary of the *Holy* Spirit,

— make us temples of your Spir*it* for ever.

Our Father . . .

Prayer

Eternal Father,

you inspired the Virgin Mary, mother of your Son,

to visit Elizabeth and assist her in her need.

Keep us open to the working of your Spirit,

and with Mary may we praise you for ever.

We ask this through our Lord Jesus Christ, your Son,

who lives and reigns with you and the Holy Spirit,

one God, for ever and ever.

May 31

Evening Prayer

HYMN

Concito gressu. (11.11.11.5)

Concito gressu petis alta montis,
Virgo, quam matrem Deus ipse fecit,
ut seni matri studios*i* amoris
    pignora promas.

Swifty you journey to the hills of Juda,
Virgin and Mother, treasuring your secret,
Eager to render service to another
    Favored by heaven.

Cum salutantis capit illa vocem,
abditus gestit puer exsilire,
te parens dicit dominam, salutat
    teque beatam.

Your words of greeting thrilled the little Baptist,
Stirred by the coming of the unborn Savior,
Prompting his mother to declare you blessèd
    Far beyond others.

Ipsa prædicis fore te beatam
Spiritu fervens penitus loquente,
ac Deum cantu celebras amœno
    magn*a* operantem.

Filled with the Spirit, you foretell the future,
All generations will proclaim you blessèd,
He who is mighty did great things within you,
    Choosing his Mother.

Teque felicem populi per orbem
semper, o mater, recitant ovantes
atque te credunt Domini favorum
    esse ministram.

Peoples and nations ever sing your praises,
Mother of Jesus, and their mother also,
Trusting as children in your intercession
    For their well-being.

Quæ, ferens Christum, nova semper affers
dona, tu nobis fer opes salutis,
qui pie tecum Triadem supernam
    magnificamus. Amen.

Mother of Jesus, you bestow great favors,
Give us the graces needed for salvation,
So that in heaven we may praise the God-head
    With you for ever. Amen.

PSALMODY

Ant. 1   Mary entered the house of Ze*ch*ariah, * and greet*ed* Elizabeth, (*al*leluia).

Psalms and canticles from the common of the Blessed Virgin Mary, 1196.

Ant. 2   When your greeting sounded *in* my ears, * the infant in my womb leaped *for* joy, (all*el*uia).

Ant. 3   Blessèd are you a*mong* women, * and blessèd is the fruit of *your* womb, (all*el*uia).

READING   1 Peter 5:5b-7

In your relations with one another, clothe yourselves with humility, because God "is stern with the arrogant but to the humble he shows kindness." Bow humbly under God's mighty hand, so that in due time he may lift you high. Cast all your cares on him because he cares for you.

RESPONSORY (VI F)

Hail Mary, *full* of grace, * the Lord is *with* you.
— Hail Mary, *full* of grace, * the Lord is *with* you.

Blessèd are you among women, and blessèd is the fruit *of* your womb.
— The Lord is *with* you.
Glory to the Father, and *to* the Son, * and to the Ho*ly* Spirit.
— Hail Mary, *full* of grace, * the Lord is *with* you.

Easter:
Hail Mary, full of grace, † the Lord *is* with you, * alleluia, al*le*luia.
— Hail Mary, full of grace, † the Lord *is* with you, * alleluia, al*le*luia.
Blessèd are you among women, and blessèd is the fruit *of* your womb,
— alleluia, al*le*luia.
Glory to the Father, and *to* the Son, * and to the Ho*ly* Spirit.
— Hail Mary, full of grace, † the Lord *is* with you, * alleluia, al*le*luia.

CANTICLE OF MARY
Ant. All generations will *call* me blessèd; * the Lord has looked with favor on his low*ly* servant (al*le*luia).

INTERCESSIONS (VI F)
Let us praise God our almighty Father, who wished that Mary, his Son's mother, be celebrated by each *gen*eration. * Now in *need* we ask:
Mary, full of grace, intercede for *us.*
O God, worker of miracles, you made the Immaculate Virgin Mary share, body and soul, in your Son's glo*ry* in heaven,
— direct the hearts of your children to *that* same glory.
Lord, make your Church one in mind and heart, united *in* your love,
— and keep Christians united in prayer with Mary, the moth*er* of Jesus.
You made Mary the moth*er* of mercy,
— may all who are faced with trials feel her moth*er*ly love.
You wished Mary to be the mother of the family in the home of Je*sus* and Joseph,
— may all mothers of families foster love and holiness through her *in*tercession.
You crowned Mary *queen* of heaven,
— may all the dead rejoice in your kingdom with the *saints* for ever.

Our Father . . .

Prayer

Eternal Father,
you inspired the Virgin Mary, mother of your Son,
to visit Elizabeth and assist her in her need.
Keep us open to the working of your Spirit,
and with Mary may we praise you for ever.
We ask this through our Lord Jesus Christ, your Son,
who lives and reigns with you and the Holy Spirit,
one God, for ever and ever.

Saturday following the Second Sunday after Pentecost
IMMACULATE HEART OF MARY
From the common of the Blessed Virgin Mary, 1192, except for the following:

Morning Prayer

CANTICLE OF ZECHARIAH

Ant.   My heart *and* my flesh * rejoice in the liv*ing* God.

Prayer

Father,
you prepared the heart of the Virgin Mary
to be a fitting home for your Holy Spirit.
By her prayers
may we become a more worthy temple of your glory.
Grant this through our Lord Jesus Christ, your Son,
who lives and reigns with you and the Holy Spirit,
one God, for ever and ever.

Evening Prayer

CANTICLE OF MARY

Ant.   My heart rejoices *in* the Lord, * for the almighty has done great
                         things *for* me.

June 1
JUSTIN, MARTYR
Memorial
From the common of one martyr, 1228.

Morning Prayer

CANTICLE OF ZECHARIAH

Ant.   In every sacrifice let us praise the Creator *of* all things * through
                         his Son Jesus Christ and through the Ho*ly* Spirit (al*le*luia).

Prayer

Father,
through the folly of the cross
you taught Saint Justin the sublime wisdom of Jesus Christ.
May we too reject falsehood
and remain loyal to the faith.
We ask this through our Lord Jesus Christ, your Son,
who lives and reigns with you and the Holy Spirit,
one God, for ever and ever.

Evening Prayer

CANTICLE OF MARY

Ant.   Suddenly my soul caught fire, † and I became filled with love *for* the prophets * and those men who are the friends *of* Christ (al*le*luia).

June 2
MARCELLINUS AND PETER, MARTYRS

From the common of several martyrs, 1214.

Prayer

Father,
may we benefit from the example
of your martyrs Marcellinus and Peter,
and be supported by their prayers.
Grant this through our Lord Jesus Christ, your Son,
who lives and reigns with you and the Holy Spirit,
one God, for ever and ever.

June 3
CHARLES LWANGA AND COMPANIONS, MARTYRS
Memorial

From the common of several martyrs, 1214.

Prayer

Father,
you have made the blood of the martyrs
the seed of Christians.
May the witness of Saint Charles and his companions
and their loyalty to Christ in the face of torture
inspire countless men and women
to live the Christian faith.
We ask this through our Lord Jesus Christ, your Son,
who lives and reigns with you and the Holy Spirit,
one God, for ever and ever.

June 5
BONIFACE, BISHOP AND MARTYR
Memorial

From the common of one martyr, 1228, or of pastors, 1238.

Prayer

Lord,
you martyr Boniface
spread the faith by his teaching
and witnessed to it with his blood.
By the help of his prayers
keep us loyal to our faith
and give us courage to profess it in our lives.
Grant this through our Lord Jesus Christ, your Son,
who lives and reigns with you and the Holy Spirit,
one God, for ever and ever.

June 6
NORBERT, BISHOP

From the common of pastors, 1238.

Prayer

Father,
you made the bishop, Norbert
an outstanding minister of your Church,
renowned for his preaching and pastoral zeal.
Always grant to your Church faithful shepherds
to lead your people to eternal salvation.
We ask this through our Lord Jesus Christ, your Son,
who lives and reigns with you and the Holy Spirit,
one God, for ever and ever.

June 9
EPHREM, DEACON AND DOCTOR

From the common of doctors, 1246.

Prayer

Lord,
in your love fill our hearts with the Holy Spirit,
who inspired the deacon Ephrem to sing the praise of your mysteries
and gave him strength to serve you alone.
Grant this through our Lord Jesus Christ, your Son,
who lives and reigns with you and the Holy Spirit,
one God, for ever and ever.

June 11
BARNABAS, APOSTLE
Memorial

From the common of apostles, 1206.

Morning Prayer

HYMN

Barnabæ clarum. (11.11.11.5)

Barnabæ clarum colimus tropæum,	With the Apostles, Barnabas the levite
quo micat celsus merita corona,	Shines in the glory won by many labors,
multa pro Christi vehementer usque	Through love of Jesus, he despised as nothing
passus amore.	All that he suffered.
Abdicans agro, generosus urget	Land and possessions he abandoned also,
ut, fide vivax ope caritatis,	Charity's ardor marked his earnest teaching;
nominis plebes nova christiani	Antioch's concerts won the name of Christians,
læta virescat.	Proof of their fervor.
Quam libens noscit, petit atque defert	Quickly perceiving Paul's sincere conversion,
maximum Paulum, socio labore	Gladly he welcomed such a keen companion,
Spiritus nutu peragrans fidelis	By divine choosing, many miles they travelled,
litora multa!	Spreading the Gospel.
Nil sibi parcit cupidusque Christo	Tireless and eager, he would spare no effort,
plurimos affert, bonus atque pascit,	Preaching Christ Jesus by his words and goodness,
donec effuso rutila probatur	'Til martyr's glory sealed his never failing
sanguine palma.	Life-long devotion.
Da, Deus, tanto famulo rogante,	Lord God Almighty, through the intercession
nos sequi fortes iter ad salutem,	Of your great servant, give us strength to labor
ut domo æterna tibi concinamus	For our salvation, that we may in heaven
cantica laudis. Amen.	Praise you for ever. Amen.

READING   1 Corinthians 15:1-2a, 3-4

Brothers, I want to remind you of the gospel I preached to you, which you received and in which you stand firm. You are being saved by it at this very moment. I handed on to you first of all what I myself received, that Christ died for our sins in accordance with the Scriptures; that he was buried and, in accordance with the Scriptures, rose on the third day.

RESPONSORY (VI F)

They proclaimed *the* Lord's praises * and his sav*ing* power.
— They proclaimed *the* Lord's praises * and his sav*ing* power.
They spoke of the wonders *he* had worked,
— and his sav*ing* power.
Glory to the Father, and *to* the Son, * and to the Ho*ly* Spirit.
— They proclaimed *the* Lord's praises * and his sav*ing* power.

Easter:

They proclaimed the Lord's praises and his *saving* power, * alleluia, al*le*luia.
—They proclaimed the Lord's praises and his *saving* power, * alleluia, al*le*luia.
They spoke of the wonders *he* had worked,
—alleluia, al*le*luia.
Glory to the Father, and *to* the Son, * and to the Ho*ly* Spirit.
—They proclaimed the Lord's praises and his *saving* power, * alleluia, al*le*luia.

CANTICLE OF ZECHARIAH

Ant.   Barnabas set *out* for Tarsus * to look *for* Paul.
                        Once he found him, he brought him to Antioch † where they
                        met *with* the church * and instructed a great number *of* people
                        (al*le*luia).

NTERCESSIONS (VI F)

Let us sing a song of praise to our Savior, who destroyed the power of death and
    made clear the path to life and immortality *through* the Gospel; * and let us
    petition him in humble *sup*plication:
Strengthen your Church in faith and love.
You gave wonderful guidance to your Church through her holy and dis*tin*-
    guished teachers,
— may Christians rejoice always in the splendid legacy given *to* your Church.
When their holy pastors prayed to you, as Moses had done, you forgave the sins
    of the people,
— through the intercession of these holy pastors continue to sanctify and puri*fy*
    your Church.
You anointed your holy ones in the midst of their brothers and called the Holy
    Spirit *down* upon them,
— fill all the leaders of your people with the *Holy* Spirit.
You yourself are the sole possession of your *holy* pastors,
— grant that those you have redeemed with your blood may remain al*ways* in
    you.

Our Father . . .

Prayer

God our Father,
    you filled Saint Barnabas with faith and the Holy Spirit
    and sent him to convert the nations.
    Help us to proclaim the gospel by word and deed.
    We ask this through our Lord Jesus Christ, your Son,
    who lives and reigns with you and the Holy Spirit,
    one God, for ever and ever.

Evening Prayer

READING   Colossians 1:3-6a

We always give thanks to God, the Father of our Lord Jesus Christ, in our prayers for you because we have heard of your faith in Christ Jesus and the love you bear toward all the saints— moved as you are by the hope held in store for you in heaven. You have heard of this hope through the message of truth, the gospel, which has come to you, has borne fruit, and has continued to grow in your midst, as it has everywhere in the world.

RESPONSORY (VI F)

Tell *all* the nations * how glorious *God* is.
— Tell *all* the nations * how glorious *God* is.
Make known his wonders to *every* people.
— How glorious *God* is.
Glory to the Father, and *to* the Son, * and to the Ho*ly* Spirit.
— Tell *all* the nations * how glorious *God* is.

Easter:

Tell all the nations how glor*ious* God is, * alleluia, al*le*luia.
— Tell all the nations how glor*ious* God is, * alleluia, al*le*luia.
Make known his wonders to *every* people.
— Alleluia, al*le*luia.
Glory to the Father, and *to* the Son, * and to the Ho*ly* Spirit.
— Tell all the nations how glor*ious* God is, * alleluia, al*le*luia.

CANTICLE OF MARY

Ant.   The whole assem*bly* fell silent, * and they listened to Barnabas *and* Paul
describing all the *signs* and wonders * God had worked through them among *the* Gentiles (al*le*luia).

INTERCESSIONS (VI F)

Our God is Father of light. Through the good news of his Son he has called us
    to believe *in* the truth. * We pray now for his chosen people *as* we say:
*Remember your holy peo*ple, Lord.
Father, you raised your Son, our Good Shepherd, *from* the dead,
— make us his witnesses to the very ends *of* the earth.
You sent your Son to bring good news *to* the poor,
— give us courage to bring that good news to *every* creature.
You sent your Son to sow the *word* of life,
— help us to sow his word and to reap its har*vest* with joy.
You sent your Son to make the world one *through* his blood,
— may all of us work together *for* this unity.

You set your Son at your right hand *in* the heavens,
— open the gates of your kingdom to those *who* have died.

Our Father . . .

Prayer

God our Father,
you filled Saint Barnabas with faith and the Holy Spirit
and sent him to convert the nations.
Help us to proclaim the gospel by word and deed.
We ask this through our Lord Jesus Christ, your Son,
who lives and reigns with you and the Holy Spirit,
one God, for ever and ever.

June 13
ANTHONY OF PADUA, PRIEST AND DOCTOR
Memorial

From the common of pastors, 1238, or of doctors, 1246, or of holy men: religious, 1282.

Prayer

Almighty God,
you have given Saint Anthony to your people
as an outstanding preacher
and a ready helper in time of need.
With his assistance may we follow the gospel of Christ
and know the help of your grace in every difficulty.
Grant this through our Lord Jesus Christ, your Son,
who lives and reigns with you and the Holy Spirit,
one God, for ever and ever.

June 19
ROMUALD, ABBOT

From the common of holy men: religious, 1282.

Prayer

Father,
through Saint Romuald
your renewed the life of solitude and prayer in your Church.
By our self-denial as we follow Christ
bring us the joy of heaven.
We ask this through our Lord Jesus Christ, your Son,
who lives and reigns with you and the Holy Spirit,
one God, for ever and ever.

June 21
ALOYSIUS GONZAGA, RELIGIOUS
Memorial

From the common of holy men, 1263.

Prayer

Father of love, giver of all good things,
in Saint Aloysius you combined remarkable innocence
with the spirit of penance.
By the help of his prayers
may we who have not followed his innocence
follow his example of penance.
Grant this through our Lord Jesus Christ, your Son,
who lives and reigns with you and the Holy Spirit,
one God, for ever and ever.

June 22
PAULINUS OF NOLA, BISHOP

From the common of pastors, 1238.

Prayer

Lord, you made Saint Paulinus
renowned for his love of poverty
and concern for his people.
May we who celebrate his witness to the gospel
imitate his example of love for others.
We ask this through our Lord Jesus Christ, your Son,
who lives and reigns with you and the Holy Spirit,
one God, for ever and ever.

On the same day, June 22
JOHN FISHER, BISHOP AND MARTYR, AND THOMAS MORE, MARTYR

From the common of several martyrs, 1214.

Prayer

Father,
you confirm the true faith
with the crown of martyrdom.
May the prayers of Saints John Fisher and Thomas More
give us the courage to proclaim our faith
by the witness of our lives.
Grant this through our Lord Jesus Christ, your Son,
who lives and reigns with you and the Holy Spirit,
one God, for ever and ever.

June 24
BIRTH OF JOHN THE BAPTIST
Solemnity

Evening Prayer I

HYMN

Ut queant laxis. (11.11.11.5)

Ut queant laxis resonare fibris	Preacher of penance, great Saint John the Baptist,
mira gestorum famuli tuorum,	Cleanse us poor sinners that our tongues may praise you,
solve polluti labii reatum,	Joyfully singing with a new-found fervor
sanctæ Ioannes.	On this your feast day.
Nuntius cælo veniens supreme,	Angel from heaven told your honored father
te patri magnum fore nasciturum,	Of coming wonder, destined to delight him,
nomen et vitæ seriem gerendæ	Son of his old age, John, the greatest prophet,
ordine promit.	Such he foretold you.
Ille promissi dubius superni	Zachary doubted, trusted not the message,
perdidit promptæ modulos loquelæ;	And in atonement not a word could utter,
sed reformasti genitus peremptæ	'Til he received you in his arms as father,
organa vocis.	Humbly rejoicing.
Ventris obstruso positus cubili	Hidden and waiting for your future mission,
senseras regem thalamo manentem;	You leapt to welcome the unborn Messiah,
hinc parens nati meritis uterque	So that your mother knew of heaven's secrets
abdita pandit.	Through her son's merits.
Laudibus cives celebrant superni	Trinity holy, One, Almighty Godhead,
te, Deus simplex pariterque trine;	All saints in heaven celebrate your praises;
supplices ac nos veniam precamur:	Humbly we beg you, spare and grant us pardon
parce redemptis. Amen.	Through the Redemption. Amen.

PSALMODY

Ant. 1   Elizabeth, the wife of Zechariah, † gave birth to a great man, *John* the Baptist, * who prepared the way *for* the Lord.

Psalms and canticle from the common of holy men, 1260.

Ant. 2   John, the forerunner *of* the Lord, * was born of an old and child*less* couple.

Ant. 3   There is no man born *of* woman * greater than John *the* Baptist.

READING   Acts 13:23-25

According to his promise, God has brought forth from David's descendants Jesus, a savior for Israel. John heralded the coming of Jesus by proclaiming a baptism of repentance to all the people of Israel. As John's career was coming to an end, he would say, "What you suppose me to be I am not. Rather, look for the one who comes after me. I am not worthy to unfasten the sandals on his feet."

RESPONSORY (VI F)
Prepare the way *of* the Lord; * make straight *his* paths.
— Prepare the way *of* the Lord; * make straight *his* paths.
He who is to come after me exist*ed* before me.
— Make straight *his* paths.
Glory to the Father, and *to* the Son, * and to the Ho*ly* Spirit.
— Prepare the way *of* the Lord; * make straight *his* paths.

CANTICLE OF MARY

Ant.   Zechariah entered the temple of the Lord, † and the angel
              Gabriel ap*peared* to him, * standing on the right of the altar *of*
              incense.

INTERCESSIONS (VI F)
Let us pray joyfully to *God* our Father * who called John the Baptist to proclaim
the coming of the king*dom* of Christ:
O Lord, guide our feet into the way of *peace.*
You called John the Baptist from his mother's womb to prepare the way *of* your
    Son,
— help us to follow in that path which the Baptist opened before *the* Lord
    Jesus.
May your Church, in imitation of the Baptist, fearlessly point out the *Lamb* of
    God,
— so that people in every age may acknowledge that the Lord *comes* to them.
John the Baptist did not exalt himself but acknowledged his role as forerunner
    of the Christ,
— teach us to acknowledge that you are the giver of all our good gifts and that
    we must use them *in* your service.
You called John the Baptist to give testimony to you by his life and even *by* his
    death,
— help us to imitate his unceasing witness *to* your truth.
Remember those *who* have died,
— give them a place of light, happi*ness* and peace.

Our Father . . .

Prayer

    All-powerful God,
    help your people to walk the path to salvation.
    By following the teaching of John the Baptist,
    may we come to your Son, our Lord Jesus Christ,
    who lives and reigns with you and the Holy Spirit,
    one God, for ever and ever.

Morning Prayer

HYMN

O nimis felix. (11.11.11.5)

O nimis felix meritique celsi,	Most truly happy, of exalted virtue,
nesciens labem nivei pudoris,	Purest of heralds of the Sun of Justice,
præpotens martyr eremique cultor,	Martyr intrepid, dweller in the desert,
maxime vatum.	Greatest of prophets!
Nunc potens nostri meritis opimis	Now by your merits and compelling virtue,
pectoris duros lapides repelle,	From our souls' pathway take the stones of harshness,
asperum planas iter, et reflexos	Make smooth the rugged, straighten out the crooked,
dirige calles,	Gently prepare us.
Ut pius mundi sator et redemptor,	So that our Maker and the world's Redeemer
mentibus pulsa macula politis,	May find us ready, purified and loving,
rite dignetur veniens sacratos	Happy to welcome even smallest imprint
ponere gressus.	Of feet so sacred.
Laudibus cives celebrant superni	Trinity holy, One, Almighty Godhead,
te, Deus simplex pariterque trine;	All saints in heaven celebrate your praises;
supplices ac nos veniam precamur:	Humbly we beg you, spare and grant us pardon
parce redemptis. Amen.	Through the Redemption. Amen.

PSALMODY

Ant. 1   You shall name *the* child John, * and many will rejoice *at* his birth.

Psalms and canticle from Sunday, Week I, 606.

Ant. 2   In the spirit and power of Elijah, † he will go be*fore* the Lord * to prepare a people worthy *of* him.

Ant. 3   You, my child, shall be called the prophet of *the* Most High, * for you will go before the Lord to prepare *his* way.

READING   Malachi 3:23-24

Lo, I will send you
    Elijah, the prophet,
Before the day of the Lord comes,
    the great and terrible day,
To turn the hearts of fathers to their children,
    and the hearts of children to their fathers,
Lest I come and strike
    the land with doom.

RESPONSORY (VI F)

He will be great in the eyes *of* the Lord * and he will be filled with the Ho*ly*
Spirit.
— He will be great in the eyes *of* the Lord * and he will be filled with the Ho*ly*
Spirit.
He will go before the Lord to prepare a people worth*y* of him.
— And he will be filled with the Ho*ly* Spirit.
Glory to the Father, and *to* the Son, * and to the Ho*ly* Spirit.
— He will be great in the eyes *of* the Lord * and he will be filled with the Ho*ly*
Spirit.

CANTICLE OF ZECHARIAH

Ant.   The mouth of Zechariah was opened, † and he *spoke* this
              prophecy: * Blessèd be the Lord, the God *of* Israel.

INTERCESSIONS (VI F)

In faith let us call upon Christ *who* sent John * to prepare *for* his coming:
Dawn from on high, break up*on us.*
Your coming caused John the Baptist to leap for joy in his *mo*ther's womb,
— help us to rejoice at your com*ing* among us.
Through the life and preaching of the Baptist you showed us the way *to*
    repentance,
— turn our hearts to follow the commandments *of* your kingdom.
You willed that your coming among men should be announced by *John* the
    Baptist,
— send new heralds to proclaim you through*out* the world.
You wished to be baptized by John in the Jordan to fulfill all that the Fa*ther*
    required,
— help us to do the *Fa*ther's will.

Our Father . . .

Prayer

    God our Father,
    you raised up John the Baptist
    to prepare a perfect people for Christ the Lord.
    Give your Church joy in spirit
    and guide those who believe in you
    into the way of salvation and peace.
    We ask this through our Lord Jesus Christ, your Son,
    who lives and reigns with you and the Holy Spirit,
    one God, for ever and ever.

Evening Prayer II

HYMN, as in Evening Prayer I, 986.

PSALMODY

Ant. 1   There was a man *sent* by God * whose *name* was John.

Psalms and canticle from the common of holy men, 1268.

Ant. 2   He came *to* bear witness * to *the* truth.

Ant. 3   John *was* like * a brilliantly shin*ing* light.

READING   Acts 13:23-25

According to his promise, God has brought forth from David's descendants Jesus, a savior for Israel. John heralded the coming of Jesus by proclaiming a baptism of repentance to all the people of Israel. As John's career was coming to an end, he would say, "What you suppose me to be I am not. Rather, look for the one who comes after me. I am not worthy to unfasten the sandals on his feet."

RESPONSORY (VI F)

Prepare the way *of* the Lord; * make straight *his* paths.
— Prepare the way *of* the Lord; * make straight *his* paths.
He who is to come after me exist*ed* before me.
— Make straight *his* paths.
Glory to the Father, and *to* the Son, * and to the Ho*ly* Spirit.
— Prepare the way *of* the Lord; * make straight *his* paths.

CANTICLE OF MARY

Ant.   This child, born to us, is greater than any prophet; † the Savior *said* of him: * There is no man born of woman greater than John *the* Baptist.

INTERCESSIONS (VI F)

Let us pray joyfully to *God* our Father * who called John the Baptist to proclaim the coming of the king*dom* of Christ:
O Lord, guide our feet into the way of peace.
You called John the Baptist from his mother's womb to prepare the way *of* your Son,
— help us to follow in that path which the Baptist opened before *the* Lord Jesus.
May your Church, in imitation of the Baptist, fearlessly point out the *Lamb* of God,
— so that people in every age may acknowledge that the Lord *comes* to them.

John the Baptist did not exalt himself but acknowledged his role as forerunner *of* the Christ,
— teach us to acknowledge that you are the giver of all our good gifts and that we must use them *in* your service.
You called John the Baptist to give testimony to you by his life and even *by* his death,
— help us to imitate his unceasing witness *to* your truth.
Remember those *who* have died,
— give them a place of light, happi*ness* and peace.

Our Father . . .

Prayer

God our Father,
you raised up John the Baptist
to prepare a perfect people for Christ the Lord.
Give your Church joy in spirit
and guide those who believe in you
into the way of salvation and peace.
We ask this through our Lord Jesus Christ, your Son,
who lives and reigns with you and the Holy Spirit,
one God, for ever and ever.

June 27
CYRIL OF ALEXANDRIA, BISHOP AND DOCTOR

From the common of pastors, 1238, or of doctors, 1246.

Prayer

Father,
the bishop Cyril courageously taught
that Mary was the Mother of God.
May we who cherish this belief
receive salvation through the incarnation of Christ your Son,
who lives and reigns with you and the Holy Spirit,
one God, for ever and ever.

June 28
IRENÆUS, BISHOP AND MARTYR
Memorial

From the common of one martyr, 1228, or of pastors, 1238.

Morning Prayer

CANTICLE OF ZECHARIAH

Ant.   Irenæus, true to his name, † made peace the aim and object *of his life,* * and he labored strenuously for the peace of *the* Church.

Prayer

Father,
you called Saint Irenæus to uphold your truth
and bring peace to your Church.
By his prayers renew us in faith and love
that we may always be intent
on fostering unity and peace.
Grant this through our Lord Jesus Christ, your Son,
who lives and reigns with you and the Holy Spirit,
one God, for ever and ever.

June 29
PETER AND PAUL, APOSTLES
Solemnity

Evening Prayer I

HYMN

Aurea luce. Mode I (12.12.12.12)

Aurea luce et decore roseo,	Light of the Godhead, shining from eternity
lux lucis, omne perfudisti sæculum,	You bless the heavens with a golden radiance,
decorans cælos inclito martyrio	For this great feast day on which we commemorate
hac sacra die, quæ dat reis veniam.	Martyred Apostles, winning grace for penitents.
Ianitor cæli, doctor orbis pariter,	Keys of the Kingdom prove one great supremacy,
iudices sæcli, vera mundi lumina,	Teacher of nations was Saint Paul's activity;
per crucem alter, alter ense triumphans,	Cross for Saint Peter, sword for Paul, meant victory.
vitæ senatum laureati possident.	They shine as judges crowned for all eternity.
O Roma felix, quæ tantorum principum	Rome, favored city, your soil had the privilege
es purpurata pretioso sanguine,	Of being purpled by such leaders' martyrdom,
non laude tua, sed ipsorum meritis	Not for your merits, but by their great fortitude,
excellis omnem mundi pulchritudinem.	You can claim beauty, passing all in excellence.

Olivæ binæ pietatis unicæ,	Mystical olives, one in sacred tenderness,
fide devotos, spe robustos maxime,	Pray for us always, gain for us true happiness,
fonte repletos caritatis geminæ	When the things hoped for, clung to with fidelity,
post mortem carnis impetrate vivere.	Blossom in merits won by twofold charity.
Sit Trinitati sempiterna gloria,	Praise be unending, homage and all reverence,
honor, potestas atque iubilatio,	Glory and honor, now and through eternity,
in unitate, cui manet imperium	Joyful thanksgiving to the Blessèd Trinity,
ex tunc et modo per æterna sæcula. Amen.	Reigning for ever in Their perfect unity. Amen.

PSALMODY

Ant. 1   You are the Christ, the Son of the *li*ving God. * Blessèd are you
               Simon, *son* of John!

VIIIg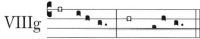

Psalm 117

O praise the Lord, *all* you nations, * acclaim him, *all* you peoples!
Strong is his *love* for us; * he is faith*ful* for ever.

Glory to the Father, and *to* the Son, * and to the *Ho*ly Spirit:
as it was in the begin*ning*, is now, * and will be for ev*er*. Amen.

Antiphon   You are the Christ, the Son of the *li*ving God. * Blessèd are you
               Simon, *son* of John!

Ant. 2   You are Peter, and *on* this rock * I will build *my* Church.

IIA

Psalm 147:12-20

O praise the *Lord*, Jerusalem! * Zion, praise *your* God!
He has strengthened the bars *of* your gates, * he has blessed the children *with*in you.
He established peace *on* your borders, * he feeds you with fin*est* wheat.
He sends out his word *to* the earth * and swiftly runs his *com*mand.
He showers down snow *white* as wool, * he scatters hoar-frost *like* ashes.
He hurls down hail*stones* like crumbs. * The waters are frozen at *his* touch;

he sends forth his word *and* it melts them: * at the breath of his mouth the wa*ters* flow.
He makes his word *known* to Jacob, * to Israel his laws and de*crees.*
He has not dealt thus with *other* nations; * he has not taught them his de*crees.*
Glory to the Father, and *to* the Son, * and to the Ho*ly* Spirit:
as it was in the begin*ning*, is now, * and will be for ever. *A*men.

Antiphon   You are Peter, and *on* this rock * I will build *my* Church.

Ant. 3   You are the chosen vessel of God, † blessèd apos*tle* Paul; * you
                preached the truth throughout the *whole* world.

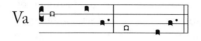

Va

                              Canticle   Ephesians 1:3-10

Praised be the God *and* Father * of
   our Lord Je*sus* Christ,
who has bestowed on us *in* Christ *
   every spiritual blessing in *the* heavens.
God chose us in him † before the
   world *be*gan * to be holy and blameless in *his* sight.
He predestined us † to be his adopted
   sons through Je*sus* Christ, * such was
   his will *and* pleasure,
that all might praise the glori*ous* favor *
   he has bestowed on us in his *be*lovèd.
In him and through his blood, † we
   have been *re*deemed, * and our sins

*for*given,
so immeasura*bly* generous * is God's
   favor *to* us.
God has given us the wisdom † to
   understand fully *the* mystery, * the
   plan he was pleased to decree *in*
   Christ.
A plan to be carried out *in* Christ, * in
   the fullness *of* time,
to bring all things into one *in* him, * in
   the heavens and *on* earth.
Glory to the Father, and to *the* Son, *
   and to the Ho*ly* Spirit:
as it was in the beginning, *is* now, * and
   will be for ever. *A*men.

Antiphon   You are the chosen vessel of God, † blessèd apos*tle* Paul; * you
                preached the truth throughout the *whole* world.

READING   Romans 1:1-2, 7
     Greetings from Paul, a servant of Christ Jesus, called to be an apostle and set
     apart to proclaim the gospel of God which he promised long ago through
     his prophets, as the holy Scriptures record— the gospel concerning his
     Son—to all in Rome, beloved of God and called to holiness, grace and peace
     from God our Father and the Lord Jesus Christ.

RESPONSORY (VI F)
The apostles proclaimed the *word* of God * and preached *it* faithfully.
— The apostles proclaimed the *word* of God * and preached *it* faithfully.
They bore witness to the resurrection of *Jesus* Christ.
— And preached *it* faithfully.
Glory to the Father, and *to* the Son, * and to the Ho*ly* Spirit.
— The apostles proclaimed the *word* of God * and preached *it* faithfully.

CANTICLE OF MARY

Ant. How glorious are the apostles of Christ; † in life they loved *one* another; * in death they rejoice together *for* ever.

INTERCESSIONS (VI F)

The Lord Jesus built his holy people on the foundation of the apos*tles* and prophets. * In faith *let* us pray:
Lord, come to the aid of your people.
You once called Simon, the fisherman, *to* catch men,
— now summon new workers who will bring the message of salvation *to* all peoples.
You calmed the waves so that your followers would *not* be drowned,
— guard your Church, protect it *from* all dangers.
You gathered your scattered flock around Peter after the *resurrection*,
— good Shepherd, bring all your people together *as* one flock.
You sent Paul as apostle to preach the good news *to* the Gentiles,
— let the word of salvation be proclaimed to *all* mankind.
You gave the keys of your kingdom into the hands of your *ho*ly Church,
— open the gates of that kingdom to all who trusted in your mercy *while* on earth.

Our Father . . .

Prayer

Lord our God,
encourage us through the prayers of Saints Peter and Paul.
May the apostles who strengthened the faith of the infant Church
help us on our way to salvation.
We ask this through our Lord Jesus Christ, your Son,
who lives and reigns with you and the Holy Spirit,
one God, for ever and ever.

Morning Prayer

HYMN

Apostolorum passio. (L.M.)

Apostolorum passio	This happy day is sanctified
diem sacravit sæculi,	As Martyrs' glory we recall;
Petri triumphum nobilem,	The cross bedewed with Peter's blood,
Pauli coronam præferens.	The sword that won a crown for Paul.
Coniunxit æquales viros	The triumph of their martyrdom
cruor triumphalis necis;	United these great souls in death,
Deum secutos præsulem	Whose faith in Christ had crowned their lives
Christi coronavit fides.	In service to their final breath.

Primus Petrus apostolus; nec Paulus impar gratia, electionis vas sacræ Petri adæquavit fidem.	Saint Peter held the primacy, Saint Paul would equal him in grace, When once, as chosen instrument The cause of Christ he would embrace.
Verso crucis vestigio Simon, honorem dans Deo, suspensus ascendit, dati non immemor oraculi.	Once, Simon, leaving Rome, turned back, To give, by death, full praise to God, That by the cross he too should tread The self-same path his Master trod.
Hinc Roma celsum verticem devotionis extulit, fundata tali sanguine et vate tanto nobilis.	Now Rome exults, as well she may, And strives to give devotion's due To one who sealed with his own blood His work as priest and pastor true.
Huc ire quis mundum putet, concurrere plebem poli: electa gentium caput, sedes magistri gentium.	And who can count the crowds that come As loving children to her gate, Where nations' Teacher, holy Paul Once dwelt and gladly met his fate.
Horum, Redemptor, quæsumus, ut principum consortio iungas precantes servulos in sempiterna sæcula. Amen.	Grant us, O Lord, the final grace Of sharing in their joy above, That with such princes we may praise Your bounty and undying love. Amen.

PSALMODY

Ant. 1   I know the one whom I have trusted † and I am certain that he, *the* just judge, * has power to keep safe what he has entrusted to me un*til* that Day.

Psalms and canticle from Sunday, Week I, 606.

Ant. 2   God's grace in me has not been *with*out fruit; * it is always at work *in* me.

Ant. 3   I have fought the good fight; † I have run the race to *the* finish; * I have kept *the* faith.

READING   1 Peter 4:13-14
Beloved, rejoice in the measure that you share Christ's sufferings. When his glory is revealed, you will rejoice exultantly. Happy are you when you are insulted for the sake of Christ, for then God's Spirit in its glory has come to rest on you.

RESPONSORY (VI F)
They gave *up* their lives * for the name of our Lord Je*sus* Christ.
— They gave *up* their lives * for the name of our Lord Je*sus* Christ.

They went forth rejoicing † because they have been found worthy to *suffer* insult,
— for the name of our Lord Je*sus* Christ.
Glory to the Father, and *to* the Son, * and to the Ho*ly* Spirit.
— They gave *up* their lives * for the name of our Lord Je*sus* Christ.

CANTICLE OF ZECHARIAH

Antiphon   Simon Peter said: Lord to whom *shall* we go? * You have the words of eter*nal* life;
and we believe and we are convinced † that you *are* the Christ, *
the Son of God, al*le*luia.

INTERCESSIONS (VI F)

The Lord Jesus built his holy people on the foundation of the apos*tles* and prophets. * In faith *let* us pray:
Bless your Church, O Lord.
You prayed that the faith of Peter *would* not fail,
— strengthen the faith *of* your Church.
You appeared to Peter after your resurrection and you appeared to Saul on the road *to* Damascus,
— strengthen our faith, so that we may steadfastly proclaim that you have risen *from* the dead.
You chose Paul as an apostle to preach your message *to* the Gentiles,
— make us faithful preachers *of* your Gospel.
You mercifully forgave Pe*ter's* denials,
— forgive us all *of* our sins.

Our Father . . .

Prayer

God our Father,
today you give us the joy
of celebrating the feast of the apostles Peter and Paul.
Through them your Church first received the faith.
Keep us true to their teaching.
We ask this through our Lord Jesus Christ, your Son,
who lives and reigns with you and the Holy Spirit,
one God, for ever and ever.

Evening Prayer II

HYMN

O Roma felix. Mode I (12.12.12.12)

O Roma felix, quæ tantorum principum	Rome, favored city, your soil had the privilege
es purpurata pretioso sanguine!	Of being purpled by such leaders' martyrdom,
Excellis omnem mundi pulchritudinem	You can claim beauty, passing all in excellence.
non laude tua, sed sanctorum meritis,	Not for your merits, but by deeds and sanctity
quos cruentatis iugulasti gladiis.	Of these Apostles whom you killed so cruelly.
Vos ergo modo, gloriosi martyres,	Glorious Martyrs, we beg with humility:
Petre beate, Paule, mundi lilium,	Peter, Christ's Vicar, Paul his chosen instrument,
cælestis aulæ triumphales milites,	Soldiers triumphant in the realm of blessèdness,
precibus almis vestris nos ab omnibus	Shield us from evil that no harm may injure us,
munite malis, ferte super æthera.	Bring us to heaven by your prayer's sollicitude.
Gloria Patri per immensa sæcula,	Praise to the Father, now and through eternity,
sit tibi, Nate, decus et imperium,	And to you, Jesus, glory and dominion,
honor, potestas Sanctoque Spiritui;	And to the Spirit, adoration's reverence,
sit Trinitati salus individua	So that due homage to the Blessèd Trinity
per infinita sæculorum sæcula. Amen.	May be continued where delight is infinite. Amen.

PSALMODY

Ant. 1   I have prayed for you, Peter, that your faith may not fail; † and when you have *turned* to me, * you must strengthen the faith *of* your brothers.

VIIIg

Psalm 116: 10-19

I trusted, even *when* I said, * "I am sore*ly* afflicted,"
and when I said in *my* alarm: * "No man *can* be trusted."
How can I re*pay* the Lord * for his good*ness* to me?
The cup of salvation *I* will raise; * I will call *on* the Lord's name.
My vows to the Lord I *will* fulfill * before *all* his people.
O precious in the eyes *of* the Lord * is the death *of* his faithful.

Your servant, Lord, † your serv*ant* am I; * you have loos*ened* my bonds.
A thanksgiving sacri*fice* I make: * I will call *on* the Lord's name.
My vows to the Lord I *will* fulfill * before *all* his people,
in the courts of the house *of* the Lord, * in your midst, O Jerusalem.
Glory to the Father, and *to* the Son, * and to the *Holy* Spirit:
as it was in the begin*ning*, is now, * and will be for ev*er.* Amen.

Antiphon   I have prayed for you, Peter, that your faith may not fail; † and when you have *turned* to me, * you must strengthen the faith *of* your brothers.

Ant. 2   Willingly I boast *of* my weaknesses, * that the power of Christ
may live *in* me.

IIA

Psalm 126

When the Lord delivered *Zion*
from bondage, * it seemed like
a dream.
Then was our mouth *filled* with
laughter, * on our lips there *were*
songs.
The heathens themselves *said*: "What
marvels * the Lord worked *for* them!"
What marvels the Lord *worked* for us!
* Indeed we *were* glad.
Deliver us, O Lord, *from* our bondage *

as streams in *dry* land.
Those who are sow*ing* in tears * will
sing when *they* reap.
They go out, they go out, *full* of tears, *
carrying seed for *the* sowing:
they come back, they come back, *full* of
song, * carrying *their* sheaves.
Glory to the Father, and *to* the Son, *
and to the Ho*ly* Spirit:
as it was in the begin*ning*, is now, *
and will be for ever. *A*men.

Antiphon   Willingly I boast *of* my weaknesses, * that the power of Christ
may live *in* me.

Ant. 3   You are shepherd of the flock, † the prince of the *a*postles; * to
you were entrusted the keys of the kingdom *of* heaven.

Va

Canticle   Ephesians 1:3-10

Praised be the God *and* Father * of
our Lord Je*sus* Christ,
who has bestowed on us *in* Christ *
every spiritual blessing in *the* heavens.
God chose us in him † before the
world *be*gan * to be holy and blameless in *his* sight.
He predestined us † to be his adopted
sons through Je*sus* Christ, * such was
his will *and* pleasure,
that all might praise the glori*ous* favor *
he has bestowed on us in his *be*lovèd.

In him and through his blood, † we
have been *re*deemed, * and our sins
*for*given,
so immeasura*bly* generous * is God's
favor *to* us.
God has given us the wisdom † to
understand fully *the* mystery, * the
plan he was pleased to decree *in*
Christ.
A plan to be carried out *in* Christ, * in
the fullness *of* time,
to bring all things into one *in* him, * in
the heavens and *on* earth.

Glory to the Father, and to *the* Son, * and to the Ho*ly* Spirit: | as it was in the beginning, *is* now, * and will be for ever. *A*men.

Antiphon   You are shepherd of the flock, † the prince of the *a*postles; * to you were entrusted the keys of the kingdom *of* heaven.

READING   1 Corinthians 15:3-5, 8a

I handed on to you first of all what I myself received, that Christ died for our sins in accordance with the Scriptures; that he was buried and, in accordance with the Scriptures, rose on the third day; that he was seen by Cephas, then by the Twelve. Last of all he was seen by me.

RESPONSORY (VI F)

The apostles proclaimed the *word* of God * and preached *it* faithfully.
— The apostles proclaimed the *word* of God * and preached *it* faithfully.
They testified to the resurrection of *Jes*us Christ.
— And preached *it* faithfully.
Glory to the Father, and *to* the Son, * and to the Ho*ly* Spirit.
— The apostles proclaimed the *word* of God * and preached *it* faithfully.

CANTICLE OF MARY

Antiphon   Peter the apostle † and Paul the teacher *of* the Gentiles * taught us your law, O Lord.

INTERCESSIONS (VI F)

The Lord Jesus built his holy people on the foundation of the apos*tles* and prophets. * In faith *let* us pray:
Lord, come to the aid of your *people.*
You once called Simon, the fisherman, *to* catch men,
— now summon new workers who will bring the message of salvation *to* all peoples.
You calmed the waves so that your followers would *not* be drowned,
— guard your Church, protect it *from* all dangers.
You gathered your scattered flock around Peter after the *res*urrection,
— good Shepherd, bring all your people together *as* one flock.
You sent Paul as apostle to preach the good news *to* the Gentiles,
— let the word of salvation be proclaimed to *all* mankind.
You gave the keys of your kingdom into the hands of your *holy* Church,
— open the gates of that kingdom to all who trusted in your mercy *while* on earth.

Our Father . . .

Prayer

Lord our God,
encourage us through the prayers of Saints Peter and Paul.
May the apostles who strengthened the faith of the infant Church
help us on our way to salvation.
We ask this through our Lord Jesus Christ, your Son,
who lives and reigns with you and the Holy Spirit,
one God, for ever and ever.

June 30
FIRST MARTYRS OF THE CHURCH OF ROME

From the common of several martyrs, 1214.

Morning Prayer

CANTICLE OF ZECHARIAH

Ant.   The great numbers of martyrs stood firm in their love for *one*
another * because they shared the same spirit and the *same* faith.

Prayer

Father,
you sanctified the Church of Rome
with the blood of its first martyrs.
May we find strength from their courage
and rejoice in their triumph.
We ask this through our Lord Jesus Christ, your Son,
who lives and reigns with you and the Holy Spirit,
one God, for ever and ever.

Evening Prayer

CANTICLE OF MARY

Ant.   They loved Christ in this life † and imitated him *in* their death;
* and so they will rejoice with him *for* ever.

July 1
BLESSED JUNIPERO SERRA, PRIEST

From the common of pastors: missionary, 1238.

Prayer

God most high,
your servant Junipero Serra
brought the gospel of Christ
to the peoples of Mexico and California
and firmly established the Church among them.

By his intercession,
and through the example of his evangelical zeal,
inspire us to be faithful witnesses of Jesus Christ,
who lives and reigns with you and the Holy Spirit,
one God, for ever and ever.

July 3
THOMAS, APOSTLE
Feast

From the common of apostles, 1206, except for the following:

Morning Prayer
HYMN

Qui luce. (L.M.)

Qui luce splendes ordinis apostolorum maxima, Thoma, benignus accipe laudes tibi quas pangimus.	Saint Thomas, whom the Savior chose When here on earth, as special friend, Accept our joyous hymn of praise, And to our earnest prayer attend.
Te lucidis in sedibus amore Christus collocat; amore promptus expetis tu pro Magistro commori.	Your love for Christ made you desire To die with him and share his plight; His love for you gave you a throne Of glory in his realm of light.
Te torquet et dilectio narrantibus cum fratribus vis certus esse, visere, palpare Iesu vulnera.	Your tortured love could not believe The Ten had seen him, as they said; But you must touch his hands and feet To prove him risen from the dead.
Quantoque cordis gaudio ipsum misertum conspicis, Deumque dicis credulus, fervore adorans pectoris!	And later when you saw him too With joy, his mercy you adored, Acclaiming his as truly God, And worshiping your risen Lord.
Nobisque qui non vidimus per te fides fit acrior, fit æstus et potentior quo Christi amorem quærimus.	As you once grew to know our Lord, Give us more faith, both strong and firm, And make our love grow deeper yet For Jesus whom we have not seen.
Christo sit omnis gloria, qui te rogante præbeat nobis fide ambulantibus ipsum videre perpetim. Amen.	All glory be to Christ, our Lord, Who by your prayer will grant us grace, When we have blindly walked in faith, To see the glory of his face. Amen.

PSALMODY

Ant. 1   Lord, we do not know where *you* are going; * how can we *know* the way?
Jesus replied: I *am* the way, * the truth *and* the life.

Psalms and canticle from Sunday, Week I, 606.

Ant. 2   Thomas, who was called the Twin, *was* not present * when Jesus appeared to the *a*postles;
so they told him: We have *seen* the Lord, * al*le*luia.

Ant. 3   With your hand, touch the mark of *the* nails; * doubt no longer, but believe, al*le*luia.

READING   Ephesians 2:19-22

You are strangers and aliens no longer. No, you are fellow citizens of the saints and members of the household of God. You form a building which rises on the foundation of the apostles and prophets, with Christ Jesus himself as the capstone. Through him the whole structure is fitted together and takes shape as a holy temple in the Lord; in him you are being built into this temple, to become a dwelling place for God in the Spirit.

RESPONSORY (VI F)

You have *made* them rulers * over all *the* earth.
— You have *made* them rulers * over all *the* earth.
They will always remember your *name*, O Lord,
— over all *the* earth.
Glory to the Father, and *to* the Son, * and to the Ho*ly* Spirit.
— You have *made* them rulers * over all *the* earth.

CANTICLE OF ZECHARIAH

Ant.   Because you have seen me, Thomas, † you *have* believed; * blessèd are they who have not seen me and yet *be*lieve.

INTERCESSIONS (VI F)

Belovèd friends, we have inherited heaven along with *the* apostles. * Let us give thanks to the Father for *all* his gifts:
The company of apostles praises you, O Lord.
Praise be to you, Lord, for the banquet of Christ's body and blood given us through *the* apostles,
— which refreshes us and *gives* us life.
The company of apostles praises you, O Lord.
Praise be to you, Lord, for the feast of your word prepared for us by *the* apostles,
— giving us *light* and joy.

The company of apostles praises you, O Lord.
Praise be to you, Lord, for your holy Church, founded on *the* apostles,
— where we are gathered together into *your* community.
The company of apostles praises you, O Lord.
Praise be to you, Lord, for the cleansing power of baptism and penance that you
   have entrusted to *your* apostles,
— through which we are cleansed *of* our sins.
The company of apostles praises you, O Lord.

Our Father . . .

Prayer

   Almighty Father,
   as we honor Thomas the apostle,
   let us always experience the help of his prayers.
   May we have eternal life by believing in Jesus,
   who Thomas acknowledged as Lord,
   for he lives and reigns with you and the Holy Spirit,
   one God, for ever and ever.

Evening Prayer

HYMN, psalms and canticle from the common of apostles, 1208.
Antiphons, as in Morning Prayer, 1003.

READING   Ephesians 4:11-13
   Christ gave apostles, prophets, evangelists, pastors and teachers in roles of
   service for the faithful to build up the body of Christ, till we become one in
   faith and in the knowledge of God's Son, and form that perfect man who is
   Christ come to full stature.

RESPONSORY (VI F)
Tell *all* the nations * how glorious *God* is.
— Tell *all* the nations * how glorious *God* is.
Make known his wonders to *every* people.
— How glorious *God* is.
Glory to the Father, and *to* the Son, * and to the Ho*ly* Spirit.
— Tell *all* the nations * how glorious *God* is.

CANTICLE OF MARY
Ant.   I touched the mark of the nails with my fingers; † I put my
                    hand into his *side* and said: * My Lord and my God, al*le*luia.

INTERCESSIONS (VI F)

My brothers, we build on the foundation of *the* apostles. * Let us pray to our
almighty Father for his holy peo*ple* and say:

Be mindful of your Church, O Lord.

Father, you wanted your Son to be seen first by the apostles after the
resurrection *from* the dead,

— we ask you to make us his witnesses to the farthest corners *of* the world.

You sent your Son to preach the good news *to* the poor,

— help us to preach the Gospel to *every* creature.

You sent your Son to sow the seed of un*end*ing life,

— grant that we who work at sowing the seed may share the joy *of* the harvest.

You sent your Son to reconcile all men to you *through* his blood,

— help us all to work toward achieving this recon*cili*ation.

Your Son sits at your right *hand* in heaven,

— let the dead enter your king*dom* of joy.

Our Father . . .

Prayer

Almighty Father,
as we honor Thomas the apostle,
let us always experience the help of his prayers.
May we have eternal life by believing in Jesus,
who Thomas acknowledged as Lord,
for he lives and reigns with you and the Holy Spirit,
one God, for ever and ever.

July 4
ELIZABETH OF PORTUGAL

From the common of holy women: those who worked for the underprivileged, 1284.

Prayer

Father of peace and love,
you gave Saint Elizabeth the gift of reconciling enemies.
By the help of her prayers
give us the courage to work for peace among men,
that we may be called the sons of God.
We ask this through our Lord Jesus Christ, your Son,
who lives and reigns with you and the Holy Spirit,
one God, for ever and ever.

July 5
ANTHONY MARY ZACCARIA, PRIEST

From the common of pastors, 1238, or of holy men: teachers, 1285, or religious, 1282.

Prayer

Lord,
enable us to grasp in the spirit of Saint Paul,
the sublime wisdom of Jesus Christ,
the wisdom which inspired Saint Anthony Zaccaria
to preach the message of salvation in your Church.
Grant this through our Lord Jesus Christ, your Son,
who lives and reigns with you and the Holy Spirit,
one God, for ever and ever.

July 6
MARIA GORETTI, VIRGIN AND MARTYR

From the common of one martyr, 1228, or of virgins, 1253.

Prayer

Father,
source of innocence and lover of chastity,
you gave Saint Maria Goretti the privilege
of offering her life in witness to Christ.
As you gave her the crown of martyrdom,
let her prayers keep us faithful to your teaching.
We ask this through our Lord Jesus Christ, your Son,
who lives and reigns with you and the Holy Spirit,
one God, for ever and ever.

July 9
AUGUSTINE ZHAO RONG, PRIEST,
AND COMPANIONS, MARTYRS

From the common of several martyrs, 1214.

Prayer

Father,
we celebrate the memory of St. Augustine and his companions
who died for their faithful witnessing to Christ.
Give us the strength to follow their example,
loyal and faithful to the end.
We ask this through our Lord Jesus Christ, your Son,
who lives and reigns with you and the Holy Spirit,
one God, for ever and ever.

July 11
BENEDICT, ABBOT
Memorial
From the common of holy men: religious, 1282, except for the following:

Morning Prayer

CANTICLE OF ZECHARIAH
Ant.   He lived a *holy* life; * Benedict, blessèd in name and *in* grace.

Prayer
God our Father,
you made Saint Benedict an outstanding guide
to teach men how to live in your service.
Grant that by preferring your love to everything else,
we may walk in the way of your commandments.
We ask this through our Lord Jesus Christ, your Son,
who lives and reigns with you and the Holy Spirit,
one God, for ever and ever.

Evening Prayer

CANTICLE OF MARY
Ant.   He received the Lord's blessing † and the merciful saving pow*er*
of God; * such is the fortune of those who seek *the* Lord.

July 13
HENRY
From the common of holy men, 1263.

Prayer
Lord,
you filled Saint Henry with your love
and raised him from the cares of an earthly kingdom
to eternal happiness in heaven.
In the midst of the changes of this world,
may his prayers keep us free from sin
and help us on our way toward you.
Grant this through our Lord Jesus Christ, your Son,
who lives and reigns with you and the Holy Spirit,
one God, for ever and ever.

July 14
BLESSED KATERI TEKAKWITHA, VIRGIN
Memorial

From the common of virgins, 1253.

Prayer

Lord God,
you called the virgin, blessèd Kateri Tekakwitha,
to shine among the Indian people
as an example of innocent life.
Through her intercession,
may all peoples of every tribe, tongue, and nation,
having been gathered into your Church,
proclaim your greatness
in one song of praise.
We ask this through our Lord Jesus Christ, your Son,
who lives and reigns with you and the Holy Spirit,
one God, for ever and ever.

July 15
BONAVENTURE, BISHOP AND DOCTOR
Memorial

From the common of pastors, 1238, or of doctors, 1246.

Prayer

All-powerful Father,
may we who celebrate the feast of Saint Bonaventure
always benefit from his wisdom
and follow the example of his love.
Grant this through our Lord Jesus Christ, your Son,
who lives and reigns with you and the Holy Spirit,
one God, for ever and ever.

July 16
OUR LADY OF MOUNT CARMEL
From the common of the Blessed Virgin Mary, 1192.

Morning Prayer

CANTICLE OF ZECHARIAH

Ant.   I have openly sought wisdom *in* my prayers, * and it has blos-
                        somed like ear*ly* grapes.

Prayer

Father,
may the prayers of the Virgin Mary protect us
and help us to reach Christ her Son
who lives and reigns with you and the Holy Spirit,
one God, for ever and ever.

Evening Prayer

CANTICLE OF MARY

Ant.   Mary heard the word of *God* and kept it; * she pondered it in
her heart.

July 18
CAMILLUS DE LELLIS, PRIEST

From the common of holy men: those who worked for the underprivileged, 1284.

Prayer

Father,
you gave Saint Camillus a special love for the sick.
Through his prayers inspire us with your grace,
so that by serving you in our brothers and sisters
we may come safely to you at the end of our lives.
We ask this through our Lord Jesus Christ, your Son,
who lives and reigns with you and the Holy Spirit,
one God, for ever and ever.

July 20
APOLLINARIS, BISHOP AND MARTYR

From the common of one martyr, 1228, or of pastors, 1238.

Prayer

God of power and mercy,
you gave St. Apollinaris, your martyr, victory over pain and suffering.
Strengthen us who celebrate this day of triumph
and help us to be victorious over the evils that threaten us.
Grant this through our Lord Jesus Christ, your Son,
who lives and reigns with you and the Holy Spirit,
one God, for ever and ever.

July 21
LAWRENCE OF BRINDISI, PRIEST AND DOCTOR

From the common of pastors, 1238, or of doctors, 1246.

Prayer

Lord,
for the glory of your name and the salvation of our souls
you gave Lawrence of Brindisi
courage and right judgment.
By his prayers,
help us to know what we should do
and give us the courage to do it.
We ask this through our Lord Jesus Christ, your Son,
who lives and reigns with you and the Holy Spirit,
one God, for ever and ever.

July 22
MARY MAGDALENE
Memorial

From the common of holy women, 1274, except for the following:

Morning Prayer
HYMN
Aurora surgit. (L.M.)

Aurora surgit lucida Christi triumphos afferens, cum corpus eius visere, Maria, vis et ungere.	The golden dawn is breaking fast, And Christ is risen from the tomb, When, Mary, you arrive in haste With spices to embalm him dead.
Anhela curris; angelus at ecce lætus prædocet mortis refractis postibus redisse quem desideras.	With breathless speed you reach the spot, To find an angel full of joy, Who tells you that the one you seek Has broken all the bonds of death.
Sed te manet iucundius intacti amoris præmium, cum, voce plusans vilicum, tuum Magistrum conspicis.	But greater happiness is yours, Reward of love's fidelity, As speaking to the gardener, Behold! It is your smiling Lord.
Quæ cum dolenti Virgine hæsisti acerbo stipiti, tu prima vivi ab inferis es testis atque nuntia.	You shared the Virgin Mother's woe, And watched beside the bitter Cross, You were the first to hear the news That Christ had risen from the dead.

O flos venuste Magdalæ,	O fairest flow'r of Magdala,
o Christi amore saucia,	Aflame with deepest love for Christ,
tu caritatis ignibus	Enkindle in our hearts that fire
fac nostra corda ferveant.	Of charity that counts no cost.
Da, Christe, tantæ servulæ	Lord Jesus, grant us too the grace
dilectionem persequi,	To imitate such ardent love,
et nos ut incælestibus	That we may your great mercy sing
tibi canamus gloriam. Amen.	In joy with Magdalen above. Amen.

PSALMODY

Ant. 1   Very early in the morning after the sabbath, † Mary
               Magdalene came *to* the tomb, * just as the *sun* was rising.

Psalms and canticle from Sunday, Week I, 606.

Ant. 2   My heart burns within me; I long to see my Lord; † I *look* for
               him, * but I cannot find where they have put him, al*le*luia.

Ant. 3   While Mary was weeping she bent down to look into the
               tomb; † she saw two angels seat*ed* there, * clothed in white,
               al*le*luia.

READING   Romans 12:1-2
     Brothers, I beg you through the mercy of God to offer your bodies as a
     living sacrifice holy and acceptable to God, your spiritual worship. Do not
     conform yourselves to this age but be transformed by the renewal of your
     mind, so that you may judge what is God's will, what is good, pleasing and
     perfect.

RESPONSORY (VI F)
Mary, *do* not weep; * the Lord is risen from *the* dead.
— Mary, *do* not weep; * the Lord is risen from *the* dead.
Go to my brothers and *say* to them:
— The Lord is risen from *the* dead.
Glory to the Father, and *to* the Son, * and to the Ho*ly* Spirit.
— Mary, *do* not weep; * the Lord is risen from *the* dead.

CANTICLE OF ZECHARIAH
Ant.   When Jesus had risen from the dead on the morning after the
               sabbath, † he appeared first to *Mary* Magdalene, * from whom
               he had cast out sev*en* devils.

INTERCESSIONS, from the common of holy women, 1276, or from the weekday.

Prayer

Father,
your Son first entrusted to Mary Magdalene
the joyful news of his resurrection.
By her prayers and example
may we proclaim Christ as our living Lord
and one day see him in glory,
for he lives and reigns with you and the Holy Spirit,
one God, for ever and ever.

Evening Prayer

HYMN

Magalæ sidus. (11.11.11.5)

Magdalæ sidus, mulier beata,	Magdala's glory, light of holy women,
te pio cultu veneramur omnes,	Healed and forgiven by our gracious Savior,
quam sibi Christus sociavit arcti	Your true repentance, binding your to Jesus,
fœder*e* amoris.	Gladly we honor.
Cum tib*i* illius patefit potestas	Once he had shown you his supreme dominion
dæmonum vires abigens tremenda,	Over all evil, demons' pow'r expelling,
tu fide gaudes potiore necti	Joy bound you to him with a faith the stronger,
grata medenti.	Grateful for healing.
Hæret hinc urgens tibi caritatis	Love and repentance urge you on hence forward,
vis ut insistas pedibus Magistri,	Nought will withdraw you from the Master's service,
fervidis illum comitata semper	Never intruding, but alert and constant,
sedula curis.	Following always.
Tuque comploras Dominum, crucique	Close to your Savior in his hours of anguish,
impetu flagrans pietatis astas;	Mourning and weeping by the Cross of Jesus,
membra tu terges studios*a* et ungis	Richly anointing sacred limbs then destined
danda sepulcro.	For their entombment.
Quos amor Christi peperit, triumphis	Make us companions of your love and sorrow,
nos fac adiungi socios per ævum,	Since Christ accepts us through his bitter Passion,
atque Dilecto simul affluenter	So that together we may praise for ever
pangere laudes. Amen.	Jesus our Savior. Amen.

Ant. 1   Jesus said to Mary: † Woman, why *are* you weeping? * Whom *do* you seek?

Psalms and canticle from the common of holy women, 1279.

Ant. 2   They have taken my *Lord* away, * and I do not know where they *have* put him.

Ant. 3   Jesus said: Mary. † She turned to him and said: *Rab*boni, * which *means* teacher.

READING   Romans 8:28-30

We know that God makes all things work together for the good of those who have been called according to his decree. Those whom he foreknew he predestined to share the image of his Son, that the Son might be the first-born of many brothers. Those he predestined he likewise called; those he called he also justified; and those he justified he in turn glorified.

RESPONSORY (VI F)

Mary, *do* not weep; * the Lord is risen from *the* dead.
— Mary, *do* not weep; * the Lord is risen from *the* dead.
Go to my brothers and *say* to them:
— The Lord is risen from *the* dead.
Glory to the Father, and *to* the Son, * and to the Ho*ly* Spirit.
— Mary, *do* not weep; * the Lord is risen from *the* dead.

CANTICLE OF MARY

Ant.   Mary ran and told *the* disciples * that she had seen the Lord, al*le*luia.

INTERCESSIONS, from the common of holy women as in Morning Prayer, 1276, or from the current weekday.
Prayer, as in Morning Prayer, 1012.

July 23
BRIDGET OF SWEDEN, RELIGIOUS

From the common of holy women: religious, 1282.

Prayer

Lord our God,
you revealed the secrets of heaven to Saint Bridget
as she meditated on the suffering and death of your Son.
May your people rejoice in the revelation of your glory.
Grant this through our Lord Jesus Christ, your Son,
who lives and reigns with you and the Holy Spirit,
one God, for ever and ever.

July 24
SHARBEL MAKHLUF, PRIEST

From the common of pastors, 1238, or of holy men: religious, 1282.

Prayer

God our Father,
in St. Sharbel Makhluf, you gave a light to your faithful people.
You made him a pastor of the Church

to feed your sheep with his word
and to teach them by his example.
Help us by his prayers to keep the faith he taught
and follow the way of life he showed us.
Grant this through our Lord Jesus Christ, your Son,
who lives and reigns with you and the Holy Spirit,
one God, for ever and ever.

July 25
JAMES, APOSTLE
Feast
From the common of apostles, 1206, except for the following:

Morning Prayer
HYMN
Te nostra. (L.M.)

Te nostra lætis laudibus,	With joyous song we greet your feast,
Iacobe, tollunt cantica,	Saint James, apostle of our Lord,
quem Christus art*e* ex retium	Who called you from a fisher's nets
ad tanta vexit culmina.	To gain far higher a reward.
Ipso vocante, concitus	His call to leave all things and come,
cum fratre linquis omnia,	Your younger brother also heard,
ipsius et fis nominis	And eagerly you both became
verbique præco fervidus.	Most fervent preachers of his word.
Testis potentis dexteræ	You saw the Son of Man indeed
præclarus alta conspicis,	Transfigured on the mountain height,
in monte celsam gloriam,	You saw his bitter agony
tristes in hort*o* angustias.	Enshrouded by the gloom of night.
Qui promptus exstas, poscitur	You once declared your eagerness
cum passionis poculum,	To share your Master's pow'r and fame,
tu primus ex apostolis	And of the Twelve you were the first
pro Christ*i* amore plecteris.	To suffer for his holy name.
Iesu fidelis assecla	O faithful follower of Christ,
satorque lucis cælicæ,	And sower of the Gospel's light,
mentes fide clarescere,	Enrich our minds with living faith
da spe foveri pectora.	And hope that guides our steps aright.
Christi sequi da sedulos	Enable us to keep God's law,
præcepta nos in sæculo,	Observing his command to love,
hymnos ut olim gloriæ	That we may ever sing his praise
fundamus illi perpetim. Amen.	In joy and happiness above. Amen.

Ant. 1   As he was walking along, † Jesus saw James, the *son* of Zebedee, * and his brother John, *and* he called them.

Psalms and canticle from Sunday, Week I, 606.

Ant. 2   Immediately they left their nets *and* their father * and fol*lowed* him.

Ant. 3   You shall drink from the cup that I *shall* drink from * and you shall be baptized as I *am* baptized.

READING   Ephesians 2:19-22

You are strangers and aliens no longer. No, you are fellow citizens of the saints and members of the household of God. You form a building which rises on the foundation of the apostles and prophets, with Christ Jesus himself as the capstone. Through him the whole structure is fitted together and takes shape as a holy temple in the Lord; in him you are being built into this temple, to become a dwelling place for God in the Spirit.

RESPONSORY (VI F)

You have *made* them rulers * over all *the* earth.
— You have *made* them rulers * over all *the* earth.
They will always remember your *name*, O Lord,
— over all *the* earth.
Glory to the Father, and *to* the Son, * and to the Ho*ly* Spirit.
— You have *made* them rulers * over all *the* earth.

CANTICLE OF ZECHARIAH

Ant.   Jesus took Peter, James and his brother John † and led them up a high mountain where they could *be* alone, * and he was transfigured *be*fore them.

INTERCESSIONS (VI F)

Belovèd friends, we have inherited heaven along with *the* apostles. * Let us give thanks to the Father for *all* his gifts:
The company of apostles praises you, O Lord.
Praise be to you, Lord, for the banquet of Christ's body and blood given us through *the* apostles,
— which refreshes us and *gives* us life.
The company of apostles praises you, O Lord.
Praise be to you, Lord, for the feast of your word prepared for us by *the* apostles,
— giving us *light* and joy.
The company of apostles praises you, O Lord.
Praise be to you, Lord, for your holy Church, founded on *the* apostles,
— where we are gathered together into *your* community.

The company of apostles praises you, O Lord.
Praise be to you, Lord, for the cleansing power of baptism and penance that you
    have entrusted to *your* apostles,
— through which we are cleansed *of* our sins.
The company of apostles praises you, O Lord.

Our Father . . .

Prayer

Almighty Father,
by the martyrdom of Saint James
you blessed the work of the early Church.
May his profession of faith give us courage
and his prayers bring us strength.
We ask this through our Lord Jesus Christ, your Son,
who lives and reigns with you and the Holy Spirit,
one God, for ever and ever.

Evening Prayer

HYMN, from the common of apostles, 1203.

Ant. 1   Jesus took Peter, James and *John* with him, * and he became
                 fearful and be*gan* to tremble.

Psalms and canticle from the common of the apostles, 1208.

Ant. 2   Then he said to them: *Stay* awake * and pray that you may not
                 be tempted.

Ant. 3   King Herod began presecuting certain members of *the* Church.
                 * He beheaded James, the brother *of* John.

READING   Ephesians 4:11-13
    Christ gave apostles, prophets, evangelists, pastors and teachers in roles of
    service for the faithful to build up the body of Christ, till we become one in
    faith and in the knowledge of God's Son, and form that perfect man who is
    Christ come to full stature.

RESPONSORY (VI F)
Tell *all* the nations * how glorious *God* is.
— Tell *all* the nations * how glorious *God* is.
Make known his wonders to *every* people.
— How glorious *God* is.
Glory to the Father, and *to* the Son, * and to the Ho*ly* Spirit.
— Tell *all* the nations * how glorious *God* is.

CANTICLE OF MARY

Ant.   Whoever wishes to be great among you must *be* your servant; *
        whoever wishes to be first among you must be the slave *of* all.

INTERCESSIONS (VI F)

My brothers, we build on the foundation of *the* apostles. * Let us pray to our
    almighty Father for his holy peo*ple* and say:
Be mindful of your Church, O Lord.
Father, you wanted your Son to be seen first by the apostles after the
    resurrection *from* the dead,
— we ask you to make us his witnesses to the farthest corners *of* the world.
You sent your Son to preach the good news *to* the poor,
— help us to preach the Gospel to *every* creature.
You sent your Son to sow the seed of un*end*ing life,
— grant that we who work at sowing the seed may share the joy *of* the harvest.
You sent your Son to reconcile all men to you *through* his blood,
— help us all to work toward achieving this recon*cili*ation.
Your Son sits at your right *hand* in heaven,
— let the dead enter your king*dom* of joy.

Our Father . . .

Prayer

Almighty Father,
by the martyrdom of Saint James
you blessed the work of the early Church.
May his profession of faith give us courage
and his prayers bring us strength.
We ask this through our Lord Jesus Christ, your Son,
who lives and reigns with you and the Holy Spirit,
one God, for ever and ever.

July 26
JOACHIM AND ANN, PARENTS OF MARY
Memorial
From the common of holy men,1263, except for the following:

Morning Prayer
HYMN
Nocti succedit. (L.M.)

Nocti succedit lucifer,	The morning star will pierce the night,
quem mox aurora sequitur,	Then rosy tints of dawn appear,
solis ortum prænuntians	Announcing that the sun will rise
mundum lustrantis lumine.	To bathe the world in luster clear.
Christus sol est iustitiæ,	The Sun of Justice is our Lord,
aurora Mater gratiæ,	The Dawn is Mary, full of grace,
quam, Anna, præis rutilans	Saint Ann the fair and gleaming star,
legis propellens tenebras.	Before whom ancient Law gives place.
Anna, radix uberrima,	Saint Ann, you were the fruitful root,
arbor tu salutifera,	The tree that would salvation bring,
virgam producens floridam	By bearing her, the chosen stem,
quæ Christum nobis attulit.	The Mother of our Lord and King.
O matris Christi genetrix	Most holy parents of the one
tuque parens sanctissime,	Who is our loving Mother too,
natæ favente merito,	With her, now pray for us who fall:
nobis rogate veniam.	Our pardon win, our strength renew.
Iesu, tibi sit gloria,	All glory, Jesus, be to you
qui natus est de Virgine,	Once born of Virgin undefiled,
cum Patre et almo Spiritu,	Who, with the Spirit of your Love
in sempiterna sæcula. Amen.	And God the Father, ever reign. Amen.

READING   Isaiah 55:33

> Come to me heedfully,
>   listen that you may have life.
> I will renew with you the everlasting covenant,
>   the benefits assured to David.

RESPONSORY (VI F)

In the tender compassion *of* our God, * the Lord has come *to* us.
— In the tender compassion *of* our God, * the Lord has come *to* us.
He has raised up Je*sus,* our savior.
— The Lord has come *to* us.
Glory to the Father, and *to* the Son, * and to the Ho*ly* Spirit.
— In the tender compassion *of* our God, * the Lord has come *to* us.

CANTICLE OF ZECHARIAH

Ant.   Blessèd be the Lord, the God of Israel; † he has raised up for us
                   a *mighty* savior, * born of the house of his ser*vant* David.

INTERCESSIONS, from the common of holy men, 1265, or from the weekday.

Prayer

God of our fathers,
you gave Saints Joachim and Ann
the privilege of being the parents of Mary,
the mother of your incarnate Son.
May their prayers help us to attain
the salvation you have promised to your people.
Grant this through our Lord Jesus Christ, your Son,
who lives and reigns with you and the Holy Spirit,
one God, for ever and ever.

Evening Prayer

HYMN

Dum tuas festo. (11.11.11.5)

Dum tuas festo, pater o colende,
cantico laudes habet hæc corona,
vocis ac mentis, Ioachim, benigne
    accipe munus.

Longa te regum series avorum
Abrahæ prolem tulit atque David;
clarior mundi domina coruscas
    prole Maria.

Sic tuum germen benedict*a* ab Anna
editum, patrum repetita vota
implet, et mæsto properat referre
    gaudia mundo.

Laus tibi, Prolis Pater increatæ;
laus tibi, summi Suboles Parentis;
summa laus, compar, tibi sit per omne,
    Spiritus, ævum. Amen.

Joachim favored with a special mission
In the divine plan as a chosen parent,
Graciously hear us as we humbly praise you,
    Most favored father.

Ancestors royal, patriarchs and prophets,
Abraham, David, none would have such glory;
You and no other would deserve the title,
    Father of Mary.

Ann's gentle daughter would fulfil the promise
Of a redeemer born in time of woman;
Her prompt acceptance of the angel's message
    Gladdens us always.

Praise to you, Father of the Word Eternal,
Praise to you, Jesus, Son and Word Incarnate,
And to the Spirit from their love proceeding,
    Praise be for ever. Amen.

READING   Romans 9:4-5

To the Israelites belonged the adoption, the glory, the covenants, the lawgiving, the worship, and the promises; theirs were the patriarchs, and from
them came the Messiah (I speak of his human origins). Blessed forever be
God who is over all! Amen.

RESPONSORY (VI F)

He has come to the help of his *ser*vant Israel; * he has remembered his promise
  of mercy.
— He has come to the help of his *ser*vant Israel; * he has remembered his
  promise *of* mercy.
According to the promise he made *to* our fathers,
— he has remembered his promise *of* mercy.
Glory to the Father, and *to* the Son, * and to the Ho*ly* Spirit.
— He has come to the help of his *ser*vant Israel; * he has remembered his
  promise *of* mercy.

CANTICLE OF MARY

Ant.   From the noble stem of Jesse a branch has sprung, † and from
                       this branch a beau*ti*ful flower, * rich in scent, *has* blossomed.

INTERCESSIONS, from the common of holy men, 1270, or from weekday.
Prayer, as in Morning Prayer, 1019.

July 29
MARTHA
Memorial
From the common of holy women, 1275, except for the following:

Morning Prayer
HYMN
Quas tibi laudes. (11.11.11.5)

Quas tibi laudes ferimusque vota,	O blessèd Martha, honored friend of Jesus,
nos tuis possint meritis iuvare,	May our rejoicing over all your merits
Martha, quam mire sibi corde iungit	Help us to labor with a pure intention,
Christus amico.	Just for his glory.
Te frequens visit Dominus tuaque	Often the Master, wearied by his labors,
in domo degit placida quiete	Sought rest and refuge in your peaceful household,
ac tuis verbis studiisque lætans	Thanking and blessing for her words and service,
teque ministra.	Handmaid so eager.
Tu prior fratrem quereris perisse,	First you lamented he had not been present
cumque germana lacrimata multum,	Prompt in compassion, sure to save your brother,
aspicis vitæ subita Magistri	But you and Mary, from the grave received him,
voce redire.	Summoned by Jesus.
Quæ fide prompta stabilem fateris	Firmly believing in our resurrection
spem resurgendi, Domino probante,	You word so steadfast won our Lord's approval;
impetra nobis cupid*e* in perenne	Graciously win us by your intercession
pergerer regnum.	Access to heaven.

Laus Deo Patri, Genitoque virtus,	Praise to the Father, to the Son all honor,
Flamini Sancto parilis potestas,	Homage and service to the Holy Spirit,
gloriam quorum petimus per ævum	Whose equal glory we desire to worship
cernere tecum. Amen.	With you for ever. Amen.

CANTICLE OF ZECHARIAH

Ant. Martha said to Jesus: † You are the Christ, the Son of the *liv*ing God: * he who is to come into *the* world.

Prayer

Father,
your Son honored Saint Martha
by coming to her home as a guest.
By her prayers
may we serve Christ in our brothers and sisters
and be welcomed by you into heaven, our true home.
We ask this through our Lord Jesus Christ, your Son,
who lives and reigns with you and the Holy Spirit,
one God, for ever and ever.

Evening Prayer

HYMN

Te gratulantes. (L.M.)

Te gratulantes pangimus,	Saint Martha, we recall the joy
Martha, beata mulier,	Of which your energy gave proof,
quæ meruisti sæpius	When opportunity was yours
Christum domi recipere.	To welcome Christ beneath your roof.
Tantum libenter hospitem	Alert and eager with much care,
curis ornabas sedulis,	Your ardent soul could find no rest,
in plurima sollicita	In many things sollicitous
amoris dulci stimulo.	To please so greatly loved a Guest.
Pascis dum læta Dominum,	While you prepare a festal board
soror ac frater avide	At which he will have honored place,
possunt ab illo gratiæ	Your brother and your sister draw
vitæque cibum sumere.	From him the food of life and grace.
Capturo mortis tramitem	And when his death is drawing near,
dante sorore aromata,	The Hour he always had in view,
extremi tu servitii	Your sister's perfume was the sign
vigil donasti munera.	Of your devotion and service too.

Magistri felix hospita,	O favored hostess of your Lord,
corda fac nostra ferveant,	Make our hearts ready like your own,
ut illi gratæ iugiter	To welcome him to their abode
sint sedes amicitiæ.	To find in them true friendship's throne.
Sit Trinitati gloria,	All glory to the Trinity
quæ nos in domum cælicam	Whom we implore with earnest voice,
admitti tandem tribuat	To let us join you up above
tecumque laudes canere. Amen.	Where all in gratitude rejoice. Amen.

CANTICLE OF MARY

Ant.　　　　　Jesus loved Mar*tha* and Mary * and their bro*ther* Lazarus.

Prayer, as in Morning Prayer, 1021.

July 30
PETER CHRYSOLOGUS, BISHOP AND DOCTOR

From the common of pastors, 1238, or of doctors, 1246.

Prayer

Father,
you made Peter Chrysologus
an outstanding preacher of your incarnate Word.
May the prayers of Saint Peter help us to cherish
the mystery of our salvation
and make its meaning clear in our love for others.
Grant this through our Lord Jesus Christ, your Son,
who lives and reigns with you and the Holy Spirit,
one God, for ever and ever.

July 31
IGNATIUS OF LOYOLA, PRIEST
Memorial

From the common of pastors, 1238, or of holy men: religious, 1282.

Morning Prayer
HYMN
Magnæ cohortis. (L.M.)

Magnæ cohortis pincipem	Courageous leader in the fight,
Ignatium laus concinat,	Ignatius merits earnest praise,
clarum loquelis, actibus	Raised up by God in time of need,
ducem cientem milites.	In troubled and in war-like days.

Regi supremo cælitum
amore vinctus unico,
eius fovenda gloria
nil censuit iucundius.

Hinc se suosque devovet,
urgentis instar agminis,
ut iura Christi vindicet,
erroris umbras dissipet.

Sancto monente Spiritu,
certam salutis semitam
scrutator altus sæculis
doctorque prudens denotat.

Suis alumnis dissita
missis in orbis litora,
Ecclesiam quot expetit
frondere lætam gentibus!

Sit Trinitati gloria,
quæ nos det huius militis
exempla fortes persequi
in Christi honorem perpetim. Amen.

Once conquered by the love of God,
He found security and peace
In working for high heaven's King,
His greater glory to increase.

The ardor of his little band
No dangers and no threats could quell,
To vindicate the law of Christ
And error's darkness to dispel.

The Holy Spirit's gifts of grace,
Much penance and long hours of prayer
Made him a wise and prudent guide
For souls who came beneath his care.

To ev'ry corner of the earth
His eager sons will gladly go,
To bring all nations to the Church
That Christ's sweet message they may know.

All glory to the Trinity
Who graciously will strength accord
To fight as this great soldier fought
In loyal service to our Lord. Amen.

CANTICLE OF ZECHARIAH

Ant.   Would that I might know Christ † and the power of his
*res*urrection * and that I might share in *his* sufferings.

Prayer

Father,
you gave Saint Ignatius of Loyola to your Church
to bring greater glory to your name.
May we follow his example on earth
and share the crown of life in heaven.
We ask this through our Lord Jesus Christ, your Son,
who lives and reigns with you and the Holy Spirit,
one God, for ever and ever.

Evening Prayer

CANTICLE OF MARY

Ant.   Of what use is it to a man to gain *the* whole world, * if he pays
for it by losing *his* soul?

August 1
ALPHONSUS LIGUORI, BISHOP AND DOCTOR
Memorial
From the common of pastors, 1238, or of doctors, 1246.

Prayer

Father,
you constantly build up your Church
by the lives of your saints.
Give us grace to follow Saint Alphonsus
in his loving concern for the salvation of men,
and so come to share his reward in heaven.
Grant this through our Lord Jesus Christ, your Son,
who lives and reigns with you and the Holy Spirit,
one God, for ever and ever.

August 2
EUSEBIUS OF VERCELLI, BISHOP
From the common of pastors, 1238.

Prayer

Lord God,
Saint Eusebius affirmed the divinity of your Son.
By keeping the faith he taught,
may we come to share the eternal life of Christ,
who lives and reigns with you and the Holy Spirit,
one God, for ever and ever.

On the same day, August 2
PETER JULIAN EYMARD, PRIEST
From the common of pastors, 1238. or of holy men: religious, 1282.

Prayer

Lord God,
you kept St. Peter faithful to Christ's pattern of poverty and humility.
May his prayers help us to live in fidelity to our calling
and bring us to the perfection you have shown us in your Son,
who lives and reigns with you and the Holy Spirit,
one God, for ever and ever.

August 4
JOHN VIANNEY, PRIEST
Memorial

From the common of pastors, 1238.

Prayer

Father of mercy,
you made Saint JohnVianney outstanding
in his priestly zeal and concern for your people.
By his example and prayer,
enable us to win our brothers and sisters
to the love of Christ and come with them to eternal glory.
Grant this through our Lord Jesus Christ, your Son,
who lives and reigns with you and the Holy Spirit,
one God, for ever and ever.

August 5
DEDICATION OF ST. MARY MAJOR
Commemoration

From the common of the Blessed Virgin Mary, 1192, except for the following:

Morning Prayer

CANTICLE OF ZECHARIAH

Ant.   Holy Mary, ever Virgin, Mother of God, † blessèd are you
among women * and blessed is the fruit of *your* womb.

Prayer

Lord,
pardon the sins of your people.
May the prayers of Mary, the mother of your Son,
help to save us, for by ourselves we cannot please you.
Grant this through our Lord Jesus Christ, your Son,
who lives and reigns with you and the Holy Spirit,
one God, for ever and ever.

CANTICLE OF MARY

Ant.   Holy Mary, Mother of God, † pray *for* us sinners, * now and at
the hour of *our* death.

August 6
TRANSFIGURATION
Feast

Evening Prayer I
(when this feast occurs on Sunday)

HYMN

O nata lux. (L.M.)

O nata lux de lumine,	O Jesus, Light of very Light,
Iesu, redemptor sæculi,	Redeemer of our fallen race,
dignare clemens supplicum	Receive our earnest prayers and praise,
laudes precesque sumere.	Extend to us your mercy's grace.
Præ sole vultu flammeus,	You once were seen by chosen three
ut nix amictu candidus,	Upon the mount, your face aglow
in monte dignis testibus	With splendor to outshine the sun,
apparuisti conditor.	And garments bright as purest snow.
Vates alumnis abditos	The three Apostles grew in faith
novis vetustos conferens,	As this great vision they adored,
utrisque te divinitus	While prophets of the ancient Law
Deum dedisti credere.	Bore witness to their God and Lord.
Te vox paterna cælitus	And then the Father's voice on high,
suum vocavit Filium,	Proclaimed you as his Son most dear;
quem nos fideli pectore	Our grateful hearts acclaim you King,
regem fatemur cælitum.	Our minds desire your words to hear.
Qui carne quondam contegi	You once consented for our sake,
dignatus es pro perditis,	Our lowly mortal state to bear,
nos membra confer effici	To raise us up, condemned by sin,
tui beati corporis.	That we your life divine may share.
Laudes tibi nos pangimus,	O God our Father, with the Son
dilectus es qui Filius,	And Spirit, ever reigning One,
quem Patris atque Spiritus	Be present with us here below
splendor revelat inclitus. Amen.	That future glory we may know. Amen.

PSALMODY

Ant. 1   Jesus took his disciples and went *up* the mountain * where he
was transfig*ured* before them.

VIIIg
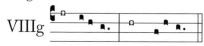

Psalm 113

Praise, O servants *of* the Lord, *
   praise the name *of* the Lord!
May the name of the *Lord* be blessed *
   both now and for *evermore*!
From the rising of the sun *to* its setting
   * praised be the name *of* the Lord!
High above all nations *is* the Lord, *
   above the heav*ens* his glory.
Who is like the *Lord*, our God, * who
   has risen on high *to* his throne
yet stoops from the heights *to* look
   down, * to look down upon heav*en*

and earth?
From the dust he lifts *up* the lowly, *
   from his misery he rais*es* the poor
to set him in the compan*y* of princes, *
   yes, with the princes *of* his people.
To the childless wife he *gives* a home *
   and gladdens her *heart* with children.
Glory to the Father, and *to* the Son, *
   and to the *Holy* Spirit:
as it was in the begin*ning*, is now, * and
   will be for ev*er*. Amen.

Antiphon   Jesus took his disciples and went *up* the mountain * where he
            was transfig*ured* before them.

Ant. 2   Suddenly Moses and Elijah appeared *be*fore them * and began
            talking *with* Jesus.

IIA

Psalm 117

O praise the Lord, *all* you nations,
   * acclaim him, all *you* peoples!
Strong is his *love* for us; * he is faithful
   for ever.

Glory to the Father, and *to* the Son, *
   and to the Ho*ly* Spirit:
as it was in the begin*ning*, is now, * and
   will be for ever. *A*men.

Antiphon   Suddenly Moses and Elijah appeared *be*fore them * and began
            talking *with* Jesus.

Ant. 3   Lord, how good it is for us to be here; † if you wish, let us build
            three tents here, † one for you, one for Moses and one for
            *E*lijah, * alleluia, alleluia.

** al- le- lu- ia, al- le- lu- ia.

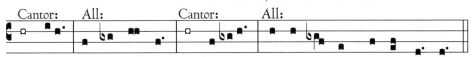

*Al- le- lu- ia.   ** al- le- lu- ia,   al- le - lu- ia.

Canticle   See Revelation 19:1-7

Salvation, glory, and power to *our* God:
   * Alleluia.
his judgments are hon*est* and true.
** Alleluia, alleluia.

Sing praise to our God, all you *his* servants,
* Alleluia.
all who worship him reverently, *great* and small.
** Alleluia, alleluia.

The Lord our all-powerful God *is* King;
* Alleluia.
let us rejoice, sing praise, and *give* him glory.
** Alleluia, alleluia.

The wedding feast of the Lamb has *be*gun,
* Alleluia.
and his bride is pre*pared* to welcome him.
** Alleluia, alleluia.

Glory to the Father, and to the Son, †
and to the Ho*ly* Spirit.
* Alleluia.
As it was in the beginning, is now, †
and will be for ev*er*. Amen.
** Alleluia, alleluia.

Antiphon   Lord, how good it is for us to be here; † if you wish, let us build
                three tents here, † one for you, one for Moses and one for
                *E*lijah, * alleluia, alleluia.

READING   Philippians 3:20-21

We have our citizenship in heaven; it is from there that we eagerly await the
coming of our Savior, the Lord Jesus Christ. He will give a new form to this
lowly body of ours and remake it according to the pattern of his glorified
body, by his power to subject everything to himself.

RESPONSORY (VI F)

You have appeared in glory be*fore* the Lord, * alleluia, al*le*luia.
— You have appeared in glory be*fore* the Lord, * alleluia, al*le*luia.
The Lord has clothed *you* in splendor,
— alleluia, al*le*luia.
Glory to the Father, and *to* the Son, * and to the Ho*ly* Spirit.
— You have appeared in glory be*fore* the Lord, * alleluia, al*le*luia.

CANTICLE OF MARY

Antiphon   Christ Jesus, you are the splendor of the Father † and the
                  perfect image of his being; † you sustain all creation with your
                  powerful word * and cleanse us of all *our* sins.
                  On this day you were exalt*ed* in glory * upon the *high* mountain.

INTERCESSIONS

In the presence of his disciples our Savior was wonderfully transfigured *on*
     Mount Tabor. * Let us pray to *him* with confidence:
Lord, in your light may we see light.
O Christ, before your passion and death you revealed the resurrection to your
     disciples on Mount Tabor; we pray for your Church which labors amid the
     cares and anxieties *of* this world,
— that in its trials it may always be transfigured by the joy *of* your victory.
O Christ, you took Peter, James and John and led them up a high mountain by
     themselves; we pray for our *pope* and bishops,
— that they may inspire in your people the hope of being transfigured at *the* last
     day.
O Christ, upon the mountaintop you let the light of your face shine over Moses
     and Elijah,
— we ask your blessing upon the Jewish people, of old you called them to be
     your *chos*en nation.
O Christ, you gave light to the world when the glory of the Creator arose *over*
     you,
— we pray for men of good will that they may walk *in* your light.
O Christ, you will reform our lowly body and make it *like* your glorious one,
— we pray for our brothers and sisters who have died that they may share in
     your glo*ry* for ever.

Our Father . . .

Prayer

     God our Father,
     in the transfigured glory of Christ your Son,
     you strengthen our faith
     by confirming the witness of your prophets,
     and show us the splendor of your belovèd sons and daughters.
     As we listen to the voice of your Son,
     help us to become heirs to eternal life with him
     who lives and reigns with you and the Holy Spirit,
     one God, for ever and ever.

Morning Prayer

HYMN

Dulci Jesu memoria. (L.M.)

Dulcis Iesu memoria, dans vera cordi gaudia, sed super mel et omnia eius dulcis præsentia.	The very thought of Jesus Christ To troubled soul brings peace and cheer, Beyond all honey and delights It is to feel his presence near.
Nil canitur suavius, auditur nil iucundius, nil cogitatur dulcius quam Iesus Dei Filius.	No sweeter Name the voice can sing, More pleasing sound the ear finds none, No better thought can come to mind Than that of Jesus, God the Son.
Iesu, dulcedo cordium, fons veri, lumen mentium, excedis omne gaudium et omne desiderium.	O Jesus, joy of ev'ry heart, True fount of life and sacred fire, The thought of you surpasses all Our longings and the soul's desire.
Quando cor nostrum visitas, tunc lucet ei veritas, mundi vilescit vanitas et intus fervet caritas.	And when you visit us unseen, Our hearts are bathed in truth and light, The joys of earth grow cold and dim As love for you asserts its right.
Da nobis largus veniam, amoris tui copiam; da nobis per prasentiam tuam videre gloriam.	Increase the ardor of our love, And heal our wounds with pardon blest; May we one day your glory see And ever in your presence rest.
Laudes tibi nos pangimus, dilectus es qui Filius, quem Patris atque Spiritus splendor revelat inclitus. Amen.	Christ Jesus Lord, we praise your Name, Belovèd Son, for us you died, But with the Spirit now you reign For ever by the Father's side. Amen.

PSALMODY

Ant. 1   Today the Lord Jesus Christ shone with splendor *on* the mountain, * his face like the sun and his clothes *white* as snow.

Psalms and canticle from Sunday, Week I, 606.

Ant. 2   Today the Lord was transfigured and the voice of the Father bore witness to him; † Moses and Elijah appeared with *him* in glory * and spoke with him about the death he was to un*der*go.

Ant. 3   The law was given through Moses and prophecy through Elijah. † Radiant in the di*vine* majesty, * they were seen speaking with *the* Lord.

READING   Revelation 21: 10, 23

The angel carried me away in spirit to the top of a very high mountain and showed me the holy city Jerusalem coming down out of heaven from God. The city had no need of sun or moon, for the glory of God gave it light, and its lamp was the Lamb.

RESPONSORY (VI F)

With glo*ry* and honor, * Lord, you *have* crowned him.
— With glo*ry* and honor, * Lord, you *have* crowned him.
You set him over the works *of* your hands.
— Lord, you *have* crowned him.
Glory to the Father, and *to* the Son, * and to the Ho*ly* Spirit.
— With glo*ry* and honor, * Lord, you *have* crowned him.

CANTICLE OF ZECHARIAH

Antiphon   A voice spoke from the cloud: † This is my belovèd Son in
                  whom I *am* well pleased; * listen *to* him.

INTERCESSIONS

In the presence of his disciples our Savior was wonderfully transfigured *on*
    Mount Tabor. * Let us pray to *him* with confidence:
Lord, in your light may we see light.
Father of mercies, you glorified your heavenly Son and revealed yourself in *the*
    bright cloud,
— grant that we may listen in faith to the *word* of Christ.
O God, you have filled your chosen people with the bounty *of* your house,
— grant that we may always find the source of our life in the bo*dy* of Christ.
O God, you have scattered the darkness with your light and have poured your
    light into our hearts so that we might look upon the radiant face of *Jesus*
    Christ,
— nourish in us the desire to contemplate your be*lov*èd Son.
O God, according to your plan, you have called us to holiness by your grace
    which you have revealed in *Jesus* Christ,
— through your Gospel show to all mankind the glorious splendor of un*end*ing
    life.
Loving Father, you have so loved us that we have been called to be *sons* of God,
— when Christ comes grant that we may *be* like him.

Our Father . . .

Prayer

God our Father,
in the transfigured glory of Christ your Son,
you strengthen our faith

by confirming the witness of your prophets,
and show us the splendor of your belovèd sons and daughters.
As we listen to the voice of your Son,
help us to become heirs to eternal life with him
who lives and reigns with you and the Holy Spirit,
one God, for ever and ever.

Evening Prayer II

HYMN, as in Evening Prayer I, 1026.

PSALMODY

Ant. 1   Jesus took Peter, James and his brother John † and led them up
               a high mountain † where they could *be* alone, * and he was
               tranfig*ured* before them.

VIIIg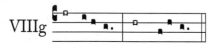

Psalm 110:1-5, 7

The Lord's revelation to my Master:
† "Sit *on* my right: * your foes I
will put be*neath* your feet."
The Lord will wield from Zion † your
scep*ter* of power: * rule in the midst
of *all* your foes.
A prince from the day of your birth †
on the *ho*ly mountains; * from the
womb before the dawn *I* begot you.
The Lord has sworn an oath he will
not change. † "You are a *priest* for
ever, * a priest like Melchize*dek* of

old."
The Master standing at *your* right
hand * will shatter kings in the day
of *his* great wrath.
He shall drink from the stream *by* the
wayside * and therefore he shall lift
up his head.
Glory to the Father, and *to* the Son, *
and to the *Ho*ly Spirit:
as it was in the begin*ning*, is now, * and
will be for ev*er*. Amen.

Antiphon   Jesus took Peter, James and his brother John † and led them up
               a high mountain † where they could *be* alone, * and he was
               tranfig*ured* before them.

Ant. 2   A bright cloud overshadowed them † and suddenly a voice
               spoke from the cloud: † This is my belovèd Son in whom I *am*
               well pleased; * listen *to* him.

IIA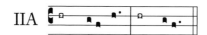

Psalm 121

I lift up my eyes *to* the mountains; *
from where shall come *my* help?

My help shall come *from* the Lord *
who made heaven *and* earth.

May he never allow *you* to stumble! *
Let him sleep not, *your* guard.

No, he sleeps *not* nor slumbers, *
Isra*el's* guard.

The Lord is your guard *and* your
shade; * at your right side *he* stands.

By day the sun *shall* not smite you *
nor the moon in *the* night.

The Lord will guard *you* from evil, * he
will guard *your* soul.

The Lord will guard your go*ing* and
coming * both now and *for* ever.

Glory to the Father, and *to* the Son, *
and to the Ho*ly* Spirit:

as it was in the begin*ning*, is now, * and
will be for ever. *A*men.

Antiphon   A bright cloud overshadowed them † and suddenly a voice
                spoke from the cloud: † This is my belovèd Son in whom I *am*
                well pleased; * listen *to* him.

Ant. 3   As they came down from the mountain Jesus commanded them:
                † Tell no one of *the* vision * until the Son of Man has risen from
                the dead.

                          Canticle   See 1 Timothy 3:16

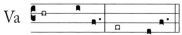

Va

℟. Praise *the* Lord, * all *you* nations.

Christ manifested in *the* flesh, *
Christ justified in *the* Spirit.

℟. Praise *the* Lord, * all *you* nations.

Christ contemplated by *the* angels, *
Christ proclaimed by *the* pagans.

℟. Praise *the* Lord, * all *you* nations.

Christ who is believed in *the* world, *
Christ exalted *in* glory.

℟. Praise *the* Lord, * all *you* nations.

Glory to the Father, and to *the* Son, *
and to the Ho*ly* Spirit:

as it was in the beginning, *is* now, * and
will be for ever. *A*men.

Antiphon   As they came down from the mountain Jesus commanded them:
                † Tell no one of *the* vision * until the Son of Man has risen from
                the dead.

READING   Romans 8:16-17
    The Spirit himself gives witness with our spirit that we are children of God.
    But if we are children, we are heirs as well: heirs of God, heirs with Christ, if
    only we suffer with him so as to be glorified with him.

RESPONSORY (VI F)
Beauty and *wealth* surround him, * alleluia, al*le*luia.
— Beauty and *wealth* surround him, * alleluia, al*le*luia.

Richness and splendor adorn his *ho*ly place.
— Alleluia, al*le*luia.
Glory to the Father, and *to* the Son, * and to the Ho*ly* Spirit.
— Beauty and *wealth* surround him, * alleluia, al*le*luia.

CANTICLE OF MARY

Antiphon   When they heard the voice *from* the cloud, * the disciples fell on
their faces, overcome *with* fear;
Jesus came up to them, † touched *them* and said: * Stand up. Do
not be *a*fraid.

INTERCESSIONS

In the presence of his disciples our Savior was wonderfully transfigured *on*
Mount Tabor. * Let us pray to *him* with confidence:
Lord, in your light may we see light.
O Christ, before your passion and death you revealed the resurrection to your
disciples on Mount Tabor; we pray for your Church which labors amid the
cares and anxieties *of* this world,
— that in its trials it may always be transfigured by the joy *of* your victory.
O Christ, you took Peter, James and John and led them up a high mountain by
themselves; we pray for our *pope* and bishops,
— that they may inspire in your people the hope of being transfigured at *the* last
day.
O Christ, upon the mountaintop you let the light of your face shine over Moses
and Elijah,
— we ask your blessing upon the Jewish people, of old you called them to be
your *cho*sen nation.
O Christ, you gave light to the world when the glory of the Creator arose *o*ver you,
— we pray for men of good will that they may walk *in* your light.
O Christ, you will reform our lowly body and make it *like* your glorious one,
— we pray for our brothers and sisters who have died that they may share in
your glo*ry* for ever.

Our Father . . .

Prayer

God our Father,
in the transfigured glory of Christ your Son,
you strengthen our faith
by confirming the witness of your prophets,
and show us the splendor of your belovèd sons and daughters.
As we listen to the voice of your Son,
help us to become heirs to eternal life with him
who lives and reigns with you and the Holy Spirit,
one God, for ever and ever.

August 7
SIXTUS II, POPE AND MARTYR, AND COMPANIONS, MARTYRS

From the common of several martyrs, 1214.

Prayer

Father,
by the power of the Holy Spirit,
you enabled Saint Sixtus and his companions to lay down their lives
for your word in witness to Jesus.
Give us the grace to believe in you
and the courage to profess our faith.
We ask this through our Lord Jesus Christ, your Son,
who lives and reigns with you and the Holy Spirit,
one God, for ever and ever.

On the same day, August 7
CAJETAN, PRIEST

From the common of pastors, 1238, or of holy men: religious, 1282.

Prayer

Lord,
you helped Saint Cajetan
to imitate the apostolic way of life.
By his example and prayers
may we trust in you always
and be faithful in seeking your kingdom.
Grant this through our Lord Jesus Christ, your Son,
who lives and reigns with you and the Holy Spirit,
one God, for ever and ever.

August 8
DOMINIC, PRIEST
Memorial

From the common of pastors, 1238, or of holy men: religious, 1282.

HYMN

Novus athleta. (L.M.)

Novus athleta Domini	Saint Dominic fulfills his name
collaudetur Dominicus,	As tireless athlete for his Lord,
qui rem conformat nomini,	In preaching and in making known
vir factus evangelicus.	The word of God, the Spirit's sword.

Conservans sine macula	Preserving heart and conscience pure,
virginitatis lilium,	From evil he kept far away,
ardebat quasi facula	Though burning like a flaming torch
pro zelo pereuntium.	With zeal to save those gone astray.
Mundum calcans sub pedibus	He spurned the honors of this world,
accinxit cor ad proelia,	To all he strove the truth to show,
nudus occurrens hostibus,	Supported by the grace of Christ
Christi suffultus gratia.	He went unarmed to meet the foe.
Pugnat verbo, miraculis,	To words he added prodigies
missis per orbem fratribus,	With earnest tears and constant prayer,
crebros adiungens sedulis	While sending his companions out
fletus orationibus.	To spread the Gospel ev'rywhere.
Sit trino Deo et simplici	All honor, glory, homage, praise
laus, honor, decus, gloria,	To God Almighty, One in Three,
qui nos prece Dominici	Who by the prayers of Dominic
ducat ad cæli gaudia. Amen.	Will give us joy eternally. Amen.

Prayer

Lord,
let the holiness and teaching of Saint Dominic
come to the aid of your Church.
May he help us now with his prayers
as he once inspired people by his preaching.
We ask this through our Lord Jesus Christ, your Son,
who lives and reigns with you and the Holy Spirit,
one God, for ever and ever.

August 9
TERESA BENEDICTA OF THE CROSS,
VIRGIN AND MARTYR

From the common of one martyr, 1228, or of virgins, 1253.

Prayer

God our Father,
you give us joy each year
in honoring the memory of St. Teresa Benedicta of the Cross.
May her prayers be a source of help for us,
and may her example of courage and chastity be our inspiration.
Grant this through our Lord Jesus Christ, your Son,
who lives and reigns with you and the Holy Spirit,
one God, for ever and ever.

August 10
LAWRENCE, DEACON AND MARTYR
Feast

Morning Prayer
HYMN

In martyris. (L.M.)

In martyris Laurentii non incruento prœlio, armata pugnavit Fides proprii cruoris prodiga.	When Lawrence was led out to die, Love made him prodigal of life, No armor would he use but faith Against the persecutor's strife.
Hic primus e septem viris qui stant ad aram proximi, levita sublimis gradu et ceteris præstantior.	The first of seven chosen men Selected at the Pope's behest, A deacon's office to fulfil, In virtue he surpassed the rest.
Hic dimicans fortissimus non ense præcinxit latus, hostile sed ferrum retro torquens in auctorem tulit.	He was a leader in the fight, Although no sword hung by his side, And with a smile in face of death, He could the torturer deride.
Sic, sancte Laurenti, tuam nos passionem quærimus; quod quisque supplex postulat, fert impetratum prospere,	We praise your triumph here on earth, So, holy Lawrence, lend your aid, May each of us your favor feel, Receiving grace for which we prayed.
Dum cæli inenarrabili allectus urbi municeps, æternæ in arce curiæ gestas coronam civicam.	For all the care with which your served And loved the city's poor in Rome, what luster must enhance your crown For ever in the Father's home!
Honor Patri cum Filio et Spiritu Paraclito, qui nos tuis suffragiis ditent perenni laurea. Amen.	To Father, Son, and Spirit too, Be honor, homage and renown, Who will reward your prayers for us By granting an eternal crown. Amen.

PSALMODY

Ant. 1   My soul clings to *you*, my God, * because I endured death by
fire *for* your sake.

Psalms and canticle from Sunday, Week I, 606.

Ant. 2   The Lord sent his angel to free me *from* the fire, * and I escaped
the flames *un*harmed.

Ant. 3   Blessèd Lawrence prayed: † I thank you, Lord, for permit*ting*
me * to enter the gates of *your* kingdom.

READING   2 Corinthians 1:3-5

Praised be God, the Father of our Lord Jesus Christ, the Father of mercies, and the God of all consolation! He comforts us in all our afflictions and thus enables us to comfort those who are in trouble, with the same consolation we have received from him. As we have shared much in the sufferings of Christ, so through Christ do we share abundantly in his consolation.

RESPONSORY (VI F)

The Lord *is* my strength, * and I shall sing *his* praise.
— The Lord *is* my strength, * and I shall sing *his* praise.
The Lord *is* my savior,
— and I shall sing *his* praise.
Glory to the Father, and *to* the Son, * and to the Ho*ly* Spirit.
— The Lord *is* my strength, * and I shall sing *his* praise.

CANTICLE OF ZECHARIAH

Antiphon   Do not be afraid, my son, for I am with you; † if you should walk through the fire, † the flames *will* not harm you, * nor will the odor of burning cling *to* you.

INTERCESSIONS, from the common of one martyr, 1229.

Prayer

Father,
you called Saint Lawrence to serve you by love
and crowned his life with glorious martyrdom.
Help us to be like him
in loving you and doing your work.
Grant this through our Lord Jesus Christ, your Son,
who lives and reigns with you and the Holy Spirit,
one God, for ever and ever.

Evening Prayer

HYMN

Martyris Christi. (11.11.11.5)

Martyris Christi colimus triumphum,
dona qui mundi peritura spernit,
fert opem nudis, alimenta, nummos
     tradit egenis.

Igne torquetur, stabili tenore
cordis accensus superat minaces
ignium flammas in amore vitæ
     semper opimæ.

Lawrence the deacon spent himself in service,
Aiding the needy, wealth of earth despising,
Then as a martyr for the name of Jesus,
     Joyfully triumphed.

Fire's bitter torment he endured serenely,
Even to jesting as the flame grew fiercer,
Nothing could conquer love so bent on reaching
     Joys everlasting.

Spiritum sumpsit chorus angelorum,
intulit cælo bene laureandum,
ut scelus laxet hominum, precando
          omnipotentem.

Welcoming angels bore his happy spirit,
Swiftly to heaven to be crowned for ever,
Where he would always intercede for sinners,
          With the Almighty.

Supplici voto rogitamus ergo
omnibus, martyr, veniam preceris,
cordis ardores, fidei tenacem
          usque vigorem.

Most holy martyr, humbly we implore you,
Pray for us daily, winning us forgiveness,
Make us more fervent, by our faith and morals
          Bearing full witness.

Gloriam Patri resonemus omnes,
eius et Nato modulemur apte,
cum quibus regnat simul et creator
          Spiritus almus. Amen.

Praise to the Father let us sing with gladness,
Praise to our Savior, God the Son, Incarnate,
Reigning for ever with the Holy Spirit,
          God and Creator. Amen.

PSALMODY

Ant. 1   By his martyrdom Lawrence gave witness to our Lord *Jesus*
               Christ * and gained the re*ward* of heaven.

Psalms and canticle from the common of one martyr, 1232.

Ant. 2   Blessèd Lawrence cried out: † I rejoice greatly because I have
               been con*sid*ered worthy * to be a sacrificial victim *for* Christ.

Ant. 3   I thank you, Lord Je*sus* Christ, * for permitting me to enter the
               gates of *your* kingdom.

READING   1 Peter 4:13-14
          Rejoice, beloved, in the measure that you share Christ's sufferings. When his
          glory is revealed, you will rejoice exultantly. Happy are you when you are
          insulted for the sake of Christ, for then God's Spirit in its glory has come to
          rest on you.

RESPONSORY (VI F)
You have tried us by *fire*, O God, * then led us to a place of re*fresh*ment.
— You have tried us by *fire*, O God, * then led us to a place of re*fresh*ment.
You refined us as silver *in* the furnace,
— then led us to a place of re*fresh*ment.
Glory to the Father, and *to* the Son, * and to the Ho*ly* Spirit.
— You have tried us by *fire*, O God, * then led us to a place of re*fresh*ment.

CANTICLE OF MARY
Antiphon   Blessèd Lawrence said: † The night is not *dark* for me; * all
                  things shine as in the noon*day* light.

INTERCESSIONS, from the common of one martyr, 1234.

Prayer, as in Morning Prayer, 1038.

August 11
CLARE, VIRGIN
Memorial

From the common of virgins, 1253, or of holy women: religious, 1282.

Prayer

God of mercy,
you inspired Saint Clare with the love of poverty.
By the help of her prayers
may we follow Christ in poverty of spirit
and come to the joyful vision of your glory
in the kingdom of heaven.
We ask this through our Lord Jesus Christ, your Son,
who lives and reigns with you and the Holy Spirit,
one God, for ever and ever.

August 13
PONTIAN, POPE AND MARTYR, AND
HIPPOLYTUS, PRIEST AND MARTYR

From the common of several martyrs, 1214, or of pastors, 1238.

Prayer

Lord,
may the loyal suffering of your saints, Pontian and Hippolytus,
fill us with your love,
and make our hearts steadfast in faith.
Grant this through our Lord Jesus Christ, your Son,
who lives and reigns with you and the Holy Spirit,
one God, for ever and ever.

August 14
MAXIMILIAN MARY KOLBE, PRIEST AND MARTYR
Memorial

From the common of pastors: missionary, 1238, or from the common of one martyr, 1228, except for the following:

Morning Prayer

CANTICLE OF ZECHARIAH

Ant. Christ will be exalted in me whether I *live* or die. * For to me to live is Christ and to die *is* gain.

Prayer

Gracious God,
you filled your priest and martyr,
Saint Maximilian Kolbe,
with zeal for your house and love for his neighbor.
Through the prayers of this devoted servant of Mary Immaculate,
grant that in our efforts to serve others for your glory
we too may become like Christ your Son,
who loved his own in the world even to the end,
and now lives and reigns with you and the Holy Spirit,
one God, for ever and ever.

Evening Prayer

CANTICLE OF MARY

Ant.   By this we have come to know the meaning of God's love: †
Christ laid down his *life* for us, * and we should lay down our
lives *for* others.

August 15
ASSUMPTION
Solemnity

Evening Prayer I

HYMN

Gaudium mundi. (11.11.11.5)

Gaudium mundi, nova stella cæli,
procreans solem, pariens parentem,
da manum lapsis, fer opem caducis,
　　　virgo Maria.

Joy of poor sinners, fairest Star of heaven,
Sun of true justice chose you as his mother;
Save us who perish, raise the sadly fallen,
　　　Mary, pure Virgin.

Te Deo factam liquet esse scalam
qua tenens summa petit Altus ima;
nos ad excelsi remeare cæli
　　　culmina dona.

You were the ladder by which God descended,
Through you the Highest came to seek the lowest;
By your protection, help us as we journey
　　　Onwards to heaven.

Te beatorum chorus angelorum,
te prophetarum et apostolorum
ordo prælatam sibi crenit unam
　　　post Deitatem.

Choirs of bright angels throng with joy to meet you,
Saints of the Old Law, prophets and apostles,
Hasten to lead you to your throne of glory
　　　Next to the Godhead.

Laus sit excelsæ Triadi perennis,
quæ tibi, Virgo ,tribuit coronam,
atque reginam statuitque nostram
　　　provida matrem. Amen.

Praise be for ever Trinity most holy,
Who crowned you, Mary, Virgin pure and sinless,
And gave you to us, Queen and loving Mother,
　　　Now and for ever. Amen.

PSALMODY

Ant. 1   Christ ascended into heaven † and prepared an ever*last*ing place * for his immaculate Mother, a*l*leluia.

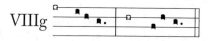

VIIIg

Psalm 113

Praise, O servants *of* the Lord, *
  praise the name *of* the Lord!
May the name of the *Lord* be blessed *
  both now and for *ever*more!
From the rising of the sun *to* its setting
  * praised be the name *of* the Lord!
High above all nations *is* the Lord, *
  above the heav*ens* his glory.
Who is like the *Lord,* our God, * who
  has risen on high *to* his throne
yet stoops from the heights *to* look
  down, * to look down upon heav*en*

and earth?
From the dust he lifts *up* the lowly, *
  from his misery he rais*es* the poor
to set him in the company of princes, *
  yes, with the princes *of* his people.
To the childless wife he *gives* a home *
  and gladdens her *heart* with children.
Glory to the Father, and *to* the Son, *
  and to the *Holy* Spirit:
as it was in the begin*ning,* is now, * and
  will be for ev*er.* Amen.

Antiphon   Christ ascended into heaven † and prepared an ever*last*ing place * for his immaculate Mother, a*l*leluia.

Ant. 2   Through Eve the gates of heaven were closed to all mankind; † through the Virgin Mother they were opened *wide* again, * al*l*eluia.

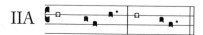

IIA

Psalm 147:12-20

O praise the *Lord,* Jerusalem! *
  Zion, praise *your* God!
He has strengthened the bars *of* your
  gates, * he has blessed the children
  *with*in you.
He established peace *on* your borders, *
  he feeds you with fin*est* wheat.
He sends out his word *to* the earth *
  and swiftly runs his *com*mand.
He showers down snow *white* as wool, *
  he scatters hoar-frost *like* ashes.

He hurls down hail*stones* like crumbs. *
  The waters are frozen at *his* touch;
he sends forth his word *and* it melts
  them: * at the breath of his mouth
  the wa*ters* flow.
He makes his word *known* to Jacob, *
  to Israel his laws and *de*crees.
He has not dealt thus with *other*
  nations; * he has not taught them his
  *de*crees.
Glory to the Father, and *to* the Son, *

and to the Ho*ly* Spirit: will be for ever. *A*men.
as it was in the begin*ning*, is now, * and

Antiphon   Through Eve the gates of heaven were closed to all mankind; †
                through the Virgin Mother they were opened *wide* again, *
                al*le*luia.

Ant. 3   The Virgin Mary has been exalted above all the heavens; †
                come, let all men glorify Christ *the* King, * whose kingdom will
                endure for ever, al*le*luia.

Canticle   Ephesians 1:3-10

Praised be the God *and* Father * of
    our Lord Je*sus* Christ,
who has bestowed on us *in* Christ *
    every spiritual blessing in *the* heav-
    ens.
God chose us in him † before the
    world *be*gan * to be holy and blame-
    less in *his* sight.
He predestined us † to be his adopted
    sons through Je*sus* Christ, * such was
    his will *and* pleasure,
that all might praise the glori*ous* favor *
    he has bestowed on us in his *be*lovèd.
In him and through his blood, † we
    have been *re*deemed, * and our sins

forgiven,
so immeasura*bly* generous * is God's
    favor *to* us.
God has given us the wisdom † to
    understand fully *the* mystery, * the
    plan he was pleased to decree *in*
    Christ.
A plan to be carried out *in* Christ, * in
    the fullness *of* time,
to bring all things into one *in* him, * in
    the heavens and *on* earth.
Glory to the Father, and to *the* Son, *
    and to the Ho*ly* Spirit:
as it was in the beginning, *is* now, * and
    will be for ever. *A*men.

Antiphon   The Virgin Mary has been exalted above all the heavens; †
                come, let all men glorify Christ *the* King, * whose kingdom will
                endure for ever, al*le*luia.

READING   Romans 8:30
    Those God predestined he likewise called; those he called he also justified;
    and those he justified he in turn glorified.

RESPONSORY (VI F)
As Mary is taken *up* to heaven, * the angels of God re*joice.*
— As Mary is taken *up* to heaven, * the angels of God re*joice.*
They worship the Lord and *sing* his praises.
— The angels of God re*joice.*

Glory to the Father, and *to* the Son, * and to the Ho*ly* Spirit.
— As Mary is taken *up* to heaven, * the angels of God *re*joice.

CANTICLE OF MARY

Ant.   All generations will *call* me blessèd: * the Almighty has done
                        great things for me, al*le*luia.

INTERCESSIONS

Let us praise God our almighty Father, who wished that Mary, his Son's mother,
    be celebrated by each *gen*eration. * Now in *need* we ask:
Mary, full of grace, intercede for us.
O God, worker of miracles, you made the Immaculate Virgin Mary share, body
    and soul, in your Son's glo*ry* in heaven,
— direct the hearts of your children to *that* same glory.
You made Mary our mother. Through her intercession grant strength to the
    weak, comfort to the sorrowing, par*don* to sinners,
— salvation and *peace* to all.
You made Mary *full* of grace,
— grant all men the joyful abundance *of* your grace.
Make your Church of one mind and one *heart* in love,
— and help all those who believe to be one in prayer with Mary, the mo*ther* of
    Jesus.
You crowned Mary *queen* of heaven,
— may all the dead rejoice in your kingdom with the *saints* for ever.

Our Father . . .

                              Prayer
        Almighty God,
        you gave a humble virgin
        the privilege of being the mother of your Son,
        and crowned her with the glory of heaven.
        May the prayers of the Virgin Mary
        bring us to the salvation of Christ
        and raise us up to eternal life.
        We ask this through our Lord Jesus Christ, your Son,
        who lives and reigns with you and the Holy Spirit,
        one God, for ever and ever.

Morning Prayer

HYMN

Solis, o Virgo. (11.11.11.5)

Solis, o Virgo, radiis amicta,	O Virgin Mary, words cannot describe you,
bis caput senis redimita stellis,	Clothed with the beauty of the sun at noonday,
luna cui præbet pedibus scabellum,	Twelve stars to crown you, and the moon beneath you,
inclita fulges.	Queen of creation.
Mortis, inferni domitrixque culpæ,	Through your submission, death and hell were conquered,
assides Christo studiosa nostri,	Now you are seated by your Son and Savior,
teque reginam celebrat potentem	Strong to protect us by your intercession,
terra polusque.	As we entreat you.
Asseclas diæ fidei tuere;	Guard and watch over those within the sheepfold,
dissitos adduc ad ovile sacrum;	Lead to the Shepherd those who are far distant,
quas diu gentes tegit umbra mortis	Pity the nations groping in the darkness,
undique coge.	Graciously guide them.
Sontibus mitis veniam precare,	Tenderly pleading, win us all forgiveness,
adiuva flentes, inopes et ægros,	Help those in trouble, poverty or sickness;
spes mica cunctis per acuta vitæ	Hope of salvation, as a star to pilgrims
certa salutis.	Shine through the darkness.
laus sit excelsæ Triadi perennis,	Praise be for ever Trinity Almighty,
quæ tibi, Virgo, tribuit coronam,	Who crowned you, Mary, ever spotless Virgin,
atque reginam statuitque nostram	Making you also Queen of men and angels,
provida matrem. Amen.	Most loving Mother. Amen.

PSALMODY

Ant. 1   Blessèd are you, O Mary, † for the world's salvation came *forth* through you; * now in glory, you rejoice for ever *with* the Lord.

VIIIg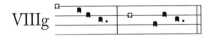

Psalm 63:2-9

O God, you are my God, for *you* I long; * for you my *soul* is thirsting.
My body *pines* for you * like a dry,
   weary land *with*out water.
So I gaze on you *in* the sanctuary * to
   see your strength *and* your glory.
For your love is bet*ter* than life, * my
   lips will *speak* your praise.
So I will bless you *all* my life, * in your
   name I will lift *up* my hands.

My soul shall be filled as *with* a
   banquet, * my mouth shall praise *you*
   with joy.
On my bed I re*member* you. * On you
   I muse *through* the night
for you have *been* my help; * in the
   shadow of your wings *I* rejoice.
My soul *clings* to you; * your right hand
   holds me fast.
Glory to the Father, and *to* the Son, *

and to the *Ho*ly Spirit:
as it was in the begin*ning*, is now, *

and will be for e*ver*. Amen.

Antiphon　　Blessèd are you, O Mary, † for the world's salvation came *forth* through you; * now in glory, you rejoice for ever *with* the Lord.

Ant. 2　　The Virgin Mary is exalted above the *choirs* of angels; * let all believers rejoice and bless *the* Lord.

Canticle　　　　　　　　　　Daniel 3:57-88; 56

Bless the Lord, all you works *of* the Lord. * Praise and exalt him above all *for*ever.

Angels of the Lord, *bless* the Lord, * You heavens, bless *the* Lord.

All you waters above the heavens, *bless* the Lord. * All you hosts of the Lord, bless *the* Lord.

Sun and moon, *bless* the Lord. * Stars of heaven, bless *the* Lord.

Every shower and dew, *bless* the Lord. * All you winds, bless *the* Lord.

Fire and heat, *bless* the Lord. * Cold and chill, bless *the* Lord.

Dew and rain, *bless* the Lord. * Frost and chill, bless *the* Lord.

Ice and snow, *bless* the Lord. * Nights and days, bless *the* Lord.

Light and darkness, *bless* the Lord. * Lightnings and clouds, bless *the* Lord.

Let the earth *bless* the Lord. * Praise and exalt him above all *for*ever.

Mountains and hills, *bless* the Lord. * Everything growing from the earth, bless *the* Lord.

You springs, *bless* the Lord. * Seas and rivers, bless *the* Lord.

You dolphins and all water creatures, *bless* the Lord. * All you birds of the air, bless *the* Lord.

All you beasts, wild and tame, *bless* the Lord. * You sons of men, bless *the* Lord.

O Israel, *bless* the Lord. * Praise and exalt him above all *for*ever.

Priests of the Lord, *bless* the Lord. * Servants of the Lord, bless *the* Lord.

Spirits and souls of the just, *bless* the Lord. * Holy men of humble heart, bless *the* Lord.

Hananiah, Azariah, Mishael, *bless* the Lord. * Praise and exalt him above all *for*ever.

Let us bless the Father, and the Son, and the *Ho*ly Spirit. * Let us praise and exalt him above all *for*ever.

Blessèd are you in the firma*ment* of heaven. * Praiseworthy and glorious and exalted above all *for*ever.

Antiphon　　The Virgin Mary is exalted above the *choirs* of angels; * let all believers rejoice and bless *the* Lord.

Ant. 3   The Lord has made you *so* glorious * that your praise will never cease to resound *among* men.

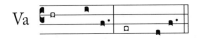

Va

Psalm 149

Sing a new song to *the* Lord, *
his praise in the assembly of *the* faithful.
Let Israel rejoice in *its* Maker, * let
Zion's sons exult in *their* king.
Let them praise his name *with* dancing * and make music with timbrel *and* harp.
For the Lord takes delight in *his* people. * He crowns the poor with *sal*vation.
Let the faithful rejoice in *their* glory, * shout for joy and take *their* rest.

Let the praise of God be on *their* lips * and a two-edged sword in *their* hand,
to deal out vengeance to *the* nations * and punishment on all *the* peoples;
to bind their kings *in* chains * and their nobles in fetters *of* iron;
to carry out the sentence pre-*or*dained: * this honor is for all *his* faithful.
Glory to the Father, and to *the* Son, * and to the Ho*ly* Spirit:
as it was in the beginning, *is* now, * and will be for ever. *A*men.

Antiphon   The Lord has made you *so* glorious * that your praise will never cease to resound *among* men.

READING   See Isaiah 61:10

I rejoice heartily in the Lord,
    in my God is the joy of my soul;
For he has clothed me with a robe of salvation,
    and wrapped me in a mantle of justice,
    like a bride bedecked with her jewels.

RESPONSORY (VI F)

Today the *Vir*gin Mary * was taken up *to* heaven.
— Today the *Vir*gin Mary * was taken up *to* heaven.
For all eternity she shares the victo*ry* of Christ.
— The Virgin Mary was taken up *to* heaven.
Glory to the Father, and *to* the Son, * and to the Ho*ly* Spirit.
— Today the *Vir*gin Mary * was taken up *to* heaven.

CANTICLE OF ZECHARIAH

Antiphon   The daugher of Jerusalem is love*ly* and beautiful * as she ascends to heaven like the rising sun *at* daybreak.

INTERCESSIONS (VI F)

Let us glorify our Savior, who chose the Virgin Mary *for* his mother. * *Let* us ask him:

May your mother intercede for us, *Lord.*

Eternal Word, you chose Mary as the uncorrupted ark of your *dwell*ing place,
— free us from the corrup*tion* of sin.

You are our redeemer, who made the immaculate Virgin Mary your purest home and the sanctuary of the *Ho*ly Spirit,
— make us temples of your Spir*it* for ever.

King of kings, you lifted up your mother, body and soul, *into* heaven;
— help us to fix our thoughts on *things* above.

Lord of heaven and earth, you crowned Mary and set her at your right *hand* as queen,
— make us worthy to *share* this glory.

Our Father . . .

Prayer

All-powerful and ever-living God,
you raised the sinless Virgin Mary,
mother of your Son,
body and soul to the glory of heaven.
May we see heaven as our final goal
and come to share her glory.
We ask this through our Lord Jesus Christ, your Son,
who lives and reigns with you and the Holy Spirit,
one God, for ever and ever.

Evening Prayer II

HYMN, as in Evening Prayer I, 1041.

Ant. 1   Mary has been taken up to heaven; † the an*gels* rejoice. * They
               bless the Lord and *sing* his praises.

VIIIg

Psalm 122

I rejoiced when I *heard* them say: *
"Let us go *to* God's house."
And now our *feet* are standing * within
your gates, O Jerusalem.

Jerusalem is built *as* a city * strong*ly*
compact.
It is there that the *tribes* go up, * the
tribes *of* the Lord.

For Israel's *law* it is, * there to praise
  the Lord's name.
There were set the *thrones* of judgment
  * of the *house* of David.
For the peace of Jeru*sa*lem pray: *
  "Peace be *to* your homes!
May peace reign *in* your walls, * in
  your pa*la*ces, peace!"

For love of my bre*thren* and friends * I
  say: "*Peace* upon you!"
For love of the house *of* the Lord * I
  will ask *for* your good.
Glory to the Father, and *to* the Son, *
  and to the *Ho*ly Spirit:
as it was in the begin*ning*, is now, * and
  will be for ev*er*. Amen.

Antiphon   Mary has been taken up to heaven; † the an*gels* rejoice. * They
                bless the Lord and *sing* his praises.

Ant. 2   The Virgin Mary was taken up to the heavenly *brid*al chamber *
                where the King of kings is seated on a star*ry* throne.

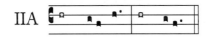

Psalm 127

If the Lord does not *build* the house,
  * in vain do its build*ers* labor;
if the Lord does not watch *over* the
  city, * in vain does the watchman
  keep vigil.
In vain is your ear*lier* rising, * your
  going later *to* rest,
you who toil for the *bread* you eat: *
  when he pours gifts on his belovèd
  while *they* slumber.
Truly sons are a gift *from* the Lord, * a
  blessing, the fruit of *the* womb.

Indeed the *sons* of youth * are like
  arrows in the hand of *a* warrior.
O the happiness *of* the man * who has
  filled his quiver with *these* arrows!
He will have no *cause* for shame * when
  he disputes with his foes in *the*
  gateways.
Glory to the Father, and *to* the Son, *
  and to the *Ho*ly Spirit:
as it was in the begin*ning*, is now, * and
  will be for ever. *A*men.

Antiphon   The Virgin Mary was taken up to the heavenly *brid*al chamber *
                where the King of kings is seated on a star*ry* throne.

Ant. 3   We share the fruit of life *through* you, * O daughter blessed by
                the Lord.

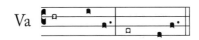

Canticle   Ephesians 1:3-10

Praised be the God *and* Father * of
  our Lord Je*sus* Christ,

who has bestowed on us *in* Christ *
  every spiritual blessing in *the* heavens.

God chose us in him † before the world began * to be holy and blameless in *his* sight.

He predestined us † to be his adopted sons through Je*sus* Christ, * such was his will *and* pleasure,

that all might praise the glori*ous* favor * he has bestowed on us in his *be*lovèd.

In him and through his blood, † we have been *re*deemed, * and our sins *for*given,

so immeasura*bly* generous * is God's favor *to* us.

God has given us the wisdom † to understand fully *the* mystery, * the plan he was pleased to decree *in* Christ.

A plan to be carried out *in* Christ, * in the fullness *of* time,

to bring all things into one *in* him, * in the heavens and *on* earth.

Glory to the Father, and to *the* Son, * and to the Ho*ly* Spirit:

as it was in the beginning, *is* now, * and will be for ever. *A*men.

Antiphon   We share the fruit of life *through* you, * O daughter blessed by *the* Lord.

READING   1 Corinthians 15:22-23

Just as in Adam all die, so in Christ all will come to life again, but each one in proper order: Christ the first fruits and then, at his coming, all those who belong to him.

RESPONSORY (VI F)

The Virgin Mary *is* exalted * above the choirs *of* angels.

— The Virgin Mary *is* exalted * above the choirs *of* angels.

Blessèd is the Lord who has *raised* her up.

— Above the choirs *of* angels.

Glory to the Father, and *to* the Son, * and to the Ho*ly* Spirit.

— The Virgin Mary *is* exalted * above the choirs *of* angels.

CANTICLE OF MARY

Ant.   Today the Virgin Mary was taken *up* to heaven; * rejoice, for she reigns with Christ *for* ever.

INTERCESSIONS (VI F)

Let us praise God our almighty Father, who wished that Mary, his Son's mother, be celebrated by each *gen*eration. * Now in *need* we ask:

Mary, full of grace, intercede for *us.*

O God, worker of miracles, you made the Immaculate Virgin Mary share, body and soul, in your Son's glo*ry* in heaven,

— direct the hearts of your children to *that* same glory.

You made Mary our mother. Through her intercession grant strength to the weak, comfort to the sorrowing, par*don* to sinners,

— salvation and *peace* to all.

You made Mary *full* of grace,
— grant all men the joyful abundance *of* your grace.
Make your Church of one mind and one *heart* in love,
— and help all those who believe to be one in prayer with Mary, the mo*ther* of
    Jesus.
You crowned Mary *queen* of heaven,
— may all the dead rejoice in your kingdom with the *saints* for ever.

Our Father . . .

Prayer

All-powerful and ever-living God,
you raised the sinless Virgin Mary,
mother of your Son,
body and soul to the glory of heaven.
May we see heaven as our final goal
and come to share her glory.
We ask this through our Lord Jesus Christ, your Son,
who lives and reigns with you and the Holy Spirit,
one God, for ever and ever.

At the end of Night prayer on this day, it is appropriate to recite or sing the *Ave, Regina cælorum*, 1344.

August 16
STEPHEN OF HUNGARY
Memorial

From the common of holy men, 1263.

Prayer

Almighty Father,
grant that Saint Stephen of Hungary,
who fostered the growth of your Church on earth,
may continue to be our powerful helper in heaven.
We ask this through our Lord Jesus Christ, your Son,
who lives and reigns with you and the Holy Spirit,
one God, for ever and ever.

August 18
JANE FRANCES DE CHANTAL, RELIGIOUS

From the common of holy women: religious, 1282, except for the following:

Prayer

Lord,
you chose Saint Jane Frances to serve you

both in marriage and in religious life.
By her prayers
help us to be faithful in our vocation
and always to be the light of the world.
We ask this through our Lord Jesus Christ, your Son,
who lives and reigns with you and the Holy Spirit,
one God, for ever and ever.

August 19
JOHN EUDES, PRIEST

From the common of pastors, 1238, or of holy men: religious, 1282.

Prayer

Father,
you chose the priest John Eudes
to preach the infinite riches of Christ.
By his teaching and example
help us to know you better
and live faithfully in the light of the gospel.
Grant this through our Lord Jesus Christ, your Son,
who lives and reigns with you and the Holy Spirit,
one God, for ever and ever.

August 20
BERNARD, ABBOT AND DOCTOR

Memorial

From the common of doctors, 1246, or of holy men: religious, 1282.

HYMN

Bernarde, gemma. (L.M.)

Bernarde, gemma cælitum,	Saint Bernard, jewel in the crown
laudes, tibi quas pangimus,	Of Mother Church you loved so well,
in nostra verte gaudia	Repay our lowly praise with grace
salutis atque munera.	To earn the joy no tongue can tell.
Te Christus ussit intimo	Christ wounded your pure heart with love
dilectionis vulnere	To which all other fire must yield,
Sponsæque fecit providus	That you might serve his Bride the Church,
scutum, columnam, lampada.	As pillar, gleaming light, and shield.
Almus dedit te Spiritus	The Holy Spirit blessed your lips,
os veritatis profluum	That words of truth from them should flow,
et angelorum pabuli	As sweet as honey to the taste,
arcana mella proferens.	Yet burning with a seraph's glow.

Amoris æstu candidi	The Virgin Mother filled your heart

Amoris æstu candidi
te Virgo Mater imbuit,
quam nemo te facundius
vel prædicavit altius.

Te quæsierunt arbitrum
reges, magistri, præsules,
cultorque solitudinis
fama replesti sæculum.

Sit Trinitati gloria,
quæ se videndam largiens,
tecum benigna gaudio
nos det perenni perfui. Amen.

The Virgin Mother filled your heart
With ardor for her Son alone;
No preacher ever spoke of her
In words more tender than your own.

A lover of deep solitude,
The world was filled with your repute,
So that great leaders, teachers, kings,
Sought your solutions in dispute.

All glory to the Trinity,
Who will the wondrous grace bestow
Of joining you before the throne
Eternal happiness to know. Amen.

Morning Prayer

CANTICLE OF ZECHARIAH

Ant. Blessèd Bernard, your life, flooded by the splendor of the divine Word, † illumines the Church * with the light of true faith and doctrine.

Prayer

Heavenly Father,
Saint Bernard was filled with zeal for your house
and was a radiant light in your Church.
By his prayers
may we be filled with this spirit of zeal
and walk always as children of light.
We ask this through our Lord Jesus Christ, your Son,
who lives and reigns with you and the Holy Spirit,
one God, for ever and ever.

Evening Prayer

CANTICLE OF MARY

Ant. Bernard, eloquent doctor of the Church, † friend of Christ the Bridegroom, † eminent preacher of the Virgin Mother's glory, * at Clairvaux you became the illustrious shepherd of your followers.

August 21
PIUX X, POPE
Memorial

From the common of pastors: for a pope, 1238.

Prayer

Father,
to defend the Catholic faith

and to make all things new in Christ,
you filled Saint Pius X
with heavenly wisdom and apostolic courage.
May his example and teaching
lead us to the reward of eternal life.
Grant this through our Lord Jesus Christ, your Son,
who lives and reigns with you and the Holy Spirit,
one God, for ever and ever.

August 22
QUEENSHIP OF MARY
Memorial
From the common of the Blessed Virgin Mary, 1192.

Morning Prayer
HYMN
Rerum supremo. Mode II (11.11.11.11)

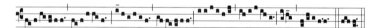

O quam glorifica luce coruscas,	Glorious majesty, pure light unfailing,
stirpis Davidicæ regia proles,	Shines as your diadem, sweet Virgin Mary,
sublimis residens, virgo Maria,	Daughter of David's race, further exalted
supra caligenas ætheris omnes.	Over angelic hosts, close to the Godhead.
Tu, cum virgineo mater honore,	Virginal purity stays with you always,
cælorum Domino pectoris aulam	Honor of Motherhood adds to your glory,
sacris visceribus casta parasti;	You were the resting place of the Eternal;
natus hinc Deus est corpore Christus:	Of the Almighty one, King of the angels.
Quem cunctus venerans orbis adorat,	Whom the earth venerates, humbly adoring,
cui nunc rite genu flectitur omne,	To whose almighty love knees bend in worship,
a quo te petimus subveniente	May he assist us all on our life's journey
abiectis tenebris gaudia lucis.	To win true happiness, casting off darkness.
Hoc largire, Pater luminis omnis,	Hear us tender Father, Light uncreated,
Natum per proprium, Flamine Sancto,	Through your belovèd Son and through the Spirit,
qui tecum nitida vivit in æthra	Who ever reigns with you, guiding and ruling,
regnans ac moderans sæcula cuncta. Amen.	For all eternity in your bright kingdom. Amen.

CANTICLE OF ZECHARIAH

Ant.   Mary, ever-virgin, most honored Queen *of* the world, * you gave
               birth to our Savior, Christ *the* Lord.

Prayer
Father,
you have given us the mother of your Son
to be our queen and mother.
With the support of her prayers

may we come to share the glory of your children
in the kingdom of heaven.
We ask this through our Lord Jesus Christ, your Son,
who lives and reigns with you and the Holy Spirit,
one God, for ever and ever.

Evening Prayer

HYMN

Mole gravati. (L.M.)

Mole gravati criminum	O Queen of heaven and of earth,
ad te, regina cælitum,	Weighed down by sin we cry to you,
confugientes, poscimus	The hope of those who refuge seek
nostris ut adsis precibus.	Hear now our lowly prayer for aid.
Æternæ vitæ ianua,	You are the gate to endless life,
aurem nobis accommoda,	Lend gracious ear to us who call,
per quam spes vitæ rediit,	You took away Eve's sad reproach
quam Eva peccans abstulit.	By bringing hope of life to all.
Tu princeps, mater Principis,	Dear Mother of our Lord and King,
vitam desposce famulis,	Implore for us the grace of life,
et pænitendi spatia	That we may strive to make amends
nobis indulgens impetra.	For all the faults of bygone years.
Orante te, sanctissima,	Most holy Mary, when you pray
sanctorum orant agmina;	The saints in heaven intercede;
tuis, regina, precibus	A word from you as suppliant
concilietur Dominus.	Will reconcile us with the Lord.
Regnatrix mater omnium,	Our Mother and most pow'rful Queen,
vota comple fidelium,	Fulfil your children's chief desire,
ac vitam nos post fragilem	And bring us when this life is done
ad veram perduc requiem.	To everlasting joy and peace.
Sit laus Patri cum Filio	We praise the Father and the Son,
et Spiritu Paraclito,	Due homage to the Spirit pay,
qui te præ cunctis cælica	For raising you as heaven's Queen
exornaverunt gloria. Amen.	Above all angels and all saints. Amen.

CANTICLE OF MARY

Ant.   Blessèd are you, Virgin Mary, † because you believed that the
                    Lord's words to you would *be* fulfilled; * now you reign with
                    Christ *for* ever.

At the end of Night prayer on this day, it is appropriate to recite or sing the *Ave, Regina
cælorum*, 1344.

August 23
ROSE OF LIMA, VIRGIN

From the common of virgins, 1253, or of holy women: religious, 1282.

Prayer

God our Father,
for love of you
Saint Rose gave up everything
to devote herself to a life of penance.
By the help of her prayers
may we imitate her selfless way of life on earth
and enjoy the fullness of your blessings in heaven.
Grant this through our Lord Jesus Christ, your Son,
who lives and reigns with you and the Holy Spirit,
one God, for ever and ever.

August 24
BARTHOLOMEW, APOSTLE
Feast

From the common of apostles, 1206.

Morning Prayer
HYMN

Reluccas inter. (L.M.)

Relucens inter principes
immensæ Dei curiæ,
Bartholomæe, laudibus
nostrisque intende precibus.

Great saint of God, Bartholomew,
Apostle now enthroned above,
Our lowly supplications hear,
Accept our hymn of praise and love.

In te convertit Dominus
dilectionis oculos,
quem pura insignem conspicit
sinceritate pectoris.

With tender eyes Christ welcomed you,
Among his Twelve you would have part;
You wondered as he greatly praised
Your deep sincerity of heart.

Prophetæ quem cecinerant,
quem longa clamant tempora,
Messias en mirifice
tibi lætanti proditur.

He whom the prophets had foretold,
Foreshadowed too in many ways,
The great Messiah, come at last,
Smiled back to greet your joyous gaze.

Teque sibi conglutinat
sequelæ talis fœdere,
qua petat crucis aspera,
cæli sedes retribuat.

Heart spoke to heart, and from that day,
Your faith and love in strength would gain,
For you would follow him in death
And then for ever with him reign.

Christi, qui sæclis imperat,	Apostle and close friend of Christ
amicus et apostolus,	Who rules beyond the chain of time,
Magistro vivis homines	You share in joy your Master's life,
Magistri vita refoves.	And help us from that fount sublime.
Sit ipsi laus et gloria,	To him be glory and all praise
qui, te iuvante meritis,	Who by your help and loving prayer,
æternis nos in patria	Will grant that we in heaven's home
frui concedat gaudiis. Amen.	Your everlasting joy may share. Amen.

Prayer

Lord,
sustain within us the faith
which made Saint Bartholomew every loyal to Christ.
Let your Church be the sign of salvation for all the nations of the world.
We ask this through our Lord Jesus Christ, your Son,
who lives and reigns with you and the Holy Spirit,
one God, for ever and ever.

August 25
LOUIS OF FRANCE

From the common of holy men, 1263.

Prayer

Father,
you raised Saint Louis
from the cares of earthly rule
to the glory of your heavenly kingdom.
By the help of his prayers
may we come to your eternal kingdom
by our work here on earth.
Grant this through our Lord Jesus Christ, your Son,
who lives and reigns with you and the Holy Spirit,
one God, for ever and ever.

On the same day, August 25
JOSEPH CALASANZ, PRIEST

From the common of holy men: teachers, 1285, or of pastors, 1238.

Prayer

Lord,
you blessed Saint Joseph Calasanz
with such charity and patience
that he dedicated himself

to the formation of Christian youth.
As we honor this teacher of wisdom
may we follow his example in working for truth.
We ask this through our Lord Jesus Christ, your Son,
who lives and reigns with you and the Holy Spirit,
one God, for ever and ever.

August 27
MONICA
Memorial

From the common of holy women, 1274.

Morning Prayer

CANTICLE OF ZECHARIAH

Ant.   You answered her prayer, O Lord, † you did not disre*gard* her
tears * which fell upon the earth wherever *she* prayed.

Prayer

God of mercy,
comfort of those in sorrow,
the tears of Saint Monica moved you
to convert her son Saint Augustine to the faith of Christ.
By their prayers, help us to turn from our sins
and to find your loving forgiveness.
Grant this through our Lord Jesus Christ, your Son,
who lives and reigns with you and the Holy Spirit,
one God, for ever and ever.

Evening Prayer

CANTICLE OF MARY

Ant.   While in this world, Monica lived in Christ; † the goodness of
her life was so evident that the name *of* the Lord * was praised in
her faith and in *her* works.

August 28
AUGUSTINE, BISHOP AND DOCTOR
Memorial

From the common of pastors, 1238, or of doctors, 1246.

HYMN

Fulget in cælis. (11.11.11.5)

Fulget in cælis celebris sacerdos,
stella doctorum rutilat corusca,
lumen intactum fidei per orbis
    climata spargens.

Those who teach others sound and sacred doctrine
Shine, say the Scriptures, as the stars of heaven,
Such is Augustine, shedding light unfailing
    Down through the ages.

Cive tam claro, Sion o superna,
læta dic laudes Domino salutis,
qui modis miris sibi vinxit ipsum
    lumine complens.

City of Zion in the joys of heaven,
Praise the almighty Lord of true salvation,
Who led Augustine through much restless seeking
    Safe to your heaven.

Hic fidem sacram vigil usque firmat,
arma et errorum subigit potenter,
sordidos mores lavat et repellit
    dogmate claro.

Earnest defender of the faith he treasured,
Dauntlessly checking all attacks of error,
Morals and virtue grew in strength and luster
    From his clear teaching.

Qui, gregis Christi speculator almus,
enites clero monachisque forma,
tu Dei nobis faciem benignam
    fac prece semper.

Vigilant pastor of your flock as bishop,
Light and example for both monks and clerics,
Pray for us always, so that God our Father
    Ever may bless us.

Laus, honor, virtus Triadi beatæ,
cuius in terris studuisti amanter
alta scrutari nitidaque in astris
    luce potiris. Amen.

Praise to the Godhead, Trinity most holy,
Whose divine Essence formed your chosen study
Even while earth-bound, what must be your rapture
    Now in high heaven! Amen.

Morning Prayer

CANTICLE OF ZECHARIAH

Ant.   You inspire us, O Lord, to delight in praising you, † because you made us *for* yourself; * our hearts are restless until they rest *in* you.

Prayer

Lord,
renew in your Church
the spirit you gave Saint Augustine.
Filled with this spirit,
may we thirst for you alone as the fountain of wisdom
and seek you as the source of eternal love.
We ask this through our Lord Jesus Christ, your Son,
who lives and reigns with you and the Holy Spirit,
one God, for ever and ever.

Evening Prayer

CANTICLE OF MARY

Ant.   Late have I loved you, O Beauty ever ancient, ever new, † late
                    have I loved you. * You called, you shouted and you shattered
                    my deafness.

August 29
THE MARTYRDOM OF JOHN THE BAPTIST
Memorial

From the common of one martyr, 1228.

Morning Prayer

HYMN, as on June 24, 988.

PSALMODY

Ant. 1   The Lord extended his hand and *touched* my lips; * he ordered
                    me to prophesy *to* the nations.

Psalms and canticle from Sunday, Week I, 606.

Ant. 2   Herod feared John, † knowing him to be a good and *ho*ly man, *
                    and guarded *him* carefully.

Ant. 3   Although John's words disturbed *him* greatly, * Herod enjoyed
                    listening *to* John.

READING   Isaiah 49:1b-2

The Lord called me from birth,
    from my mother's womb he gave me my name.
He made me a sharp-edged sword
    and concealed me in the shadow of his arm.
He made me a polished arrow,
    in his quiver he hid me.

RESPONSORY (VI F)

You sent your disci*ples* to John, * and he gave witness to *the* truth.
— You sent your disci*ples* to John, * and he gave witness to *the* truth.
He was like a brightly *shin*ing light.
— And he gave witness to *the* truth.
Glory to the Father, and *to* the Son, * and to the Ho*ly* Spirit.
— You sent your disci*ples* to John, * and he gave witness to *the* truth.

CANTICLE OF ZECHARIAH

Antiphon   The friend of the bridegroom, † who waits and listens for his
                return, † rejoices when he *hears* his voice: * so now my joy is
                *com*plete.

INTERCESSIONS (VI F)

In faith let us call upon Christ *who* sent John * to prepare *for* his coming:
Dawn from on high, break up*on us.*
Your coming caused John the Baptist to leap for joy in his *mo*ther's womb,
— help us to rejoice at your com*ing* among us.
Through the life and preaching of the Baptist you showed us the way *to*
    repentance,
— turn our hearts to follow the commandments *of* your kingdom.
You willed that your coming among men should be announced by *John* the
    Baptist,
— send new heralds to proclaim you through*out* the world.
You wished to be baptized by John in the Jordan to fulfill all that the Fa*ther*
    required,
— help us to do the *Fa*ther's will.

Our Father . . .

                                Prayer

        God our Father,
        you called John the Baptist
        to be the herald of your Son's birth and death.
        As he gave his life in witness to truth and justice,
        so may we strive to profess our faith in your gospel.
        Grant this through our Lord Jesus Christ, your Son,
        who lives and reigns with you and the Holy Spirit,
        one God, for ever and ever.

                        Evening Prayer

                            HYMN
                    Præcessor almus. (L.M.)

Præcessor almus gratiæ   Saint John was like a flaming torch,
et veritatis angelus,   Evangelist of coming Light,
lucerna Christi et perpetis   forerunner of the reign of grace,
evangelista luminis,   And messenger of Truth's full right.

Latin	English
Prophetiæ præconia, quæ voce, vita et actibus cantaverat, hæc astruit mortis sacræ signaculo.	John's voice and life and ev'ry deed Portrayed the perfect prophet's zeal, And on his mission when fulfilled A martyr's death set holy seal.
Nam nasciturum sæculis, nascendo quem prævenerat, sed et datorem proprii monstraverat baptismatis,	By birth he came before the One In Whom both God and Man combine; And later on he would baptize The very Source of life divine.
Huiusce mortem innoxiam, qua vita mundo est reddita, signat sui præsagio baptista martyr sanguinis.	As he who was to save the world Would conquer through a death of shame, So did the Baptist shed his blood To seal the work for which he came.
Præsta, Pater piissime, sequi Ioannis semitas, metamus ut plenissime æterna Christi munera. Amen.	Most tender Father, grant us grace In John's straight way our feet to keep, That fully in the living Christ Eternal joys we too may reap. Amen.

PSALMODY

Ant. 1   Do not be afraid to face them, * for I am with you, says the Lord.

Psalms and canticle from the common of one martyr, 1232.

Ant. 2   He sent an executioner * to behead John who was in prison.

Ant. 3   The disciples of John came and took his body * and laid it in a tomb.

READING   Acts 13:23-25
According to his promise, God has brought forth from David's descendants Jesus, a savior for Israel. John heralded the coming of Jesus by proclaiming a baptism of repentance to all the people of Israel. As John's career was coming to an end, he would say, "What you suppose me to be I am not. Rather, look for the one who comes after me. I am not worthy to unfasten the sandals on his feet."

RESPONSORY (VI F)
The friend of the bridegroom rejoices, * upon hearing the bridegroom's voice.
— The friend of the bridegroom rejoices, * upon hearing the bridegroom's voice.
Now my joy is complete,
— upon hearing the bridegroom's voice.
Glory to the Father, and to the Son, * and to the Holy Spirit.
— The friend of the bridegroom rejoices, * upon hearing the bridegroom's voice.

CANTICLE OF MARY

Antiphon I am not the Christ; † I have been sent before him to pre*pare* his way. * He must increase, and I *must* decrease.

INTERCESSIONS (VI F)

Let us pray joyfully to *God* our Father * who called John the Baptist to proclaim the coming of the king*dom* of Christ:

O Lord, guide our feet into the way of peace.

You called John the Baptist from his mother's womb to prepare the way *of* your Son,

— help us to follow in that path which the Baptist opened before *the* Lord Jesus.

May your Church, in imitation of the Baptist, fearlessly point out the *Lamb* of God,

— so that people in every age may acknowledge that the Lord *comes* to them.

John the Baptist did not exalt himself but acknowledged his role as forerunner *of* the Christ,

— teach us to acknowledge that you are the giver of all our good gifts and that we must use them *in* your service.

You called John the Baptist to give testimony to you by his life and even *by* his death,

— help us to imitate his unceasing witness *to* your truth.

Remember those *who* have died,

— give them a place of light, happi*ness* and peace.

Our Father . . .

Prayer

God our Father,
you called John the Baptist
to be the herald of your Son's birth and death.
As he gave his life in witness to truth and justice,
so may we strive to profess our faith in your gospel.
Grant this through our Lord Jesus Christ, your Son,
who lives and reigns with you and the Holy Spirit,
one God, for ever and ever.

September 3
GREGORY THE GREAT, POPE AND DOCTOR
Memorial
From the common of pastors, 1238, or of doctors, 1246.

HYMN
Anglorum jam apostolus. (L.M.)

Anglorum iam apostolus,	Apostle of the English race,
nunc angelorum socius,	Athirst to bring them life and grace,
ut tunc, Gregori, gentibus,	The joy of angels now you share,
succurre iam credentibus.	Extend to us your loving care.
Tu largas opum copias	Saint Gregory, you gave no thought
omnemque mundi gloriam	To honors, setting wealth at nought;
spernis, ut inops inopem	One thing alone your heart would seek,
Iesum sequaris principem.	To follow Christ both poor and meek.
Te celsus Christus pontifex	His will it was that you should hold
suæ præfert Ecclesiæ;	His place as Shepherd of the Fold;
sic Peter gradum percipis,	When raised to Peter's high estate
cuius et normam sequeris.	His zeal you strove to imitate.
Scipturæ sacræ mystica	The depths the Sacred Books contain
mire solvis ænigmata,	You could both fathom and explain;
excelsaque mysteria	The Spirit of all truth indeed
te docet ipsa Veritas.	Enlightened you in hours of need.
O pontifex egregie,	Great Pontiff in the days gone by,
lux et decus Ecclesiæ,	Protect the Church, to you we cry;
non sinas in periculis	We glory in your teaching still,
quos tot mandatis instruis.	With light and strength your children fill.
Sit Patri laus ingenito,	To God the Father glory be,
sit decus Unigenito,	Both now and in eternity,
sit utriusque parili	Be praised the Spirit and the Son
maiestas summa Flamini. Amen.	Who in the Trinity are one. Amen.

Morning Prayer

CANTICLE OF ZECHARIAH

Antiphon   Gregory, an outstanding pastor of the Church, † has left us a splendid example and *rule* of life, * a guide for all who shepherd *God's* people.

Prayer

Father,
you guide your people with kindness

and govern us with love.
By the prayers of Saint Gregory
give the spirit of wisdom
to those you have called to lead your Church.
May the growth of your people in holiness
be the eternal joy of our shepherds.
We ask this through our Lord Jesus Christ, your Son,
who lives and reigns with you and the Holy Spirit,
one God, for ever and ever.

Evening Prayer

CANTICLE OF MARY

Antiphon   Gregory put into practice all that he preached † so that he
               might be a liv*ing* example * of the spiritual message he
               *pro*claimed.

September 8
NATIVITY OF THE BLESSED VIRGIN MARY
Feast

Morning Prayer

HYMN

O Sancta. (L.M.)

O sancta mundi domina,
regina cæli inclita,
o stella maris fulgida,
virgo mater mirifica,

Appare, dulcis filia,
nitesce iam, virguncula,
florem latura nobilem,
Christum Deum et hominem.

Natalis tui annua
en colimus sollemnia,
quo stirpe delectissima
mundo fulsisti genita.

Per te sumus, terrigenæ
simulque iam cæligenæ,
pacati pace nobili,
more non æstimabili.

Sit Trinitati gloria
per sæculorum sæcula,
cuius vocaris mundere
mater beat*a* Ecclesiæ. Amen.

O Mary, Mistress of the world,
And Queen of heaven's blissful court,
O gleaming Star on life's wide sea,
And Virgin Mother, pure as snow.

To our poor earth, fair daughter, come,
In all your virgin glory, shine,
For you will bear most noble Flow'r,
When God the Son comes down as man.

Your birth from David's chosen stem,
We venerate with joy this day
You form our hope of Light to come,
To gladden and relieve our woe.

We dwell on earth, but through your prayer
Access to heaven we can win,
Once ransomed by the sacrifice
Of Christ your Son in which we share.

For ever glory and all praise
Be rendered to the Trinity,
Who gave to you a mother's place
Within the Church in name and grace. Amen.

PSALMODY

Ant. 1   We commemorate the birth of the blessèd Virgin Mary, † a
               descen*dant* of Abraham, * born of the tribe of Judah and of
               *Da*vid's seed.

Psalms and canticles from Sunday, Week I, 606.

Ant. 2   When the most holy Virgin was born, † the whole world *was*
               made radiant; * blessèd is the branch and blessèd is the stem
               which bore such ho*ly* fruit.

Ant. 3   Let us joyfully celebrate the birth of bless*èd* Mary * so that she
               may intercede for us before Jesus Christ *the* Lord.

READING   Isaiah 11:1-3
        A shoot shall sprout from the stump of Jesse,
            and from its roots a bud shall blossom.
        The spirit of the Lord shall rest upon him:
            a spirit of wisdom and of understanding,
        A spirit of counsel and of strength,
            a spirit of knowledge and of fear of the Lord,
            and his delight shall be the fear of the Lord.

RESPONSORY (VI F)
The *Lord* has chosen her, * his loved one from the *be*ginning.
— The *Lord* has chosen her, * his loved one from the *be*ginning.
He has taken her to *live* with him,
— his loved one from the *be*ginning.
Glory to the Father, and *to* the Son, * and to the Ho*ly* Spirit.
— The *Lord* has chosen her, * his loved one from the *be*ginning.

CANTICLE OF ZECHARIAH
Ant.   Your birth, O Virgin Mother of God, † proclaims joy to *the*
               whole world, * for from you arose the glorious Sun of Justice,
               Christ *our* God;
                   he freed us from the age-old curse and filled *us* with holiness; *
                   he destroyed death and gave us eter*nal* life.

INTERCESSIONS (VI F)
Let us glorify our Savior, who chose the Virgin Mary *for* his mother. * *Let* us ask
    him:
May your mother intercede for us, *Lord.*
Sun of Justice, the Immaculate Virgin was the white dawn announc*ing* your
    rising,
— grant that we may always live in the light *of* your coming.

Eternal Word, you chose Mary as the uncorrupted ark *of* your dwelling place,
— free us from the corrup*tion* of sin.
Savior of mankind, your mother stood at the foot *of* your cross,
— grant, through her intercession, that we may rejoice to share *in* your passion.
With ultimate generosity and love, you gave Mary as a mother to your belov*èd*
   disciple,
— help us to live as worthy sons of so no*ble* a mother.

Our Father . . .

Prayer

Father of mercy,
give your people help and strength from heaven.
The birth of the Virgin Mary's Son
was the dawn of our salvation.
May this celebration of her birthday
bring us closer to lasting peace.
Grant this through our Lord Jesus Christ, your Son,
who lives and reigns with you and the Holy Spirit,
one God, for ever and ever.

Evening Prayer

HYMN

Beata Dei genetrix. (L.M.)

Beata Dei genetrix;	O Blessèd Mother of our Lord,
nitor humani generis,	And glory of the human race,
per quam de servis liberi	Through you no longer are we slaves,
lucisque sumus filii;	But children of God's light and grace.
Maria, virgo regia,	Less noble is your dignity
David stirpe progenita,	As one of David's royal line,
non tam paterna nobilis	Than that bestowed on you by God
quam dignitate subolis,	As Mother of his Son divine.
Tu nos, avulso veteri,	Destroy in us the roots of ill,
complanta novo germini;	Increase in us the good begun,
per te sit genus hominum	That Christians all may fully share
regale sacerdotium.	The royal priesthood of your Son.
Tu nos culparum nexibus	For us, by your most pow'rful prayer
sacris absolve precibus;	Obtain the pardon we implore,
tua promentes merita	That we who now your praises sing
ad cæli transfer præmia.	May gain reward for evermore.
Sit Trinitati gloria,	All glory to the Trinity
o Virgo nobilissima,	Endowing you with gifts so rare,
quæ te suorum munerum	To be the cause of all our joy,
thesaurum dat magnificum. Amen.	Most holy Mary, Virgin fair! Amen.

PSALMODY

Ant. 1   The Virgin Mary came forth from the *root* of Jesse, * and the Spirit of the Most High came to dwell *in* her heart.

Psalms and canticles from the common of the Blessed Virgin Mary, 1196.

Ant. 2   Today we commemorate the birth of the *Vir*gin Mary. * God saw her beauty and visited her in *her* lowliness.

Ant. 3   Blessèd and worthy of our praise is the holy Virgin Mary, † the Mother *of* God. * We celebrate her birth, that she might intercede for us before *the* Lord.

READING   Romans 9:4-5

To the Israelites belonged the adoption, the glory, the covenants, the lawgiving, the worship, and the promises; theirs were the patriarchs, and from them came the Messiah (I speak of his human origins). Blessed forever be God who is over all! Amen.

RESPONSORY (VI F)

Hail Mary, *full* of grace, * the Lord is *with* you.
— Hail Mary, *full* of grace, * the Lord is *with* you.
Blessèd are you among women † and blessèd is the fruit *of* your womb.
— The Lord is *with* you.
Glory to the Father, and *to* the Son, * and to the Ho*ly* Spirit.
— Hail Mary, *full* of grace, * the Lord is *with* you.

CANTICLE OF MARY

Ant.   Let us commemorate the illustrious birth of the glorious *Vir*gin Mary, * for the Lord has looked with favor on his low*ly* servant. He sent his angel to an*nounce* to her * that she would conceive the Savior of *the* world.

INTERCESSIONS (VI F)

Let us praise God our almighty Father, who wished that Mary, his Son's mother, be celebrated by each *gener*ation. * Now in *need* we ask:
Mary, full of grace, intercede for us.
O God, worker of miracles, you made the Immaculate Virgin Mary share, body and soul, in your Son's glo*ry* in heaven,
— direct the hearts of your children to *that* same glory.
You made Mary our mother. Through her intercession grant strength to the weak, comfort to the sorrowing, pard*on* to sinners,
— salvation and *peace* to all.

You made Mary *full* of grace,
— grant all men the joyful abundance *of* your grace.
Make your Church of one mind and one *heart* in love,
— and help all those who believe to be one in prayer with Mary, the mo*ther* of
  Jesus.
You crowned Mary *queen* of heaven,
— may all the dead rejoice in your kingdom with the *saints* for ever.

Our Father . . .

Prayer

Father of mercy,
give your people help and strength from heaven.
The birth of the Virgin Mary's Son
was the dawn of our salvation.
May this celebration of her birthday
bring us closer to lasting peace.
Grant this through our Lord Jesus Christ, your Son,
who lives and reigns with you and the Holy Spirit,
one God, for ever and ever.

[In the dioceses of the United States]
September 9
PETER CLAVER, PRIEST
Memorial

From the common of pastors, 1238, or of holy men: those who worked with the underprivileged, 1284.

Prayer

God of mercy and love,
you offer all peoples
the dignity of sharing in your life.
By the example and prayers of Saint Peter Claver,
strengthen us to overcome all racial hatreds
and to love each other as brothers and sisters.
We ask this through our Lord Jesus Christ, your Son,
who lives and reigns with you and the Holy Spirit,
one God, for ever and ever.

September 12
THE MOST HOLY NAME OF THE BLESSED VIRGIN MARY

From the common of the Blessed Virgin Mary, 1192.

Prayer

Lord our God,
when your Son was dying on the altar of the cross,
he gave us as our mother
the one he had chosen to be his own mother,
the Blessed Virgin Mary;
grant that we who call upon the holy name of Mary, our mother,
with confidence in her protection
may receive strength and comfort in all our needs.
We ask this through our Lord Jesus Christ, your Son,
who lives and reigns with you and the Holy Spirit,
one God, for ever and ever.

September 13
JOHN CHRYSOSTOM, BISHOP AND DOCTOR
Memorial
From the common of pastors, 1238, or of doctors, 1246.

HYMN
Laude te cives. (11.11.11.5)

Laude te cives superi coronant,
magne Ioannes, sociusque noster
iungitur cantus, generose præsul,
    celse magister.

Generous leader, John the faithful shepherd,
Crowned and triumphant now among the blessèd,
To their rejoicing we would join our voices,
    Paying you honor.

Aureo profers vehementer ore
verba quæ dives facilisque amoris
vena progignit, feriunt vel acri
    vulnere noxas.

Eloquent preacher, even called "The Golden,"
Such was the beauty of your clear discourses,
Strong against evil, yet both deep and tender
    In their persuasion.

Ipse virtutum speculum nitescis
ac tuæ plebi meritis coruscas,
omnibus, Pauli velut æmulator,
    omnia factus.

You were a model for the Christian people;
Paul the Apostle you revered devoutly,
Earnestly striving to become as he did,
    All things to all men.

Nemo te frangit, nihil imperantum
te domant iræ rutilæque honorem
obtines palmæ venerandus exsul,
    pectore martyr.

Fearless and upright in the face of tyrants,
Threats could not break you, nor the rage of rulers,
Banished in exile, you remained undaunted,
    Brave as a martyr.

Nunc tuis valde precibus iuvemur,	Lovingly help us with your intercession,
ut Dei sedem celeres petamus,	That we may swiftly see God's wondrous glory,
dulcibus tecum sonituri amoris	And duly praise him with our heart's devotion,
vocibus hymnos. Amen.	With you for ever. Amen.

Prayer

Father,
the strength of all who trust in you,
you made John Chrysostom
renowned for his eloquence
and heroic in his sufferings.
May we learn from his teaching
and gain courage from his patient endurance.
We ask this through our Lord Jesus Christ, your Son,
who lives and reigns with you and the Holy Spirit,
one God, for ever and ever.

September 14
THE EXALTATION OF THE HOLY CROSS
Feast
Evening Prayer I
(when this feast occurs on Sunday)

HYMN, as in Evening Prayer II, 1076.

PSALMODY

Ant. 1   Our crucified and *ris*en Lord * has redeemed us, *al*leluia.

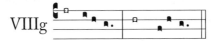

VIIIg

Psalm 147:1-11

Praise the Lord for he is good; †
  sing to our God for *he* is loving: *
to him our *praise* is due.
The Lord builds *up* Jerusalem * and
  brings back Is*ra*el's exiles,
he heals the *bro*ken-hearted, * he binds
  up *all* their wounds.
He fixes the number *of* the stars; * he
  calls each one *by* its name.
Our Lord is great *and* almighty; * his
  wisdom can ne*ver* be measured.
The Lord rais*es* the lowly; * he humbles the wicked *to* the dust.

O sing to the Lord, *giving* thanks; *
  sing psalms to our God *with* the
  harp.
He covers the heav*ens* with clouds; * he
  prepares the rain *for* the earth,
making mountains *sprout* with grass *
  and with plants to *serve* man's needs.
He provides the beasts *with* their food
  * and young ravens that *call* upon
  him.
His delight is *not* in horses * nor his
  pleasure in warriors' strength.
The Lord delights in those *who* revere

him, * in those who wait *for* his love.
Glory to the Father, and *to* the Son, *
  and to the *Ho*ly Spirit:

as it was in the begin*ning*, is now, * and
  will be for e*ver.* Amen.

Antiphon   Our crucified and *ris*en Lord * has redeemed us, *al*leluia.

Ant. 2   The tree of life flourished in the midst of the holy city *of*
                Jerusalem, * and its leaves had power to save all the nations,
                al*le*luia.

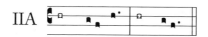

Psalm 147:12-20

O praise the *Lord*, Jerusalem! *
  Zion, praise *your* God!
He has strengthened the bars *of* your
  gates, * he has blessed the children
  *with*in you.
He established peace *on* your borders, *
  he feeds you with fin*est* wheat.
He sends out his word *to* the earth *
  and swiftly runs his com*mand*.
He showers down snow *white* as wool, *
  he scatters hoar-frost *like* ashes.
He hurls down hail*stones* like crumbs. *
  The waters are frozen at *his* touch;

he sends forth his word *and* it melts
  them: * at the breath of his mouth
  the wat*ers* flow.
He makes his word *known* to Jacob, *
  to Israel his laws and *de*crees.
He has not dealt thus with *other*
  nations; * he has not taught them his
  *de*crees.
Glory to the Father, and *to* the Son, *
  and to the Ho*ly* Spirit:
as it was in the begin*ning*, is now, * and
  will be for ever. *A*men.

Antiphon   The tree of life flourished in the midst of the holy city *of*
                Jerusalem, * and its leaves had power to save all the nations,
                al*le*luia.

Ant. 3   We must glory in *the* cross * of our Lord Je*sus* Christ.

Canticle   Philippians 2:6-11

Though he was in the form of God,
  † Jesus did not deem equality
  with God * something to *be* grasped
  at.
Rather, he emptied himself † and took
  the form of *a* slave, * being born in

the likeness *of* men.
He was known to be of human *estate*, *
  and it was thus that *he* humbled
  himself,
obediently accepting e*ven* death, *
  death on *a* cross!

Because of this, God highly *exalted* him * and bestowed on him the name above every oth*er* name,
So that at Jesus' name every knee *must* bend * in the heavens, on the earth, and under *the* earth,
and every tongue proclaim to the glory of God *the* Father: * JESUS CHRIST *IS* LORD!
Glory to the Father, and to *the* Son, * and to the Ho*ly* Spirit:
as it was in the beginning, *is* now, * and will be for ever. *A*men.

Antiphon   We must glory in *the* cross * of our Lord Je*sus* Christ.

READING   1 Corinthians 1:23-24

We preach a Christ crucified— a stumbling block to Jews, and an absurdity to Gentiles; but to those who are called, Jews and Greeks alike, Christ the power of God and the wisdom of God.

RESPONSORY (VI F)
This sign will appear *in* the heavens * when the *Lord* comes.
— This sign will appear *in* the heavens * when the *Lord* comes.
Lift up your heads, your salvation *is* at hand.
— When the *Lord* comes.
Glory to the Father, and *to* the Son, * and to the Ho*ly* Spirit.
— This sign will appear *in* the heavens * when the *Lord* comes.

CANTICLE OF MARY
Ant.   It was ordained that *Christ* should suffer, * and on the third day rise from *the* dead.

INTERCESSIONS (VI F)
Let us pray with confi*dence* to Christ * who endured the *cross* to save us:
Lord, through your cross bring us to the glory of your kingdom.
O Christ, you emptied yourself, taking the form of a servant and being *made* like us,
— grant that your people may follow the example of *your* humility.
O Christ, you humbled yourself and became obedient unto death, even death *on* a cross,
— grant that your servants may imitate your obedience and willing accept*ance* of trials.
O Christ, you were raised up by the Father and given the name that is above all *o*ther names,
— may your people, strengthened in the hope of a heavenly resurrection, perse*vere* to the end.
O Christ, at your name every knee in heaven, on earth, and under the earth will bend in *ad*oration,
— pour out your love upon all men that they may join together in proclaim*ing* your glory.

O Christ, every tongue shall confess that you are Lord to the glory of *God* the Father,

— welcome our brothers and sisters who have died into the unfailing joy *of* your kingdom.

Our Father . . .

Prayer

God our Father,
in obedience to you
your only Son accepted death on the cross
for the salvation of mankind.
We acknowledge the mystery of the cross on earth.
May we receive the gift of redemption in heaven.
We ask this through our Lord Jesus Christ, your Son,
who lives and reigns with you and the Holy Spirit,
one God, for ever and ever.

Morning Prayer

HYMN

Signum salutis. (L.M.)

Signum crucis mirabile
totum per orbem prænitet,
in qua pependit innocens
Christus, redemptor omnium.

The Holy Cross shines through the world,
To bless us with the sign of grace,
Bestowed upon our guilty race
For whom our Lord and Savior died.

Hæc arbor est sublimior
cedris, habet quas Libanus,
quæ poma nescit noxia,
sed ferre vitæ præmia.

No cedar tree of Lebanon
Can boast the glory that it claims,
No harmful fruit its branches bore,
But promise of eternal life.

Te, Christe, rex piissime,
huius crucis signaculo
horis, momentis omnibus
munire nos non abnuas,

Lord Jesus Christ, most tender King,
As ev'ry day and hour goes by,
Protect us with the sacred sign
Of your great love and sacrifice.

Ut ore tibi consono
et corde devotissimo
possimus omni tempore
laudes referre debitas.

So that we may throughout our lives
Rejoice to praise you as we should,
Our will inspiring mind and voice
To serve you with our heart's delight.

Patri, tibi, Paraclito
sit æque, Iesu, gloria
qui nos crucis victoria
concedis usque perfrui. Amen.

With Father and the Spirit One,
All glory, Jesus, be to you,
Who by the triumph of the Cross
Will lead us to eternal life. Amen.

PSALMODY

Ant. 1   To destroy the power of hell Christ died up*on* the cross; *
          clothed in strength and glory, he triumphed *over* death.

Psalms and canticles from Sunday, Week I, 606.

Ant. 2   The Lord hung upon the cross to wash away our sins in *his* own
          blood. * How splendid is that bless*èd* cross.

Ant. 3   How radiant is that precious cross which brought us our salva-
          tion. † In the cross we are victorious, † through the cross we
          shall reign, * by the cross all evil is destroyed, al*le*luia.

READING   Hebrews 2:9-10
    We see Jesus crowned with glory and honor because he suffered death, that
    through God's gracious will he might taste death for the sake of all men.
    Indeed, it was fitting that when bringing many sons to glory God, for
    whom and through whom all things exist, should make their leader in the
    work of salvation perfect through suffering.

RESPONSORY (VI F)
We adore *you*, O Christ, * and *we* bless you.
— We adore *you*, O Christ, * and *we* bless you.
By your holy cross you have re*deemed* the world.
— And *we* bless you.
Glory to the Father, and *to* the Son, * and to the Ho*ly* Spirit.
— We adore *you*, O Christ, * and *we* bless you.

CANTICLE OF ZECHARIAH
Ant.   We worship your cross, O Lord, † and we praise and glorify
          your holy *resurrection, * for the wood of the cross has brought
          joy to *the* world.

INTERCESSIONS (VI F)
Let us pray with confi*dence* to Christ * who endured the cross *to* redeem us:
Save us through your cross, O Lord.
Son of God, you healed the people of Israel when they looked upon *the* bronze
    serpent,
— protect us this day from the deadly *wound* of sin.
Son of Man, just as Moses raised up the serpent in the desert, so you were lifted
    up on the cross in the sight of *all* the nations,
— raise us up to share in the triumph *of* your cross.
Only-begotten Son of the Father, you were sent into the world so that those
    who believe in you *might* not perish,
— grant unending life to all who long to see you *face* to face.

Belovèd Son of the Father, you were not sent to judge the world *but* to save it,
— grant faith to our brothers and sisters and bring them on the last day to the *joy* of heaven.

Eternal Son of the Father, you came to cast fire on the earth and you longed to see its flame kindled in the hearts *of* all men,
— grant that through holiness of life we may come to share in the undying light *of* your glory.

Our Father . . .

Prayer

God our Father,
in obedience to you
your only Son accepted death on the cross
for the salvation of mankind.
We acknowledge the mystery of the cross on earth.
May we receive the gift of redemption in heaven.
We ask this through our Lord Jesus Christ, your Son,
who lives and reigns with you and the Holy Spirit,
one God, for ever and ever.

Evening Prayer II

HYMN

Vexilla Regis. Mode I. (L.M.)

Vexilla regis prodeunt,	Behold the standard of the King,
fulget crucis mysterium,	The Cross gleams forth its mystery;
quo carne carnis conditor	On it the Son of God as Man
suspensus est patibulo;	Atoned on earth for sinners all.
Quo, vulneratus insuper	His side was pierced by cruel lance
mucrone diro lanceæ,	That drew out water with his Blood,
ut nos lavaret crimine,	To cleanse our souls from ev'ry stain,
manavit unda et sanguine.	And nourish them with its pure stream.
Arbor decora et fulgida,	O Tree that shines with beauty rare,
ornata regis purpura,	Ennobled by Christ's precious Blood,
electa digno stipite	He chose you as the royal bed
tam sancta membra tangere!	To rest his sacred limbs in death.
Beata, cuius bracchiis	O blessèd were your rugged arms,
sæcli pependit pretium;	From which the whole world's ransom hung,
statera facta est corporis	You bore the weight of sacrifice
prædam tulitque tartari.	That snatched from greedy hell its prey.

Salve, ara, salve, victima,	Hail, holy altar, Victim hail,
de passionis gloria,	For all the glory of that Cross,
que Vita mortem pertulit	By which Life chose and welcomed death,
et morte vitam reddidit!	And dying gave us life once more.
O crux, ave, spes unica!	Hail, holy Cross, our only hope,
in hac triumphi gloria	Wash all our guilt and crimes away,
piis adauge gratiam	Increase our grace while we adore
reisque dele crimina.	In honor of your victory.
Te, fons salutis, Trinitas,	Let ev'ry soul sing in your praise,
collaudet omnis spiritus;	Salvation's Fount, O Trinity,
quos per crucis mysterium	For ever cherish those redeemed
salvas, fove per sæcula. Amen.	Through that great mystery, the Cross. Amen.

PSALMODY

Ant. 1   What a great *work* of charity! * Death itself died when life was
              slain *on* the tree.

VIIIg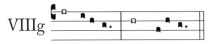

Psalm 110:1-5, 7

The Lord's revelation to my Master:
  † "Sit *on* my right: * your foes I
will put be*neath* your feet."
The Lord will wield from Zion † your
  scep*ter* of power: * rule in the midst
  of *all* your foes.
A prince from the day of your birth †
  on the *holy* mountains; * from the
  womb before the dawn *I* begot you.
The Lord has sworn an oath he will
  not change. † "You are a *priest* for
ever, * a priest like Melchize*dek* of

old."
The Master standing at *your* right
  hand * will shatter kings in the day
  of *his* great wrath.
He shall drink from the stream *by* the
  wayside * and therefore he shall lift
  up his head.
Glory to the Father, and *to* the Son, *
  and to the *Holy* Spirit:
as it was in the begin*ning*, is now, * and
  will be for ev*er*. Amen.

Antiphon   What a great *work* of charity! * Death itself died when life was
              slain *on* the tree.

Ant. 2   We worship your cross, O Lord, † and we commemorate your
              glorious passion. † You suf*fered* for us; * have mercy *on* us.

IIA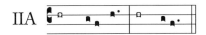

Psalm 116:10-19

I trusted, even *when* I said, * "I am
sorely *afflicted*,"
and when I said in *my* alarm: * "No
man can *be* trusted."
How can I re*pay* the Lord * for his
goodness *to* me?
The cup of salvation *I* will raise; * I
will call on *the* Lord's name.
My vows to the Lord I *will* fulfill *
before all *his* people.
O precious in the eyes *of* the Lord * is
the death of *his* faithful.

Your servant, Lord, your ser*vant* am I;
* you have loosened *my* bonds.
A thanksgiving sacri*fice* I make: * I will
call on *the* Lord's name.
My vows to the Lord I *will* fulfill *
before all *his* people,
in the courts of the house *of* the Lord, *
in your midst, O *Jerusalem*.
Glory to the Father, and *to* the Son, *
and to the Ho*ly* Spirit:
as it was in the begin*ning*, is now, * and
will be for ever. *Amen*.

Antiphon   We worship your cross, O Lord, † and we commemorate your
                  glorious passion. † You suf*fered* for us; * have mercy *on* us.

Ant. 3   We adore you, O Christ, and *we* bless you, * for by your holy
                  cross you have redeemed *the* world.

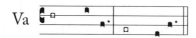

Canticle   Revelation 4:11; 5:9, 10, 12

O Lord our God, you *are* worthy *
to receive glory and honor *and*
power.
For you have created *all* things; * by
your will they came to be and *were*
made.
Worthy are you, *O* Lord, * to receive
the scroll and break open *its* seals.
For you *were* slain; * with your blood
you purchased *for* God
men of every race *and* tongue, * of
every people *and* nation.

You made of them a kingdom, † and
priests to serve *our* God, * and they
shall reign on *the* earth.
Worthy is the Lamb that *was* slain * to
receive power *and* riches,
wisdom *and* strength, * honor and
glory *and* praise.
Glory to the Father, and to *the* Son, *
and to the Ho*ly* Spirit:
as it was in the beginning, *is* now, * and
will be for ever. *Amen*.

Antiphon   We adore you, O Christ, and *we* bless you, * for by your holy
                  cross you have redeemed *the* world.

READING   1 Corinthians 1:23-24
      We preach a Christ crucified— a stumbling block to Jews, and an absurdity
      to Gentiles; but to those who are called, Jews and Greeks alike, Christ the
      power of God and the wisdom of God.

RESPONSORY (VI F)

O glo*ri*ous cross, * on you the King of angels was *vic*torious.

— O glo*ri*ous cross, * on you the King of angels was *vic*torious.

And he has washed away our sins in *his* own blood.

— On you the King of angels was *vic*torious.

Glory to the Father, and *to* the Son, * and to the Ho*ly* Spirit.

— O glo*ri*ous cross, * on you the King of angels was *vic*torious.

CANTICLE OF MARY

Ant.　　　　　O cross, you are the glorious sign *of* our victory. * Through your power may we share in the triumph of *Christ* Jesus.

INTERCESSIONS (VI F)

Let us pray with confi*dence* to Christ * who endured the *cross* to save us:

Lord, through your cross bring us to the glory of your kingdom.

O Christ, you emptied yourself, taking the form of a servant and being *made* like us,

— grant that your people may follow the example of *your* humility.

O Christ, you humbled yourself and became obedient unto death, even death *on* a cross,

— grant that your servants may imitate your obedience and willing accept*ance* of trials.

O Christ, you were raised up by the Father and given the name that is above all *o*ther names,

— may your people, strengthened in the hope of a heavenly resurrection, perse*vere* to the end.

O Christ, at your name every knee in heaven, on earth, and under the earth will bend in *ado*ration,

— pour out your love upon all men that they may join together in proclaim*ing* your glory.

O Christ, every tongue shall confess that you are Lord to the glory of *God* the Father,

— welcome our brothers and sisters who have died into the unfailing joy *of* your kingdom.

Our Father . . .

Prayer, as in Morning Prayer, 1076.

September 15
OUR LADY OF SORROWS
Memorial

Morning Prayer
HYMN

Stabat Mater. (cont.) (8.8.7)

Eia, mater, fons amoris,	Mother, fount of love and pity
me sentire vim doloris	Make me feel, if for a moment,
fac, ut tecum lugeam.	Something of your depths of woe.
Fac ut ardeat cor meum	Fill my heart with true devotion,
in amando Christum Deum,	That my love for God increasing,
ut sibi complaceam.	I may ever please him more.
Sancta mater, istud agas,	Holy Mother, I implore you,
Crucifixi fige plagas	Print the sacred wounds of Jesus
cordi meo valide.	Firmly in my inmost heart.
Tui Nati vulnerati,	Share with me the fearful torments
tam dignati pro me pati	Of your Son thus lacerated,
pœnas mecum divide.	Glad to die for love of me.
Fac me vere tecum flere,	By your tears, O Mother sinless,
Crucifixo condolere,	Win me grace of deep contrition,
donec ego vixero.	Which will grow as life goes on.
Iuxta crucem tecum stare	Keep my heart united always
ac me tibi sociare	To your sorrow and your courage,
in planctu desidero.	As you stood beside the Cross.
Quando corpus morietur,	When this mortal life is ended,
fac ut animæ donetur	May my soul enjoy the glory
paradisi gloria. Amen.	Of the vision of my Lord. Amen.

PSALMODY

Ant. 1   My soul *clings* to you, * Lord *Je*sus Christ.

Psalms and canticles from Sunday, Week I, 606.

Ant. 2   Let *us* rejoice * that we have been made sharers in *Christ's* passion.

Ant. 3   It has pleased the Father to reconcile all creation in *him*self * through the blood *of* Christ.

READING   Colossians 1:24-25

Even now I find my joy in the suffering I endure for you. In my own flesh I fill up what is lacking in the sufferings of Christ for the sake of his body, the church. I became a minister of this church through the commission God gave me to preach among you his word in its fullness.

RESPONSORY (VI F)

Through you we drink from the wellsprings *of* salvation, * O Bless*è*d Vir*gin* Mary.
— Through you we drink from the wellsprings *of* salvation, * O Bless*è*d Vir*gin* Mary.
From the sacred *wounds* of Christ,
— O Bless*è*d Vir*gin* Mary.
Glory to the Father, and *to* the Son, * and to the Ho*ly* Spirit.
    Through you we drink from the wellsprings *of* salvation, * O Bless*è*d Vir*gin* Mary.

CANTICLE OF ZECHARIAH

Ant.   Rejoice, O sorrowful Mother; † after your great sufferings, you shine *forth* as Queen, * enthroned beside *your* Son.

INTERCESSIONS (VI F)

Let us glorify our Savior, who chose the Virgin Mary *for* his mother. * *Let* us ask him:
May your mother intercede for us, Lord.
Sun of Justice, the Immaculate Virgin was the white dawn announc*ing* your rising,
— grant that we may always live in the light *of* your coming.
Eternal Word, you chose Mary as the uncorrupted ark *of* your dwelling place,
— free us from the corrup*tion* of sin.
Savior of mankind, your mother stood at the foot *of* your cross,
— grant, through her intercession, that we may rejoice to share *in* your passion.
With ultimate generosity and love, you gave Mary as a mother to your belov*è*d disciple,
— help us to live as worthy sons of so no*ble* a mother.

Our Father . . .

                              Prayer

Father,
    as your Son was raised on the cross,
    his mother Mary stood by him, sharing his sufferings.
    May your Church be united with Christ
    in his suffering and death

and so come to share in his rising to new life,
where he lives and reigns with you and the Holy Spirit,
one God, for ever and ever.

Evening Prayer

HYMN

Stabat Mater. (cont.) (8.8.7)

Virgo virginum præclara, mihi iam non sis amara; fac me tecum plangere.	Virgin of all virgins favored, Do not turn from me though sinful, Let me mourn and weep with you.
Fac ut portem Christi mortem, passionis fac me sortem et plagas recolere.	Made me bear the death of Jesus In my very soul's recesses, And his sacred wounds adore.
Fac me plagis vulnerari, cruce hac inebriari et cruore Filii.	By his wounds may I be strengthened, May the Blood he shed to save me Be as wine unto my soul.
Flammis urar ne succensus, per te, Virgo, sim defensus in die iudicii.	On the searching day of Judgment, Holy Virgin Mary help me, Let me not be cast away.
Fac me cruce custodiri, morte Christi præmuniri, confoveri gratia.	Make the Cross my sure salvation, With Christ's death as my protection May I pass from grace to grace.
Quando corpus morietur, fac ut animæ donetur paradisi gloria. Amen.	When this mortal life is ended, May my soul enjoy the glory Of the vision of my Lord. Amen.

PSALMODY

Ant. 1   Through his cross, *Christ* our peace * has reconciled *us* to God.

Psalms and canticles from the common of the Blessed Virgin Mary, 1196.

Ant. 2   We have come to the city of the *living* God, * and to Jesus,
                mediator of the *new* Covenant.

Ant. 3   In Christ we have *re*demption * through *his* blood.

READING   2 Timothy 2:10-12a
    I bear with all this for the sake of those whom God has chosen, in order that
they may obtain the salvation to be found in Christ Jesus and with it eternal
glory. You can depend on this:
        If we have died with him

we shall also live with him;
If we hold out to the end
we shall also reign with him.

RESPONSORY (VI F)

Holy Mary, heaven's Queen *and* our Lady, * you stood by the cross of *the* Lord.
— Holy Mary, heaven's Queen *and* our Lady, * you stood by the cross of *the* Lord.
Happy is she, who without dying has won the *mar*tyr's crown.
— You stood by the cross of *the* Lord.
Glory to the Father, and *to* the Son, * and to the Ho*ly* Spirit.
— Holy Mary, heaven's Queen *and* our Lady, * you stood by the cross of *the* Lord.

CANTICLE OF MARY

Ant.   When Jesus saw his mother standing beside the cross † with the disciple *whom* he loved, * he said to her: Woman, behold *your* son.
Then he said to *the* disciple: * Behold *your* mother.

INTERCESSIONS (VI F)

Let us glorify our Savior, who chose the Virgin Mary *for* his mother. * *Let* us ask him:
May your mother intercede for us, *Lord.*
Sun of Justice, the Immaculate Virgin was the white dawn announc*ing* your rising,
— grant that we may always live in the light *of* your coming.
Eternal Word, you chose Mary as the uncorrupted ark *of* your dwelling place,
— free us from the corrup*tion* of sin.
Savior of mankind, your mother stood at the foot *of* your cross,
— grant, through her intercession, that we may rejoice to share *in* your passion.
With ultimate generosity and love, you gave Mary as a mother to your belov*èd* disciple,
— help us to live as worthy sons of so no*ble* a mother.

Our Father . . .

Prayer, as in Morning Prayer, 1081.

September 16
CORNELIUS, POPE AND MARTYR,
AND CYPRIAN, BISHOP AND MARTYR
Memorial

From the common of several martyrs, 1214, or of pastors, 1238.

Morning Prayer

CANTICLE OF ZECHARIAH

Ant.　　　　How precious the death of those who purchased e*ter*nal life *
by shedding *their* blood.

Prayer

God our Father,
in Saints Cornelius and Cyprian
you have given your people an inspiring example
of dedication to the pastoral ministry
and constant witness to Christ in their suffering.
May their prayers and faith give us courage
to work for the unity of your Church.
Grant this through our Lord Jesus Christ, your Son,
who lives and reigns with you and the Holy Spirit,
one God, for ever and ever.

Evening Prayer

CANTICLE OF MARY

Ant.　　　　O *bless*èd Church, * the blood of martyrs has made *you* glorious.

September 17
ROBERT BELLARMINE, BISHOP AND DOCTOR
From the common of pastors, 1238, or of doctors, 1246.

Prayer

God our Father,
you gave Robert Bellarmine wisdom and goodness
to defend the faith of your Church.
By his prayers
may we always rejoice in the profession of our faith.
We ask this through our Lord Jesus Christ, your Son,
who lives and reigns with you and the Holy Spirit,
one God, for ever and ever.

September 19
JANUARIUS, BISHOP AND MARTYR

From the common of one martyr, 1228, or of pastors, 1238.

Prayer

God our Father,
enable us who honor the memory of Saint Januarius
to share with him the joy of eternal life.
Grant this through our Lord Jesus Christ, your Son,
who lives and reigns with you and the Holy Spirit,
one God, for ever and ever.

September 20
ANDREW KIM TAEGON, PRIEST AND MARTYR
PAUL CHONG HASANG, AND COMPANIONS, MARTYRS
Memorial

From the common of several martyrs, 1214.

Prayer

O God,
you have created all nations
and you are their salvation.
In the land of Korea
your call to Catholic faith formed a people of adoption,
whose growth you nurtured
by the blood of Andrew, Paul, and their companions.
Through their martyrdom and their intercession
grant us strength
that we too may remain faithful to your commandments
even until death.
We ask this through our Lord Jesus Christ, your Son,
who lives and reigns with you and the Holy Spirit,
one God, for ever and ever.

September 21
MATTHEW, APOSTLE AND EVANGELIST
Feast

From the common of apostles, 1206, except for the following:

Morning Prayer
HYMN

Præclara qua. (L.M.)

Præclara qua tu gloria,	The glory that surrounds your name,
Levi beate, cingeris,	O blessèd Levi, is a proof
laus est Dei clementiæ,	Of God's all loving clemency
spes nostra ad indulgentiam.	Besides a sign of hope for us.
Teloneo quando assidens	While seated at your counting board,
nummis inhæres anxius,	O Matthew, Christ just bade you come,
Matthæe, Christus advocans	Without a word of all the wealth
opes tibi quas præparat!	Of grace he had in store for you.
Iam cordis ardens impetu	Your heart no hesitation knew,
curris, Magistrum suscipis,	From then your house became his own,
sermone factus inclito	In following, you gave up all
princeps in urbe cælica.	To earn the triumph of the Twelve.
Tu verba vitæ colligens	The life the Son of David led,
Davidque facta Filii,	The words he spoke, you stored as gold,
per scripta linquis aurea	Which, handed down the centuries,
cæleste mundo pabulum.	Have fed and taught the Christian world.
Christum per orbem nuntians	You spread the Gospel fearlessly,
confessus atque sanguine,	Until at last you shed your blood,
dilectionis vividæ	In witness to your faith in Christ
supremo honoras pignore.	And pledge of your undying love.
O martyr atque apostole,	Apostle and evangelist
evangelista nobilis,	With martyrdom as final crown,
tecum fac omne in sæculum	Bring us to heaven, that with you
Christo canamus gloriam. Amen.	God's praises we may ever sing. Amen.

CANTICLE OF ZECHARIAH

Ant.   The Lord saw a man named Matthew sitting at the tax collector's office † and said to him: *Fol*low me. * Matthew got up and fol*lowed* him.

Prayer

God of mercy,
you chose a tax collector, Saint Matthew,
to share the dignity of the apostles.
By his example and prayers

help us to follow Christ
and remain faithful in your service.
We ask this through our Lord Jesus Christ, your Son,
who lives and reigns with you and the Holy Spirit,
one God, for ever and ever.

Evening Prayer

CANTICLE OF MARY
Ant.   I desire mercy *and* not sacrifice. * I did not come to call the
virtuous *but* sinners.

September 23
PIO OF PIETRELCINA, PRIEST

From the common of pastors, 1238.

Prayer

God our Father,
in Saint Padre Pio
you gave a light to your faithful people.
You made him a pastor of the Church
to feed your sheep with his word
and to teach them by his example.
Help us by his prayers to keep the faith he taught
and follow the way of life he showed us.
Grant this through our Lord Jesus Christ, your Son,
who lives and reigns with you and the Holy Spirit,
one God, for ever and ever.

September 26
COSMAS AND DAMIAN, MARTYRS

From the common of several martyrs, 1214.

Prayer

Lord,
we honor the memory of Saints Cosmas and Damian.
Accept our grateful praise
for raising them to eternal glory
and for giving us your fatherly care.
We ask this through our Lord Jesus Christ, your Son,
who lives and reigns with you and the Holy Spirit,
one God, for ever and ever.

September 27
VINCENT DE PAUL, PRIEST
Memorial

From the common of pastors, 1238, or of holy men: those who worked for the underprivileged, 1284, except for the following:

Morning Prayer

CANTICLE OF ZECHARIAH

Ant.   Vincent consoled the sorrowful, † defended the *rights* of orphans
                     * and generously aid*ed* widows.

Prayer

God our Father,
you gave Vincent de Paul
the courage and holiness of an apostle
for the well-being of the poor
and the formation of the clergy.
Help us to be zealous in continuing his work.
Grant this through our Lord Jesus Christ, your Son,
who lives and reigns with you and the Holy Spirit,
one God, for ever and ever.

Evening Prayer

CANTICLE OF MARY

Ant.   Whatever you do for the least *of* my brothers, * you do *for* me.

September 28
WENCESLAUS, MARTYR

From the common of one martyr, 1228.

Prayer

Lord,
you taught your martyr Wenceslaus
to prefer the kingdom of heaven
to all that the earth has to offer.
May his prayers free us from our self-seeking
and help us to serve you with all our hearts.
We ask this through our Lord Jesus Christ, your Son,
who lives and reigns with you and the Holy Spirit,
one God, for ever and ever.

On the same day, September 28
LAWRENCE RUIZ AND COMPANIONS, MARTYRS
From the common of several martyrs, 1214.

Prayer

Lord God,
in our service to you and to our neighbor
give us the patience of the holy martyrs,
Lawrence and his companions;
for those who suffer persecution for justice's sake
are blessèd in the Kingdom of heaven.
We ask this through our Lord Jesus Christ, your Son,
who lives and reigns with you and the Holy Spirit,
one God, for ever and ever.

September 29
MICHAEL, GABRIEL AND RAPHAEL, ARCHANGELS
Feast

Morning Prayer
HYMN
Tibi Christe. (87.87.87)

Tibi, Christe, splendor Patris,
vita, virtus cordium,
in conspectu angelorum
votis, voce psallimus;
alternantes concrepando
melos damus vocibus.

Collaudamus venerantes
inclitos archangelos,
sed præcipue primatem
cælestis exercitus,
Michælem in virtute
conterentem Satanam.

Quo custode procul pelle,
rex Christe piissime,
omne nefas inimici;
mundos corde et corpore
paradiso redde tuo
nos sola clementia.

Jesus, Splendor of the Father,
Life and strength of ev'ry heart,
In the presence of the angels,
In their praise we would take part,
Making melody to echo
What they sing both day and night.

We extol with veneration
Great archangels round the throne;
First, their leader, holy Michael,
Prince of all angelic hosts,
Who with Satan entered combat,
And in conflict overcame.

By his guardianship we pray you,
Christ our King and gracious Lord,
Drive the evil tempter from us,
Soul and body, keep us pure,
Unto Paradise restore us
By your wondrous clemency.

Gloriam Patri melodis	Let us sing with joyful voices
personemus vocibus,	Glory to our Father, God,
gloriam Christo canamus,	Glory be to Christ our Savior,
gloriam Paraclito,	Glory to the Spirit blest,
qui Deus trinus et unus	Reigning in three Persons perfect,
exstat ante sæcula. Amen.	Yet for ever Godhead One. Amen.

PSALMODY

Ant. 1   Let us join the angels in praising the Lord, † as the cherubim
               and seraphim sing: * Holy, holy, holy.

Psalms and canticles from Sunday, Week I, 606.

Ant. 2   Angels of the Lord, * sing praise to the Lord for ever.

Ant. 3   All the angels in heaven praise you, O Lord, † and with one
               voice they say: * To you we owe our hymn of praise, O God.

READING   Genesis 28:12-13a
   Jacob had a dream: a stairway rested on the ground, with its top reaching to
   the heavens; and God's messengers were going up and down on it. And there
   was the Lord standing beside him and saying: "I, the Lord, am the God of
   your forefather Abraham and the God of Isaac."

RESPONSORY (VI F)
An angel stood * by the altar.
— An angel stood * by the altar.
And held a golden censer,
— by the altar.
Glory to the Father, and to the Son, * and to the Holy Spirit.
— An angel stood * by the altar.

CANTICLE OF ZECHARIAH
Ant.   Truly I say to you: † You will see the heavens open up, * and the
               angels of God ascending and descending upon the Son of Man.

INTERCESSIONS (VI F)
With one voice the choirs of angels sing their unceasing praise of the Lord. * Let
   us join in their worship as we proclaim:
Angels of the Lord, bless the Lord.
You commanded your angels to guard us in all our ways,
— keep us from sin as you lead us in your path this day.
Father, the angels stand for ever before your face,
— nourish in us a never-failing hope of coming at last into your presence.

Your children will be like the an*gels* in heaven,
— grant us chastity in both *mind* and body.
Send Michael, the prince of the heavenly hosts, to the aid *of* your people,
— may he defend them against Satan and his angels on the *day* of battle.

Our Father . . .

Prayer

God our Father,
in a wonderful way you guide the work of angels and men.
May those who serve you constantly in heaven
keep our lives safe from all harm on earth.
Grant this through our Lord Jesus Christ, your Son,
who lives and reigns with you and the Holy Spirit,
one God, for ever and ever.

Evening Prayer

HYMN

Angelum pacis. (11.11.11.5)

Angelus pacis Michæl ad istam,
Christe, demitti rogitamus aulam,
cuncta quo crebro veniente crescant
    prospera nobis.

Lord of the angels, Christ our loving Savior,
Send holy Michael down among your people,
That he may bring us peace and true assistance
    On our life's journey.

Angelus fortis Gabriel, ut hostem
pellat antiquum, volitet superne,
sæpius templus cupiens favendo
    visere nostrum.

Gabriel's presence, strong, unseen and gentle,
Surely protects us if you will but send him
Into this temple, ever glad to help us,
    Shielding from evil.

Angelum nobis medicum salutis
mitte de cælis Raphæl, ut omnes
sanet ægrotos pariterque nostros
    dirigat actus.

Send holy Raphael tenderly to heal us,
Bringing salvation from our hidden blindness,
And by his counsel may he guide our actions,
    Each day and always.

Christe, sanctorum decus angelorum,
adsit illorum chorus usque nobis,
ut simul tandem Triadi per ævum
    carmina demus. Amen.

May all the angels constantly attend us,
That we may join them praising the one Godhead;
This we implore you, Jesus ever reigning,
    Joy of the angels. Amen.

PSALMODY

Ant. 1   Your majesty is praised *above* the heavens, * O King *of* the angels.

VIIIg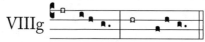

Psalm 8

How great is your name, O *Lord* our God, * through *all* the earth!

Your majesty is praised a*bove* the heavens; * on the lips of children *and* of babes

you have found praise to *foil* your enemy, * to silence the foe *and* the rebel.

When I see the heavens, the work *of* your hands, * the moon and the stars which *you* arranged,

what is man that you should keep *him* in mind, * mortal man that you *care* for him?

Yet you have made him little less *than* a god; * with glory and ho*nor* you crowned him,

gave him power over the works *of* your hand, * put all things un*der* his feet.

All of them, *sheep* and cattle, * yes, even the *savage* beasts,

birds of the *air*, and fish * that make their way *through* the waters.

How great is your name, O *Lord* our God, * through *all* the earth!

Glory to the Father, and *to* the Son, * and to the *Holy* Spirit:

as it was in the begin*ning*, is now, * and will be for e*ver*. Amen.

Antiphon   Your majesty is praised a*bove* the heavens, * O King *of* the angels.

Ant. 2   In the company *of* the angels * I will sing psalms to you, *my* God.

IIA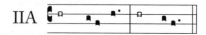

Psalm 138

I thank you, Lord, with *all* my heart, * you have heard the words of *my* mouth.

In the presence of the angels *I* will bless you. * I will adore before your ho*ly* temple.

I thank you for your faithful*ness* and love * which excel all we ever knew *of* you.

On the day I *called*, you answered; * you increased the strength of *my* soul.

All earth's *kings* shall thank you * when they hear the words of *your* mouth.

They shall sing *of* the Lord's ways: * "How great is the glory of *the* Lord!"

The Lord is high yet he looks *on* the lowly * and the haughty he knows from *a*far.

Though I walk in the midst *of* affliction * you give me life and frustrate
my foes.

You stretch out your *hand* and save me,
* your hand will do all things *for* me.

Your love, O Lord, *is* eternal, * discard
not the work of *your* hands.

Glory to the Father, and *to* the Son, *
and to the Ho*ly* Spirit:

as it was in the begin*ning*, is now, * and
will be for ever. *A*men.

Antiphon   In the company *of* the angels * I will sing psalms to you, *my*
God.

Ant. 3   I saw the Lamb, which appeared to have been slain, † standing
in the center of *the* throne, * and I heard the sound of angelic
choirs around *the* throne.

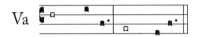

Va

Canticle   Colossians 1:12-20

Let us give thanks to the Father †
for having made *you* worthy * to
share the lot of the saints *in* light.

He rescued us from the power *of*
darkness * and brought us into the
kingdom of his belovèd Son.

Through him we have *re*demption, *
the forgiveness of *our* sins.

He is the image of the invisi*ble* God, *
the first-born of *all* creatures.

In him everything in heaven and on
earth was *cre*ated, * things visible and
*in*visible.

All were created *through* him; * all were
created *for* him.

He is before all else *that* is. * In him

everything continues *in* being.

It is he who is head of the body, *the*
church! * he who is the beginning,

the first-born of *the* dead, * so that
primacy may be his *in* everything.

It pleased God to make absolute
fullness reside *in* him * and, by
means of him, to reconcile everything in *his* person,

both on earth and in *the* heavens, *
making peace through the blood of
his cross.

Glory to the Father, and to *the* Son, *
and to the Ho*ly* Spirit:

as it was in the beginning, *is* now, * and
will be for ever. *A*men.

Antiphon   I saw the Lamb, which appeared to have been slain, † standing
in the center of *the* throne, * and I heard the sound of angelic
choirs around *the* throne.

READING   Revelation 1:4b-5

Grace and peace—from him who is and who was and who is to come, and
from the seven spirits before his throne, and from Jesus Christ the faithful
witness, the first-born from the dead and ruler of the kings of earth, who
loves us and freed us from our sins by his own blood.

RESPONSORY (VI F)

Clouds of *in*cense rose * in the presence of *the* Lord.

— Clouds of *in*cense rose * in the presence of *the* Lord.

From the hand of the angel *in*cense rose

— in the presence of *the* Lord.

Glory to the Father, and *to* the Son, * and to the Ho*ly* Spirit.

— Clouds of *in*cense rose * in the presence of *the* Lord.

CANTICLE OF MARY

Ant.   The angel Gabriel spoke to Mary and said: † "You will conceive and *bear* a son, * and you shall name *him* Jesus.

INTERCESSIONS

The angels carry *out* God's will. * Let us pray that we too may listen carefully for his voice and hear his call, *as* we say:

We beg you, *hear us.*

That our prayers may rise like a pleasant frag*rance* before you,

— through the hands *of* your angels.

We beg you, *hear us.*

That our prayers may be brought to your al*tar* on high,

— through the hands *of* your angels.

We beg you, *hear us.*

That we may proclaim glory to God in the highest and peace to his peo*ple* on earth,

— with the multitude of the hea*ven*ly armies.

We beg you, *hear us.*

That the angels may receive us at the end *of* our days,

— and lead us *home* to paradise.

We beg you, *hear us.*

That the holy standard-bearer, Michael, may bring into the light *of* your presence,

— the souls of those *who* have died.

We beg you, *hear us.*

Our Father . . .

Prayer

God our Father,
in a wonderful way you guide the work of angels and men.
May those who serve you constantly in heaven
keep our lives safe from all harm on earth.
Grant this through our Lord Jesus Christ, your Son,
who lives and reigns with you and the Holy Spirit,
one God, for ever and ever.

September 30
JEROME, PRIEST AND DOCTOR
Memorial

From the common of doctors, 1246, except for the following:

From the common of doctors, 1246, except for the following:

HYMN

Festiva canimus. (11.11.11.5)

Festiva canimus laude Hieronymum,	Jerome the ardent, strong and keen ascetic,
qui nobis radiat sidus ut eminens	Eminent scholar, steeped in erudition,
doctrinæ meritis ac simul actibus	Greatly we praise him since all ages profit
vitæ fortis et asperæ.	By his wide knowledge.
Hic verbum fidei sanctaque dogmata	Learnèd and tireless, nothing could deter him
scrutando studuit pandere lucide,	From patient study, though when critics pressed him,
aut hostes, vehemens ut leo, concitus	Fierce as a lion, he would swiftly answer
acri voce refellere.	In refutation.
Insudans alacer prata virentia	Sparing no labor, he explored with relish
Scripturæ coluit cælitus editæ;	Scripture's green pastures, digging for its treasure,
ex his et locuples dulcia protulit	That in its pages many should find graces
cunctis pabula gratiæ.	Rich and abundant.
Deserti cupiens grata silentia,	Seeking the silence of the lonely desert
ad cunas Domini pervigil astitit,	Christ's lowly birth place won his predilection;
ut carnem crucians se daret intime	There to his labors and his prayer he added
Patri munus et hostiam.	Penance and fasting.
Tanti nos, petimus te, Deus optime,	Lord God our Father, humbly we implore you,
doctoris precibus difige, confove,	Guide and protect us through his intercession,
ut lætas liceat nos tib*i* in omnia	So that rejoicing we may sing your praises
laudes pangere sæcula. Amen.	In light eternal. Amen.

Prayer

Father,
you gave Saint Jerome delight
in his study of holy scripture.
May your people find in your word
the food of salvation and the fountain of life.
We ask this through our Lord Jesus Christ, your Son,
who lives and reigns with you and the Holy Spirit,
one God, for ever and ever.

October 1
THERESA OF THE CHILD JESUS, VIRGIN
Memorial

From the common of virgins, 1253, except for the following:

Morning Prayer

CANTICLE OF ZECHARIAH

Ant.   Truly I say to you, † unless you change your lives and become like *lit*tle children, * you will not enter the kingdom *of* heaven.

Prayer

God our Father,
you have promised your kingdom
to those who are willing to become like little children.
Help us to follow the way of Saint Theresa with confidence
so that by her prayers
we may come to know your eternal glory.
Grant this through our Lord Jesus Christ, your Son,
who lives and reigns with you and the Holy Spirit,
one God, for ever and ever.

Evening Prayer

CANTICLE OF MARY

Ant.   Rejoice *and* be glad, * for your names are written *in* heaven.

October 2
GUARDIAN ANGELS
Memorial

Morning Prayer
HYMN
Orbis patrator. (L.M.)

Orbis patrator optime,	O great Creator of the world,
quæcumque sunt qui dextera	You hand divine has fashioned all,
magna creasti, nec regis	And with an equal providence
minore providentia,	You guard us lest we fail and fall.
Adesto supplicantium	Be present with us while we pray,
tibi reorum cœtui,	Poor sinners, but your children too,
lucisque sub crepusculum	From dawn to dusk, most loving Lord,
lucem novam da mentibus.	Enrich our souls with light anew.

Tuusque nobis angelus,
signatus ad custodiam,
hic adsit, a contagio
qui criminum nos protegat.

Each angel whom you have assigned
To help and guide us night and day,
Be present, also, pure and strong,
To keep all harm and sin away.

Nobis draconis æmuli
caluminias exterminet,
ne rete fraudulentiæ
incauta nectat pectora.

May he be ever at our side
To bid the hostile fiend depart,
Lest he ensnare with his deceits
The heedless and unwary heart.

Metum repellat hostium
nostris procul de finibus;
pacem secundet civium
fugetque pestilentiam.

And may he shield us from the fear
Of enemies and constant strife,
Averting pestilence and woe
That peace may truly bless our life.

Deo Patri sit gloria,
qui, quos redemit Filius
et Sanctus unxit Spiritus,
per angelos custodiat. Amen.

All glory to the Father be,
Who by his angels fear dispels,
From souls whom God the Son redeemed,
In whom the Holy Spirit dwells. Amen.

PSALMODY

Ant. 1   The Lord will send his angel *to* accompany you * and to guide you safely *on* your way.

Psalms and canticles from Sunday, Week I, 606.

Ant. 2   Blessèd be God who *sent* his angels * to rescue his faith*ful* servants.

Ant. 3   Praise *the* Lord, * all you heavenly hosts *of* angels.

READING   Exodus 23:20-21a
See, I am sending an angel before you, to guard you on the way and bring you to the place I have prepared. Be attentive to him and heed his voice.

RESPONSORY (VI F)
In the presence *of* the angels, * I will sing to you, *my* God.
— In the presence *of* the angels, * I will sing to you, *my* God.
I will *praise* your name.
— I will sing to you, *my* God.
Glory to the Father, and *to* the Son, * and to the Ho*ly* Spirit.
— In the presence *of* the angels, * I will sing to you, *my* God.

CANTICLE OF ZECHARIAH
Ant.   They are all minis*ter*ing spirits, * sent to care for those on the way to *sal*vation.

INTERCESSIONS

With one voice the choirs of angels sing their unceasing praise *of* the Lord. * Let
us join in their worship as *we* proclaim:
Angels of the Lord, bless the Lord.
You commanded your angels to guard us in *all* our ways,
— keep us from sin as you lead us in your *path* this day.
Father, the angels stand for ever be*fore* your face,
— nourish in us a never-failing hope of coming at last in*to* your presence.
Your children will be like the an*gels* in heaven,
— grant us chastity in both *mind* and body.
Send Michael, the prince of the heavenly hosts, to the aid *of* your people,
— may he defend them against Satan and his angels on the *day* of battle.

Our Father . . .

Prayer

God our Father,
in your loving providence
you send your holy angels to watch over us.
Hear our prayers,
defend us always by their protection
and let us share your life with them for ever.
We ask this through our Lord Jesus Christ, your Son,
who lives and reigns with you and the Holy Spirit,
one God, for ever and ever.

Evening Prayer

HYMN

Custodes hominum. (11.11.11.5)

Custodes hominum psallimus angelos,	Let us sing gratefully praising the guardians
naturæ fragili quos Pater addidit	Whom God's own providence gives to protect us all,
cælestis comites, insidiantibus	For they watch over us lest we are led astray
ne succumberet hostibus.	By the wiles of the enemy.
Nam quod corruerit proditor angelus,	For since proud Lucifer, banished from heaven's court
concessis merito pulsus honoribus,	Became a rebel prince, keen to avenge himself,
ardens invidia pellere nititur	His bitter jealousy seeks to prevent our race
quos cælo Deus advocat.	From attaining its destiny.
Huc, custos, igitur pervigil advola,	Hasten to succour us, watchful custodian;
avertens partia de tibi credita	Keep all calamities from those who trust in you;
tam morbos animi quam requiescere	Let nothing trouble us, dangers, anxieties,
quicquid non sinit incolas.	Counsel us in perplexity.

Sanctæ sit Triadi laus pia iugiter,
cuius perpetuo numine machina
triplex hæc regitur, cuius in omnia
    regnat gloria sæcula. Amen.
	All praise eternally be to the Trinity,
	Whose one Omnipotence rules all created things,
	Whose glory infinite reigns in supremacy
	    Outside time and the centuries. Amen.

Ant. 1   The angel of the Lord encamps around *those* who fear him, * to
              *res*cue them.

VIIIg

Psalm 34
I

I will bless the Lord *at* all times, *
his praise always *on* my lips;
in the Lord my soul shall *make* its
    boast. * The humble shall hear *and* be
    glad.
Glorify the *Lord* with me. * Together let
    us *praise* his name.
I sought the Lord *and* he answered me;
    * from all my terrors he *set* me free.
Look towards him *and* be radiant; * let
    your faces not *be* abashed.
This poor man called; *the* Lord heard
    him * and rescued him from all *his*
    distress.

The angel of the Lord is encamped
    around those *who* revere him, * to
    *res*cue them.
Taste and see that the *Lord* is good. *
    He is happy who seeks re*fuge* in him.
Revere the Lord, *you* his saints. * They
    lack nothing, those *who* revere him.
Strong lions suffer want *and* go hungry
    * but those who seek the Lord *lack*
    no blessing.
Glory to the Father, and *to* the Son, *
    and to the *Ho*ly Spirit:
as it was in the begin*ning,* is now, * and
    will be for ev*er.* Amen.

Antiphon   The angel of the Lord encamps around *those* who fear him, * to
              *res*cue them.

Ant. 2   Our God is a *liv*ing God, * for his angel has *pro*tected me.

IIA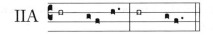

II

C ome, chil*dren,* and hear me *
that I may teach you the fear of
    the Lord.
Who is he who *longs* for life * and
    many days, to enjoy his *pros*perity?
Then keep your *tongue* from evil * and
    your lips from speaking *de*ceit.

Turn aside from evil *and* do good; *
    seek and strive af*ter* peace.
The Lord turns his face a*gainst* the
    wicked * to destroy their remem-
    brance from *the* earth.
The Lord turns his eyes *to* the just *
    and his ears to their *ap*peal.

They call and *the* Lord hears * and
rescues them in all their *dis*tress.
The Lord is close to the *broken-*
hearted; * those whose spirit is
crushed he *will* save.
Many are the trials *of* the just man *
but from them all the Lord will
res*cue* him.
He will keep guard over *all* his bones, *
not one of his bones shall *be* broken.

Evil brings death *to* the wicked; * those
who hate the good *are* doomed.
The Lord ransoms the souls *of* his
servants. * Those who hide in him
shall not be con*demned*.
Glory to the Father, and *to* the Son, *
and to the Ho*ly* Spirit:
as it was in the begin*ning*, is now, * and
will be for ever. *A*men.

Antiphon   Our God is a *living* God, * for his angel has *pro*tected me.

Ant. 3   Glorify the God of heaven, † sing praise to him before all liv*ing*
creatures, * for he has shown you such *great* mercy.

Canticle   Revelation 11:17-18; 12:10b-12a

We praise you, the Lord God
Almighty, * who is and *who* was.
You have assumed your *great* power, *
you have begun *your* reign.
The nations have raged in anger, † but
then came your day *of* wrath * and the
moment to judge *the* dead:
the time to reward your servants the
prophets † and the holy ones who
re*vere* you, * the great and the small
a*like*.
Now have salvation and po*wer* come, *
the reign of our God and the authority of his *A*nointed One.

For the accuser of our brothers is *cast*
out, * who night and day accused
them be*fore* God.
They defeated him by the blood of the
Lamb † and by the word of *their*
testimony; * love for life did not deter
them *from* death.
so rejoice, *you* heavens, * and you that
dwell *there*in!
Glory to the Father, and to *the* Son, *
and to the Ho*ly* Spirit:
as it was in the beginning, *is* now, * and
will be for ever. *A*men.

Antiphon   Glorify the God of heaven, † sing praise to him before all liv*ing*
creatures, * for he has shown you such *great* mercy.

READING   Revelation 8:3-4

An angel came in holding a censer of gold. He took his place at the altar of
incense and was given large amounts of incense to deposit on the altar of gold
in front of the throne, together with the prayers of all God's holy ones. From
the angel's hand the smoke of the incense went up before God, and with it
the prayers of God's people.

RESPONSORY (VI F)

God *gave* his angels * charge o*ver* you.

— God *gave* his angels * charge o*ver* you.

To protect you in *all* your ways.

— God gave his angels charge o*ver* you.

Glory to the Father, and *to* the Son, * and to the Ho*ly* Spirit.

— God *gave* his angels * charge o*ver* you.

CANTICLE OF MARY

Ant.　　　The angels will *al*ways see * the face of my heaven*ly* Father.

INTERCESSIONS

The angels carry *out* God's will. * Let us pray that we too may listen carefully for his voice and hear his call, *as* we say:

With the angels we sing of your glory.

O God, you made the angels messengers of your mar*ve*lous works,

— help us to proclaim your wonderful deeds *to* all men.

The angels unceasingly proclaim that you are holy *and* exalted,

— may your people on earth join their voices to the angelic *song* of praise.

You commanded your angels to watch over your servants in *all* their ways,

— guide those who are traveling and bring them home safely in joy *and* in peace.

You gave the angels the mission of announcing *peace* to men,

— inspire counsels of peace in the hearts of leaders and peoples *of* all nations.

When you send forth the angels to gather together your chosen people from every corner *of* the earth,

— do not let them pass over any of your children, but bring them all to the unending gladness *of* your kingdom.

Our Father . . .

Prayer

God our Father,
in your loving providence
you send your holy angels to watch over us.
Hear our prayers,
defend us always by their protection
and let us share your life with them for ever.
We ask this through our Lord Jesus Christ, your Son,
who lives and reigns with you and the Holy Spirit,
one God, for ever and ever.

October 4
FRANCIS OF ASSISI, RELIGIOUS
Memorial
From the common of holy men: religious, 1282., except for the following:

Morning Prayer
HYMN
In cælesti collegio. (L.M.)

In cælesti collegio	Among the happy throng above
Franciscus fulget gloria,	St. Francis shines with luster rare,
insigni privilegio	While yet on earth he had the grace
Christi portans insignia.	The wound of Jesus Christ to bear.
Hic cœtus apostolici	Apostle's lot he gladly chose,
est factus consors pauperis,	A wand'ring life of poverty,
crucem in se dominici	To preach to all the cross of Christ,
signum reportans fœderis.	And bear it with serenity.
Hic martyr desiderio	The joy of martyrs now he shares
crucem post Iesum baiulat,	Who proved their love for Christ by death;
quem martyrum consortio	He was a martyr in desire,
Christus in cælis copulat.	And suffered till his latest breath.
Crucem per abstinentiam	The Cross of Christ he daily bore,
Franciscus ferens iugiter,	In abnegation's rugged ways;
iam confessorum gloriam	Confessor's glory thus he won,
adeptus est feliciter.	And sings their special hymn of praise.
Candens decore niveo,	The gentle choir of virgins too
passum hic sequens Dominum,	Can claim for him their own reward,
nunc castitatis præmio	For Francis in all purity
gaudet in choro virginum.	Pursued with love his suff'ring Lord.
Pater, Natus cum Flamine	May God the Father with the Son
nos per Francisci vulnera	And Holy Spirit grant us grace,
lustrent divino lumine,	through the stigmata Francis bore,
æterna dantes munera. Amen.	To win above our lasting place. Amen.

CANTICLE OF ZECHARIAH

Ant.   Francis left this earth a poor and lowly man; † he enters heaven rich *in* God's favor, * greeted with songs of *re*joicing.

Prayer

Father,
you helped Saint Francis to reflect the image of Christ
through a life of poverty and humility.

May we follow your Son
by walking in the footsteps of Francis of Assisi,
and by imitating his joyful love.
Grant this through our Lord Jesus Christ, your Son,
who lives and reigns with you and the Holy Spirit,
one God, for ever and ever.

Evening Prayer

CANTICLE OF MARY

Ant.   God forbid that I should boast † except in the cross of our Lord
                Jesus Christ; * for I bear the marks of Jesus on *my* body.

October 6
BRUNO, PRIEST

From the common of pastors, 1238, or of holy men: religious, 1282, except for the following:

Prayer

Father,
you called Saint Bruno to serve you in solitude.
In answer to his prayers
help us to remain faithful to you
amid the changes of this world.
We ask this through our Lord Jesus Christ, your Son,
who lives and reigns with you and the Holy Spirit,
one God, for ever and ever.

[In the dioceses of the United States]
On the same day, October 6
BLESSED MARIE-ROSE DUROCHER, VIRGIN

From the common of virgins, 1253.

Prayer

Lord,
you enkindled in the heart of blessèd Marie-Rose Durocher
the flame of ardent charity
and a great desire to collaborate, as teacher,
in the mission of the Church.
Grant us that same active love,
so that in responding to the needs of the world today,
we may lead our brothers and sisters to eternal life.
We ask this through our Lord Jesus Christ, your Son,
who lives and reigns with you and the Holy Spirit,
one God, for ever and ever.

October 7
OUR LADY OF THE ROSARY
Memorial
From the common of the Blessed Virgin Mary, 1192, except for the following:

Morning Prayer

Ant. 1   Mary gave *birth* to Jesus, * who is *called* the Christ.

Psalms and canticles from Sunday, Week I, 606.

Ant. 2   Holy Mother, † on the cross Christ entrusted us to you *as* your
children. * Today we join with you in prais*ing* him.

Ant. 3   The Virgin Mary, crowned with a diadem of *twelve* stars, * is
exalted above the choirs *of* angels.

READING   See Isaiah 61:10
I rejoice heartily in the Lord,
in my God is the joy of my soul;
For he has clothed me with a robe of salvation,
and wrapped me in a mantle of justice,
like a bride bedecked with her jewels.

RESPONSORY (VI F)
Hail Mary, *full* of grace, * the Lord is *with* you.
— Hail Mary, *full* of grace, * the Lord is *with* you.
Blessèd are you among women, and blessèd is the fruit *of* your womb.
— The Lord is *with* you.
Glory to the Father, and *to* the Son, * and to the Ho*ly* Spirit.
— Hail Mary, *full* of grace, * the Lord is *with* you.

CANTICLE OF ZECHARIAH
Ant.   Holy and immaculate Virgin Mary, † you are the glorious
Queen *of* the world; * may all who celebrate your feastday know
the help of *your* prayers.

INTERCESSIONS from the common of the Blessed Virgin Mary, 1193.

Prayer
Lord,
fill our hearts with your love,
and as you revealed to us by an angel
the coming of your Son as man,
so lead us through his suffering and death

to the glory of his resurrection,
who lives and reigns with you and the Holy Spirit,
one God, for ever and ever.

Evening Prayer

Ant. 1   The angel Gabriel brought God's mess*age* to Mary, * and she
            conceived by the power of the *Ho*ly Spirit.

Psalms and canticles from the common of the Blessed Virgin Mary, 1196.

Ant. 2   His *moth*er stood * beside *the* cross.

Ant. 3   Rejoice, O Vir*gin* Mother; * Christ has risen from the dead,
            al*le*luia.

READING   Galatians 4:4-5
   When the designated time had come, God sent forth his Son born of a
   woman, born under the law, to deliver from the law those who were subjected
   to it, so that we might receive our status as adopted sons.

RESPONSORY (VI F)
Hail Mary, *full* of grace, * the Lord is *with* you.
— Hail Mary, *full* of grace, * the Lord is *with* you.
Blessèd are you among women, and blessèd is the fruit *of* your womb.
— The Lord is *with* you.
Glory to the Father, and *to* the Son, * and to the Ho*ly* Spirit.
— Hail Mary, *full* of grace, * the Lord is *with* you.

CANTICLE OF MARY
Ant.   Mary heard the *word* of God * and cherished it in *her* heart.

INTERCESSIONS from the common of the Blessed Virgin Mary, 1199.
Prayer, as in Morning Prayer, 1104.

October 9
DENIS, BISHOP AND MARTYR, AND COMPANIONS, MARTYRS
From the common of several martyrs, 1214.

Prayer

Father,
you sent Saint Denis and his companions
to preach your glory to the nations,
and you gave them strength
to be steadfast in their sufferings for Christ.
Grant that we may learn from their example

to reject the power and wealth of this world
and to brave all earthly trials.
We ask this through our Lord Jesus Christ, your Son,
who lives and reigns with you and the Holy Spirit,
one God, for ever and ever.

On the same day, October 9
JOHN LEONARDI, PRIEST

From the common of pastors, 1238, or of holy men: those who worked for the underprivileged, 1284.

Prayer

Father,
giver of all good things,
you proclaimed the good news to countless people
through the ministry of Saint John Leonardi.
By the help of his prayers
may the true faith continue to grow.
Grant this through our Lord Jesus Christ, your Son,
who lives and reigns with you and the Holy Spirit,
one God, for ever and ever.

October 14
CALLISTUS I, POPE AND MARTYR

From the common of one martyr, 1228, or of pastors, 1238.

Prayer

God of mercy,
hear the prayers of your people
that we may be helped by Saint Callistus,
whose martyrdom we celebrate with joy.
We ask this through our Lord Jesus Christ, your Son,
who lives and reigns with you and the Holy Spirit,
one God, for ever and ever.

October 15
TERESA OF JESUS, VIRGIN AND DOCTOR
Memorial

From the common of virgins, 1253, or of doctors, 1246, except for the following:

Morning Prayer
HYMN

Regis superni. (L.M.)

Regis superni nuntia	Teresa, yet a child in years,
domum paternam deseris,	You left your home with heart afire,
terris, Teresia, barbaris	To spread abroad the faith in Christ,
Christum datura aut sanguinem.	A martyr, ready in desire.
Sed te manet suavior	A death more gentle will be yours,
mors, pœna poscit dulcior:	With pain far sweeter, yet more keen,
divini amoris cuspide	For wound divine will pierce your soul
in vulnus icta concides.	With its consuming flame serene.
O caritatis victima,	O victim of undying love,
tu corda nostra concrema,	Make our poor hearts in fervor grow;
tibique gentes creditas	Protect all those who trust in you,
inferni ab igne libera.	And save us from eternal woe.
Te, sponse, Iesu, virginum,	O Jesus, Spouse of virgins pure,
beati adorent ordines,	Their happy ranks your praises sing
et nuptiali cantico	For ever, with that melody
laudent per omne sæculum. Amen.	Known but to virgins and their King. Amen.

Prayer

Father,
by your Spirit you raised up Saint Teresa of Avila
to show your Church the way to perfection.
May her inspired teaching
awaken in us a longing for true holiness.
Grant this through our Lord Jesus Christ, your Son,
who lives and reigns with you and the Holy Spirit,
one God, for ever and ever.

Evening Prayer
HYMN

Hæc est. (L.M.)

Hæc est dies, qua candidæ	Upon this day Teresa's soul
instar columbæ, cælitum	Like gentle dove, no more to roam,
ad sacra templa spiritus	Found peace within the mansions blest
se transtulit Teresiæ,	Of our eternal Father's home.

Sponsique voces audiit:	At last she heard the Bridegroom's voice:
« Veni, soror, de vertice	"My loved one, come from Carmel's height,
Carmel*i* ad Agni nuptias ;	The spotless Lamb awaits his bride,
ven*i* ad coronam gloriæ ».	Receive your crown in glory's light."
Te, sponse, Iesu, virginum,	O Jesus, Spouse of virgins pure,
beat*i* adorent ordines,	Their happy ranks your praises sing
et nuptiali cantico	For ever, with that melody
laudent per omne sæculum. Amen.	Known but to virgins and their King. Amen.

October 16
HEDWIG, RELIGIOUS

From the common of holy women: those who worked for the underprivileged, 1284, or religious, 1282.

Prayer

All-powerful God,
may the prayers of Saint Hedwig bring us your help
and may her life of remarkable humility
be an example to us all.
We ask this through our Lord Jesus Christ, your Son,
who lives and reigns with you and the Holy Spirit,
one God, for ever and ever.

On the same day, October 16
MARGARET MARY ALACOQUE, VIRGIN

From the common of virgins, 1253, or of holy women: religious, 1282.

Prayer

Lord,
pour out on us the riches of the Spirit
which you bestowed on Saint Margaret Mary.
May we come to know the love of Christ,
which surpasses all human understanding,
and be filled with the fullness of God.
Grant this through our Lord Jesus Christ, your Son,
who lives and reigns with you and the Holy Spirit,
one God, for ever and ever.

October 17
IGNATIUS OF ANTIOCH, BISHOP AND MARTYR
Memorial
From the common of one martyr, 1228, or of pastors, 1238, except for the following:

Morning Prayer

CANTICLE OF ZECHARIAH

Ant.   I seek him who *died* for us; * I long for him who rose for *our* sake.

Prayer

All-powerful and ever-living God,
you ennoble your Church
with the heroic witness of all
who give their lives for Christ.
Grant that the victory of Saint Ignatius of Antioch
may bring us your constant help
as it brought him eternal glory.
We ask this through our Lord Jesus Christ, your Son
who lives and reigns with you and the Holy Spirit,
one God, for ever and ever.

Evening Prayer

CANTICLE OF MARY

Ant.   I hunger for the bread of God, the flesh of *Je*sus Christ, * born
of *Da*vid's seed;
I long to drink *of* his blood, * the gift of his unend*ing* love.

October 18
LUKE, EVANGELIST
Feast
HYMN

Pausibus, Luca. (11.11.11.5)

Plausibus, Luca, canimus, triumphum
quo nites fuso rutilo cruore,
atque præcelsis meritis adeptam
    rite coronam.
	Holy and learnèd, great Saint Luke, we praise you,
	Closely you followed in the steps of Jesus;
	As supreme witness to his life and teaching
	    Shedding your life-blood.

Spiritus ductu, studiosus orbi
mira quæ pastor docuit supernus
Christus ac fecit miserans amore,
    tradis amanter.
	Under the guidance of the Holy Spirit,
	You left in writing, for all time to study
	Stories unrivaled for their depth and beauty,
	    Christ's love revealing.

Providus chartis perhibes venustis	Yours are the records which we read with pleasure
gesta quæ Iesu celebrant alumnos,	Of the beginning of the Church so fervent,
eius et gentis nova quæ patescunt	Under the impulse of the true and living
in nova sæcla.	Spirit of Jesus.

Providus chartis perhibes venustis
gesta quæ Iesu celebrant alumnos,
eius et gentis nova quæ patescunt
                    in nova sæcla.

O comes Pauli, speculator alti
cordis illius sed et æmulator,
caritas Christi fac ut usque nostrum
                    pectus adurat.

Tu malis nostris medicus fer artem,
confer et lætum fidei levamen,
ut Deo tandem potiamur, ipsi
                    semper ovantes. Amen.

Yours are the records which we read with pleasure
Of the beginning of the Church so fervent,
Under the impulse of the true and living
                    Spirit of Jesus.

Paul's earnest helper, sharer in his travels,
Zealous as he was, with a heart as loving;
Make our souls also steadfast and devoted
                    To the Lord Jesus.

Tender physician, use your gift of healing,
Comfort our weakness with a faith unswerving,
So that rejoicing we may praise for ever
                    God the Almighty. Amen.

Morning Prayer

Ant. 1   The holy evangelists searched the wisdom *of* past ages. *
              Through their gospels they confirmed the words *of* the proph-
              ets.

Psalms and canticles from Sunday, Week I, 606.

Ant. 2   Through the Gospel † God called us to believe *in* the truth *
              and to share the glory of our Lord Je*sus* Christ.

Ant. 3   Many will praise *their* wisdom; * it shall be remembered *for* ever.

READING   1 Corinthians 15:1-2a, 3-4
    Brothers, I want to remind you of the gospel I preached to you, which you
    received and in which you stand firm. You are being saved by it at this very
    moment. I handed on to you first of all what I myself received, that Christ
    died for our sins in accordance with the Scriptures; that he was buried and,
    in accordance with the Scriptures, rose on the third day.

RESPONSORY (VI F)
They proclaimed *the* Lord's praises, * told of his power *to* save.
— They proclaimed *the* Lord's praises, * told of his power *to* save.
And of the wonders *he* had worked.
— They told of his power *to* save.
Glory to the Father, and *to* the Son, * and to the Ho*ly* Spirit.
— They proclaimed *the* Lord's praises, * told of his power *to* save.

CANTICLE OF ZECHARIAH
Ant.   Saint Luke gave us the *gospel* message * and proclaimed Christ
              as the dawn from *on* high.

INTERCESSIONS

Let us sing a song of praise to our Savior, who destroyed the power of death and made clear the path to life and immortality *through* the Gospel; * and let us petition him in humble *sup*plication:

Strengthen your Church in faith and *love.*

You gave wonderful guidance to your Church through her holy and dis*tin*-guished teachers,

— may Christians rejoice always in the splendid legacy given *to* your Church.

When their holy pastors prayed to you, as Moses had done, you forgave the sins *of* the people,

— through the intercession of these holy pastors continue to sanctify and puri*fy* your Church.

You anointed your holy ones in the midst of their brothers and called the Holy Spirit *down* upon them,

— fill all the leaders of your people with the *Ho*ly Spirit.

You yourself are the sole possession of your *ho*ly pastors,

— grant that those you have redeemed with your blood may remain al*ways* in you.

Our Father . . .

Prayer

Father,
you chose Luke the evangelist to reveal
by preaching and writing
the mystery of your love for the poor.
Unite in one heart and spirit
all who glory in your name,
and let all nations come to see your salvation.
Grant this through our Lord Jesus Christ, your Son,
who lives and reigns with you and the Holy Spirit,
one God, for ever and ever.

Evening Prayer

HYMN, as in Morning Prayer, 1109.

Ant. 1   My life is at the service *of* the Gospel; * God have given me this gift *of* his grace.

Psalms and canticles from the common of apostles, 1208.

Ant. 2   I do all this for the sake *of* the Gospel, * in order to share in its *re*wards.

Ant. 3   This grace has been given *to* me: * to proclaim to the nations the
                infinite riches *of* Christ.

READING   Colossians 11:3-6a

We always give thanks to God, the Father of our Lord Jesus Christ, in our
prayers for you because we have heard of your faith in Christ Jesus and the
love you bear toward all the saints— moved as you are by the hope held in
store for you in heaven. You heard of this hope through the message of
truth, the gospel, which has come to you, has borne fruit, and has continued
to grow in your midst, as it has everywhere in the world.

RESPONSORY (VI F)

Tell *all* the nations * how glorious *God* is.
— Tell *all* the nations * how glorious *God* is.
Make known his wonders to *every* people.
— How glorious *God* is.
Glory to the Father, and *to* the Son, * and to the Ho*ly* Spirit.
— Tell *all* the nations * how glorious *God* is.

CANTICLE OF MARY

Ant.   The holy evangelist Luke is worthy of praise *in* the Church, *
                for he has proclaimed the tender compassion *of* Christ.

[In the dioceses of the United States: Memorial]

October 19
ISAAC JOGUES AND JOHN DE BREBEUF, PRIESTS
AND MARTYRS, AND COMPANIONS, MARTYRS

From the common of several martyrs, 1214, or of pastors, 1238.

Prayer

Father,
you consecrated the first beginnings
of the faith in North America
by the preaching and martyrdom
of Saints John and Isaac and their companions.
By the help of their prayers
may the Christian faith continue to grow
throughout the world.
We ask this through our Lord Jesus Christ, your Son,
who lives and reigns with you and the Holy Spirit,
one God, for ever and ever.

[In the dioceses of the United States]
October 20
PAUL OF THE CROSS, PRIEST
From the common of pastors, 1238, or of holy men: religious, 1282.

Prayer

Father,
you gave your priest Saint Paul
a special love for the cross of Christ.
May his example inspire us
to embrace our own cross with courage.
Grant this through our Lord Jesus Christ, your Son,
who lives and reigns with you and the Holy Spirit,
one God, for ever and ever.

October 23
JOHN OF CAPISTRANO, PRIEST
From the common of pastors, 1238.

Prayer

Lord,
you raised up Saint John of Capistrano
to give your people comfort in their trials.
May your Church enjoy unending peace
and be secure in your protection.
We ask this through our Lord Jesus Christ, your Son,
who lives and reigns with you and the Holy Spirit,
one God, for ever and ever.

October 24
ANTHONY MARY CLARET, BISHOP
From the common of pastors, 1238.

Prayer

Father,
you endowed Anthony Claret
with the strength of love and patience
to preach the gospel to many nations.
By the help of his prayers
may we work generously for your kingdom
and gain our brothers and sisters for Christ,
who lives and reigns with you and the Holy Spirit,
one God, for ever and ever.

October 28
SIMON AND JUDE, APOSTLES
Feast

From the common of apostles, 1206, except for the following:

Morning Prayer
HYMN

Commune vos. (L.M.)

Commune vos, apostoli,	One joyful hymn of praise must greet
extollat hymni iubilum,	Apostles whom we always find
quos advocat par gratia,	Together in the Gospel's page,
coronat una gloria.	By faithful love and zeal combined.
Ardore pulsus cælico,	To follow Christ in early youth
Christi premis vestigia,	Was surely Simon's joy and pride,
Simon, et illum nuntias	Before the Zealot would set forth
zelo peractus impigro.	To preach His Name both far and wide.
Tu carne frater, assecla	Saint Jude, a kinsman of our Lord,
fraterque Christi spiritu,	In heart and mind yet closer still,
Iuda, Magistrum prædicas	Your words remain until this day
scriptisque fratres erudis.	With hope and love our souls to fill.
Nec pertimescit sanguinem	As brothers both in life and death,
uterque purum fundere,	A martyr's crown was your reward,
ut veritatis enitens	As shining witnesses to truth
sit testis atque victima.	And victims worthy of your Lord.
O summa cæli sidera,	O gleaming stars in heaven's light
nos detis ut per aspera,	Help us to tread our thorny way,
fide valentes integra,	That with our faith alert and strong
tendamus ad cælestia.	We may attain to glory's day.
Patri per ævum gloria	Be praised the Father evermore,
Natoque cum Paraclito,	The Holy Spirit and the Son,
quorum supernis gaudiis	May we rejoice before God's throne
simul fruemur perpetim. Amen.	Eternally when life is done. Amen.

Prayer

Father,
you revealed yourself to us
through the preaching of your apostles Simon and Jude.
By their prayers,
give your Church continued growth
and increase the number of those who believe in you.
Grant this through our Lord Jesus Christ, your Son,
who lives and reigns with you and the Holy Spirit,
one God, for ever and ever.

November 1
ALL SAINTS
Solemnity

Evening Prayer I

HYMN

Christe, Redemptor omnium. (L.M.)

Christe, redémptor omnium,	Most dear Redeemer of us all,
conserva tuos famulos,	Protect your servants in their need,
beatae semper Virginis	Accept the Blessèd Virgin's prayers,
placatus sanctis précibus.	Who deigns for us to intercede.
Beata quoque agmina	All choirs of holy Angels too,
caeléstium spirituum,	Who praise our God both night and day,
praeterita, praeséntia,	Both past and present woes dispel,
futura mala pellite.	All future evils keep away.
Vates aeterni iudicis	Great prophets of the Judge supreme,
apostolique Domini,	And keen Apostles of our Lord,
suppliciter exposcimus	We humbly beg the pow'rful aid
salvari vestris précibus.	Your intercession will afford.
Martyres Dei incliti	All martyrs for God's holy Name,
confessorésque lucidi,	Who gloried in Christ's death to share,
vestris orationibus	And those whose lives have honored him,
nos ferte in caeléstibus.	Bring us to heaven by your prayer.
Chori sanctarum virginum	All monks and nuns who reap in joy
monachorumque omnium,	The fruits of ardent toil and praise,
simul cum sanctis omnibus	Help us to earn our sight of God
consortes Christi facite.	With contemplation's purest gaze.
Sit Trinitati gloria,	Give glory to the Trinity,
vestrasque voces iungite	And join your voices to our own,
ut illi laudes débitas	That fittingly our eager praise
persolvamus alacriter. Amen.	May mount before God's holy throne. Amen.

PSALMODY

Ant. 1   Eternal light will shine upon your *saints*, O Lord, * and they
will live for ever, *al*leluia.

VIIIg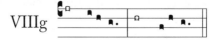

Psalm 113

Praise, O servants *of* the Lord, * praise the name *of* the Lord!	May the name of the *Lord* be blessed * both now and for *ev*ermore!

From the rising of the sun *to* its setting
 * praised be the name *of* the Lord!
High above all nations *is* the Lord, *
 above the heav*ens* his glory.
Who is like the *Lord,* our God, * who
 has risen on high *to* his throne
yet stoops from the heights *to* look
 down, * to look down upon heav*en*
 and earth?
From the dust he lifts *up* the lowly, *

from his misery he rais*es* the poor
 to set him in the company of princes, *
 yes, with the princes *of* his people.
To the childless wife he *gives* a home *
 and gladdens her *heart* with children.
Glory to the Father, and *to* the Son, *
 and to the *Holy* Spirit:
as it was in the begin*ning,* is now, * and
 will be for ev*er.* Amen.

Antiphon   Eternal light will shine upon your *saints,* O Lord, * and they
                will live for ever, a*l*leluia.

Ant. 2   Jerusalem, city *of* God, * you will rejoice *in* your children,
                for they shall all *be* blessed * and gathered together with the
                Lord, a*l*leluia.

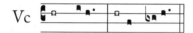

Psalm 147:12-20

O praise the Lord, *Jerusalem!* *
 Zion, *praise* your God!
He has strengthened the bars of *your*
 gates, * he has blessed the chil*dren*
 within you.
He established peace on *your* borders, *
 he feeds you with *fin*est wheat.
He sends out his word to *the* earth *
 and swiftly runs *his* command.
He showers down snow white *as* wool, *
 he scatters hoar-*frost* like ashes.
He hurls down hailstones *like* crumbs.
 * The waters are frozen *at* his touch;

he sends forth his word and *it* melts
 them: * at the breath of his mouth the
 wat*ers* flow.
 He makes his word known *to* Jacob, *
 to Israel his laws *and* decrees.
He has not dealt thus with o*ther*
 nations; * he has not taught them *his*
 decrees.
Glory to the Father, and to *the* Son, *
 and to the *Holy* Spirit:
as it was in the beginning, *is* now, * and
 will be for ev*er.* Amen.

Antiphon   Jerusalem, city *of* God, * you will rejoice *in* your children,
                for they shall all *be* blessed * and gathered together with the
                Lord, a*l*leluia.

Ant. 3 Before the throne of God and the Lamb † the saints will sing a new song; † their voices will resound throughout *the* earth, * alleluia, alleluia.

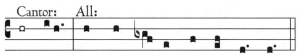

** al- le- lu- ia, al- le- lu- ia.

*Al- le- lu- ia.   ** al- le- lu- ia, al- le - lu- ia.

Canticle   See Revelation 19:1-7

Salvation, glory, and power to *our* God:
* Alleluia.
his judgments are hon*est* and true.
** Alleluia, alleluia.
Sing praise to our God, all you *his* servants,
* Alleluia.
all who worship him reverently, *great* and small.
** Alleluia, alleluia.

The Lord our all-powerful God *is* King;
* Alleluia.
let us rejoice, sing praise, and *give* him glory.
** Alleluia, alleluia.

The wedding feast of the Lamb has *be*gun,
* Alleluia.
and his bride is pre*pared* to welcome him.
** Alleluia, alleluia.

Glory to the Father, and to the Son, †
and to the Ho*ly* Spirit.
* Alleluia.
As it was in the beginning, is now, †
and will be for ev*er*. Amen.
** Alleluia, alleluia.

Antiphon Before the throne of God and the Lamb † the saints will sing a new song; † their voices will resound throughout *the* earth, * alleluia, alleluia.

READING   Hebrews 12:22-24

You have drawn near to Mount Zion and the city of the living God, the
heavenly Jerusalem, to myriads of angels in festal gathering, to the assembly
of the first-born enrolled in heaven, to God the judge of all, to the spirits of
just men made perfect, to Jesus, the mediator of a new covenant, and to the
sprinkled blood which speaks more eloquently than that of Abel.

RESPONSORY

The just *shall* rejoice * in the presence of *the* Lord.
— The just *shall* rejoice * in the presence of *the* Lord.
They shall *sing* for joy
— in the presence of *the* Lord.
Glory to the Father, and *to* the Son, * and to the Ho*ly* Spirit.
— The just *shall* rejoice * in the presence of *the* Lord.

CANTICLE OF MARY

Antiphon   The glorious company of apostles praises you, † the noble
                    fellowship of prophets *prais*es you, * the white-robed army of
                    martyrs prais*es* you,
                    all the saints together *sing* your glory, * O Holy Trinity, *one* God.

M y soul ✠ proclaims the greatness
   of the Lord, * my spirit rejoices
   in God *my* savior
for he has *looked* with favor * on his
   low*ly* servant.
From this day all *gen*erations * will call
   me blessèd:
the Almighty has done great *things* for
   me, * and holy is *his* Name.
He has mercy on *those* who fear him *
   in every gen*er*ation.
He has shown the strength *of* his arm, *
   he has scattered the proud in their
   *con*ceit.
He has cast down the mighty *from*

their thrones, * and has lifted up *the*
   lowly.
He has filled the hungry *with* good
   things, * and the rich he has sent
   a*way* empty.
He has come to the help of his *ser*vant
   Israel * for he has remembered his
   promise *of* mercy,
the promise he made *to* our fathers, * to
   Abraham and his children *for* ever.
Glory to the Father, and *to* the Son, *
   and to the Ho*ly* Spirit:
as it was in the begin*ning*, is now, * and
   will be for ever. *A*men.

Antiphon   The glorious company of apostles praises you, † the noble
                    fellowship of prophets *prais*es you, * the white-robed army of
                    martyrs prais*es* you,
                    all the saints together *sing* your glory, * O Holy Trinity, *one*
                    God.

INTERCESSIONS

God is the reward of *all* the saints. * Let us joyfully *call* upon him:
Lord, save your *people.*

O God, through your Son Jesus Christ you built your Church on the foundation of *the* apostles,
— keep their teaching secure among your *faith*ful people.

You made the martyrs powerful witnesses even to the point of giving *up* their lives,
— help all Christians to give faithful witness *to* your Son.

You gave holy virgins the gift of imitating the virgini*ty* of Christ,
— may those consecrated to virginity be steadfast witnesses to the coming *of* your kingdom.

Your saints now see you *face* to face,
 keep alive in our hearts the hope of coming at last in*to* your presence.

Bring all who have died into the company of heaven with Mary, Joseph and *all* your saints,
— and give us also a place in the unending fellowship *of* your kingdom.

Our Father . . .

Prayer

Father, all-powerful and ever-living God,
today we rejoice in the holy men and women
of every time and place.
May their prayers bring us your forgiveness and love.
We ask this through our Lord Jesus Christ, your Son,
who lives and reigns with you and the Holy Spirit,
one God, for ever and ever.

Morning Prayer

HYMN

Jesu, salvator sæculi. (L.M.)

Iesu, salvator sæculi,	O Jesus, Savior of the world,
redémptis ope subveni,	Assist the souls you have redeemed;
et, pia Dei génetrix,	And gentle Mother of our Lord,
salutem posce miseris.	For us poor sinners pardon win.
Coetus omnes angélici,	May all the gleaming Angel hosts
patriarcharum cunei	And patient Patriarchs serene,
ac prophetarum mérita	And Prophets faithful unto death,
nobis precéntur véniam.	Make supplication for the world.

Baptista tui praevius	May John, fore-runner of our Light,
et claviger aethéreus	And he who holds the keys above,
cum céteris apostolis	And all Apostles of our Lord,
nos solvant nexu criminis.	Absolve us from the stains of sin.
Chorus sacratus martyrum,	And may the Martyrs countless throng,
sacerdotum conféssio	And Priests devoted to their Lord,
et virginalis castitas	And holy virgins' merits too,
nos a peccatis abluant.	Obtain remission for our falls.
Monachorum suffragia	May pure monastic prayer above,
omnésque cives caelici	United with all Saints on high,
annuant votis supplicum	Accept our lowly sighs on earth,
et vitae poscant praeminum.	And gain for us eternal life.
Sit, Christe, tibi gloria	All glory, Jesus, be to you,
cum Patre et Sancto Spiritu,	The Father and the Spirit, too,
quorum luce mirifica	Whose wondrous light is cause of joy
sancti congaudent pérpetim. Amen.	For all the Saints eternally. Amen.

PSALMODY

Ant. 1   The saints find their home in the king*dom* of heaven; * their life
               is eternal peace, *a*lleluia.

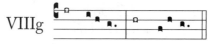

VIIIg

Psalm 63:2-9

O God, you are my God, for *you* I
long; * for you my *soul* is thirsting.
My body *pines* for you * like a dry,
weary land *with*out water.
So I gaze on you *in* the sanctuary * to
see your strength *and* your glory.
For your love is bet*ter* than life, * my
lips will *speak* your praise.
So I will bless you *all* my life, * in your
name I will lift *up* my hands.
My soul shall be filled as *with* a

banquet, * my mouth shall praise *you*
with joy.
On my bed I re*mem*ber you. * On you
I muse *through* the night
for you have *been* my help; * in the
shadow of your wings *I* rejoice.
My soul *clings* to you; * your right
hand *holds* me fast.
Glory to the Father, and *to* the Son, *
and to the *Holy* Spirit:
as it was in the begin*ning*, is now, * and
will be for *ever*. Amen.

Antiphon   The saints find their home in the king*dom* of heaven; * their life
             is eternal peace, *a*lleluia.

Ant. 2   Saints *of* the Lord, * sing praise to the Lord *for* ever.

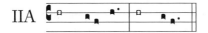

                        Canticle   Daniel 3:57-88; 56

Bless the Lord, all you works *of* the
Lord. * Praise and exalt him above
all *for*ever.

Angels of the Lord, *bless* the Lord, *
You heavens, bless *the* Lord.

All you waters above the heavens, *bless*
the Lord. * All you hosts of the
Lord, bless *the* Lord.

Sun and moon, *bless* the Lord. * Stars
of heaven, bless *the* Lord.

Every shower and dew, *bless* the Lord. *
All you winds, bless *the* Lord.

Fire and heat, *bless* the Lord. * Cold
and chill, bless *the* Lord.

Dew and rain, *bless* the Lord. * Frost
and chill, bless *the* Lord.

Ice and snow, *bless* the Lord. * Nights
and days, bless *the* Lord.

Light and darkness, *bless* the Lord. *
Lightnings and clouds, bless *the*
Lord.

Let the earth *bless* the Lord. * Praise
and exalt him above all *for*ever.

Mountains and hills, *bless* the Lord. *
Everything growing from the earth,
bless *the* Lord.

You springs, *bless* the Lord. * Seas and
rivers, bless *the* Lord.

You dolphins and all water creatures,
bless the Lord. * All you birds of the
air, bless *the* Lord.

All you beasts, wild and tame, *bless* the
Lord. * You sons of men, bless *the*
Lord.

O Israel, *bless* the Lord. * Praise and
exalt him above all *for*ever.

Priests of the Lord, *bless* the Lord. *
Servants of the Lord, bless *the* Lord.

Spirits and souls of the just, *bless* the
Lord. * Holy men of humble heart,
bless *the* Lord.

Hananiah, Azariah, Mishael, *bless* the
Lord. * Praise and exalt him above all
*for*ever.

Let us bless the Father, and the Son,
and the *Ho*ly Spirit. * Let us praise
and exalt him above all *for*ever.

Bless̀ed are you in the firma*ment* of
heaven. * Praiseworthy and glorious
and exalted above all *for*ever.

Antiphon   Saints *of* the Lord, * sing praise to the Lord *for* ever.

Ant. 3   Sing a hymn of praise in honor of the saints, † the children of
                Israel whom God has chosen as *his* own; * celebrate the glory of
                all *his* holy ones.

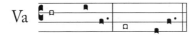

Psalm 149

Sing a new song to *the* Lord, *
his praise in the assembly of *the*
faithful.
Let Israel rejoice in *its* Maker, * let
Zion's sons exult in *their* king.
Let them praise his name *with* dancing
* and make music with timbrel *and*
harp.
For the Lord takes delight in *his* people.
* He crowns the poor with *sal*vation.
Let the faithful rejoice in *their* glory, *
shout for joy and take *their* rest.

Let the praise of God be on *their* lips *
and a two-edged sword in *their* hand,
to deal out vengeance to *the* nations *
and punishment on all *the* peoples;
to bind their kings *in* chains * and their
nobles in fetters *of* iron;
to carry out the sentence pre-*or*dained:
* this honor is for all *his* faithful.
Glory to the Father, and to *the* Son, *
and to the Ho*ly* Spirit:
as it was in the beginning, *is* now, * and
will be for ever. *A*men.

Antiphon   Sing a hymn of praise in honor of the saints, † the children of
Israel whom God has chosen as *his* own; * celebrate the glory of
all *his* holy ones.

READING   Ephesians 1:17-18

May the God of our Lord Jesus Christ, the Father of glory, grant you a
spirit of wisdom and insight to know him clearly. May he enlighten your
innermost vision that you may know the great hope to which he has called
you, the wealth of his glorious heritage to be distributed among the members of the church.

RESPONSORY

Let the *just* rejoice * and sing for joy in *the* Lord.
— Let the *just* rejoice * and sing for joy in *the* Lord.
Delight in his love, you *pure* of heart,
— and sing for joy in *the* Lord.
Glory to the Father, and *to* the Son, * and to the Ho*ly* Spirit.
— Let the *just* rejoice * and sing for joy in *the* Lord.

CANTICLE OF ZECHARIAH

Antiphon   The saints will shine *like* the sun * in the kingdom of their
Father, al*le*luia.

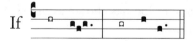

Blessèd ✠ be the Lord, the *God* of
Israel; * he has come to his people
and set *them* free.
He has raised up for us a *migh*ty savior,
* born of the house of his ser*vant*

David.
Through his holy prophets he promised of old † that he would save us
from our enemies, * from the hands
of all *who* hate us.

He promised to show mercy *to* our
fathers * and to remember his ho*ly*
covenant.
This was the oath he swore to our
*fath*er Abraham: * to set us free from
the hands of *our* enemies,
free to worship him without fear, † holy
and righteous *in* his sight * all the
days of *our* life.
You, my child, shall be called the
prophet *of* the Most High; * for you
will go before the Lord to prepare *his*
way,

to give his people knowledge *of* salvation * by the forgiveness of *their* sins.
In the tender compassion *of* our God *
the dawn from on high shall break
*up*on us,
to shine on those who dwell in darkness
and the sha*dow* of death, * and to
guide our feet into the way *of* peace.
Glory to the Father, and *to* the Son, *
and to the Ho*ly* Spirit:
as it was in the begin*ning*, is now, * and
will be for ever. *A*men.

Antiphon   The saints will shine *like* the sun * in the kingdom of their
Father, al*le*luia.

INTERCESSIONS
God is the reward of *all* the saints. * Let us joyfully *call* upon him:
Lord, save your *people.*
O God, source of all that is holy, you have let your holiness shine in many
marvelous ways through the lives *of* your saints,
— help us to celebrate your great*ness* in them.
The lives of your saints have given testimony to your Son, *Jesus* Christ,
— through their example may we draw clos*er* to him.
King of heaven, through your saints you have given us the courage to follow af*ter*
your Son,
— help us to imitate the example of the saints who show us the *way* to Christ.
Father, in the eucharistic sacrifice you unite us more fully with those who now
live *in* your kingdom,
— by our frequent sharing in the body and blood of your Son bring us to the
company of the e*ter*nal banquet.

Our Father . . .

Prayer
Father, all-powerful and ever-living God,
today we rejoice in the holy men and women
of every time and place.
May their prayers bring us your forgiveness and love.
We ask this through our Lord Jesus Christ, your Son,
who lives and reigns with you and the Holy Spirit,
one God, for ever and ever.

Evening Prayer II

HYMN, as in Evening Prayer I, 1115.

PSALMODY

Ant. 1   I saw a vast crowd of countless numbers † from *every* nation, *
              standing be*fore* the throne.

VIIIg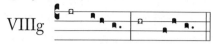

Psalm 110:1-5, 7

The Lord's revelation to my
    Master: † "Sit *on* my right: * your
foes I will put be*neath* your feet."
The Lord will wield from Zion † your
    scep*ter* of power: * rule in the midst
    of *all* your foes.
A prince from the day of your birth †
    on the *holy* mountains; * from the
    womb before the dawn *I* begot you.
The Lord has sworn an oath he will
    not change. † "You are a *priest* for
    ever, * a priest like Melchize*dek* of

old."
The Master standing at *your* right
    hand * will shatter kings in the day
    of *his* great wrath.
He shall drink from the stream *by* the
    wayside * and therefore he shall lift
    up his head.
Glory to the Father, and *to* the Son, *
    and to the *Holy* Spirit:
as it was in the begin*ning*, is now, * and
    will be for ev*er*. Amen.

Antiphon   I saw a vast crowd of countless numbers † from *every* nation, *
              standing be*fore* the throne.

Ant. 2   God tried them and found them worthy *of* himself; * they shall
              receive a crown of glory from *the* Lord.

IIA

Psalm 116: 10-19

I trusted, even *when* I said, * "I am
    sorely *afflicted*,"
and when I said in *my* alarm: * "No man
    can *be* trusted."
How can I re*pay* the Lord * for his
    goodness *to* me?
The cup of salvation *I* will raise; * I will
    call on *the* Lord's name.
My vows to the Lord I *will* fulfill *

before all *his* people.
O precious in the eyes *of* the Lord * is
    the death of *his* faithful.
Your servant, Lord, your ser*vant* am I; *
    you have loosened *my* bonds.
A thanksgiving sacri*fice* I make: * I will
    call on *the* Lord's name.
My vows to the Lord I *will* fulfill *
    before all *his* people,

in the courts of the house *of* the Lord, * | and to the Ho*ly* Spirit:
  in your midst, O *Je*rusalem. | as it was in the begin*ning*, is now, * and
Glory to the Father, and *to* the Son, * | will be for ever. *A*men.

Antiphon   God tried them and found them worthy *of* himself; * they shall
                receive a crown of glory from *the* Lord.

Ant. 3   By your own blood, Lord, † you brought us back *to* God; * from
                every tribe *and* tongue,
                and people *and* nation, * you made us a kingdom for *our* God.

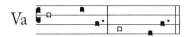

Canticle   Revelation 4:11; 5:9, 10, 12

O Lord our God, you *are*
  worthy * to receive glory and
honor *and* power.
For you have created *all* things; * by
  your will they came to be and *were*
  made.
Worthy are you, O Lord, * to receive
  the scroll and break open *its* seals.
For you *were* slain; * with your blood
  you purchased *for* God
men of every race *and* tongue, * of every
  people *and* nation.

You made of them a kingdom, † and
  priests to serve *our* God, * and they
  shall reign on *the* earth.
Worthy is the Lamb that *was* slain * to
  receive power *and* riches,
wisdom *and* strength, * honor and glory
  and praise.
Glory to the Father, and to *the* Son, *
  and to the Ho*ly* Spirit:
as it was in the beginning, *is* now, * and
  will be for ever. *A*men.

Antiphon   By your own blood, Lord, † you brought us back *to* God; * from
                every tribe *and* tongue,
                and people *and* nation, * you made us a kingdom for *our* God.

READING   2 Corinthians 6:16b; 7:1
    You are the temple of the living God, just as God has said:
        "I will dwell with them and walk among them.
        I will be their God
        and they shall be my people."
    Since we have these promises, beloved, let us purify ourselves from every
defilement of flesh and spirit, and in the fear of God strive to fulfill our
consecration perfectly.

RESPONSORY

Let the *saints* rejoice, * rejoice in *the* Lord.
— Let the *saints* rejoice, * rejoice in *the* Lord.
God has chosen you *as* his own;
— rejoice in *the* Lord.
Glory to the Father, and *to* the Son, * and to the Ho*ly* Spirit.
— Let the *saints* rejoice, * rejoice in *the* Lord.

CANTICLE OF MARY

Antiphon   How glorious is that kingdom † where all the saints rejoice with
                  Christ; † clothed *in* white robes, * they follow the Lamb wher-
                  ever *he* goes.

M y soul ✠ proclaims the greatness
    of the Lord, * my spirit rejoices
in God *my* savior
for he has *looked* with favor * on his
    low*ly* servant.
From this day all *gen*erations * will call
    me bless*èd*:
the Almighty has done great *things* for
    me, * and holy is *his* Name.
He has mercy on *those* who fear him *
    in every gen*er*ation.
He has shown the strength *of* his arm, *
    he has scattered the proud in their
    *con*ceit.

He has cast down the mighty *from* their
    thrones, * and has lifted up *the* lowly.
He has filled the hungry *with* good
    things, * and the rich he has sent
    a*way* empty.
He has come to the help of his *ser*vant
    Israel * for he has remembered his
    promise *of* mercy,
the promise he made *to* our fathers, * to
    Abraham and his children *for* ever.
Glory to the Father, and *to* the Son, *
    and to the Ho*ly* Spirit:
as it was in the begin*ning*, is now, * and
    will be for ever. *A*men.

Antiphon   How glorious is that kingdom † where all the saints rejoice with
                  Christ; † clothed *in* white robes, * they follow the Lamb wher-
                  ever *he* goes.

INTERCESSIONS

God is the reward of *all* the saints. * Let us joyfully *call* upon him:
Lord, save your *people.*
O God, through your Son Jesus Christ you built your Church on the foundation
    of *the* apostles,
— keep their teaching secure among your *faith*ful people.
You made the martyrs powerful witnesses even to the point of giving *up* their
    lives,
— help all Christians to give faithful witness *to* your Son.
You gave holy virgins the gift of imitating the virgin*ity* of Christ,
— may those consecrated to virginity be steadfast witnesses to the coming *of* your
    kingdom.

Your saints now see you *face* to face,

— keep alive in our hearts the hope of coming at last in*to* your presence.

Bring all who have died into the company of heaven with Mary, Joseph and *all* your saints,

— and give us also a place in the unending fellowship *of* your kingdom.

Our Father . . .

Prayer

Father, all-powerful and ever-living God,
today we rejoice in the holy men and women
of every time and place.
May their prayers bring us your forgiveness and love.
We ask this through our Lord Jesus Christ, your Son,
who lives and reigns with you and the Holy Spirit,
one God, for ever and ever.

November 2
THE COMMEMORATION OF ALL THE FAITHFUL DEPARTED

When November 2 occurs on Sunday, even though the Mass for All Souls Day may be celebrated, the office is taken from the current Sunday in Ordinary Time; the Office for the Dead is not said. However, when Morning Prayer and Evening Prayer are celebrated with the people, these hours may be taken from the Office for the Dead.

As in the Office for the Dead, 1288.

Prayer

Merciful Father,
hear our prayers and console us.
As we renew our faith in your Son,
whom you raised from the dead,
strengthen our hope that all our departed brothers and sisters
will share in his resurrection,
who lives and reigns with you and the Holy Spirit,
one God, for ever and ever.

November 3
MARTIN DE PORRES, RELIGIOUS

From the common of holy men: religious, 1282.

Morning Prayer

CANTICLE OF ZECHARIAH

Ant.   Blessèd be the Lord, for he has set all *nations* free. * He has called us out of darkness into his own wonder*ful* light.

Prayer

Lord,
you led Martin de Porres by a life of humility
to eternal glory.
May we follow his example
and be exalted with him in the kingdom of heaven.
Grant this through our Lord Jesus Christ, your Son,
who lives and reigns with you and the Holy Spirit,
one God, for ever and ever.

Evening Prayer

CANTICLE OF MARY

Ant.   Let us proclaim the greatness *of* the Lord, * for with heavenly
gifts he has raised up his lowly ser*vant* Martin.

November 4
CHARLES BORROMEO, BISHOP
Memorial

From the common of pastors, 1238.

Prayer

Father,
keep in your people the spirit
which filled Charles Borromeo.
Let your Church be continually renewed
and show the image of Christ to the world
by being conformed to his likeness,
who lives and reigns with you and the Holy Spirit,
one God, for ever and ever.

November 9
DEDICATION OF THE LATERAN BASILICA IN ROME
Feast

From the common of the dedication of a church, 1177, except for the following:

Prayer

God our Father,
from living stones, your chosen people,
you built an eternal temple to your glory.
Increase the spiritual gifts you have given to your Church
that your faithful people may continue to grow
into the new and eternal Jerusalem.

We ask this through our Lord Jesus Christ, your Son,
who lives and reigns with you and the Holy Spirit,
one God, for ever and ever.

or:

Father,
you called your people to be your Church.
As we gather together in your name,
may we love, honor, and follow you
to eternal life in the kingdom you promise.
Grant this through our Lord Jesus Christ, your Son,
who lives and reigns with you and the Holy Spirit,
one God, for ever and ever.

November 10
LEO THE GREAT, POPE AND DOCTOR
Memorial

From the common of pastors, 1238, or of doctors, 1246, except for the following:

Morning Prayer

CANTICLE OF ZECHARIAH

Ant.   Strengthened by Christ, † blessèd Peter has remained steadfast
                as a rock * in his guidance of *the* Church.

Prayer

God our Father,
you will never allow the power of hell
to prevail against your Church,
founded on the rock of the apostle Peter.
Let the prayers of Pope Leo the Great
keep us faithful to your truth
and secure in your peace.
We ask this through our Lord Jesus Christ, your Son,
who lives and reigns with you and the Holy Spirit,
one God, for ever and ever.

Evening Prayer

CANTICLE OF MARY

Ant.   Day after day Peter proclaims to *the* whole Church: * You are
                Christ, the Son of the liv*ing* God.

November 11
MARTIN OF TOURS, BISHOP
Memorial

From the common of pastors, 1238.

Morning Prayer
HYMN

Marine par. (L.M.)

Martine, par apostolis,	Saint Martin, with Apostles' zeal,
festum coléntes tu fove;	You were prepared to live or die
qui vivere discipulis	As pleased God best; smile down on us,
aut mori vis, nos réspice.	As lovingly to you we cry.
Fac nunc quod olim gésseras,	In spirit walk the earth once more,
nunc praesules clarifica,	Guide shepherds and their flocks as well,
auge decus Ecclésiae,	Increase the beauty of God's Church,
fraudes relide Satanae.	Restrain and curb the pow'rs of hell.
Qui ter chaos evisceras,	Three times you stole from death its prey,
mersos reatu suscita;	So now raise up those fallen low;
diviseras ut chlamydem,	And as you shared your cloak on earth,
nos indue iustitiam.	True virtue on our souls bestow.
Ut specialis gloriae	Remember how a prelate's word
quondam tuae memineris,	Was cherished in the days of old;
pontificum nunc ordini	And now assist all bishops' work,
pio favore subveni.	Their efforts foster and uphold.
Sit Trinitati gloria,	All glory to the Trinity
Martinus ut conféssus est,	In whom our hope and love find rest;
eius fidem qui iugiter	May Martin win us grace to prove
in nos per actus inserat. Amen.	By deeds the faith which he professed. Amen.

Ant. 1   Martin, *priest* of God, * the kingdom of my heavenly Father lies o*pen* before you.

Psalms and canticles from Sunday, Week I, 606.

Ant. 2   With hands and eyes raised *up* to heaven, * Martin never ceased praying, al*le*luia.

Ant. 3   Filled with joy, Martin was welcomed by Abraham. † Martin left this life a poor and low*ly* man * and entered heaven rich in God's favor, al*le*luia.

READING   Hebrews 13:7-8

Remember your leaders who spoke the word of God to you; consider how their lives ended, and imitate their faith. Jesus Christ is the same yesterday, today, and forever.

RESPONSORY (VI F)

On your *walls* Jerusalem, * I have set my watchmen *to* guard you.
— On your *walls* Jerusalem, I have set my watchmen *to* guard you.
Day or night, they will not cease to proclaim the name *of* the Lord.
— I have set my watchmen *to* guard you.
Glory to the Father, and *to* the Son, * and to the Ho*ly* Spirit.
— On your *walls* Jerusalem, I have set my watchmen *to* guard you.

CANTICLE OF ZECHARIAH

Ant.   How happy is that man whose soul gains paradise! † Angels rejoice, archan*gels* sing praise, * the company of vir*gins* welcomes him,
                choirs of saints call *out* to him: * Stay with us *for* ever.

Prayer

Father,
by his life and death
Martin of Tours offered you worship and praise.
Renew in our hearts the power of your love,
so that neither death nor life may separate us from you.
Grant this through our Lord Jesus Christ, your Son,
who lives and reigns with you and the Holy Spirit,
one God, for ever and ever.

Evening Prayer

HYMN

Iste confessor (11.11.11.5)

Iste conféssor Domini sacratus,	God's holy people celebrates with honor
festa plebs cuius célebrat per orbem,	This great Confessor truly dedicated
hodie laetus méruit secréta	To the Lord's service, who this day was summoned
scandere caeli.	Into his presence.
Qui pius, prudens, humilis, pudicus,	Throughout his lifetime in our world so troubled,
sobrius, castus fuit et quiétus,	He was devoted both to prayer and penance,
vita dum praesens vegetavit eius	Prudent in action, firm while yet remaining
corporis artus.	Humble and peaceful.
Ad sacrum cuius tumulum frequénter	Pilgrims uncounted to his tomb came flocking,
membra lanuéntum modo sanitati,	Health and protection through his intercession
quolibet morbo fuerint gravati,	Daily were sought for, and of these petitions
restituuntur.	None went unanswered.

Under nunc noster chorus in honorem
ipsius, hymnum canit hunc libénter,
ut piis eius méritis iuvémur
    omne per aevum.

Sit salus illi, decus atque virtus,
qui supra caeli résidens cacumen,
totius mundi machinam gubérnat
    trinus et unus. Amen.

This makes us bolder to implore assistance
From such a patron glorious in merits,
That he may help us to fulfil the mission
    To us entrusted.

Praise and all glory, honor ever growing
Be to the God-head reigning in high heaven,
Ruling creations with all loving wisdom,
    One in three Persons. Amen.

Ant. 1   Here is a man that words cannot describe. † Death could not defeat him nor *toil* dismay him. * He did not fear death, nor did he re*fuse* to live.

Psalms and canticles from the common of pastors, 1242.

Ant. 2   Lord, if your people still need me, † I am ready *for* the task; * your will *be* done.

Ant. 3   Bishop Martin has left this world; † a shining light a*mong* priests, * now he lives with Christ *for* ever.

READING   1 Peter 5:1-4

To the elders among you I, a fellow elder, a witness of Christ's sufferings and sharer in the glory that is to be revealed, make this appeal. God's flock is in your midst; give it a shepherd's care. Watch over it willingly as God would have you do, not under constraint; and not for shameful profit either, but generously. Be examples to the flock, not lording it over those assigned to you, so that when the chief Shepherd appears you will win for yourselves the unfading crown of glory.

RESPONSORY (VI F)

This is a man who *loved* his brethren * and ever prayed *for* them.
— This is a man who *loved* his brethren * and ever prayed *for* them.
He spent himself *in* their service,
— and ever prayed *for* them.
Glory to the Father, and *to* the Son, * and to the Ho*ly* Spirit.
— This is a man who *loved* his brethren * and ever prayed *for* them.

CANTICLE OF MARY

Ant.   This blessèd bishop loved Christ with *all* his strength * and had no fear of earth*ly* rulers;
    though he did not die a *martyr's* death, * this holy confessor won the mar*tyr's* palm.

Prayer, as in Morning Prayer; 1131.

November 12
JOSAPHAT, BISHOP AND MARTYR
Memorial

From the common of one martyr, 1228, or of pastors, 1238.

Prayer

Lord,
fill your Church with the Spirit
that gave Saint Josaphat courage
to lay down his life for his people.
By his prayers
may your Spirit make us strong
and willing to offer our lives
for our brothers and sisters.
We ask this through our Lord Jesus Christ, your Son,
who lives and reigns with you and the Holy Spirit,
one God, for ever and ever.

[In the dioceses of the United States]
November 13
FRANCES XAVIER CABRINI, VIRGIN
Memorial

From the common of virgins, 1253, or of holy women: religious, 1282, or those who worked for
the underprivileged, 1284.

Prayer

God our Father,
you called Frances Xavier Cabrini from Italy
to serve the immigrants of America.
By her example teach us concern for the stranger,
the sick, and the frustrated.
By her prayers help us to see Christ
in all the men and women we meet.
Grant this through our Lord Jesus Christ, your Son,
who lives and reigns with you and the Holy Spirit,
one God, for ever and ever.

November 15
ALBERT THE GREAT, BISHOP AND DOCTOR

From the common of pastors, 1238, or of doctors, 1246.

Prayer

God our Father,
you endowed Saint Albert with the talent

of combining human wisdom with divine faith.
Keep us true to his teachings
that the advance of human knowledge
may deepen our knowledge and love of you.
Grant this through our Lord Jesus Christ, your Son,
who lives and reigns with you and the Holy Spirit,
one God, for ever and ever.

November 16
MARGARET OF SCOTLAND

From the common of virgins, 1253, or of holy women, 1274, or those who worked for the underprivileged, 1284.

Prayer

Lord,
you gave Saint Margaret of Scotland
a special love for the poor.
Let her example and prayers
help us to become a living sign of your goodness.
We ask this through our Lord Jesus Christ, your Son,
who lives and reigns with you and the Holy Spirit,
one God, for ever and ever.

On the same day, November 16
GERTRUDE, VIRGIN

From the common of virgins, 1253, or of holy women: religious, 1282.

Prayer

Father,
you filled the heart of Saint Gertrude
with the presence of your love.
Bring light into our darkness
and let us experience the joy of your presence
and the power of your grace.
Grant this through our Lord Jesus Christ, your Son,
who lives and reigns with you and the Holy Spirit,
one God, for ever and ever.

November 17
ELIZABETH OF HUNGARY, RELIGIOUS
Memorial

From the common of holy women: those who worked for the underprivileged, 1284.

Prayer

Father,
you helped Elizabeth of Hungary
to recognize and honor Christ
in the poor of this world.
Let her prayers help us to serve our brothers and sisters
in time of trouble and need.
We ask this through our Lord Jesus Christ, your Son,
who lives and reigns with you and the Holy Spirit,
one God, for ever and ever.

November 18
DEDICATION OF THE CHURCHES OF PETER AND PAUL, APOSTLES

From the common of apostles, 1206.

Morning Prayer

CANTICLE OF ZECHARIAH

Ant.   Peter the apostle and Paul the teacher *of* the Gentiles * taught us
              your law, O Lord.

Prayer

Lord,
give your Church the protection of the apostles.
From them it first received the faith of Christ.
May they help your Church to grow in your grace
until the end of time.
Grant this through our Lord Jesus Christ, your Son,
who lives and reigns with you and the Holy Spirit,
one God, for ever and ever.

Evening Prayer

CANTICLE OF MARY

Ant.   The bodies of the saints have been bur*ied* in peace, * but their
              names live on *for* ever.

[In the dioceses of the United States]
On the same day, November 18
ROSE PHILIPPINE DUCHESNE, VIRGIN
From the common of virgins, 1253.

Prayer

Gracious God,
you filled the heart of Philippine Duchesne
with charity and missionary zeal,
and gave her the desire
to make you known among all peoples.
Fill us, who honor her memory today,
with that same love and zeal
to extend your kingdom to the ends of the earth.
We ask this through our Lord Jesus Christ, your Son,
who lives and reigns with you and the Holy Spirit,
one God, for ever and ever.

November 21
THE PRESENTATION OF THE BLESSED VIRGIN MARY
Memorial
From the common of the Blessed Virgin Mary, 1192.

Morning Prayer
HYMN
Maria, Virgo regia. (L.M.)

Maria, virgo regia,	O Mary, royal virgin pure,
sponsa regis et filia,	Both spouse and daughter of the King,
te Dei sapientia	God's wisdom chose you for his own
elegit ante sæcula.	Before the world and time began.
Puella carens macula,	O Virgin, without smallest taint,
Dei domus eburnea,	God's peerless tower of ivory
te dedicavit cælitus	The Holy Spirit from above
missus ab eo Spiritus.	Selected you as sanctuary.
Caritatis signaculum,	You are the image of all good,
totius boni speculum,	And seal of love most beautiful,
aurora veri luminis,	The dawn indeed of very light,
arca divini seminis,	The ark containing manna true.
In domo summi principis	Within the house of God Most High
tu affluis deliciis;	You overflow with His delights,
virga Iesse florigera,	The flow'ring rod from Jesse's root,
repleris Dei gratia.	Your soul is filled with grace untold.

O margarita candida
et stella mundi splendida,
fac puris esse moribus
nos vera templa Spiritus.

Sit Trinitati gloria,
o Virgo nobilissima,
quæ te suorum munerum
thesaurum dat magnificum. Amen.

O Pearl, far fairer than the rest,
O Star with luster all your own,
Make us true temples of the Lord
In whom the Spirit loves to dwell.

All glory to the Trinity,
O Virgin of all virgins blest,
Who shed on you with lavish love
Such treasury of gifts and grace. Amen.

CANTICLE OF ZECHARIAH

Ant.   Blessèd are you, Mary, † because you believed that the Lord's
                words to you * would be fulfilled, al*le*luia.

Prayer

Eternal Father,
we honor the holiness and glory of the Virgin Mary.
May her prayers bring us the fullness of your life and love.
We ask this through our Lord Jesus Christ, your Son,
who lives and reigns with you and the Holy Spirit,
one God, for ever and ever.

Evening Prayer

CANTICLE OF MARY

Ant.   Holy Mother of God, Mary ever-Virgin, † you are the temple *of*
                the Lord * and the dwelling place of the Ho*ly* Spirit.
                Be*yond* all others * you were pleasing to our Lord Je*sus* Christ.

November 22
CECILIA, VIRGIN AND MARTYR
Memorial
From the common of one martyr, 1228, or of virgins, 1253.

Morning Prayer

CANTICLE OF ZECHARIAH

Ant.   At daybreak, Cecilia cried out: † Come, soldiers of Christ, cast
                off the *works* of darkness, * and clothe yourselves in the armor *of*
                light.

Prayer

Lord of mercy,
be close to those who call upon you.
With Saint Cecilia to help us hear and answer our prayers.

Grant this through our Lord Jesus Christ, your Son,
who lives and reigns with you and the Holy Spirit,
one God, for ever and ever.

Evening Prayer

CANTICLE OF MARY

Ant.   Saint Cecilia kept the Gospel of Christ ever *near* her heart; * day
or night she never ceased praying and speaking *with* God.

November 23
CLEMENT I, POPE AND MARTYR

From the common of one martyr, 1228, or of pastors, 1238.

Prayer

All-powerful and ever-living God,
we praise your power and glory
revealed to us in the lives of all your saints.
Give us joy on this feast of Saint Clement,
the priest and martyr
who bore witness with his blood to the love he proclaimed
and the gospel he preached.
We ask this through our Lord Jesus Christ, your Son,
who lives and reigns with you and the Holy Spirit,
one God, for ever and ever.

On the same day, November 23
COLUMBAN, ABBOT

From the common of pastors, 1238, or of holy men: religious, 1282.

Prayer

Lord,
you called Saint Columban to live the monastic life
and to preach the gospel with zeal.
May his prayers and example
help us to seek you above all things
and to work with all our hearts
for the spread of the faith.
Grant this through our Lord Jesus Christ, your Son,
who lives and reigns with you and the Holy Spirit,
one God, for ever and ever.

[In the dioceses of the United States]
On the same day, November 23
BLESSED MIGUEL AGUSTIN PRO, PRIEST AND MARTYR
From the common of one martyr, 1228, or of pastors, 1238.

Prayer
God our Father, you gave your servant Miguel Agustín
the grace to seek ardently your greater glory
and the salvation of your people.
Grant that, through his intercession
and following his exmple,
we may serve you and glorify you
by performing our daily duties with fidelity and joy
and effectively helping our neighbor.
We ask this through our Lord Jesus Christ, your Son,
who lives and reigns with you and the Holy Spirit,
one God, for ever and ever.

November 24
ANDREW DUNG-LAC, PRIEST, AND COMPANIONS, MARTYRS
Memorial
From the common of several martyrs, 1214.

Prayer
O God, the source and origin of all fatherhood,
you kept the blessèd martyrs Andrew and his companions
faithful to the cross of your Son
even to the shedding of their blood.
Through their intercession
enable us to spread your love
among our brothers and sisters,
that we may be called and may truly be your children.
We ask this through our Lord Jesus Christ, your Son,
who lives and reigns with you and the Holy Spirit,
one God, for ever and ever.

November 25
CATHERINE OF ALEXANDRIA, VIRGIN AND MARTYR
From the common of one martyr, 1228, or of virgins, 1253.

Prayer
God of power and mercy,
you gave St. Catherine of Alexandria, your martyr,

victory over pain and suffering.
Strengthen us who celebrate this day of her triumph
and help us to be victorious over the evils that threaten us.
Grant this through our Lord Jesus Christ, your Son,
who lives and reigns with you and the Holy Spirit,
one God, for ever and ever.

November 30
ANDREW, APOSTLE
Feast
From the common of apostles, 1206, except for the following:

Morning Prayer
HYMN

Captator olim (L.M.)

Captator olim piscium,	Saint Andrew, who once cast your nets
Iam nunc piscator hominum,	Upon the lake of Galilee,
Tuis, Andrea, retibus	Show now your skill in catching souls,
Mundi nos rape fluctibus.	And save us from the world's wild sea.
Germanus Petri corpore	Saint Peter's brother during life,
Nec mortis dispar ordine;	Not even death your souls could part,
Quos una caro genuit,	Since both endured the bitter cross
Crux caelo fratres edidit.	With patient and courageous heart.
O germen venerabile,	True brothers in your work on earth,
O par corona gloriae!	Your crown of glory is the same,
Ecclesiae patres pii	Both fathers of the infant Church,
Crucis sunt aeque filii.	Both crucified for Jesus' Name.
Ad Iesum fratri praevius,	You were the first to find Our Lord,
Indexque vitae strenuus,	And led your brother to his feet,
Et nobis esto miseris	So help us on life's weary way,
Beati dux itineris.	Befriend us in its dust and heat.
Fratris comes egergius,	Companion of your brother's toil,
Ecclesias impensius	Preserve the Church in charity,
Da caritate exercitas	That with Saint Peter, shepherd true,
Pastori Petro subditas.	We may serve God in unity.
Vir Christo dilectissime,	Belovèd Saint, so dear to Christ,
Amore fac nos currere,	Help us to run the path of love,
Ut laeti adepti patriam	That we may all God's praises sing,
Deo canamus gloriam. Amen.	United in full joy above. Amen.

Ant. 1   Two men followed the Lord from *the* beginning; * one of these was Andrew, the brother of *Si*mon Peter.

Psalms and canticle from Sunday, Week I, 606.

Ant. 2   The *Lord* loved Andrew * and cherished *his* friendship.

Ant. 3   Andrew said to his bro*ther* Simon: * We have found the Messiah, and he brought him *to* Jesus.

READING   Ephesians 2:19-20

You are strangers and aliens no longer. No, you are fellow citizens of the saints and members of the household of God. You form a building which rises on the foundation of the apostles and prophets, with Christ Jesus himself as the capstone. Through him the whole structure is fitted together and takes shape as a holy temple in the Lord; in him you are being built into this temple, to become a dwelling place for God in the Spirit.

RESPONSORY (VI F)
You have *made* them rulers * over all *the* earth.
— You have *made* them rulers * over all *the* earth.
They will always remember your *name*, O Lord,
— over all *the* earth.
Glory to the Father, and *to* the Son, * and to the Ho*ly* Spirit.
— You have *made* them rulers * over all *the* earth.

CANTICLE OF ZECHARIAH
Antiphon   I bow before the cross made precious by *Christ*, my Master. * I embrace it as his *dis*ciple.

INTERCESSIONS (VI F)
Belovèd friends, we have inherited heaven along with *the* apostles. * Let us give thanks to the Father for *all* his gifts:
The company of apostles praises you, O Lord.
Praise be to you, Lord, for the banquet of Christ's body and blood given us through *the* apostles,
— which refreshes us and *gives* us life.
The company of apostles praises you, O Lord.
Praise be to you, Lord, for the feast of your word prepared for us by *the* apostles,
— giving us *light* and joy.
The company of apostles praises you, O Lord.
Praise be to you, Lord, for your holy Church, founded on *the* apostles,
— where we are gathered together into *your* community.
The company of apostles praises you, O Lord.

Praise be to you, Lord, for the cleansing power of baptism and penance that you have entrusted to *your* apostles,
— through which we are cleansed *of* our sins.
The company of apostles praises you, O Lord.

Our Father . . .

Prayer

Lord,
in your kindness hear our petitions.
You called Andrew the apostle
to preach the Gospel and guide your Church in faith.
May he always be our friend in your presence
to help us with his prayers.
We ask this through our Lord Jesus Christ, your Son,
who lives and reigns with you and the Holy Spirit,
one God, for ever and ever.

Evening Prayer

Ant. 1   The Lord saw Pet*er* and Andrew; * he called them to *fo*llow him.

Psalms and canticle from the common of apostles, 1208.

Ant. 2   Come, follow me, *said* the Lord. * I will make you fishers *of* men.

Ant. 3   They left their nets to fol*low* Christ, * their Lord and *Re*deemer.

READING   Ephesians 4:11-13
Christ gave apostles, prophets, evangelists, pastors and teachers in roles of service for the faithful to build up the body of Christ, till we become one in faith and in the knowledge of God's Son, and form that perfect man who is Christ come to full stature.

RESPONSORY (VI F)
Tell *all* the nations * how glorious *God* is.
— Tell *all* the nations * how glorious *God* is.
They will always remember your *name*, O Lord.
— How glorious *God* is.
Glory to the Father, and *to* the Son, * and to the Ho*ly* Spirit.
— Tell *all* the nations * how glorious *God* is.

CANTICLE OF MARY
Antiphon   Andrew served Christ and loyally *preached* the Gospel; * with his brother Peter, he laid down his life *for* God.

INTERCESSIONS (VI F)

My brothers, we build on the foundation of *the* apostles. * Let us pray to our
  almighty Father for his holy peo*ple* and say:
Be mindful of your Church, O Lord.
Father, you wanted your Son to be seen first by the apostles after the
  resurrection *from* the dead,
— we ask you to make us his witnesses to the farthest corners *of* the world.
You sent your Son to preach the good news *to* the poor,
— help us to preach the Gospel to *every* creature.
You sent your Son to sow the seed of un*end*ing life,
— grant that we who work at sowing the seed may share the joy *of* the harvest.
You sent your Son to reconcile all men to you *through* his blood,
— help us all to work toward achieving this recon*cili*ation.
Your Son sits at your right *hand* in heaven,
— let the dead enter your king*dom* of joy.

Our Father . . .

Prayer

Lord,
in your kindness hear our petitions.
You called Andrew the apostle
to preach the Gospel and guide your Church in faith.
May he always be our friend in your presence
to help us with his prayers.
We ask this through our Lord Jesus Christ, your Son,
who lives and reigns with you and the Holy Spirit,
one God, for ever and ever.

<h2 align="center">December 3
FRANCIS XAVIER, PRIEST</h2>
Memorial

From the common of pastors, 1238.

Prayer

God our Father,
by the preaching of Francis Xavier
you brought many nations to yourself.
Give his zeal for the faith to all who believe in you,
that your Church may rejoice in continued growth
throughout the world.
Grant this through our Lord Jesus Christ, your Son,
who lives and reigns with you and the Holy Spirit,
one God, for ever and ever.

December 4
JOHN OF DAMASCUS, PRIEST AND DOCTOR

From the common of pastors, 1238, or of doctors, 1246.

Prayer

Lord,
may the prayers of Saint John Damascene help us,
and may the true faith he taught so well
always be our light and our strength.
We ask this through our Lord Jesus Christ, your Son,
who lives and reigns with you and the Holy Spirit,
one God, for ever and ever.

December 6
NICHOLAS, BISHOP

From the common of pastors, 1238.

Prayer

Father,
hear our prayers for mercy,
and by the help of Saint Nicholas
keep us safe from all danger, and guide us on the way of salvation.
Grant this through our Lord Jesus Christ, your Son,
who lives and reigns with you and the Holy Spirit,
one God, for ever and ever.

December 7
AMBROSE, BISHOP AND DOCTOR
Memorial

From the common of doctors, 1246.

HYMN

Fortem piumque. (L.M.)

Fortem piumque præsulem canamus omnes, turbidas qui fluctuantis sæculi terris procellas expulit.	This gentle prelate let us praise And to his courage tribute pay, For he both conquered and dispelled The raging tempests of his day.
Non sceptra concussus timet, non imperantem feminam, temploque, clausis postibus, arcet cruentum cæsarem.	God's law in all things he upheld, Resisting might's oppression base, Forbidding entrance to the church To ruler bearing crime's disgrace.
Arcana sacræ paginæ altus magister explicat; divina pandens dogmata, mira nitet facundia.	The mysteries the Scriptures hold He loved to fathom and explain; He taught with flowing eloquence The truth and doctrine they contain.

Fide ciente spiritum,
præclara fundit carmina;
fide coæquans martyres,
deprendit artus martyrum.

His ardent mind, aglow with faith
Composed new hymns for sacred rites;
His eager search for martyr's tombs
Some holy relics brought to light.

Iam nunc furentem tartari
lupum flagello submove;
scientiæ nos lumine
fove, tuere iugiter.

Assist us now, most gracious Saint,
The wolves of hell drive far away
And with your learning's gleaming light
Protect and guard us ev'ry day.

Sit Trinitati gloria,
quam, te rogante prospere,
hymnis in aula cælica
laudemus usquæ in sæculum. Amen.

All glory to the Trinity,
Whom, by your kindly help and prayer,
We hope to worship with the saints
And in their endless praise to share. Amen.

Prayer

Lord, you made Saint Ambrose
an outstanding teacher of the Catholic faith
and gave him the courage of an apostle.
Raise up in your Church more leaders after your own heart,
to guide us with courage and wisdom.
We ask this through our Lord Jesus Christ, your Son,
who lives and reigns with you and the Holy Spirit,
one God, for ever and ever.

December 8
IMMACULATE CONCEPTION
Solemnity

Evening Prayer I

HYMN

Praeclara custos. (L.M.)

Præclara custos virginum	O Virgin of all virgins blest,
Deique mater innuba,	Predestined Mother of Our Lord,
cælestis aulæ ianua,	The golden gate of heaven's court,
spes nostra, cæli gaudium;	Our hope, and joy of all the saints.
Inter rubeta lilium,	You are the lily among thorns
columba formosissima,	The fairest dove of purity,
e stirpe virga germinans	The root producing branch divine,
nostro medelam vulneri;	The remedy for our deep wound.
Turris draconi impervia,	O Tow'r defying Satan's guile,
amica stella naufragis,	Consoling Star on life's rough sea,
defende nos a fraudibus	Defend us in the hour of need,
tuaque luce dirige.	And lead us by your gentle light.
Erroris umbras discute,	Dark error's shadows drive away,
syrtes dolosas amove,	The shifting sands of doubt dispel
fluctus tot inter, deviis	From us, storm-tossed upon the waves;
tutam reclude semitam.	In safety bring us to the shore.
Quæ labe nostræ originis	You shine with privilege of grace,
intacta splendes unica,	Have never known our fallen state,
serpentis artes æmuli	So graciously avenge our race
elude vindex inclita.	And bring the serpent's wiles to nought.
Patri sit et Paraclito	To God the Father and the Son,
tuoque Nato gloria,	And to the Spirit, glory be,
qui sanctitatis unicæ	Who gave you gifts beyond compare
te munerarunt gratia. Amen.	Of holiness and purity. Amen.

PSALMODY

Ant. 1   I will make you enemies, you *and* the woman, * your off*spring* and hers.

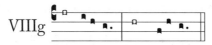

VIIIg

Psalm 113

Praise, O servants *of* the Lord, *
    praise the name *of* the Lord!
May the name of the *Lord* be blessed *
    both now and for ever*more*!
From the rising of the sun *to* its setting
    * praised be the name *of* the Lord!
High above all nations *is* the Lord, *
    above the heav*ens* his glory.
Who is like the *Lord*, our God, * who
    has risen on high *to* his throne
yet stoops from the heights *to* look
    down, * to look down upon heav*en*

and earth?
From the dust he lifts *up* the lowly, *
    from his misery he rais*es* the poor
to set him in the compan*y* of princes, *
    yes, with the princes *of* his people.
To the childless wife he *gives* a home *
    and gladdens her *heart* with children.
Glory to the Father, and *to* the Son, *
    and to the *Ho*ly Spirit:
as it was in the begin*ning*, is now, * and
    will be for ev*er*. Amen.

Antiphon   I will make you enemies, you *and* the woman, * your off*spring* and hers.

Ant. 2   The Lord has clothed me with garments *of* salvation; * he has covered me with a robe *of* justice.

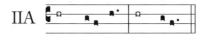

IIA

Psalm 147:12-20

O praise the *Lord*, Jerusalem! *
    Zion, praise *your* God!
He has strengthened the bars *of* your
    gates, * he has blessed the children
    *with*in you.
He established peace *on* your borders, *
    he feeds you with fin*est* wheat.
He sends out his word *to* the earth *
    and swiftly runs his *com*mand.
He showers down snow *white* as wool, *
    he scatters hoar-frost *like* ashes.
He hurls down hail*stones* like crumbs. *
    The waters are frozen at *his* touch;

he sends forth his word *and* it melts
    them: * at the breath of his mouth
    the wa*ters* flow.
He makes his word *known* to Jacob, *
    to Israel his laws and *de*crees.
He has not dealt thus with *other*
    nations; * he has not taught them his
    *de*crees.
Glory to the Father, and *to* the Son, *
    and to the Ho*ly* Spirit:
as it was in the begin*ning*, is now, * and
    will be for ever. *A*men.

Antiphon   The Lord has clothed me with garments *of* salvation; * he has covered me with a robe *of* justice.

Ant. 3   Hail Mary, full *of* grace; * the Lord is *with* you.

                                    Canticle   Ephesians 1:3-10

Praised be the God *and* Father * of our Lord Je*sus* Christ,
who has bestowed on us *in* Christ * every spiritual blessing in *the* heavens.
God chose us in him † before the world *be*gan * to be holy and blameless in *his* sight.
He predestined us † to be his adopted sons through Je*sus* Christ, * such was his will *and* pleasure,
that all might praise the glori*ous* favor * he has bestowed on us in his *be*lovèd.
In him and through his blood, † we have been *re*deemed, * and our sins

*for*given,
so immeasura*bly* generous * is God's favor *to* us.
God has given us the wisdom † to understand fully *the* mystery, * the plan he was pleased to decree *in* Christ.
A plan to be carried out *in* Christ, * in the fullness *of* time,
to bring all things into one *in* him, * in the heavens and *on* earth.
Glory to the Father, and to *the* Son, * and to the Ho*ly* Spirit:
as it was in the beginning, *is* now, * and will be for ever. *A*men.

Antiphon   Hail Mary, full *of* grace; * the Lord is *with* you.

READING   Romans 8:29-30
    Those whom God foreknew he predestined to share the image of his Son. Those he predestined he likewise called; those he called he also justified.

RESPONSORY (VI F)
I shall glori*fy* you, Lord, * for you have res*cued* me.
— I shall glori*fy* you, Lord, * for you have res*cued* me.
You have not let my enemies rejoice *over* me.
— For you have res*cued* me.
Glory to the Father, and *to* the Son, * and to the Ho*ly* Spirit.
— I shall glori*fy* you, Lord, * for you have res*cued* me.

CANTICLE OF MARY

Ant.   All generations will *call* me blessèd: * the Almighty has done
            great things *for* me.

If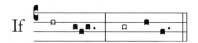

My soul ✠ proclaims the greatness
of the Lord, * my spirit rejoices
in God *my* savior
for he has *looked* with favor * on his
lowly servant.
From this day all *gen*erations * will call
me blessèd:
the Almighty has done great *things* for
me, * and holy is *his* Name.
He has mercy on *those* who fear him *
in every gen*er*ation.
He has shown the strength *of* his arm, *
he has scattered the proud in their
*con*ceit.

He has cast down the mighty *from* their
thrones, * and has lifted up *the* lowly.
He has filled the hungry *with* good
things, * and the rich he has sent
a*way* empty.
He has come to the help of his *ser*vant
Israel * for he has remembered his
promise *of* mercy,
the promise he made *to* our fathers, * to
Abraham and his children *for* ever.
Glory to the Father, and *to* the Son, *
and to the Ho*ly* Spirit:
as it was in the begin*ning*, is now, * and
will be for ever. *A*men.

Antiphon   All generations will *call* me blessèd: * the Almighty has done
            great things *for* me.

INTERCESSIONS

Let us praise God our almighty Father, who wished that Mary, his Son's mother,
be celebrated by each *gen*eration. * Now in *need* we ask:
Mary, full of grace, intercede for *us.*
O God, worker of miracles, you made the Immaculate Virgin Mary share, body
and soul, in your Son's glo*ry* in heaven,
— direct the hearts of your children to *that* same glory.
You made Mary our mother. Through her intercession grant strength to the
weak, comfort to the sorrowing, par*don* to sinners,
— salvation and *peace* to all.
You made Mary the mo*ther* of mercy,
— may all who are faced with trials feel her mo*ther*ly love.
You wished Mary to be the mother of the family in the home of Je*sus* and
Joseph,
— may all mothers of families foster love and holiness through her *in*tercession.
You crowned Mary *queen* of heaven,
— may all the dead rejoice in your kingdom with the *saints* for ever.

Our Father . . .

Prayer

Father,
you prepared the Virgin Mary
to be the worthy mother of your Son.
You let her share beforehand
in the salvation Christ would bring by his death,
and kept her sinless from the first moment of her conception.
Help us by her prayers
to live in your presence without sin.
We ask this through our Lord Jesus Christ, your Son,
who lives and reigns with you and the Holy Spirit,
one God, for ever and ever.

Morning Prayer

HYMN
In plausu. (L.M.)

In plausu grati carminis adsit nova lætitia, dum Dei matris Virginis sumit vita principia.	With joyful song we celebrate New happiness unknown to earth, Conceived immaculate is she Who will be mother of her Lord.
Maria, mundi gloria, lucis æternæ filia, te præservavit Filius ab omni labe penitus.	O Mary, glory of the world, And daughter of eternal light, Your Son preserved you from the first From ev'ry taint, result of sin.
Originalis macula cuncta respersit sæcula ; sola post Natum vitiis numquam contacta diceris.	The guilty stain of Adam's fall Afflicts each member of his race; The sinless Son whom you would bear Redeemed you by his foreseen grace.
Caput serpentis callidi tuo pede conteritur ; fastus gigantis perfidi David funda devincitur.	The cruel serpent's crafty head Is crushed beneath your virgin foot, As David conquered with his sling The giant's arrogance and pride.
Columba mitis, humilis, fers, carens felle criminis, signum Dei clementiæ, ramum virentis gratiæ.	O dove of dazzling innocence, The lowly handmaid of the Lord, You bring his sign of clemency The olive branch of peace and grace.
Parti sit et Paraclito tuoque Nato gloria, qui sanctitatis unicæ te munerarunt gratia. Amen.	To God the Father and the Son, And to the Spirit, glory be, Who gave you gifts beyond compare Of holiness and purity. Amen.

PSALMODY

Ant. 1   O Mother, how pure you are, † you are un*touched* by sin; *
                yours was the privilege to carry *God* within you.

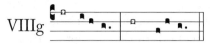

VIIIg

Psalm 63:2-9

O God, you are my God, for *you* I long; * for you my *soul* is thirsting.

My body *pines* for you * like a dry, weary land *without* water.

So I gaze on you *in* the sanctuary * to see your strength *and* your glory.

For your love is bet*ter* than life, * my lips will *speak* your praise.

So I will bless you *all* my life, * in your name I will lift *up* my hands.

My soul shall be filled as *with* a banquet, * my mouth shall praise *you* with joy.

On my bed I re*mem*ber you. * On you I muse *through* the night

for you have *been* my help; * in the shadow of your wings *I* rejoice.

My soul *clings* to you; * your right hand *holds* me fast.

Glory to the Father, and *to* the Son, * and to the *Holy* Spirit:

as it was in the begin*ning*, is now, * and will be for ev*er*. Amen.

Antiphon   O Mother, how pure you are, † you are un*touched* by sin; *
                yours was the privilege to carry *God* within you.

Ant. 2   The Lord God Most High has blessed you, *Vir*gin Mary, *
                above all the women of *the* earth.

IIA

Canticle   Daniel 3:57-88; 56

Bless the Lord, all you works *of* the Lord. * Praise and exalt him above all *for*ever.

Angels of the Lord, *bless* the Lord, * You heavens, bless *the* Lord.

All you waters above the heavens, *bless* the Lord. * All you hosts of the Lord, bless *the* Lord.

Sun and moon, *bless* the Lord. * Stars of heaven, bless *the* Lord.

Every shower and dew, *bless* the Lord. * All you winds, bless *the* Lord.

Fire and heat, *bless* the Lord. * Cold and chill, bless *the* Lord.

Dew and rain, *bless* the Lord. * Frost and chill, bless *the* Lord.

Ice and snow, *bless* the Lord. * Nights and days, bless *the* Lord.

Light and darkness, *bless* the Lord. * Lightnings and clouds, bless *the* Lord.

Let the earth *bless* the Lord. * Praise and exalt him above all *for*ever.

Mountains and hills, *bless* the Lord. *

Everything growing from the earth, bless *the* Lord.

You springs, *bless* the Lord. * Seas and rivers, bless *the* Lord.

You dolphins and all water creatures, *bless* the Lord. * All you birds of the air, bless *the* Lord.

All you beasts, wild and tame, *bless* the Lord. * You sons of men, bless *the* Lord.

O Israel, *bless* the Lord. * Praise and exalt him above all *fore*ver.

Priests of the Lord, *bless* the Lord. *

Servants of the Lord, bless *the* Lord.

Spirits and souls of the just, *bless* the Lord. * Holy men of humble heart, bless *the* Lord.

Hananiah, Azariah, Mishael, *bless* the Lord. * Praise and exalt him above all *fore*ver.

Let us bless the Father, and the Son, and the *Ho*ly Spirit. * Let us praise and exalt him above all *fore*ver.

Blessèd are you in the firma*ment* of heaven. * Praiseworthy and glorious and exalted above all *fore*ver.

Antiphon   The Lord God Most High has blessed you, *Vir*gin Mary, * above all the women of *the* earth.

Ant. 3   Sinless Virgin, let us follow joyfully in *your* footsteps; * draw us after you in the fragrance of *your* holiness.

Va

Psalm 149

Sing a new song to *the* Lord, * his praise in the assembly of *the* faithful.

Let Israel rejoice in *its* Maker, * let Zion's sons exult in *their* king.

Let them praise his name *with* dancing * and make music with timbrel *and* harp.

For the Lord takes delight in *his* people. * He crowns the poor with sal*va*tion.

Let the faithful rejoice in *their* glory, * shout for joy and take *their* rest.

Let the praise of God be on *their* lips * and a two-edged sword in *their* hand,

to deal out vengeance to *the* nations * and punishment on all *the* peoples;

to bind their kings *in* chains * and their nobles in fetters *of* iron;

to carry out the sentence pre-*or*dained: * this honor is for all *his* faithful.

Glory to the Father, and to *the* Son, * and to the Ho*ly* Spirit:

as it was in the beginning, *is* now, * and will be for ever. *A*men.

Antiphon   Sinless Virgin, let us follow joyfully in *your* footsteps; * draw us after you in the fragrance of *your* holiness.

READING   Isaiah 43:1

> But now, thus says the Lord,
>> who created you, O Jacob,
>> and formed you, O Israel;
> Fear not, for I have redeemed you;
>> I have called you by name: you are mine.

RESPONSORY (VI F)

The *God* of power * has given me *his* strength.
— The *God* of power * has given me *his* strength.
He has kept me in the *way* of holiness.
— And has given me *his* strength.
Glory to the Father, and *to* the Son, * and to the Ho*ly* Spirit.
— The *God* of power * has given me *his* strength.

CANTICLE OF ZECHARIAH

Antiphon   The Lord God said *to* the serpent: * I will make *you* enemies,
you and the woman, † your offspring *and* her offspring; * she
will crush your head, al*le*luia.

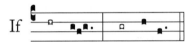

B lessèd ✠ be the Lord, the *God* of
Israel; * he has come to his people
and set *them* free.
He has raised up for us a *mighty* savior,
* born of the house of his ser*vant*
David.
Through his holy prophets he promised of old † that he would save us
from our enemies, * from the hands
of all *who* hate us.
He promised to show mercy *to* our
fathers * and to remember his ho*ly*
covenant.
This was the oath he swore to our
*fath*er Abraham: * to set us free from
the hands of *our* enemies,
free to worship him without fear, †
holy and righteous *in* his sight * all

the days of *our* life.
You, my child, shall be called the
prophet *of* the Most High; * for you
will go before the Lord to prepare *his*
way,
to give his people knowledge *of* salvation * by the forgiveness of *their* sins.
In the tender compassion *of* our God *
the dawn from on high shall break
*up*on us,
to shine on those who dwell in darkness and the sha*dow* of death, * and
to guide our feet into the way *of*
peace.
Glory to the Father, and *to* the Son, *
and to the Ho*ly* Spirit:
as it was in the begin*ning*, is now, * and
will be for ever. *A*men.

Antiphon   The Lord God said *to* the serpent: * I will make *you* enemies,
you and the woman, † your offspring *and* her offspring; * she
will crush your head, al*le*luia.

INTERCESSIONS (VI F)

Let us glorify our Savior, who chose the Virgin Mary *for* his mother. * *Let* us ask
    him:

May your mother intercede for us, *Lord.*

Sun of Justice, the Immaculate Virgin was the white dawn announc*ing* your
    rising,

— grant that we may always live in the light *of* your coming.

Savior of the world, by your redeeming might you preserved your mother
    beforehand from all *stain* of sin,

— keep watch over us, *lest* we sin.

You are our redeemer, who made the Immaculate Virgin Mary your purest
    home and the sanctuary of the *Holy* Spirit,

— make us temples of your Spir*it* for ever.

King of kings, you lifted up your mother, body and soul, *into* heaven,

— help us to fix our thoughts on *things* above.

Our Father . . .

Prayer

Father,
    you prepared the Virgin Mary
    to be the worthy mother of your Son.
    You let her share beforehand
    in the salvation Christ would bring by his death,
    and kept her sinless from the first moment of her conception.
    Help us by her prayers
    to live in your presence without sin.
    We ask this through our Lord Jesus Christ, your Son,
    who lives and reigns with you and the Holy Spirit,
    one God, for ever and ever.

Evening Prayer II

HYMN, as in Evening Prayer I, 1146.

PSALMODY

Ant. 1   You are all beauti*ful*, O Mary; * in you there is no trace of
                 orig*inal* sin.

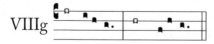

VIIIg

Psalm 122

I rejoiced when I *heard* them say: *   And now our *feet* are standing * within
   "Let us go *to* God's house."   your gates, *O* Jerusalem.

Jerusalem is built *as* a city * strong*ly* compact.

It is there that the *tribes* go up, * the tribes *of* the Lord.

For Israel's *law* it is, * there to praise *the* Lord's name.

There were set the *thrones* of judgment * of the *house* of David.

For the peace of Jeru*sa*lem pray: * "Peace be *to* your homes!

May peace reign *in* your walls, * in your pal*a*ces, peace!"

For love of my bre*thren* and friends * I say: "*Peace* upon you!"

For love of the house *of* the Lord * I will ask *for* your good.

Glory to the Father, and *to* the Son, * and to the *Holy* Spirit:

as it was in the begin*ning*, is now, * and will be for ev*er*. Amen.

Antiphon   You are all beauti*ful*, O Mary; * in you there is no trace of orig*i*nal sin.

Ant. 2   You are the glory of Jerusalem, † the *joy* of Israel; * you are the fairest honor of *our* race.

IIA

Psalm 127

If the Lord does not *build* the house, * in vain do its build*ers* labor;

if the Lord does not watch ov*er* the city, * in vain does the watchman *keep* vigil.

In vain is your ear*lier* rising, * your going later *to* rest,

you who toil for the *bread* you eat: * when he pours gifts on his belovèd while *they* slumber.

Truly sons are a gift *from* the Lord, * a blessing, the fruit of *the* womb.

Indeed the *sons* of youth * are like arrows in the hand of *a* warrior.

O the happiness *of* the man * who has filled his quiver with *these* arrows!

He will have no *cause* for shame * when he disputes with his foes in *the* gateways.

Glory to the Father, and *to* the Son, * and to the Ho*ly* Spirit:

as it was in the begin*ning*, is now, * and will be for ever. *A*men.

Antiphon   You are the glory of Jerusalem, † the *joy* of Israel; * you are the fairest honor of *our* race.

Ant. 3   The robe you wear is white as spot*less* snow; * your face is radiant like *the* sun.

Va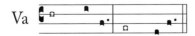

Canticle   Ephesians 1:3-10

Praised be the God *and* Father * of
our Lord Je*sus* Christ,
who has bestowed on us *in* Christ *
every spiritual blessing in *the* heavens.
God chose us in him † before the
world *began* * to be holy and blameless in *his* sight.
He predestined us † to be his adopted
sons through Je*sus* Christ, * such was
his will *and* pleasure,
that all might praise the glori*ous* favor *
he has bestowed on us in his *be*lovèd.
In him and through his blood, † we
have been *re*deemed, * and our sins

forgiven,
so immeasura*bly* generous * is God's
favor *to* us.
God has given us the wisdom † to
understand fully *the* mystery, * the
plan he was pleased to decree *in*
Christ.
A plan to be carried out *in* Christ, * in
the fullness *of* time,
to bring all things into one in him, * in
the heavens and *on* earth.
Glory to the Father, and to *the* Son, *
and to the Ho*ly* Spirit:
as it was in the beginning, *is* now, * and
will be for ever. *A*men.

Antiphon   The robe you wear is white as spot*less* snow; * your face is
                  radiant like *the* sun.

READING   Romans 5:20-21
    Despite the increase of sin, grace has far surpassed it, so that, as sin reigned
    through death, grace may reign by way of justice leading to eternal life,
    through Jesus Christ our Lord.

RESPONSORY (VI F)
By *this* I know * you have chos*en* me.
— By *this* I know * you have chos*en* me.
You have not let my enemy triumph *over* me.
— You have chos*en* me.
Glory to the Father, and *to* the Son, * and to the Ho*ly* Spirit.
— By *this* I know * you have chos*en* me.

CANTICLE OF MARY

Ant.   Hail Mary, full of grace; the Lord is with you; † blessèd are you among women, * and blessèd is the fruit of your womb, al*le*luia.

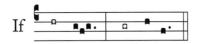

My soul ✠ proclaims the greatness *of* the Lord, * my spirit rejoices in God *my* savior

for he has *looked* with favor * on his low*ly* servant.

From this day all *gen*erations * will call *me* blessèd:

the Almighty has done great *things* for me, * and holy is *his* Name.

He has mercy on *those* who fear him * in every gen*er*ation.

He has shown the strength *of* his arm, * he has scattered the proud in their *con*ceit.

He has cast down the mighty *from*

their thrones, * and has lifted up *the* lowly.

He has filled the hungry *with* good things, * and the rich he has sent a*way* empty.

He has come to the help of his *ser*vant Israel * for he has remembered his promise *of* mercy,

the promise he made *to* our fathers, * to Abraham and his children *for* ever.

Glory to the Father, and *to* the Son, * and to the Ho*ly* Spirit:

as it was in the begin*ning*, is now, * and will be for ever. *A*men.

Antiphon   Hail Mary, full of grace; the Lord is with you; † blessèd are you among women, * and blessèd is the fruit of your womb, al*le*luia.

INTERCESSIONS

Let us praise God our almighty Father, who wished that Mary, his Son's mother, be celebrated by each *gen*eration. * Now in *need* we ask:

Mary, full of grace, intercede for us.

O God, worker of miracles, you made the Immaculate Virgin Mary share, body and soul, in your Son's glo*ry* in heaven,

— direct the hearts of your children to *that* same glory.

You made Mary our mother. Through her intercession grant strength to the weak, comfort to the sorrowing, par*don* to sinners,

— salvation and *peace* to all.

You made Mary the mo*ther* of mercy,

— may all who are faced with trials feel her mo*ther*ly love.

You wished Mary to be the mother of the family in the home of Je*sus* and Joseph,

— may all mothers of families foster love and holiness through her *in*tercession.

You crowned Mary *queen* of heaven,

— may all the dead rejoice in your kingdom with the *saints* for ever.

Our Father . . .

Prayer

Father,
you prepared the Virgin Mary
to be the worthy mother of your Son.
You let her share beforehand
in the salvation Christ would bring by his death,
and kept her sinless from the first moment of her conception.
Help us by her prayers
to live in your presence without sin.
We ask this through our Lord Jesus Christ, your Son,
who lives and reigns with you and the Holy Spirit,
one God, for ever and ever.

December 9
JUAN DIEGO, HERMIT
Memorial

From the common of holy men, 1263.

Prayer

Lord God,
through blessèd Juan Diego
you made known the love of Our Lady of Guadalupe
toward your people.
Grant by his intercession
that we who follow the counsel of Mary, our Mother,
may strive continually to do your will.
We ask this through our Lord Jesus Christ, your Son,
who lives and reigns with you and the Holy Spirit,
one God, for ever and ever.

December 11
DAMASUS I, POPE

From the common of pastors, 1238.

Prayer

Father,
as Saint Damasus loved and honored your martyrs,
so may we continue to celebrate their witness for Christ
who lives and reigns with you and the Holy Spirit,
one God, for ever and ever.

[In the dioceses of the United States]
December 12
OUR LADY OF GUADALUPE
Feast

From the common of the Blessed Virgin Mary, 1192.

Prayer

God of power and mercy,
you blessed the Americas at Tepeyac
with the presence of the Virgin Mary at Guadalupe.
May her prayers help all men and women
to accept each other as brothers and sisters.
Through your justice present in our hearts
may your peace reign in the world.
We ask this through our Lord Jesus Christ, your Son,
who lives and reigns with you and the Holy Spirit,
one God, for ever and ever.

December 13
LUCY, VIRGIN AND MARTYR
Memorial

From the common of one martyr, 1228, or of virgins, 1253.

Morning Prayer

CANTICLE OF ZECHARIAH

Ant.   I am the Lord's poor servant; † to him alone, the *livi*ng God, * I
have offered all *in* sacrifice;
I have nothing *else* to give; * I offer him *my*self.

Prayer

Lord,
give us courage through the prayers of Saint Lucy.
As we celebrate her entrance into eternal glory,
we ask to share her happiness in the life to come.
Grant this through our Lord Jesus Christ, your Son,
who lives and reigns with you and the Holy Spirit,
one God, for ever and ever.

Evening Prayer

Ant.   Lucy, *bride* of Christ, * by your suffering you have gained the
         mastery of *your* soul.
         You have despised the *world*ly values * and now you are glorious
         among *the* angels.
         With *your* own blood * you have triumphed over *the* enemy.

December 14
JOHN OF THE CROSS, PRIEST AND DOCTOR
Memorial

From the common of doctors, 1246.

Prayer

Father,
you endowed John of the Cross with a spirit of self-denial
and a love of the cross.
By following his example,
may we come to the eternal vision of your glory.
We ask this through our Lord Jesus Christ, your Son,
who lives and reigns with you and the Holy Spirit,
one God, for ever and ever.

December 21
PETER CANISIUS, PRIEST AND DOCTOR
Commemoration

Morning Prayer

Ant.   Those who are learnèd will be as radiant *as* the sky * in all *its*
         beauty;
         those who instruct the peo*ple* in goodness * will shine like the
         stars for all *e*ternity.

Prayer

Lord,
you gave Saint Peter Canisius
wisdom and courage to defend the Catholic faith.
By the help of his prayers
may all who seek the truth rejoice in finding you
and may all who believe in you

be loyal in professing their faith.
Grant this through our Lord Jesus Christ, your Son,
who lives and reigns with you and the Holy Spirit,
one God, for ever and ever.

Evening Prayer

CANTICLE OF MARY
Ant.   O blessèd doctor, Saint Peter, † light of holy Church and lover
              of God's law, * pray to the Son of God *for* us.

December 23
JOHN OF KANTY, PRIEST
Commemoration

Morning Prayer

CANTICLE OF ZECHARIAH
Ant.   All the world will recognize you as *my* disciples * when they see
              the love you have for one *an*other.

Prayer
Almighty Father,
through the example of John of Kanty
may we grow in the wisdom of the saints.
As we show understanding and kindness to others,
my we receive your forgiveness.
We ask this through our Lord Jesus Christ, your Son,
who lives and reigns with you and the Holy Spirit,
one God, for ever and ever.

Evening Prayer

CANTICLE OF MARY
Ant.   I tell *you* most solemnly, * what you did for the least of men you
              did *for* me.
              Come, my Father delights in you; † receive the kingdom
              pre*pared* for you * from the foundation of *the* world.

December 26
STEPHEN, FIRST MARTYR
Feast

Morning Prayer
HYMN

Christus est. (11.11.11.5)

Christus est vita	Jesus the Christ-Child
veniens in orbem,	brought new life to all men,
qui ferens vulnus	And in his Manhood
removensque mortem,	conquered death and evil,
ad Patris dextram	Risen, triumphant,
repetendo, regnat	in the Father's glory
sede superna.	He reigns for ever.
Hunc sequens primus	Stephen the Deacon
Stephanus minister	was the first to follow
sortis illate	Christ's great example,
titulo est decorus,	done to death by sinners,
quam dedit spirans	Though all his actions
Domini benignus	and his words were prompted
Spiritus illi.	By the Lord's Spirit.
Saxeo nimbo	Enemies' anger
lapidatus instat,	destined him to perish,
sustinet mortis	Stoned by his hearers,
rabiem profanam,	victim of their fury,
hostibu quærit	Yet like his Savior,
veniam misertus	in his dying moments
pectore grato.	Pleading their pardon.
Quæsumus flentes,	Witness to Jesus,
benedicte prime	help us, holy Stephen,
martyr et civis	Mourning and contrite
sociate iustis:	to attain the Kingdom;
cælitus, claræ	Gain us the graces
regionis heres,	which we need to bring us
mitte favores.	Safely to heaven.
Gloriæ laudes	Of the same nature
Triadi beatæ	as the blessed martyrs;
martyrum læti	Let us sing praises
comites canamus,	to our God Almighty,
quæ dedit primas	Who honored Stephen
Stephano ex agone	with a martyr's glory,
ferre coronas. Amen.	First among thousands. Amen.

Ant. 1   My soul has held fast to *you*, my God; * for your sake I suffered *death* by stoning.

Psalms and canticle from Sunday, Week I, 606.

Ant. 2   Stephen saw the heavens open; † he saw and *en*tered in. * Happy the man to whom the heav*ens* opened.

Ant. 3   Behold I see the heav*ens* open, * and Jesus standing at the right hand of the almigh*ty* God.

READING   Acts 6:2b-5a

"It is not right for us to neglect the word of God in order to wait on tables. Look around your own number, brothers, for seven men acknowledged to be deeply spiritual and prudent, and we shall appoint them to this task. This will permit us to concentrate on prayer and the ministry of the word." The proposal was unanimously accepted by the community.

RESPONSORY (VI F)

The Lord *is* my strength, * and I shall sing *his* praise.
— The Lord *is* my strength, * and I shall sing *his* praise.
The Lord *is* my savior,
— and I shall sing *his* praise.
Glory to the Father, and *to* the Son, * and to the Ho*ly* Spirit.
— The Lord *is* my strength, * and I shall sing *his* praise.

CANTICLE OF ZECHARIAH

Antiphon   The gates of heaven opened out to *bless*èd Stephen, * and he was crowned first *of* martyrs.

INTERCESSIONS (VI F)

Our Savior's faithfulness is mirrored in the fidelity of his witnesses who shed their blood for the *word* of God. * Let us praise him in remem*brance* of them:
You redeemed us by your *blood.*
Your martyrs freely embraced death in bearing witness *to* the faith,
— give us the true freedom of the Spir*it*, O Lord.
Your martyrs professed their faith by shed*ding* their blood,
— give us a faith, O Lord, that is con*stant* and pure.
Your martyrs followed in your footsteps by carry*ing* the cross,
— help us to endure courageously the misfort*unes* of life.
Your martyrs washed their garments in the blood *of* the Lamb,
— help us to avoid the weaknesses of the flesh and world*ly* allurements.

Our Father . . .

Prayer

Lord,
today we celebrate the entrance of Saint Stephen
into eternal glory.
He died praying for those who killed him.
Help us to imitate his goodness
and to love our enemies.
We ask this through our Lord Jesus Christ, your Son,
who lives and reigns with you and the Holy Spirit,
one God, for ever and ever.

Evening Prayer

Everything is taken from the octave of Christmas as on December 26.

If the feast of Saint Stephen is observed as a solemnity: the hymn, antiphons, readings and responsory are taken from Morning Prayer; psalms, canticle and intercessions from the common of martyrs, 1232.

December 27
JOHN, APOSTLE AND EVANGELIST
Feast

Morning Prayer
HYMN
Cohors beata. (L.M.)

Cohors beáta Séraphim
quem Christus arcte díligit
laudet, chorúsque cánticis
noster resúltet æmulis.

Hic discit, almus édocet
hic unde Verbum pródeat,
sinúmque matris ímpleat,
sinum Patris non déserens.

Felix Ioánnes, déligit
et te Magíster próvidus,
ut clara Thabor lúmina
hortíque cernas tædia.

Tu, raptus in sublímia,
arcána cæli cónspicis,
Agni sed et mystéria
Ecclesiæque pércipis.

May all the shining Seraphim
Praise him whom Christ so dearly loved,
And may our lowly hymns resound
In echo to angelic songs.

The Fount of Wisdom was his school,
To teach the glory of the Word,
Who with the Father ever dwells
Yet filled his Virgin Mother's womb.

The Master's love selected you,
O happy John, great things to see;
The glory shown on Tabor's height,
The Garden's bitter agony.

Caught up in ecstasies sublime,
You were allowed to contemplate
The triumph of the spotless Lamb
And of the Church, his chosen Bride.

O digne fili Vírgine,	When dying, Jesus gave to you
succéssor alti nóminis,	His Virgin Mother as your own;
nos adde Matri fílios,	Make us her loving children too,
nos conde Christi in péctore.	And hide us in the Heart of Christ.
Verbo sit ingens glória,	All glory to the Word Divine
caro quod est et créditur,	Who took our flesh as truly Man,
cum Patre et almo Spíritu	Who with the Father reigns on high
in sempitérna sæcula. Amen.	For ever with their Spirit's Love. Amen.

Ant. 1   John, the apostle and evangelist, † a virgin chosen *by* the Lord, *
was loved by the Lord a*bove* the others.

Psalms and canticle from Sunday, Week I, 606.

Ant. 2   To the virgin John, Christ, dying *on* the cross, * entrusted his
vir*gin* mother.

Ant. 3   The disciple who Jesus loved *cried* out: * It is the Lord, al*le*luia.

READING   Acts 4:19-20

Peter and John answered, "Judge for yourselves whether it is right in God's
sight for us to obey you rather than God. Surely we cannot help speaking of
what we have heard and seen."

RESPONSORY (VI F)

You have *made* them rulers * over all *the* earth.
— You have *made* them rulers * over all *the* earth.
They will always remember your *name*, O Lord,
— over all *the* earth.
Glory to the Father, and *to* the Son, * and to the Ho*ly* Spirit.
— You have *made* them rulers * over all *the* earth.

CANTICLE OF ZECHARIAH

Antiphon   The Word was made flesh and *lived* among us, * and we have
seen *his* glory.

INTERCESSIONS (VI F)

My brothers, we build on the foundation of *the* apostles. * Let us pray to our
almighty Father for his holy peo*ple* and say:
Be mindful of your Church, O Lord.
Father, you wanted your Son to be seen first by the apostles after the
resurrection *from* the dead,
— we ask you to make us his witnesses to the farthest corners *of* the world.
You sent your Son to preach the good news *to* the poor,
— help us to preach the Gospel to *every* creature.

You sent your Son to sow the seed of un*end*ing life,
— grant that we who work at sowing the seed may share the joy *of* the harvest.
You sent your Son to reconcile all men to you *through* his blood,
— help us all to work toward achieving this recon*cili*ation.

Our Father . . .

Prayer

God our Father,
you have revealed the mysteries of your Word
through John the apostle.
By prayer and reflection
may we come to understand the wisdom he taught.
Grant this through our Lord Jesus Christ, your Son,
who lives and reigns with you and the Holy Spirit,
one God, for ever and ever.

Evening Prayer

Everything is taken from the octave of Christmas as on December 27.

If the feast of Saint John is observed as a solemnity: the hymn, antiphons, readings and responsory are taken from Morning Prayer; psalms, canticle and intercessions from the common of apostles, 1208.

December 28
HOLY INNOCENTS, MARTYRS
Feast

Morning Prayer

HYMN

Audit tyrranus (L.M.)

Audit tyrannus anxius	The anxious tyrant's troubled ears
adesse regum principem,	Have heard that there is born the King,
qui nomen Israel regat	Appointed to fill David's place
teneatque David regiam.	And rule the land of Israel.
Exclamat amens nuntio,	In guilty madness he exclaims:
"Successor instat, pellimur;	"We must protect our threatened throne!
satelles i, ferrum rape,	Go, servant, draw a ruthless sword,
perfunde cunas sanguine."	And stain the cradles red with blood."
Quid proficit tantum nefas,	What profit brings this craven deed?
quid crimen Herodem iuvat?	Where, cruel Herod, is your gain?
unus tot inter funera	In safety from your evil schemes
impune Christus tollitur.	The Infant Christ is borne away.

Salvete, flores martyrum,	Hail, fairest flow'rs of martyrdom,
quos lucis ips*o* in limine	Sweet roses in their early bud,
Christ*i* insecutor sustulit	But plucked by enemy of Christ,
ceu turbo nascentes rosas.	When on the threshold of your life.
Vos prima Christi victima,	A little flock of tender lambs,
grex immolatorum tener,	You were the first oblations pure;
aram sub ipsam simplices	Beneath the altar-throne of Christ
palm*a* et coronis luditis.	You gaily play with palms and crowns.
Iesu, tibi sit gloria,	All glory, Jesus, be to you
qui natus es de Virgine,	Born of a Virgin undefiled,
cum Patr*e* et almo Spiritu,	Who with the Spirit of your Love
in sempiterna sæcula. Amen.	And God the Father, ever reign. Amen.

Ant. 1   Clothed in white robes, † they will walk with me, *says* the Lord, * for *they* are worthy.

Psalms and canticle from Sunday, Week I, 606.

Ant. 2   These children cry out their praises to the Lord; † by their death they *have* proclaimed * what they could not preach with their in*fant* voices.

Ant. 3   From the mouths of children and babies at *the* breast * you have found praise to foil *your* enemies.

READING   Jeremiah 31:15

> In Ramah is heard the sound of moaning,
>   of bitter weeping!
> Rachel mourns her children,
>   she refuses to be consoled
>   because her children are no more.

RESPONSORY (VI F)

The just are the *friends* of God. * They live with him *for* ever.
— The just are the *friends* of God. * They live with him *for* ever.
God himself is *their* reward.
— They live with him *for* ever.
Glory to the Father, and *to* the Son, * and to the Ho*ly* Spirit.
— The just are the *friends* of God. * They live with him *for* ever.

CANTICLE OF ZECHARIAH

Antiphon   At the king's command these innocent babies and *lit*tle children * were put *to* death;
                    they died for Christ, and now in the glory of heaven † as they follow him, the *sin*less Lamb, * they sing for ever: Glory to you, O Lord.

INTERCESSIONS (VI F)

We rejoice in the glory of Jesus Christ, who conquered the enemy not by force
of arms but with a white-robed army of children, * and *we* cry out:
The white-robed army of martyrs praises you.

The Holy Innocents gave witness not by words but by *their* life's blood,
— give us strength to be your witnesses before men, both by words *and* by
actions.

They were not ready for battle but you made them fit to win the *palm* of
victory,
— now that we are prepared for victory, do not let *us* despair.

You washed the robes of the Innocents *in* your blood;
— cleanse us *from* all sin.

You rewarded the child martyrs with the first share *in* your kingdom,
— do not let us be cast out from the unending hea*ven*ly banquet.

You knew persecution and exile *as* a child,
— protect all children whose lives are in danger from famine, war *and* disasters.

Our Father . . .

Prayer

Father,
the Holy Innocents offered you praise
by the death they suffered for Christ.
May our lives bear witness
to the faith we profess with our lips.
We ask this through our Lord Jesus Christ, your Son,
who lives and reigns with you and the Holy Spirit,
one God, for ever and ever.

Evening Prayer

Everything is taken from the octave of Christmas as on December 28.

If the feast of the Holy Innocents is observed as a solemnity: the hymn, antiphons, readings
and responsory are taken from Morning Prayer; psalms, canticle and intercessions from the
common of martyrs, 1232.

December 29
THOMAS BECKET, BISHOP AND MARTYR
Commemoration

Morning Prayer

CANTICLE OF ZECHARIAH

Ant.   Whoever hates his life *in* this world * keeps it safe for life
                  ev*er*lasting.

Prayer

Almighty God,
you granted the martyr Thomas
the grace to give his life for the cause of justice.
By his prayers
make us willing to renounce for Christ
our life in this world
so that we may find it in heaven.
We ask this through our Lord Jesus Christ, your Son,
who lives and reigns with you and the Holy Spirit,
one God, for ever and ever.

Evening Prayer

CANTICLE OF MARY

Ant.   The saints find their home in the king*dom* of heaven; * their life
is eter*nal* peace.

December 31
SYLVESTER I, POPE
Commemoration

Morning Prayer

CANTICLE OF ZECHARIAH

Ant.   What you say of me does not come *from* yourselves; * it is the
Spirit of my Father speak*ing* in you.

Prayer

Lord,
help and sustain your people
by the prayers of Pope Sylvester.
Guide us always in this present life
and bring us to the joy that never ends.
We ask this through our Lord Jesus Christ, your Son,
who lives and reigns with you and the Holy Spirit,
one God, for ever and ever.

Commons

COMMON OF THE DEDICATION
OF A CHURCH

Evening Prayer I

HYMN, as in Evening Prayer II, 1182.

PSALMODY

Ant. 1   The streets of Jerusalem will ring with *re*joicing; * they will
resound with the song of praise: *Al*leluia.

Lent: In the temple of the Lord all peoples *will* say: * Glory to you.

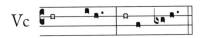

Psalm 147:1-11

Praise the Lord for he is good; †
sing to our God for he *is* loving: *
to him our *praise* is due.
The Lord builds up *Je*rusalem * and
brings back Is*rae*l's exiles,
he heals the bro*ken*-hearted, * he binds
up *all* their wounds.
He fixes the number of *the* stars; * he
calls each one *by* its name.
Our Lord is great and *al*mighty; * his
wisdom can ne*ver* be measured.
The Lord raises *the* lowly; * he humbles the wicked *to* the dust.
O sing to the Lord, giv*ing* thanks; *
sing psalms to our God *with* the

harp.
He covers the heavens *with* clouds; * he
prepares the rain *for* the earth,
making mountains sprout *with* grass *
and with plants to *serve* man's needs.
He provides the beasts with *their* food *
and young ravens that *call* upon him.
His delight is not *in* horses * nor his
pleasure in warriors' strength.
The Lord delights in those who *re*vere
him, * in those who wait *for* his love.
Glory to the Father, and to *the* Son, *
and to the *Ho*ly Spirit:
as it was in the beginning, *is* now, * and
will be for *e*ver. Amen.

Antiphon   The streets of Jerusalem will ring with *re*joicing; * they will
resound with the song of praise: *Al*leluia.

Lent: In the temple of the Lord all peoples *will* say: * Glory to you.

Ant. 2   How safe a dwelling the Lord *has* made you; * how blessed the
children with*in* your walls (*al*leluia).

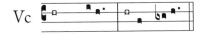

Psalm 147:12-20

O praise the Lord, *Jerusalem*! *
Zion, *praise* your God!
He has strengthened the bars of *your*
gates, * he has blessed the child*ren*
within you.
He established peace on *your* borders, *
he feeds you with *finest* wheat.
He sends out his word to *the* earth *
and swiftly runs *his* command.
He showers down snow white *as* wool,
* he scatters hoar-*frost* like ashes.
He hurls down hailstones *like* crumbs.
* The waters are frozen *at* his touch;

he sends forth his word and *it* melts
them: * at the breath of his mouth
the *wat*ers flow.
He makes his word known *to* Jacob, *
to Israel his laws *and* decrees.
He has not dealt thus with o*ther*
nations; * he has not taught them *his*
decrees.
Glory to the Father, and to *the* Son, *
and to the *Holy* Spirit:
as it was in the beginning, *is* now, * and
will be for e*ver*. Amen.

Antiphon   How safe a dwelling the Lord *has* made you; * how blessed the
children with*in* your walls (a*l*leluia).

Ant. 3   In the holy city, throngs of saints make jubilee; † angels pour
out their songs of praise before the throne *of* God, * alleluia,
alleluia.

** al- le- lu- ia, al- le- lu- ia.

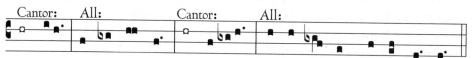

*Al- le- lu- ia.   ** al- le- lu- ia, al- le - lu- ia.

Canticle   See Revelation 19:1-7

Salvation, glory, and power to *our* God:
* Alleluia.
his judgments are hon*est* and true.
** Alleluia, alleluia.
Sing praise to our God, all you *his* servants,
* Alleluia.
all who worship him reverently, *great* and small.
** Alleluia, alleluia.

The Lord our all-powerful God *is* King;
* Alleluia.
let us rejoice, sing praise, and *give* him glory.
** Alleluia, alleluia.

The wedding feast of the Lamb has *be*gun,
* Alleluia.
and his bride is pre*pared* to welcome him.
** Alleluia, alleluia.

Glory to the Father, and to the Son, †
and to the Ho*ly* Spirit.
* Alleluia.
As it was in the beginning, is now, †
and will be for ev*er.* Amen.
** Alleluia, alleluia.

Antiphon   In the holy city, throngs of saints make jubilee; † angels pour out
            their songs of praise before the throne *of* God, * alleluia, alleluia.

Lent: Through Je*sus* Christ, * may your Church, O *Lord,* give glory.

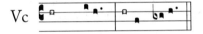

Canticle   Colossians 1:12-20

Let us give thanks to the Father †
for having made *you* worthy * to
share the lot of the *saints* in light.
He rescued us from the power *of*
darkness * and brought us into the
kingdom of his be*lovèd* Son.
Through him we have *re*demption, *
the forgiveness *of* our sins.
He is the image of the invisi*ble* God, *
the first-born *of* all creatures.
In him everything in heaven and on
earth was *cre*ated, * things visible *and*
invisible.
All were created *through* him; * all were
creat*ed* for him.
He is before all else *that* is. * In him

everything contin*ues* in being.
It is he who is head of the body, the
church! † he who is the beginning,
the first-born of *the* dead, * so that
primacy may be *his* in everything.
It pleased God to make absolute
fullness reside *in* him * and, by
means of him, to reconcile everything *in* his person,
both on earth and in *the* heavens, *
making peace through the blood *of*
his cross.
Glory to the Father, and to *the* Son, *
and to the *Ho*ly Spirit:
as it was in the beginning, *is* now, * and
will be for ev*er.* Amen.

Antiphon   Through Je*sus* Christ, * may your Church, O *Lord,* give glory.

READING   Ephesians 2:19-20

You are strangers and aliens no longer. No, you are fellow citizens of the saints and members of the household of God. You form a building which rises on the foundation of the apostles and prophets, with Christ Jesus himself as the capstone. Through him the whole structure is fitted together and takes shape as a holy temple in the Lord; in him you are being built into this temple, to become a dwelling place for God in the Spirit.

RESPONSORY (VI F)

Your house, O Lord, must always be a *holy* place * alleluia, al*le*luia.
— Your house, O Lord, must always be a *holy* place * alleluia, al*le*luia.
For ev*er* and ever,
— alleluia, al*le*luia.
Glory to the Father, and *to* the Son, * and to the Ho*ly* Spirit.
— Your house, O Lord, must always be a *holy* place * alleluia, al*le*luia.

Lent:

Your house, O Lord, must *al*ways be * a ho*ly* place.
— Your house, O Lord, must *al*ways be * a ho*ly* place.
For ev*er* and ever,
— a ho*ly* place.
Glory to the Father, and *to* the Son, * and to the Ho*ly* Spirit.
— Your house, O Lord, must *al*ways be * a ho*ly* place.

CANTICLE OF MARY

Ant.   All you who *love* Jerusalem, * rejoice with her *for* ever (al*le*luia).

Weeks I and III   Weeks II and IV

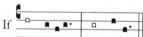

Mʏ soul ✠ proclaims the greatness *of* the Lord, * my spirit rejoices in God *my* savior
for he has *looked* with favor * on his low*ly* servant.
From this day all *gen*erations * will call *me* blessèd:
the Almighty has done great *things* for me, * and holy is *his* Name.
He has mercy on *those* who fear him * in every gen*er*ation.
He has shown the strength *of* his arm, * he has scattered the proud in their *con*ceit.

He has cast down the mighty *from* their thrones, * and has lifted up *the* lowly.
He has filled the hungry *with* good things, * and the rich he has sent a*way* empty.
He has come to the help of his *servant* Israel * for he has remembered his promise *of* mercy,
the promise he made *to* our fathers, * to Abraham and his children *for* ever.
Glory to the Father, and *to* the Son, * and to the Ho*ly* Spirit:
as it was in the begin*ning*, is now, * and will be for ever. *A*men.

Antiphon   All you who *love* Jerusalem, * rejoice with her *for* ever (al*le*luia).

INTERCESSIONS (VI F)

Our Savior laid down his life so that all God's scattered children might be
     ga*thered* together. * In our need let *us* cry out:
Remember your Church, O Lord.
Lord Jesus, you built your house up*on* a rock,
— strengthen your Church with solid and *last*ing faith.
Lord Jesus, blood and water flowed *from* your side,
— give new life to your Church through the sacrament of your new and un*end*-
     ing covenant.
Lord Jesus, you are in the midst of those who gather *in* your name,
— hear the prayers of your uni*ver*sal Church.
Lord Jesus, you prepare a dwelling-place in your Father's house for *all* who love
     you,
— help your Church to grow in *di*vine love.
Lord Jesus, you never cast out anyone who *comes* to you,
— open your Father's house to all those *who* have died.

Our Father . . .

Prayer, as in Morning Prayer.

Morning Prayer

HYMN

Angularis fundamentum. (87.87.87)

Angularis fundamentum	Christ the Cornerstone from heaven,
lapis Christus missus est,	Came to make the arch complete,
qui parietum compage	Ancient Sion gently moulding
in utroque nectitur,	Into his new Law of Love.
quem Sion sancta suscepti,	Souls sincere, with faith received him
in quo credens permanet.	Founding thus his Church on earth.
Omnis illa Deo sacra	Now that loved and loving city
et dilecta civitas,	Sings to God with all its might,
plena modulis in laude	Filled with melody and praises,
et canore iubilo,	It proclaims its earnest faith
trinum Deum unicumque	In its Lord the ever holy,
cum fervore praedicat.	In the God both One and Three.
Hoc in templo, summe Deus,	God most holy, we implore you,
exoratus adveni,	In this temple, hear our prayer,
et clementi bonitate	And with all your loving kindness
precumvota suscipe;	Unto us incline your ear:
largam benedictionem	Ever pour a lavish blessing
hic infunde iugiter.	On your servants gathered here.

Hic promereantur omnes	May all humble supplications
petita acquirere	Win the grace they truly seek;
et adepta possidere	Reaping all their labours' merits
cum sanctis perenniter,	In your Paradise above,
paradisum introire	With the Saints at last united
translati in requiem.	In abiding peace and love.
Gloria et honor Deo	Glory, honor everlasting,
usquequaque altissimo,	Be to God, our Lord Most High,
una Patri Filioque	To the Son and Holy Spirit,
atque Sancto Flamini,	With the Father, Three in One,
quibus laudes et potestas	Praise and homage be for ever,
per aeterna saecula. Amen.	While unending ages run. Amen.

PSALMODY

Ant. 1   My house *will* be called * a *house* of prayer (*al*leluia).

Psalm 63:2-9

O God, you are my God, for *you* I long; * for you my *soul* is thirsting.
My body *pines* for you * like a dry, weary land *with*out water.
So I gaze on you *in* the sanctuary * to see your strength *and* your glory.
For your love is bet*ter* than life, * my lips will *speak* your praise.
So I will bless you *all* my life, * in your name I will lift *up* my hands.
My soul shall be filled as *with* a banquet, * my mouth shall praise *you* with joy.
On my bed I re*mem*ber you. * On you I muse *through* the night
for you have *been* my help; * in the shadow of your wings *I* rejoice.
My soul *clings* to you; * your right hand *holds* me fast.
Glory to the Father, and *to* the Son, * and to the *Ho*ly Spirit:
as it was in the begin*ning*, is now, * and will be for *ev*er. Amen.

Antiphon   My house *will* be called * a *house* of prayer (*al*leluia).

Ant. 2   Blessèd are *you*, O Lord, * in your ho*ly* temple (al*le*luia).

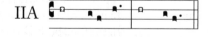

Canticle   Daniel 3:57-88; 56

Bless the Lord, all you works *of* the Lord. * Praise and exalt him above all *for*ever.
Angels of the Lord, *bless* the Lord, *
You heavens, bless *the* Lord.
All you waters above the heavens, *bless* the Lord. * All you hosts of the Lord, bless *the* Lord.

Sun and moon, *bless* the Lord. * Stars
of heaven, bless *the* Lord.

Every shower and dew, *bless* the Lord. *
All you winds, bless *the* Lord.

Fire and heat, *bless* the Lord. * Cold
and chill, bless *the* Lord.

Dew and rain, *bless* the Lord. * Frost
and chill, bless *the* Lord.

Ice and snow, *bless* the Lord. * Nights
and days, bless *the* Lord.

Light and darkness, *bless* the Lord. *
Lightnings and clouds, bless *the*
Lord.

Let the earth *bless* the Lord. * Praise
and exalt him above all *for*ever.

Mountains and hills, *bless* the Lord. *
Everything growing from the earth,
bless *the* Lord.

You springs, *bless* the Lord. * Seas and
rivers, bless *the* Lord.

You dolphins and all water creatures,
bless the Lord. * All you birds of the
air, bless *the* Lord.

All you beasts, wild and tame, *bless* the
Lord. * You sons of men, bless *the*
Lord.

O Israel, *bless* the Lord. * Praise and
exalt him above all *for*ever.

Priests of the Lord, *bless* the Lord. *
Servants of the Lord, bless *the* Lord.

Spirits and souls of the just, *bless* the
Lord. * Holy men of humble heart,
bless *the* Lord.

Hananiah, Azariah, Mishael, *bless* the
Lord. * Praise and exalt him above all
*for*ever.

Let us bless the Father, and the Son,
and the *Ho*ly Spirit. * Let us praise
and exalt him above all *for*ever.

Blessèd are you in the firma*ment* of
heaven. * Praiseworthy and glorious
and exalted above all *for*ever.

Antiphon   Blessèd are *you*, O Lord, * in your ho*ly* temple   (al*le*luia).

Ant. 3   Praise *the* Lord * in the assembly of his ho*ly* people (al*le*luia).

Va

Psalm 149

Sing a new song to *the* Lord, * his
praise in the assembly of *the*
faithful.

Let Israel rejoice in *its* Maker, * let
Zion's sons exult in *their* king.

Let them praise his name *with* dancing
* and make music with timbrel *and*
harp.

For the Lord takes delight in *his*
people. * He crowns the poor with
sal*va*tion.

Let the faithful rejoice in *their* glory, *
shout for joy and take *their* rest.

Let the praise of God be on *their* lips *
and a two-edged sword in *their* hand,

to deal out vengeance to *the* nations *
and punishment on all *the* peoples;

to bind their kings *in* chains * and their
nobles in fetters *of* iron;

to carry out the sentence pre-*or*dained:
* this honor is for all *his* faithful.

Glory to the Father, and to *the* Son, *
and to the Ho*ly* Spirit:

as it was in the beginning, *is* now, * and
will be for ever. *A*men.

Antiphon   Praise *the* Lord * in the assembly of his ho*ly* people (al*le*luia).

READING   Isaiah 56:7

Them I will bring to my holy mountain;
  and make joyful in my house of prayer;
Their holocausts and sacrifices
  will be acceptable on my altar,
For my house shall be called
  a house of prayer for all peoples.

RESPONSORY (VI F)

The Lord is great beyond all telling, † he ex*ceeds* all praise * alleluia, al*le*luia.
— The Lord is great beyond all telling, † he ex*ceeds* all praise * alleluia, al*le*luia.
In the city of our God and on his *holy* mountain,
— alleluia, al*le*luia.
Glory to the Father, and *to* the Son, * and to the Ho*ly* Spirit.
— The Lord is great beyond all telling, † he ex*ceeds* all praise * alleluia, al*le*luia.

Lent:
The Lord is great be*yond* all telling, * he exceeds *all* praise.
— The Lord is great be*yond* all telling, * he exceeds *all* praise.
In the city of our God and on his *holy* mountain,
— he exceeds *all* praise.
Glory to the Father, and *to* the Son, * and to the Ho*ly* Spirit.
— The Lord is great be*yond* all telling, * he exceeds *all* praise.

CANTICLE OF ZECHARIAH

Antiphon   Zacchaeus, *hur*ry down, * I mean to stay with you *to*day.
He hurried down † and welcomed *Christ* with joy, * for this day
salvation had come to *his* house (al*le*luia).

Weeks I and III   Weeks II and IV

   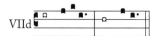

Blessèd ✠ be the Lord, the *God* of Israel; * he has come to his people and set *them* free.
He has raised up for us a *mighty* savior, * born of the house of his ser*vant* David.
Through his holy prophets he promised of old † that he would save us *from* our enemies, * from the hands of all *who* hate us.

He promised to show mercy *to* our fathers * and to remember his ho*ly* covenant.
This was the oath he swore to our *fath*er Abraham: * to set us free from the hands of *our* enemies,
free to worship him without fear, † holy and righteous *in* his sight * all the days of *our* life.
You, my child, shall be called the

prophet *of* the Most High; * for you will go before the Lord to prepare *his* way,
to give his people knowledge *of* salvation * by the forgiveness of *their* sins.
In the tender compassion *of* our God * the dawn from on high shall break *up*on us,
to shine on those who dwell in darkness and the sha*dow* of death, * and to guide our feet into the way *of* peace.
Glory to the Father, and *to* the Son, * and to the Ho*ly* Spirit:
as it was in the begin*ning*, is now, * and will be for ever. *A*men.

Antiphon   Zacchaeus, *hur*ry down, * I mean to stay with you *to*day. He hurried down † and welcomed *Christ* with joy, * for this day salvation had come to *his* house (al*le*luia).

INTERCESSIONS (VI F)

We are the living stones, laid upon the cornerstone *that* is Christ. * Let us pray to our all-powerful Father for his Son's belovèd Church, professing our faith in her *as* we say:
This is the house of God and the gate of *heaven.*
Father, like the farmer, prune your vineyard, protect it and in*crease* its yield,
— until it extends before you through*out* the world.
Eternal shepherd, protect and in*crease* your flock,
— that all the sheep may be gathered into one flock under your Son, *the* one shepherd.
All-powerful sower, plant the word *in* your field,
— that it may yield a hundredfold for your e*ter*nal harvest.
Wise builder, sanctify your home *and* your family,
— that the heavenly city, the new Jerusalem, your spouse, may appear before all as your glo*ri*ous bride.

Our Father . . .

Prayer

In the dedicated church:
Father,
each year we recall the dedication of this church to your service.
Let our worship always be sincere
and help us to find your saving love in this church.
Grant this through our Lord Jesus Christ, your Son,
who lives and reigns with you and the Holy Spirit,
one God, for ever and ever.

Outside the dedicated church:

> God our Father,
> from living stones, your chosen people,
> you built an eternal temple to your glory.
> Increase the spiritual gifts you have given to your Church
> that your faithful people may continue to grow
> into the new and eternal Jerusalem.
> We ask this through our Lord Jesus Christ, your Son,
> who lives and reigns with you and the Holy Spirit,
> one God, for ever and ever.

Or:

> Father,
> you called your people to be your Church.
> As we gather together in your name,
> may we love, honor, and follow you
> to eternal life in the kingdom you promise.
> Grant this through our Lord Jesus Christ, your Son,
> who lives and reigns with you and the Holy Spirit,
> one God, for ever and ever.

Evening Prayer II

HYMN

Urbs Jerusalem. (87.87.87)

Urbs Ierusalem beata,
dicta pacis visio,
quae construitur in caelis
vivis ex lapidibus,
angelisque coronata
sicut sponsa comite,

Realms of light were seen in vision
As a new Jerusalem,
Filled with Christ's own peace and glory,
Built of living stones above,
And with angel hosts encircled,
As a bride's fair diadem.

Nova veniens e caelo,
nuptiali thalamo
praeparata, ut intacta
copuletur Domino.
Plateae et muri eius
ex auro purissimo;

Seen as coming down from heaven,
And adorned in bright array,
Eager for the great espousals
With the sov'reign Lord and king.
All its walls, its streets and byways
Shimmer with the purest gold.

Portae nitent margaritis
adytis patentibus,
et virtute meritorum
illuc introducitur
omnis qui ob Christi nomen
hic in mundo premitur.

Pearls most precious form its portals,
Open wide to welcome in
Those whose virtues and whose merits
Have attained that grace to win,
Who have suffered pain and sorrow
For the name of Christ their Lord.

Tunsionibus, pressuris	Stones of every hue and beauty
expoliti lapides	Sparkle from its sacred walls,
suis coaptantur locis	Tested, polished to perfection
per manum artificis;	By the Artist's Hand divine;
disponuntur permansuri	Placed with love in their position,
sacris aedificiis.	There for evermore to shine:
Gloria et honor Deo	Glory, honor everlasting,
usquequaque altissimo,	Be to God, our Lord Most High,
una Pari Filioque	To the Son and Holy Spirit,
atque Sancto Flamini,	With the Father, Three in One,
quibus laudes et potestas	Praise and homage be for ever,
per aeterna saecula. Amen.	While unending ages run. Amen.

PSALMODY

Ant 1   This is God's dwelling place † and he has *made* it holy, * it will stand for ev*er* firm (al*le*luia).

Psalm 46

God is for us a re*fuge* and strength, * a helper close at hand, in time of *dis*tress:

so we shall not fear though the *earth* should rock, * though the mountains fall into the depths of *the* sea,

even though its waters *rage* and foam, * even though the mountains be shaken by *its* waves.

The Lord of *hosts* is with us: * the God of Jacob is *our* stronghold.

The waters of a river give joy *to* God's city, * the holy place where the Most *High* dwells.

God is within, it can*not* be shaken; * God will help it at the dawning of *the* day.

Nations are in tumult, king*doms* are shaken: * he lifts his voice, the earth shrinks *a*way.

The Lord of *hosts* is with us: * the God of Jacob is *our* stronghold.

Come, consider the works *of* the Lord, * the redoubtable deeds he has done on *the* earth.

He puts an end to wars over all the earth; † the bow he breaks, the *spear* he snaps. * He burns the shields *with* fire.

"Be still and know that *I* am God, * supreme among the nations, supreme on *the* earth!"

The Lord of *hosts* is with us: * the God of Jacob is *our* stronghold.

Glory to the Father, and *to* the Son, * and to the Ho*ly* Spirit:

as it was in the begin*ning*, is now, * and will be for ever. *A*men.

Antiphon   This is God's dwelling place † and he has *made* it holy; * it will stand for ev*er* firm (al*le*luia).

Ant. 2   Let us go up with re*joic*ing * to the house of *the* Lord (al*le*luia).

VIIIa

Psalm 122

I rejoiced when I heard them *say*: *
"Let us go to *God's* house."

And now our feet are *stand*ing * within
your gates, O *Je*rusalem.

Jerusalem is built as a *city* * strongly
*com*pact.

It is there that the tribes go *up*, * the
tribes of *the* Lord.

For Israel's law it *is*, * there to praise *the*
Lord's name.

There were set the thrones of *judg*ment
* of the house *of* David.

For the peace of Jerusalem *pray*: *
"Peace be to *your* homes!

May peace reign in your *walls*, * in
your palac*es*, peace!"

For love of my brethren and *friends* * I
say: "Peace up*on* you!"

For love of the house of the *Lord* * I
will ask for *your* good.

Glory to the Father, and to the *Son*, *
and to the Ho*ly* Spirit:

as it was in the beginning, is *now*, * and
will be for ever. *A*men.

Antiphon   Let us go up with re*joic*ing * to the house of *the* Lord (al*le*luia).

Ant. 3   All you his saints, † sing out the praises of *our* God, * alleluia,
alleluia.

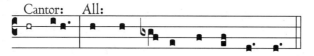

** al- le- lu- ia, al- le- lu- ia.

*Al- le- lu- ia.   ** al- le- lu- ia, al- le - lu- ia.

Canticle   See Revelation 19:1-7

S alvation, glory, and power to *our* God:
* Alleluia.

his judgments are hon*est* and true.
** Alleluia, alleluia.

Sing praise to our God, all you *his* servants,
* Alleluia.

all who worship him reverently, *great* and small.
** Alleluia, alleluia.

The Lord our all-powerful God *is* King;
* Alleluia.
let us rejoice, sing praise, and *give* him glory.
** Alleluia, alleluia.

The wedding feast of the Lamb has *be*gun,
* Alleluia.
and his bride is pre*pared* to welcome him.
** Alleluia, alleluia.

Glory to the Father, and to the Son, †
and to the Ho*ly* Spirit.
* Alleluia.
As it was in the beginning, is now, †
and will be for *ever*. Amen.
** Alleluia, alleluia.

Antiphon All you his saints, † sing out the praises of *our* God, * alleluia,
alleluia.

Lent: People of eve*ry* nation * shall come and worship *you*, O Lord.

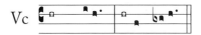

Vc

Canticle   Revelation 15:3-4

Mighty and wonderful are *your*
works, * Lord *God* Almighty!
Righteous and true are *your* ways, * O
King *of* the nations!
Who would dare refuse *you* honor, * or
the glory due your *name*, O Lord?
Since you alone *are* holy, * all nations
shall come and worship *in* your
presence.
Your mighty deeds * are *clear*ly seen.
Glory to the Father, and to *the* Son, *
and to the *Holy* Spirit:
as it was in the beginning, *is* now, * and
will be for *ever*. Amen.

Antiphon People of eve*ry* nation * shall come and worship *you*, O Lord.

READING   Revelation 21:2-3, 22, 27

I saw a new Jerusalem, the holy city, coming down out of heaven from God,
beautiful as a bride prepared to meet her husband. I heard a loud voice from
the throne cry out: "This is God's dwelling among men. He shall dwell with
them and they shall be his people and he shall be their God who is always
with them." I saw no temple in the city. The Lord, God the Almighty, is its
temple— he and the Lamb. But nothing profane shall enter it, nor anyone

who is a liar or has done a detestable act. Only those shall enter whose names are inscribed in the book of the living kept by the Lamb.

RESPONSORY (VI F)

Blessèd are they who dwell in your *house*, O Lord, * alleluia, al*le*luia.
— Blessèd are they who dwell in your *house*, O Lord, * alleluia, al*le*luia.
They will praise *you* for ever,
— alleluia, al*le*luia.
Glory to the Father, and *to* the Son, * and to the Ho*ly* Spirit.
— Blessèd are they who dwell in your *house*, O Lord, * alleluia, al*le*luia.

Lent:
Blessèd are *they* who dwell * in your house, O Lord.
— Blessèd are *they* who dwell * in your house, O Lord.
They will praise *you* for ever,
— in your house, O Lord.
Glory to the Father, and *to* the Son, * and to the Ho*ly* Spirit.
— Blessèd are *they* who dwell * in your house, O Lord.

CANTICLE OF MARY

Ant.   This is God's dwelling place and he has made it holy; † here we call on his name, for *Scrip*ture says: * There you *will* find me (al*le*luia).

Weeks I and III   Weeks II and IV

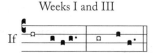   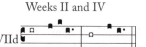

My soul ✠ proclaims the greatness *of* the Lord, * my spirit rejoices in God *my* savior
for he has *looked* with favor * on his low*ly* servant.
From this day all *gen*erations * will call *me* blessèd:
the Almighty has done great *things* for me, * and holy is *his* Name.
He has mercy on *those* who fear him * in every gen*er*ation.
He has shown the strength *of* his arm, * he has scattered the proud in their *con*ceit.

He has cast down the mighty *from* their thrones, * and has lifted up *the* lowly.
He has filled the hungry *with* good things, * and the rich he has sent a*way* empty.
He has come to the help of his *ser*vant Israel * for he has remembered his promise *of* mercy,
the promise he made *to* our fathers, * to Abraham and his children *for* ever.
Glory to the Father, and *to* the Son, * and to the Ho*ly* Spirit:
as it was in the begin*ning*, is now, * and will be for ever. *A*men.

Antiphon   This is God's dwelling place and he has made it holy; † here we call on his name, for *Scrip*ture says: * There you *will* find me (al*le*luia).

INTERCESSIONS (VI F)

Our Savior laid down his life so that all God's scattered children might be ga*thered* together. * In our need let *us* cry out:

Remember your Church, O Lord.

Lord Jesus, you built your house up*on* a rock,
— strengthen your Church with solid and *last*ing faith.

Lord Jesus, blood and water flowed *from* your side,
— give new life to your Church through the sacrament of your new and un*end*-ing covenant.

Lord Jesus, you are in the midst of those who gather *in* your name,
— hear the prayers of your uni*ver*sal Church.

Lord Jesus, you prepare a dwelling-place in your Father's house for *all* who love you,
— help your Church to grow in *di*vine love.

Lord Jesus, you never cast out anyone who *comes* to you,
— open your Father's house to all those *who* have died.

Our Father . . .

Prayer, as in Morning Prayer, 1181.

COMMON OF THE BLESSED VIRGIN MARY

Evening Prayer I

HYMN

Maria, quæ mortalium. (L.M.)

Quem terra, pontus, æthera	He whom the earth, the sea and sky
colunt, adorant, prædicant	By their own beauty can proclaim,
trinam regentem machinam,	Whom they thus serve and venerate,
claustrum Mariæ baiulat.	Enshrines himself in Mary's womb.
Cui luna, sol et omnia	He whom the sun, the moon, the stars
deserviunt per tempora,	Obey as centuries pass by,
perfusa cæli gratia	Lies hid within a Virgin's womb
gestant puellæ visera.	Made fruitful by divine decree.
Beata mater munere,	The mighty God who made the world,
cuius, supernus artifex,	And lovingly sustains it still,
mundum pugillo continens,	Selects as mother, maiden pure
ventris sub arca clausus est.	And rests within her chaste abode.
Beata cæli nuntio,	The angels calls her full of grace,
fecunda Sancto Spiritu,	As chosen by the Spirit's love,
desideratus gentibus	For she will soon enrich the world
cuius per alvum fusus est.	With him whom ev'ry heart desires.
Iesu, tibi sit gloria,	All glory, Jesus, be to you
qui natus es de Virgine,	Once born of Virgin undefiled,
cum Patre et almo Spiritu,	Who, with the Spirit of your Love
in sepiterna sæcula. Amen.	And God the Father, ever reign. Amen.

PSALMODY

Ant. 1   Blessèd are you, O *Vir*gin Mary, * for you carried the Creator of
the world *in* your womb (*al*leluia).

VIIIg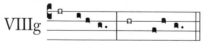

Psalm 113

Praise, O servants *of* the Lord, *	Who is like the *Lord,* our God, * who
praise the name *of* the Lord!	has risen on high *to* his throne
May the name of the *Lord* be blessed *	yet stoops from the heights *to* look
both now and for *ever*more!	down, * to look down upon heav*en*
From the rising of the sun *to* its setting	and earth?
* praised be the name *of* the Lord!	From the dust he lifts *up* the lowly, *
High above all nations *is* the Lord, *	from his misery he rai*ses* the poor
above the heav*ens* his glory.	to set him in the compan*y* of princes, *

yes, with the princes *of* his people. | and to the *Holy* Spirit:
To the childless wife he *gives* a home * | as it was in the begin*ning*, is now, * and
  and gladdens her *heart* with children. | will be for ev*er*. Amen.
Glory to the Father, and *to* the Son, * |

Antiphon   Blessèd are you, O *Vir*gin Mary, * for you carried the Creator of
the world *in* your womb (*al*leluia).

Ant. 2   You are the mother *of* your Maker, * yet you remain a virgin *for*
ever (al*le*luia).

IIA

Psalm 147:12-20

O praise the *Lord*, Jerusalem! *
  Zion, praise *your* God!
He has strengthened the bars *of* your
  gates, * he has blessed the children
  *with*in you.
He established peace *on* your borders, *
  he feeds you with fin*est* wheat.
He sends out his word *to* the earth *
  and swiftly runs his *com*mand.
He showers down snow *white* as wool, *
  he scatters hoar-frost *like* ashes.
He hurls down hail*stones* like crumbs. *
  The waters are frozen at *his* touch;

he sends forth his word *and* it melts
  them: * at the breath of his mouth
  the wa*ters* flow.
He makes his word *known* to Jacob, *
  to Israel his laws and *de*crees.
He has not dealt thus with *other*
  nations; * he has not taught them his
  *de*crees.
Glory to the Father, and *to* the Son, *
  and to the Ho*ly* Spirit:
as it was in the begin*ning*, is now, * and
  will be for ever. *A*men.

Antiphon   You are the mother *of* your Maker, * yet you remain a virgin *for*
ever (al*le*luia).

Ant. 3   We share the fruit of life *through* you, * O daughter blessed by
the Lord (al*le*luia).

Va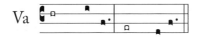

Canticle   Ephesians 1:3-10

Praised be the God *and* Father * of
  our Lord Je*sus* Christ,
who has bestowed on us *in* Christ *
  every spiritual blessing in *the* heavens.

God chose us in him † before the
  world *be*gan * to be holy and blameless in *his* sight.
He predestined us † to be his adopted
  sons through Je*sus* Christ, * such was

his will *and* pleasure,
that all might praise the glori*ous* favor *
    he has bestowed on us in his *belovèd.*
In him and through his blood, † we
    have been *re*deemed, * and our sins
    *for*given,
so immeasura*bly* generous * is God's
    favor *to* us.
God has given us the wisdom † to
    understand fully *the* mystery, * the

plan he was pleased to decree *in*
    Christ.
A plan to be carried out *in* Christ, * in
    the fullness *of* time,
to bring all things into one *in* him, * in
    the heavens and *on* earth.
Glory to the Father, and to *the* Son, *
    and to the Ho*ly* Spirit:
as it was in the beginning, *is* now, * and
    will be for ever. *A*men.

Antiphon   We share the fruit of life *through* you, * O daughter blessed by *the* Lord (al*le*luia).

READING   Galatians 4:4-5

When the designated time had come, God sent forth his Son born of a woman, born under the law, to deliver from the law those who were subjected to it, so that we might receive our status as adopted sons.

RESPONSORY (VI F)
After the birth *of* your son, * you remained *a* virgin.
— After the birth *of* your son, * you remained *a* virgin.
Mother of God, inter*cede* for us;
— you remained *a* virgin.
Glory to the Father, and *to* the Son, * and to the Ho*ly* Spirit.
— After the birth *of* your son, * you remained *a* virgin.

Easter:
After the birth of your son, you re*mained* a virgin, * alleluia, al*le*luia.
— After the birth of your son, you re*mained* a virgin, * alleluia, al*le*luia.
Mother of God, inter*cede* for us;
— alleluia, al*le*luia.
Glory to the Father, and *to* the Son, * and to the Ho*ly* Spirit.
— After the birth of your son, you re*mained* a virgin, * alleluia, al*le*luia.

CANTICLE OF MARY
Ant.   The Lord has looked with favor on his *lowly* servant; * the Almighty has done great things *for* me (al*le*luia).

Or: All generations will *call* me blessèd: * the Lord has looked with favor on his low*ly* servant (al*le*luia).

INTERCESSIONS

Let us praise God our almighty Father, who wished that Mary, his Son's mother, be celebrated by each *gen*eration. * Now in *need* we ask:

Mary, full of grace, intercede for *us.*

O God, worker of miracles, you made the Immaculate Virgin Mary share, body and soul, in your Son's glo*ry* in heaven,

— direct the hearts of your children to *that* same glory.

You made Mary our mother. Through her intercession grant strength to the weak, comfort to the sorrowing, par*don* to sinners,

— salvation and *peace* to all.

You made Mary *full* of grace,

— grant all men the joyful abundance *of* your grace.

Make your Church of one mind and one *heart* in love,

— and help all those who believe to be one in prayer with Mary, the mo*ther* of Jesus.

You crowned Mary *queen* of heaven,

— may all the dead rejoice in your kingdom with the *saints* for ever.

Or:

Let us praise God our almighty Father, who wished that Mary, his Son's mother, be celebrated by each *gen*eration. * Now in *need* we ask:

Mary, full of grace, intercede for *us.*

You made Mary the moth*er* of mercy,

— may all who are faced with trials feel her moth*er*ly love.

You wished Mary to be the mother of the family in the home of Je*sus* and Joseph,

— may all mothers of families foster love and holiness through her *in*tercession.

You gave Mary strength at the foot of the cross and filled her with joy at the resurrection *of* your Son,

— lighten the hardships of those who are burdened and deepen their *sense* of hope.

You made Mary open to your word and faithful *as* your servant,

— through her intercession make us servants and true followers *of* your Son.

You crowned Mary *queen* of heaven,

— may all the dead rejoice in your kingdom with the *saints* for ever.

Our Father . . .

Prayer, as in Morning Prayer, 1194.

Morning Prayer

HYMN
O gloriosa Domina. (L.M.)

O gloriosa domina excelsa super sidera, qui te creavit provide, lactas sacrato ubere.	O glorious Lady, throned in rest, Amidst the starry host above, Who gavest nurture from thy breast To God, with pure maternal love.
Quod Eva tristis abstulit, tu reddis almo germine; intrent ut astra flebiles, sternis benigna semitam.	What we had lost through sinful Eve The Blossom sprung from thee restores, And, granting bliss to souls that grieve, Unbars the everlasting doors.
Tu regis alti ianua et porta lucis fulgida; vitam datam per Virginem, gentes redemptæ, plaudite.	O Gate, through which hath passed the King, O Hall, whence Light shone through the gloom; The ransomed nations praise and sing Life given from the Virgin womb.
Patri sit Paraclito tuoque Nato gloria, qui veste te mirabili circumdederunt gratiæ. Amen.	All honor, laud and glory be, O Jesus, Virgin born, to thee! All glory, as is ever meet, To Father and to Paraclete. Amen.

PSALMODY

Ant. 1   Blessèd are *you*, O Mary, * for the world's salvation came *forth* from you;
now in glory, † you rejoice for ever *with* the Lord. * Intercede for us *with* your Son (*al*leluia).

Psalms and canticle from Sunday, Week I, 606.

Ant. 2   You are the glory of Jerusalem, † the *joy* of Israel; * you are the fairest honor of *our* race (al*le*luia).

Ant. 3   O Virgin Mary, how great your cause *for* joy; * God found you worthy to bear Christ *our* Savior (al*le*luia).

READING   See Isaiah 61:10
I rejoice heartily in the Lord,
in my God is the joy of my soul;
For he has clothed me with a robe of salvation,
and wrapped me in a mantle of justice,
like a bride bedecked with her jewels.

RESPONSORY (VI F)

The Lord has *chos*en her, * his loved one from the *beg*inning.
— The Lord has *chos*en her, * his loved one from the *beg*inning.
He has taken her to *live* with him,
— his loved one from the *beg*inning.
Glory to the Father, and *to* the Son, * and to the Ho*ly* Spirit.
— The Lord has *chos*en her, * his loved one from the *beg*inning.

Easter:

The Lord has chosen her, † his loved one from *the* beginning, * alleluia, al*le*luia.
— The Lord has chosen her, † his loved one from *the* beginning, * alleluia, al*le*luia.
He has taken her to *live* with him,
— alleluia, al*le*luia.
Glory to the Father, and *to* the Son, * and to the Ho*ly* Spirit.
— The Lord has chosen her, † his loved one from *the* beginning, * alleluia, al*le*luia.

CANTICLE OF ZECHARIAH

Antiphon   Eve shut all her children *out* of Paradise; * the Virgin Mary
           opened wide *its* gates (al*le*luia).

INTERCESSIONS (VI F)

Let us glorify our Savior, who chose the Virgin Mary *for* his mother. * *Let* us ask
   him:
May your mother intercede for us, *Lord.*
Sun of Justice, the immaculate Virgin was the white dawn announc*ing* your
   rising,
   — grant that we may always live in the light *of* your coming.
Eternal Word, you chose Mary as the uncorrupted ark of your *dwell*ing place,
   — free us from the corrup*tion* of sin.
Savior of mankind, your mother stood at the foot *of* your cross,
   — grant, through her intercession, that we may rejoice to share *in* your passion.
With ultimate generosity and love, you gave Mary as a mother to your belov*èd*
   disciple,
   — help us to live as worthy sons of so no*ble* a mother.

Or:

Let us glorify our Savior, who chose the Virgin Mary *for* his mother. * *Let* us ask him:
May your mother intercede for us, *Lord.*
Savior of the world, by your redeeming might you preserved your mother beforehand from all
   stain of sin,
   — keep watch over us, *lest* we sin.
You are our redeemer, who made the immaculate Virgin Mary your purest home and the
   sanctuary of the *Ho*ly Spirit,
   — make us temples of your Spir*it* for ever.

Eternal Word, you taught your mother to choose the *bet*ter part,
— grant that in imitating her we may seek the food that brings life *ev*erlasting.
King of kings, you lifted up your mother, body and soul, *in*to heaven;
— help us to fix our thoughts on *things* above.
Lord of heaven and earth, you crowned Mary and set her at your right *hand* as queen,
— make us worthy to *share* this glory.

Our Father . . .

Prayer
If there is no proper prayer, one of the following is said:

Advent:

>Father,
>in your plan for our salvation
>your Word became man,
>announced by an angel and born of the Virgin Mary.
>May we who believe that she is the Mother of God
>receive the help of her prayers.
>We ask this through our Lord Jesus Christ, your Son,
>who lives and reigns with you and the Holy Spirit,
>one God, for ever and ever.

Christmas:

>Father,
>you gave the human race eternal salvation
>through the motherhood of the Virgin Mary.
>May we experience the help of her prayers in our lives,
>for through her we received the very source of life,
>your Son, our Lord Jesus Christ,
>who lives and reigns with you and the Holy Spirit,
>one God, for ever and ever.

Lent:

>Lord,
>fill our hearts with your love,
>and as you revealed to us by an angel
>the coming of your Son as man,
>so lead us through his suffering and death
>to the glory of his resurrection,
>for he lives and reigns with you and the Holy Spirit,
>one God, for ever and ever.

Or (also for Ordinary Time):

> Lord,
> take away the sins of your people.
> May the prayers of Mary the mother of your Son help us,
> for alone and unaided we cannot hope to please you.
> We ask this through our Lord Jesus Christ, your Son,
> who lives and reigns with you and the Holy Spirit,
> one God, for ever and ever.

Easter:

> God our Father,
> you give joy to the world
> by the resurrection of your Son, our Lord Jesus Christ.
> Through the prayers of his mother, the Virgin Mary,
> bring us to the happiness of eternal life.
> We ask this through our Lord Jesus Christ, your Son,
> who lives and reigns with you and the Holy Spirit,
> one God, for ever and ever.

Or:

> God our Father,
> you gave the Holy Spirit to your apostles
> as they joined in prayer with Mary, the mother of Jesus.
> By the help of her prayers
> keep us faithful in your service
> and let our words and actions be so inspired
> as to bring glory to your name.
> Grant this through our Lord Jesus Christ, your Son,
> who lives and reigns with you and the Holy Spirit,
> one God, for ever and ever.

Ordinary Time:

> Lord God,
> give to your people the joy
> of continual health in mind and body.
> With the prayers of the Virgin Mary to help us,
> guide us through the sorrows of this life
> to eternal happiness in the life to come.
> Grant this through our Lord Jesus Christ, your Son,
> who lives and reigns with you and the Holy Spirit,
> one God, for ever and ever.

Or:

> God of mercy,
> give us strength.
> May we who honor the memory of the Mother of God
> rise above our sins and failings with the help of her prayers.

Grant this through our Lord Jesus Christ, your Son,
who lives and reigns with you and the Holy Spirit,
one God, for ever and ever.

Or:

Lord,
may the prayers of the Virgin Mary
bring us protection from danger
and freedom from sin
that we may come to the joy of your peace.
We ask this through our Lord Jesus Christ, your Son,
who lives and reigns with you and the Holy Spirit,
one God, for ever and ever.

Or:

Lord, as we honor the glorious memory of the Virgin Mary,
we ask that by the help of her prayers
we too may come to share the fullness of your grace.
Grant this through our Lord Jesus Christ, your Son,
who lives and reigns with you and the Holy Spirit,
one God, for ever and ever.

Or:

Lord Jesus Christ,
you chose the Virgin Mary to be your mother,
a worthy home in which to dwell.
By her prayers keep us from danger
and bring us to the joy of heaven,
where you live and reign with the Father and the Holy Spirit,
one God, for ever and ever.

Evening Prayer II

HYMN, as in Evening Prayer I, 1188.

PSALMODY

Ant. 1   Hail, Mary, *full* of grace, * the Lord *is* with you (*al*leluia).

VIIIg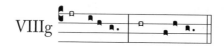

Psalm 122

I rejoiced when I *heard* them say: *   │ And now our *feet* are standing * within
"Let us go *to* God's house."   │   your gates, O Jerusalem.

Jerusalem is built *as* a city * strong*ly* compact.

It is there that the *tribes* go up, * the tribes *of* the Lord.

For Israel's *law* it is, * there to praise *the* Lord's name.

There were set the *thrones* of judgment * of the *house* of David.

For the peace of Jerus*a*lem pray: * "Peace be *to* your homes!

May peace reign *in* your walls, * in your pal*aces*, peace!"

For love of my bre*thren* and friends * I say: "*Peace* upon you!"

For love of the house *of* the Lord * I will ask *for* your good.

Glory to the Father, and *to* the Son, * and to the *Holy* Spirit:

as it was in the begin*ning*, is now, * and will be for ev*er*. Amen.

Antiphon   Hail, Mary, *full* of grace, * the Lord *is* with you (*al*leluia).

Ant. 2   I am the handmaid *of* the Lord. * Let it be done to me as you *have* said (al*le*luia).

Psalm 127

If the Lord does not *build* the house, * in vain do its build*ers* labor;

if the Lord does not watch *over* the city, * in vain does the watchman *keep* vigil.

In vain is your ear*lier* rising, * your going later *to* rest,

you who toil for the *bread* you eat: * when he pours gifts on his belovèd while *they* slumber.

Truly sons are a gift *from* the Lord, * a blessing, the fruit of *the* womb.

Indeed the *sons* of youth * are like arrows in the hand of *a* warrior.

O the happiness *of* the man * who has filled his quiver with *these* arrows!

He will have no *cause* for shame * when he disputes with his foes in *the* gateways.

Glory to the Father, and *to* the Son, * and to the Ho*ly* Spirit:

as it was in the begin*ning*, is now, * and will be for ever. *A*men.

Antiphon   I am the handmaid *of* the Lord. * Let it be done to me as you *have* said (al*le*luia).

Ant. 3   Blessèd are you a*mong* women, * and blessèd is the fruit of *your* womb (al*le*luia).

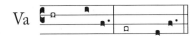

Canticle   Ephesians 1:3-10

Praised be the God *and* Father * of
our Lord Je*sus* Christ,
who has bestowed on us *in* Christ *
every spiritual blessing in *the* heavens.
God chose us in him † before the
world *be*gan * to be holy and blameless in *his* sight.
He predestined us † to be his adopted
sons through Je*sus* Christ, * such was
his will *and* pleasure,
that all might praise the glori*ous* favor *
he has bestowed on us in his *be*lovèd.
In him and through his blood, † we
have been *re*deemed, * and our sins

*for*given,
so immeasura*bly* generous * is God's
favor *to* us.
God has given us the wisdom † to
understand fully *the* mystery, * the
plan he was pleased to decree *in*
Christ.
A plan to be carried out *in* Christ, * in
the fullness *of* time,
to bring all things into one *in* him, * in
the heavens and *on* earth.
Glory to the Father, and to *the* Son, *
and to the Ho*ly* Spirit:
as it was in the beginning, *is* now, * and
will be for ever. *A*men.

Antiphon   Blessèd are you a*mong* women, * and blessèd is the fruit of *your*
womb (al*le*luia).

READING   Galatians 4:4-5
When the designated time had come, God sent forth his Son born of a
woman, born under the law, to deliver from the law those who were subjected to it, so that we might receive our status as adopted sons.

RESPONSORY (VI F)
Hail Mary, *full* of grace, * the Lord is *with* you.
— Hail Mary, *full* of grace, * the Lord is *with* you.
Blessèd are you among women † and blessèd is the fruit *of* your womb.
— The Lord is *with* you.
Glory to the Father, and *to* the Son, * and to the Ho*ly* Spirit.
— Hail Mary, *full* of grace, * the Lord is *with* you.

Easter:
Hail Mary, full of grace, the Lord *is* with you, * alleluia, al*le*luia.
— Hail Mary, full of grace, the Lord *is* with you, * alleluia, al*le*luia.
Blessèd are you among women † and blessèd is the fruit *of* your womb.
— alleluia, al*le*luia.
Glory to the Father, and *to* the Son, * and to the Ho*ly* Spirit.
— Hail Mary, full of grace, the Lord *is* with you, * alleluia, al*le*luia.

CANTICLE OF MARY
Ant.   Blessèd are you, O Virgin Mary, for *your* great faith; * all that
                        the Lord promised you will come to pass *through* you (al*l*eluia).

INTERCESSIONS (VI F)
Let us praise God our almighty Father, who wished that Mary, his Son's mother,
    be celebrated by each *gen*eration. * Now in *need* we ask:
Mary, full of grace, intercede for *us.*
O God, worker of miracles, you made the Immaculate Virgin Mary share, body
    and soul, in your Son's glo*ry* in heaven,
— direct the hearts of your children to *that* same glory.
You made Mary our mother. Through her intercession grant strength to the
    weak, comfort to the sorrowing, par*don* to sinners,
— salvation and *peace* to all.
You made Mary *full* of grace,
— grant all men the joyful abundance *of* your grace.
Make your Church of one mind and one *heart* in love,
— and help all those who believe to be one in prayer with Mary, the mo*ther* of
    Jesus.
You crowned Mary *queen* of heaven,
— may all the dead rejoice in your kingdom with the *saints* for ever.

Or:
Let us praise God our almighty Father, who wished that Mary, his Son's mother, be cel-
    ebrated by each *gen*eration. * Now in *need* we ask:
Mary, full of grace, intercede for *us.*
You made Mary the moth*er* of mercy,
— may all who are faced with trials feel her moth*er*ly love.
You wished Mary to be the mother of the family in the home of Je*sus* and Joseph,
— may all mothers of families foster love and holiness through her *in*tercession.
You gave Mary strength at the foot of the cross and filled her with joy at the resurrection *of*
    your Son,
— lighten the hardships of those who are burdened and deepen their *sense* of hope.
You made Mary open to your word and faithful *as* your servant,
— through her intercession make us servants and true followers *of* your Son.
You crowned Mary *queen* of heaven,
— may all the dead rejoice in your kingdom with the *saints* for ever.

Our Father . . .

Prayer, as in Morning Prayer, 1194.

MEMORIAL OF THE BLESSED VIRGIN MARY
ON SATURDAY

HYMN
Quæ caritatis. (L.M.)

Quæ caritatis fulgidum es astrum, Virgo, superis, spei nobis mortalibus fons vivax es et profluus.	What gleaming star of charity, You are, O Mary, for the saints! To us on earth, you are the fount Of hope that cannot fade or fail.
Sic vales, celsa Domina, in Nati cor piissimi, ut qui fidenter postulat, per te securus impetret.	Your pow'r such, exalted Queen, To win the heart of Christ your Son, That what we ask in faith, through you, We know we surely shall obtain.
Opem tua benignitas non solum fert poscentibus, sed et libenter sæpius precantum vota prævenit.	Your loving tenderness will aid Not only those who pray and plead, But sometimes favors yet unasked Are granted to the souls in need.
In te misericordia, in te magnificentia; tu bonitatis cumulas quicquid creata possident.	Within your heart true mercy dwells, In you are glory, greatness, pow'r; All goodness that creation holds Is found with plenitude in you.
Patri sit et Paraclito tuoque Nato gloria, qui veste te mirabili cirumdederunt gratiæ. Amen.	To God the Father glory be, The Spirit and the Son be praised, Who clothed you with a robe of grace, Immaculate, untouched by sin. Amen.

The antiphons and psalms are from the current Saturday.

READING   Galatians 4:4-5

When the designated time had come, God sent forth his Son born of a
woman, born under the law, to deliver from the law those who were subjected to it, so that we might receive our status as adopted sons.

RRESPONSORY (VI F)

After the birth *of* your son, * you remained *a* virgin.

— After the birth *of* your son, * you remained *a* virgin.

Mother of God, inter*cede* for us;

— you remained *a* virgin.

Glory to the Father, and *to* the Son, * and to the Ho*ly* Spirit.

— After the birth *of* your son, * you remained *a* virgin.

CANTICLE OF ZECHARIAH

Ant.   Let us celebrate with great devotion this day in memory of the Blessèd *Vir*gin Mary; * may she intercede for us with the Lord Je*sus* Christ.

INTERCESSIONS (VI F)

Let us glorify our Savior, who chose the Virgin Mary *for* his mother. * *Let* us ask him:

May your mother intercede for us, *Lord.*

Sun of Justice, the immaculate Virgin was the white dawn announc*ing* your rising,

— grant that we may always live in the light *of* your coming.

Eternal Word, you chose Mary as the uncorrupted ark of your *dwel*ling place,

— free us from the corrup*tion* of sin.

Savior of mankind, your mother stood at the foot *of* your cross,

— grant, through her intercession, that we may rejoice to share *in* your passion.

With ultimate generosity and love, you gave Mary as a mother to your belov*èd* disciple,

— help us to live as worthy sons of so no*ble* a mother.

Our Father . . .

Prayer

The prayer is chosen from one of the following:

Lord God,
give to your people the joy
of continual health in mind and body.
With the prayers of the Virgin Mary to help us,
guide us through the sorrows of this life
to eternal happiness in the life to come.
Grant this through our Lord Jesus Christ, your Son,
who lives and reigns with you and the Holy Spirit,
one God, for ever and ever.

Or:

Lord,
take away the sins of your people.
May the prayers of Mary the mother of your Son help us,
for alone and unaided we cannot hope to please you.
We ask this through our Lord Jesus Christ, your Son,
who lives and reigns with you and the Holy Spirit,
one God, for ever and ever.

Or:

God of mercy,
give us strength.
May we who honor the memory of the Mother of God
rise above our sins and failings with the help of her prayers.
Grant this through our Lord Jesus Christ, your Son,
who lives and reigns with you and the Holy Spirit,
one God, for ever and ever.

Or:

Lord,
may the prayers of the Virgin Mary
bring us protection from danger
and freedom from sin
that we may come to the joy of your peace.
We ask this through our Lord Jesus Christ, your Son,
who lives and reigns with you and the Holy Spirit,
one God, for ever and ever.

Or:

Lord, as we honor the glorious memory of the Virgin Mary,
we ask that by the help of her prayers
we too may come to share the fullness of your grace.
Grant this through our Lord Jesus Christ, your Son,
who lives and reigns with you and the Holy Spirit,
one God, for ever and ever.

Or:

All-powerful God,
we rejoice in the protection of the holy Virgin Mary.
May her prayers help to free us from all evils here on earth
and lead us to eternal joy in heaven.
Grant this through our Lord Jesus Christ, your Son,
who lives and reigns with you and the Holy Spirit,
one God, for ever and ever.

COMMON OF APOSTLES

Evening Prayer I

HYMN

Exsultet cælum. (L.M.)

Exsultet cælum laudibus,	Let heaven now resound with praise,
resultet terra gaudiis:	And earth re-echo with its joy,
Apostolorum gloriam	To celebrate with melody
sacra canunt sollemnia.	The triumph of the chosen Twelve.
Vos, sæcli iusti iudices	O holy judges of the world,
et vera mundi lumina,	Its truest light and trusted guides,
votis precamur cordium,	Incline your ears to our poor prayer
audite preces supplicum.	Arising from our grateful hearts.
Qui cælum verbo clauditis	To you entrusted was the pow'r
serasque eius solvitis,	Of binding and of loosing sin,
nos a peccatis omnibus	With but a word, we humbly pray,
solvite iussu, quæsumus.	From bonds of trespass set us free.
Quorum præcepto subditur	All maladies and evil harm
salus et languor omnium,	At your command were soon dispelled,
sanate ægros moribus,	Restore our health of soul anew
nos reddentes virtutibus,	Enrich us with all virtue's grace.
Ut, cum iudex advenerit	So that when Christ our Judge shall come
Christus in fine sæculi,	And time and space shall be no more,
nos sempiterni gaudii	He may bestow on us a share
faciat esse compotes.	Of heaven's bliss that has no end.
Deo sint laudes gloriæ,	All glory to the Father be,
qui dat nos evangelicis	All glory to his only Son,
per vos doctrinis instrui	And to the Holy Spirit blest,
et prosequi cælestia. Amen.	Both now and in eternity. Amen.

PSALMODY

Ant. 1   Of those whom he called to follow him, † Je*sus* chose twelve, *
and made them *his* apostles (*al*leluia).

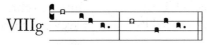

VIIIg

Psalm 117

O praise the Lord, *all* you nations, *
    * acclaim him, *all* you peoples!
Strong is his *love* for us; * he is faith*ful*
    for ever.

Glory to the Father, and *to* the Son, *
    and to the *Holy* Spirit:
as it was in the begin*ning*, is now, * and
    will be for ev*er*. Amen.

Antiphon   Of those whom he called to follow him, † Je*sus* chose twelve, *
            and made them *his* apostles (*al*leluia).

Ant. 2   They *left* their nets * to follow the Lord and *Re*deemer (al*le*luia).

IIA

Psalm 147:12-20

O praise the *Lord*, Jerusalem! *
  Zion, praise *your* God!
He has strengthened the bars *of* your
  gates, * he has blessed the children
  *with*in you.
He established peace *on* your borders, *
  he feeds you with fin*est* wheat.
He sends out his word *to* the earth *
  and swiftly runs his *com*mand.
He showers down snow *white* as wool, *
  he scatters hoar-frost *like* ashes.
He hurls down hail*stones* like crumbs. *
  The waters are frozen at *his* touch;

he sends forth his word *and* it melts
  them: * at the breath of his mouth
  the wa*ters* flow.
He makes his word *known* to Jacob, *
  to Israel his laws and *de*crees.
He has not dealt thus with *oth*er
  nations; * he has not taught them his
  *de*crees.
Glory to the Father, and *to* the Son, *
  and to the Ho*ly* Spirit:
as it was in the begin*ning,* is now, * and
  will be for ever. *A*men.

Antiphon   They *left* their nets * to follow the Lord and *Re*deemer (al*le*luia).

Ant. 3   You are *my* friends, * for you have remained steadfast in *my* love
            (al*le*luia).

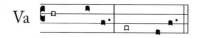

Va

Canticle   Ephesians 1:3-10

P raised be the God *and* Father * of
  our Lord Je*sus* Christ,
who has bestowed on us *in* Christ *
  every spiritual blessing in *the* heavens.
God chose us in him † before the
  world *began* * to be holy and blameless in *his* sight.
He predestined us † to be his adopted
  sons through Je*sus* Christ, * such was
  his will *and* pleasure,

that all might praise the glori*ous* favor *
  he has bestowed on us in his *be*lovèd.
In him and through his blood, † we
  have been *re*deemed, * and our sins
  *for*given,
so immeasura*bly* generous * is God's
  favor *to* us.
God has given us the wisdom † to
  understand fully *the* mystery, * the
  plan he was pleased to decree *in*
  Christ.

A plan to be carried out *in* Christ, * in the fullness *of* time,
to bring all things into one *in* him, * in the heavens and *on* earth.

Glory to the Father, and to *the* Son, * and to the Ho*ly* Spirit:
as it was in the beginning, *is* now, * and will be for ever. *A*men.

Antiphon   You are *my* friends, * for you have remained steadfast in *my* love (al*le*luia).

READING   Acts 2:42-45

They devoted themselves to the apostles' instruction and the communal life, to the breaking of bread and the prayers. A reverent fear overtook them all, for many wonders and signs were performed by the apostles. Those who believed shared all things in common; they would sell their property and goods, dividing everything on the basis of each one's need.

RESPONSORY (VI F)

All the *world* will know, * you are living as *I* taught you.
— All the *world* will know, * you are living as *I* taught you.
If you love *one* another,
— you are living as *I* taught you.
Glory to the Father, and *to* the Son, * and to the Ho*ly* Spirit.
— All the *world* will know, * you are living as *I* taught you.

Easter:
All the world will know, † you are living *as* I taught you, * alleluia, al*le*luia.
— All the world will know, † you are living *as* I taught you, * alleluia, al*le*luia.
If you love *one* another,
— alleluia, al*le*luia.
Glory to the Father, and *to* the Son, * and to the Ho*ly* Spirit.
— All the world will know, † you are living *as* I taught you, * alleluia, al*le*luia.

CANTICLE OF MARY

Antiphon   You did not choose me, † but *I* chose you * to go forth and bear fruit that will last *for* ever (al*le*luia).

INTERCESSIONS (VI F)

My brothers, we build on the foundation of *the* apostles. * Let us pray to our almighty Father for his holy peo*ple* and say:
Be mindful of your Church, O Lord.
Father, you wanted your Son to be seen first by the apostles after the resurrection *from* the dead,
— we ask you to make us his witnesses to the farthest corners *of* the world.
You sent your Son to preach the good news *to* the poor,
— help us to preach the Gospel to *every* creature.

You sent your Son to sow the seed of un*end*ing life,
— grant that we who work at sowing the seed may share the joy *of* the harvest.
You sent your Son to reconcile all men to you *through* his blood,
— help us all to work toward achieving this recon*cil*iation.
Your Son sits at your right *hand* in heaven,
— let the dead enter your king*dom* of joy.

Our Father . . .

Prayer, as in the Proper of Saints.

Morning Prayer

HYMN, as in the Proper of Saints, or: (L.M.)

Christ Jesus Lord, true Light of Light,
Begotten Son of God most high,
You sent the Twelve afar to teach
And spread the faith throughout the world.

You gave them special gifts and grace,
And sent them out the world to win,
To bring the Gospel's truth to all
Its seed to scatter far and wide.

Appeased by your Apostles' prayer,
Be gracious to us, Lord, we pray,
Smile down on us as we rejoice
To celebrate their feast today.

By their great merits keep us safe
From ev'ry snare of sin and death,
Since we preserve in faithful hearts
The holy teaching they proclaimed.

With face serene look down on us,
Correct us with your loving gaze,
That we may conquer by your grace
The evils that beset our way.

All glory be to you, O Lord,
Beyond the limits of all time,
Who by your true Apostles' words
Lead us, your children, safely home. Amen.

PSALMODY

Ant. 1   My commandment is this: † love *one* another * as I *have* loved
                you (*al*leluia).

Psalms and canticle from Sunday, Week I, 606.

Ant. 2   There is no greater love † than to lay *down* your life * for *your*
                friends (al*le*luia).

Ant. 3   You are my friends, says *the* Lord, * if you do what I *com*mand
                you (al*le*luia).

READING   Ephesians 2:19-20
        You are strangers and aliens no longer. No, you are fellow citizens of the
        saints and members of the household of God. You form a building which
        rises on the foundation of the apostles and prophets, with Christ Jesus
        himself as the capstone. Through him the whole structure is fitted together

and takes shape as a holy temple in the Lord; in him you are being built into this temple, to become a dwelling place for God in the Spirit.

RESPONSORY (VI F)

You have *made* them rulers * over all *the* earth.
— You have *made* them rulers * over all *the* earth.
They will always remember your *name*, O Lord,
— Over all *the* earth.
Glory to the Father, and *to* the Son, * and to the Ho*ly* Spirit.
— You have *made* them rulers * over all *the* earth.

Easter:
You have made them rulers over *all* the earth, * alleluia, al*le*luia.
— You have made them rulers over *all* the earth, * alleluia, al*le*luia.
They will always remember your *name*, O Lord,
    alleluia, al*le*luia.
Glory to the Father, and *to* the Son, * and to the Ho*ly* Spirit.
— You have made them rulers over *all* the earth, * alleluia, al*le*luia.

CANTICLE OF ZECHARIAH

Antiphon   On the foundation stones of the heaven*ly* Jerusalem, * the
                names of the twelve apostles of the Lamb *are* written;
                the *Lamb* of God * is the light of that ho*ly* city (al*le*luia).

INTERCESSIONS (VI F)

Belovèd friends, we have inherited heaven along with *the* apostles. * Let us give
    thanks to the Father for *all* his gifts:
The company of apostles praises you, O Lord.
Praise be to you, Lord, for the banquet of Christ's body and blood given us
    through *the* apostles,
— which refreshes us and *gives* us life.
The company of apostles praises you, O Lord.
Praise be to you, Lord, for the feast of your word prepared for us by *the* apostles,
— giving us *light* and joy.
The company of apostles praises you, O Lord.
Praise be to you, Lord, for your holy Church, founded on *the* apostles,
— where we are gathered together into *your* community.
The company of apostles praises you, O Lord.
Praise be to you, Lord, for the cleansing power of baptism and penance that you
    have entrusted to *your* apostles,
— through which we are cleansed *of* our sins.
The company of apostles praises you, O Lord.

Our Father . . .

Prayer, as in the Proper of Saints.

Evening Prayer II

HYMN, as in Evening Prayer I, 1203.

PSALMODY

Ant. 1 You are the men who *have* stood by me * in my *time* of trial
(*a*lleluia).

VIIIg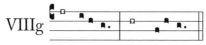

Psalm 116: 10-19

I trusted, even *when* I said, * "I am
sore*ly* afflicted,"
and when I said in *my* alarm: * "No
man *can* be trusted."
How can I re*pay* the Lord * for his
good*ness* to me?
The cup of salvation *I* will raise; * I
will call *on* the Lord's name.
My vows to the Lord I *will* fulfill *
before *all* his people.
O precious in the eyes *of* the Lord * is
the death *of* his faithful.

Your servant, Lord, your ser*vant* am I;
* you have loos*ened* my bonds.
A thanksgiving sacri*fice* I make: * I will
call *on* the Lord's name.
My vows to the Lord I *will* fulfill *
before *all* his people,
in the courts of the house *of* the Lord, *
in your midst, O Jerusalem.
Glory to the Father, and *to* the Son, *
and to the *Ho*ly Spirit:
as it was in the begin*ning*, is now, * and
will be for ev*er*. Amen.

Antiphon You are the men who *have* stood by me * in my *time* of trial
(*a*lleluia).

Ant. 2 I have *lived* among you * as one who ministers *to* others
(al*le*luia).

IIA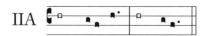

Psalm 126

When the Lord delivered *Zion*
from bondage, * it seemed like
a dream.
Then was our mouth *filled* with
laughter, * on our lips there *were*
songs.
The heathens *them*selves said: *
"What marvels the Lord worked *for*
them!"

What marvels the Lord *worked* for us!
* Indeed we *were* glad.
Deliver us, O Lord, *from* our bondage *
as streams in *dry* land.
Those who are sow*ing* in tears * will
sing when *they* reap.
They go out, they go out, *full* of tears, *
carrying seed for *the* sowing:
they come back, they come back, *full* of

song, * carrying *their* sheaves.
Glory to the Father, and *to* the Son, *
and to the Ho*ly* Spirit:

as it was in the begin*ning*, is now, * and
will be for ever. *A*men.

Antiphon   I have *lived* among you * as one who ministers *to* others
(al*le*luia).

Ant. 3   I no longer call you servants, but my friends, † for I have shared
with you * everything I have heard from *my* Father (al*le*luia).

Canticle   Ephesians 1:3-10

Praised be the God *and* Father * of
our Lord Je*sus* Christ,
who has bestowed on us *in* Christ *
every spiritual blessing in *the* heavens.
God chose us in him † before the
world *be*gan * to be holy and blameless in *his* sight.
He predestined us † to be his adopted
sons through Je*sus* Christ, * such was
his will *and* pleasure,
that all might praise the glori*ous* favor *
he has bestowed on us in his *be*lovèd.
In him and through his blood, † we
have been *re*deemed, * and our sins

*for*given,
so immeasura*bly* generous * is God's
favor *to* us.
God has given us the wisdom † to
understand fully *the* mystery, * the
plan he was pleased to decree *in*
Christ.
A plan to be carried out *in* Christ, * in
the fullness *of* time,
to bring all things into one *in* him, * in
the heavens and *on* earth.
Glory to the Father, and to *the* Son, *
and to the Ho*ly* Spirit:
as it was in the beginning, *is* now, * and
will be for ever. *A*men.

Antiphon   I no longer call you servants, but my friends, † for I have shared
with you * everything I have heard from *my* Father (al*le*luia).

READING   Ephesians 4:11-13
Christ gave apostles, prophets, evangelists, pastors and teachers in roles of
service for the faithful to build up the body of Christ, till we become one in
faith and in the knowledge of God's Son, and form that perfect man who is
Christ come to full stature.

RESPONSORY (VI F)
Tell *all* the nations * how glorious *God* is.
— Tell *all* the nations * how glorious *God* is.

They will always remember your *name*, O Lord,
— How glorious *God* is.
Glory to the Father, and *to* the Son, * and to the Ho*ly* Spirit.
— Tell *all* the nations * how glorious *God* is.

Easter:
Tell all the nations how glor*ious* God is, * alleluia, al*le*luia.
— Tell all the nations how glor*ious* God is, * alleluia, al*le*luia.
Make known his wonders to *every* people,
— alleluia, al*le*luia.
Glory to the Father, and *to* the Son, * and to the Ho*ly* Spirit.
— Tell all the nations how glor*ious* God is, * alleluia, al*le*luia.

CANTICLE OF MARY

Antiphon   When all things are made new, † and the Son of Man is en-*throned* in majesty, * you will sit in judgment over the twelve tribes *of* Israel (al*le*luia).

INTERCESSIONS (VI F)
My brothers, we build on the foundation of *the* apostles. * Let us pray to our almighty Father for his holy peo*ple* and say:
Be mindful of your Church, O Lord.
Father, you wanted your Son to be seen first by the apostles after the resurrection *from* the dead,
— we ask you to make us his witnesses to the farthest corners *of* the world.
You sent your Son to preach the good news *to* the poor,
— help us to preach the Gospel to *every* creature.
You sent your Son to sow the seed of un*end*ing life,
— grant that we who work at sowing the seed may share the joy *of* the harvest.
You sent your Son to reconcile all men to you *through* his blood,
— help us all to work toward achieving this reconc*il*iation.
Your Son sits at your right *hand* in heaven,
— let the dead enter your king*dom* of joy.

Our Father . . .

Prayer, as in the Proper of Saints.

COMMON OF MARTYRS
FOR SEVERAL MARTYRS
Evening Prayer I

HYMN, as in Evening Prayer II, 1220.

PSALMODY

Ant. 1   The saints endured *many* torments * to gain the *ma*rtyr's crown
(*a*lleluia).

VIIIg

Psalm 118

I

Give thanks to the Lord for *he* is good, * for his love en*dures* for ever.

Let the sons of Is*ra*el say: * "His love en*dures* for ever."

Let the sons of *Aa*ron say: * "His love en*dures* for ever."

Let those who fear *the* Lord say: * "His love en*dures* for ever."

I called to the Lord in *my* distress; * he an*swered* and freed me.

The Lord is at my side; I *do* not fear. * What can man *do* against me?

The Lord is at my side *as* my helper: * I shall look down *on* my foes.

It is better to take refuge *in* the Lord * than to *trust* in men:

it is better to take refuge *in* the Lord * than to *trust* in princes.

The nations *all* encompassed me; * in the Lord's *name* I crushed them.

They compassed me, compassed *me* about; * in the Lord's *name* I crushed them.

They compassed me about like bees; †
they blazed like a fire *a*mong thorns.
* In the Lord's *name* I crushed them.

I was hard-pressed *and* was falling * but the Lord *came* to help me.

The Lord is my strength *and* my song; * he *is* my savior.

There are shouts of *joy* and victory * in the tents *of* the just.

The Lord's right *hand* has triumphed; * his *right* hand raised me.

The Lord's right hand has triumphed; † I *shall* not die, * I shall live and re*count* his deeds.

I was punished, I was punished *by* the Lord, * but not *doomed* to die.

Glory to the Father, and *to* the Son, * and to the *Ho*ly Spirit:

as it was in the begin*ning*, is now, * and will be for ev*er*. Amen.

Antiphon   The saints endured *many* torments * to gain the *ma*rtyr's crown
(*a*lleluia).

Ant. 2   Triumphant, the saints *reach* the kingdom, * to be wreathed in splendor by the hand *of* God (al*le*luia).

IIA

II

Open to me the *gates* of holiness: * I will enter and *give* thanks.

This is the *Lord's* own gate * where the just *may* enter.

I will thank you for *you* have answered * and you are *my* savior.

The stone which the build*ers* rejected * has become *the* corner stone.

This is the work *of* the Lord, * a marvel in *our* eyes.

This day was made *by* the Lord; * we rejoice and *are* glad.

O Lord, grant *us* salvation; * O Lord, grant *success.*

Blessèd in the name *of* the Lord * is he *who* comes.

We bless you from the house *of* the Lord; * the Lord God is *our* light.

Go forward in proces*sion* with branch-es * even to *the* altar.

You are my *God*, I thank you.* My God, *I* praise you.

Give thanks to the Lord for *he* is good; * for his love endures *for* ever.

Glory to the Father, and *to* the Son, * and to the Ho*ly* Spirit:

as it was in the begin*ning*, is now, * and will be for ever. *A*men.

Antiphon   Triumphant, the saints *reach* the kingdom, * to be wreathed in splendor by the hand *of* God (al*le*luia).

Ant. 3   The martyrs died *for* Christ * and received the gift of eter*nal* life (al*le*luia).

Va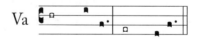

Canticle   1 Peter 2:21-24

Christ suffered for you, † and left you an ex*am*ple * to have you follow in *his* footsteps.

He did *no* wrong; * no deceit was found in *his* mouth.

When he was *in*sulted * he returned *no* insult.

When he was made *to* suffer, * he did not counter *with* threats.

Instead he delivered him*self* up * to the

One who judg*es* justly.

In his *own* body * he brought his sins to *the* cross,

so that all of us, dead *to* sin, * could live in accord with *God's* will.

By *his* wounds * you *were* healed.

Glory to the Father, and to *the* Son, * and to the Ho*ly* Spirit:

as it was in the beginning, *is* now, * and will be for ever. *A*men.

Antiphon   The martyrs died *for* Christ * and received the gift of eter*nal* life
                 (al*le*luia).

READING   Romans 8:35, 37-39

Who will separate us from the love of Christ? Trial or distress, or persecution, or hunger, or nakedness, or danger, or the sword? Yet in all this we are
more than conquerors because of him who has loved us. For I am certain
that neither death nor life, neither angels nor principalities, neither height
nor depth nor any other creature, will be able to separate us from the love of
God that comes to us in Christ Jesus, our Lord.

In the Easter Season: Revelation 3:10-12

Because you have kept my plea to stand fast, I will keep you safe in the time of trial
which is coming on the whole world, to test all men on earth. I am coming soon. Hold
fast to what you have lest someone rob you of your crown. I will make the victor a pillar
in the temple of my God and he shall never leave it. I will inscribe on him the name of
my God and the name of the city of my God, the new Jerusalem which he will send
down from heaven, and my own name which is new.

RESPONSORY (VI F)

These are the *friends* of God; * they lie safe in *his* hands.
— These are the *friends* of God; * they lie safe in *his* hands.
Nothing can *harm* them now,
— they lie safe in *his* hands.
Glory to the Father, and *to* the Son, * and to the Ho*ly* Spirit.
— These are the *friends* of God; * they lie safe in *his* hands.

In the Easter Season:

Let the just rejoice *in* the Lord, * alleluia, al*le*luia.
— Let the just rejoice *in* the Lord, * alleluia, al*le*luia.
God has chosen you as *his* own people,
— alleluia, al*le*luia.
Glory to the Father, and *to* the Son, * and to the Ho*ly* Spirit.
— Let the just rejoice *in* the Lord, * alleluia, al*le*luia.

CANTICLE OF MARY

Antiphon   Renouncing all this *world* could offer, * these martyrs are now in
                 God's kingdom;
                 with their robes washed clean in the blood *of* the Lamb, * they
                 share his joy *for* ever.

In the Easter Season:
Antiphon   The everlasting light of *end*less days * will shine upon your saints, O
                 Lord, al*le*luia.

INTERCESSIONS (VI F)

This is the hour when the King of Martyrs offered his life in the upper room
   and laid it down *on* the cross. * Let us thank *him* and say:
> *We praise you, O Lord.*

We praise you, O Lord, our Savior, inspiration and example for *eve*ry martyr, *
   for loving us *to* the end:
> *We praise you, O Lord.*

For calling all re*pent*ant sinners * to the re*wards* of life:
> *We praise you, O Lord.*

For entrusting to your Church the blood of the new and ever*last*ing covenant *
   poured out for the remis*sion* of sin:
> *We praise you, O Lord.*

For our *per*severance * in your *grace* today:
> *We praise you, O Lord.*

For incorporating our dead broth*ers* and sisters * into your own *death* today:
> *We praise you, O Lord.*

Our Father . . .

Prayer, as in Morning Prayer.

Morning Prayer

HYMN

Æterna Christi munera. (L.M.)

Æterna Christi munera,	With souls alert for happiness
et martyrum victorias,	We sing the praises which are due
laudes ferentes debitas,	To honor every martyr's crown,
lætis canamus mentibus.	Eternal gift from Christ our Lord.
Ecclesiarum principes,	As shining lights before the world,
belli triumphales duces,	And leaders of the Church of God,
cælestis aulæ milites,	They head the ranks of those who fight
et vera mundi lumina.	As soldiers in the cause of right.
Terrore victo sæculi,	They conquered fear of ev'ry kind,
pœnisque spretis corporis,	Despising anguish and all pain,
mortis sacræ compendio,	That through their constancy in death
lucem beatam possident.	Eternal light they would obtain.
Tortoris insani manu	Their dedicated blood was shed
sanguis sacratus funditur,	By torture's cruel, craven hand,
sed permanent immobiles	Their dauntless courage was upheld
vitæ perennis gratia.	By grace of life that has no end.

Devota sanctorum fides,	Devoted faith of all the saints,
invicta spes credentium;	Believers' hope that never wanes,
perfecta Christi charitas,	The perfect charity of Christ,
mundi triumphat principem.	The prince of darkness soon defeat.
In his paterna gloria,	In them the Father's glory shines,
in his voluntas Spiritus,	In them the Holy Spirit's will
exsultat in his Filius,	Exsults with all the joy of Christ
cælum repletur gaudiis.	That fills the courts of bliss above.
Te nunc, Redemptor, quæsumus,	Redeemer of all men, we pray,
ut martyrum consortio	Permit your lowly servants here
iungas precantes servulos,	To share the martyrs' fellowship
in sempiterna sæcula. Amen.	For ever in your realm of light. Amen.

PSALMODY

Ant. 1   The martyrs fixed their eyes on heaven, † and cried out *in* their
                torments: * Come, Lord, be with us *in* this hour (*al*leluia).

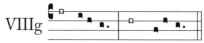

VIIIg

Psalm 63:2-9

O God, you are my God, for *you* I
long; * for you my *soul* is thirsting.
My body *pines* for you * like a dry,
weary land *with*out water.
So I gaze on you *in* the sanctuary * to
see your strength *and* your glory.
For your love is bet*ter* than life, * my
lips will *speak* your praise.
So I will bless you *all* my life, * in your
name I will lift *up* my hands.
My soul shall be filled as *with* a
banquet, * my mouth shall praise *you*
with joy.
On my bed I re*mem*ber you. * On you
I muse *through* the night
for you have *been* my help; * in the
shadow of your wings *I* rejoice.
My soul *clings* to you; * your right
hand *holds* me fast.
Glory to the Father, and *to* the Son, *
and to the *Holy* Spirit:
as it was in the begin*ning*, is now, * and
will be for ev*er*. Amen.

Antiphon   The martyrs fixed their eyes on heaven, † and cried out *in* their
                  torments: * Come, Lord, be with us *in* this hour (*al*leluia).

Ant. 2   Blessèd spirits and souls *of* the just, * pour out your songs of
                praise to the Lord, al*le*luia.

Lent: Martyrs *of* the Lord, * bless the Lord *for* ever.

IIA

Canticle   Daniel 3:57-88; 56

Bless the Lord, all you works *of* the
Lord. * Praise and exalt him above
all *for*ever.

Angels of the Lord, *bless* the Lord, *
You heavens, bless *the* Lord.

All you waters above the heavens, *bless*
the Lord. * All you hosts of the
Lord, bless *the* Lord.

Sun and moon, *bless* the Lord. * Stars
of heaven, bless *the* Lord.

Every shower and dew, *bless* the Lord. *
All you winds, bless *the* Lord.

Fire and heat, *bless* the Lord. * Cold
and chill, bless *the* Lord.

Dew and rain, *bless* the Lord. * Frost
and chill, bless *the* Lord.

Ice and snow, *bless* the Lord. * Nights
and days, bless *the* Lord.

Light and darkness, *bless* the Lord. *
Lightnings and clouds, bless *the*
Lord.

Let the earth *bless* the Lord. * Praise
and exalt him above all *for*ever.

Mountains and hills, *bless* the Lord. *
Everything growing from the earth,

bless *the* Lord.

You springs, *bless* the Lord. * Seas and
rivers, bless *the* Lord.

You dolphins and all water creatures,
bless the Lord. * All you birds of the
air, bless *the* Lord.

All you beasts, wild and tame, *bless* the
Lord. * You sons of men, bless *the*
Lord.

O Israel, *bless* the Lord. * Praise and
exalt him above all *for*ever.

Priests of the Lord, *bless* the Lord. *
Servants of the Lord, bless *the* Lord.

Spirits and souls of the just, *bless* the
Lord. * Holy men of humble heart,
bless *the* Lord.

Hananiah, Azariah, Mishael, *bless* the
Lord. * Praise and exalt him above all
*for*ever.

Let us bless the Father, and the Son,
and the *Ho*ly Spirit. * Let us praise
and exalt him above all *for*ever.

Blessed are you in the firma*ment* of
heaven. * Praiseworthy and glorious
and exalted above all *for*ever.

Antiphon   Blessèd spirits and souls *of* the just, * pour out your songs of
                  praise to the Lord, al*le*luia.

Lent: Martyrs *of* the Lord, * bless the Lord *for* ever.

Ant. 3   You throng *of* martyrs, * give endless praise to God *on* high
              (al*le*luia).

Va

Psalm 149

Sing a new song to *the* Lord, * his
praise in the assembly of *the*
faithful.

Let Israel rejoice in *its* Maker, * let
Zion's sons exult in *their* king.

Let them praise his name *with* dancing
* and make music with timbrel *and*
harp.

For the Lord takes delight in *his*
people. * He crowns the poor with
sal*va*tion.

Let the faithful rejoice in *their* glory, *
shout for joy and take *their* rest.

Let the praise of God be on *their* lips *
and a two-edged sword in *their* hand,

to deal out vengeance to *the* nations *
and punishment on all *the* peoples;

to bind their kings *in* chains * and their
nobles in fetters *of* iron;

to carry out the sentence pre-*or*dained:
* this honor is for all *his* faithful.

Glory to the Father, and to *the* Son, *
and to the Ho*ly* Spirit:

as it was in the beginning, *is* now, * and
will be for ever. *A*men.

Antiphon   You throng *of* martyrs, * give endless praise to God *on* high
              (al*le*luia).

READING   2 Corinthians 1:3-5

Praised be God, the Father of our Lord Jesus Christ, the Father of mercies,
and the God of all consolation! He comforts us in all our afflictions and
thus enables us to comfort those who are in trouble, with the same consolation we have received from him. As we have shared much in the suffering of
Christ, so through Christ do we share abundantly in his consolation.

In the Easter Season: 1 John 5:3-5

The love of God consists in this:
that we keep his commandments—
and his commandments are not burdensome.
Everyone begotten of God conquers the world,
and the power that has conquered the world
is this faith of ours.
Who, then, is conqueror of the world?
The one who believes that Jesus is the Son of God.

RESPONSORY (VI F)

The just are the *friends* of God. * They live with him *for* ever.

— The just are the *friends* of God. * They live with him *for* ever.

God himself is *their* reward.
— They live with him *for* ever.
Glory to the Father, and *to* the Son, * and to the Ho*ly* Spirit.
— The just are the *friends* of God. * They live with him *for* ever.

In the Easter Season:
They will be crowned with ever*last*ing joy, * alleluia, al*le*luia.
— They will be crowned with ever*last*ing joy, * alleluia, al*le*luia.
Gladness and rejoicing will be *their* inheritance,
— alleluia, al*le*luia.
Glory to the Father, and *to* the Son, * and to the Ho*ly* Spirit.
— They will be crowned with ever*last*ing joy, * alleluia, al*le*luia.

CANTICLE OF ZECHARIAH
Antiphon Blessèd are those who suffer persecution for the *sake* of justice; * the kingdom of heaven *is* theirs.

In the Easter Season:
Antiphon Rejoice and be glad, *all* you saints, * for your reward is great in heaven, al*le*luia.

INTERCESSIONS (VI F)
Our Savior's faithfulness is mirrored in the fidelity of his witnesses who shed their blood for the *word* of God. * Let us praise him in remem*brance* of them:
You redeemed us by your *blood.*
Your martyrs freely embraced death in bearing witness *to* the faith,
— give us the true freedom of the Spir*it*, O Lord.
Your martyrs professed their faith by shed*ding* their blood,
— give us a faith, O Lord, that is con*stant* and pure.
Your martyrs followed in your footsteps by carry*ing* the cross,
— help us to endure courageously the misfor*tunes* of life.
Your martyrs washed their garments in the blood *of* the Lamb,
— help us to avoid the weaknesses of the flesh and world*ly* allurements.

Our Father . . .

Prayer
If there is no proper prayer, one of the following is said:
All-powerful, ever-living God,
turn our weakness into strength.
As you gave your martyrs, N. and N.
the courage to suffer death for Christ,
give us courage to live in faithful witness to you.
Grant this through our Lord Jesus Christ, your Son,

who lives and reigns with you and the Holy Spirit,
one God, for ever and ever.
Or:
Lord, hear the prayers of the martyrs N. and N.
and give us courage to bear witness to your truth.
Grant this through our Lord Jesus Christ, your Son,
who lives and reigns with you and the Holy Spirit,
one God, for ever and ever.

During the Easter Season:
God our all-powerful Father,
you strengthen our faith
and take away our weakness.
Let the prayers and example of your martyrs N. and N. help us
to share in the passion and resurrection of Christ
and bring us to eternal joy with all your saints.
We ask this through our Lord Jesus Christ, your Son,
who lives and reigns with you and the Holy Spirit,
one God, for ever and ever.
Or:
Lord, you gave your martyrs N. and N.
the privilege of shedding their blood
in boldly proclaiming the death and resurrection of your Son.
May this celebration of their victory
give them honor among your people.
We ask this through our Lord Jesus Christ, your Son,
who lives and reigns with you and the Holy Spirit,
one God, for ever and ever.

For virgin martyrs:
God our Father, you give us joy each year
in honoring the memory of Saints N. and N.
May their prayers be a source of help for us,
and may their example of courage and chastity be our inspiration.
Grant this through our Lord Jesus Christ, your Son,
who lives and reigns with you and the Holy Spirit,
one God, for ever and ever.

For holy women:
Father, in our weakness your power reaches perfection.
You gave Saints N. and N. the strength
to defeat the power of sin and evil.
May we who celebrate their glory share in their triumph.
We ask this through our Lord Jesus Christ, your Son,
who lives and reigns with you and the Holy Spirit,
one God, for ever and ever.

Evening Prayer II

HYMN

Sanctorum meritis. Mode II (12.12.12.8)

Sanctorum meritis inclita gaudia
pangamus socii gestaque fortia ;
nam gliscit animus promere cantibus
    victorum genus optimum.

Pro sanctis viris :

Hi sunt quos retinens mundus inhorruit,
ipsum nam sterili flore peraridum
sprevere penitus teque secuti sunt,
    rex, Christe, bone cælitum.

Pro sanctis mulieribus:

Hæ sunt, quas retienes mundus inhorruit,
ipsum nam sterili flore peraridum
sprevere penitus teque secutæ sunt,
    rex, Christe, bone cælitum.

Hi (Hæ) pro te furias sævaque sustinent;
non murmur resonat, non querimonia,
sed corde tacito mens bene conscia
    conservat patientiam.

Quæ vox, quæ poterit lingua retexere
quæ tu martyribus munera præparas?
Rubri nam fluido sanguine laureis
    ditantur bene fulgidis.

Te, trina Deitas unaque, poscimus,
ut culpas abluas, noxia subtrahas,
des pacem famulis, nos quoque gloriam
    per cuncta tibi sæcula. Amen.

Come, let us celebrate ever more joyfully
How through the centuries martyrs so glorious
Laid down their lives for you, Jesus, our King and Lord,
    Enduring all courageously.

The world enticing them to its apostasy,
They braved its mockery, setting its threats at nought;
Their love upholding them, nothing could hinder them
    From imitating their Leader.

Brave men and women too, suffered for love of you;
No sound or murmuring broke from their tortured lips,
Their souls' tranquility, gay in its fortitude
    Could bear such anguish patiently.

What voice or tongue e'er can tell of the happiness
You have in readiness for those who die for you;
Their robes are beautiful, dyed in their sacrifice,
    Their crowns are rich beyond measure.

Most holy Trinity, humbly we beg of you,
Forgive our sinfulness, danger avert from us,
Grant us serenity till in the world to come
    We may delight in your glory. Amen.

PSALMODY

Ant. 1   The mortal bodies of God's saints lie bur*ied* in peace, * but they
          themselves live with *God* for ever (a*l*leluia).

VIIIg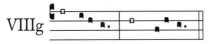

Psalm 116:1-9

I love the Lord for *he* has heard * the
cry of *my* appeal;
for he turned his *ear* to me * in the day
when I called him.
They surrounded me, the *snares* of
death, * with the anguish *of* the
tomb;
they caught me, sorrow *and* distress. * I
called *on* the Lord's name.
O *Lord* my God, * de*liv*er me!
How gracious is the *Lord*, and just; *
our God *has* compassion.
The Lord protects the *simple* hearts; *
I was helpless *so* he saved me.
Turn back, my soul, *to* your rest * for
the Lord *has* been good;
he has kept my soul from death, † my
eyes from tears * and my *feet* from
stumbling.
I will walk in the presence *of* the Lord
* in the land *of* the living.
Glory to the Father, and *to* the Son, *
and to the *Ho*ly Spirit:
as it was in the begin*ning*, is now, * and
will be for ev*er*. Amen.

Antiphon   The mortal bodies of God's saints lie bur*ied* in peace, * but they
           themselves live with *God* for ever (a*l*leluia).

Ant. 2   I saw the souls of those put to death for the *word* of God * and
          for their faith*ful* witness (al*le*luia).

IIA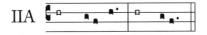

Psalm 116: 10-19

I trusted, even *when* I said, * "I am
sorely *afflicted*,"
and when I said in *my* alarm: * "No
man can *be* trusted."
How can I re*pay* the Lord * for his
goodness *to* me?
The cup of salvation *I* will raise; * I
will call on *the* Lord's name.
My vows to the Lord I *will* fulfill *
before all *his* people.
O precious in the eyes *of* the Lord * is
the death of *his* faithful.
Your servant, Lord, your serv*ant* am I;
* you have loosened *my* bonds.
A thanksgiving sacri*fice* I make: * I will
call on *the* Lord's name.
My vows to the Lord I *will* fulfill *
before all *his* people,
in the courts of the house *of* the Lord, *
in your midst, O *Je*rusalem.
Glory to the Father, and *to* the Son, *
and to the Ho*ly* Spirit:
as it was in the begin*ning*, is now, * and
will be for ever. *A*men.

Antiphon   I saw the souls of those put to death for the *word* of God * and for their faith*ful* witness (al*le*luia).

Ant. 3   These are the saints who surrendered *their* bodies * in witness to *God's* covenant;

they have washed *their* robes * in the blood of *the* Lamb (al*le*luia).

Va

Canticle   Revelation 4:11; 5:9, 10, 12

O Lord our God, you *are* worthy * to receive glory and honor *and* power.

For you have created *all* things; * by your will they came to be and *were* made.

Worthy are you, O Lord, * to receive the scroll and break open *its* seals.

For you *were* slain; * with your blood you purchased *for* God

men of every race *and* tongue, * of every people *and* nation.

You made of them a kingdom, † and priests to serve *our* God, * and they shall reign on *the* earth.

Worthy is the Lamb that *was* slain * to receive power *and* riches,

wisdom *and* strength, * honor and glory *and* praise.

Glory to the Father, and to *the* Son, * and to the Ho*ly* Spirit:

as it was in the beginning, *is* now, * and will be for ever. *A*men.

Antiphon   These are the saints who surrendered *their* bodies * in witness to *God's* covenant;

they have washed *their* robes * in the blood of *the* Lamb (al*le*luia).

READING   1 Peter 4:13-14

Dearly beloved: Rejoice in the measure that you share Christ's sufferings. When his glory is revealed, you will rejoice exultantly. Happy are you when you are insulted for the sake of Christ, for then God's Spirit in its glory has come to rest on you.

In the Easter Season: Revelation 7:14b-17

These are the ones who have survived the great period of trial; they have washed their robes and made them white in the blood of the Lamb.

It was this that brought them before God's throne:
    day and night they minister to him in his temple;
    he who sits on the throne will give them shelter.
Never again shall they know hunger or thirst,
    nor shall the sun or its heat beat down on them,
    for the Lamb on the throne will shepherd them.
He will lead them to springs of life-giving water,
    and God will wipe every tear from their eyes.

RESPONSORY (VI F)

Let the *just* rejoice * and sing for joy in *the* Lord.
— Let the *just* rejoice * and sing for joy in *the* Lord.
Delight in his love, you *pure* of heart,
— and sing for joy in *the* Lord.
Glory to the Father, and *to* the Son, * and to the Ho*ly* Spirit.
— Let the *just* rejoice * and sing for joy in *the* Lord.

In the Easter Season:
The splendor of the just will shine *be*fore God, * alleluia, al*le*luia.
— The splendor of the just will shine *be*fore God, * alleluia, al*le*luia.
The upright of heart *will* rejoice,
— alleluia, al*le*luia.
Glory to the Father, and *to* the Son, * and to the Ho*ly* Spirit.
— The splendor of the just will shine *be*fore God, * alleluia, al*le*luia.

CANTICLE OF MARY

Antiphon   The holy friends of Christ re*joice* in heaven; * they followed in his footsteps to *the* end.
They have shed their blood for *love* of him * and will reign with him *for* ever.

In the Easter Season:
Antiphon   Rejoice, all you saints, before the Lamb; † for the kingdom has been pre*pared* for you * from the beginning of the world, al*le*luia.

INTERCESSIONS (VI F)

This is the hour when the King of Martyrs offered his life in the upper room and laid it down *on* the cross. * Let us thank *him* and say:
          We praise you, O Lord.
We praise you, O Lord, our Savior, inspiration and example for *eve*ry martyr, *
     for loving us *to* the end:
          We praise you, O Lord.
For calling all re*pen*tant sinners * to the re*wards* of life:
          We praise you, O Lord.
For entrusting to your Church the blood of the new and ever*last*ing covenant *
     poured out for the remis*sion* of sin:
          We praise you, O Lord.
For our *per*severance * in your *grace* today:
          We praise you, O Lord.
For incorporating our dead broth*ers* and sisters * into your own *death* today:
We praise you, O Lord.

Our Father . . .

Prayer, as in Morning Prayer.

FOR ONE MARTYR
Evening Prayer I

HYMN, as in Evening Prayer II, 1231.

PSALMODY

Ant. 1   If anyone declares himself for me *be*fore men, * I will declare myself for him be*fore* my Father (*al*leluia).

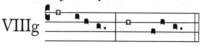

VIIIg

Psalm 118
I

Give thanks to the Lord for *he* is good, * for his love en*dures* for ever.

Let the sons of Is*ra*el say: * "His love en*dures* for ever."

Let the sons of *Aar*on say: * "His love en*dures* for ever."

Let those who fear *the* Lord say: * "His love en*dures* for ever."

I called to the Lord in *my* distress; * he an*swered* and freed me.

The Lord is at my side; I *do* not fear. * What can man *do* against me?

The Lord is at my side *as* my helper: * I shall look down *on* my foes.

It is better to take refuge *in* the Lord * than to *trust* in men:

it is better to take refuge *in* the Lord * than to *trust* in princes.

The nations *all* encompassed me; * in the Lord's *name* I crushed them.

They compassed me, compassed *me* about; * in the Lord's *name* I crushed them.

They compassed me about like bees; †
they blazed like a fire *among* thorns.
* In the Lord's *name* I crushed them.

I was hard-pressed *and* was falling * but the Lord *came* to help me.

The Lord is my strength *and* my song; * he *is* my savior.

There are shouts of *joy* and victory * in the tents *of* the just.

The Lord's right *hand* has triumphed; * his *right* hand raised me.

The Lord's right hand has triumphed; † I *shall* not die, * I shall live and re*count* his deeds.

I was punished, I was punished *by* the Lord, * but not *doomed* to die.

Glory to the Father, and *to* the Son, * and to the *Ho*ly Spirit:

as it was in the begin*ning*, is now, * and will be for *ev*er. Amen.

Antiphon   If anyone declares himself for me *be*fore men, * I will declare myself for him be*fore* my Father (*al*leluia).

Ant. 2   Whoever follows me does not walk *in* the dark; * he will have
          the light *of* life (al*le*luia).

IIA

II

Open to me the *gates* of holiness: *
I will enter and *give* thanks.
This is the *Lord's* own gate * where the
just *may* enter.
I will thank you for *you* have answered
* and you are *my* savior.
The stone which the build*ers* rejected *
has become *the* corner stone.
This is the work *of* the Lord, * a marvel
in *our* eyes.
This day was made *by* the Lord; * we
rejoice and *are* glad.
O Lord, grant *us* salvation; * O Lord,
grant *success.*

Bless*èd* in the name *of* the Lord * is he
who comes.
We bless you from the house *of* the
Lord; * the Lord God is *our* light.
Go forward in proces*sion* with branch-
es * even to *the* altar.
You are my *God*, I thank you.* My
God, *I* praise you.
Give thanks to the Lord for *he* is good;
* for his love endures *for* ever.
Glory to the Father, and *to* the Son, *
and to the Ho*ly* Spirit:
as it was in the begin*ning*, is now, * and
will be for ever. *A*men.

Antiphon   Whoever follows me does not walk *in* the dark; * he will have
            the light *of* life (al*le*luia).

Ant. 3   If we share fully in the sufferings of Christ, † through Christ
          we *shall* know * the fullness of his conso*la*tion (al*le*luia).

Va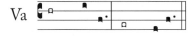

Canticle   1 Peter 2:21-24

Christ suffered for you, † and left
you an *ex*ample * to have you
follow in *his* footsteps.
He did *no* wrong; * no deceit was
found in *his* mouth.
When he was *in*sulted * he returned *no*
insult.
When he was made *to* suffer, * he did
not counter *with* threats.
Instead he delivered him*self* up * to the

One who judg*es* justly.
In his *own* body * he brought his sins
to *the* cross,
so that all of us, dead *to* sin, * could live
in accord with *God's* will.
By *his* wounds * you *were* healed.
Glory to the Father, and to *the* Son, *
and to the Ho*ly* Spirit:
as it was in the beginning, *is* now, * and
will be for ever. *A*men.

Antiphon   If we share fully in the sufferings of Christ, † through Christ
                we *shall* know * the fullness of his con*so*lation (al*le*luia).

READING   Romans 8:35, 37-39
Who will separate us from the love of Christ? Trial or distress, or persecution, or hunger, or nakedness, or danger, or the sword? Yet in all this we are
more than conquerors because of him who has loved us. For I am certain
that neither death nor life, neither angels nor principalities, neither the
present nor the future, nor powers, neither height nor depth nor any other
creature, will be able to separate us from the love of God that comes to us in
Christ Jesus, our Lord.

In the Easter Season: Revelation 3:10-12
Because you have kept my plea to stand fast, I will keep you safe in the time of trial
which is coming on the whole world, to test all men on earth. I am coming soon. Hold
fast to what you have lest someone rob you of your crown. I will make the victor a pillar
in the temple of my God and he shall never leave it. I will inscribe on him the name of
my God and the name of the city of my God, the new Jerusalem which he will send
down from heaven, and my own name which is new.

RESPONSORY (VI F)
For a man:
With glo*ry* and honor, * Lord, you *have* crowned him.
— With glo*ry* and honor, * Lord, you *have* crowned him.
You set him over the works *of* your hands.
— Lord, you *have* crowned him.
Glory to the Father, and *to* the Son, * and to the Ho*ly* Spirit.
— With glo*ry* and honor, * Lord, you *have* crowned him.

For a woman:
The Lord has *cho*sen her, * his loved one from the *be*ginning.
— The Lord has *cho*sen her, * his loved one from the *be*ginning.
He has taken her to *live* with him,
— his loved one from the *be*ginning.
Glory to the Father, and *to* the Son, * and to the Ho*ly* Spirit.
— The Lord has *cho*sen her, * his loved one from the *be*ginning.

In the Easter Season:
Let the just rejoice *in* the Lord, * alleluia, al*le*luia.
— Let the just rejoice *in* the Lord, * alleluia, al*le*luia.
God has chosen you as *his* own people,
— alleluia, al*le*luia.
Glory to the Father, and *to* the Son, * and to the Ho*ly* Spirit.
— Let the just rejoice *in* the Lord, * alleluia, al*le*luia.

CANTICLE OF MARY

For a man:

Antiphon   For the *law* of God * this holy man engaged in combat *to* death.
His faith was founded on *so*lid rock; * he feared no wick*ed*
threats.

For a woman:

Antiphon   She has girded herself with strength † and made *her* arms
sturdy. * The light she has kindled will never *go* out.

In the Easter Season:

Antiphon   The everlasting light of *end*less days * will shine upon your saints, O
Lord, al*le*luia.

INTERCESSIONS (VI F)

This is the hour when the King of martyrs offered his life in the upper room
and laid it down *on* the cross. * Let us thank *him* and say:
We praise you, O Lord.
We praise you, O *Lord*, our Savior, * inspiration and example for every martyr,
for loving us *to* the end:
We praise you, O Lord.
For calling all re*pen*tant sinners * to the re*wards* of life:
We praise you, O Lord.
For entrusting to your Church the blood of the new and ever*last*ing covenant *
poured out for the remis*sion* of sin:
We praise you, O Lord.
For our *per*severance * in your *grace* today:
We praise you, O Lord.
For incorporating our dead broth*ers* and sisters * into your own *death* today:
We praise you, O Lord.

Our Father . . .

Prayer, as in Morning Prayer.

Morning Prayer

HYMN

Martyr Dei qui unicum. (L.M.)

Martyr Dei, qui (quæ) unicum	God's holy martyr, who disdained
Patris sequendo Filium	And overcame all pains and death,
victis triumphas hostibus,	Your faithful following of Christ
victor (victrix) fruens cælestibus,	Has led you to the Father's home.
Tui precatus munere	By your incessant prayer for us,
nostrum reatum dilue,	Obtain forgiveness for our sins;
arcens mali contagium,	Protect us from the pow'rs of ill,
vitae repellens tædium.	Relieve us in our daily cares.
Soluta sunt iam vincula	For you are free from ev'ry bond
tui sacrati corporis;	That bound you once to things of earth,
nos solve vinclis sæculi	By your own ardent love for Christ,
amore Filii Dei.	Free us from all that drags us down.
Honor Patri cum Filio	All honor to our Father, God,
et Spiritu Paraclito,	Who with the Spirit and the Son,
qui te corona perpeti	Awarded you a deathless crown,
cingunt in aula gloriæ. Amen.	In heaven's court of glory blest. Amen.

PSALMODY

Ant. 1   My lips will praise you, Lord, † for sweet*er* than life * is your mer*ci*ful love (*al*leluia).

Psalms and canticle from Sunday, Week I, 606.

Ant. 2   Martyrs *of* the Lord, * bless the Lord *for* ever (al*le*luia).

Ant. 3   I will make the man who is *vic*torious, * a pillar in my temple, says *the* Lord (al*le*luia).

READING   2 Corinthians 1:3-5

Praised be God, the Father of our Lord Jesus Christ, the Father of mercies, and the God of all consolation! He comforts us in all our afflictions and thus enables us to comfort those who are in trouble, with the same consolation we have received from him. As we have shared much in the suffering of Christ, so through Christ do we share abundantly in his consolation.

In the Easter Season: 1 John 5:3-5

The love of God consists in this:
that we keep his commandments—
and his commandments are not burdensome.
Everyone begotten of God conquers the world,
and the power that has conquered the world

is this faith of ours.
Who, then, is conqueror of the world?
The one who believes that Jesus is the Son of God.

RESPONSORY (VI F)

The Lord *is* my strength, * and I shall sing *his* praise.
— The Lord *is* my strength, * and I shall sing *his* praise.
The Lord *is* my savior,
— and I shall sing *his* praise.
Glory to the Father, and *to* the Son, * and to the Ho*ly* Spirit.
— The Lord *is* my strength, * and I shall sing *his* praise.

In the Easter Season:
They will be crowned with ever*last*ing joy, * alleluia, al*le*luia.
— They will be crowned with ever*last*ing joy, * alleluia, al*le*luia.
Gladness and rejoicing will be *their* inheritance,
— alleluia, al*le*luia.
Glory to the Father, and *to* the Son, * and to the Ho*ly* Spirit.
— They will be crowned with ever*last*ing joy, * alleluia, al*le*luia.

CANTICLE OF ZECHARIAH

Antiphon   Whoever hates his life *in* this world * keeps it safe for life
                ev*er*lasting.

In the Easter Season:
Antiphon   Rejoice and be glad, *all* you saints, * for your reward is great in heaven,
                al*le*luia.

INTERCESSIONS (VI F)

Our Savior's faithfulness is mirrored in the fidelity of his witnesses who shed
    their blood for the *word* of God. * Let us praise him in remem*brance* of them:
You redeemed us by your *blood.*
Your martyrs freely embraced death in bearing witness *to* the faith,
— give us the true freedom of the Spir*it*, O Lord.
Your martyrs professed their faith by shed*ding* their blood,
— give us a faith, O Lord, that is con*stant* and pure.
Your martyrs followed in your footsteps by carry*ing* the cross,
— help us to endure courageously the misfort*unes* of life.
Your martyrs washed their garments in the blood *of* the Lamb,
— help us to avoid the weaknesses of the flesh and world*ly* allurements.

Our Father . . .

Prayer

If there is no proper prayer, one of the following is said:

God of power and mercy,
you gave N., your martyr, victory over pain and suffering.

Strengthen us who celebrate this day of his triumph
and help us to be victorious over the evils that threaten us.
Grant this through our Lord Jesus Christ, your Son,
who lives and reigns with you and the Holy Spirit,
one God, for ever and ever.

Or:

All-powerful, ever-living God,
you gave Saint N. the courage to witness to the gospel of Christ
even to the point of giving his life for it.
By his prayers help us to endure all suffering for love of you
and to seek you with all our hearts,
for you alone are the source of life.
Grant this through our Lord Jesus Christ, your Son,
who lives and reigns with you and the Holy Spirit,
one God, for ever and ever.

For a virgin martyr:

God our Father,
you give us joy each year
in honoring the memory of Saint N.
May her prayers be a source of help for us,
and may her example of courage and chastity be our inspiration.
Grant this through our Lord Jesus Christ, your Son,
who lives and reigns with you and the Holy Spirit,
one God, for ever and ever.

For a holy woman:

Father,
in our weakness your power reaches perfection.
You gave Saint N. the strength
to defeat the power of sin and evil.
May we who celebrate her glory share in her triumph.
We ask this through our Lord Jesus Christ, your Son,
who lives and reigns with you and the Holy Spirit,
one God, for ever and ever.

In the Easter Season:

God our Father,
you have honored the Church
with the victorious witness of Saint N., who died for his faith.
As he imitated the sufferings and death of the Lord,
may we follow in his footsteps and come to eternal joy.
We ask this through our Lord Jesus Christ, your Son,
who lives and reigns with you and the Holy Spirit,
one God, for ever and ever.

Or.

Lord,
hear the prayers of those who praise your mighty power.
As Saint N. was ready to follow Christ in suffering and death,
so may he be ready to help us in our weakness.
We ask this through our Lord Jesus Christ, your Son,
who lives and reigns with you and the Holy Spirit,
one God, for ever and ever.

Evening Prayer II
HYMN

Deus tuorum militum. (L.M.)

Deus, tuorum militum	O God, the Crown and great Reward
sors et corona, præmium,	Of all your soldiers brave and true,
laudes canentes martyris	Absolve us from all bonds of sin,
absolve nexu criminis	Who sing your loyal martyr's praise.
Hic (Hæc) testis ore protulit	S/He spoke up fearlessly to prove
quod cordis arca credidit,	The steadfast faith deep in her/his heart,
Christum sequendo repperit	So closely following our Lord,
effusione sanguinis.	Like him, s/he gladly shed her/his blood.
Hic (Hæc) nempe mundi gaudia	Despising all the world could give,
et blandimenta noxia	Its pleasures which can lead to harm,
caduca rite deputans,	Quite rightly counting them as dross,
precenit ad cælestia.	S/he chose full happiness above.
Poenas cucurrit fortiter	With strength and courage s/he endured
et sustulit viriliter;	The horrors of a cruel death,
pro te refundens sanguinem,	And gave her/his life with joy to prove
æterna dona possidet.	Her/his love for you, and life to gain.
Ob hoc precatu supplici	Because of her/his great constancy,
te poscimus, piissime ;	We humbly beg, O Father kind,
in hoc triumpho martyris	On this, your martyr's festal day,
dimitte noxam servulis,	Forgive our failings and our falls.
Ut consequamur muneris	That we at last may also share
ipsius et consortia,	All martyrs' company on high,
lætemur ac perenniter	Rejoicing with them evermore,
iuncti polorum sedibus.	Enthroned with them in realms of light.
Laud et perennis gloria	All praise and glory without end,
tibi, Pater, cum Filio,	Be yours, O Father, with the Son,
Sancto simul Paraclito	And with the Holy Spirit too,
in sæculorum sæcula. Amen.	In time and in eternity. Amen.

PSALMODY

Ant. 1   If anyone wishes to come after me, he must de*ny* himself, * take
              up his cross, and *fo*llow me (*a*lleluia).

VIIIg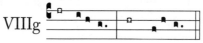

Psalm 116:1-9

I love the Lord for *he* has heard * the
cry of *my* appeal;

for he turned his *ear* to me * in the day
when I called him.

They surrounded me, the *snares* of
death, * with the anguish *of* the
tomb;

they caught me, sorrow *and* distress. * I
called *on* the Lord's name.

O *Lord* my God, * de*liver* me!

How gracious is the *Lord*, and just; *
our God *has* compassion.

The Lord protects the *sim*ple hearts; *

I was helpless *so* he saved me.

Turn back, my soul, *to your* rest * for
the Lord *has* been good;

he has kept my soul from death, † my
eyes from tears * and my *feet* from
stumbling.

I will walk in the presence *of* the Lord
* in the land *of* the living.

Glory to the Father, and *to* the Son, *
and to the *Holy* Spirit:

as it was in the begin*ning*, is now, * and
will be for *ever*. Amen.

Antiphon   If anyone wishes to come after me, he must de*ny* himself, * take
             up his cross, and *fo*llow me (*a*lleluia).

Ant. 2   Who*ev*er serves me * will be honored by my Father *in* heaven
              (al*le*luia).

IIA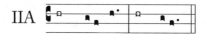

Psalm 116: 10-19

I trusted, even *when* I said: * "I am
sorely *af*flicted,"

and when I said in *my* alarm: * "No
man can *be* trusted."

How can I re*pay* the Lord * for his
goodness *to* me?

The cup of salvation *I* will raise; * I
will call on *the* Lord's name.

My vows to the Lord I *will* fulfill *
before all *his* people.

O precious in the eyes *of* the Lord * is
the death of *his* faithful.

Your servant, Lord, your ser*vant* am I;
* you have loosened *my* bonds.

A thanksgiving sacri*fice* I make: * I will
call on *the* Lord's name.

My vows to the Lord I *will* fulfill *
before all *his* people,

in the courts of the house *of* the Lord, *
in your midst, O *Je*rusalem.

Glory to the Father, and *to* the Son, * | as it was in the begin*ning*, is now, * and
and to the Ho*ly* Spirit: | will be for ever. *A*men.

Antiphon   Who*ev*er serves me * will be honored by my Father *in* heaven
(al*le*luia).

Ant. 3   He who loses his life because *of* me * will find it *for*ever (al*le*luia).

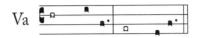

Canticle   Revelation 4:11; 5:9, 10, 12

O Lord our God, you *are* worthy *
to receive glory and honor *and*
power.
For you have created *all* things; * by
your will they came to be and *were*
made.
Worthy are you, O Lord, * to receive
the scroll and break open *its* seals.
For you *were* slain. * With your blood
you purchased *for* God
men of every race *and* tongue, * of
every people *and* nation.

You made of them a kingdom, † and
priests to serve *our* God, * and they
shall reign on *the* earth.
Worthy is the Lamb that *was* slain * to
receive power *and* riches,
wisdom *and* strength, * honor and
glory *and* praise.
Glory to the Father, and to *the* Son, *
and to the Ho*ly* Spirit:
as it was in the beginning, *is* now, * and
will be for ever. *A*men.

Antiphon   He who loses his life because *of* me * will find it *for*ever (al*le*luia).

READING   1 Peter 4:13-14
Rejoice in the measure that you share Christ's sufferings. When his glory is
revealed, you will rejoice exultantly. Happy are you when you are insulted
for the sake of Christ, for then God's Spirit in its glory has come to rest on
you.

In the Easter Season: Revelation 7:14b-17
These are the ones who have survived the great period of trial; they have washed their
robes and made them white in the blood of the Lamb.

It was this that brought them before God's throne:
day and night they minister to him in his temple;
he who sits on the throne will give them shelter.
Never again shall they know hunger or thirst,
nor shall the sun or its heat beat down on them,
for the Lamb on the throne will shepherd them.
He will lead them to springs of life-giving water,
and God will wipe every tear from their eyes.

RESPONSORY (VI F)

Let the *just* rejoice * and sing for joy in *the* Lord.
— Let the *just* rejoice * and sing for joy in *the* Lord.
Delight in his love, you *pure* of heart,
— and sing for joy in *the* Lord.
Glory to the Father, and *to* the Son, * and to the Ho*ly* Spirit.
— Let the *just* rejoice * and sing for joy in *the* Lord.

In the Easter Season:

The splendor of the just will shine *be*fore God, * alleluia, al*le*luia.
—The splendor of the just will shine *be*fore God, * alleluia, al*le*luia.
The upright of heart *will* rejoice,
— alleluia, al*le*luia.
Glory to the Father, and *to* the Son, * and to the Ho*ly* Spirit.
—The splendor of the just will shine *be*fore God, * alleluia, al*le*luia.

CANTICLE OF MARY

Antiphon   The holy friends of Christ re*joice* in heaven; * they followed in his footsteps to *the* end.
            They have shed their blood for *love* of him * and will reign with him *for* ever.

In the Easter Season:

Antiphon   Rejoice, all you saints, before the Lamb; † for the kingdom has been pre*pared* for you * from the beginning of the world, al*le*luia.

INTERCESSIONS (VI F)

This is the hour when the King of martyrs offered his life in the upper room and laid it down *on* the cross. * Let us thank *him* and say:
        We praise you, O Lord.
We praise you, O *Lord*, our Savior, * inspiration and example for every martyr, for loving us *to* the end:
        We praise you, O Lord.
For calling all re*pen*tant sinners * to the re*wards* of life:
        We praise you, O Lord.
For entrusting to your Church the blood of the new and ever*last*ing covenant * poured out for the remis*sion* of sin:
        We praise you, O Lord.
For our *per*severance * in your *grace* today:
        We praise you, O Lord.
For incorporating our dead broth*ers* and sisters * into your own *death* today:
        We praise you, O Lord.

Our Father . . .

Prayer, as in Morning Prayer.

COMMON OF PASTORS

Evening Prayer I

HYMN, as in Evening Prayer II, 1242.

PSALMODY

Ant. 1 I will give you shepherd after *my* own heart; * they will nourish you with knowledge *and* sound teaching (*a*lleluia).

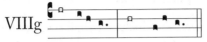

VIIIg

Psalm 113

Praise, O servants *of* the Lord, *
 praise the name *of* the Lord!
May the name of the *Lord* be blessed *
 both now and for *ev*ermore!
From the rising of the sun *to* its setting
 * praised be the name *of* the Lord!
High above all nations *is* the Lord, *
 above the heav*ens* his glory.
Who is like the *Lord*, our God, * who
 has risen on high *to* his throne
yet stoops from the heights *to* look
 down, * to look down upon heav*en*

and earth?
From the dust he lifts *up* the lowly, *
 from his misery he rais*es* the poor
to set him in the company of princes, *
 yes, with the princes *of* his people.
To the childless wife he *gives* a home *
 and gladdens her *heart* with children.
Glory to the Father, and *to* the Son, *
 and to the *Ho*ly Spirit:
as it was in the begin*ning*, is now, * and
 will be for *ev*er. Amen.

Antiphon I will give you shepherd after *my* own heart; * they will nourish you with knowledge *and* sound teaching (*a*lleluia).

Ant. 2 I shall feed my flock; † I shall search *for* the lost * and lead back those who *have* strayed (al*le*luia).

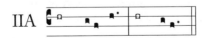

IIA

Psalm 146

My soul, give praise to the Lord; †
 I will praise the Lord *all* my
days, * make music to my God while
I live.
Put no *trust* in princes, * in mortal men
 in whom there is *no* help.
Take their breath, they re*turn* to clay *
 and their plans that day come *to*

nothing.
He is happy who is helped by *Jacob's*
 God, * whose hope is in the Lord *his*
 God,
who alone made heav*en* and earth, * the
 seas and all they con*tain*.
It is he who keeps *faith* for ever, * who
 is just to those who are *op*pressed.

It is he who gives bread *to* the hungry,
 * the Lord, who sets prison*ers* free,
the Lord who gives sight *to* the blind, *
 who raises up those who are *bowed*
 down,
the Lord, who pro*tects* the stranger *
 and upholds the widow *and* orphan.
It is the Lord who *loves* the just * but
thwarts the path of *the* wicked.
The Lord will *reign* for ever, * Zion's
 God, from age *to* age.
Glory to the Father, and *to* the Son, *
 and to the Ho*ly* Spirit:
as it was in the begin*ning*, is now, * and
 will be for ever. *A*men.

Antiphon   I shall feed my flock; † I shall search *for* the lost * and lead back
                those who *have* strayed (al*le*luia).

Ant. 3   The Good Shepherd laid down *his* life * for *his* sheep (al*le*luia).

Va

                                Canticle   Ephesians 1:3-10

Praised be the God *and* Father * of
  our Lord Je*sus* Christ,
who has bestowed on us *in* Christ *
 every spiritual blessing in *the* heavens.
God chose us in him † before the
 world *began* * to be holy and blameless in *his* sight.
He predestined us † to be his adopted
 sons through Je*sus* Christ, * such was
 his will *and* pleasure,
that all might praise the glori*ous* favor *
 he has bestowed on us in his *beloved*.
In him and through his blood, † we
 have been *redeemed*, * and our sins
for*given*,
so immeasura*bly* generous * is God's
 favor *to* us.
God has given us the wisdom † to
 understand fully *the* mystery, * the
 plan he was pleased to decree *in*
 Christ.
A plan to be carried out *in* Christ, * in
 the fullness *of* time,
to bring all things into one *in* him, * in
 the heavens and *on* earth.
Glory to the Father, and to *the* Son, *
 and to the Ho*ly* Spirit:
as it was in the beginning, *is* now, * and
 will be for ever. *A*men.

Antiphon   The Good Shepherd laid down *his* life * for *his* sheep (al*le*luia).

READING   1 Peter 5:1-4
    To the elders among you I, a fellow elder, a witness of Christ's sufferings
    and sharer in the glory that is to be revealed, make this appeal. God's flock is
    in your midst; give it a shepherd's care. Watch over it willingly as God
    would have you do, not under constraint; and not for shameful profit either,
    but generously. Be examples to the flock, not lording it over those assigned
    to you, so that when the chief Shepherd appears you will win for yourselves
    the unfading crown of glory.

RESPONSORY (VI F)

Priests *of* the Lord, * give thanks and praise to *the* Lord.

— Priests *of* the Lord, * give thanks and praise to *the* Lord.

You of holy and humble heart, ac*claim* your Lord.

— Give thanks and praise to *the* Lord.

Glory to the Father, and *to* the Son, * and to the Ho*ly* Spirit.

— Priests *of* the Lord, * give thanks and praise to *the* Lord.

Easter:

Priests of the Lord, give thanks and praise *to* the Lord, * alleluia, al*le*luia.

— Priests of the Lord, give thanks and praise *to* the Lord, * alleluia, al*le*luia.

You of holy and humble heart, ac*claim* your Lord.

— alleluia, al*le*luia.

Glory to the Father, and *to* the Son, * and to the Ho*ly* Spirit.

—Priests of the Lord, give thanks and praise *to* the Lord, * alleluia, al*le*luia.

CANTICLE OF MARY

For a pope or bishop:

Ant.   Priest of the Most High God and mirror of goodness, † you were a good shepherd *to* your people * and pleasing to *the* Lord (al*le*luia).

For a priest: I became all things *to* all men, * that all might find sa*l*vation (al*le*luia).

INTERCESSIONS

Jesus Christ is worthy of all praise, for he was appointed high priest among men and their representative *be*fore God. * We honor him and in our weak*ness* we pray:

*Bring salvation to your peo*ple, *Lord.*

You marvelously illuminated your Church through distinguished leaders and holy *men* and women,

— let Christians rejoice always *in* such splendor.

You forgave the sins of your people when their holy leaders like Moses sought *your* compassion,

— through their intercession continue to purify and sanctify your *holy* people.

In the midst of their brothers and sisters you anointed your holy ones and filled them with the *Holy* Spirit,

— fill all the leaders of your people with *the* same Spirit.

You yourself are the only visible possession of our *holy* pastors,

— let none of them, won at the price of your blood, remain *far* from you.

The shepherds of your Church keep your flock from being snatched out of your hand. Through them you give your flock e*ter*nal life,

— save those who have died, those for whom you gave *up* your life.

Our Father . . .

Prayer, as in Morning Prayer.

Morning Prayer
HYMN
Inclitus rector. (11.11.11.5)

Inclitus rector pater atque prudens,	This prudent leader, father to his people,
cuius insignem colimus triumphum,	Whose final triumph we rejoice to honor,
iste confessor sine fine lætus	Rich in true merits, endless joy attaining
regnat in astris.	Now reigns in heaven.

Pro papa:

Qui Petri summa cathedra residens,
præsul immensi gregis et magister,
regna per claves Domini potenter
cælica pandit.

For a pope:

Once elevated to the see of Peter,
Pastor of shepherds, Servant of God's servants,
He was entrusted with those mystic symbols,
Keys of the Kingdom.

Pro episcopo:

Qui sacerdotis, ducis ac magistri
munus insumpsit populis sacratum,
præsul et vitæ sapiens paravit
dona beatæ.

For a bishop:

He held the office, sacred and exalted
Of chosen pastor to confirm and strengthen,
Teaching as master by his own example,
Virtue and learning.

Pro presbytero:

Ipse dux clarus fuit et magister,
exhibens sacræ documenta vitæ
ac Deo semper satagens placere
pectore mundo.

For a priest:

Generous leader and a zealous master,
His holy teaching showed the path of virtue,
Seeking to please God with a pure intention
At every moment.

Nunc eum nisu rogitemus omnes,
abluat nostrum pius ut reatum,
et sua ducat prece nos ad alta
culmina cæli.

Now let us ask him for his intercession
That his compassion may win us forgiveness,
Leading us sinners, penitent and contrite
Home to the Father.

Sit Deo soli decus et potestas,
laud in excelsis, honor ac perennis,
qui suis totum moderans gubernat
legibus orbem. Amen.

Glory and honor be to God Almighty,
Praise in the highest, power and dominion,
Who in his wisdom rules and governs all things
His love created. Amen.

PSALMODY

Ant. 1   You are the light *of* the world; * a city set on a hill can*not* be
                hidden (*a/*leluia).

Psalms and canticle from Sunday, Week I, 606.

Ant. 2   Let your light shine before men, † that they may see *your* good
                works * and give glory to *your* Father (al*e*luia).

Ant. 3   God's word is alive; it strikes to *the* heart. * It pierces more
                surely than a two-*edged* sword (al*e*luia).

READING   Hebrews 13:7-9a
    Remember your leaders who spoke the word of God to you; consider how
    their lives ended, and imitate their faith. Jesus Christ is the same yesterday,
    today, and forever. Do not be carried away by all kinds of strange teaching.

RESPONSORY (VI F)
On your *walls*, Jerusalem, * I have set my watchmen *to* guard you.
— On your *walls*, Jerusalem, * I have set my watchmen *to* guard you.
Day or night, they will not cease to proclaim the name *of* the Lord.
— I have set my watchmen *to* guard you.
Glory to the Father, and *to* the Son, * and to the Ho*ly* Spirit.
— On your *walls*, Jerusalem, * I have set my watchmen *to* guard you.

Easter:
On your walls, Jerusalem, † I have set my watch*men* to guard you, * alleluia, al*e*luia.
— On your walls, Jerusalem, † I have set my watch*men* to guard you, * alleluia, al*e*luia.
Day or night, they will not cease to proclaim the name *of* the Lord.
— alleluia, al*e*luia.
Glory to the Father, and *to* the Son, * and to the Ho*ly* Spirit.
— On your walls, Jerusalem, † I have set my watch*men* to guard you, * alleluia, al*e*luia.

CANTICLE OF ZECHARIAH
Antiphon   What you say of me does not come *from* yourselves; * it is the
                Spirit of my Father speaking *in* you (al*e*luia).

INTERCESSIONS (VI F)
Christ is the Good Shepherd who laid down his life *for* his sheep. * Let us praise
    and thank him *as* we pray:
*Nourish your peo*ple, *Lord.*
Christ, you decided to show your merciful love through your *holy* shepherds,
— let your mercy always reach *us* through them.
Through your vicars you continue to perform the ministry of shep*herd* of souls,
— direct us always *through* our leaders.

Through your holy ones, the leaders of your people, you served as physician of
 our bodies *and* our spirits,
— continue to fulfill your ministry of life and holi*ness* in us.
You taught your flock through the prudence and love *of* your saints,
— grant us continual growth in holiness under the direction *of* our pastors.

Our Father . . .

Prayer

If there is no proper prayer, one of the following is said:

For a pope:

> All-powerful and ever-living God,
> you called Saint N. to guide your people
> by his word and example.
> With him we pray to you:
> watch over the pastors of your Church
> with the people entrusted to their care,
> and lead them to salvation.
> We ask this through our Lord Jesus Christ, your Son,
> who lives and reigns with you and the Holy Spirit,
> one God, for ever and ever.

For a bishop:

> Lord God,
> you counted Saint N. among your holy pastors,
> renowned for faith and love which conquered evil in this world.
> By the help of his prayers
> keep us strong in faith and love
> and let us come to share his glory.
> Grant this through our Lord Jesus Christ, your Son,
> who lives and reigns with you and the Holy Spirit,
> one God, for ever and ever.

For the founder of a church:

> Lord, you called our fathers to the light of the gospel
> by the preaching of Saint N.
> By his prayers help us to grow in the love and knowledge of your Son, our
> Lord Jesus Christ,
> who lives and reigns with you and the Holy Spirit,
> one God, for ever and ever.

For a pastor:

> God our Father,
> in Saint N. you gave
> a light to your faithful people.
> You made him a pastor of the Church

to feed your sheep with his word
and to teach them by his example.
Help us by his prayers to keep the faith he taught
and follow the way of life he showed us.
Grant this through our Lord Jesus Christ, your Son,
who lives and reigns with you and the Holy Spirit,
one God, for ever and ever.

Or:

Lord God,
you gave your Saint N.
the spirit of truth and love
to shepherd your people.
May we who honor him on this feast
learn from his example
and be helped by his prayers.
We ask this through our Lord Jesus Christ, your Son,
who lives and reigns with you and the Holy Spirit,
one God, for ever and ever.

For a missionary:

God of mercy,
you gave us Saint N. to proclaim the riches of Christ.
By the help of his prayers
may we grow in knowledge of you,
be eager to do good,
and learn to walk before you
by living the truth of the gospel.
Grant this through our Lord Jesus Christ, your Son,
who lives and reigns with you and the Holy Spirit,
one God, for ever and ever.

Evening Prayer II

HYMN

Vir celse. (L.M.)

Mode 8

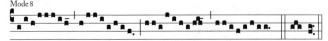

Vir celse, forma fulgida	Resplendent model for us all,
virtutis, hymnum suscipe,	Receive the humble praise we sing,
qui iure dum te prædicat,	For while we spread your great renown
Dei canit magnalia.	We praise God's wondrous work of grace.
Qui sempiternus Pontifex	For our eternal Priest and Lord
stirpem Deo mortalium	Restored to God our fallen race,
revinxit, atque reddidit	And by his death as mortal man,
paci novo nos fœdere,	Atoned for us, became our peace.
Te fecit ipse providum	Christ chose you in his tender love,
sui ministrum muneris,	To be the steward of his grace,
Patri daturum gloriam	To give his Father glory due,
eiusque vitam plebibus.	And to all peoples lasting life.
Pro papa:	For a pope:
Tu Petri ovile cælitus	The sheepfold's keys were in your care,
sumptis regebas clavibus,	Elected to hold Peter's place,
gregemque verbo gratiæ,	You led Christ's flock by worthy deeds,
puris fovebas actibus.	Instructing it with words of grace.
Pro episcopo :	For a bishop:
Virtute factus ditior	Made richer by the Spirit's grace,
te consecrantis Spiritus,	Who consecrated you apart,
præsul, salutis pinguia	You nourished all Christ's little ones
tu tradidisti pabula.	On food for everlasting life.
Pro presbytero:	For a priest:
Regalis huius culminis	He raised you to the royal height
adeptus altitudinem,	Of teacher, priest, oblation too,
verbo fuisti et moribus	That by your ev'ry word and work
doctor, sacerdos, hostia.	His image should be seen in you.
Locatus in cælestibus,	From your high throne in heaven's light,
sanctae memento Ecclesiæ,	Remember holy Church's needs,
oves ut omnes pascua	That all Christ's sheep may follow him
Christi petant felicia.	To pastures of eternal bliss.
Sit Trinitati gloria,	All glory to the Trinity,
quae sancti honoris munia	Who crowns you with your merit's joy,
tibi ministro sedulo	Who have deserved the recompense
dignis coronat gaudiis. Amen.	Of servant worthy of his Lord. Amen.

PSALMODY

Ant. 1   My life is at the service *of* the Gospel; * God has given me this gift *of* his grace (*al*leluia).

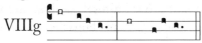

VIIIg

Psalm 15

Lord, who shall be admitted *to* your tent * and dwell on your *holy* mountain?

He who walks *with*out fault; * he who *acts* with justice

and speaks the truth *from* his heart; * he who does not slander *with* his tongue;

he who does no wrong *to* his brother, * who casts no slur *on* his neighbor,

who holds the godless *in* disdain, * but honors those who *fear* the Lord;

he who keeps his pledge, *come* what may; * who takes no interest *on* a loan

and accepts no bribes *against* the innocent. * Such a man will stand *firm* for ever.

Glory to the Father, and *to* the Son, * and to the *Holy* Spirit:

as it was in the begin*ning*, is now, * and will be for ev*er*. Amen.

Antiphon   My life is at the service *of* the Gospel; * God has given me this gift *of* his grace (*al*leluia).

Ant. 2   This servant proved himself faith*ful* and wise; * the Lord entrusted the care of his household *to* him (al*le*luia).

IIA

Psalm 112

Happy the man who *fears* the Lord, * who takes delight in all his *com*mands.

His sons will be power*ful* on earth; * the children of the upright *are* blessèd.

Riches and wealth are *in* his house; * his justice stands firm *for* ever.

He is a light in the darkness *for* the upright: * he is generous, merciful *and* just.

The good man takes pi*ty* and lends, * he conducts his affairs *with* honor.

The just man will *nev*er waver: * he will be remembered *for* ever.

He has no fear of *evil* news; * with a firm heart he trusts in *the* Lord.

With a steadfast heart he *will* not fear; * he will see the downfall of *his* foes.

Open-handed, he gives to the poor; † his justice stands *firm* for ever. * His head will be raised *in* glory.

The wicked man sees and is angry, † grinds his teeth and *fades* away; * the

desire of the wicked leads *to* doom.
Glory to the Father, and *to* the Son, *
and to the Ho*ly* Spirit:

as it was in the begin*ning*, is now, * and
will be for ever. *A*men.

Antiphon   This servant proved himself faith*ful* and wise; * the Lord
entrusted the care of his household *to* him (al*le*luia).

Ant. 3   My sheep will hear *my* voice; * and there shall be one fold and
one shepherd (al*le*luia).

Va

Canticle   Revelation 15:3-4

Mighty and wonderful are *your*
works, * Lord God *Al*mighty!
Righteous and true are *your* ways, * O
King of *the* nations!
Who would dare refuse *you* honor, * or
the glory due your name, O Lord?
Since you alone *are* holy, * all nations

shall come and worship in *your*
presence.
Your migh*ty* deeds * are clear*ly* seen.
Glory to the Father, and to *the* Son, *
and to the Ho*ly* Spirit:
as it was in the beginning, *is* now, * and
will be for ever. *A*men.

Antiphon   My sheep will hear *my* voice; * and there shall be one fold and
one shepherd (al*le*luia).

READING   1 Peter 5:1-4

To the elders among you I, a fellow elder, a witness of Christ's sufferings
and sharer in the glory that is to be revealed, make this appeal. God's flock is
in your midst; give it a shepherd's care. Watch over it willingly as God
would have you do, not under constraint; and not for shameful profit either,
but generously. Be examples to the flock, not lording it over those assigned
to you, so that when the chief Shepherd appears you will win for yourselves
the unfading crown of glory.

RESPONSORY (VI F)
This is a man who *loved* his brethren * and ever prayed *for* them.
— This is a man who *loved* his brethren * and ever prayed *for* them.
He spent himself *in* their service,
— and ever prayed *for* them.
Glory to the Father, and *to* the Son, * and to the Ho*ly* Spirit.
— This is a man who *loved* his brethren * and ever prayed *for* them.

Easter:

This is a man who loved his brethren and ever *prayed* for them, * alleluia, al*le*luia.

— This is a man who loved his brethren and ever *prayed* for them, * alleluia, al*le*luia.

He spent himself *in* their service,

— alleluia, al*le*luia.

Glory to the Father, and *to* the Son, * and to the Ho*ly* Spirit.

— This is a man who loved his brethren and ever *prayed* for them, * alleluia, al*le*luia.

CANTICLE OF MARY

Antiphon   This is a faithful and wise steward: † the Lord entrusted the
                    care of his house*hold* to him, * so that he might give them their
                    portion of food at the prop*er* season (al*le*luia).

Or: O Christ, Good Shepherd, I thank you for leading me to glory;
                    † I pray that the flock you have entrusted *to* my care * will share
                    with me in your glory *for* ever (al*le*luia).

INTERCESSIONS (VI F)

Jesus Christ is worthy of all praise, for he was appointed high priest among men
    and their representative *be*fore God. * We honor him and in our weak*ness* we
    pray:

*Bring salvation to your peo*ple, *Lord.*

You marvelously illuminated your Church through distinguished leaders and
    holy *men* and women,

— let Christians rejoice always *in* such splendor.

You forgave the sins of your people when their holy leaders like Moses sought
    your compassion,

— through their intercession continue to purify and sanctify your *holy* people.

In the midst of their brothers and sisters you anointed your holy ones and filled
    them with the *Ho*ly Spirit,

— fill all the leaders of your people with *the* same Spirit.

You yourself are the only visible possession of our *holy* pastors,

— let none of them, won at the price of your blood, remain *far* from you.

The shepherds of your Church keep your flock from being snatched out of your
    hand. Through them you give your flock e*ter*nal life,

— save those who have died, those for whom you gave *up* your life.

Our Father . . .

Prayer, as in Morning Prayer.

COMMON OF DOCTORS OF THE CHURCH

Everything is taken from the common of pastors, 1235, except for the following:

Evening Prayer I

HYMN, as in Evening Prayer II, 1248.

READING James 3:17-18

Wisdom from above is first of all innocent. It is also peaceable, lenient, docile, rich in sympathy and the kindly deeds that are its fruits, impartial and sincere. The harvest of justice is sown in peace for those who cultivate peace.

RESPONSORY (VI F)

The just *man* will speak * the wisdom he has pondered in *his* heart.
— The just *man* will speak * the wisdom he has pondered in *his* heart.
Truth will come *from* his lips,
— the wisdom he has pondered in *his* heart.
Glory to the Father, and *to* the Son, * and to the Ho*ly* Spirit.
— The just *man* will speak * the wisdom he has pondered in *his* heart.

Easter:
The just man will speak the wisdom he has pondered *in* his heart, * alleluia, al*le*luia.
— The just man will speak the wisdom he has pondered *in* his heart, * alleluia, al*le*luia.
Truth will come *from* his lips,
— alleluia, al*le*luia.
Glory to the Father, and *to* the Son, * and to the Ho*ly* Spirit.
— The just man will speak the wisdom he has pondered *in* his heart, * alleluia, al*le*luia.

CANTICLE OF MARY

Antiphon   The man who not only teaches but does *what* is right * will be counted great in the kingdom *of* God (al*le*luia).

Prayer, as in Morning Prayer.

Morning Prayer

HYMN

Doctor aeternus. (11.11.11.5)

Doctor æternus coleris piusque,
 Christe, qui leges aperis salutis,
 verba qui vitæ merito putaris
      solus habere.
	Jesus, our Teacher, loving Lord and Master,
	 In adoration we acclaim your precepts,
	 You alone offer words of life eternal,
	      Laws of salvation.

Teque clamamus, bone Pastor orbis,
 cælitus semper solidasse Sponsæ
 verba, constanter quibus illa mundo
      lumen adesset.
	Humbly we thank you, Shepherd through the ages,
	 For the protection to your Church extended,
	 Constantly guiding, that all souls may find there
	      Light in the darkness.

Ipse quin præbes famulos coruscos,
aureas stellas velut emicantes,
certa qui nobis reserent beatæ
    dogmata vitæ.

Unde te laudes recinant, Magister,
Spiritus fundis bona qui stupenda
ore doctorum, tua quo potenter
    lux patet alma.

Quique nunc iustus celebratur, instet
ut tuam plebem per amœna lucis
des gradi, donec tibi dicat hymnos
    lumine pleno. Amen.

Masters of learning were your eager servants,
Stars of great splendour with but one ambition,
Deeper to fathom and explain the wonders
    Of revelation.

All tongues should praise you, Jesus, divine Master,
Who lavish treasures from your Holy Spirit,
Through words and writings of the Church's doctors,
    Flame ever fruitful.

May this day's patron whom we gladly honor,
Ever be near us, leading on your people,
Till we all praise you, faith and hope rewarded,
    In light eternal. Amen.

READING   Wisdom 7:13-14

Simply I learned about Wisdom, and ungrudingly do I share—
    her riches I do not hide away;
For to men she is an unfailing treasure;
    those who gain this treasure win the friendship of God,
    to whom the gifts they have from discipline commend them.

RESPONSORY (VI F)

Let the peo*ples* proclaim * the wisdom of *the* saints.
— Let the peo*ples* proclaim * the wisdom of *the* saints.
With joyful praise let the *Church* tell forth
— the wisdom of *the* saints.
Glory to the Father, and *to* the Son, * and to the Ho*ly* Spirit.
— Let the peo*ples* proclaim * the wisdom of *the* saints.

Easter:

Let the peoples proclaim the wisdom *of* the saints, * alleluia, al*le*luia.
— Let the peoples proclaim the wisdom *of* the saints, * alleluia, al*le*luia.
With joyful praise let the *Church* tell forth
— alleluia, al*le*luia.
Glory to the Father, and *to* the Son, * and to the Ho*ly* Spirit.
— Let the peoples proclaim the wisdom *of* the saints, * alleluia, al*le*luia.

CANTICLE OF ZECHARIAH

Antiphon   Those *who* are learnèd * will be as radiant as the sky in all *its*
                beauty;
                those who instruct the peo*ple* in goodness * will shine like the
                stars for all *e*ternity (al*le*luia).

Prayer

If there is no proper prayer, the following is said:

Lord God,
you filled Saint N. with heavenly wisdom.
By his help may we remain true to his teaching
and put it into practice.
We ask this through our Lord Jesus Christ, your Son,
who lives and reigns with you and the Holy Spirit,
one God, for ever and ever.

Evening Prayer II

HYMN

Æterne Sol. (L.M.)

Æterne sol, qui lumine
creata comples omnia,
suprema lux et mentium,
te corda nostra concinunt.

Eternal Sun, true Light Divine,
Whose wisdom fills creation's plan,
We sing to you with joy this day,
The Light supreme of ev'ry soul.

Tu fovente Spiritu,
hic viva luminaria
fulsere, per quæ sæculis
patent salutis semitæ.

Your Holy Spirit's ardent fire
Inspired some chosen master minds,
To shed bright rays upon the world
And open up salvation's way.

Quod verba missa cælitus,
nativa mens quod exhibet,
per hos ministros gratiæ
novo nitore claruit.

Both inspiration from on high,
And efforts of deep human thought,
Have worked in harmony of grace
Developing our holy Faith.

Horum coronæ particeps,
doctrina honestus lucida,
hir vir beatus splenduit
quem prædicamus laudibus.

This saint and doctor whom we praise,
Shines out with lustre all her/his own,
A jewel in the favored crown
Of those who spread true doctrine's light.

Ipsum favente, quæsumus,
nobis Deus, percurrere
da veritatis tramitem,
possimus ut te consequi.

May her/his assistance help us too,
Unswerving path of truth to read,
That we at last may gaze on you,
Our God, for all eternity.

Præsta, Pater piissime,
Patrique compar Unice,
cum Spiritu Paraclito
regnans per omne sæculum. Amen.

Most tender Father, hear our prayer,
Whom we adore, with Christ the Lord,
And Holy Spirit of them both,
Bless us who praise your Trinity. Amen.

READING   James 3:17-18

Wisdom from above is first of all innocent. It is also peaceable, lenient, docile, rich in sympathy and the kindly deeds that are its fruits, impartial and sincere. The harvest of justice is sown in peace for those who cultivate peace.

RESPONSORY (VI F)

In the midst *of* the Church * he spoke *with* eloquence.
— In the midst *of* the Church * he spoke *with* eloquence.
The Lord filled him with the spirit of wisdom and *un*derstanding.
— He spoke *with* eloquence.
Glory to the Father, and *to* the Son, * and to the Ho*ly* Spirit.
— In the midst *of* the Church * he spoke *with* eloquence.

Easter:

In the midst of the Church he *spoke* with eloquence, * alleluia, al*le*luia.
— In the midst of the Church he *spoke* with eloquence,* alleluia, al*le*luia.
The Lord filled him with the spirit of wisdom and *un*derstanding,
— alleluia, al*le*luia.
Glory to the Father, and *to* the Son, * and to the Ho*ly* Spirit.
— In the midst of the Church he *spoke* with eloquence,* alleluia, al*le*luia.

CANTICLE OF MARY

Antiphon   O blessèd doctor, Saint N., † light of holy Church and lover *of* God's law, * pray to the Son of God *for* us (al*le*luia).

Prayer, as in Morning Prayer.

COMMON OF VIRGINS

Evening Prayer I

HYMN, as in Evening Prayer II, 1256.

PSALMODY

Ant. 1   Come, daughters, draw close *to* the Lord, * and share the splendor *of* his light (*al*leluia).

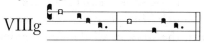

VIIIg

Psalm 113

Praise, O servants *of* the Lord, *
   praise the name *of* the Lord!
May the name of the *Lord* be blessed *
   both now and for *ever*more!
From the rising of the sun *to* its setting
   * praised be the name *of* the Lord!
High above all nations *is* the Lord, *
   above the heav*ens* his glory.
Who is like the *Lord*, our God, * who
   has risen on high *to* his throne
yet stoops from the heights *to* look
   down, * to look down upon heav*en*

and earth?
From the dust he lifts *up* the lowly, *
   from his misery he rais*es* the poor
to set him in the compa*ny* of princes, *
   yes, with the princes *of* his people.
To the childless wife he *gives* a home *
   and gladdens her *heart* with children.
Glory to the Father, and *to* the Son, *
   and to the *Holy* Spirit:
as it was in the begin*ning*, is now, * and
   will be for ev*er*. Amen.

Antiphon   Come, daughters, draw close *to* the Lord, * and share the splendor *of* his light (*al*leluia).

Ant. 2   With all our heart we follow you in awe; † we long to see you *face* to face. * Lord, do not disappoint *our* hope (al*l*eluia).

IIA

Psalm 147:12-20

O praise the *Lord*, Jerusalem! *
   Zion, praise *your* God!
He has strengthened the bars *of* your
   gates, * he has blessed the children
   *with*in you.
He established peace *on* your borders, *
   he feeds you with fin*est* wheat.
He sends out his word *to* the earth *

and swiftly runs his *com*mand.
He showers down snow *white* as wool, *
   he scatters hoar-frost *like* ashes.
He hurls down hail*stones* like crumbs. *
   The waters are frozen at *his* touch;
he sends forth his word *and* it melts
   them: * at the breath of his mouth
   the wa*ters* flow.

He makes his word *known* to Jacob, *
to Israel his laws and *de*crees.
He has not dealt thus with *o*ther
nations; * he has not taught them his
*de*crees.

Glory to the Father, and *to* the Son, *
and to the Ho*ly* Spirit:
as it was in the begin*ning*, is now, * and
will be for ever. *A*men.

Antiphon   With all our heart we follow you in awe; † we long to see you
face to face. * Lord, do not disappoint *our* hope (al*le*luia).

Ant. 3   Sing for joy, virgins *of* Christ; * he is your spouse for all *e*ternity
(al*le*luia).

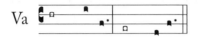

Va

Canticle   Ephesians 1:3-10

Praised be the God *and* Father * of
our Lord Je*sus* Christ,
who has bestowed on us *in* Christ *
every spiritual blessing in *the* heavens.
God chose us in him † before the
world *be*gan * to be holy and blameless in *his* sight.
He predestined us † to be his adopted
sons through Je*sus* Christ, * such was
his will *and* pleasure,
that all might praise the glori*ous* favor *
he has bestowed on us in his *be*lovèd.
In him and through his blood, † we
have been *re*deemed, * and our sins

*for*given,
so immeasura*bly* generous * is God's
favor *to* us.
God has given us the wisdom † to
understand fully *the* mystery, * the
plan he was pleased to decree *in*
Christ.
A plan to be carried out *in* Christ, * in
the fullness *of* time,
to bring all things into one *in* him, * in
the heavens and *on* earth.
Glory to the Father, and to *the* Son, *
and to the Ho*ly* Spirit:
as it was in the beginning, *is* now, * and
will be for ever. *A*men.

Antiphon   Sing for joy, virgins *of* Christ; * he is your spouse for all *e*ternity
(al*le*luia).

READING   1 Corinthians 7: 32b, 34a
The unmarried man is busy with the Lord's affairs, concerned with pleasing
the Lord. The virgin— indeed, any unmarried woman— is concerned with
things of the Lord, in pursuit of holiness in body and spirit.

RESPONSORY (VI F)
The Lord is *my* inheritance; * this I know in *my* heart.
— The Lord is *my* inheritance; * this I know in *my* heart.

The Lord is good to *those* who seek him;
— this I know in *my* heart.
Glory to the Father, and *to* the Son, * and to the Ho*ly* Spirit.
— The Lord is *my* inheritance; * this I know in *my* heart.

Easter:
The Lord is my inheritance; this I know *in* my heart, * alleluia, al*le*luia.
— The Lord is my inheritance; this I know *in* my heart, * alleluia, al*le*luia.
The Lord is good to *those* who seek him;
— alleluia, al*le*luia.
Glory to the Father, and *to* the Son, * and to the Ho*ly* Spirit.
— The Lord is my inheritance; this I know *in* my heart, * alleluia, al*le*luia.

CANTICLE OF MARY
For a virgin and martyr:

Antiphon   With courageous heart she fol*lowed* the Lamb, * who was
crucified for love *of* us;
she of*fered* herself * as a chaste and spot*less* victim (al*le*luia).

For a virgin:

Antiphon   When the Bridegroom came, † he found the wise *virgin* ready *
to enter the wedding feast *with* him (al*le*luia).

For several virgins:

Antiphon   Keep watch with love, wise virgins, with your lamps alight. †
See, the *Bride*groom comes; * go out *to* welcome him (al*le*luia).

INTERCESSIONS (VI F)
Christ extolled those who practiced virginity for the sake *of* the kingdom. * Let
     us praise him joyfully and *pray* to him:
*Jesus, example of vir*gins, *hear us.*
Christ, you presented the Church to yourself as a chaste virgin *to* her spouse,
— keep her holy *and* inviolate.
Christ, the holy virgins went out to meet you with their *lamps* alight,
— keep the fidelity of your consecrated handmaids *burn*ing brightly.
Lord, your virgin Church has always kept its faith whole *and* untarnished,
— grant all Christians a whole and un*tarn*ished faith.
You have given your people joy in celebrating the feast of your holy Virgin N.,
— give us contant joy through her *in*tercession.
You have admitted the holy virgins to your *mar*riage banquet,
— in your mercy lead the dead to your heaven*ly* feast.

Our Father . . .

Prayer, as in Morning Prayer.

Morning Prayer

HYMN

Aptata, virgo. (L.M.)

For several virgins, use *Iesu, corona virginum*, 1256.

Apata, virgo, lampade ad nuptias ingressa es æterni regis gloriæ, quem laudant turbæ cælicæ.	Your lamp of virtue, work and prayer, O virgin, pleasing to the King, Has won you favor in his sight, Whose glory all the angels sing.
Grata conviva superis, cælesti sponso iungeris, amplexu casti foederis, pudoris dives meritis.	As chosen bride of Spouse divine, The saints rejoice your face to see, His love has kept you for his own, By treasured grace of chastity.
Normam vivendi instrue, nos prece tua confove, possimus ut resistere hostis nostri versutiæ.	Teach us to live true Christian lives And help us with your fervent prayers That we may val'antly resist The wicked tempter's evil snares.
Exemplar vitæ virginum, Maria roget Filium, ut eius adiutorium nos iuvet per exsilium.	True model of a virgin's life, May holy Mary beg her Son To help us exiles here below Until our course on earth is run.
Sit Deitati gloria per infinita sæcula pro virginis victoria, qua gaudet cæli curia. Amen.	All glory be to God on high, Beyond the realms of time and space, Who added to the bliss above This virgin's triumph won by grace. Amen.

PSALMODY

Ant. 1   With my whole being I *wor*ship Christ; * I long for him and desire to be with *him* for ever (*al*leluia).

Psalms and canticle from Sunday, Week I, 606.

Ant. 2   O virgins, praise the Lord with all your heart. † He sowed the seeds *of* your virtue; * he crowned the fruits of your life with *his* gifts (al*le*luia).

Ant. 3   The saints will sing for joy in heav*en's* glory; * radiant is their victory over hu*man* frailties (al*le*luia).

READING   Song of Songs 8:7
    Deep waters cannot quench love,
        nor floods sweep it away.
    Were one to offer all he owns to purchase love,
        he would be roundly mocked.

RESPONSORY (VI F)

My heart is *ever* pleading, * show me *your* face.
— My heart is *ever* pleading, * show me *your* face.
I long to gaze up*on* you, Lord.
— Show me *your* face.
Glory to the Father, and *to* the Son, * and to the Ho*ly* Spirit.
— My heart is *ever* pleading, * show me *your* face.

Easter:

My heart is ever pleading, show *me* your face, * alleluia, al*le*luia.
— My heart is ever pleading, show *me* your face, * alleluia, al*le*luia.
I long to gaze up*on* you, Lord.
— alleluia, al*le*luia.
Glory to the Father, and *to* the Son, * and to the Ho*ly* Spirit.
— My heart is ever pleading, show *me* your face, * alleluia, al*le*luia.

CANTICLE OF ZECHARIAH

For a virgin martyr:

Antiphon   Happy the virgin who denied herself and took up her cross. †
                She imitat*ed* the Lord, * the spouse of virgins and prince *of*
                martyrs (al*le*luia).

For a virgin:

Antiphon   Now this wise virgin has gone to Christ. † Among the *choirs* of
                virgins * she is radiant as the sun in *the* heavens (al*le*luia).

For several virgins:

Antiphon   Virgins *of* the Lord, * bless the Lord *for* ever (al*le*luia).

INTERCESSIONS (VI F)

Christ is the spouse and crowning glo*ry* of virgins. * Let us praise him with joy
    in our voices and pray to him with sincerity *in* our hearts:
Jesus, crown of virgins, hear us.
Christ, the holy virgins loved you as their *one* true spouse,
    — grant that nothing may separate us *from* your love.
You crowned Mary, your mother, *queen* of virgins,
    — through her intercession, let us continually serve you *with* pure hearts.
Your handmaids were always careful to love you with whole and undivided
    attention, that they might be holy in bo*dy* and spirit,
    — through their intercession grant that the lure of this passing world may not
    distract our atten*tion* from you.
Lord Jesus, you are the spouse whose coming was anticipated by *the* wise virgins,
    — grant that we may wait for you in hope and *ex*pectation.

Through the intercession of Saint N., who was one of the wise and *prudent* virgins,
— grant us wisdom and inno*cence* of life.

Our Father . . .

Prayer

If there is no proper prayer, one of the following is said:

Lord,
you have told us that you live for ever
in the hearts of the chaste.
By the prayers of the virgin N.,
help us to live by your grace
and remain a temple of your Spirit.
Grant this through our Lord Jesus Christ, your Son,
who lives and reigns with you and the Holy Spirit,
one God, for ever and ever.

Or:

Lord,
hear the prayers of those who recall the devoted life of the virgin N.
Guide us on our way and help us to grow
in love and devotion as long as we live.
We ask this through our Lord Jesus Christ, your Son,
who lives and reigns with you and the Holy Spirit,
one God, for ever and ever.

For several virgins:

Lord, increase in us your gift of mercy and forgiveness.
May we who rejoice at this celebration in honor of the virgins N. and N.
receive the joy of sharing eternal life with them.
We ask this through our Lord Jesus Christ, your Son,
who lives and reigns with you and the Holy Spirit,
one God, for ever and ever.

Evening Prayer II

HYMN

Jesu, corona virginum. (L.M.)

Iesu, corona virginum,	O Crown of Virgins, Jesus Lord,
quem Mater illa concipit	Whom once a Virgin pure conceived,
quæ sola virgo parturit,	Whom Virgin Mary bore with joy,
hæc vota clemens accipe,	In mercy now receive our prayer.
Qui pascis inter lilia	As Spouse, of beauty past compare,
sæptus choreis virginum,	You feed among the lilies fair,
sponsus decorus gloria	Surrounded by those virgin souls
sponsisque reddens præmia.	Who dedicated all to you.
Quocumque pergis, virgines	They follow in a happy band
sequuntur, atque laudibus	Wherever you may choose to go,
post te canentes cursitant	And sing a canticle of joy,
hymnosque dulces personant.	A melody no others know.
Te deprecamur, largius	In tender pity hear our cry,
nostris adauge mentibus	Give us the graces that we need,
nescire prorsus omnia	Our hearts and minds to purify,
corruptionis vulnera.	To serve you in both word and deed.
Iesu, tibi sit gloria,	All honor, glory, virtue, praise
qui natus es de Virgine,	Resound to God in Persons Three,
cum Patre et almo Spiritu,	To Father, Son, and Spirit too,
in sempiterna sæcula. Amen.	In time and in eternity. Amen.

PSALMODY

Ant. 1   I have kept myself for you alone, † and now with *lamp* alight * I run to *meet* my Spouse (*al*leluia).

VIIIg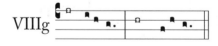

Psalm 122

I rejoiced when I *heard* them say: *
"Let us go *to* God's house."
And now our *feet* are standing * within
    your gates, O Jerusalem.
Jerusalem is built *as* a city * strong*ly*
    compact.
It is there that the *tribes* go up, * the
    tribes *of* the Lord.

For Israel's *law* it is, * there to praise
    the Lord's name.
There were set the *thrones* of judgment
    * of the *house* of David.
For the peace of Jerus*a*lem pray: *
    "Peace be *to* your homes!
May peace reign *in* your walls, * in
    your pal*a*ces, peace!"

For love of my bre*thren* and friends * I
  say: "*Peace* upon you!"
For love of the house *of* the Lord * I
  will ask *for* your good.

Glory to the Father, and *to* the Son, *
  and to the *Ho*ly Spirit:
as it was in the begin*ning*, is now, * and
  will be for ev*er*. Amen.

Antiphon   I have kept myself for you alone, † and now with *lamp* alight * I
             run to *meet* my Spouse (*al*leluia).

Ant. 2   Blessèd are the *pure* of heart, * for they shall *see* God (al*le*luia).

Psalm 127

If the Lord does not *build* the house,
  * in vain do its buil*ders* labor;
if the Lord does not watch ov*er* the
  city, * in vain does the watchman
  keep vigil.
In vain is your ear*lier* rising, * your
  going later *to* rest,
you who toil for the *bread* you eat: *
  when he pours gifts on his belovèd
  while *they* slumber.
Truly sons are a gift *from* the Lord, * a
  blessing, the fruit of *the* womb.

Indeed the *sons* of youth * are like
  arrows in the hand of *a* warrior.
O the happiness *of* the man * who has
  filled his quiver with *these* arrows!
He will have no *cause* for shame * when
  he disputes with his foes in *the*
  gateways.
Glory to the Father, and *to* the Son, *
  and to the Ho*ly* Spirit:
as it was in the begin*ning*, is now, * and
  will be for ever. *A*men.

Antiphon   Blessèd are the *pure* of heart, * for they shall *see* God (al*le*luia).

Ant. 3   My faith is firmly *es*tablished, * for I have built my life *on*
             Christ (al*le*luia).

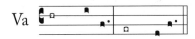

Canticle   Ephesians 1:3-10

Praised be the God *and* Father * of
  our Lord Je*sus* Christ,
who has bestowed on us *in* Christ *
  every spiritual blessing in *the* heavens.
God chose us in him † before the
  world *began* * to be holy and blame-

less in *his* sight.
He predestined us † to be his adopted
  sons through Je*sus* Christ, * such was
  his will *and* pleasure,
that all might praise the glor*ious* favor *
  he has bestowed on us in his *be*lovèd.
In him and through his blood, † we

have been *re*deemed, * and our sins *for*given,

so immeasura*bly* generous * is God's favor *to* us.

God has given us the wisdom † to understand fully *the* mystery, * the plan he was pleased to decree *in* Christ.

A plan to be carried out *in* Christ, * in the fullness *of* time,

to bring all things into one *in* him, * in the heavens and *on* earth.

Glory to the Father, and to *the* Son, * and to the Ho*ly* Spirit:

as it was in the beginning, *is* now, * and will be for ever. *A*men.

Antiphon   My faith is firmly *es*tablished, * for I have built my life *on* Christ (al*le*luia).

READING   1 Corinthians 7: 32b, 34a

The unmarried man is busy with the Lord's affairs, concerned with pleasing the Lord. The virgin— indeed, any unmarried woman— is concerned with things of the Lord, in pursuit of holiness in body and spirit.

RESPONSORY (VI F)

The virgins are led into the presence *of* the King, * amid gladness *and* joy.
— The virgins are led into the presence *of* the King, * amid gladness *and* joy.
They are brought into the King's *dwell*ing place,
— amid gladness *and* joy.
Glory to the Father, and *to* the Son, * and to the Ho*ly* Spirit.
— The virgins are led into the presence *of* the King, * amid gladness *and* joy.

Easter:

The virgins are led into the presence of the King, † amid glad*ness* and joy, * alleluia, al*le*luia.
— The virgins are led into the presence of the King, † amid glad*ness* and joy, * alleluia, al*le*luia.
The Lord is good to *those* who seek him;
— alleluia, al*le*luia.
Glory to the Father, and *to* the Son, * and to the Ho*ly* Spirit.
— The virgins are led into the presence of the King, † amid glad*ness* and joy, * alleluia, al*le*luia.

CANTICLE OF MARY

For a virgin and martyr:

Antiphon   In this one victim we hail the double crown of purity and devotion; † hers the glory *of* virginity, * hers the palm *of* martyrdom (al*le*luia).

For a virgin:

Antiphon   Come, spouse of Christ, † receive the crown the Lord has pre*pared* for you * from all *e*ternity (al*le*luia).

For several virgins:

Antiphon   These holy ones *seek* the Lord; * they long to see him face *to* face
                (al*le*luia).

INTERCESSIONS (VI F)

Christ extolled those who practiced virginity for the sake *of* the kingdom. * Let
  us praise him joyfully and *pray* to him:

Jesus, example of virgins, hear us.

Christ, you presented the Church to yourself as a chaste virgin *to* her spouse,
  — keep her holy *and* inviolate.

Christ, the holy virgins went out to meet you with their *lamps* alight,
  — keep the fidelity of your consecrated handmaids *burn*ing brightly.

Lord, your virgin Church has always kept its faith whole *and* untarnished,
  — grant all Christians a whole and un*tarn*ished faith.

You have given your people joy in celebrating the feast of your holy Virgin N.,
  — give us contant joy through her *in*tercession.

You have admitted the holy virgins to your *mar*riage banquet,
  — in your mercy lead the dead to your heav*en*ly feast.

Our Father . . .

Prayer, as in Morning Prayer.

COMMON OF HOLY MEN

Evening Prayer I

HYMN, as in Evening Prayer II, 1267.

PSALMODY

Ant. 1   All *you* saints sing, * sing praise *to* our God (*al*leluia).

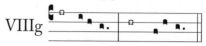

VIIIg

Psalm 113

Praise, O servants *of* the Lord, *
praise the name *of* the Lord!
May the name of the *Lord* be blessed *
both now and for *ev*ermore!
From the rising of the sun *to* its
setting * praised be the name *of* the
Lord!
High above all nations *is* the Lord, *
above the heav*ens* his glory.
Who is like the *Lord*, our God, * who
has risen on high *to* his throne
yet stoops from the heights *to* look

down, * to look down upon heav*en*
and earth?
From the dust he lifts *up* the lowly, *
from his misery he rais*es* the poor
to set him in the compan*y* of princes, *
yes, with the princes *of* his people.
To the childless wife he *gives* a home *
and gladdens her *heart* with children.
Glory to the Father, and *to* the Son, *
and to the *Ho*ly Spirit:
as it was in the begin*ning*, is now, * and
will be for *ev*er. Amen.

Antiphon   All *you* saints sing, * sing praise *to* our God (*al*leluia).

Ant. 2   Bless*èd* are they who hunger and *thirst* for holiness; * they will
be sat*is*fied (al*le*luia).

IIA

Psalm 146

My soul, give praise to the Lord; †
I will praise the Lord *all* my
days, * make music to my God while
I live.
Put no *trust* in princes, * in mortal men
in whom there is *no* help.
Take their breath, they re*turn* to clay *
and their plans that day come *to*
nothing.
He is happy who is helped by *Jacob's*

God, * whose hope is in the Lord *his*
God,
who alone made heav*en* and earth, * the
seas and all they *con*tain.
It is he who keeps *faith* for ever, * who
is just to those who are *op*pressed.
It is he who gives bread *to* the hungry,
* the Lord, who sets prison*ers* free,
the Lord who gives sight *to* the blind, *
who raises up those who are *bowed*

down,
the Lord, who pro*tects* the stranger *
 and upholds the widow *and* orphan.
It is the Lord who *loves* the just * but
 thwarts the path of *the* wicked.
The Lord will *reign* for ever, * Zion's

God, from age *to* age.
Glory to the Father, and *to* the Son, *
 and to the Ho*ly* Spirit:
as it was in the begin*ning*, is now, * and
 will be for ever. *A*men.

Antiphon   Blessèd are they who hunger and *thirst* for holiness; * they will
                 be sat*is*fied (al*le*luia).

Ant. 3   Blessèd be God! † He has chosen us to live *in* love, * holy and
                 without blemish in *his* sight (al*le*luia).

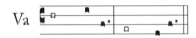

Canticle   Ephesians 1:3-10

Praised be the God *and* Father * of
 our Lord Je*sus* Christ,
who has bestowed on us *in* Christ *
 every spiritual blessing in *the* heavens.
God chose us in him † before the
 world *began* * to be holy and blameless in *his* sight.
He predestined us † to be his adopted
 sons through Je*sus* Christ, * such was
 his will *and* pleasure,
that all might praise the glori*ous* favor *
 he has bestowed on us in his be*lov*èd.
In him and through his blood, † we
 have been *re*deemed, * and our sins

for*gi*ven,
so immeasura*bly* generous * is God's
 favor *to* us.
God has given us the wisdom † to
 understand fully *the* mystery, * the
 plan he was pleased to decree *in*
 Christ.
A plan to be carried out *in* Christ, * in
 the fullness *of* time,
to bring all things into one *in* him, * in
 the heavens and *on* earth.
Glory to the Father, and to *the* Son, *
 and to the Ho*ly* Spirit:
as it was in the beginning, *is* now, * and
 will be for ever. *A*men.

Antiphon   Blessèd be God! † He has chosen us to live *in* love, * holy and
                 without blemish in *his* sight (al*le*luia).

READING   Philippians 3:7-8
   Those things I used to consider gain I have now reappraised as loss in the
   light of Christ. I have come to rate all as loss in the light of the surpassing
   knowledge of my Lord Jesus Christ. For his sake I have forfeited everything;
   I have accounted all else rubbish so that Christ may be my wealth.

RESPONSORY (VI F)

The *Lord* loved him, * and shared with him *his* glory.
— The *Lord* loved him, * and shared with him *his* glory.
He wrapped him in a *splen*did robe,
— and shared with him *his* glory.
Glory to the Father, and *to* the Son, * and to the Ho*ly* Spirit.
— The *Lord* loved him, * and shared with him *his* glory.

Easter:

The Lord loved him, and shared with *him* his glory, * alleluia, al*le*luia.
— The Lord loved him, and shared with *him* his glory, * alleluia, al*le*luia.
He wrapped him in a *splen*did robe,
— alleluia, al*le*luia.
Glory to the Father, and *to* the Son, * and to the Ho*ly* Spirit.
— The Lord loved him, and shared with *him* his glory, * alleluia, al*le*luia.

CANTICLE OF MARY

Antiphon   He is like *the* wise man * who built his house up*on* rock (al*le*-
                luia).

For several holy men:

Antiphon   The eyes of the Lord are on *those* who fear him, * on those who
                hope in *his* mercy (al*le*luia).

INTERCESSIONS (VI F)

Let us pray to the Father, the source *of* all holiness, * and ask him to lead us to
    holiness of life through the example and intercession *of* his saints:
May we be holy as you are *holy.*
Holy Father, you want us to be called your sons and truly *to* be such,
— grant that your holy Church may proclaim you through*out* the world.
Holy Father, you want us to walk worthily and please you in *all* we do,
— let us abound in do*ing* good works.
Holy Father, you have reconciled us to your*self* through Christ,
— preserve us in your name so that all *may* be one.
Holy Father, you have called us to a heaven*ly* banquet,
— through the bread that came down from heaven make us worthy to grow in
    *per*fect love.
Holy Father, forgive the offenses of *every* sinner,
— let the dead perceive the light *of* your countenance.

Our Father . . .

Prayer, as in Morning Prayer.

Morning Prayer

HYMN

Jesu, corona celsior. (L.M.)

Iesu, corona celsior	O Jesus, Crown of all, Most High,
et veritas sublimior,	And Truth sublime, surpassing all,
qui confitenti servulo	You give reward that has no end
reddis perenne præmium,	To those that love and praise your Name.
Da supplicanti cœtui,	Through intercession of this Saint,
huius rogatu cælitis,	Give unto us who grace implore
remissionem criminum	Remission of our daily sins,
rumpendo nexum vinculi.	And break the bonds that hold us fast.
Nil vanitatis diligens,	He gave no thought to vanities,
terrena sic exercuit,	But lived and toiled while here below,
ut mente tota fervidus	To please you only, day by day
tibi placeret unice.	While love for you inspir'd each deed.
Te, Christe, rex piissime,	Most gracious King, Lord Jesus Christ,
hic confitendo iugiter,	By ever clinging to your law,
calcavit hostem fortiter	He overcame the demon proud,
superbum ac satellitem.	By strength you gave him for the fight.
Virtute clarus et fide,	Made perfect by deep faith and prayer,
orationi sedulus	And virtue's constant energy,
ac membra servans sobria,	Your love has summoned him to share
dapes supernas obtinet.	The joyous festival above.
Deo Patri sit gloria	To God the Father glory be,
tibique soli Filio	And glory to his only Son,
cum Spiritu Paraclito,	The Holy Spirit too be praised
in sempiterna sæcula. Amen.	Both now and for eternity. Amen.

Or, for several holy men:

Beata cæli gaudia. (L.M.)

Beata cæli gaudia,	Most faithful followers of Christ,
confessionis præmium,	And keen disciples of our Lord,
Christi o fideles asseclæ,	In heaven's bliss and endless peace
iam possidetis affatim.	You now enjoy a full reward.
Laudes benignis auribus	Our minds and hearts in unison,
audite, quas effundimus	In sacred canticle we raise,
nos exsules de patria	With kindly ear for exiles' prayer,
vobis sacrato cantico.	Accept our lowly hymn of praise.

Amore Christi perciti	Led on by ardent love for Christ,
crucem tulistis asperam,	The rugged Cross you bravely bore,
obœdientes, impigri	With diligence, obedient,
et caritate fervidi.	With charity as ruling law.
Sprevistis artes dæmonum	You spurned proud Satan and his fiends,
fallaciasque sæculi;	And all that earth would call delight;
Christum fatendo moribus	Confessing Christ, you entrance won
migrastis inter sidera.	To realms of everlasting light.
Iam nunc potiti gloria	The glory that you now possess,
adeste votis omnium	Help us, your followers, to gain,
ardenter exoptantium	That eager in the path you trod,
exempla vestra prosequi.	Eternal life they may obtain.
Sit Trinitati gloria,	All glory to the Trinity,
quæ pro sua clementia	Who with the Godhead's boundless love,
vobisque suffragantibus	In answer to your earnest prayers,
nos ducat ad cælestia. Amen.	Will lead us to our home above. Amen.

PSALMODY

Ant. 1   The Lord has given them un*end*ing glory; * their name shall be in everlast*ing* remembrance (*al*leluia).

Psalms and canticle from Sunday, Week I, 606.

Ant. 2   Servants *of* the Lord, * bless the Lord *for* ever (al*l*eluia).

Ant. 3   The saints will exult in glory; † they will sing *for* joy * as they bow down before *the* Lord (al*l*eluia).

READING   Romans 12:1-2

Brothers, I beg you through the mercy of God to offer your bodies as a living sacrifice holy and acceptable to God, your spiritual worship. Do not conform yourselves to this age but be transformed by the renewal of your mind, so that you may judge what is God's will, what is good, pleasing and perfect.

RESPONSORY (VI F)

In the depths *of* his heart, * the law of God is *his* guide.
— In the depths *of* his heart, * the law of God is *his* guide.
He will never *lose* his way;
— the law of God is *his* guide.
Glory to the Father, and *to* the Son, * and to the Ho*ly* Spirit.
— In the depths *of* his heart, * the law of God is *his* guide.

Easter:
In the depths of his heart, † the law of God *is* his guide, * alleluia, al*l*eluia.
— In the depths of his heart, † the law of God *is* his guide, * alleluia, al*l*eluia.
He will never *lose* his way;
— alleluia, al*l*eluia.
Glory to the Father, and *to* the Son, * and to the Ho*ly* Spirit.
— In the depths of his heart, † the law of God *is* his guide, * alleluia, al*l*eluia.

For several holy men:
Let the *just* rejoice * in the presence *of* God.
— Let the *just* rejoice * in the presence *of* God.
Let them be *filled* with gladness,
— Let the *just* rejoice * in the presence *of* God.
Glory to the Father, and *to* the Son, * and to the Ho*ly* Spirit.
— Let the *just* rejoice * in the presence *of* God

For several holy men, in the Easter Season:
Let the just rejoice in the pres*ence* of God, * alleluia, al*l*eluia.
— Let the just rejoice in the pres*ence* of God, * alleluia, al*l*eluia.
Let them be *filled* with gladness,
— alleluia, al*l*eluia.
Glory to the Father, and *to* the Son, * and to the Ho*ly* Spirit.
— Let the just rejoice in the pres*ence* of God, * alleluia, al*l*eluia.

CANTICLE OF ZECHARIAH
Antiphon   The man of God wel*comes* the light * that searches his deeds and finds *them* true (al*l*eluia).

For several holy men:
Antiphon   Blessèd are the peacemakers, † and blessèd are the *pure* of heart; * they shall *see* God (al*l*eluia).

INTERCESSIONS (VI F)
My brothers, let us praise Christ, asking to serve him and to be holy and righteous in his sight all the days *of* our life. * Let *us* acclaim him:
Lord, you alone are the holy one.
You desired to experience everything we experi*ence* but sin,
— have mercy on *us*, Lord Jesus.
You called us *to* love perfectly,
— make us ho*ly*, Lord Jesus.
You commissioned us to be the salt of the earth and the light *of* the world,
— let your light shine on *us*, Lord Jesus.
You desired to serve, not *to* be served,
— help us, Lord Jesus, to give humble service to you and *to* our neighbors.

You are in the form of God sharing in the splendor *of* the Father,
— Lord Jesus, let us see the glory *of* your face.

Our Father . . .

Prayer

If there is no proper prayer, one of the following is said:

> God our Father,
> you alone are holy;
> without you nothing is good.
> Trusting in the prayers of Saint N.
> we ask you to help us
> to become the holy people you call us to be.
> Never let us be found undeserving
> of the glory you have prepared for us.
> We ask this through our Lord Jesus Christ, your Son,
> who lives and reigns with you and the Holy Spirit,
> one God, for ever and ever.

Or:

> All-powerful God,
> help us who celebrate the memory of Saint N.
> to imitate his way of life.
> May the example of your saints
> be our challenge to live holier lives.
> Grant this through our Lord Jesus Christ, your Son,
> who lives and reigns with you and the Holy Spirit,
> one God, for ever and ever.

For several holy men:

> Ever-living God,
> the signs of your love are manifest
> in the honor you give your saints.
> May their prayers and their example encourage us
> to follow your Son more faithfully.
> Grant this through our Lord Jesus Christ, your Son,
> who lives and reigns with you and the Holy Spirit,
> one God, for ever and ever.

For a religious:

> Lord God,
> you kept Saint N. faithful to Christ's pattern of poverty and humility.
> May his prayers help us to live in fidelity to our calling
> and bring us to the perfection you have shown us in your Son,
> who lives and reigns with you and the Holy Spirit,
> one God, for ever and ever.

For one who worked for the underprivileged:

Lord God,
you teach us that the commandments of heaven
are summarized in love of you and love of our neighbor.
By following the example of Saint N.
in practicing works of charity
may we be counted among the blessèd in your kingdom.
Grant this through our Lord Jesus Christ, your Son,
who lives and reigns with you and the Holy Spirit,
one God, for ever and ever.

For a teacher:

Lord God,
you called Saint N. to serve you in the Church
by teaching his fellow man the way of salvation.
Inspire us by his example:
help us to follow Christ our teacher,
and lead us to our brothers and sisters in heaven.
We ask this through our Lord Jesus Christ, your Son,
who lives and reigns with you and the Holy Spirit,
one God, for ever and ever.

Evening Prayer II

HYMN

Iesu, redemptor omnium. (L.M.)

Iesu, redemptor omnium,
perpes corona cælitum,
in ac die clementius
nostris faveto vocibus,

Sacre tui qua nominis
confessor almus claruit,
cuius celebrat annua
devota plebs sollemnia.

Per illa quæ sunt sæculi
gressu sereno transiit,
tibi fidelis iugiter
iter salutis persequens.

At rite mundi gaudiis
non cor caducis applicans,
cum angelis cælestibus
lætus potitur præmiis.

O Jesus, man's Redeemer kind,
Eternal Crown of all the saints,
Upon this joyful festal day
Heed yet more graciously our prayer.

For we, your People, celebrate
The feast of one who loved you well,
And for the honor of your Name
Sought first your Kingdom of all good.

Through all the snares the world presents
He passed unruffled and unharmed,
Pursuing true salvation's path,
Remaining faithful to the last.

He dallied not with things of earth,
Nor set his heart on passing joys,
And now with angels choirs above
He joyously obtains reward.

Huius benignus annue	Grant us the grace we beg and pray,
nobis sequi vestigia;	To follow in his footsteps sure,
huius precatu servulis	And by his intercession too,
dimitte noxam criminis.	Forgive us when we go astray.

Sit, Christe, rex piissime,	O Christ our King and tender Lord,
tibi Patrique gloria	All glory ever be to you,
cum Spiritu Paraclito,	Who with the Holy Spirit reign
in sempiterna sæcula. Amen.	With God the Father's might supreme. Amen.

PSALMODY

Ant. 1   God found him *pure* and strong; * he will have ever*last*ing glory
(*al*leluia).

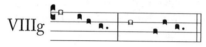

VIIIg

Psalm 15

Lord, who shall be admitted *to* your tent * and dwell on your *holy* mountain?	honors those who *fear* the Lord;
He who walks *with*out fault; * he who *acts* with justice	he who keeps his pledge, *come* what may; * who takes no interest *on* a loan
and speaks the truth *from* his heart; * he who does not slander *with* his tongue;	and accepts no bribes *against* the innocent. * Such a man will stand *firm* for ever.
he who does no wrong *to* his brother, * who casts no slur *on* his neighbor,	Glory to the Father, and *to* the Son, * and to the *Holy* Spirit:
who holds the godless *in* disdain, * but	as it was in the begin*ning*, is now, * and will be for ev*er*. Amen.

Antiphon   God found him *pure* and strong; * he will have ever*last*ing glory
(*al*leluia).

Ant. 2   God's saints will be filled with his *love* and mercy; * he watches
over his cho*sen* ones (al*le*luia).

IIA

Psalm 112

| Happy the man who *fears* the Lord, * who takes delight in all his *com*mands. | the children of the upright *are* blessèd. |
| His sons will be power*ful* on earth; * | Riches and wealth are *in* his house; * his justice stands firm *for* ever. |

He is a light in the darkness *for* the
   upright: * he is generous, merciful
   and just.
The good man takes pi*ty* and lends, *
   he conducts his affairs *with* honor.
The just man will *never* waver: * he
   will be remembered *for* ever.
He has no fear of *evil* news; * with a
   firm heart he trusts in *the* Lord.
With a steadfast heart he *will* not fear;
   * he will see the downfall of *his* foes.

Open-handed, he gives to the poor; †
   his justice stands *firm* for ever. * His
   head will be raised *in* glory.
The wicked man sees and is angry, †
   grinds his teeth and *fades* away; * the
   desire of the wicked leads *to* doom.
Glory to the Father, and *to* the Son, *
   and to the Ho*ly* Spirit:
as it was in the begin*ning*, is now, * and
   will be for ever. *A*men.

Antiphon   God's saints will be filled with his *love* and mercy; * he watches
              over his chos*en* ones (al*le*luia).

Ant. 3   The whole earth echoes with the melody of heaven † where the
              saints *are* singing * before the throne of God and *the* Lamb
              (al*le*luia).

Va

                        Canticle   Revelation 15:3-4

Mighty and wonderful are *your*
   works, * Lord God *Al*mighty!
Righteous and true are *your* ways, * O
   King of *the* nations!
Who would dare refuse *you* honor, * or
   the glory due your name, O Lord?
Since you alone *are* holy, * all nations

shall come and worship in *your*
   presence.
Your mighty deeds * are clear*ly* seen.
Glory to the Father, and to *the* Son, *
   and to the Ho*ly* Spirit:
as it was in the beginning, *is* now, * and
   will be for ever. *A*men.

Antiphon   The whole earth echoes with the melody of heaven † where the
              saints *are* singing * before the throne of God and *the* Lamb
              (al*le*luia).

READING   Romans 8:28-30
   We know that God makes all things work together for the good of those
   who have been called according to his decree. Those whom he foreknew he
   predestined to share the image of his Son, that the Son might be the first-
   born of many brothers. Those he predestined he likewise called; those he
   called he also justified; and those he justified he in turn glorified.

RESPONSORY (VI F)
Just *is* the Lord, * in justice he *de*lights.
—Just *is* the Lord, * in justice he *de*lights.

He looks with favor on the *up*right man;
— in justice he *de*lights.
Glory to the Father, and *to* the Son, * and to the Ho*ly* Spirit.
— Just *is* the Lord, * in justice he *de*lights.

Easter:
Just is the Lord, in justice *he* delights, * alleluia, al*le*luia.
— Just is the Lord, in justice *he* delights, * alleluia, al*le*luia.
He looks with favor on the *up*right man;
— alleluia, al*le*luia.
Glory to the Father, and *to* the Son, * and to the Ho*ly* Spirit.
— Just is the Lord, in justice *he* delights, * alleluia, al*le*luia.

CANTICLE OF MARY
Antiphon   Good and *faith*ful servant, * enter into the joy of *your* Lord
                (al*le*luia).

For several holy men:
Antiphon   These holy ones persevered even *un*to death; * the Lord has
                bestowed on them the crown *of* life (al*le*luia).

INTERCESSIONS (VI F)
Let us pray to the Father, the source *of* all holiness, * and ask him to lead us to
    holiness of life through the example and intercession *of* his saints:
May we be holy as you are *holy.*
Holy Father, you want us to be called your sons and truly *to* be such,
    — grant that your holy Church may proclaim you through*out* the world.
Holy Father, you want us to walk worthily and please you in *all* we do,
    — let us abound in do*ing* good works.
Holy Father, you have reconciled us to your*self* through Christ,
    — preserve us in your name so that all *may* be one.
Holy Father, you have called us to a heaven*ly* banquet,
    — through the bread that came down from heaven make us worthy to grow in
    *per*fect love.
Holy Father, forgive the offenses of *every* sinner,
    — let the dead perceive the light *of* your countenance.

Our Father . . .

Prayer, as in Morning Prayer.

COMMON OF HOLY WOMEN

Evening Prayer I

HYMN, as in Evening Prayer II, 1278.

PSALMODY

Ant. 1   Blessèd *be* the Lord; * he has filled his handmaid *with* his mercy (*al*leluia).

VIIIg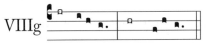

Psalm 113

Praise, O servants *of* the Lord, *
    praise the name *of* the Lord!
May the name of the *Lord* be blessed *
    both now and for *ever*more!
From the rising of the sun *to* its setting
    * praised be the name *of* the Lord!
High above all nations *is* the Lord, *
    above the heav*ens* his glory.
Who is like the *Lord*, our God, * who
    has risen on high *to* his throne
yet stoops from the heights *to* look
    down, * to look down upon heav*en*

and earth?
From the dust he lifts *up* the lowly, *
    from his misery he rais*es* the poor
to set him in the company of princes, *
    yes, with the princes *of* his people.
To the childless wife he *gives* a home *
    and gladdens her *heart* with children.
Glory to the Father, and *to* the Son, *
    and to the *Holy* Spirit:
as it was in the begin*ning*, is now, * and
    will be for *ever*. Amen.

Antiphon   Blessèd *be* the Lord; * he has filled his handmaid *with* his mercy (*al*leluia).

Ant. 2   Give glory to the *Lord*, Jerusalem; * he has blessed every child *with*in you (al*le*luia).

IIA

Psalm 147:12-20

O praise the *Lord*, Jerusalem! *
    Zion, praise *your* God!
He has strengthened the bars *of* your
    gates, * he has blessed the children
    *with*in you.
He established peace *on* your borders, *
    he feeds you with fin*est* wheat.
He sends out his word *to* the earth *

and swiftly runs his *com*mand.
He showers down snow *white* as wool, *
    he scatters hoar-frost *like* ashes.
He hurls down hail*stones* like crumbs. *
    The waters are frozen at *his* touch;
he sends forth his word *and* it melts
    them: * at the breath of his mouth
    the wa*ters* flow.

He makes his word *known* to Jacob, *
to Israel his laws and *de*crees.
He has not dealt thus with *o*ther
nations; * he has not taught them his
*de*crees.

Glory to the Father, and *to* the Son, *
and to the Ho*ly* Spirit:
as it was in the begin*ning*, is now, * and
will be for ever. *A*men.

Antiphon   Give glory to the *Lord*, Jerusalem; * he has blessed every child *with*in you (al*le*luia).

Ant. 3   The Lord delights *in* you; * you are the joy of *his* heart (al*le*luia).

Va

Canticle
Ephesians 1:3-10

Praised be the God *and* Father * of
our Lord Je*sus* Christ,
who has bestowed on us *in* Christ *
every spiritual blessing in *the* heavens.
God chose us in him † before the
world *be*gan * to be holy and blameless in *his* sight.
He predestined us † to be his adopted
sons through Je*sus* Christ, * such was
his will *and* pleasure,
that all might praise the glori*ous* favor *
he has bestowed on us in his *be*lovèd.
In him and through his blood, † we
have been *re*deemed, * and our sins

*for*given,
so immeasura*bly* generous * is God's
favor *to* us.
God has given us the wisdom † to
understand fully *the* mystery, * the
plan he was pleased to decree *in*
Christ.
A plan to be carried out *in* Christ, * in
the fullness *of* time,
to bring all things into one *in* him, * in
the heavens and *on* earth.
Glory to the Father, and to *the* Son, *
and to the Ho*ly* Spirit:
as it was in the beginning, *is* now, * and
will be for ever. *A*men.

Antiphon   The Lord delights *in* you; * you are the joy of *his* heart (al*le*luia).

READING   Philippians 3:7-8

Those things I used to consider gain I have now reappraised as loss in the light of Christ. I have come to rate all as loss in the light of the surpassing knowledge of my Lord Jesus Christ. For his sake I have forfeited everything; I have accounted all else rubbish so that Christ may be my wealth.

RESPONSORY (VI F)

Joy and gladness *fill* my heart; * the Lord has been merciful *to* me.
— Joy and gladness *fill* my heart; * the Lord has been merciful *to* me.

He has looked with favor on his *lowly* servant.
— The Lord has been merciful *to* me.
Glory to the Father, and *to* the Son, * and to the Ho*ly* Spirit.
— Joy and gladness *fill* my heart; * the Lord has been merciful *to* me.

Easter:
Joy and gladness fill my heart; † the Lord has been merci*ful* to me, * alleluia, al*le*luia.
— Joy and gladness fill my heart; † the Lord has been merci*ful* to me, * alleluia, al*le*luia.
The Lord has been merciful *to* me.
— alleluia, al*le*luia.
Glory to the Father, and *to* the Son, * and to the Ho*ly* Spirit.
— Joy and gladness fill my heart; † the Lord has been merci*ful* to me, * alleluia, al*le*luia.

CANTICLE OF MARY
Antiphon   Give her the reward *of* her deeds; * they will proclaim as she
               enters *the* gates (al*le*luia).

For several holy women:
Antiphon   Praise the holy name *of* the Lord; * the heart that seeks him will
               re*joice* (al*le*luia).

INTERCESSIONS (VI F)
Through the intercession of *holy* women, * let us pray for the Church *in* these
     words:
Be mindful of your Church, O Lord.
Through all the women martyrs who have conquered bodily death *by* their
     courage,
— strengthen your Church in the *hour* of trial.
Through married women who have advanced in grace by *holy* matrimony,
— make the apostolic mission of *your* Church fruitful.
Through widows who eased their loneliness and sanctified it by prayer and
     *hos*pitality,
— help your Church reveal the mystery of your love *to* the world.
Through mothers who have borne children for the kingdom of God and the
     hu*man* community,
— help your Church bring all men and women to a rebirth in life *and* salva-
     tion.
Through all your holy women who have been worthy to contemplate the light *of*
     your countenance,
— let the deceased members of your Church exult in that same *vision* for ever.

Our Father . . .

Prayer, as in Morning Prayer.

Morning Prayer

HYMN

Nobilem Christi. (11.11.11.5)

Nobilem Christi famulam diserta
voce cantemus, decus æmulatam
feminæ fortis, sacra cui profudit
pagina laudes.

Cui fides vivax, pia spes amorque
in Deum fervens, operum bonorum
fertilis radix amor unde fratrum
nascitur ultro.

Motus illius meritis, remitte,
sontibus nobis scelus omne, Iesu,
ut tibi puro resonemus æquas
pectore laudes.

Sit Patri summo decus atque virtus,
laus tibi Nato celebrisque cultus,
Flamini Sancto parilis potestas
nunc et in ævum. Amen.

Eloquent praises let us sing together,
Following Scripture which extols the virtues
Proved by the actions of a valiant woman
Strong and yet gentle.

Hope that was equal to her faith deep rooted,
Urged her to love God and to serve her neighbor,
Charity prompting her to works of mercy,
Root of all virtues.

Moved by her merits, Jesus, we implore you,
Pardon our failings, smile upon the guilty,
That we may praise you with a fervor equal
To her intentions.

Praise to the Father, honor and all glory,
Praise to you, Jesus, God the Son, our Savior,
Praise to the Spirit, with our deepest homage,
Now and for ever. Amen.

Or, for several holy women:

Nobiles Christi famulas diserta
voce cantemus, decus æmulatas
feminæ fortis, sacra cui profudit
pagina laudes.

Non eas mundus laqueis revincit,
iussa quæ Patris subeunt volentes,
ut bonum Christi satagant ubique
spargere odorem.

Edomant corpus, precibusque mentem
nutriunt sanctis; peritura temnunt
lucra, ut inquirant sibi permanentis
præmia vitæ.

Sit Deo soli decus et potestas,
laus in excelsis honor ac perennis,
qui suis totum moderans gubernat
legibus orbem. Amen.

Eloquent praises let us sing together,
Following Scripture which extols the virtues
Proved by the actions of these valiant women
Strong and yet gentle.

Worldly attractions never could ensnare them,
Steadfast and earnest to obey the Father,
Their sole endeavor was to spread the fragrance
Christ's law diffuses.

By self-denial, over coming nature,
Bravely they conquered all desire for riches,
Prayer led them onward, to its lofty summits,
Longing for heaven.

Glory and honor be to God Almighty,
Praise in the highest, power and dominion,
Who in his wisdom rules and governs all things
His love created. Amen.

PSALMODY

Ant. 1   My soul *clings* to you; * with your right hand you have *raised* me up (*al*leluia).

Psalms and canticle from Sunday, Week I, 606.

Ant. 2   The hand of the Lord has giv*en* you strength; * you will be
                praised *for* ever (al*le*luia).

Ant. 3   Lord, I shall rejoice and *be* glad, * for you have been merciful *to*
                me (al*le*luia).

READING   Romans 12:1-2

Brothers, I beg you through the mercy of God to offer your bodies as a
living sacrifice holy and acceptable to God, your spiritual worship. Do not
conform yourselves to this age but be transformed by the renewal of your
mind, so that you may judge what is God's will, what is good, pleasing and
perfect.

RESPONSORY (VI F)

The *Lord* will help her; * his loving presence will *be* with her.
— The *Lord* will help her; * his loving presence will *be* with her.
He dwells in her; she *will* not falter.
— His loving presence will *be* with her.
Glory to the Father, and *to* the Son, * and to the Ho*ly* Spirit.
— The *Lord* will help her; * his loving presence will *be* with her.

Easter:
The Lord will help her; † his loving presence *will* be with her, * alleluia, al*le*luia.
— The Lord will help her; † his loving presence *will* be with her, * alleluia, al*le*luia.
He dwells in her; she *will* not falter,
— alleluia, al*le*luia.
Glory to the Father, and *to* the Son, * and to the Ho*ly* Spirit.
— The Lord will help her; † his loving presence *will* be with her, * alleluia, al*le*luia.

For several holy women:
Let the *just* rejoice * in the presence *of* God.
— Let the *just* rejoice * in the presence *of* God.
Let them be *filled* with gladness,
— in the presence *of* God.
Glory to the Father, and *to* the Son, * and to the Ho*ly* Spirit.
— Let the *just* rejoice * in the presence *of* God.

For several holy women, in the Easter Season:
Let the just rejoice in the pres*ence* of God, * alleluia, al*le*luia.
— Let the just rejoice in the pres*ence* of God, * alleluia, al*le*luia.
Let them be *filled* with gladness,
— alleluia, al*le*luia.
Glory to the Father, and *to* the Son, * and to the Ho*ly* Spirit.
— Let the just rejoice in the pres*ence* of God, * alleluia, al*le*luia.

CANTICLE OF ZECHARIAH

Antiphon   The kingdom of heaven is like a merchant seeking fine pearls; †
he finds one *of* great value * and gives all that he has to *pos*sess it
(al*le*luia).

INTERCESSIONS (VI F)

My brothers and sisters with all the holy women, * let us profess our faith in
our Savior and *call* upon him:

Come, Lord *Jesus.*

Lord Jesus, you forgave the sinful woman because *she* loved much,
— forgive us *who* have sinned much.

Lord Jesus, the holy women ministered to your needs dur*ing* your journeys,
— help us to fol*low* your footsteps.

Lord Jesus, Master, Mary listened to your words while Martha *served* your
needs,
— help us to serve you with love *and* devotion.

Lord Jesus, you call everyone who does your will your brother, sis*ter* and mother,
— help us to do what is pleasing to you in *word* and action.

Our Father . . .

Prayer

If there is no proper prayer, one of the following is said:

God our Father,
every year you give us joy on this feast of Saint N.
As we honor her memory by this celebration,
may we follow the example of her holy life.
We ask this through our Lord Jesus Christ, your Son,
who lives and reigns with you and the Holy Spirit,
one God, for ever and ever.

Or:

Lord,
pour upon us the spirit of wisdom and love
with which you filled your servant Saint N.
By serving you as she did,
may we please you with our faith and our actions.
Grant this through our Lord Jesus Christ, your Son,
who lives and reigns with you and the Holy Spirit,
one God, for ever and ever.

For several holy women:

All-powerful God,
may the prayers of Saints N. and N. bring us help from heaven
as their lives have already given us

an example of holiness.
We ask this through our Lord Jesus Christ, your Son,
who lives and reigns with you and the Holy Spirit,
one God, for ever and ever.

For a religious:
Lord God,
you kept Saint N. faithful to Christ's pattern of poverty and humility.
May her prayers help us to live in fidelity to our calling
and bring us to the perfection you have shown us in your Son,
who lives and reigns with you and the Holy Spirit,
one God, for ever and ever.

For one who worked for the underpriviledged:
Lord God,
you teach us that the commandments of heaven
are summarized in love of you and love of our neighbor.
By following the example of Saint N.
in practicing works of charity
may we be counted among the blessèd in your kingdom.
Grant this through our Lord Jesus Christ, your Son,
who lives and reigns with you and the Holy Spirit,
one God, for ever and ever.

For a teacher:
Lord God,
you called Saint N. to serve you in the Church
by teaching her fellow man the way of salvation.
Inspire us by her example:
help us to follow Christ our teacher,
and lead us to our brothers and sisters in heaven.
We ask this through our Lord Jesus Christ, your Son,
who lives and reigns with you and the Holy Spirit,
one God, for ever and ever.

Evening Prayer II

HYMN

Fortem virili pectore. (L.M.)

Fortem virili pectore laudemus omnes feminam, quæ sanctitatis gloria ubique fuget inclita.	A valiant woman, strong by grace, Unites us all in praise this day, The glory of her holiness Sheds far and wide its sacred ray.
Hæc sancto amore saucia, huius caduca sæculi dum calcat, ad cælestia iter peregit arduum.	Her heart aglow with holy love, The glamour of this earth she spurned, And chose the hard and narrow way To reach the home for which she yearned.
Carnem domans ieiuniis, dulcique mentem pabulo orationis nutriens, cæli potitur gaudiis.	By fasts and prayer she overcame Our fallen nature's downward trend, She fed her soul with constant prayer That heavenwards her mind should tend.
Rex Christe, virtus fortium, qui magna solus efficis, huius precatu, quæsumus, audi benignus supplices.	O Jesus, King and Source of strength, Great things are done by You alone, So to her supplication's praise We humbly strive to join our own.
Iesu, tibi sit gloria, qui nos beatæ servulæ sperare das suffragia et sempiterna præmia. Amen.	All glory, Jesus, be to you, For through your holy handmaid's love, You give us hope for our reward And everlasting joy above. Amen.

Or for several holy women: (11.11.11.5)

Christe, cunctorum sator et redemptor,
siderum, terræ, maris atque rector
omnium laudes tibi personantum
    solve reatum,
	Christ, our Redeemer, Ruler of creation,
	Bright constellations sparkle for your glory,
	Land and sea worship, pardon us your creatures,
	    Singing your praises.

Vase qui gemmas fragili recondis,
viribus fluxas animo pudicas
feminas reddens faciensque claros
    ferre triumphos.
	Frail are the caskets chosen by your mercy,
	As humble settings for your fairest jewels,
	Making pure women strong against temptation,
	    Conquering evil.

Quas et in sensu teneras videmus,
prærogativa meriti coronas,
incolas regni facis et perennes
    esse superni.
	Those whom the world sees as unarmed for combat,
	You crown with merits won by grace and effort,
	Sharing the Kingdom of eternal glory,
	    Promised for ever.

Sit Patri summo decus atque virtus,
laud tibi Nato celebrisque cultus,
Flamini Sancto parilis potestas
    nune et in ævum. Amen.
	Praise to the Father, honor and all glory,
	Praise to you, Jesus, God the Son, and Savior,
	Praise to the Spirit, with our deepest homage,
	    Now and for ever. Amen.

PSALMODY

Ant. 1   Now your servant re*joices*, Lord, * for *you* have saved her
                         (*a*lleluia).

VIIIg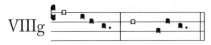

Psalm 122

I rejoiced when I *heard* them say: *
"Let us go *to* God's house."
And now our *feet* are standing * within
your gates, *O* Jerusalem.
Jerusalem is built *as* a city * strong*ly*
compact.
It is there that the *tribes* go up, * the
tribes *of* the Lord.
For Israel's *law* it is, * there to praise
the Lord's name.
There were set the *thrones* of judgment
* of the *house* of David.

For the peace of Jeru*sa*lem pray: *
"Peace be *to* your homes!
May peace reign *in* your walls, * in
your pala*ces*, peace!"
For love of my bre*thren* and friends * I
say: *"Peace* upon you!"
For love of the house *of* the Lord * I
will ask *for* your good.
Glory to the Father, and *to* the Son, *
and to the *Ho*ly Spirit:
as it was in the begin*ning*, is now, * and
will be for ev*er*. Amen.

Antiphon   Now your servant re*joices*, Lord, * for *you* have saved her
                      (*a*lleluia).

Ant. 2   Like a house built on enduring rock, † so the command*ments* of
                God * will remain firm in the heart of a ho*ly* woman (al*le*luia).

IIA

Psalm 127

If the Lord does not *build* the house,
* in vain do its build*ers* labor;
if the Lord does not watch *over* the
city, * in vain does the watchman
keep vigil.
In vain is your ear*li*er rising, * your
going later *to* rest,
you who toil for the *bread* you eat: *
when he pours gifts on his belovèd
while *they* slumber.
Truly sons are a gift *from* the Lord, * a
blessing, the fruit of *the* womb.

Indeed the *sons* of youth * are like
arrows in the hand of *a* warrior.
O the happiness *of* the man * who has
filled his quiver with *these* arrows!
He will have no *cause* for shame * when
he disputes with his foes in *the*
gateways.
Glory to the Father, and *to* the Son, *
and to the Ho*ly* Spirit:
as it was in the begin*ning*, is now, * and
will be for ever. *A*men.

Antiphon   Like a house built on enduring rock, † so the command*ments* of
                God * will remain firm in the heart of a ho*ly* woman (al*le*luia).

Ant. 3   The hand of the Lord has given *her* strength; * she will be
                praised *for* ever (al*le*luia).

Va

                            Canticle   Ephesians 1:3-10

Praised be the God *and* Father * of   *for*given,
our Lord Je*sus* Christ,   so immeasura*bly* generous * is God's
who has bestowed on us *in* Christ *   favor *to* us.
  every spiritual blessing in *the* heav- God has given us the wisdom † to
  ens.   understand fully *the* mystery, * the
God chose us in him † before the   plan he was pleased to decree *in*
  world *be*gan * to be holy and blame-   Christ.
  less in *his* sight.   A plan to be carried out *in* Christ, * in
He predestined us † to be his adopted   the fullness *of* time,
  sons through Je*sus* Christ, * such was   to bring all things into one *in* him, * in
  his will *and* pleasure,   the heavens and *on* earth.
that all might praise the glori*ous* favor * Glory to the Father, and to *the* Son, *
  he has bestowed on us in his *be*lovèd.   and to the Ho*ly* Spirit:
In him and through his blood, † we   as it was in the beginning, *is* now, * and
  have been *re*deemed, * and our sins   will be for ever. *A*men.

Antiphon   The hand of the Lord has given *her* strength; * she will be
                praised *for* ever (al*le*luia).

READING   Romans 8:28-30
    We know that God makes all things work together for the good of those
    who have been called according to his decree. Those whom he foreknew he
    predestined to share the image of his Son, that the Son might be the first-
    born of many brothers. Those he predestined he likewise called; those he
    called he also justified; and those he justified he in turn glorified.

RESPONSORY (VI F)
The Lord has *cho*sen her, * his loved one from the *be*ginning.
— The Lord has *cho*sen her, * his loved one from the *be*ginning.
He has taken her to *live* with him,
— his loved one from the *be*ginning.
Glory to the Father, and *to* the Son, * and to the Ho*ly* Spirit.
— The Lord has *cho*sen her, * his loved one from the *be*ginning.

Easter:

The Lord has chosen her, † his loved one from *the* beginning, * alleluia, al*l*eluia.

— The Lord has chosen her, † his loved one from *the* beginning, * alleluia, al*l*eluia.

He has taken her to *live* with him,

— alleluia, al*l*eluia.

Glory to the Father, and *to* the Son, * and to the Ho*ly* Spirit.

— The Lord has chosen her, † his loved one from *the* beginning, * alleluia, al*l*eluia.

CANTICLE OF MARY

Antiphon   My heart sings for joy and over*flows* with gladness, * for the
Lord is *my* Savior (al*l*eluia).

INTERCESSIONS (VI F)

Through the intercession of *holy* women, * let us pray for the Church *in* these
words:

Be mindful of your Church, O Lord.

Through all the women martyrs who have conquered bodily death *by* their
courage,

— strengthen your Church in the *hour* of trial.

Through married women who have advanced in grace by *holy* matrimony,

— make the apostolic mission of *your* Church fruitful.

Through widows who eased their loneliness and sanctified it by prayer and
*ho*spitality,

— help your Church reveal the mystery of your love *to* the world.

Through mothers who have borne children for the kingdom of God and the
hu*man* community,

— help your Church bring all men and women to a rebirth in life *and* salvation.

Through all your holy women who have been worthy to contemplate the light *of*
your countenance,

— let the deceased members of your Church exult in that same vi*sion* for ever.

Our Father . . .

Prayer, as in Morning Prayer.

FOR RELIGIOUS

Everything is taken from the common of holy men, 1260, or of holy women, 1271, except for the following:

Evening Prayer I

CANTICLE OF MARY
Antiphon   Unless you give all *you* possess, * you cannot be my disciple, says *the* Lord (al*l*eluia).

Or, for a man:

Antiphon   This man will receive blessings and compassion † from the Lord *God*, his Savior, * for this is the reward of those who seek *the* Lord (al*l*eluia).

Or, for a woman:

Antiphon   The Lord chose her for his spouse † with a loyal, compas*sio*nate love * that will last *for* ever (al*l*eluia).

Prayer, as in Morning Prayer.

Morning Prayer

CANTICLE OF ZECHARIAH

Antiphon   Whoever does my Father's will, *says* the Lord, * he is my brother, my sister and *my* mother (al*l*eluia).

Or, for a man:

Antiphon   The Lord is *my* inheritance; * he is good to those *who* seek him (al*l*eluia).

Prayer

If there is no proper prayer, one of the following is said:

Lord God,
you kept Saint N. faithful to Christ's pattern of poverty and humility.
May his (her) prayers help us to live in fidelity to our calling
and bring us to the perfection you have shown us in your Son,
who lives and reigns with you and the Holy Spirit,
one God, for ever and ever.

For an abbot:

Lord,
in your abbot N.
you give an example of the gospel lived to perfection.
Help us to follow him
by keeping before us the things of heaven
amid all the changes of this world.
Grant this through our Lord Jesus Christ, your Son,

who lives and reigns with you and the Holy Spirit,
one God, for ever and ever.

Evening Prayer II

CANTICLE OF MARY

Antiphon   You have left everything to follow me; † you will have it all
            returned a *hun*dredfold * and will inherit eter*nal* life (al*le*luia).

Or:

Antiphon   Where brothers praise *God* together, * there the Lord will
            shower *his* graces (al*le*luia).

Prayer, as in Morning Prayer.

FOR THOSE WHO WORKED FOR THE UNDERPRIVILEGED

Everything is taken from the common of holy men, 1260, or of holy women, 1271, except for the following:

Evening Prayer I

CANTICLE OF MARY

Antiphon   How blessèd the man whose heart goes out to the poor; † those who trust *in* the Lord * delight in show*ing* mercy (al*le*luia).

Prayer, as in Morning Prayer.

Morning Prayer

CANTICLE OF ZECHARIAH

Antiphon   All the world will recognize you as *my* disciples * when they see the love you have for one *an*other (al*le*luia).

Prayer

If there is no proper prayer, the following is said:

Lord God,
you teach us that the commandments of heaven
are summarized in love of you and love of our neighbor.
By following the example of Saint N.
in practicing works of charity
may we be counted among the blessèd in your kingdom.
Grant this through our Lord Jesus Christ, your Son,
who lives and reigns with you and the Holy Spirit,
one God, for ever and ever.

Evening Prayer II

CANTICLE OF MARY

Antiphon   I tell *you* most solemnly, * what you did for the least of men you did *for* me.
Come, my Father delights in you; † receive the kingdom pre*pared* for you * from the foundation of *the* world (al*le*luia).

Prayer, as in Morning Prayer.

FOR TEACHERS

Everything is taken from the common of holy men, 1260, or of holy women, 1271, except for the following:

Evening Prayer I

CANTICLE OF MARY

Antiphon   My son, observe your father's commands † and do not reject your *mo*ther's precepts; * keep them close to *your* heart (al*le*luia).

Prayer, as in Morning Prayer.

Morning Prayer

CANTICLE OF ZECHARIAH

Antiphon   The man of compassion guides and teach*es* his brothers * with the gentle care of the good shepherd for *his* sheep (al*le*luia).

Prayer

If there is no proper prayer, the following is said:

Lord God,
you called Saint N. to serve you in the Church
by teaching his (her) fellow man the way of salvation.
Inspire us by his (her) example:
help us to follow Christ our teacher,
and lead us to our brothers and sisters in heaven.
We ask this through our Lord Jesus Christ, your Son,
who lives and reigns with you and the Holy Spirit,
one God, for ever and ever.

Evening Prayer II

CANTICLE OF MARY

Antiphon   Let the little children *come* to me, * for they are at home in my Fa*ther's* kingdom (al*le*luia).

Prayer, as in Morning Prayer.

Office for the Dead

Morning Prayer

HYMN

Spes, Christe. (L.M.)

Spes, Christe, nostræ veniæ,	O Christ, our Pardon and our Hope,
tu vita, resurrectio;	Our Resurrection and our Life,
ad te sunt corda et oculi	All eyes and hearts to you must turn
cum mortis dolor ingruit.	When saddened by approaching death.
Tu quoque mortis tædia	You also bore its dreadful pangs,
passus dirosque stimulos,	In suff'rings deeper far than ours,
Patri, inclinato capite,	Into the the Father's loving hands
mitis dedisti spiritum.	With head bowed low your spirit fled.
Vere nostros excipiens	Good Shepherd, merciful and kind,
languores, pastor miserens,	Who knew our fragile, human state,
tecum donasti compati	You give us grace your death to share,
Patrisque in sinu commori.	And in the Father's love to die.
Apertis pendens bracchiis,	Your arms extended on the Cross,
incor transixum pertrahis	Your heart pierced through by bitter lance,
quos morituros aggravat	Encourage those who pass away
morbus vel mæror anxius.	In sorrow's anguish or in pain.
Qui portis fractis inferi	Since you once broke the gates of hell,
victor pandisti cælicas,	And opened heaven's portal wide,
nos nunc dolentes erige,	Raise up our hope as now we mourn,
post obitum vivifica.	As you will raise us after death.
Sed et qui frater corpore	May this (these) our brother/sister (broth-
nunc dormit pacis requie,	ers) who now sleeps (sleep)
iam te beante vigilet	In everlasting rest and peace,
tibique laudes referat. Amen.	By your sweet favor live to you,
	And sing your praises ever more. Amen.

PSALMODY

Ant. 1   The bones *that* were crushed * shall leap for joy before *the* Lord.

Psalm 51

Have mercy on me, God, *in* your kindness. * In your compassion blot out my *off*ense.	Against you, you alone, *have* I sinned; * what is evil in your sight I *have* done.
O wash me more and more *from* my guilt * and cleanse me from *my* sin.	That you may be justified when *you* give sentence * and be without reproach when *you* judge,
My offenses tru*ly* I know them; * my sin is always *be*fore me.	O see, in guilt *I* was born, * a sinner was I *con*ceived.

Indeed you love truth *in* the heart; *
then in the secret of my heart teach
me wisdom.
O purify me, then I *shall* be clean; * O
wash me, I shall be whiter *than* snow.
Make me hear rejoi*cing* and gladness, *
that the bones you have crushed may
re*vive.*
From my sins turn a*way* your face * and
blot out all *my* guilt.
A pure heart create for *me*, O God, *
put a steadfast spirit *with*in me.
Do not cast me away *from* your presence, " nor deprive me of your ho*ly*
spirit.
Give me again the joy *of* your help; *
with a spirit of fervor *sus*tain me,
that I may teach transgres*sors* your ways
* and sinners may return *to* you.

O rescue me, *God*, my helper, * and my
tongue shall ring out *your* goodness.
O Lord, o*pen* my lips * and my mouth
shall declare *your* praise.
For in sacrifice you take *no* delight, *
burnt offering from me you would
re*fuse,*
my sacrifice, a con*trite* spirit. * A
humbled, contrite heart you will *not*
spurn.
In your goodness, show fa*vor* to Zion: *
rebuild the walls of *Je*rusalem.
Then you will be pleased with *lawful*
sacri*fice*, * holocausts offered on *your*
altar.
Glory to the Father, and *to* the Son, *
and to the Ho*ly* Spirit:
as it was in the begin*ning*, is now, * and
will be for ever. *A*men.

Antiphon   The bones *that* were crushed * shall leap for joy before *the* Lord.

Ant. 2   At the very threshold of *death*, * rescue *me*, Lord.

Canticle   Isaiah 38:10-14, 17-20

Once I *said*, * "In the noontime of
life I must de*part!*
To the gates of the nether *world* * I
shall be consigned for the rest of *my*
years."
I said, "I shall see the Lord no *more* * in
the land of *the* living.
No longer shall I behold my fellow *men*
* among those who dwell in *the*
world."
My dwelling, like a shepherd's *tent*, * is
struck down and borne away *from* me;
you have folded up my *life*, * like a
weaver who severs the *last* thread.
Day and night you give me over to

*tor*ment; * I cry out until *the* dawn.
Like a lion he breaks all my *bones*; * day
and night you give me over *to* torment.
Like a swallow I utter shrill *cries*; * I
moan like *a* dove.
My eyes grow weak, gazing *heaven*-
ward: * O Lord, I am in straits; be *my*
surety!
You have preserved my life from the pit
of des*truction*, * when you cast
behind your back all *my* sins.
For it is not the nether world that gives
you *thanks*, * nor death that prais*es*
you;

neither do those who do down into the
pit await your *kind*ness. * The living,
the living give you thanks, as I do
*to*day.
Fathers declare to their *sons*, * O God,
your faithfulness.
The Lord is our *savior*; * we shall sing
to *string*ed instruments
in the house of the *Lord* * all the days of
our life.
Glory to the Father, and to the *Son*, *
and to the Ho*ly* Spirit:
as it was in the beginning, is *now*, * and
will be for ever. *A*men.

Antiphon   At the very threshold of *death*, * rescue *me*, Lord.

Ant. 3   I will *praise* my God * all the days *of* my life.

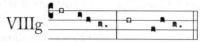

Psalm 146

My soul, give praise to the Lord; †
I will praise the Lord *all* my
days, * make music to my God *while* I
live.
Put no *trust* in princes, * in mortal men
in whom there *is* no help.
Take their breath, they re*turn* to clay *
and their plans that day *come* to
nothing.
He is happy who is helped by *Jacob's*
God, * whose hope is in the *Lord* his
God,
who alone made hea*ven* and earth, * the
seas and all *they* contain.
It is he who keeps *faith* for ever, * who
is just to those who *are* oppressed.

It is he who gives bread *to* the hungry, *
the Lord, who sets pris*on*ers free,
the Lord, who gives sight *to* the blind, *
who raises up those who *are* bowed
down,
the Lord, who pro*tects* the stranger *
and upholds the wi*dow* and orphan.
It is the Lord who *loves* the just * but
thwarts the path *of* the wicked.
The Lord will *reign* for ever, * Zion's
God, from *age* to age.
Glory to the Father, and *to* the Son, *
and to the *Ho*ly Spirit:
as it was in the begin*ning*, is now, * and
will be for e*ver*. Amen.

Antiphon   I will *praise* my God * all the days *of* my life.
Or:
Ant. 3   Let every*thing* that breathes * give praise *to* the Lord.

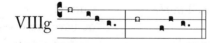

Psalm 150

Praise God in his *holy* place, *
praise him in his *mighty* heavens.
Praise him for his po*wer*ful deeds, *
praise his sur*pass*ing greatness.

O praise him with *sound* of trumpet, *
  praise him with *lute* and harp.
Praise him with tim*brel* and dance, *
  praise him with *strings* and pipes.
O praise him with re*sound*ing cymbals,
  * praise him with clash*ing* of cymbals.

Let everything that lives *and* that
  breathes * give praise *to* the Lord.
Glory to the Father, and *to* the Son, *
  and to the *Ho*ly Spirit:
as it was in the begin*ning*, is now, * and
  will be for e*ver*. Amen.

Antiphon   Let every*thing* that breathes * give praise *to* the Lord.

READING   1 Thessalonians 4:14
  If we believe that Jesus died and rose, God will bring forth with him from the
  dead those also who have fallen asleep believing in him.

RESPONSORY
I will *praise* you, Lord, * for you have res*cued* me.
— I will *praise* you, Lord, * for you have res*cued* me.
You turned my sorrow *in*to joy,
— for you have res*cued* me.
Glory to the Father, and *to* the Son, * and to the Ho*ly* Spirit.
— I will *praise* you, Lord, * for you have res*cued* me.

CANTICLE OF ZECHARIAH
Antiphon   I am the Resurrection, I am the Life; † to believe in me means
                  life, in *spite* of death, * and all who believe and live in me shall
                  ne*ver* die.

Or, during the Easter Season:
                  The splendor of Christ risen *from* the dead * has shone on the
                  people redeemed by his blood, al*le*luia.

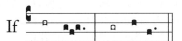

Blessèd ✠ be the Lord, the *God* of
  Israel; * he has come to his people
  and set *them* free.
He has raised up for us a *mighty* savior,
  * born of the house of his ser*vant*
  David.
Through his holy prophets he promised
  of old † that he would save us *from*
  our enemies, * from the hands of all
  who hate us.
He promised to show mercy *to* our

fathers * and to remember his ho*ly*
  covenant.
This was the oath he swore to our
  *fath*er Abraham: * to set us free from
  the hands of *our* enemies,
free to worship him without fear, † holy
  and righteous *in* his sight * all the
  days of *our* life.
You, my child, shall be called the
  prophet *of* the Most High; * for you
  will go before the Lord to prepare *his*

way,
to give his people knowledge *of* salvation * by the forgiveness of *their* sins.
In the tender compassion *of* our God *
the dawn from on high shall break
*up*on us,
to shine on those who dwell in darkness

and the sha*dow* of death, * and to
guide our feet into the way *of* peace.
Glory to the Father, and *to* the Son, *
and to the Ho*ly* Spirit:
as it was in the begin*ning*, is now, * and
will be for ever. *A*men.

Antiphon   I am the Resurrection, I am the Life; † to believe in me means
life, in *spite* of death, * and all who believe and live in me shall
ne*ver* die.

Or, during the Easter Season:

The splendor of Christ risen *from* the dead * has shone on the
people redeemed by his blood, al*le*luia.

INTERCESSIONS

Let us pray to the all-powerful Father who raised Jesus *from* the dead * and gives
new life to our mortal bodies, and *say* to him:
Lord, give us new life in *Christ.*
Father, through baptism we have been buried with your Son and have risen with
him in his *re*surrection,
— grant that we may walk in newness of life so that when we die, we may live
with *Christ* for ever.
Provident Father, you have given us the living bread that has come down from
heaven and which should always be *eat*en worthily,
— grant that we may eat this bread worthily and be raised up to eternal life on *the*
last day.
Lord, you sent an angel to comfort your Son *in* his agony,
— give us the hope of your consolation when *death* draws near.
You delivered the three youths from the *fie*ry furnace,
— free your faithful ones from the punishment they suffer *for* their sins.
God of the living and the dead, you raised Jesus *from* the dead,
— raise up those who have died and grant that we may share eternal glo*ry* with
them.

Our Father . . .

Prayer
Lord, hear our prayers.
By raising your Son from the dead, you have given us faith.
Strengthen hope that N., our brother (sister),
will share in his resurrection.
We ask this through our Lord Jesus Christ, your Son,

who lives and reigns with you and the Holy Spirit,
one God, for ever and ever.
Or:
Lord God, you are the glory of believers
and the life of the just.
Your Son redeemed us
by dying and rising to life again.
Our brother (sister) N. was faithful
and believed in our own resurrection.
Give to him (her) the joy and blessings
of the life to come.
We ask this through our Lord Jesus Christ, your Son,
who lives and reigns with you and the Holy Spirit,
one God, for ever and ever.
Or, during the Easter Season:
Almighty and merciful God,
may our brother (sister) N. share the victory of Christ
who loved us so much that he died and rose again
to bring us new life.
We ask this through our Lord Jesus Christ, your Son,
who lives and reigns with you and the Holy Spirit,
one God, for ever and ever.
Or:
Lord of mercy,
hear our prayer.
May our brother (sister) N.,
whom you called your son (daughter) on earth,
enter the kingdom of peace and light,
where your saints live in glory.
We ask this through our Lord Jesus Christ, your Son,
who lives and reigns with you and the Holy Spirit,
one God, for ever and ever.
For several people:
God, our creator and redeemer,
by your power Christ conquered death
and returned to you in glory.
May all your people (N. and N.),
who have gone before us in faith share his victory
and enjoy the vision of your glory for ever,
where Christ lives and reigns with you and the Holy Spirit,
one God, for ever and ever.

For relatives, friends, and benefactors:

> Father,
> source of forgiveness and salvation for all mankind,
> hear our prayer.
> By the prayers of the ever-virgin Mary,
> may our friends, relatives, and benefactors
> who have gone from this world
> come to share eternal happiness with all your saints.
> We ask this through our Lord Jesus Christ, your Son,
> who lives and reigns with you and the Holy Spirit,
> one God, for ever and ever.

Evening Prayer

HYMN

Immensæ Rex. (L.M.)

Immensa rex potentiæ,	O Christ our King, supreme in power,
Christe, tu Patris gloriam	The Father's glory and delight,
nostrumque decus moliens,	Our fallen nature you restored,
mortis fregisti iacula.	By dying you defeated death.
Infirma nostra subiens	You bore our sorrows and our griefs,
magnumque petens prœlium,	And sought a sterner conflict yet,
mortem qua serpens vicerat,	By death you crushed the serpent's head
victor calcasti moriens.	Who conquered us and caused our death.
Surgens fortis e tumulo,	In triumph risen from the tomb
paschali nos mysterio	You bring your people back to life
peccato rursus mortuos	Through your great Paschal mystery,
ad vitam semper innovas.	We who were dead and lost by sin.
Vitam largire gratiæ,	Increase in us the life of grace
ut, sponsus cum redieris,	That when as Bridegroom you return,
ornata nos cum lampade	With lamps well trimmed we be prepared
iam promptos cælo invenias.	To follow you at once with joy.
In lucem nos et requiem	Receive us as a judge serene
serenus iudex accipe,	Into the realms of peace and light,
quos fides sanctæ Triadi	Whom faith and love have bound to you,
devinxit atque caritas.	Adoring your great Trinity.
Tuumque voca famulum,	Your servant(s) who has (have) left this world
qui nunc exutus corpore	With soul from body now set free,
in regna Patris inhiat,	Call swiftly to our Father's home
ut te collaudet perpetim. Amen.	To praise you for eternity. Amen.

PSALMODY

Ant. 1   The Lord will keep you *from* all evil. * He will guard *your* soul.

Psalm 121

I lift up my eyes *to* the mountains: *
from where shall come *my* help?
My help shall come *from* the Lord *
who made heaven *and* earth.
May he never allow *you* to stumble! *
Let him sleep not, *your* guard.
No, he sleeps *not* nor slumbers, * Isra*el's*
guard.
The Lord is your guard *and* your shade;
* at your right side *he* stands.

By day the sun *shall* not smite you * nor
the moon in *the* night.
The Lord will guard *you* from evil, * he
will guard *your* soul.
The Lord will guard your go*ing* and
coming * both now and *for*ever.
Glory to the Father, and *to* the Son, *
and to the Ho*ly* Spirit:
as it was in the begin*ning*, is now, * and
will be for ever. *A*men.

Antiphon   The Lord will keep you *from* all evil. * He will guard *your* soul.

Ant. 2   If you kept a record *of* our sins, * Lord, who could escape con-
               *dem*nation?

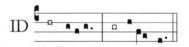

Psalm 130

O ut of the depths I cry to *you,*
O Lord, * Lord, hear *my* voice!
O let your ears *be* attentive * to the
voice of *my* pleading.
If you, O Lord, should *mark* our guilt, *
Lord, who would *sur*vive?
But with you is *found* forgiveness: * for
this we *re*vere you.
My soul is waiting *for* the Lord, * I
count on *his* word.
My soul is longing *for* the Lord * more

than watchman *for* daybreak.
Let the watchman *count* on daybreak *
and Israel on *the* Lord.
Because with the Lord *there* is mercy *
and fullness of *re*demption,
Israel indeed he *will* redeem * from all
its in*iquity.
Glory to the Father, and *to* the Son, *
and to the Ho*ly* Spirit:
as it was in the begin*ning*, is now, * and
will be for ever. *A*men.

Antiphon   If you kept a record *of* our sins, * Lord, who could escape con-
               *dem*nation?

Ant. 3   As the Father raises the dead and gives them *life*, * so the Son gives life to whom *he* wills.

VIIIa

                   Canticle   Philippians 2:6-11

Though he was in the form of God, † Jesus did not deem equality with God * something to *be* grasped at.

Rather, he emptied himself † and took the form of a *slave*, * being born in the likeness *of* men.

He was known to be of human e*state*, * and it was thus that he humbled *him*self,

obediently accepting even *death*, * death on *a* cross!

Because of *this*, * God highly exalt*ed* him

and bestowed on him the *name* * above every o*ther* name,

so that at Jesus' name every knee must *bend* * in the heavens, on the earth, and under *the* earth,

and every tongue proclaim to the glory of God the *Fa*ther: * JESUS CHRIST *IS* LORD!

Glory to the Father, and to the *Son*, * and to the Ho*ly* Spirit:

as it was in the beginning, is *now*, * and will be for ever. *A*men.

Antiphon   As the Father raises the dead and gives them *life*, * so the Son gives life to whom *he* wills.

READING   1 Corinthians 15:55-57

O death, where is your victory? O death, where is your sting? The sting of death is sin, and sin gets its sting from the law. But thanks be to God who has given us the victory through our Lord Jesus Christ.

RESPONSORY (VI F)

In you, Lord, *is* our hope. * We shall never hope *in* vain.

— In you, Lord, *is* our hope. * We shall never hope *in* vain.

We shall dance and rejoice *in* your mercy.

— We shall never hope *in* vain.

Glory to the Father, and *to* the Son, * and to the Ho*ly* Spirit.

— In you, Lord, *is* our hope. * We shall never hope *in* vain.

Or:

Lord, in your *stead*fast love, * give them eter*nal* rest.

— Lord, in your *stead*fast love, * give them eter*nal* rest.

You will come to judge the living *and* the dead.

— Give them eter*nal* rest.

Glory to the Father, and *to* the Son, * and to the Ho*ly* Spirit.
— Lord, in your *stead*fast love, * give them eter*nal* rest.

GOSPEL CANTICLE   Luke 1:46-55
Antiphon   All that the Father gives me will *come* to me, * and whoever
                comes to me I shall not turn *away*.

Or, during the Easter Season:
Antiphon   Our crucified and *ris*en Lord * has redeemed us, al*le*luia.

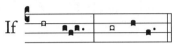

My soul ✠ proclaims the greatness
of the Lord, * my spirit rejoices
  in God *my* savior
for he has *looked* with favor * on his
  low*ly* servant.
From this day all *gen*erations * will call
  me blessèd:
the Almighty has done great *things* for
  me, * and holy is *his* Name.
He has mercy on *those* who fear him *
  in every gen*er*ation.
He has shown the strength *of* his arm, *
  he has scattered the proud in their
  *con*ceit.

He has cast down the mighty *from* their
  thrones, * and has lifted up *the* lowly.
He has filled the hungry *with* good
  things, * and the rich he has sent
  a*way* empty.
He has come to the help of his *ser*vant
  Israel * for he has remembered his
  promise *of* mercy,
the promise he made *to* our fathers, * to
  Abraham and his children *for* ever.
Glory to the Father, and *to* the Son, *
  and to the Ho*ly* Spirit:
as it was in the begin*ning*, is now, * and
  will be for ever. *A*men.

Antiphon   All that the Father gives me will *come* to me, * and whoever
                comes to me I shall not turn *away*.

Or, during the Easter Season:
Antiphon   Our crucified and *ris*en Lord * has redeemed us, al*le*luia.

INTERCESSIONS
We acknowledge Christ the Lord through whom we hope that our *lowly* bodies *
  will be made like his in glory, *and* we say:
*Lord, you are our life and res*urrection.
Christ, Son of the living God, who raised up Lazarus, your friend, *from* the dead,
— raise up to life and glory the dead whom you have redeemed by your *precious*
  blood.
Christ, consoler of those who mourn, you dried the tears of the family of
  Lazarus, of the widow's son, and the daugh*ter* of Jairus,
— comfort those who mourn *for* the dead.

Christ, Savior, destroy the reign of sin in our earthly bodies, so that just as
  through sin we *de*served punishment,
— so through you we may gain e*ter*nal life.
Christ, Redeemer, look on those who have no hope because they *do* not know
  you,
— may they receive faith in the resurrection and in the life of the *world* to come.
You revealed yourself to the blind man who begged for the light *of* his eyes,
— show your face to the dead who are still deprived *of* your light.
When at last our earthly home *is* dissolved,
— give us a home, not of earthly making, but built of eterni*ty* in heaven.

Our Father . . .

Prayer, as in Morning Prayer.

Hymnal
for the
Liturgy of the Hours

O Kind Creator of the Stars

Conditor alme siderum. Mode IV (L.M.)

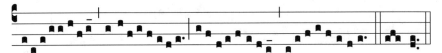

Conditor alme siderum,
æterna lux credentium,
Christe, redemptor omnium,
exaudi preces supplicum.

Creator of the stars of night,
Thy people's everlasting light,
O Christ, Redeemer, save us all,
And hear thy servants when they call.

Qui condolens interitu
mortis perire sæculum,
salvasti mundum languidum,
donans reis remedium.

Thou, grieving that the ancient curse
Should doom to death a universe,
Hast found the medicine full of grace
To save and heal a ruined race.

Vergente mundi vespere,
uti sponsus de thalamo,
egressus honestissima
Virginis matris clausula.

Thou cam'st, the Bridegroom of the bride,
As drew the world to evening-tide;
Proceeding from a virgin shrine,
The spotless Victim all divine:

Cuius forti potentiæ
genu curvantur omnia;
cælestia, terrestria
nutu fatentur subdita.

At whose dread Name majestic now,
All knees must bend, all hearts must bow;
And things celestial thee shall own,
And things terrestrial, Lord alone.

Te, Sancte, fide quæsumus,
venture iudex sæculi,
conserva nos in tempore
hostis a telo perfidi.

O thou whose coming is with dread
To judge and doom the quick and dead,
Preserve us, while we dwell below,
From every insult of the foe.

Sit, Christe, rex piissime,
tibi Patrique gloria
cum Spiritu Paraclito,
in sempiterna sæcula. Amen.

To God the Father, God the Son,
And God the Spirit, Three in One,
Laud, honor, might, and glory be
From age to age eternally. Amen.

Hark! A Herald Voice Is Calling

Vox clara ecce intonat. Mode V (87.87)

Vox clara ecce intonat,
obscura quæque increpat:
procul fugentur somnia;
ab æthre Christus promicat.

Hark! a herald voice is calling:
"Christ is nigh" it seems to say;
"Cast away the dreams of darkness,
O ye children of the day."

Mens iam resurgat torpida
quæ sorde exstat saucia;
sidus refulget iam novum,
ut tollat omne noxium.

Startled at the solemn warning,
Let the earth-bound soul arise;
Christ, her Sun, all sloth dispelling,
Shines upon the morning sky.

E sursum Agnus mittitur
laxare gratis debitum;
omnes pro indulgentia
vocem demus cum lacrimis,

Lo! the Lamb so long expected,
Comes with pardon down from heav'n;
Let us haste, with tears of sorrow,
One and all to be forgiv'n;

Secundo ut cum fulserit
mundumque horror cinxerit,
non pro reatu puniat,
sed nos pius tunc protegat.

So when next he comes in glory,
Wrapping all the earth in fear,
May he then as our defender
On the clouds of heav'n appear.

Summo Parenti gloria
Natoque sit victoria,
et Flamini laus debita
per sæculorum sæcula. Amen.

Honor, glory, virtue, merit
To the Father and the Son,
With the co-eternal Spirit,
While unending ages run. Amen.

O Mary, Blessed Virgin Pure

Verbum salutis. Mode IV (L.M.)

Verbum salutis omnium,
Patris ab ore prodiens,
Virgo beata, suscipe
casta, Maria, viscere.

Te nunc illustrat cælitus
umbra fecundi Spiritus,
gestes ut Christum Dominum,
æqualem Patri Filium.

Hæc est sacrati ianua
templi serata iugiter,
soli supremo Principi
pandens beata limina.

Olim promissus vatibus,
natus ante luciferum,
quem Gabriel annuntiat,
terris descendit Dominus.

Lætentur simul angeli,
omnes exsultent populi:
excelsus venit humilis
salvare quod perierat.

Sit, Christe, rex piissime,
tibi Patrique gloria
cum Spiritu Parclito,
in sempiterna sæcula. Amen.

O Mary, blessèd Virgin pure,
Receive within your spotless womb
The Word, Salvation for us all,
Proceeding from the Father's mouth.

The Holy Spirit's fruitful cloud
Has overshadowed you with love,
That you may bring forth Christ our Lord,
The Father's Ever-equal Son.

Here is the holy Temple's gate
For ever sealed from use profane,
Whose sacred portal is reserved
To open for the King alone.

To prophets promised long ago,
And born before the birth of light,
Whom Gabriel announced with joy,
The Lord himself comes down to earth.

Let all the angels gladly sing,
All peoples of the earth exult,
In lowly guise the Most High comes
To save the world which sin had lost.

O Christ our King and tender Lord,
All glory ever be to you,
Who with the Holy Spirit reign
With God the Father's might supreme. Amen.

Of Old the Prophets Cried Aloud

Magnis prophetæ vocibus. (L.M.)

Magnis prophetæ vocibus
venire Christum nuntiant,
lætæ salutis prævia,
qua nos redemit, gratia.

Of old the prophets cried aloud,
Foretelling Christ would surely come,
Theirs was the special grace to know
That man's redemption was at hand.

Hinc mane nostrum promicat
ex corda læta exæstuant,
cum vox fidelis personat
prænuntiatrix gloriæ.

Hence radiates our joy at dawn,
Our happy hearts rejoice and sing,
Proclaiming now our earnest faith
In glory long since promised us.

Adventus hic primus fuit,
punire quo non sæculum
venit, sed ulcus tergere,
salvando quod perierat.

This humble Coming known to few,
Was not to judge a sinful world,
But all our wounds to tend and heal
By saving what had gone astray.

At nos secundus præmonet
adesse Christum ianuis,
sanctis coronas reddere
cælique regna pandere.

His second Coming will declare
That Christ is at our very doors,
To crown all those who love him well,
And welcome them to lasting bliss.

Æterna lux promittitur
sidusque salvans promitur;
iam nos iubar præfulgidum
ad ius vocat cælestium.

Eternal light is promised us,
The star of our salvation shines,
Already its bright, gleaming rays
Call us to keep the law of love.

Te, Christe, solum quærimus
videre, sicut es Deus,
ut perpes hæc sit visio
perenne laudis canticum. Amen.

Lord Jesus Christ, we seek but you,
To see you, God yet truly man,
So that this vision blest may be
Our never ending hymn of praise. Amen.

O Merciful Creator hear!

Audi, benigne Conditor. Mode II (L.M.)

Audi, benigne Conditor,
nostras preces cum fletibus,
sacrata in abstinentia
fusas quadragenaria.

Scrutator alme cordium,
infirma tu scis virium,
ad te reversis exhibe
remissionis gratiam.

Multum quidem peccavimus,
sed parce confitentibus,
tuique laude nominis
confer medelam languidis.

Sic corpus extra conteri
dona per abstinentiam,
ieiunet ut mens sobria
a labe prorsus criminum.

Praesta, beata Trinitas,
concede, simplex Unitas,
ut fructuosa sint tuis
haec parcitatis munera. Amen.

O Merciful Creator, hear!
To us in pity bow Thine ear:
Accept the tearful prayer we raise
In this our fast of forty days.

Our hearts are open, Lord, to Thee:
Thou knowest our infirmity;
Pour out on all who seek Thy face
Abundance of Thy pard'ning grace.

Our sins are many, this we know;
Spare us, good Lord, Thy mercy show;
And for the honor of Thy name
Our fainting souls to life reclaim.

Give us self-control that springs
From discipline of outward things,
That fasting inward secretly
The soul may purely dwell with Thee.

We pray Thee, Holy Trinity,
One God, unchanging Unity,
That we from this our abstinence
May reap the fruits of penitence. Amen.

In Prayer Together Let Us Fall

Precemur omnes cernui. Mode II (L.M.)

Precemur omnes cernui,	In prayer together let us fall,
clamemus atque singuli,	And cry for mercy, one and all,
ploremus ante iudicem,	And weep before the Judge's feet,
flectamus iram vindicem:	And His avenging wrath entreat.
Nostris malis offendimus	Thy grace have we offended sore,
tuam, Deus, clementiam;	By sins, O God, which we deplore;
effunde nobis desuper,	But pour upon us from on high,
remissor, indulgentiam.	O pard'ning One, Thy clemency.
Memento quod sumus tui,	Remember Thou, though frail we be,
licet caduci, plasmatis;	That yet Thine handiwork are we;
ne des honorem nominis	Nor let the honor of Thy Name
tui, precamur, alteri.	Be by another put to shame.
Laxa malum quod fecimus,	Forgive the sin that we have wrought;
auge bonum quod poscimus,	Increase the good that we have sought:
placere quo tandem tibi	That we at length, our wanderings o'er,
possimus hic et perpetim.	May please Thee here and evermore.
Praesta, beata Trinitas,	Blest Three in One, and One in Three,
concede, simplex Unitas,	Almighty God, we pray to Thee,
ut fructuosa sint tuis	That this our fast of forty days
haec parcitatis munera. Amen.	May work our profit and Thy praise. Amen.

The Glory of These Forty Days

Iesu, quadragenariæ. Mode II (L.M.)

Iesu, quadragenariæ
dicator abstientiæ,
qui ob salutem mentium
praeceperas ieiunium,

Adesto nunc Ecclesiæ,
adesto paenitentiae,
qua supplicamus cernui
peccata nostra dilui.

Tu retroacta crimina
tua remitte gratia
et a futuris adhibe
custodiam mitissime,

Ut, expiati annuis
compunctionis actibus,
tendamus ad paschalia
digne colenda gaudia.

Te rerum universitas,
clemens, adoret, Trinitas,
et nos novi per veniam
novum canamus canticum. Amen.

The glory of these forty days
We celebrate with songs of praise;
For Christ, by whom all things were made,
Himself has fasted and has prayed.

Alone and fasting Moses saw
The loving God who gave the law;
And to Elijah, fasting, came
The steed and chariots of flame.

So Daniel trained his mystic sight,
Deliver'd from the lions' might;
And John, the Bridegroom's friend, became
The herald of Messiah's name.

Then grant us, Lord, like them to do
Such things as bring great praise to you;
Our spirits strengthen with your grace
And give us joy to see your face.

O Father, Son and Spirit blest,
To you be every prayer addressed
And by all mankind be adored,
From age to age, the only Lord. Amen.

Now Christ, Thou Sun of Righteousness

Iam, Christe, sol iustitiæ. (L.M.)

Iam, Christe, sol iustitiæ,
mentis dehiscant tenebræ,
virtutum ut lux redeat,
terris diem cum reparas.

Dans tempus acceptabile
et pænitens cor tribue,
convertat ut benignitas
quos longa suffert pietas.

Quiddamque paenitentiæ
da ferre, quo fit demptio,
maiore tuo munere,
culparum quamvis grandium.

Dies venit, dies tua,
per quam reflorent omnia;
laetemur in hac ut tuæ
per hanc reducti gratiæ.

Te rerum universitas,
clemens, adoret, Trinitas,
et nos novi per veniam
novum canamus canticum. Amen.

Now Christ, Thou Sun of righteousness,
Let dawn our darkened spirits bless:
The light of grace to us restore
While day to earth returns once more.

Thou who dost give th'accepted time,
Give, too, a heart that mourns for crime,
Let those by mercy now be cured
Whom loving kindness long endured.

Spare not, we pray, to send us here
Some penance kindly but severe,
So let Thy gift of pard'ning grace
Our grievous sinfulness efface.

Soon will that day, Thy day, appear
And all things with its brightness cheer:
We will rejoice in it, as we
Return thereby to grace, and Thee.

Let all the world from shore to shore
Thee, gracious Trinity, adore;
Right soon Thy loving pardon grant,
That we our new-made song may chant. Amen.

The Lamb's High Banquet We Await

Ad cenam Agni providi. Mode VIII (L.M.)

Ad cenam Agni providi,
Stolis salutis candidi,
Post transitum maris Rubri
Christo canamus principi.

The Lamb's high banquet we await
In snow-white robes of royal state;
And now, the Red Sea's channel past,
To Christ, our Prince, we sing at last.

Cuius corpus sanctissimum
In ara crucis torridum,
Sed et cruorem roseum
Gustando, Dei vivimus.

Upon the altar of the Cross
His body hath redeemed our loss,
And tasting of his life-red Blood
Our life is hid with him in God.

Protecti paschae vespero
A devastante angelo,
De Pharaonis aspero
Sumus erepti imperio.

That Paschal eve God's arm was bared;
The devastating Angel spared:
By strength of hand our hosts went free
From Pharoah's ruthless tyranny.

Iam pascha nostrum Christus est,
Agnus occisus innocens;
Sinceritatis azyma
Qui carnem suam obtulit.

Now Christ, our Paschal Lamb, is slain,
The Lamb of God that knows no stain;
The true Oblation offered here,
Our own unleavened Bread sincere.

O vera, digna hostia,
Per quam franguntur tartara,
Captiva plebs redimitur,
Redduntur vitae praemia!

O thou from whom hell's monarch flies,
O great, O very Sacrifice,
Thy captive people are set free,
And endless life restored in thee.

Consurgit Christus tumulo,
Victor redit de barathro,
Tyrannum trudens vinculo
Et paradisum reserans.

For Christ arising from the dead,
From conquered hell victorious sped;
He thrusts the tyrant down to chains,
And Paradise for man regains.

Esto perenne mentibus
Paschale, Iesu, gaudium
Et nos renatos gratiae
Tuis triumphis aggrega.

Maker of all, to thee we pray,
Fulfil in us thy joy today;
When death assails, grant, Lord, that we
May share the Paschal victory.

Iesu, tibi sit gloria,
Qui morte victa praenites,
Cum Patre et almo Spiritu,
In sempiterna saecula. Amen.

To thee, who dead, again dost live,
All glory, Lord, thy people give;
All glory as is ever meet,
To Father and to Paraclete. Amen.

The Morn Had Spread Her Crimson Rays

Aurora lucis rutilat. Mode VIII (L.M.)

Aurora lucis rutilat,	The morn had spread her crimson rays,
Cælum resultat laudibus,	When rang the skies with shouts of praise;
Mundus exsultans iubilat,	Earth joined the joyful hymn to swell,
Gemens infernus ululat.	That brought despair to vanquished hell.
Cum rex ille fortissimus,	He comes victorious from the grave,
Mortis confractis viribus,	The Lord omnipotent to save,
Pede conculcans tartara	And brings with him to light of day
Solvit catena miseros.	The Saints who long imprisoned lay.
Ille, quem clausum lapide	Vain is the cavern's threefold ward—
Miles custodit acriter,	The stone, the seal, the armèd guard;
Triumphans pompa nobili	O death, no more thine arm we fear,
Victor surgit de funere.	The Victor's tomb is now thy bier.
Inferni iam gemitibus	Enough of death, enough of tears,
solutis et doloribus,	Enough of sorrows and of fears!
Quia surrexit Dominus	O hear yon white-robed angel cry,
Resplendens clamat angelus.	Death's Conqueror lives, no more to die.
Esto perenne mentibus	Grant, Lord, in thee each faithful mind
Paschale, Iesu, gaudium,	Unceasing Paschal joy may find;
Et nos renatos gratie	And from the death of sin set free
Tuis triumphis aggrega.	Souls newly born to life by thee.
Iesu, tibi sit gloria,	To thee, once dead, who now dost live,
Qui morte victa prænites,	All glory, Lord, thy people give,
Cum Patre et almo Spiritu,	Whom, with the Father we adore,
In sempiterna sæcula. Amen.	And Holy Ghost for evermore. Amen.

Creator of the Earth and Sky

Deus, Creator omnium. Mode II.

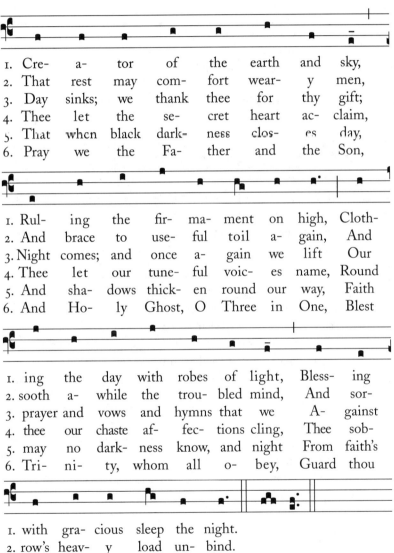

1. Cre- a- tor of the earth and sky,
2. That rest may com- fort wear- y men,
3. Day sinks; we thank thee for thy gift;
4. Thee let the se- cret heart ac- claim,
5. That when black dark- ness clos- es day,
6. Pray we the Fa- ther and the Son,

1. Rul- ing the fir- ma- ment on high, Cloth-
2. And brace to use- ful toil a- gain, And
3. Night comes; and once a- gain we lift Our
4. Thee let our tune- ful voic- es name, Round
5. And sha- dows thick- en round our way, Faith
6. And Ho- ly Ghost, O Three in One, Blest

1. ing the day with robes of light, Bless- ing
2. sooth a- while the trou- bled mind, And sor-
3. prayer and vows and hymns that we A- gainst
4. thee our chaste af- fec- tions cling, Thee sob-
5. may no dark- ness know, and night From faith's
6. Tri- ni- ty, whom all o- bey, Guard thou

1. with gra- cious sleep the night.
2. row's heav- y load un- bind.
3. all ills may shield- èd be.
4. er rea- son own as King.
5. clear beam may bor- row light.
6. thy sheep by night and day. A- men.

Eternal Maker of the World

Æterne rerum Conditor. Mode I.

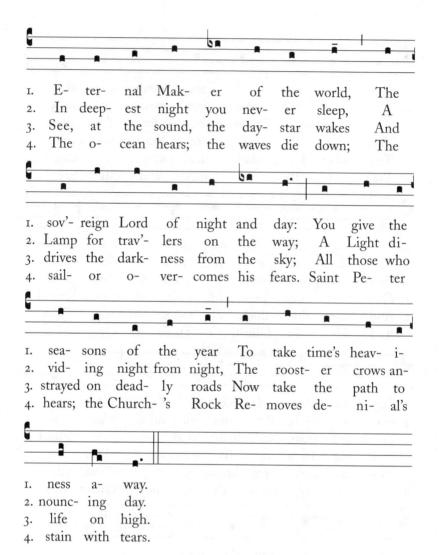

1. E- ter- nal Mak- er of the world, The
2. In deep- est night you nev- er sleep, A
3. See, at the sound, the day- star wakes And
4. The o- cean hears; the waves die down; The

1. sov'- reign Lord of night and day: You give the
2. Lamp for trav'- lers on the way; A Light di-
3. drives the dark- ness from the sky; All those who
4. sail- or o- ver- comes his fears. Saint Pe- ter

1. sea- sons of the year To take time's heav- i-
2. vid- ing night from night, The roost- er crows an-
3. strayed on dead- ly roads Now take the path to
4. hears; the Church- 's Rock Re- moves de- ni- al's

1. ness a- way.
2. nounc- ing day.
3. life on high.
4. stain with tears.

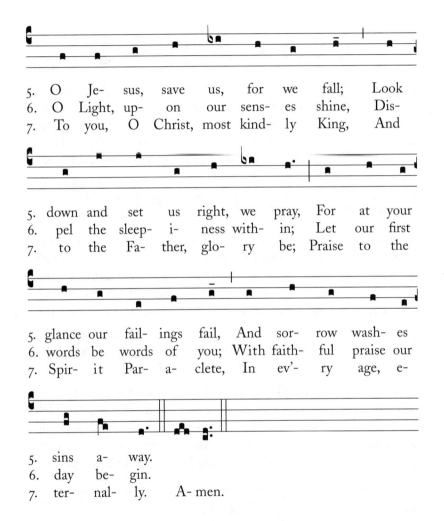

5. O   Je- sus, save   us,   for   we   fall;   Look
6. O   Light, up- on   our   sens- es   shine,   Dis-
7. To   you, O   Christ, most kind- ly   King,   And

5. down and   set   us   right, we   pray, For   at   your
6. pel   the sleep- i-   ness with- in;   Let   our   first
7. to   the Fa- ther, glo- ry   be; Praise to   the

5. glance our fail- ings fail, And sor- row wash- es
6. words be   words of   you; With faith- ful praise our
7. Spir- it Par- a- clete, In   ev'- ry   age, e-

5. sins   a- way.
6. day   be- gin.
7. ter- nal- ly.   A- men.

O Blest Creator of the Light

Lucis Creator optime. Mode VIII.

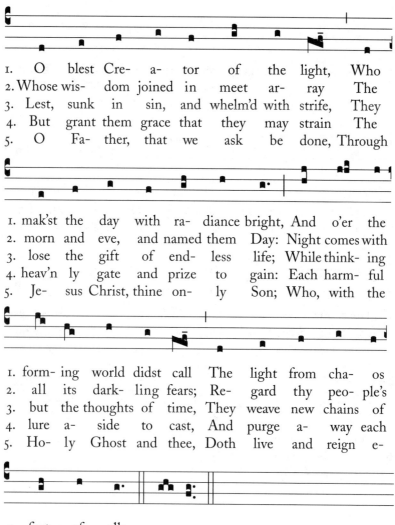

1. O blest Cre- a- tor of the light, Who
2. Whose wis- dom joined in meet ar- ray The
3. Lest, sunk in sin, and whelm'd with strife, They
4. But grant them grace that they may strain The
5. O Fa- ther, that we ask be done, Through

1. mak'st the day with ra- diance bright, And o'er the
2. morn and eve, and named them Day: Night comes with
3. lose the gift of end- less life; While think- ing
4. heav'n ly gate and prize to gain: Each harm- ful
5. Je- sus Christ, thine on- ly Son; Who, with the

1. form- ing world didst call The light from cha- os
2. all its dark- ling fears; Re- gard thy peo- ple's
3. but the thoughts of time, They weave new chains of
4. lure a- side to cast, And purge a- way each
5. Ho- ly Ghost and thee, Doth live and reign e-

1. first of all;
2. prayers and tears,
3. woe and crime.
4. er- ror past.
5. ter- nal- ly. A- men.

O Splendor of God's Glory Bright

Splendor paternæ gloriæ. Mode VI.

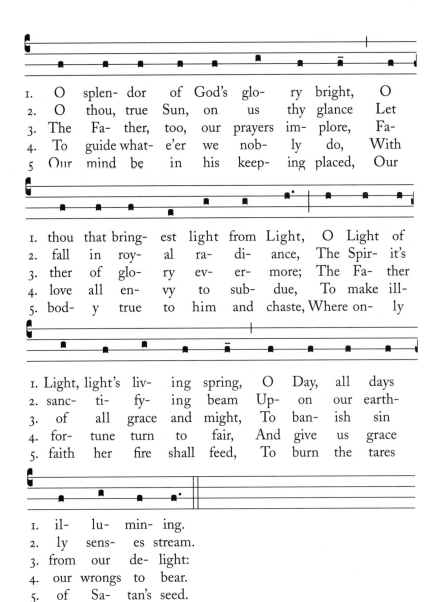

1. O splen- dor of God's glo- ry bright, O
2. O thou, true Sun, on us thy glance Let
3. The Fa- ther, too, our prayers im- plore, Fa-
4. To guide what- e'er we nob- ly do, With
5. Our mind be in his keep- ing placed, Our

1. thou that bring- est light from Light, O Light of
2. fall in roy- al ra- di- ance, The Spir- it's
3. ther of glo- ry ev- er- more; The Fa- ther
4. love all en- vy to sub- due, To make ill-
5. bod- y true to him and chaste, Where on- ly

1. Light, light's liv- ing spring, O Day, all days
2. sanc- ti- fy- ing beam Up- on our earth-
3. of all grace and might, To ban- ish sin
4. for- tune turn to fair, And give us grace
5. faith her fire shall feed, To burn the tares

1. il- lu- min- ing.
2. ly sens- es stream.
3. from our de- light:
4. our wrongs to bear.
5. of Sa- tan's seed.

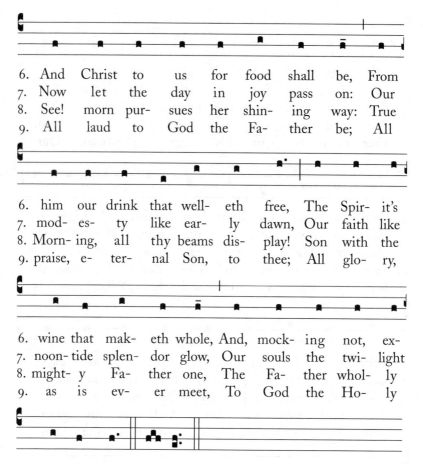

6. And Christ to us for food shall be, From
7. Now let the day in joy pass on: Our
8. See! morn pur- sues her shin- ing way: True
9. All laud to God the Fa- ther be; All

6. him our drink that well- eth free, The Spir- it's
7. mod- es- ty like ear- ly dawn, Our faith like
8. Morn- ing, all thy beams dis- play! Son with the
9. praise, e- ter- nal Son, to thee; All glo- ry,

6. wine that mak- eth whole, And, mock- ing not, ex-
7. noon- tide splen- dor glow, Our souls the twi- light
8. might- y Fa- ther one, The Fa- ther whol- ly
9. as is ev- er meet, To God the Ho- ly

6. alts the soul.
7. nev- er know.
8. in the Son.
9. Par- a-clete. A- men.

O Boundless Wisdom, God Most High

Immense cæli Conditor. Mode VIII.

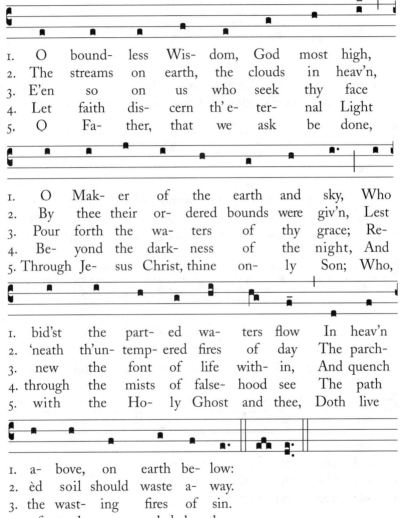

1. O bound- less Wis- dom, God most high,
2. The streams on earth, the clouds in heav'n,
3. E'en so on us who seek thy face
4. Let faith dis- cern th' e- ter- nal Light
5. O Fa- ther, that we ask be done,

1. O Mak- er of the earth and sky, Who
2. By thee their or- dered bounds were giv'n, Lest
3. Pour forth the wa- ters of thy grace; Re-
4. Be- yond the dark- ness of the night, And
5. Through Je- sus Christ, thine on- ly Son; Who,

1. bid'st the part- ed wa- ters flow In heav'n
2. 'neath th'un- temp- ered fires of day The parch-
3. new the font of life with- in, And quench
4. through the mists of false- hood see The path
5. with the Ho- ly Ghost and thee, Doth live

1. a- bove, on earth be- low:
2. èd soil should waste a- way.
3. the wast- ing fires of sin.
4. of truth re- vealed by thee.
5. and reign e- ter- nal- ly. A- men.

The Beauty of the Rising Sun

Pergrata mundo nuntiat. Mode IV.

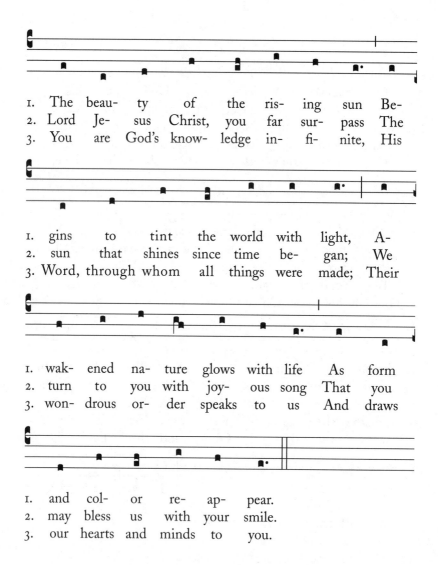

1. The beau- ty of the ris- ing sun Be-
2. Lord Je- sus Christ, you far sur- pass The
3. You are God's know- ledge in- fi- nite, His

1. gins to tint the world with light, A-
2. sun that shines since time be- gan; We
3. Word, through whom all things were made; Their

1. wak- ened na- ture glows with life As form
2. turn to you with joy- ous song That you
3. won- drous or- der speaks to us And draws

1. and col- or re- ap- pear.
2. may bless us with your smile.
3. our hearts and minds to you.

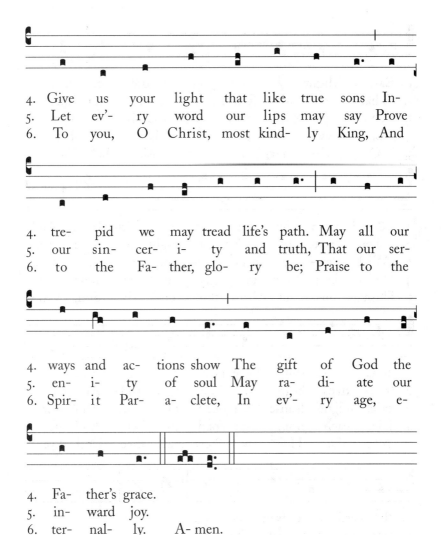

4. Give us your light that like true sons In-
5. Let ev'- ry word our lips may say Prove
6. To you, O Christ, most kind- ly King, And

4. tre- pid we may tread life's path. May all our
5. our sin- cer- i- ty and truth, That our ser-
6. to the Fa- ther, glo- ry be; Praise to the

4. ways and ac- tions show The gift of God the
5. en- i- ty of soul May ra- di- ate our
6. Spir- it Par- a- clete, In ev'- ry age, e-

4. Fa- ther's grace.
5. in- ward joy.
6. ter- nal- ly. A- men.

Earth's Mighty Maker, Whose Command

Telluris ingens Conditor. Mode VIII.

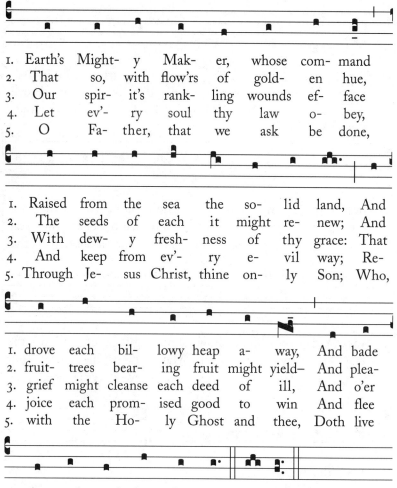

1. Earth's Might- y Mak- er, whose com- mand
2. That so, with flow'rs of gold- en hue,
3. Our spir- it's rank- ling wounds ef- face
4. Let ev'- ry soul thy law o- bey,
5. O Fa- ther, that we ask be done,

1. Raised from the sea the so- lid land, And
2. The seeds of each it might re- new; And
3. With dew- y fresh- ness of thy grace: That
4. And keep from ev'- ry e- vil way; Re-
5. Through Je- sus Christ, thine on- ly Son; Who,

1. drove each bil- lowy heap a- way, And bade
2. fruit- trees bear- ing fruit might yield— And plea-
3. grief might cleanse each deed of ill, And o'er
4. joice each prom- ised good to win And flee
5. with the Ho- ly Ghost and thee, Doth live

1. the earth stand firm for aye:
2. sant pas- ture of the field.
3. each lust might tri- umph still.
4. from ev'- ry mor- tal sin.
5. and reign e- ter- nal- ly. A- men.

When Breaks the Day and Dawn Grows Bright

Nox et tenebræ et nubila. Mode II.

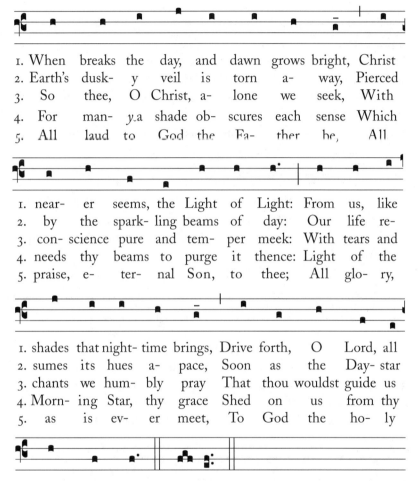

1. When breaks the day, and dawn grows bright, Christ
2. Earth's dusk- y veil is torn a- way, Pierced
3. So thee, O Christ, a- lone we seek, With
4. For man- y a shade ob- scures each sense Which
5. All laud to God the Fa- ther be, All

1. near- er seems, the Light of Light: From us, like
2. by the spark- ling beams of day: Our life re-
3. con- science pure and tem- per meek: With tears and
4. needs thy beams to purge it thence: Light of the
5. praise, e- ter- nal Son, to thee; All glo- ry,

1. shades that night- time brings, Drive forth, O Lord, all
2. sumes its hues a- pace, Soon as the Day- star
3. chants we hum- bly pray That thou wouldst guide us
4. Morn- ing Star, thy grace Shed on us from thy
5. as is ev- er meet, To God the ho- ly

1. dark- some things.
2. shows his face.
3. through each day.
4. cloud- less face.
5. Par- a- clete. A- men.

O God, Whose Hand Hath Spread the Sky

Cæli Deus sanctissime. Mode VIII.

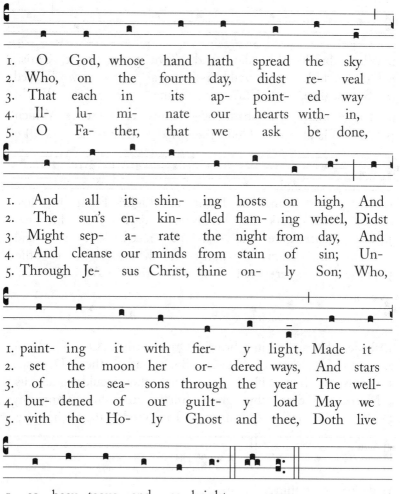

1. O God, whose hand hath spread the sky
2. Who, on the fourth day, didst re- veal
3. That each in its ap- point- ed way
4. Il- lu- mi- nate our hearts with- in,
5. O Fa- ther, that we ask be done,

1. And all its shin- ing hosts on high, And
2. The sun's en- kin- dled flam- ing wheel, Didst
3. Might sep- a- rate the night from day, And
4. And cleanse our minds from stain of sin; Un-
5. Through Je- sus Christ, thine on- ly Son; Who,

1. paint- ing it with fier- y light, Made it
2. set the moon her or- dered ways, And stars
3. of the sea- sons through the year The well-
4. bur- dened of our guilt- y load May we
5. with the Ho- ly Ghost and thee, Doth live

1. so beau- teous and so bright;
2. their ev- er wind- ing maze;
3. re- mem- bered signs de- clare:
4. un- fet- tered serve our God.
5. and reign e- ter- nal- ly. A- men.

Behold, the Golden Dawn Arise

Sol ecce surgit aurea. Mode II.

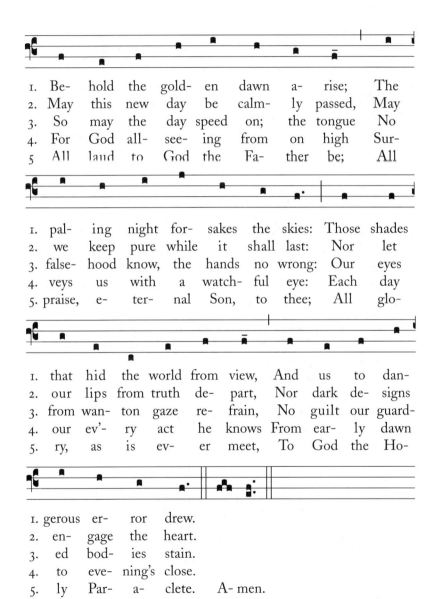

1. Be- hold the gold- en dawn a- rise; The
2. May this new day be calm- ly passed, May
3. So may the day speed on; the tongue No
4. For God all- see- ing from on high Sur-
5. All land to God the Fa- ther be; All

1. pal- ing night for- sakes the skies: Those shades
2. we keep pure while it shall last: Nor let
3. false- hood know, the hands no wrong: Our eyes
4. veys us with a watch- ful eye: Each day
5. praise, e- ter- nal Son, to thee; All glo-

1. that hid the world from view, And us to dan-
2. our lips from truth de- part, Nor dark de- signs
3. from wan- ton gaze re- frain, No guilt our guard-
4. our ev'- ry act he knows From ear- ly dawn
5. ry, as is ev- er meet, To God the Ho-

1. gerous er- ror drew.
2. en- gage the heart.
3. ed bod- ies stain.
4. to eve- ning's close.
5. ly Par- a- clete. A- men.

Almighty God, Whose Will Supreme

Magnæ Deus potentiæ. Mode VIII.

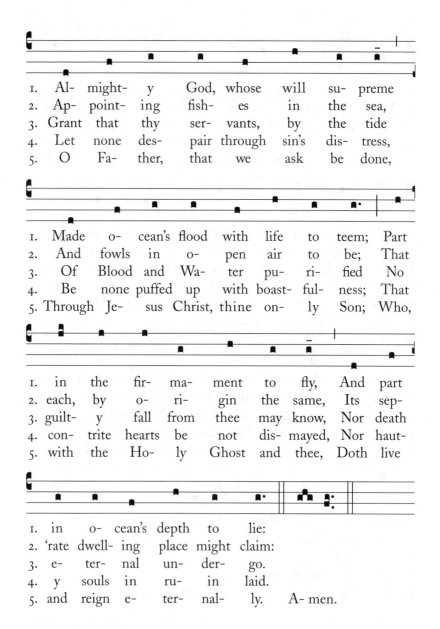

1. Al- might- y God, whose will su- preme
2. Ap- point- ing fish- es in the sea,
3. Grant that thy ser- vants, by the tide
4. Let none des- pair through sin's dis- tress,
5. O Fa- ther, that we ask be done,

1. Made o- cean's flood with life to teem; Part
2. And fowls in o- pen air to be; That
3. Of Blood and Wa- ter pu- ri- fied No
4. Be none puffed up with boast- ful- ness; That
5. Through Je- sus Christ, thine on- ly Son; Who,

1. in the fir- ma- ment to fly, And part
2. each, by o- ri- gin the same, Its sep-
3. guilt- y fall from thee may know, Nor death
4. con- trite hearts be not dis- mayed, Nor haut-
5. with the Ho- ly Ghost and thee, Doth live

1. in o- cean's depth to lie:
2. 'rate dwell- ing place might claim:
3. e- ter- nal un- der- go.
4. y souls in ru- in laid.
5. and reign e- ter- nal- ly. A- men.

Eternal Glory of the Sky

Æterna cæli gloria. Mode VI.

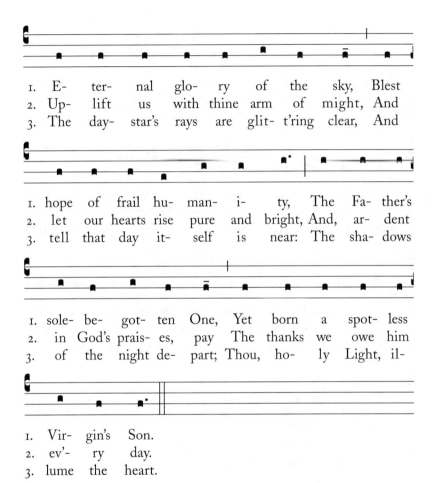

1. E- ter- nal glo- ry of the sky, Blest
2. Up- lift us with thine arm of might, And
3. The day- star's rays are glit- t'ring clear, And

1. hope of frail hu- man- i- ty, The Fa- ther's
2. let our hearts rise pure and bright, And, ar- dent
3. tell that day it- self is near: The sha- dows

1. sole- be- got- ten One, Yet born a spot- less
2. in God's prais- es, pay The thanks we owe him
3. of the night de- part; Thou, ho- ly Light, il-

1. Vir- gin's Son.
2. ev'- ry day.
3. lume the heart.

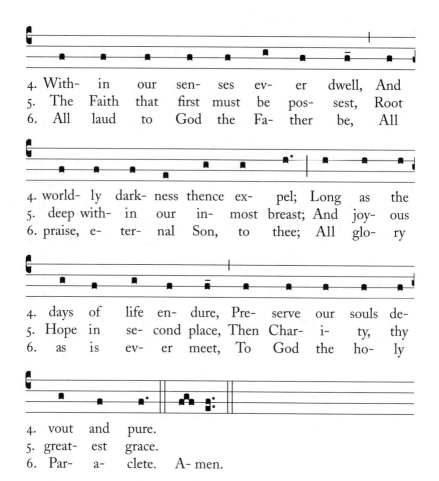

4. With- in our sen- ses ev- er dwell, And
5. The Faith that first must be pos- sest, Root
6. All laud to God the Fa- ther be, All

4. world- ly dark- ness thence ex- pel; Long as the
5. deep with- in our in- most breast; And joy- ous
6. praise, e- ter- nal Son, to thee; All glo- ry

4. days of life en- dure, Pre- serve our souls de-
5. Hope in se- cond place, Then Char- i- ty, thy
6. as is ev- er meet, To God the ho- ly

4. vout and pure.
5. great- est grace.
6. Par- a- clete. A- men.

Maker of Men, Who from Thy Throne

Plasmator hominis, Deus. Mode II.

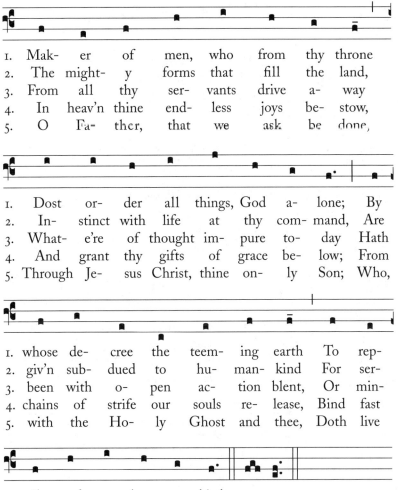

1. Mak- er of men, who from thy throne
2. The might- y forms that fill the land,
3. From all thy ser- vants drive a- way
4. In heav'n thine end- less joys be- stow,
5. O Fa- ther, that we ask be done,

1. Dost or- der all things, God a- lone; By
2. In- stinct with life at thy com- mand, Are
3. What- e're of thought im- pure to- day Hath
4. And grant thy gifts of grace be- low; From
5. Through Je- sus Christ, thine on- ly Son; Who,

1. whose de- cree the teem- ing earth To rep-
2. giv'n sub- dued to hu- man- kind For ser-
3. been with o- pen ac- tion blent, Or min-
4. chains of strife our souls re- lease, Bind fast
5. with the Ho- ly Ghost and thee, Doth live

1. tile and to beast gave birth:
2. vice in their rank as- signed.
3. gled with the heart's in- tent.
4. the gen- tle bands of peace.
5. and reign e- ter- nal- ly. A-men.

The Dawn Is Sprinkling in the East

Aurora iam spargit polum. Mode IV.

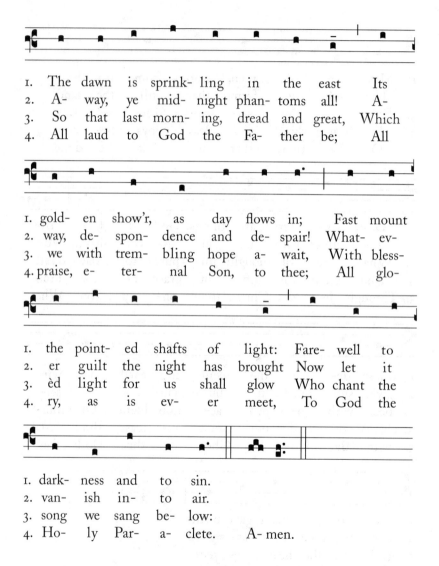

1. The dawn is sprink- ling in the east Its
2. A- way, ye mid- night phan- toms all! A-
3. So that last morn- ing, dread and great, Which
4. All laud to God the Fa- ther be; All

1. gold- en show'r, as day flows in; Fast mount
2. way, de- spon- dence and de- spair! What- ev-
3. we with trem- bling hope a- wait, With bless-
4. praise, e- ter- nal Son, to thee; All glo-

1. the point- ed shafts of light: Fare- well to
2. er guilt the night has brought Now let it
3. èd light for us shall glow Who chant the
4. ry, as is ev- er meet, To God the

1. dark- ness and to sin.
2. van- ish in- to air.
3. song we sang be- low:
4. Ho- ly Par- a- clete. A- men.

O God, the Source and Fount of Life

Rerum, Deus, fons omnium. Mode II.

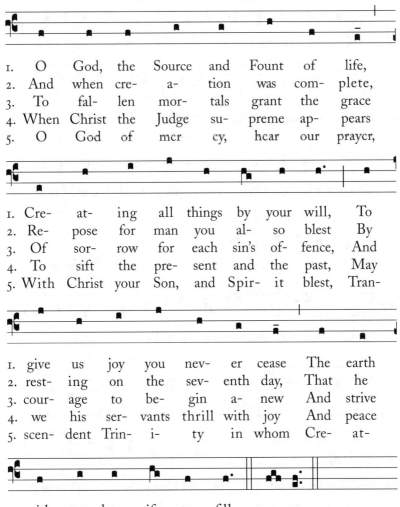

1. O God, the Source and Fount of life,
2. And when cre- a- tion was com- plete,
3. To fal- len mor- tals grant the grace
4. When Christ the Judge su- preme ap- pears
5. O God of mer cy, hear our prayer,

1. Cre- at- ing all things by your will, To
2. Re- pose for man you al- so blest By
3. Of sor- row for each sin's of- fence, And
4. To sift the pre- sent and the past, May
5. With Christ your Son, and Spir- it blest, Tran-

1. give us joy you nev- er cease The earth
2. rest- ing on the sev- enth day, That he
3. cour- age to be- gin a- new And strive
4. we his ser- vants thrill with joy And peace
5. scen- dent Trin- i- ty in whom Cre- at-

1. with won- drous gifts to fill.
2. might toil a- gain re- freshed.
3. for vir- tue's re- com- pense.
4. to gaze on him at last.
5. ed things all come to rest. A- men.

Lo! The Dim Shadows

Ecce iam noctis. Mode IV.

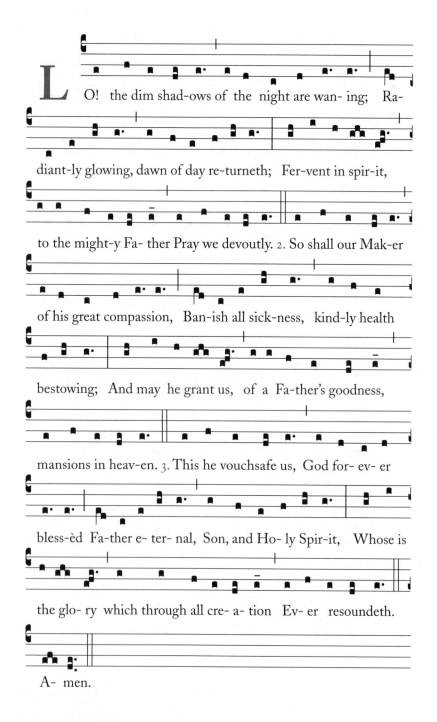

LO! the dim shad-ows of the night are wan- ing; Ra-

diant-ly glowing, dawn of day re-turneth; Fer-vent in spir-it,

to the might-y Fa- ther Pray we devoutly. 2. So shall our Mak-er

of his great compassion, Ban-ish all sick-ness, kind-ly health

bestowing; And may he grant us, of a Fa-ther's goodness,

mansions in heav-en. 3. This he vouchsafe us, God for- ev- er

bless-èd Fa-ther e- ter- nal, Son, and Ho- ly Spir-it, Whose is

the glo- ry which through all cre- a- tion Ev- er resoundeth.

A- men.

O Trinity of Blessed Light

O Lux, beata Trinitas. Mode VIII.

1. O Trin- i- ty of bless- èd light, O U-
2. To thee our morn- ing song of praise, To thee
3. All laud to God the Fa- ther be; All praise,

1. ni- ty of prince- ly might, The fier- y sun now
2. our eve- ning prayer we raise; Thy glo- ry sup- pliant
3. e- ter- nal Son, to thee; All glo- ry as is

1. goes his way; Shed thou with- in our hearts thy ray.
2. we a- dore For ev- er and for ev- er- more.
3. ev- er meet, To God the Ho- ly Par- a- clete.

A- men.

O Lavish Giver of the Light

Lucis largitor splendide. Mode II.

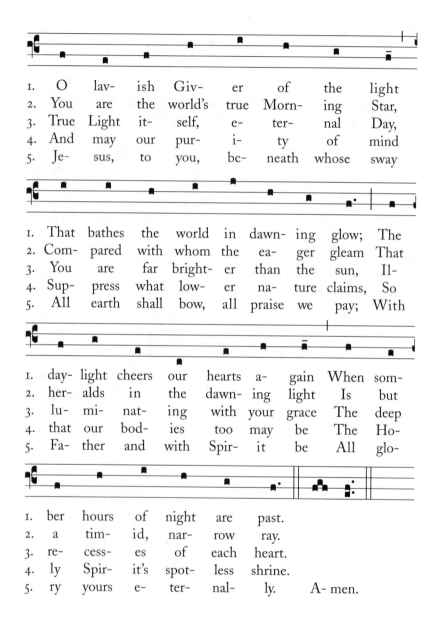

1. O lav- ish Giv- er of the light
2. You are the world's true Morn- ing Star,
3. True Light it- self, e- ter- nal Day,
4. And may our pur- i- ty of mind
5. Je- sus, to you, be- neath whose sway

1. That bathes the world in dawn- ing glow; The
2. Com- pared with whom the ea- ger gleam That
3. You are far bright- er than the sun, Il-
4. Sup- press what low- er na- ture claims, So
5. All earth shall bow, all praise we pay; With

1. day- light cheers our hearts a- gain When som-
2. her- alds in the dawn- ing light Is but
3. lu- mi- nat- ing with your grace The deep
4. that our bod- ies too may be The Ho-
5. Fa- ther and with Spir- it be All glo-

1. ber hours of night are past.
2. a tim- id, nar- row ray.
3. re- cess- es of each heart.
4. ly Spir- it's spot- less shrine.
5. ry yours e- ter- nal- ly. A- men.

O Fount of Light, True Light Itself

Luminis fons, lux et origo lucis. Mode VIII.

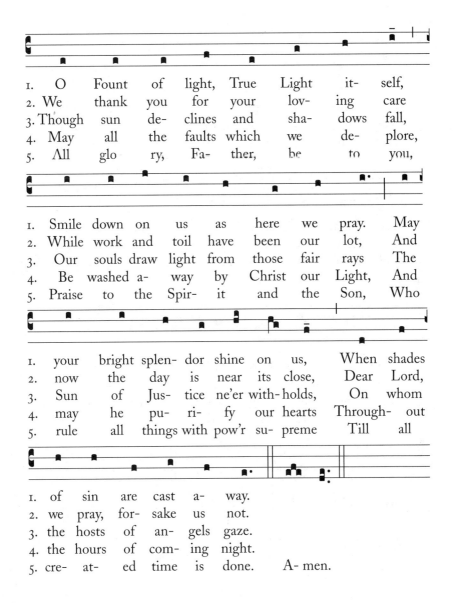

1. O Fount of light, True Light itself,
2. We thank you for your lov-ing care
3. Though sun de-clines and sha-dows fall,
4. May all the faults which we de-plore,
5. All glo-ry, Fa-ther, be to you,

1. Smile down on us as here we pray. May
2. While work and toil have been our lot, And
3. Our souls draw light from those fair rays The
4. Be washed a-way by Christ our Light, And
5. Praise to the Spir-it and the Son, Who

1. your bright splen-dor shine on us, When shades
2. now the day is near its close, Dear Lord,
3. Sun of Jus-tice ne'er with-holds, On whom
4. may he pu-ri-fy our hearts Through-out
5. rule all things with pow'r su-preme Till all

1. of sin are cast a-way.
2. we pray, for-sake us not.
3. the hosts of an-gels gaze.
4. the hours of com-ing night.
5. cre-at-ed time is done. A-men.

Eternal Maker of the Light

Æterne lucis conditor. Mode IV.

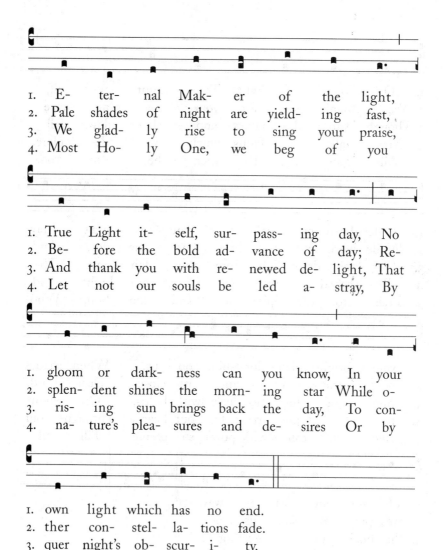

1. E- ter- nal Mak- er of the light,
2. Pale shades of night are yield- ing fast,
3. We glad- ly rise to sing your praise,
4. Most Ho- ly One, we beg of you

1. True Light it- self, sur- pass- ing day, No
2. Be- fore the bold ad- vance of day; Re-
3. And thank you with re- newed de- light, That
4. Let not our souls be led a- stray, By

1. gloom or dark- ness can you know, In your
2. splen- dent shines the morn- ing star While o-
3. ris- ing sun brings back the day, To con-
4. na- ture's plea- sures and de- sires Or by

1. own light which has no end.
2. ther con- stel- la- tions fade.
3. quer night's ob- scur- i- ty.
4. the world's de- ceiv- ing glare.

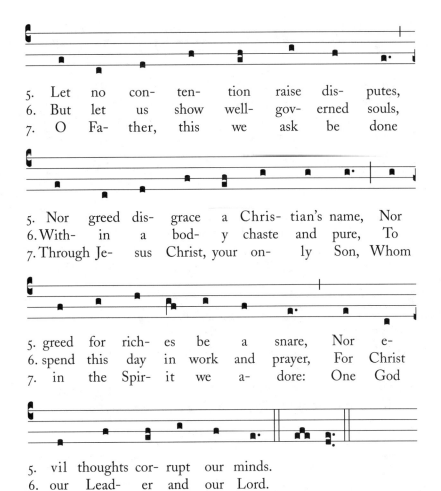

5. Let no con- ten- tion raise dis- putes,
6. But let us show well- gov- erned souls,
7. O Fa- ther, this we ask be done

5. Nor greed dis- grace a Chris- tian's name, Nor
6. With- in a bod- y chaste and pure, To
7. Through Je- sus Christ, your on- ly Son, Whom

5. greed for rich- es be a snare, Nor e-
6. spend this day in work and prayer, For Christ
7. in the Spir- it we a- dore: One God

5. vil thoughts cor- rupt our minds.
6. our Lead- er and our Lord.
7. who reigns for ev- er- more. A- men.

Great Ruler of All Space and Time

Sator princepsque temporum. Mode VIII.

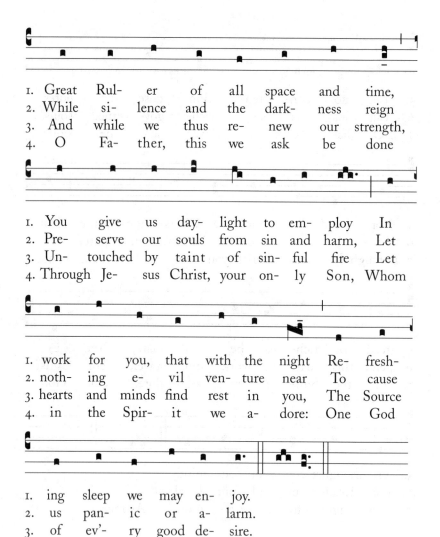

1. Great Rul- er of all space and time,
2. While si- lence and the dark- ness reign
3. And while we thus re- new our strength,
4. O Fa- ther, this we ask be done

1. You give us day- light to em- ploy In
2. Pre- serve our souls from sin and harm, Let
3. Un- touched by taint of sin- ful fire Let
4. Through Je- sus Christ, your on- ly Son, Whom

1. work for you, that with the night Re- fresh-
2. noth- ing e- vil ven- ture near To cause
3. hearts and minds find rest in you, The Source
4. in the Spir- it we a- dore: One God

1. ing sleep we may en- joy.
2. us pan- ic or a- larm.
3. of ev'- ry good de- sire.
4. who reigns for ev- er- more. A- men.

Creator of the Skies Above

Fulgentis auctor ætheris. Mode II.

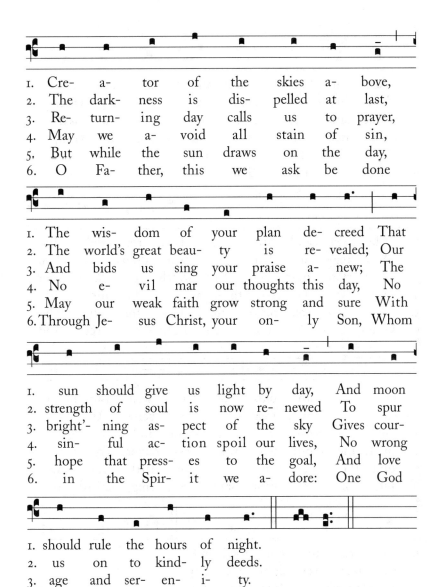

1. Cre- a- tor of the skies a- bove,
2. The dark- ness is dis- pelled at last,
3. Re- turn- ing day calls us to prayer,
4. May we a- void all stain of sin,
5. But while the sun draws on the day,
6. O Fa- ther, this we ask be done

1. The wis- dom of your plan de- creed That
2. The world's great beau- ty is re- vealed; Our
3. And bids us sing your praise a- new; The
4. No e- vil mar our thoughts this day, No
5. May our weak faith grow strong and sure With
6. Through Je- sus Christ, your on- ly Son, Whom

1. sun should give us light by day, And moon
2. strength of soul is now re- newed To spur
3. bright'- ning as- pect of the sky Gives cour-
4. sin- ful ac- tion spoil our lives, No wrong
5. hope that press- es to the goal, And love
6. in the Spir- it we a- dore: One God

1. should rule the hours of night.
2. us on to kind- ly deeds.
3. age and ser- en- i- ty.
4. or i- dle words of- fend.
5. u- nites us all to Christ.
6. who reigns for ev- er- more. A- men.

As Sun Declines and Shadows Fall

Sol, ecce, lentus occidens. Mode VIII.

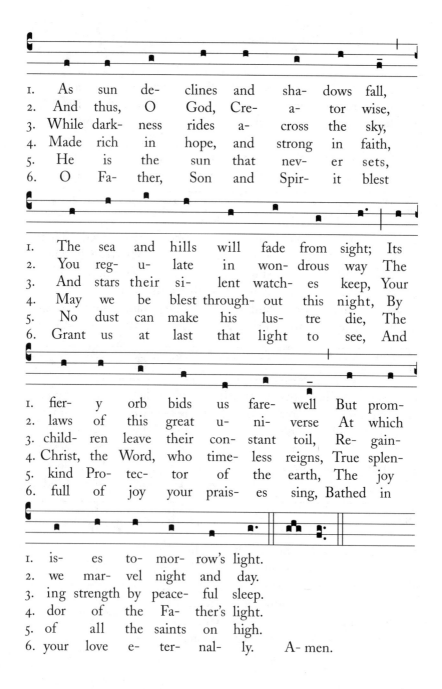

1. As sun de- clines and sha- dows fall,
2. And thus, O God, Cre- a- tor wise,
3. While dark- ness rides a- cross the sky,
4. Made rich in hope, and strong in faith,
5. He is the sun that nev- er sets,
6. O Fa- ther, Son and Spir- it blest

1. The sea and hills will fade from sight; Its
2. You reg- u- late in won- drous way The
3. And stars their si- lent watch- es keep, Your
4. May we be blest through- out this night, By
5. No dust can make his lus- tre die, The
6. Grant us at last that light to see, And

1. fier- y orb bids us fare- well But prom-
2. laws of this great u- ni- verse At which
3. child- ren leave their con- stant toil, Re- gain-
4. Christ, the Word, who time- less reigns, True splen-
5. kind Pro- tec- tor of the earth, The joy
6. full of joy your prais- es sing, Bathed in

1. is- es to- mor- row's light.
2. we mar- vel night and day.
3. ing strength by peace- ful sleep.
4. dor of the Fa- ther's light.
5. of all the saints on high.
6. your love e- ter- nal- ly. A- men.

Now that the Daylight Fills the Sky

Iam lucis orto sidere. Mode II.

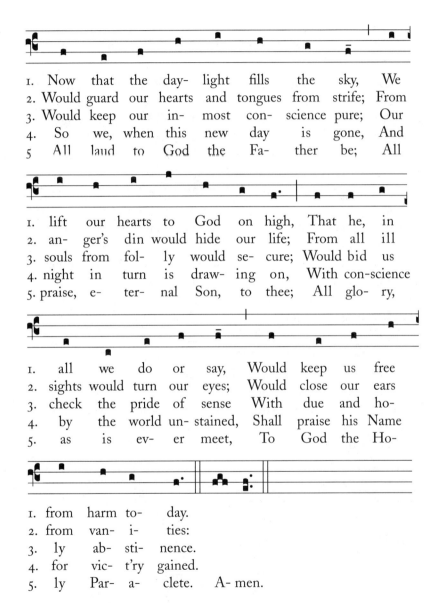

1. Now that the day- light fills the sky, We
2. Would guard our hearts and tongues from strife; From
3. Would keep our in- most con- science pure; Our
4. So we, when this new day is gone, And
5. All laud to God the Fa- ther be; All

1. lift our hearts to God on high, That he, in
2. an- ger's din would hide our life; From all ill
3. souls from fol- ly would se- cure; Would bid us
4. night in turn is draw- ing on, With con-science
5. praise, e- ter- nal Son, to thee; All glo- ry,

1. all we do or say, Would keep us free
2. sights would turn our eyes; Would close our ears
3. check the pride of sense With due and ho-
4. by the world un- stained, Shall praise his Name
5. as is ev- er meet, To God the Ho-

1. from harm to- day.
2. from van- i- ties:
3. ly ab- sti- nence.
4. for vic- t'ry gained.
5. ly Par- a- clete. A- men.

O Lord Our God, Who Made the Day

Deus, qui claro lumine. Mode VIII.

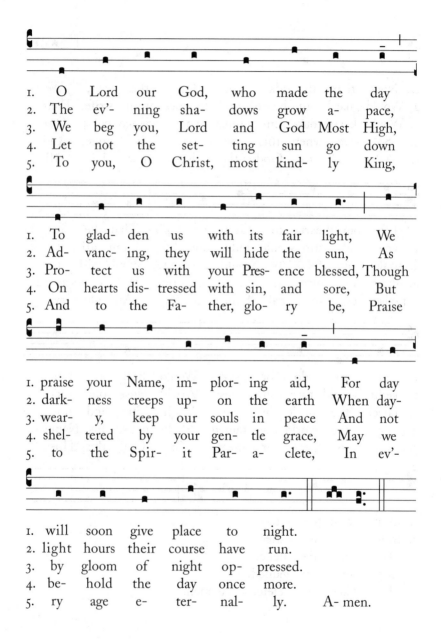

1. O Lord our God, who made the day
2. The ev'- ning sha- dows grow a- pace,
3. We beg you, Lord and God Most High,
4. Let not the set- ting sun go down
5. To you, O Christ, most kind- ly King,

1. To glad- den us with its fair light, We
2. Ad- vanc- ing, they will hide the sun, As
3. Pro- tect us with your Pres- ence blessed, Though
4. On hearts dis- tressed with sin, and sore, But
5. And to the Fa- ther, glo- ry be, Praise

1. praise your Name, im- plor- ing aid, For day
2. dark- ness creeps up- on the earth When day-
3. wear- y, keep our souls in peace And not
4. shel- tered by your gen- tle grace, May we
5. to the Spir- it Par- a- clete, In ev'-

1. will soon give place to night.
2. light hours their course have run.
3. by gloom of night op- pressed.
4. be- hold the day once more.
5. ry age e- ter- nal- ly. A- men.

O God, the Lamp of Heaven High

Deus, qui cæli lumen es. Mode VI.

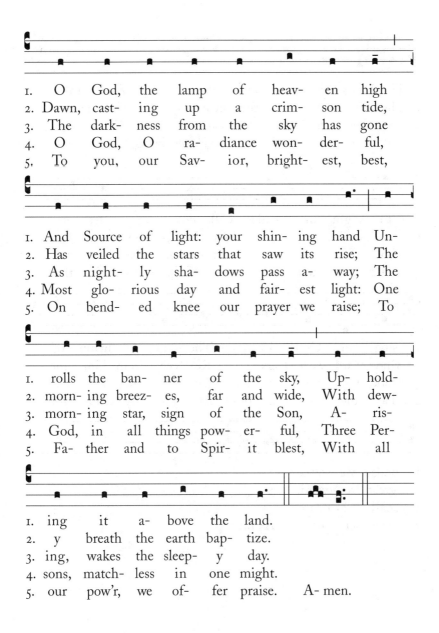

1. O God, the lamp of heav- en high
2. Dawn, cast- ing up a crim- son tide,
3. The dark- ness from the sky has gone
4. O God, O ra- diance won- der- ful,
5. To you, our Sav- ior, bright- est, best,

1. And Source of light: your shin- ing hand Un-
2. Has veiled the stars that saw its rise; The
3. As night- ly sha- dows pass a- way; The
4. Most glo- rious day and fair- est light: One
5. On bend- ed knee our prayer we raise; To

1. rolls the ban- ner of the sky, Up- hold-
2. morn- ing breez- es, far and wide, With dew-
3. morn- ing star, sign of the Son, A- ris-
4. God, in all things pow- er- ful, Three Per-
5. Fa- ther and to Spir- it blest, With all

1. ing it a- bove the land.
2. y breath the earth bap- tize.
3. ing, wakes the sleep- y day.
4. sons, match- less in one might.
5. our pow'r, we of- fer praise. A- men.

The Hours Are Passing Swiftly By

Horis peractis undecim. Mode II.

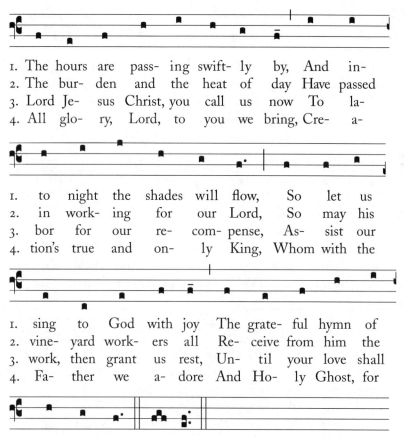

1. The hours are pass- ing swift- ly by, And in-
2. The bur- den and the heat of day Have passed
3. Lord Je- sus Christ, you call us now To la-
4. All glo- ry, Lord, to you we bring, Cre- a-

1. to night the shades will flow, So let us
2. in work- ing for our Lord, So may his
3. bor for our re- com- pense, As- sist our
4. tion's true and on- ly King, Whom with the

1. sing to God with joy The grate- ful hymn of
2. vine- yard work- ers all Re- ceive from him the
3. work, then grant us rest, Un- til your love shall
4. Fa- ther we a- dore And Ho- ly Ghost, for

1. praise we owe.
2. great re- ward.
3. call us hence.
4. ev- er- more. A- men.

As Light of Day Returns Once More

Diei luce reddita. Mode II.

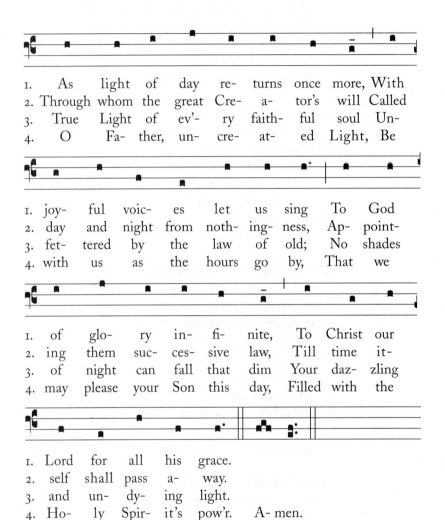

1. As light of day re- turns once more, With
2. Through whom the great Cre- a- tor's will Called
3. True Light of ev'- ry faith- ful soul Un-
4. O Fa- ther, un- cre- at- ed Light, Be

1. joy- ful voic- es let us sing To God
2. day and night from noth- ing- ness, Ap- point-
3. fet- tered by the law of old; No shades
4. with us as the hours go by, That we

1. of glo- ry in- fi- nite, To Christ our
2. ing them suc- ces- sive law, Till time it-
3. of night can fall that dim Your daz- zling
4. may please your Son this day, Filled with the

1. Lord for all his grace.
2. self shall pass a- way.
3. and un- dy- ing light.
4. Ho- ly Spir- it's pow'r. A- men.

ANTIPHONS IN HONOR OF THE BLESSED VIRGIN MARY

Alma Redemptoris Mater, quæ pervia cæli
    porta manes, et stella maris succurre cadenti,
surgere qui curat, populo: tu quæ genuisti,
    natura mirante, tuum sanctum Genitorem,
Virgo prius ac posterius, Gabrielis ab ore
    sumens illud Ave, peccatorum miserere.

Or:

Ave Regina cœlorum,
    ave Domina Angelorum,
salve radix, salve, porta
    ex qua mundo lux est orta.
Gaude, Virgo gloriosa,
    super omnes speciosa;
vale, o valde decora,
    et pro nobis Christum exora.

Or:

Salve Regina, Mater misericordiæ;
    vita dulcedo et spes nostra salve,
Ad te clamamus, exsules filii Evæ.
Ad te suspiramus, gementes et flentes
    in hac lacrimarum valle.
Eia ergo, advocata nostra,
    illos tuos misericordes oculos
    ad nos converte.
Et Jesum, benedictum fructum ventris tui,
    nobis post hoc exsilium ostende.
O clemens, o pia, o dulcis Virgo Maria.

Or:

Regina cæli, lætare, alleluia,
    quia quem meruisti portare, alleluia,
resurrexit sicut dixit, alleluia;
    ora pro nobis Deum, alleluia.

Gaude et lætare, Virgo Maria, alleluia.
Quia surrexit Dominus vere, alleluia.